Less managing. More teaching. Greater learning.

INSTRUCTORS...

Would you like your **students** to show up for class **more prepared**? *(Let's face it, class is much more fun if everyone is engaged and prepared...)*

Want an **easy way to assign** homework online and track student **progress**? *(Less time grading means more time teaching...)*

Want an **instant view** of student or class performance relative to learning objectives? *(No more wondering if students understand...)*

Need to **collect data and generate reports** required for administration or accreditation? *(Say goodbye to manually tracking student learning outcomes...)*

Want to **record and post your lectures** for students to view online?

With McGraw-Hill's *Connect™ Plus Accounting*,

INSTRUCTORS GET:

- Simple **assignment management**, allowing you to spend more time teaching.
- **Auto-graded** assignments, quizzes, and tests.
- **Detailed Visual Reporting** where student and section results can be viewed and analyzed.
- Sophisticated **online testing** capability.
- A **filtering and reporting** function that allows you to easily assign and report on materials that are correlated to accreditation standards, learning outcomes, and Bloom's taxonomy.
- An easy-to-use **lecture capture** tool.
- The option to **upload course documents** for student access.

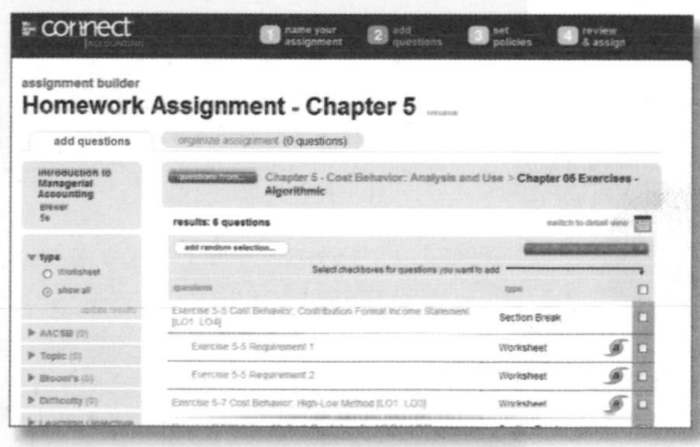

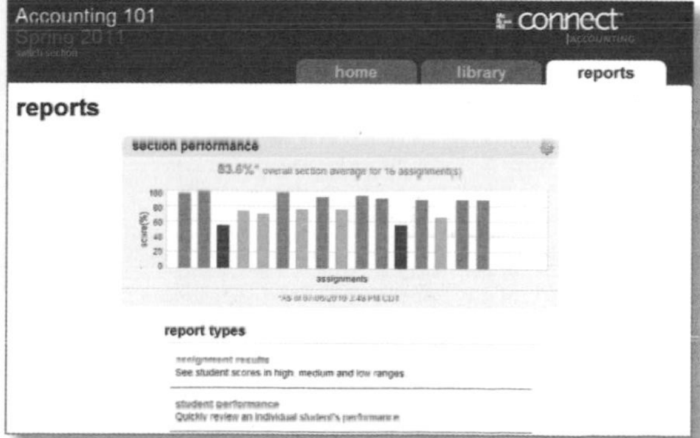

Want an online, **searchable version** of your textbook?

Wish your textbook could be **available online** while you're doing your assignments?

Connect™ Plus Accounting eBook

If you choose to use *Connect™ Plus Accounting*, you have an affordable and searchable online version of your book integrated with your other online tools.

Connect™ Plus Accounting eBook offers features like:

- Topic search
- Direct links from assignments
- Adjustable text size
- Jump to page number
- Print by section

Want to get more **value** from your textbook purchase?

Think learning accounting should be a bit more **interesting**?

Check out the STUDENT RESOURCES section under the *Connect™* Library tab.

Here you'll find a wealth of resources designed to help you achieve your goals in the course. You'll find things like **quizzes, PowerPoints, and Internet activities** to help you study. Every student has different needs, so explore the STUDENT RESOURCES to find the materials best suited to you.

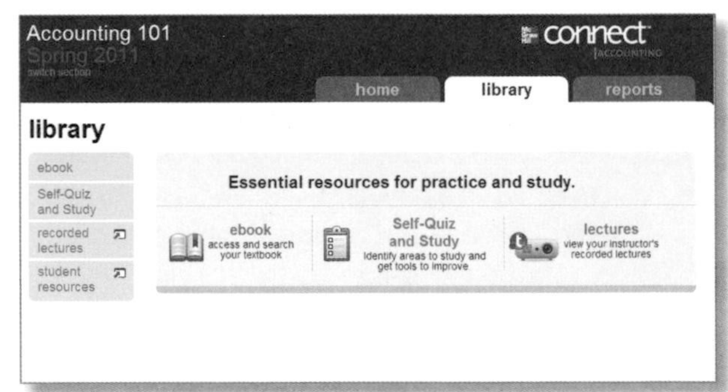

Fundamental Accounting Principles

20th edition

Volume 1, Chapters 1–12

John J. Wild
University of Wisconsin at Madison

Ken W. Shaw
University of Missouri at Columbia

Barbara Chiappetta
Nassau Community College

McGraw-Hill Irwin

To my students and family, especially **Kimberly, Jonathan, Stephanie,** and **Trevor.**
To my wife **Linda** and children, **Erin, Emily,** and **Jacob.**
To my mother, husband **Bob,** and sons **Michael** and **David.**

FUNDAMENTAL ACCOUNTING PRINCIPLES
Published by McGraw-Hill/Irwin, a business unit of The McGraw-Hill Companies, Inc., 1221 Avenue of the Americas, New York, NY, 10020.

This book is printed on acid-free paper.

1 2 3 4 5 6 7 8 9 0 DOW/DOW 1 0 9 8 7 6 5 4 3 2 1 0

ISBN-13: 978-0-07-811087-0 (combined edition)
ISBN-10: 0-07-811087-4 (combined edition)
ISBN-13: 978-0-07-733825-1 (volume 1, chapters 1-12)
ISBN-10: 0-07-733825-1 (volume 1, chapters 1-12)
ISBN-13: 978-0-07-733824-4 (volume 2, chapters 12-25)
ISBN-10: 0-07-733824-3 (volume 2, chapters 12-25)
ISBN-13: 978-0-07-733826-8 (with working papers volume 1, chapters 1-12)
ISBN-10: 0-07-733826-X (with working papers volume 1, chapters 1-12)
ISBN-13: 978-0-07-733827-5 (with working papers volume 2, chapters 12-25)
ISBN-10: 0-07-733827-8 (with working papers volume 2, chapters 12-25)
ISBN-13: 978-0-07-733823-7 (principles, chapters 1-17)
ISBN-10: 0-07-733823-5 (principles, chapters 1-17)

Vice president and editor-in-chief: *Brent Gordon*
Editorial director: *Stewart Mattson*
Publisher: *Tim Vertovec*
Executive editor: *Steve Schuetz*
Director of development: *Ann Torbert*
Senior development editor: *Christina A. Sanders*
Vice president and director of marketing: *Robin J. Zwettler*
Marketing director: *Brad Parkins*
Marketing manager: *Michelle Heaster*
Vice president of editing, design, and production: *Sesha Bolisetty*
Managing editor: *Lori Koetters*
Senior buyer: *Carol A. Bielski*
Lead designer: *Matthew Baldwin*
Senior photo research coordinator: *Jeremy Cheshareck*
Photo researcher: *Sarah Evertson*
Lead media project manager: *Brian Nacik*
Media project manager: *Ron Nelms*
Interior and cover design: *Laurie Entringer*
Cover image: © *Getty Images*
Typeface: *10.5/12 Times Roman*
Compositor: *Aptara®, Inc.*
Printer: *R. R. Donnelley*

The Library of Congress has cataloged the single volume edition of this work as follows

Wild, John J.
Fundamental accounting principles / John J. Wild, Ken W. Shaw, Barbara Chiappetta.—20th ed.
p. cm.
Includes index.
ISBN-13: 978-0-07-811087-0 (combined edition : alk. paper)
ISBN-10: 0-07-811087-4 (combined edition : alk. paper)
ISBN-13: 978-0-07-733825-1 (volume 1 ch. 1-12 : alk. paper)
ISBN-10: 0-07-733825-1 (volume 1 ch. 1-12 : alk. paper)
[etc.]
1. Accounting. I. Shaw, Ken W. II. Chiappetta, Barbara. III. Title.
HF5636.W675 2011
657—dc22

2010026205

www.mhhe.com

Dear Colleagues/Friends,

As we roll out the new edition of *Fundamental Accounting Principles*, we thank each of you who provided suggestions to improve our textbook. As teachers, we know how important it is to select the right book for our course. This new edition reflects the advice and wisdom of many dedicated reviewers, symposium and workshop participants, students, and instructors. Our book consistently rates number one in customer loyalty because of you. Together, we have created the most readable, concise, current, accurate, and innovative accounting book available today.

Throughout the writing process, we steered this book in the manner you directed. Reviewers, instructors, and students say this book's enhanced presentation, graphics, and technology cater to different learning styles and helps students better understand accounting. *Connect Accounting Plus* offers new features to improve student learning and to assist instructor teaching and grading. Our iPod content lets students study on the go, while our Algorithmic Test Bank provides an infinite variety of exam problems. You and your students will find all these tools easy to apply.

We owe the success of this book to our colleagues who graciously took time to help us focus on the changing needs of today's instructors and students. We feel fortunate to have witnessed our profession's extraordinary devotion to teaching. Your feedback and suggestions are reflected in everything we write. Please accept our heartfelt thanks for your dedication in helping today's students learn, understand, and appreciate accounting.

With kindest regards,

John J. Wild Ken W. Shaw Barbara Chiappetta

About the Authors

JOHN J. WILD is a distinguished professor of accounting at the University of Wisconsin at Madison. He previously held appointments at Michigan State University and the University of Manchester in England. He received his BBA, MS, and PhD from the University of Wisconsin.

Professor Wild teaches accounting courses at both the undergraduate and graduate levels. He has received numerous teaching honors, including the Mabel W. Chipman Excellence-in-Teaching Award, the departmental Excellence-in-Teaching Award, and the Teaching Excellence Award from the 2003 and 2005 business graduates at the University of Wisconsin. He also received the Beta Alpha Psi and Roland F. Salmonson Excellence-in-Teaching Award from Michigan State University. Professor Wild has received several research honors and is a past KPMG Peat Marwick National Fellow and is a recipient of fellowships from the American Accounting Association and the Ernst and Young Foundation.

Professor Wild is an active member of the American Accounting Association and its sections. He has served on several committees of these organizations, including the Outstanding Accounting Educator Award, Wildman Award, National Program Advisory, Publications, and Research Committees. Professor Wild is author of Financial Accounting, Managerial Accounting, and College Accounting, each published by McGraw-Hill/Irwin. His research articles on accounting and analysis appear in The Accounting Review, Journal of Accounting Research, Journal of Accounting and Economics, Contemporary Accounting Research, Journal of Accounting, Auditing and Finance, Journal of Accounting and Public Policy, and other journals. He is past associate editor of Contemporary Accounting Research and has served on several editorial boards including The Accounting Review.

In his leisure time, Professor Wild enjoys hiking, sports, travel, people, and spending time with family and friends.

KEN W. SHAW is an associate professor of accounting and the Deloitte Professor at the University of Missouri. He previously was on the faculty at the University of Maryland at College Park. He received an accounting degree from Bradley University and an MBA and PhD from the University of Wisconsin. He is a Certified Public Accountant with work experience in public accounting.

Professor Shaw teaches financial accounting at the undergraduate and graduate levels. He received the Williams-Keepers LLC Teaching Excellence award in 2007, was voted the "Most Influential Professor" by the 2005, 2006, and 2010 School of Accountancy graduating classes, and is a two-time recipient of the O'Brien Excellence in Teaching Award. He is the advisor to his School's chapter of the Association of Certified Fraud Examiners.

Professor Shaw is an active member of the American Accounting Association and its sections. He has served on many committees of these organizations and presented his research papers at national and regional meetings. Professor Shaw's research appears in The Accounting Review; Journal of Accounting Research; Contemporary Accounting Research; Journal of Financial and Quantitative Analysis; Journal of the American Taxation Association; Journal of Accounting, Auditing, and Finance; Journal of Financial Research; Research in Accounting Regulation; and other journals. He has served on the editorial boards of Issues in Accounting Education, the Journal of Business Research, and Research in Accounting Regulation. Professor Shaw is co-author of Financial and Managerial Accounting and College Accounting, both published by McGraw-Hill.

In his leisure time, Professor Shaw enjoys tennis, cycling, music, and coaching his children's sports teams.

BARBARA CHIAPPETTA received her BBA in Accountancy and MS in Education from Hofstra University and is a tenured full professor at Nassau Community College. For the past two decades, she has been an active executive board member of the Teachers of Accounting at Two-Year Colleges (TACTYC), serving 10 years as vice president and as president from 1993 through 1999. As an active member of the American Accounting Association, she has served on the Northeast Regional Steering Committee, chaired the Curriculum Revision Committee of the Two-Year Section, and participated in numerous national committees. Professor Chiappetta has been inducted into the American Accounting Association Hall of Fame for the Northeast Region. She had also received the Nassau Community College dean of instruction's Faculty Distinguished Achievement Award. Professor Chiappetta was honored with the State University of New York Chancellor's Award for Teaching Excellence in 1997. As a confirmed believer in the benefits of the active learning pedagogy, Professor Chiappetta has authored Student Learning Tools, an active learning workbook for a first-year accounting course, published by McGraw-Hill/Irwin.

In her leisure time, Professor Chiappetta enjoys tennis and participates on a U.S.T.A. team. She also enjoys the challenge of bridge. Her husband, Robert, is an entrepreneur in the leisure sport industry. She has two sons—Michael, a lawyer, specializing in intellectual property law in New York, and David, a composer, pursuing a career in music for film in Los Angeles.

Helping Students Achieve Peak Performance

Fundamental Accounting Principles 20e

Great performances result from pushing the limits through quality practices and reinforcing feedback to strengthen abilities and motivation. Assist your students in achieving their peak performance by giving them what they need to succeed in today's accounting principles course.

Whether the goal is to become an accountant or a businessperson, or simply to be an informed consumer of accounting information, *Fundamental Accounting Principles (FAP)* has helped generations of students succeed by giving them support in the form of leading-edge accounting content that engages students, paired with state-of-the-art technology that elevates their understanding of key accounting principles.

With *FAP* on your side, you'll be provided with **engaging content** in a **motivating style** to help students see the relevance of accounting. Students are motivated when reading materials that are clear and pertinent. *FAP* excels at engaging students. Its chapter-opening vignettes showcase dynamic, successful entrepreneurial individuals and companies guaranteed to **interest and excite students**. This edition's featured companies—**Research In Motion** (maker of BlackBerry), **Apple**, **Nokia**, and **Palm**—captivate students with their products and annual reports, which are a pathway for learning financial statements. Further, this book's coverage of the accounting cycle fundamentals is widely praised for its clarity and effectiveness.

FAP also delivers innovative technology to help student performance. ***Connect Accounting*** provides students with instant grading and feedback for assignments that are completed online. ***Connect Accounting Plus*** integrates an online version of the textbook with *Connect Accounting*. Our algorithmic test bank offers infinite variations of numerical test bank questions. The Self-Quiz and Study, Interactive Presentations, and LearnSmart all provide additional support to help reinforce concepts and keep students motivated.

We're confident you'll agree that ***FAP* will help your students achieve peak performance**.

Your Students' Connection to

McGraw-Hill *Connect Accounting* is an online assignment and assessment solution that connects your students with the tools and resources needed to achieve success through faster learning, more efficient studying, and higher retention of knowledge.

Online Assignments: *Connect Accounting* helps students learn more efficiently by providing feedback and practice material when they need it, where they need it. *Connect* grades homework automatically and gives immediate feedback on any questions students may have missed.

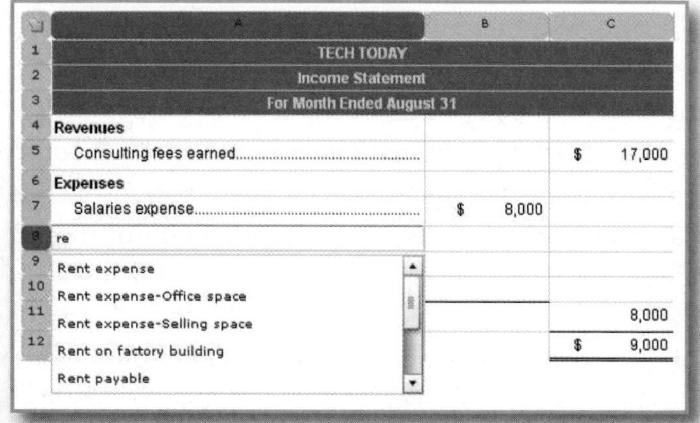

A
B
C
TECH TODAY
Income Statement
For Month Ended August 31
Revenues
Consulting fees earned
$ 17,000
Expenses
Salaries expense
$ 8,000
re
Rent expense
Rent expense-Office space
Rent expense-Selling space
Rent on factory building
Rent payable
8,000
$ 9,000

Interactive Presentations: The interactive presentations provide engaging narratives of all chapter learning objectives in an interactive online format. The presentations are tied specifically to *Fundamental Accounting Principles*, 20e. They follow the structure of the text and are organized to match the learning objectives within each chapter. While the interactive presentations are not meant to replace the textbook in this course, they provide additional explanation and enhancement of material from the text chapter, allowing students to learn, study, and practice with instant feedback at their own pace.

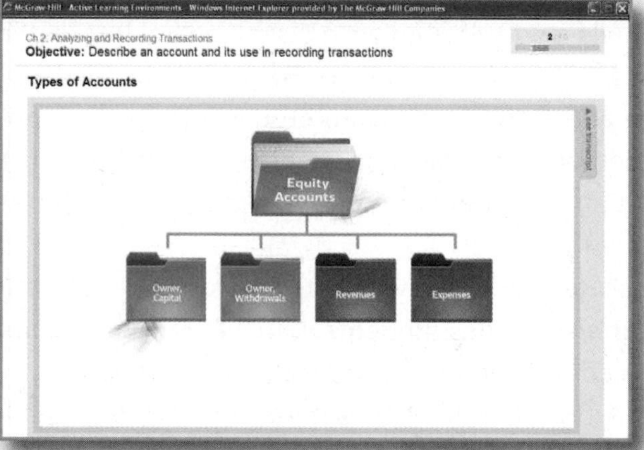

Student Resource Library: The *Connect Accounting* Student Study Center gives access to additional resources such as recorded lectures, online practice materials, an eBook, and more.

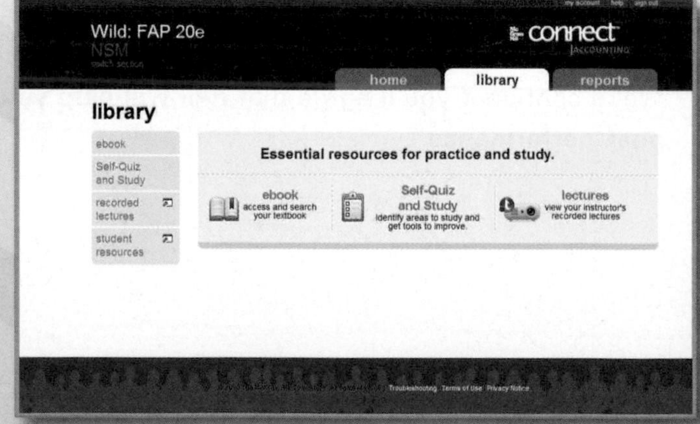

Reach Peak Performance!

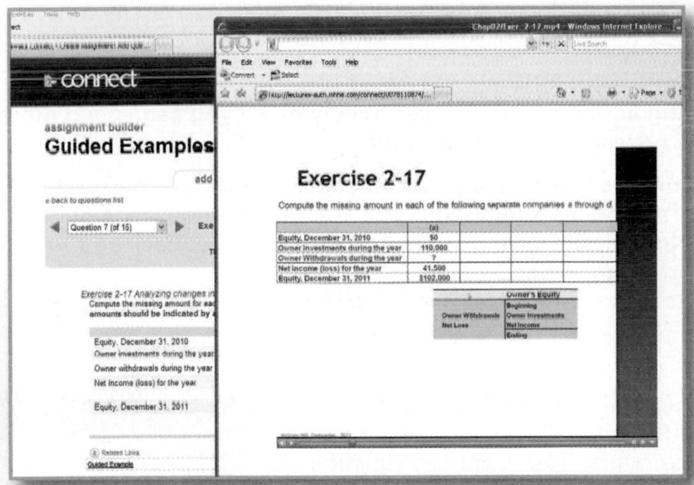

Guided Examples: The Guided Examples in *Connect Accounting* provide a narrated, animated, step-by-step walk-through of select exercises similar to those assigned. These short presentations provide reinforcement when students need it most.

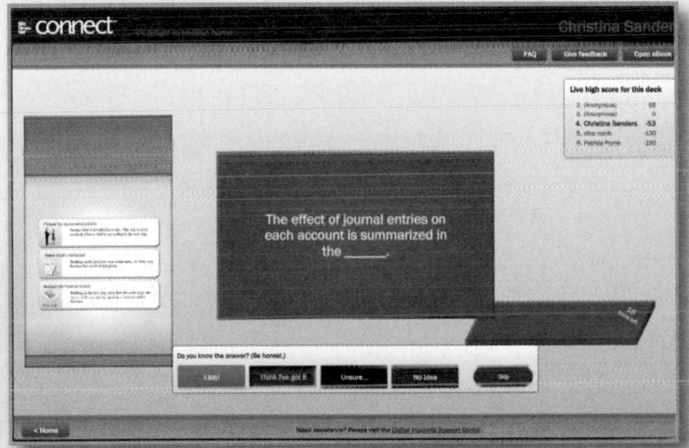

LearnSmart: LearnSmart adaptive self-study technology within *Connect Accounting* helps students make the best use of their study time. LearnSmart provides a seamless combination of practice, assessment, and remediation for every concept in the textbook. LearnSmart's intelligent software adapts to students by supplying questions on a new concept when they are ready to learn it. With LearnSmart, students will spend less time on topics they understand and practice more on those they have yet to master.

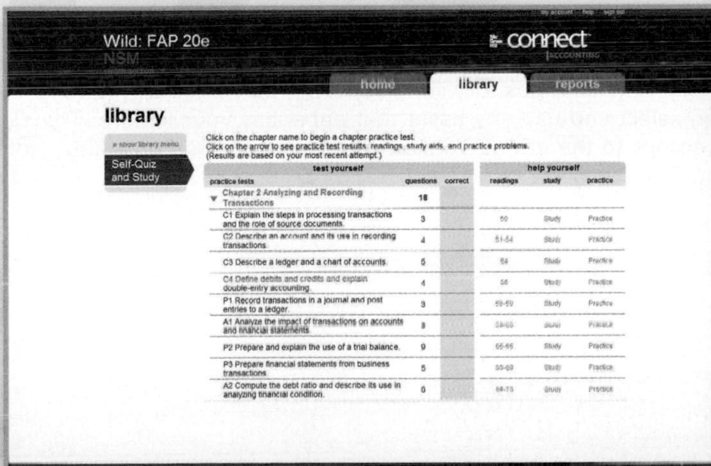

Self-Quiz and Study: The Self-Quiz and Study (SQS) connects students to the learning resources students need to succeed in the course. For each chapter, students can take a practice quiz and immediately see how well they performed. A study plan then recommends specific readings from the text, supplemental study material, and practice exercises that will improve students' understanding and mastery of each learning objective.

Connect Accounting

Connect Accounting offers a number of powerful tools and features to make managing assignments easier, so faculty can spend more time teaching. With *Connect Accounting*, students can engage with their coursework anytime and anywhere, making the learning process more accessible and efficient. (Please see previous page for a description of the student tools available within *Connect Accounting*.)

Simple Assignment Management and Smart Grading

With *Connect Accounting,* creating assignments is easier than ever, so you can spend more time teaching and less time managing. *Connect Accounting* enables you to:

- Create and deliver assignments easily with select end-of-chapter questions and test bank items.
- Go paperless with the eBook and online submission and grading of student assignments.
- Have assignments scored automatically, giving students immediate feedback on their work and side-by-side comparisons with correct answers.
- Reinforce classroom concepts with practice tests and instant quizzes.

Student Reporting

Connect Accounting keeps instructors informed about how each student, section, and class is performing, allowing for more productive use of lecture and office hours. The reporting function enables you to:

- View scored work immediately and track individual or group performance with assignment and grade reports.
- Access an instant view of student or class performance relative to learning objectives.
- Collect data and generate reports required by many accreditation organizations, such as AACSB and AICPA.

© Svetlana Gryankina; iStockphoto

Instructor Library

The *Connect Accounting* Instructor Library is your repository for additional resources to improve student engagement in and out of class. You can select and use any asset that enhances your lecture. The *Connect Accounting* Instructor Library includes: access to the eBook version of the text, PowerPoint files, Solutions Manual, Instructor Resource Manual, and Test Bank.

© David Pedre; iStockphoto

Tools for Instructors

McGraw-Hill *Connect Plus Accounting*

McGraw-Hill reinvents the textbook learning experience for the modern student with *Connect Plus Accounting.* A seamless integration of an eBook and *Connect Accounting, Connect Plus Accounting* provides all of the *Connect Accounting* features plus:

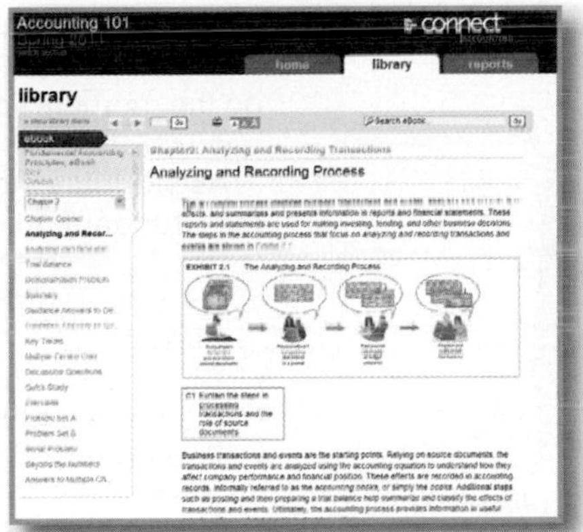

- An integrated eBook, allowing for anytime, anywhere access to the textbook.
- Dynamic links between the problems or questions you assign to your students and the location in the eBook where that problem or question is covered.
- A powerful search function to pinpoint and connect key concepts in a snap.

For more information about *Connect*, go to **www.mcgrawhillconnect.com**, or contact your local McGraw-Hill sales representative.

Tegrity Campus: Lectures 24/7

Tegrity Campus is a service that makes class time available 24/7 by automatically capturing every lecture. With a simple one-click start-and-stop process, you capture all computer screens and corresponding audio in a format that is easily searchable, frame by frame. Students can replay any part of any class with easy-to-use browser-based viewing on a PC or Mac, an iPod, or other mobile device.

Educators know that the more students can see, hear, and experience class resources, the better they learn. In fact, studies prove it. Tegrity Campus's unique search feature helps students efficiently find what they need, when they need it, across an entire semester of class recordings. Help turn your students' study time into learning moments immediately supported by your lecture. With Tegrity Campus, you also increase intent listening and class participation by easing students' concerns about note-taking. Lecture Capture will make it more likely you will see students' faces, not the tops of their heads.

To learn more about Tegrity watch a two-minute Flash demo at **http://tegritycampus.mhhe.com**.

McGraw-Hill Customer Care Contact Information

At McGraw-Hill, we understand that getting the most from new technology can be challenging. That's why our services don't stop after you purchase our products. You can e-mail our Product Specialists 24 hours a day to get product training online. Or you can search our knowledge bank of Frequently Asked Questions on our support Website. For Customer Support, call 800-331-5094 or visit **www.mhhe.com/support**. One of our Technical Support Analysts will be able to assist you in a timely fashion.

How Can Text-Related Web Resources Enrich My Course?

Online Learning Center (OLC)

© Okea; iStockphoto

We offer an Online Learning Center (OLC) that follows *Fundamental Accounting Principles* chapter by chapter. It doesn't require any building or maintenance on your part. It's ready to go the moment you and your students type in the URL:
www.mhhe.com/wildFAP20e

As students study and learn from *Fundamental Accounting Principles*, they can visit the Student Edition of the OLC Website to work with a multitude of helpful tools:

- Generic Template Working Papers
- Chapter Learning Objectives
- Interactive Chapter Quizzes
- PowerPoint® Presentations
- Narrated PowerPoint® Presentations*
- Video Library
- Excel Template Assignments
- iPod Content*

* indicates Premium Content

A secured Instructor Edition stores essential course materials to save you prep time before class. Everything you need to run a lively classroom and an efficient course is included. All resources available to students, plus . . .

- Instructor's Resource Manual
- Solutions Manual
- Solutions to Excel Template Assignments
- Test Bank
- Solutions to CYGL, Peachtree, and QuickBooks templates

The OLC Website also serves as a doorway to other technology solutions, like course management systems.

"There are numerous materials and resources available for the instructor. I love how everything is on one Website and there is no need for a CD or different supplements/materials that need to be carried around."

—Jeanine Metzler, Northampton Community College, on the OLC

eCollege℠

Online Course Management

No matter what online course management system you use (WebCT, BlackBoard, or eCollege), we have a course content ePack available for *FAP* 20e. Our new ePacks are specifically designed to make it easy for students to navigate and access content online. They are easier than ever to install on the latest version of the course management system available today.

Don't forget that you can count on the highest level of service from McGraw-Hill. Our online course management specialists are ready to assist you with your online course needs. They provide training and will answer any questions you have throughout the life of your adoption. So try our new ePack for *FAP* 20e and make online course content delivery easy and fun.

CourseSmart

CourseSmart is a new way to find and buy eTextbooks. CourseSmart has the largest selection of eTextbooks available anywhere, offering thousands of the most commonly adopted textbooks from a wide variety of higher education publishers. CourseSmart eTextbooks are available in one standard online reader with full text search, notes, and highlighting, and email tools for sharing between classmates. Visit **www.CourseSmart.com** for more information on ordering.

How Students Can Study On the Go Using Their iPods

iPod Content

Harness the power of one of the most popular technology tools students use today—the Apple iPod. Our innovative approach allows students to download audio and video presentations right into their iPod and take learning materials with them wherever they go. Students just need to visit the Online Learning Center at **www.mhhe.com/wildFAP20e** to download our iPod content. For each chapter of the book they will be able to download audio narrated lecture presentations for use on various versions of iPods. iPod Touch users can even access self-quizzes.

It makes review and study time as easy as putting on headphones.

How Can McGraw-Hill Help Teach My Course Online?

Improve Student Learning Outcomes and Save Instructor Time with ALEKS®

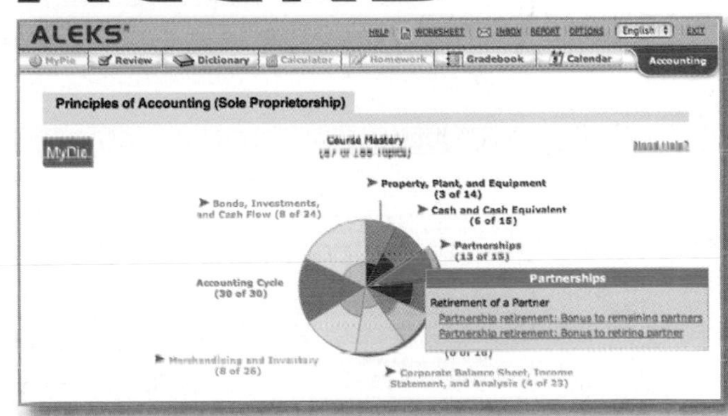

ALEKS is an assessment and learning program that provides individualized instruction in accounting. Available online in partnership with McGraw-Hill/Irwin, ALEKS interacts with students much like a skilled human tutor, with the ability to assess precisely a student's knowledge and provide instruction on the exact topics the student is most ready to learn. By providing topics to meet individual students' needs, allowing students to move between explanation and practice, correcting and analyzing errors, and defining terms, ALEKS helps students to master course content quickly and easily.

ALEKS also includes an Instructor Module with powerful, assignment-driven features and extensive content flexibility. The complimentary Instructor Module provides a course calendar, a customizable gradebook with automatically graded homework, textbook integration, and dynamic reports to monitor student and class progress. ALEKS simplifies course management and allows instructors to spend less time with administrative tasks and more time directing student learning.

To learn more about ALEKS, visit **www.aleks.com/highered/business.**

ALEKS is a registered trademark of ALEKS Corporation.

Innovative Textbook Features

Using Accounting for Decisions

Whether we prepare, analyze, or apply accounting information, one skill remains essential: decision-making. To help develop good decision-making habits and to illustrate the relevance of accounting, our book uses a unique pedagogical framework we call the Decision Center. This framework is comprised of a variety of approaches and subject areas, giving students insight into every aspect of business decision-making; see three examples to the right and one below. Answers to Decision Maker and Ethics boxes are at the end of each chapter.

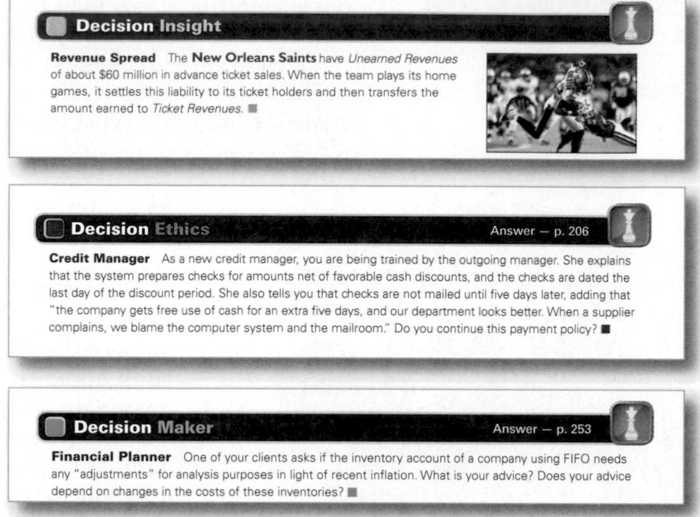

Decision Insight

Revenue Spread The **New Orleans Saints** have *Unearned Revenues* of about $60 million in advance ticket sales. When the team plays its home games, it settles this liability to its ticket holders and then transfers the amount earned to *Ticket Revenues*. ■

Decision Ethics Answer — p. 206

Credit Manager As a new credit manager, you are being trained by the outgoing manager. She explains that the system prepares checks for amounts net of favorable cash discounts, and the checks are dated the last day of the discount period. She also tells you that checks are not mailed until five days later, adding that "the company gets free use of cash for an extra five days, and our department looks better. When a supplier complains, we blame the computer system and the mailroom." Do you continue this payment policy? ■

Decision Maker Answer — p. 253

Financial Planner One of your clients asks if the inventory account of a company using FIFO needs any "adjustments" for analysis purposes in light of recent inflation. What is your advice? Does your advice depend on changes in the costs of these inventories? ■

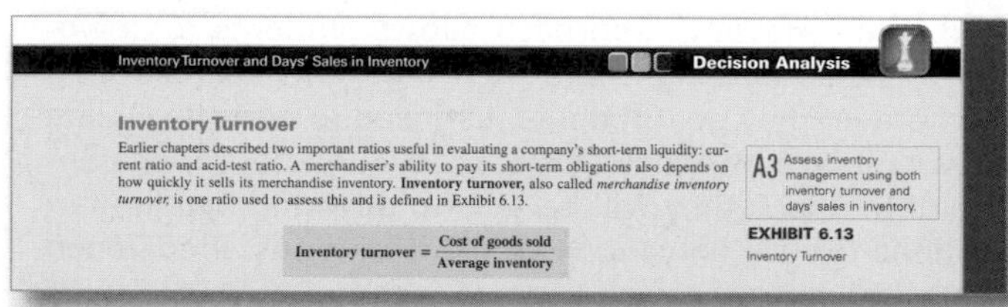

Inventory Turnover and Days' Sales in Inventory — **Decision Analysis**

Inventory Turnover

Earlier chapters described two important ratios useful in evaluating a company's short-term liquidity: current ratio and acid-test ratio. A merchandiser's ability to pay its short-term obligations also depends on how quickly it sells its merchandise inventory. **Inventory turnover,** also called *merchandise inventory turnover,* is one ratio used to assess this and is defined in Exhibit 6.13.

A3 Assess inventory management using both inventory turnover and days' sales in inventory.

$$\text{Inventory turnover} = \frac{\text{Cost of goods sold}}{\text{Average inventory}}$$

EXHIBIT 6.13
Inventory Turnover

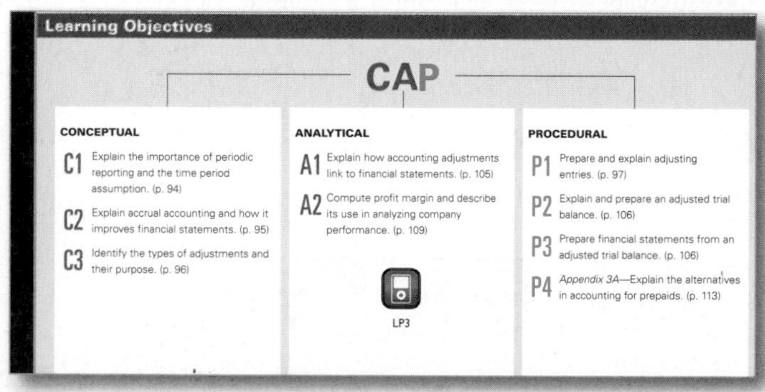

Learning Objectives

CAP

CONCEPTUAL	ANALYTICAL	PROCEDURAL
C1 Explain the importance of periodic reporting and the time period assumption. (p. 94)	A1 Explain how accounting adjustments link to financial statements. (p. 105)	P1 Prepare and explain adjusting entries. (p. 97)
C2 Explain accrual accounting and how it improves financial statements. (p. 95)	A2 Compute profit margin and describe its use in analyzing company performance. (p. 109)	P2 Explain and prepare an adjusted trial balance. (p. 106)
C3 Identify the types of adjustments and their purpose. (p. 96)	LP3	P3 Prepare financial statements from an adjusted trial balance. (p. 106)
		P4 *Appendix 3A*—Explain the alternatives in accounting for prepaids. (p. 113)

CAP Model

The Conceptual/Analytical/Procedural (CAP) Model allows courses to be specially designed to meet your teaching needs or those of a diverse faculty. This model identifies learning objectives, textual materials, assignments, and test items by C, A, or P, allowing different instructors to teach from the same materials, yet easily customize their courses toward a conceptual, analytical, or procedural approach (or a combination thereof) based on personal preferences.

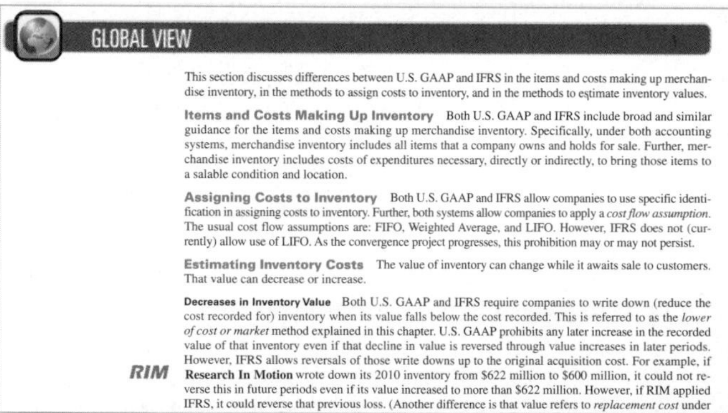

GLOBAL VIEW

This section discusses differences between U.S. GAAP and IFRS in the items and costs making up merchandise inventory, in the methods to assign costs to inventory, and in the methods to estimate inventory values.

Items and Costs Making Up Inventory Both U.S. GAAP and IFRS include broad and similar guidance for the items and costs making up merchandise inventory. Specifically, under both accounting systems, merchandise inventory includes all items that a company owns and holds for sale. Further, merchandise inventory includes costs of expenditures necessary, directly or indirectly, to bring those items to a salable condition and location.

Assigning Costs to Inventory Both U.S. GAAP and IFRS allow companies to use specific identification in assigning costs to inventory. Further, both systems allow companies to apply a *cost flow assumption*. The usual cost flow assumptions are: FIFO, Weighted Average, and LIFO. However, IFRS does not (currently) allow use of LIFO. As the convergence project progresses, this prohibition may or may not persist.

Estimating Inventory Costs The value of inventory can change while it awaits sale to customers. That value can decrease or increase.

Decreases in Inventory Value Both U.S. GAAP and IFRS require companies to write down (reduce the cost recorded for) inventory when its value falls below the cost recorded. This is referred to as the *lower of cost or market* method explained in this chapter. U.S. GAAP prohibits any later increase in the recorded value of that inventory even if that decline in value is reversed through value increases in later periods. However, IFRS allows reversals of those write downs up to the original acquisition cost. For example, if **Research In Motion** wrote down its 2010 inventory from $622 million to $600 million, it could not reverse this in future periods even if its value increased to more than $622 million. However, if RIM applied IFRS, it could reverse that previous loss. (Another difference is that value refers to *replacement cost* under

RIM

New Global View

This section explains international accounting practices relating to the material covered in that chapter. This section is purposefully located at the end of each chapter so that each instructor can decide what emphasis, if at all, is to be assigned to it. The aim of this Global View section is to describe accounting practices and to identify the similarities and differences in international accounting practices versus that in the U.S. As we move toward global convergence in accounting practices, and as we witness the likely conversion of U.S. GAAP to IFRS, the importance of student familiarity with international accounting grows. This innovative section helps us begin down that path of learning and teaching global accounting practices.

"...the chapter openers are absolutely excellent and include entrepreneurs that the students can easily relate to. This helps the students understand the need/importance of accounting in a small business."

—**Michelle Grant, Bossier Parish Community College**

Bring Accounting To Life

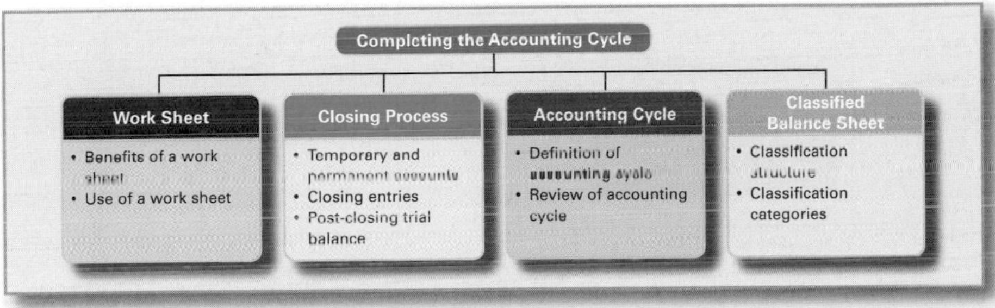

Chapter Preview With Flowchart

This feature provides a handy textual/visual guide at the start of every chapter. Students can now begin their reading with a clear understanding of what they will learn and when, allowing them to stay more focused and organized along the way.

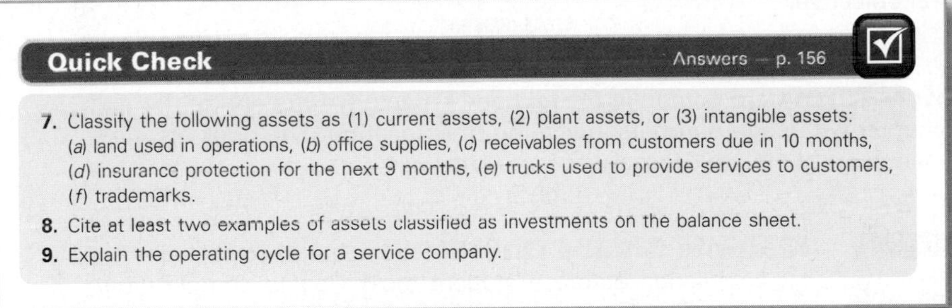

Quick Check Answers — p. 156

7. Classify the following assets as (1) current assets, (2) plant assets, or (3) intangible assets: (*a*) land used in operations, (*b*) office supplies, (*c*) receivables from customers due in 10 months, (*d*) insurance protection for the next 9 months, (*e*) trucks used to provide services to customers, (*f*) trademarks.
8. Cite at least two examples of assets classified as investments on the balance sheet.
9. Explain the operating cycle for a service company.

Quick Check

These short question/answer features reinforce the material immediately preceding them. They allow the reader to pause and reflect on the topics described, then receive immediate feedback before going on to new topics. Answers are provided at the end of each chapter.

"The author(s) are doing an excellent job of using learning and study aids. The examples are real-world and easy to understand. I cannot think of anything else that I would add."

—**Shirly Kleiner, Johnson County Community College**

g transactions is to post journal entries to
ledger is up-to-date, entries are posted as
en time permits. All entries must be posted
l to ensure that account balances are up-to-
bits in journal entries are transferred into

Point: Computerized systems often provide a code beside a balance such as *dr.* or *cr.* to identify its balance. Posting is automatic and immediate with accounting software.

Marginal Student Annotations

These annotations provide students with additional hints, tips, and examples to help them more fully understand the concepts and retain what they have learned. The annotations also include notes on global implications of accounting and further examples.

Outstanding Assignment Material

Once a student has finished reading the chapter, how well he or she retains the material can depend greatly on the questions, exercises, and problems that reinforce it. This book leads the way in comprehensive, accurate assignments.

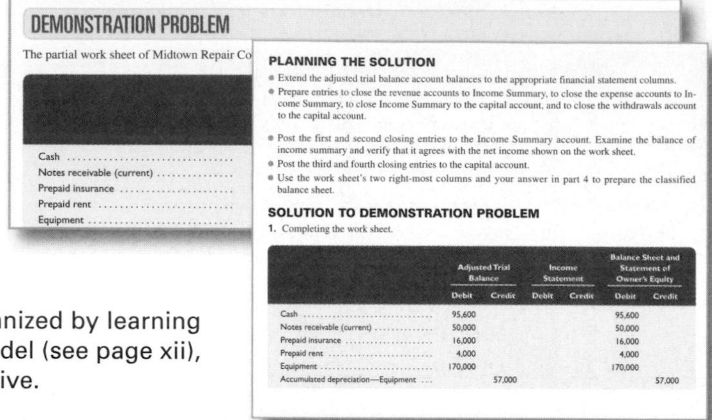

DEMONSTRATION PROBLEM

The partial work sheet of Midtown Repair Co

PLANNING THE SOLUTION

- Extend the adjusted trial balance account balances to the appropriate financial statement columns.
- Prepare entries to close the revenue accounts to Income Summary, to close the expense accounts to Income Summary, to close Income Summary to the capital account, and to close the withdrawals account to the capital account.
- Post the first and second closing entries to the Income Summary account. Examine the balance of income summary and verify that it agrees with the net income shown on the work sheet.
- Post the third and fourth closing entries to the capital account.
- Use the work sheet's two right-most columns and your answer in part 4 to prepare the classified balance sheet.

SOLUTION TO DEMONSTRATION PROBLEM

1. Completing the work sheet.

	Adjusted Trial Balance		Income Statement		Balance Sheet and Statement of Owner's Equity	
	Debit	Credit	Debit	Credit	Debit	Credit
Cash	95,600				95,600	
Notes receivable (current)	50,000				50,000	
Prepaid insurance	16,000				16,000	
Prepaid rent	4,000				4,000	
Equipment	170,000				170,000	
Accumulated depreciation—Equipment		57,000				57,000

Demonstration Problems present both a problem and a complete solution, allowing students to review the entire problem-solving process and achieve success.

Chapter Summaries provide students with a review organized by learning objectives. Chapter Summaries are a component of the CAP model (see page xii), which recaps each conceptual, analytical, and procedural objective.

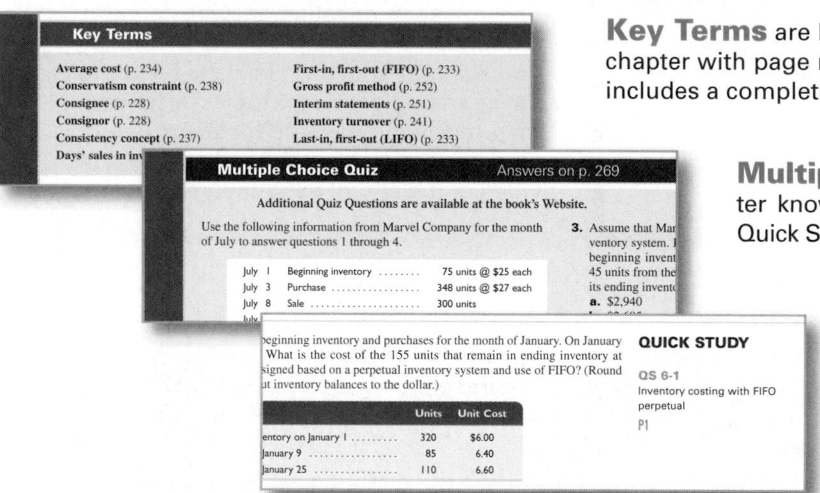

Key Terms

Average cost (p. 234)
Conservatism constraint (p. 238)
Consignee (p. 228)
Consignor (p. 228)
Consistency concept (p. 237)
Days' sales in in
First-in, first-out (FIFO) (p. 233)
Gross profit method (p. 252)
Interim statements (p. 251)
Inventory turnover (p. 241)
Last-in, first-out (LIFO) (p. 233)

Multiple Choice Quiz — Answers on p. 269

Additional Quiz Questions are available at the book's Website.

Use the following information from Marvel Company for the month of July to answer questions 1 through 4.

July 1	Beginning inventory	75 units @ $25 each
July 3	Purchase	348 units @ $27 each
July 8	Sale	300 units

3. Assume that Mar ventory system. beginning invent 45 units from the its ending invento
a. $2,940

QUICK STUDY

QS 6-1
Inventory costing with FIFO perpetual
P1

beginning inventory and purchases for the month of January. On January What is the cost of the 155 units that remain in ending inventory at signed based on a perpetual inventory system and use of FIFO? (Round it inventory balances to the dollar.)

	Units	Unit Cost
entory on January 1	320	$6.00
January 9	85	6.40
January 25	110	6.60

Key Terms are bolded in the text and repeated at the end of the chapter with page numbers indicating their location. The book also includes a complete Glossary of Key Terms.

Multiple Choice Quiz Questions quickly test chapter knowledge before a student moves on to complete Quick Studies, Exercises, and Problems.

Quick Study assignments are short exercises that often focus on one learning objective. Most are included in *Connect Accounting*. There are usually 8-10 Quick Study assignments per chapter.

Exercises are one of this book's many strengths and a competitive advantage. There are about 10-15 per chapter and most are included in *Connect Accounting*.

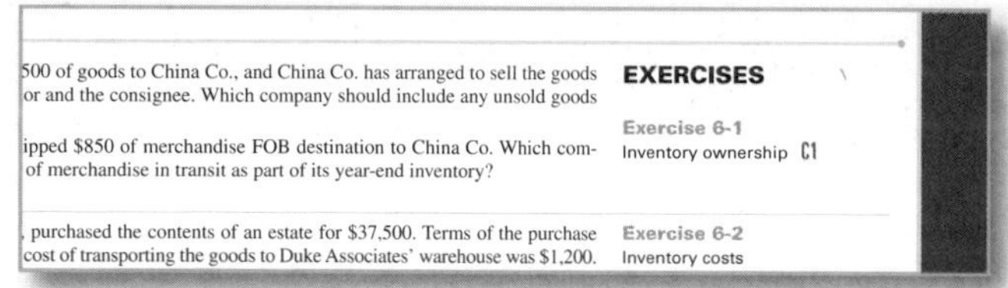

EXERCISES

500 of goods to China Co., and China Co. has arranged to sell the goods or and the consignee. Which company should include any unsold goods

Exercise 6-1
Inventory ownership C1

ipped $850 of merchandise FOB destination to China Co. Which com- of merchandise in transit as part of its year-end inventory?

purchased the contents of an estate for $37,500. Terms of the purchase cost of transporting the goods to Duke Associates' warehouse was $1,200.

Exercise 6-2
Inventory costs

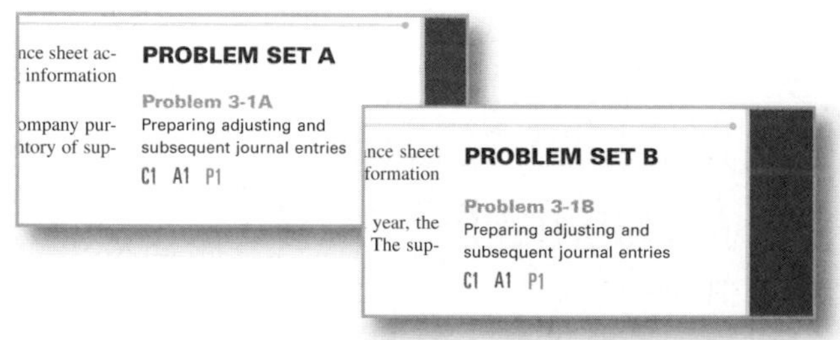

PROBLEM SET A

nce sheet ac- information

ompany pur- ntory of sup-

Problem 3-1A
Preparing adjusting and subsequent journal entries
C1 A1 P1

PROBLEM SET B

nce sheet formation

year, the The sup-

Problem 3-1B
Preparing adjusting and subsequent journal entries
C1 A1 P1

Problem Sets A & B are proven problems that can be assigned as homework or for in-class projects. All problems are coded according to the CAP model (see page xii), and Set A is included in *Connect Accounting.*

PUT AWAY YOUR RED PEN!

We pride ourselves on the accuracy of this book's assignment materials. Independent research reports that instructors and reviewers point to the accuracy of this book's assignment materials as one of its key competitive advantages.

Helps Students Master Key Concepts

Beyond the Numbers exercises ask students to use accounting figures and understand their meaning. Students also learn how accounting applies to a variety of business situations. These creative and fun exercises are all new or updated, and are divided into sections:

- Reporting in Action
- Comparative Analysis
- Ethics Challenge
- Communicating in Practice
- Taking It To The Net
- Teamwork in Action
- Hitting the Road
- Entrepreneurial Decision
- Global Decision

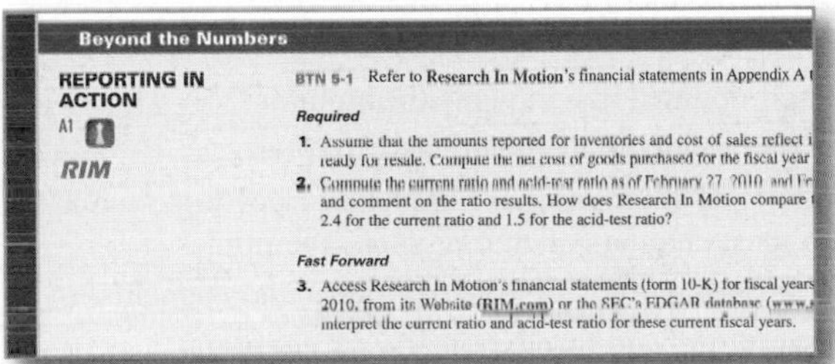
Beyond the Numbers

REPORTING IN ACTION
A1
RIM

BTN 5-1 Refer to **Research In Motion**'s financial statements in Appendix A t

Required

1. Assume that the amounts reported for inventories and cost of sales reflect i ready for resale. Compute the net cost of goods purchased for the fiscal year
2. Compute the current ratio and acid-test ratio as of February 27, 2010, and Fe and comment on the ratio results. How does Research In Motion compare t 2.4 for the current ratio and 1.5 for the acid-test ratio?

Fast Forward

3. Access Research In Motion's financial statements (form 10-K) for fiscal years 2010, from its Website (RIM.com) or the SEC's EDGAR database (www. interpret the current ratio and acid-test ratio for these current fiscal years.

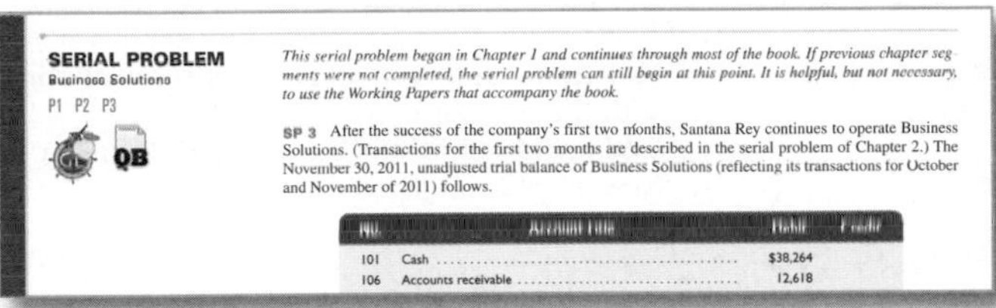
SERIAL PROBLEM
Business Solutions
P1 P2 P3

This serial problem began in Chapter 1 and continues through most of the book. If previous chapter segments were not completed, the serial problem can still begin at this point. It is helpful, but not necessary, to use the Working Papers that accompany the book.

SP 3 After the success of the company's first two months, Santana Rey continues to operate Business Solutions. (Transactions for the first two months are described in the serial problem of Chapter 2.) The November 30, 2011, unadjusted trial balance of Business Solutions (reflecting its transactions for October and November of 2011) follows.

No.	Account Title	Debit	Credit
101	Cash	$38,264	
106	Accounts receivable	12,618	

Serial Problem uses a continuous running case study to illustrate chapter concepts in a familiar context. The Serial Problem can be followed continuously from the first chapter or picked up at any later point in the book; enough information is provided to ensure students can get right to work.

> "Well planned, and very organized. A very thorough coverage of all topics. Easy to read and comprehend."
>
> **— Linda Bolduc, Mount Wachusett Community College**

The End of the Chapter Is Only the Beginning Our valuable and proven assignments aren't just confined to the book. From problems that require technological solutions to materials found exclusively online, this book's end-of-chapter material is fully integrated with its technology package.

- Quick Studies, Exercises, and Problems available in *Connect* are marked with an icon.

- Problems supported by the General Ledger Application Software, Peachtree, or Quickbooks are marked with an icon.

- Online Learning Center (OLC) includes Interactive Quizzes, Excel template assignments, and more.

- Problems supported with Microsoft Excel template assignments are marked with an icon.

- Material that receives additional coverage (slide shows, videos, audio, etc.) available in iPod ready format are marked with an icon.

- Assignments that focus on global accounting practices and companies are often identified with an icon.

The authors extend a special thanks to accuracy checkers Barbara Schnathorst, The Write Solution, Inc.; Helen Roybark, Radford University; Beth Woods, CPA, Accuracy Counts; and David Krug, Johnson County Community College.

Enhancements in This Edition

This edition's revisions are driven by instructors and students. General revisions to the entire book follow (including chapter-by-chapter revisions):

- Revised and updated assignments throughout
- Updated ratio (tool) analyses for each chapter
- New material on International Financial Reporting Standards (IFRS) in most chapters, including global examples
- New and revised entrepreneurial examples and elements
- Revised serial problem through nearly all chapters
- New art program, visual info-graphics and text layout
- New Research In Motion (maker of BlackBerry) annual report with comparisons to Apple, Palm, and Nokia (IFRS) with new assignments
- Updated graphics added to each chapter's analysis section
- New technology content integrated and referenced in the book
- New Global View section in each chapter referencing international accounting including examples using global companies
- New assignments covering international accounting

Chapter 1

Facebook NEW opener with new entrepreneurial assignment
Streamlined and consolidated learning objectives
New section on International Standards and convergence
Revised section on accounting principles, assumptions, and constraints
New visual layouts for conceptual framework and the building blocks of GAAP
New discussion of conceptual framework linked to IFRSs
New graphic discussing fraud control in accounting
Updated compensation data in exhibit

Chapter 2

CitySlips NEW opener with new entrepreneurial assignment
Reorganized and streamlined learning objectives
Revised introduction of double-entry accounting
New 4-step process for analyzing, recording, and posting transactions
Revised layout for transaction analysis
New discussion on accounting quality

Chapter 3

Cheezburger Network NEW opener with new entrepreneurial assignment
Updated 3-step process for adjusting accounts
Enhanced and streamlined presentation of accounting adjustments
Revised info-graphics for adjusting entries
Enhanced exhibit on steps in preparing financial statements
Expanded discussion of global accounting

Chapter 4

Gamer Grub NEW opener with new entrepreneurial assignment
Slightly revised steps 1 and 2 of work sheet
Enhanced graphics for closing process
Enhanced details for general ledger after the closing process
Updated color-coded work sheet

Chapter 5

Heritage Link Brands NEW opener with new entrepreneurial assignment
Streamlined learning objectives
New 2-step presentation for recording merchandise sales and its costs
Revised presentation on purchase returns
New discussion on fraud and invoices
Revised discussion of gross margin

Chapter 6

Fitness Anywhere NEW opener with new entrepreneurial assignment
Streamlined presentation for lower of cost or market (LCM)
Color-coded graphic for introducing cost flow assumptions
Enhanced graphics for learning inventory errors
Expanded discussion on inventory controls
Expanded explanation of inventory accounting under IFRS

Chapter 7

New Belgium Brewing Company NEW opener with new entrepreneurial assignment
Streamlined learning objectives
Enhanced graphics for special journals
Detailed four benefits from subsidiary ledgers
Updated ERP presentation
Revised discussion of segment returns

Chapter 8

Dylan's Candy Bar REVISED opener with new entrepreneurial assignment
Enhanced SOX discussion of controls, including the role of COSO
Streamlined learning objectives
New material on drivers of human fraud
New graphic introducing a bank reconciliation with links to bank and book balances
Updated graphic on frequent cyber frauds
New graphic on drivers of financial misconduct

Chapter 9

LaserMonks NEW opener with new entrepreneurial assignment
Streamlined learning objectives
Reorganized recording of credit sales
Further clarification of interest formula
Enhanced graphics for bad debts estimation

Chapter 10

Games2U NEW opener with new entrepreneurial assignment
Reorganized learning objectives
Added entry to record impairment
Enhanced discussion of asset sales
Expanded explanation of asset valuation under IFRS
Updated all real world examples and graphics

Chapter 11

SnorgTees NEW opener with new entrepreneurial assignment
Updated tax illustrations and assignments using most recent government rates
New data on frauds involving employee payroll
New entry to reclassify long- to short-term debt
Updated all real world examples and graphics

Chapter 12

Kids Konserve NEW opener with new entrepreneurial assignment
New 3-step process for partnership liquidation
New *statement of liquidation* introduced
Enhanced discussion of partnership liquidation

For Better Learning

Chapter 13

Clean Air Lawn Care NEW opener with new entrepreneurial assignment
Streamlined learning objectives
Inserted numerous key margin computations for entries involving equity
Updated statement of stockholders' equity
Updated all real world examples and graphics
Explained accounting for equity under IFRS

Chapter 14

CakeLove NEW opener with new entrepreneurial assignment
Enhanced graphics for bonds and notes
Revised discussion of debt-to-equity
Enhanced explanation of how U.S. GAAP and IFRS determine fair value
New arrow lines linking effective interest amortization tables to journal entries

Chapter 15

Blackboard NEW opener with new entrepreneurial assignment
Streamlined learning objectives
Phrase "fair value" used in lieu of "market value"
Enhanced exhibit summarizing accounting for securities
Revised explanation of investments in securities with significant influence
New, enhanced section on comprehensive income

Chapter 16

Animoto NEW opener with new entrepreneurial assignment
Streamlined learning objectives
Enhanced graphics on cash inflows and outflows involving operating, investing, and financing
Highlighted 5-step process to prepare the statement of cash flows
New discussion of different classifications for certain cash flows under IFRS
Increased number and range of assignments

Chapter 17

Motley Fool REVISED opener with new entrepreneurial assignment
Streamlined learning objectives
New companies— Research In Motion, Apple, Palm and Nokia—data throughout the chapter, exhibits, and illustrations
Enhanced horizontal and vertical analysis using new company and industry data
Enhanced discussion of common-size graphics
Enhanced ratio analysis using new company and industry data

Chapter 18

Hot Box Cookies NEW opener with new entrepreneurial assignment
Revised learning objectives
Enhanced discussion of trends in managerial accounting, including e-commerce and role of services
New exhibit and discussion of the value chain
Discussion of fraud and ethics in managerial accounting moved to earlier in chapter
New discussion of global trends in managerial accounting

Chapter 19

Liberty Tax Service NEW opener with new entrepreneurial assignment
Enhanced explanation of events in job order costing, including new 3-step process
Added new arrow lines to exhibits as learning aids
Enhanced discussion of adjusting factory overhead
New factory overhead T-account exhibit
New exhibit on entries to adjust factory overhead account
Added several new assignments

Chapter 20

IdeaPaint NEW opener with new entrepreneurial assignment
Streamlined learning objectives
Updated list of companies applying process operations
Enhanced several exhibits for better learning
New section on trends in process operations, including discussion of just-in-time, automation, role of services, and customer focus
Increased number and range of assignments

Chapter 21

Skullcandy NEW opener with new entrepreneurial assignment
Streamlined learning objectives
Enhanced activity-based costing exhibits
Revised discussion and exhibits for comparisons between activity-based costing and two-stage cost allocation
Added summary of cost allocation methods with exhibit
Deleted section on departmental reporting and analysis
Added Serial Problem to end of chapter assignments

Chapter 22

Johnny Cupcakes NEW opener with new entrepreneurial assignment
Streamlined learning objectives
Revised cost exhibits for added clarity and learning
New discussion on global use of contribution margin

Chapter 23

Smathers and Branson NEW opener with new entrepreneurial assignment
Reorganized learning objectives
New discussion on potential outcomes of participatory budgeting
Enhanced discussion and exhibits for cash budgets
New exhibit on general formula for preparing the cash budget
Added Decision Insight box on Apple's cash cushion
Enhanced discussion of computing cash disbursements for purchases, including new exhibit
Increased number and range of assignments

Chapter 24

SewWhat? NEW opener with new entrepreneurial assignment
Streamlined learning objectives
Simplified presentation of overhead variances to focus on controllable and volume variances
Moved detailed overhead variances and standard cost system journal entries to (new) Appendix 24A
Increased number and range of assignments

Chapter 25

Dogswell NEW opener with new entrepreneurial assignment
Streamlined learning objectives
Updated graphic on industry cost of capital estimates
Added section and assignments on decision to keep or replace equipment
Increased number and range of assignments

Instructor Supplements

Instructor's Resource CD-ROM

Chapters 1-25
ISBN13: 978007338107
ISBN10: 0077338103

This is your all-in-one resource. It allows you to create custom presentations from your own materials or from the following text-specific materials provided in the CD's asset library:

- **Instructor's Resource Manual**
  Written by Barbara Chiappetta, Nassau Community College, and Patricia Walczak, Lansing Community College.
  This manual contains (for each chapter) a Lecture Outline, a chart linking all assignment materials to Learning Objectives, a list of relevant active learning activities, and additional visuals with transparency masters.
- **Solutions Manual**
- **Test Bank, Computerized Test Bank**
- **PowerPoint® Presentations**
  Prepared by Jon Booker, Charles Caldwell, Cindy Rooney, and Susan Galbreth.
  Presentations allow for revision of lecture slides, and includes a viewer, allowing screens to be shown with or without the software.
- **Link to PageOut**

Test Bank

Vol. 1, Chapters 1-12
ISBN13: 9780077338183
ISBN10: 0077338189

Vol. 2, Chapters 13-25
ISBN13: 9780077338190
ISBN10: 0077338197

Revised by Barbara Gershowitz, Nashville State Technical Community College.

Solutions Manual

Vol. 1, Chapters 1-12
ISBN13: 9780077338152
ISBN10: 0077338154

Vol. 2, Chapters 13-25
ISBN13: 9780077338145
ISBN10: 0077338146

Written by John J. Wild, Ken W. Shaw, and Anita Kroll, University of Wisconsin–Madison.

Student Supplements

Excel Working Papers CD

ISBN13: 9780077338084
ISBN10: 0077338081

Written by John J. Wild.

Working Papers (for Chapters 1-25) delivered in Excel spreadsheets. These Excel Working Papers are available on CD-ROM and can be bundled with the printed Working Papers; see your representative for information.

Working Papers

Vol. 1, Chapters 1-12
ISBN13: 9780077338220
ISBN10: 0077338227

Vol. 2, Chapters 12-25
ISBN13: 9780077338206
ISBN10: 0077338200

Principles of Financial Accounting Chapters 1-17
ISBN13: 9780077338213
ISBN10: 0077338219

Written by John J. Wild.

Study Guide

Vol. 1, Chapters 1-12
ISBN13: 9780077338169
ISBN10: 0077338162

Vol. 2, Chapters 12-25
ISBN13: 9780077338176
ISBN10: 0077338170

Written by Barbara Chiapetta, Nassau Community College, and Patricia Walczak, Lansing Community College.

Covers each chapter and appendix with reviews of the learning objectives, outlines of the chapters, summaries of chapter materials, and additional problems with solutions.

Carol Yacht's General Ledger CD-ROM

ISBN13: 9780077338039
ISBN10: 0077338030

The CD-ROM includes fully functioning versions of McGraw-Hill's own General Ledger Application software. Problem templates prepared by Carol Yacht and student user guides are included that allow you to assign text problems for working in Yacht's General Ledger or Peachtree.

QuickBooks Pro 2011 Student Guide and Templates

ISBN13: 9780077455309
ISBN10: 0077455304

Prepared by Carol Yacht.

To better prepare students for accounting in the real world, select end-of-chapter material in the text is tied to QuickBooks software. The accompanying student guide provides a step-by-step walkthrough for students on how to complete the problem in the software.

Assurance of Learning Ready

Many educational institutions today are focused on the notion of assurance of learning, an important element of some accreditation standards. *Fundamental Accounting Principles* is designed specifically to support your assurance of learning initiatives with a simple, yet powerful solution. Each test bank question for *Fundamental Accounting Principles* maps to a specific chapter learning objective listed in the text. You can use our test bank software, EZ Test and EZ Test Online, or *Connect Accounting* to easily query for learning objectives that directly relate to the learning objectives for your course. You can then use the reporting features of EZ Test to aggregate student results in similar fashion, making the collection and presentation of assurance of learning data simple and easy.

"Best on the market! Great examples, complete coverage of principle's topics, and great resources!"

— **David Alldredge, Salt Lake Community College**

AACSB Statement

The McGraw-Hill Companies is a proud corporate member of AACSB International. Understanding the importance and value of AACSB accreditation, *Fundamental Accounting Principles* recognizes the curricula guidelines detailed in the AACSB standards for business accreditation by connecting selected questions in the test bank to the six general knowledge and skill guidelines in the AACSB standards. The statements contained in *Fundamental Accounting Principles* are provided only as a guide for the users of this textbook. The AACSB leaves content coverage and assessment within the purview of individual schools, the mission of the school, and the faculty. While *Fundamental Accounting Principles* and the teaching package make no claim of any specific AACSB qualification or evaluation, we have within *Fundamental Accounting Principles* labeled select questions according to the six general knowledge and skills areas.

The authors extend a special thanks to our contributing and technology supplement authors:
Contributing Author: Anita Kroll, University of Wisconsin–Madison
LearnSmart Authors: Anna Boulware, St. Charles Community College; Brenda Mattison, Tri County Technical College; and Dominique Svarc, William Rainey Harper College
Online Quizzes: Gina Jones, Aims County Community College
Connect Self-Quiz and Study: Jeannine Metzler, Northampton Community College
Interactive Presentations: Kathleen O'Donnell, Onongada Community College, and Jeannie Folk, College of DuPage

Acknowledgments

John J. Wild, Ken W. Shaw, Barbara Chiappetta, and McGraw-Hill/Irwin would like to recognize the following instructors for their valuable feedback and involvement in the development of *Fundamental Accounting Principles* 20e. We are thankful for their suggestions, counsel, and encouragement.

Nelson Alino, Quinnipiac University

David Alldredge, Salt Lake Community College

Sheila Ammons, Austin Community College

Victoria Badura, Chadron State College

Susan Baker, University of Michigan-Dearborn

Charles Scott Barhight, Northampton Community College

Robert Beebe, Morrisville State University

Teri Bernstein, Santa Monica College

Swati Bhandarkar, University of Georgia

Jaswinder Bhangal, Chabot College

Linda Bolduc, Mount Wachusett Community College

Anna Boulware, St. Charles Community College

Philip Brown, Harding University

Jay Buchanon, Burlington County College-Pemberton

Mary Burnell, Fairmont State University

Nathaniel Calloway, University of Maryland

Sal Cardiel, Chaffey College

Lloyd Carroll, Borough of Manhattan Community College

Hong Chen, Northeastern Illinois University

Stanley Chu, Borough of Manhattan Community College

Kwang-Hyun Chung, Pace University

Shiefei Chung, Rowan University

Robert Churchman, Harding University

Marilyn Ciolino, Delgado Community College

Lisa Cole, Johnson County Community College

Howard A. Collins, SUNY at Stony Brook

William Cooper, North Carolina A &T University

Suzie Cordes, Johnson County Community College

James Cosby, John Tyler Community College

Richard Culp, Ball State University

Alan Czyzewski, Indiana State University-Terre Haute

Judy Daulton, Piedmont Technical College

Walter DeAguero, Saddleback College

Mike Deschamps, Mira Costa College

Rosemond Desir, Colorado State University

Vincent Dicalogero, Suffolk County Community College

Roger Dorsey, University of Arkansas-Little Rock

Jap Efendi, University of Texas-Arlington

Terry Elliott Morehead State University

James M. Emig, Villanova University

Steven Englert, Ivy Tech Community College

Caroline Falconetti, Nassau Community College

Stephanie Farewell, University of Arkansas-Little Rock

Laura Farrell, Wagner College

Charles Fazzi, Saint Vincent College

Ronald A. Feinberg, Suffolk Community College

Kathleen Fitzpatrick, University of Toledo-Scott Park

Jeannie Folk, College of DuPage

Mary Foster, Illinois Central College

Mitchell Franklin, Syracuse University

Paul Franklin, Kaplan University Online

Kim Gatzke, Delgado Community College

Rich Geglien, Ivy Tech Community College

Barbara Gershowitz, Nashville State Technical Community College

Richard Gordon, Columbia Southern

Michelle Grant, Bossier Parish Community College

Richard P. Green II, Texas A& M University

Tony Greig, Purdue University

Joyce Griffin, Kansas City Kansas Community College

Lillian Grose, Delgado Community College

Denise Guest, Germanna Community College

Amy Haas, Kingsborough Community College

Betty Habiger, New Mexico State University

Francis Haggerty, Lee College

Betty Harper, Middle Tennessee State University

Jeannie Harrington, Middle Tennessee State University

John L. Haverty, St. Joseph's University

Laurie Hays, Western Michigan University

Shelley Henke, Fox Valley Technical College

Geoffrey Heriot, Greenville Technical College

Lyle Hicks, Danville Area Community College

Cecil Hill, Jackson State University

Patricia Holmes, Des Moines Area Community College

Margaret Houston, Wright State University

Constance Hylton, George Mason University

Gary Allen Hypes, Mount Aloysius College

Catherine Jeppson, Caifornia State University–Northridge

Gina M. Jones, Aims Community College

Rita Jones, Columbus State University

Christine Jonick, Gainesville State College

Thomas Kam, Hawaii Pacific University

Jack Karbens, Hawaii Pacific University

Connie Kelt, San Juan College

Karen Kettelson, Western Technical College

Randy Kidd, Longview Community College

Irene Kim, George Washington University

James Kinard, Ohio State University-Columbus

Rita Kingery-Cook, University of Delaware

Frank Klaus, Cleveland State University

Shirly A. Kleiner, Johnson County Community College

Robert F. Koch, Saint Peter's College

Phillip Korb, University of Baltimore

David Krug, Johnson County Community College

Jill Kolody, Anne Arundel Community College

Charles Lacey, Henry Ford Community College

Tara Laken, Joliet Junior College

Beth Lasky, Delgado Community College
Phillip Lee, Nashville State Technical Community College
Jerry Lehman, Madison Area Technical College
Frederic Lerner, New York University
Roger Lewis, West Virginia University-Parkersburg
Eric Lindquist, Lansing Community College
Jeannie Liu, Chaffey College
Rebecca Lohmann, Southeast Missouri State University
Debra Luna, El Paso Community College
Sylvester A. Maorino, SUNY Westchester Community College
Thomas S. Marsh, Northern Virginia Community College-Annadale
Stacie Mayes, Rose State College
Brenda Mattison, Tri-County Technical College
Jeanine Metzler, Northampton Community College
Kathleen Michele, Prairieville University
Tim Miller, El Camino College
Roger L. Moore, Arkansas State University-Beebe
Robbie Morse, Ivy Tech Community College
Linda Muren, Cuyahoga Community College—West Campus
Andrea Murowski, Brookdale Community College
Ramesh Narasimhan, Montclair State University
Mary Beth Nelson, North Shore Community College
Deborah Niemer, Oakland Community College
Kathleen O'Donnell, Onongada Community College
Ahmed Omar, Burlington County College
Deborah Pauly, Loras College
Joel Peralto, Hawaii Community College
Yvonne Phang, Borough of Manhattan Community College
Gary Pieroni, Diablo Valley College
Susan Pope, University of Akron
Jean Price, Marshall University
Debbie Rankin, Lincoln University
Susan Reeves, University of South Carolina
Jenny Resnick, Santa Monica College
Ruthie Reynolds, Howard University
Carla Rich, Pensacola Junior College
Paul Rivers, Bunker Hill Community College
Jill Roberts, Campbellsville University
Karen Robinson, Morgan State University
Richard Roding, Red Rocks Community College
Joel Rosenfeld, New York University
Pamela Rouse, Butler University
Helen Roybark, Radford University
Alphonse Ruggiero, Suffolk County Community College
Martin Sabo, Community College of Denver
Judith Sage, Texas A&M International University
Nathaniel Samba, Ivy Tech Community College
Linda Schain, Hoefstra University
Christine Schalow, University of Wisconsin-Stevens Point
Bunney Schmidt, Keiser University
Geeta Shankhar, University of Dayton
Regina Shea, Community College of Baltimore County—Essex
Jay Siegel, Union County College
Lois Slutsky, Broward College-South
Gerald Smith, University of Northern Iowa
Kathleen Sobieralski, University of Maryland
Charles Spector, State University of New York College
Jane Stam, Onondaga Community College
Douglas P. Stives, Monmouth University
Jacqueline Stoute, Baruch University
Beverly Strachan, Troy University
John Suckow, Lansing Community College
Dominique Svarc, William Rainey Harper College
Anthony Teng, Saddleback College
Sue Terizan, Wright State University
Leslie Thysell, John Tyler Community College
Michael Ulinski, Pace University-Pleasantville
Bob Urell, Irvine Valley College
Alonda Vaughn, Strayer University Tampa East
Ari Vega, Fashion Institute of Technology
Adam Vitalis, University of Wisconsin
Patricia Walczak, Lansing Community College
Li Wang, University of Akron
Doris Warmflash, SUNY Westchester Community College
David Welch, Franklin University
Jean Wells, Howard University
Robert A. Widman, Brooklyn College CUNY
Christopher Widmer, Tidewater Community College
Jane Wiese, Valencia Community College
Kenneth L. Wild, University of London
Scott Williams, County College of Morris
Wanda Wong, Chabot College
Darryl Woolley, University of Idaho
Gloria Worthy, Southwest Tennessee Community College-Macon
Lorenzo Ybarra, West Los Angeles College
Laura Young, University of Central Arkansas
Judy Zander, Grossmont College

In addition to the helpful and generous colleagues listed above, we thank the entire McGraw-Hill/Irwin *Fundamental Accounting Principles* 20e team, including Stewart Mattson, Tim Vertovec, Steve Schuetz, Christina Sanders, Aaron Downey of Matrix Productions, Lori Koetters, Matthew Baldwin, Carol Bielski, Patricia Plumb, and Brian Nacik. We also thank the great marketing and sales support staff, including Michelle Heaster, Kathleen Klohr, and Simi Dutt. Many talented educators and professionals worked hard to create the supplements for this book, and for their efforts we're grateful. Finally, many more people we either did not meet or whose efforts we did not personally witness nevertheless helped to make this book everything that it is, and we thank them all.

John J. Wild *Ken W. Shaw* *Barbara Chiappetta*

Brief Contents

Contents

We Has Too
KTHXBAI!!

10 Plant Assets, Natural Resources, and Intangibles 392

11 Current Liabilities and Payroll Accounting 434

Fundamental Accounting Principles

Volume 1, Chapters 1–12

1 Accounting in Business

A Look at This Chapter

Accounting is crucial in our information age. In this chapter, we discuss the importance of accounting to different types of organizations and describe its many users and uses. We explain that ethics are essential to accounting. We also explain business transactions and how they are reflected in financial statements.

A Look Ahead

Chapter 2 describes and analyzes business transactions. We explain the analysis and recording of transactions, the ledger and trial balance, and the double-entry system. More generally, Chapters 2 through 4 show (via the accounting cycle) how financial statements reflect business activities.

Learning Objectives

***Learning Objectives** are classified as conceptual, analytical, or procedural.*

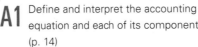

CONCEPTUAL

C1 Explain the purpose and importance of accounting. (p. 4)

C2 Identify users and uses of, and opportunities in, accounting. (p. 5)

C3 Explain why ethics are crucial to accounting. (p. 8)

C4 Explain generally accepted accounting principles and define and apply several accounting principles. (p. 9)

C5 *Appendix 1B*—Identify and describe the three major activities of organizations. (p. 26)

ANALYTICAL

A1 Define and interpret the accounting equation and each of its components. (p. 14)

A2 Compute and interpret return on assets. (p. 22)

A3 *Appendix 1A*—Explain the relation between return and risk. (p. 26)

LP1

PROCEDURAL

P1 Analyze business transactions using the accounting equation. (p. 15)

P2 Identify and prepare basic financial statements and explain how they interrelate. (p. 19)

Decision Insight

*A **Decision Feature** launches each chapter showing the relevance of accounting for a real entrepreneur. An **Entrepreneurial Decision** problem at the end of the assignments returns to this feature with a mini-case.*

Accounting for Facebook

"We are focused on . . . helping people share information"

—MARK ZUCKERBERG

PALO ALTO, CA—"Open Society" conjures up philosophical thoughts and political ideologies. However, for Mark Zuckerberg, his vision of an open society "is to give people the power to share and make the world more open and connected." That vision led Mark to create **Facebook (Facebook.com)** from his college dorm. Today, Facebook is the highest-profile social networking site. Along the way, Mark had to learn accounting and the details of preparing and interpreting financial statements.

"It's all been very interesting," says Mark. Important questions involving business formation, transaction analysis, and financial reporting arose. Mark answered them and in the process has set his company apart. "I'm here to build something for the long term," declares Mark. "Anything else is a distraction."

Information is the focus—both within Facebook and within its accounting records. Mark recalls that when he launched his business, there were "all these reasons why they could not aggregate this [personal] information." He took a similar tactic in addressing accounting information. "There's an intense focus on . . . information, as both an ideal and a practical strategy to get things done," insists Mark. This includes using accounting information to make key business decisions.

While Facebook is the language of social networking, accounting is the language of business networking. "As a company we are very focused on what we are building," says Mark. "We are adding a certain amount of value to people's lives if we build a very good product." That value is reflected in its financial statements, which are based on transaction analysis and accounting concepts.

Facebook's success is reflected in its revenues, which continue to grow and exhibit what people call the monetizing of social networking. "Social Ads are doing pretty well," asserts Mark. "We are happy with how we are doing in terms of numbers of advertisers and revenue." Facebook also tracks its expenses and asset purchases. "We expect to achieve . . . profitability next year," states Mark. "It means we will be able to fund all of our operations and server purchases from the cash we generate." This is saying a lot as Facebook's operating expenditures must support nearly 1 billion photo uploads and 8 million video uploads per day.

Mark emphasizes that his financial house must be in order for Facebook to realize its full potential—and that potential is in his sights. "We believe really deeply that if people are sharing more, then the world will be a more open place where people can understand what is going on with the people around them."

[Sources: *Facebook Website,* January 2011; *CNN,* October 2008; *Mercury News,* April 2009; *VentureBeat,* March 2008; *FastCompany.com,* May 2007; *Wired,* June 2009]

Chapter Preview

*A **Preview** opens each chapter with a summary of topics covered.*

Today's world is one of information—its preparation, communication, analysis, and use. Accounting is at the core of this information age. Knowledge of accounting gives us career opportunities and the insight to take advantage of them. This book introduces concepts, procedures, and analyses that help us make better decisions, including career choices. In this chapter we describe accounting, the users and uses of accounting information, the forms and activities of organizations, and several accounting principles. We also introduce transaction analysis and financial statements.

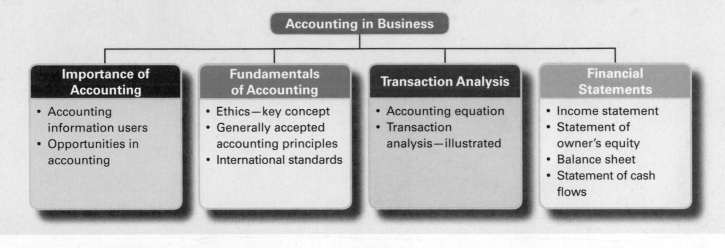

Accounting in Business

Importance of Accounting	Fundamentals of Accounting	Transaction Analysis	Financial Statements
• Accounting information users • Opportunities in accounting	• Ethics—key concept • Generally accepted accounting principles • International standards	• Accounting equation • Transaction analysis—illustrated	• Income statement • Statement of owner's equity • Balance sheet • Statement of cash flows

IMPORTANCE OF ACCOUNTING

C1 Explain the purpose and importance of accounting.

Why is accounting so popular on campuses? Why are there so many accounting jobs for graduates? Why is accounting so important to companies? Why do politicians and business leaders focus on accounting regulations? The answer is that we live in an information age, where that information, and its reliability, impacts the financial well-being of us all.

Accounting is an information and measurement system that identifies, records, and communicates relevant, reliable, and comparable information about an organization's business activities. *Identifying* business activities requires selecting transactions and events relevant to an organization. Examples are the sale of iPhones by **Apple** and the receipt of ticket money by **TicketMaster**. *Recording* business activities requires keeping a chronological log of transactions and events measured in dollars and classified and summarized in a useful format. *Communicating* business activities requires preparing accounting reports such as financial statements. It also requires analyzing and interpreting such reports. (The financial statements and notes of **Research In Motion**, the maker of *BlackBerry*, are shown in Appendix A near the end of this book. This appendix also shows the financial statements of **Apple**, **Palm**, and **Nokia**.) Exhibit 1.1 summarizes accounting activities.

***Real company names** are printed in bold magenta.*

We must guard against a narrow view of accounting. Our most common contact with accounting is through credit approvals, checking accounts, tax forms, and payroll. These experiences are limited and tend to focus on the recordkeeping parts of accounting. **Recordkeeping,** or **bookkeeping,** is the recording of transactions and events, either manually or electronically. This is just one part of accounting. Accounting also identifies and communicates information on transactions and events, and it includes the crucial processes of analysis and interpretation.

EXHIBIT 1.1

Accounting Activities

Technology is a key part of modern business and plays a major role in accounting. Technology reduces the time, effort, and cost of recordkeeping while improving clerical accuracy. Some small organizations continue to perform various accounting tasks manually, but even they are impacted by technology. As technology has changed the way we store, process, and summarize masses of data, accounting has been freed to expand. Consulting, planning, and other financial services are now closely linked to accounting. These services require sorting through data, interpreting their meaning, identifying key factors, and analyzing their implications.

Point: Technology is only as useful as the accounting data available, and users' decisions are only as good as their understanding of accounting. The best software and recordkeeping cannot make up for lack of accounting knowledge.

***Margin notes** further enhance the textual material.*

Users of Accounting Information

Accounting is often called the *language of business* because all organizations set up an accounting information system to communicate data to help people make better decisions. Exhibit 1.2 shows that the accounting information system serves many kinds of users (this is a partial listing) who can be divided into two groups: external users and internal users.

EXHIBIT 1.2

Users of Accounting Information

External users

- Lenders
- Shareholders
- Governments
- Consumer groups
- External auditors
- Customers

Internal users

- Officers
- Managers
- Internal auditors
- Sales staff
- Budget officers
- Controllers

***Infographics** reinforce key concepts through visual learning.*

C2 Identify users and uses of, and opportunities in, accounting.

External Information Users External users of accounting information are *not* directly involved in running the organization. They include shareholders (investors), lenders, directors, customers, suppliers, regulators, lawyers, brokers, and the press. External users have limited access to an organization's information. Yet their business decisions depend on information that is reliable, relevant, and comparable.

Financial accounting is the area of accounting aimed at serving external users by providing them with *general-purpose financial statements*. The term *general-purpose* refers to the broad range of purposes for which external users rely on these statements.

Each external user has special information needs depending on the types of decisions to be made. *Lenders* (creditors) loan money or other resources to an organization. Banks, savings and loans, co-ops, and mortgage and finance companies are lenders. Lenders look for information to help them assess whether an organization is likely to repay its loans with interest. *Shareholders* (investors) are the owners of a corporation. They use accounting reports in deciding whether to buy, hold, or sell stock. Shareholders typically elect a *board of directors* to oversee their interests in an organization. Since directors are responsible to shareholders, their information needs are similar. *External* (independent) *auditors* examine financial statements to verify that they are prepared according to generally accepted accounting principles. *Nonexecutive employees* and *labor unions* use financial statements to judge the fairness of wages, assess job prospects, and bargain for better wages. *Regulators* often have legal authority over certain activities of organizations. For example, the Internal Revenue Service (IRS) and other tax authorities require organizations to file accounting reports in computing taxes. Other regulators include utility boards that use accounting information to set utility rates and securities regulators that require reports for companies that sell their stock to the public.

Accounting serves the needs of many other external users. *Voters, legislators,* and *government officials* use accounting information to monitor and evaluate government receipts and expenses. *Contributors* to nonprofit organizations use accounting information to evaluate the use and impact of their donations. *Suppliers* use accounting information to judge the soundness of a customer before making sales on credit, and *customers* use financial reports to assess the staying power of potential suppliers.

Internal Information Users **Internal users** of accounting information are those directly involved in managing and operating an organization. They use the information to help improve the efficiency and effectiveness of an organization. **Managerial accounting** is the area of accounting that serves the decision-making needs of internal users. Internal reports are not subject to the same rules as external reports and instead are designed with the special needs of internal users in mind.

There are several types of internal users, and many are managers of key operating activities. *Research and development managers* need information about projected costs and revenues of any proposed changes in products and services. *Purchasing managers* need to know what, when, and how much to purchase. *Human resource managers* need information about employees' payroll, benefits, performance, and compensation. *Production managers* depend on information to monitor costs and ensure quality. *Distribution managers* need reports for timely, accurate, and efficient delivery of products and services. *Marketing managers* use reports about sales and costs to target consumers, set prices, and monitor consumer needs, tastes, and price concerns. *Service managers* require information on the costs and benefits of looking after products and services. Decisions of these and other internal users depend on accounting reports.

Both internal and external users rely on internal controls to monitor and control company activities. *Internal controls* are procedures set up to protect company property and equipment, ensure reliable accounting reports, promote efficiency, and encourage adherence to company policies. Examples are good records, physical controls (locks, passwords, guards), and independent reviews.

***Decision Insight** boxes highlight relevant items from practice.*

Decision Insight

Virtuous Returns Virtue is not always its own reward. Compare the S&P 500 with the Domini Social Index (DSI), which covers 400 companies that have especially good records of social responsibility. We see that returns for companies with socially responsible behavior are at least as high as those of the S&P 500. ■

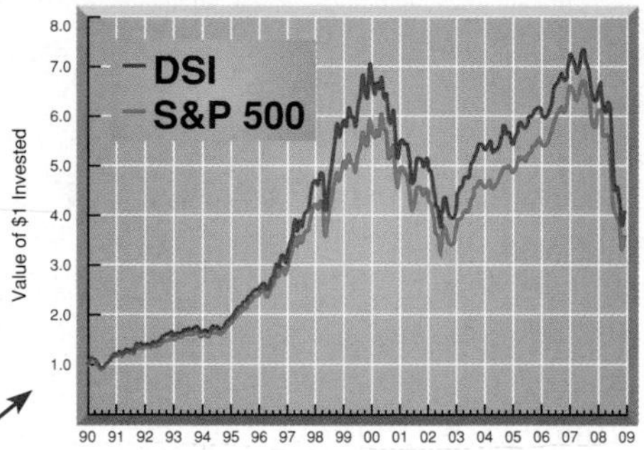

***Graphical displays** are often used to illustrate key points.*

Opportunities in Accounting

Accounting information affects many aspects of our lives. When we earn money, pay taxes, invest savings, budget earnings, and plan for the future, we are influenced by accounting. Accounting has four broad areas of opportunities: financial, managerial, taxation, and accounting-related. Exhibit 1.3 lists selected opportunities in each area.

EXHIBIT 1.3

Accounting Opportunities

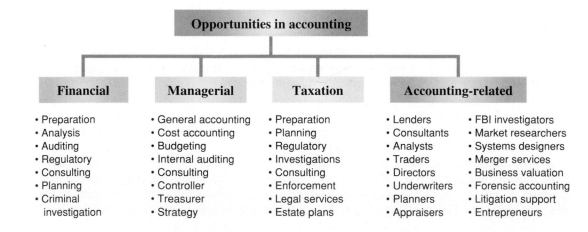

Opportunities in accounting

Financial	Managerial	Taxation	Accounting-related	
• Preparation	• General accounting	• Preparation	• Lenders	• FBI investigators
• Analysis	• Cost accounting	• Planning	• Consultants	• Market researchers
• Auditing	• Budgeting	• Regulatory	• Analysts	• Systems designers
• Regulatory	• Internal auditing	• Investigations	• Traders	• Merger services
• Consulting	• Consulting	• Consulting	• Directors	• Business valuation
• Planning	• Controller	• Enforcement	• Underwriters	• Forensic accounting
• Criminal investigation	• Treasurer	• Legal services	• Planners	• Litigation support
	• Strategy	• Estate plans	• Appraisers	• Entrepreneurs

The majority of accounting opportunities are in *private accounting,* which are employees working for businesses, as shown in Exhibit 1.4. *Public accounting* offers the next largest number of opportunities, which involve services such as auditing and tax advice to a vast range of businesses. Still other opportunities exist in government and not-for-profit agencies, including business regulation and investigation of law violations.

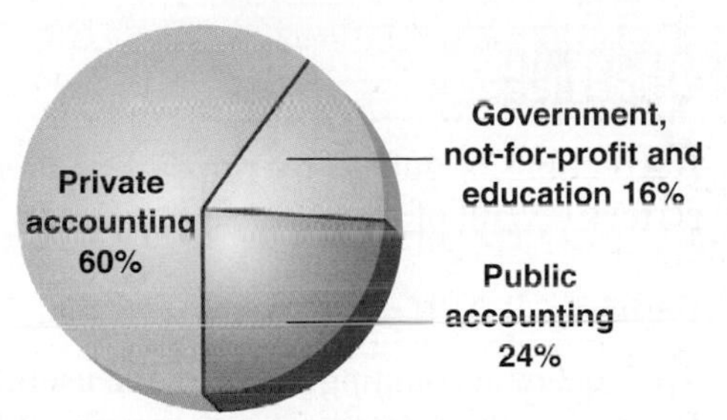

EXHIBIT 1.4

Accounting Jobs by Area

Accounting specialists are highly regarded. Their professional standing often is denoted by a certificate. Certified public accountants (CPAs) must meet education and experience requirements, pass an examination, and exhibit ethical character. Many accounting specialists hold certificates in addition to or instead of the CPA. Two of the most common are the certificate in management accounting (CMA) and the certified internal auditor (CIA). Employers also look for specialists with designations such as certified bookkeeper (CB), certified payroll professional (CPP), personal financial specialist (PFS), certified fraud examiner (CFE), and certified forensic accountant (CrFA).

Point: The largest accounting firms are Deloitte, Ernst & Young, KPMG, and PricewaterhouseCoopers.

Individuals with accounting knowledge are always in demand as they can help with financial analysis, strategic planning, e-commerce, product feasibility analysis, information technology, and financial management. Benefit packages can include flexible work schedules, telecommuting options, career path alternatives, casual work environments, extended vacation time, and child and elder care.

Demand for accounting specialists is strong. Exhibit 1.5 reports average annual salaries for several accounting positions. Salary variation depends on location, company size, professional designation, experience, and other factors. For example, salaries for chief financial officers (CFO) range from under $75,000 to more than $1 million per year. Likewise, salaries for bookkeepers range from under $30,000 to more than $80,000.

Point: Census Bureau (2009) reports that for workers 18 and over, higher education yields higher average pay:

Advanced degree	$80,977
Bachelor's degree..........	57,181
High school degree	31,286
No high school degree......	21,484

EXHIBIT 1.5

Accounting Salaries for Selected Fields

Field	Title (experience)	2009 Salary	2014 Estimate*
Public Accounting	Partner	$191,000	$211,000
	Manager (6–8 years)	94,500	104,000
	Senior (3–5 years)..................	72,000	79,500
	Junior (0–2 years)	51,500	57,000
Private Accounting	CFO	232,000	256,000
	Controller/Treasurer	147,500	163,000
	Manager (6–8 years)	87,500	96,500
	Senior (3–5 years)..................	72,500	80,000
	Junior (0–2 years)	49,000	54,000
Recordkeeping	Full-charge bookkeeper	57,500	63,500
	Accounts manager..................	51,000	56,500
	Payroll manager	54,500	60,000
	Accounting clerk (0–2 years)	37,500	41,500

* Estimates assume a 2% compounded annual increase over current levels (rounded to nearest $500).

Point: For updated salary information:
Abbott-Langer.com
www.AICPA.org
Kforce.com

Quick Check

Answers — p. 28

1. What is the purpose of accounting?
2. What is the relation between accounting and recordkeeping?
3. Identify some advantages of technology for accounting.
4. Who are the internal and external users of accounting information?
5. Identify at least five types of managers who are internal users of accounting information.
6. What are internal controls and why are they important?

***Quick Check** is a chance to stop and reflect on key points.*

FUNDAMENTALS OF ACCOUNTING

Accounting is guided by principles, standards, concepts, and assumptions. This section describes several of these key fundamentals of accounting.

Ethics—A Key Concept

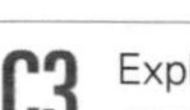
Explain why ethics are crucial to accounting.

The goal of accounting is to provide useful information for decisions. For information to be useful, it must be trusted. This demands ethics in accounting. **Ethics** are beliefs that distinguish right from wrong. They are accepted standards of good and bad behavior.

Identifying the ethical path is sometimes difficult. The preferred path is a course of action that avoids casting doubt on one's decisions. For example, accounting users are less likely to trust an auditor's report if the auditor's pay depends on the success of the client's business. To avoid such concerns, ethics rules are often set. For example, auditors are banned from direct investment in their client and cannot accept pay that depends on figures in the client's reports. Exhibit 1.6 gives guidelines for making ethical decisions.

Point: **Sarbanes-Oxley Act** requires each issuer of securities to disclose whether it has adopted a code of ethics for its senior financial officers and the contents of that code.

EXHIBIT 1.6

Guidelines for Ethical Decision Making

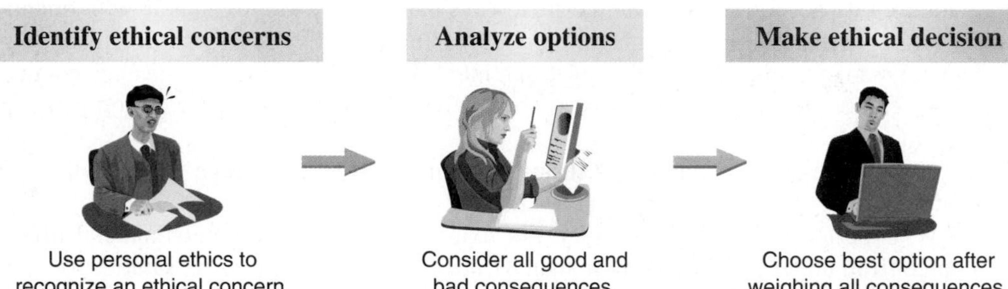
Identify ethical concerns
Analyze options
Make ethical decision
Use personal ethics to recognize an ethical concern.
Consider all good and bad consequences.
Choose best option after weighing all consequences.

Providers of accounting information often face ethical choices as they prepare financial reports. These choices can affect the price a buyer pays and the wages paid to workers. They can even affect the success of products and services. Misleading information can lead to a wrongful closing of a division that harms workers, customers, and suppliers. There is an old saying: *Good ethics are good business.*

Some people extend ethics to *social responsibility,* which refers to a concern for the impact of actions on society. An organization's social responsibility can include donations to hospitals, colleges, community programs, and law enforcement. It also can include programs to reduce pollution, increase product safety, improve worker conditions, and support continuing education. These programs are not limited to large companies. For example, many small businesses offer discounts to students and senior citizens. Still others help sponsor events such as the Special Olympics and summer reading programs.

Point: The American Institute of Certified Public Accountants' *Code of Professional Conduct* is available at **www.AICPA.org**.

Decision Insight

They Fought the Law Our economic and social welfare depends on reliable accounting. Some individuals forgot that and are now paying their dues. They include Bernard Madoff (in photo) of **Madoff Investment Securities**, convicted of falsifying securities records; Bernard Ebbers of **WorldCom**, convicted of an $11 billion accounting scandal; Andrew Fastow of **Enron**, guilty of hiding debt and inflating income; and Ramalinga Raju of **Satyam Computers**, accused of overstating assets by $1.5 billion. ■

Generally Accepted Accounting Principles

Financial accounting practice is governed by concepts and rules known as **generally accepted accounting principles (GAAP).** To use and interpret financial statements effectively, we need to understand these principles, which can change over time in response to the demands of users.

GAAP aims to make information in financial statements *relevant, reliable,* and *comparable.* Relevant information affects the decisions of its users. Reliable information is trusted by users. Comparable information is helpful in contrasting organizations.

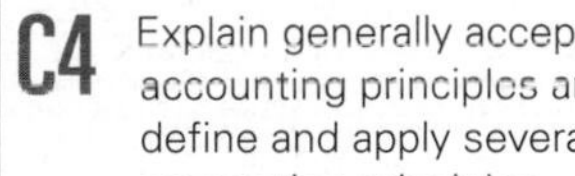

C4 Explain generally accepted accounting principles and define and apply several accounting principles.

In the United States, the **Securities and Exchange Commission (SEC),** a government agency, has the legal authority to set GAAP. The SEC also oversees proper use of GAAP by companies that raise money from the public through issuances of their stock and debt. Those companies that issue their stock on U.S. exchanges include both *U.S. SEC registrants* (companies incorporated in the United States) and *non-U.S. SEC registrants* (companies incorporated under non-U.S. laws). The SEC has largely delegated the task of setting U.S. GAAP to the **Financial Accounting Standards Board (FASB),** which is a private-sector group that sets both broad and specific principles.

Point: State ethics codes require CPAs who audit financial statements to disclose areas where those statements fail to comply with GAAP. If CPAs fail to report noncompliance, they can lose their licenses and be subject to criminal and civil actions and fines.

International Standards

In today's global economy, there is increased demand by external users for comparability in accounting reports. This demand often arises when companies wish to raise money from lenders and investors in different countries. To that end, the **International Accounting Standards Board (IASB),** an independent group (consisting of individuals from many countries), issues **International Financial Reporting Standards (IFRS)** that identify preferred accounting practices.

If standards are harmonized, one company can potentially use a single set of financial statements in all financial markets. Differences between U.S. GAAP and IFRS are slowly fading as the FASB and IASB pursue a *convergence* process aimed to achieve a single set of accounting standards for global use. More than 115 countries now require or permit companies to prepare financial reports following IFRS. Further, non-U.S. SEC registrants can use IFRS in financial reports filed with the SEC (with no reconciliation to U.S. GAAP). This means there are *two* sets of accepted accounting principles in the United States: (1) U.S. GAAP for U.S. SEC registrants and (2) either IFRS or U.S. GAAP for non-U.S. SEC registrants.

The convergence process continues and, in late 2008, the SEC set a roadmap for use of IFRS by publicly traded U.S. companies. This roadmap proposes that large U.S. companies adopt IFRS by 2014, with midsize and small companies following in 2015 and 2016, respectively. Early adoption is permitted for large multinationals that meet certain criteria. For updates on this roadmap, we can check with the AICPA (**IFRS.com**), FASB (**FASB.org**), and IASB (**IASB.org.uk**).

IFRS

Like the FASB, the IASB uses a conceptual framework to aid in revising or drafting new standards. However, unlike the FASB, the IASB's conceptual framework is used as a reference when specific guidance is lacking. The IASB also requires that transactions be accounted for according to their substance (not only their legal form), and that financial statements give a fair presentation, whereas the FASB narrows that scope to fair presentation *in accordance with U.S. GAAP.* ■

Conceptual Framework and Convergence

The FASB and IASB are attempting to converge and enhance the **conceptual framework** that guides standard setting. The framework consists broadly of the following:

- **Objectives**—to provide information useful to investors, creditors, and others.
- **Qualitative Characteristics**—to require information that is relevant, reliable, and comparable.
- **Elements**—to define items that financial statements can contain.
- **Recognition and Measurement**—to set criteria that an item must meet for it to be recognized as an element; and how to measure that element.

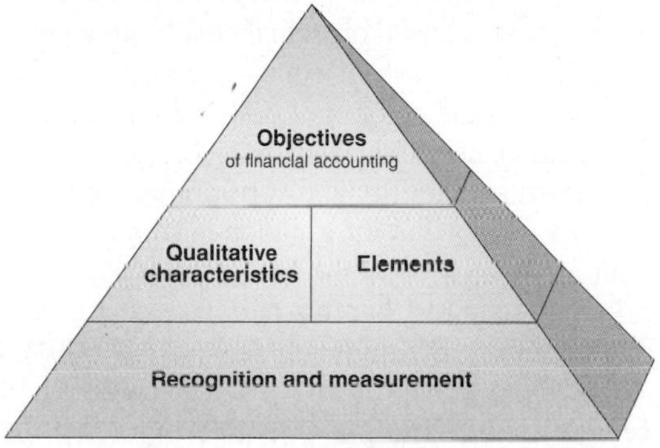

For updates on this joint FASB and IASB conceptual framework convergence we can check with FASB.org or IASB.org.uk Websites. We must remember that U.S. GAAP and IFRS are two similar, but not identical, systems. However, their similarities greatly outweigh any differences. The remainder of this section describes key principles and assumptions of accounting.

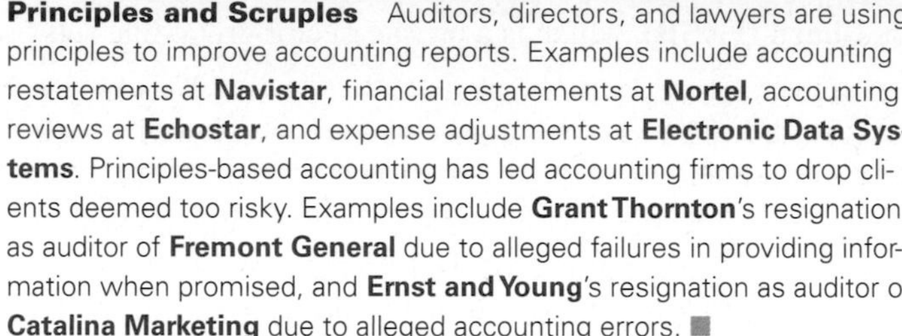

Principles and Scruples Auditors, directors, and lawyers are using principles to improve accounting reports. Examples include accounting restatements at **Navistar**, financial restatements at **Nortel**, accounting reviews at **Echostar**, and expense adjustments at **Electronic Data Systems**. Principles-based accounting has led accounting firms to drop clients deemed too risky. Examples include **Grant Thornton**'s resignation as auditor of **Fremont General** due to alleged failures in providing information when promised, and **Ernst and Young**'s resignation as auditor of **Catalina Marketing** due to alleged accounting errors. ■

Principles and Assumptions of Accounting Accounting principles (and assumptions) are of two types. *General principles* are the basic assumptions, concepts, and guidelines for preparing financial statements. *Specific principles* are detailed rules used in reporting business transactions and events. General principles stem from long-used accounting practices. Specific principles arise more often from the rulings of authoritative groups.

EXHIBIT 1.7

Building Blocks for GAAP

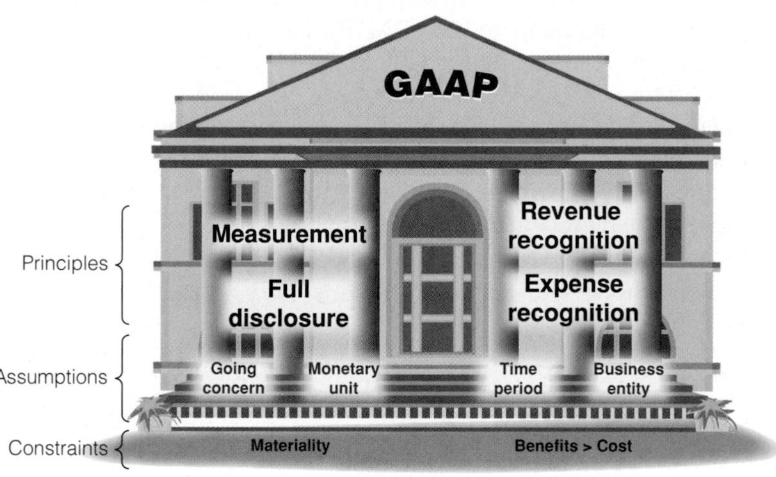

We need to understand both general and specific principles to effectively use accounting information. Several general principles are described in this section that are relied on in later chapters. General principles (in purple font with white shading) and assumptions (in red font with yellow shading) are portrayed as building blocks of GAAP in Exhibit 1.7. The specific principles are described as we encounter them in the book.

Accounting Principles General principles consist of at least four basic principles, four assumptions, and two constraints.

Point: The cost principle is also called the *historical cost principle*.

The **measurement principle,** also called the **cost principle,** usually means that accounting information is based on actual cost (with a potential for subsequent adjustments to market). Cost is measured on a cash or equal-to-cash basis. This means if cash is given for a service, its cost is measured as the amount of cash paid. If something besides cash is exchanged (such as a car traded for a truck), cost is measured as the cash value of what is given up or received. The cost principle emphasizes reliability and verifiability, and information based on cost is considered objective. *Objectivity* means that information is supported by independent, unbiased evidence; it demands more than a person's opinion. To illustrate, suppose a company pays $5,000 for equipment. The cost principle requires that this purchase be recorded at a cost of $5,000. It makes no difference if the owner thinks this equipment is worth $7,000. Later in the book we introduce *fair value* measures.

Revenue (sales) is the amount received from selling products and services. The **revenue recognition principle** provides guidance on when a company must recognize revenue. To *recognize* means to record it. If revenue is recognized too early, a company would look more profitable than it is. If revenue is recognized too late, a company would look less profitable than it is.

Three concepts are important to revenue recognition. (1) *Revenue is recognized when earned.* The earnings process is normally complete when services are performed or a seller transfers ownership of products to the buyer. (2) *Proceeds from selling products and services need not be in cash.* A common noncash proceed received by a seller is a customer's promise to pay at a future date, called *credit sales.* (3) *Revenue is measured by the cash received plus the cash value of any other items received.*

Example: When a bookstore sells a textbook on credit is its earnings process complete? *Answer:* A bookstore can record sales for these books minus an amount expected for returns.

The **expense recognition principle,** also called the **matching principle,** prescribes that a company record the expenses it incurred to generate the revenue reported. The principles of matching and revenue recognition are key to modern accounting.

The **full disclosure principle** prescribes that a company report the details behind financial statements that would impact users' decisions. Those disclosures are often in footnotes to the statements.

Decision Insight

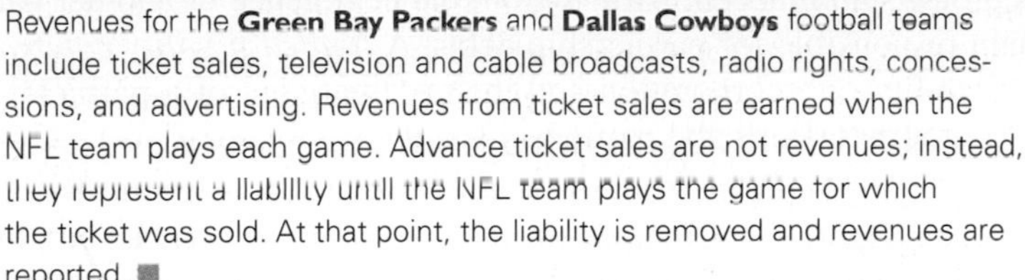

Revenues for the **Green Bay Packers** and **Dallas Cowboys** football teams include ticket sales, television and cable broadcasts, radio rights, concessions, and advertising. Revenues from ticket sales are earned when the NFL team plays each game. Advance ticket sales are not revenues; instead, they represent a liability until the NFL team plays the game for which the ticket was sold. At that point, the liability is removed and revenues are reported. ■

Accounting Assumptions There are four accounting assumptions: the going concern assumption, the monetary unit assumption, the time period assumption, and the business entity assumption.

The **going-concern assumption** means that accounting information reflects a presumption that the business will continue operating instead of being closed or sold. This implies, for example, that property is reported at cost instead of, say, liquidation values that assume closure.

The **monetary unit assumption** means that we can express transactions and events in monetary, or money, units. Money is the common denominator in business. Examples of monetary units are the dollar in the United States, Canada, Australia, and Singapore; and the peso in Mexico, the Philippines, and Chile. The monetary unit a company uses in its accounting reports usually depends on the country where it operates, but many companies today are expressing reports in more than one monetary unit.

Point: For currency conversion: xe.com

The **time period assumption** presumes that the life of a company can be divided into time periods, such as months and years, and that useful reports can be prepared for those periods.

The **business entity assumption** means that a business is accounted for separately from other business entities, including its owner. The reason for this assumption is that separate information about each business is necessary for good decisions. A business entity can take one of three legal forms: *proprietorship, partnership,* or *corporation.*

Point: Abuse of the entity assumption was a main culprit in **Enron**'s collapse.

1. A **sole proprietorship,** or simply **proprietorship,** is a business owned by one person. No special legal requirements must be met to start a proprietorship. It is a separate entity for accounting purposes, but it is *not* a separate legal entity from its owner. This means, for example, that a court can order an owner to sell personal belongings to pay a proprietorship's debt. This *unlimited liability* of a proprietorship is a disadvantage. However, an advantage is that a proprietorship's income is not subject to a business income tax but is instead reported and taxed on the owner's personal income tax return. Proprietorship attributes are summarized in Exhibit 1.8, including those for partnerships and corporations.
2. A **partnership** is a business owned by two or more people, called *partners*. Like a proprietorship, no special legal requirements must be met in starting a partnership. The only

EXHIBIT 1.8

Attributes of Businesses

Attribute Present	Proprietorship	Partnership	Corporation
One owner allowed	yes	no	yes
Business taxed	no	no	yes
Limited liability	no*	no*	yes
Business entity	yes	yes	yes
Legal entity	no	no	yes
Unlimited life	no	no	yes

* Proprietorships and partnerships that are set up as LLCs provide limited liability.

requirement is an agreement between partners to run a business together. The agreement can be either oral or written and usually indicates how income and losses are to be shared. A partnership, like a proprietorship, is *not* legally separate from its owners. This means that each partner's share of profits is reported and taxed on that partner's tax return. It also means *unlimited liability* for its partners. However, at least three types of partnerships limit liability. A *limited partnership* (*LP*) includes a general partner(s) with unlimited liability and a limited partner(s) with liability restricted to the amount invested. A *limited liability partnership* (*LLP*) restricts partners' liabilities to their own acts and the acts of individuals under their control. This protects an innocent partner from the negligence of another partner, yet all partners remain responsible for partnership debts. A *limited liability company* (*LLC*) offers the limited liability of a corporation and the tax treatment of a partnership (and proprietorship). Most proprietorships and partnerships are now organized as LLCs.

Point: Proprietorships and partnerships are usually managed by their owners. In a corporation, the owners (shareholders) elect a board of directors who appoint managers to run the business.

3. A **corporation** is a business legally separate from its owners, meaning it is responsible for its own acts and its own debts. Separate legal status means that a corporation can conduct business with the rights, duties, and responsibilities of a person. A corporation acts through its managers, who are its legal agents. Separate legal status also means that its owners, who are called **shareholders** (or **stockholders**), are not personally liable for corporate acts and debts. This limited liability is its main advantage. A main disadvantage is what's called *double taxation*—meaning that (1) the corporation income is taxed and (2) any distribution of income to its owners through dividends is taxed as part of the owners' personal income, usually at the 15% rate. (For lower income taxpayers, the dividend tax is less than 15%, and in some cases zero.) An *S corporation,* a corporation with special attributes, does not owe corporate income tax. Owners of S corporations report their share of corporate income with their personal income. Ownership of all corporations is divided into units called **shares** or **stock.** When a corporation issues only one class of stock, we call it **common stock** (or *capital stock*).

Decision Ethics boxes are role-playing exercises that stress ethics in accounting and business.

Decision Ethics Answer — p. 27

Entrepreneur You and a friend develop a new design for in-line skates that improves speed by 25% to 30%. You plan to form a business to manufacture and market those skates. You and your friend want to minimize taxes, but your prime concern is potential lawsuits from individuals who might be injured on these skates. What form of organization do you set up? ■

Accounting Constraints There are two basic constraints on financial reporting. The **materiality constraint** prescribes that only information that would influence the decisions of a reasonable person need be disclosed. This constraint looks at both the importance and relative size of an amount. The **cost-benefit constraint** prescribes that only information with benefits of disclosure greater than the costs of providing it need be disclosed.

Sarbanes–Oxley (SOX)

Point: An **audit** examines whether financial statements are prepared using GAAP. It does *not* attest to absolute accuracy of the statements.

Congress passed the **Sarbanes–Oxley Act,** also called *SOX,* to help curb financial abuses at companies that issue their stock to the public. SOX requires that these public companies apply both accounting oversight and stringent internal controls. The desired results include more transparency, accountability, and truthfulness in reporting transactions.

Compliance with SOX requires documentation and verification of internal controls and increased emphasis on internal control effectiveness. Failure to comply can yield financial penalties, stock market delisting, and criminal prosecution of executives. Management must issue a report stating that internal controls are effective. CEOs and CFOs who knowingly sign off on bogus accounting reports risk millions of dollars in fines and years in prison. **Auditors** also must verify the effectiveness of internal controls.

A listing of some of the more publicized accounting scandals in recent years follows.

Point: *BusinessWeek* reports that external audit costs run about $35,000 for start-ups, up from $15,000 pre-SOX.

Company	Alleged Accounting Abuses
Enron	Inflated income, hid debt, and bribed officials
WorldCom	Understated expenses to inflate income and hid debt
Fannie Mae	Inflated income
Adelphia Communications	Understated expenses to inflate income and hid debt
AOL Time Warner	Inflated revenues and income
Xerox	Inflated income
Bristol-Myers Squibb	Inflated revenues and income
Nortel Networks	Understated expenses to inflate income
Global Crossing	Inflated revenues and income
Tyco	Hid debt, and CEO evaded taxes
Halliburton	Inflated revenues and income
Qwest Communications	Inflated revenues and income

To reduce the risk of accounting fraud, companies set up *governance systems.* A company's governance system includes its owners, managers, employees, board of directors, and other important stakeholders, who work together to reduce the risk of accounting fraud and increase confidence in accounting reports.

The impact of SOX regulations for accounting and business is discussed throughout this book. Ethics and investor confidence are key to company success. Lack of confidence in accounting numbers impacts company value as evidenced by huge stock price declines for **Enron**, **WorldCom**, **Tyco**, and **ImClone** after accounting misconduct was uncovered.

Decision Insight

Economic Downturn, Fraud Upturn? Executives polled show that 80% believe that the economic downturn has or will have a significant impact on fraud control in their companies (Deloitte 2009). The top three responses to the question "What activity would best counter this increased fraud risk?" are tallied in the graphic to the right. ■

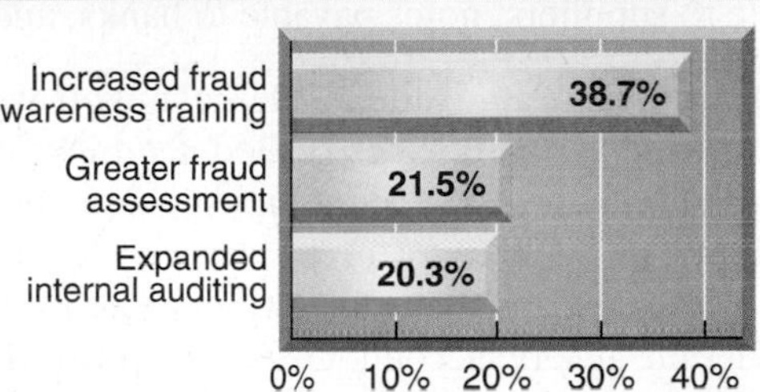

Quick Check

Answers — p. 28

7. What three-step guidelines can help people make ethical decisions?
8. Why are ethics and social responsibility valuable to organizations?
9. Why are ethics crucial in accounting?
10. Who sets U.S. accounting rules?
11. How are U.S. companies affected by international accounting standards?
12. How are the objectivity concept and cost principle related?
13. Why is the business entity assumption important?
14. Why is the revenue recognition principle important?
15. What are the three basic forms of business organization?
16. Identify the owners of corporations and the terminology for ownership units.

TRANSACTION ANALYSIS AND THE ACCOUNTING EQUATION

To understand accounting information, we need to know how an accounting system captures relevant data about transactions, and then classifies, records, and reports data.

Accounting Equation

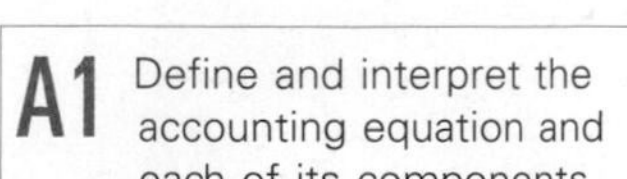
A1 Define and interpret the accounting equation and each of its components.

The accounting system reflects two basic aspects of a company: what it owns and what it owes. *Assets* are resources a company owns or controls. Examples are cash, supplies, equipment, and land, where each carries expected benefits. The claims on a company's assets—what it owes—are separated into owner and nonowner claims. *Liabilities* are what a company owes its nonowners (creditors) in future payments, products, or services. *Equity* (also called owner's equity or capital) refers to the claims of its owner(s). Together, liabilities and equity are the source of funds to acquire assets. The relation of assets, liabilities, and equity is reflected in the following **accounting equation:**

Assets = Liabilities + Equity

Liabilities are usually shown before equity in this equation because creditors' claims must be paid before the claims of owners. (The terms in this equation can be rearranged; for example, Assets − Liabilities = Equity.) The accounting equation applies to all transactions and events, to all companies and forms of organization, and to all points in time. For example, **Research In Motion**'s assets equal \$10,204,409, its liabilities equal \$2,601,746, and its equity equals \$7,602,663 (\$ in thousands). Let's now look at the accounting equation in more detail.

Assets **Assets** are resources a company owns or controls. These resources are expected to yield future benefits. Examples are Web servers for an online services company, musical instruments for a rock band, and land for a vegetable grower. The term *receivable* is used to refer to an asset that promises a future inflow of resources. A company that provides a service or product on credit is said to have an account receivable from that customer.

Point: The phrases "on credit" and "on account" imply that cash payment will occur at a future date.

Liabilities **Liabilities** are creditors' claims on assets. These claims reflect company obligations to provide assets, products or services to others. The term *payable* refers to a liability that promises a future outflow of resources. Examples are wages payable to workers, accounts payable to suppliers, notes payable to banks, and taxes payable to the government.

Equity **Equity** is the owner's claim on assets. Equity is equal to assets minus liabilities. This is the reason equity is also called *net assets* or *residual equity*.

Equity for a noncorporate entity—commonly called owner's equity—increases and decreases as follows: owner investments and revenues *increase* equity, whereas owner withdrawals and expenses *decrease* equity. **Owner investments** are assets an owner puts into the company and are included under the generic account **Owner, Capital. Revenues** are sales of products or services to customers. Revenues increase equity (via net income) and result from a company's earnings activities. Examples are consulting services provided, sales of products, facilities rented to others, and commissions from services. **Owner withdrawals** are assets an owner takes from the company for personal use. **Expenses** are the costs necessary to earn revenues. Expenses decrease equity. Examples are costs of employee time, use of supplies, and advertising, utilities, and insurance services from others. In sum, equity is the accumulated revenues and owner investments less the accumulated expenses and withdrawals since the company began. This breakdown of equity yields the following **expanded accounting equation.**

*Key **terms** are printed in bold and defined again in the end-of-book **glossary.***

$$\text{Assets} = \text{Liabilities} + \overbrace{\text{Owner, Capital} - \text{Owner, Withdrawals} + \text{Revenues} - \text{Expenses}}^{\text{Equity}}$$

Net income occurs when revenues exceed expenses. Net income increases equity. A **net loss** occurs when expenses exceed revenues, which decreases equity.

Decision Insight

Web Info Most organizations maintain Websites that include accounting data—see **Research in Motion (RIM.com)** as an example. The SEC keeps an online database called **EDGAR (www.sec.gov/edgar.shtml)**, which has accounting information for thousands of companies that issue stock to the public (EDGAR is being upgraded and renamed **IDEA**). Information services such as Finance.Google.com and Finance.Yahoo.com offer additional online data and analysis. ■

Transaction Analysis

P1 Analyze business transactions using the accounting equation.

Business activities can be described in terms of transactions and events. **External transactions** are exchanges of value between two entities, which yield changes in the accounting equation. An example is the sale of ad space by **Facebook**. **Internal transactions** are exchanges within an entity, which may or may not affect the accounting equation. An example is Facebook's use of its supplies, which are reported as expenses when used. **Events** refer to happenings that affect the accounting equation *and* are reliably measured. They include business events such as changes in the market value of certain assets and liabilities and natural events such as floods and fires that destroy assets and create losses. They do not include, for example, the signing of service or product contracts, which by themselves do not impact the accounting equation.

This section uses the accounting equation to analyze 11 selected transactions and events of FastForward, a start-up consulting (service) business, in its first month of operations. Remember that each transaction and event leaves the equation in balance and that assets *always* equal the sum of liabilities and equity.

Transaction 1: Investment by Owner On December 1, Chas Taylor forms a consulting business, named FastForward and set up as a proprietorship, that focuses on assessing the performance of footwear and accessories. Taylor owns and manages the business. The marketing plan for the business is to focus primarily on publishing online reviews and consulting with clubs, athletes, and others who place orders for footwear and accessories with manufacturers. Taylor personally invests $30,000 cash in the new company and deposits the cash in a bank account opened under the name of FastForward. After this transaction, the cash (an asset) and the owner's equity each equal $30,000. The source of increase in equity is the owner's investment, which is included in the column titled C. Taylor, Capital. (Owner investments are always included under the title *'Owner name,' Capital.*) The effect of this transaction on FastForward is reflected in the accounting equation as follows:

Point: There are 3 basic types of company operations: (1) **Services**—providing customer services for profit, (2) **Merchandisers**—buying products and re-selling them for profit, and (3) **Manufacturers**—creating products and selling them for profit.

	Assets	=	Liabilities	+	Equity
	Cash	=			**C. Taylor, Capital**
(1)	**+$30,000**	=			**+$30,000**

Transaction 2: Purchase Supplies for Cash FastForward uses $2,500 of its cash to buy supplies of brand name footwear for performance testing over the next few months. This transaction is an exchange of cash, an asset, for another kind of asset, supplies. It merely changes the form of assets from cash to supplies. The decrease in cash is exactly equal to the increase in supplies. The supplies of footwear are assets because of the expected future benefits from the test results of their performance. This transaction is reflected in the accounting equation as follows:

	Assets			=	Liabilities	+	Equity
	Cash	+	**Supplies**	=			**C. Taylor, Capital**
Old Bal.	$30,000			=			$30,000
(2)	**−2,500**	+	**$2,500**				
New Bal.	$27,500	+	$ 2,500	=			$30,000
		$30,000				$30,000	

Transaction 3: Purchase Equipment for Cash FastForward spends $26,000 to acquire equipment for testing footwear. Like transaction 2, transaction 3 is an exchange of one asset, cash, for another asset, equipment. The equipment is an asset because of its expected future benefits from testing footwear. This purchase changes the makeup of assets but does not change the asset total. The accounting equation remains in balance.

	Assets					=	Liabilities	+	Equity
	Cash	+	**Supplies**	+	**Equipment**	=			**C. Taylor, Capital**
Old Bal.	$27,500	+	$2,500			=			$30,000
(3)	**−26,000**			+	**$26,000**				
New Bal.	$ 1,500	+	$2,500	+	$ 26,000	=			$30,000
			$30,000					$30,000	

Example: If FastForward pays $500 cash in transaction 4, how does this partial payment affect the liability to CalTech? What would be FastForward's cash balance? *Answers:* The liability to CalTech would be reduced to $6,600 and the cash balance would be reduced to $1,000.

Transaction 4: Purchase Supplies on Credit Taylor decides more supplies of footwear and accessories are needed. These additional supplies total $7,100, but as we see from the accounting equation in transaction 3, FastForward has only $1,500 in cash. Taylor arranges to purchase them on credit from CalTech Supply Company. Thus, FastForward acquires supplies in exchange for a promise to pay for them later. This purchase increases assets by $7,100 in supplies, and liabilities (called *accounts payable* to CalTech Supply) increase by the same amount. The effects of this purchase follow:

	Assets					=	Liabilities	+	Equity
	Cash	+	**Supplies**	+	**Equipment**	=	**Accounts Payable**	+	**C. Taylor, Capital**
Old Bal.	$1,500	+	$2,500	+	$26,000	=			$30,000
(4)		+	**7,100**				**+$7,100**		
New Bal.	$1,500	+	$9,600	+	$26,000	=	$ 7,100	+	$30,000
			$37,100					$37,100	

Transaction 5: Provide Services for Cash FastForward earns revenues by selling online ad space to manufacturers and by consulting with clients about test results on footwear and accessories. It earns net income only if its revenues are greater than its expenses incurred in earning them. In one of its first jobs, FastForward provides consulting services to a power-walking club and immediately collects $4,200 cash. The accounting equation reflects this increase in cash of $4,200 and in equity of $4,200. This increase in equity is identified in the far right column under Revenues because the cash received is earned by providing consulting services.

	Assets					=	Liabilities	+	Equity		
	Cash	+	**Supplies**	+	**Equipment**	=	**Accounts Payable**	+	**C. Taylor, Capital**	+	**Revenues**
Old Bal.	$1,500	+	$9,600	+	$26,000	=	$7,100	+	$30,000		
(5)	**+4,200**									+	**$4,200**
New Bal.	$5,700	+	$9,600	+	$26,000	=	$7,100	+	$30,000	+	$ 4,200
			$41,300						$41,300		

Transactions 6 and 7: Payment of Expenses in Cash FastForward pays $1,000 rent to the landlord of the building where its facilities are located. Paying this amount allows FastForward to occupy the space for the month of December. The rental payment is reflected in the following accounting equation as transaction 6. FastForward also pays the biweekly $700 salary of the company's only employee. This is reflected in the accounting equation as transaction 7. Both transactions 6 and 7 are December expenses for FastForward. The costs of both rent and salary are expenses, as opposed to assets, because their benefits are used in December (they have no future benefits after December). These transactions also use up an asset (cash) in carrying out FastForward's operations. The accounting equation shows that both transactions reduce cash and equity. The far right column identifies these decreases as Expenses.

By definition, increases in expenses yield decreases in equity.

	Assets					=	Liabilities	+	Equity				
	Cash	+	**Supplies**	+	**Equipment**	=	**Accounts Payable**	+	**C. Taylor, Capital**	+	**Revenues**	−	**Expenses**
Old Bal.	$5,700	+	$9,600	+	$26,000	=	$7,100	+	$30,000	+	$4,200		
(6)	−1,000											−	$1,000
Bal.	4,700	+	9,600	+	26,000	=	7,100	+	30,000	+	4,200	−	1,000
(7)	− 700											−	700
New Bal.	$4,000	+	$9,600	+	$26,000	=	$7,100	+	$30,000	+	$4,200	−	$ 1,700
			$39,600						$39,600				

Transaction 8: Provide Services and Facilities for Credit FastForward provides consulting services of $1,600 and rents its test facilities for $300 to a podiatric services center. The rental involves allowing members to try recommended footwear and accessories at FastForward's testing area. The center is billed for the $1,900 total. This transaction results in a new asset, called *accounts receivable,* from this client. It also yields an increase in equity from the two revenue components reflected in the Revenues column of the accounting equation:

	Assets							=	Liabilities	+	Equity				
	Cash	+	**Accounts Receivable**	+	**Supplies**	+	**Equipment**	=	**Accounts Payable**	+	**C. Taylor, Capital**	+	**Revenues**	−	**Expenses**
Old Bal.	$4,000	+		+	$9,600	+	$26,000	=	$7,100	+	$30,000	+	$4,200	−	$1,700
(8)		+	$1,900									+	1,600		
												+	300		
New Bal.	$4,000	+	$ 1,900	+	$9,600	+	$26,000	=	$7,100	+	$30,000	+	$6,100	−	$1,700
				$41,500							$41,500				

Transaction 9: Receipt of Cash from Accounts Receivable The client in transaction 8 (the podiatric center) pays $1,900 to FastForward 10 days after it is billed for consulting services. This transaction 9 does not change the total amount of assets and does not affect liabilities or equity. It converts the receivable (an asset) to cash (another asset). It does not create new revenue. Revenue was recognized when FastForward rendered the services in transaction 8, not when the cash is now collected. This emphasis on the earnings process instead of cash flows is a goal of the revenue recognition principle and yields useful information to users. The new balances follow:

Point: Receipt of cash is not always a revenue.

	Assets							=	Liabilities	+	Equity				
	Cash	+	**Accounts Receivable**	+	**Supplies**	+	**Equipment**	=	**Accounts Payable**	+	**C. Taylor, Capital**	+	**Revenues**	−	**Expenses**
Old Bal.	$4,000	+	$1,900	+	$9,600	+	$26,000	=	$7,100	+	$30,000	+	$6,100	−	$1,700
(9)	+1,900	−	1,900												
New Bal.	$5,900	+	$ 0	+	$9,600	+	$26,000	=	$7,100	+	$30,000	+	$6,100	−	$1,700
				$41,500							$41,500				

Transaction 10: Payment of Accounts Payable FastForward pays CalTech Supply $900 cash as partial payment for its earlier $7,100 purchase of supplies (transaction 4), leaving $6,200 unpaid. The accounting equation shows that this transaction decreases FastForward's cash by $900 and decreases its liability to CalTech Supply by $900. Equity does not change. This event does not create an expense even though cash flows out of FastForward (instead the expense is recorded when FastForward derives the benefits from these supplies).

	Assets				= Liabilities	+	Equity	
	Cash	+ Accounts Receivable	+ Supplies	+ Equipment	= Accounts Payable	+ C. Taylor, Capital	+ Revenues	− Expenses
Old Bal.	$5,900	+ $ 0	+ $9,600	+ $26,000	= $7,100	+ $30,000	+ $6,100	− $1,700
(10)	**− 900**				**− 900**			
New Bal.	$5,000	+ $ 0	+ $9,600	+ $26,000	= $6,200	+ $30,000	+ $6,100	− $1,700
	$40,600				$40,600			

Transaction 11: Withdrawal of Cash by Owner The owner of FastForward withdraws $200 cash for personal use. Withdrawals (decreases in equity) are not reported as expenses because they are not part of the company's earnings process. Since withdrawals are not company expenses, they are not used in computing net income.

By definition, increases in withdrawals yield decreases in equity.

	Assets				= Liabilities	+	Equity		
	Cash	+ Accounts Receivable	+ Supplies	+ Equipment	= Accounts Payable	+ C. Taylor, Capital	− C. Taylor, Withdrawals	+ Revenues	− Expenses
Old Bal.	$5,000	+ $ 0	+ $9,600	+ $26,000	= $6,200	+ $30,000		+ $6,100	− $1,700
(11)	**− 200**						**− $200**		
New Bal.	$4,800	+ $ 0	+ $9,600	+ $26,000	= $6,200	+ $30,000	− $200	+ $6,100	− $1,700
	$40,400				$40,400				

Summary of Transactions

We summarize in Exhibit 1.9 the effects of these 11 transactions of FastForward using the accounting equation. First, we see that the accounting equation remains in balance after each transaction. Second, transactions can be analyzed by their effects on components of the

EXHIBIT 1.9

Summary of Transactions Using the Accounting Equation

	Assets				= Liabilities	+	Equity		
	Cash	+ Accounts Receivable	+ Supplies	+ Equipment	= Accounts Payable	+ C. Taylor, Capital	− C. Taylor, Withdrawals	+ Revenues	− Expenses
(1)	**$30,000**				=	**$30,000**			
(2)	**− 2,500**		**+ $2,500**						
Bal.	27,500		+ 2,500		=	30,000			
(3)	**−26,000**			**+ $26,000**					
Bal.	1,500		+ 2,500	+ 26,000	=	30,000			
(4)			**+ 7,100**		**+$7,100**				
Bal.	1,500		+ 9,600	+ 26,000	= 7,100	+ 30,000			
(5)	**+ 4,200**							**+ $4,200**	
Bal.	5,700		+ 9,600	+ 26,000	= 7,100	+ 30,000		+ 4,200	
(6)	**− 1,000**								**− $1,000**
Bal.	4,700		+ 9,600	+ 26,000	= 7,100	+ 30,000		+ 4,200	− 1,000
(7)	**− 700**								**− 700**
Bal.	4,000		+ 9,600	+ 26,000	= 7,100	+ 30,000		+ 4,200	− 1,700
(8)		**+ $1,900**						**+ 1,600**	
								+ 300	
Bal.	4,000	+ 1,900	+ 9,600	+ 26,000	= 7,100	+ 30,000		+ 6,100	− 1,700
(9)	**+ 1,900**	**− 1,900**							
Bal.	5,900	+ 0	+ 9,600	+ 26,000	= 7,100	+ 30,000		+ 6,100	− 1,700
(10)	**− 900**				**− 900**				
Bal.	5,000	+ 0	+ 9,600	+ 26,000	= 6,200	+ 30,000		+ 6,100	− 1,700
(11)	**− 200**						**− $200**		
Bal.	$ 4,800	+ $ 0	+ $ 9,600	+ $ 26,000	= $ 6,200	+ $ 30,000	− $200	+ $6,100	− $1,700

accounting equation. For example, in transactions 2, 3, and 9, one asset increased while another asset decreased by equal amounts.

Point: Knowing how financial statements are prepared improves our analysis of them. We develop the skills for analysis of financial statements throughout the book. Chapter 17 focuses on financial statement analysis.

Quick Check Answers — p. 28

17. When is the accounting equation in balance, and what does that mean?
18. How can a transaction not affect any liability and equity accounts?
19. Describe a transaction increasing equity and one decreasing it.
20. Identify a transaction that decreases both assets and liabilities.

FINANCIAL STATEMENTS

This section introduces us to how financial statements are prepared from the analysis of business transactions. The four financial statements and their purposes are:

P2 Identify and prepare basic financial statements and explain how they interrelate.

1. **Income statement**—describes a company's revenues and expenses along with the resulting net income or loss over a period of time due to earnings activities.
2. **Statement of owner's equity**—explains changes in equity from net income (or loss) and from any owner investments and withdrawals over a period of time.
3. **Balance sheet**—describes a company's financial position (types and amounts of assets, liabilities, and equity) at a point in time.
4. **Statement of cash flows**—identifies cash inflows (receipts) and cash outflows (payments) over a period of time.

We prepare these financial statements, in this order, using the 11 selected transactions of FastForward. (These statements are technically called *unadjusted*—we explain this in Chapters 2 and 3.)

Income Statement

FastForward's income statement for December is shown at the top of Exhibit 1.10. Information about revenues and expenses is conveniently taken from the Equity columns of Exhibit 1.9. Revenues are reported first on the income statement. They include consulting revenues of $5,800 from transactions 5 and 8 and rental revenue of $300 from transaction 8. Expenses are reported after revenues. (For convenience in this chapter, we list larger amounts first, but we can sort expenses in different ways.) Rent and salary expenses are from transactions 6 and 7. Expenses reflect the costs to generate the revenues reported. Net income (or loss) is reported at the bottom of the statement and is the amount earned in December. Owner's investments and withdrawals are *not* part of income.

Point: Net income is sometimes called *earnings* or *profit.*

Statement of Owner's Equity

The statement of owner's equity reports information about how equity changes over the reporting period. This statement shows beginning capital, events that increase it (owner investments and net income), and events that decrease it (withdrawals and net loss). Ending capital is computed in this statement and is carried over and reported on the balance sheet. FastForward's statement of owner's equity is the second report in Exhibit 1.10. The beginning capital balance is measured as of the start of business on December 1. It is zero because FastForward did not exist before then. An existing business reports a beginning balance equal to that as of the end of the prior reporting period (such as from November 30). FastForward's statement of owner's equity shows that Taylor's initial investment created $30,000 of equity. It also shows the $4,400 of net income earned during the period. This links the income statement to the statement of owner's equity (see line ①). The statement also reports Taylor's $200 cash withdrawal and FastForward's end-of-period capital balance.

Point: The statement of owner's equity is also called the *statement of changes in owner's equity.* Note: Beg. Capital + Net Income − Withdrawals = Ending Capital

EXHIBIT 1.10

Financial Statements and Their Links

Point: A statement's heading identifies the company, the statement title, and the date or time period.

Point: Arrow lines show how the statements are linked. ① Net income is used to compute equity. ② Owner capital is used to prepare the balance sheet. ③ Cash from the balance sheet is used to reconcile the statement of cash flows.

Point: The income statement, the statement of owner's equity, and the statement of cash flows are prepared for a *period* of time. The balance sheet is prepared as of a *point* in time.

Point: A single ruled line denotes an addition or subtraction. Final totals are double underlined. Negative amounts are often in parentheses.

FASTFORWARD
Income Statement
For Month Ended December 31, 2011

Revenues		
Consulting revenue ($4,200 + $1,600)	$ 5,800	
Rental revenue	300	
Total revenues		$ 6,100
Expenses		
Rent expense	1,000	
Salaries expense	700	
Total expenses		1,700
Net income		**$ 4,400**

①

FASTFORWARD
Statement of Owner's Equity
For Month Ended December 31, 2011

C. Taylor, Capital, December 1, 2011		$ 0
Plus: Investments by owner	$30,000	
Net income	4,400	34,400
		34,400
Less: Withdrawals by owner		200
C. Taylor, Capital, December 31, 2011		**$34,200**

②

FASTFORWARD
Balance Sheet
December 31, 2011

Assets		Liabilities	
Cash	**$ 4,800**	Accounts payable	$ 6,200
Supplies	9,600	Total liabilities	6,200
Equipment	26,000		
		Equity	
		C. Taylor, Capital	34,200
Total assets	$ 40,400	Total liabilities and equity	$ 40,400

③

FASTFORWARD
Statement of Cash Flows
For Month Ended December 31, 2011

Cash flows from operating activities		
Cash received from clients ($4,200 + $1,900)	$ 6,100	
Cash paid for supplies ($2,500 + $900)	(3,400)	
Cash paid for rent	(1,000)	
Cash paid to employee	(700)	
Net cash provided by operating activities		$ 1,000
Cash flows from investing activities		
Purchase of equipment	(26,000)	
Net cash used by investing activities		(26,000)
Cash flows from financing activities		
Investments by owner	30,000	
Withdrawals by owner	(200)	
Net cash provided by financing activities		29,800
Net increase in cash		$ 4,800
Cash balance, December 1, 2011		0
Cash balance, December 31, 2011		**$ 4,800**

Balance Sheet

FastForward's balance sheet is the third report in Exhibit 1.10. This statement refers to Fast-Forward's financial condition at the close of business on December 31. The left side of the balance sheet lists FastForward's assets: cash, supplies, and equipment. The upper right side of the balance sheet shows that FastForward owes $6,200 to creditors. Any other liabilities (such as a bank loan) would be listed here. The equity (capital) balance is $34,200. Line ② shows the link between the ending balance of the statement of owner's equity and the equity balance on the balance sheet. (This presentation of the balance sheet is called the *account form:* assets on the left and liabilities and equity on the right. Another presentation is the *report form:* assets on top, followed by liabilities and then equity at the bottom. Either presentation is acceptable.) As always, we see the accounting equation applies: Assets of $40,400 = Liabilities of $6,200 + Equity of $34,200.

***Decision Maker** boxes are role-playing exercises that stress the relevance of accounting.*

Decision Maker

Answer — p. 28

Retailer You open a wholesale business selling entertainment equipment to retail outlets. You find that most of your customers demand to buy on credit. How can you use the balance sheets of these customers to help you decide which ones to extend credit to? ■

Statement of Cash Flows

FastForward's statement of cash flows is the final report in Exhibit 1.10. The first section reports cash flows from *operating activities*. It shows the $6,100 cash received from clients and the $5,100 cash paid for supplies, rent, and employee salaries. Outflows are in parentheses to denote subtraction. Net cash provided by operating activities for December is $1,000. If cash paid exceeded the $5,100 cash received, we would call it "cash used by operating activities." The second section reports *investing activities,* which involve buying and selling assets such as land and equipment that are held for *long-term use* (typically more than one year). The only investing activity is the $26,000 purchase of equipment. The third section shows cash flows from *financing activities,* which include the *long-term* borrowing and repaying of cash from lenders and the cash investments from, and withdrawals by, the owner. FastForward reports $30,000 from the owner's initial investment and the $200 cash withdrawal. The net cash effect of all financing transactions is a $29,800 cash inflow. The final part of the statement shows FastForward increased its cash balance by $4,800 in December. Since it started with no cash, the ending balance is also $4,800—see line ③. We see that cash flow numbers are different from income statement (*accrual*) numbers, which is common.

Point: Statement of cash flows has three main sections: operating, investing, and financing.

Point: Payment for supplies is an operating activity because supplies are expected to be used up in short-term operations (typically less than one year).

Point: Investing activities refer to long-term asset investments by the company, *not* to owner investments.

Quick Check

Answers — p. 28

21. Explain the link between the income statement and the statement of owner's equity.
22. Describe the link between the balance sheet and the statement of owner's equity.
23. Discuss the three major sections of the statement of cash flows.

GLOBAL VIEW

Accounting according to U.S. GAAP is similar, but not identical, to IFRS. Throughout the book we use this last section to identify major similarities and differences between IFRS and U.S. GAAP for the materials in each chapter.

Basic Principles Both U.S. GAAP and IFRS include broad and similar guidance for accounting. However, neither system specifies particular account names nor the detail required. (A typical *chart of accounts* is shown near the end of this book.) IFRS does require certain minimum line items be reported in the balance sheet along with other minimum disclosures that U.S. GAAP does not. On the other hand, U.S. GAAP requires disclosures for the current and prior two years for the income statement, statement of cash flows, and statement of retained earnings (equity), while IFRS requires disclosures for the current and prior year. Still, the basic principles behind these two systems are similar.

Transaction Analysis Both U.S. GAAP and IFRS apply transaction analysis identically as shown in this chapter. Although some variations exist in revenue and expense recognition and other principles, all of the transactions in this chapter are accounted for identically under these two systems. It is often said that U.S. GAAP is more *rules-based* whereas IFRS is more *principles-based.* The main difference on the rules versus principles focus is with the approach in deciding how to account for certain transactions. Under U.S. GAAP, the approach is more focused on strictly following the accounting rules; under IFRS, the approach is more focused on a review of the situation and how accounting can best reflect it. This difference typically impacts advanced topics beyond the introductory course.

NOKIA

Financial Statements Both U.S. GAAP and IFRS prepare the same four basic financial statements. To illustrate, a condensed version of **Nokia**'s income statement follows (numbers are in Euros millions). Nokia is a leader in mobile technology, from smartphones to mobile computers. Similar condensed versions can be prepared for the other three statements.

NOKIA
Income Statement (in € millions)
For Year Ended December 31, 2009

Net sales	40,984
Cost of sales	27,720
Research, selling, administrative, and other expenses	12,302
Taxes	702
Net income (profit)	260

Decision Analysis (a section at the end of each chapter) introduces and explains ratios helpful in decision making using real company data. Instructors can skip this section and cover all ratios in Chapter 17.

Decision Analysis

Return on Assets

A2 Compute and interpret return on assets.

A *Decision Analysis* section at the end of each chapter is devoted to financial statement analysis. We organize financial statement analysis into four areas: (1) liquidity and efficiency, (2) solvency, (3) profitability, and (4) market prospects—Chapter 17 has a ratio listing with definitions and groupings by area. When analyzing ratios, we need benchmarks to identify good, bad, or average levels. Common benchmarks include the company's prior levels and those of its competitors.

This chapter presents a profitability measure: return on assets. Return on assets is useful in evaluating management, analyzing and forecasting profits, and planning activities. **Dell** has its marketing department compute return on assets for *every* order. **Return on assets (ROA),** also called *return on investment (ROI)*, is defined in Exhibit 1.11.

EXHIBIT 1.11
Return on Assets

$$\textbf{Return on assets} = \frac{\textbf{Net income}}{\textbf{Average total assets}}$$

Net income is from the annual income statement, and average total assets is computed by adding the beginning and ending amounts for that same period and dividing by 2. To illustrate, **Best Buy** reports net income of $1,317 million for fiscal year 2010. At the beginning of fiscal 2010, its total assets are $15,826 million and at the end of fiscal 2010, they total $18,302 million. Best Buy's return on assets for fiscal 2010 is:

$$\text{Return on assets} = \frac{\$1{,}317 \text{ million}}{(\$15{,}826 \text{ million} + \$18{,}302 \text{ million})/2} = 7.7\%$$

Is a 7.7% return on assets good or bad for Best Buy? To help answer this question, we compare (benchmark) Best Buy's return with its prior performance, the returns of competitors (such as **RadioShack**, **Conn's**, and **Rex Stores**), and the returns from alternative investments. Best Buy's return for each of the prior five years is in the second column of Exhibit 1.12, which ranges from 7.0% to 10.8%.

EXHIBIT 1.12

Best Buy and Industry Returns

Fiscal Year	Return on Assets Best Buy	Return on Assets Industry
2010	7.7%	2.9%
2009	7.0	2.5
2008	10.7	3.4
2007	10.8	3.5
2006	10.3	3.3

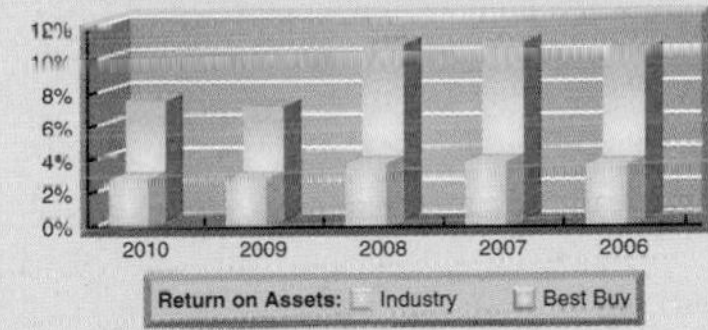

Best Buy shows a fairly stable pattern of good returns that reflect its productive use of assets. There is a decline in its 2009 return reflecting the recessionary period. We compare Best Buy's return to the normal return for similar merchandisers of electronic products (third column). Industry averages are available from services such as **Dun & Bradstreet's** *Industry Norms and Key Ratios* and **The Risk Management Association's** *Annual Statement Studies*. When compared to the industry, Best Buy performs well.

Each ***Decision Analysis*** *section ends with a role-playing scenario to show the usefulness of ratios.*

Decision Maker Answer — p. 28

Business Owner You own a small winter ski resort that earns a 21% return on its assets. An opportunity to purchase a winter ski equipment manufacturer is offered to you. This manufacturer earns a 19% return on its assets. The industry return for this manufacturer is 14%. Do you purchase this manufacturer? ■

The ***Demonstration Problem*** *is a review of key chapter content. The* Planning the Solution *offers strategies in solving the problem.*

DEMONSTRATION PROBLEM

After several months of planning, Jasmine Worthy started a haircutting business called Expressions. The following events occurred during its first month of business.

a. On August 1, Worthy invested $3,000 cash and $15,000 of equipment in Expressions.
b. On August 2, Expressions paid $600 cash for furniture for the shop.
c. On August 3, Expressions paid $500 cash to rent space in a strip mall for August.
d. On August 4, it purchased $1,200 of equipment on credit for the shop (using a long-term note payable).
e. On August 5, Expressions opened for business. Cash received from haircutting services in the first week and a half of business (ended August 15) was $825.
f. On August 15, it provided $100 of haircutting services on account.
g. On August 17, it received a $100 check for services previously rendered on account.
h. On August 17, it paid $125 cash to an assistant for hours worked during the grand opening.
i. Cash received from services provided during the second half of August was $930.
j. On August 31, it paid a $400 installment toward principal on the note payable entered into on August 4.
k. On August 31, Worthy made a $900 cash withdrawal from the company for personal use.

Required

1. Arrange the following asset, liability, and equity titles in a table similar to the one in Exhibit 1.9: Cash; Accounts Receivable; Furniture; Store Equipment; Note Payable; J. Worthy, Capital; J. Worthy, Withdrawals; Revenues; and Expenses. Show the effects of each transaction using the accounting equation.
2. Prepare an income statement for August.
3. Prepare a statement of owner's equity for August.
4. Prepare a balance sheet as of August 31.
5. Prepare a statement of cash flows for August.
6. Determine the return on assets ratio for August.

PLANNING THE SOLUTION

- Set up a table like Exhibit 1.9 with the appropriate columns for accounts.
- Analyze each transaction and show its effects as increases or decreases in the appropriate columns. Be sure the accounting equation remains in balance after each transaction.
- Prepare the income statement, and identify revenues and expenses. List those items on the statement, compute the difference, and label the result as *net income* or *net loss.*
- Use information in the Equity columns to prepare the statement of owner's equity.
- Use information in the last row of the transactions table to prepare the balance sheet.
- Prepare the statement of cash flows; include all events listed in the Cash column of the transactions table. Classify each cash flow as operating, investing, or financing.
- Calculate return on assets by dividing net income by average assets.

SOLUTION TO DEMONSTRATION PROBLEM

1.

	Assets							=	Liabilities	+	Equity						
	Cash	+	**Accounts Receivable**	+	**Furniture**	+	**Store Equipment**	=	**Note Payable**	+	**J. Worthy, Capital**	−	**J. Worthy, Withdrawals**	+	**Revenues**	−	**Expenses**
a.	$3,000						$15,000				$18,000						
b.	− 600			+	$600												
Bal.	2,400	+		+	600	+	15,000	=			18,000						
c.	− 500															−	$500
Bal.	1,900	+		+	600	+	15,000	=			18,000					−	500
d.						+	1,200		+$1,200								
Bal.	1,900	+		+	600	+	16,200	=	1,200	+	18,000					−	500
e.	+ 825													+	$ 825		
Bal.	2,725	+		+	600	+	16,200	=	1,200	+	18,000			+	825	−	500
f.		+	$100											+	100		
Bal.	2,725	+	100	+	600	+	16,200	=	1,200	+	18,000			+	925	−	500
g.	+ 100	−	100														
Bal.	2,825	+	0	+	600	+	16,200	=	1,200	+	18,000			+	925	−	500
h.	− 125															−	125
Bal.	2,700	+	0	+	600	+	16,200	=	1,200	+	18,000			+	925	−	625
i.	+ 930													+	930		
Bal.	3,630	+	0	+	600	+	16,200	=	1,200	+	18,000			+	1,855	−	625
j.	− 400								− 400								
Bal.	3,230	+	0	+	600	+	16,200	=	800	+	18,000			+	1,855	−	625
k.	− 900											−	$900				
Bal.	$ 2,330	+	0	+	$600	+	$ 16,200	=	$ 800	+	$ 18,000	−	$900	+	$1,855	−	$625

2.

EXPRESSIONS
Income Statement
For Month Ended August 31

Revenues		
Haircutting services revenue		$1,855
Expenses		
Rent expense	$500	
Wages expense	125	
Total expenses		625
Net Income		$1,230

3.

EXPRESSIONS Statement of Owner's Equity For Month Ended August 31		
J. Worthy, Capital, August 1*		$ 0
Plus: Investments by owner	$18,000	
Net income.	1,230	19,230
		19,230
Less: Withdrawals by owner.		900
J. Worthy, Capital, August 31.		$18,330

* If Expressions had been an existing business from a prior period, the beginning capital balance would equal the Capital account balance from the end of the prior period.

4.

EXPRESSIONS Balance Sheet August 31			
Assets		**Liabilities**	
Cash	$ 2,330	Note payable	$ 800
Furniture	600	**Equity**	
Store equipment	16,200	J. Worthy, Capital	18,330
Total assets	$19,130	Total liabilities and equity	$19,130

5.

EXPRESSIONS Statement of Cash Flows For Month Ended August 31		
Cash flows from operating activities		
Cash received from customers	$1,855	
Cash paid for rent	(500)	
Cash paid for wages	(125)	
Net cash provided by operating activities		$1,230
Cash flows from investing activities		
Cash paid for furniture		(600)
Cash flows from financing activities		
Cash investments by owner.	3,000	
Cash withdrawals by owner	(900)	
Partial repayment of (long-term) note payable	(400)	
Net cash provided by financing activities		1,700
Net increase in cash.		$2,330
Cash balance, August 1		0
Cash balance, August 31.		$2,330

6. Return on assets $= \frac{\text{Net income}}{\text{Average assets}} = \frac{\$1{,}230}{(\$18{,}000^* + \$19{,}130)/2} = \frac{\$1{,}230}{\$18{,}565} = \mathbf{6.63\%}$

* Uses the initial $18,000 investment as the beginning balance for the *start-up period only*.

APPENDIX

1A Return and Risk Analysis

A3 Explain the relation between return and risk.

This appendix explains return and risk analysis and its role in business and accounting.

Net income is often linked to **return.** Return on assets (ROA) is stated in ratio form as income divided by assets invested. For example, banks report return from a savings account in the form of an interest return such as 4%. If we invest in a savings account or in U.S. Treasury bills, we expect a return of around 2% to 7%. We could also invest in a company's stock, or even start our own business. How do we decide among these investment options? The answer depends on our trade-off between return and risk.

Risk is the uncertainty about the return we will earn. All business investments involve risk, but some investments involve more risk than others. The lower the risk of an investment, the lower is our expected return. The reason that savings accounts pay such a low return is the low risk of not being repaid with interest (the government guarantees most savings accounts from default). If we buy a share of eBay or any other company, we might obtain a large return. However, we have no guarantee of any return; there is even the risk of loss.

EXHIBIT 1A.1

Average Returns for Bonds with Different Risks

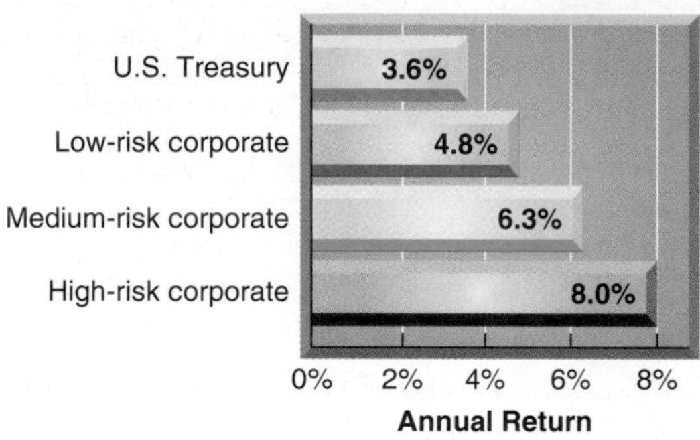

The bar graph in Exhibit 1A.1 shows recent returns for 10-year bonds with different risks. *Bonds* are written promises by organizations to repay amounts loaned with interest. U.S. Treasury bonds provide a low expected return, but they also offer low risk since they are backed by the U.S. government. High-risk corporate bonds offer a much larger potential return but with much higher risk.

The trade-off between return and risk is a normal part of business. Higher risk implies higher, but riskier, expected returns. To help us make better decisions, we use accounting information to assess both return and risk.

APPENDIX

1B Business Activities and the Accounting Equation

C5 Identify and describe the three major activities of organizations.

This appendix explains how the accounting equation is derived from business activities.

There are three major types of business activities: financing, investing, and operating. Each of these requires planning. *Planning* involves defining an organization's ideas, goals, and actions. Most public corporations use the *Management Discussion and Analysis* section in their annual reports to communicate plans. However, planning is not cast in stone. This adds *risk* to both setting plans and analyzing them.

Financing *Financing activities* provide the means organizations use to pay for resources such as land, buildings, and equipment to carry out plans. Organizations are careful in acquiring and managing financing activities because they can determine success or failure. The two sources of financing are owner and nonowner. *Owner financing* refers to resources contributed by the owner along with any income the owner leaves in the organization. *Nonowner* (or *creditor*) *financing* refers to resources contributed by creditors (lenders). *Financial management* is the task of planning how to obtain these resources and to set the right mix between owner and creditor financing.

Point: Management must understand accounting data to set financial goals, make financing and investing decisions, and evaluate operating performance.

Investing *Investing activities* are the acquiring and disposing of resources (assets) that an organization uses to acquire and sell its products or services. Assets are funded by an organization's financing. Organizations differ on the amount and makeup of assets. Some require land and factories to operate. Others need only an office. Determining the amount and type of assets for operations is called *asset management*. Invested amounts are referred to as *assets.* Financing is made up of creditor and owner financing, which hold claims on assets. Creditors' claims are called *liabilities,* and the owner's claim is called *equity.* This basic equality is called the *accounting equation* and can be written as: Assets = Liabilities + Equity.

Point: Investing (assets) and financing (liabilities plus equity) totals are *always* equal.

Operating *Operating activities* involve using resources to research, develop, purchase, produce, distribute, and market products and services. Sales and revenues are the inflow of assets from selling products and services. Costs and expenses are the outflow of assets to support operating activities. *Strategic management* is the process of determining the right mix of operating activities for the type of organization, its plans, and its market.

Exhibit 1B.1 summarizes business activities. Planning is part of each activity and gives them meaning and focus. Investing (assets) and financing (liabilities and equity) are set opposite each other to stress their balance. Operating activities are below investing and financing activities to show that operating activities are the result of investing and financing.

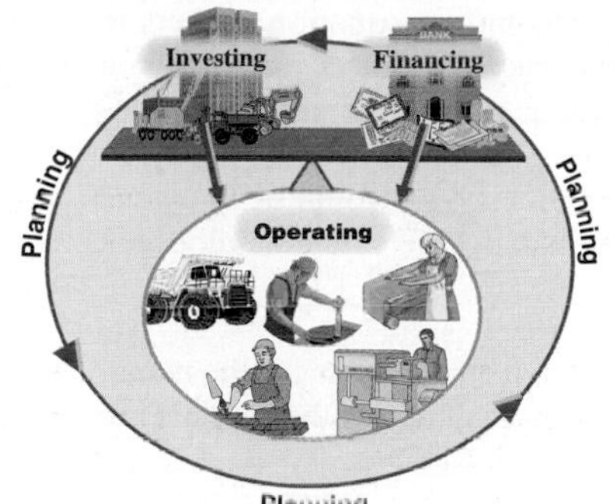

EXHIBIT 1B.1

Activities of Organizations

Summary

*A **Summary** organized by learning objectives concludes each chapter.*

C1 Explain the purpose and importance of accounting. Accounting is an information and measurement system that aims to identify, record, and communicate relevant, reliable, and comparable information about business activities. It helps assess opportunities, products, investments, and social and community responsibilities.

C2 Identify users and uses of, and opportunities in, accounting. Users of accounting are both internal and external. Some users and uses of accounting include (a) managers in controlling, monitoring, and planning; (b) lenders for measuring the risk and return of loans; (c) shareholders for assessing the return and risk of stock; (d) directors for overseeing management; and (e) employees for judging employment opportunities. Opportunities in accounting include financial, managerial, and tax accounting. They also include accounting-related fields such as lending, consulting, managing, and planning.

C3 Explain why ethics are crucial to accounting. The goal of accounting is to provide useful information for decision making. For information to be useful, it must be trusted. This demands ethical behavior in accounting.

C4 Explain generally accepted accounting principles and define and apply several accounting principles. Generally accepted accounting principles are a common set of standards applied by accountants. Accounting principles aid in producing relevant, reliable, and comparable information. Four principles underlying financial statements were introduced: cost, revenue recognition, matching, and full disclosure. Financial statements also reflect four assumptions: going-concern, monetary unit, time period, and business entity.

C5B Identify and describe the three major activities of organizations. Organizations carry out three major activities: financing, investing, and operating. Financing is the means used to pay for resources such as land, buildings, and machines. Investing refers to the buying and selling of resources used in acquiring and selling products and services. Operating activities are those necessary for carrying out the organization's plans.

A1 Define and interpret the accounting equation and each of its components. The accounting equation is: Assets = Liabilities + Equity. Assets are resources owned by a company. Liabilities are creditors' claims on assets. Equity is the owner's claim on assets (*the residual*). The expanded accounting equation is: Assets = Liabilities + [Owner Capital − Owner Withdrawals + Revenues − Expenses].

A2 Compute and interpret return on assets. Return on assets is computed as net income divided by average assets. For example, if we have an average balance of $100 in a savings account and it earns $5 interest for the year, the return on assets is $5/$100, or 5%.

A3A Explain the relation between return and risk. *Return* refers to income, and *risk* is the uncertainty about the return we hope to make. All investments involve risk. The lower the risk of an investment, the lower is its expected return. Higher risk implies higher, but riskier, expected return.

P1 Analyze business transactions using the accounting equation. A *transaction* is an exchange of economic consideration between two parties. Examples include exchanges of products, services, money, and rights to collect money. Transactions always have at least two effects on one or more components of the accounting equation. This equation is always in balance.

P2 Identify and prepare basic financial statements and explain how they interrelate. Four financial statements report on an organization's activities: balance sheet, income statement, statement of owner's equity, and statement of cash flows.

Guidance Answers to Decision Maker and Decision Ethics

Entrepreneur (p. 12) You should probably form the business as a corporation if potential lawsuits are of prime concern. The corporate form of organization protects your personal property from lawsuits directed at the business and places only the corporation's resources at risk. A downside of the corporate form is double taxation: The corporation must pay taxes on its income, and you normally must pay taxes on any money distributed to you from the business (even though the corporation already paid taxes on this money). You should also examine the ethical and socially responsible aspects of starting a business in which you anticipate injuries to others. Formation as an LLC or S corp. should also be explored.

Retailer (p. 21) You can use the accounting equation (Assets = Liabilities + Equity) to help identify risky customers to whom you would likely not want to extend credit. A balance sheet provides amounts for each of these key components. The lower a customer's equity is relative to liabilities, the less likely you would be to extend credit. A low equity means the business has little value that does not already have creditor claims to it.

Business Owner (p. 23) The 19% return on assets for the manufacturer exceeds the 14% industry return (and many others). This is a positive factor for a potential purchase. Also, the purchase of this manufacturer is an opportunity to spread your risk over two businesses as opposed to one. Still, you should hesitate to purchase a business whose return of 19% is lower than your current resort's return of 21%. You are probably better off directing efforts to increase investment in your resort, assuming you can continue to earn a 21% return.

Guidance Answers to Quick Checks

1. Accounting is an information and measurement system that identifies, records, and communicates relevant information to help people make better decisions.
2. Recordkeeping, also called *bookkeeping,* is the recording of financial transactions and events, either manually or electronically. Recordkeeping is essential to data reliability; but accounting is this and much more. Accounting includes identifying, measuring, recording, reporting, and analyzing business events and transactions.
3. Technology offers increased accuracy, speed, efficiency, and convenience in accounting.
4. External users of accounting include lenders, shareholders, directors, customers, suppliers, regulators, lawyers, brokers, and the press. Internal users of accounting include managers, officers, and other internal decision makers involved with strategic and operating decisions.
5. Internal users (managers) include those from research and development, purchasing, human resources, production, distribution, marketing, and servicing.
6. Internal controls are procedures set up to protect assets, ensure reliable accounting reports, promote efficiency, and encourage adherence to company policies. Internal controls are crucial for relevant and reliable information.
7. Ethical guidelines are threefold: (1) identify ethical concerns using personal ethics, (2) analyze options considering all good and bad consequences, and (3) make ethical decisions after weighing all consequences.
8. Ethics and social responsibility yield good behavior, and they often result in higher income and a better working environment.
9. For accounting to provide useful information for decisions, it must be trusted. Trust requires ethics in accounting.
10. Two major participants in setting rules include the SEC and the FASB. (*Note:* Accounting rules reflect society's needs, not those of accountants or any other single constituency.)
11. Most U.S. companies are not directly affected by international accounting standards. International standards are put forth as preferred accounting practices. However, stock exchanges and other parties are increasing the pressure to narrow differences in worldwide accounting practices. International accounting standards are playing an important role in that process.
12. The objectivity concept and cost principle are related in that most users consider information based on cost as objective. Information prepared using both is considered highly reliable and often relevant.
13. Users desire information about the performance of a specific entity. If information is mixed between two or more entities, its usefulness decreases.
14. The revenue recognition principle gives preparers guidelines on when to recognize (record) revenue. This is important; for example, if revenue is recognized too early, the statements report revenue sooner than it should and the business looks more profitable than it is. The reverse is also true.
15. The three basic forms of business organization are sole proprietorships, partnerships, and corporations.
16. Owners of corporations are called *shareholders* (or *stockholders*). Corporate ownership is divided into units called *shares* (or *stock*). The most basic of corporate shares is common stock (or capital stock).
17. The accounting equation is: Assets = Liabilities + Equity. This equation is always in balance, both before and after each transaction.
18. A transaction that changes the makeup of assets would not affect liability and equity accounts. FastForward's transactions 2 and 3 are examples. Each exchanges one asset for another.
19. Earning revenue by performing services, as in FastForward's transaction 5, increases equity (and assets). Incurring expenses while servicing clients, such as in transactions 6 and 7, decreases equity (and assets). Other examples include owner investments that increase equity and withdrawals that decrease equity.
20. Paying a liability with an asset reduces both asset and liability totals. One example is FastForward's transaction 10 that reduces a payable by paying cash.
21. An income statement reports a company's revenues and expenses along with the resulting net income or loss. A statement of owner's equity shows changes in equity, including that from net income or loss. Both statements report transactions occurring over a period of time.
22. The balance sheet describes a company's financial position (assets, liabilities, and equity) at a point in time. The equity amount in the balance sheet is obtained from the statement of owner's equity.
23. Cash flows from operating activities report cash receipts and payments from the primary business the company engages in. Cash flows from investing activities involve cash transactions from buying and selling long-term assets. Cash flows from financing activities include long-term cash borrowings and repayments to lenders and the cash investments from and withdrawals by the owner.

A list of key terms with page references concludes each chapter (a complete glossary is at the end of the book and also on the book's Website).

Key Terms

mhhe.com/wildFAP20e

Accounting (p. 4)
Accounting equation (p. 14)
Assets (p. 14)
Audit (p. 12)
Auditors (p. 13)
Balance sheet (p. 19)
Bookkeeping (p. 4)
Business entity assumption (p. 11)
Common stock (p. 12)
Conceptual framework (p. 9)
Corporation (p. 12)
Cost-benefit constraint (p. 12)
Cost principle (p. 10)
Equity (p. 14)
Ethics (p. 8)
Events (p. 15)
Expanded accounting equation (p. 14)
Expense recognition principle (p. 11)
Expenses (p. 14)
External transactions (p. 15)
External users (p. 5)
Financial accounting (p. 5)
Financial Accounting Standards Board (FASB) (p. 9)
Full disclosure principle (p. 11)
Generally accepted accounting principles (GAAP) (p. 8)
Going-concern assumption (p. 11)
Income statement (p. 19)
Internal transactions (p. 15)
Internal users (p. 6)
International Accounting Standards Board (IASB) (p. 9)
International Financial Reporting Standards (IFRS) (p. 9)
Liabilities (p. 14)
Managerial accounting (p. 6)
Matching principle (p. 11)
Materiality constraint (p. 12)
Measurement principle (p. 10)
Monetary unit assumption (p. 11)
Net income (p. 14)
Net loss (p. 14)
Owner, Capital (p. 14)
Owner investment (p. 14)
Owner withdrawals (p. 14)
Partnership (p. 11)
Proprietorship (p. 11)
Recordkeeping (p. 4)
Return (p. 26)
Return on assets (p. 22)
Revenue recognition principle (p. 10)
Revenues (p. 14)
Risk (p. 26)
Sarbanes–Oxley Act (p. 12)
Securities and Exchange Commission (SEC) (p. 9)
Shareholders (p. 12)
Shares (p. 12)
Sole proprietorship (p. 11)
Statement of cash flows (p. 19)
Statement of owner's equity (p. 19)
Stock (p. 12)
Stockholders (p. 12)
Time period assumption (p. 11)
Withdrawals (p. 14)

Multiple Choice Quiz

Answers on p. 47

mhhe.com/wildFAP20e

Additional Quiz Questions are available at the book's Website.

1. A building is offered for sale at $500,000 but is currently assessed at $400,000. The purchaser of the building believes the building is worth $475,000, but ultimately purchases the building for $450,000. The purchaser records the building at:
- **a.** $50,000
- **b.** $400,000
- **c.** $450,000
- **d.** $475,000
- **e.** $500,000

2. On December 30, 2010, **KPMG** signs a $150,000 contract to provide accounting services to one of its clients in 2011. KPMG has a December 31 year-end. Which accounting principle or assumption requires KPMG to record the accounting services revenue from this client in 2011 and not 2010?
- **a.** Business entity assumption
- **b.** Revenue recognition principle
- **c.** Monetary unit assumption
- **d.** Cost principle
- **e.** Going-concern assumption

3. If the assets of a company increase by $100,000 during the year and its liabilities increase by $35,000 during the same year, then the change in equity of the company during the year must have been:
- **a.** An increase of $135,000.
- **b.** A decrease of $135,000.
- **c.** A decrease of $65,000.
- **d.** An increase of $65,000.
- **e.** An increase of $100,000.

4. **Brunswick** borrows $50,000 cash from Third National Bank. How does this transaction affect the accounting equation for Brunswick?
- **a.** Assets increase by $50,000; liabilities increase by $50,000; no effect on equity.
- **b.** Assets increase by $50,000; no effect on liabilities; equity increases by $50,000.
- **c.** Assets increase by $50,000; liabilities decrease by $50,000; no effect on equity.
- **d.** No effect on assets; liabilities increase by $50,000; equity increases by $50,000.
- **e.** No effect on assets; liabilities increase by $50,000; equity decreases by $50,000.

5. **Geek Squad** performs services for a customer and bills the customer for $500. How would Geek Squad record this transaction?
   - **a.** Accounts receivable increase by $500; revenues increase by $500.
   - **b.** Cash increases by $500; revenues increase by $500.
   - **c.** Accounts receivable increase by $500; revenues decrease by $500.
   - **d.** Accounts receivable increase by $500; accounts payable increase by $500.
   - **e.** Accounts payable increase by $500; revenues increase by $500.

A(B) *Superscript letter A (B) denotes assignments based on Appendix 1A (1B).*
Icon denotes assignments that involve decision making.

Discussion Questions

1. What is the purpose of accounting in society?
2. Technology is increasingly used to process accounting data. Why then must we study and understand accounting?
3. Identify four kinds of external users and describe how they use accounting information.
4. What are at least three questions business owners and managers might be able to answer by looking at accounting information?
5. Identify three actual businesses that offer services and three actual businesses that offer products.
6. Describe the internal role of accounting for organizations.
7. Identify three types of services typically offered by accounting professionals.
8. What type of accounting information might be useful to the marketing managers of a business?
9. Why is accounting described as a service activity?
10. What are some accounting-related professions?
11. How do ethics rules affect auditors' choice of clients?
12. What work do tax accounting professionals perform in addition to preparing tax returns?
13. What does the concept of *objectivity* imply for information reported in financial statements? Why?
14. A business reports its own office stationery on the balance sheet at its $400 cost, although it cannot be sold for more than $10 as scrap paper. Which accounting principle and/or assumption justifies this treatment?
15. Why is the revenue recognition principle needed? What does it demand?
16. Describe the three basic forms of business organization and their key attributes.
17. Define (*a*) *assets,* (*b*) *liabilities,* (*c*) *equity,* and (*d*) *net assets.*
18. What events or transactions change equity?
19. Identify the two main categories of accounting principles.
20. What do accountants mean by the term *revenue?*
21. Define *net income* and explain its computation.
22. Identify the four basic financial statements of a business.
23. What information is reported in an income statement?
24. Give two examples of expenses a business might incur.
25. What is the purpose of the statement of owner's equity?
26. What information is reported in a balance sheet?
27. The statement of cash flows reports on what major activities?
28. Define and explain return on assets.
29.[A] Define return and risk. Discuss the trade-off between them.
30.[B] Describe the three major business activities in organizations.
31.[B] Explain why investing (assets) and financing (liabilities and equity) totals are always equal.
32. Refer to the financial statements of **Research In Motion** in Appendix A near the end of the book. To what level of significance are dollar amounts rounded? What time period does its income statement cover? RIM
33. Identify the dollar amounts of **Apple**'s 2009 assets, liabilities, and equity as reported in its statements in Appendix A near the end of the book. Apple
34. Refer to **Nokia**'s balance sheet in Appendix A near the end of the book. Confirm that its total assets equal its total liabilities plus total equity. NOKIA
35. Access the SEC EDGAR database (**www.SEC.gov**) and retrieve **Palm**'s 2009 10-K (filed July 24, 2009). Identify its auditor. What responsibility does its independent auditor claim regarding Palm's financial statements? Palm

Connect *reproduces assignments online, in static or algorithmic mode, which allows instructors to monitor, promote, and assess student learning. It can be used for practice, homework, or exams.*

Quick Study *exercises give readers a brief test of key elements.*

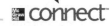

connect

QUICK STUDY

QS 1-1
Identifying accounting terms C1

Reading and interpreting accounting reports requires some knowledge of accounting terminology. (*a*) Identify the meaning of these accounting-related acronyms: GAAP, SEC, FASB, IASB and IFRS. (*b*) Briefly explain the importance of the knowledge base or organization that is referred to for each of the accounting-related acronyms.

QS 1-2 Explaining internal control C1

An important responsibility of many accounting professionals is to design and implement internal control procedures for organizations. Explain the purpose of internal control procedures. Provide two examples of internal controls applied by companies.

QS 1-3 Identifying accounting users C2

Identify the following users as either external users (E) or internal users (I).

a. Lenders	**d.** Sales staff	**g.** Brokers	**j.** Managers
b. Controllers	**e.** FBI and IRS	**h.** Suppliers	**k.** Business press
c. Shareholders	**f.** Consumer group	**i.** Customers	**l.** District attorney

QS 1-4 Accounting opportunities C2

There are many job opportunities for those with accounting knowledge. Identify at least three main areas of opportunities for accounting professionals. For each area, identify at least three job possibilities linked to accounting.

QS 1-5 Identifying ethical concerns C3

This icon highlights assignments that enhance decision-making skills.

Accounting professionals must sometimes choose between two or more acceptable methods of accounting for business transactions and events. Explain why these situations can involve difficult matters of ethical concern.

QS 1-6 Identifying accounting principles C4

Identify which accounting principle or assumption best describes each of the following practices:

a. If $51,000 cash is paid to buy land, the land is reported on the buyer's balance sheet at $51,000.

b. Alissa Kees owns both Sailing Passions and Dockside Supplies. In preparing financial statements for Dockside Supplies, Kees makes sure that the expense transactions of Sailing Passions are kept separate from Dockside's transactions and financial statements.

c. In December 2010, Ace Landscaping received a customer's order and cash prepayment to install sod at a new house that would not be ready for installation until March 2011. Ace should record the revenue from the customer order in March 2011, not in December 2010.

QS 1-7 Applying the accounting equation A1

a. Total assets of Caldwell Company equal $40,000 and its equity is $10,000. What is the amount of its liabilities?

b. Total assets of Waterworld equal $55,000 and its liabilities and equity amounts are equal to each other. What is the amount of its liabilities? What is the amount of its equity?

QS 1-8 Applying the accounting equation A1

Use the accounting equation to compute the missing financial statement amounts (*a*), (*b*), and (*c*).

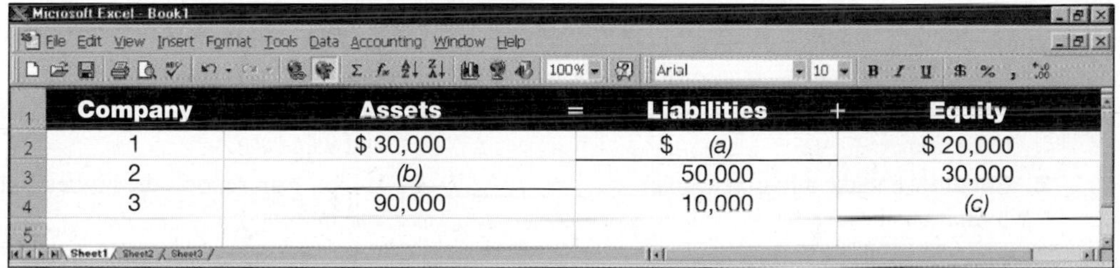

Company	Assets	=	Liabilities	+	Equity
1	$ 30,000		$ (a)		$ 20,000
2	(b)		50,000		30,000
3	90,000		10,000		(c)

QS 1-9 Identifying transactions and events P1

Accounting provides information about an organization's business transactions and events that both affect the accounting equation and can be reliably measured. Identify at least two examples of both (*a*) business transactions and (*b*) business events that meet these requirements.

QS 1-10 Identifying and computing assets, liabilities, and equity P1

Use **Apple**'s September 26, 2009, financial statements, in Appendix A near the end of the book, to answer the following:

a. Identify the dollar amounts of Apple's 2009 (1) assets, (2) liabilities, and (3) equity.

b. Using Apple's amounts from part *a*, verify that Assets = Liabilities + Equity.

QS 1-11
Computing and interpreting return on assets
A2

In a recent year's financial statements, **Home Depot** reported the following results. Compute and interpret Home Depot's return on assets (assume competitors average a 5% return on assets).

Sales	$71,288 million
Net income	2,260 million
Average total assets	42,744 million

QS 1-12
Identifying items with financial statements
P2

Indicate in which financial statement each item would most likely appear: income statement (I), balance sheet (B), statement of owner's equity (OE), or statement of cash flows (CF).

a. Assets
b. Revenues
c. Liabilities
d. Equipment
e. Withdrawals
f. Expenses
g. Total liabilities and equity
h. Cash from operating activities
i. Net decrease (or increase) in cash

QS 1-13
International accounting standards C4

This icon highlights assignments that focus on IFRS-related content.

Answer each of the following questions related to international accounting standards.

a. The International Accounting Standards Board (IASB) issues preferred accounting practices that are referred to as what?
b. The FASB and IASB are working on a convergence process for what purpose?
c. The SEC has proposed a roadmap for use of IFRS by U.S. companies. What is the proposed adoption date for large U.S. companies to adopt IFRS?

Mc Graw Hill connect

EXERCISES

Exercise 1-1
Classifying activities reflected in the accounting system
C1

Accounting is an information and measurement system that identifies, records, and communicates relevant, reliable, and comparable information about an organization's business activities. Classify the following activities as part of the identifying (I), recording (R), or communicating (C) aspects of accounting.

_____ **1.** Determining employee tasks behind a service.
_____ **2.** Establishing revenues generated from a product.
_____ **3.** Maintaining a log of service costs.
_____ **4.** Measuring the costs of a product.
_____ **5.** Preparing financial statements.
_____ **6.** Analyzing and interpreting reports.
_____ **7.** Presenting financial information.

Exercise 1-2
Identifying accounting users and uses
C2

Part A. Identify the following users of accounting information as either an internal (I) or an external (E) user.

_____ **1.** Shareholders
_____ **2.** Creditors
_____ **3.** Nonexecutive employee
_____ **4.** Research and development director
_____ **5.** Purchasing manager
_____ **6.** Human resources director
_____ **7.** Production supervisors
_____ **8.** Distribution managers

Part B. Identify the following questions as most likely to be asked by an internal (I) or an external (E) user of accounting information.

_____ **1.** What are the costs of our service to customers?
_____ **2.** Should we make a five-year loan to that business?
_____ **3.** Should we spend further research on our product?
_____ **4.** Do income levels justify the current stock price?
_____ **5.** What are reasonable payroll benefits and wages?
_____ **6.** Which firm reports the highest sales and income?
_____ **7.** What are the costs of our product's ingredients?

Exercise 1-3
Describing accounting responsibilities
C2

Many accounting professionals work in one of the following three areas:

A. Managerial accounting **B.** Financial accounting **C.** Tax accounting

Identify the area of accounting that is most involved in each of the following responsibilities:

_____ **1.** Reviewing reports for SEC compliance.
_____ **2.** Planning transactions to minimize taxes.
_____ **3.** Investigating violations of tax laws.
_____ **4.** Preparing external financial statements.
_____ **5.** Budgeting.
_____ **6.** Cost accounting.
_____ **7.** External auditing.
_____ **8.** Internal auditing.

Exercise 1-4
Identifying ethical concerns
C3 

Assume the following role and describe a situation in which ethical considerations play an important part in guiding your decisions and actions:

a. You are a student in an introductory accounting course.
b. You are an accounting professional with audit clients that are competitors in business.
c. You are an accounting professional preparing tax returns for clients.
d. You are a manager with responsibility for several employees.

Exercise 1-5
Learning the language of business
C1–C3

Match each of the numbered descriptions with the term or phrase it best reflects. Indicate your answer by writing the letter for the term or phrase in the blank provided.

A. Audit	**C.** Ethics	**E.** SEC	**G.** Net income
B. GAAP	**D.** Tax accounting	**F.** Public accountants	**H.** IASB

_____ **1.** Amount a business earns after paying all expenses and costs associated with its sales and revenues.
_____ **2.** An examination of an organization's accounting system and records that adds credibility to financial statements.
_____ **3.** Principles that determine whether an action is right or wrong.
_____ **4.** Accounting professionals who provide services to many clients.
_____ **5.** An accounting area that includes planning future transactions to minimize taxes paid.

Exercise 1-6
Identifying accounting principles and assumptions
C4

Match each of the numbered descriptions with the principle or assumption it best reflects. Enter the letter for the appropriate principle or assumption in the blank space next to each description.

A. Cost principle	**E.** General accounting principle
B. Matching principle	**F.** Business entity assumption
C. Specific accounting principle	**G.** Revenue recognition principle
D. Full disclosure principle	**H.** Going-concern assumption

_____ **1.** Revenue is recorded only when the earnings process is complete.
_____ **2.** Information is based on actual costs incurred in transactions.
_____ **3.** Usually created by a pronouncement from an authoritative body.
_____ **4.** Financial statements reflect the assumption that the business continues operating.
_____ **5.** A company reports details behind financial statements that would impact users' decisions.
_____ **6.** A company records the expenses incurred to generate the revenues reported.
_____ **7.** Derived from long-used and generally accepted accounting practices.
_____ **8.** Every business is accounted for separately from its owner or owners.

Exercise 1-7
Distinguishing business organizations
C4

The following describe several different business organizations. Determine whether the description refers to a sole proprietorship, partnership, or corporation.

a. A-1 pays its own income taxes and has two owners.
b. Ownership of Zeller Company is divided into 1,000 shares of stock.
c. Waldron is owned by Mary Malone, who is personally liable for the company's debts.
d. Micah Douglas and Nathan Logan own Financial Services, a financial services provider. Neither Douglas nor Logan has personal responsibility for the debts of Financial Services.
e. Bailey and Kay own Squeaky Clean, a cleaning service. Both are personally liable for the debts of the business.
f. Plasto Products does not pay income taxes and has one owner.
g. Ian LLC does not have separate legal existence apart from the one person who owns it.

Exercise 1-8
Using the accounting equation
A1 P1 

Answer the following questions. (*Hint:* Use the accounting equation.)

a. Office Mart has assets equal to $123,000 and liabilities equal to $53,000 at year-end. What is the total equity for Office Mart at year-end?
b. At the beginning of the year, Logan Company's assets are $200,000 and its equity is $150,000. During the year, assets increase $70,000 and liabilities increase $30,000. What is the equity at the end of the year?
c. At the beginning of the year, Keller Company's liabilities equal $60,000. During the year, assets increase by $80,000, and at year-end assets equal $180,000. Liabilities decrease $10,000 during the year. What are the beginning and ending amounts of equity?

Check (c) Beg. equity, $40,000

Exercise 1-9
Using the accounting equation
A1

Determine the missing amount from each of the separate situations *a*, *b*, and *c* below.

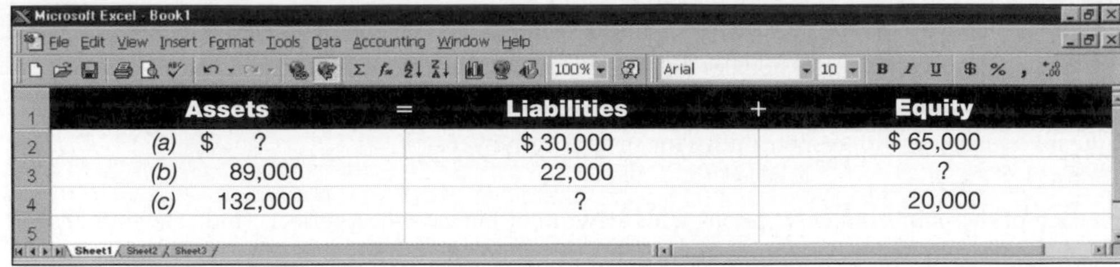

	Assets	=	Liabilities	+	Equity
(a)	$?		$ 30,000		$ 65,000
(b)	89,000		22,000		?
(c)	132,000		?		20,000

Exercise 1-10
Identifying effects of transactions on the accounting equation
P1

Provide an example of a transaction that creates the described effects for the separate cases *a* through *g*.

a. Increases an asset and decreases an asset.
b. Decreases an asset and decreases a liability.
c. Decreases a liability and increases a liability.
d. Increases an asset and increases a liability.
e. Decreases an asset and decreases equity.
f. Increases a liability and decreases equity.
g. Increases an asset and increases equity.

Exercise 1-11
Identifying effects of transactions using the accounting equation
P1 

Lena Gold began a professional practice on June 1 and plans to prepare financial statements at the end of each month. During June, Gold (the owner) completed these transactions:

a. Owner invested $50,000 cash in the company along with equipment that had a $10,000 market value.
b. The company paid $1,600 cash for rent of office space for the month.
c. The company purchased $12,000 of additional equipment on credit (payment due within 30 days).
d. The company completed work for a client and immediately collected the $2,000 cash earned.
e. The company completed work for a client and sent a bill for $7,000 to be received within 30 days.
f. The company purchased additional equipment for $8,000 cash.
g. The company paid an assistant $2,400 cash as wages for the month.
h. The company collected $5,000 cash as a partial payment for the amount owed by the client in transaction *e*.
i. The company paid $12,000 cash to settle the liability created in transaction *c*.
j. Owner withdrew $500 cash from the company for personal use.

Required

Check Net income, $5,000

Create a table like the one in Exhibit 1.9, using the following headings for columns: Cash; Accounts Receivable; Equipment; Accounts Payable; L. Gold, Capital; L. Gold, Withdrawals; Revenues; and Expenses. Then use additions and subtractions to show the effects of the transactions on individual items of the accounting equation. Show new balances after each transaction.

Exercise 1-12
Analysis using the accounting equation
P1 

Zelda began a new consulting firm on January 5. The accounting equation showed the following balances after each of the company's first five transactions. Analyze the accounting equation for each transaction and describe each of the five transactions with their amounts.

	Assets							=	Liabilities	+	Equity		
Transaction	Cash	+	Accounts Receivable	+	Office Supplies	+	Office Furniture	=	Accounts Payable	+	Zelda, Capital	+	Revenues
a.	$20,000	+	$ 0	+	$ 0	+	$ 0	=	$ 0	+	$20,000	+	$ 0
b.	19,000	+	0	+	1,500	+	0	=	500	+	20,000	+	0
c.	11,000	+	0	+	1,500	+	8,000	=	500	+	20,000	+	0
d.	11,000	+	3,000	+	1,500	+	8,000	=	500	+	20,000	+	3,000
e.	11,500	+	3,000	+	1,500	+	8,000	=	500	+	20,000	+	3,500

The following table shows the effects of five transactions (*a* through *e*) on the assets, liabilities, and equity of Vera's Boutique. Write short descriptions of the probable nature of each transaction.

Exercise 1-13
Identifying effects of transactions on accounting equation
P1 

	Assets				=	Liabilities	+	Equity	
	Cash	+ Accounts Receivable	+ Office Supplies	+ Land	=	Accounts Payable	+	Vera, Capital	+ Revenues
	$ 10,500	+ $ 0	+ $1,500	+ $ 9,500	=	$ 0	+	$21,500	+ $ 0
a.	− 2,000			+ 2,000					
b.			+ 500			+500			
c.		+ 950							+ 950
d.	− 500					−500			
e.	+ 950	− 950							
	$ 8,950	+ $ 0	+ $2,000	+ $11,500	=	$ 0	+	$21,500	+ $950

On October 1, Natalie King organized Real Solutions, a new consulting firm. On October 31, the company's records show the following items and amounts. Use this information to prepare an October income statement for the business.

Exercise 1-14
Preparing an income statement
P2

Cash	$ 2,000	Cash withdrawals by owner	$ 3,360
Accounts receivable	13,000	Consulting fees earned	15,000
Office supplies	4,250	Rent expense	2,550
Land	36,000	Salaries expense	6,000
Office equipment	28,000	Telephone expense	660
Accounts payable	7,500	Miscellaneous expenses	680
Owner investments	74,000		

Check Net income, $5,110

Use the information in Exercise 1-14 to prepare an October statement of owner's equity for Real Solutions.

Exercise 1-15
Preparing a statement of owner's equity P2

Use the information in Exercise 1-14 (if completed, you can also use your solution to Exercise 1-15) to prepare an October 31 balance sheet for Real Solutions.

Exercise 1-16
Preparing a balance sheet P2

Use the information in Exercise 1-14 to prepare an October 31 statement of cash flows for Real Solutions. Also assume the following:

a. The owner's initial investment consists of $38,000 cash and $36,000 in land.
b. The company's $28,000 equipment purchase is paid in cash.
c. The accounts payable balance of $7,500 consists of the $4,250 office supplies purchase and $3,250 in employee salaries yet to be paid.
d. The company's rent, telephone, and miscellaneous expenses are paid in cash.
e. $2,000 has been collected on the $15,000 consulting fees earned.

Exercise 1-17
Preparing a statement of cash flows
P2  

Check Net increase in cash, $2,000

Geneva Group reports net income of $20,000 for 2011. At the beginning of 2011, Geneva Group had $100,000 in assets. By the end of 2011, assets had grown to $150,000. What is Geneva Group's 2011 return on assets? How would you assess its performance if competitors average a 10% return on assets?

Exercise 1-18
Analysis of return on assets
A2 

Indicate the section where each of the following would appear on the statement of cash flows.

A. Cash flows from operating activity
B. Cash flows from investing activity
C. Cash flows from financing activity

_______	**1.** Cash paid for wages	_______	**5.** Cash paid on an account payable
_______	**2.** Cash withdrawal by owner	_______	**6.** Cash investment by owner
_______	**3.** Cash purchase of equipment	_______	**7.** Cash received from clients
_______	**4.** Cash paid for advertising	_______	**8.** Cash paid for rent

Exercise 1-19
Identifying sections of the statement of cash flows
P2

Exercise 1-20[B]
Identifying business activities
C5

Match each transaction or event to one of the following activities of an organization: financing activities (F), investing activities (I), or operating activities (O).

1. ______ An owner contributes resources to the business.
2. ______ An organization purchases equipment.
3. ______ An organization advertises a new product.
4. ______ The organization borrows money from a bank.
5. ______ An organization sells some of its land.

Exercise 1-21
Preparing an income statement for a global company
P2 

Nintendo Company reports the following income statement accounts for the year ended March 31, 2009. (Japanese yen in millions.)

Net sales	¥1,838,622
Cost of sales	1,044,981
Selling, general and administrative expenses	238,378
Other expenses	276,174

Use this information to prepare Nintendo's income statement for the year ended March 31, 2009.

***Problem Set B** located at the end of **Problem Set A** is provided for each problem to reinforce the learning process.*

PROBLEM SET A

Problem 1-1A
Identifying effects of transactions on financial statements
A1 P1 

Identify how each of the following separate transactions affects financial statements. For the balance sheet, identify how each transaction affects total assets, total liabilities, and total equity. For the income statement, identify how each transaction affects net income. For the statement of cash flows, identify how each transaction affects cash flows from operating activities, cash flows from financing activities, and cash flows from investing activities. For increases, place a "+" in the column or columns. For decreases, place a "−" in the column or columns. If both an increase and a decrease occur, place a "+/−" in the column or columns. The first transaction is completed as an example.

		Balance Sheet			Income Statement	Statement of Cash Flows		
	Transaction	Total Assets	Total Liab.	Total Equity	Net Income	Operating Activities	Financing Activities	Investing Activities
1	Owner invests cash in business	+		+			+	
2	Incurs legal costs on credit							
3	Pays cash for employee wages							
4	Borrows cash by signing long-term note payable							
5	Receives cash for services provided							
6	Buys land by signing note payable							
7	Buys office equipment for cash							
8	Provides services on credit							
9	Collects cash on receivable from (8)							
10	Owner withdraws cash							

Problem 1-2A
Computing missing information using accounting knowledge
A1 P1 

The following financial statement information is from five separate companies:

	Company A	Company B	Company C	Company D	Company E
December 31, 2010					
Assets	$45,000	$35,000	$29,000	$80,000	$123,000
Liabilities	23,500	22,500	14,000	38,000	?
December 31, 2011					
Assets	48,000	41,000	?	125,000	112,500
Liabilities	?	27,500	19,000	64,000	75,000
During year 2011					
Owner investments	5,000	1,500	7,750	?	4,500
Net income (loss)	7,500	?	9,000	12,000	18,000
Owner cash withdrawals	2,500	3,000	3,875	0	9,000

Required

1. Answer the following questions about Company A:
   a. What is the amount of equity on December 31, 2010?
   b. What is the amount of equity on December 31, 2011?
   c. What is the amount of liabilities on December 31, 2011?
2. Answer the following questions about Company B:
   a. What is the amount of equity on December 31, 2010?
   b. What is the amount of equity on December 31, 2011?
   c. What is net income for year 2011?
3. Calculate the amount of assets for Company C on December 31, 2011.
4. Calculate the amount of owner investments for Company D during year 2011.
5. Calculate the amount of liabilities for Company E on December 31, 2010.

Check (1*b*) $31,500

(2*c*) $2,500

(3) $46,875

Problem 1-3A
Preparing a balance sheet
P2

The following is selected financial information for Affiliated Company as of December 31, 2011: liabilities, $34,000; equity, $56,000; assets, $90,000.

Required

Prepare the balance sheet for Affiliated Company as of December 31, 2011.

Problem 1-4A
Preparing an income statement
P2

The following is selected financial information for Sun Energy Company for the year ended December 31, 2011: revenues, $65,000; expenses, $50,000; net income, $15,000.

Required

Prepare the 2011 calendar-year income statement for Sun Energy Company.

Problem 1-5A
Preparing a statement of owner's equity
P2

Following is selected financial information for Boardwalk for the year ended December 31, 2011.

B. Walk, Capital, Dec. 31, 2011	$15,000	B. Walk, Withdrawals	$2,000
Net income	9,000	B. Walk, Capital, Dec. 31, 2010	8,000

Required

Prepare the 2011 statement of owner's equity for Boardwalk.

Problem 1-6A
Preparing a statement of cash flows
P2

Following is selected financial information of Trimark for the year ended December 31, 2011.

Cash used by investing activities	$(3,000)
Net increase in cash	200
Cash used by financing activities	(3,800)
Cash from operating activities	7,000
Cash, December 31, 2010	3,300

Check Cash balance, Dec. 31, 2011, $3,500

Required

Prepare the 2011 statement of cash flows for Trimark Company.

Problem 1-7A
Analyzing effects of transactions
C4 P1 P2 A1

Miranda Right started Right Consulting, a new business, and completed the following transactions during its first year of operations.

a. M. Right invests $60,000 cash and office equipment valued at $30,000 in the company.
b. The company purchased a $300,000 building to use as an office. Right paid $50,000 in cash and signed a note payable promising to pay the $250,000 balance over the next ten years.
c. The company purchased office equipment for $6,000 cash.
d. The company purchased $4,000 of office supplies and $1,000 of office equipment on credit.
e. The company paid a local newspaper $1,000 cash for printing an announcement of the office's opening.
f. The company completed a financial plan for a client and billed that client $4,000 for the service.
g. The company designed a financial plan for another client and immediately collected an $8,000 cash fee.
h. M. Right withdrew $1,800 cash from the company for personal use.
i. The company received $3,000 cash as partial payment from the client described in transaction *f*.
j. The company made a partial payment of $500 cash on the equipment purchased in transaction *d*.
k. The company paid $2,500 cash for the office secretary's wages for this period.

Required

Check (2) Ending balances: Cash, $9,200; Expenses, $3,500; Notes Payable, $250,000
(3) Net income, $8,500

1. Create a table like the one in Exhibit 1.9, using the following headings for the columns: Cash; Accounts Receivable; Office Supplies; Office Equipment; Building; Accounts Payable; Notes Payable; M. Right, Capital; M. Right, Withdrawals; Revenues; and Expenses.
2. Use additions and subtractions within the table created in part *1* to show the dollar effects of each transaction on individual items of the accounting equation. Show new balances after each transaction.
3. Once you have completed the table, determine the company's net income.

Problem 1-8A
Analyzing transactions and preparing financial statements
C4 P1 P2

mhhe.com/wildFAP20e

J. D. Simpson started The Simpson Co., a new business that began operations on May 1. The Simpson Co. completed the following transactions during its first month of operations.

May 1	J. D. Simpson invested $60,000 cash in the company.
1	The company rented a furnished office and paid $3,200 cash for May's rent.
3	The company purchased $1,680 of office equipment on credit.
5	The company paid $800 cash for this month's cleaning services.
8	The company provided consulting services for a client and immediately collected $4,600 cash.
12	The company provided $3,000 of consulting services for a client on credit.
15	The company paid $850 cash for an assistant's salary for the first half of this month.
20	The company received $3,000 cash payment for the services provided on May 12.
22	The company provided $2,800 of consulting services on credit.
25	The company received $2,800 cash payment for the services provided on May 22.
26	The company paid $1,680 cash for the office equipment purchased on May 3.
27	The company purchased $60 of advertising in this month's (May) local paper on credit; cash payment is due June 1.
28	The company paid $850 cash for an assistant's salary for the second half of this month.
30	The company paid $200 cash for this month's telephone bill.
30	The company paid $480 cash for this month's utilities.
31	J. D. Simpson withdrew $1,200 cash from the company for personal use.

Required

1. Arrange the following asset, liability, and equity titles in a table like Exhibit 1.9: Cash; Accounts Receivable; Office Equipment; Accounts Payable; J. D. Simpson, Capital; J. D. Simpson, Withdrawals; Revenues; and Expenses.

2. Show effects of the transactions on the accounts of the accounting equation by recording increases and decreases in the appropriate columns. Do not determine new account balances after each transaction. Determine the final total for each account and verify that the equation is in balance.

Check (2) Ending balances: Cash, $61,140; Expenses, $6,440

3. Prepare an income statement for May, a statement of owner's equity for May, a May 31 balance sheet, and a statement of cash flows for May.

(3) Net income, $3,960; Total assets, $62,820

Problem 1-9A
Analyzing transactions and preparing financial statements
C4 P1 P2

eXcel
mhhe.com/wildFAP20e

Curtis Hamilton started a new business and completed these transactions during December.

Dec. 1 Curtis Hamilton transferred $56,000 cash from a personal savings account to a checking account in the name of Hamilton Electric.
2 The company rented office space and paid $800 cash for the December rent.
3 The company purchased $14,000 of electrical equipment by paying $3,200 cash and agreeing to pay the $10,800 balance in 30 days.
5 The company purchased office supplies by paying $900 cash.
6 The company completed electrical work and immediately collected $1,000 cash for these services.
8 The company purchased $3,800 of office equipment on credit.
15 The company completed electrical work on credit in the amount of $4,000.
18 The company purchased $500 of office supplies on credit.
20 The company paid $3,800 cash for the office equipment purchased on December 8.
24 The company billed a client $600 for electrical work completed; the balance is due in 30 days.
28 The company received $4,000 cash for the work completed on December 15.
29 The company paid the assistant's salary of $1,200 cash for this month.
30 The company paid $440 cash for this month's utility bill.
31 C. Hamilton withdrew $700 cash from the company for personal use.

Required

1. Arrange the following asset, liability, and equity titles in a table like Exhibit 1.9: Cash; Accounts Receivable; Office Supplies; Office Equipment; Electrical Equipment; Accounts Payable; C. Hamilton, Capital; C. Hamilton, Withdrawals; Revenues; and Expenses.
2. Use additions and subtractions to show the effects of each transaction on the accounts in the accounting equation. Show new balances after each transaction.
3. Use the increases and decreases in the columns of the table from part 2 to prepare an income statement, a statement of owner's equity, and a statement of cash flows—each of these for the current month. Also prepare a balance sheet as of the end of the month.

Check (2) Ending balances: Cash, $49,960, Accounts Payable, $11,300

(3) Net income, $3,160; Total assets, $69,760

Analysis Component

4. Assume that the owner investment transaction on December 1 was $40,000 cash instead of $56,000 and that Hamilton Electric obtained another $16,000 in cash by borrowing it from a bank. Explain the effect of this change on total assets, total liabilities, and total equity.

Problem 1-10A
Determining expenses, liabilities, equity, and return on assets
A1 A2 

Nolan manufactures, markets, and sells cellular telephones. The average total assets for Nolan is $250,000. In its most recent year, Nolan reported net income of $55,000 on revenues of $455,000.

Required

1. What is Nolan's return on assets?
2. Does return on assets seem satisfactory for Nolan given that its competitors average a 12% return on assets?
3. What are total expenses for Nolan in its most recent year?
4. What is the average total amount of liabilities plus equity for Nolan?

Check (3) $400,000
(4) $250,000

Problem 1-11A
Computing and interpreting return on assets
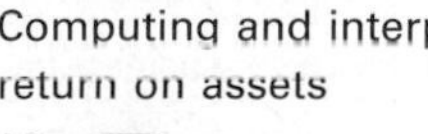
A2 

Coca-Cola and **PepsiCo** both produce and market beverages that are direct competitors. Key financial figures (in $ millions) for these businesses over the past year follow.

Key Figures ($ millions)	Coca-Cola	PepsiCo
Sales	$30,990	$43,232
Net income	6,906	5,979
Average assets	44,595	37,921

Check (1*a*) 15.5%; (1*b*) 15.8%

Required

1. Compute return on assets for (*a*) Coca-Cola and (*b*) PepsiCo.
2. Which company is more successful in its total amount of sales to consumers?
3. Which company is more successful in returning net income from its assets invested?

Analysis Component

4. Write a one-paragraph memorandum explaining which company you would invest your money in and why. (Limit your explanation to the information provided.)

Problem 1-12A[A]
Identifying risk and return
A3

All business decisions involve aspects of risk and return.

Required

Identify both the risk and the return in each of the following activities:

1. Investing $1,000 in a 4% savings account.
2. Placing a $1,000 bet on your favorite sports team.
3. Investing $10,000 in Yahoo! stock.
4. Taking out a $10,000 college loan to earn an accounting degree.

Problem 1-13A[B]
Describing organizational activities C5

An organization undertakes various activities in pursuit of business success. Identify an organization's three major business activities, and describe each activity.

Problem 1-14A[B]
Describing organizational activities
C5

A start-up company often engages in the following transactions in its first year of operations. Classify those transactions in one of the three major categories of an organization's business activities.

F. Financing **I.** Investing **O.** Operating

_______ **1.** Owner investing land in business.
_______ **2.** Purchasing a building.
_______ **3.** Purchasing land.
_______ **4.** Borrowing cash from a bank.
_______ **5.** Purchasing equipment.
_______ **6.** Selling and distributing products.
_______ **7.** Paying for advertising.
_______ **8.** Paying employee wages.

PROBLEM SET B

Problem 1-1B
Identifying effects of transactions on financial statements A1 P1

Identify how each of the following separate transactions affects financial statements. For the balance sheet, identify how each transaction affects total assets, total liabilities, and total equity. For the income statement, identify how each transaction affects net income. For the statement of cash flows, identify how each transaction affects cash flows from operating activities, cash flows from financing activities, and cash flows from investing activities. For increases, place a "+" in the column or columns. For decreases, place a "−" in the column or columns. If both an increase and a decrease occur, place "+/−" in the column or columns. The first transaction is completed as an example.

		Balance Sheet			Income Statement	Statement of Cash Flows		
	Transaction	Total Assets	Total Liab.	Total Equity	Net Income	Operating Activities	Financing Activities	Investing Activities
1	Owner invests cash in business	+		+			+	
2	Buys building by signing note payable							
3	Pays cash for salaries incurred							
4	Provides services for cash							
5	Pays cash for rent incurred							
6	Incurs utilities costs on credit							
7	Buys store equipment for cash							
8	Owner withdraws cash							
9	Provides services on credit							
10	Collects cash on receivable from (9)							

The following financial statement information is from five separate companies.

Problem 1-2B
Computing missing information using accounting knowledge
A1 P1 

	Company V	Company W	Company X	Company Y	Company Z
December 31, 2010					
Assets	$45,000	$70,000	$121,500	$82,500	$124,000
Liabilities	30,000	50,000	58,500	61,500	?
December 31, 2011					
Assets	49,000	90,000	136,500	?	160,000
Liabilities	26,000	?	55,500	72,000	52,000
During year 2011					
Owner investments	6,000	10,000	?	38,100	40,000
Net income or (loss)	?	30,000	16,500	24,000	32,000
Owner cash withdrawals	4,500	2,000	0	18,000	6,000

Required

1. Answer the following questions about Company V:
   a. What is the amount of equity on December 31, 2010?
   b. What is the amount of equity on December 31, 2011?
   c. What is the net income or loss for the year 2011?
2. Answer the following questions about Company W:
   a. What is the amount of equity on December 31, 2010?
   b. What is the amount of equity on December 31, 2011?
   c. What is the amount of liabilities on December 31, 2011?
3. Calculate the amount of owner investments for Company X during 2011.
4. Calculate the amount of assets for Company Y on December 31, 2011.
5. Calculate the amount of liabilities for Company Z on December 31, 2010.

Check (1*b*) $23,000

(2*c*) $32,000

(4) $137,100

The following is selected financial information for RWB Company as of December 31, 2011.

Problem 1-3B
Preparing a balance sheet
P2

Liabilities	$74,000	Equity	$40,000	Assets	$114,000

Required

Prepare the balance sheet for RWB Company as of December 31, 2011.

Selected financial information for Online Co. for the year ended December 31, 2011, follows.

Problem 1-4B
Preparing an income statement
P2

Revenues	$58,000	Expenses	$30,000	Net income	$28,000

Required

Prepare the 2011 income statement for Online Company.

Following is selected financial information of ComEx for the year ended December 31, 2011.

Problem 1-5B
Preparing a statement of owner's equity
P2

C. Tex, Capital, Dec. 31, 2011	$47,000	C. Tex, Withdrawals	$ 8,000
Net income	6,000	C. Tex, Capital, Dec. 31, 2010	49,000

Required

Prepare the 2011 statement of owner's equity for ComEx.

Problem 1-6B
Preparing a statement of cash flows
P2

Selected financial information of BuyRight Co. for the year ended December 31, 2011, follows.

Cash from investing activities	$2,600
Net increase in cash	1,400
Cash from financing activities	2,800
Cash used by operating activities	(4,000)
Cash, December 31, 2010	1,300

Required

Prepare the 2011 statement of cash flows for BuyRight Company.

Problem 1-7B
Analyzing effects of transactions
C4 P1 P2 A1

Tiana Moore started a new business, Tiana's Solutions, and completed the following transactions during its first year of operations.

a. T. Moore invests $95,000 cash and office equipment valued at $20,000 in the company.
b. The company purchased a $120,000 building to use as an office. It paid $20,000 in cash and signed a note payable promising to pay the $100,000 balance over the next ten years.
c. The company purchased office equipment for $20,000 cash.
d. The company purchased $1,400 of office supplies and $3,000 of office equipment on credit.
e. The company paid a local newspaper $400 cash for printing an announcement of the office's opening.
f. The company completed a financial plan for a client and billed that client $1,800 for the service.
g. The company designed a financial plan for another client and immediately collected a $2,000 cash fee.
h. T. Moore withdrew $5,000 cash from the company for personal use.
i. The company received $1,800 cash from the client described in transaction *f*.
j. The company made a payment of $2,000 cash on the equipment purchased in transaction *d*.
k. The company paid $2,000 cash for the office secretary's wages.

Required

1. Create a table like the one in Exhibit 1.9, using the following headings for the columns: Cash; Accounts Receivable; Office Supplies; Office Equipment; Building; Accounts Payable; Notes Payable; T. Moore, Capital; T. Moore, Withdrawals; Revenues; and Expenses.
2. Use additions and subtractions within the table created in part *1* to show the dollar effects of each transaction on individual items of the accounting equation. Show new balances after each transaction.
3. Once you have completed the table, determine the company's net income.

Check (2) Ending balances: Cash, $49,400; Expenses, $2,400; Notes Payable, $100,000
(3) Net income, $1,400

Problem 1-8B
Analyzing transactions and preparing financial statements
C4 P1 P2

Ken Stone launched a new business, Ken's Maintenance Co., that began operations on June 1. The following transactions were completed by the company during that first month.

June	1	K. Stone invested $120,000 cash in the company.
	2	The company rented a furnished office and paid $4,500 cash for June's rent.
	4	The company purchased $2,400 of equipment on credit.
	6	The company paid $1,125 cash for this month's advertising of the opening of the business.
	8	The company completed maintenance services for a customer and immediately collected $750 cash.
	14	The company completed $6,300 of maintenance services for City Center on credit.
	16	The company paid $900 cash for an assistant's salary for the first half of the month.
	20	The company received $6,300 cash payment for services completed for City Center on June 14.
	21	The company completed $3,500 of maintenance services for Skyway Co. on credit.
	24	The company completed $825 of maintenance services for Comfort Motel on credit.
	25	The company received $3,500 cash payment from Skyway Co. for the work completed on June 21.
	26	The company made payment of $2,400 cash for equipment purchased on June 4.
	28	The company paid $900 cash for an assistant's salary for the second half of this month.
	29	K. Stone withdrew $2,000 cash from the company for personal use.
	30	The company paid $120 cash for this month's telephone bill.
	30	The company paid $525 cash for this month's utilities.

Required

1. Arrange the following asset, liability, and equity titles in a table like Exhibit 1.9: Cash; Accounts Receivable; Equipment; Accounts Payable; K. Stone, Capital; K. Stone, Withdrawals; Revenues; and Expenses.

2. Show the effects of the transactions on the accounts of the accounting equation by recording increases and decreases in the appropriate columns. Do not determine new account balances after each transaction. Determine the final total for each account and verify that the equation is in balance.
3. Prepare a June income statement, a June statement of owner's equity, a June 30 balance sheet, and a June statement of cash flows.

Check (2) Ending balances: Cash, $118,080; Expenses, $8,070

(3) Net income, $3,305; Total assets, $121,305

Problem 1-9B
Analyzing transactions and preparing financial statements
C4 P1 P2

Swender Excavating Co., owned by Patrick Swender, began operations in July and completed these transactions during that first month of operations.

July 1 P. Swender invested $60,000 cash in the company.
2 The company rented office space and paid $500 cash for the July rent.
3 The company purchased excavating equipment for $4,000 by paying $800 cash and agreeing to pay the $3,200 balance in 30 days.
6 The company purchased office supplies for $500 cash.
8 The company completed work for a customer and immediately collected $2,200 cash for the work.
10 The company purchased $3,800 of office equipment on credit.
15 The company completed work for a customer on credit in the amount of $2,400.
17 The company purchased $1,920 of office supplies on credit.
23 The company paid $3,800 cash for the office equipment purchased on July 10.
25 The company billed a customer $5,000 for work completed; the balance is due in 30 days.
28 The company received $2,400 cash for the work completed on July 15.
30 The company paid an assistant's salary of $1,260 cash for this month.
31 The company paid $260 cash for this month's utility bill.
31 P. Swender withdrew $1,200 cash from the company for personal use.

Required

1. Arrange the following asset, liability, and equity titles in a table like Exhibit 1.9: Cash; Accounts Receivable; Office Supplies; Office Equipment; Excavating Equipment; Accounts Payable; P. Swender, Capital; P. Swender, Withdrawals; Revenues; and Expenses.
2. Use additions and subtractions to show the effects of each transaction on the accounts in the accounting equation. Show new balances after each transaction.
3. Use the increases and decreases in the columns of the table from part 2 to prepare an income statement, a statement of owner's equity, and a statement of cash flows—each of these for the current month. Also prepare a balance sheet as of the end of the month.

Check (2) Ending balances: Cash, $56,280; Accounts Payable, $5,120

(3) Net income, $7,580; Total assets, $71,500

Analysis Component

4. Assume that the $4,000 purchase of excavating equipment on July 3 was financed from an owner investment of another $4,000 cash in the business (instead of the purchase conditions described in the transaction). Explain the effect of this change on total assets, total liabilities, and total equity.

Problem 1-10B
Determining expenses, liabilities, equity, and return on assets
A1 A2 

Aspen Company manufactures, markets, and sells ATV and snowmobile equipment and accessories. The average total assets for Aspen is $2,000,000. In its most recent year, Aspen reported net income of $100,000 on revenues of $1,200,000.

Required

1. What is Aspen Company's return on assets?
2. Does return on assets seem satisfactory for Aspen given that its competitors average a 9.5% return on assets?
3. What are the total expenses for Aspen Company in its most recent year?
4. What is the average total amount of liabilities plus equity for Aspen Company?

Check (3) $1,100,000

(4) $2,000,000

Problem 1-11B
Computing and interpreting return on assets
A2  

AT&T and **Verizon** produce and market telecommunications products and are competitors. Key financial figures (in $ millions) for these businesses over the past year follow.

Key Figures ($ millions)	AT&T	Verizon
Sales	$123,018	$107,808
Net income	12,535	10,358
Average assets	266,999	214,937

Check (1*a*) 4.7%; (1*b*) 4.8%

Required

1. Compute return on assets for (*a*) AT&T and (*b*) Verizon.
2. Which company is more successful in the total amount of sales to consumers?
3. Which company is more successful in returning net income from its assets invested?

Analysis Component

4. Write a one-paragraph memorandum explaining which company you would invest your money in and why. (Limit your explanation to the information provided.)

Problem 1-12B[A]
Identifying risk and return
A3 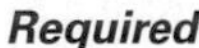

All business decisions involve aspects of risk and return.

Required

Identify both the risk and the return in each of the following activities:

1. Stashing $1,000 cash under your mattress.
2. Placing a $500 bet on a horse running in the Kentucky Derby.
3. Investing $10,000 in Nike stock.
4. Investing $10,000 in U.S. Savings Bonds.

Problem 1-13B[B]
Describing organizational activities C5

Identify in outline format the three major business activities of an organization. For each of these activities, identify at least two specific transactions or events normally undertaken by the business's owners or its managers.

Problem 1-14B[B]
Describing organizational activities
C5

A start-up company often engages in the following activities during its first year of operations. Classify each of the following activities into one of the three major activities of an organization.

A. Financing **B.** Investing **C.** Operating

______	**1.** Providing client services.	______	**5.** Supervising workers.
______	**2.** Obtaining a bank loan.	______	**6.** Owner investing money in business.
______	**3.** Purchasing machinery.	______	**7.** Renting office space.
______	**4.** Research for its products.	______	**8.** Paying utilities expenses.

This serial problem starts in this chapter and continues throughout most chapters of the book. It is most readily solved if you use the Working Papers that accompany this book (but working papers are not required).

SERIAL PROBLEM

Business Solutions
C4 P1

SP 1 On October 1, 2011, Santana Rey launched a computer services company, **Business Solutions,** that is organized as a proprietorship and provides consulting services, computer system installations, and custom program development. Rey adopts the calendar year for reporting purposes and expects to prepare the company's first set of financial statements on December 31, 2011.

Required

Create a table like the one in Exhibit 1.9 using the following headings for columns: Cash; Accounts Receivable; Computer Supplies; Computer System; Office Equipment; Accounts Payable; S. Rey, Capital; S. Rey, Withdrawals; Revenues; and Expenses. Then use additions and subtractions within the table created to show the dollar effects for each of the following October transactions for Business Solutions on the individual items of the accounting equation. Show new balances after each transaction.

Oct.	1	S. Rey invested $45,000 cash, a $20,000 computer system, and $8,000 of office equipment in the company.
	3	The company purchased $1,420 of computer supplies on credit from Harris Office Products.
	6	The company billed Easy Leasing $4,800 for services performed in installing a new Web server.
	8	The company paid $1,420 cash for the computer supplies purchased from Harris Office Products on October 3.
	10	The company hired Lyn Addie as a part-time assistant for $125 per day, as needed.
	12	The company billed Easy Leasing another $1,400 for services performed.
	15	The company received $4,800 cash from Easy Leasing as partial payment toward its account.
	17	The company paid $805 cash to repair computer equipment damaged when moving it.
	20	The company paid $1,728 cash for advertisements published in the local newspaper.
	22	The company received $1,400 cash from Easy Leasing toward its account.
	28	The company billed IFM Company $5,208 for services performed.
	31	The company paid $875 cash for Lyn Addie's wages for seven days of work this month.
	31	S. Rey withdrew $3,600 cash from the company for personal use.

Check Ending balances: Cash, $42,772; Revenues, $11,408; Expenses, $3,408

Beyond the Numbers (BTN) *is a special problem section aimed to refine communication, conceptual, analysis, and research skills. It includes many activities helpful in developing an active learning environment.*

Beyond the Numbers

REPORTING IN ACTION
A1 A2 A3 
RIM

BTN 1-1 Key financial figures for **Research In Motion**'s fiscal year ended February 27, 2010, follow.

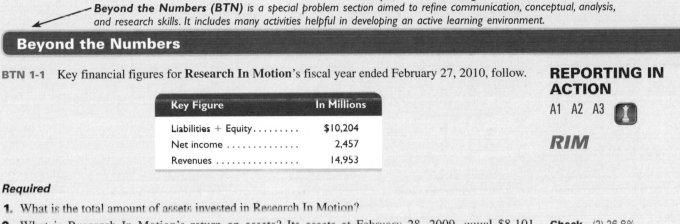

Key Figure	In Millions
Liabilities + Equity	$10,204
Net income	2,457
Revenues	14,953

Required

1. What is the total amount of assets invested in Research In Motion?
2. What is Research In Motion's return on assets? Its assets at February 28, 2009, equal $8,101 (in millions).
3. How much are total expenses for Research In Motion for the year ended February 27, 2010?
4. Does Research In Motion's return on assets seem satisfactory if competitors average an 18% return?

Check (2) 26.8%

Fast Forward

5. Access Research In Motion's financial statements (Form 10-K) for fiscal years ending after February 27, 2010, from its Website (**RIM.com**) or from the SEC Website (**www.SEC.gov**) and compute its return on assets for those fiscal years. Compare the February 27, 2010, fiscal year-end return on assets to any subsequent years' returns you are able to compute, and interpret the results.

COMPARATIVE ANALYSIS
A1 A2 A3 
RIM
Apple

BTN 1-2 Key comparative figures ($ millions) for both **Research In Motion** and **Apple** follow.

Key Figure	Research In Motion	Apple
Liabilities + Equity	$10,204	$47,501
Net income	2,457	8,235
Revenues and sales	14,953	42,905

Required

1. What is the total amount of assets invested in (*a*) Research In Motion and (*b*) Apple?
2. What is the return on assets for (*a*) Research In Motion and (*b*) Apple? Research In Motion's beginning-year assets equal $8,101 (in millions) and Apple's beginning-year assets equal $36,171 (in millions).
3. How much are expenses for (*a*) Research In Motion and (*b*) Apple?
4. Is return on assets satisfactory for (*a*) Research In Motion and (*b*) Apple? (Assume competitors average an 18% return.)
5. What can you conclude about Research In Motion and Apple from these computations?

Check (2b) 19.7%

ETHICS CHALLENGE
C3 C4 

BTN 1-3 Madison Thorne works in a public accounting firm and hopes to eventually be a partner. The management of Allnet Company invites Thorne to prepare a bid to audit Allnet's financial statements. In discussing the audit fee, Allnet's management suggests a fee range in which the amount depends on the reported profit of Allnet. The higher its profit, the higher will be the audit fee paid to Thorne's firm.

Required

1. Identify the parties potentially affected by this audit and the fee plan proposed.
2. What are the ethical factors in this situation? Explain.
3. Would you recommend that Thorne accept this audit fee arrangement? Why or why not?
4. Describe some ethical considerations guiding your recommendation.

COMMUNICATING IN PRACTICE

A1 C2

BTN 1-4 Refer to this chapter's opening feature about **Facebook**.® Assume that Mark Zuckerberg desires to expand his online services to meet people's demands. He decides to meet with his banker to discuss a loan to allow Facebook to expand.

Required

1. Prepare a half-page report outlining the information you would request from Mark Zuckerberg if you were the loan officer.
2. Indicate whether the information you request and your loan decision are affected by the form of business organization for Facebook.

TAKING IT TO THE NET

A2

BTN 1-5 Visit the EDGAR database at (**www.sec.gov**). Access the Form 10-K report of **Rocky Mountain Chocolate Factory** (ticker RMCF) filed on May 26, 2009, covering its 2009 fiscal year.

Required

1. Item 6 of the 10-K report provides comparative financial highlights of RMCF for the years 2005–2009. How would you describe the revenue trend for RMCF over this five-year period?
2. Has RMCF been profitable (see net income) over this five-year period? Support your answer.

TEAMWORK IN ACTION

C1

BTN 1-6 Teamwork is important in today's business world. Successful teams schedule convenient meetings, maintain regular communications, and cooperate with and support their members. This assignment aims to establish support/learning teams, initiate discussions, and set meeting times.

Required

1. Form teams and open a team discussion to determine a regular time and place for your team to meet between each scheduled class meeting. Notify your instructor via a memorandum or e-mail message as to when and where your team will hold regularly scheduled meetings.
2. Develop a list of telephone numbers and/or e-mail addresses of your teammates.

ENTREPRENEURIAL DECISION

A1 P1

BTN 1-7 Refer to this chapter's opening feature about **Facebook**. Assume that Mark Zuckerberg decides to open a new Website devoted to social networking for accountants and those studying accounting. This new company will be called AccountBook.

Required

1. AccountBook obtains a $500,000 loan and Mark Zuckerberg contributes $250,000 of his own assets in exchange for common stock in the new company.
   a. What is the new company's total amount of liabilities plus equity?
   b. What is the new company's total amount of assets?
2. If the new company earns $80,000 in net income in the first year of operation, compute its return on asset (assume average assets equal $750,000). Assess its performance if competitors average a 10% return.

Check (2) 10.7%

HITTING THE ROAD

C2

BTN 1-8 You are to interview a local business owner. (This can be a friend or relative.) Opening lines of communication with members of the business community can provide personal benefits of business networking. If you do not know the owner, you should call ahead to introduce yourself and explain your position as a student and your assignment requirements. You should request a thirty minute appointment for a face-to-face or phone interview to discuss the form of organization and operations of the business. Be prepared to make a good impression.

Required

1. Identify and describe the main operating activities and the form of organization for this business.
2. Determine and explain why the owner(s) chose this particular form of organization.
3. Identify any special advantages and/or disadvantages the owner(s) experiences in operating with this form of business organization.

BTN 1-9 **Nokia** (www.Nokia.com) is a leading manufacturer of mobile devices and services, and it competes to some extent with both **Research In Motion** and **Apple**. Key financial figures for Nokia follow.

GLOBAL DECISION

A1 A2 A3  

NOKIA

RIM

Apple

Key Figure*	Euro (EUR) in Millions
Average assets	37,660
Net income	260
Revenue	40,984
Return on assets	0.7%

* Figures prepared in accordance with International Financial Reporting Standards.

Required

1. Identify any concerns you have in comparing Nokia's income and revenue figures to those of Research In Motion and Apple (in BTN 1-2) for purposes of making business decisions.
2. Identify any concerns you have in comparing Nokia's return on assets ratio to those of Research In Motion and Apple (computed for BTN 1-2) for purposes of making business decisions.

ANSWERS TO MULTIPLE CHOICE QUIZ

1. c; $450,000 is the actual cost incurred.
2. b; revenue is recorded when earned.
3. d;

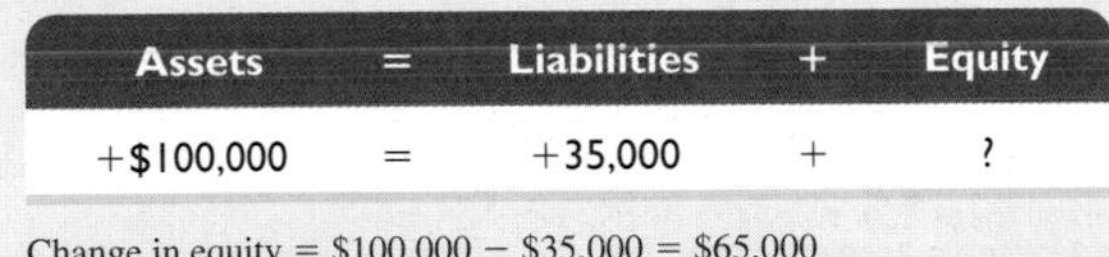

Assets	=	Liabilities	+	Equity
+$100,000	=	+35,000	+	?

Change in equity = $100,000 − $35,000 = $65,000

4. a
5. a

2 Analyzing and Recording Transactions

A Look Back

Chapter 1 defined accounting and introduced financial statements. We described forms of organizations and identified users and uses of accounting. We defined the accounting equation and applied it to transaction analysis.

A Look at This Chapter

This chapter focuses on the accounting process. We describe transactions and source documents, and we explain the analysis and recording of transactions. The accounting equation, T-account, general ledger, trial balance, and debits and credits are key tools in the accounting process.

A Look Ahead

Chapter 3 extends our focus on processing information. We explain the importance of adjusting accounts and the procedures in preparing financial statements.

Learning Objectives

CAP

CONCEPTUAL

C1 Explain the steps in processing transactions and the role of source documents. (p. 50)

C2 Describe an account and its use in recording transactions. (p. 51)

C3 Describe a ledger and a chart of accounts. (p. 54)

C4 Define *debits* and *credits* and explain double-entry accounting. (p. 55)

ANALYTICAL

A1 Analyze the impact of transactions on accounts and financial statements. (p. 59)

A2 Compute the debt ratio and describe its use in analyzing financial condition. (p. 69)

LP2

PROCEDURAL

P1 Record transactions in a journal and post entries to a ledger. (p. 56)

P2 Prepare and explain the use of a trial balance. (p. 65)

P3 Prepare financial statements from business transactions. (p. 66)

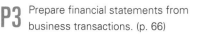

Decision Insight

Sole Sisters

"Every way we can cut costs, we do!"
—**SUSIE LEVITT** (on right)

NEW YORK—"High heels were killing our feet, but we didn't want to give them up because we aren't the tallest people out there," insists Susie Levitt, who stands no taller than 5′2″. "So we came up with the idea of emergency footwear." Susie, along with Katie Shea, designed a stylish, foldable slip-on ballet flat with a pouch that is readily tucked into a handbag and pulled out when their feet cry for mercy. The empty pouch then expands into a tote bag to hold their "killer" heels for carrying home. Launched from their college apartment, Susie and Katie invested "less than $10,000" for the cost of their first order of 1,000 pairs, including Website design, to launch **CitySlips (www.cityslips.com).**

To pursue their business ambitions, Susie and Katie took business courses, including accounting. They learned and applied recordkeeping processes, transaction analysis, inventory accounting, and financial statement reporting. We were careful to get a handle on our financial situation, says Katie. Today, the two are running a profitable business and have a reliable accounting system to help them make good business decisions.

We had to account for product costs, design expenses, supplier payments, patent fees, and other expenses, says Susie. At the same time, the two have grown sales and expanded their product line. "It was all done online," says Susie. "We became nocturnal!"

The two insist that it is crucial to track and account for all revenues and expenses, and what is invested in the business. They maintain that success requires proper accounting for and analysis of the financial side. Susie also suggests that young entrepreneurs "network with your professors and other staff members. They have years of experience and can often help you, or introduce you to people who can help you, with your business."

The bigger message of our company, says Susie, is promoting comfort and confidence for women. Adds Katie, "Regardless of what your business is, the story of starting while in college, differentiates you from the beginning!"

[Sources: *CitySlips Website,* January 2011; *Entrepreneur,* December 2009; *Examiner.com*, December 2009; *CNN.com*, August 2009; *Daily News*, May 2009.]

Chapter Preview

Financial statements report on the financial performance and condition of an organization. Knowledge of their preparation, organization, and analysis is important. A main goal of this chapter is to illustrate how transactions are recorded, how they are reflected in financial statements, and how they impact analysis of financial statements. Debits and credits are introduced and identified as a tool in helping analyze and process transactions.

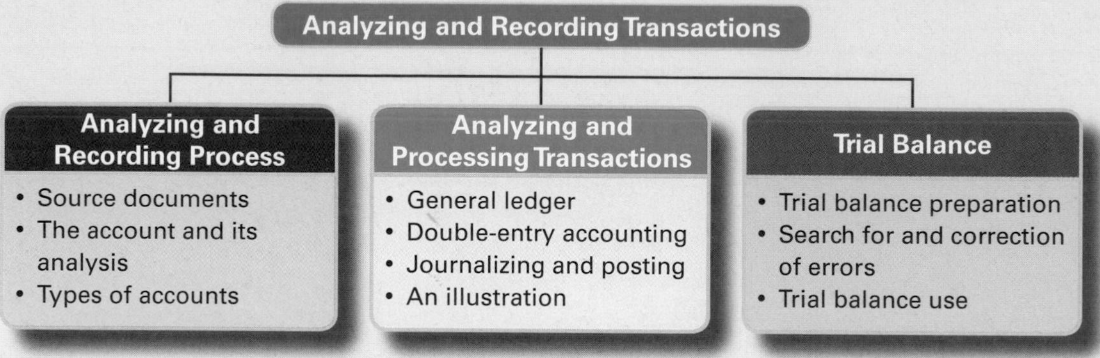

Analyzing and Recording Transactions
Analyzing and Recording Process
• Source documents
• The account and its analysis
• Types of accounts
Analyzing and Processing Transactions
• General ledger
• Double-entry accounting
• Journalizing and posting
• An illustration
Trial Balance
• Trial balance preparation
• Search for and correction of errors
• Trial balance use

ANALYZING AND RECORDING PROCESS

The accounting process identifies business transactions and events, analyzes and records their effects, and summarizes and presents information in reports and financial statements. These reports and statements are used for making investing, lending, and other business decisions. The steps in the accounting process that focus on *analyzing and recording* transactions and events are shown in Exhibit 2.1.

EXHIBIT 2.1

The Analyzing and Recording Process

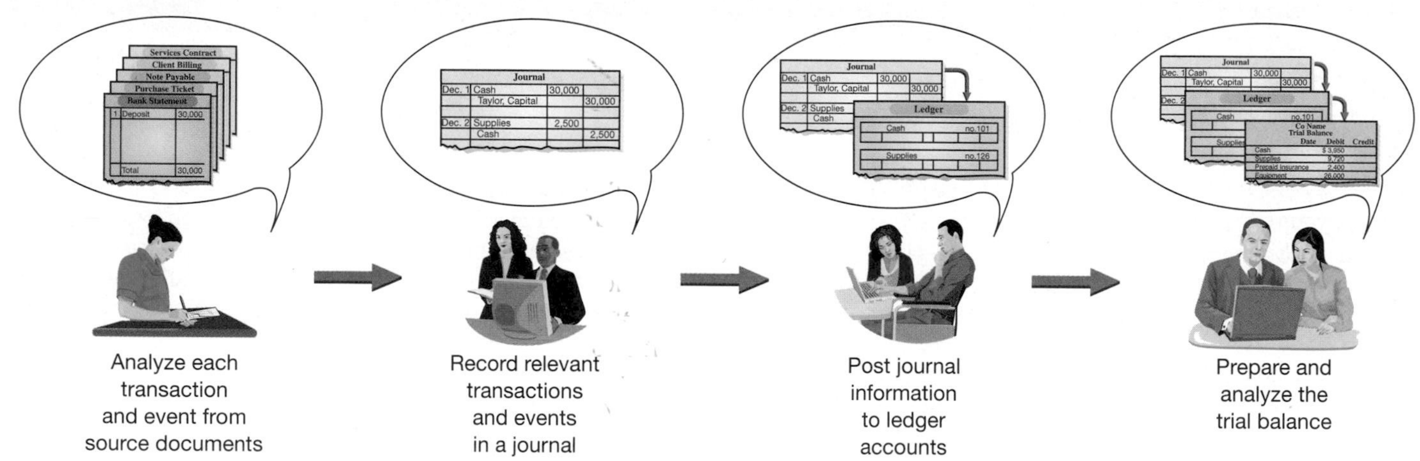

C1 Explain the steps in processing transactions and the role of source documents.

Business transactions and events are the starting points. Relying on source documents, the transactions and events are analyzed using the accounting equation to understand how they affect company performance and financial position. These effects are recorded in accounting records, informally referred to as the *accounting books,* or simply the *books*. Additional steps such as posting and then preparing a trial balance help summarize and classify the effects of transactions and events. Ultimately, the accounting process provides information in useful reports or financial statements to decision makers.

Source Documents

Source documents identify and describe transactions and events entering the accounting process. They are the sources of accounting information and can be in either hard copy or electronic form. Examples are sales tickets, checks, purchase orders, bills from suppliers, employee earnings records, and bank statements. To illustrate, when an item is purchased on credit, the seller usually prepares at least two copies of a sales invoice. One copy is given to the buyer. Another copy, often sent electronically, results in an entry in the seller's information system to record the sale. Sellers use invoices for recording sales and for control; buyers use them for recording purchases and for monitoring purchasing activity. Many cash registers record information for each sale on a tape or electronic file locked inside the register. This record can be used as a source document for recording sales in the accounting records. Source documents, especially if obtained from outside the organization, provide objective and reliable evidence about transactions and events and their amounts.

Point: To ensure that all sales are rung up on the register, most sellers require customers to have their receipts to exchange or return purchased items.

Cashier Your manager requires that you, as cashier, immediately enter each sale. Recently, lunch hour traffic has increased and the assistant manager asks you to avoid delays by taking customers' cash and making change without entering sales. The assistant manager says she will add up cash and enter sales after lunch. She says that, in this way, the register will always match the cash amount when the manager arrives at three o'clock. What do you do? ■

The Account and Its Analysis

C2 Describe an account and its use in recording transactions.

An **account** is a record of increases and decreases in a specific asset, liability, equity, revenue, or expense item. Information from an account is analyzed, summarized, and presented in reports and financial statements. The **general ledger,** or simply **ledger,** is a record containing all accounts used by a company. The ledger is often in electronic form. While most companies' ledgers contain similar accounts, a company often uses one or more unique accounts because of its type of operations. As shown in Exhibit 2.2, accounts are classified into three general categories based on the accounting equation: asset, liability, or equity.

EXHIBIT 2.2

Accounts Organized by the Accounting Equation

Asset Accounts Assets are resources owned or controlled by a company and that have expected future benefits. Most accounting systems include (at a minimum) separate accounts for the assets described here.

A *Cash* account reflects a company's cash balance. All increases and decreases in cash are recorded in the Cash account. It includes money and any medium of exchange that a bank accepts for deposit (coins, checks, money orders, and checking account balances).

Accounts receivable are held by a seller and refer to promises of payment from customers to sellers. These transactions are often called *credit sales* or *sales on account* (or *on credit*). Accounts receivable are increased by credit sales and are decreased by customer payments. A company needs a separate record for each customer, but for now, we use the simpler practice of recording all increases and decreases in receivables in a single account called Accounts Receivable.

Point: Customers and others who owe a company are called its **debtors.**

A *note receivable,* or promissory note, is a written promise of another entity to pay a definite sum of money on a specified future date to the holder of the note. A company holding a promissory note signed by another entity has an asset that is recorded in a Note (or Notes) Receivable account.

Prepaid accounts (also called *prepaid expenses*) are assets that represent prepayments of future expenses (*not* current expenses). When the expenses are later incurred, the amounts in prepaid accounts are transferred to expense accounts. Common examples of prepaid accounts include prepaid insurance, prepaid rent, and prepaid services (such as club memberships). Prepaid accounts expire with the passage of time (such as with rent) or through use (such as with prepaid meal tickets). When financial statements are prepared, prepaid accounts are adjusted so that (1) all expired and used prepaid accounts are recorded as regular expenses and (2) all unexpired and unused prepaid accounts are recorded as assets (reflecting future use in

Point: A college parking fee is a prepaid account from the student's standpoint. At the beginning of the term, it represents an asset that entitles a student to park on or near campus. The benefits of the parking fee expire as the term progresses. At term-end, prepaid parking (asset) equals zero as it has been entirely recorded as parking expense.

Point: Prepaid accounts that apply to current and future periods are assets. These assets are adjusted at the end of each period to reflect only those amounts that have not yet expired, and to record as expenses those amounts that have expired.

future periods). To illustrate, when an insurance fee, called a *premium,* is paid in advance, the cost is typically recorded in the asset account Prepaid Insurance. Over time, the expiring portion of the insurance cost is removed from this asset account and reported in expenses on the income statement. Any unexpired portion remains in Prepaid Insurance and is reported on the balance sheet as an asset. (An exception exists for prepaid accounts that will expire or be used before the end of the current accounting period when financial statements are prepared. In this case, the prepayments *can* be recorded immediately as expenses.)

Supplies are assets until they are used. When they are used up, their costs are reported as expenses. The costs of unused supplies are recorded in a Supplies asset account. Supplies are often grouped by purpose—for example, office supplies and store supplies. *Office supplies* include stationery, paper, toner, and pens. *Store supplies* include packaging materials, plastic and paper bags, gift boxes and cartons, and cleaning materials. The costs of these unused supplies can be recorded in an Office Supplies or a Store Supplies asset account. When supplies are used, their costs are transferred from the asset accounts to expense accounts.

Point: Some assets are described as *intangible* because they do not have physical existence or their benefits are highly uncertain. A recent balance sheet for **Coca-Cola Company** shows nearly $1 billion in intangible assets.

Equipment is an asset. When equipment is used and gets worn down, its cost is gradually reported as an expense (called depreciation). Equipment is often grouped by its purpose—for example, office equipment and store equipment. *Office equipment* includes computers, printers, desks, chairs, and shelves. Costs incurred for these items are recorded in an Office Equipment asset account. The Store Equipment account includes the costs of assets used in a store, such as counters, showcases, ladders, hoists, and cash registers.

Buildings such as stores, offices, warehouses, and factories are assets because they provide expected future benefits to those who control or own them. Their costs are recorded in a Buildings asset account. When several buildings are owned, separate accounts are sometimes kept for each of them.

The cost of *land* owned by a business is recorded in a Land account. The cost of buildings located on the land is separately recorded in one or more building accounts.

Decision Insight

Women Entrepreneurs The Center for Women's Business Research reports that women-owned businesses, such as **CitySlips**, are growing and that they:

- Total approximately 11 million and employ nearly 20 million workers.
- Generate $2.5 trillion in annual sales and tend to embrace technology.
- Are philanthropic—70% of owners volunteer at least once per month.
- Are more likely funded by individual investors (73%) than venture firms (15%). ■

Liability Accounts Liabilities are claims (by creditors) against assets, which means they are obligations to transfer assets or provide products or services to others. **Creditors** are individuals and organizations that have rights to receive payments from a company. If a company fails to pay its obligations, the law gives creditors a right to force the sale of that company's assets to obtain the money to meet creditors' claims. When assets are sold under these conditions, creditors are paid first, but only up to the amount of their claims. Any remaining money, the residual, goes to the owners of the company. Creditors often use a balance sheet to help decide whether to loan money to a company. A loan is less risky if the borrower's liabilities are small in comparison to assets because this means there are more resources than claims on resources. Common liability accounts are described here.

Point: Accounts payable are also called *trade payables.*

Accounts payable refer to oral or implied promises to pay later, which usually arise from purchases of merchandise. Payables can also arise from purchases of supplies, equipment, and services. Accounting systems keep separate records about each creditor. We describe these individual records in Chapter 5.

A *note payable* refers to a formal promise, usually denoted by the signing of a promissory note, to pay a future amount. It is recorded in either a short-term Note Payable account or a long-term Note Payable account, depending on when it must be repaid. We explain details of short- and long-term classification in Chapter 3.

Unearned revenue refers to a liability that is settled in the future when a company delivers its products or services. When customers pay in advance for products or services (before revenue is earned), the revenue recognition principle requires that the seller consider this payment as unearned revenue. Examples of unearned revenue include magazine subscriptions collected in advance by a publisher, sales of gift certificates by stores, and season ticket sales by sports teams. The seller would record these in liability accounts such as Unearned Subscriptions, Unearned Store Sales, and Unearned Ticket Revenue. When products and services are later delivered, the earned portion of the unearned revenue is transferred to revenue accounts such as Subscription Fees, Store Sales, and Ticket Sales.[1]

Point: If a subscription is canceled, the publisher is expected to refund the unused portion to the subscriber.

Accrued liabilities are amounts owed that are not yet paid. Examples are wages payable, taxes payable, and interest payable. These are often recorded in separate liability accounts by the same title. If they are not large in amount, one or more ledger accounts can be added and reported as a single amount on the balance sheet. (Financial statements often have amounts reported that are a summation of several ledger accounts.)

Decision Insight

Revenue Spread The **New Orleans Saints** have *Unearned Revenues* of about $60 million in advance ticket sales. When the team plays its home games, it settles this liability to its ticket holders and then transfers the amount earned to *Ticket Revenues.* ■

Equity Accounts The owner's claim on a company's assets is called *equity* or *owner's equity.* Equity is the owner's *residual interest* in the assets of a business after deducting liabilities. Equity is impacted by four types of accounts: owner's capital, owner's withdrawals, revenues, and expenses. We show this visually in Exhibit 2.3 by expanding the accounting equation.

Point: Equity is also called *net assets.*

EXHIBIT 2.3

Expanded Accounting Equation

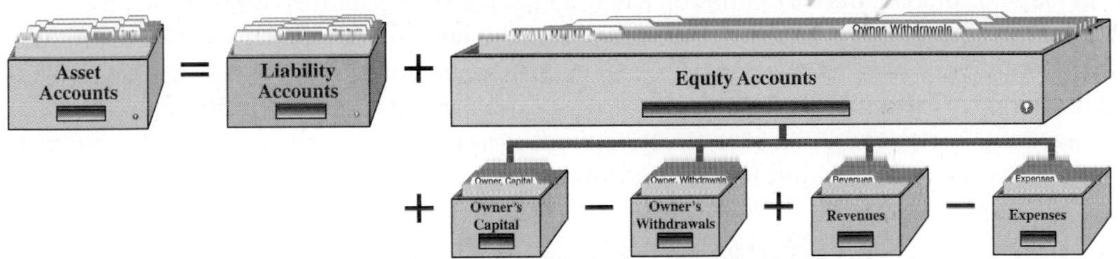

When an owner invests in a company, the invested amount is recorded in an account titled Owner, Capital (where the owner's name is inserted in place of "owner"). The account titled *C. Taylor, Capital* is used for FastForward. Any further owner investments are recorded in this account. When an owner withdraws assets for personal use it decreases both company assets and total equity. Withdrawals are not expenses of the business; they are simply the opposite of owner investments. The Owner, Withdrawals account is used to record asset distributions to the owner. The account titled *C. Taylor, Withdrawals* is used for FastForward. (Owners of proprietorships cannot receive company salaries because they are not legally separate from their companies, and they cannot enter into company contracts with themselves.)

Point: The Owner's Withdrawals account is a *contra equity* account because it reduces the normal balance of equity.

Point: The withdrawal of assets by the owners of a corporation is called a *dividend.*

Revenues and expenses also impact equity. Examples of revenue accounts are Sales, Commissions Earned, Professional Fees Earned, Rent Revenue, and Interest Revenue. *Revenues increase equity* and result from products and services provided to customers. Examples of expense accounts are Advertising Expense, Store Supplies Expense, Office Salaries Expense, Office Supplies Expense, Rent Expense, Utilities Expense, and Insurance Expense. *Expenses decrease equity* and result from assets and services used in a company's operations. The variety of revenues and expenses can be seen by looking at the *chart of accounts* that follows the index at the

[1] In practice, account titles vary. As one example, Subscription Fees is sometimes called Subscription Fees Revenue, Subscription Fees Earned, or Earned Subscription Fees. As another example, Rent Earned is sometimes called Rent Revenue, Rental Revenue, or Earned Rent Revenue. We must use good judgment when reading financial statements because titles can differ even within the same industry. For example, product sales are called *revenue* at **Research In Motion**, but *net sales* at **Apple**. Generally, the term *revenues* or *fees* is more commonly used with service businesses, and *net sales* or *sales* with product businesses.

back of this book. (Different companies sometimes use different account titles than those in this book's chart of accounts. For example, some might use Interest Revenue instead of Interest Earned, or Rental Expense instead of Rent Expense. It is important only that an account title describe the item it represents.)

Decision Insight

Sporting Accounts The **Los Angeles Lakers** and the other NBA teams have the following major revenue and expense accounts:

Revenues	**Expenses**
Basketball ticket sales	Team salaries
TV & radio broadcast fees	Game costs
Advertising revenues	NBA franchise costs
Basketball playoff receipts	Promotional costs ■

ANALYZING AND PROCESSING TRANSACTIONS

This section explains several tools and processes that comprise an accounting system. These include a ledger, T-account, debits and credits, double-entry accounting, journalizing, and posting.

Ledger and Chart of Accounts

C3 Describe a ledger and a chart of accounts.

The collection of all accounts and their balances for an information system is called a *ledger* (or *general ledger*). If accounts are in files on a hard drive, the sum of those files is the ledger. If the accounts are pages in a file, that file is the ledger. A company's size and diversity of operations affect the number of accounts needed. A small company can get by with as few as 20 or 30 accounts; a large company can require several thousand. The **chart of accounts** is a list of all ledger accounts and includes an identification number assigned to each account. A small business might use the following numbering system for its accounts:

101–199	Asset accounts
201–299	Liability accounts
301–399	Equity accounts
401–499	Revenue accounts
501–699	Expense accounts

These numbers provide a three-digit code that is useful in recordkeeping. In this case, the first digit assigned to asset accounts is a 1, the first digit assigned to liability accounts is a 2, and so on. The second and third digits relate to the accounts' subcategories. Exhibit 2.4 shows a partial chart of accounts for FastForward, the focus company of Chapter 1. (Please review the more complete chart of accounts that follows the index at the back of this book.)

EXHIBIT 2.4

Partial Chart of Accounts for FastForward

Acct. No.	Account Name	Acct. No.	Account Name	Acct. No.	Account Name
101	Cash	236	Unearned consulting revenue	622	Salaries expense
106	Accounts receivable	301	C. Taylor, Capital	637	Insurance expense
126	Supplies	302	C. Taylor, Withdrawals	640	Rent expense
128	Prepaid insurance	403	Consulting revenue	652	Supplies expense
167	Equipment	406	Rental revenue	690	Utilities expense
201	Accounts payable				

Debits and Credits

C4 Define *debits* and *credits* and explain double-entry accounting.

A **T-account** represents a ledger account and is a tool used to understand the effects of one or more transactions. Its name comes from its shape like the letter **T**. The layout of a T-account, shown in Exhibit 2.5, is (1) the account title on top, (2) a left, or debit side, and (3) a right, or credit, side.

EXHIBIT 2.5

The T-Account

Account Title	
(Left side) *Debit*	(Right side) *Credit*

The left side of an account is called the **debit** side, often abbreviated *Dr*. The right side is called the **credit** side, abbreviated *Cr*.[2] To enter amounts on the left side of an account is to *debit* the account. To enter amounts on the right side is to *credit* the account. Do not make the error of thinking that the terms *debit* and *credit* mean increase or decrease. Whether a debit or a credit is an increase or decrease depends on the account. For an account where a debit is an increase, the credit is a decrease; for an account where a debit is a decrease, the credit is an increase. The difference between total debits and total credits for an account, including any beginning balance, is the **account balance.** When the sum of debits exceeds the sum of credits, the account has a *debit balance*. It has a *credit balance* when the sum of credits exceeds the sum of debits. When the sum of debits equals the sum of credits, the account has a *zero balance*.

Point: Think of *debit* and *credit* as accounting directions for left and right.

Double-Entry Accounting

Double-entry accounting requires that for each transaction:

- At least two accounts are involved, with at least one debit and one credit.
- The total amount debited must equal the total amount credited.
- The accounting equation must not be violated.

"Total debits equal total credits for each entry."

This means the sum of the debits for all entries must equal the sum of the credits for all entries, and the sum of debit account balances in the ledger must equal the sum of credit account balances.

The system for recording debits and credits follows from the usual accounting equation—see Exhibit 2.6. Two points are important here. First, like any simple mathematical relation, net increases or decreases on one side have equal net effects on the other side. For example, a net increase in assets must be accompanied by an identical net increase on the liabilities and equity side. Recall that some transactions affect only one side of the equation, meaning that two or more accounts on one side are affected, but their net effect on this one side is zero. Second, the left side is the *normal balance* side for assets, and the right side is the *normal balance* side for liabilities and equity. This matches their layout in the accounting equation where assets are on the left side of this equation, and liabilities and equity are on the right.

EXHIBIT 2.6

Debits and Credits in the Accounting Equation

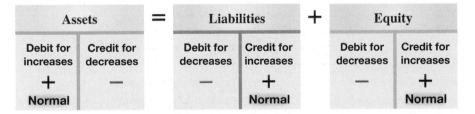

Assets		=	Liabilities		+	Equity	
Debit for increases	Credit for decreases		Debit for decreases	Credit for increases		Debit for decreases	Credit for increases
+	−		−	+		−	+
Normal				Normal			Normal

Recall that equity increases from revenues and owner investments and it decreases from expenses and owner withdrawals. These important equity relations are conveyed by expanding the accounting equation to include debits and credits in double-entry form as shown in Exhibit 2.7.

Increases (credits) to owner's capital and revenues *increase* equity; increases (debits) to withdrawals and expenses *decrease* equity. The normal balance of each account (asset, liability, capital, withdrawals, revenue, or expense) refers to the left or right (debit or credit) side where

Point: Debits and credits do not mean favorable or unfavorable. A debit to an asset increases it, as does a debit to an expense. A credit to a liability increases it, as does a credit to a revenue.

[2] These abbreviations are remnants of 18th century English recordkeeping practices where the terms *debitor* and *creditor* were used instead of *debit* and *credit*. The abbreviations use the first and last letters of these terms, just as we still do for Saint (St.) and Doctor (Dr.).

EXHIBIT 2.7

Debit and Credit Effects for Component Accounts

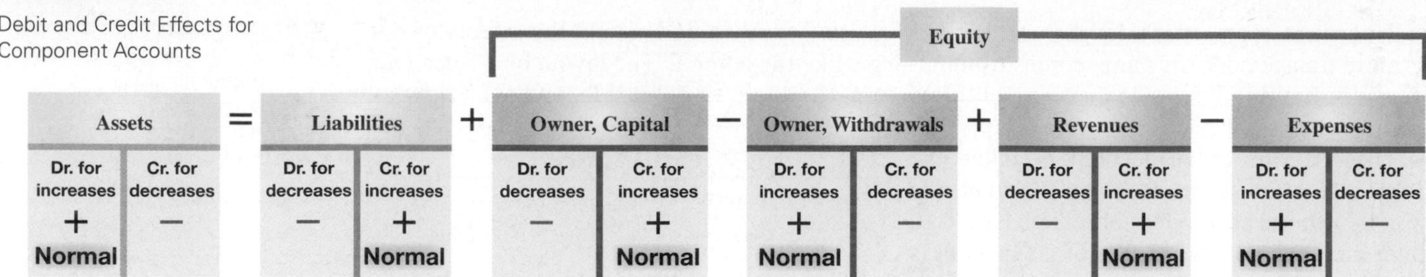

increases are recorded. Understanding these diagrams and rules is required to prepare, analyze, and interpret financial statements.

The T-account for FastForward's Cash account, reflecting its first 11 transactions (from Exhibit 1.9), is shown in Exhibit 2.8. The total increases in its Cash account are $36,100, the total decreases are $31,300, and the account's debit balance is $4,800. (We illustrate use of T-accounts later in this chapter.)

EXHIBIT 2.8

Computing the Balance for a T-Account

Point: The ending balance is on the side with the larger dollar amount. Also, a plus (+) and minus (−) are not used in a T-account.

Cash			
Receive investment by owner	30,000	Purchase of supplies	2,500
Consulting services revenue earned	4,200	Purchase of equipment	26,000
Collection of account receivable	1,900	Payment of rent	1,000
		Payment of salary	700
		Payment of account payable	900
		Withdrawal by owner	200
Balance	**4,800**		

Quick Check Answers — p. 75 

1. Identify examples of accounting source documents.
2. Explain the importance of source documents.
3. Identify each of the following as either an asset, a liability, or equity: (*a*) Prepaid Rent, (*b*) Unearned Fees, (*c*) Building, (*d*) Wages Payable, and (*e*) Office Supplies.
4. What is an account? What is a ledger?
5. What determines the number and types of accounts a company uses?
6. Does *debit* always mean increase and *credit* always mean decrease?
7. Describe a chart of accounts.

Journalizing and Posting Transactions

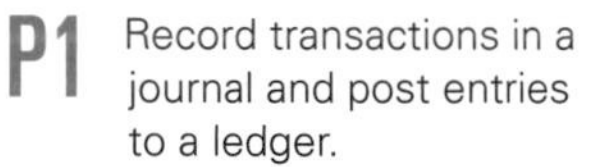

P1
Record transactions in a journal and post entries to a ledger.

Processing transactions is a crucial part of accounting. The four usual steps of this process are depicted in Exhibit 2.9. Steps 1 and 2—involving transaction analysis and the accounting equation—were introduced in prior sections. This section extends that discussion and focuses on steps 3 and 4 of the accounting process. Step 3 is to record each transaction chronologically in a journal. A **journal** gives a complete record of each transaction in one place. It also shows debits and credits for each transaction. The process of recording transactions in a journal is called **journalizing.** Step 4 is to transfer (or *post*) entries from the journal to the ledger. The process of transferring journal entry information to the ledger is called **posting.**

Journalizing Transactions The process of journalizing transactions requires an understanding of a journal. While companies can use various journals, every company uses a **general journal.** It can be used to record any transaction and includes the following information about each transaction: ⓐ date of transaction, ⓑ titles of affected accounts, ⓒ dollar amount of each

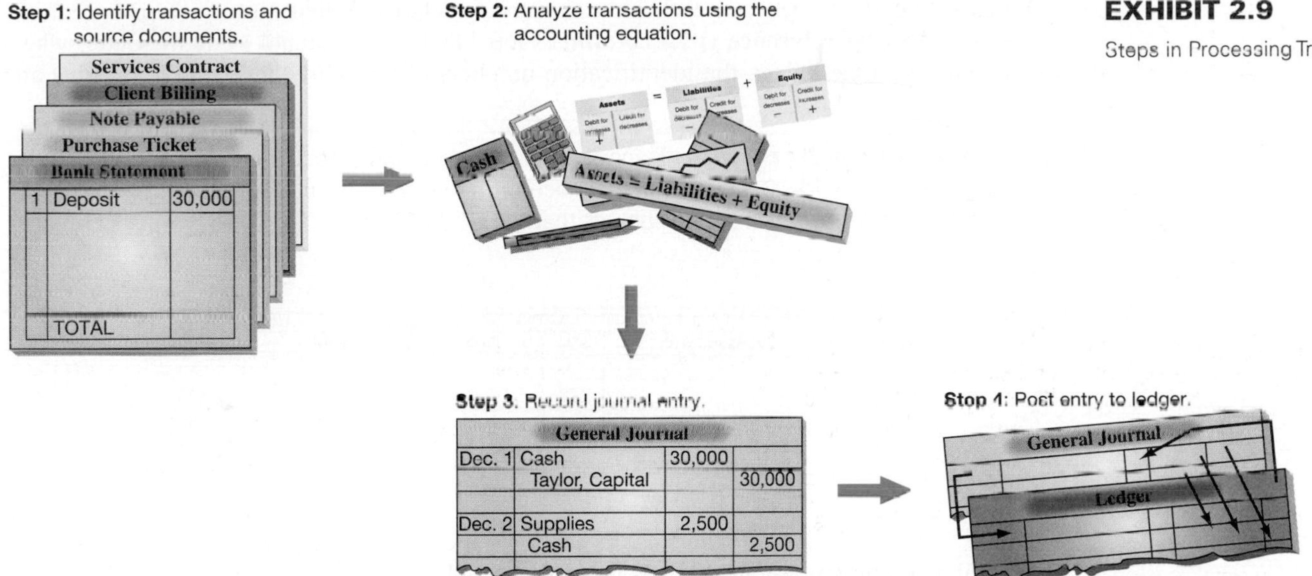

EXHIBIT 2.9

Steps in Processing Transactions

debit and credit, and ⓓ explanation of the transaction. Exhibit 2.10 shows how the first two transactions of FastForward are recorded in a general journal. This process is similar for manual and computerized systems. Computerized journals are often designed to look like a manual journal page, and also include error-checking routines that ensure debits equal credits for each entry. Shortcuts allow recordkeepers to select account names and numbers from pull-down menus.

EXHIBIT 2.10

Partial General Journal for FastForward

General Journal Entry

File Edit Go To Window Help

Close New List Save Print Delete Recur Row Reports Help

Journal Entry

Date: Dec 1, 2011 Reference: ☐ Reverse Transaction

Date	Account Titles and Explanation	PR	Debit	Credit
2011 ⓐ				
Dec. 1	ⓑ Cash		30,000	ⓒ
	C. Taylor, Capital			30,000
	Receive investment by owner. ⓓ			
Dec. 2	Supplies		2,500	
	Cash			2,500
	Purchase supplies for cash.			

To record entries in a general journal, apply these steps; refer to the entries in Exhibit 2.10 when reviewing these steps. (1) Date the transaction: Enter the year at the top of the first column and the month and day on the first line of each journal entry. (2) Enter titles of accounts debited and then enter amounts in the Debit column on the same line. Account titles are taken from the chart of accounts and are aligned with the left margin of the Account Titles and Explanation column. (3) Enter titles of accounts credited and then enter amounts in the Credit column on the same line. Account titles are from the chart of accounts and are indented from the left margin of the Account Titles and Explanation column to distinguish them from debited accounts. (4) Enter a brief explanation of the transaction on the line below the entry (it often references a source document). This explanation is indented about half as far as the credited account titles to avoid confusing it with accounts, and it is italicized.

Point: There are no exact rules for writing journal entry explanations. An explanation should be short yet describe why an entry is made.

IFRS

IFRS requires that companies report the following four basic financial statements with explanatory notes:

- Balance sheet
- Income statement
- Statement of changes in equity (or statement of recognized revenue and expense)
- Statement of cash flows

IFRS does not prescribe specific formats; and comparative information is required for the preceding period only. ■

A blank line is left between each journal entry for clarity. When a transaction is first recorded, the **posting reference (PR) column** is left blank (in a manual system). Later, when posting entries to the ledger, the identification numbers of the individual ledger accounts are entered in the PR column.

Balance Column Account T-accounts are simple and direct means to show how the accounting process works. However, actual accounting systems need more structure and therefore use **balance column accounts,** such as that in Exhibit 2.11.

EXHIBIT 2.11

Cash Account in Balance Column Format

		Cash		Account No. 101	
Date	**Explanation**	**PR**	**Debit**	**Credit**	**Balance**
2011					
Dec. 1		G1	30,000		30,000
Dec. 2		G1		2,500	27,500
Dec. 3		G1		26,000	1,500
Dec. 10		G1	4,200		5,700

The balance column account format is similar to a T-account in having columns for debits and credits. It is different in including transaction date and explanation columns. It also has a column with the balance of the account after each entry is recorded. To illustrate, FastForward's Cash account in Exhibit 2.11 is debited on December 1 for the $30,000 owner investment, yielding a $30,000 debit balance. The account is credited on December 2 for $2,500, yielding a $27,500 debit balance. On December 3, it is credited again, this time for $26,000, and its debit balance is reduced to $1,500. The Cash account is debited for $4,200 on December 10, and its debit balance increases to $5,700; and so on.

Point: Explanations are typically included in ledger accounts only for unusual transactions or events.

The heading of the Balance column does not show whether it is a debit or credit balance. Instead, an account is assumed to have a *normal balance*. Unusual events can sometimes temporarily

EXHIBIT 2.12

Posting an Entry to the Ledger

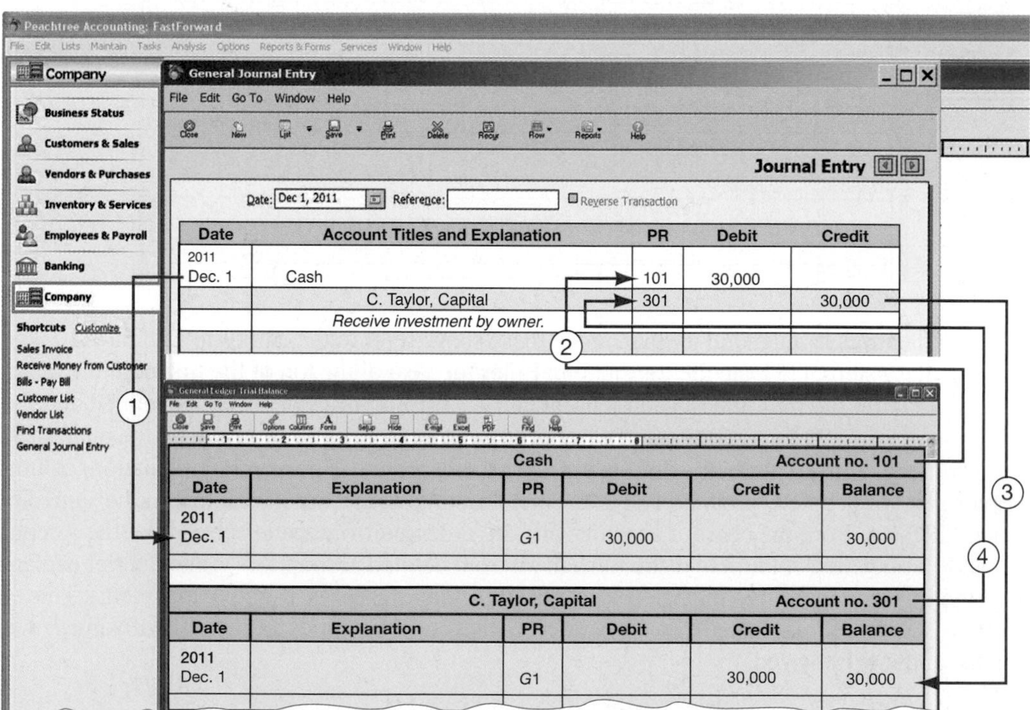

Key: (1) Identify debit account in Ledger: enter date, journal page, amount, and balance.
(2) Enter the debit account number from the Ledger in the PR column of the journal.
(3) Identify credit account in Ledger: enter date, journal page, amount, and balance.
(4) Enter the credit account number from the Ledger in the PR column of the journal.

Point: The fundamental concepts of a manual (pencil-and-paper) system are identical to those of a computerized information system.

give an account an abnormal balance. An *abnormal balance* refers to a balance on the side where decreases are recorded. For example, a customer might mistakenly overpay a bill. This gives that customer's account receivable an abnormal (credit) balance. An abnormal balance is often identified by circling it or by entering it in red or some other unusual color. A zero balance for an account is usually shown by writing zeros or a dash in the Balance column to avoid confusion between a zero balance and one omitted in error.

Posting Journal Entries Step 4 of processing transactions is to post journal entries to ledger accounts (see Exhibit 2.9). To ensure that the ledger is up-to-date, entries are posted as soon as possible. This might be daily, weekly, or when time permits. All entries must be posted to the ledger before financial statements are prepared to ensure that account balances are up-to-date. When entries are posted to the ledger, the debits in journal entries are transferred into ledger accounts as debits, and credits are transferred into ledger accounts as credits. Exhibit 2.12 shows the *four steps to post a journal entry*. First, identify the ledger account that is debited in the entry; then, in the ledger, enter the entry date, the journal and page in its PR column, the debit amount, and the new balance of the ledger account. (The letter *G* shows it came from the General Journal.) Second, enter the ledger account number in the PR column of the journal. Steps 3 and 4 repeat the first two steps for credit entries and amounts. The posting process creates a link between the ledger and the journal entry. This link is a useful cross-reference for tracing an amount from one record to another.

Point: Computerized systems often provide a code beside a balance such as *dr.* or *cr.* to identify its balance. Posting is automatic and immediate with accounting software.

Point: A journal is often referred to as the *book of original entry*. The ledger is referred to as the *book of final entry* because financial statements are prepared from it.

Analyzing Transactions—An Illustration

We return to the activities of FastForward to show how double-entry accounting is useful in analyzing and processing transactions. Analysis of each transaction follows the four steps of Exhibit 2.9.

A1 Analyze the impact of transactions on accounts and financial statements.

Step 1 Identify the transaction and any source documents.

Step 2 Analyze the transaction using the accounting equation.

Step 3 Record the transaction in journal entry form applying double-entry accounting.

Step 4 Post the entry (for simplicity, we use T-accounts to represent ledger accounts).

Study each transaction thoroughly before proceeding to the next. The first 11 transactions are from Chapter 1, and we analyze five additional December transactions of FastForward (numbered 12 through 16) that were omitted earlier.

FASTforward

1. Receive investment by Owner

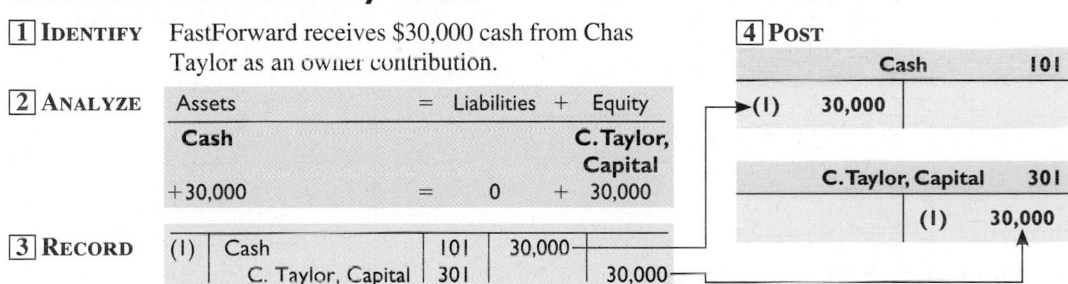

2. Purchase Supplies for Cash

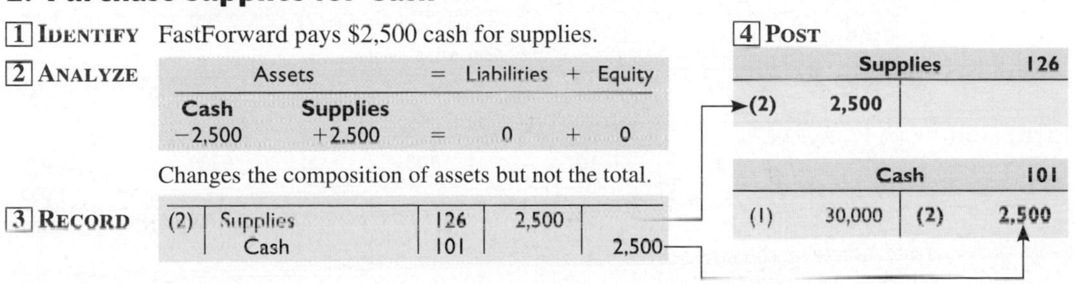

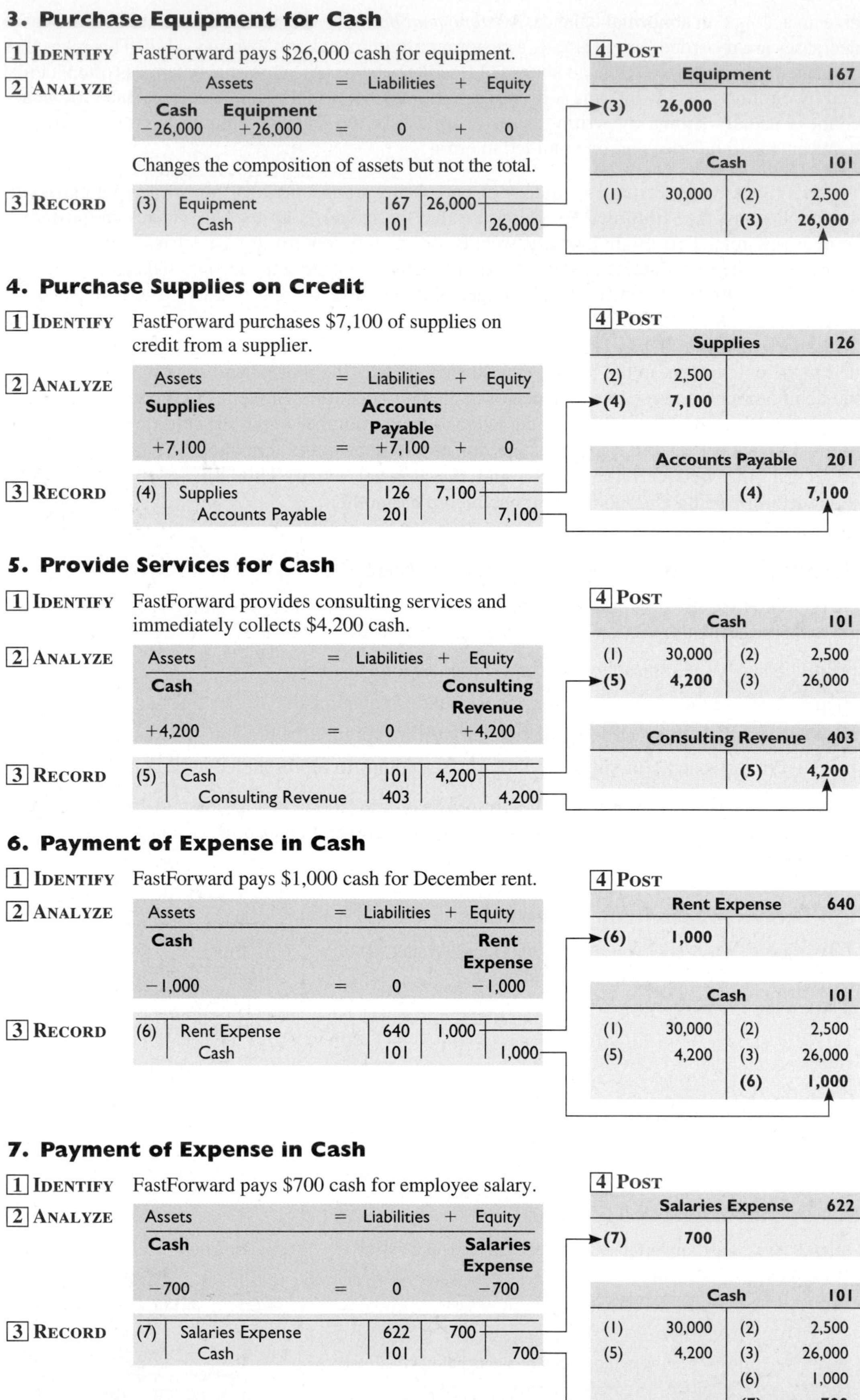

3. Purchase Equipment for Cash

1 IDENTIFY FastForward pays $26,000 cash for equipment.

2 ANALYZE

Assets		=	Liabilities	+	Equity
Cash	Equipment				
−26,000	+26,000	=	0	+	0

Changes the composition of assets but not the total.

3 RECORD

(3)	Equipment	167	26,000	
	Cash	101		26,000

4 POST

Equipment			167
(3)	26,000		

Cash			101
(1)	30,000	(2)	2,500
		(3)	26,000

4. Purchase Supplies on Credit

1 IDENTIFY FastForward purchases $7,100 of supplies on credit from a supplier.

2 ANALYZE

Assets	=	Liabilities	+	Equity
Supplies		Accounts Payable		
+7,100	=	+7,100	+	0

3 RECORD

(4)	Supplies	126	7,100	
	Accounts Payable	201		7,100

4 POST

Supplies			126
(2)	2,500		
(4)	7,100		

Accounts Payable			201
		(4)	7,100

5. Provide Services for Cash

1 IDENTIFY FastForward provides consulting services and immediately collects $4,200 cash.

2 ANALYZE

Assets	=	Liabilities	+	Equity
Cash				Consulting Revenue
+4,200	=	0		+4,200

3 RECORD

(5)	Cash	101	4,200	
	Consulting Revenue	403		4,200

4 POST

Cash			101
(1)	30,000	(2)	2,500
(5)	4,200	(3)	26,000

Consulting Revenue			403
		(5)	4,200

6. Payment of Expense in Cash

1 IDENTIFY FastForward pays $1,000 cash for December rent.

2 ANALYZE

Assets	=	Liabilities	+	Equity
Cash				Rent Expense
−1,000	=	0		−1,000

3 RECORD

(6)	Rent Expense	640	1,000	
	Cash	101		1,000

4 POST

Rent Expense			640
(6)	1,000		

Cash			101
(1)	30,000	(2)	2,500
(5)	4,200	(3)	26,000
		(6)	1,000

7. Payment of Expense in Cash

1 IDENTIFY FastForward pays $700 cash for employee salary.

2 ANALYZE

Assets	=	Liabilities	+	Equity
Cash				Salaries Expense
−700	=	0		−700

3 RECORD

(7)	Salaries Expense	622	700	
	Cash	101		700

4 POST

Salaries Expense			622
(7)	700		

Cash			101
(1)	30,000	(2)	2,500
(5)	4,200	(3)	26,000
		(6)	1,000
		(7)	700

Point: *Salary* usually refers to compensation for an employee who receives a fixed amount for a given time period, whereas *wages* usually refers to compensation based on time worked.

8. Provide Consulting and Rental Services on Credit

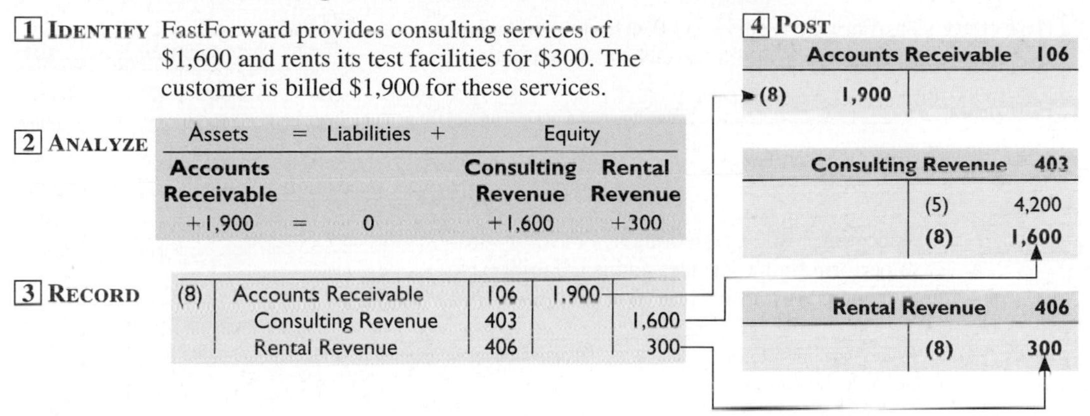

1 IDENTIFY
FastForward provides consulting services of $1,600 and rents its test facilities for $300. The customer is billed $1,900 for these services.
2 ANALYZE
Assets = Liabilities + Equity
Accounts Receivable
Consulting Revenue
Rental Revenue
+1,900 = 0 +1,600 +300
3 RECORD
(8) Accounts Receivable 106 1,900
Consulting Revenue 403 1,600
Rental Revenue 406 300
4 POST
Accounts Receivable 106
(8) 1,900
Consulting Revenue 403
(5) 4,200
(8) 1,600
Rental Revenue 406
(8) 300

Point: Transaction 8 is a **compound journal entry,** which affects three or more accounts.

9. Receipt of Cash on Account

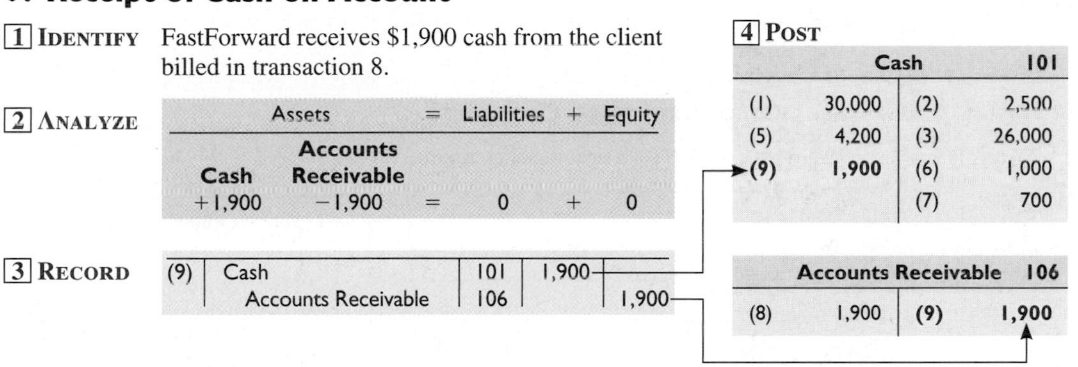

1 IDENTIFY
FastForward receives $1,900 cash from the client billed in transaction 8.
2 ANALYZE
Assets = Liabilities + Equity
Cash
Accounts Receivable
+1,900 −1,900 = 0 + 0
3 RECORD
(9) Cash 101 1,900
Accounts Receivable 106 1,900
4 POST
Cash 101
(1) 30,000 (2) 2,500
(5) 4,200 (3) 26,000
(9) 1,900 (6) 1,000
(7) 700
Accounts Receivable 106
(8) 1,900 (9) 1,900

Point: The *revenue recognition principle* requires revenue to be recognized when earned, which is when the company provides products and services to a customer. This is not necessarily the same time that the customer pays. A customer can pay before or after products or services are provided.

10. Partial Payment of Accounts Payable

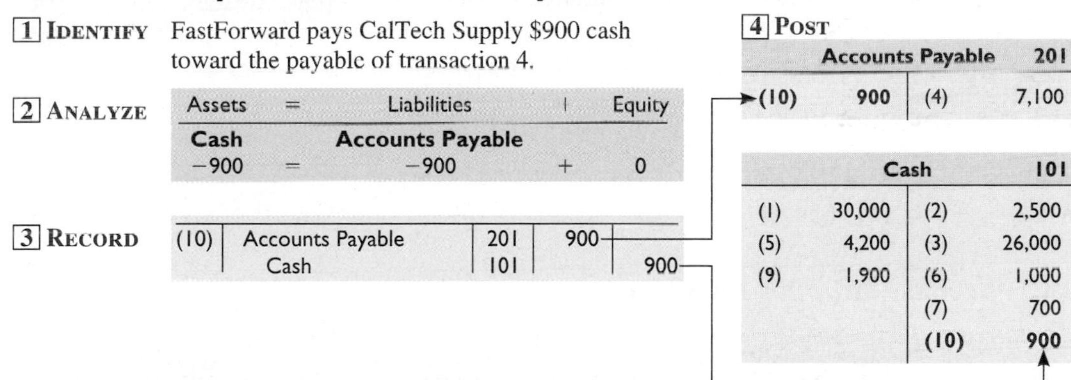

1 IDENTIFY
FastForward pays CalTech Supply $900 cash toward the payable of transaction 4.
2 ANALYZE
Assets = Liabilities + Equity
Cash
Accounts Payable
−900 = −900 + 0
3 RECORD
(10) Accounts Payable 201 900
Cash 101 900
4 POST
Accounts Payable 201
(10) 900 (4) 7,100
Cash 101
(1) 30,000 (2) 2,500
(5) 4,200 (3) 26,000
(9) 1,900 (6) 1,000
(7) 700
(10) 900

11. Withdrawal of Cash by Owner

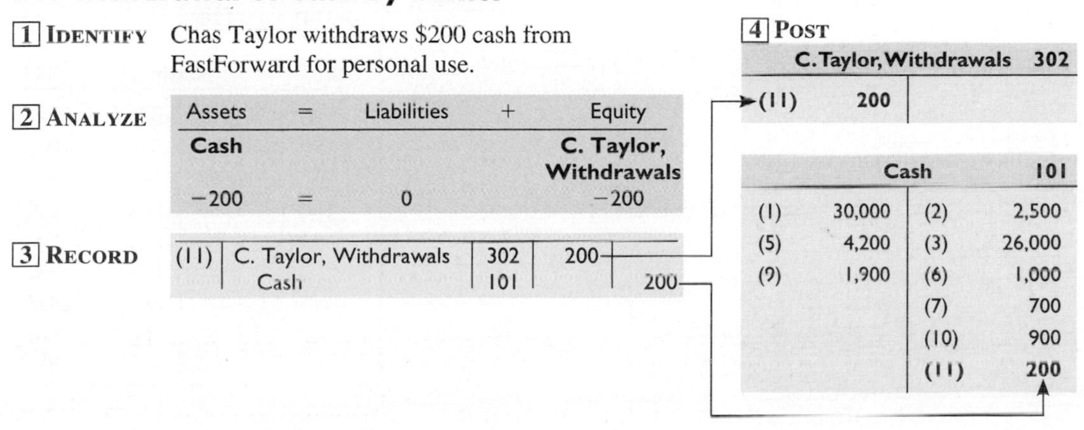

1 IDENTIFY
Chas Taylor withdraws $200 cash from FastForward for personal use.
2 ANALYZE
Assets = Liabilities + Equity
Cash
C. Taylor, Withdrawals
−200 = 0 −200
3 RECORD
(11) C. Taylor, Withdrawals 302 200
Cash 101 200
4 POST
C. Taylor, Withdrawals 302
(11) 200
Cash 101
(1) 30,000 (2) 2,500
(5) 4,200 (3) 26,000
(9) 1,900 (6) 1,000
(7) 700
(10) 900
(11) 200

Point: Luca Pacioli, a 15th-century monk, is considered a pioneer in accounting and the first to devise double-entry accounting.

12. Receipt of Cash for Future Services

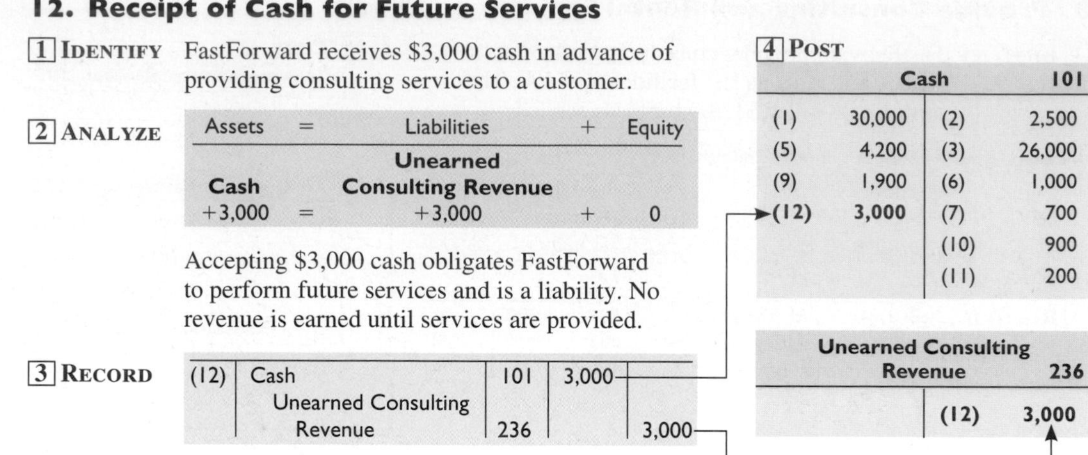

1 IDENTIFY FastForward receives $3,000 cash in advance of providing consulting services to a customer.

2 ANALYZE

Assets	=	Liabilities	+	Equity
Cash		**Unearned Consulting Revenue**		
+3,000	=	+3,000	+	0

Accepting $3,000 cash obligates FastForward to perform future services and is a liability. No revenue is earned until services are provided.

3 RECORD

(12)	Cash	101	3,000	
	Unearned Consulting Revenue	236		3,000

4 POST

Cash			101
(1)	30,000	(2)	2,500
(5)	4,200	(3)	26,000
(9)	1,900	(6)	1,000
(12)	**3,000**	(7)	700
		(10)	900
		(11)	200

Unearned Consulting Revenue			236
		(12)	**3,000**

13. Pay Cash for Future Insurance Coverage

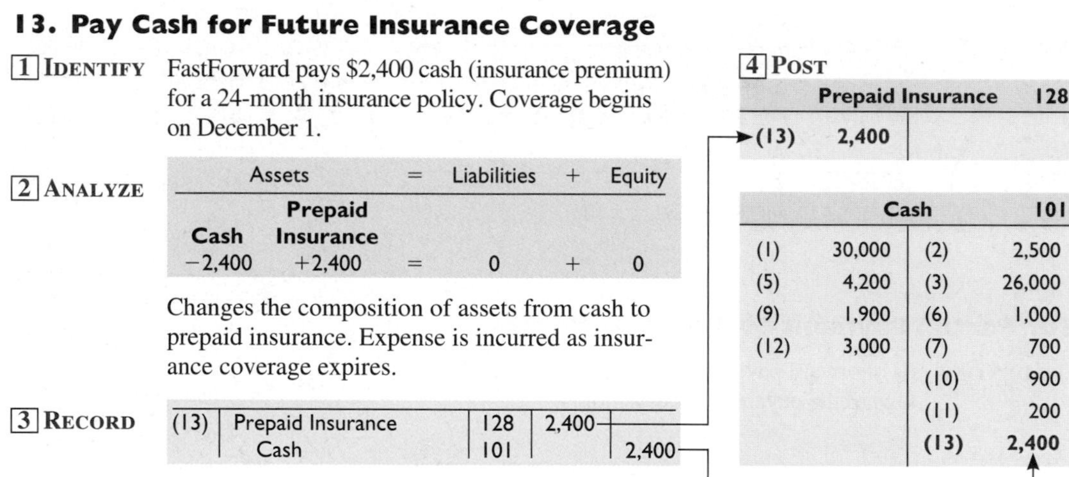

1 IDENTIFY FastForward pays $2,400 cash (insurance premium) for a 24-month insurance policy. Coverage begins on December 1.

2 ANALYZE

Assets		=	Liabilities	+	Equity
Cash	**Prepaid Insurance**				
−2,400	+2,400	=	0	+	0

Changes the composition of assets from cash to prepaid insurance. Expense is incurred as insurance coverage expires.

3 RECORD

(13)	Prepaid Insurance	128	2,400	
	Cash	101		2,400

4 POST

Prepaid Insurance			128
(13)	**2,400**		

Cash			101
(1)	30,000	(2)	2,500
(5)	4,200	(3)	26,000
(9)	1,900	(6)	1,000
(12)	3,000	(7)	700
		(10)	900
		(11)	200
		(13)	**2,400**

14. Purchase Supplies for Cash

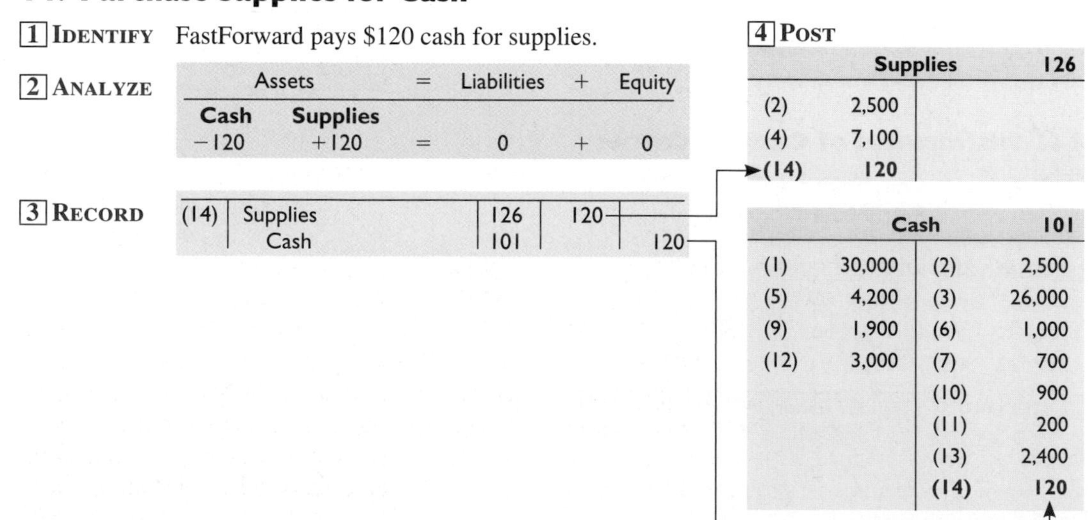

1 IDENTIFY FastForward pays $120 cash for supplies.

2 ANALYZE

Assets		=	Liabilities	+	Equity
Cash	**Supplies**				
−120	+120	=	0	+	0

3 RECORD

(14)	Supplies	126	120	
	Cash	101		120

4 POST

Supplies			126
(2)	2,500		
(4)	7,100		
(14)	**120**		

Cash			101
(1)	30,000	(2)	2,500
(5)	4,200	(3)	26,000
(9)	1,900	(6)	1,000
(12)	3,000	(7)	700
		(10)	900
		(11)	200
		(13)	2,400
		(14)	**120**

15. Payment of Expense in Cash

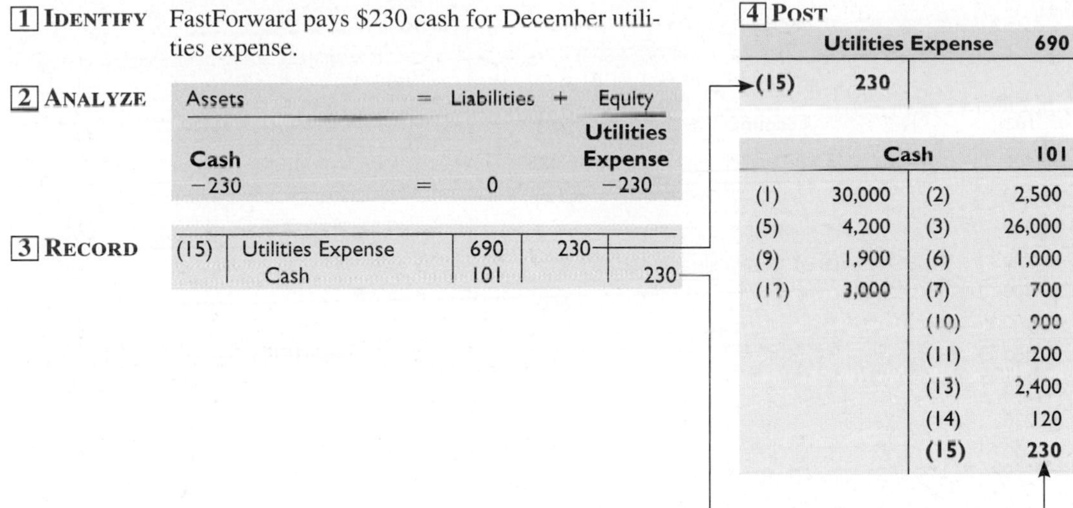

16. Payment of Expense in Cash

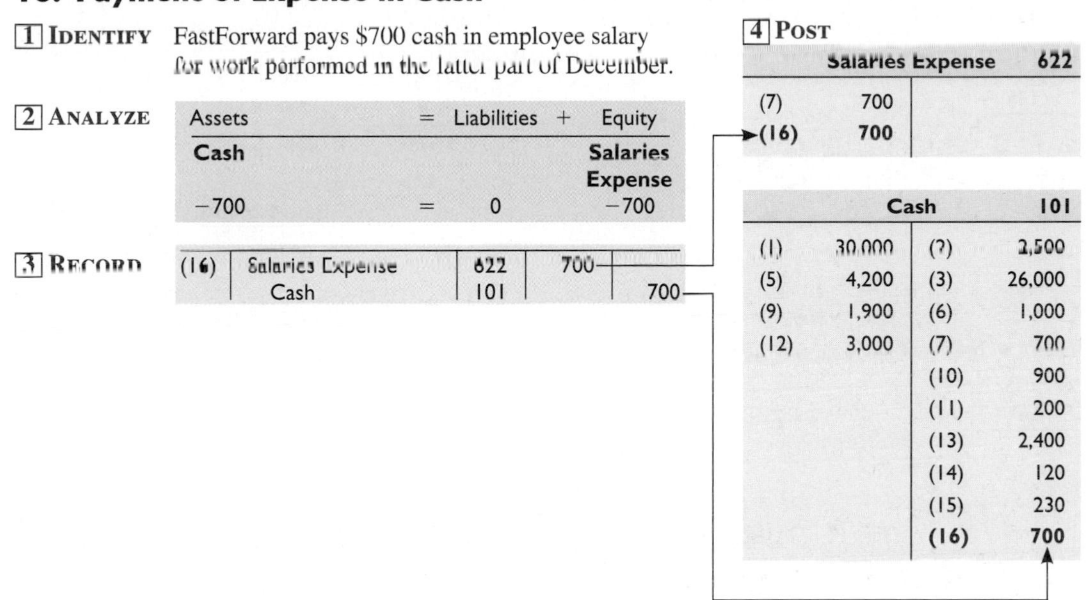

Point: We could merge transactions 15 and 16 into one *compound entry.*

Accounting Equation Analysis

Exhibit 2.13 shows the ledger accounts (in T-account form) of FastForward after all 16 transactions are recorded and posted and the balances computed. The accounts are grouped into three major columns corresponding to the accounting equation: assets, liabilities, and equity. Note several important points. First, as with each transaction, the totals for the three columns must obey the accounting equation. Specifically, assets equal $42,470 ($4,350 + $0 + $9,720 + $2,400 + $26,000); liabilities equal $9,200 ($6,200 + $3,000); and equity equals $33,270 ($30,000 − $200 + $5,800 + $300 − $1,400 − $1,000 − $230). These numbers prove the accounting equation: Assets of $42,470 = Liabilities of $9,200 + Equity of $33,270. Second, the capital, withdrawals, revenue, and expense accounts reflect the transactions that change equity. These account categories underlie the statement of owner's equity. Third, the revenue and expense account balances will be summarized and reported in the income statement. Fourth, increases and decreases in the cash account make up the elements reported in the statement of cash flows.

Debit and Credit Rules

Accounts	Increase (normal bal.)	Decrease
Asset	Debit	Credit
Liability	Credit	Debit
Capital	Credit	Debit
Withdrawals	Debit	Credit
Revenue	Credit	Debit
Expense	Debit	Credit

Point: Technology does not provide the judgment required to analyze most business transactions. Analysis requires the expertise of skilled and ethical professionals.

EXHIBIT 2.13

Ledger for FastForward (in T-Account Form)

Assets = Liabilities + Equity

Assets

Cash			101
(1)	30,000	(2)	2,500
(5)	4,200	(3)	26,000
(9)	1,900	(6)	1,000
(12)	3,000	(7)	700
		(10)	900
		(11)	200
		(13)	2,400
		(14)	120
		(15)	230
		(16)	700
Balance	**4,350**		

Accounts Receivable			106
(8)	1,900	(9)	1,900
Balance	**0**		

Supplies			126
(2)	2,500		
(4)	7,100		
(14)	120		
Balance	**9,720**		

Prepaid Insurance			128
(13)	**2,400**		

Equipment			167
(3)	**26,000**		

Liabilities

Accounts Payable			201
(10)	900	(4)	7,100
		Balance	**6,200**

Unearned Consulting Revenue			236
		(12)	**3,000**

Equity

C. Taylor, Capital			301
		(1)	**30,000**

C. Taylor, Withdrawals			302
(11)	**200**		

Consulting Revenue			403
		(5)	4,200
		(8)	1,600
		Balance	**5,800**

Rental Revenue			406
		(8)	**300**

Salaries Expense			622
(7)	700		
(16)	700		
Balance	**1,400**		

Rent Expense			640
(6)	**1,000**		

Utilities Expense			690
(15)	**230**		

Accounts in this white area reflect those reported on the income statement.

$42,470 = $9,200 + $33,270

Quick Check

Answers — p. 75

8. What types of transactions increase equity? What types decrease equity?
9. Why are accounting systems called *double-entry?*
10. For each transaction, double-entry accounting requires which of the following? (*a*) Debits to asset accounts must create credits to liability or equity accounts, (*b*) a debit to a liability account must create a credit to an asset account, or (*c*) total debits must equal total credits.
11. An owner invests $15,000 cash along with equipment having a market value of $23,000 in a company. Prepare the necessary journal entry.
12. Explain what a compound journal entry is.
13. Why are posting reference numbers entered in the journal when entries are posted to ledger accounts?

TRIAL BALANCE

Double-entry accounting requires the sum of debit account balances to equal the sum of credit account balances. A trial balance is used to confirm this. A **trial balance** is a list of accounts and their balances at a point in time. Account balances are reported in their appropriate debit or credit columns of a trial balance. A trial balance can be used to confirm this and to follow up on any abnormal or unusual balances. Exhibit 2.14 shows the trial balance for FastForward after its 16 entries have been posted to the ledger. (This is an *unadjusted* trial balance—Chapter 3 explains the necessary adjustments.)

EXHIBIT 2.14

Trial Balance (Unadjusted)

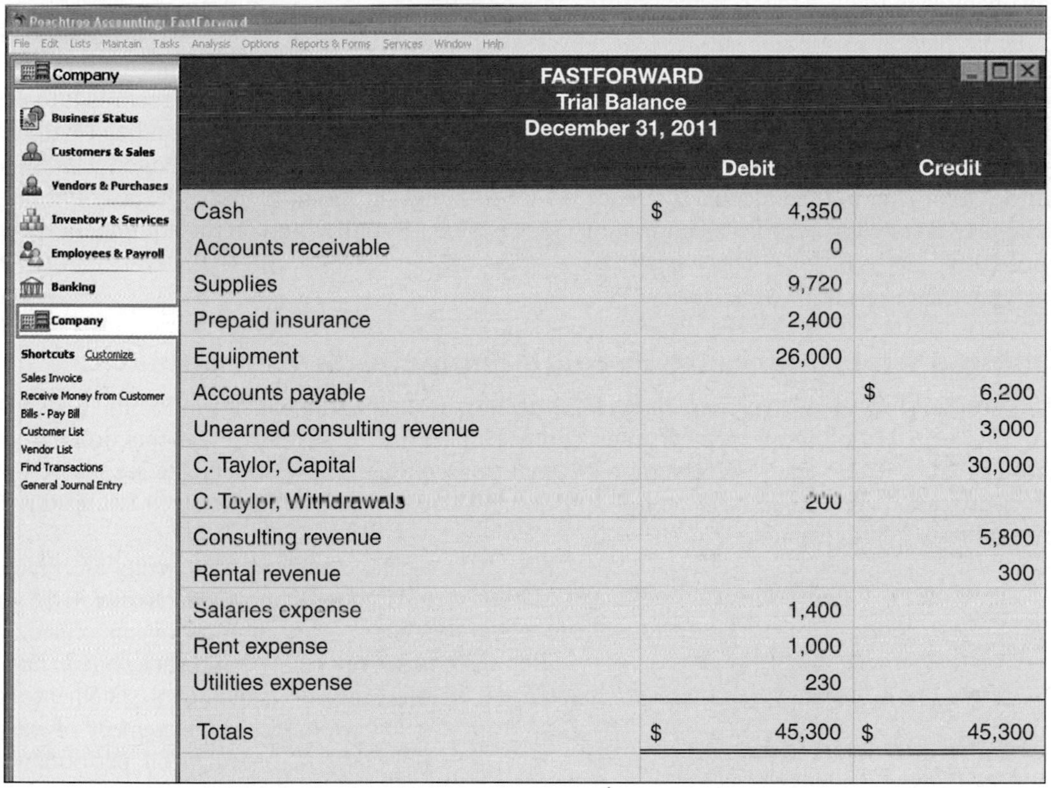

Peachtree Accounting: FastForward

File Edit Lists Maintain Tasks Analysis Options Reports & Forms Services Window Help

Company: Business Status; Customers & Sales; Vendors & Purchases; Inventory & Services; Employees & Payroll; Banking; Company

Shortcuts Customize: Sales Invoice; Receive Money from Customer; Bills - Pay Bill; Customer List; Vendor List; Find Transactions; General Journal Entry

FASTFORWARD
Trial Balance
December 31, 2011

	Debit	Credit
Cash	$ 4,350	
Accounts receivable	0	
Supplies	9,720	
Prepaid insurance	2,400	
Equipment	26,000	
Accounts payable		$ 6,200
Unearned consulting revenue		3,000
C. Taylor, Capital		30,000
C. Taylor, Withdrawals	200	
Consulting revenue		5,800
Rental revenue		300
Salaries expense	1,400	
Rent expense	1,000	
Utilities expense	230	
Totals	$ 45,300	$ 45,300

Point: The ordering of accounts in a trial balance typically follows their identification number from the chart of accounts.

Preparing a Trial Balance

P2 Prepare and explain the use of a trial balance.

Preparing a trial balance involves three steps:

1. List each account title and its amount (from ledger) in the trial balance. If an account has a zero balance, list it with a zero in its normal balance column (or omit it entirely).
2. Compute the total of debit balances and the total of credit balances.
3. Verify (*prove*) total debit balances equal total credit balances.

The total of debit balances equals the total of credit balances for the trial balance in Exhibit 2.14. Equality of these two totals does not guarantee that no errors were made. For example, the column totals still will be equal when a debit or credit of a correct amount is made to a wrong account. Another error that does not cause unequal column totals occurs when equal debits and credits of an incorrect amount are entered.

Point: A trial balance is *not* a financial statement but a mechanism for checking equality of debits and credits in the ledger. Financial statements do not have debit and credit columns.

Searching for and Correcting Errors If the trial balance does not balance (when its columns are not equal), the error (or errors) must be found and corrected. An efficient

Example: If a credit to Unearned Revenue was incorrectly posted from the journal as a credit to the Revenue ledger account, would the ledger still balance? Would the financial statements be correct? *Answers:* The ledger would balance, but liabilities would be understated, equity would be overstated, and income would be overstated (all because of overstated revenues).

way to search for an error is to check the journalizing, posting, and trial balance preparation in *reverse order.* Step 1 is to verify that the trial balance columns are correctly added. If step 1 fails to find the error, step 2 is to verify that account balances are accurately entered from the ledger. Step 3 is to see whether a debit (or credit) balance is mistakenly listed in the trial balance as a credit (or debit). A clue to this error is when the difference between total debits and total credits equals twice the amount of the incorrect account balance. If the error is still undiscovered, Step 4 is to recompute each account balance in the ledger. Step 5 is to verify that each journal entry is properly posted. Step 6 is to verify that the original journal entry has equal debits and credits. At this point, the errors should be uncovered.[3]

If an error in a journal entry is discovered before the error is posted, it can be corrected in a manual system by drawing a line through the incorrect information. The correct information is written above it to create a record of change for the auditor. Many computerized systems allow the operator to replace the incorrect information directly.

Point: The IRS requires companies to keep records that can be audited.

If an error in a journal entry is not discovered until after it is posted, we do not strike through both erroneous entries in the journal and ledger. Instead, we correct this error by creating a *correcting entry* that removes the amount from the wrong account and records it to the correct account. As an example, suppose a $100 purchase of supplies is journalized with an incorrect debit to Equipment, and then this incorrect entry is posted to the ledger. The Supplies ledger account balance is understated by $100, and the Equipment ledger account balance is overstated by $100. The correcting entry is: debit Supplies and credit Equipment (both for $100).

Using a Trial Balance to Prepare Financial Statements

P3 Prepare financial statements from business transactions.

This section shows how to prepare *financial statements* from the trial balance in Exhibit 2.14 and from information on the December transactions of FastForward. These statements differ from those in Chapter 1 because of several additional transactions. These statements are also more precisely called *unadjusted statements* because we need to make some further accounting adjustments (described in Chapter 3).

EXHIBIT 2.15

Links between Financial Statements across Time

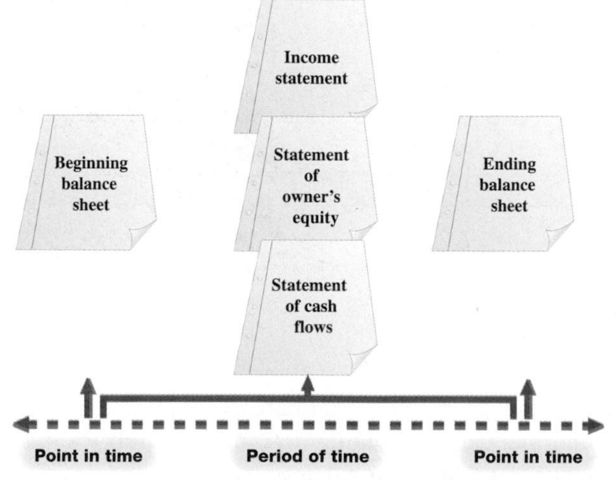

How financial statements are linked in time is illustrated in Exhibit 2.15. A balance sheet reports on an organization's financial position at a *point in time.* The income statement, statement of owner's equity, and statement of cash flows report on financial performance over a *period of time*. The three statements in the middle column of Exhibit 2.15 link balance sheets from the beginning to the end of a reporting period. They explain how financial position changes from one point to another.

Preparers and users (including regulatory agencies) determine the length of the reporting period. A one-year, or

[3] *Transposition* occurs when two digits are switched, or transposed, within a number. If transposition is the only error, it yields a difference between the two trial balance totals that is evenly divisible by 9. For example, assume that a $691 debit in an entry is incorrectly posted to the ledger as $619. Total credits in the trial balance are then larger than total debits by $72 ($691 − $619). The $72 error is *evenly* divisible by 9 (72/9 = 8). The first digit of the quotient (in our example it is 8) equals the difference between the digits of the two transposed numbers (the 9 and the 1). The number of digits in the quotient also tells the location of the transposition, starting from the right. The quotient in our example had only one digit (8), so it tells us the transposition is in the first digit. Consider another example where a transposition error involves posting $961 instead of the correct $691. The difference in these numbers is $270, and its quotient is 30 (270/9). The quotient has two digits, so it tells us to check the second digit from the right for a transposition of two numbers that have a difference of 3.

annual, reporting period is common, as are semiannual, quarterly, and monthly periods. The one-year reporting period is known as the *accounting,* or *fiscal, year.* Businesses whose accounting year begins on January 1 and ends on December 31 are known as *calendar-year* companies. Many companies choose a fiscal year ending on a date other than December 31. **Research In Motion** is a *noncalendar-year* company as reflected in the headings of its February 27 year-end financial statements in Appendix A near the end of the book.

Point: A statement's heading lists the 3 W's: **Who**—name of organization, **What**—name of statement, **When**—statement's point in time or period of time.

Income Statement An income statement reports the revenues earned less the expenses incurred by a business over a period of time. FastForward's income statement for December is shown at the top of Exhibit 2.16. Information about revenues and expenses is conveniently taken from the trial balance in Exhibit 2.14. Net income of $3,470 is reported at the bottom of the statement. Owner investments and withdrawals are *not* part of income.

Statement of Owner's Equity The statement of owner's equity reports information about how equity changes over the reporting period. FastForward's statement of owner's equity is the second report in Exhibit 2.16. It shows the $30,000 owner investment, the $3,470 of net income, the $200 withdrawal, and the $33,270 end-of-period (capital) balance. (The beginning

EXHIBIT 2.16

Financial Statements and Their Links

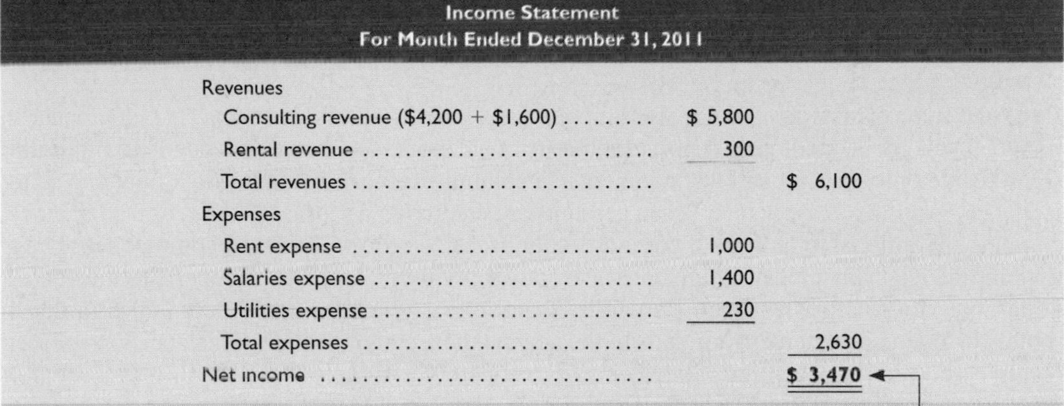

FASTFORWARD
Income Statement
For Month Ended December 31, 2011

Revenues		
Consulting revenue ($4,200 + $1,600)	$ 5,800	
Rental revenue	300	
Total revenues		$ 6,100
Expenses		
Rent expense	1,000	
Salaries expense	1,400	
Utilities expense	230	
Total expenses		2,630
Net income		$ 3,470

Point: Arrow lines show how the statements are linked.

FASTFORWARD
Statement of Owner's Equity
For Month Ended December 31, 2011

C. Taylor, Capital, December 1, 2011		$ 0
Plus: Investments by owner	$30,000	
Net income	3,470	33,470
		33,470
Less: Withdrawals by owner		200
C. Taylor, Capital, December 31, 2011		$33,270

FASTFORWARD
Balance Sheet
December 31, 2011

Assets		Liabilities	
Cash	$ 4,350	Accounts payable	$ 6,200
Supplies	9,720	Unearned revenue	3,000
Prepaid insurance	2,400	Total liabilities	9,200
Equipment	26,000	**Equity**	
		C. Taylor, Capital	33,270
Total assets	$42,470	Total liabilities and equity	$ 42,470

Point: To *foot* a column of numbers is to add them.

balance in the statement of owner's equity is rarely zero; an exception is for the first period of operations. The beginning capital balance in January 2012 is $33,270, which is December's ending balance.)

Point: An income statement is also called an *earnings statement, a statement of operations,* or a *P&L* (profit and loss) *statement.* A balance sheet is also called a *statement of financial position.*

Point: While revenues increase equity, and expenses decrease equity, the amounts are not reported in detail in the statement of owner's equity. Instead, their effects are reflected through net income.

Balance Sheet The balance sheet reports the financial position of a company at a point in time, usually at the end of a month, quarter, or year. FastForward's balance sheet is the third report in Exhibit 2.16. This statement refers to financial condition at the close of business on December 31. The left side of the balance sheet lists its assets: cash, supplies, prepaid insurance, and equipment. The upper right side of the balance sheet shows that it owes $6,200 to creditors and $3,000 in services to customers who paid in advance. The equity section shows an ending balance of $33,270. Note the link between the ending balance of the statement of owner's equity and the capital balance. (Recall that this presentation of the balance sheet is called the *account form:* assets on the left and liabilities and equity on the right. Another presentation is the *report form:* assets on top, followed by liabilities and then equity. Either presentation is acceptable.)

Decision Maker Answer — p. 74 

Entrepreneur You open a wholesale business selling entertainment equipment to retail outlets. You find that most of your customers demand to buy on credit. How can you use the balance sheets of these customers to decide which ones to extend credit to? ■

Point: Knowing how financial statements are prepared improves our analysis of them.

Presentation Issues Dollar signs are not used in journals and ledgers. They do appear in financial statements and other reports such as trial balances. The usual practice is to put dollar signs beside only the first and last numbers in a column. **Research In Motion**'s financial statements in Appendix A show this. When amounts are entered in a journal, ledger, or trial balance, commas are optional to indicate thousands, millions, and so forth. However, commas are always used in financial statements. Companies also commonly round amounts in reports to the nearest dollar, or even to a higher level. Research In Motion is typical of many companies in that it rounds its financial statement amounts to the nearest thousand or million. This decision is based on the perceived impact of rounding for users' business decisions.

off the mark.com by Mark Parisi
COULD YOU PLEASE STOP TOUCHING THINGS FOR ONE MOMENT?! I CAN'T KEEP UP!
offthemark.com
KING MIDAS' ACCOUNTANT

Quick Check Answers — p. 75 

14. Where are dollar signs typically entered in financial statements?

15. If a $4,000 debit to Equipment in a journal entry is incorrectly posted to the ledger as a $4,000 credit, and the ledger account has a resulting debit balance of $20,000, what is the effect of this error on the Trial Balance column totals?

16. Describe the link between the income statement and the statement of owner's equity.

17. Explain the link between the balance sheet and the statement of owner's equity.

18. Define and describe revenues and expenses.

19. Define and describe assets, liabilities, and equity.

GLOBAL VIEW

Financial accounting according to U.S. GAAP is similar, but not identical, to IFRS. This section discusses differences in analyzing and recording transactions, and with the preparation of financial statements.

Analyzing and Recording Transactions Both U.S. GAAP and IFRS include broad and similar guidance for financial accounting. As the FASB and IASB work toward a common conceptual framework over the next few years, even those differences will fade. Further, both U.S. GAAP and IFRS apply transaction analysis and recording as shown in this chapter—using the same debit and credit system and accrual accounting. Although some variations exist in revenue and expense recognition and other accounting principles, all of the transactions in this chapter are accounted for identically under these two systems.

Financial Statements Both U.S. GAAP and IFRS prepare the same four basic financial statements. A few differences within each statement do exist and we will discuss those throughout the book. For example, both U.S. GAAP and IFRS require balance sheets to separate current items from noncurrent items. However, while U.S. GAAP balance sheets report current items first, IFRS balance sheets normally (but are not required to) present noncurrent items first, and equity before liabilities. To illustrate, a condensed version of **Nokia**'s balance sheet follows (numbers using Euros in millions).

NOKIA

NOKIA
Balance Sheet (in EUR millions)
December 31, 2009

Assets		Equity and Liabilities	
Noncurrent assets	12,125	Total equity	14,749
Current assets	23,613	Noncurrent liabilities	5,801
		Current liabilities	15,188
Total assets	35,738	Total equity and liabilities	35,738

Accounting Controls and Assurance Accounting systems depend on control procedures that assure the proper principles were applied in processing accounting information. The passage of SOX legislation strengthened U.S. control procedures in recent years. However, global standards for control are diverse and so are enforcement activities. Consequently, while global accounting standards are converging, their application in different countries can yield different outcomes depending on the quality of their auditing standards and enforcement.

Decision Insight

Accounting Control Recording valid transactions, and not recording fraudulent transactions, enhances the quality of financial statements. The graph here shows the percentage of employees in information technology that report observing specific types of misconduct within the past year. ■

[Source: KPMG 2009]

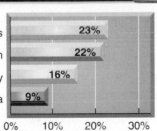

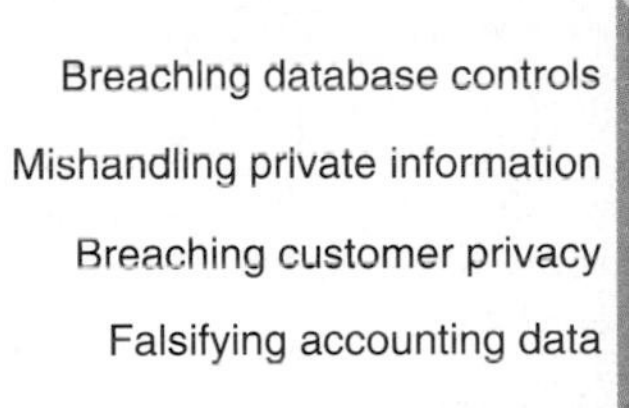

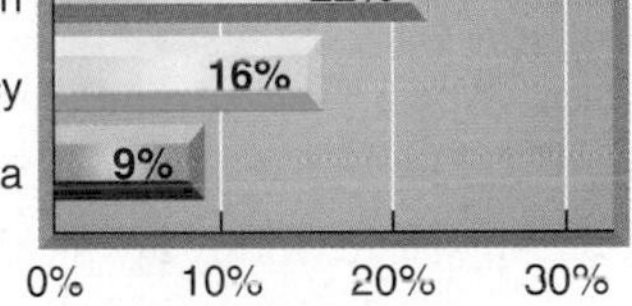

Debt Ratio

Decision Analysis

A2 Compute the debt ratio and describe its use in analyzing financial condition.

An important business objective is gathering information to help assess a company's risk of failing to pay its debts. Companies finance their assets with either liabilities or equity. A company that finances a relatively large portion of its assets with liabilities is said to have a high degree of *financial leverage*. Higher financial leverage involves greater risk because liabilities must be repaid and often require regular interest payments (equity financing does not). The risk that a company might not be able to meet such required payments is higher if it has more liabilities (is more highly leveraged). One way to assess the risk associated with a company's use of liabilities is to compute the **debt ratio** as in Exhibit 2.17.

EXHIBIT 2.17
Debt Ratio

$$\textbf{Debt ratio} = \frac{\textbf{Total liabilities}}{\textbf{Total assets}}$$

Point: Compare the equity amount to the liability amount to assess the extent of owner versus nonowner financing.

To see how to apply the debt ratio, let's look at **Skechers**'s liabilities and assets. The company designs, markets, and sells footwear for men, women, and children under the Skechers brand. Exhibit 2.18 computes and reports its debt ratio at the end of each year from 2005 to 2009.

EXHIBIT 2.18

Computation and Analysis of Debt Ratio

$ in millions	2009	2008	2007	2006	2005
Total liabilities	$246	$204	$201	$288	$238
Total assets	$996	$876	$828	$737	$582
Debt ratio	**0.25**	**0.23**	**0.24**	**0.39**	**0.41**
Industry debt ratio	0.51	0.50	0.46	0.48	0.47

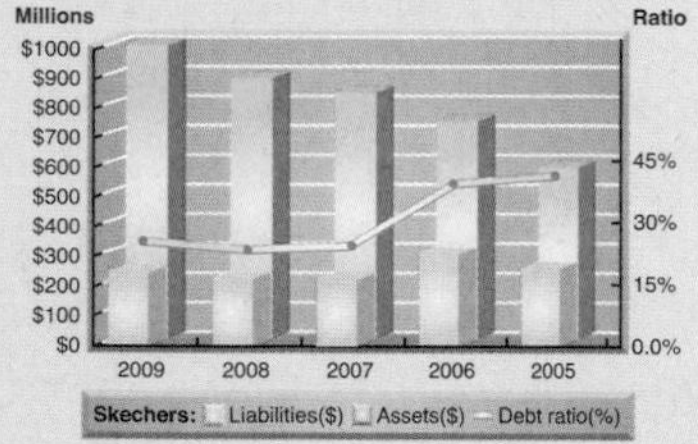

Skechers's debt ratio ranges from a low of 0.23 to a high of 0.41—also, see graph in margin. Its ratio is lower, and has been generally declining, compared with the industry ratio. This analysis implies a low risk from its financial leverage. Is financial leverage good or bad for Skechers? To answer that question we need to compare the company's return on the borrowed money to the rate it is paying creditors. If the company's return is higher, it is successfully borrowing money to make more money. A company's success with making money from borrowed money can quickly turn unprofitable if its own return drops below the rate it is paying creditors.

Decision Maker Answer — p. 74

Investor You consider buying stock in **Converse**. As part of your analysis, you compute its debt ratio for 2009, 2010, and 2011 as: 0.35, 0.74, and 0.94, respectively. Based on the debt ratio, is Converse a low-risk investment? Has the risk of buying Converse stock changed over this period? (The industry debt ratio averages 0.40.) ■

DEMONSTRATION PROBLEM

(This problem extends the demonstration problem of Chapter 1.) After several months of planning, Jasmine Worthy started a haircutting business called Expressions. The following events occurred during its first month.

a. On August 1, Worthy invested $3,000 cash and $15,000 of equipment in Expressions.
b. On August 2, Expressions paid $600 cash for furniture for the shop.
c. On August 3, Expressions paid $500 cash to rent space in a strip mall for August.
d. On August 4, it purchased $1,200 of equipment on credit for the shop (using a long-term note payable).
e. On August 5, Expressions opened for business. Cash received from haircutting services in the first week and a half of business (ended August 15) was $825.
f. On August 15, it provided $100 of haircutting services on account.
g. On August 17, it received a $100 check for services previously rendered on account.
h. On August 17, it paid $125 to an assistant for hours worked during the grand opening.
i. Cash received from services provided during the second half of August was $930.
j. On August 31, it paid a $400 installment toward principal on the note payable entered into on August 4.
k. On August 31, Worthy withdrew $900 cash for personal use.

Required

1. Open the following ledger accounts in balance column format (account numbers are in parentheses): Cash (101); Accounts Receivable (102); Furniture (161); Store Equipment (165); Note Payable (240); J. Worthy, Capital (301); J. Worthy, Withdrawals (302); Haircutting Services Revenue (403); Wages Expense (623); and Rent Expense (640). Prepare general journal entries for the transactions.
2. Post the journal entries from (1) to the ledger accounts.

3. Prepare a trial balance as of August 31.
4. Prepare an income statement for August.
5. Prepare a statement of owner's equity for August.
6. Prepare a balance sheet as of August 31.
7. Determine the debt ratio as of August 31.

Extended Analysis

8. In the coming months, Expressions will experience a greater variety of business transactions. Identify which accounts are debited and which are credited for the following transactions. (*Hint:* We must use some accounts not opened in part 1.)
   a. Purchase supplies with cash.
   b. Pay cash for future insurance coverage.
   c. Receive cash for services to be provided in the future.
   d. Purchase supplies on account.

PLANNING THE SOLUTION

- Analyze each transaction and use the debit and credit rules to prepare a journal entry for each.
- Post each debit and each credit from journal entries to their ledger accounts and cross-reference each amount in the posting reference (PR) columns of the journal and ledger.
- Calculate each account balance and list the accounts with their balances on a trial balance.
- Verify that total debits in the trial balance equal total credits.
- To prepare the income statement, identify revenues and expenses. List those items on the statement, compute the difference, and label the result as *net income* or *net loss*.
- Use information in the ledger to prepare the statement of owner's equity.
- Use information in the ledger to prepare the balance sheet.
- Calculate the debt ratio by dividing total liabilities by total assets.
- Analyze the future transactions to identify the accounts affected and apply debit and credit rules.

SOLUTION TO DEMONSTRATION PROBLEM

1. General journal entries:

General Journal Entry

Page 1

Date	Account Titles and Explanation	PR	Debit	Credit
Aug. 1	Cash	101	3,000	
	Store Equipment	165	15,000	
	J. Worthy, Capital	301		18,000
	Owner's investment.			
2	Furniture	161	600	
	Cash	101		600
	Purchased furniture for cash.			
3	Rent Expense	640	500	
	Cash	101		500
	Paid rent for August.			
4	Store Equipment	165	1,200	
	Note Payable	240		1,200
	Purchased additional equipment on credit.			
15	Cash	101	825	
	Haircutting Services Revenue	403		825
	Cash receipts from first half of August.			

[continued on next page]

[continued from previous page]

15	Accounts Receivable	102	100	
	Haircutting Services Revenue	403		100
	To record revenue for services provided on account.			
17	Cash	101	100	
	Accounts Receivable	102		100
	To record cash received as payment on account.			
17	Wages Expense	623	125	
	Cash	101		125
	Paid wages to assistant.			
31	Cash	101	930	
	Haircutting Services Revenue	403		930
	Cash receipts from second half of August.			
31	Note Payable	240	400	
	Cash	101		400
	Paid an installment on the note payable.			
31	J. Worthy, Withdrawals	302	900	
	Cash	101		900
	Cash withdrawal by owner.			

2. Post journal entries from part 1 to the ledger accounts:

General Ledger

Cash **Account No. 101**

Date	PR	Debit	Credit	Balance
Aug. 1	G1	3,000		3,000
2	G1		600	2,400
3	G1		500	1,900
15	G1	825		2,725
17	G1	100		2,825
17	G1		125	2,700
31	G1	930		3,630
31	G1		400	3,230
31	G1		900	2,330

Accounts Receivable **Account No. 102**

Date	PR	Debit	Credit	Balance
Aug. 15	G1	100		100
17	G1		100	0

Furniture **Account No. 161**

Date	PR	Debit	Credit	Balance
Aug. 2	G1	600		600

Store Equipment **Account No. 165**

Date	PR	Debit	Credit	Balance
Aug. 1	G1	15,000		15,000
4	G1	1,200		16,200

Note Payable **Account No. 240**

Date	PR	Debit	Credit	Balance
Aug. 4	G1		1,200	1,200
31	G1	400		800

J. Worthy, Capital **Account No. 301**

Date	PR	Debit	Credit	Balance
Aug. 1	G1		18,000	18,000

J. Worthy, Withdrawals **Account No. 302**

Date	PR	Debit	Credit	Balance
Aug. 31	G1	900		900

Haircutting Services Revenue **Account No. 403**

Date	PR	Debit	Credit	Balance
Aug. 15	G1		825	825
15	G1		100	925
31	G1		930	1,855

Wages Expense **Account No. 623**

Date	PR	Debit	Credit	Balance
Aug. 17	G1	125		125

Rent Expense **Account No. 640**

Date	PR	Debit	Credit	Balance
Aug. 3	G1	500		500

3. Prepare a trial balance from the ledger:

EXPRESSIONS
Trial Balance
August 31

	Debit	Credit
Cash	$ 2,330	
Accounts receivable	0	
Furniture	600	
Store equipment	16,200	
Note payable		$ 800
J. Worthy, Capital		18,000
J. Worthy, Withdrawals	900	
Haircutting services revenue		1,855
Wages expense	125	
Rent expense	500	
Totals	$20,655	$20,655

4.

EXPRESSIONS
Income Statement
For Month Ended August 31

Revenues		
Haircutting services revenue		$1,855
Operating expenses		
Rent expense	$500	
Wages expense	125	
Total operating expenses		625
Net income		$1,230

5.

EXPRESSIONS
Statement of Owner's Equity
For Month Ended August 31

J. Worthy, Capital, August 1		$ 0
Plus: Investments by owner	$18,000	
Net income	1,230	19,230
		19,230
Less: Withdrawals by owner		900
J. Worthy, Capital, August 31		$18,330

6.

EXPRESSIONS
Balance Sheet
August 31

Assets		**Liabilities**	
Cash	$ 2,330	Note payable	$ 800
Furniture	600	**Equity**	
Store equipment	16,200	J. Worthy, Capital	18,330
Total assets	$19,130	Total liabilities and equity	$19,130

7. Debt ratio $= \dfrac{\text{Total liabilities}}{\text{Total assets}} = \dfrac{\$800}{\$19{,}130} = \underline{\underline{4.18\%}}$

8a. Supplies *debited*
Cash *credited*

8b. Prepaid Insurance *debited*
Cash *credited*

8c. Cash *debited*
Unearned Services Revenue *credited*

8d. Supplies *debited*
Accounts Payable *credited*

Summary

C1 Explain the steps in processing transactions and the role of source documents. The accounting process identifies business transactions and events, analyzes and records their effects, and summarizes and prepares information useful in making decisions. Transactions and events are the starting points in the accounting process. Source documents identify and describe transactions and events. Examples are sales tickets, checks, purchase orders, bills, and bank statements. Source documents provide objective and reliable evidence, making information more useful. The effects of transactions and events are recorded in journals. Posting along with a trial balance helps summarize and classify these effects.

C2 Describe an account and its use in recording transactions. An account is a detailed record of increases and decreases in a specific asset, liability, equity, revenue, or expense. Information from accounts is analyzed, summarized, and presented in reports and financial statements for decision makers.

C3 Describe a ledger and a chart of accounts. The ledger (or general ledger) is a record containing all accounts used by a company and their balances. It is referred to as the *books*. The chart of accounts is a list of all accounts and usually includes an identification number assigned to each account.

C4 Define *debits* and *credits* and explain double-entry accounting. *Debit* refers to left, and *credit* refers to right. Debits increase assets, expenses, and withdrawals while credits decrease them. Credits increase liabilities, owner capital, and revenues; debits decrease them. Double-entry accounting means each transaction affects at least two accounts and has at least one debit and one credit. The system for recording debits and credits follows from the accounting equation. The left side of an account is the normal balance for assets, withdrawals, and expenses, and the right side is the normal balance for liabilities, capital, and revenues.

A1 Analyze the impact of transactions on accounts and financial statements. We analyze transactions using concepts of double-entry accounting. This analysis is performed by determining a transaction's effects on accounts. These effects are recorded in journals and posted to ledgers.

A2 Compute the debt ratio and describe its use in analyzing financial condition. A company's debt ratio is computed as total liabilities divided by total assets. It reveals how much of the assets are financed by creditor (nonowner) financing. The higher this ratio, the more risk a company faces because liabilities must be repaid at specific dates.

P1 Record transactions in a journal and post entries to a ledger. Transactions are recorded in a journal. Each entry in a journal is posted to the accounts in the ledger. This provides information that is used to produce financial statements. Balance column accounts are widely used and include columns for debits, credits, and the account balance.

P2 Prepare and explain the use of a trial balance. A trial balance is a list of accounts from the ledger showing their debit or credit balances in separate columns. The trial balance is a summary of the ledger's contents and is useful in preparing financial statements and in revealing recordkeeping errors.

P3 Prepare financial statements from business transactions. The balance sheet, the statement of owner's equity, the income statement, and the statement of cash flows use data from the trial balance (and other financial statements) for their preparation.

Guidance Answers to Decision Maker and Decision Ethics

Cashier The advantages to the process proposed by the assistant manager include improved customer service, fewer delays, and less work for you. However, you should have serious concerns about internal control and the potential for fraud. In particular, the assistant manager could steal cash and simply enter fewer sales to match the remaining cash. You should reject her suggestion without the manager's approval. Moreover, you should have an ethical concern about the assistant manager's suggestion to ignore store policy.

Entrepreneur We can use the accounting equation (Assets = Liabilities + Equity) to help us identify risky customers to whom we would likely not want to extend credit. A balance sheet provides amounts for each of these key components. The lower a customer's equity is relative to liabilities, the less likely you would extend credit. A low equity means the business has little value that does not already have creditor claims to it.

Investor The debt ratio suggests the stock of Converse is of higher risk than normal and that this risk is rising. The average industry ratio of 0.40 further supports this conclusion. The 2011 debt ratio for Converse is twice the industry norm. Also, a debt ratio approaching 1.0 indicates little to no equity.

Guidance Answers to Quick Checks

1. Examples of source documents are sales tickets, checks, purchase orders, charges to customers, bills from suppliers, employee earnings records, and bank statements.
2. Source documents serve many purposes, including recordkeeping and internal control. Source documents, especially if obtained from outside the organization, provide objective and reliable evidence about transactions and their amounts.
3.

Assets	Liabilities	Equity
a,c,e	b,d	—

4. An account is a record in an accounting system that records and stores the increases and decreases in a specific asset, liability, equity, revenue, or expense. The ledger is a collection of all the accounts of a company.
5. A company's size and diversity affect the number of accounts in its accounting system. The types of accounts depend on information the company needs to both effectively operate and report its activities in financial statements.
6. No. Debit and credit both can mean increase or decrease. The particular meaning in a circumstance depends on the *type of account*. For example, a debit increases the balance of asset, withdrawals, and expense accounts, but it decreases the balance of liability, capital, and revenue accounts.
7. A chart of accounts is a list of all of a company's accounts and their identification numbers.
8. Equity is increased by revenues and by owner investments. Equity is decreased by expenses and owner withdrawals.
9. The name *double-entry* is used because all transactions affect at least two accounts. There must be at least one debit in one account and at least one credit in another account.
10. The answer is (*c*).
11.

Cash	15,000	
Equipment	23,000	
Owner, Capital		38,000
Investment by owner of cash and equipment.		

12. A compound journal entry affects three or more accounts.
13. Posting reference numbers are entered in the journal when posting to the ledger as a cross-reference that allows the recordkeeper or auditor to trace debits and credits from one record to another.
14. At a minimum, dollar signs are placed beside the first and last numbers in a column. It is also common to place dollar signs beside any amount that appears after a ruled line to indicate that an addition or subtraction has occurred.
15. The Equipment account balance is incorrectly reported at $20,000—it should be $28,000. The effect of this error understates the trial balance's Debit column total by $8,000. This results in an $8,000 difference between the column totals.
16. An income statement reports a company's revenues and expenses along with the resulting net income or loss. A statement of owner's equity reports changes in equity, including that from net income or loss. Both statements report transactions occurring over a period of time.
17. The balance sheet describes a company's financial position (assets, liabilities, and equity) at a point in time. The capital amount in the balance sheet is obtained from the statement of owner's equity.
18. Revenues are inflows of assets in exchange for products or services provided to customers as part of the main operations of a business. Expenses are outflows or the using up of assets that result from providing products or services to customers.
19. Assets are the resources a business owns or controls that carry expected future benefits. Liabilities are the obligations of a business, representing the claims of others against the assets of a business. Equity reflects the owner's claims on the assets of the business after deducting liabilities.

Key Terms

mhhe.com/wildFAP20e

Account (p. 51)
Account balance (p. 55)
Balance column account (p. 58)
Chart of accounts (p. 54)
Compound journal entry (p. 61)
Credit (p. 55)
Creditors (p. 52)
Debit (p. 55)
Debtors (p. 51)
Debt ratio (p. 69)
Double-entry accounting (p. 55)
General journal (p. 56)
General ledger (p. 51)
Journal (p. 56)
Journalizing (p. 56)
Ledger (p. 51)
Posting (p. 56)
Posting reference (PR) column (p. 58)
Source documents (p. 50)
T-account (p. 55)
Trial balance (p. 65)
Unearned revenue (p. 52)

Multiple Choice Quiz

Answers on p. 91

mhhe.com/wildFAP20e

Additional Quiz Questions are available at the book's Website.

1. Amalia Company received its utility bill for the current period of $700 and immediately paid it. Its journal entry to record this transaction includes a
   - a. Credit to Utility Expense for $700.
   - b. Debit to Utility Expense for $700.
   - c. Debit to Accounts Payable for $700.
   - d. Debit to Cash for $700.
   - e. Credit to capital for $700.
2. On May 1, Mattingly Lawn Service collected $2,500 cash from a customer in advance of five months of lawn service. Mattingly's journal entry to record this transaction includes a
   - a. Credit to Unearned Lawn Service Fees for $2,500.
   - b. Debit to Lawn Service Fees Earned for $2,500.
   - c. Credit to Cash for $2,500.
   - d. Debit to Unearned Lawn Service Fees for $2,500.
   - e. Credit to capital for $2,500.
3. Liang Shue contributed $250,000 cash and land worth $500,000 to open his new business, Shue Consulting. Which of the following journal entries does Shue Consulting make to record this transaction?

		Debit	Credit
a.	Cash Assets	750,000	
	L. Shue, Capital		750,000
b.	L. Shue, Capital	750,000	
	Assets		750,000
c.	Cash	250,000	
	Land	500,000	
	L. Shue, Capital		750,000
d.	L. Shue, Capital	750,000	
	Cash		250,000
	Land		500,000

4. A trial balance prepared at year-end shows total credits exceed total debits by $765. This discrepancy could have been caused by
   - a. An error in the general journal where a $765 increase in Accounts Payable was recorded as a $765 decrease in Accounts Payable.
   - b. The ledger balance for Accounts Payable of $7,650 being entered in the trial balance as $765.
   - c. A general journal error where a $765 increase in Accounts Receivable was recorded as a $765 increase in Cash.
   - d. The ledger balance of $850 in Accounts Receivable was entered in the trial balance as $85.
   - e. An error in recording a $765 increase in Cash as a credit.
5. Bonaventure Company has total assets of $1,000,000, liabilities of $400,000, and equity of $600,000. What is its debt ratio (rounded to a whole percent)?
   - a. 250%
   - b. 167%
   - c. 67%
   - d. 150%
   - e. 40%

Icon denotes assignments that involve decision making.

Discussion Questions

1. Provide the names of two (*a*) asset accounts, (*b*) liability accounts, and (*c*) equity accounts.
2. What is the difference between a note payable and an account payable?
3. Discuss the steps in processing business transactions.
4. What kinds of transactions can be recorded in a general journal?
5. Are debits or credits typically listed first in general journal entries? Are the debits or the credits indented?
6. If assets are valuable resources and asset accounts have debit balances, why do expense accounts also have debit balances?
7. Should a transaction be recorded first in a journal or the ledger? Why?
8. Why does the recordkeeper prepare a trial balance?
9. If an incorrect amount is journalized and posted to the accounts, how should the error be corrected?
10. Identify the four financial statements of a business.
11. What information is reported in an income statement?
12. Why does the user of an income statement need to know the time period that it covers?
13. What information is reported in a balance sheet?
14. Define (*a*) *assets,* (*b*) *liabilities,* (*c*) *equity,* and (*d*) *net assets.*
15. Which financial statement is sometimes called the *statement of financial position?*
16. Review the **Research in Motion** balance sheet in Appendix A. Identify three accounts on its balance sheet that carry debit balances and three accounts on its balance sheet that carry credit balances. **RIM**
17. Review the **Apple** balance sheet in Appendix A. Identify an asset with the word *receivable* in its account title and a liability with the word *payable* in its account title. Apple
18. Locate **Palm**'s income statement in Appendix A. What is the title of its revenue account? **Palm**
19. Refer to **Nokia**'s balance sheet in Appendix A. What does Nokia title its current asset referring to merchandise available for sale? **NOKIA**

connect

QUICK STUDY

QS 2-1
Identifying financial statement items
C2 P3

Identify the financial statement(s) where each of the following items appears. Use I for income statement, E for statement of owner's equity, and B for balance sheet.

a. Accounts payable
b. Cash
c. Rent expense
d. Office supplies
e. Prepaid insurance
f. Revenue
g. Office equipment
h. Cash withdrawal by owner
i. Unearned rent revenue

QS 2-2
Identifying source documents
C1

Identify the items from the following list that are likely to serve as source documents.

a. Bank statement
b. Sales ticket
c. Income statement
d. Trial balance
e. Telephone bill
f. Invoice from supplier
g. Company revenue account
h. Balance sheet
i. Prepaid rent

QS 2-3
Analyzing debit or credit by account
A1 

Identify whether a debit or credit yields the indicated change for each of the following accounts.

a. To increase Store Equipment
b. To increase Land
c. To decrease Cash
d. To increase Utilities Expense
e. To increase Fees Earned
f. To decrease Unearned Revenue
g. To decrease Prepaid Insurance
h. To increase Notes Payable
i. To decrease Accounts Receivable
j. To increase Owner Capital

QS 2-4
Identifying normal balance
C4

Identify the normal balance (debit or credit) for each of the following accounts.

a. Equipment
b. Wages Expense
c. Repair Services Revenue
d. Office Supplies
e. Owner Withdrawals
f. Accounts Receivable
g. Prepaid Insurance
h. Wages Payable
i. Owner Capital

QS 2-5
Linking debit or credit with normal balance
C4

Indicate whether a debit or credit *decreases* the normal balance of each of the following accounts.

a. Land
b. Service Revenue
c. Interest Payable
d. Accounts Receivable
e. Salaries Expense
f. Owner Capital
g. Prepaid Insurance
h. Buildings
i. Interest Revenue
j. Owner Withdrawals
k. Unearned Revenue
l. Accounts Payable

QS 2-6
Preparing journal entries
P1

Prepare journal entries for each of the following selected transactions.

a. On January 15, Kolby Anderson opens a remodeling company called Fancy Kitchens by investing $75,000 cash along with equipment having a $30,000 value.
b. On January 21, Fancy Kitchens purchases office supplies on credit for $650.
c. On January 25, Fancy Kitchens receives $8,700 cash for performing remodeling services.
d. On January 30, Fancy Kitchens receives $4,000 cash in advance of providing remodeling services to a customer.

QS 2-7
Identifying a posting error
P2 

A trial balance has total debits of $20,000 and total credits of $24,500. Which one of the following errors would create this imbalance? Explain.

a. A $2,250 debit posting to Accounts Receivable was posted mistakenly to Cash.
b. A $4,500 debit posting to Equipment was posted mistakenly to Supplies.
c. An entry debiting Cash and crediting Accounts Payable for $4,500 was mistakenly not posted.
d. A $2,250 credit to Revenue in a journal entry is incorrectly posted to the ledger as a $2,250 debit, leaving the Revenue account with a $6,300 credit balance.
e. A $4,500 debit to Rent Expense in a journal entry is incorrectly posted to the ledger as a $4,500 credit, leaving the Rent Expense account with a $750 debit balance.
f. A $2,250 debit to Utilities Expense in a journal entry is incorrectly posted to the ledger as a $2,250 credit, leaving the Utilities Expense account with a $3,000 debit balance.

QS 2-8
Classifying accounts in financial statements
P3

Indicate the financial statement on which each of the following items appears. Use I for income statement, E for statement of owner's equity, and B for balance sheet.

a. Buildings
b. Interest Expense
c. Owner Withdrawals
d. Office Supplies
e. Rental Revenue
f. Insurance Expense
g. Services Revenue
h. Interest Payable
i. Accounts Receivable
j. Salaries Expense
k. Equipment
l. Prepaid Insurance

QS 2-9
International accounting standards
C4 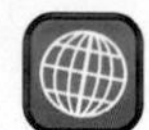

Answer each of the following questions related to international accounting standards.

a. What type of entry system is applied when accounting follows IFRS?
b. Identify the number and usual titles of the financial statements prepared under IFRS.
c. How do differences in accounting controls and enforcement impact accounting reports prepared across different countries?

connect

EXERCISES

Exercise 2-1
Steps in analyzing and recording transactions C1

Order the following steps in the accounting process that focus on analyzing and recording transactions.

__2__ **a.** Record relevant transactions in a journal.
__4__ **b.** Prepare and analyze the trial balance.
__1__ **c.** Analyze each transaction from source documents.
__3__ **d.** Post journal information to ledger accounts.

Exercise 2-2
Identifying and classifying accounts
C2

Enter the number for the item that best completes each of the descriptions below.

1. Account **3.** Asset **5.** Equity
2. Three **4.** Liability

a. Owner, capital and owner, withdrawals are examples of ______ accounts.
b. Accounts payable, unearned revenue, and note payable are examples of ______ accounts.
c. Accounts receivable, prepaid accounts, supplies, and land are examples of ______ accounts.
d. Accounts are arranged into ______ general categories
e. An ______ is a record of increases and decreases in a specific asset, liability, equity, revenue, or expense item.

Exercise 2-3
Identifying a ledger and chart of accounts
C3

Enter the number for the item that best completes each of the descriptions below.

1. General ledger **2.** Chart

a. The ______ is a record containing all accounts used by a company.
b. A ______ of accounts is a list of all accounts a company uses.

Exercise 2-4
Identifying type and normal balances of accounts
C4

For each of the following (1) identify the type of account as an asset, liability, equity, revenue, or expense, (2) identify the normal balance of the account, and (3) enter *debit* (*Dr.*) or *credit* (*Cr.*) to identify the kind of entry that would increase the account balance.

a. Fees Earned
b. Equipment
c. Notes Payable
d. Owner Capital
e. Cash
f. Legal Expense
g. Prepaid Insurance
h. Land
i. Accounts Receivable
j. Owner Withdrawals
k. License Fee Revenue
l. Unearned Revenue

Exercise 2-5
Analyzing effects of transactions on accounts
A1 

Taylor Co. bills a client $48,000 for services provided and agrees to accept the following three items in full payment: (1) $7,500 cash, (2) computer equipment worth $75,000, and (3) to assume responsibility for a $34,500 note payable related to the computer equipment. The entry Taylor makes to record this transaction includes which one or more of the following?

a. $34,500 increase in a liability account
b. $7,500 increase in the Cash account
c. $7,500 increase in a revenue account
d. $48,000 increase in an asset account
e. $48,000 increase in a revenue account
f. $34,500 increase in an equity account

Exercise 2-6
Analyzing account entries and balances
A1

Use the information in each of the following separate cases to calculate the unknown amount.

a. During October, Shandra Company had $97,500 of cash receipts and $101,250 of cash disbursements. The October 31 Cash balance was $16,800. Determine how much cash the company had at the close of business on September 30.

b. On September 30, Mordish Co. had a $97,500 balance in Accounts Receivable. During October, the company collected $88,950 from its credit customers. The October 31 balance in Accounts Receivable was $100,500. Determine the amount of sales on account that occurred in October.

c. Nasser Co. had $147,000 of accounts payable on September 30 and $136,500 on October 31. Total purchases on account during October were $270,000. Determine how much cash was paid on accounts payable during October.

Exercise 2-7
Preparing general journal entries
P1

Prepare general journal entries for the following transactions of a new company called Pose for Pics.

Aug.	1	Kasey Madison, the owner, invested $7,500 cash and $32,500 of photography equipment in the company.
	2	The company paid $3,000 cash for an insurance policy covering the next 24 months.
	5	The company purchased office supplies for $1,400 cash.
	20	The company received $2,650 cash in photography fees earned.
	31	The company paid $875 cash for August utilities.

Exercise 2-8
Preparing T-accounts (ledger) and a trial balance P2

Use the information in Exercise 2-7 to prepare an August 31 trial balance for Pose for Pics. Begin by opening these T-accounts: Cash; Office Supplies; Prepaid Insurance; Photography Equipment; K. Madison, Capital; Photography Fees Earned; and Utilities Expense. Then, post the general journal entries to these T-accounts (which will serve as the ledger), and prepare the trial balance.

Exercise 2-9
Recording effects of transactions in T-accounts
A1

Prepare general journal entries to record the transactions below for Dexter Company by using the following accounts: Cash; Accounts Receivable, Office Supplies, Office Equipment, Accounts Payable, M. Dexter, Capital; M. Dexter, Withdrawals; Fees Earned; and Rent Expense. Use the letters beside each transaction to identify entries. After recording the transactions, post them to T-accounts, which serves as the general ledger for this assignment. Determine the ending balance of each T-account.

a. Macy Dexter, owner, invested $12,750 cash in the company.

b. The company purchased office supplies for $375 cash.

c. The company purchased $7,050 of office equipment on credit.

d. The company received $1,500 cash as fees for services provided to a customer.

e. The company paid $7,050 cash to settle the payable for the office equipment purchased in transaction *c*.

f. The company billed a customer $2,700 as fees for services provided.

g. The company paid $525 cash for the monthly rent.

h. The company collected $1,125 cash as partial payment for the account receivable created in transaction *f*.

i. Macy Dexter withdrew $1,000 cash from the company for personal use.

Check Cash ending balance, $6,425

Exercise 2-10
Preparing a trial balance P2

After recording the transactions of Exercise 2-9 in T-accounts and calculating the balance of each account, prepare a trial balance. Use May 31, 2011, as its report date.

Exercise 2-11
Analyzing and journalizing revenue transactions
A1 P1 

Examine the following transactions and identify those that create revenues for Jade Services, a company owned by Mia Jade. Prepare general journal entries to record those revenue transactions and explain why the other transactions did not create revenues.

a. Mia Jade invests $38,250 cash in the company.

b. The company provided $1,350 of services on credit.

c. The company provided services to a client and immediately received $1,575 cash.

d. The company received $9,150 cash from a client in payment for services to be provided next year.

e. The company received $4,500 cash from a client in partial payment of an account receivable.

f. The company borrowed $150,000 cash from the bank by signing a promissory note.

Exercise 2-12
Analyzing and journalizing expense transactions
A1 P1 

Examine the following transactions and identify those that create expenses for Jade Services. Prepare general journal entries to record those expense transactions and explain why the other transactions did not create expenses.

a. The company paid $14,100 cash for payment on a 14-month old liability for office supplies.
b. The company paid $1,125 cash for the just completed two-week salary of the receptionist.
c. The company paid $45,000 cash for equipment purchased.
d. The company paid $930 cash for this month's utilities.
e. Owner (Jade) withdrew $5,000 cash from the company for personal use.

Exercise 2-13
Preparing an income statement
C3 P3

Dominick Lopez operates a consulting firm called Tech Today. On August 31, the company's records show the following accounts and amounts for the month of August. Use this information to prepare an August income statement for the business.

Cash	$ 8,360	D. Lopez, Withdrawals	$ 3,000
Accounts receivable	17,000	Consulting fees earned	17,000
Office supplies	3,250	Rent expense	4,550
Land	46,000	Salaries expense	8,000
Office equipment	18,000	Telephone expense	560
Accounts payable	8,000	Miscellaneous expenses	280
D. Lopez, Capital, July 31	4,000	Owner investments	80,000

Check Net income, $3,610

Exercise 2-14
Preparing a statement of owner's equity P3
Check End. Capital, $84,610

Use the information in Exercise 2-13 to prepare an August statement of owner's equity for Tech Today. (The owner invested $84,000 cash in the company during the first week of August.)

Exercise 2-15
Preparing a balance sheet P3

Use the information in Exercise 2-13 (if completed, you can also use your solution to Exercise 2-14) to prepare an August 31 balance sheet for Tech Today.

Exercise 2-16
Computing net income
A1

A sole proprietorship had the following assets and liabilities at the beginning and end of this year.

	Assets	Liabilities
Beginning of the year	$ 70,000	$30,000
End of the year	115,000	46,000

Determine the net income earned or net loss incurred by the business during the year for each of the following *separate* cases:

a. Owner made no investments in the business and no withdrawals were made during the year.
b. Owner made no investments in the business but withdrew $1,250 cash per month for personal use.
c. Owner made no withdrawals during the year but did invest an additional $45,000 cash.
d. Owner withdrew $1,250 cash per month for personal use and invested an additional $25,000 cash.

Exercise 2-17
Analyzing changes in a company's equity
P3 

Compute the missing amount for each of the following separate companies *a* through *d*.

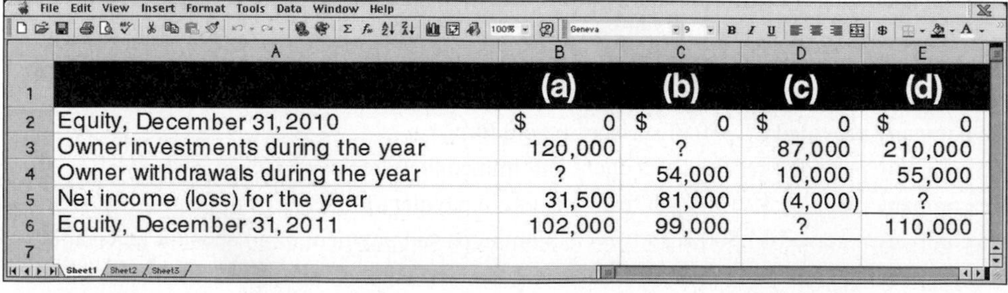

	(a)	(b)	(c)	(d)
Equity, December 31, 2010	$ 0	$ 0	$ 0	$ 0
Owner investments during the year	120,000	?	87,000	210,000
Owner withdrawals during the year	?	54,000	10,000	55,000
Net income (loss) for the year	31,500	81,000	(4,000)	?
Equity, December 31, 2011	102,000	99,000	?	110,000

Exercise 2-18
Interpreting and describing transactions from T-accounts
A1 

Assume the following T-accounts reflect Joy Co.'s general ledger and that seven transactions *a* through *g* are posted to them. Provide a short description of each transaction. Include the amounts in your descriptions.

Cash

	Debit		Credit
(a)	7,000	(b)	3,600
(e)	2,500	(c)	600
		(f)	2,400
		(g)	700

Office Supplies

	Debit		Credit
(c)	600		
(d)	200		

Prepaid Insurance

	Debit		Credit
(b)	3,600		

Equipment

	Debit		Credit
(a)	5,600		
(d)	9,400		

Automobiles

	Debit		Credit
(a)	11,000		

Accounts Payable

	Debit		Credit
(f)	2,400	(d)	9,600

D. Joy, Capital

	Debit		Credit
		(a)	23,600

Delivery Services Revenue

	Debit		Credit
		(e)	2,500

Gas and Oil Expense

	Debit		Credit
(g)	700		

Exercise 2-19
Preparing general journal entries
P1

Use information from the T-accounts in Exercise 2-18 to prepare general journal entries for each of the seven transactions *a* through *g*.

Exercise 2-20
Identifying effects of posting errors on the trial balance
A1 P2

Posting errors are identified in the following table. In column (1), enter the amount of the difference between the two trial balance columns (debit and credit) due to the error. In column (2), identify the trial balance column (debit or credit) with the larger amount if they are not equal. In column (3), identify the account(s) affected by the error. In column (4), indicate the amount by which the account(s) in column (3) is under- or overstated. Item (a) is completed as an example.

	Description of Posting Error	(1) Difference between Debit and Credit Columns	(2) Column with the Larger Total	(3) Identify Account(s) Incorrectly Stated	(4) Amount that Account(s) Is Over- or Understated
a.	$2,400 debit to Rent Expense is posted as a $1,590 debit.	$810	Credit	Rent Expense	Rent Expense understated $810
b.	$4,050 credit to Cash is posted twice as two credits to Cash.				
c.	$9,900 debit to the Withdrawals account is debited to Owner's Capital.				
d.	$2,250 debit to Prepaid Insurance is posted as a debit to Insurance Expense.				
e.	$42,000 debit to Machinery is posted as a debit to Accounts Payable.				
f.	$4,950 credit to Services Revenue is posted as a $495 credit.				
g.	$1,440 debit to Store Supplies is not posted.				

Exercise 2-21
Analyzing a trial balance error
A1 P2

You are told the column totals in a trial balance are not equal. After careful analysis, you discover only one error. Specifically, a correctly journalized credit purchase of a computer for $16,950 is posted from the journal to the ledger with a $16,950 debit to Office Equipment and another $16,950 debit to Accounts Payable. The Office Equipment account has a debit balance of $40,100 on the trial balance. Answer each of the following questions and compute the dollar amount of any misstatement.

a. Is the debit column total of the trial balance overstated, understated, or correctly stated?
b. Is the credit column total of the trial balance overstated, understated, or correctly stated?
c. Is the Office Equipment account balance overstated, understated, or correctly stated in the trial balance?
d. Is the Accounts Payable account balance overstated, understated, or correctly stated in the trial balance?
e. If the debit column total of the trial balance is $360,000 before correcting the error, what is the total of the credit column before correction?

Exercise 2-22
Interpreting the debt ratio and return on assets
A2 

a. Calculate the debt ratio and the return on assets using the year-end information for each of the following six separate companies ($ thousands).

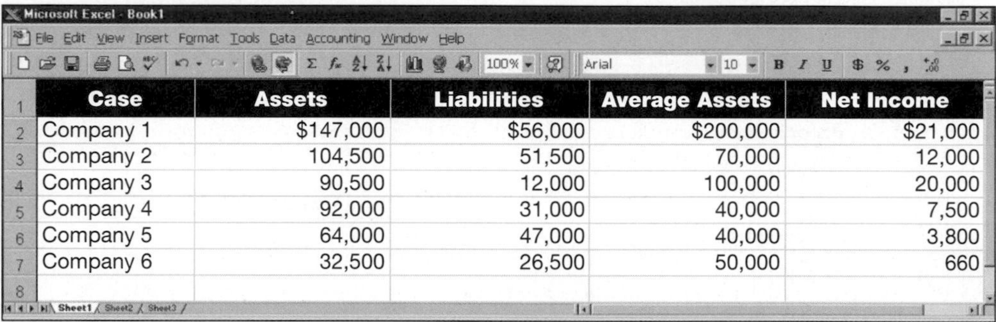

Case	Assets	Liabilities	Average Assets	Net Income
Company 1	$147,000	$56,000	$200,000	$21,000
Company 2	104,500	51,500	70,000	12,000
Company 3	90,500	12,000	100,000	20,000
Company 4	92,000	31,000	40,000	7,500
Company 5	64,000	47,000	40,000	3,800
Company 6	32,500	26,500	50,000	660

b. Of the six companies, which business relies most heavily on creditor financing?
c. Of the six companies, which business relies most heavily on equity financing?
d. Which two companies indicate the greatest risk?
e. Which two companies earn the highest return on assets?
f. Which one company would investors likely prefer based on the risk–return relation?

Exercise 2-23
Preparing a balance sheet following IFRS
P3 

BMW reports the following balance sheet accounts for the year ended December 31, 2009 (euro in millions). Prepare the balance sheet for this company as of December 31, 2009, following the usual IFRS formats.

Current liabilities	€ 8,350	Noncurrent liabilities	€10,943
Current assets	17,663	Noncurrent assets	6,984
Total equity	5,354		

connect

PROBLEM SET A

Problem 2-1A
Preparing and posting journal entries; preparing a trial balance
C3 C4 A1 P1 P2

mhhe.com/wildFAP20e

Gary Bauer opens a computer consulting business called Technology Consultants and completes the following transactions in April.

April 1 Bauer invested $100,000 cash along with $24,000 in office equipment in the company.
2 The company prepaid $7,200 cash for twelve months' rent for an office. (*Hint:* Debit Prepaid Rent for $7,200.)
3 The company made credit purchases of office equipment for $12,000 and office supplies for $2,400. Payment is due within 10 days.
6 The company completed services for a client and immediately received $2,000 cash.
9 The company completed an $8,000 project for a client, who must pay within 30 days.
13 The company paid $14,400 cash to settle the account payable created on April 3.
19 The company paid $6,000 cash for the premium on a 12-month insurance policy. (*Hint:* Debit Prepaid Insurance for $6,000.)
22 The company received $6,400 cash as partial payment for the work completed on April 9.
25 The company completed work for another client for $2,640 on credit.
28 Bauer withdrew $6,200 cash from the company for personal use.
29 The company purchased $800 of additional office supplies on credit.
30 The company paid $700 cash for this month's utility bill.

Required

1. Prepare general journal entries to record these transactions (use the account titles listed in part 2).
2. Open the following ledger accounts—their account numbers are in parentheses (use the balance column format): Cash (101); Accounts Receivable (106); Office Supplies (124); Prepaid Insurance (128);

Prepaid Rent (131); Office Equipment (163); Accounts Payable (201); G. Bauer, Capital (301); G. Bauer, Withdrawals (302); Services Revenue (403); and Utilities Expense (690). Post the journal entries from part 1 to the ledger accounts and enter the balance after each posting.

3. Prepare a trial balance as of the end of April.

Check (2) Ending balances: Cash, $73,900; Accounts Receivable, $4,240; Accounts Payable, $800

(3) Total debits, $137,440

Problem 2-2A
Preparing and posting journal entries; preparing a trial balance

C3 C4 A1 P1 P2

Shelton Engineering completed the following transactions in the month of June.

a. Shana Shelton, the owner, invested $105,000 cash, office equipment with a value of $6,000, and $45,000 of drafting equipment to launch the company.
b. The company purchased land worth $54,000 for an office by paying $5,400 cash and signing a long-term note payable for $48,600.
c. The company purchased a portable building with $75,000 cash and moved it onto the land acquired in *b*.
d. The company paid $6,000 cash for the premium on an 18-month insurance policy.
e. The company completed and delivered a set of plans for a client and collected $5,700 cash.
f. The company purchased $22,500 of additional drafting equipment by paying $10,500 cash and signing a long-term note payable for $12,000.
g. The company completed $12,000 of engineering services for a client. This amount is to be received in 30 days.
h. The company purchased $2,250 of additional office equipment on credit.
i. The company completed engineering services for $18,000 on credit.
j. The company received a bill for rent of equipment that was used on a recently completed job. The $1,200 rent cost must be paid within 30 days.
k. The company collected $7,200 cash in partial payment from the client described in transaction *g*.
l. The company paid $1,500 cash for wages to a drafting assistant.
m. The company paid $2,250 cash to settle the account payable created in transaction *h*.
n. The company paid $675 cash for minor maintenance of its drafting equipment.
o. S. Shelton withdrew $9,360 cash from the company for personal use.
p. The company paid $1,500 cash for wages to a drafting assistant.
q. The company paid $3,000 cash for advertisements in the local newspaper during June.

Required

1. Prepare general journal entries to record these transactions (use the account titles listed in part 2).
2. Open the following ledger accounts—their account numbers are in parentheses (use the balance column format): Cash (101); Accounts Receivable (106); Prepaid Insurance (108); Office Equipment (163); Drafting Equipment (164); Building (170); Land (172); Accounts Payable (201); Notes Payable (250); S. Shelton, Capital (301); S. Shelton, Withdrawals (302); Engineering Fees Earned (402); Wages Expense (601); Equipment Rental Expense (602); Advertising Expense (603); and Repairs Expense (604). Post the journal entries from part 1 to the accounts and enter the balance after each posting.
3. Prepare a trial balance as of the end of June.

Check (2) Ending balances: Cash, $2,715; Accounts Receivable, $22,800; Accounts Payable, $1,200

(3) Trial balance totals, $253,500

Problem 2-3A
Computing net income from equity analysis, preparing a balance sheet, and computing the debt ratio

C2 A1 A2 P3 

mhhe.com/wildFAP20e

The accounting records of Fabiano Distribution show the following assets and liabilities as of December 31, 2010 and 2011.

December 31	2010	2011
Cash	$ 52,500	$ 18,750
Accounts receivable	28,500	22,350
Office supplies	4,500	3,300
Office equipment	138,000	147,000
Trucks	54,000	54,000
Building	0	180,000
Land	0	45,000
Accounts payable	7,500	37,500
Note payable	0	105,000

Late in December 2011, the business purchased a small office building and land for $225,000. It paid $120,000 cash toward the purchase and a $105,000 note payable was signed for the balance. Mr. Fabiano had to invest $35,000 cash in the business to enable it to pay the $120,000 cash. Mr. Fabiano withdraws $3,000 cash per month for personal use.

Required

1. Prepare balance sheets for the business as of December 31, 2010 and 2011. (*Hint:* Report only total equity on the balance sheet and remember that total equity equals the difference between assets and liabilities.)
2. By comparing equity amounts from the balance sheets and using the additional information presented in this problem, prepare a calculation to show how much net income was earned by the business during 2011.
3. Compute the 2011 year-end debt ratio for the business.

Check (2) Net income, $58,900

(3) Debt ratio, 30.29%

Problem 2-4A
Preparing and posting journal entries; preparing a trial balance
C3 C4 A1 P1 P2

Santo Birch opens a Web consulting business called Show-Me-the-Money and completes the following transactions in its first month of operations.

March	1	Birch invests $150,000 cash along with office equipment valued at $22,000 in the company.
	2	The company prepaid $6,000 cash for twelve months' rent for office space. (*Hint:* Debit Prepaid Rent for $6,000.)
	3	The company made credit purchases for $3,000 in office equipment and $1,200 in office supplies. Payment is due within 10 days.
	6	The company completed services for a client and immediately received $4,000 cash.
	9	The company completed a $7,500 project for a client, who must pay within 30 days.
	13	The company paid $4,200 cash to settle the account payable created on March 3.
	19	The company paid $5,000 cash for the premium on a 12-month insurance policy. (*Hint:* Debit Prepaid Insurance for $5,000.)
	22	The company received $3,500 cash as partial payment for the work completed on March 9.
	25	The company completed work for another client for $3,820 on credit.
	29	Birch withdrew $5,100 cash from the company for personal use.
	30	The company purchased $600 of additional office supplies on credit.
	31	The company paid $200 cash for this month's utility bill.

Required

1. Prepare general journal entries to record these transactions (use account titles listed in part 2).
2. Open the following ledger accounts—their account numbers are in parentheses (use the balance column format): Cash (101); Accounts Receivable (106); Office Supplies (124); Prepaid Insurance (128); Prepaid Rent (131); Office Equipment (163); Accounts Payable (201); S. Birch, Capital (301); S. Birch, Withdrawals (302); Services Revenue (403); and Utilities Expense (690). Post journal entries from part 1 to the ledger accounts and enter the balance after each posting.
3. Prepare a trial balance as of April 30.

Check (2) Ending balances: Cash, $137,000; Accounts Receivable, $7,820; Accounts Payable, $600

(3) Total debits, $187,920

Problem 2-5A
Recording transactions; posting to ledger; preparing a trial balance
C3 A1 P1 P2

Business transactions completed by Eric Pense during the month of September are as follows.

a. Pense invested $23,000 cash along with office equipment valued at $12,000 in a new sole proprietorship named EP Consulting.
b. The company purchased land valued at $8,000 and a building valued at $33,000. The purchase is paid with $15,000 cash and a long-term note payable for $26,000.
c. The company purchased $600 of office supplies on credit.
d. Pense invested his personal automobile in the company. The automobile has a value of $7,000 and is to be used exclusively in the business.
e. The company purchased $1,100 of additional office equipment on credit.
f. The company paid $800 cash salary to an assistant.
g. The company provided services to a client and collected $2,700 cash.
h. The company paid $430 cash for this month's utilities.
i. The company paid $600 cash to settle the account payable created in transaction *c*.
j. The company purchased $4,000 of new office equipment by paying $4,000 cash.
k. The company completed $2,400 of services for a client, who must pay within 30 days.
l. The company paid $800 cash salary to an assistant.
m. The company received $1,000 cash in partial payment on the receivable created in transaction *k*.
n. Pense withdrew $1,050 cash from the company for personal use.

Required

1. Prepare general journal entries to record these transactions (use account titles listed in part 2).
2. Open the following ledger accounts—their account numbers are in parentheses (use the balance column format): Cash (101); Accounts Receivable (106); Office Supplies (108); Office Equipment (163); Automobiles (164); Building (170); Land (172); Accounts Payable (201); Notes Payable (250); E. Pense, Capital (301); E. Pense, Withdrawals (302); Fees Earned (402); Salaries Expense (601); and Utilities Expense (602). Post the journal entries from part 1 to the ledger accounts and enter the balance after each posting.
3. Prepare a trial balance as of the end of September.

Check (2) Ending balances: Cash, $4,020; Office Equipment, $17,100

(3) Trial balance totals, $74,200

Problem 2-6A
Analyzing account balances and reconstructing transactions
C1 C3 A1 P2 

Carlos Beltran started an engineering firm called Beltran Engineering. He began operations and completed seven transactions in May, which included his initial investment of $17,000 cash. After those seven transactions, the ledger included the following accounts with normal balances.

Cash	$26,660
Office supplies	660
Prepaid insurance	3,200
Office equipment	16,500
Accounts payable	16,500
C. Beltran, Capital	17,000
C. Beltran, Withdrawals	3,740
Engineering fees earned	24,000
Rent expense	6,740

Required

1. Prepare a trial balance for this business as of the end of May.

Check (1) Trial balance totals, $57,500

Analysis Components

2. Analyze the accounts and their balances and prepare a list that describes each of the seven most likely transactions and their amounts.
3. Prepare a report of cash received and cash paid showing how the seven transactions in part 2 yield the $26,660 ending Cash balance.

(3) Cash paid, $14,340

PROBLEM SET B

Problem 2-1B
Preparing and posting journal entries; preparing a trial balance
C3 C4 A1 P1 P2

Shaw Management Services opens for business and completes these transactions in November.

Nov. 1	Kita Shaw, the owner, invested $30,000 cash along with $15,000 of office equipment in the company.
2	The company prepaid $4,500 cash for six months' rent for an office. (*Hint:* Debit Prepaid Rent for $4,500.)
4	The company made credit purchases of office equipment for $2,500 and of office supplies for $600. Payment is due within 10 days.
8	The company completed work for a client and immediately received $3,400 cash.
12	The company completed a $10,200 project for a client, who must pay within 30 days.
13	The company paid $3,100 cash to settle the payable created on November 4.
19	The company paid $1,800 cash for the premium on a 24-month insurance policy.
22	The company received $5,200 cash as partial payment for the work completed on November 12.
24	The company completed work for another client for $1,750 on credit.
28	K. Shaw withdrew $5,300 cash from the company for personal use.
29	The company purchased $249 of additional office supplies on credit.
30	The company paid $531 cash for this month's utility bill.

Required

1. Prepare general journal entries to record these transactions (use account titles listed in part 2).
2. Open the following ledger accounts—their account numbers are in parentheses (use the balance column format): Cash (101); Accounts Receivable (106); Office Supplies (124); Prepaid Insurance (128); Prepaid Rent (131); Office Equipment (163); Accounts Payable (201); K. Shaw, Capital (301); K. Shaw, Withdrawals (302); Services Revenue (403); and Utilities Expense (690). Post the journal entries from part 1 to the ledger accounts and enter the balance after each posting.
3. Prepare a trial balance as of the end of November.

Check (2) Ending balances: Cash, $23,369; Accounts Receivable, $6,750; Accounts Payable, $249

(3) Total debits, $60,599

Problem 2-2B
Preparing and posting journal entries; preparing a trial balance
C3 C4 A1 P1 P2

At the beginning of April, Brooke Gable launched a custom computer solutions company called Softways. The company had the following transactions during April.

a. Brooke Gable invested $45,000 cash, office equipment with a value of $4,500, and $28,000 of computer equipment in the company.
b. The company purchased land worth $24,000 for an office by paying $4,800 cash and signing a long-term note payable for $19,200.
c. The company purchased a portable building with $21,000 cash and moved it onto the land acquired in *b*.
d. The company paid $6,600 cash for the premium on a two-year insurance policy.
e. The company provided services to a client and immediately collected $3,200 cash.
f. The company purchased $3,500 of additional computer equipment by paying $700 cash and signing a long-term note payable for $2,800.
g. The company completed $3,750 of services for a client. This amount is to be received within 30 days.
h. The company purchased $750 of additional office equipment on credit.
i. The company completed client services for $9,200 on credit.
j. The company received a bill for rent of a computer testing device that was used on a recently completed job. The $320 rent cost must be paid within 30 days.
k. The company collected $4,600 cash in partial payment from the client described in transaction *i*.
l. The company paid $1,600 cash for wages to an assistant.
m. The company paid $750 cash to settle the payable created in transaction *h*.
n. The company paid $425 cash for minor maintenance of the company's computer equipment.
o. B. Gable withdrew $3,875 cash from the company for personal use.
p. The company paid $1,600 cash for wages to an assistant.
q. The company paid $800 cash for advertisements in the local newspaper during April.

Required

1. Prepare general journal entries to record these transactions (use account titles listed in part 2).
2. Open the following ledger accounts—their account numbers are in parentheses (use the balance column format): Cash (101); Accounts Receivable (106); Prepaid Insurance (108); Office Equipment (163); Computer Equipment (164); Building (170); Land (172); Accounts Payable (201); Notes Payable (250); B. Gable, Capital (301); B. Gable, Withdrawals (302); Fees Earned (402); Wages Expense (601); Computer Rental Expense (602); Advertising Expense (603); and Repairs Expense (604). Post the journal entries from part 1 to the accounts and enter the balance after each posting.
3. Prepare a trial balance as of the end of April.

Check (2) Ending balances: Cash, $10,650; Accounts Receivable, $8,350; Accounts Payable, $320

(3) Trial balance totals, $115,970

Problem 2-3B
Computing net income from equity analysis, preparing a balance sheet, and computing the debt ratio
C2 A1 A2 P3 

The accounting records of Schmit Co. show the following assets and liabilities as of December 31, 2010 and 2011.

December 31	2010	2011
Cash	$14,000	$ 10,000
Accounts receivable	25,000	30,000
Office supplies	10,000	12,500
Office equipment	60,000	60,000
Machinery	30,500	30,500
Building	0	260,000
Land	0	65,000
Accounts payable	5,000	15,000
Note payable	0	260,000

Late in December 2011, the business purchased a small office building and land for $325,000. It paid $65,000 cash toward the purchase and a $260,000 note payable was signed for the balance. Janet Schmit, the owner, had to invest an additional $25,000 cash to enable it to pay the $65,000 cash toward the purchase. The owner withdraws $1,000 cash per month for personal use.

Required

1. Prepare balance sheets for the business as of December 31, 2010 and 2011. (*Hint:* Report only total equity on the balance sheet and remember that total equity equals the difference between assets and liabilities.)

2. By comparing equity amounts from the balance sheets and using the additional information presented in the problem, prepare a calculation to show how much net income was earned by the business during 2011.

3. Calculate the December 31, 2011, debt ratio for the business.

Check (2) Net income, $45,500

(3) Debt ratio, 58.76%

Problem 2-4B
Preparing and posting journal entries; preparing a trial balance
C3 C4 A1 P1 P2

Lummus Management Services opens for business and completes these transactions in September.

Sept. 1 Rhonda Lummus, the owner, invests $28,000 cash along with office equipment valued at $25,000 in the company.
2 The company prepaid $10,500 cash for 12 months' rent for office space. (*Hint:* Debit Prepaid Rent for $10,500.)
4 The company made credit purchases for $9,000 in office equipment and $1,200 in office supplies. Payment is due within 10 days.
8 The company completed work for a client and immediately received $2,600 cash.
12 The company completed a $13,400 project for a client, who must pay within 30 days.
13 The company paid $10,200 cash to settle the payable created on September 4.
19 The company paid $5,200 cash for the premium on an 18-month insurance policy. (*Hint:* Debit Prepaid Insurance for $5,200.)
22 The company received $7,800 cash as partial payment for the work completed on September 12.
24 The company completed work for another client for $1,900 on credit.
28 Lummus withdrew $5,300 cash from the company for personal use.
29 The company purchased $1,700 of additional office supplies on credit.
30 The company paid $460 cash for this month's utility bill.

Required

1. Prepare general journal entries to record these transactions (use account titles listed in part 2).

2. Open the following ledger accounts—their account numbers are in parentheses (use the balance column format): Cash (101); Accounts Receivable (106); Office Supplies (124); Prepaid Insurance (128); Prepaid Rent (131); Office Equipment (163); Accounts Payable (201); R. Lummus, Capital (301); R. Lummus, Withdrawals (302); Service Fees Earned (401); and Utilities Expense (690). Post journal entries from part 1 to the ledger accounts and enter the balance after each posting.

3. Prepare a trial balance as of the end of September.

Check (2) Ending balances: Cash, $6,740; Accounts Receivable, $7,500; Accounts Payable, $1,700

(3) Total debits, $72,600

Problem 2-5B
Recording transactions; posting to ledger; preparing a trial balance
C3 A1 P1 P2

Cooke Consulting completed the following transactions during June.

a. Chris Cooke, the owner, invested $80,000 cash along with office equipment valued at $30,000 in the new company.
b. The company purchased land valued at $30,000 and a building valued at $170,000. The purchase is paid with $40,000 cash and a long-term note payable for $160,000.
c. The company purchased $2,400 of office supplies on credit.
d. C. Cooke invested his personal automobile in the company. The automobile has a value of $18,000 and is to be used exclusively in the business.
e. The company purchased $6,000 of additional office equipment on credit.
f. The company paid $1,500 cash salary to an assistant.
g. The company provided services to a client and collected $6,000 cash.
h. The company paid $800 cash for this month's utilities.
i. The company paid $2,400 cash to settle the payable created in transaction *c*.
j. The company purchased $20,000 of new office equipment by paying $20,000 cash.
k. The company completed $5,200 of services for a client, who must pay within 30 days.
l. The company paid $1,500 cash salary to an assistant.
m. The company received $3,800 cash in partial payment on the receivable created in transaction *k*.
n. C. Cooke withdrew $6,400 cash from the company for personal use.

Required

1. Prepare general journal entries to record these transactions (use account titles listed in part 2).

2. Open the following ledger accounts—their account numbers are in parentheses (use the balance column format): Cash (101); Accounts Receivable (106); Office Supplies (108); Office Equipment (163); Automobiles (164); Building (170); Land (172); Accounts Payable (201); Notes Payable (250); C. Cooke, Capital (301); C. Cooke, Withdrawals (302); Fees Earned (402); Salaries Expense (601); and Utilities Expense (602). Post the journal entries from part 1 to the ledger accounts and enter the balance after each posting.

3. Prepare a trial balance as of the end of June.

Check (2) Ending balances: Cash, $17,200; Office Equipment, $56,000

(3) Trial balance totals, $305,200

Problem 2-6B
Analyzing account balances and reconstructing transactions
C1 C3 A1 P2 

Michael Gould started a Web consulting firm called Gould Solutions. He began operations and completed seven transactions in April that resulted in the following accounts, which all have normal balances.

Cash	$12,485
Office supplies	560
Prepaid rent	1,500
Office equipment	11,450
Accounts payable	11,450
M. Gould, Capital	10,000
M. Gould, Withdrawals	6,200
Consulting fees earned	16,400
Operating expenses	5,655

Required

Check (1) Trial balance total, $37,850

1. Prepare a trial balance for this business as of the end of April.

Analysis Component

2. Analyze the accounts and their balances and prepare a list that describes each of the seven most likely transactions and their amounts.

(3) Cash paid, $13,915

3. Prepare a report of cash received and cash paid showing how the seven transactions in part 2 yield the $12,485 ending Cash balance.

SERIAL PROBLEM
Business Solutions
A1 P1 P2

(This serial problem started in Chapter 1 and continues through most of the chapters. If the Chapter 1 segment was not completed, the problem can begin at this point. It is helpful, but not necessary, to use the Working Papers that accompany this book.)

SP 2 On October 1, 2011, Santana Rey launched a computer services company called **Business Solutions,** which provides consulting services, computer system installations, and custom program development. Rey adopts the calendar year for reporting purposes and expects to prepare the company's first set of financial statements on December 31, 2011. The company's initial chart of accounts follows.

Account	No.	Account	No.
Cash	101	S. Rey, Capital	301
Accounts Receivable	106	S. Rey, Withdrawals	302
Computer Supplies	126	Computer Services Revenue	403
Prepaid Insurance	128	Wages Expense	623
Prepaid Rent	131	Advertising Expense	655
Office Equipment	163	Mileage Expense	676
Computer Equipment	167	Miscellaneous Expenses	677
Accounts Payable	201	Repairs Expense—Computer	684

Required

1. Prepare journal entries to record each of the following transactions for Business Solutions.

Oct. 1 S. Rey invested $45,000 cash, a $20,000 computer system, and $8,000 of office equipment in the company.
2 The company paid $3,300 cash for four months' rent. (*Hint:* Debit Prepaid Rent for $3,300.)
3 The company purchased $1,420 of computer supplies on credit from Harris Office Products.
5 The company paid $2,220 cash for one year's premium on a property and liability insurance policy. (*Hint:* Debit Prepaid Insurance for $2,220.)
6 The company billed Easy Leasing $4,800 for services performed in installing a new Web server.
8 The company paid $1,420 cash for the computer supplies purchased from Harris Office Products on October 3.
10 The company hired Lyn Addie as a part-time assistant for $125 per day, as needed.
12 The company billed Easy Leasing another $1,400 for services performed.

15 The company received $4,800 cash from Easy Leasing as partial payment on its account.
17 The company paid $805 cash to repair computer equipment that was damaged when moving it.
20 The company paid $1,728 cash for advertisements published in the local newspaper.
22 The company received $1,400 cash from Easy Leasing on its account.
28 The company billed IFM Company $5,208 for services performed.
31 The company paid $875 cash for Lyn Addie's wages for seven days' work.
31 S. Rey withdrew $3,600 cash from the company for personal use.
Nov. 1 The company reimbursed S. Rey in cash for business automobile mileage allowance (Rey logged 1,000 miles at $0.32 per mile).
2 The company received $4,633 cash from Liu Corporation for computer services performed.
5 The company purchased computer supplies for $1,125 cash from Harris Office Products.
8 The company billed Gomez Co. $5,668 for services performed.
13 The company received notification from Alex's Engineering Co. that Business Solutions' bid of $3,950 for an upcoming project is accepted.
18 The company received $2,208 cash from IFM Company as partial payment of the October 28 bill.
22 The company donated $250 cash to the United Way in the company's name.
24 The company completed work for Alex's Engineering Co. and sent it a bill for $3,950.
25 The company sent another bill to IFM Company for the past-due amount of $3,000.
28 The company reimbursed S. Rey in cash for business automobile mileage (1,200 miles at $0.32 per mile).
30 The company paid $1,750 cash for Lyn Addie's wages for 14 days' work.
30 S. Rey withdrew $2,000 cash from the company for personal use.

2. Open ledger accounts (in balance column format) and post the journal entries from part 1 to them.
3. Prepare a trial balance as of the end of November.

Check (2) Cash, Nov. 30 bal., $38,204
(3) Trial bal. totals, $98,659

Beyond the Numbers

REPORTING IN ACTION
A1 A2
RIM

BTN 2-1 Refer to **Research In Motion**'s financial statements in Appendix A for the following questions.

Required

1. What amount of total liabilities does it report for each of the fiscal years ended February 28, 2009, and February 27, 2010?
2. What amount of total assets does it report for each of the fiscal years ended February 28, 2009, and February 27, 2010?
3. Compute its debt ratio for each of the fiscal years ended February 28, 2009, and February 27, 2010.
4. In which fiscal year did it employ more financial leverage (February 28, 2009, or February 27, 2010)? Explain.

Fast Forward

5. Access its financial statements (10-K report) for a fiscal year ending after February 27, 2010, from its Website (RIM.com) or the SEC's EDGAR database (www.SEC.gov). Recompute its debt ratio for any subsequent year's data and compare it with the debt ratio for 2009 and 2010.

COMPARATIVE ANALYSIS
A1 A2 
RIM
Apple

BTN 2-2 Key comparative figures for **Research In Motion** and **Apple** follow.

	Research In Motion		Apple	
($ millions)	Current Year	Prior Year	Current Year	Prior Year
Total liabilities	$ 2,602	$ 2,227	$15,861	$13,874
Total assets	10,204	8,101	47,501	36,171

1. What is the debt ratio for Research In Motion in the current year and for the prior year?
2. What is the debt ratio for Apple in the current year and for the prior year?
3. Which of the two companies has the higher degree of financial leverage? What does this imply?

ETHICS CHALLENGE

C1

BTN 2-3 Review the *Decision Ethics* case from the first part of this chapter involving the cashier. The guidance answer suggests that you should not comply with the assistant manager's request.

Required

Propose and evaluate two other courses of action you might consider, and explain why.

COMMUNICATING IN PRACTICE

C1 C2 A1 P3 

BTN 2-4 Mora Stanley is an aspiring entrepreneur and your friend. She is having difficulty understanding the purposes of financial statements and how they fit together across time.

Required

Write a one-page memorandum to Stanley explaining the purposes of the four financial statements and how they are linked across time.

TAKING IT TO THE NET

A1  

BTN 2-5 Access EDGAR online (**www.SEC.gov**) and locate the 2009 year 10-K report of **Amazon.com** (ticker AMZN) filed on January 29, 2010. Review its financial statements reported for years ended 2009, 2008, and 2007 to answer the following questions.

Required

1. What are the amounts of its net income or net loss reported for each of these three years?
2. Does Amazon's operating activities provide cash or use cash for each of these three years?
3. If Amazon has a 2009 net income of more than $900 million and 2009 operating cash flows of more than $3,000 million, how is it possible that its cash balance at December 31, 2009, increases by less than $700 million relative to its balance at December 31, 2008?

TEAMWORK IN ACTION

C1 C2 C4 A1

BTN 2-6 The expanded accounting equation consists of assets, liabilities, capital, withdrawals, revenues, and expenses. It can be used to reveal insights into changes in a company's financial position.

Required

1. Form *learning teams* of six (or more) members. Each team member must select one of the six components and each team must have at least one expert on each component: (*a*) assets, (*b*) liabilities, (*c*) capital, (*d*) withdrawals, (*e*) revenues, and (*f*) expenses.
2. Form *expert teams* of individuals who selected the same component in part 1. Expert teams are to draft a report that each expert will present to his or her learning team addressing the following:
   a. Identify for its component the (i) increase and decrease side of the account and (ii) normal balance side of the account.
   b. Describe a transaction, with amounts, that increases its component.
   c. Using the transaction and amounts in (*b*), verify the equality of the accounting equation and then explain any effects on the income statement and statement of cash flows.
   d. Describe a transaction, with amounts, that decreases its component.
   e. Using the transaction and amounts in (*d*), verify the equality of the accounting equation and then explain any effects on the income statement and statement of cash flows.
3. Each expert should return to his/her learning team. In rotation, each member presents his/her expert team's report to the learning team. Team discussion is encouraged.

ENTREPRENEURIAL DECISION

A1 A2 P3  

BTN 2-7 Assume Susie Levitt and Katie Shea of **CitySlips** plan on expanding their business to accommodate more product lines. They are considering financing their expansion in one of two ways: (1) contributing more of their own funds to the business or (2) borrowing the funds from a bank.

Required

Identify at least two issues that Susie and Katie should consider when trying to decide on the method for financing their expansion.

ENTREPRENEURIAL DECISION

A1 A2 P3  

BTN 2-8 Lisa Langely is a young entrepreneur who operates Langely Music Services, offering singing lessons and instruction on musical instruments. Langely wishes to expand but needs a $15,000 loan. The bank requests Langely to prepare a balance sheet and key financial ratios. Langely has not kept formal records but is able to provide the following accounts and their amounts as of December 31, 2011.

Cash	$ 1,800	Accounts Receivable	$4,800	Prepaid Insurance	$ 750
Prepaid Rent	4,700	Store Supplies	3,300	Equipment	25,000
Accounts Payable	1,100	Unearned Lesson Fees . . .	7,800	Total Equity*	31,450
Annual net income . . .	20,000				

* The total equity amount reflects all owner investments, withdrawals, revenues, and expenses as of December 31, 2011.

Required

1. Prepare a balance sheet as of December 31, 2011, for Langely Music Services. (Report only the total equity amount on the balance sheet.)
2. Compute Langely's debt ratio and its return on assets (the latter ratio is defined in Chapter 1). Assume average assets equal its ending balance.
3. Do you believe the prospects of a $15,000 bank loan are good? Why or why not?

HITTING THE ROAD

C1

BTN 2-9 Obtain a recent copy of the most prominent newspaper distributed in your area. Research the classified section and prepare a report answering the following questions (attach relevant classified clippings to your report). Alternatively, you may want to search the Web for the required information. One suitable Website is **CareerOneStop (www.CareerOneStop.org)**. For documentation, you should print copies of Websites accessed.

1. Identify the number of listings for accounting positions and the various accounting job titles.
2. Identify the number of listings for other job titles, with examples, that require or prefer accounting knowledge/experience but are not specifically accounting positions.
3. Specify the salary range for the accounting and accounting-related positions if provided.
4. Indicate the job that appeals to you, the reason for its appeal, and its requirements.

GLOBAL DECISION

A2  

RIM

Apple

BTN 2-10 **Nokia (www.Nokia.com)** is a leading global manufacturer of mobile devices and services, and it competes to some extent with both **Research In Motion** and **Apple**. Key financial ratios for the current fiscal year follow.

Key Figure	Nokia	Research In Motion	Apple
Return on assets	0.7%	26.8%	19.7%
Debt ratio	58.7%	25.5%	33.4%

Required

1. Which company is most profitable according to its return on assets?
2. Which company is most risky according to the debt ratio?
3. Which company deserves increased investment based on a joint analysis of return on assets and the debt ratio? Explain.

ANSWERS TO MULTIPLE CHOICE QUIZ

1. b; debit Utility Expense for $700, and credit Cash for $700.
2. a; debit Cash for $2,500, and credit Unearned Lawn Service Fees for $2,500.
3. c; debit Cash for $250,000, debit Land for $500,000, and credit L. Shue, Capital for $750,000.
4. d
5. e; Debt ratio = $400,000/$1,000,000 = 40%

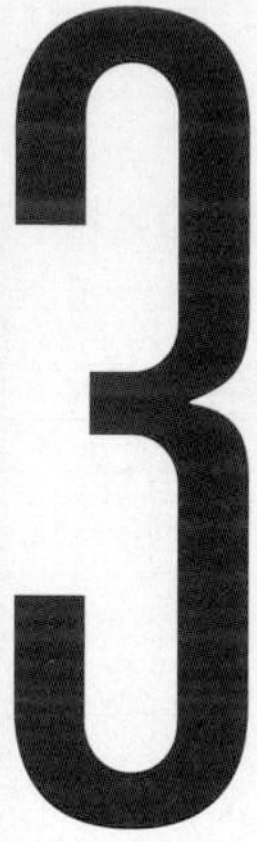

Adjusting Accounts and Preparing Financial Statements

A Look Back

Chapter 2 explained the analysis and recording of transactions. We showed how to apply and interpret company accounts, T-accounts, double-entry accounting, ledgers, postings, and trial balances.

A Look at This Chapter

This chapter explains the timing of reports and the need to adjust accounts. Adjusting accounts is important for recognizing revenues and expenses in the proper period. We describe the adjusted trial balance and how it is used to prepare financial statements.

A Look Ahead

Chapter 4 highlights the completion of the accounting cycle. We explain the important final steps in the accounting process. These include closing procedures, the post-closing trial balance, and reversing entries.

Learning Objectives

CAP

CONCEPTUAL

C1 Explain the importance of periodic reporting and the time period assumption. (p. 94)

C2 Explain accrual accounting and how it improves financial statements. (p. 95)

C3 Identify the types of adjustments and their purpose. (p. 96)

ANALYTICAL

A1 Explain how accounting adjustments link to financial statements. (p. 105)

A2 Compute profit margin and describe its use in analyzing company performance. (p. 109)

LP3

PROCEDURAL

P1 Prepare and explain adjusting entries. (p. 97)

P2 Explain and prepare an adjusted trial balance. (p. 106)

P3 Prepare financial statements from an adjusted trial balance. (p. 106)

P4 *Appendix 3A*—Explain the alternatives in accounting for prepaids. (p. 113)

Decision Insight

Huh? Yes!

"Make sure that whatever commitment you make . . . you keep"
—BEN HUH

SEATTLE—"When we were starting this thing, people asked who was going to run it, and I said, 'I will, and my wife.' And they said, 'You're crazy.' And I said, 'Yes!' " Meet Ben Huh. His thing? **Cheezburger Network (Cheezburger.com/sites),** which controls over 30 Websites devoted to Internet memes. (Memes are running gags, usually in JPEG or video format, which spawn and spread on the Web.) His sites include ICanHasCheezburger?, FailBlog, IHasAHotdog!, ROFLrazzi, and TotallyLooksLike. Since launching his company just a few years ago, his network has nearly 200 million page views per month and annual revenue in the millions. Revenue comes from display ads, along with some merchandise sales.

Ben explains that he set up an accounting system early on to account for all business activities, including cash, revenues, receivables, and payables. He also had to learn about the deferral and accrual of revenues and expenses. Setting up a good accounting system is an important part of success, explains Ben. "I learned how to keep costs low."

In spite of his quirky business, Ben insists "it is very serious business." He also seriously monitors the adjusting of accounts so that revenues and expenses are properly reported so that good decisions are made. Adds Ben, "No matter how strange or ridiculous a business looks, those fundamentals still need to be there."

Financial statement preparation and analysis is a process that Ben emphasizes. Although he insists on timely and accurate accounting reports, Ben says "we're just having fun . . . we've always been very much counterculture." To achieve the fun part, Ben first took time to understand accounting adjustments and their effects. It is part of the larger picture. We "make people happy for five minutes every day." But, for Ben to do that, he insists that a reliable accounting system is necessary . . . otherwise his business would fail.

"We'd like to continue to do what we do . . . build bigger communities and just kind of evangelize the idea that the user is great at creating excellent content," says Ben. "The market is far more efficient than any one company . . . but we haven't applied that theory to [Web] content."

[Sources: *Cheezburger Website* and *BenHuh Website,* January 2011; *Entrepreneur,* August 2009; *Wired,* February 2010; *The New York Times,* April 2009; *Time,* August 2009]

Chapter Preview

Financial statements reflect revenues when earned and expenses when incurred. This is known as *accrual accounting,* which was the focus of Chapter 2. We showed how companies use accounting systems to collect information about *external* transactions and events. We also explained how journals, ledgers, and other tools are useful in preparing financial statements. This chapter describes the accounting process for producing useful information involving *internal* transactions and events. An important part of this process is adjusting the account balances so that financial statements at the end of a reporting period reflect the effects of all transactions. We then explain the important steps in preparing financial statements.

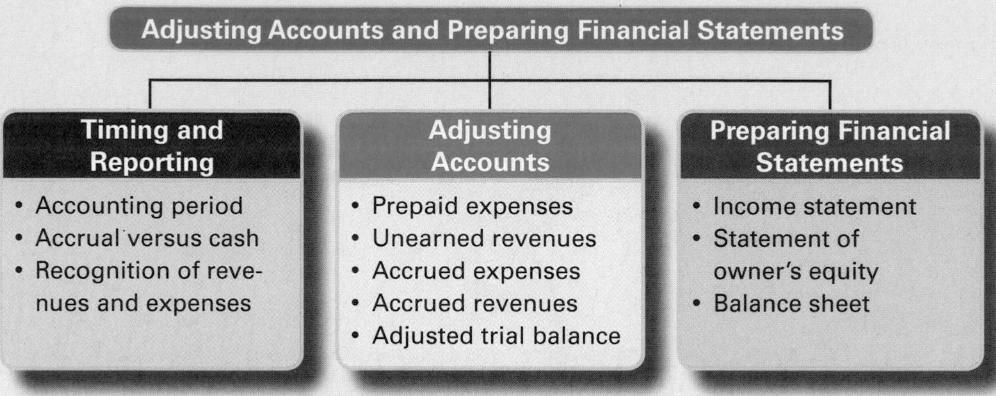

Adjusting Accounts and Preparing Financial Statements
Timing and Reporting
• Accounting period
• Accrual versus cash
• Recognition of revenues and expenses
Adjusting Accounts
• Prepaid expenses
• Unearned revenues
• Accrued expenses
• Accrued revenues
• Adjusted trial balance
Preparing Financial Statements
• Income statement
• Statement of owner's equity
• Balance sheet

TIMING AND REPORTING

This section describes the importance of reporting accounting information at regular intervals and its impact for recording revenues and expenses.

The Accounting Period

C1 Explain the importance of periodic reporting and the time period assumption.

The value of information is often linked to its timeliness. Useful information must reach decision makers frequently and promptly. To provide timely information, accounting systems prepare reports at regular intervals. This results in an accounting process impacted by the time period (or periodicity) assumption. The **time period assumption** presumes that an organization's activities can be divided into specific time periods such as a month, a three-month quarter, a six-month interval, or a year. Exhibit 3.1 shows various **accounting,** or *reporting,* **periods.** Most organizations use a year as their primary accounting period. Reports covering a one-year period are known as **annual financial statements.** Many organizations also prepare **interim financial statements** covering one, three, or six months of activity.

"RIM announces annual income of . . ."

EXHIBIT 3.1

Accounting Periods

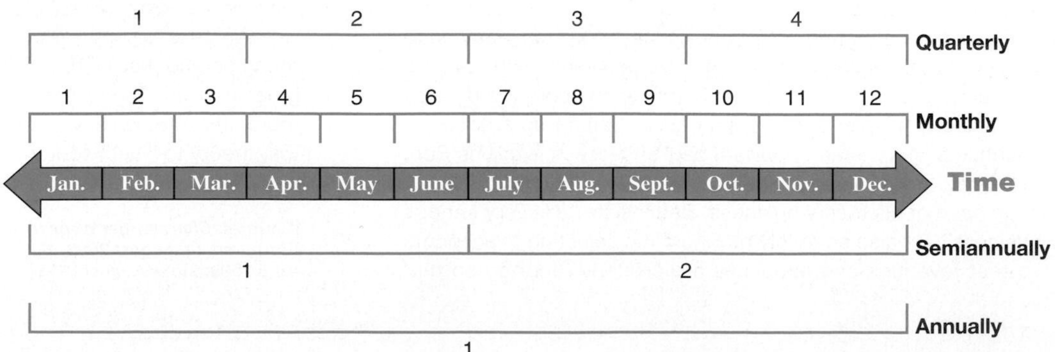

The annual reporting period is not always a calendar year ending on December 31. An organization can adopt a **fiscal year** consisting of any 12 consecutive months. It is also acceptable to adopt an annual reporting period of 52 weeks. For example, **Gap**'s fiscal year consistently ends the final week of January or the first week of February each year.

Companies with little seasonal variation in sales often choose the calendar year as their fiscal year. The financial statements of **The Kellogg Company** (the company that controls characters such as Tony the Tiger, Snap! Crackle! Pop!, and Keebler Elf) reflect a fiscal year that ends on the Saturday nearest December 31. Companies experiencing seasonal variations in sales often choose a **natural business year** end, which is when sales activities are at their lowest level for the year. The natural business year for retailers such as **Walmart**, **Target**, and **Macy's** usually ends around January 31, after the holiday season.

Accrual Basis versus Cash Basis

C2 Explain accrual accounting and how it improves financial statements.

After external transactions and events are recorded, several accounts still need adjustments before their balances appear in financial statements. This need arises because internal transactions and events remain unrecorded. **Accrual basis accounting** uses the adjusting process to recognize revenues when earned and expenses when incurred (matched with revenues).

Cash basis accounting recognizes revenues when cash is received and records expenses when cash is paid. This means that cash basis net income for a period is the difference between cash receipts and cash payments. Cash basis accounting is not consistent with generally accepted accounting principles (neither U.S. GAAP nor IFRS).

It is commonly held that accrual accounting better reflects business performance than information about cash receipts and payments. Accrual accounting also increases the *comparability* of financial statements from one period to another. Yet cash basis accounting is useful for several business decisions—which is the reason companies must report a statement of cash flows.

To see the difference between these two accounting systems, let's consider FastForward's Prepaid Insurance account. FastForward paid $2,400 for 24 months of insurance coverage that began on December 1, 2011. Accrual accounting requires that $100 of insurance expense be reported on December 2011's income statement. Another $1,200 of expense is reported in year 2012, and the remaining $1,100 is reported as expense in the first 11 months of 2013. Exhibit 3.2 illustrates this allocation of insurance cost across these three years. Any unexpired premium is reported as a Prepaid Insurance asset on the accrual basis balance sheet.

EXHIBIT 3.2

Accrual Accounting for Allocating Prepaid Insurance to Expense

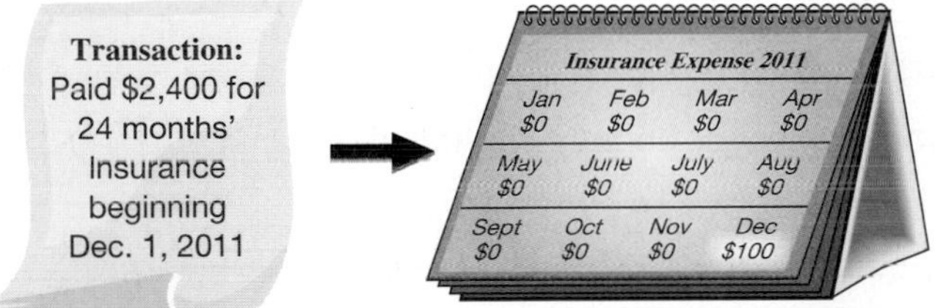

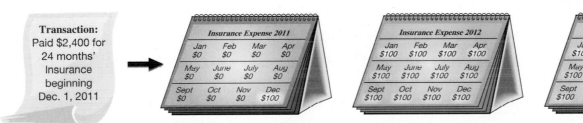

Alternatively, a cash basis income statement for December 2011 reports insurance expense of $2,400, as shown in Exhibit 3.3. The cash basis income statements for years 2012 and 2013 report no insurance expense. The cash basis balance sheet never reports an insurance asset because it is immediately expensed. This shows that cash basis income for 2011–2013 fails to match the cost of insurance with the insurance benefits received for those years and months.

EXHIBIT 3.3

Cash Accounting for Allocating Prepaid Insurance to Expense

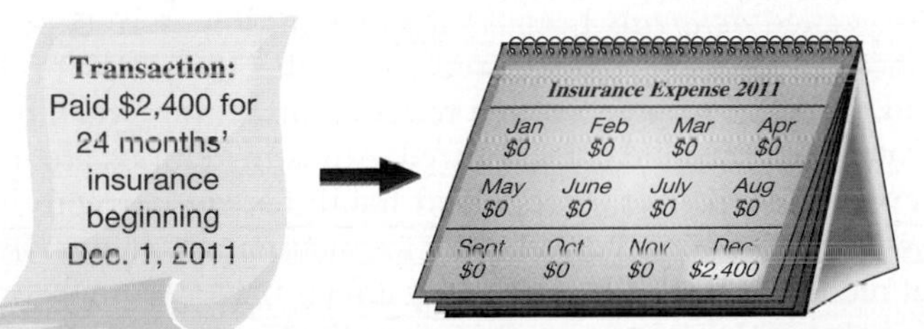

Recognizing Revenues and Expenses

Point: Recording revenue early overstates current-period revenue and income; recording it late understates current-period revenue and income.

Point: Recording expense early overstates current-period expense and understates current-period income; recording it late understates current-period expense and overstates current-period income.

We use the time period assumption to divide a company's activities into specific time periods, but not all activities are complete when financial statements are prepared. Thus, adjustments often are required to get correct account balances.

We rely on two principles in the adjusting process: revenue recognition and expense recognition (the latter is often referred to as matching). Chapter 1 explained that the *revenue recognition principle* requires that revenue be recorded when earned, not before and not after. Most companies earn revenue when they provide services and products to customers. A major goal of the adjusting process is to have revenue recognized (reported) in the time period when it is earned. The **expense recognition** (or **matching**) **principle** aims to record expenses in the same accounting period as the revenues that are earned as a result of those expenses. This matching of expenses with the revenue benefits is a major part of the adjusting process.

Matching expenses with revenues often requires us to predict certain events. When we use financial statements, we must understand that they require estimates and therefore include measures that are not precise. **Walt Disney**'s annual report explains that its production costs from movies, such as *Alice in Wonderland,* are matched to revenues based on a ratio of current revenues from the movie divided by its predicted total revenues.

Quick Check

Answers — p. 116

1. Describe a company's annual reporting period.
2. Why do companies prepare interim financial statements?
3. What two accounting principles most directly drive the adjusting process?
4. Is cash basis accounting consistent with the matching principle? Why or why not?
5. If your company pays a $4,800 premium on April 1, 2011, for two years' insurance coverage, how much insurance expense is reported in 2012 using cash basis accounting?

ADJUSTING ACCOUNTS

Adjusting accounts is a 3-step process:

Step 1: **Determine what the current account balance *equals*.**

Step 2: **Determine what the current account balance *should equal*.**

Step 3: **Record an adjusting entry to get from step *1* to step *2*.**

Framework for Adjustments

C3 Identify the types of adjustments and their purpose.

Adjustments are necessary for transactions and events that extend over more than one period. It is helpful to group adjustments by the timing of cash receipt or cash payment in relation to the recognition of the related revenues or expenses. Exhibit 3.4 identifies four types of adjustments.

Point: Source documents provide information for most daily transactions, and in many businesses the recordkeepers record them. Adjustments require more knowledge and are usually handled by senior accounting professionals.

The upper half of this exhibit shows prepaid expenses (including depreciation) and unearned revenues, which reflect transactions when cash is paid or received *before* a related expense or revenue is recognized. They are also called *deferrals* because the recognition of an expense (or revenue) is *deferred* until after the related cash is paid (or received). The lower half of this exhibit shows accrued expenses and accrued revenues, which reflect transactions when cash is paid or received *after* a related expense or revenue is recognized. Adjusting entries are necessary for each of these so that revenues, expenses, assets, and liabilities are correctly reported. Specifically, an **adjusting entry** is made at the end of an accounting period to reflect a transaction or event that is not yet recorded. Each adjusting entry affects one or more income statement accounts *and* one or more balance sheet accounts (but never the Cash account).

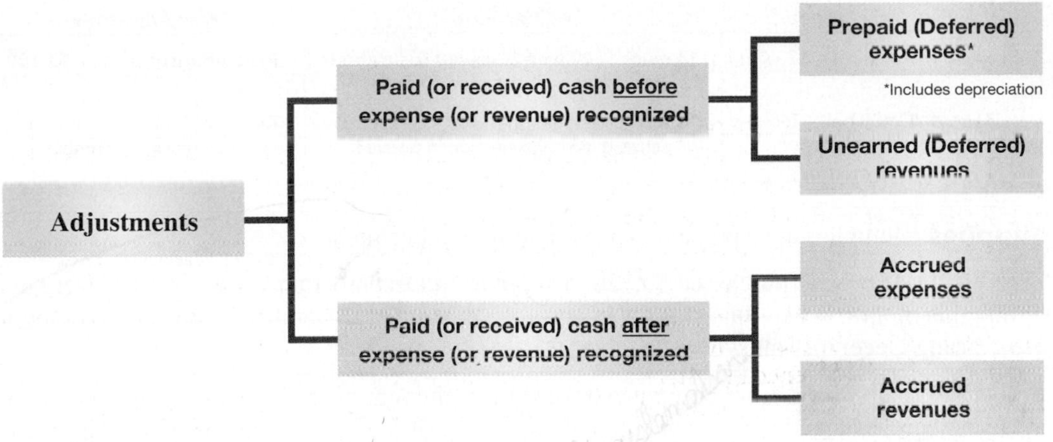

EXHIBIT 3.4

Types of Adjustments

Prepaid (Deferred) Expenses

P1 Prepare and explain adjusting entries.

Prepaid expenses refer to items *paid for* in advance of receiving their benefits. Prepaid expenses are assets. When these assets are used, their costs become expenses. Adjusting entries for prepaids increase expenses and decrease assets as shown in the T-accounts of Exhibit 3.5. Such adjustments reflect transactions and events that use up prepaid expenses (including passage of time). To illustrate the accounting for prepaid expenses, we look at prepaid insurance, supplies, and depreciation.

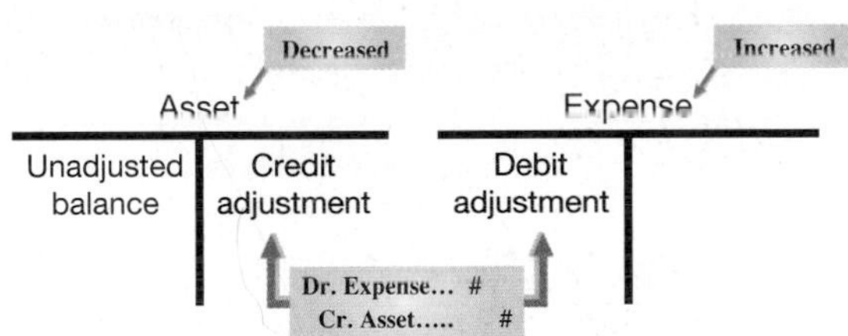

EXHIBIT 3.5

Adjusting for Prepaid Expenses

Prepaid Insurance We use our 3-step process for this and all accounting adjustments.

Step 1: We determine that the current balance of FastForward's prepaid insurance is equal to its $2,400 payment for 24 months of insurance benefits that began on December 1, 2011.

Step 2: With the passage of time, the benefits of the insurance gradually expire and a portion of the Prepaid Insurance asset becomes expense. For instance, one month's insurance coverage expires by December 31, 2011. This expense is $100, or 1/24 of $2,400, which leaves $2,300.

Step 3: The adjusting entry to record this expense and reduce the asset, along with T-account postings, follows:

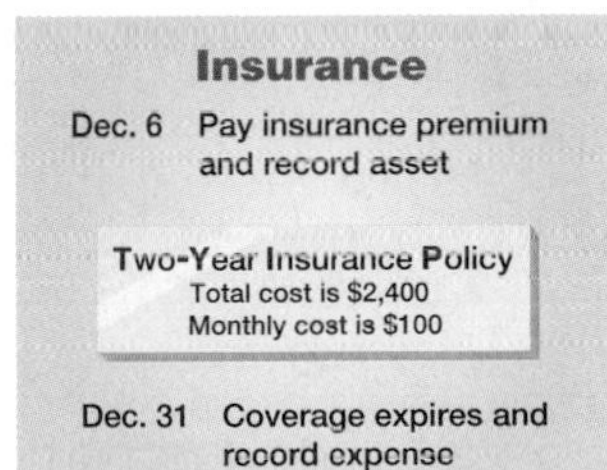

Insurance
Dec. 6 Pay insurance premium and record asset
Two-Year Insurance Policy
Total cost is $2,400
Monthly cost is $100
Dec. 31 Coverage expires and record expense

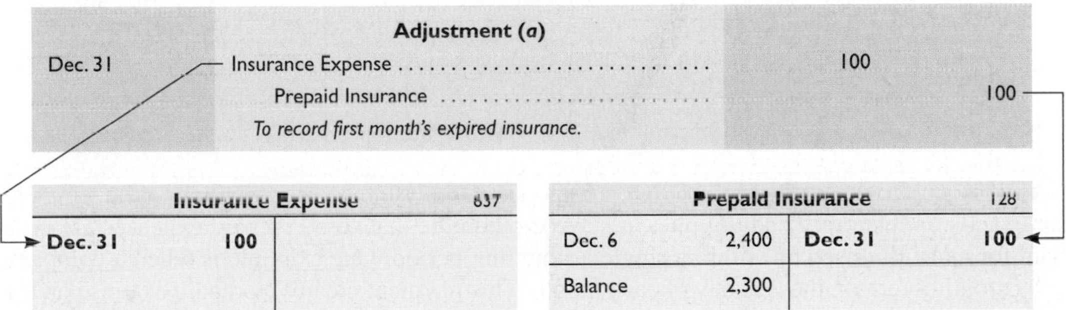

Adjustment (*a*)

		Debit	Credit
Dec. 31	Insurance Expense	100	
	Prepaid Insurance		100
	To record first month's expired insurance.		

Insurance Expense 637

Dec. 31	100		

Prepaid Insurance 128

Dec. 6	2,400	Dec. 31	100
Balance	2,300		

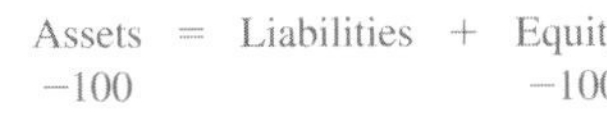

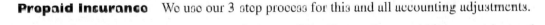

Explanation After adjusting and posting, the $100 balance in Insurance Expense and the $2,300 balance in Prepaid Insurance are ready for reporting in financial statements. *Not* making the adjustment on or before December 31 would (1) understate expenses by $100 and overstate net income by $100 for the December income statement and (2) overstate both prepaid insurance (assets) and equity (because of net income) by $100 in the December 31 balance sheet. (Exhibit 3.2 showed that 2012's adjustments must transfer a total of $1,200 from Prepaid Insurance to Insurance Expense, and 2013's adjustments must transfer the remaining $1,100 to Insurance Expense.) The following table highlights the December 31, 2011, adjustment for prepaid insurance.

Point: Many companies record adjusting entries only at the end of each year because of the time and cost necessary.

Before Adjustment	Adjustment	After Adjustment
Prepaid Insurance = $2,400	**Deduct $100 from Prepaid Insurance Add $100 to Insurance Expense**	**Prepaid Insurance = $2,300**
Reports $2,400 policy for 24-months' coverage.	Record current month's $100 insurance expense and $100 reduction in prepaid amount.	Reports $2,300 in coverage for remaining 23 months.

Supplies Supplies are a prepaid expense requiring adjustment.

Step 1: FastForward purchased $9,720 of supplies in December and some of them were used during this month. When financial statements are prepared at December 31, the cost of supplies used during December must be recognized.

Step 2: When FastForward computes (takes physical count of) its remaining unused supplies at December 31, it finds $8,670 of supplies remaining of the $9,720 total supplies. The $1,050 difference between these two amounts is December's supplies expense.

Step 3: The adjusting entry to record this expense and reduce the Supplies asset account, along with T-account postings, follows:

Assets	=	Liabilities	+	Equity
−1,050				−1,050

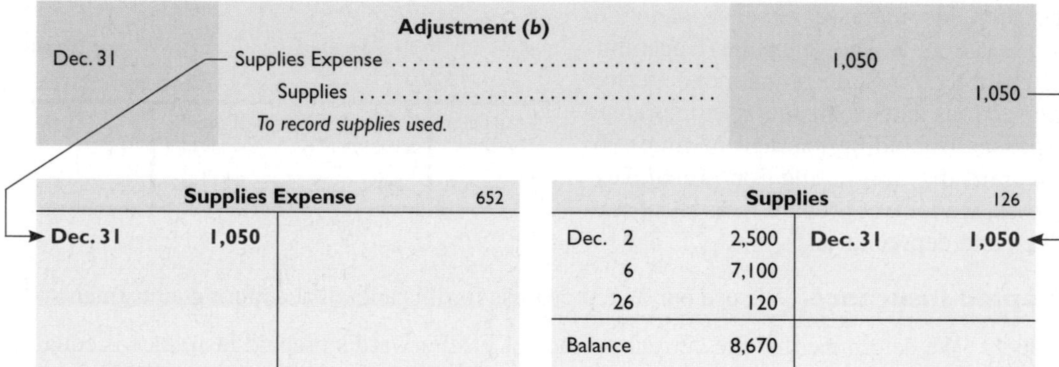

	Adjustment (*b*)		
Dec. 31	Supplies Expense	1,050	
	Supplies		1,050
	To record supplies used.		

Supplies Expense 652

Dec. 31	**1,050**	

Supplies 126

Dec. 2	2,500	**Dec. 31**	**1,050**
6	7,100		
26	120		
Balance	8,670		

Explanation The balance of the Supplies account is $8,670 after posting—equaling the cost of the remaining supplies. *Not* making the adjustment on or before December 31 would (1) understate expenses by $1,050 and overstate net income by $1,050 for the December income statement and (2) overstate both supplies and equity (because of net income) by $1,050 in the December 31 balance sheet. The following table highlights the adjustment for supplies.

Before Adjustment	Adjustment	After Adjustment
Supplies = $9,720	**Deduct $1,050 from Supplies Add $1,050 to Supplies Expense**	**Supplies = $8,670**
Reports $9,720 in supplies.	Record $1,050 in supplies used and $1,050 as supplies expense.	Reports $8,670 in supplies.

Other Prepaid Expenses Other prepaid expenses, such as Prepaid Rent, are accounted for exactly as Insurance and Supplies are. We should note that some prepaid expenses are both paid for and fully used up within a single accounting period. One example is when a company pays monthly rent on the first day of each month. This payment creates a prepaid expense on the first day of each month that fully expires by the end of the month. In these special cases, we can record the cash paid with a debit to an expense account instead of an asset account. This practice is described more completely later in the chapter.

Point: We assume that prepaid and unearned items are recorded in balance sheet accounts. An alternative is to record them in income statement accounts; Appendix 3A discusses this alternative. The adjusted financial statements are identical.

Decision Maker Answer — p. 115

Investor A small publishing company signs a well-known athlete to write a book. The company pays the athlete $500,000 to sign plus future book royalties. A note to the company's financial statements says that "prepaid expenses include $500,000 in author signing fees to be matched against future expected sales." Is this accounting for the signing bonus acceptable? How does it affect your analysis? ■

Depreciation A special category of prepaid expenses is **plant assets,** which refers to long-term tangible assets used to produce and sell products and services. Plant assets are expected to provide benefits for more than one period. Examples of plant assets are buildings, machines, vehicles, and fixtures. All plant assets, with a general exception for land, eventually wear out or decline in usefulness. The costs of these assets are deferred but are gradually reported as expenses in the income statement over the assets' useful lives (benefit periods). **Depreciation** is the process of allocating the costs of these assets over their expected useful lives. Depreciation expense is recorded with an adjusting entry similar to that for other prepaid expenses.

Point: Plant assets are also called *Plant & Equipment*, or *Property, Plant & Equipment*.

Point: Depreciation does not necessarily measure decline in market value.

Point: An asset's expected value at the end of its useful life is called *salvage value*.

Step 1: Recall that FastForward purchased equipment for $26,000 in early December to use in earning revenue. This equipment's cost must be depreciated.

Step 2: The equipment is expected to have a useful life (benefit period) of four years and to be worth about $8,000 at the end of four years. This means the *net* cost of this equipment over its useful life is $18,000 ($26,000 − $8,000). We can use any of several methods to allocate this $18,000 net cost to expense. FastForward uses a method called **straight-line depreciation,** which allocates equal amounts of the asset's net cost to depreciation during its useful life. Dividing the $18,000 net cost by the 48 months in the asset's useful life gives a monthly cost of $375 ($18,000/48).

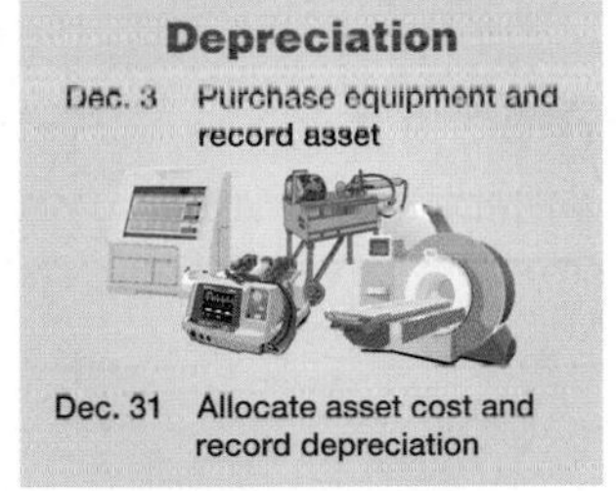

Depreciation
Dec. 3 Purchase equipment and record asset
Dec. 31 Allocate asset cost and record depreciation

Step 3: The adjusting entry to record monthly depreciation expense, along with T-account postings, follows:

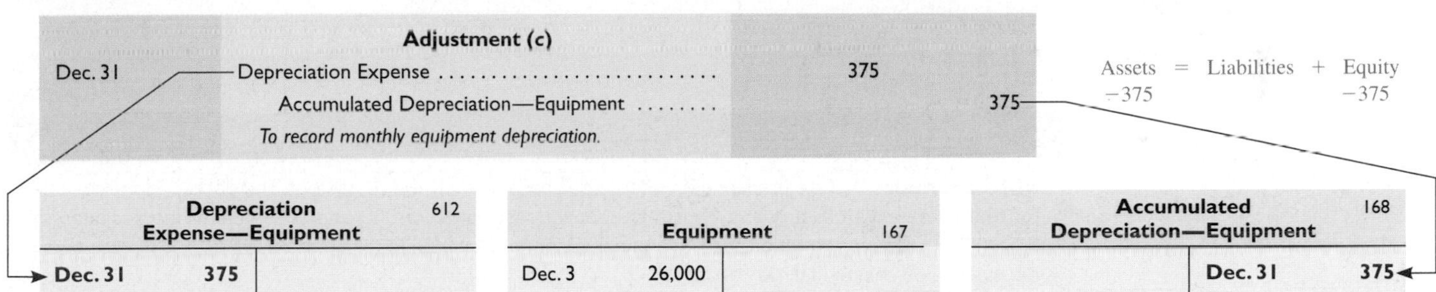

Adjustment (c)
Dec. 31 Depreciation Expense 375
Accumulated Depreciation—Equipment 375
To record monthly equipment depreciation.
Depreciation Expense—Equipment 612
Dec. 31 375
Equipment 167
Dec. 3 26,000
Accumulated Depreciation—Equipment 168
Dec. 31 375

Assets = Liabilities + Equity
−375 −375

Explanation After posting the adjustment, the Equipment account ($26,000) less its Accumulated Depreciation ($375) account equals the $25,625 net cost (made up of $17,625 for the 47 remaining months in the benefit period plus the $8,000 value at the end of that time). The $375 balance in the Depreciation Expense account is reported in the December income statement. *Not* making the adjustment at December 31 would (1) understate expenses by $375 and overstate net income by $375 for the December income statement and (2) overstate both assets and equity (because of income) by $375 in the December 31 balance sheet. The following table highlights the adjustment for depreciation.

Before Adjustment	Adjustment	After Adjustment
Equipment, net = $26,000	**Deduct $375 from Equipment, net Add $375 to Depreciation Expense**	**Equipment, net = $25,625**
Reports $26,000 in equipment.	Record $375 in depreciation and $375 as accumulated depreciation, which is deducted from equipment.	Reports $25,625 in equipment, net of accumulated depreciation.

Accumulated depreciation is kept in a separate contra account. A **contra account** is an account linked with another account, it has an opposite normal balance, and it is reported as a subtraction from that other account's balance. For instance, FastForward's contra account of Accumulated Depreciation—Equipment is subtracted from the Equipment account in the balance sheet (see Exhibit 3.7). This contra account allows balance sheet readers to know both the full costs of assets and the total depreciation.

The title of the contra account, *Accumulated Depreciation,* reveals that this account includes total depreciation expense for all prior periods for which the asset was used. To illustrate, the Equipment and the Accumulated Depreciation accounts appear as in Exhibit 3.6 on February 28, 2012, after three months of adjusting entries. The $1,125 balance in the accumulated depreciation account can be subtracted from its related $26,000 asset cost. The difference ($24,875) between these two balances is the cost of the asset that has not yet been depreciated. This difference is

Point: The cost principle requires an asset to be initially recorded at acquisition cost. Depreciation causes the asset's book value (cost less accumulated depreciation) to decline over time.

EXHIBIT 3.6

Accounts after Three Months of Depreciation Adjustments

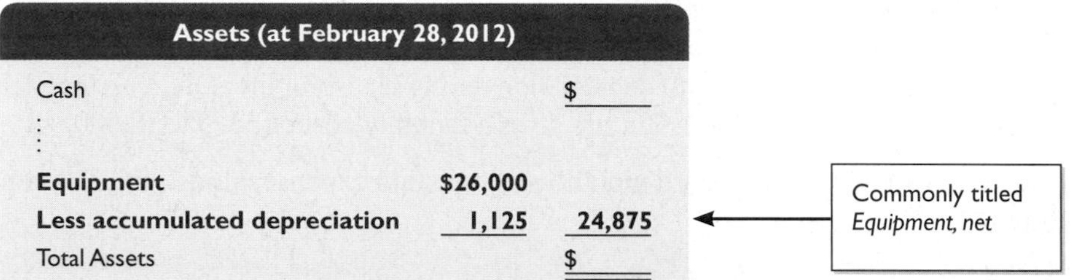

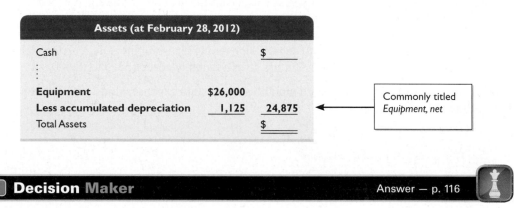

Equipment			167
Dec. 3	26,000		

Accumulated Depreciation—Equipment			168
		Dec. 31	375
		Jan. 31	375
		Feb. 28	375
		Balance	**1,125**

Point: The net cost of equipment is also called the *depreciable basis.*

called the **book value,** or the *net amount,* which equals the asset's costs less its accumulated depreciation.

These account balances are reported in the assets section of the February 28 balance sheet in Exhibit 3.7.

EXHIBIT 3.7

Equipment and Accumulated Depreciation on February 28 Balance Sheet

Assets (at February 28, 2012)		
Cash		$
⋮		
Equipment	**$26,000**	
Less accumulated depreciation	**1,125**	**24,875**
Total Assets		$

← Commonly titled *Equipment, net*

Entrepreneur You are preparing an offer to purchase a family-run restaurant. The depreciation schedule for the restaurant's building and equipment shows costs of $175,000 and accumulated depreciation of $155,000. This leaves a net for building and equipment of $20,000. Is this information useful in helping you decide on a purchase offer? ■

Unearned (Deferred) Revenues

The term **unearned revenues** refers to cash received in advance of providing products and services. Unearned revenues, also called *deferred revenues,* are liabilities. When cash is accepted, an obligation to provide products or services is accepted. As products or services are provided, the unearned revenues become *earned* revenues. Adjusting entries for unearned revenues involve increasing revenues and decreasing unearned revenues, as shown in Exhibit 3.8.

EXHIBIT 3.8

Adjusting for Unearned Revenues

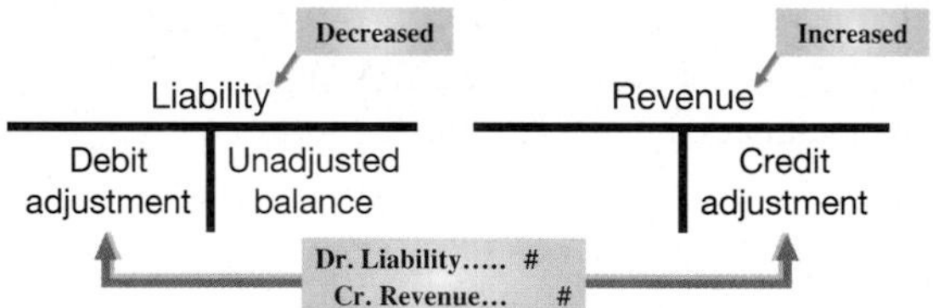

Point: To *defer* is to postpone. We postpone reporting amounts received as revenues until they are earned.

An example of unearned revenues is from **The New York Times Company**, which reports unexpired (unearned) subscriptions of $81 million: "Proceeds from ... subscriptions are deferred at the time of sale and are recognized in earnings on a pro rata basis over the terms of the subscriptions." Unearned revenues are nearly 10% of the current liabilities for the Times. Another example comes from the **Boston Celtics**. When the Celtics receive cash from advance ticket sales and broadcast fees, they record it in an unearned revenue account called *Deferred Game Revenues.* The Celtics recognize this unearned revenue with adjusting entries on a game-by-game basis. Since the NBA regular season begins in October and ends in April, revenue recognition is mainly limited to this period. For a recent season, the Celtics' quarterly revenues were $0 million for July–September; $34 million for October–December; $48 million for January–March; and $17 million for April–June.

Unearned Revenues
Dec. 26 Cash received in advance and record liability
Thanks for cash in advance. I'll work now through Feb. 24
Dec. 31 Provided services and record revenue

Returning to FastForward, it also has unearned revenues. It agreed on December 26 to provide consulting services to a client for a fixed fee of $3,000 for 60 days.

Step 1: On December 26, the client paid the 60-day fee in advance, covering the period December 27 to February 24. The entry to record the cash received in advance is

Dec. 26	Cash	3,000	
	Unearned Consulting Revenue		3,000
	Received advance payment for services over the next 60 days.		

Assets = Liabilities + Equity
+3,000 +3,000

This advance payment increases cash and creates an obligation to do consulting work over the next 60 days.

Step 2: As time passes, FastForward earns this payment through consulting. By December 31, it has provided five days' service and earned 5/60 of the $3,000 unearned revenue. This amounts to $250 ($3,000 × 5/60). The *revenue recognition principle* implies that $250 of unearned revenue must be reported as revenue on the December income statement.

Step 3: The adjusting entry to reduce the liability account and recognize earned revenue, along with T-account postings, follows:

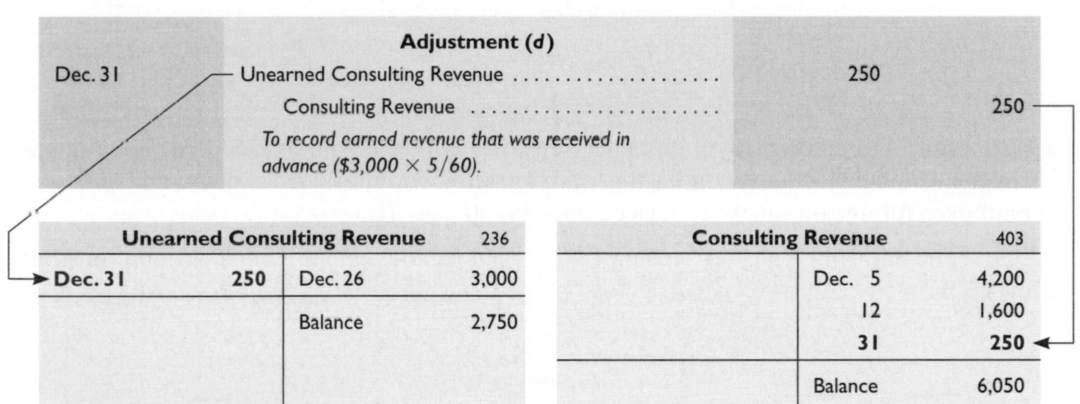

Adjustment (d)

Dec. 31	Unearned Consulting Revenue	250	
	Consulting Revenue		250
	To record earned revenue that was received in advance ($3,000 × 5/60).		

Unearned Consulting Revenue			236
Dec. 31	**250**	Dec. 26	3,000
		Balance	2,750

Consulting Revenue			403
		Dec. 5	4,200
		12	1,600
		31	**250**
		Balance	6,050

Assets = Liabilities + Equity
−250 +250

Explanation The adjusting entry transfers $250 from unearned revenue (a liability account) to a revenue account. *Not* making the adjustment (1) understates revenue and net income by $250 in the December income statement and (2) overstates unearned revenue and understates equity by $250 on the December 31 balance sheet. The following highlights the adjustment for unearned revenue.

Before Adjustment	Adjustment	After Adjustment
Unearned Consulting Revenue = $3,000	**Deduct $250 from Unearned Consulting Revenue Add $250 to Consulting Revenue**	**Unearned Consulting Revenue = $2,750**
Reports $3,000 in unearned revenue for consulting services promised for 60 days.	Record 5 days of earned consulting revenue, which is 5/60 of unearned amount.	Reports $2,750 in unearned revenue for consulting services owed over next 55 days.

Accounting for unearned revenues is crucial to many companies. For example, the **National Retail Federation** reports that gift card sales, which are unearned revenues for sellers, exceed $20 billion annually. Gift cards are now the top selling holiday gift.

Accrued Expenses

Accrued expenses refer to costs that are incurred in a period but are both unpaid and unrecorded. Accrued expenses must be reported on the income statement of the period when incurred. Adjusting entries for recording accrued expenses involve increasing expenses and increasing liabilities as shown in Exhibit 3.9. This adjustment recognizes expenses incurred in a period but not yet paid. Common examples of accrued expenses are salaries, interest, rent, and taxes. We use salaries and interest to show how to adjust accounts for accrued expenses.

Point: Accrued expenses are also called accrued liabilities.

EXHIBIT 3.9
Adjusting for Accrued Expenses

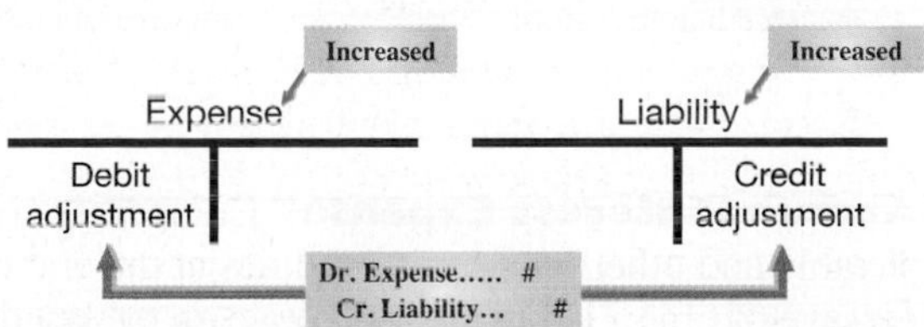

Accrued Salaries Expense FastForward's employee earns $70 per day, or $350 for a five-day workweek beginning on Monday and ending on Friday.

Step 1: Its employee is paid every two weeks on Friday. On December 12 and 26, the wages are paid, recorded in the journal, and posted to the ledger.

Step 2: The calendar in Exhibit 3.10 shows three working days after the December 26 payday (29, 30, and 31). This means the employee has earned three days' salary by the close of business on Wednesday, December 31, yet this salary cost has not been paid or recorded. The financial statements would be incomplete if FastForward fails to report the added expense and liability to the employee for unpaid salary from December 29, 30, and 31.

EXHIBIT 3.10

Salary Accrual and Paydays

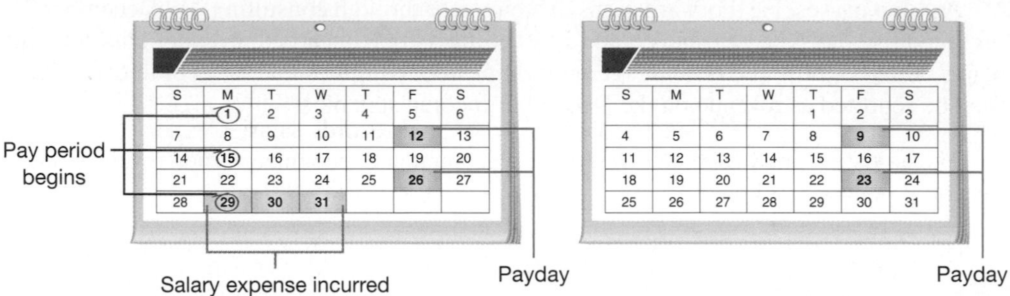

Point: An employer records salaries expense and a vacation pay liability when employees earn vacation pay.

Step 3: The adjusting entry to account for accrued salaries, along with T-account postings, follows:

Assets = Liabilities + Equity
+210 −210

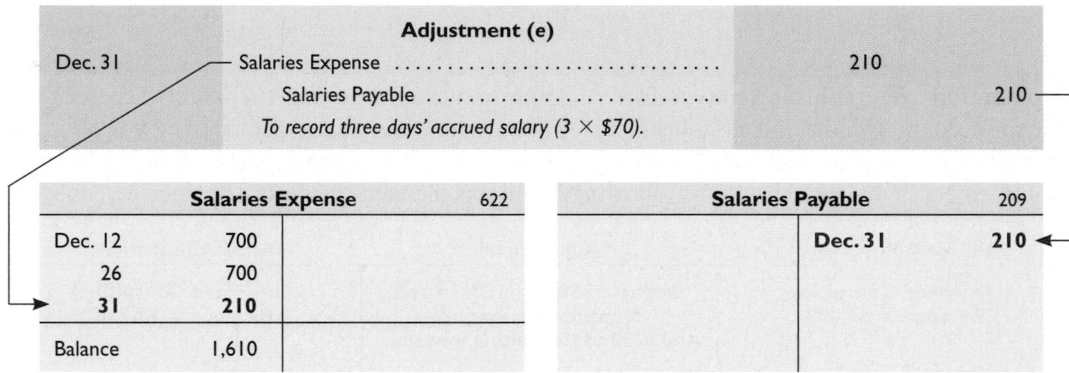

Adjustment (e)

		Debit	Credit
Dec. 31	Salaries Expense	210	
	Salaries Payable		210
	To record three days' accrued salary (3 × $70).		

Salaries Expense 622

	Debit	Credit
Dec. 12	700	
26	700	
31	**210**	
Balance	1,610	

Salaries Payable 209

Debit		Credit
	Dec. 31	**210**

Explanation Salaries expense of $1,610 is reported on the December income statement and $210 of salaries payable (liability) is reported in the balance sheet. *Not* making the adjustment (1) understates salaries expense and overstates net income by $210 in the December income statement and (2) understates salaries payable (liabilities) and overstates equity by $210 on the December 31 balance sheet. The following highlights the adjustment for salaries incurred.

Before Adjustment	Adjustment	After Adjustment
Salaries Payable = $0	**Add $210 to Salaries Payable** **Add $210 to Salaries Expense**	**Salaries Payable = $210**
Reports $0 from employee salaries incurred but not yet paid in cash.	Record 3 days' salaries owed to employee, but not yet paid, at $70 per day.	Reports $210 salaries payable to employee but not yet paid.

Accrued Interest Expense Companies commonly have accrued interest expense on notes payable and other long-term liabilities at the end of a period. Interest expense is incurred with the passage of time. Unless interest is paid on the last day of an accounting period, we need to adjust for interest expense incurred but not yet paid. This means we must accrue interest cost from the most recent payment date up to the end of the period. The formula for computing accrued interest is:

Principal amount owed × Annual interest rate × Fraction of year since last payment date.

To illustrate, if a company has a $6,000 loan from a bank at 6% annual interest, then 30 days' accrued interest expense is $30—computed as $6,000 × 0.06 × 30/360. The adjusting entry would be to debit Interest Expense for $30 and credit Interest Payable for $30.

Point: Interest computations assume a 360-day year; known as the *bankers' rule*.

Future Payment of Accrued Expenses Adjusting entries for accrued expenses foretell cash transactions in future periods. Specifically, accrued expenses at the end of one accounting period result in *cash payment* in a *future period*(s). To illustrate, recall that FastForward recorded accrued salaries of $210. On January 9, the first payday of the next period, the following entry settles the accrued liability (salaries payable) and records salaries expense for seven days of work in January:

Jan. 9	Salaries Payable (3 days at $70 per day)	210	
	Salaries Expense (7 days at $70 per day)	490	
	Cash		700
	Paid two weeks' salary including three days accrued in December.		

Assets	=	Liabilities	+	Equity
−700		−210		−490

The $210 debit reflects the payment of the liability for the three days' salary accrued on December 31. The $490 debit records the salary for January's first seven working days (including the New Year's Day holiday) as an expense of the new accounting period. The $700 credit records the total amount of cash paid to the employee.

Accrued Revenues

The term **accrued revenues** refers to revenues earned in a period that are both unrecorded and not yet received in cash (or other assets). An example is a technician who bills customers only when the job is done. If one-third of a job is complete by the end of a period, then the technician must record one-third of the expected billing as revenue in that period—even though there is no billing or collection. The adjusting entries for accrued revenues increase assets and increase revenues as shown in Exhibit 3.11. Accrued revenues commonly arise from services, products, interest, and rent. We use service fees and interest to show how to adjust for accrued revenues.

Point: Accrued revenues are also called *accrued assets*.

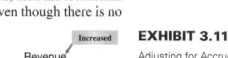

EXHIBIT 3.11

Adjusting for Accrued Revenues

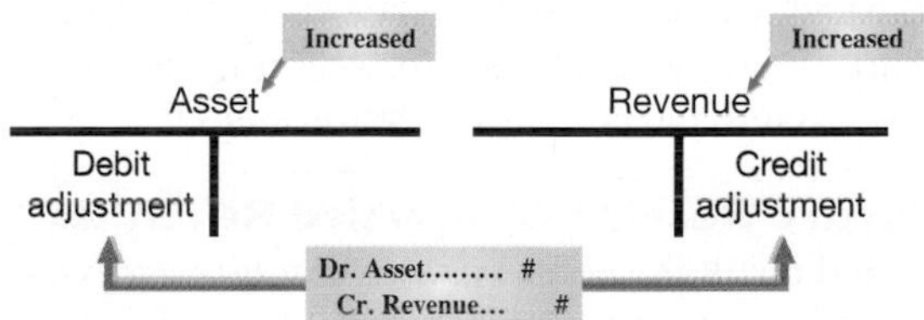

Accrued Services Revenue Accrued revenues are not recorded until adjusting entries are made at the end of the accounting period. These accrued revenues are earned but unrecorded because either the buyer has not yet paid for them or the seller has not yet billed the buyer. FastForward provides an example.

Step 1: In the second week of December, it agreed to provide 30 days of consulting services to a local fitness club for a fixed fee of $2,700. The terms of the initial agreement call for FastForward to provide services from December 12, 2011, through January 10, 2012, or 30 days of service. The club agrees to pay FastForward $2,700 on January 10, 2012, when the service period is complete.

Step 2: At December 31, 2011, 20 days of services have already been provided. Since the contracted services have not yet been entirely provided, FastForward has neither billed the club nor recorded the services already provided. Still, FastForward has earned two-thirds of the 30-day fee, or $1,800 ($2,700 × 20/30). The *revenue recognition principle* implies that it must report the $1,800 on the December income statement. The balance sheet also must report that the club owes FastForward $1,800.

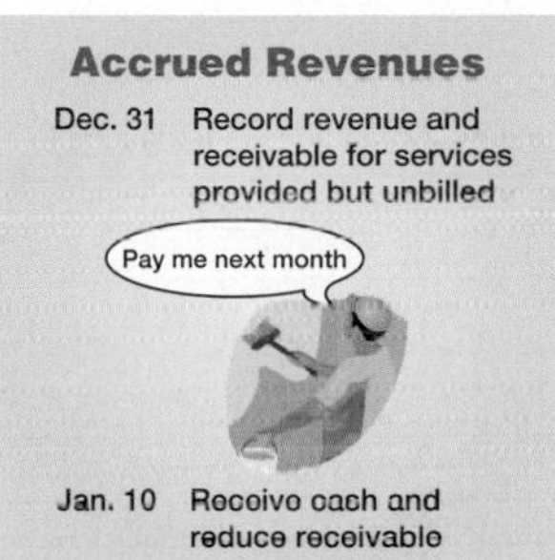

Accrued Revenues
Dec. 31 Record revenue and receivable for services provided but unbilled
Pay me next month
Jan. 10 Receive cash and reduce receivable

Step 3: The year-end adjusting entry to account for accrued services revenue is

Assets	=	Liabilities	+	Equity
+1,800				+1,800

	Adjustment (*f*)		
Dec. 31	Accounts Receivable	1,800	
	Consulting Revenue		1,800
	To record 20 days' accrued revenue.		

Accounts Receivable			106
Dec. 12	1,900	Dec. 22	1,900
31	**1,800**		
Balance	1,800		

Consulting Revenue			403
		Dec. 5	4,200
		12	1,600
		31	250
		31	**1,800**
		Balance	7,850

Example: What is the adjusting entry if the 30-day consulting period began on December 22? *Answer:* One-third of the fee is earned:
Accounts Receivable 900
Consulting Revenue 900

Explanation Accounts receivable are reported on the balance sheet at $1,800, and the $7,850 total of consulting revenue is reported on the income statement. *Not* making the adjustment would understate (1) both consulting revenue and net income by $1,800 in the December income statement and (2) both accounts receivable (assets) and equity by $1,800 on the December 31 balance sheet. The following table highlights the adjustment for accrued revenue.

Before Adjustment	Adjustment	After Adjustment
Accounts Receivable = $0	**Add $1,800 to Accounts Receivable** **Add $1,800 to Consulting Revenue**	**Accounts Receivable = $1,800**
Reports $0 from revenue earned but not yet received in cash.	Record 20 days of earned consulting revenue, which is 20/30 of total contract amount.	Reports $1,800 in accounts receivable from consulting services provided.

Accrued Interest Revenue In addition to the accrued interest expense we described earlier, interest can yield an accrued revenue when a debtor owes money (or other assets) to a company. If a company is holding notes or accounts receivable that produce interest revenue, we must adjust the accounts to record any earned and yet uncollected interest revenue. The adjusting entry is similar to the one for accruing services revenue. Specifically, we debit Interest Receivable (asset) and credit Interest Revenue.

Future Receipt of Accrued Revenues Accrued revenues at the end of one accounting period result in *cash receipts* in a *future period*(s). To illustrate, recall that FastForward made an adjusting entry for $1,800 to record 20 days' accrued revenue earned from its consulting contract. When FastForward receives $2,700 cash on January 10 for the entire contract amount, it makes the following entry to remove the accrued asset (accounts receivable) and recognize the revenue earned in January. The $2,700 debit reflects the cash received. The $1,800 credit reflects the removal of the receivable, and the $900 credit records the revenue earned in January.

Assets	=	Liabilities	+	Equity
+2,700				+900
−1,800				

Jan. 10	Cash	2,700	
	Accounts Receivable (20 days at $90 per day)		1,800
	Consulting Revenue (10 days at $90 per day)		900
	Received cash for the accrued asset and recorded earned consulting revenue for January.		

Answer — p. 116

Loan Officer The owner of an electronics store applies for a business loan. The store's financial statements reveal large increases in current-year revenues and income. Analysis shows that these increases are due to a promotion that let consumers buy now and pay nothing until January 1 of next year. The store recorded these sales as accrued revenue. Does your analysis raise any concerns? ■

Links to Financial Statements

A1 Explain how accounting adjustments link to financial statements.

The process of adjusting accounts is intended to bring an asset or liability account balance to its correct amount. It also updates a related expense or revenue account. These adjustments are necessary for transactions and events that extend over more than one period. (Adjusting entries are posted like any other entry.)

Exhibit 3.12 summarizes the four types of transactions requiring adjustment. Understanding this exhibit is important to understanding the adjusting process and its importance to financial statements. Remember that each adjusting entry affects one or more income statement accounts *and* one or more balance sheet accounts (but never cash).

EXHIBIT 3.12

Summary of Adjustments and Financial Statement Links

	BEFORE Adjusting		
Category	**Balance Sheet**	**Income Statement**	**Adjusting Entry**
Prepaid expenses†	Asset overstated Equity overstated	Expense understated	**Dr. Expense** **Cr. Asset***
Unearned revenues†	Liability overstated Equity understated	Revenue understated	**Dr. Liability** **Cr. Revenue**
Accrued expenses	Liability understated Equity overstated	Expense understated	**Dr. Expense** **Cr. Liability**
Accrued revenues	Asset understated Equity understated	Revenue understated	**Dr. Asset** **Cr. Revenue**

* For depreciation, the credit is to Accumulated Depreciation (contra asset).

† Exhibit assumes that prepaid expenses are initially recorded as assets and that unearned revenues are initially recorded as liabilities.

Information about some adjustments is not always available until several days or even weeks after the period-end. This means that some adjusting and closing entries are recorded later than, but dated as of, the last day of the period. One example is a company that receives a utility bill on January 10 for costs incurred for the month of December. When it receives the bill, the company records the expense and the payable as of December 31. Other examples include long-distance phone usage and costs of many Web billings. The December income statement reflects these additional expenses incurred, and the December 31 balance sheet includes these payables, although the amounts were not actually known on December 31.

Decision Ethics

Answer — p. 116

Financial Officer At year-end, the president instructs you, the financial officer, not to record accrued expenses until next year because they will not be paid until then. The president also directs you to record in current-year sales a recent purchase order from a customer that requires merchandise to be delivered two weeks after the year-end. Your company would report a net income instead of a net loss if you carry out these instructions. What do you do? ■

Quick Check

Answers — p. 116

6. If an adjusting entry for accrued revenues of $200 at year-end is omitted, what is this error's effect on the year-end income statement and balance sheet?
7. What is a contra account? Explain its purpose.
8. What is an accrued expense? Give an example.
9. Describe how an unearned revenue arises. Give an example.

Adjusted Trial Balance

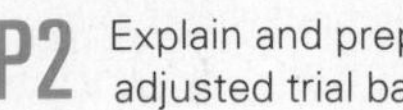

Explain and prepare an adjusted trial balance.

An **unadjusted trial balance** is a list of accounts and balances prepared *before* adjustments are recorded. An **adjusted trial balance** is a list of accounts and balances prepared *after* adjusting entries have been recorded and posted to the ledger.

Exhibit 3.13 shows both the unadjusted and the adjusted trial balances for FastForward at December 31, 2011. The order of accounts in the trial balance is usually set up to match the order in the chart of accounts. Several new accounts arise from the adjusting entries.

EXHIBIT 3.13

Unadjusted and Adjusted Trial Balances

FASTFORWARD
Trial Balances
December 31, 2011

Acct. No.	Account Title	Unadjusted Trial Balance		Adjustments		Adjusted Trial Balance	
		Dr.	Cr.	Dr.	Cr.	Dr.	Cr.
101	Cash	$ 4,350				$ 4,350	
106	Accounts receivable	0		(f) $1,800		1,800	
126	Supplies	9,720			(b) $1,050	8,670	
128	Prepaid insurance	2,400			(a) 100	2,300	
167	Equipment	26,000				26,000	
168	Accumulated depreciation—Equip.		$ 0		(c) 375		$ 375
201	Accounts payable		6,200				6,200
209	Salaries payable		0		(e) 210		210
236	Unearned consulting revenue		3,000	(d) 250			2,750
301	C. Taylor, Capital		30,000				30,000
302	C. Taylor, Withdrawals	200				200	
403	Consulting revenue		5,800		(d) 250		7,850
					(f) 1,800		
406	Rental revenue		300				300
612	Depreciation expense—Equip.	0		(c) 375		375	
622	Salaries expense	1,400		(e) 210		1,610	
637	Insurance expense	0		(a) 100		100	
640	Rent expense	1,000				1,000	
652	Supplies expense	0		(b) 1,050		1,050	
690	Utilities expense	230				230	
	Totals	$45,300	$45,300	$3,785	$3,785	$47,685	$47,685

Each adjustment (see middle columns) is identified by a letter in parentheses that links it to an adjusting entry explained earlier. Each amount in the Adjusted Trial Balance columns is computed by taking that account's amount from the Unadjusted Trial Balance columns and adding or subtracting any adjustment(s). To illustrate, Supplies has a $9,720 Dr. balance in the unadjusted columns. Subtracting the $1,050 Cr. amount shown in the adjustments columns yields an adjusted $8,670 Dr. balance for Supplies. An account can have more than one adjustment, such as for Consulting Revenue. Also, some accounts might not require adjustment for this period, such as Accounts Payable.

PREPARING FINANCIAL STATEMENTS

P3 Prepare financial statements from an adjusted trial balance.

Point: **Sarbanes-Oxley Act** requires that financial statements filed with the SEC be certified by the CEO and CFO, including a declaration that the statements fairly present the issuer's operations and financial condition. Violators can receive fines and/or prison terms.

We can prepare financial statements directly from information in the *adjusted* trial balance. An adjusted trial balance (see the right-most columns in Exhibit 3.13) includes all accounts and balances appearing in financial statements, and is easier to work from than the entire ledger when preparing financial statements.

Exhibit 3.14 shows how revenue and expense balances are transferred from the adjusted trial balance to the income statement (red lines). The net income and the withdrawals amount are then used to prepare the statement of owner's equity (black lines). Asset and liability balances on the adjusted trial balance are then transferred to the balance sheet (blue lines). The ending capital is determined on the statement of owner's equity and transferred to the balance sheet (green lines).

EXHIBIT 3.14

Preparing Financial Statements (Adjusted Trial Balance from Exhibit 3.13)

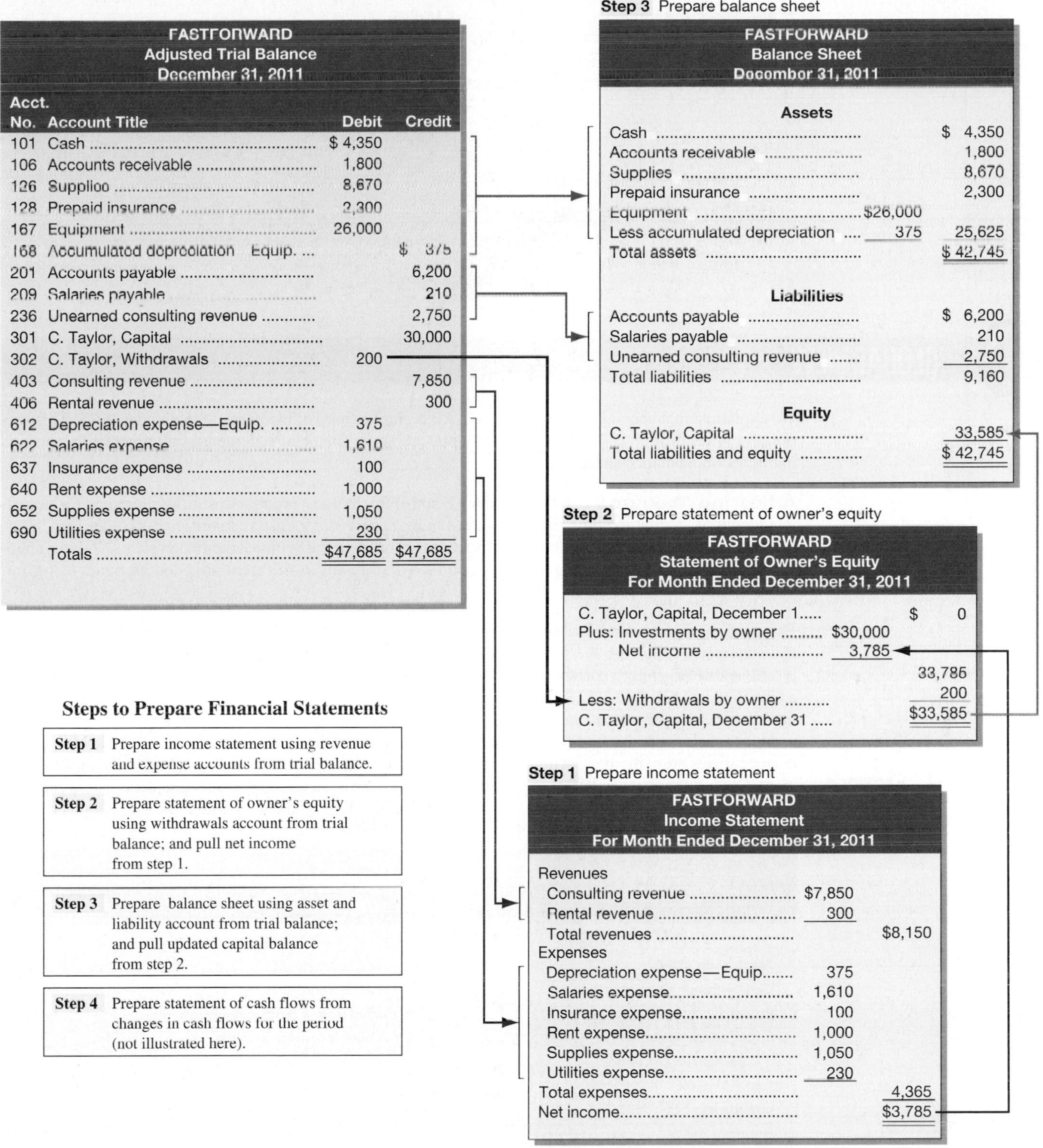

FASTFORWARD
Adjusted Trial Balance
December 31, 2011

Acct. No.	Account Title	Debit	Credit
101	Cash	$ 4,350	
106	Accounts receivable	1,800	
126	Supplies	8,670	
128	Prepaid insurance	2,300	
167	Equipment	26,000	
168	Accumulated depreciation—Equip.		$ 375
201	Accounts payable		6,200
209	Salaries payable		210
236	Unearned consulting revenue		2,750
301	C. Taylor, Capital		30,000
302	C. Taylor, Withdrawals	200	
403	Consulting revenue		7,850
406	Rental revenue		300
612	Depreciation expense—Equip.	375	
622	Salaries expense	1,610	
637	Insurance expense	100	
640	Rent expense	1,000	
652	Supplies expense	1,050	
690	Utilities expense	230	
	Totals	$47,685	$47,685

Step 3 Prepare balance sheet

FASTFORWARD
Balance Sheet
December 31, 2011

Assets		
Cash		$ 4,350
Accounts receivable		1,800
Supplies		8,670
Prepaid insurance		2,300
Equipment	$26,000	
Less accumulated depreciation	375	25,625
Total assets		$ 42,745
Liabilities		
Accounts payable		$ 6,200
Salaries payable		210
Unearned consulting revenue		2,750
Total liabilities		9,160
Equity		
C. Taylor, Capital		33,585
Total liabilities and equity		$ 42,745

Step 2 Prepare statement of owner's equity

FASTFORWARD
Statement of Owner's Equity
For Month Ended December 31, 2011

C. Taylor, Capital, December 1		$ 0
Plus: Investments by owner	$30,000	
Net income	3,785	33,785
Less: Withdrawals by owner		200
C. Taylor, Capital, December 31		$33,585

Step 1 Prepare income statement

FASTFORWARD
Income Statement
For Month Ended December 31, 2011

Revenues		
Consulting revenue	$7,850	
Rental revenue	300	
Total revenues		$8,150
Expenses		
Depreciation expense—Equip.	375	
Salaries expense	1,610	
Insurance expense	100	
Rent expense	1,000	
Supplies expense	1,050	
Utilities expense	230	
Total expenses		4,365
Net income		$3,785

Steps to Prepare Financial Statements

Step 1	Prepare income statement using revenue and expense accounts from trial balance.
Step 2	Prepare statement of owner's equity using withdrawals account from trial balance; and pull net income from step 1.
Step 3	Prepare balance sheet using asset and liability account from trial balance; and pull updated capital balance from step 2.
Step 4	Prepare statement of cash flows from changes in cash flows for the period (not illustrated here).

We prepare financial statements in the following order: income statement, statement of owner's equity, and balance sheet. This order makes sense because the balance sheet uses information from the statement of owner's equity, which in turn uses information from the income statement. The statement of cash flows is usually the final statement prepared.

Point: Each trial balance amount is used in only *one* financial statement and, when financial statements are completed, each account will have been used once.

Quick Check

Answers — p. 116

10. Music-Mart records $1,000 of accrued salaries on December 31. Five days later, on January 5 (the next payday), salaries of $7,000 are paid. What is the January 5 entry?
11. Jordan Air has the following information in its unadjusted and adjusted trial balances. What are the adjusting entries that Jordan Air likely recorded?

	Unadjusted		Adjusted	
	Debit	Credit	Debit	Credit
Prepaid insurance	$6,200		$5,900	
Salaries payable		$ 0		$1,400

12. What accounts are taken from the adjusted trial balance to prepare an income statement?
13. In preparing financial statements from an adjusted trial balance, what statement is usually prepared second?

GLOBAL VIEW

We explained that accounting under U.S. GAAP is similar, but not identical, to that under IFRS. This section discusses differences in adjusting accounts, preparing financial statements, and reporting assets and liabilities on a balance sheet.

Adjusting Accounts Both U.S. GAAP and IFRS include broad and similar guidance for adjusting accounts. Although some variations exist in revenue and expense recognition and other principles, all of the adjustments in this chapter are accounted for identically under the two systems. In later chapters we describe how certain assets and liabilities can result in different adjusted amounts using fair value measurements.

Preparing Financial Statements Both U.S. GAAP and IFRS prepare the same four basic financial statements following the same process discussed in this chapter. Chapter 2 explained how both U.S. GAAP and IFRS require current items to be separated from noncurrent items on the balance sheet (yielding a classified balance sheet). U.S. GAAP balance sheets report current items first. Assets are listed from most liquid to least liquid, where liquid refers to the ease of converting an asset to cash. Liabilities are listed from nearest to maturity to furthest from maturity, maturity refers to the nearness of paying off the liability. IFRS balance sheets normally present noncurrent items first (and equity before liabilities), but this is not a requirement. Other differences with financial statements exist, which we identify in later chapters. **Nokia** provides the following example of IFRS reporting for its assets, liabilities, and equity within the balance sheet:

NOKIA

NOKIA
Balance Sheet (in EUR millions)
December 31, 2009

Assets		Equity and Liabilities	
Noncurrent assets		Total equity	14,749
Goodwill and other intangibles	8,076	Noncurrent liabilities	
Property, plant and equipment	1,867	Long-term interest-bearing liabilities	4,432
Other noncurrent assets	2,182	Other long-term liabilities	1,369
Total noncurrent assets	12,125	Total noncurrent liabilities	5,801
Current assets		Current liabilities	
Inventories	1,865	Current portion of long-term loans........	44
Accounts receivable, net	7,981	Short-term borrowings and other liabilities ...	972
Prepaid expenses and accrued income	4,551	Accounts payable	4,950
Other current assets	8,074	Accrued expenses	6,504
Cash	1,142	Provisions	2,718
Total current assets	23,613	Total current liabilities	15,188
Total assets	35,738	Total equity and liabilities	35,738

IFRS

Revenue and expense recognition are key to recording accounting adjustments. IFRS tends to be more *principles-based* relative to U.S. GAAP, which is viewed as more *rules-based*. A principles-based system depends heavily on control procedures to reduce the potential for fraud or misconduct. Failure in judgment led to improper accounting adjustments at **Fannie Mae**, **Xerox**, **WorldCom**, and others. A KPMG 2009 survey of accounting and finance employees found that 13% of them had witnessed falsification or manipulation of accounting data within the past year. Internal controls and governance processes are directed at curtailing such behavior. ■

Profit Margin — Decision Analysis

A2 Compute profit margin and describe its use in analyzing company performance.

A useful measure of a company's operating results is the ratio of its net income to net sales. This ratio is called **profit margin,** or *return on sales,* and is computed as in Exhibit 3.15.

EXHIBIT 3.15

Profit Margin

$$\textbf{Profit margin} = \frac{\textbf{Net income}}{\textbf{Net sales}}$$

This ratio is interpreted as reflecting the percent of profit in each dollar of sales. To illustrate how we compute and use profit margin, let's look at the results of **Limited Brands, Inc.**, in Exhibit 3.16 for its fiscal years 2006 through 2010.

EXHIBIT 3.16

Limited Brands' Profit Margin

$ in millions	2010	2009	2008	2007	2006
Net income	$ 448	$ 220	$ 718	$ 676	$ 683
Net sales	$8,632	$9,043	$10,134	$10,671	$9,699
Profit margin	**5.2%**	**2.4%**	**7.1%**	**6.3%**	**7.0%**
Industry profit margin	0.9%	0.3%	1.1%	1.6%	1.5%

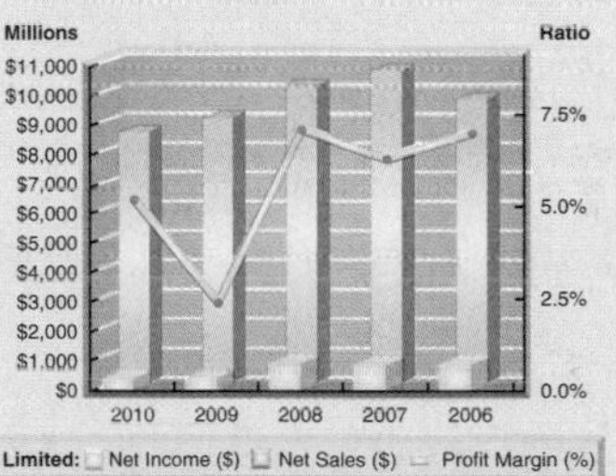

The Limited's average profit margin is 5.6% during this 5-year period. This favorably compares to the average industry profit margin of 1.1%. However, Limited's profit margin has declined in the most recent two years—from 7.1% in 2008 to 2.4% and 5.2% for the recent recessionary periods (see margin graph). Future success depends on Limited maintaining its market share and increasing its profit margin.

DEMONSTRATION PROBLEM 1

The following information relates to Fanning's Electronics on December 31, 2011. The company, which uses the calendar year as its annual reporting period, initially records prepaid and unearned items in balance sheet accounts (assets and liabilities, respectively).

a. The company's weekly payroll is $8,750, paid each Friday for a five-day workweek. Assume December 31, 2011, falls on a Monday, but the employees will not be paid their wages until Friday, January 4, 2012.

b. Eighteen months earlier, on July 1, 2010, the company purchased equipment that cost $20,000. Its useful life is predicted to be five years, at which time the equipment is expected to be worthless (zero salvage value).

c. On October 1, 2011, the company agreed to work on a new housing development. The company is paid \$120,000 on October 1 in advance of future installation of similar alarm systems in 24 new homes. That amount was credited to the Unearned Services Revenue account. Between October 1 and December 31, work on 20 homes was completed.

d. On September 1, 2011, the company purchased a 12-month insurance policy for \$1,800. The transaction was recorded with an \$1,800 debit to Prepaid Insurance.

e. On December 29, 2011, the company completed a \$7,000 service that has not been billed and not recorded as of December 31, 2011.

Required

1. Prepare any necessary adjusting entries on December 31, 2011, in relation to transactions and events *a* through *e*.
2. Prepare T-accounts for the accounts affected by adjusting entries, and post the adjusting entries. Determine the adjusted balances for the Unearned Revenue and the Prepaid Insurance accounts.
3. Complete the following table and determine the amounts and effects of your adjusting entries on the year 2011 income statement and the December 31, 2011, balance sheet. Use up (down) arrows to indicate an increase (decrease) in the Effect columns.

Entry	Amount in the Entry	Effect on Net Income	Effect on Total Assets	Effect on Total Liabilities	Effect on Total Equity

PLANNING THE SOLUTION

- Analyze each situation to determine which accounts need to be updated with an adjustment.
- Calculate the amount of each adjustment and prepare the necessary journal entries.
- Show the amount of each adjustment in the designated accounts, determine the adjusted balance, and identify the balance sheet classification of the account.
- Determine each entry's effect on net income for the year and on total assets, total liabilities, and total equity at the end of the year.

SOLUTION TO DEMONSTRATION PROBLEM 1

1. Adjusting journal entries.

(*a*) Dec. 31	Wages Expense	1,750	
	Wages Payable		1,750
	To accrue wages for the last day of the year (\$8,750 × 1/5).		
(*b*) Dec. 31	Depreciation Expense—Equipment	4,000	
	Accumulated Depreciation—Equipment		4,000
	To record depreciation expense for the year (\$20,000/5 years = \$4,000 per year).		
(*c*) Dec. 31	Unearned Services Revenue	100,000	
	Services Revenue		100,000
	To recognize services revenue earned (\$120,000 × 20/24).		
(*d*) Dec. 31	Insurance Expense	600	
	Prepaid Insurance		600
	To adjust for expired portion of insurance (\$1,800 × 4/12).		
(*e*) Dec. 31	Accounts Receivable	7,000	
	Services Revenue		7,000
	To record services revenue earned.		

2. T-accounts for adjusting journal entries *a* through *e*.

Wages Expense

(a)	1,750		

Wages Payable

		(a)	1,750

Depreciation Expense—Equipment

(b)	4,000		

Accumulated Depreciation—Equipment

		(b)	4,000

Unearned Revenue

		Unadj. Bal.	120,000
(c)	100,000		
		Adj. Bal.	20,000

Services Revenue

		(c)	100,000
		(e)	7,000
		Adj. Bal.	107,000

Insurance Expense

(d)	600		

Prepaid Insurance

Unadj. Bal.	1,800		
		(d)	600
Adj. Bal.	1,200		

Accounts Receivable

(e)	7,000		

3. Financial statement effects of adjusting journal entries.

Entry	Amount in the Entry	Effect on Net Income	Effect on Total Assets	Effect on Total Liabilities	Effect on Total Equity
a	$ 1,750	$ 1,750 ↓	No effect	$ 1,750 ↑	$ 1,750 ↓
b	4,000	4,000 ↓	$4,000 ↓	No effect	4,000 ↓
c	100,000	100,000 ↑	No effect	$100,000 ↓	100,000 ↑
d	600	600 ↓	$ 600 ↓	No effect	600 ↓
e	7,000	7,000 ↑	$7,000 ↑	No effect	7,000 ↑

DEMONSTRATION PROBLEM 2

Use the following adjusted trial balance to answer questions 1–3.

CHOI COMPANY
Adjusted Trial Balance
December 31

	Debit	Credit
Cash	$ 3,050	
Accounts receivable	400	
Prepaid insurance	830	
Supplies	80	
Equipment	217,200	
Accumulated depreciation—Equipment		$ 29,100
Wages payable		880

[continued on next page]

[continued from previous page]

Interest payable		3,600
Unearned rent		460
Long-term notes payable		150,000
M. Choi, Capital		40,340
M. Choi, Withdrawals	21,000	
Rent earned		57,500
Wages expense	25,000	
Utilities expense	1,900	
Insurance expense	3,200	
Supplies expense	250	
Depreciation expense—Equipment	5,970	
Interest expense	3,000	
Totals	$281,880	$281,880

1. Prepare the annual income statement from the adjusted trial balance of Choi Company.

Answer:

CHOI COMPANY
Income Statement
For Year Ended December 31

Revenues		
Rent earned		$57,500
Expenses		
Wages expense	$25,000	
Utilities expense	1,900	
Insurance expense	3,200	
Supplies expense	250	
Depreciation expense—Equipment	5,970	
Interest expense	3,000	
Total expenses		39,320
Net income		$18,180

2. Prepare a statement of owner's equity from the adjusted trial balance of Choi Company. Choi's capital account balance of $40,340 consists of a $30,340 balance from the prior year-end, plus a $10,000 owner investment during the current year.

Answer:

CHOI COMPANY
Statement of Owner's Equity
For Year Ended December 31

M. Choi, Capital, December 31 prior year-end		$30,340
Plus: Owner investments	$10,000	
Net income	18,180	28,180
		58,520
Less: Withdrawals by owner		21,000
M. Choi, Capital, December 31 current year-end		$37,520

3. Prepare a balance sheet from the adjusted trial balance of Choi Company.

Answer:

CHOI COMPANY Balance Sheet December 31		
Assets		
Cash		$ 3,050
Accounts receivable		400
Prepaid insurance		830
Supplies		80
Equipment	$217,200	
Less accumulated depreciation	29,100	188,100
Total assets		$192,460
Liabilities		
Wages payable		$ 880
Interest payable		3,600
Unearned rent		460
Long-term notes payable		150,000
Total liabilities		154,940
Equity		
M. Choi, Capital		37,520
Total liabilities and equity		$192,460

APPENDIX

Alternative Accounting for Prepayments 3A

This appendix explains an alternative in accounting for prepaid expenses and unearned revenues.

P4 Explain the alternatives in accounting for prepaids.

Recording Prepayment of Expenses in Expense Accounts An alternative method is to record *all* prepaid expenses with debits to expense accounts. If any prepaids remain unused or unexpired at the end of an accounting period, then adjusting entries must transfer the cost of the unused portions from expense accounts to prepaid expense (asset) accounts. This alternative method is acceptable. The financial statements are identical under either method, but the adjusting entries are different. To illustrate the differences between these two methods, let's look at FastForward's cash payment of December 6 for 24 months of insurance coverage beginning on December 1. FastForward recorded that payment with a debit to an asset account, but it could have recorded a debit to an expense account. These alternatives are shown in Exhibit 3A.1.

EXHIBIT 3A.1

Alternative Initial Entries for Prepaid Expenses

		Payment Recorded as Asset		Payment Recorded as Expense	
Dec. 6	Prepaid Insurance	2,400			
	Cash		2,400		
Dec. 6	Insurance Expense			2,400	
	Cash				2,400

At the end of its accounting period on December 31, insurance protection for one month has expired. This means $100 ($2,400/24) of insurance coverage expired and is an expense for December. The adjusting entry depends on how the original payment was recorded. This is shown in Exhibit 3A.2.

EXHIBIT 3A.2

Adjusting Entry for Prepaid Expenses for the Two Alternatives

		Payment Recorded as Asset		Payment Recorded as Expense	
Dec. 31	Insurance Expense	100			
	Prepaid Insurance		100		
Dec. 31	Prepaid Insurance			2,300	
	Insurance Expense				2,300

When these entries are posted to the accounts in the ledger, we can see that these two methods give identical results. The December 31 adjusted account balances in Exhibit 3A.3 show Prepaid Insurance of $2,300 and Insurance Expense of $100 for both methods.

EXHIBIT 3A.3

Account Balances under Two Alternatives for Recording Prepaid Expenses

Payment Recorded as Asset

Prepaid Insurance			128
Dec. 6	2,400	Dec. 31	100
Balance	**2,300**		

Insurance Expense			637
Dec. 31	**100**		

Payment Recorded as Expense

Prepaid Insurance			128
Dec. 31	**2,300**		

Insurance Expense			637
Dec. 6	2,400	Dec. 31	2,300
Balance	**100**		

Recording Prepayment of Revenues in Revenue Accounts As with prepaid expenses, an alternative method is to record *all* unearned revenues with credits to revenue accounts. If any revenues are unearned at the end of an accounting period, then adjusting entries must transfer the unearned portions from revenue accounts to unearned revenue (liability) accounts. This alternative method is acceptable. The adjusting entries are different for these two alternatives, but the financial statements are identical. To illustrate the accounting differences between these two methods, let's look at FastForward's December 26 receipt of $3,000 for consulting services covering the period December 27 to February 24. FastForward recorded this transaction with a credit to a liability account. The alternative is to record it with a credit to a revenue account, as shown in Exhibit 3A.4.

EXHIBIT 3A.4

Alternative Initial Entries for Unearned Revenues

		Receipt Recorded as Liability		Receipt Recorded as Revenue	
Dec. 26	Cash	3,000			
	Unearned Consulting Revenue		3,000		
Dec. 26	Cash			3,000	
	Consulting Revenue				3,000

By the end of its accounting period on December 31, FastForward has earned $250 of this revenue. This means $250 of the liability has been satisfied. Depending on how the initial receipt is recorded, the adjusting entry is as shown in Exhibit 3A.5.

EXHIBIT 3A.5

Adjusting Entry for Unearned Revenues for the Two Alternatives

		Receipt Recorded as Liability		Receipt Recorded as Revenue	
Dec. 31	Unearned Consulting Revenue	250			
	Consulting Revenue		250		
Dec. 31	Consulting Revenue			2,750	
	Unearned Consulting Revenue				2,750

After adjusting entries are posted, the two alternatives give identical results. The December 31 adjusted account balances in Exhibit 3A.6 show unearned consulting revenue of $2,750 and consulting revenue of $250 for both methods.

EXHIBIT 3A.6

Account Balances under Two Alternatives for Recording Unearned Revenues

Receipt Recorded as Liability

Unearned Consulting Revenue			236
Dec. 31	250	Dec. 26	3,000
		Balance	**2,750**

Consulting Revenue			403
		Dec. 31	**250**

Receipt Recorded as Revenue

Unearned Consulting Revenue			236
		Dec. 31	**2,750**

Consulting Revenue			403
Dec. 31	2,750	Dec. 26	3,000
		Balance	**250**

Summary

C1 Explain the importance of periodic reporting and the time period assumption. The value of information is often linked to its timeliness. To provide timely information, accounting systems prepare periodic reports at regular intervals. The time period assumption presumes that an organization's activities can be divided into specific time periods for periodic reporting.

C2 Explain accrual accounting and how it improves financial statements. Accrual accounting recognizes revenue when earned and expenses when incurred—not necessarily when cash inflows and outflows occur. This information is valuable in assessing a company's financial position and performance.

C3 Identify the types of adjustments and their purpose. Adjustments can be grouped according to the timing of cash receipts and cash payments relative to when they are recognized as revenues or expenses as follows: prepaid expenses, unearned revenues, accrued expenses, and accrued revenues. Adjusting entries are necessary so that revenues, expenses, assets, and liabilities are correctly reported.

A1 Explain how accounting adjustments link to financial statements. Accounting adjustments bring an asset or liability account balance to its correct amount. They also update related expense or revenue accounts. Every adjusting entry affects one or more income statement accounts *and* one or more balance sheet accounts. An adjusting entry never affects cash.

A2 Compute profit margin and describe its use in analyzing company performance. *Profit margin* is defined as the reporting period's net income divided by its net sales. Profit margin reflects on a company's earnings activities by showing how much income is in each dollar of sales.

P1 Prepare and explain adjusting entries. *Prepaid expenses* refer to items paid for in advance of receiving their benefits. Prepaid expenses are assets. Adjusting entries for prepaids involve increasing (debiting) expenses and decreasing (crediting) assets. *Unearned* (or *prepaid*) *revenues* refer to cash received in advance of providing products and services. Unearned revenues are liabilities. Adjusting entries for unearned revenues involve increasing (crediting) revenues and decreasing (debiting) unearned revenues. *Accrued expenses* refer to costs incurred in a period that are both unpaid and unrecorded. Adjusting entries for recording accrued expenses involve increasing (debiting) expenses and increasing (crediting) liabilities. *Accrued revenues* refer to revenues earned in a period that are both unrecorded and not yet received in cash. Adjusting entries for recording accrued revenues involve increasing (debiting) assets and increasing (crediting) revenues.

P2 Explain and prepare an adjusted trial balance. An adjusted trial balance is a list of accounts and balances prepared after recording and posting adjusting entries. Financial statements are often prepared from the adjusted trial balance.

P3 Prepare financial statements from an adjusted trial balance. Revenue and expense balances are reported on the income statement. Asset, liability, and equity balances are reported on the balance sheet. We usually prepare statements in the following order: income statement, statement of owner's equity, balance sheet, and statement of cash flows.

P4^A Explain the alternatives in accounting for prepaids. Charging all prepaid expenses to expense accounts when they are purchased is acceptable. When this is done, adjusting entries must transfer any unexpired amounts from expense accounts to asset accounts. Crediting all unearned revenues to revenue accounts when cash is received is also acceptable. In this case, the adjusting entries must transfer any unearned amounts from revenue accounts to unearned revenue accounts.

Guidance Answers to Decision Maker and Decision Ethics

Investor Prepaid expenses are items paid for in advance of receiving their benefits. They are assets and are expensed as they are used up. The publishing company's treatment of the signing bonus is acceptable provided future book sales can at least match the $500,000 expense. As an investor, you are concerned about the risk of future book sales. The riskier the likelihood of future book sales is, the more likely your analysis is to treat the $500,000, or a portion of it, as an expense, not a prepaid expense (asset).

Entrepreneur Depreciation is a process of cost allocation, not asset valuation. Knowing the depreciation schedule is not especially useful in your estimation of what the building and equipment are currently worth. Your own assessment of the age, quality, and usefulness of the building and equipment is more important.

Loan Officer Your concern in lending to this store arises from analysis of current-year sales. While increased revenues and income are fine, your concern is with collectibility of these promotional sales. If the owner sold products to customers with poor records of paying bills, then collectibility of these sales is low. Your analysis must assess this possibility and recognize any expected losses.

Financial Officer Omitting accrued expenses and recognizing revenue early can mislead financial statement users. One action is to request a second meeting with the president so you can explain that accruing expenses when incurred and recognizing revenue when earned are required practices. If the president persists, you might discuss the situation with legal counsel and any auditors involved. Your ethical action might cost you this job, but the potential pitfalls for falsification of statements, reputation and personal integrity loss, and other costs are too great.

Guidance Answers to Quick Checks

1. An annual reporting (or accounting) period covers one year and refers to the preparation of annual financial statements. The annual reporting period is not always a calendar year that ends on December 31. An organization can adopt a fiscal year consisting of any consecutive 12 months or 52 weeks.
2. Interim financial statements (covering less than one year) are prepared to provide timely information to decision makers.
3. The revenue recognition principle and the matching principle lead most directly to the adjusting process.
4. No. Cash basis accounting is not consistent with the matching principle because it reports revenue when received, not necessarily when earned, and expenses when paid, not necessarily in the period when the expenses were incurred as a result of the revenues earned.
5. No expense is reported in 2012. Under cash basis accounting, the entire $4,800 is reported as an expense in April 2011 when the premium is paid.
6. If the accrued revenues adjustment of $200 is not made, then both revenues and net income are understated by $200 on the current year's income statement, and both assets and equity are understated by $200 on the balance sheet.
7. A contra account is an account that is subtracted from the balance of a related account. Use of a contra account provides more information than simply reporting a net amount.
8. An accrued expense is a cost incurred in a period that is both unpaid and unrecorded prior to adjusting entries. One example is salaries earned but not yet paid at period-end.
9. An unearned revenue arises when a firm receives cash (or other assets) from a customer before providing the services or products to the customer. A magazine subscription paid in advance is one example; season ticket sales is another.
10.

Salaries Payable	1,000	
Salaries Expense	6,000	
Cash		7,000
Paid salary including accrual from December.		

11. The probable adjusting entries of Jordan Air are:

Insurance Expense	300	
Prepaid Insurance		300
To record insurance expired.		
Salaries Expense	1,400	
Salaries Payable		1,400
To record accrued salaries.		

12. Revenue accounts and expense accounts.
13. Statement of owner's equity.

Key Terms

mhhe.com/wildFAP20e

Accounting period (p. 94)
Accrual basis accounting (p. 95)
Accrued expenses (p. 101)
Accrued revenues (p. 103)
Adjusted trial balance (p. 106)
Adjusting entry (p. 96)
Annual financial statements (p. 94)
Book value (p. 100)
Cash basis accounting (p. 95)
Contra account (p. 99)
Depreciation (p. 99)
Expense recognition (or **matching**) **principle** (p. 96)
Fiscal year (p. 95)
Interim financial statements (p. 94)
Natural business year (p. 95)
Plant assets (p. 99)
Prepaid expenses (p. 97)
Profit margin (p. 109)
Straight-line depreciation method (p. 99)
Time period assumption (p. 94)
Unadjusted trial balance (p. 106)
Unearned revenues (p. 100)

Multiple Choice Quiz

Answers on p. 135 mhhe.com/wildFAP20e

Additional Quiz Questions are available at the book's Website.

1. A company forgot to record accrued and unpaid employee wages of $350,000 at period-end. This oversight would
   a. Understate net income by $350,000.
   b. Overstate net income by $350,000.
   c. Have no effect on net income.
   d. Overstate assets by $350,000.
   e. Understate assets by $350,000.
2. Prior to recording adjusting entries, the Supplies account has a $450 debit balance. A physical count of supplies shows $125 of unused supplies still available. The required adjusting entry is:
   a. Debit Supplies $125; Credit Supplies Expense $125.
   b. Debit Supplies $325; Credit Supplies Expense $325.
   c. Debit Supplies Expense $325; Credit Supplies $325.
   d. Debit Supplies Expense $325; Credit Supplies $125.
   e. Debit Supplies Expense $125; Credit Supplies $125.
3. On May 1, 2011, a two-year insurance policy was purchased for $24,000 with coverage to begin immediately. What is the amount of insurance expense that appears on the company's income statement for the year ended December 31, 2011?
   a. $4,000
   b. $8,000
   c. $12,000
   d. $20,000
   e. $24,000
4. On November 1, 2011, Stockton Co. receives $3,600 cash from Hans Co. for consulting services to be provided evenly over the period November 1, 2011, to April 30, 2012—at which time Stockton credited $3,600 to Unearned Consulting Fees. The adjusting entry on December 31, 2011 (Stockton's year-end) would include a
   a. Debit to Unearned Consulting Fees for $1,200.
   b. Debit to Unearned Consulting Fees for $2,400.
   c. Credit to Consulting Fees Earned for $2,400.
   d. Debit to Consulting Fees Earned for $1,200.
   e. Credit to Cash for $3,600.
5. If a company had $15,000 in net income for the year, and its sales were $300,000 for the same year, what is its profit margin?
   a. 20%
   b. 2,000%
   c. $285,000
   d. $315,000
   e. 5%

[A] *Superscript letter A denotes assignments based on Appendix 3A.*
Icon denotes assignments that involve decision making.

Discussion Questions

1. What is the difference between the cash basis and the accrual basis of accounting?
2. Why is the accrual basis of accounting generally preferred over the cash basis?
3. What type of business is most likely to select a fiscal year that corresponds to its natural business year instead of the calendar year?
4. What is a prepaid expense and where is it reported in the financial statements?
5. What type of assets require adjusting entries to record depreciation?
6. What contra account is used when recording and reporting the effects of depreciation? Why is it used?
7. **Apple** has unearned revenue. What is unearned revenue and where is it reported in financial statements? Apple
8. What is an accrued revenue? Give an example.
9. [A] If a company initially records prepaid expenses with debits to expense accounts, what type of account is debited in the adjusting entries for those prepaid expenses?
10. Review the balance sheet of **Research In Motion** in Appendix A. Identify one asset account that requires adjustment before annual financial statements can be prepared. What would be the effect on the income statement if this asset account were not adjusted? RIM
11. Review the balance sheet of **Nokia** in Appendix A. Identify the amount for property, plant, and equipment. What adjusting entry is necessary (no numbers required) for this account when preparing financial statements? NOKIA
12. Refer to **Palm**'s balance sheet in Appendix A. If it made an adjustment for unpaid wages at year-end, where would the accrued wages be reported on its balance sheet? Palm

connect

QUICK STUDY

QS 3-1
Identifying accounting adjustments
P1

Classify the following adjusting entries as involving prepaid expenses (PE), unearned revenues (UR), accrued expenses (AE), or accrued revenues (AR).

a. ______ To record revenue earned that was previously received as cash in advance.
b. ______ To record annual depreciation expense.
c. ______ To record wages expense incurred but not yet paid (nor recorded).
d. ______ To record revenue earned but not yet billed (nor recorded).
e. ______ To record expiration of prepaid insurance.

QS 3-2
Adjusting prepaid expenses
P1

a. On July 1, 2011, Baxter Company paid $1,800 for six months of insurance coverage. No adjustments have been made to the Prepaid Insurance account, and it is now December 31, 2011. Prepare the journal entry to reflect expiration of the insurance as of December 31, 2011.

b. Tyrell Company has a Supplies account balance of $1,000 on January 1, 2011. During 2011, it purchased $3,000 of supplies. As of December 31, 2011, a supplies inventory shows $1,300 of supplies available. Prepare the adjusting journal entry to correctly report the balance of the Supplies account and the Supplies Expense account as of December 31, 2011.

QS 3-3
Adjusting for depreciation
P1

a. Carlos Company purchases $30,000 of equipment on January 1, 2011. The equipment is expected to last five years and be worth $5,000 at the end of that time. Prepare the entry to record one year's depreciation expense of $5,000 for the equipment as of December 31, 2011.

b. Chaves Company purchases $40,000 of land on January 1, 2011. The land is expected to last indefinitely. What depreciation adjustment, if any, should be made with respect to the Land account as of December 31, 2011?

QS 3-4
Adjusting for unearned revenues
A1 P1 

a. Eager Co. receives $20,000 cash in advance for 4 months of legal services on October 1, 2011, and records it by debiting Cash and crediting Unearned Revenue both for $20,000. It is now December 31, 2011, and Eager has provided legal services as planned. What adjusting entry should Eager make to account for the work performed from October 1 through December 31, 2011?

b. Rutherford Co. started a new publication called *Contest News*. Its subscribers pay $48 to receive 12 issues. With every new subscriber, Rutherford debits Cash and credits Unearned Subscription Revenue for the amounts received. The company has 100 new subscribers as of July 1, 2011. It sends *Contest News* to each of these subscribers every month from July through December. Assuming no changes in subscribers, prepare the journal entry that Rutherford must make as of December 31, 2011, to adjust the Subscription Revenue account and the Unearned Subscription Revenue account.

QS 3-5
Accruing salaries
A1 P1

Marsha Moder employs one college student every summer in her coffee shop. The student works the five weekdays and is paid on the following Monday. (For example, a student who works Monday through Friday, June 1 through June 5, is paid for that work on Monday, June 8.) Moder adjusts her books monthly, if needed, to show salaries earned but unpaid at month-end. The student works the last week of July—Friday is August 1. If the student earns $100 per day, what adjusting entry must Moder make on July 31 to correctly record accrued salaries expense for July?

QS 3-6
Recording and analyzing adjusting entries
A1

Adjusting entries affect at least one balance sheet account and at least one income statement account. For the following entries, identify the account to be debited and the account to be credited. Indicate which of the accounts is the income statement account and which is the balance sheet account.

a. Entry to record revenue earned that was previously received as cash in advance.
b. Entry to record annual depreciation expense.
c. Entry to record wage expenses incurred but not yet paid (nor recorded).
d. Entry to record revenue earned but not yet billed (nor recorded).
e. Entry to record expiration of prepaid insurance.

QS 3-7
Computing accrual and cash income
P1 C2 

In its first year of operations, Harden Co. earned $39,000 in revenues and received $33,000 cash from these customers. The company incurred expenses of $22,500 but had not paid $2,250 of them at year-end. The company also prepaid $3,750 cash for expenses that would be incurred the next year. Calculate the first year's net income under both the cash basis and the accrual basis of accounting.

QS 3-8
Interpreting adjusting entries
C2 P2

The following information is taken from Cruz Company's unadjusted and adjusted trial balances.

	Unadjusted		Adjusted	
	Debit	Credit	Debit	Credit
Prepaid insurance.	$4,100		$3,700	
Interest payable		$ 0		$800

Given this information, which of the following is likely included among its adjusting entries?

a. A $400 credit to Prepaid Insurance and an $800 debit to Interest Payable.
b. A $400 debit to Insurance Expense and an $800 debit to Interest Payable.
c. A $400 debit to Insurance Expense and an $800 debit to Interest Expense.

QS 3-9
Determining effects of adjusting entries
C3 A1 

In making adjusting entries at the end of its accounting period, Gomez Consulting failed to record $1,600 of insurance coverage that had expired. This $1,600 cost had been initially debited to the Prepaid Insurance account. The company also failed to record accrued salaries expense of $1,000. As a result of these two oversights, the financial statements for the reporting period will [choose one] (1) understate assets by $1,600; (2) understate expenses by $2,600; (3) understate net income by $1,000; or (4) overstate liabilities by $1,000.

QS 3-10
Preparing adjusting entries
C3 P1

During the year, Lyle Co. recorded prepayments of expenses in asset accounts, and cash receipts of unearned revenues in liability accounts. At the end of its annual accounting period, the company must make three adjusting entries: (1) accrue salaries expense, (2) adjust the Unearned Services Revenue account to recognize earned revenue, and (3) record services revenue earned for which cash will be received the following period. For each of these adjusting entries (1), (2), and (3), indicate the account from *a* through *i* to be debited and the account to be credited.

a. Prepaid Salaries	**d.** Salaries Payable	**g.** Unearned Services Revenue
b. Salaries Expense	**e.** Equipment	**h.** Accounts Receivable
c. Services Revenue	**f.** Cash	**i.** Accounts Payable

QS 3-11
Analyzing profit margin
A2

Yang Company reported net income of $37,925 and net sales of $390,000 for the current year. Calculate the company's profit margin and interpret the result. Assume that its competitors earn an average profit margin of 15%.

QS 3-12[A]
Preparing adjusting entries
C3 P4

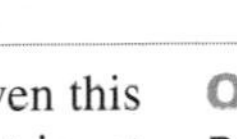

Diego Consulting initially records prepaid and unearned items in income statement accounts. Given this company's accounting practices, which of the following applies to the preparation of adjusting entries at the end of its first accounting period?

a. Earned but unbilled (and unrecorded) consulting fees are recorded with a debit to Unearned Consulting Fees and a credit to Consulting Fees Earned.
b. Unpaid salaries are recorded with a debit to Prepaid Salaries and a credit to Salaries Expense.
c. The cost of unused office supplies is recorded with a debit to Supplies Expense and a credit to Office Supplies.
d. Unearned fees (on which cash was received in advance earlier in the period) are recorded with a debit to Consulting Fees Earned and a credit to Unearned Consulting Fees.

QS 3-13
International accounting standards

Answer each of the following questions related to international accounting standards.

a. Do financial statements prepared under IFRS normally present assets from least liquid to most liquid or vice-versa?
b. Do financial statements prepared under IFRS normally present liabilities from furthest from maturity to nearest to maturity or vice-versa?

EXERCISES

Exercise 3-1
Classifying adjusting entries
C3

In the blank space beside each adjusting entry, enter the letter of the explanation *A* through *F* that most closely describes the entry.

A. To record this period's depreciation expense.
B. To record accrued salaries expense.
C. To record this period's use of a prepaid expense.
D. To record accrued interest revenue.
E. To record accrued interest expense.
F. To record the earning of previously unearned income.

		Account	Debit	Credit
B	1.	Salaries Expense	13,280	
		Salaries Payable		13,280
E	2.	Interest Expense	2,208	
		Interest Payable		2,208
C	3.	Insurance Expense	3,180	
		Prepaid Insurance		3,180
F	4.	Unearned Professional Fees	19,250	
		Professional Fees Earned		19,250
D	5.	Interest Receivable	3,300	
		Interest Revenue		3,300
A	6.	Depreciation Expense	38,217	
		Accumulated Depreciation		38,217

Exercise 3-2
Preparing adjusting entries
P1

For each of the following separate cases, prepare adjusting entries required of financial statements for the year ended (date of) December 31, 2011. (Assume that prepaid expenses are initially recorded in asset accounts and that fees collected in advance of work are initially recorded as liabilities.)

a. One-third of the work related to $30,000 cash received in advance is performed this period.
b. Wages of $9,000 are earned by workers but not paid as of December 31, 2011.
c. Depreciation on the company's equipment for 2011 is $19,127.
d. The Office Supplies account had a $480 debit balance on December 31, 2010. During 2011, $5,349 of office supplies are purchased. A physical count of supplies at December 31, 2011, shows $587 of supplies available.
e. The Prepaid Insurance account had a $5,000 balance on December 31, 2010. An analysis of insurance policies shows that $2,200 of unexpired insurance benefits remain at December 31, 2011.
f. The company has earned (but not recorded) $750 of interest from investments in CDs for the year ended December 31, 2011. The interest revenue will be received on January 10, 2012.
g. The company has a bank loan and has incurred (but not recorded) interest expense of $3,500 for the year ended December 31, 2011. The company must pay the interest on January 2, 2012.

Check (*e*) Dr. Insurance Expense, $2,800; (*f*) Cr. Interest Revenue, $750

Exercise 3-3
Preparing adjusting entries
P1

Prepare adjusting journal entries for the year ended (date of) December 31, 2011, for each of these separate situations. Assume that prepaid expenses are initially recorded in asset accounts. Also assume that fees collected in advance of work are initially recorded as liabilities.

a. Depreciation on the company's equipment for 2011 is computed to be $16,000.
b. The Prepaid Insurance account had a $7,000 debit balance at December 31, 2011, before adjusting for the costs of any expired coverage. An analysis of the company's insurance policies showed that $1,040 of unexpired insurance coverage remains.
c. The Office Supplies account had a $300 debit balance on December 31, 2010; and $2,680 of office supplies were purchased during the year. The December 31, 2011, physical count showed $354 of supplies available.
d. One-half of the work related to $10,000 of cash received in advance was performed this period.
e. The Prepaid Insurance account had a $5,600 debit balance at December 31, 2011, before adjusting for the costs of any expired coverage. An analysis of insurance policies showed that $4,600 of coverage had expired.
f. Wage expenses of $4,000 have been incurred but are not paid as of December 31, 2011.

Check (*c*) Dr. Office Supplies Expense, $2,626; (*e*) Dr. Insurance Expense, $4,600

Exercise 3-4
Adjusting and paying accrued expenses
A1 P1

The following three separate situations require adjusting journal entries to prepare financial statements as of April 30. For each situation, present both the April 30 adjusting entry and the subsequent entry during May to record the payment of the accrued expenses.

a. On April 1, the company retained an attorney for a flat monthly fee of $2,500. This amount is paid to the attorney on the 12th day of the following month in which it was earned.

b. A $780,000 note payable requires 9.6% annual interest, or $6,240 to be paid at the 20th day of each month. The interest was last paid on April 20 and the next payment is due on May 20. As of April 30, $2,080 of interest expense has accrued.

c. Total weekly salaries expense for all employees is $9,000. This amount is paid at the end of the day on Friday of each five-day workweek. April 30 falls on Tuesday of this year, which means that the employees had worked two days since the last payday. The next payday is May 3.

Check (*b*) May 20 Dr. Interest Expense, $4,160

Exercise 3-5
Determining cost flows through accounts
C1 A1 P1

Determine the missing amounts in each of these four separate situations *a* through *d*.

	a	b	c	d
Supplies available—prior year-end	$ 300	$1,600	$1,360	?
Supplies purchased during the current year	2,100	5,400	?	$6,000
Supplies available—current year-end	750	?	1,840	800
Supplies expense for the current year	?	1,300	9,600	6,575

Exercise 3-6
Adjusting and paying accrued wages
C1 P1

Pablo Management has five part-time employees, each of whom earns $100 per day. They are normally paid on Fridays for work completed Monday through Friday of the same week. They were paid in full on Friday, December 28, 2011. The next week, the five employees worked only four days because New Year's Day was an unpaid holiday. Show (*a*) the adjusting entry that would be recorded on Monday, December 31, 2011, and (*b*) the journal entry that would be made to record payment of the employees' wages on Friday, January 4, 2012.

Exercise 3-7
Analyzing and preparing adjusting entries
A1 P1 P3 

Following are two income statements for Kendall Co. for the year ended December 31. The left column is prepared before any adjusting entries are recorded, and the right column includes the effects of adjusting entries. The company records cash receipts and payments related to unearned and prepaid items in balance sheet accounts. Analyze the statements and prepare the eight adjusting entries that likely were recorded. (*Note:* 30% of the $6,000 adjustment for Fees Earned has been earned but not billed, and the other 70% has been earned by performing services that were paid for in advance.)

KENDALL CO.
Income Statements
For Year Ended December 31

	Unadjusted	Adjusted
Revenues		
Fees earned	$24,000	$30,000
Commissions earned	42,500	42,500
Total revenues	66,500	72,500
Expenses		
Depreciation expense—Computers	0	1,500
Depreciation expense—Office furniture	0	1,750
Salaries expense	12,500	14,950
Insurance expense	0	1,300
Rent expense	4,500	4,500
Office supplies expense	0	480
Advertising expense	3,000	3,000
Utilities expense	1,250	1,320
Total expenses	21,250	28,800
Net income	$45,250	$43,700

Exercise 3-8
Determining assets and expenses for accrual and cash accounting
C2

On March 1, 2009, a company paid a $16,200 premium on a 36-month insurance policy for coverage beginning on that date. Refer to that policy and fill in the blanks in the following table.

Balance Sheet Prepaid Insurance Asset Using			Insurance Expense Using		
	Accrual Basis	Cash Basis		Accrual Basis	Cash Basis
Dec. 31, 2009	$______	$______	2009	$______	$______
Dec. 31, 2010	______	______	2010	______	______
Dec. 31, 2011	______	______	2011	______	______
Dec. 31, 2012	______	______	2012	______	______
			Total	$______	$______

Check 2011 insurance expense: Accrual, $5,400; Cash, $0. Dec. 31, 2011, asset: Accrual, $900; Cash, $0.

Exercise 3-9
Computing and interpreting profit margin
A2 

Use the following information to compute profit margin for each separate company *a* through *e*.

	Net Income	Net Sales		Net Income	Net Sales
a.	$ 5,390	$ 44,830	**d.**	$55,234	$1,458,999
b.	87,644	398,954	**e.**	70,158	435,925
c.	93,385	257,082			

Which of the five companies is the most profitable according to the profit margin ratio? Interpret that company's profit margin ratio.

Exercise 3-10A
Recording and reporting revenues received in advance
P4

Corbel Company experienced the following events and transactions during July.

July 1 Received $2,000 cash in advance of performing work for Beth Oker.
6 Received $8,400 cash in advance of performing work for Lisa Poe.
12 Completed the job for Oker.
18 Received $7,500 cash in advance of performing work for Henry Coe.
27 Completed the job for Poe.
31 None of the work for Coe has been performed.

a. Prepare journal entries (including any adjusting entries as of the end of the month) to record these events using the procedure of initially crediting the Unearned Fees account when payment is received from a customer in advance of performing services.

b. Prepare journal entries (including any adjusting entries as of the end of the month) to record these events using the procedure of initially crediting the Fees Earned account when payment is received from a customer in advance of performing services.

c. Under each method, determine the amount of earned fees reported on the income statement for July and the amount of unearned fees reported on the balance sheet as of July 31.

Check (*c*) Fees Earned—using entries from part *b*, $10,400

Exercise 3-11A
Adjusting for prepaids recorded as expenses and unearned revenues recorded as revenues
P4

On-The-Mark Construction began operations on December 1. In setting up its accounting procedures, the company decided to debit expense accounts when it prepays its expenses and to credit revenue accounts when customers pay for services in advance. Prepare journal entries for items *a* through *d* and the adjusting entries as of its December 31 period-end for items *e* through *g*.

a. Supplies are purchased on December 1 for $3,000 cash.
b. The company prepaid its insurance premiums for $1,440 cash on December 2.
c. On December 15, the company receives an advance payment of $12,000 cash from a customer for remodeling work.
d. On December 28, the company receives $3,600 cash from another customer for remodeling work to be performed in January.

e. A physical count on December 31 indicates that On-The-Mark has $1,920 of supplies available.

f. An analysis of the insurance policies in effect on December 31 shows that $240 of insurance coverage had expired.

g. As of December 31, only one remodeling project has been worked on and completed. The $6,300 fee for this project had been received in advance.

Check (*f*) Cr. Insurance Expense, $1,200; (*g*) Dr. Remodeling Fees Earned, $9,300

Exercise 3-12
Preparing a balance sheet following IFRS
P3

adidas AG reports the following balance sheet accounts for the year ended December 31, 2009 (euros in millions). Prepare the balance sheet for this company as of December 31, 2009, following usual IFRS practices.

Tangible and other assets	€1,410	Intangible assets	€2,980
Total equity	3,776	Total current liabilities	2,836
Receivables and financial assets	1,753	Inventories	1,471
Total noncurrent liabilities	2,263	Total liabilities	5,099
Cash and cash equivalents	775	Other current assets	486
Total current assets	4,485	Total noncurrent assets	4,390

connect

PROBLEM SET A

Problem 3-1A
Preparing adjusting and subsequent journal entries
C1 A1 P1

Meyer Co. follows the practice of recording prepaid expenses and unearned revenues in balance sheet accounts. The company's annual accounting period ends on December 31, 2011. The following information concerns the adjusting entries to be recorded as of that date.

a. The Office Supplies account started the year with a $3,000 balance. During 2011, the company purchased supplies for $12,400, which was added to the Office Supplies account. The inventory of supplies available at December 31, 2011, totaled $2,640.

b. An analysis of the company's insurance policies provided the following facts.

Policy	Date of Purchase	Months of Coverage	Cost
A	April 1, 2010	24	$15,840
B	April 1, 2011	36	13,068
C	August 1, 2011	12	2,700

The total premium for each policy was paid in full (for all months) at the purchase date, and the Prepaid Insurance account was debited for the full cost. (Year-end adjusting entries for Prepaid Insurance were properly recorded in all prior years.)

c. The company has 15 employees, who earn a total of $2,100 in salaries each working day. They are paid each Monday for their work in the five-day workweek ending on the previous Friday. Assume that December 31, 2011, is a Tuesday, and all 15 employees worked the first two days of that week. Because New Year's Day is a paid holiday, they will be paid salaries for five full days on Monday, January 6, 2012.

d. The company purchased a building on January 1, 2011. It cost $855,000 and is expected to have a $45,000 salvage value at the end of its predicted 30-year life. Annual depreciation is $27,000.

e. Since the company is not large enough to occupy the entire building it owns, it rented space to a tenant at $2,400 per month, starting on November 1, 2011. The rent was paid on time on November 1, and the amount received was credited to the Rent Earned account. However, the tenant has not paid the December rent. The company has worked out an agreement with the tenant, who has promised to pay both December and January rent in full on January 15. The tenant has agreed not to fall behind again.

f. On November 1, the company rented space to another tenant for $2,175 per month. The tenant paid five months' rent in advance on that date. The payment was recorded with a credit to the Unearned Rent account.

Check (1*b*) Dr. Insurance Expense, $12,312 (1*d*) Dr. Depreciation Expense, $27,000

Required

1. Use the information to prepare adjusting entries as of December 31, 2011.
2. Prepare journal entries to record the first subsequent cash transaction in 2012 for parts *c* and *e*.

Problem 3-2A
Identifying adjusting entries with explanations
C3 P1

For each of the following entries, enter the letter of the explanation that most closely describes it in the space beside each entry. (You can use letters more than once.)

A. To record receipt of unearned revenue.
B. To record this period's earning of prior unearned revenue.
C. To record payment of an accrued expense.
D. To record receipt of an accrued revenue.
E. To record an accrued expense.
F. To record an accrued revenue.
G. To record this period's use of a prepaid expense.
H. To record payment of a prepaid expense.
I. To record this period's depreciation expense.

		Account	Debit	Credit
______	1.	Rent Expense	2,000	
		Prepaid Rent		2,000
______	2.	Interest Expense	1,000	
		Interest Payable		1,000
______	3.	Depreciation Expense	4,000	
		Accumulated Depreciation		4,000
______	4.	Unearned Professional Fees	3,000	
		Professional Fees Earned		3,000
______	5.	Insurance Expense	4,200	
		Prepaid Insurance		4,200
______	6.	Salaries Payable	1,400	
		Cash		1,400
______	7.	Prepaid Rent	4,500	
		Cash		4,500
______	8.	Salaries Expense	6,000	
		Salaries Payable		6,000
______	9.	Interest Receivable	5,000	
		Interest Revenue		5,000
______	10.	Cash	9,000	
		Accounts Receivable (from consulting)		9,000
______	11.	Cash	7,500	
		Unearned Professional Fees		7,500
______	12.	Cash	2,000	
		Interest Receivable		2,000

Problem 3-3A
Preparing adjusting entries, adjusted trial balance, and financial statements
A1 P1 P2 P3

mhhe.com/wildFAP20e

Watson Technical Institute (WTI), a school owned by Tom Watson, provides training to individuals who pay tuition directly to the school. WTI also offers training to groups in off-site locations. Its unadjusted trial balance as of December 31, 2011, follows. WTI initially records prepaid expenses and unearned revenues in balance sheet accounts. Descriptions of items *a* through *h* that require adjusting entries on December 31, 2011, follow.

Additional Information Items

a. An analysis of WTI's insurance policies shows that $3,000 of coverage has expired.
b. An inventory count shows that teaching supplies costing $2,600 are available at year-end 2011.
c. Annual depreciation on the equipment is $12,000.
d. Annual depreciation on the professional library is $6,000.
e. On November 1, WTI agreed to do a special six-month course (starting immediately) for a client. The contract calls for a monthly fee of $2,200, and the client paid the first five months' fees in advance. When the cash was received, the Unearned Training Fees account was credited. The fee for the sixth month will be recorded when it is collected in 2012.

f. On October 15, WTI agreed to teach a four-month class (beginning immediately) for an individual for $3,000 tuition per month payable at the end of the class. The class started on October 15, but no payment has yet been received. (WTI's accruals are applied to the nearest half-month; for example, October recognizes one-half month accrual.)

g. WTI's two employees are paid weekly. As of the end of the year, two days' salaries have accrued at the rate of $100 per day for each employee.

h. The balance in the Prepaid Rent account represents rent for December.

	A	B	C
1	**WATSON TECHNICAL INSTITUTE** **Unadjusted Trial Balance** **December 31, 2011**		
2		**Debit**	**Credit**
3	Cash	$ 26,000	
4	Accounts receivable	0	
5	Teaching supplies	10,000	
6	Prepaid insurance	15,000	
7	Prepaid rent	2,000	
8	Professional library	30,000	
9	Accumulated depreciation—Professional library		$ 9,000
10	Equipment	70,000	
11	Accumulated depreciation—Equipment		16,000
12	Accounts payable		36,000
13	Salaries payable		0
14	Unearned training fees		11,000
15	T. Watson, Capital		63,600
16	T. Watson, Withdrawals	40,000	
17	Tuition fees earned		102,000
18	Training fees earned		38,000
19	Depreciation expense—Professional library	0	
20	Depreciation expense—Equipment	0	
21	Salaries expense	48,000	
22	Insurance expense	0	
23	Rent expense	22,000	
24	Teaching supplies expense	0	
25	Advertising expense	7,000	
26	Utilities expense	5,600	
27	Totals	$ 275,600	$ 275,600
28			

Required

1. Prepare T-accounts (representing the ledger) with balances from the unadjusted trial balance.

2. Prepare the necessary adjusting journal entries for items *a* through *h* and post them to the T-accounts. Assume that adjusting entries are made only at year-end.

3. Update balances in the T-accounts for the adjusting entries and prepare an adjusted trial balance.

4. Prepare Watson Technical Institute's income statement and statement of owner's equity for the year 2011 and prepare its balance sheet as of December 31, 2011.

Check (2*e*) Cr. Training Fees Earned, $4,400; (2*f*) Cr. Tuition Fees Earned, $7,500; (3) Adj. Trial balance totals, $301,500; (4) Net income, $38,500; Ending T. Watson, Capital $62,100

Problem 3-4A
Interpreting unadjusted and adjusted trial balances, and preparing financial statements
C3 A1 P1 P2 P3 

mhhe.com/wildFAP20e

A six-column table for JJW Company follows. The first two columns contain the unadjusted trial balance for the company as of July 31, 2011. The last two columns contain the adjusted trial balance as of the same date.

Required

Analysis Component

1. Analyze the differences between the unadjusted and adjusted trial balances to determine the eight adjustments that likely were made. Show the results of your analysis by inserting these adjustment amounts in the table's two middle columns. Label each adjustment with a letter *a* through *h* and provide a short description of it at the bottom of the table.

Preparation Component

Check (2) Net income, $37,020; J. Winner, Capital (7/31/2011), $55,440; Total assets, $131,340

2. Use the information in the adjusted trial balance to prepare the company's (*a*) income statement and its statement of owner's equity for the year ended July 31, 2011 (*note:* J. Winner, Capital at July 31, 2010, was $28,420, and the current-year withdrawals were $10,000), and (*b*) the balance sheet as of July 31, 2011.

	Unadjusted Trial Balance		Adjustments		Adjusted Trial Balance	
Cash	$ 27,000				$ 27,000	
Accounts receivable	12,000				22,460	
Office supplies	18,000				3,000	
Prepaid insurance	7,320				4,880	
Office equipment	92,000				92,000	
Accum. depreciation—Office equip.		$ 12,000				$ 18,000
Accounts payable		9,300				10,200
Interest payable		0				800
Salaries payable		0				6,600
Unearned consulting fees		16,000				14,300
Long-term notes payable		44,000				44,000
J. Winner, Capital		28,420				28,420
J. Winner, Withdrawals	10,000				10,000	
Consulting fees earned		156,000				168,160
Depreciation expense—Office equip.	0				6,000	
Salaries expense	71,000				77,600	
Interest expense	1,400				2,200	
Insurance expense	0				2,440	
Rent expense	13,200				13,200	
Office supplies expense	0				15,000	
Advertising expense	13,800				14,700	
Totals	$265,720	$265,720			$290,480	$290,480

Problem 3-5A
Preparing financial statements from the adjusted trial balance and calculating profit margin
P3 A1 A2

The adjusted trial balance for Callahay Company as of December 31, 2011, follows.

	Debit	Credit
Cash	$ 22,000	
Accounts receivable	44,000	
Interest receivable	10,000	
Notes receivable (due in 90 days)	160,000	
Office supplies	8,000	
Automobiles	160,000	
Accumulated depreciation—Automobiles		$ 42,000
Equipment	130,000	
Accumulated depreciation—Equipment		10,000
Land	70,000	
Accounts payable		88,000
Interest payable		12,000
Salaries payable		11,000
Unearned fees		22,000
Long-term notes payable		130,000
J. Callahay, Capital		247,800
J. Callahay, Withdrawals	38,000	

[continued on next page]

[continued from previous page]

Fees earned		420,000
Interest earned		16,000
Depreciation expense—Automobiles	18,000	
Depreciation expense—Equipment	10,000	
Salaries expense	180,000	
Wages expense	32,000	
Interest expense	24,000	
Office supplies expense	26,000	
Advertising expense	50,000	
Repairs expense—Automobiles	16,800	
Totals	$998,800	$998,800

Required

1. Use the information in the adjusted trial balance to prepare (*a*) the income statement for the year ended December 31, 2011; (*b*) the statement of owner's equity for the year ended December 31, 2011; and (*c*) the balance sheet as of December 31, 2011.
2. Calculate the profit margin for year 2011.

Check (1) Total assets, $552,000

Problem 3-6A[A]
Recording prepaid expenses and unearned revenues
P1 P4

Quisp Co. had the following transactions in the last two months of its year ended December 31.

Nov.	1	Paid $1,500 cash for future newspaper advertising.
	1	Paid $2,160 cash for 12 months of insurance through October 31 of the next year.
	30	Received $3,300 cash for future services to be provided to a customer.
Dec.	1	Paid $2,700 cash for a consultant's services to be received over the next three months.
	15	Received $7,650 cash for future services to be provided to a customer.
	31	Of the advertising paid for on November 1, $900 worth is not yet used.
	31	A portion of the insurance paid for on November 1 has expired. No adjustment was made in November to Prepaid Insurance.
	31	Services worth $1,200 are not yet provided to the customer who paid on November 30.
	31	One-third of the consulting services paid for on December 1 have been received.
	31	The company has performed $3,000 of services that the customer paid for on December 15.

Required

1. Prepare entries for these transactions under the method that records prepaid expenses as assets and records unearned revenues as liabilities. Also prepare adjusting entries at the end of the year.
2. Prepare entries for these transactions under the method that records prepaid expenses as expenses and records unearned revenues as revenues. Also prepare adjusting entries at the end of the year.

Analysis Component

3. Explain why the alternative sets of entries in requirements 1 and 2 do not result in different financial statement amounts.

PROBLEM SET B

Problem 3-1B
Preparing adjusting and subsequent journal entries
C1 A1 P1

Nomo Co. follows the practice of recording prepaid expenses and unearned revenues in balance sheet accounts. The company's annual accounting period ends on October 31, 2011. The following information concerns the adjusting entries that need to be recorded as of that date.

a. The Office Supplies account started the fiscal year with a $500 balance. During the fiscal year, the company purchased supplies for $3,650, which was added to the Office Supplies account. The supplies available at October 31, 2011, totaled $700.

b. An analysis of the company's insurance policies provided the following facts.

Policy	Date of Purchase	Months of Coverage	Cost
A	April 1, 2010	24	$3,000
B	April 1, 2011	36	3,600
C	August 1, 2011	12	660

The total premium for each policy was paid in full (for all months) at the purchase date, and the Prepaid Insurance account was debited for the full cost. (Year-end adjusting entries for Prepaid Insurance were properly recorded in all prior fiscal years.)

c. The company has four employees, who earn a total of $800 for each workday. They are paid each Monday for their work in the five-day workweek ending on the previous Friday. Assume that October 31, 2011, is a Monday, and all four employees worked the first day of that week. They will be paid salaries for five full days on Monday, November 7, 2011.

d. The company purchased a building on November 1, 2010, that cost $155,000 and is expected to have a $20,000 salvage value at the end of its predicted 25-year life. Annual depreciation is $5,400.

e. Since the company does not occupy the entire building it owns, it rented space to a tenant at $600 per month, starting on September 1, 2011. The rent was paid on time on September 1, and the amount received was credited to the Rent Earned account. However, the October rent has not been paid. The company has worked out an agreement with the tenant, who has promised to pay both October and November rent in full on November 15. The tenant has agreed not to fall behind again.

f. On September 1, the company rented space to another tenant for $525 per month. The tenant paid five months' rent in advance on that date. The payment was recorded with a credit to the Unearned Rent account.

Required

Check (1*b*) Dr. Insurance Expense, $2,675; (1*d*) Dr. Depreciation Expense, $5,400.

1. Use the information to prepare adjusting entries as of October 31, 2011.

2. Prepare journal entries to record the first subsequent cash transaction in November 2011 for parts *c* and *e*.

Problem 3-2B
Identifying adjusting entries with explanations

C3 P1

For each of the following entries, enter the letter of the explanation that most closely describes it in the space beside each entry. (You can use letters more than once.)

A. To record payment of a prepaid expense.
B. To record this period's use of a prepaid expense.
C. To record this period's depreciation expense.
D. To record receipt of unearned revenue.
E. To record this period's earning of prior unearned revenue.
F. To record an accrued expense.
G. To record payment of an accrued expense.
H. To record an accrued revenue.
I. To record receipt of accrued revenue.

		Account	Debit	Credit
_____	1.	Unearned Professional Fees	6,000	
		Professional Fees Earned		6,000
_____	2.	Interest Receivable	3,500	
		Interest Revenue		3,500
_____	3.	Salaries Payable	9,000	
		Cash		9,000
_____	4.	Depreciation Expense	8,000	
		Accumulated Depreciation		8,000
_____	5.	Cash	9,000	
		Unearned Professional Fees		9,000
_____	6.	Insurance Expense	4,000	
		Prepaid Insurance		4,000
_____	7.	Interest Expense	5,000	
		Interest Payable		5,000
_____	8.	Cash	1,500	
		Accounts Receivable (from services)		1,500
_____	9.	Salaries Expense	7,000	
		Salaries Payable		7,000
_____	10.	Cash	1,000	
		Interest Receivable		1,000
_____	11.	Prepaid Rent	3,000	
		Cash		3,000
_____	12.	Rent Expense	7,500	
		Prepaid Rent		7,500

Problem 3-3B
Preparing adjusting entries, adjusted trial balance, and financial statements
A1 P1 P2 P3

Following is the unadjusted trial balance for Alcorn Institute as of December 31, 2011, which initially records prepaid expenses and unearned revenues in balance sheet accounts. The Institute provides one-on-one training to individuals who pay tuition directly to the business and offers extension training to groups in off-site locations. Shown after the trial balance are items *a* through *h* that require adjusting entries as of December 31, 2011.

ALCORN INSTITUTE Unadjusted Trial Balance December 31, 2011		
	Debit	**Credit**
Cash	$ 50,000	
Accounts receivable	0	
Teaching supplies	60,000	
Prepaid insurance	18,000	
Prepaid rent	2,600	
Professional library	10,000	
Accumulated depreciation—Professional library		$ 1,500
Equipment	30,000	
Accumulated depreciation—Equipment		16,000
Accounts payable		12,200
Salaries payable		0
Unearned training fees		27,600
M. Alcorn, Capital		68,500
M. Alcorn, Withdrawals	20,000	
Tuition fees earned		105,000
Training fees earned		62,000
Depreciation expense—Professional library	0	
Depreciation expense—Equipment	0	
Salaries expense	40,200	
Insurance expense	0	
Rent expense	28,600	
Teaching supplies expense	0	
Advertising expense	18,000	
Utilities expense	12,400	
Totals	$ 292,800	$292,800

Additional Information Items

a. An analysis of the Institute's insurance policies shows that $6,400 of coverage has expired.

b. An inventory count shows that teaching supplies costing $2,500 are available at year-end 2011.

c. Annual depreciation on the equipment is $4,000.

d. Annual depreciation on the professional library is $2,000.

e. On November 1, the Institute agreed to do a special four-month course (starting immediately) for a client. The contract calls for a $4,600 monthly fee, and the client paid the first two months' fees in advance. When the cash was received, the Unearned Training Fees account was credited. The last two month's fees will be recorded when collected in 2012.

f. On October 15, the Institute agreed to teach a four-month class (beginning immediately) to an individual for $2,200 tuition per month payable at the end of the class. The class started on October 15, but no payment has yet been received. (Alcorn's accruals are applied to the nearest half-month; for example, October recognizes one-half month accrual.)

g. The Institute's only employee is paid weekly. As of the end of the year, three days' salaries have accrued at the rate of $180 per day.

h. The balance in the Prepaid Rent account represents rent for December.

Check (2*e*) Cr. Training Fees Earned, $9,200; (2*f*) Cr. Tuition Fees Earned, $5,500; (3) Adj. trial balance totals, $304,840; (4) Net income, $6,460; Ending M. Alcorn, Capital, $54,960

Required

1. Prepare T-accounts (representing the ledger) with balances from the unadjusted trial balance.
2. Prepare the necessary adjusting journal entries for items *a* through *h*, and post them to the T-accounts. Assume that adjusting entries are made only at year-end.
3. Update balances in the T-accounts for the adjusting entries and prepare an adjusted trial balance.
4. Prepare the company's income statement and statement of owner's equity for the year 2011, and prepare its balance sheet as of December 31, 2011.

Problem 3-4B
Interpreting unadjusted and adjusted trial balances, and preparing financial statements
C3 A1 P1 P2 P3 

A six-column table for Daxu Consulting Company follows. The first two columns contain the unadjusted trial balance for the company as of December 31, 2011, and the last two columns contain the adjusted trial balance as of the same date.

	Unadjusted Trial Balance		Adjustments		Adjusted Trial Balance	
Cash	$ 48,000				$ 48,000	
Accounts receivable	70,000				76,660	
Office supplies	30,000				7,000	
Prepaid insurance	13,200				8,600	
Office equipment	150,000				150,000	
Accumulated depreciation—Office equip.		$ 30,000				$ 40,000
Accounts payable		36,000				42,000
Interest payable		0				1,600
Salaries payable		0				11,200
Unearned consulting fees		30,000				17,800
Long-term notes payable		80,000				80,000
D. Chen, Capital		70,200				70,200
D. Chen, Withdrawals	10,000				10,000	
Consulting fees earned		264,000				282,860
Depreciation expense—Office equip.	0				10,000	
Salaries expense	115,600				126,800	
Interest expense	6,400				8,000	
Insurance expense	0				4,600	
Rent expense	24,000				24,000	
Office supplies expense	0				23,000	
Advertising expense	43,000				49,000	
Totals	$510,200	$510,200			$545,660	$545,660

Required

Analysis Component

1. Analyze the differences between the unadjusted and adjusted trial balances to determine the eight adjustments that likely were made. Show the results of your analysis by inserting these adjustment amounts in the table's two middle columns. Label each adjustment with a letter *a* through *h* and provide a short description of it at the bottom of the table.

Preparation Component

Check (2) Net income, $37,460; D. Chen, Capital (12/31/11), $97,660; Total assets, $250,260

2. Use the information in the adjusted trial balance to prepare this company's (*a*) income statement and its statement of owner's equity for the year ended December 31, 2011 (*note:* D. Chen, Capital at December 31, 2010, was $70,200, and the current-year withdrawals were $10,000), and (*b*) the balance sheet as of December 31, 2011.

Problem 3-5B
Preparing financial statements from the adjusted trial balance and calculating profit margin
P3 A1 A2

The adjusted trial balance for Lightning Courier as of December 31, 2011, follows.

	Debit	Credit
Cash	$ 48,000	
Accounts receivable	110,000	
Interest receivable	6,000	
Notes receivable (due in 90 days)	200,000	
Office supplies	12,000	
Trucks	124,000	
Accumulated depreciation—Trucks		$ 48,000
Equipment	260,000	
Accumulated depreciation—Equipment		190,000
Land	90,000	
Accounts payable		124,000
Interest payable		22,000
Salaries payable		30,000
Unearned delivery fees		110,000
Long-term notes payable		190,000
J. Hallam, Capital		115,000
J. Hallam, Withdrawals	40,000	
Delivery fees earned		580,000
Interest earned		24,000
Depreciation expense—Trucks	24,000	
Depreciation expense—Equipment	46,000	
Salaries expense	64,000	
Wages expense	290,000	
Interest expense	25,000	
Office supplies expense	33,000	
Advertising expense	26,400	
Repairs expense—Trucks	34,600	
Totals	$1,433,000	$1,433,000

Required

1. Use the information in the adjusted trial balance to prepare (*a*) the income statement for the year ended December 31, 2011, (*b*) the statement of owner's equity for the year ended December 31, 2011, and (*c*) the balance sheet as of December 31, 2011.
2. Calculate the profit margin for year 2011.

Check (1) Total assets, $612,000

Problem 3-6B[A]
Recording prepaid expenses and unearned revenues
P1 P4

Quake Co. had the following transactions in the last two months of its fiscal year ended May 31.

Apr.	1	Paid $3,450 cash to an accounting firm for future consulting services.
	1	Paid $2,700 cash for 12 months of insurance through March 31 of the next year.
	30	Received $7,500 cash for future services to be provided to a customer.
May	1	Paid $3,450 cash for future newspaper advertising.
	23	Received $9,450 cash for future services to be provided to a customer.
	31	Of the consulting services paid for on April 1, $1,500 worth has been received.
	31	A portion of the insurance paid for on April 1 has expired. No adjustment was made in April to Prepaid Insurance.
	31	Services worth $3,600 are not yet provided to the customer who paid on April 30.
	31	Of the advertising paid for on May 1, $1,050 worth is not yet used.
	31	The company has performed $4,500 of services that the customer paid for on May 23.

Required

1. Prepare entries for these transactions under the method that records prepaid expenses and unearned revenues in balance sheet accounts. Also prepare adjusting entries at the end of the year.

2. Prepare entries for these transactions under the method that records prepaid expenses and unearned revenues in income statement accounts. Also prepare adjusting entries at the end of the year.

Analysis Component

3. Explain why the alternative sets of entries in parts 1 and 2 do not result in different financial statement amounts.

SERIAL PROBLEM

Business Solutions

P1 P2 P3

This serial problem began in Chapter 1 and continues through most of the book. If previous chapter segments were not completed, the serial problem can still begin at this point. It is helpful, but not necessary, to use the Working Papers that accompany the book.

SP 3 After the success of the company's first two months, Santana Rey continues to operate Business Solutions. (Transactions for the first two months are described in the serial problem of Chapter 2.) The November 30, 2011, unadjusted trial balance of Business Solutions (reflecting its transactions for October and November of 2011) follows.

No.	Account Title	Debit	Credit
101	Cash	$38,264	
106	Accounts receivable	12,618	
126	Computer supplies	2,545	
128	Prepaid insurance	2,220	
131	Prepaid rent	3,300	
163	Office equipment	8,000	
164	Accumulated depreciation—Office equipment		$ 0
167	Computer equipment	20,000	
168	Accumulated depreciation—Computer equipment		0
201	Accounts payable		0
210	Wages payable		0
236	Unearned computer services revenue		0
301	S. Rey, Capital		73,000
302	S. Rey, Withdrawals	5,600	
403	Computer services revenue		25,659
612	Depreciation expense—Office equipment	0	
613	Depreciation expense—Computer equipment	0	
623	Wages expense	2,625	
637	Insurance expense	0	
640	Rent expense	0	
652	Computer supplies expense	0	
655	Advertising expense	1,728	
676	Mileage expense	704	
677	Miscellaneous expenses	250	
684	Repairs expense—Computer	805	
	Totals	$98,659	$98,659

Business Solutions had the following transactions and events in December 2011.

Dec. 2 Paid $1,025 cash to Hillside Mall for Business Solutions' share of mall advertising costs.
3 Paid $500 cash for minor repairs to the company's computer.
4 Received $3,950 cash from Alex's Engineering Co. for the receivable from November.
10 Paid cash to Lyn Addie for six days of work at the rate of $125 per day.
14 Notified by Alex's Engineering Co. that Business Solutions' bid of $7,000 on a proposed project has been accepted. Alex's paid a $1,500 cash advance to Business Solutions.
15 Purchased $1,100 of computer supplies on credit from Harris Office Products.
16 Sent a reminder to Gomez Co. to pay the fee for services recorded on November 8.
20 Completed a project for Liu Corporation and received $5,625 cash.
22–26 Took the week off for the holidays.
28 Received $3,000 cash from Gomez Co. on its receivable.

29 Reimbursed S. Rey for business automobile mileage (600 miles at $0.32 per mile).
31 S. Rey withdrew $1,500 cash from the company for personal use.

The following additional facts are collected for use in making adjusting entries prior to preparing financial statements for the company's first three months:

a. The December 31 inventory count of computer supplies shows $580 still available.
b. Three months have expired since the 12-month insurance premium was paid in advance.
c. As of December 31, Lyn Addie has not been paid for four days of work at $125 per day.
d. The company's computer is expected to have a four-year life with no salvage value.
e. The office equipment is expected to have a five-year life with no salvage value.
f. Three of the four months' prepaid rent has expired.

Required

1. Prepare journal entries to record each of the December transactions and events for Business Solutions. Post those entries to the accounts in the ledger.
2. Prepare adjusting entries to reflect *a* through *f*. Post those entries to the accounts in the ledger.
3. Prepare an adjusted trial balance as of December 31, 2011.
4. Prepare an income statement for the three months ended December 31, 2011.
5. Prepare a statement of owner's equity for the three months ended December 31, 2011.
6. Prepare a balance sheet as of December 31, 2011.

Check (3) Adjusted trial balance totals, $109,034

(6) Total assets, $83,160

Beyond the Numbers

REPORTING IN ACTION
C1 C2 A1 A2 
RIM

BTN 3-1 Refer to **Research In Motion**'s financial statements in Appendix A to answer the following.

1. Identify and write down the revenue recognition principle as explained in the chapter.
2. Review Research In Motion's footnotes to discover how it applies the revenue recognition principle and when it recognizes revenue. Report what you discover.
3. What is Research In Motion's profit margin for fiscal years ended February 28, 2009, and February 27, 2010.

Fast Forward

4. Access RIM's annual report (10-K) for fiscal years ending after February 27, 2010, at its Website (<u>RIM.com</u>) or the SEC's EDGAR database (**<u>www.SEC.gov</u>**). Assess and compare the February 27, 2010, fiscal year profit margin to any subsequent year's profit margin that you compute.

COMPARATIVE ANALYSIS
A2 
RIM
Apple

BTN 3-2 Key figures for the recent two years of both **Research In Motion** and **Apple** follow.

	Research In Motion		Apple	
($ millions)	Current Year	Prior Year	Current Year	Prior Year
Net income	$ 2,457	$ 1,893	$ 8,235	$ 6,119
Net sales	14,953	11,065	42,905	37,491
Current assets	5,813	4,842	31,555	30,006
Current liabilities	2,432	2,115	11,506	11,361

Required

1. Compute profit margins for (*a*) Research In Motion and (*b*) Apple for the two years of data shown.
2. Which company is more successful on the basis of profit margin? Explain.

ETHICS CHALLENGE
C1 C2 A1 

BTN 3-3 Jackie Bergez works for Sea Biscuit Co. She and Bob Welch, her manager, are preparing adjusting entries for annual financial statements. Bergez computes depreciation and records it as

Depreciation Expense—Equipment	123,000	
Accumulated Depreciation—Equipment		123,000

Welch agrees with her computation but says the credit entry should be directly to the Equipment account. Welch argues that while accumulated depreciation is technically correct, "it is less hassle not to use a contra account and just credit the Equipment account directly. And besides, the balance sheet shows the same amount for total assets under either method."

Required

1. How should depreciation be recorded? Do you support Bergez or Welch?
2. Evaluate the strengths and weaknesses of Welch's reasons for preferring his method.
3. Indicate whether the situation Bergez faces is an ethical problem. Explain.

COMMUNICATING IN PRACTICE

C1 A2 

BTN 3-4 The class should be divided into teams. Teams are to select an industry (such as automobile manufacturing, airlines, defense contractors), and each team member is to select a different company in that industry. Each team member is to acquire the annual report of the company selected. Annual reports can be downloaded from company Websites or from the SEC's EDGAR database at **(www.SEC.gov).**

Required

1. Use the annual report to compute the return on assets, debt ratio, and profit margin.
2. Communicate with team members via a meeting, e-mail, or telephone to discuss the meaning of the ratios, how different companies compare to each other, and the industry norm. The team must prepare a single memo reporting the ratios for each company and identifying the conclusions or consensus of opinion reached during the team's discussion. The memo is to be copied and distributed to the instructor and all classmates.

TAKING IT TO THE NET

C1 A2  

BTN 3-5 Access EDGAR online **(www.SEC.gov)** and locate the 10-K report of **The Gap, Inc.,** (ticker GPS) filed on March 26, 2010. Review its financial statements reported for the year ended January 30, 2010, to answer the following questions.

Required

1. What are Gap's main brands?
2. What is Gap's fiscal year-end?
3. What is Gap's net sales for the period ended January 30, 2010?
4. What is Gap's net income for the period ended January 30, 2010?
5. Compute Gap's profit margin for the year ended January 30, 2010.
6. Do you believe Gap's decision to use a year-end of late January or early February relates to its natural business year? Explain.

TEAMWORK IN ACTION

C3 A1 P1 

BTN 3-6 Four types of adjustments are described in the chapter: (1) prepaid expenses, (2) unearned revenues, (3) accrued expenses, and (4) accrued revenues.

Required

1. Form *learning teams* of four (or more) members. Each team member must select one of the four adjustments as an area of expertise (each team must have at least one expert in each area).
2. Form *expert teams* from the individuals who have selected the same area of expertise. Expert teams are to discuss and write a report that each expert will present to his or her learning team addressing the following:
   - **a.** Description of the adjustment and why it's necessary.
   - **b.** Example of a transaction or event, with dates and amounts, that requires adjustment.
   - **c.** Adjusting entry(ies) for the example in requirement *b*.
   - **d.** Status of the affected account(s) before and after the adjustment in requirement *c*.
   - **e.** Effects on financial statements of not making the adjustment.
3. Each expert should return to his or her learning team. In rotation, each member should present his or her expert team's report to the learning team. Team discussion is encouraged.

BTN 3-7 Review the opening feature of this chapter dealing with **Cheezburger Network**.

ENTREPRENEURIAL DECISION

A2  

Required

1. Assume that Cheezburger Network sells a $300 gift certificate to a customer, collecting the $300 cash in advance. Prepare the journal entry for the (*a*) collection of the cash for delivery of the gift certificate to the customer and (*b*) revenue from the subsequent delivery of merchandise when the gift certificate is used.
2. How can keeping less inventory help to improve Cheezburger Network's profit margin?
3. Ben Huh understands that many companies carry considerable inventory, and Ben is thinking of carrying additional inventory of merchandise for sale. Ben desires your advice on the pros and cons of carrying such inventory. Provide at least one reason for and one reason against carrying additional inventory.

BTN 3-8 Visit the Website of a major company that interests you. Use the Investor Relations link at the Website to obtain the toll-free telephone number of the Investor Relations Department. Call the company, ask to speak to Investor Relations, and request a copy of the company's most recent annual report. You should receive the requested report within one to two weeks. Once you have received your report, use it throughout the term to see that the principles you are learning in class are being applied in practice.

HITTING THE ROAD

C1

BTN 3-9 **Nokia** (www.Nokia.com) is a leading global manufacturer of mobile devices and services.

GLOBAL DECISION

A2 C1 C2  

NOKIA

Required

1. Locate the notes to its December 31, 2009, financial statements at the company's Website, and read note *1 Accounting Principles—Revenue Recognition,* first paragraph only. When is revenue recognized by Nokia?
2. Refer to Nokia's financials in Appendix A. What is Nokia's profit margin for the year ended December 31, 2009?

ANSWERS TO MULTIPLE CHOICE QUIZ

1. b; the forgotten adjusting entry is: *dr.* Wages Expense, *cr.* Wages Payable.
2. c; Supplies used = $450 − $125 = $325
3. b; Insurance expense = $24,000 × (8/24) = $8,000; adjusting entry is: *dr.* Insurance Expense for $8,000, *cr.* Prepaid Insurance for $8,000.
4. a; Consulting fees earned = $3,600 × (2/6) = $1,200; adjusting entry is: *dr.* Unearned Consulting Fee for $1,200, *cr.* Consulting Fees Earned for $1,200.
5. e; Profit margin = $15,000/$300,000 = 5%

4 Completing the Accounting Cycle

A Look Back

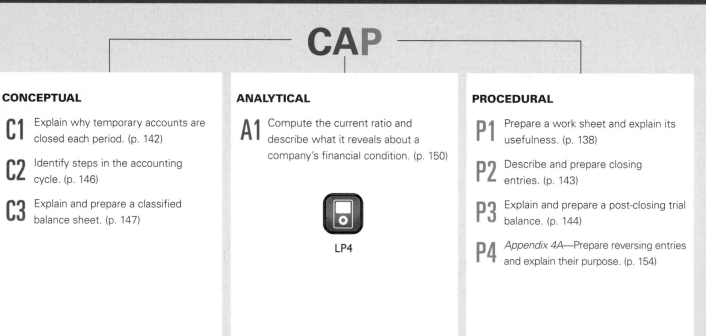

Chapter 3 explained the timing of reports. We described why adjusting accounts is key for recognizing revenues and expenses in the proper period. We prepared an adjusted trial balance and used it to prepare financial statements.

A Look at This Chapter

This chapter emphasizes the final steps in the accounting process and reviews the entire accounting cycle. We explain the closing process, including accounting procedures and the use of a post-closing trial balance. We show how a work sheet aids in preparing financial statements.

A Look Ahead

Chapter 5 looks at accounting for merchandising activities. We describe the sale and purchase of merchandise and their implications for preparing and analyzing financial statements.

Learning Objectives

CONCEPTUAL

C1 Explain why temporary accounts are closed each period. (p. 142)

C2 Identify steps in the accounting cycle. (p. 146)

C3 Explain and prepare a classified balance sheet. (p. 147)

ANALYTICAL

A1 Compute the current ratio and describe what it reveals about a company's financial condition. (p. 150)

LP4

PROCEDURAL

P1 Prepare a work sheet and explain its usefulness. (p. 138)

P2 Describe and prepare closing entries. (p. 143)

P3 Explain and prepare a post-closing trial balance. (p. 144)

P4 *Appendix 4A*—Prepare reversing entries and explain their purpose. (p. 154)

Decision Insight

Gamer Grub!

"Be in front of your customer . . . [and] have a little bit of an edge"
—**KEITH MULLIN** (far left)

SAN DIEGO—"I have been battling greasy fingers and keyboard crumbs," complained gamer Keith Mullin. "I thought '*there has to be a better way*!'" So, Keith-the-gamer morphed into Keith-the-entrepreneur. In 2008, Keith set up what he calls his "garage startup" and introduced **Gamer Grub® (GamerGrub.com),** which is performance snack food for gamers. "I got tired of wiping my hands on my jeans," laughs Keith. "And, I like to multi-task."

Success, however, requires Keith to monitor and minimize costs. "I made the first Gamer Grub prototypes in my mom's kitchen," explains Keith. He eventually set up an accounting system to track costs and match them with revenues. But, Keith says, it is a constant struggle as his business has been tripling in revenues each month. He explains that properly applying the accounting cycle, preparing classified financial statements, and acting on that information has helped in his success. However, admits Keith, "it is more of a collaborative effort."

To date, Keith has successfully controlled his costs while monitoring both revenues and customer needs. "You need to be in front of your customer, watch them taste it, watch them understand what you're doing," says Keith. "You have to be out there . . . we have given out at least 16,000 samples!" Keith adds that he applies the accounting cycle, including closing entries, to help identify and match costs with revenues for specific time periods. He also relies on classified balance sheets to plan payment schedules. But, what keeps him going, admits Keith, is knowing that he offers "different ways to snack while you're computer gaming or multi-tasking."

Keith is on a mission. What motivates him, explains Keith, is the "Wow! If you get that 'Wow' reaction, that's a really good thing." To make that happen, he tracks the accounting numbers to be sure his "Wow food" is a money-making venture. "Gamer Grub allows gamers to consume healthy, game-enhancing snacks," insists Keith. "Without greasy fingers or keyboard crumbs!"

[Sources: *GamerGrub* Website, January 2011; *Entrepreneur,* October 2009; *Business Wire,* September 2008; *MGC* Website, January 2010]

Chapter Preview

Many of the important steps leading to financial statements were explained in earlier chapters. We described how transactions and events are analyzed, journalized, and posted. This chapter explains the closing process that readies revenue, expense, and withdrawal accounts for the next reporting period and updates the capital account. A work sheet is shown to be a useful tool for these final steps and in preparing financial statements. It also explains how accounts are classified on a balance sheet to increase their usefulness to decision makers.

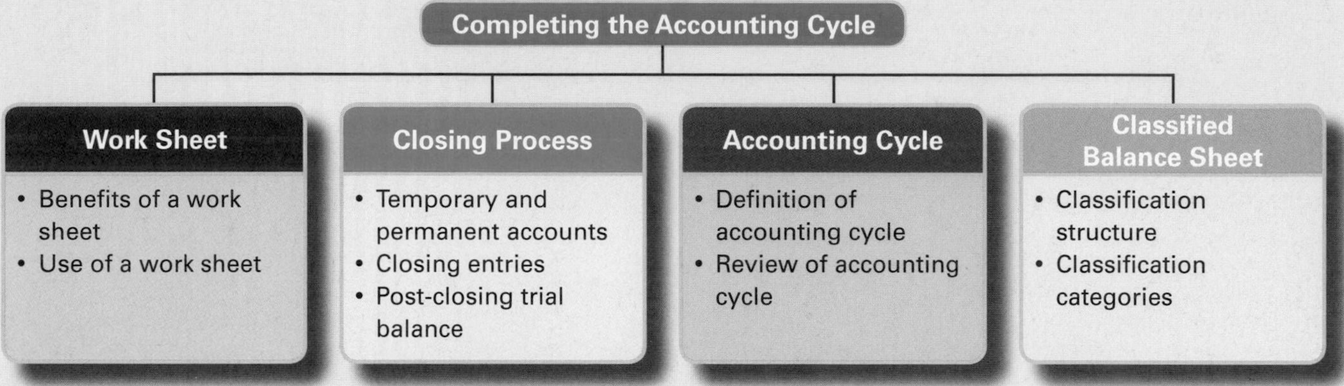

Completing the Accounting Cycle
Work Sheet
• Benefits of a work sheet
• Use of a work sheet
Closing Process
• Temporary and permanent accounts
• Closing entries
• Post-closing trial balance
Accounting Cycle
• Definition of accounting cycle
• Review of accounting cycle
Classified Balance Sheet
• Classification structure
• Classification categories

WORK SHEET AS A TOOL

Information preparers use various analyses and internal documents when organizing information for internal and external decision makers. Internal documents are often called **working papers.** One widely used working paper is the **work sheet,** which is a useful tool for preparers in working with accounting information. It is usually not available to external decision makers.

Benefits of a Work Sheet (Spreadsheet)

P1 Prepare a work sheet and explain its usefulness.

A work sheet is *not* a required report, yet using a manual or electronic work sheet has several potential benefits. Specifically, a work sheet

- Aids the preparation of financial statements.
- Reduces the possibility of errors when working with many accounts and adjustments.
- Links accounts and adjustments to their impacts in financial statements.
- Assists in planning and organizing an audit of financial statements—as it can be used to reflect any adjustments necessary.
- Helps in preparing interim (monthly and quarterly) financial statements when the journalizing and posting of adjusting entries are postponed until year-end.
- Shows the effects of proposed or "what-if" transactions.

Decision Insight

High-Tech Work Sheet An electronic work sheet using spreadsheet software such as Excel allows us to easily change numbers, assess the impact of alternative strategies, and quickly prepare financial statements at less cost. It can also increase the available time for analysis and interpretation. ■

Use of a Work Sheet

Point: Since a work sheet is *not* a required report or an accounting record, its format is flexible and can be modified by its user to fit his/her preferences.

When a work sheet is used to prepare financial statements, it is constructed at the end of a period before the adjusting process. The complete work sheet includes a list of the accounts, their balances and adjustments, and their sorting into financial statement columns. It provides two columns each for the unadjusted trial balance, the adjustments, the adjusted trial balance, the income statement, and the balance sheet (including the statement of owner's equity). To describe and interpret the work sheet, we use the information from FastForward. Preparing the work sheet has five important steps. Each step, 1 through 5, is color-coded and explained with reference to Exhibits 4.1 and 4.2.

1 Step 1. Enter Unadjusted Trial Balance

Refer to Exhibit 4.1 The first step in preparing a work sheet is to list the title of every account and its account number that is expected to appear on its financial statements. This includes all accounts in the ledger plus any new ones from adjusting entries. Most adjusting entries—including expenses from salaries, supplies, depreciation, and insurance—are predictable and recurring. The unadjusted balance for each account is then entered in the appropriate Debit or Credit column of the unadjusted trial balance columns. The totals of these two columns must be equal. Exhibit 4.1 shows FastForward's work sheet after completing this first step. Sometimes blank lines are left on the work sheet based on past experience to indicate where lines will be needed for adjustments to certain accounts. Exhibit 4.1 shows Consulting Revenue as one example. An alternative is to squeeze adjustments on one line or to combine the effects of two or more adjustments in one amount. In the unusual case when an account is not predicted, we can add a new line for such an account following the *Totals* line.

2 Step 2. Enter Adjustments

Refer to Exhibit 4.1a (turn over first transparency). The second step in preparing a work sheet is to enter adjustments in the Adjustments columns. The adjustments shown are the same ones shown in Exhibit 3.13. An identifying letter links the debit and credit of each adjusting entry. This is called *keying* the adjustments. After preparing a work sheet, adjusting entries must still be entered in the journal and posted to the ledger. The Adjustments columns provide the information for those entries.

Point: A recordkeeper often can complete the procedural task of journalizing and posting adjusting entries by using a work sheet and the guidance that *keying* provides.

3 Step 3. Prepare Adjusted Trial Balance

Refer to Exhibit 4.1b (turn over second transparency). The adjusted trial balance is prepared by combining the adjustments with the unadjusted balances for each account. As an example, the Prepaid Insurance account has a $2,400 debit balance in the Unadjusted Trial Balance columns. This $2,400 debit is combined with the $100 credit in the Adjustments columns to give Prepaid Insurance a $2,300 debit in the Adjusted Trial Balance columns. The totals of the Adjusted Trial Balance columns confirm the equality of debits and credits.

Point: To avoid omitting the transfer of an account balance, start with the first line (cash) and continue in account order.

4 Step 4. Sort Adjusted Trial Balance Amounts to Financial Statements

Refer to Exhibit 4.1c (turn over third transparency). This step involves sorting account balances from the adjusted trial balance to their proper financial statement columns. Expenses go to the Income Statement Debit column and revenues to the Income Statement Credit column. Assets and withdrawals go to the Balance Sheet & Statement of Owner's Equity Debit column. Liabilities and owner's capital go to the Balance Sheet & Statement of Owner's Equity Credit column.

5 Step 5. Total Statement Columns, Compute Income or Loss, and Balance Columns

Refer to Exhibit 4.1d (turn over fourth transparency). Each financial statement column (from Step 4) is totaled. The difference between the totals of the Income Statement columns is net income or net loss. This occurs because revenues are entered in the Credit column and expenses in the Debit column. If the Credit total exceeds the Debit total, there is net income. If the Debit total exceeds the Credit total, there is a net loss. For FastForward, the Credit total exceeds the Debit total, giving a $3,785 net income.

The net income from the Income Statement columns is then entered in the Balance Sheet & Statement of Owner's Equity Credit column. Adding net income to the last Credit column implies that it is to be added to owner's capital. If a loss occurs, it is added to the Debit column. This implies that it is to be subtracted from owner's capital. The ending balance of owner's capital does not appear in the last two columns as a single amount, but it is computed in the statement of owner's equity using these account balances. When net income or net loss is added

[continued on p. 142]

EXHIBIT 4.1

Work Sheet with Unadjusted Trial Balance

FastForward
Work Sheet
For Month Ended December 31, 2011

(1)

No.	Account	Unadjusted Trial Balance Dr.	Unadjusted Trial Balance Cr.	Adjustments Dr.	Adjustments Cr.	Adjusted Trial Balance Dr.	Adjusted Trial Balance Cr.	Income Statement Dr.	Income Statement Cr.	Balance Sheet & Statement of Owner's Equity Dr.	Balance Sheet & Statement of Owner's Equity Cr.
101	Cash	4,350									
126	Supplies	9,720									
128	Prepaid insurance	2,400									
167	Equipment	26,000									
201	Accounts payable		6,200								
236	Unearned consulting revenue		3,000								
301	C. Taylor, Capital		30,000								
302	C. Taylor, Withdrawals	200									
403	Consulting revenue		5,800								
406	Rental revenue		300								
622	Salaries expense	1,400									
640	Rent expense	1,000									
690	Utilities expense	230									
	Totals	45,300	45,300								

List all accounts from the ledger (can include those expected to arise from adjusting entries).

Enter all amounts available from ledger accounts. Column totals must be equal.

A work sheet collects and summarizes information used to prepare adjusting entries, financial statements, and closing entries.

EXHIBIT 4.1

Work Sheet with Unadjusted Trial Balance

File Edit View Insert Format Tools Data Window Help

FastForward
Work Sheet
For Month Ended December 31, 2011

①

No.	Account	Unadjusted Trial Balance Dr.	Unadjusted Trial Balance Cr.	Adjustments Dr.	Adjustments Cr.	Adjusted Trial Balance Dr.	Adjusted Trial Balance Cr.	Income Statement Dr.	Income Statement Cr.	Balance Sheet & Statement of Owner's Equity Dr.	Balance Sheet & Statement of Owner's Equity Cr.
101	Cash	4,350									
120	Supplies	9,720									
128	Prepaid insurance	2,400									
167	Equipment	26,000									
201	Accounts payable		6,200								
236	Unearned consulting revenue		3,000								
301	C. Taylor, Capital		30,000								
302	C. Taylor, Withdrawals	200									
403	Consulting revenue		5,800								
406	Rental revenue		300								
622	Salaries expense	1,400									
640	Rent expense	1,000									
690	Utilities expense	230									
	Totals	45,300	45,300								

Sheet1 / Sheet2 / Sheet3

List all accounts from the ledger (can include those expected to arise from adjusting entries).

Enter all amounts available from ledger accounts. Column totals must be equal.

A work sheet collects and summarizes information used to prepare adjusting entries, financial statements, and closing entries.

work sheet, we use the information from FastForward. Preparing the work sheet has five important steps. Each step, 1 through 5, is color-coded and explained with reference to Exhibits 4.1 and 4.2.

1 Step 1. Enter Unadjusted Trial Balance

Refer to Exhibit 4.1. The first step in preparing a work sheet is to list the title of every account and its account number that is expected to appear on its financial statements. This includes all accounts in the ledger plus any new ones from adjusting entries. Most adjusting entries—including expenses from salaries, supplies, depreciation, and insurance—are predictable and recurring. The unadjusted balance for each account is then entered in the appropriate Debit or Credit column of the unadjusted trial balance columns. The totals of these two columns must be equal. Exhibit 4.1 shows FastForward's work sheet after completing this first step. Sometimes blank lines are left on the work sheet based on past experience to indicate where lines will be needed for adjustments to certain accounts. Exhibit 4.1 shows Consulting Revenue as one example. An alternative is to squeeze adjustments on one line or to combine the effects of two or more adjustments in one amount. In the unusual case when an account is not predicted, we can add a new line for such an account following the *Totals* line.

2 Step 2. Enter Adjustments

Refer to Exhibit 4.1a (turn over first transparency). The second step in preparing a work sheet is to enter adjustments in the Adjustments columns. The adjustments shown are the same ones shown in Exhibit 3.13. An identifying letter links the debit and credit of each adjusting entry. This is called *keying* the adjustments. After preparing a work sheet, adjusting entries must still be entered in the journal and posted to the ledger. The Adjustments columns provide the information for those entries.

Point: A recordkeeper often can complete the procedural task of journalizing and posting adjusting entries by using a work sheet and the guidance that *keying* provides.

3 Step 3. Prepare Adjusted Trial Balance

Refer to Exhibit 4.1b (turn over second transparency). The adjusted trial balance is prepared by combining the adjustments with the unadjusted balances for each account. As an example, the Prepaid Insurance account has a $2,400 debit balance in the Unadjusted Trial Balance columns. This $2,400 debit is combined with the $100 credit in the Adjustments columns to give Prepaid Insurance a $2,300 debit in the Adjusted Trial Balance columns. The totals of the Adjusted Trial Balance columns confirm the equality of debits and credits.

Point: To avoid omitting the transfer of an account balance, start with the first line (cash) and continue in account order.

4 Step 4. Sort Adjusted Trial Balance Amounts to Financial Statements

Refer to Exhibit 4.1c (turn over third transparency). This step involves sorting account balances from the adjusted trial balance to their proper financial statement columns. Expenses go to the Income Statement Debit column and revenues to the Income Statement Credit column. Assets and withdrawals go to the Balance Sheet & Statement of Owner's Equity Debit column. Liabilities and owner's capital go to the Balance Sheet & Statement of Owner's Equity Credit column.

5 Step 5. Total Statement Columns, Compute Income or Loss, and Balance Columns

Refer to Exhibit 4.1d (turn over fourth transparency). Each financial statement column (from Step 4) is totaled. The difference between the totals of the Income Statement columns is net income or net loss. This occurs because revenues are entered in the Credit column and expenses in the Debit column. If the Credit total exceeds the Debit total, there is net income. If the Debit total exceeds the Credit total, there is a net loss. For FastForward, the Credit total exceeds the Debit total, giving a $3,785 net income.

The net income from the Income Statement columns is then entered in the Balance Sheet & Statement of Owner's Equity Credit column. Adding net income to the last Credit column implies that it is to be added to owner's capital. If a loss occurs, it is added to the Debit column. This implies that it is to be subtracted from owner's capital. The ending balance of owner's capital does not appear in the last two columns as a single amount, but it is computed in the statement of owner's equity using these account balances. When net income or net loss is added

[continued on p. 142]

EXHIBIT 4.2

Financial Statements Prepared from the Work Sheet

FASTFORWARD
Income Statement
For Month Ended December 31, 2011

Revenues		
Consulting revenue	$ 7,850	
Rental revenue	300	
Total revenues		$ 8,150
Expenses		
Depreciation expense—Equipment	375	
Salaries expense	1,610	
Insurance expense	100	
Rent expense	1,000	
Supplies expense	1,050	
Utilities expense	230	
Total expenses		4,365
Net income		$ 3,785

FASTFORWARD
Statement of Owner's Equity
For Month Ended December 31, 2011

C. Taylor, Capital, December 1		$ 0
Add: Investment by owner	$30,000	
Net income	3,785	33,785
		33,785
Less: Withdrawals by owner		200
C. Taylor, Capital, December 31		$33,585

FASTFORWARD
Balance Sheet
December 31, 2011

Assets		
Cash		$ 4,350
Accounts receivable		1,800
Supplies		8,670
Prepaid insurance		2,300
Equipment	$26,000	
Accumulated depreciation—Equipment	(375)	25,625
Total assets		$42,745
Liabilities		
Accounts payable		$ 6,200
Salaries payable		210
Unearned consulting revenue		2,750
Total liabilities		9,160
Equity		
C. Taylor, Capital		33,585
Total liabilities and equity		$42,745

to the proper Balance Sheet & Statement of Owner's Equity column, the totals of the last two columns must balance. If they do not, one or more errors have been made. The error can either be mathematical or involve sorting one or more amounts to incorrect columns.

Decision Maker Answer — p. 156 

Entrepreneur You make a printout of the electronic work sheet used to prepare financial statements. There is no depreciation adjustment, yet you own a large amount of equipment. Does the absence of depreciation adjustment concern you? ■

Work Sheet Applications and Analysis

A work sheet does not substitute for financial statements. It is a tool we can use at the end of an accounting period to help organize data and prepare financial statements. FastForward's financial statements are shown in Exhibit 4.2. Its income statement amounts are taken from the Income Statement columns of the work sheet. Similarly, amounts for its balance sheet and its statement of owner's equity are taken from the Balance Sheet & Statement of Owner's Equity columns of the work sheet.

Information from the Adjustments columns of a work sheet can be used to journalize adjusting entries. It is important to remember that a work sheet is not a journal. This means that even when a work sheet is prepared, it is necessary to both journalize adjustments and post them to the ledger.

Work sheets are also useful in analyzing the effects of proposed, or what-if, transactions. This is done by entering financial statement amounts in the Unadjusted (what-if) columns. Proposed transactions are then entered in the Adjustments columns. We then compute "adjusted" amounts from these proposed transactions. The extended amounts in the financial statement columns show the effects of these proposed transactions. These financial statement columns yield **pro forma financial statements** because they show the statements *as if* the proposed transactions occurred.

Quick Check Answers — p. 156 

1. Where do we get the amounts to enter in the Unadjusted Trial Balance columns of a work sheet?
2. What are the advantages of using a work sheet to help prepare adjusting entries?
3. What are the overall benefits of a work sheet?

CLOSING PROCESS

C1 Explain why temporary accounts are closed each period.

The **closing process** is an important step at the end of an accounting period *after* financial statements have been completed. It prepares accounts for recording the transactions and the events of the *next* period. In the closing process we must (1) identify accounts for closing, (2) record and post the closing entries, and (3) prepare a post-closing trial balance. The purpose of the closing process is twofold. First, it resets revenue, expense, and withdrawals account balances to zero at the end of each period. This is done so that these accounts can properly measure income and withdrawals for the next period. Second, it helps in summarizing a period's revenues and expenses. This section explains the closing process.

Temporary Accounts
(closed at period-end)
Revenues
Expenses
Owner Withdrawals
Income Summary

Permanent Accounts
(not closed at period-end)
Assets
Liabilities
Owner Capital

Temporary and Permanent Accounts

Temporary (or *nominal*) **accounts** accumulate data related to one accounting period. They include all income statement accounts, the withdrawals account, and the Income Summary account. They are temporary because the accounts are opened at the beginning of a period, used to record transactions and events for that period, and then closed at the end of the period. *The closing process applies only to temporary accounts.* **Permanent** (or *real*) **accounts** report on activities related to one or more future accounting periods. They carry their ending balances into the next period and generally consist of all balance sheet accounts. These asset, liability, and equity accounts are not closed.

Recording Closing Entries

To record and post **closing entries** is to transfer the end-of-period balances in revenue, expense, and withdrawals accounts to the permanent capital account. Closing entries are necessary at the end of each period after financial statements are prepared because

- Revenue, expense, and withdrawals accounts must begin each period with zero balances.
- Owner's capital must reflect prior periods' revenues, expenses, and withdrawals.

An income statement aims to report revenues and expenses for a *specific accounting period*. The statement of owner's equity reports similar information, including withdrawals. Since revenue, expense, and withdrawals accounts must accumulate information separately for each period, they must start each period with zero balances. To close these accounts, we transfer their balances first to an account called *Income Summary*. **Income Summary** is a temporary account (only used for the closing process) that contains a credit for the sum of all revenues (and gains) and a debit for the sum of all expenses (and losses). Its balance equals net income or net loss and it is transferred to the capital account. Next the withdrawals account balance is transferred to the capital account. After these closing entries are posted, the revenue, expense, withdrawals, and Income Summary accounts have zero balances. These accounts are then said to be *closed* or *cleared*.

Point: To understand the closing process, focus on its *outcomes*—*updating* the capital account balance to its proper ending balance, and getting *temporary accounts* to show *zero balances* for purposes of accumulating data for the next period.

Exhibit 4.3 uses the adjusted account balances of FastForward (from the Adjusted Trial Balance columns of Exhibit 4.1 or from the left side of Exhibit 4.4) to show the four steps necessary to close its temporary accounts. We explain each step.

EXHIBIT 4.3

Four-Step Closing Process

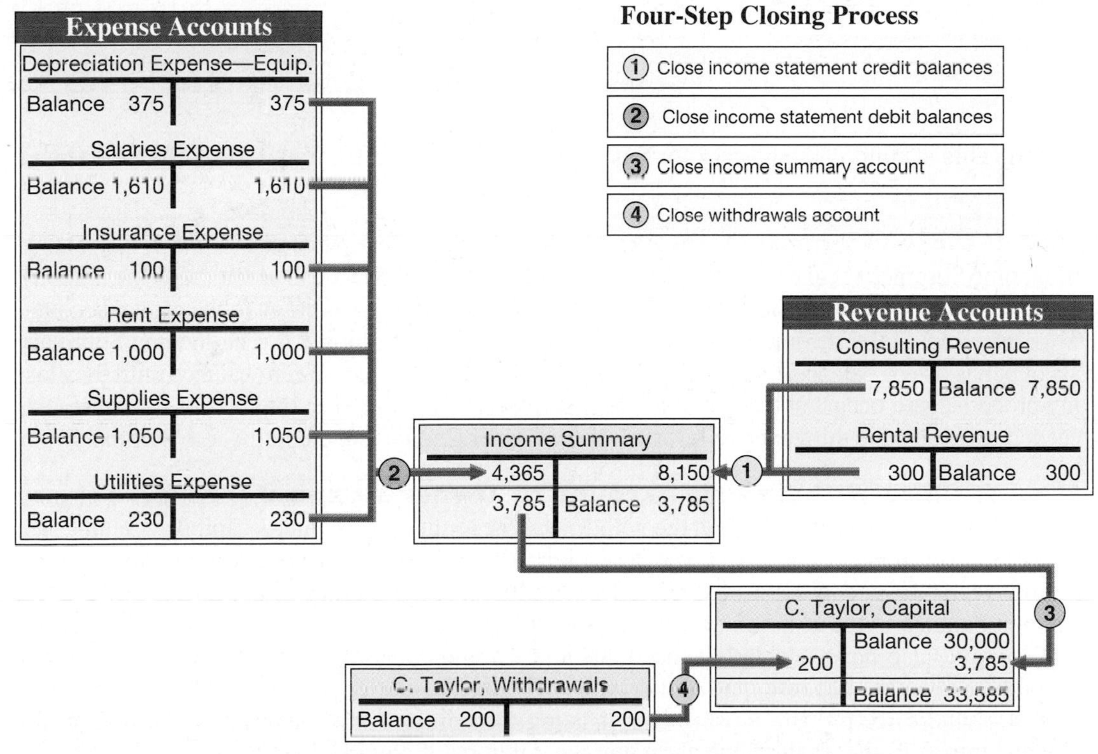

Point: C. Taylor, Capital is the only *permanent account* in Exhibit 4.3.

Step 1: Close Credit Balances in Revenue Accounts to Income Summary The first closing entry transfers credit balances in revenue (and gain) accounts to the Income Summary account. We bring accounts with credit balances to zero by debiting them. For FastForward, this journal entry is step 1 in Exhibit 4.4. This entry closes revenue accounts and leaves them with zero balances. The accounts are now ready to record revenues when they occur in the next period. The $8,150 credit entry to Income Summary equals total revenues for the period.

P2 Describe and prepare closing entries.

Step 2: Close Debit Balances in Expense Accounts to Income Summary The second closing entry transfers debit balances in expense (and loss) accounts to the Income Summary account. We bring expense accounts' debit balances to zero by crediting them. With a balance of zero, these accounts are ready to accumulate a record of expenses for the next

Point: It is possible to close revenue and expense accounts directly to owner's capital. Computerized accounting systems do this.

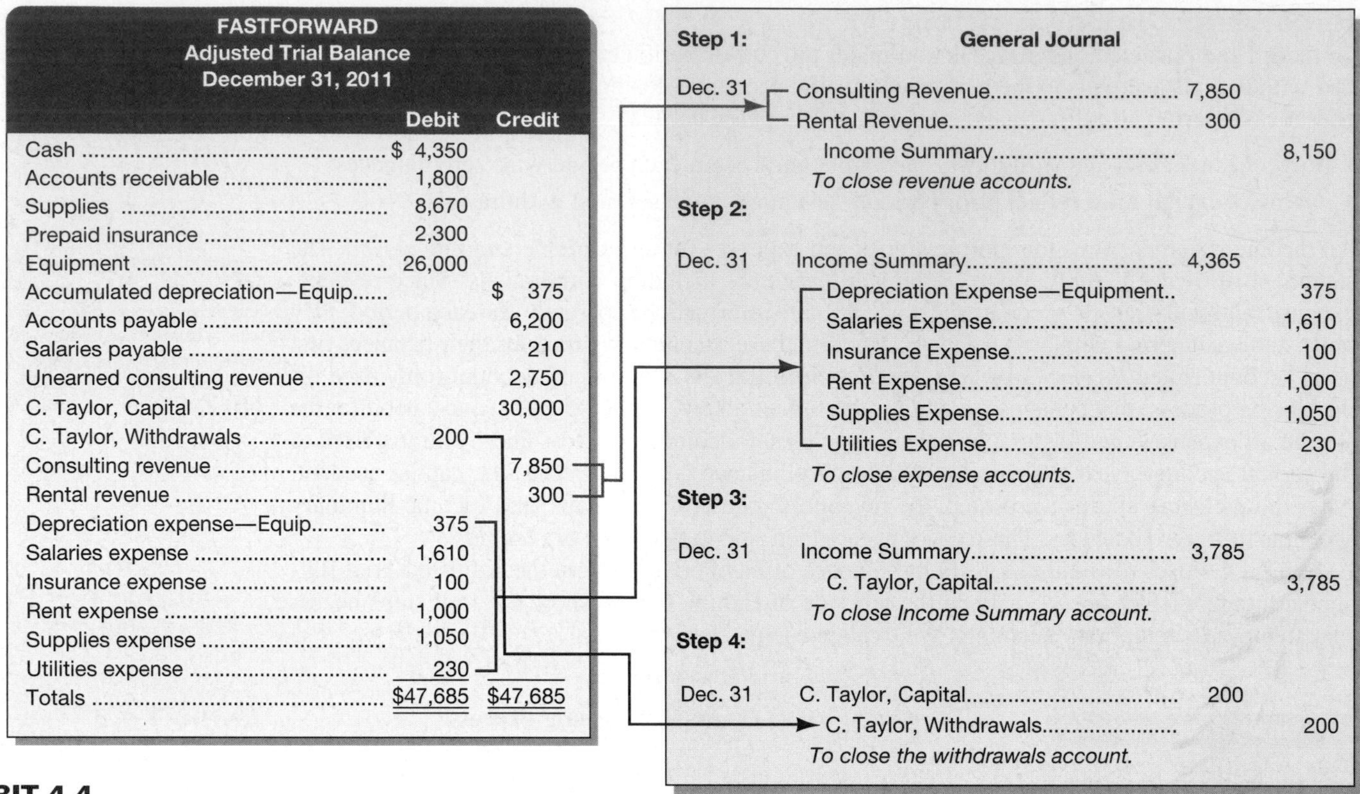

FASTFORWARD
Adjusted Trial Balance
December 31, 2011

	Debit	Credit
Cash	$ 4,350	
Accounts receivable	1,800	
Supplies	8,670	
Prepaid insurance	2,300	
Equipment	26,000	
Accumulated depreciation—Equip.		$ 375
Accounts payable		6,200
Salaries payable		210
Unearned consulting revenue		2,750
C. Taylor, Capital		30,000
C. Taylor, Withdrawals	200	
Consulting revenue		7,850
Rental revenue		300
Depreciation expense—Equip.	375	
Salaries expense	1,610	
Insurance expense	100	
Rent expense	1,000	
Supplies expense	1,050	
Utilities expense	230	
Totals	$47,685	$47,685

General Journal

Step 1:			
Dec. 31	Consulting Revenue	7,850	
	Rental Revenue	300	
	Income Summary		8,150
	To close revenue accounts.		
Step 2:			
Dec. 31	Income Summary	4,365	
	Depreciation Expense—Equipment		375
	Salaries Expense		1,610
	Insurance Expense		100
	Rent Expense		1,000
	Supplies Expense		1,050
	Utilities Expense		230
	To close expense accounts.		
Step 3:			
Dec. 31	Income Summary	3,785	
	C. Taylor, Capital		3,785
	To close Income Summary account.		
Step 4:			
Dec. 31	C. Taylor, Capital	200	
	C. Taylor, Withdrawals		200
	To close the withdrawals account.		

EXHIBIT 4.4

Preparing Closing Entries

period. This second closing entry for FastForward is step 2 in Exhibit 4.4. Exhibit 4.3 shows that posting this entry gives each expense account a zero balance.

Step 3: Close Income Summary to Owner's Capital After steps 1 and 2, the balance of Income Summary is equal to December's net income of $3,785 ($8,150 credit less $4,365 debit). The third closing entry transfers the balance of the Income Summary account to the capital account. This entry closes the Income Summary account–see step 3 in Exhibit 4.4. The Income Summary account has a zero balance after posting this entry. It continues to have a zero balance until the closing process again occurs at the end of the next period. (If a net loss occurred because expenses exceeded revenues, the third entry is reversed: debit Owner Capital and credit Income Summary.)

Step 4: Close Withdrawals Account to Owner's Capital The fourth closing entry transfers any debit balance in the withdrawals account to the owner's capital account—see step 4 in Exhibit 4.4. This entry gives the withdrawals account a zero balance, and the account is now ready to accumulate next period's withdrawals. This entry also reduces the capital account balance to the $33,585 amount reported on the balance sheet.

We could also have selected the accounts and amounts needing to be closed by identifying individual revenue, expense, and withdrawals accounts in the ledger. This is illustrated in Exhibit 4.4 where we prepare closing entries using the adjusted trial balance.[1] (Information for closing entries is also in the financial statement columns of a work sheet.)

Post-Closing Trial Balance

P3 Explain and prepare a post-closing trial balance.

Exhibit 4.5 shows the entire ledger of FastForward as of December 31 after adjusting and closing entries are posted. (The transaction and adjusting entries are in Chapters 2 and 3.) The temporary accounts (revenues, expenses, and withdrawals) have ending balances equal to zero.

[1] The closing process has focused on proprietorships. It is identical for partnerships with the exception that each owner has separate capital and withdrawals accounts (for steps 3 and 4). The closing process for a corporation is similar with the exception that it uses a Retained Earnings account instead of a Capital account, and a Dividend account instead of a Withdrawals account.

EXHIBIT 4.5

General Ledger after the Closing Process for FastForward

Asset Accounts

Cash — Acct. No. 101

Date	Explan.	PR	Debit	Credit	Balance
2011					
Dec. 1	(1)	G1	30,000		30,000
2	(2)	G1		2,500	27,500
3	(3)	G1		26,000	1,500
5	(5)	G1	4,200		5,700
6	(13)	G1		2,400	3,300
12	(6)	G1		1,000	2,300
12	(7)	G1		700	1,600
22	(9)	G1	1,900		3,500
24	(10)	G1		900	2,600
24	(11)	G1		200	2,400
26	(12)	G1	3,000		5,400
26	(14)	G1		120	5,280
26	(15)	G1		230	5,050
26	(16)	G1		700	**4,350**

Accounts Receivable — Acct. No. 106

Date	Explan.	PR	Debit	Credit	Balance
2011					
Dec. 12	(8)	G1	1,900		1,900
22	(9)	G1		1,900	0
31	Adj.(f)	G1	1,800		**1,800**

Supplies — Acct. No. 126

Date	Explan.	PR	Debit	Credit	Balance
2011					
Dec. 2	(2)	G1	2,500		2,500
6	(4)	G1	7,100		9,600
26	(14)	G1	120		9,720
31	Adj.(b)	G1		1,050	**8,670**

Prepaid Insurance — Acct. No. 128

Date	Explan.	PR	Debit	Credit	Balance
2011					
Dec. 6	(13)	G1	2,400		2,400
31	Adj.(a)	G1		100	**2,300**

Equipment — Acct. No. 167

Date	Explan.	PR	Debit	Credit	Balance
2011					
Dec. 3	(3)	G1	26,000		**26,000**

Accumulated Depreciation—Equipment — Acct. No. 168

Date	Explan.	PR	Debit	Credit	Balance
2011					
Dec. 31	Adj.(c)	G1		375	**375**

Liability and Equity Accounts

Accounts Payable — Acct. No. 201

Date	Explan.	PR	Debit	Credit	Balance
2011					
Dec. 6	(4)	G1		7,100	7,100
24	(10)	G1	900		**6,200**

Salaries Payable — Acct. No. 209

Date	Explan.	PR	Debit	Credit	Balance
2011					
Dec. 31	Adj.(e)	G1		210	**210**

Unearned Consulting Revenue — Acct. No. 236

Date	Explan.	PR	Debit	Credit	Balance
2011					
Dec. 26	(12)	G1		3,000	3,000
31	Adj.(d)	G1	250		**2,750**

C. Taylor, Capital — Acct. No. 301

Date	Explan.	PR	Debit	Credit	Balance
2011					
Dec. 1	(1)	G1		30,000	**30,000**
31	**Clos.(3)**	**G1**		**3,785**	**33,785**
31	**Clos.(4)**	**G1**	**200**		**33,585**

C. Taylor, Withdrawals — Acct. No. 302

Date	Explan.	PR	Debit	Credit	Balance
2011					
Dec. 24	(11)	G1	200		**200**
31	**Clos.(4)**	**G1**		**200**	**0**

Revenue and Expense Accounts (Including Income Summary)

Consulting Revenue — Acct. No. 403

Date	Explan.	PR	Debit	Credit	Balance
2011					
Dec. 5	(5)	G1		4,200	4,200
12	(8)	G1		1,600	5,800
31	Adj.(d)	G1		250	6,050
31	Adj.(f)	G1		1,800	**7,850**
31	**Clos.(1)**	**G1**	**7,850**		**0**

Rental Revenue — Acct. No. 406

Date	Explan.	PR	Debit	Credit	Balance
2011					
Dec. 12	(8)	G1		300	**300**
31	**Clos.(1)**	**G1**	**300**		**0**

Depreciation Expense—Equipment — Acct. No. 612

Date	Explan.	PR	Debit	Credit	Balance
2011					
Dec. 31	Adj.(c)	G1	375		**375**
31	**Clos.(2)**	**G1**		**375**	**0**

Salaries Expense — Acct. No. 622

Date	Explan.	PR	Debit	Credit	Balance
2011					
Dec. 12	(7)	G1	700		700
26	(16)	G1	700		1,400
31	Adj.(e)	G1	210		**1,610**
31	**Clos.(2)**	**G1**		**1,610**	**0**

Insurance Expense — Acct. No. 637

Date	Explan.	PR	Debit	Credit	Balance
2011					
Dec. 31	Adj.(a)	G1	100		**100**
31	**Clos.(2)**	**G1**		**100**	**0**

Rent Expense — Acct. No. 640

Date	Explan.	PR	Debit	Credit	Balance
2011					
Dec. 12	(6)	G1	1,000		**1,000**
31	**Clos.(2)**	**G1**		**1,000**	**0**

Supplies Expense — Acct. No. 652

Date	Explan.	PR	Debit	Credit	Balance
2011					
Dec. 31	Adj.(b)	G1	1,050		**1,050**
31	**Clos.(2)**	**G1**		**1,050**	**0**

Utilities Expense — Acct. No. 690

Date	Explan.	PR	Debit	Credit	Balance
2011					
Dec. 26	(15)	G1	230		**230**
31	**Clos.(2)**	**G1**		**230**	**0**

Income Summary — Acct. No. 901

Date	Explan.	PR	Debit	Credit	Balance
2011					
Dec. 31	**Clos.(1)**	**G1**		**8,150**	**8,150**
31	**Clos.(2)**	**G1**	**4,365**		**3,785**
31	**Clos.(3)**	**G1**	**3,785**		**0**

A **post-closing trial balance** is a list of permanent accounts and their balances from the ledger after all closing entries have been journalized and posted. It lists the balances for all accounts not closed. These accounts comprise a company's assets, liabilities, and equity, which are identical to those in the balance sheet. The aim of a post-closing trial balance is to verify that (1) total debits equal total credits for permanent accounts and (2) all temporary accounts have zero balances. FastForward's post-closing trial balance is shown in Exhibit 4.6. The post-closing trial balance usually is the last step in the accounting process.

EXHIBIT 4.6

Post-Closing Trial Balance

FASTFORWARD
Post-Closing Trial Balance
December 31, 2011

	Debit	Credit
Cash	$ 4,350	
Accounts receivable	1,800	
Supplies	8,670	
Prepaid insurance	2,300	
Equipment	26,000	
Accumulated depreciation—Equipment		$ 375
Accounts payable		6,200
Salaries payable		210
Unearned consulting revenue		2,750
C. Taylor, Capital		33,585
Totals	$43,120	$43,120

ACCOUNTING CYCLE

C2 Identify steps in the accounting cycle.

The term **accounting cycle** refers to the steps in preparing financial statements. It is called a *cycle* because the steps are repeated each reporting period. Exhibit 4.7 shows the 10 steps in the cycle, beginning with analyzing transactions and ending with a post-closing trial balance or

EXHIBIT 4.7

Steps in the Accounting Cycle*

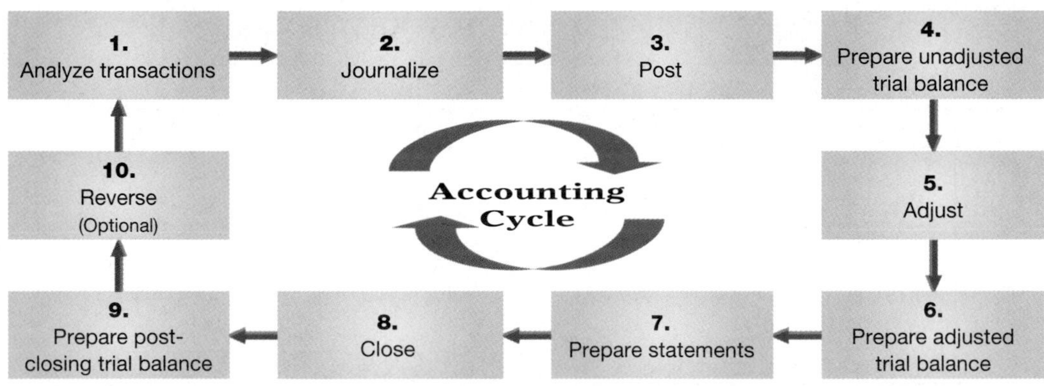

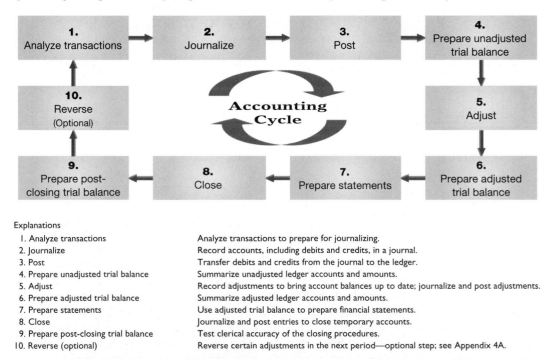

Explanations

1. Analyze transactions	Analyze transactions to prepare for journalizing.
2. Journalize	Record accounts, including debits and credits, in a journal.
3. Post	Transfer debits and credits from the journal to the ledger.
4. Prepare unadjusted trial balance	Summarize unadjusted ledger accounts and amounts.
5. Adjust	Record adjustments to bring account balances up to date; journalize and post adjustments.
6. Prepare adjusted trial balance	Summarize adjusted ledger accounts and amounts.
7. Prepare statements	Use adjusted trial balance to prepare financial statements.
8. Close	Journalize and post entries to close temporary accounts.
9. Prepare post-closing trial balance	Test clerical accuracy of the closing procedures.
10. Reverse (optional)	Reverse certain adjustments in the next period—optional step; see Appendix 4A.

* Steps 4, 6, and 9 can be done on a work sheet. A work sheet is useful in planning adjustments, but adjustments (step 5) must always be journalized and posted. Steps 3, 4, 6, and 9 are automatic with a computerized system.

reversing entries. Steps 1 through 3 usually occur regularly as a company enters into transactions. Steps 4 through 9 are done at the end of a period. *Reversing entries* in step 10 are optional and are explained in Appendix 4A.

Quick Check Answers — p. 156 

4. What are the major steps in preparing closing entries?
5. Why are revenue and expense accounts called *temporary?* Identify and list the types of temporary accounts.
6. What accounts are listed on the post-closing trial balance?

CLASSIFIED BALANCE SHEET

C3 Explain and prepare a classified balance sheet.

Our discussion to this point has been limited to unclassified financial statements. This section describes a classified balance sheet. The next chapter describes a classified income statement. An **unclassified balance sheet** is one whose items are broadly grouped into assets, liabilities, and equity. One example is FastForward's balance sheet in Exhibit 4.2. A **classified balance sheet** organizes assets and liabilities into important subgroups that provide more information to decision makers.

Classification Structure

A classified balance sheet has no required layout, but it usually contains the categories in Exhibit 4.8. One of the more important classifications is the separation between current and noncurrent items for both assets and liabilities. Current items are those expected to come due (either collected or owed) within one year or the company's operating cycle, whichever is longer. The **operating cycle** is the time span from when *cash is used* to acquire goods and services until *cash is received* from the sale of goods and services. "Operating" refers to company operations and "cycle" refers to the circular flow of cash used for company inputs and then cash received from its outputs. The length of a company's operating cycle depends on its activities. For a service company, the operating cycle is the time span between (1) paying employees who perform the services and (2) receiving cash from customers. For a merchandiser selling products, the operating cycle is the time span between (1) paying suppliers for merchandise and (2) receiving cash from customers.

EXHIBIT 4.8

Typical Categories in a Classified Balance Sheet

Assets	Liabilities and Equity
Current assets	Current liabilities
Noncurrent assets	Noncurrent liabilities
Long-term investments	Equity
Plant assets	
Intangible assets	

Most operating cycles are less than one year. This means most companies use a one-year period in deciding which assets and liabilities are current. A few companies have an operating cycle longer than one year. For instance, producers of certain beverages (wine) and products (ginseng) that require aging for several years have operating cycles longer than one year. A balance sheet lists current assets before noncurrent assets and current liabilities before noncurrent liabilities. This consistency in presentation allows users to quickly identify current assets that are most easily converted to cash and current liabilities that are shortly coming due. Items in current assets and current liabilities are listed in the order of how quickly they will be converted to, or paid in, cash.

EXHIBIT 4.9

Example of a Classified Balance Sheet

SNOWBOARDING COMPONENTS Balance Sheet January 31, 2011		
Assets		
Current assets		
Cash	$ 6,500	
Short-term investments	2,100	
Accounts receivable, net	4,400	
Merchandise inventory	27,500	
Prepaid expenses	2,400	
Total current assets		$ 42,900
Long-term investments		
Notes receivable	1,500	
Investments in stocks and bonds	18,000	
Land held for future expansion	48,000	
Total long-term investments		67,500
Plant assets		
Equipment and buildings	203,200	
Less accumulated depreciation	53,000	
Equipment and buildings, net		150,200
Land		73,200
Total plant assets		223,400
Intangible assets		10,000
Total assets		$343,800
Liabilities		
Current liabilities		
Accounts payable	$ 15,300	
Wages payable	3,200	
Notes payable	3,000	
Current portion of long-term liabilities	7,500	
Total current liabilities		$ 29,000
Long-term liabilities (net of current portion)		150,000
Total liabilities		179,000
Equity		
T. Hawk, Capital		164,800
Total liabilities and equity		$343,800

Classification Categories

This section describes the most common categories in a classified balance sheet. The balance sheet for Snowboarding Components in Exhibit 4.9 shows the typical categories. Its assets are classified as either current or noncurrent. Its noncurrent assets include three main categories: long-term investments, plant assets, and intangible assets. Its liabilities are classified as either current or long-term. Not all companies use the same categories of assets and liabilities for their balance sheets. **K2 Inc.**, a manufacturer of snowboards, reported a balance sheet with only three asset classes: current assets; property, plant and equipment; and other assets.

Current Assets **Current assets** are cash and other resources that are expected to be sold, collected, or used within one year or the company's operating cycle, whichever is longer. Examples are cash, short-term investments, accounts receivable, short-term notes receivable, goods for sale (called *merchandise* or *inventory*), and prepaid expenses. The individual prepaid expenses of a company are usually small in amount compared to many other assets and are often combined and shown as a single item. The prepaid expenses in Exhibit 4.9 likely include items such as prepaid insurance, prepaid rent, office supplies, and store supplies. Prepaid expenses are usually listed last because they will not be converted to cash (instead, they are used).

Point: Current is also called *short-term,* and noncurrent is also called *long-term.*

Long-Term Investments A second major balance sheet classification is **long-term** (or *noncurrent*) **investments.** Notes receivable and investments in stocks and bonds are long-term assets when they are expected to be held for more than the longer of one year or the operating cycle. Land held for future expansion is a long-term investment because it is *not* used in operations.

Plant Assets Plant assets are tangible assets that are both *long-lived* and *used to produce* or *sell products and services.* Examples are equipment, machinery, buildings, and land that are used to produce or sell products and services. The order listing for plant assets is usually from most liquid to least liquid such as equipment and machinery to buildings and land.

Point: Plant assets are also called *fixed assets; property, plant and equipment;* or *long-lived assets.*

Intangible Assets **Intangible assets** are long-term resources that benefit business operations, usually lack physical form, and have uncertain benefits. Examples are patents, trademarks, copyrights, franchises, and goodwill. Their value comes from the privileges or rights granted to or held by the owner. **K2, Inc.**, reported intangible assets of $228 million, which is nearly 20 percent of its total assets. Its intangibles included trademarks, patents, and licensing agreements.

Current Liabilities **Current liabilities** are obligations due to be paid or settled within one year or the operating cycle, whichever is longer. They are usually settled by paying out current assets such as cash. Current liabilities often include accounts payable, notes payable, wages payable, taxes payable, interest payable, and unearned revenues. Also, any portion of a long-term liability due to be paid within one year or the operating cycle, whichever is longer, is a current liability. Unearned revenues are current liabilities when they will be settled by delivering products or services within one year or the operating cycle, whichever is longer. Current liabilities are reported in the order of those to be settled first.

Point: Many financial ratios are distorted if accounts are not classified correctly.

Long-Term Liabilities **Long-term liabilities** are obligations *not* due within one year or the operating cycle, whichever is longer. Notes payable, mortgages payable, bonds payable, and lease obligations are common long-term liabilities. If a company has both short- and long term items in each of these categories, they are commonly separated into two accounts in the ledger.

Point: Only assets and liabilities are classified as current or noncurrent.

Equity Equity is the owner's claim on assets. For a proprietorship, this claim is reported in the equity section with an owner's capital account. (For a partnership, the equity section reports a capital account for each partner. For a corporation, the equity section is divided into two main subsections, common stock and retained earnings.)

Quick Check Answers — p. 156 

7. Classify the following assets as (1) current assets, (2) plant assets, or (3) intangible assets: (*a*) land used in operations, (*b*) office supplies, (*c*) receivables from customers due in 10 months, (*d*) insurance protection for the next 9 months, (*e*) trucks used to provide services to customers, (*f*) trademarks.
8. Cite at least two examples of assets classified as investments on the balance sheet.
9. Explain the operating cycle for a service company.

GLOBAL VIEW

We explained that accounting under U.S. GAAP is similar, but not identical, to that under IFRS. This section discusses differences in the closing process and in reporting assets and liabilities on a balance sheet.

Closing Process The closing process is identical under U.S. GAAP and IFRS. Although unique accounts can arise under either system, the closing process remains the same.

Reporting Assets and Liabilities The definition of an asset is similar under U.S. GAAP and IFRS and involves three basic criteria: (1) the company owns or controls the right to use the item, (2) the right arises from a past transaction or event, and (3) the item can be reliably measured. Both systems define the initial asset value as historical cost for nearly all assets. After acquisition, one of two asset measurement systems is applied: historical cost or fair value. Generally, U.S. GAAP defines fair value as the amount to be received in an orderly sale. IFRS defines fair value as *exchange value*—either replacement cost or selling price. We describe these differences, and the assets to which they apply, in later chapters.

The definition of a liability is similar under U.S. GAAP and IFRS and involves three basic criteria: (1) the item is a *present* obligation requiring a probable future resource outlay, (2) the obligation arises from a past transaction or event, and (3) the obligation can be reliably measured. As with assets, both systems apply one of two measurement systems to liabilities: historical cost or fair value. Later chapters discuss specific differences.

Decision Analysis  Current Ratio

A1 Compute the current ratio and describe what it reveals about a company's financial condition.

An important use of financial statements is to help assess a company's ability to pay its debts in the near future. Such analysis affects decisions by suppliers when allowing a company to buy on credit. It also affects decisions by creditors when lending money to a company, including loan terms such as interest rate, due date, and collateral requirements. It can also affect a manager's decisions about using cash to pay debts when they come due. The **current ratio** is one measure of a company's ability to pay its short-term obligations. It is defined in Exhibit 4.10 as current assets divided by current liabilities.

EXHIBIT 4.10
Current Ratio

$$\textbf{Current ratio} = \frac{\textbf{Current assets}}{\textbf{Current liabilities}}$$

Using financial information from **Limited Brands, Inc.**, we compute its current ratio for the recent four-year period. The results are in Exhibit 4.11.

EXHIBIT 4.11
Limited Brands' Current Ratio

$ in millions	2010	2009	2008	2007	2006
Current assets	$3,250	$2,867	$2,919	$2,771	$2,784
Current liabilities	$1,322	$1,255	$1,374	$1,709	$1,575
Current ratio	**2.5**	**2.3**	**2.1**	**1.6**	**1.8**
Industry current ratio	1.9	2.0	2.1	2.3	2.4

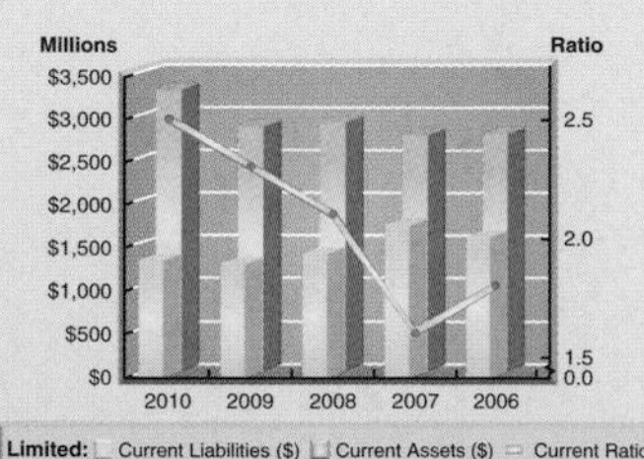

Limited Brands' current ratio averaged 2.1 for its fiscal years 2006 through 2010. The current ratio for each of these years suggests that the company's short-term obligations can be covered with its short-term assets. However, if its ratio would approach 1.0, Limited would expect to face challenges in covering liabilities. If the ratio were *less* than 1.0, current liabilities would exceed current assets, and the company's ability to pay short-term obligations could be in doubt.

Decision Maker Answer — p. 156

Analyst You are analyzing the financial condition of a company to assess its ability to meet upcoming loan payments. You compute its current ratio as 1.2. You also find that a major portion of accounts receivable is due from one client who has not made any payments in the past 12 months. Removing this receivable from current assets lowers the current ratio to 0.7. What do you conclude? ■

DEMONSTRATION PROBLEM

The partial work sheet of Midtown Repair Company at December 31, 2011, follows.

	Adjusted Trial Balance		Income Statement		Balance Sheet and Statement of Owner's Equity	
	Debit	Credit	Debit	Credit	Debit	Credit
Cash	95,600					
Notes receivable (current)	50,000					
Prepaid insurance	16,000					
Prepaid rent	4,000					
Equipment	170,000					
Accumulated depreciation—Equipment		57,000				
Accounts payable		52,000				
Long-term notes payable		63,000				
C. Trout, Capital		178,500				
C. Trout, Withdrawals	30,000					
Repair services revenue		180,800				
Interest revenue		7,500				
Depreciation expense—Equipment	28,500					
Wages expense	85,000					
Rent expense	48,000					
Insurance expense	6,000					
Interest expense	5,700					
Totals	538,800	538,800				

Required

1. Complete the work sheet by extending the adjusted trial balance totals to the appropriate financial statement columns.
2. Prepare closing entries for Midtown Repair Company.
3. Set up the Income Summary and the C. Trout, Capital account in the general ledger (in balance column format) and post the closing entries to these accounts.
4. Determine the balance of the C. Trout, Capital account to be reported on the December 31, 2011, balance sheet.
5. Prepare an income statement, statement of owner's equity, and classified balance sheet (in report form) as of December 31, 2011.

PLANNING THE SOLUTION

- Extend the adjusted trial balance account balances to the appropriate financial statement columns.
- Prepare entries to close the revenue accounts to Income Summary, to close the expense accounts to Income Summary, to close Income Summary to the capital account, and to close the withdrawals account to the capital account.

- Post the first and second closing entries to the Income Summary account. Examine the balance of income summary and verify that it agrees with the net income shown on the work sheet.
- Post the third and fourth closing entries to the capital account.
- Use the work sheet's two right-most columns and your answer in part 4 to prepare the classified balance sheet.

SOLUTION TO DEMONSTRATION PROBLEM

1. Completing the work sheet.

	Adjusted Trial Balance		Income Statement		Balance Sheet and Statement of Owner's Equity	
	Debit	Credit	Debit	Credit	Debit	Credit
Cash	95,600				95,600	
Notes receivable (current)	50,000				50,000	
Prepaid insurance	16,000				16,000	
Prepaid rent	4,000				4,000	
Equipment	170,000				170,000	
Accumulated depreciation—Equipment		57,000				57,000
Accounts payable		52,000				52,000
Long-term notes payable		63,000				63,000
C. Trout, Capital		178,500				178,500
C. Trout, Withdrawals	30,000				30,000	
Repair services revenue		180,800		180,800		
Interest revenue		7,500		7,500		
Depreciation expense—Equipment	28,500		28,500			
Wages expense	85,000		85,000			
Rent expense	48,000		48,000			
Insurance expense	6,000		6,000			
Interest expense	5,700		5,700			
Totals	538,800	538,800	173,200	188,300	365,600	350,500
Net income			15,100			15,100
Totals			188,300	188,300	365,600	365,600

2. Closing entries.

Dec. 31	Repair Services Revenue	180,800	
	Interest Revenue	7,500	
	Income Summary		188,300
	To close revenue accounts.		
Dec. 31	Income Summary	173,200	
	Depreciation Expense—Equipment		28,500
	Wages Expense		85,000
	Rent Expense		48,000
	Insurance Expense		6,000
	Interest Expense		5,700
	To close expense accounts.		
Dec. 31	Income Summary	15,100	
	C. Trout, Capital		15,100
	To close the Income Summary account.		
Dec. 31	C. Trout, Capital	30,000	
	C. Trout, Withdrawals		30,000
	To close the withdrawals account.		

3. Set up the Income Summary and the capital ledger accounts and post the closing entries.

Income Summary					Account No. 901
Date	Explanation	PR	Debit	Credit	Balance
2011					
Jan. 1	Beginning balance				0
Dec. 31	Close revenue accounts			188,300	188,300
31	Close expense accounts		173,200		15,100
31	Close income summary		15,100		0

C. Trout, Capital					Account No. 301
Date	Explanation	PR	Debit	Credit	Balance
2011					
Jan. 1	Beginning balance				178,500
Dec. 31	Close Income Summary			15,100	193,600
31	Close C. Trout, Withdrawals		30,000		163,600

4. The final capital balance of $163,600 (from part 3) will be reported on the December 31, 2011, balance sheet. The final capital balance reflects the increase due to the net income earned during the year and the decrease for the owner's withdrawals during the year.

5.

MIDTOWN REPAIR COMPANY Income Statement For Year Ended December 31, 2011		
Revenues		
Repair services revenue	$180,800	
Interest revenue	7,500	
Total revenues		$188,300
Expenses		
Depreciation expense—Equipment	28,500	
Wages expense	85,000	
Rent expense	48,000	
Insurance expense	6,000	
Interest expense	5,700	
Total expenses		173,200
Net income		$ 15,100

MIDTOWN REPAIR COMPANY Statement of Owner's Equity For Year Ended December 31, 2011		
C. Trout, Capital, December 31, 2010		$178,500
Add: Investment by owner	$ 0	
Net income	15,100	15,100
		193,600
Less: Withdrawals by owner		30,000
C. Trout, Capital, December 31, 2011		$163,600

MIDTOWN REPAIR COMPANY Balance Sheet December 31, 2011		
Assets		
Current assets		
Cash		$ 95,600
Notes receivable		50,000
Prepaid insurance		16,000
Prepaid rent		4,000
Total current assets		165,600
Plant assets		
Equipment	$170,000	
Less: Accumulated depreciation—Equipment	(57,000)	
Total plant assets		113,000
Total assets		$278,600
Liabilities		
Current liabilities		
Accounts payable		$ 52,000
Long-term liabilities		
Long-term notes payable		63,000
Total liabilities		115,000
Equity		
C. Trout, Capital		163,600
Total liabilities and equity		$278,600

APPENDIX

4A Reversing Entries

Reversing entries are optional. They are recorded in response to accrued assets and accrued liabilities that were created by adjusting entries at the end of a reporting period. The purpose of reversing entries is to simplify a company's recordkeeping. Exhibit 4A.1 shows an example of FastForward's reversing entries. The top of the exhibit shows the adjusting entry FastForward recorded on December 31 for its employee's earned but unpaid salary. The entry recorded three days' salary of $210, which increased December's total salary expense to $1,610. The entry also recognized a liability of $210. The expense is reported on December's income statement. The expense account is then closed. The ledger on January 1, 2012, shows a $210 liability and a zero balance in the Salaries Expense account. At this point, the choice is made between using or not using reversing entries.

Point: As a general rule, adjusting entries that create new asset or liability accounts are likely candidates for reversing.

Accounting *without* Reversing Entries The path down the left side of Exhibit 4A.1 is described in the chapter. To summarize here, when the next payday occurs on January 9, we record payment with a compound entry that debits both the expense and liability accounts and credits Cash. Posting that entry creates a $490 balance in the expense account and reduces the liability account balance to zero because the debt has been settled. The disadvantage of this approach is the slightly more complex entry required on January 9. Paying the accrued liability means that this entry differs from the routine entries made on all other paydays. To construct the proper entry on January 9, we must recall the effect of the December 31 adjusting entry. Reversing entries overcome this disadvantage.

P4 Prepare reversing entries and explain their purpose.

Accounting *with* Reversing Entries The right side of Exhibit 4A.1 shows how a reversing entry on January 1 overcomes the disadvantage of the January 9 entry when not using reversing entries. A reversing entry is the exact opposite of an adjusting entry. For FastForward, the Salaries Payable liability account is debited for $210, meaning that this account now has a zero balance after the entry is posted. The Salaries Payable account temporarily understates the liability, but this is not a problem since

EXHIBIT 4A.1

Reversing Entries for an Accrued Expense

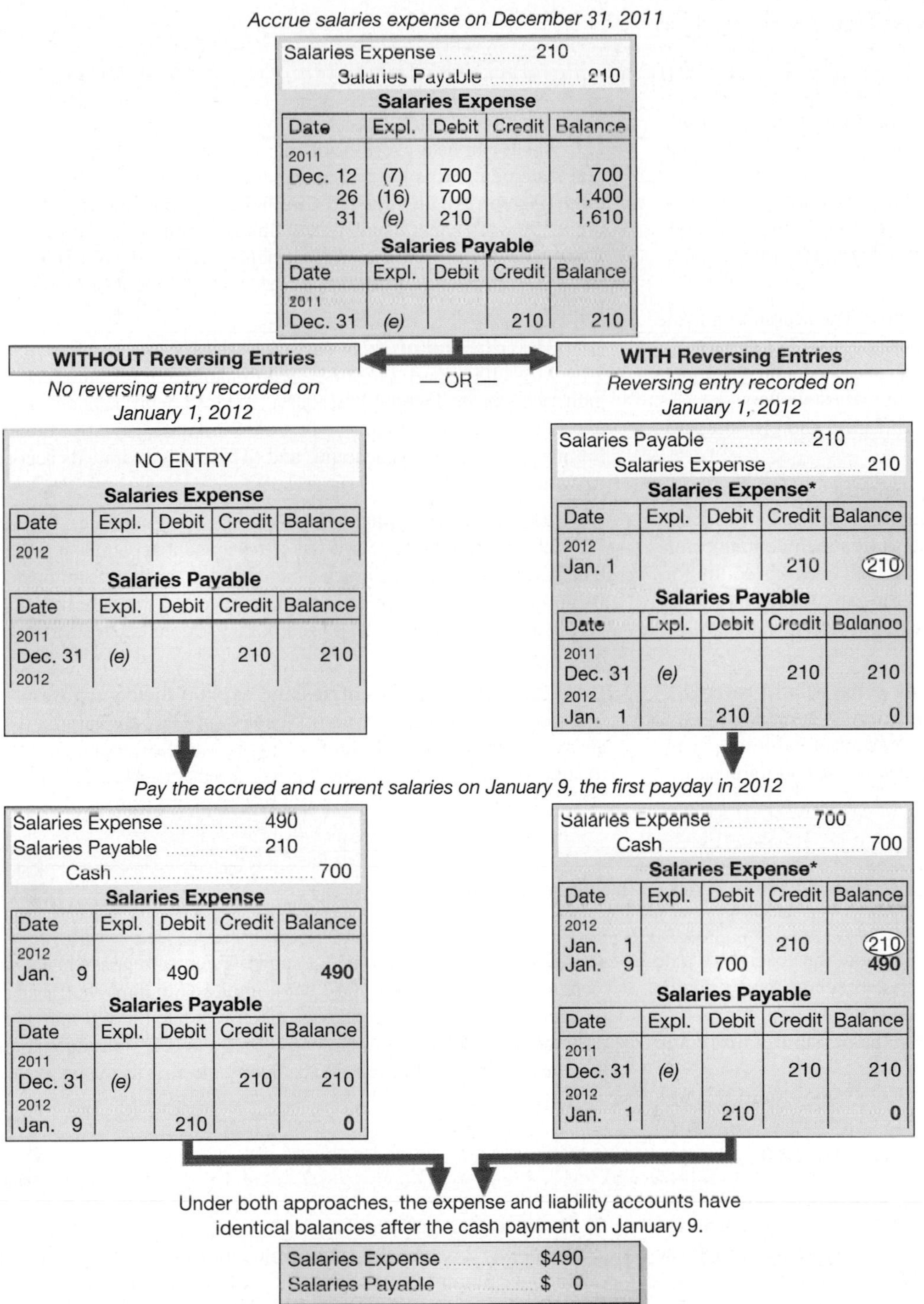

*Circled numbers in the *Balance* column indicate abnormal balances.

financial statements are not prepared before the liability is settled on January 9. The credit to the Salaries Expense account is unusual because it gives the account an *abnormal credit balance.* We highlight an abnormal balance by circling it. Because of the reversing entry, the January 9 entry to record payment is straightforward. This entry debits the Salaries Expense account and credits Cash for the full $700 paid. It is the same as all other entries made to record 10 days' salary for the employee. Notice that after the payment entry is posted, the Salaries Expense account has a $490 balance that reflects seven days' salary of $70 per day (see the lower right side of Exhibit 4A.1). The zero balance in the Salaries Payable account is now correct. The lower section of Exhibit 4A.1 shows that the expense and liability accounts have exactly the same balances whether reversing entries are used or not. This means that both approaches yield identical results.

Summary

C1 Explain why temporary accounts are closed each period. Temporary accounts are closed at the end of each accounting period for two main reasons. First, the closing process updates the capital account to include the effects of all transactions and events recorded for the period. Second, it prepares revenue, expense, and withdrawals accounts for the next reporting period by giving them zero balances.

C2 Identify steps in the accounting cycle. The accounting cycle consists of 10 steps: (1) analyze transactions, (2) journalize, (3) post, (4) prepare an unadjusted trial balance, (5) adjust accounts, (6) prepare an adjusted trial balance, (7) prepare statements, (8) close, (9) prepare a post-closing trial balance, and (10) prepare (optional) reversing entries.

C3 Explain and prepare a classified balance sheet. Classified balance sheets report assets and liabilities in two categories: current and noncurrent. Noncurrent assets often include long-term investments, plant assets, and intangible assets. Owner's equity for proprietorships (and partnerships) report the capital account balance. A corporation separates equity into common stock and retained earnings.

A1 Compute the current ratio and describe what it reveals about a company's financial condition. A company's current ratio is defined as current assets divided by current liabilities. We use it to evaluate a company's ability to pay its current liabilities out of current assets.

P1 Prepare a work sheet and explain its usefulness. A work sheet can be a useful tool in preparing and analyzing financial statements. It is helpful at the end of a period in preparing adjusting entries, an adjusted trial balance, and financial statements. A work sheet usually contains five pairs of columns: Unadjusted Trial Balance, Adjustments, Adjusted Trial Balance, Income Statement, and Balance Sheet & Statement of Owner's Equity.

P2 Describe and prepare closing entries. Closing entries involve four steps: (1) close credit balances in revenue (and gain) accounts to Income Summary, (2) close debit balances in expense (and loss) accounts to Income Summary, (3) close Income Summary to the capital account, and (4) close withdrawals account to owner's capital.

P3 Explain and prepare a post-closing trial balance. A post-closing trial balance is a list of permanent accounts and their balances after all closing entries have been journalized and posted. Its purpose is to verify that (1) total debits equal total credits for permanent accounts and (2) all temporary accounts have zero balances.

P4A Prepare reversing entries and explain their purpose. Reversing entries are an optional step. They are applied to accrued expenses and revenues. The purpose of reversing entries is to simplify subsequent journal entries. Financial statements are unaffected by the choice to use or not use reversing entries.

Guidance Answers to Decision Maker and Decision Ethics

Entrepreneur Yes, you are concerned about the absence of a depreciation adjustment. Equipment does depreciate, and financial statements must recognize this occurrence. Its absence suggests an error or a misrepresentation (there is also the possibility that equipment is fully depreciated).

Analyst A current ratio of 1.2 suggests that current assets are sufficient to cover current liabilities, but it implies a minimal buffer in case of errors in measuring current assets or current liabilities. Removing the past due receivable reduces the current ratio to 0.7. Your assessment is that the company will have some difficulty meeting its loan payments.

Guidance Answers to Quick Checks

1. Amounts in the Unadjusted Trial Balance columns are taken from current account balances in the ledger. The balances for new accounts expected to arise from adjusted entries can be left blank or set at zero.
2. A work sheet offers the advantage of listing on one page all necessary information to make adjusting entries.
3. A work sheet can help in (a) accounting efficiency and avoiding errors, (b) linking transactions and events to their effects in financial statements, (c) showing adjustments for audit purposes, (d) preparing interim financial statements, and (e) showing effects from proposed, or what-if, transactions.
4. The major steps in preparing closing entries are to close (1) credit balances in revenue accounts to Income Summary, (2) debit balances in expense accounts to Income Summary, (3) Income Summary to owner's capital, and (4) any withdrawals account to owner's capital.
5. Revenue (and gain) and expense (and loss) accounts are called *temporary* because they are opened and closed each period. The Income Summary and owner's withdrawals accounts are also temporary.
6. Permanent accounts make up the post-closing trial balance, which consist of asset, liability, and equity accounts.
7. Current assets: (*b*), (*c*), (*d*). Plant assets: (*a*), (*e*). Item (*f*) is an intangible asset.
8. Investment in common stock, investment in bonds, and land held for future expansion.
9. For a service company, the operating cycle is the usual time between (1) paying employees who do the services and (2) receiving cash from customers for services provided.

Key Terms

mhhe.com/wildFAP20e

Accounting cycle (p. 146)
Classified balance sheet (p. 147)
Closing entries (p. 143)
Closing process (p. 142)
Current assets (p. 148)
Current liabilities (p. 149)
Current ratio (p. 150)
Income summary (p. 143)
Intangible assets (p. 149)
Long-term investments (p. 149)
Long-term liabilities (p. 149)
Operating cycle (p. 147)
Permanent accounts (p. 142)
Post-closing trial balance (p. 146)
Pro forma financial statements (p. 142)
Reversing entries (p. 154)
Temporary accounts (p. 142)
Unclassified balance sheet (p. 147)
Working papers (p. 138)
Work sheet (p. 138)

Multiple Choice Quiz

Answers on p. 177

mhhe.com/wildFAP20e

Additional Quiz Questions are available at the book's Website.

1. G. Venda, owner of Venda Services, withdrew $25,000 from the business during the current year. The entry to close the withdrawals account at the end of the year is:

a.	G. Venda, Withdrawals	25,000	
	G. Venda, Capital		25,000
b.	Income Summary	25,000	
	G. Venda, Capital		25,000
c.	G. Venda, Withdrawals	25,000	
	Cash		25,000
d.	G. Venda, Capital	25,000	
	Salary Expense		25,000
e.	G. Venda, Capital	25,000	
	G. Venda, Withdrawals		25,000

2. The following information is available for the R. Kandamil Company before closing the accounts. After all of the closing entries are made, what will be the balance in the R. Kandamil, Capital account?

Total revenues	$300,000
Total expenses	195,000
R. Kandamil, Capital	100,000
R. Kandamil, Withdrawals	45,000

a. $360,000
b. $250,000
c. $160,000
d. $150,000
e. $60,000

3. Which of the following errors would cause the balance sheet and statement of owner's equity columns of a work sheet to be out of balance?

a. Entering a revenue amount in the balance sheet and statement of owner's equity debit column.
b. Entering a liability amount in the balance sheet and statement of owner's equity credit column.
c. Entering an expense account in the balance sheet and statement of owner's equity debit column.
d. Entering an asset account in the income statement debit column.
e. Entering a liability amount in the income statement credit column.

4. The temporary account used only in the closing process to hold the amounts of revenues and expenses before the net difference is added or subtracted from the owner's capital account is called the

a. Closing account.
b. Nominal account.
c. Income Summary account.
d. Balance Column account.
e. Contra account.

5. Based on the following information from Repicor Company's balance sheet, what is Repicor Company's current ratio?

Current assets	$ 75,000
Investments	30,000
Plant assets	300,000
Current liabilities	50,000
Long-term liabilities	60,000
D. Repicor, Capital	295,000

a. 2.10
b. 1.50
c. 1.00
d. 0.95
e. 0.67

A *Superscript letter A denotes assignments based on Appendix 4A.*
Icon denotes assignments that involve decision making.

Discussion Questions

1. What accounts are affected by closing entries? What accounts are not affected?
2. What two purposes are accomplished by recording closing entries?
3. What are the steps in recording closing entries?
4. What is the purpose of the Income Summary account?
5. Explain whether an error has occurred if a post-closing trial balance includes a Depreciation Expense account.
6. What tasks are aided by a work sheet?
7. Why are the debit and credit entries in the Adjustments columns of the work sheet identified with letters?
8. What is a company's operating cycle?
9. What classes of assets and liabilities are shown on a typical classified balance sheet?
10. How is unearned revenue classified on the balance sheet?
11. What are the characteristics of plant assets?
12.A How do reversing entries simplify recordkeeping?
13.A If a company recorded accrued salaries expense of $500 at the end of its fiscal year, what reversing entry could be made? When would it be made?
14. Refer to the balance sheet for **Research In Motion** in Appendix A. What five main noncurrent asset categories are used on its classified balance sheet? RIM
15. Refer to **Nokia**'s balance sheet in Appendix A. Identify and list its 9 current assets. NOKIA
16. Refer to **Apple**'s balance sheet in Appendix A. Identify the three accounts listed as current liabilities. Apple
17. Refer to **Palm**'s financial statements in Appendix A. What journal entry was likely recorded as of May 31, 2009, to close its Income Summary account? Palm

connect

QUICK STUDY

QS 4-1
Identifying the accounting cycle
C2

List the following steps of the accounting cycle in their proper order.

a. Preparing the post-closing trial balance.
b. Posting the journal entries.
c. Journalizing and posting adjusting entries.
d. Preparing the adjusted trial balance.
e. Journalizing and posting closing entries.
f. Analyzing transactions and events.
g. Preparing the financial statements.
h. Preparing the unadjusted trial balance.
i. Journalizing transactions and events.

QS 4-2
Explaining temporary and permanent accounts
C1

Complete the following descriptions related to temporary and permanent accounts.

1. Temporary accounts accumulate data related to ______ accounting period.
2. Permanent accounts report on activities related to ______ future accounting periods, and they carry their ending balances into the next period.
3. ______ accounts include all income statement accounts, the withdrawals account, and the Income Summary account.
4. ______ accounts generally consist of all balance sheet accounts, and these accounts are not closed.

QS 4-3
Identifying current accounts and computing the current ratio
A1

Compute Jamar Company's current ratio using the following information.

Accounts receivable	$15,000	Long-term notes payable	$20,000
Accounts payable	10,000	Office supplies	1,800
Buildings	42,000	Prepaid insurance	2,500
Cash	6,000	Unearned services revenue	4,000

QS 4-4
Classifying balance sheet items
C3

The following are common categories on a classified balance sheet.

A. Current assets
B. Long-term investments
C. Plant assets
D. Intangible assets
E. Current liabilities
F. Long-term liabilities

For each of the following items, select the letter that identifies the balance sheet category where the item typically would appear.

_____ **1.** Trademarks
_____ **2.** Accounts receivable
_____ **3.** Land not currently used in operations
_____ **4.** Notes payable (due in three years)
_____ **5.** Cash
_____ **6.** Wages payable
_____ **7.** Store equipment
_____ **8.** Accounts payable

QS 4-5
Applying a work sheet
P1

In preparing a work sheet, indicate the financial statement Debit column to which a normal balance in the following accounts should be extended. Use IS for the Income Statement Debit column and BS for the Balance Sheet and Statement of Owner's Equity Debit column.

_IS_ **a.** Insurance expense
_BS_ **b.** Equipment
_OE_ **c.** Owner, Withdrawals
_IS_ **d.** Depreciation expense—Equipment
_BS_ **e.** Prepaid rent
_BS_ **f.** Accounts receivable

QS 4-6
Ordering work sheet steps
P1

List the following steps in preparing a work sheet in their proper order by writing numbers 1–5 in the blank spaces provided.

a. _____ Prepare an adjusted trial balance on the work sheet.
b. _____ Prepare an unadjusted trial balance on the work sheet.
c. _____ Enter adjustments data on the work sheet.
d. _____ Extend adjusted balances to appropriate financial statement columns.
e. _____ Total the statement columns, compute net income (loss), and complete work sheet.

QS 4-7
Interpreting a work sheet
P1

The following selected information is taken from the work sheet for Wayman Company as of December 31, 2011. Using this information, determine the amount for K. Wayman, Capital, that should be reported on its December 31, 2011, balance sheet.

	Income Statement		Balance Sheet and Statement of Owner's Equity	
	Dr.	Cr.	Dr.	Cr.
⋮				
K. Wayman, Capital				65,000
K. Wayman, Withdrawals			32,000	
⋮				
Totals	115,000	174,000		

QS 4-8
Preparing a partial work sheet
P1

The ledger of Terrel Company includes the following unadjusted normal balances: Prepaid Rent $800, Services Revenue $11,600, and Wages Expense $5,000. Adjusting entries are required for **(a)** accrued rent expense $240; **(b)** accrued services revenue $180; and **(c)** accrued wages expense $160. Enter these unadjusted balances and the necessary adjustments on a work sheet and complete the work sheet for these accounts. *Note:* Also include the following accounts: Accounts Receivable, Wages Payable, and Rent Expense.

QS 4-9
Prepare closing entries from the ledger P2

The ledger of Avril Company includes the following accounts with normal balances: L. Avril, Capital $6,000; L. Avril, Withdrawals $400; Services Revenue $10,000; Wages Expense $5,200; and Rent Expense $800. Prepare the necessary closing entries from the available information at December 31.

QS 4-10
Identify post-closing accounts P3

Identify the accounts listed in QS 4-9 that would be included in a post-closing trial balance.

QS 4-11[A]
Reversing entries
P4

On December 31, 2010, Lester Co. prepared an adjusting entry for $6,700 of earned but unrecorded management fees. On January 16, 2011, Lester received $15,500 cash in management fees, which included the accrued fees earned in 2010. Assuming the company uses reversing entries, prepare the January 1, 2011, reversing entry and the January 16, 2011, cash receipt entry.

QS 4-12
International accounting standards P2

Answer each of the following questions related to international accounting standards.

a. Explain how the closing process is different between accounting under IFRS versus U.S. GAAP.

b. What basic principle do U.S. GAAP and IFRS rely upon in recording the initial acquisition value for nearly all assets?

EXERCISES

Exercise 4-1
Preparing and posting closing entries
P2

Use the March 31 fiscal year-end information from the following ledger accounts (assume that all accounts have normal balances) to prepare closing journal entries and then post those entries to the appropriate ledger accounts.

Check M. Mallon, Capital (ending balance), $38,900

General Ledger

M. Mallon, Capital Acct. No. 301

Date	PR	Debit	Credit	Balance
Mar. 31	G2			42,000

M. Mallon, Withdrawals Acct. No. 302

Date	PR	Debit	Credit	Balance
Mar. 31	G2			25,000

Services Revenue Acct. No. 401

Date	PR	Debit	Credit	Balance
Mar. 31	G2			74,000

Depreciation Expense Acct. No. 603

Date	PR	Debit	Credit	Balance
Mar. 31	G2			17,000

Salaries Expense Acct. No. 622

Date	PR	Debit	Credit	Balance
Mar. 31	G2			21,000

Insurance Expense Acct. No. 637

Date	PR	Debit	Credit	Balance
Mar. 31	G2			4,500

Rent Expense Acct. No. 640

Date	PR	Debit	Credit	Balance
Mar. 31	G2			9,600

Income Summary Acct. No. 901

Date	PR	Debit	Credit	Balance

Exercise 4-2
Preparing closing entries and a post-closing trial balance
P2 P3

The adjusted trial balance for Sundance Marketing Co. follows. Complete the four right-most columns of the table by first entering information for the four closing entries (keyed *1* through *4*) and second by completing the post-closing trial balance.

No.	Account Title	Adjusted Trial Balance		Closing Entry Information		Post-Closing Trial Balance	
		Dr.	Cr.	Dr.	Cr.	Dr.	Cr.
101	Cash	$ 8,200					
106	Accounts receivable	24,000					
153	Equipment	41,000					
154	Accumulated depreciation—Equipment		$ 16,500				
193	Franchise	30,000					
201	Accounts payable		14,000				
209	Salaries payable		3,200				
233	Unearned fees		2,600				
301	H. Sundance, Capital		64,500				
302	H. Sundance, Withdrawals	14,400					
401	Marketing fees earned		79,000				
611	Depreciation expense—Equipment	11,000					
622	Salaries expense	31,500					
640	Rent expense	12,000					
677	Miscellaneous expenses	7,700					
901	Income summary						
	Totals	$179,800	$179,800				

Exercise 4-3
Preparing closing entries and a post-closing trial balance
P2 P3

The following adjusted trial balance contains the accounts and balances of Showers Company as of December 31, 2011, the end of its fiscal year. (1) Prepare the December 31, 2011, closing entries for Showers Company. (2) Prepare the December 31, 2011, post-closing trial balance for Showers Company.

No.	Account Title	Debit	Credit
101	Cash	$18,000	
126	Supplies	12,000	
128	Prepaid insurance	2,000	
167	Equipment	23,000	
168	Accumulated depreciation—Equipment		$ 6,500
301	R. Showers, Capital		46,600
302	R. Showers, Withdrawals	6,000	
404	Services revenue		36,000
612	Depreciation expense—Equipment	2,000	
622	Salaries expense	21,000	
637	Insurance expense	1,500	
640	Rent expense	2,400	
652	Supplies expense	1,200	
	Totals	$89,100	$89,100

Check (2) R. Showers, Capital (ending), $48,500; Total debits, $55,000

Exercise 4-4
Preparing the financial statements
C2

Use the following adjusted trial balance of Webb Trucking Company to prepare the (1) income statement and (2) statement of owner's equity, for the year ended December 31, 2011. The K. Webb, Capital, account balance is $161,000 at December 31, 2010.

Account Title	Debit	Credit
Cash	$ 7,000	
Accounts receivable	16,500	
Office supplies	2,000	
Trucks	170,000	
Accumulated depreciation—Trucks		$ 35,000
Land	75,000	
Accounts payable		11,000
Interest payable		3,000
Long-term notes payable		52,000
K. Webb, Capital		161,000
K. Webb, Withdrawals	19,000	
Trucking fees earned		128,000
Depreciation expense—Trucks	22,500	
Salaries expense	60,000	
Office supplies expense	7,000	
Repairs expense—Trucks	11,000	
Totals	$390,000	$390,000

Exercise 4-5
Preparing a classified balance sheet C3

Use the information in the adjusted trial balance reported in Exercise 4-4 to prepare Webb Trucking Company's classified balance sheet as of December 31, 2011.

Check Total assets, $235,500; K. Webb, Capital, $169,500

Exercise 4-6
Computing the current ratio
A1 

Use the information in the adjusted trial balance reported in Exercise 4-4 to compute the current ratio as of the balance sheet date (round the ratio to two decimals). Interpret the current ratio for the Webb Trucking Company. (Assume that the industry average for the current ratio is 1.5.)

Exercise 4-7
Computing and analyzing the current ratio
A1 

Calculate the current ratio in each of the following separate cases (round the ratio to two decimals). Identify the company case with the strongest liquidity position. (These cases represent competing companies in the same industry.)

	Current Assets	Current Liabilities
Case 1	$ 78,000	$31,000
Case 2	104,000	75,000
Case 3	44,000	48,000
Case 4	84,500	80,600
Case 5	60,000	99,000

Exercise 4-8
Extending adjusted account balances on a work sheet
P1

These 16 accounts are from the Adjusted Trial Balance columns of a company's 10-column work sheet. In the blank space beside each account, write the letter of the appropriate financial statement column (A, B, C, or D) to which a normal account balance is extended.

A. Debit column for the Income Statement columns.
B. Credit column for the Income Statement columns.
C. Debit column for the Balance Sheet and Statement of Owner's Equity columns.
D. Credit column for the Balance Sheet and Statement of Owner's Equity columns.

_______ **1.** Office Supplies
_______ **2.** Accounts Payable
_______ **3.** Owner, Capital
_______ **4.** Wages Payable
_______ **5.** Machinery
_______ **6.** Interest Receivable
_______ **7.** Interest Expense
_______ **8.** Owner, Withdrawals
_______ **9.** Service Fees Revenue
_______ **10.** Insurance Expense
_______ **11.** Accumulated Depreciation
_______ **12.** Interest Revenue
_______ **13.** Accounts Receivable
_______ **14.** Rent Expense
_______ **15.** Depreciation Expense
_______ **16.** Cash

Exercise 4-9
Preparing adjusting entries from a work sheet P1

Use the following information from the Adjustments columns of a 10-column work sheet to prepare the necessary adjusting journal entries (*a*) through (*e*).

	A	B	C	D	E	F	G	H	I	J	K	L
1											Balance Sheet	
2			Unadjusted				Adjusted		Income		and Statement of	
3			Trial Balance		Adjustments		Trial Balance		Statement		Owner's Equity	
4	No.	Account Title	Dr.	Cr.	Dr.	Cr.	Dr.	Cr.	Dr.	Cr.	Dr.	Cr.
5	109	Interest receivable					(d) $ 580					
6	124	Office supplies						(b) $1,650				
7	128	Prepaid insurance						(a) 900				
8	164	Accumulated depreciation—Office equipment						(c) 3,300				
9	209	Salaries payable						(e) 660				
10	409	Interest revenue						(d) 580				
11	612	Depreciation expense—Office equipment					(c) 3,300					
12	620	Office salaries expense					(e) 660					
13	636	Insurance expense—Office equipment					(a) 432					
14	637	Insurance expense—Store equipment					(a) 468					
15	650	Office supplies expense					(b) 1,650					
16		Totals					$7,090	$7,090				
17												

Exercise 4-10
Extending accounts in a work sheet P1

The Adjusted Trial Balance columns of a 10-column work sheet for Propel Company follow. Complete the work sheet by extending the account balances into the appropriate financial statement columns and by entering the amount of net income for the reporting period.

	A	B	C	D	E	F	G	H	I	J	K	L
1											Balance Sheet and	
2			Unadjusted				Adjusted		Income		Statement of	
3			Trial Balance		Adjustments		Trial Balance		Statement		Owner's Equity	
4	No.	Account Title	Dr.	Cr.	Dr.	Cr.	Dr.	Cr.	Dr.	Cr.	Dr.	Cr.
5	101	Cash					$ 6,000					
6	106	Accounts receivable					26,200					
7	153	Trucks					41,000					
8	154	Accumulated depreciation—Trucks						$ 16,500				
9	183	Land					30,000					
10	201	Accounts payable						14,000				
11	209	Salaries payable						3,200				
12	233	Unearned fees						2,600				
13	301	J. Propel, Capital						64,500				
14	302	J. Propel, Withdrawals					14,400					
15	401	Plumbing fees earned						79,000				
16	611	Depreciation expense—Trucks					5,500					
17	622	Salaries expense					37,000					
18	640	Rent expense					12,000					
19	677	Miscellaneous expenses					7,700					
20		Totals					$179,000	$179,000				
21												
22												

Check Net income, $16,800

Exercise 4-11
Completing the income statement columns and preparing closing entries
P1 P2

These partially completed Income Statement columns from a 10-column work sheet are for Welch's Red Sail Rental Company. (1) Use the information to determine the amount that should be entered on the net income line of the work sheet. (2) Prepare the company's closing entries. The owner, L. Welch, did not make any withdrawals this period.

Account Title	Debit	Credit
Rent earned		102,000
Salaries expense	45,300	
Insurance expense	6,400	
Dock rental expense	15,000	
Boat supplies expense	3,200	
Depreciation expense—Boats	19,500	
Totals		
Net income		
Totals		

Check Net income, $12,600

Exercise 4-12
Preparing a work sheet and recording closing entries
P1 P2

The following unadjusted trial balance contains the accounts and balances of Dalton Delivery Company as of December 31, 2011, its first year of operations.

(1) Use the following information about the company's adjustments to complete a 10-column work sheet.

a. Unrecorded depreciation on the trucks at the end of the year is $35,000.

b. The total amount of accrued interest expense at year-end is $8,000.

c. The cost of unused office supplies still available at the year-end is $1,000.

(2) Prepare the year-end closing entries for this company, and determine the capital amount to be reported on its year-end balance sheet.

	A	B	C
1		Unadjusted Trial Balance	
2	Account Title	Debit	Credit
3	Cash	$ 14,000	
4	Accounts receivable	33,000	
5	Office supplies	4,000	
6	Trucks	340,000	
7	Accumulated depreciation—Trucks		$70,000
8	Land	150,000	
9	Accounts payable		22,000
10	Interest payable		6,000
11	Long-term notes payable		104,000
12	V. Dalton, Capital		322,000
13	V. Dalton, Withdrawals	38,000	
14	Delivery fees earned		256,000
15	Depreciation expense—Truck	45,000	
16	Salaries expense	120,000	
17	Office supplies expense	14,000	
18	Interest expense	6,000	
19	Repairs expense—Trucks	16,000	
20	Totals	$780,000	$780,000
21			

Check Adj. trial balance totals, $817,000; Net income, $15,000

Exercise 4-13^A
Preparing reversing entries
P4

The following two events occurred for Tanger Co. on October 31, 2011, the end of its fiscal year.

a. Tanger rents a building from its owner for $3,200 per month. By a prearrangement, the company delayed paying October's rent until November 5. On this date, the company paid the rent for both October and November.

b. Tanger rents space in a building it owns to a tenant for $750 per month. By prearrangement, the tenant delayed paying the October rent until November 8. On this date, the tenant paid the rent for both October and November.

Required

1. Prepare adjusting entries that the company must record for these events as of October 31.

2. Assuming Tanger does *not* use reversing entries, prepare journal entries to record Tanger's payment of rent on November 5 and the collection of rent on November 8 from Tanger's tenant.

3. Assuming that the company uses reversing entries, prepare reversing entries on November 1 and the journal entries to record Tanger's payment of rent on November 5 and the collection of rent on November 8 from Tanger's tenant.

Exercise 4-14^A
Preparing reversing entries
P4

Hinson Company records prepaid assets and unearned revenues in balance sheet accounts. The following information was used to prepare adjusting entries for the company as of August 31, the end of the company's fiscal year.

a. The company has earned $5,000 in service fees that were not yet recorded at period-end.

b. The expired portion of prepaid insurance is $2,700.

c. The company has earned $1,900 of its Unearned Service Fees account balance.

d. Depreciation expense for office equipment is $2,300.

e. Employees have earned but have not been paid salaries of $2,400.

Prepare any necessary reversing entries for the accounting adjustments *a* through *e* assuming that the company uses reversing entries in its accounting system.

Exercise 4-15
Determining effects of closing entries
C1  

Argosy Company began the current period with a $14,000 credit balance in the D. Argosy, Capital account. At the end of the period, the company's adjusted account balances include the following temporary accounts with normal balances.

Service fees earned	$35,000	Interest revenue	$3,500
Salaries expense	19,000	D. Argosy, Withdrawals	6,000
Depreciation expense	4,000	Utilities expense	2,300

After closing the revenue and expense accounts, what will be the balance of the Income Summary account? After all closing entries are journalized and posted, what will be the balance of the D. Argosy, Capital account?

Exercise 4-16
Preparing closing entries
P2

Following are **Nintendo**'s revenue and expense accounts for a recent calendar year (yen in millions). Prepare the company's closing entries for its revenues and its expenses.

Net sales	¥1,838,622
Cost of sales	1,044,981
Advertising expense	117,308
Other expense, net	397,244

Exercise 4-17
Completing a worksheet
P1

The following data are taken from the unadjusted trial balance of the Madison Company at December 31, 2011. Each account carries a normal balance and the accounts are shown here in alphabetical order.

Accounts Payable	$ 2	Prepaid Insurance	$ 6	T. Madison, Withdrawals	$2
Accounts Receivable	4	Revenue	25	Unearned Revenue	4
Accumulated Depreciation—Equip.	5	Salaries Expense	6	Utilities Expense	4
Cash	7	Supplies	8		
Equipment	13	T. Madison, Capital	14		

1. Use the data above to prepare a worksheet. Enter the accounts in proper order and enter their balances in the correct debit or credit column.
2. Use the following adjustment information to complete the worksheet.
   a. Depreciation on equipment, $1
   b. Accrued salaries, $2
   c. The $4 of unearned revenue has been earned
   d. Supplies available at December 31, 2011, $5
   e. Expired insurance, $5

connect

PROBLEM SET A

Problem 4-1A
Determining balance sheet classifications
C3

In the blank space beside each numbered balance sheet item, enter the letter of its balance sheet classification. If the item should not appear on the balance sheet, enter a *Z* in the blank.

A. Current assets
B. Long-term investments
C. Plant assets
D. Intangible assets
E. Current liabilities
F. Long-term liabilities
G. Equity

_____ **1.** Office equipment
_____ **2.** Office supplies
_____ **3.** Buildings
_____ **4.** Store supplies
_____ **5.** Accumulated depreciation—Trucks
_____ **6.** Land (used in operations)
_____ **7.** Repairs expense
_____ **8.** Cash
_____ **9.** Current portion of long-term note payable
_____ **10.** Long-term investment in stock
_____ **11.** Depreciation expense—Building
_____ **12.** Prepaid rent
_____ **13.** Interest receivable
_____ **14.** Taxes payable
_____ **15.** Automobiles
_____ **16.** Notes payable (due in 3 years)
_____ **17.** Accounts payable
_____ **18.** Prepaid insurance
_____ **19.** Owner, Capital
_____ **20.** Unearned services revenue

Problem 4-2A
Applying the accounting cycle
C1 C2 P2 P3

mhhe.com/wildFAP20e

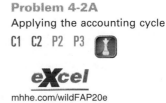

On April 1, 2011, Jennifer Stafford created a new travel agency, See-It-Now Travel. The following transactions occurred during the company's first month.

April	1	Stafford invested $20,000 cash and computer equipment worth $40,000 in the company.
	2	The company rented furnished office space by paying $1,700 cash for the first month's (April) rent.
	3	The company purchased $1,100 of office supplies for cash.
	10	The company paid $3,600 cash for the premium on a 12-month insurance policy. Coverage begins on April 11.
	14	The company paid $1,800 cash for two weeks' salaries earned by employees.
	24	The company collected $7,900 cash on commissions from airlines on tickets obtained for customers.
	28	The company paid $1,800 cash for two weeks' salaries earned by employees.
	29	The company paid $250 cash for minor repairs to the company's computer.
	30	The company paid $650 cash for this month's telephone bill.
	30	Stafford withdrew $1,500 cash from the company for personal use.

The company's chart of accounts follows:

101	Cash	405	Commissions Earned
106	Accounts Receivable	612	Depreciation Expense—Computer Equip.
124	Office Supplies	622	Salaries Expense
128	Prepaid Insurance	637	Insurance Expense
167	Computer Equipment	640	Rent Expense
168	Accumulated Depreciation—Computer Equip.	650	Office Supplies Expense
209	Salaries Payable	684	Repairs Expense
301	J. Stafford, Capital	688	Telephone Expense
302	J. Stafford, Withdrawals	901	Income Summary

Required

1. Use the balance column format to set up each ledger account listed in its chart of accounts.
2. Prepare journal entries to record the transactions for April and post them to the ledger accounts. The company records prepaid and unearned items in balance sheet accounts.
3. Prepare an unadjusted trial balance as of April 30.
4. Use the following information to journalize and post adjusting entries for the month:
   a. Two-thirds of one month's insurance coverage has expired.
   b. At the end of the month, $700 of office supplies are still available.
   c. This month's depreciation on the computer equipment is $600.
   d. Employees earned $320 of unpaid and unrecorded salaries as of month-end.
   e. The company earned $1,650 of commissions that are not yet billed at month-end.
5. Prepare the income statement and the statement of owner's equity for the month of April and the balance sheet at April 30, 2011.
6. Prepare journal entries to close the temporary accounts and post these entries to the ledger.
7. Prepare a post-closing trial balance.

Check (3) Unadj. trial balance totals, $67,900

(4*a*) Dr. Insurance Expense, $200

(5) Net income, $1,830; J. Stafford, Capital (4/30/2011), $60,330; Total assets, $60,650

(7) P-C trial balance totals, $61,250

Problem 4-3A
Preparing trial balances, closing entries, and financial statements
C3 P2 P3

mhhe.com/wildFAP20e

The adjusted trial balance of Kobe Repairs on December 31, 2011, follows.

KOBE REPAIRS
Adjusted Trial Balance
December 31, 2011

No.	Account Title	Debit	Credit
101	Cash	$ 13,000	
124	Office supplies	1,200	
128	Prepaid insurance	1,950	
167	Equipment	48,000	
168	Accumulated depreciation—Equipment		$ 4,000
201	Accounts payable		12,000
210	Wages payable		500
301	S. Kobe, Capital		40,000
302	S. Kobe, Withdrawals	15,000	
401	Repair fees earned		77,750
612	Depreciation expense—Equipment	4,000	
623	Wages expense	36,500	
637	Insurance expense	700	
640	Rent expense	9,600	
650	Office supplies expense	2,600	
690	Utilities expense	1,700	
	Totals	$134,250	$134,250

Required

1. Prepare an income statement and a statement of owner's equity for the year 2011, and a classified balance sheet at December 31, 2011. There are no owner investments in 2011.

Check (1) Ending capital balance, $47,650; net income, $22,650

2. Enter the adjusted trial balance in the first two columns of a six-column table. Use columns three and four for closing entry information and the last two columns for a post-closing trial balance. Insert an Income Summary account as the last item in the trial balance.
3. Enter closing entry information in the six-column table and prepare journal entries for it.

(2) P-C trial balance totals, $64,150

Analysis Component

4. Assume for this part only that
   a. None of the $700 insurance expense had expired during the year. Instead, assume it is a prepayment of the next period's insurance protection.
   b. There are no earned and unpaid wages at the end of the year. (*Hint:* Reverse the $500 wages payable accrual.)

   Describe the financial statement changes that would result from these two assumptions.

Problem 4-4A
Preparing closing entries, financial statements, and ratios
C3 A1 P2

The adjusted trial balance for Sharp Construction as of December 31, 2011, follows.

SHARP CONSTRUCTION
Adjusted Trial Balance
December 31, 2011

No.	Account Title	Debit	Credit
101	Cash	$ 4,000	
104	Short-term investments	22,000	
126	Supplies	7,100	
128	Prepaid insurance	6,000	
167	Equipment	39,000	
168	Accumulated depreciation—Equipment		$ 20,000
173	Building	130,000	
174	Accumulated depreciation—Building		55,000
183	Land	45,000	
201	Accounts payable		15,500
203	Interest payable		1,500
208	Rent payable		2,500
210	Wages payable		1,500
213	Property taxes payable		800
233	Unearned professional fees		6,500
251	Long-term notes payable		66,000
301	J. Sharp, Capital		82,700
302	J. Sharp, Withdrawals	12,000	
401	Professional fees earned		96,000
406	Rent earned		13,000
407	Dividends earned		1,900
409	Interest earned		1,000
606	Depreciation expense—Building	10,000	
612	Depreciation expense—Equipment	5,000	
623	Wages expense	31,000	
633	Interest expense	4,100	
637	Insurance expense	9,000	
640	Rent expense	12,400	
652	Supplies expense	6,400	
682	Postage expense	3,200	
683	Property taxes expense	4,000	
684	Repairs expense	7,900	
688	Telephone expense	2,200	
690	Utilities expense	3,600	
	Totals	$363,900	$363,900

J. Sharp invested $50,000 cash in the business during year 2011 (the December 31, 2010, credit balance of the J. Sharp, Capital account was $32,700). Sharp Construction is required to make a $6,600 payment on its long-term notes payable during 2012.

Required

Check (1) Total assets (12/31/2011), $178,100; Net income, $13,100

1. Prepare the income statement and the statement of owner's equity for the calendar year 2011 and the classified balance sheet at December 31, 2011.
2. Prepare the necessary closing entries at December 31, 2011.
3. Use the information in the financial statements to compute these ratios: (*a*) return on assets (total assets at December 31, 2010, was $200,000), (*b*) debt ratio, (*c*) profit margin ratio (use total revenues as the denominator), and (*d*) current ratio.

Problem 4-5A
Preparing a work sheet, adjusting and closing entries, and financial statements

C3 P1 P2 

The following unadjusted trial balance is for Adams Construction Co. as of the end of its 2011 fiscal year. The June 30, 2010, credit balance of the owner's capital account was $52,660, and the owner invested $25,000 cash in the company during the 2011 fiscal year.

	A	B	C	D
1		**ADAMS CONSTRUCTION CO.**		
2		**Unadjusted Trial Balance**		
3		**June 30, 2011**		
4	**No.**	**Account Title**	**Debit**	**Credit**
5	101	Cash	$ 17,500	
6	126	Supplies	8,900	
7	128	Prepaid insurance	6,200	
8	167	Equipment	131,000	
9	168	Accumulated depreciation—Equipment		$ 25,250
10	201	Accounts payable		5,800
11	203	Interest payable		0
12	208	Rent payable		0
13	210	Wages payable		0
14	213	Property taxes payable		0
15	251	Long-term notes payable		24,000
16	301	S. Adams, Capital		77,660
17	302	S. Adams, Withdrawals	30,000	
18	401	Construction fees earned		134,000
19	612	Depreciation expense—Equipment	0	
20	623	Wages expense	45,860	
21	633	Interest expense	2,640	
22	637	Insurance expense	0	
23	640	Rent expense	13,200	
24	652	Supplies expense	0	
25	683	Property taxes expense	4,600	
26	684	Repairs expense	2,810	
27	690	Utilities expense	4,000	
28		Totals	$266,710	$266,710
29				

Required

1. Prepare a 10-column work sheet for fiscal year 2011, starting with the unadjusted trial balance and including adjustments based on these additional facts.
   a. The supplies available at the end of fiscal year 2011 had a cost of $3,200.
   b. The cost of expired insurance for the fiscal year is $3,900.
   c. Annual depreciation on equipment is $8,500.
   d. The June utilities expense of $550 is not included in the unadjusted trial balance because the bill arrived after the trial balance was prepared. The $550 amount owed needs to be recorded.
   e. The company's employees have earned $1,600 of accrued wages at fiscal year-end.
   f. The rent expense incurred and not yet paid or recorded at fiscal year-end is $200.
   g. Additional property taxes of $900 have been assessed for this fiscal year but have not been paid or recorded in the accounts.

h. The long-term note payable bears interest at 12% per year. The unadjusted Interest Expense account equals the amount paid for the first 11 months of the 2011 fiscal year. The $240 accrued interest for June has not yet been paid or recorded. (The company is required to make a $5,000 payment toward the note payable during the 2012 fiscal year.)

2. Enter adjusting and closing information in the work sheet; then journalize the adjusting and closing entries.

3. Prepare the income statement and the statement of owner's equity for the year ended June 30 and the classified balance sheet at June 30, 2011.

Check (3) Total assets, $120,250; Current liabilities, $14,290; Net income, $39,300

Analysis Component

4. Analyze the following separate errors and describe how each would affect the 10-column work sheet. Explain whether the error is likely to be discovered in completing the work sheet and, if not, the effect of the error on the financial statements.

a. Assume that the adjustment for supplies used consisted of a credit to Supplies and a debit to Supplies Expense for $3,200, when the correct amount was $5,700.

b. When the adjusted trial balance in the work sheet is completed, assume that the $17,500 Cash balance is incorrectly entered in the Credit column.

Problem 4-6A[A]
Preparing adjusting, reversing, and next period entries
P4

The following six-column table for Bullseye Ranges includes the unadjusted trial balance as of December 31, 2011.

	A	B	C	D	E	F	G
1		BULLSEYE RANGES					
2		December 31, 2011					
3		Unadjusted				Adjusted	
4		Trial Balance		Adjustments		Trial Balance	
5	Account Title	Dr.	Cr.	Dr.	Cr.	Dr.	Cr.
6	Cash	$ 13,000					
7	Accounts receivable	0					
8	Supplies	5,500					
9	Equipment	130,000					
10	Accumulated depreciation—Equipment		$ 25,000				
11	Interest payable		0				
12	Salaries payable		0				
13	Unearned member fees		14,000				
14	Notes payable		50,000				
15	T. Allen, Capital		58,250				
16	T. Allen, Withdrawals	20,000					
17	Member fees earned		53,000				
18	Depreciation expense—Equipment	0					
19	Salaries expense	28,000					
20	Interest expense	3,750					
21	Supplies expense	0					
22	Totals	$200,250	$200,250				
23							

Required

1. Complete the six-column table by entering adjustments that reflect the following information.

a. As of December 31, 2011, employees had earned $900 of unpaid and unrecorded salaries. The next payday is January 4, at which time $1,600 of salaries will be paid.

b. The cost of supplies still available at December 31, 2011, is $2,700.

c. The notes payable requires an interest payment to be made every three months. The amount of unrecorded accrued interest at December 31, 2011, is $1,250. The next interest payment, at an amount of $1,500, is due on January 15, 2012.

d. Analysis of the unearned member fees account shows $5,600 remaining unearned at December 31, 2011.

e. In addition to the member fees included in the revenue account balance, the company has earned another $9,100 in unrecorded fees that will be collected on January 31, 2012. The company is also expected to collect $8,000 on that same day for new fees earned in January 2012.

f. Depreciation expense for the year is $12,500.

Check (1) Adjusted trial balance totals, $224,000

2. Prepare journal entries for the adjustments entered in the six-column table for part 1.
3. Prepare journal entries to reverse the effects of the adjusting entries that involve accruals.
4. Prepare journal entries to record the cash payments and cash collections described for January.

PROBLEM SET B

Problem 4-1B
Determining balance sheet classifications
C3

In the blank space beside each numbered balance sheet item, enter the letter of its balance sheet classification. If the item should not appear on the balance sheet, enter a *Z* in the blank.

A. Current assets
B. Long-term investments
C. Plant assets
D. Intangible assets
E. Current liabilities
F. Long-term liabilities
G. Equity

_____ **1.** Machinery
_____ **2.** Prepaid insurance
_____ **3.** Current portion of long-term note payable
_____ **4.** Interest receivable
_____ **5.** Rent receivable
_____ **6.** Land (used in operations)
_____ **7.** Copyrights
_____ **8.** Rent revenue
_____ **9.** Depreciation expense—Trucks
_____ **10.** Long-term investment in stock
_____ **11.** Office supplies
_____ **12.** Interest payable
_____ **13.** Owner, Capital
_____ **14.** Notes receivable (due in 120 days)
_____ **15.** Accumulated depreciation—Trucks
_____ **16.** Salaries payable
_____ **17.** Commissions earned
_____ **18.** Income taxes payable
_____ **19.** Office equipment
_____ **20.** Notes payable (due in 15 years)

Problem 4-2B
Applying the accounting cycle
C1 C2 P2 P3 

On July 1, 2011, Lucinda Fogle created a new self-storage business, KeepSafe Co. The following transactions occurred during the company's first month.

July	1	Fogle invested $20,000 cash and buildings worth $120,000 in the company.
	2	The company rented equipment by paying $1,800 cash for the first month's (July) rent.
	5	The company purchased $2,300 of office supplies for cash.
	10	The company paid $5,400 cash for the premium on a 12-month insurance policy. Coverage begins on July 11.
	14	The company paid an employee $900 cash for two weeks' salary earned.
	24	The company collected $8,800 cash for storage fees from customers.
	28	The company paid $900 cash for two weeks' salary earned by an employee.
	29	The company paid $850 cash for minor repairs to a leaking roof.
	30	The company paid $300 cash for this month's telephone bill.
	31	Fogle withdrew $1,600 cash from the company for personal use.

The company's chart of accounts follows:

101	Cash	401	Storage Fees Earned
106	Accounts Receivable	606	Depreciation Expense—Buildings
124	Office Supplies	622	Salaries Expense
128	Prepaid Insurance	637	Insurance Expense
173	Buildings	640	Rent Expense
174	Accumulated Depreciation—Buildings	650	Office Supplies Expense
209	Salaries Payable	684	Repairs Expense
301	L. Fogle, Capital	688	Telephone Expense
302	L. Fogle, Withdrawals	901	Income Summary

Required

1. Use the balance column format to set up each ledger account listed in its chart of accounts.
2. Prepare journal entries to record the transactions for July and post them to the ledger accounts. Record prepaid and unearned items in balance sheet accounts.
3. Prepare an unadjusted trial balance as of July 31.

Check (3) Unadj. trial balance totals, $148,800

4. Use the following information to journalize and post adjusting entries for the month:
   a. Two-thirds of one month's insurance coverage has expired.
   b. At the end of the month, $1,550 of office supplies are still available.
   c. This month's depreciation on the buildings is $1,200.
   d. An employee earned $180 of unpaid and unrecorded salary as of month-end.
   e. The company earned $950 of storage fees that are not yet billed at month-end.
5. Prepare the income statement and the statement of owner's equity for the month of July and the balance sheet at July 31, 2011.
6. Prepare journal entries to close the temporary accounts and post these entries to the ledger.
7. Prepare a post-closing trial balance.

(4a) Dr. Insurance Expense, $300

(5) Net income, $2,570; L. Fogle, Capital (7/31/2011), $140,970; Total assets, $141,150

(7) P C trial balance totals, $142,350

Problem 4-3B
Preparing trial balances, closing entries, and financial statements
C3 P2 P3 

Heel-To-Toe Shoes' adjusted trial balance on December 31, 2011, follows.

HEEL-TO-TOE SHOES
Adjusted Trial Balance
December 31, 2011

No.	Account Title	Debit	Credit
101	Cash	$ 13,450	
125	Store supplies	4,140	
128	Prepaid insurance	2,200	
167	Equipment	33,000	
168	Accumulated depreciation—Equipment		$ 9,000
201	Accounts payable		1,000
210	Wages payable		3,200
301	P. Holt, Capital		31,650
302	P. Holt, Withdrawals	16,000	
401	Repair fees earned		62,000
612	Depreciation expense—Equipment	3,000	
623	Wages expense	28,400	
637	Insurance expense	1,100	
640	Rent expense	2,400	
651	Store supplies expense	1,300	
690	Utilities expense	1,860	
	Totals	$106,850	$106,850

Required

1. Prepare an income statement and a statement of owner's equity for the year 2011, and a classified balance sheet at December 31, 2011. There are no owner investments in 2011.
2. Enter the adjusted trial balance in the first two columns of a six-column table. Use the middle two columns for closing entry information and the last two columns for a post-closing trial balance. Insert an Income Summary account (No. 901) as the last item in the trial balance.
3. Enter closing entry information in the six-column table and prepare journal entries for it.

Check (1) Ending capital balance, $39,590

(2) P C trial balance totals, $52,790

Analysis Component

4. Assume for this part only that
   a. None of the $1,100 insurance expense had expired during the year. Instead, assume it is a prepayment of the next period's insurance protection.
   b. There are no earned and unpaid wages at the end of the year. (*Hint:* Reverse the $3,200 wages payable accrual.)

   Describe the financial statement changes that would result from these two assumptions.

Problem 4-4B
Preparing closing entries, financial statements, and ratios
C3 A1 P2

The adjusted trial balance for Giovanni Co. as of December 31, 2011, follows.

GIOVANNI COMPANY
Adjusted Trial Balance
December 31, 2011

No.	Account Title	Debit	Credit
101	Cash	$ 6,400	
104	Short-term investments	10,200	
126	Supplies	3,600	
128	Prepaid insurance	800	
167	Equipment	18,000	
168	Accumulated depreciation—Equipment		$ 3,000
173	Building	90,000	
174	Accumulated depreciation—Building		9,000
183	Land	28,500	
201	Accounts payable		2,500
203	Interest payable		1,400
208	Rent payable		200
210	Wages payable		1,180
213	Property taxes payable		2,330
233	Unearned professional fees		650
251	Long-term notes payable		32,000
301	J. Giovanni, Capital		91,800
302	J. Giovanni, Withdrawals	6,000	
401	Professional fees earned		47,000
406	Rent earned		3,600
407	Dividends earned		500
409	Interest earned		1,120
606	Depreciation expense—Building	2,000	
612	Depreciation expense—Equipment	1,000	
623	Wages expense	17,500	
633	Interest expense	1,200	
637	Insurance expense	1,425	
640	Rent expense	1,800	
652	Supplies expense	900	
682	Postage expense	310	
683	Property taxes expense	3,825	
684	Repairs expense	579	
688	Telephone expense	421	
690	Utilities expense	1,820	
	Totals	$196,280	$196,280

J. Giovanni invested $30,000 cash in the business during year 2011 (the December 31, 2010, credit balance of the J. Giovanni, Capital account was $61,800). Giovanni Company is required to make a $6,400 payment on its long-term notes payable during 2012.

Required

Check (1) Total assets (12/31/2011), $145,500; Net income, $19,440

1. Prepare the income statement and the statement of owner's equity for the calendar year 2011 and the classified balance sheet at December 31, 2011.
2. Prepare the necessary closing entries at December 31, 2011.
3. Use the information in the financial statements to calculate these ratios: (*a*) return on assets (total assets at December 31, 2010, were $150,000), (*b*) debt ratio, (*c*) profit margin ratio (use total revenues as the denominator), and (*d*) current ratio.

Problem 4-5B
Preparing a work sheet, adjusting and closing entries, and financial statements

C3 P1 P2 

The following unadjusted trial balance is for Crush Demolition Company as of the end of its April 30, 2011, fiscal year. The April 30, 2010, credit balance of the owner's capital account was $36,900, and the owner invested $30,000 cash in the company during the 2011 fiscal year.

	A	B		C
1		CRUSH DEMOLITION COMPANY		
2		Unadjusted Trial Balance		
3		April 30, 2011		
4	No.	Account Title	Debit	Credit
5	101	Cash	$ 9,000	
6	126	Supplies	18,000	
7	128	Prepaid Insurance	14,600	
8	167	Equipment	140,000	
9	168	Accumulated depreciation—Equipment		$ 10,000
10	201	Accounts payable		16,000
11	203	Interest payable		0
12	208	Rent payable		0
13	210	Wages payable		0
14	213	Property taxes payable		0
15	251	Long-term notes payable		20,000
16	301	J. Bonair, Capital		66,900
17	302	J. Bonair, Withdrawals	24,000	
18	401	Demolition fees earned		177,000
19	612	Depreciation expense—Equipment	0	
20	623	Wages expense	51,400	
21	633	Interest expense	2,200	
22	637	Insurance expense	0	
23	640	Rent expense	8,800	
24	652	Supplies expense	0	
25	683	Property taxes expense	8,400	
26	684	Repairs expense	6,700	
27	690	Utilities expense	6,800	
28		Totals	$289,900	$289,900
29				

Required

1. Prepare a 10-column work sheet for fiscal year 2011, starting with the unadjusted trial balance and including adjustments based on these additional facts.
   a. The supplies available at the end of fiscal year 2011 had a cost of $8,100.
   b. The cost of expired insurance for the fiscal year is $11,500.
   c. Annual depreciation on equipment is $18,000.
   d. The April utilities expense of $700 is not included in the unadjusted trial balance because the bill arrived after the trial balance was prepared. The $700 amount owed needs to be recorded.
   e. The company's employees have earned $2,200 of accrued wages at fiscal year-end.
   f. The rent expense incurred and not yet paid or recorded at fiscal year-end is $5,360.
   g. Additional property taxes of $450 have been assessed for this fiscal year but have not been paid or recorded in the accounts.
   h. The long-term note payable bears interest at 12% per year. The unadjusted Interest Expense account equals the amount paid for the first 11 months of the 2011 fiscal year. The $200 accrued interest for April has not yet been paid or recorded. (Note that the company is required to make a $4,000 payment toward the note payable during the 2012 fiscal year.)
2. Enter adjusting and closing information in the work sheet; then journalize the adjusting and closing entries.
3. Prepare the income statement and the statement of owner's equity for the year ended April 30 and the classified balance sheet at April 30, 2011.

Check (3) Total assets, $132,200; current liabilities, $28,910; Net income, $44,390

Analysis Component

4. Analyze the following separate errors and describe how each would affect the 10-column work sheet. Explain whether the error is likely to be discovered in completing the work sheet and, if not, the effect of the error on the financial statements.
   a. Assume the adjustment for expiration of the insurance coverage consisted of a credit to Prepaid Insurance and a debit to Insurance Expense for $3,100, when the correct amount was $11,500.
   b. When the adjusted trial balance in the work sheet is completed, assume that the $6,700 Repairs Expense account balance is extended to the Debit column of the balance sheet columns.

Problem 4-6B[A]
Preparing adjusting, reversing, and next period entries
P4

The following six-column table for Solutions Co. includes the unadjusted trial balance as of December 31, 2011.

	A	B	C	D	E	F	G
1		SOLUTIONS COMPANY					
2		December 31, 2011					
3		Unadjusted				Adjusted	
4		Trial Balance		Adjustments		Trial Balance	
5	Account Title	Dr.	Cr.	Dr.	Cr.	Dr.	Cr.
6	Cash	$ 9,000					
7	Accounts receivable	0					
8	Supplies	6,600					
9	Machinery	40,100					
10	Accumulated depreciation—Machinery		$15,800				
11	Interest payable		0				
12	Salaries payable		0				
13	Unearned rental fees		5,200				
14	Notes payable		20,000				
15	G. Clay, Capital		13,200				
16	G. Clay, Withdrawals	10,500					
17	Rental fees earned		37,000				
18	Depreciation expense—Machinery	0					
19	Salaries expense	23,500					
20	Interest expense	1,500					
21	Supplies expense	0					
22	Totals	$91,200	$91,200				
23							

Required

1. Complete the six-column table by entering adjustments that reflect the following information:

a. As of December 31, 2011, employees had earned $420 of unpaid and unrecorded wages. The next payday is January 4, at which time $1,250 in wages will be paid.

b. The cost of supplies still available at December 31, 2011, is $2,450.

c. The notes payable requires an interest payment to be made every three months. The amount of unrecorded accrued interest at December 31, 2011, is $500. The next interest payment, at an amount of $600, is due on January 15, 2012.

d. Analysis of the unearned rental fees shows that $3,100 remains unearned at December 31, 2011.

e. In addition to the machinery rental fees included in the revenue account balance, the company has earned another $2,350 in unrecorded fees that will be collected on January 31, 2012. The company is also expected to collect $4,400 on that same day for new fees earned in January 2012.

f. Depreciation expense for the year is $3,800.

2. Prepare journal entries for the adjustments entered in the six-column table for part 1.

3. Prepare journal entries to reverse the effects of the adjusting entries that involve accruals.

4. Prepare journal entries to record the cash payments and cash collections described for January.

Check (1) Adjusted trial balance totals, $98,270

SERIAL PROBLEM

Business Solutions
P2 P3

(This serial problem began in Chapter 1 and continues through most of the book. If previous chapter segments were not completed, the serial problem can begin at this point. It is helpful, but not necessary, to use the Working Papers that accompany the book.)

SP 4 The December 31, 2011, adjusted trial balance of Business Solutions (reflecting its transactions from October through December of 2011) follows.

No.	Account Title	Debit	Credit
101	Cash	$ 48,372	
106	Accounts receivable	5,668	
126	Computer supplies	580	
128	Prepaid insurance	1,665	

[continued on next page]

[continued from previous page]

131	Prepaid rent	825	
163	Office equipment	8,000	
164	Accumulated depreciation—Office equipment		$ 400
167	Computer equipment	20,000	
168	Accumulated depreciation—Computer equipment		1,250
201	Accounts payable		1,100
210	Wages payable		500
236	Unearned computer services revenue		1,500
301	S. Rey, Capital		73,000
302	S. Rey, Withdrawals	7,100	
403	Computer services revenue		31,284
612	Depreciation expense—Office equipment	400	
613	Depreciation expense—Computer equipment	1,250	
623	Wages expense	3,875	
637	Insurance expense	555	
640	Rent expense	2,475	
652	Computer supplies expense	3,065	
655	Advertising expense	2,753	
676	Mileage expense	896	
677	Miscellaneous expenses	250	
684	Repairs expense—Computer	1,305	
901	Income summary		0
	Totals	$109,034	$109,034

Required

1. Record and post the necessary closing entries for Business Solutions.

2. Prepare a post-closing trial balance as of December 31, 2011.

Check Post-closing trial balance totals, $85,110

Beyond the Numbers

REPORTING IN ACTION

C1 P2 

RIM

BTN 4-1 Refer to **Research In Motion**'s financial statements in Appendix A to answer the following.

Required

1. For the fiscal year ended February 27, 2010, what amount is credited to Income Summary to summarize its revenues earned?

2. For the fiscal year ended February 27, 2010, what amount is debited to Income Summary to summarize its expenses incurred?

3. For the fiscal year ended February 27, 2010, what is the balance of its Income Summary account before it is closed?

4. In its statement of cash flows for the year ended February 27, 2010, what amount of cash is paid in dividends to common stockholders?

Fast Forward

5. Access RIM's annual report for fiscal years ending after February 27, 2010, at its Website (RIM.com) or the SEC's EDGAR database (www.SEC.gov). How has the amount of net income closed to Income Summary changed in the fiscal years ending after February 27, 2010? How has the amount of cash paid as dividends changed in the fiscal years ending after February 27, 2010?

COMPARATIVE ANALYSIS

A1

RIM

Apple

BTN 4-2 Key figures for the recent two years of **Research In Motion** and **Apple** follow.

Key Figures ($ millions)	Research In Motion		Apple	
	Current Year	Prior Year	Current Year	Prior Year
Current assets	$5,813	$4,842	$31,555	$30,006
Current liabilities	2,432	2,115	11,506	11,361

Required

1. Compute the current ratio for both years for both companies.
2. Which company has the better ability to pay short-term obligations according to the current ratio?
3. Analyze and comment on each company's current ratios for the past two years.
4. How do RIM's and Apple's current ratios compare to their industry (assumed) average ratio of 2.4?

ETHICS CHALLENGE

C2

BTN 4-3 On January 20, 2011, Tamira Nelson, the accountant for Picton Enterprises, is feeling pressure to complete the annual financial statements. The company president has said he needs up-to-date financial statements to share with the bank on January 21 at a dinner meeting that has been called to discuss Picton's obtaining loan financing for a special building project. Tamira knows that she will not be able to gather all the needed information in the next 24 hours to prepare the entire set of adjusting entries. Those entries must be posted before the financial statements accurately portray the company's performance and financial position for the fiscal period ended December 31, 2010. Tamira ultimately decides to estimate several expense accruals at the last minute. When deciding on estimates for the expenses, she uses low estimates because she does not want to make the financial statements look worse than they are. Tamira finishes the financial statements before the deadline and gives them to the president without mentioning that several account balances are estimates that she provided.

Required

1. Identify several courses of action that Tamira could have taken instead of the one she took.
2. If you were in Tamira's situation, what would you have done? Briefly justify your response.

COMMUNICATING IN PRACTICE

C1 P2

BTN 4-4 Assume that one of your classmates states that a company's books should be ongoing and therefore not closed until that business is terminated. Write a half-page memo to this classmate explaining the concept of the closing process by drawing analogies between (1) a scoreboard for an athletic event and the revenue and expense accounts of a business or (2) a sports team's record book and the capital account. (*Hint:* Think about what would happen if the scoreboard is not cleared before the start of a new game.)

TAKING IT TO THE NET

A1

BTN 4-5 Access **Motley Fool**'s discussion of the current ratio at **Fool.com/School/Valuation/CurrentAndQuickRatio.htm**. (If the page changed, search that site for the *current ratio*.)

Required

1. What level for the current ratio is generally regarded as sufficient to meet near-term operating needs?
2. Once you have calculated the current ratio for a company, what should you compare it against?
3. What are the implications for a company that has a current ratio that is too high?

TEAMWORK IN ACTION

P1 P2 P3

BTN 4-6 The unadjusted trial balance and information for the accounting adjustments of Noseworthy Investigators follow. Each team member involved in this project is to assume one of the four responsibilities listed. After completing each of these responsibilities, the team should work together to prove the accounting equation utilizing information from teammates (1 and 4). If your equation does not balance, you are to work as a team to resolve the error. The team's goal is to complete the task as quickly and accurately as possible.

Unadjusted Trial Balance

Account Title	Debit	Credit
Cash	$15,000	
Supplies	11,000	
Prepaid insurance	2,000	
Equipment	24,000	
Accumulated depreciation—Equipment		$ 6,000
Accounts payable		2,000
D. Noseworthy, Capital		31,000
D. Noseworthy, Withdrawals	5,000	
Investigation fees earned		32,000
Rent expense	14,000	
Totals	$71,000	$71,000

Additional Year-End Information

a. Insurance that expired in the current period amounts to $1,200.
b. Equipment depreciation for the period is $3,000.
c. Unused supplies total $4,000 at period-end.
d. Services in the amount of $500 have been provided but have not been billed or collected.

Responsibilities for Individual Team Members

1. Determine the accounts and adjusted balances to be extended to the balance sheet columns of the work sheet for Noseworthy. Also determine total assets and total liabilities.
2. Determine the adjusted revenue account balance and prepare the entry to close this account.
3. Determine the adjusted account balances for expenses and prepare the entry to close these accounts.
4. Prepare T-accounts for both D. Noseworthy, Capital (reflecting the unadjusted trial balance amount) and Income Summary. Prepare the third and fourth closing entries. Ask teammates assigned to parts 2 and 3 for the postings for Income Summary. Obtain amounts to complete the third closing entry and post both the third and fourth closing entries. Provide the team with the ending capital account balance.
5. The entire team should prove the accounting equation using post-closing balances.

ENTREPRENEURIAL DECISION

A1 C3 P2  

BTN 4-7 Review this chapter's opening feature involving Keith Mullin and his **Gamer Grub** business.

1. Explain how a classified balance sheet can help Keith Mullin know what bills are due when, and whether he has the resources to pay those bills.
2. Why is it important for Keith Mullin to match costs and revenues in a specific time period? How do closing entries help him in this regard?
3. What objectives are met when Keith Mullin applies closing procedures each fiscal year-end?

HITTING THE ROAD

C2 

BTN 4-8 Select a company that you can visit in person or interview on the telephone. Call ahead to the company to arrange a time when you can interview an employee (preferably an accountant) who helps prepare the annual financial statements. Inquire about the following aspects of its *accounting cycle:*

1. Does the company prepare interim financial statements? What time period(s) is used for interim statements?
2. Does the company use the cash or accrual basis of accounting?
3. Does the company use a work sheet in preparing financial statements? Why or why not?
4. Does the company use a spreadsheet program? If so, which software program is used?
5. How long does it take after the end of its reporting period to complete annual statements?

GLOBAL DECISION

A1  

NOKIA

BTN 4-9 **Nokia (www.Nokia.com)** is a leading global manufacturer of mobile devices and services. The following selected information is available from Nokia's financial statements.

(Euro millions)	Current Year	Prior Year
Current assets	23,613	24,470
Current liabilities	15,188	20,355

Required

1. Compute Nokia's current ratio for both the current year and the prior year.
2. Comment on any change from the prior year to the current year for the current ratio.

ANSWERS TO MULTIPLE CHOICE QUIZ

1. e
2. c
3. a
4. c
5. b

5

Accounting for Merchandising Operations

A Look Back

Chapters 3 and 4 focused on the final steps of the accounting process. We explained the importance of proper revenue and expense recognition and described the adjusting and closing processes. We also prepared financial statements.

A Look at This Chapter

This chapter emphasizes merchandising activities. We explain how reporting merchandising activities differs from reporting service activities. We also analyze and record merchandise purchases and sales transactions, and explain the adjustments and closing process for merchandisers.

A Look Ahead

Chapter 6 extends our analysis of merchandising activities and focuses on the valuation of inventory. Topics include the items in inventory, costs assigned, costing methods used, and inventory estimation techniques.

Learning Objectives

CAP

CONCEPTUAL

C1 Describe merchandising activities and identify income components for a merchandising company. (p. 180)

C2 Identify and explain the inventory asset and cost flows of a merchandising company. (p. 181)

ANALYTICAL

A1 Compute the acid-test ratio and explain its use to assess liquidity. (p. 196)

A2 Compute the gross margin ratio and explain its use to assess profitability. (p. 196)

LP5

PROCEDURAL

P1 Analyze and record transactions for merchandise purchases using a perpetual system. (p. 182)

P2 Analyze and record transactions for merchandise sales using a perpetual system. (p. 187)

P3 Prepare adjustments and close accounts for a merchandising company. (p. 190)

P4 Define and prepare multiple-step and single-step income statements. (p. 192)

P5 *Appendix 5A*—Record and compare merchandising transactions using both periodic and perpetual inventory systems. (p. 201)

Decision Insight

Out of Africa

"We are changing history and . . . we are all going to make a whole lot of money"

—SELENA CUFFE

LOS ANGELES—Selena Cuffe was in Johannesburg as part of a student exchange program when she discovered wine at the Soweto Wine Festival. "They have wine here?" asked a puzzled Selena. That festival unleashed Selena's passion to pursue the merchandising of wine. But not just any wine—she would import and distribute wine produced by indigenous African vintners. She and her husband, Khary, launched **Heritage Link Brands (HeritageLinkBrands.com).** Our mission, says Selena, is "to showcase the very best wines from Africa and the African Diaspora."

But the start-up was a struggle. "Our business is a family business so whatever decisions we make have to be made with the best interest of my family and those we work with," explains Selena. She describes how the business required a merchandising accounting system to account for purchases and sales transactions and to effectively track the levels of the various wines. Inventory was especially important to account for and monitor. Khary explains, "It is very easy to underestimate expenses."

To succeed, Selena and Khary needed to make smart business decisions. They set up an accounting system to capture and communicate costs and sales information. Tracking merchandising activities was necessary to set prices and to manage discounts, allowances, and returns of both sales and purchases. A perpetual inventory system enabled them to stock the right kind and amount of merchandise and to avoid the costs of out-of-stock and excess inventory. Khary stressed that they monitored current assets and current liabilities (working capital). "Understand working capital," insists Khary. "If you don't understand working capital, stop right here and open an accounting book."

Mastering accounting for merchandising is a means to an end for Selena and Khary. "My training is really about how to run a successful business," says Selena. "How to get the most profit you can out of something." Still, Selena recognizes that her merchandising business is more than profits and losses. "What we're able to do and how we're able to make an impact with this business only matters in as much as the people here and on the continent are able to be successful and thrive."

[Sources: *Heritage Link Brands Website,* January 2011; *TIME,* September 2007; *Black Enterprise,* May 2009; *Inc,* March 2009]

Chapter Preview

Buyers of merchandise expect many products, discount prices, inventory on demand, and high quality. This chapter introduces the accounting practices used by companies engaged in merchandising. We show how financial statements reflect merchandising activities and explain the new financial statement items created by merchandising activities. We also analyze and record merchandise purchases and sales, and explain the adjustments and the closing process for these companies.

Accounting for Merchandising Operations
Merchandising Activities
• Reporting income
• Reporting inventory
• Operating cycles
• Inventory systems
Merchandising Purchases
• Purchase discounts
• Purchase returns and allowances
• Transportation costs
Merchandising Sales
• Sales of merchandise
• Sales discounts
• Sales returns and allowances
Accounting Cycle
• Adjusting entries
• Preparing financial statements
• Closing entries
Financial Statement Formats
• Multiple-step income statement
• Single-step income statement
• Classified balance sheet

MERCHANDISING ACTIVITIES

C1 Describe merchandising activities and identify income components for a merchandising company.

Previous chapters emphasized the accounting and reporting activities of service companies. A merchandising company's activities differ from those of a service company. **Merchandise** consists of products, also called *goods,* that a company acquires to resell to customers. A **merchandiser** earns net income by buying and selling merchandise. Merchandisers are often identified as either wholesalers or retailers. A **wholesaler** is an *intermediary* that buys products from manufacturers or other wholesalers and sells them to retailers or other wholesalers. A **retailer** is an intermediary that buys products from manufacturers or wholesalers and sells them to consumers. Many retailers sell both products and services.

Reporting Income for a Merchandiser

Net income for a merchandiser equals revenues from selling merchandise minus both the cost of merchandise sold to customers and the cost of other expenses for the period, see Exhibit 5.1. The

EXHIBIT 5.1

Computing Income for a Merchandising Company versus a Service Company

Service Company

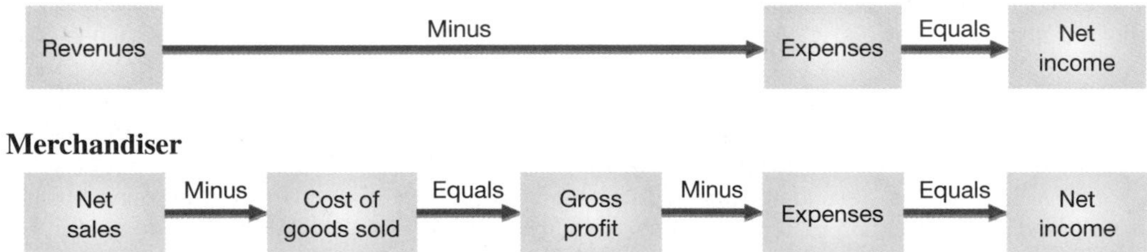

usual accounting term for revenues from selling merchandise is *sales,* and the term used for the expense of buying and preparing the merchandise is **cost of goods sold.** (Some service companies use the term *sales* instead of revenues; and cost of goods sold is also called *cost of sales.*)

The income statement for Z-Mart in Exhibit 5.2 illustrates these key components of a merchandiser's net income. The first two lines show that products are acquired at a cost of $230,400 and sold for $314,700. The third line shows an $84,300 **gross profit,** also called

Point: **Fleming, SuperValu,** and **SYSCO** are wholesalers. **Gap, Oakley, Target,** and **Walmart** are retailers.

Z-MART Income Statement For Year Ended December 31, 2011	
Net sales	$314,700
Cost of goods sold	**230,400**
Gross profit	**84,300**
Expenses	71,400
Net income	$ 12,900

EXHIBIT 5.2

Merchandiser's Income Statement

gross margin, which equals net sales less cost of goods sold. Additional expenses of $71,400 are reported, which leaves $12,900 in net income.

Point: Analysis of gross profit is important to effective business decisions, and is described later in the chapter.

Reporting Inventory for a Merchandiser

A merchandiser's balance sheet includes a current asset called *merchandise inventory,* an item not on a service company's balance sheet. **Merchandise inventory,** or simply *inventory,* refers to products that a company owns and intends to sell. The cost of this asset includes the cost incurred to buy the goods, ship them to the store, and make them ready for sale.

C2 Identify and explain the inventory asset and cost flows of a merchandising company.

Operating Cycle for a Merchandiser

A merchandising company's operating cycle begins by purchasing merchandise and ends by collecting cash from selling the merchandise. The length of an operating cycle differs across the types of businesses. Department stores often have operating cycles of two to five months. Operating cycles for grocery merchants usually range from two to eight weeks.

Exhibit 5.3 illustrates an operating cycle for a merchandiser with credit sales. The cycle moves from (*a*) cash purchases of merchandise to (*b*) inventory for sale to (*c*) credit sales to (*d*) accounts receivable to (*e*) cash. Companies try to keep their operating cycles short because assets tied up in inventory and receivables are not productive. Cash sales shorten operating cycles.

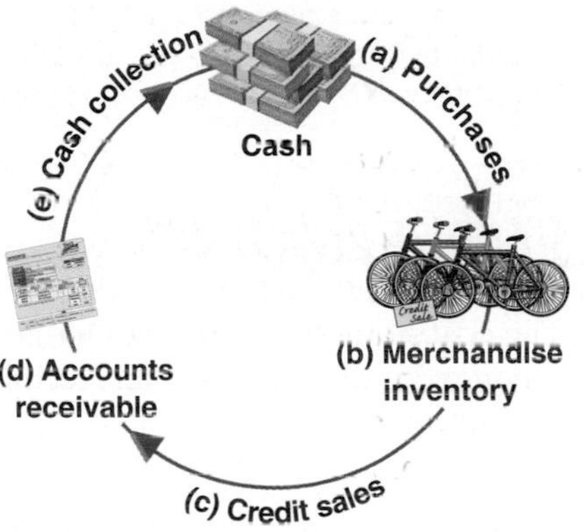

EXHIBIT 5.3

Merchandiser's Operating Cycle

Inventory Systems

Cost of goods sold is the cost of merchandise sold to customers during a period. It is often the largest single expense on a merchandiser's income statement. **Inventory** refers to products a company owns and expects to sell in its normal operations. Exhibit 5.4 shows that a company's merchandise available for sale consists of what it begins with (beginning inventory) and what it

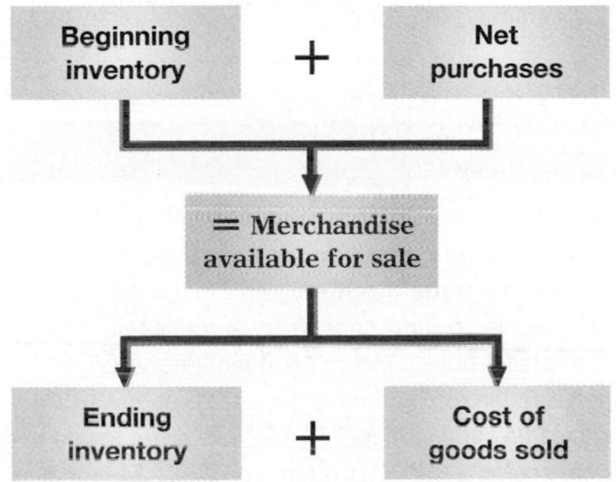

EXHIBIT 5.4

Merchandiser's Cost Flow for a Single Time Period

Point: Mathematically, Exhibit 5.4 says

BI + NP = MAS,

where BI is beginning inventory, NP is net purchases, and MAS is merchandise available for sale. Exhibit 5.4 also says

MAS = EI + COGS,

which can be rewritten as MAS − EI = COGS or MAS − COGS = EI, where EI is ending inventory and COGS is cost of goods sold.

purchases (net purchases). The merchandise available is either sold (cost of goods sold) or kept for future sales (ending inventory).

Two alternative inventory accounting systems can be used to collect information about cost of goods sold and cost of inventory: *perpetual system* or *periodic system*. The **perpetual inventory system** continually updates accounting records for merchandising transactions—specifically, for those records of inventory available for sale and inventory sold. The **periodic inventory system** updates the accounting records for merchandise transactions only at the *end of a period*. Technological advances and competitive pressures have dramatically increased the use of the perpetual system. It gives managers immediate access to detailed information on sales and inventory levels, where they can strategically react to sales trends, cost changes, consumer tastes, and so forth, to increase gross profit. (Some companies use a *hybrid* system where the perpetual system is used for tracking units available and the periodic system is used to compute cost of sales.)

Point: Growth of superstores such as **Costco** and **Sam's** is fueled by efficient use of perpetual inventory.

Quick Check Answers — p. 207 

1. Describe a merchandiser's cost of goods sold.
2. What is gross profit for a merchandising company?
3. Explain why use of the perpetual inventory system has dramatically increased.

The following sections, consisting of the next 10 pages on purchasing, selling, and adjusting merchandise, use the perpetual system. Appendix 5A uses the periodic system (with the perpetual results on the side). An instructor can choose to cover either one or both inventory systems.

ACCOUNTING FOR MERCHANDISE PURCHASES

P1 Analyze and record transactions for merchandise purchases using a perpetual system.

The cost of merchandise purchased for resale is recorded in the Merchandise Inventory asset account. To illustrate, Z-Mart records a $1,200 cash purchase of merchandise on November 2 as follows:

Assets = Liabilities + Equity
+1,200
−1,200

Nov. 2	Merchandise Inventory	1,200	
	Cash		1,200
	Purchased merchandise for cash.		

The invoice for this merchandise is shown in Exhibit 5.5. The buyer usually receives the original invoice, and the seller keeps a copy. This *source document* serves as the purchase invoice of Z-Mart (buyer) and the sales invoice for Trex (seller). The amount recorded for merchandise inventory includes its purchase cost, shipping fees, taxes, and any other costs necessary to make it ready for sale. This section explains how we compute the recorded cost of merchandise purchases.

Point: The Merchandise Inventory account reflects the cost of goods available for resale.

Decision Insight 

Trade Discounts When a manufacturer or wholesaler prepares a catalog of items it has for sale, it usually gives each item a **list price,** also called a *catalog price*. However, an item's intended *selling price* equals list price minus a given percent called a **trade discount.** The amount of trade discount usually depends on whether a buyer is a wholesaler, retailer, or final consumer. A wholesaler buying in large quantities is often granted a larger discount than a retailer buying in smaller quantities. A buyer records the net amount of list price minus trade discount. For example, in the November 2 purchase of merchandise by Z-Mart, the merchandise was listed in the seller's catalog at $2,000 and Z-Mart received a 40% trade discount. This meant that Z-Mart's purchase price was $1,200, computed as $2,000 − (40% × $2,000). ■

EXHIBIT 5.5
Invoice

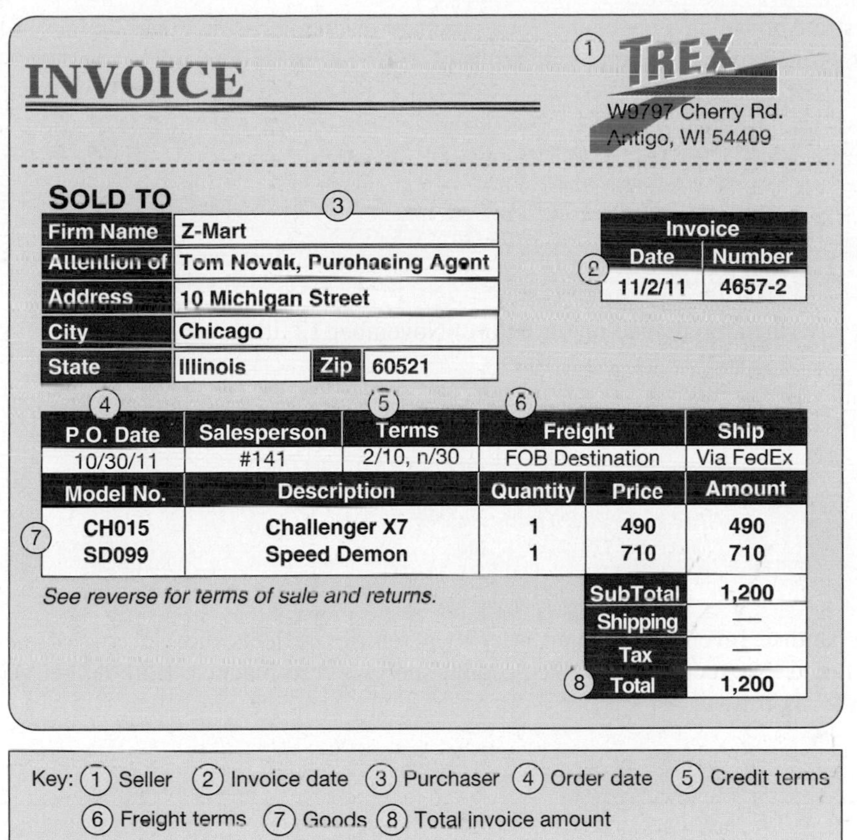
INVOICE

TREX
W9797 Cherry Rd.
Antigo, WI 54409

SOLD TO

Firm Name	Z-Mart
Attention of	Tom Novak, Purchasing Agent
Address	10 Michigan Street
City	Chicago
State	Illinois
Zip	60521

Invoice Date	Invoice Number
11/2/11	4657-2

P.O. Date	Salesperson	Terms	Freight	Ship
10/30/11	#141	2/10, n/30	FOB Destination	Via FedEx

Model No.	Description	Quantity	Price	Amount
CH015	Challenger X7	1	490	490
SD099	Speed Demon	1	710	710
			SubTotal	1,200
			Shipping	—
			Tax	—
			Total	1,200

See reverse for terms of sale and returns.

Key: (1) Seller (2) Invoice date (3) Purchaser (4) Order date (5) Credit terms (6) Freight terms (7) Goods (8) Total invoice amount

Purchase Discounts

The purchase of goods on credit requires a clear statement of expected future payments and dates to avoid misunderstandings. **Credit terms** for a purchase include the amounts and timing of payments from a buyer to a seller. Credit terms usually reflect an industry's practices. To illustrate, when sellers require payment within 10 days after the end of the month of the invoice date, the invoice will show credit terms as "n/10 EOM," which stands for net 10 days after end of month (**EOM**). When sellers require payment within 30 days after the invoice date, the invoice shows credit terms of "n/30," which stands for *net 30 days*.

Exhibit 5.6 portrays credit terms. The amount of time allowed before full payment is due is called the **credit period.** Sellers can grant a **cash discount** to encourage buyers to pay earlier. A buyer views a cash discount as a **purchase discount.** A seller views a cash discount as a **sales discount.** Any cash discounts are described in the credit terms on the invoice. For example, credit terms of "2/10, n/60" mean that full payment is due within a 60-day credit period, but the buyer can deduct 2% of the invoice amount if payment is made within 10 days of the invoice date. This reduced payment applies only for the **discount period.**

Point: Since both the buyer and seller know the invoice date, this date is used in setting the discount and credit periods.

EXHIBIT 5.6
Credit Terms

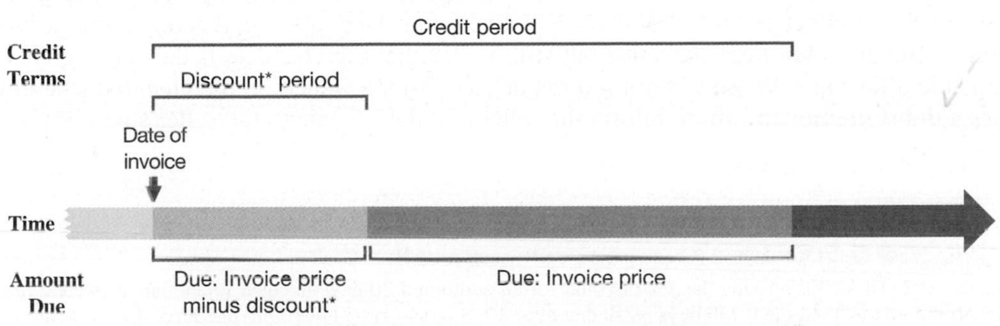

Point: Appendix 5A repeats journal entries *a* through *f* using a periodic inventory system.

To illustrate how a buyer accounts for a purchase discount, assume that Z-Mart's $1,200 purchase of merchandise is on credit with terms of 2/10, n/30. Its entry is

Assets = Liabilities + Equity
+1,200 +1,200

(a) Nov. 2	Merchandise Inventory	1,200	
	Accounts Payable		1,200
	Purchased merchandise on credit, invoice dated Nov. 2, terms 2/10, n/30.		

If Z-Mart pays the amount due on (or before) November 12, the entry is

Assets = Liabilities + Equity
−24 −1,200
−1,176

(b) Nov. 12	Accounts Payable	1,200	
	Merchandise Inventory		24
	Cash		1,176
	Paid for the $1,200 purchase of Nov. 2 less the discount of $24 (2% × $1,200).		

Point: These entries illustrate what is called the *gross method* of accounting for purchases with discount terms.

The Merchandise Inventory account after these entries reflects the net cost of merchandise purchased, and the Accounts Payable account shows a zero balance. Both ledger accounts, in T-account form, follow:

Merchandise Inventory			
Nov. 2	1,200	Nov. 12	24
Balance	1,176		

Accounts Payable			
Nov. 12	1,200	Nov. 2	1,200
		Balance	0

A buyer's failure to pay within a discount period can be expensive. To illustrate, if Z-Mart does not pay within the 10-day 2% discount period, it can delay payment by 20 more days. This delay costs Z-Mart $24, computed as 2% × $1,200. Most buyers take advantage of a purchase discount because of the usually high interest rate implied from not taking it.[1] Also, good cash management means that no invoice is paid until the last day of the discount or credit period.

Decision Maker Answer — p. 206

Entrepreneur You purchase a batch of products on terms of 3/10, n/90, but your company has limited cash and you must borrow funds at an 11% annual rate if you are to pay within the discount period. Do you take advantage of the purchase discount? ■

Purchase Returns and Allowances

Point: The sender (maker) of a *debit memorandum* will debit the account of the memo's receiver. The memo's receiver will credit the sender's account.

Purchase returns refer to merchandise a buyer acquires but then returns to the seller. A *purchase allowance* is a reduction in the cost of defective or unacceptable merchandise that a buyer acquires. Buyers often keep defective but still marketable merchandise if the seller grants an acceptable allowance. When a buyer returns or takes an allowance on merchandise, the buyer issues a **debit memorandum** to inform the seller of a debit made to the seller's account in the buyer's records.

[1] The *implied annual interest rate* formula is:

(365 days ÷ [Credit period − Discount period]) × Cash discount rate.

For terms of 2/10, n/30, missing the 2% discount for an additional 20 days is equal to an annual interest rate of 36.5%, computed as [365 days/(30 days − 10 days)] × 2% discount rate. *Favorable purchase discounts* are those with implied annual interest rates that exceed the purchaser's annual rate for borrowing money.

Purchase Allowances To illustrate purchase allowances, assume that on November 15, Z-Mart (buyer) issues a $300 debit memorandum for an allowance from Trex for defective merchandise. Z-Mart's November 15 entry to update its Merchandise Inventory account to reflect the purchase allowance is

(c) Nov. 15	Accounts Payable	300	
	Merchandise Inventory		300
	Allowance for defective merchandise.		

Assets = Liabilities + Equity
−300 −300

The buyer's allowance for defective merchandise is usually offset against the buyer's current account payable balance to the seller. When cash is refunded, the Cash account is debited instead of Accounts Payable.

Purchase Returns Returns are recorded at the net costs charged to buyers. To illustrate the accounting for returns, suppose Z-Mart purchases $1,000 of merchandise on June 1 with terms 2/10, n/60. Two days later, Z-Mart returns $100 of goods before paying the invoice. When Z-Mart later pays on June 11, it takes the 2% discount only on the $900 remaining balance. When goods are returned, a buyer can take a purchase discount on only the remaining balance of the invoice. The resulting discount is $18 (2% × $900) and the cash payment is $882 ($900 − $18). The following entries reflect this illustration.

June 1	Merchandise Inventory	1,000	
	Accounts Payable		1,000
	Purchased merchandise, invoice dated June 1, terms 2/10, n/60.		
June 3	Accounts Payable	100	
	Merchandise Inventory		100
	Returned merchandise to seller.		
June 11	Accounts Payable	900	
	Merchandise Inventory		18
	Cash		882
	Paid for $900 merchandise ($1,000 − $100) less $18 discount (2% × $900).		

Example: Assume Z-Mart pays $980 cash for $1,000 of merchandise purchased within its 2% discount period. Later, it returns $100 of the original $1,000 merchandise. The return entry is

Cash	98	
Merchandise Inventory		98

Decision Ethics Answer — p. 206

Credit Manager As a new credit manager, you are being trained by the outgoing manager. She explains that the system prepares checks for amounts net of favorable cash discounts, and the checks are dated the last day of the discount period. She also tells you that checks are not mailed until five days later, adding that "the company gets free use of cash for an extra five days, and our department looks better. When a supplier complains, we blame the computer system and the mailroom." Do you continue this payment policy? ■

Transportation Costs and Ownership Transfer

The buyer and seller must agree on who is responsible for paying any freight costs and who bears the risk of loss during transit for merchandising transactions. This is essentially the same as asking at what point ownership transfers from the seller to the buyer. The point of transfer is called the **FOB** (*free on board*) point, which determines who pays transportation costs (and often other incidental costs of transit such as insurance).

Exhibit 5.7 identifies two alternative points of transfer. (1) *FOB shipping point,* also called *FOB factory,* means the buyer accepts ownership when the goods depart the seller's place of business. The buyer is then responsible for paying shipping costs and bearing the risk of damage or loss when goods are in transit. The goods are part of the buyer's inventory when they are in transit since ownership has transferred to the buyer. **1-800-FLOWERS.COM**, a floral and gift

EXHIBIT 5.7

Ownership Transfer and Transportation Costs

	Ownership Transfers When Goods Passed to	Transportation Costs Paid by
FOB shipping point	Carrier	Buyer
FOB destination	Buyer	Seller

Point: The party not responsible for shipping costs sometimes pays the carrier. In these cases, the party paying these costs either bills the party responsible or, more commonly, adjusts its account payable or account receivable with the other party. For example, a buyer paying a carrier when terms are FOB destination can decrease its account payable to the seller by the amount of shipping cost.

merchandiser, and **Bare Escentuals**, a cosmetic manufacturer, both use FOB shipping point. (2) *FOB destination* means ownership of goods transfers to the buyer when the goods arrive at the buyer's place of business. The seller is responsible for paying shipping charges and bears the risk of damage or loss in transit. The seller does not record revenue from this sale until the goods arrive at the destination because this transaction is not complete before that point. **Kyocera**, a manufacturer, uses FOB destination.

Z-Mart's $1,200 purchase on November 2 is on terms of FOB destination. This means Z-Mart is not responsible for paying transportation costs. When a buyer is responsible for paying transportation costs, the payment is made to a carrier or directly to the seller depending on the agreement. The cost principle requires that any necessary transportation costs of a buyer (often called *transportation-in* or *freight-in*) be included as part of the cost of purchased merchandise. To illustrate, Z-Mart's entry to record a $75 freight charge from an independent carrier for merchandise purchased FOB shipping point is

Assets = Liabilities + Equity
+75
−75

(*d*) Nov. 24	Merchandise Inventory	75	
	Cash		75
	Paid freight costs on purchased merchandise.		

A seller records the costs of shipping goods to customers in a Delivery Expense account when the seller is responsible for these costs. Delivery Expense, also called *transportation-out* or *freight-out,* is reported as a selling expense in the seller's income statement.

In summary, purchases are recorded as debits to Merchandise Inventory. Any later purchase discounts, returns, and allowances are credited (decreases) to Merchandise Inventory. Transportation-in is debited (added) to Merchandise Inventory. Z-Mart's itemized costs of merchandise purchases for year 2011 are in Exhibit 5.8.

EXHIBIT 5.8

Itemized Costs of Merchandise Purchases

Z-MART
Itemized Costs of Merchandise Purchases
For Year Ended December 31, 2011

Invoice cost of merchandise purchases	$ 235,800
Less: Purchase discounts received	(4,200)
Purchase returns and allowances	(1,500)
Add: Costs of transportation-in	2,300
Total cost of merchandise purchases	**$232,400**

Point: Some companies have separate accounts for purchase discounts, returns and allowances, and transportation-in. These accounts are then transferred to Merchandise Inventory at period-end. This is a *hybrid system* of perpetual and periodic. That is, Merchandise Inventory is updated on a perpetual basis but only for purchases and cost of goods sold.

The accounting system described here does not provide separate records (accounts) for total purchases, total purchase discounts, total purchase returns and allowances, and total transportation-in. Yet nearly all companies collect this information in supplementary records because managers need this information to evaluate and control each of these cost elements. **Supplementary records,** also called *supplemental records,* refer to information outside the usual general ledger accounts.

Quick Check

Answers — p. 207

4. How long are the credit and discount periods when credit terms are 2/10, n/60?
5. Identify which items are subtracted from the *list* amount and not recorded when computing purchase price: (*a*) freight-in; (*b*) trade discount; (*c*) purchase discount; (*d*) purchase return.
6. What does *FOB* mean? What does *FOB destination* mean?

ACCOUNTING FOR MERCHANDISE SALES

P2 Analyze and record transactions for merchandise sales using a perpetual system.

Merchandising companies also must account for sales, sales discounts, sales returns and allowances, and cost of goods sold. A merchandising company such as Z-Mart reflects these items in its gross profit computation, as shown in Exhibit 5.9. This section explains how this information is derived from transactions.

EXHIBIT 5.9

Gross Profit Computation

Z-MART
Computation of Gross Profit
For Year Ended December 31, 2011

Sales		$321,000
Less: Sales discounts	$4,300	
Sales returns and allowances	2,000	6,300
Net sales		314,700
Cost of goods sold		230,400
Gross profit		**$ 84,300**

Sales of Merchandise

Each sales transaction for a seller of merchandise involves two parts.

1. **Revenue received in the form of an asset from the customer.**
2. **Recognition of the cost of merchandise sold to the customer.**

Accounting for a sales transaction under the perpetual system requires recording information about both parts. This means that each sales transaction for merchandisers, whether for cash or on credit, requires *two entries:* one for revenue and one for cost. To illustrate, Z-Mart sold $2,400 of merchandise on credit on November 3. The revenue part of this transaction is recorded as

(e) Nov. 3	Accounts Receivable	2,400	
	Sales		2,400
	Sold merchandise on credit.		

Assets	=	Liabilities	+	Equity
+2,400				+2,400

This entry reflects an increase in Z-Mart's assets in the form of accounts receivable. It also shows the increase in revenue (Sales). If the sale is for cash, the debit is to Cash instead of Accounts Receivable.

The cost part of each sales transaction ensures that the Merchandise Inventory account under a perpetual inventory system reflects the updated cost of the merchandise available for sale. For example, the cost of the merchandise Z-Mart sold on November 3 is $1,600, and the entry to record the cost part of this sales transaction is

(e) Nov. 3	Cost of Goods Sold	1,600	
	Merchandise Inventory		1,600
	To record the cost of Nov. 3 sale.		

Assets	=	Liabilities	+	Equity
−1,600				−1,600

Decision Insight 

Suppliers and Demands Large merchandising companies often bombard suppliers with demands. These include discounts for bar coding and technology support systems, and fines for shipping errors. Merchandisers' goals are to reduce inventories, shorten lead times, and eliminate errors. ■

Sales Discounts

Sales discounts on credit sales can benefit a seller by decreasing the delay in receiving cash and reducing future collection efforts. At the time of a credit sale, a seller does not know whether a customer will pay within the discount period and take advantage of a discount. This means the seller usually does not record a sales discount until a customer actually pays within the discount period. To illustrate, Z-Mart completes a credit sale for $1,000 on November 12 with terms of 2/10, n/60. The entry to record the revenue part of this sale is

Assets	= Liabilities	+ Equity
+1,000		+1,000

Nov. 12	Accounts Receivable	1,000	
	Sales		1,000
	Sold merchandise under terms of 2/10, n/60.		

This entry records the receivable and the revenue as if the customer will pay the full amount. The customer has two options, however. One option is to wait 60 days until January 11 and pay the full $1,000. In this case, Z-Mart records that payment as

Assets	= Liabilities	+ Equity
+1,000		
−1,000		

Jan. 11	Cash	1,000	
	Accounts Receivable		1,000
	Received payment for Nov. 12 sale.		

The customer's second option is to pay $980 within a 10-day period ending November 22. If the customer pays on (or before) November 22, Z-Mart records the payment as

Assets	= Liabilities	+ Equity
+980		−20
−1,000		

Nov. 22	Cash	980	
	Sales Discounts	20	
	Accounts Receivable		1,000
	Received payment for Nov. 12 sale less discount.		

Sales Discounts is a contra revenue account, meaning the Sales Discounts account is deducted from the Sales account when computing a company's net sales (see Exhibit 5.9). Management monitors Sales Discounts to assess the effectiveness and cost of its discount policy.

Sales Returns and Allowances

Point: Published income statements rarely disclose sales discounts, returns and allowances.

Sales returns refer to merchandise that customers return to the seller after a sale. Many companies allow customers to return merchandise for a full refund. *Sales allowances* refer to reductions in the selling price of merchandise sold to customers. This can occur with damaged or defective merchandise that a customer is willing to purchase with a decrease in selling price. Sales returns and allowances usually involve dissatisfied customers and the possibility of lost future sales, and managers monitor information about returns and allowances.

Sales Returns To illustrate, recall Z-Mart's sale of merchandise on November 3 for $2,400 that had cost $1,600. Assume that the customer returns part of the merchandise on

November 6, and the returned items sell for $800 and cost $600. The revenue part of this transaction must reflect the decrease in sales from the customer's return of merchandise as follows:

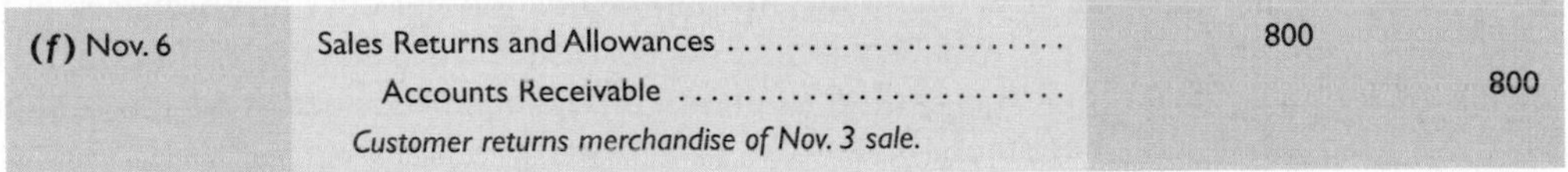

(f) Nov. 6	Sales Returns and Allowances	800	
	Accounts Receivable		800
	Customer returns merchandise of Nov. 3 sale.		

Assets = Liabilities + Equity
−800 −800

If the merchandise returned to Z-Mart is not defective and can be resold to another customer, Z-Mart returns these goods to its inventory. The entry to restore the cost of such goods to the Merchandise Inventory account is

Nov. 6	Merchandise Inventory	600	
	Cost of Goods Sold		600
	Returned goods added to inventory.		

Assets = Liabilities + Equity
+600 +600

This entry changes if the goods returned are defective. In this case the returned inventory is recorded at its estimated value, not its cost. To illustrate, if the goods (costing $600) returned to Z-Mart are defective and estimated to be worth $150, the following entry is made: Dr. Merchandise Inventory for $150, Dr. Loss from Defective Merchandise for $450, and Cr. Cost of Goods Sold for $600.

Decision Insight

Return to Sender Book merchandisers such as **Barnes & Noble**, **Borders Books**, **Books-A-Million**, and **Waldenbooks** can return unsold books to publishers at purchase price. Publishers say returns of new hardcover books run between 35% and 50%. ■

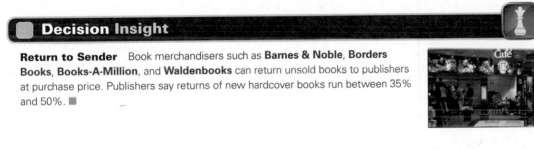

Sales Allowances To illustrate sales allowances, assume that $800 of the merchandise Z-Mart sold on November 3 is defective but the buyer decides to keep it because Z-Mart offers a $100 price reduction. Z-Mart records this allowance as follows:

Nov. 6	Sales Returns and Allowances	100	
	Accounts Receivable		100
	To record sales allowance on Nov. 3 sale.		

Assets = Liabilities + Equity
−100 −100

The seller usually prepares a credit memorandum to confirm a buyer's return or allowance. A seller's **credit memorandum** informs a buyer of the seller's credit to the buyer's Account Receivable (on the seller's books).

Point: The sender (maker) of a credit memorandum will *credit* the account of the receiver. The receiver of a credit memorandum will *debit* the sender's account.

Quick Check

Answers — p. 207

7. Why are sales discounts and sales returns and allowances recorded in contra revenue accounts instead of directly in the Sales account?
8. Under what conditions are two entries necessary to record a sales return?
9. When merchandise is sold on credit and the seller notifies the buyer of a price allowance, does the seller create and send a credit memorandum or a debit memorandum?

COMPLETING THE ACCOUNTING CYCLE

Exhibit 5.10 shows the flow of merchandising costs during a period and where these costs are reported at period-end. Specifically, beginning inventory plus the net cost of purchases is the merchandise available for sale. As inventory is sold, its cost is recorded in cost of goods sold on the income statement; what remains is ending inventory on the balance sheet. A period's ending inventory is the next period's beginning inventory.

EXHIBIT 5.10

Merchandising Cost Flow in the Accounting Cycle

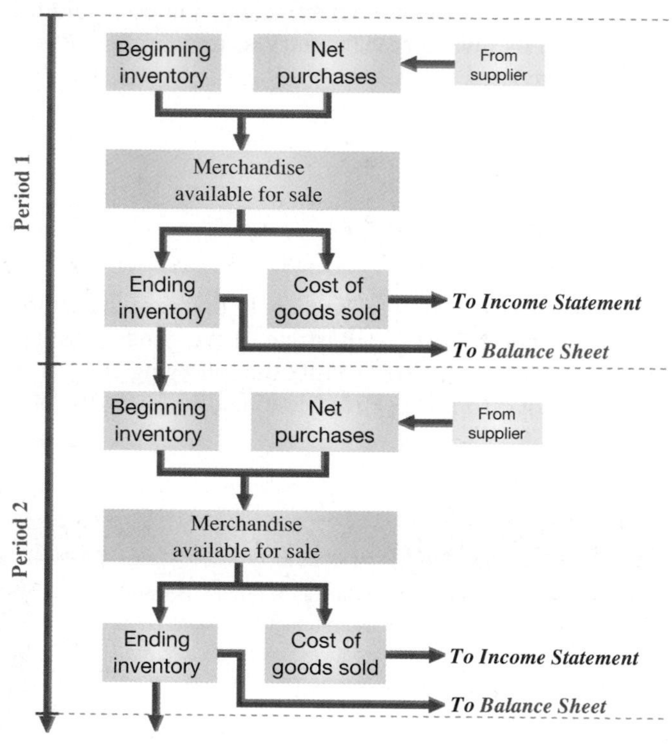

Adjusting Entries for Merchandisers

P3 Prepare adjustments and close accounts for a merchandising company.

Each of the steps in the accounting cycle described in the prior chapter for a service company applies to a merchandiser. This section and the next two further explain three steps of the accounting cycle for a merchandiser—adjustments, statement preparation, and closing.

Adjusting entries are generally the same for merchandising companies and service companies, including those for prepaid expenses (including depreciation), accrued expenses, unearned revenues, and accrued revenues. However, a merchandiser using a perpetual inventory system is usually required to make another adjustment to update the Merchandise Inventory account to reflect any loss of merchandise, including theft and deterioration. **Shrinkage** is the term used to refer to the loss of inventory and it is computed by comparing a physical count of inventory with recorded amounts. A physical count is usually performed at least once annually.

Point: About two-thirds of shoplifting losses are thefts by employees.

To illustrate, Z-Mart's Merchandise Inventory account at the end of year 2011 has a balance of $21,250, but a physical count reveals that only $21,000 of inventory exists. The adjusting entry to record this $250 shrinkage is

Assets	=	Liabilities	+	Equity
−250				−250

Dec. 31	Cost of Goods Sold	250	
	Merchandise Inventory		250
	To adjust for $250 shrinkage revealed by a physical count of inventory.		

Preparing Financial Statements

The financial statements of a merchandiser, and their preparation, are similar to those for a service company described in Chapters 2 through 4. The income statement mainly differs by the inclusion of *cost of goods sold* and *gross profit*. Also, net sales is affected by discounts, returns, and allowances, and some additional expenses are possible such as delivery expense and loss from defective merchandise. The balance sheet mainly differs by the inclusion of *merchandise inventory* as part of current assets. The statement of owner's equity is unchanged. A work sheet can be used to help prepare these statements, and one is illustrated in Appendix 5B for Z-Mart.

Point: Staples's costs of shipping merchandise to its stores is included in its costs of inventories as required by the cost principle.

Closing Entries for Merchandisers

Closing entries are similar for service companies and merchandising companies using a perpetual system. The difference is that we must close some new temporary accounts that arise from merchandising activities. Z-Mart has several temporary accounts unique to merchandisers: Sales (of goods), Sales Discounts, Sales Returns and Allowances, and Cost of Goods Sold. Their existence in the ledger means that the first two closing entries for a merchandiser are slightly different from the ones described in the prior chapter for a service company. These differences are set in **red boldface** in the closing entries of Exhibit 5.11.

Point: The Inventory account is not affected by the closing process under a perpetual system.

EXHIBIT 5.11

Closing Entries for a Merchandiser

Step 1: Close Credit Balances in Temporary Accounts to Income Summary.

Dec. 31	**Sales**	321,000	
	Income Summary		321,000
	To close credit balances in temporary accounts.		

Step 2: Close Debit Balances in Temporary Accounts to Income Summary.

Dec. 31	Income Summary	308,100	
	Sales Discounts		4,300
	Sales Returns and Allowances		2,000
	Cost of Goods Sold		230,400
	Depreciation Expense		3,700
	Salaries Expense		43,800
	Insurance Expense		600
	Rent Expense		9,000
	Supplies Expense		3,000
	Advertising Expense		11,300
	To close debit balances in temporary accounts.		

Step 3: Close Income Summary to Owner's Capital.

The third closing entry is identical for a merchandising company and a service company. The $12,900 amount is net income reported on the income statement.

Dec. 31	Income Summary	12,900	
	K. Marty, Capital		12,900
	To close the Income Summary account.		

Step 4: Close Withdrawals Account to Owner's Capital.

The fourth closing entry is identical for a merchandising company and a service company. It closes the Withdrawals account and adjusts the Owner's Capital account to the amount shown on the balance sheet.

Dec. 31	K. Marty, Capital	4,000	
	K. Marty, Withdrawals		4,000
	To close the Withdrawals account.		

Summary of Merchandising Entries

Exhibit 5.12 summarizes the key adjusting and closing entries of a merchandiser (using a perpetual inventory system) that are different from those of a service company described in prior chapters (the Demonstration Problem 2 illustrates these merchandising entries).

EXHIBIT 5.12

Summary of Merchandising Entries

	Merchandising Transactions	Merchandising Entries	Dr.	Cr.
Purchases	Purchasing merchandise for resale.	Merchandise Inventory	#	
		Cash or Accounts Payable		#
	Paying freight costs on purchases; FOB shipping point.	Merchandise Inventory	#	
		Cash		#
	Paying within discount period.	Accounts Payable	#	
		Merchandise Inventory		#
		Cash		#
	Recording purchase returns or allowances.	Cash or Accounts Payable	#	
		Merchandise Inventory		#
Sales	Selling merchandise.	Cash or Accounts Receivable	#	
		Sales		#
		Cost of Goods Sold	#	
		Merchandise Inventory		#
	Receiving payment within discount period.	Cash	#	
		Sales Discounts	#	
		Accounts Receivable		#
	Granting sales returns or allowances.	Sales Returns and Allowances	#	
		Cash or Accounts Receivable		#
		Merchandise Inventory	#	
		Cost of Goods Sold		#
	Paying freight costs on sales; FOB destination.	Delivery Expense	#	
		Cash		#

	Merchandising Events	Adjusting and Closing Entries		
Adjusting	Adjusting due to shrinkage (occurs when recorded amount larger than physical inventory).	Cost of Goods Sold	#	
		Merchandise Inventory		#
Closing	Closing temporary accounts with credit balances.	Sales	#	
		Income Summary		#
	Closing temporary accounts with debit balances.	Income Summary	#	
		Sales Returns and Allowances		#
		Sales Discounts		#
		Cost of Goods Sold		#
		Delivery Expense		#
		"Other Expenses"		#

Quick Check

Answers — p. 207

10. When a merchandiser uses a perpetual inventory system, why is it sometimes necessary to adjust the Merchandise Inventory balance with an adjusting entry?

11. What temporary accounts do you expect to find in a merchandising business but not in a service business?

12. Describe the closing entries normally made by a merchandising company.

FINANCIAL STATEMENT FORMATS

P4 Define and prepare multiple-step and single-step income statements.

Generally accepted accounting principles do not require companies to use any one presentation format for financial statements so we see many different formats in practice. This section describes two common income statement formats: multiple-step and single-step. The classified balance sheet of a merchandiser is also explained.

Multiple-Step Income Statement

A **multiple-step income statement** format shows detailed computations of net sales and other costs and expenses, and reports subtotals for various classes of items. Exhibit 5.13 shows a multiple-step income statement for Z-Mart. The statement has three main parts: (1) *gross profit,* determined by net sales less cost of goods sold, (2) *income from operations,* determined by gross profit less operating expenses, and (3) *net income,* determined by income from operations adjusted for nonoperating items.

EXHIBIT 5.13

Multiple-Step Income Statement

Z-MART
Income Statement
For Year Ended December 31, 2011

Sales		$321,000	Gross profit computation
Less: Sales discounts	$ 4,300		
Sales returns and allowances	2,000	6,300	
Net sales		314,700	
Cost of goods sold*		230,400	
Gross profit		84,300	
Operating Expenses			Income from operations computation
Selling expenses			
Depreciation expense—Store equipment	3,000		
Sales salaries expense	18,500		
Rent expense—Selling space	8,100		
Store supplies expense	1,200		
Advertising expense	11,300		
Total selling expenses	42,100		
General and administrative expenses			
Depreciation expense—Office equipment	700		
Office salaries expense	25,300		
Insurance expense	600		
Rent expense—Office space	900		
Office supplies expense	1,800		
Total general and administrative expenses	29,300		
Total operating expenses		71,400	
Income from operations		12,900	
Other revenues and gains (expenses and losses)			Nonoperating activities computation
Interest revenue	1,000		
Gain on sale of building	2,500		
Interest expense	(1,500)		
Total other revenue and gains (expenses and losses)		2,000	
Net income		$ 14,900	

*Cost of goods sold consists of the following:

Beginning inventory	$ 19,000
Cost of goods purchased	232,400
Cost of goods available for sale	251,400
Less ending inventory	21,000
Cost of goods sold	$230,400

Operating expenses are classified into two sections. **Selling expenses** include the expenses of promoting sales by displaying and advertising merchandise, making sales, and delivering goods to customers. **General and administrative expenses** support a company's overall operations and include expenses related to accounting, human resource management, and financial management. Expenses are allocated between sections when they contribute to more than one. Z-Mart allocates rent expense of $9,000 from its store building between two sections: $8,100 to selling expense and $900 to general and administrative expense.

Nonoperating activities consist of other expenses, revenues, losses, and gains that are unrelated to a company's operations. *Other revenues and gains* commonly include interest revenue,

Point: Z-Mart did not have any nonoperating activities; however, Exhibit 5.13 includes some for illustrative purposes.

dividend revenue, rent revenue, and gains from asset disposals. *Other expenses and losses* commonly include interest expense, losses from asset disposals, and casualty losses. When a company has no reportable nonoperating activities, its income from operations is simply labeled net income.

Single-Step Income Statement

Point: Many companies report interest expense and interest revenue in separate categories after operating income and before subtracting income tax expense. As one example, see **Palm**'s income statement in Appendix A.

A **single-step income statement** is another widely used format and is shown in Exhibit 5.14 for Z-Mart. It lists cost of goods sold as another expense and shows only one subtotal for total expenses. Expenses are grouped into very few, if any, categories. Many companies use formats that combine features of both the single- and multiple-step statements. Provided that income statement items are shown sensibly, management can choose the format. (In later chapters, we describe some items, such as extraordinary gains and losses, that must be reported in certain locations on the income statement.) Similar presentation options are available for the statement of owner's equity and statement of cash flows.

EXHIBIT 5.14

Single-Step Income Statement

Z-MART
Income Statement
For Year Ended December 31, 2011

Revenues		
Net sales		$314,700
Interest revenue		1,000
Gain on sale of building		2,500
Total revenues		318,200
Expenses		
Cost of goods sold	$230,400	
Selling expenses	42,100	
General and administrative expenses	29,300	
Interest expense	1,500	
Total expenses		303,300
Net income		$ 14,900

Classified Balance Sheet

The merchandiser's classified balance sheet reports merchandise inventory as a current asset, usually after accounts receivable according to an asset's nearness to liquidity. Inventory is usually less liquid than accounts receivable because inventory must first be sold before cash can be received; but it is more liquid than supplies and prepaid expenses. Exhibit 5.15 shows the current asset section of Z-Mart's classified balance sheet (other sections are as shown in Chapter 4).

EXHIBIT 5.15

Classified Balance Sheet (partial) of a Merchandiser

Z-MART
Balance Sheet (partial)
December 31, 2011

Current assets	
Cash	$ 8,200
Accounts receivable	11,200
Merchandise inventory	**21,000**
Office supplies	550
Store supplies	250
Prepaid insurance	300
Total current assets	$ 41,500

Decision Insight

Merchandising Shenanigans Accurate invoices are important to both sellers and buyers. Merchandisers rely on invoices to make certain they receive all monies for products provided—no more, no less. To achieve this, controls are set up. Still, failures arise. A survey reports that 9% of employees in sales and marketing witnessed false or misleading invoices sent to customers. Another 14% observed employees violating contract terms with customers (KPMG 2009). ■

GLOBAL VIEW

This section discusses similarities and differences between U.S. GAAP and IFRS in accounting and reporting for merchandise purchases and sales, and for the income statement.

Accounting for Merchandise Purchases and Sales Both U.S. GAAP and IFRS include broad and similar guidance for the accounting of merchandise purchases and sales. Specifically, all of the transactions presented and illustrated in this chapter are accounted for identically under the two systems. The closing process for merchandisers also is identical for U.S. GAAP and IFRS. In the next chapter we describe how inventory valuation can, in some cases, be different for the two systems.

Income Statement Presentation We explained that net income, profit, and earnings refer to the same (*bottom line*) item. However, IFRS tends to use the term *profit* more than any other term, whereas U.S. statements tend to use *net income* more than any other term. Both U.S. GAAP and IFRS income statements begin with the net sales or net revenues (*top line*) item. For merchandisers and manufacturers, this is followed by cost of goods sold. The presentation is similar for the remaining items with the following differences.

- U.S. GAAP offers little guidance about the presentation or order of expenses. IFRS requires separate disclosures for financing costs (interest expense), income tax expense, and some other special items.
- Both systems require separate disclosure of items when their size, nature, or frequency are important for proper interpretation.
- IFRS permits expenses to be presented by their function or their nature. U.S. GAAP provides no direction but the SEC requires presentation by function.
- Neither U.S. GAAP nor IFRS define *operating* income; this means classification of expenses into operating or nonoperating reflects considerable management discretion.
- IFRS permits alternative measures of income on the income statement; U.S. GAAP prohibits disclosure of alternative income measures in financial statements.

Nokia provides the following example of income statement reporting.

NOKIA

NOKIA
Income Statement (in Euros million)
For Year Ended December 31, 2009

Net sales	40,984
Cost of sales	27,720
Gross profit	13,264
Research and development expenses	5,909
Selling and marketing expenses	3,933
Administrative and general expenses	1,145
Other income and expenses	1,080
Operating profit	1,197
Financial income and expenses (and other)	235
Profit before tax	962
Tax	702
Profit	260

Balance Sheet Presentation Chapters 2 and 3 explained how both U.S. GAAP and IFRS require current items to be separated from noncurrent items on the balance sheet (yielding a *classified balance sheet*). As discussed, U.S. GAAP balance sheets report current items first. Assets are listed from most liquid to least liquid, whereas liabilities are listed from nearest to maturity to furthest from maturity. IFRS balance sheets normally present noncurrent items first (and equity before liabilities), but this is *not* a requirement. **Nokia** provides an example of IFRS reporting for the balance sheet in Appendix A.

Decision Analysis

Acid-Test and Gross Margin Ratios

Acid-Test Ratio

A1 Compute the acid-test ratio and explain its use to assess liquidity.

For many merchandisers, inventory makes up a large portion of current assets. Inventory must be sold and any resulting accounts receivable must be collected before cash is available. Chapter 4 explained that the current ratio, defined as current assets divided by current liabilities, is useful in assessing a company's ability to pay current liabilities. Because it is sometimes unreasonable to assume that inventories are a source of payment for current liabilities, we look to other measures.

One measure of a merchandiser's ability to pay its current liabilities (referred to as its *liquidity*) is the acid-test ratio. It differs from the current ratio by excluding less liquid current assets such as inventory and prepaid expenses that take longer to be converted to cash. The **acid-test ratio,** also called *quick ratio,* is defined as *quick assets* (cash, short-term investments, and current receivables) divided by current liabilities—see Exhibit 5.16.

EXHIBIT 5.16

Acid-Test (Quick) Ratio

$$\textbf{Acid-test ratio} = \frac{\textbf{Cash and cash equivalents + Short-term investments + Current receivables}}{\textbf{Current liabilities}}$$

Exhibit 5.17 shows both the acid-test and current ratios of retailer **JCPenney** for fiscal years 2007 through 2010—also see margin graph. JCPenney's acid-test ratio reveals a general increase from 2007 through 2010 that exceeds the industry average. Further, JCPenney's current ratio (never less than 1.90) suggests that its short-term obligations can be confidently covered with short-term assets.

EXHIBIT 5.17

JCPenney's Acid-Test and Current Ratios

($ millions)	2010	2009	2008	2007
Total quick assets	$3,406	$2,704	$2,845	$2,901
Total current assets	$6,652	$6,220	$6,751	$6,648
Total current liabilities	$3,249	$2,794	$3,338	$3,492
Acid-test ratio	**1.05**	**0.97**	**0.85**	**0.83**
Current ratio	**2.05**	**2.23**	**2.02**	**1.90**
Industry acid-test ratio	0.59	0.63	0.62	0.58
Industry current ratio	2.15	2.31	2.39	2.43

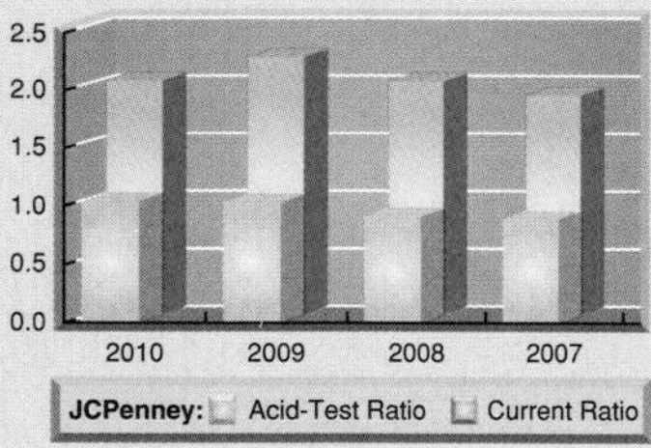

An acid-test ratio less than 1.0 means that current liabilities exceed quick assets. A rule of thumb is that the acid-test ratio should have a value near, or higher than, 1.0 to conclude that a company is unlikely to face near-term liquidity problems. A value much less than 1.0 raises liquidity concerns unless a company can generate enough cash from inventory sales or if much of its liabilities are not due until late in the next period. Similarly, a value slightly larger than 1.0 can hide a liquidity problem if payables are due shortly and receivables are not collected until late in the next period. Analysis of JCPenney shows no need for concern regarding its liquidity even though its acid-test ratio is less than one. This is because retailers such as JCPenney pay many current liabilities from inventory sales. Further, in all years, JCPenney's acid-test ratios exceed the industry norm (and its inventory is fairly liquid).

Point: Successful use of a just-in-time inventory system can narrow the gap between the acid-test ratio and the current ratio.

Decision Maker Answer — p. 206

Supplier A retailer requests to purchase supplies on credit from your company. You have no prior experience with this retailer. The retailer's current ratio is 2.1, its acid-test ratio is 0.5, and inventory makes up most of its current assets. Do you extend credit? ■

Gross Margin Ratio

A2 Compute the gross margin ratio and explain its use to assess profitability.

The cost of goods sold makes up much of a merchandiser's expenses. Without sufficient gross profit, a merchandiser will likely fail. Users often compute the gross margin ratio to help understand this relation. It differs from the profit margin ratio in that it excludes all costs except cost of goods sold. The **gross margin ratio** (also called *gross profit ratio*) is defined as *gross margin* (net sales minus cost of goods sold) divided by net sales—see Exhibit 5.18.

EXHIBIT 5.18

Gross Margin Ratio

$$\textbf{Gross margin ratio} = \frac{\textbf{Net sales} - \textbf{Cost of goods sold}}{\textbf{Net sales}}$$

Exhibit 5.19 shows the gross margin ratio of **JCPenney** for fiscal years 2007 through 2010. For JCPenney, each $1 of sales in 2010 yielded about 39.4¢ in gross margin to cover all other expenses and still produce a net income. This 39.4¢ margin is up from 39.3¢ in 2007. This slight increase is a favorable development. Success for merchandisers such as JCPenney depends on adequate gross margin. For example, the 0.1¢ increase in the gross margin ratio, computed as 39.4¢ − 39.3¢, means that JCPenney has $17.6 million more in gross margin! (This is computed as net sales of $17,556 million multiplied by the 0.1% increase in gross margin.) Management's discussion in its annual report attributes this improvement to its "strategy to sell a greater portion of merchandise at regular promotional prices and less at clearance prices."

Point: The power of a ratio is often its ability to identify areas for more detailed analysis.

EXHIBIT 5.19

JCPenney's Gross Margin Ratio

($ millions)	2010	2009	2008	2007
Gross margin	$ 6,910	$ 6,915	$ 7,671	$ 7,825
Net sales	$17,556	$18,486	$19,860	$19,903
Gross margin ratio	**39.4%**	**37.4%**	**38.6%**	**39.3%**

Financial Officer Your company has a 36% gross margin ratio and a 17% net profit margin ratio. Industry averages are 44% for gross margin and 16% for net profit margin. Do these comparative results concern you? ■

DEMONSTRATION PROBLEM 1

Use the following adjusted trial balance and additional information to complete the requirements.

KC ANTIQUES
Adjusted Trial Balance
December 31, 2011

	Debit	Credit
Cash	$ 7,000	
Accounts receivable	13,000	
Merchandise inventory	60,000	
Store supplies	1,500	
Equipment	45,600	
Accumulated depreciation—Equipment		$ 16,600
Accounts payable		9,000
Salaries payable		2,000
K. Carter, Capital		79,000
K. Carter, Withdrawals	10,000	
Sales		343,250
Sales discounts	5,000	
Sales returns and allowances	6,000	
Cost of goods sold	159,900	
Depreciation expense—Store equipment	4,100	
Depreciation expense—Office equipment	1,600	
Sales salaries expense	30,000	
Office salaries expense	34,000	
Insurance expense	11,000	
Rent expense (70% is store, 30% is office)	24,000	
Store supplies expense	5,750	
Advertising expense	31,400	
Totals	$449,850	$449,850

KC Antiques' *supplementary records* for 2011 reveal the following itemized costs for merchandising activities:

Invoice cost of merchandise purchases	$150,000
Purchase discounts received	2,500
Purchase returns and allowances	2,700
Cost of transportation-in	5,000

Required

1. Use the supplementary records to compute the total cost of merchandise purchases for 2011.
2. Prepare a 2011 multiple-step income statement. (Inventory at December 31, 2010, is $70,100.)
3. Prepare a single-step income statement for 2011.
4. Prepare closing entries for KC Antiques at December 31, 2011.
5. Compute the acid-test ratio and the gross margin ratio. Explain the meaning of each ratio and interpret them for KC Antiques.

PLANNING THE SOLUTION

- Compute the total cost of merchandise purchases for 2011.
- To prepare the multiple-step statement, first compute net sales. Then, to compute cost of goods sold, add the net cost of merchandise purchases for the year to beginning inventory and subtract the cost of ending inventory. Subtract cost of goods sold from net sales to get gross profit. Then classify expenses as selling expenses or general and administrative expenses.
- To prepare the single-step income statement, begin with net sales. Then list and subtract the expenses.
- The first closing entry debits all temporary accounts with credit balances and opens the Income Summary account. The second closing entry credits all temporary accounts with debit balances. The third entry closes the Income Summary account to the capital account, and the fourth entry closes the withdrawals account to the capital account.
- Identify the quick assets on the adjusted trial balance. Compute the acid-test ratio by dividing quick assets by current liabilities. Compute the gross margin ratio by dividing gross profit by net sales.

SOLUTION TO DEMONSTRATION PROBLEM 1

1.

Invoice cost of merchandise purchases	$150,000
Less: Purchases discounts received	2,500
Purchase returns and allowances	2,700
Add: Cost of transportation-in	5,000
Total cost of merchandise purchases	$149,800

2. Multiple-step income statement

KC ANTIQUES
Income Statement
For Year Ended December 31, 2011

Sales		$343,250
Less: Sales discounts	$ 5,000	
Sales returns and allowances	6,000	11,000
Net sales		332,250
Cost of goods sold*		159,900
Gross profit		172,350
Expenses		
Selling expenses		
Depreciation expense—Store equipment	4,100	
Sales salaries expense	30,000	
Rent expense—Selling space	16,800	
Store supplies expense	5,750	
Advertising expense	31,400	
Total selling expenses	88,050	

[continued on next page]

[continued from previous page]

General and administrative expenses		
Depreciation expense—Office equipment	1,600	
Office salaries expense	34,000	
Insurance expense	11,000	
Rent expense—Office space	7,200	
Total general and administrative expenses	53,800	
Total operating expenses		141,850
Net income		$ 30,500

* Cost of goods sold can also be directly computed (applying concepts from Exhibit 5.4):

Merchandise inventory, December 31, 2010	$ 70,100
Total cost of merchandise purchases (from part 1)	149,800
Goods available for sale	219,900
Merchandise inventory, December 31, 2011	60,000
Cost of goods sold	$159,900

3. Single-step income statement

KC ANTIQUES
Income Statement
For Year Ended December 31, 2011

Net sales		$332,250
Expenses		
Cost of goods sold	$159,900	
Selling expenses	88,050	
General and administrative expenses	53,800	
Total expenses		301,750
Net income		$ 30,500

4.

Dec. 31	Sales	343,250	
	Income Summary		343,250
	To close credit balances in temporary accounts.		
Dec. 31	Income Summary	312,750	
	Sales Discounts		5,000
	Sales Returns and Allowances		6,000
	Cost of Goods Sold		159,900
	Depreciation Expense—Store Equipment		4,100
	Depreciation Expense—Office Equipment		1,600
	Sales Salaries Expense		30,000
	Office Salaries Expense		34,000
	Insurance Expense		11,000
	Rent Expense		24,000
	Store Supplies Expense		5,750
	Advertising Expense		31,400
	To close debit balances in temporary accounts.		
Dec. 31	Income Summary	30,500	
	K. Carter, Capital		30,500
	To close the Income Summary account.		
Dec. 31	K. Carter, Capital	10,000	
	K. Carter, Withdrawals		10,000
	To close the Withdrawals account.		

5. Acid-test ratio = (Cash and equivalents + Short-term investments + Current receivables)/Current liabilities
= (Cash + Accounts receivable/(Accounts payable + Salaries payable)
= ($7,000 + $13,000)/($9,000 + $2,000) = $20,000/$11,000 = 1.82

Gross margin ratio = Gross profit/Net sales = $172,350/$332,250 = 0.52 (or 52%)

KC Antiques has a healthy acid-test ratio of 1.82. This means it has more than $1.80 in liquid assets to satisfy each $1.00 in current liabilities. The gross margin of 0.52 shows that KC Antiques spends 48¢ ($1.00 − $0.52) of every dollar of net sales on the costs of acquiring the merchandise it sells. This leaves 52¢ of every dollar of net sales to cover other expenses incurred in the business and to provide a net profit.

DEMONSTRATION PROBLEM 2

Prepare journal entries to record the following merchandising transactions for both the seller (BMX) and buyer (Sanuk).

May 4 BMX sold $1,500 of merchandise on account to Sanuk, terms FOB shipping point, n/45, invoice dated May 4. The cost of the merchandise was $900.
May 6 Sanuk paid transportation charges of $30 on the May 4 purchase from BMX.
May 8 BMX sold $1,000 of merchandise on account to Sanuk, terms FOB destination, n/30, invoice dated May 8. The cost of the merchandise was $700.
May 10 BMX paid transportation costs of $50 for delivery of merchandise sold to Sanuk on May 8.
May 16 BMX issued Sanuk a $200 credit memorandum for merchandise returned. The merchandise was purchased by Sanuk on account on May 8. The cost of the merchandise returned was $140.
May 18 BMX received payment from Sanuk for purchase of May 8.
May 21 BMX sold $2,400 of merchandise on account to Sanuk, terms FOB shipping point, 2/10, n/EOM. BMX prepaid transportation costs of $100, which were added to the invoice. The cost of the merchandise was $1,440.
May 31 BMX received payment from Sanuk for purchase of May 21, less discount (2% × $2,400).

SOLUTION TO DEMONSTRATION PROBLEM 2

	BMX (Seller)			Sanuk (Buyer)		
May 4	Accounts Receivable—Sanuk	1,500		Merchandise Inventory	1,500	
	Sales		1,500	Accounts Payable—BMX		1,500
	Cost of Goods Sold	900				
	Merchandise Inventory		900			
6	No entry.			Merchandise Inventory	30	
				Cash		30
8	Accounts Receivable—Sanuk	1,000		Merchandise Inventory	1,000	
	Sales		1,000	Accounts Payable—BMX		1,000
	Cost of Goods Sold	700				
	Merchandise Inventory		700			
10	Delivery Expense	50		No entry.		
	Cash		50			
16	Sales Returns & Allowances	200		Accounts Payable—BMX	200	
	Accounts Receivable—Sanuk		200	Merchandise Inventory		200
	Merchandise Inventory	140				
	Cost of Goods Sold		140			
18	Cash	800		Accounts Payable—BMX	800	
	Accounts Receivable—Sanuk		800	Cash		800
21	Accounts Receivable—Sanuk	2,400		Merchandise Inventory	2,500	
	Sales		2,400	Accounts Payable—BMX		2,500
	Accounts Receivable—Sanuk	100				
	Cash		100			
	Cost of Goods Sold	1,440				
	Merchandise Inventory		1,440			
31	Cash	2,452		Accounts Payable—BMX	2,500	
	Sales Discounts	48		Merchandise Inventory		48
	Accounts Receivable—Sanuk		2,500	Cash		2,452

APPENDIX

Periodic Inventory System 5A

A periodic inventory system requires updating the inventory account only at the *end of a period* to reflect the quantity and cost of both the goods available and the goods sold. Thus, during the period, the Merchandise Inventory balance remains unchanged. It reflects the beginning inventory balance until it is updated at the end of the period. During the period the cost of merchandise is recorded in a temporary *Purchases* account. When a company sells merchandise, it records revenue ***but not the cost of the goods sold.*** At the end of the period when a company prepares financial statements, it takes a *physical count of inventory* by counting the quantities and costs of merchandise available. The cost of goods sold is then computed by subtracting the ending inventory amount from the cost of merchandise available for sale.

P5 Record and compare merchandising transactions using both periodic and perpetual inventory systems.

Recording Merchandise Transactions Under a periodic system, purchases, purchase returns and allowances, purchase discounts, and transportation-in transactions are recorded in separate temporary accounts. At period-end, each of these temporary accounts is closed and the Merchandise Inventory account is updated. To illustrate, journal entries under the periodic inventory system are shown for the most common transactions (codes ***a*** through ***f*** link these transactions to those in the chapter, and we drop explanations for simplicity). For comparison, perpetual system journal entries are shown to the right of each periodic entry, where differences are in green font.

Purchases The periodic system uses a temporary *Purchases* account that accumulates the cost of all purchase transactions during each period. Z-Mart's November 2 entry to record the purchase of merchandise for $1,200 on credit with terms of 2/10, n/30 is

(*a*)

Periodic			*Perpetual*		
Purchases	1,200		Merchandise Inventory	1,200	
Accounts Payable		1,200	Accounts Payable		1,200

Purchase Discounts The periodic system uses a temporary *Purchase Discounts* account that accumulates discounts taken on purchase transactions during the period. If payment in (*a*) is delayed until after the discount period expires, the entry is to debit Accounts Payable and credit Cash for $1,200 each. However, if Z-Mart pays the supplier for the previous purchase in (*a*) within the discount period, the required payment is $1,176 ($1,200 × 98%) and is recorded as

(*b*)

Periodic			*Perpetual*		
Accounts Payable	1,200		Accounts Payable	1,200	
Purchase Discounts		24	Merchandise Inventory		24
Cash		1,176	Cash		1,176

Purchase Returns and Allowances Z-Mart returned merchandise purchased on November 2 because of defects. In the periodic system, the temporary *Purchase Returns and Allowances* account accumulates the cost of all returns and allowances during a period. The recorded cost (including discounts) of the defective merchandise is $300, and Z-Mart records the November 15 return with this entry:

(*c*)

Periodic			*Perpetual*		
Accounts Payable	300		Accounts Payable	300	
Purchase Returns and Allowances		300	Merchandise Inventory		300

Transportation-In Z-Mart paid a $75 freight charge to transport merchandise to its store. In the periodic system, this cost is charged to a temporary *Transportation-In* account.

(*d*)

Periodic			Perpetual		
Transportation-In	75		Merchandise Inventory	75	
Cash		75	Cash		75

Sales Under the periodic system, the cost of goods sold is *not* recorded at the time of each sale. (We later show how to compute total cost of goods sold at the end of a period.) Z-Mart's November 3 entry to record sales of $2,400 in merchandise on credit (when its cost is $1,600) is:

(*e*)

Periodic			Perpetual		
Accounts Receivable	2,400		Accounts Receivable	2,400	
Sales		2,400	Sales		2,400
			Cost of Goods Sold	1,600	
			Merchandise Inventory		1,600

Sales Returns A customer returned part of the merchandise from the transaction in (*e*), where the returned items sell for $800 and cost $600. (*Recall:* The periodic system records only the revenue effect, not the cost effect, for sales transactions.) Z-Mart restores the merchandise to inventory and records the November 6 return as

(*f*)

Periodic			Perpetual		
Sales Returns and Allowances	800		Sales Returns and Allowances	800	
Accounts Receivable . . .		800	Accounts Receivable		800
			Merchandise Inventory	600	
			Cost of Goods Sold		600

Sales Discounts To illustrate sales discounts, assume that the remaining $1,600 of receivables (computed as $2,400 from ***e*** less $800 for ***f***) has credit terms of 3/10, n/90 and that customers all pay within the discount period. Z-Mart records this payment as

Periodic			Perpetual		
Cash	1,552		Cash	1,552	
Sales Discounts ($1,600 × .03)	48		Sales Discounts ($1,600 × .03) . . .	48	
Accounts Receivable . . .		1,600	Accounts Receivable		1,600

Adjusting and Closing Entries The periodic and perpetual inventory systems have slight differences in adjusting and closing entries. The period-end Merchandise Inventory balance (unadjusted) is $19,000 under the periodic system and $21,250 under the perpetual system. Since the periodic system does not update the Merchandise Inventory balance during the period, the $19,000 amount is the beginning inventory. However, the $21,250 balance under the perpetual system is the recorded ending inventory before adjusting for any inventory shrinkage.

A physical count of inventory taken at the end of the period reveals $21,000 of merchandise available. The adjusting and closing entries for the two systems are shown in Exhibit 5A.1. The periodic system records the ending inventory of $21,000 in the Merchandise Inventory account (which includes

EXHIBIT 5A.1

Comparison of Adjusting and Closing Entries—Periodic and Perpetual

PERIODIC			PERPETUAL		
Adjusting Entry—Shrinkage			Adjusting Entry—Shrinkage		
None			Cost of Goods Sold	250	
			Merchandise Inventory		250

[continued on next page]

[continued from previous page]

PERIODIC			PERPETUAL		
Closing Entries			**Closing Entries**		
(1) Sales	321,000		(1) Sales	321,000	
Merchandise Inventory	**21,000**				
Purchase Discounts	**4,200**				
Purchase Returns and Allowances	**1,500**				
Income Summary		347,700	Income Summary		321,000
(2) Income Summary	334,800		(2) Income Summary	308,100	
Sales Discounts		4,300	Sales Discounts		4,300
Sales Returns and Allowances		2,000	Sales Returns and Allowances		2,000
Merchandise Inventory		**19,000**			
Purchases		**235,800**	**Cost of Goods Sold**		**230,400**
Transportation-In		**2,300**			
Depreciation Expense		3,700	Depreciation Expense		3,700
Salaries Expense		43,800	Salaries Expense		43,800
Insurance Expense		600	Insurance Expense		600
Rent Expense		9,000	Rent Expense		9,000
Supplies Expense		3,000	Supplies Expense		3,000
Advertising Expense		11,300	Advertising Expense		11,300
(3) Income Summary	12,900		(3) Income Summary	12,900	
K. Marty, Capital		12,900	K. Marty, Capital		12,900
(4) K. Marty, Capital	4,000		(4) K. Marty, Capital	4,000	
K. Marty, Withdrawals		4,000	K. Marty, Withdrawals		4,000

shrinkage) in the first closing entry and removes the $19,000 beginning inventory balance from the account in the second closing entry.[2]

By updating Merchandise Inventory and closing Purchases, Purchase Discounts, Purchase Returns and Allowances, and Transportation-In, the periodic system transfers the cost of goods sold amount to Income Summary. Review the periodic side of Exhibit 5A.1 and notice that the **boldface** items affect Income Summary as follows.

Credit to Income Summary in the first closing entry includes amounts from:	
Merchandise inventory (ending)	$ 21,000
Purchase discounts	4,200
Purchase returns and allowances	1,500
Debit to Income Summary in the second closing entry includes amounts from:	
Merchandise inventory (beginning)	(19,000)
Purchases	(235,800)
Transportation-in	(2,300)
Net effect on Income Summary	**$(230,400)**

This $230,400 effect on Income Summary is the cost of goods sold amount. The periodic system transfers cost of goods sold to the Income Summary account but without using a Cost of Goods Sold account. Also, the periodic system does not separately measure shrinkage. Instead, it computes cost of goods available

[2] This approach is called the *closing entry method.* An alternative approach, referred to as the *adjusting entry method,* would not make any entries to Merchandise Inventory in the closing entries of Exhibit 5A.1, but instead would make two adjusting entries. Using Z-Mart data, the two adjusting entries would be: (1) Dr. Income Summary and Cr. Merchandise Inventory for $19,000 each, and (2) Dr. Merchandise Inventory and Cr. Income Summary for $21,000 each. The first entry removes the beginning balance of Merchandise Inventory, and the second entry records the actual ending balance.

for sale, subtracts the cost of ending inventory, and defines the difference as cost of goods sold, which includes shrinkage.

Preparing Financial Statements The financial statements of a merchandiser using the periodic system are similar to those for a service company described in prior chapters. The income statement mainly differs by the inclusion of *cost of goods sold* and *gross profit*—of course, net sales is affected by discounts, returns, and allowances. The cost of goods sold section under the periodic system follows

Calculation of Cost of Goods Sold
For Year Ended December 31, 2011

Beginning inventory	$ 19,000
Cost of goods purchased	232,400
Cost of goods available for sale	251,400
Less ending inventory	21,000
Cost of goods sold	$230,400

The balance sheet mainly differs by the inclusion of *merchandise inventory* in current assets—see Exhibit 5.15. The statement of owner's equity is unchanged. A work sheet can be used to help prepare these statements. The only differences under the periodic system from the work sheet illustrated in Appendix 5B using the perpetual system are highlighted as follows in **blue boldface** font.

File Edit View Insert Format Tools Data Accounting Window Help

			Unadjusted Trial Balance		Adjustments		Adjusted Trial Balance		Income Statement		Balance Sheet	
1												
2	No.	Account	Dr.	Cr.	Dr.	Cr.	Dr.	Cr.	Dr.	Cr.	Dr.	Cr.
3	101	Cash	8,200				8,200				8,200	
4	106	Accounts receivable	11,200				11,200				11,200	
5	**119**	**Merchandise Inventory**	**19,000**				**19,000**		**19,000**	**21,000**	**21,000**	
6	126	Supplies	3,800			(b) 3,000	800				800	
7	128	Prepaid insurance	900			(a) 600	300				300	
8	167	Equipment	34,200				34,200				34,200	
9	168	Accumulated depr.—Equip.		3,700		(c) 3,700		7,400				7,400
10	201	Accounts payable		16,000				16,000				16,000
11	209	Salaries payable				(d) 800		800				800
12	301	K. Marty, Capital		42,600				42,600				42,600
13	302	K. Marty, Withdrawals	4,000				4,000				4,000	
14	413	Sales		321,000				321,000		321,000		
15	414	Sales returns and allowances	2,000				2,000		2,000			
16a	415	Sales discounts	4,300				4,300		4,300			
16b	**505**	**Purchases**	**235,800**				**235,800**		**235,800**			
16c	**506**	**Purchases returns & allowance**		**1,500**				**1,500**		**1,500**		
16d	**507**	**Purchases discounts**		**4,200**				**4,200**		**4,200**		
17	**508**	**Transportation-in**	**2,300**				**2,300**		**2,300**			
18	612	Depreciation expense—Equip.			(c) 3,700		3,700		3,700			
19	622	Salaries expense	43,000		(d) 800		43,800		43,800			
20	637	Insurance expense			(a) 600		600		600			
21	640	Rent expense	9,000				9,000		9,000			
22	652	Supplies expense			(b) 3,000		3,000		3,000			
23	655	Advertising expense	11,300				11,300		11,300			
24		Totals	389,000	389,000	8,100	8,100	393,500	393,500	334,800	347,700	79,700	66,800
25		Net income							12,900			12,900
26		Totals							347,700	347,700	79,700	79,700

Sheet1 / Sheet2 / Sheet3

Quick Check

Answers — p. 207 

13. What account is used in a perpetual inventory system but not in a periodic system?

14. Which of the following accounts are temporary accounts under a periodic system? (*a*) Merchandise Inventory; (*b*) Purchases; (*c*) Transportation-In.

15. How is cost of goods sold computed under a periodic inventory system?

16. Do reported amounts of ending inventory and net income differ if the adjusting entry method of recording the change in inventory is used instead of the closing entry method?

APPENDIX

Work Sheet—Perpetual System 5B

Exhibit 5B.1 shows the work sheet for preparing financial statements of a merchandiser. It differs slightly from the work sheet layout in Chapter 4—the differences are in **red boldface**. Also, the adjustments in the work sheet reflect the following: (*a*) Expiration of $600 of prepaid insurance. (*b*) Use of $3,000 of supplies. (*c*) Depreciation of $3,700 for equipment. (*d*) Accrual of $800 of unpaid salaries. (*e*) Inventory shrinkage of $250. Once the adjusted amounts are extended into the financial statement columns, the information is used to develop financial statements.

EXHIBIT 5B.1

Work Sheet for Merchandiser (using a perpetual system)

			Unadjusted Trial Balance		Adjustments		Adjusted Trial Balance		Income Statement		Balance Sheet	
1												
2	No.	Account	Dr.	Cr.	Dr.	Cr.	Dr.	Cr.	Dr.	Cr.	Dr.	Cr.
3	101	Cash	8,200				8,200				8,200	
4	106	Accounts receivable	11,200				11,200				11,200	
5	119	**Merchandise Inventory**	**21,250**			(*e*) 250	**21,000**				**21,000**	
6	126	Supplies	3,800			(*b*) 3,000	800				800	
7	128	Prepaid insurance	900			(*a*) 600	300				300	
8	167	Equipment	34,200				34,200				34,200	
9	168	Accumulated depr.—Equip.		3,700		(*c*) 3,700		7,400				7,400
10	201	Accounts payable		16,000				16,000				16,000
11	209	Salaries payable				(*d*) 800		800				800
12	301	K. Marty, Capital		42,600				42,600				42,600
13	302	K. Marty, Withdrawals	4,000				4,000				4,000	
14	413	**Sales**		**321,000**				**321,000**		**321,000**		
15	414	**Sales returns and allowances**	**2,000**				**2,000**		**2,000**			
16	415	**Sales discounts**	**4,300**				**4,300**		**4,300**			
17	502	**Cost of goods sold**	**230,150**		(*e*) 250		**230,400**		**230,400**			
18	612	Depreciation expense—Equip.			(*c*) 3,700		3,700		3,700			
19	622	Salaries expense	43,000		(*d*) 800		43,800		43,800			
20	637	Insurance expense			(*a*) 600		600		600			
21	640	Rent expense	9,000				9,000		9,000			
22	652	Supplies expense			(*b*) 3,000		3,000		3,000			
23	655	Advertising expense	11,300				11,300		11,300			
24		Totals	383,300	383,300	8,350	8,350	387,800	387,800	308,100	321,000	79,700	66,800
25		Net income							12,900			12,900
26		Totals							321,000	321,000	79,700	79,700
27												

Summary

C1 Describe merchandising activities and identify income components for a merchandising company. Merchandisers buy products and resell them. Examples of merchandisers include Walmart, Home Depot, The Limited, and Barnes & Noble. A merchandiser's costs on the income statement include an amount for cost of goods sold. Gross profit, or gross margin, equals sales minus cost of goods sold.

C2 Identify and explain the inventory asset and cost flows of a merchandising company. The current asset section of a merchandising company's balance sheet includes *merchandise inventory,* which refers to the products a merchandiser sells and are available for sale at the balance sheet date. Cost of merchandise purchases flows into Merchandise Inventory and from there to Cost of Goods Sold on the income statement. Any remaining inventory is reported as a current asset on the balance sheet.

A1 Compute the acid-test ratio and explain its use to assess liquidity. The acid-test ratio is computed as quick assets (cash, short-term investments, and current receivables) divided by current liabilities. It indicates a company's ability to pay its current liabilities with its existing quick assets. An acid-test ratio equal to or greater than 1.0 is often adequate.

A2 Compute the gross margin ratio and explain its use to assess profitability. The gross margin ratio is computed as gross margin (net sales minus cost of goods sold) divided by net sales. It indicates a company's profitability before considering other expenses.

P1 Analyze and record transactions for merchandise purchases using a perpetual system. For a perpetual inventory system, purchases of inventory (net of trade discounts) are added to the Merchandise Inventory account. Purchase discounts and purchase returns and allowances are subtracted from Merchandise Inventory, and transportation-in costs are added to Merchandise Inventory.

P2 Analyze and record transactions for merchandise sales using a perpetual system. A merchandiser records sales at list price less any trade discounts. The cost of items sold is transferred from Merchandise Inventory to Cost of Goods Sold. Refunds or credits given to customers for unsatisfactory merchandise are recorded in Sales Returns and Allowances, a contra account to Sales. If merchandise is returned and restored to inventory, the cost of this merchandise is removed from Cost of Goods Sold and transferred back to Merchandise Inventory. When cash discounts from the sales price are offered and customers pay within the discount period, the seller records Sales Discounts, a contra account to Sales.

P3 Prepare adjustments and close accounts for a merchandising company. With a perpetual system, it is often necessary to make an adjustment for inventory shrinkage. This is computed by comparing a physical count of inventory with the Merchandise Inventory balance. Shrinkage is normally charged to Cost of Goods Sold. Temporary accounts closed to Income Summary for a merchandiser include Sales, Sales Discounts, Sales Returns and Allowances, and Cost of Goods Sold.

P4 Define and prepare multiple-step and single-step income statements. Multiple-step income statements include greater detail for sales and expenses than do single-step income statements. They also show details of net sales and report expenses in categories reflecting different activities.

P5[A] Record and compare merchandising transactions using both periodic and perpetual inventory systems. A perpetual inventory system continuously tracks the cost of goods available for sale and the cost of goods sold. A periodic system accumulates the cost of goods purchased during the period and does not compute the amount of inventory or the cost of goods sold until the end of a period. Transactions involving the sale and purchase of merchandise are recorded and analyzed under both the periodic and perpetual inventory systems. Adjusting and closing entries for both inventory systems are illustrated and explained.

Guidance Answers to Decision Maker and Decision Ethics

Entrepreneur For terms of 3/10, n/90, missing the 3% discount for an additional 80 days equals an implied annual interest rate of 13.69%, computed as (365 days ÷ 80 days) × 3%. Since you can borrow funds at 11% (assuming no other processing costs), it is better to borrow and pay within the discount period. You save 2.69% (13.69% − 11%) in interest costs by paying early.

Credit Manager Your decision is whether to comply with prior policy or to create a new policy and not abuse discounts offered by suppliers. Your first step should be to meet with your superior to find out if the late payment policy is the actual policy and, if so, its rationale. If it is the policy to pay late, you must apply your own sense of ethics. One point of view is that the late payment policy is unethical. A deliberate plan to make late payments means the company lies when it pretends to make payment within the discount period. Another view is that the late payment policy is acceptable. In some markets, attempts to take discounts through late payments are accepted as a continued phase of "price negotiation." Also, your company's suppliers can respond by billing your company for the discounts not accepted because of late payments. However, this is a dubious viewpoint, especially since the prior manager proposes that you dishonestly explain late payments as computer or mail problems and since some suppliers have complained.

Supplier A current ratio of 2.1 suggests sufficient current assets to cover current liabilities. An acid-test ratio of 0.5 suggests, however, that quick assets can cover only about one-half of current liabilities. This implies that the retailer depends on money from sales of inventory to pay current liabilities. If sales of inventory decline or profit margins decrease, the likelihood that this retailer will default on its payments increases. Your decision is probably not to extend credit. If you do extend credit, you are likely to closely monitor the retailer's financial condition. (It is better to hold unsold inventory than uncollectible receivables.)

Financial Officer Your company's net profit margin is about equal to the industry average and suggests typical industry performance. However, gross margin reveals that your company is paying far more in cost of goods sold or receiving far less in sales price than competitors. Your attention must be directed to finding the problem with cost of goods sold, sales, or both. One positive note is that your company's expenses make up 19% of sales (36% − 17%). This favorably compares with competitors' expenses that make up 28% of sales (44% − 16%).

Guidance Answers to Quick Checks

1. Cost of goods sold is the cost of merchandise purchased from a supplier that is sold to customers during a specific period.
2. Gross profit (or gross margin) is the difference between net sales and cost of goods sold.
3. Widespread use of computing and related technology has dramatically increased the use of the perpetual inventory system.
4. Under credit terms of 2/10, n/60, the credit period is 60 days and the discount period is 10 days.
5. (*b*) trade discount.
6. *FOB* means "free on board." It is used in identifying the point when ownership transfers from seller to buyer. *FOB destination* means that the seller transfers ownership of goods to the buyer when they arrive at the buyer's place of business. It also means that the seller is responsible for paying shipping charges and bears the risk of damage or loss during shipment.
7. Recording sales discounts and sales returns and allowances separately from sales gives useful information to managers for internal monitoring and decision making.
8. When a customer returns merchandise *and* the seller restores the merchandise to inventory, two entries are necessary. One entry records the decrease in revenue and credits the customer's account. The second entry debits inventory and reduces cost of goods sold.
9. Credit memorandum—seller credits accounts receivable from buyer.
10. Merchandise Inventory may need adjusting to reflect shrinkage.
11. Sales (of goods), Sales Discounts, Sales Returns and Allowances, and Cost of Goods Sold (and maybe Delivery Expense).
12. Four closing entries: (1) close credit balances in temporary accounts to Income Summary, (2) close debit balances in temporary accounts to Income Summary, (3) close Income Summary to owner's capital, and (4) close withdrawals account to owner's capital.
13. Cost of Goods Sold.
14. (*b*) Purchases and (*c*) Transportation-In.
15. Under a periodic inventory system, the cost of goods sold is determined at the end of an accounting period by adding the net cost of goods purchased to the beginning inventory and subtracting the ending inventory.
16. Both methods report the same ending inventory and income.

Key Terms

mhhe.com/wildFAP20e

Acid-test ratio (p. 196)
Cash discount (p. 183)
Cost of goods sold (p. 180)
Credit memorandum (p. 189)
Credit period (p. 183)
Credit terms (p. 183)
Debit memorandum (p. 184)
Discount period (p. 183)
EOM (p. 183)
FOB (p. 185)
General and administrative expenses (p. 193)
Gross margin (p. 181)
Gross margin ratio (p. 196)
Gross profit (p. 180)
Inventory (p. 181)
List price (p. 182)
Merchandise (p. 180)
Merchandise inventory (p. 181)
Merchandiser (p. 180)
Multiple-step income statement (p. 192)
Periodic inventory system (p. 182)
Perpetual inventory system (p. 182)
Purchase discount (p. 183)
Retailer (p. 180)
Sales discount (p. 183)
Selling expenses (p. 193)
Shrinkage (p. 190)
Single-step income statement (p. 193)
Supplementary records (p. 186)
Trade discount (p. 182)
Wholesaler (p. 180)

Multiple Choice Quiz

Answers on p. 225

mhhe.com/wildFAP20e

Additional Quiz Questions are available at the book's Website.

1. A company has $550,000 in net sales and $193,000 in gross profit. This means its cost of goods sold equals
   a. $743,000
   b. $550,000
   c. $357,000
   d. $193,000
   e. $(193,000)

2. A company purchased $4,500 of merchandise on May 1 with terms of 2/10, n/30. On May 6, it returned $250 of that merchandise. On May 8, it paid the balance owed for merchandise, taking any discount it is entitled to. The cash paid on May 8 is
   a. $4,500
   b. $4,250
   c. $4,160
   d. $4,165
   e. $4,410
3. A company has cash sales of $75,000, credit sales of $320,000, sales returns and allowances of $13,700, and sales discounts of $6,000. Its net sales equal
   a. $395,000
   b. $375,300
   c. $300,300
   d. $339,700
   e. $414,700
4. A company's quick assets are $37,500, its current assets are $80,000, and its current liabilities are $50,000. Its acid-test ratio equals
   a. 1.600
   b. 0.750
   c. 0.625
   d. 1.333
   e. 0.469
5. A company's net sales are $675,000, its costs of goods sold are $459,000, and its net income is $74,250. Its gross margin ratio equals
   a. 32%
   b. 68%
   c. 47%
   d. 11%
   e. 34%

A(B) *Superscript letter A (B) denotes assignments based on Appendix 5A (5B).*

Icon denotes assignments that involve decision making.

Discussion Questions

1. In comparing the accounts of a merchandising company with those of a service company, what additional accounts would the merchandising company likely use, assuming it employs a perpetual inventory system?
2. What items appear in financial statements of merchandising companies but not in the statements of service companies?
3. Explain how a business can earn a positive gross profit on its sales and still have a net loss.
4. Why do companies offer a cash discount?
5. How does a company that uses a perpetual inventory system determine the amount of inventory shrinkage?
6. Distinguish between cash discounts and trade discounts. Is the amount of a trade discount on purchased merchandise recorded in the accounts?
7. What is the difference between a sales discount and a purchase discount?
8. Why would a company's manager be concerned about the quantity of its purchase returns if its suppliers allow unlimited returns?
9. Does the sender (maker) of a debit memorandum record a debit or a credit in the recipient's account? What entry (debit or credit) does the recipient record?
10. What is the difference between the single-step and multiple-step income statement formats?
11. Refer to the balance sheet and income statement for **Research In Motion** in Appendix A. What does the company title its inventory account? Does the company present a detailed calculation of its cost of sales? RIM
12. Refer to **Nokia**'s income statement in Appendix A. What title does it use for cost of goods sold? NOKIA
13. Refer to the income statement for **Apple** in Appendix A. What does Apple title its cost of goods sold account? Apple
14. Refer to the income statement of **Palm** in Appendix A. Does its income statement report a gross profit figure? If yes, what is the amount? Palm
15. Buyers negotiate purchase contracts with suppliers. What type of shipping terms should a buyer attempt to negotiate to minimize freight-in costs?

connect

QUICK STUDY

QS 5-1
Applying merchandising terms
C1

Enter the letter for each term in the blank space beside the definition that it most closely matches.

A. Cash discount
B. Credit period
C. Discount period
D. FOB destination
E. FOB shipping point
F. Gross profit
G. Merchandise inventory
H. Purchase discount
I. Sales discount
J. Trade discount

D 1. Ownership of goods is transferred when delivered to the buyer's place of business.
C 2. Time period in which a cash discount is available.
F 3. Difference between net sales and the cost of goods sold.
A 4. Reduction in a receivable or payable if it is paid within the discount period.
H 5. Purchaser's description of a cash discount received from a supplier of goods.
E 6. Ownership of goods is transferred when the seller delivers goods to the carrier.
J 7. Reduction below list or catalog price that is negotiated in setting the price of goods.
I 8. Seller's description of a cash discount granted to buyers in return for early payment.
B 9. Time period that can pass before a customer's payment is due.
G 10. Goods a company owns and expects to sell to its customers.

QS 5-2
Identifying inventory costs
C2

The cost of merchandise inventory includes which of the following:

a. Costs incurred to buy the goods.
b. Costs incurred to ship the goods to the store(s).
c. Costs incurred to make the goods ready for sale.
d. Both a and b.
e. a, b, and c.

QS 5-3
Recording purchases—perpetual system
P1

Prepare journal entries to record each of the following purchases transactions of a merchandising company. Show supporting calculations and assume a perpetual inventory system.

Mar. 5 Purchased 500 units of product at a cost of $5 per unit. Terms of the sale are 2/10, n/60; the invoice is dated March 5.
Mar. 7 Returned 50 defective units from the March 5 purchase and received full credit.
Mar. 15 Paid the amount due from the March 5 purchase, less the return on March 7.

QS 5-4
Recording sales—perpetual system
P2

Prepare journal entries to record each of the following sales transactions of a merchandising company. Show supporting calculations and assume a perpetual inventory system.

Apr. 1 Sold merchandise for $2,000, granting the customer terms of 2/10, EOM; invoice dated April 1. The cost of the merchandise is $1,400.
Apr. 4 The customer in the April 1 sale returned merchandise and received credit for $500. The merchandise, which had cost $350, is returned to inventory.
Apr. 11 Received payment for the amount due from the April 1 sale less the return on April 4.

QS 5-5
Computing and analyzing gross margin
A2 

Compute net sales, gross profit, and the gross margin ratio for each separate case *a* through *d*. Interpret the gross margin ratio for case *a*.

	a	b	c	d
Sales	$130,000	$512,000	$35,700	$245,700
Sales discounts	4,200	16,500	400	3,500
Sales returns and allowances	17,000	5,000	5,000	700
Cost of goods sold	76,600	326,700	21,300	125,900

QS 5-6
Accounting for shrinkage—perpetual system
P3

Nix'It Company's ledger on July 31, its fiscal year-end, includes the following selected accounts that have normal balances (Nix'It uses the perpetual inventory system).

Merchandise inventory	$ 34,800	Sales returns and allowances	$ 3,500
T. Nix, Capital	115,300	Cost of goods sold	102,000
T. Nix, Withdrawals	7,000	Depreciation expense	7,300
Sales	157,200	Salaries expense	29,500
Sales discounts	1,700	Miscellaneous expenses	2,000

A physical count of its July 31 year-end inventory discloses that the cost of the merchandise inventory still available is $32,900. Prepare the entry to record any inventory shrinkage.

QS 5-7
Closing entries P3

Refer to QS 5-6 and prepare journal entries to close the balances in temporary revenue and expense accounts. Remember to consider the entry for shrinkage that is made to solve QS 5-6.

QS 5-8
Computing and interpreting acid-test ratio
A1

Use the following information on current assets and current liabilities to compute and interpret the acid-test ratio. Explain what the acid-test ratio of a company measures.

Cash	$1,200	Prepaid expenses	$ 600
Accounts receivable	2,700	Accounts payable	4,750
Inventory	5,000	Other current liabilities	950

QS 5-9
Contrasting liquidity ratios A1

Identify similarities and differences between the acid-test ratio and the current ratio. Compare and describe how the two ratios reflect a company's ability to meet its current obligations.

QS 5-10
Multiple-step income statement
P4

The multiple-step income statement normally includes which of the following:

a. Detailed computations of net sales.
b. Detailed computations of expenses, including subtotals for various expense categories.
c. Operating expenses are usually classified into (1) selling expenses and (2) general and administrative expenses.
d. Both a and c.
e. a, b, and c.

QS 5-11[A]
Contrasting periodic and perpetual systems
P5

Identify whether each description best applies to a periodic or a perpetual inventory system.

a. Provides more timely information to managers.
b. Requires an adjusting entry to record inventory shrinkage.
c. Markedly increased in frequency and popularity in business within the past decade.
d. Records cost of goods sold each time a sales transaction occurs.
e. Updates the inventory account only at period-end.

QS 5-12[A]
Recording purchases—periodic system P5

Refer to QS 5-3 and prepare journal entries to record each of the merchandising transactions assuming that the periodic inventory system is used.

QS 5-13[A]
Recording purchases—periodic system P5

Refer to QS 5-4 and prepare journal entries to record each of the merchandising transactions assuming that the periodic inventory system is used.

QS 5-14
IFRS income statement presentation
P4

Income statement information for **adidas Group**, a German footwear, apparel, and accessories manufacturer, for the year ended December 31, 2009, follows. The company applies IFRS, as adopted by the European Union, and reports its results in millions of Euros. Prepare its calendar year 2009 (1) multiple-step income statement and (2) single-step income statement.

Net income	€ 245
Financial income	19
Financial expenses	169
Operating profit	508
Cost of sales	5,669
Income taxes	113
Income before taxes	358
Gross profit	4,712
Royalty and commission income	86
Other operating income	100
Other operating expenses	4,390
Net sales	10,381

Answer each of the following questions related to international accounting standards.

a. Explain how the accounting for merchandise purchases and sales is different between accounting under IFRS versus U.S. GAAP.

b. Income statements prepared under IFRS usually report an item titled *finance costs*. What do finance costs refer to?

c. U.S. GAAP prohibits alternative measures of income reported on the income statement. Does IFRS permit such alternative measures on the income statement?

QS 5-15
International accounting standards
C1 

connect

EXERCISES

Prepare journal entries to record the following transactions for a retail store. Assume a perpetual inventory system.

Exercise 5-1
Recording entries for merchandise purchases
P1

Apr. 2 Purchased merchandise from Blue Company under the following terms: $3,600 price, invoice dated April 2, credit terms of 2/15, n/60, and FOB shipping point.
3 Paid $200 for shipping charges on the April 2 purchase.
4 Returned to Blue Company unacceptable merchandise that had an invoice price of $600.
17 Sent a check to Blue Company for the April 2 purchase, net of the discount and the returned merchandise.
18 Purchased merchandise from Fox Corp. under the following terms: $7,500 price, invoice dated April 18, credit terms of 2/10, n/30, and FOB destination.
21 After negotiations, received from Fox a $2,100 allowance on the April 18 purchase.
28 Sent check to Fox paying for the April 18 purchase, net of the discount and allowance.

Check April 28, Cr. Cash $5,292

Taos Company purchased merchandise for resale from Tuscon Company with an invoice price of $22,000 and credit terms of 3/10, n/60. The merchandise had cost Tuscon $15,000. Taos paid within the discount period. Assume that both buyer and seller use a perpetual inventory system.

Exercise 5-2
Analyzing and recording merchandise transactions—both buyer and seller
P1 P2 

1. Prepare entries that the buyer should record for (*a*) the purchase and (*b*) the cash payment.

2. Prepare entries that the seller should record for (*a*) the sale and (*b*) the cash collection.

3. Assume that the buyer borrowed enough cash to pay the balance on the last day of the discount period at an annual interest rate of 11% and paid it back on the last day of the credit period. Compute how much the buyer saved by following this strategy. (Assume a 365-day year and round dollar amounts to the nearest cent, including computation of interest per day.)

Check (3) $338.50 savings (rounded)

The operating cycle of a merchandiser with credit sales includes the following five activities. Starting with merchandise acquisition, identify the chronological order of these five activities.

Exercise 5-3
Operating cycle for merchandiser
C2

a. _______ purchases of merchandise.
b. _______ credit sales to customers.
c. _______ inventory made available for sale.
d. _______ cash collections from customers.
e. _______ accounts receivable accounted for.

Spare Parts was organized on May 1, 2011, and made its first purchase of merchandise on May 3. The purchase was for 1,000 units at a price of $10 per unit. On May 5, Spare Parts sold 600 of the units for $14 per unit to DeSoto Co. Terms of the sale were 2/10, n/60. Prepare entries for Spare Parts to record the May 5 sale and each of the following separate transactions *a* through *c* using a perpetual inventory system.

Exercise 5-4
Recording sales returns and allowances P2

a. On May 7, DeSoto returns 200 units because they did not fit the customer's needs. Spare Parts restores the units to its inventory.

b. On May 8, DeSoto discovers that 50 units are damaged but are still of some use and, therefore, keeps the units. Spare Parts sends DeSoto a credit memorandum for $300 to compensate for the damage.

c. On May 15, DeSoto discovers that 72 units are the wrong color. DeSoto keeps 43 of these units because Spare Parts sends a $92 credit memorandum to compensate. DeSoto returns the remaining 29 units to Spare Parts. Spare Parts restores the 29 returned units to its inventory.

Check (c) Dr. Merchandise Inventory $290

Refer to Exercise 5-4 and prepare the appropriate journal entries for DeSoto Co. to record the May 5 purchase and each of the three separate transactions *a* through *c*. DeSoto is a retailer that uses a perpetual inventory system and purchases these units for resale.

Exercise 5-5
Recording purchase returns and allowances P1

Exercise 5-6
Analyzing and recording merchandise transactions—both buyer and seller
P1 P2

On May 11, Smythe Co. accepts delivery of $30,000 of merchandise it purchases for resale from Hope Corporation. With the merchandise is an invoice dated May 11, with terms of 3/10, n/90, FOB shipping point. The goods cost Hope $20,000. When the goods are delivered, Smythe pays $335 to Express Shipping for delivery charges on the merchandise. On May 12, Smythe returns $1,200 of goods to Hope, who receives them one day later and restores them to inventory. The returned goods had cost Hope $800. On May 20, Smythe mails a check to Hope Corporation for the amount owed. Hope receives it the following day. (Both Smythe and Hope use a perpetual inventory system.)

Check (1) May 20, Cr. Cash $27,936

1. Prepare journal entries that Smythe Co. records for these transactions.
2. Prepare journal entries that Hope Corporation records for these transactions.

Exercise 5-7
Sales returns and allowances
C1 

Business decision makers desire information on sales returns and allowances. (1) Explain why a company's manager wants the accounting system to record customers' returns of unsatisfactory goods in the Sales Returns and Allowances account instead of the Sales account. (2) Explain whether this information would be useful for external decision makers.

Exercise 5-8
Recording effects of merchandising activities
P1 P2

The following supplementary records summarize Titus Company's merchandising activities for year 2011. Set up T-accounts for Merchandise Inventory and Cost of Goods Sold. Then record the summarized activities in those T-accounts and compute account balances.

Cost of merchandise sold to customers in sales transactions	$186,000
Merchandise inventory, December 31, 2010	27,000
Invoice cost of merchandise purchases	190,500
Shrinkage determined on December 31, 2011	700
Cost of transportation-in	1,900
Cost of merchandise returned by customers and restored to inventory	2,200
Purchase discounts received	1,600
Purchase returns and allowances	4,100

Check Year-End Merchandise Inventory Dec. 31, $29,200

Exercise 5-9
Computing revenues, expenses, and income
C1 C2

Using your accounting knowledge, fill in the blanks in the following separate income statements *a* through *e*. Identify any negative amount by putting it in parentheses.

	a	b	c	d	e
Sales	$60,000	$42,500	$36,000	$?	$23,600
Cost of goods sold					
Merchandise inventory (beginning)	6,000	17,050	7,500	7,000	2,560
Total cost of merchandise purchases	36,000	?	?	32,000	5,600
Merchandise inventory (ending)	?	(2,700)	(9,000)	(6,600)	?
Cost of goods sold	34,050	15,900	?	?	5,600
Gross profit	?	?	3,750	45,600	?
Expenses	9,000	10,650	12,150	2,600	6,000
Net income (loss)	$?	$15,950	$ (8,400)	$43,000	$?

Exercise 5-10
Preparing adjusting and closing entries for a merchandiser
P3

The following list includes selected permanent accounts and all of the temporary accounts from the December 31, 2011, unadjusted trial balance of Deacon Co., a business owned by Julie Deacon. Use these account balances along with the additional information to journalize (*a*) adjusting entries and (*b*) closing entries. Deacon Co. uses a perpetual inventory system.

	Debit	Credit
Merchandise inventory	$ 28,000	
Prepaid selling expenses	5,000	
J. Deacon, Withdrawals	2,200	
Sales		$429,000
Sales returns and allowances	16,500	
Sales discounts	4,000	
Cost of goods sold	211,000	
Sales salaries expense	47,000	
Utilities expense	14,000	
Selling expenses	35,000	
Administrative expenses	95,000	

Additional Information

Accrued sales salaries amount to $1,600. Prepaid selling expenses of $2,000 have expired. A physical count of year-end merchandise inventory shows $27,450 of goods still available.

Check Entry to close Income Summary: Cr. J. Deacon, Capital $2,350

Exercise 5-11
Interpreting a physical count error as inventory shrinkage
A1 

A retail company recently completed a physical count of ending merchandise inventory to use in preparing adjusting entries. In determining the cost of the counted inventory, company employees failed to consider that $2,000 of incoming goods had been shipped by a supplier on December 31 under an FOB shipping point agreement. These goods had been recorded in Merchandise Inventory as a purchase, but they were not included in the physical count because they were in transit. Explain how this overlooked fact affects the company's financial statements and the following ratios: return on assets, debt ratio, current ratio, and acid-test ratio.

Exercise 5-12
Physical count error and profits
A2

Refer to the information in Exercise 5-11 and explain how the error in the physical count affects the company's gross margin ratio and its profit margin ratio.

Exercise 5-13
Computing and analyzing acid-test and current ratios
A1 

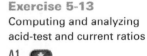

Compute the current ratio and acid-test ratio for each of the following separate cases. (Round ratios to two decimals.) Which company case is in the best position to meet short-term obligations? Explain.

	Case A	Case B	Case C
Cash	$ 800	$ 510	$3,200
Short-term investments	0	0	1,100
Current receivables	0	790	800
Inventory	2,000	1,600	1,900
Prepaid expenses	1,200	600	300
Total current assets	$4,000	$3,500	$7,300
Current liabilities	$2,200	$1,100	$3,650

Exercise 5-14
Preparing journal entries—perpetual system
P1 P2

Journalize the following merchandising transactions for CSI Systems assuming it uses a perpetual inventory system.

1. On November 1, CSI Systems purchases merchandise for $1,400 on credit with terms of 2/5, n/30, FOB shipping point; invoice dated November 1.
2. On November 5, CSI Systems pays cash for the November 1 purchase.
3. On November 7, CSI Systems discovers and returns $100 of defective merchandise purchased on November 1 for a cash refund.
4. On November 10, CSI Systems pays $80 cash for transportation costs with the November 1 purchase.
5. On November 13, CSI Systems sells merchandise for $1,500 on credit. The cost of the merchandise is $750.
6. On November 16, the customer returns merchandise from the November 13 transaction. The returned items sell for $200 and cost $100.

Exercise 5-15
Multiple-step income statement
P4

A company reports the following sales related information: Sales (gross) of $100,000; Sales discounts of $2,000; Sales returns and allowances of $8,000; Sales salaries expense of $5,000. Prepare the net sales portion only of this company's multiple-step income statement.

Exercise 5-16^A
Recording purchases—periodic system P5

Refer to Exercise 5-1 and prepare journal entries to record each of the merchandising transactions assuming that the periodic inventory system is used.

Exercise 5-17^A
Recording purchases and sales—periodic system P5

Refer to Exercise 5-2 and prepare journal entries to record each of the merchandising transactions assuming that the periodic inventory system is used by both the buyer and the seller. (Skip the part 3 requirement.)

Exercise 5-18[A]
Buyer and seller transactions—periodic system P5

Refer to Exercise 5-6 and prepare journal entries to record each of the merchandising transactions assuming that the periodic inventory system is used by both the buyer and the seller.

Exercise 5-19[A]
Recording purchases—periodic system P5

Refer to Exercise 5-14 and prepare journal entries to record each of the merchandising transactions assuming that the periodic inventory system is used.

Exercise 5-20
Preparing an income statement following IFRS
P4 

L'Oréal reports the following income statement accounts for the year ended December 31, 2009 (euros in millions). Prepare the income statement for this company for the year ended December 31, 2009, following usual IFRS practices.

Net profit	€ 1,794.9	Income tax expense	€ 676.1
Finance costs	76.0	Profit before tax expense	2,471.0
Net sales	17,472.6	Research and development expense	609.2
Gross profit	12,311.0	Selling, general and administrative expense	3,735.5
Other expense	30.6	Advertising and promotion expense	5,388.7
Cost of sales	5,161.6		

connect

PROBLEM SET A

Problem 5-1A
Preparing journal entries for merchandising activities—perpetual system
P1 P2

Prepare journal entries to record the following merchandising transactions of Stone Company, which applies the perpetual inventory system. (*Hint:* It will help to identify each receivable and payable; for example, record the purchase on August 1 in Accounts Payable—Abilene.)

Aug. 1 Purchased merchandise from Abilene Company for $6,000 under credit terms of 1/10, n/30, FOB destination, invoice dated August 1.
4 At Abilene's request, Stone paid $100 cash for freight charges on the August 1 purchase, reducing the amount owed to Abilene.
5 Sold merchandise to Lux Corp. for $4,200 under credit terms of 2/10, n/60, FOB destination, invoice dated August 5. The merchandise had cost $3,000.
8 Purchased merchandise from Welch Corporation for $5,300 under credit terms of 1/10, n/45, FOB shipping point, invoice dated August 8. The invoice showed that at Stone's request, Welch paid the $240 shipping charges and added that amount to the bill. (*Hint:* Discounts are not applied to freight and shipping charges.)
9 Paid $120 cash for shipping charges related to the August 5 sale to Lux Corp.
10 Lux returned merchandise from the August 5 sale that had cost Stone $500 and been sold for $700. The merchandise was restored to inventory.
12 After negotiations with Welch Corporation concerning problems with the merchandise purchased on August 8, Stone received a credit memorandum from Welch granting a price reduction of $800.
15 Received balance due from Lux Corp. for the August 5 sale less the return on August 10.
18 Paid the amount due Welch Corporation for the August 8 purchase less the price reduction granted.
19 Sold merchandise to Trax Co. for $3,600 under credit terms of 1/10, n/30, FOB shipping point, invoice dated August 19. The merchandise had cost $2,500.
22 Trax requested a price reduction on the August 19 sale because the merchandise did not meet specifications. Stone sent Trax a $600 credit memorandum to resolve the issue.
29 Received Trax's cash payment for the amount due from the August 19 sale.
30 Paid Abilene Company the amount due from the August 1 purchase.

Check Aug. 9, Dr. Delivery Expense, $120
Aug. 18, Cr. Cash $4,695
Aug. 29, Dr. Cash $2,970

Problem 5-2A
Preparing journal entries for merchandising activities—perpetual system
P1 P2  

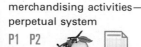

Prepare journal entries to record the following merchandising transactions of Bask Company, which applies the perpetual inventory system. (*Hint:* It will help to identify each receivable and payable; for example, record the purchase on July 1 in Accounts Payable—Black.)

July 1 Purchased merchandise from Black Company for $6,000 under credit terms of 1/15, n/30, FOB shipping point, invoice dated July 1.
2 Sold merchandise to Coke Co. for $800 under credit terms of 2/10, n/60, FOB shipping point, invoice dated July 2. The merchandise had cost $500.
3 Paid $100 cash for freight charges on the purchase of July 1.

8 Sold merchandise that had cost $1,200 for $1,600 cash.
9 Purchased merchandise from Lane Co. for $2,300 under credit terms of 2/15, n/60, FOB destination, invoice dated July 9.
11 Received a $200 credit memorandum from Lane Co. for the return of part of the merchandise purchased on July 9.
12 Received the balance due from Coke Co. for the invoice dated July 2, net of the discount.
16 Paid the balance due to Black Company within the discount period.
19 Sold merchandise that cost $900 to AKP Co. for $1,250 under credit terms of 2/15, n/60, FOB shipping point, invoice dated July 19.
21 Issued a $150 credit memorandum to AKP Co. for an allowance on goods sold on July 19.
24 Paid Lane Co. the balance due after deducting the discount.
30 Received the balance due from AKP Co. for the invoice dated July 19, net of discount.
31 Sold merchandise that cost $3,200 to Coke Co. for $5,000 under credit terms of 2/10, n/60, FOB shipping point, invoice dated July 31.

Check July 12, Dr. Cash $784
July 16, Cr. Cash $5,940
July 24, Cr. Cash $2,058
July 30, Dr. Cash $1,078

Problem 5-3A
Preparing adjusting entries and income statements; and computing gross margin, acid-test, and current ratios
A1 A2 P3 P4 

excel
mhhe.com/wildFAP20e

The following unadjusted trial balance is prepared at fiscal year-end for Rex Company.

	REX COMPANY Unadjusted Trial Balance January 31, 2011		
1		Debit	Credit
2	Cash	$ 2,200	
3	Merchandise inventory	11,500	
4	Store supplies	4,800	
5	Prepaid insurance	2,300	
6	Store equipment	41,900	
7	Accumulated depreciation—Store equipment		$ 15,000
8	Accounts payable		9,000
9	T. Rex, Capital		32,000
10	T. Rex, Withdrawals	2,000	
11	Sales		104,000
12	Sales discounts	1,000	
13	Sales returns and allowances	2,000	
14	Cost of goods sold	37,400	
15	Depreciation expense—Store equipment	0	
16	Salaries expense	31,000	
17	Insurance expense	0	
18	Rent expense	14,000	
19	Store supplies expense	0	
20	Advertising expense	9,900	
21	Totals	$160,000	$160,000
22			

Rent expense and salaries expense are equally divided between selling activities and the general and administrative activities. Rex Company uses a perpetual inventory system.

Required

1. Prepare adjusting journal entries to reflect each of the following:

a. Store supplies still available at fiscal year-end amount to $1,650.

b. Expired insurance, an administrative expense, for the fiscal year is $1,500.

c. Depreciation expense on store equipment, a selling expense, is $1,400 for the fiscal year.

d. To estimate shrinkage, a physical count of ending merchandise inventory is taken. It shows $11,100 of inventory is still available at fiscal year-end.

Check (2) Gross profit, $63,200; (3) Total expenses, $98,750; Net income, $2,250

2. Prepare a multiple-step income statement for fiscal year 2011.
3. Prepare a single-step income statement for fiscal year 2011.
4. Compute the current ratio, acid-test ratio, and gross margin ratio as of January 31, 2011.

Problem 5-4A
Computing merchandising amounts and formatting income statements
C2 P4

BizKid Company's adjusted trial balance on August 31, 2011, its fiscal year-end, follows.

	Debit	Credit
Merchandise inventory	$ 31,000	
Other (noninventory) assets	120,400	
Total liabilities		$ 35,000
N. Kidman, Capital		101,650
N. Kidman, Withdrawals	8,000	
Sales		212,000
Sales discounts	3,250	
Sales returns and allowances	14,000	
Cost of goods sold	82,600	
Sales salaries expense	29,000	
Rent expense—Selling space	10,000	
Store supplies expense	2,500	
Advertising expense	18,000	
Office salaries expense	26,500	
Rent expense—Office space	2,600	
Office supplies expense	800	
Totals	$348,650	$348,650

On August 31, 2010, merchandise inventory was $25,000. Supplementary records of merchandising activities for the year ended August 31, 2011, reveal the following itemized costs.

Invoice cost of merchandise purchases	$91,000
Purchase discounts received	1,900
Purchase returns and allowances	4,400
Costs of transportation-in	3,900

Required

1. Compute the company's net sales for the year.
2. Compute the company's total cost of merchandise purchased for the year.
3. Prepare a multiple-step income statement that includes separate categories for selling expenses and for general and administrative expenses.
4. Prepare a single-step income statement that includes these expense categories: cost of goods sold, selling expenses, and general and administrative expenses.

Check (2) $88,600; (3) Gross profit, $112,150; Net income, $22,750; (4) Total expenses, $172,000

Problem 5-5A
Preparing closing entries and interpreting information about discounts and returns
C2 P3

Use the data for BizKid Company in Problem 5-4A to complete the following requirements.

Required

1. Prepare closing entries as of August 31, 2011 (the perpetual inventory system is used).

Analysis Component

2. The company makes all purchases on credit, and its suppliers uniformly offer a 3% sales discount. Does it appear that the company's cash management system is accomplishing the goal of taking all available discounts? Explain.
3. In prior years, the company experienced a 5% returns and allowance rate on its sales, which means approximately 5% of its gross sales were eventually returned outright or caused the company to grant allowances to customers. How do this year's results compare to prior years' results?

Check (1) $22,750 Dr. to close Income Summary (3) Current-year rate, 6.6%

Problem 5-6A[B]
Preparing a work sheet for a merchandiser
P3

Refer to the data and information in Problem 5-3A.

Required

Prepare and complete the entire 10-column work sheet for Rex Company. Follow the structure of Exhibit 5B.1 in Appendix 5B.

PROBLEM SET B

Problem 5-1B
Preparing journal entries for merchandising activities—perpetual system
P1 P2

Prepare journal entries to record the following merchandising transactions of Wave Company, which applies the perpetual inventory system. (*Hint:* It will help to identify each receivable and payable; for example, record the purchase on July 3 in Accounts Payable—CAP.)

July 3 Purchased merchandise from CAP Corp. for $15,000 under credit terms of 1/10, n/30, FOB destination, invoice dated July 3.
4 At CAP's request, Wave paid $250 cash for freight charges on the July 3 purchase, reducing the amount owed to CAP.
7 Sold merchandise to Morris Co. for $10,500 under credit terms of 2/10, n/60, FOB destination, invoice dated July 7. The merchandise had cost $7,500.
10 Purchased merchandise from Murdock Corporation for $14,200 under credit terms of 1/10, n/45, FOB shipping point, invoice dated July 10. The invoice showed that at Wave's request, Murdock paid the $600 shipping charges and added that amount to the bill. (*Hint:* Discounts are not applied to freight and shipping charges.)
11 Paid $300 cash for shipping charges related to the July 7 sale to Morris Co.
12 Morris returned merchandise from the July 7 sale that had cost Wave $1,250 and been sold for $1,750. The merchandise was restored to inventory.
14 After negotiations with Murdock Corporation concerning problems with the merchandise purchased on July 10, Wave received a credit memorandum from Murdock granting a price reduction of $2,000.
17 Received balance due from Morris Co. for the July 7 sale less the return on July 12.
20 Paid the amount due Murdock Corporation for the July 10 purchase less the price reduction granted.
21 Sold merchandise to Ulsh for $9,000 under credit terms of 1/10, n/30, FOB shipping point, invoice dated July 21. The merchandise had cost $6,250.
24 Ulsh requested a price reduction on the July 21 sale because the merchandise did not meet specifications. Wave sent Ulsh a credit memorandum for $1,500 to resolve the issue.
30 Received Ulsh's cash payment for the amount due from the July 21 sale.
31 Paid CAP Corp. the amount due from the July 3 purchase.

Check July 17, Dr. Cash $8,575
July 20, Cr. Cash $12,678
July 30, Dr. Cash $7,425

Problem 5-2B
Preparing journal entries for merchandising activities—perpetual system
P1 P2

Prepare journal entries to record the following merchandising transactions of Yang Company, which applies the perpetual inventory system. (*Hint:* It will help to identify each receivable and payable; for example, record the purchase on May 2 in Accounts Payable—Bots.)

May 2 Purchased merchandise from Bots Co. for $9,000 under credit terms of 1/15, n/30, FOB shipping point, invoice dated May 2.
4 Sold merchandise to Chase Co. for $1,200 under credit terms of 2/10, n/60, FOB shipping point, invoice dated May 4. The merchandise had cost $750.
5 Paid $150 cash for freight charges on the purchase of May 2.
9 Sold merchandise that had cost $1,800 for $2,400 cash.
10 Purchased merchandise from Snyder Co. for $3,450 under credit terms of 2/15, n/60, FOB destination, invoice dated May 10.
12 Received a $300 credit memorandum from Snyder Co. for the return of part of the merchandise purchased on May 10.
14 Received the balance due from Chase Co. for the invoice dated May 4, net of the discount.
17 Paid the balance due to Bots Co. within the discount period.
20 Sold merchandise that cost $1,450 to Tex Co. for $2,800 under credit terms of 2/15, n/60, FOB shipping point, invoice dated May 20.
22 Issued a $400 credit memorandum to Tex Co. for an allowance on goods sold from May 20.
25 Paid Snyder Co. the balance due after deducting the discount.
30 Received the balance due from Tex Co. for the invoice dated May 20, net of discount and allowance.
31 Sold merchandise that cost $4,800 to Chase Co. for $7,500 under credit terms of 2/10, n/60, FOB shipping point, invoice dated May 31.

Check May 14, Dr. Cash $1,176
May 17, Cr. Cash $8,910
May 30, Dr. Cash $2,352

Problem 5-3B
Preparing adjusting entries and income statements; and computing gross margin, acid-test, and current ratios
A1 A2 P3 P4 

The following unadjusted trial balance is prepared at fiscal year-end for FAB Products Company.

	FAB PRODUCTS COMPANY Unadjusted Trial Balance October 31, 2011	Debit	Credit
2	Cash	$ 4,400	
3	Merchandise inventory	23,000	
4	Store supplies	9,600	
5	Prepaid insurance	4,600	
6	Store equipment	83,800	
7	Accumulated depreciation—Store equipment		$ 30,000
8	Accounts payable		16,000
9	A. Fab, Capital		64,000
10	A. Fab, Withdrawals	2,000	
11	Sales		208,000
12	Sales discounts	2,000	
13	Sales returns and allowances	4,000	
14	Cost of goods sold	74,800	
15	Depreciation expense—Store equipment	0	
16	Salaries expense	62,000	
17	Insurance expense	0	
18	Rent expense	28,000	
19	Store supplies expense	0	
20	Advertising expense	19,800	
21	Totals	$318,000	$318,000

Rent expense and salaries expense are equally divided between selling activities and the general and administrative activities. FAB Products Company uses a perpetual inventory system.

Required

1. Prepare adjusting journal entries to reflect each of the following.
   a. Store supplies still available at fiscal year-end amount to $3,300.
   b. Expired insurance, an administrative expense, for the fiscal year is $3,000.
   c. Depreciation expense on store equipment, a selling expense, is $2,800 for the fiscal year.
   d. To estimate shrinkage, a physical count of ending merchandise inventory is taken. It shows $22,200 of inventory is still available at fiscal year-end.
2. Prepare a multiple-step income statement for fiscal year 2011.
3. Prepare a single-step income statement for fiscal year 2011.
4. Compute the current ratio, acid-test ratio, and gross margin ratio as of October 31, 2011.

Check (2) Gross profit, $126,400; (3) Total expenses, $197,500; Net income, $4,500

Problem 5-4B
Computing merchandising amounts and formatting income statements
C1 C2 P4

Albin Company's adjusted trial balance on March 31, 2011, its fiscal year-end, follows.

	Debit	Credit
Merchandise inventory	$ 46,500	
Other (noninventory) assets	190,600	
Total liabilities		$ 52,500
R. Albin, Capital		152,475
R. Albin, Withdrawals	2,000	

[continued on next page]

[continued from previous page]

Sales		318,000
Sales discounts	4,875	
Sales returns and allowances	21,000	
Cost of goods sold	123,900	
Sales salaries expense	43,500	
Rent expense—Selling space	15,000	
Store supplies expense	3,750	
Advertising expense	27,000	
Office salaries expense	39,750	
Rent expense—Office space	3,900	
Office supplies expense	1,200	
Totals	$522,975	$522,975

On March 31, 2010, merchandise inventory was $37,500. Supplementary records of merchandising activities for the year ended March 31, 2011, reveal the following itemized costs.

Invoice cost of merchandise purchases	$136,500
Purchase discounts received	2,850
Purchase returns and allowances	6,600
Costs of transportation-in	5,850

Required

1. Calculate the company's net sales for the year.
2. Calculate the company's total cost of merchandise purchased for the year.
3. Prepare a multiple-step income statement that includes separate categories for selling expenses and for general and administrative expenses.
4. Prepare a single-step income statement that includes these expense categories: cost of goods sold, selling expenses, and general and administrative expenses.

Check (2) $132,900;
(3) Gross profit, $168,225; Net income, $34,125;
(4) Total expenses, $258,000

Problem 5-5B
Preparing closing entries and interpreting information about discounts and returns
C2 P3 

Use the data for Albin Company in Problem 5-4B to complete the following requirements.

Required

1. Prepare closing entries as of March 31, 2011 (the perpetual inventory system is used).

Analysis Component

2. The company makes all purchases on credit, and its suppliers uniformly offer a 3% sales discount. Does it appear that the company's cash management system is accomplishing the goal of taking all available discounts? Explain.
3. In prior years, the company experienced a 5% returns and allowance rate on its sales, which means approximately 5% of its gross sales were eventually returned outright or caused the company to grant allowances to customers. How do this year's results compare to prior years' results?

Check (1) $34,125 Dr. to close Income Summary
(3) Current-year rate, 6.6%

Problem 5-6B[B]
Preparing a work sheet for a merchandiser
P3

Refer to the data and information in Problem 5-3B.

Required

Prepare and complete the entire 10-column work sheet for FAB Products Company. Follow the structure of Exhibit 5B.1 in Appendix 5B.

SERIAL PROBLEM

Business Solutions

P1 P2 P3 P4

(This serial problem began in Chapter 1 and continues through most of the book. If previous chapter segments were not completed, the serial problem can begin at this point. It is helpful, but not necessary, to use the Working Papers that accompany the book.)

SP 5 Santana Rey created Business Solutions on October 1, 2011. The company has been successful, and its list of customers has grown. To accommodate the growth, the accounting system is modified to set up separate accounts for each customer. The following chart of accounts includes the account number used for each account and any balance as of December 31, 2011. Santana Rey decided to add a fourth digit with a decimal point to the 106 account number that had been used for the single Accounts Receivable account. This change allows the company to continue using the existing chart of accounts.

No.	Account Title	Dr.	Cr.
101	Cash	$48,372	
106.1	Alex's Engineering Co.	0	
106.2	Wildcat Services	0	
106.3	Easy Leasing	0	
106.4	IFM Co.	3,000	
106.5	Liu Corp.	0	
106.6	Gomez Co.	2,668	
106.7	Delta Co.	0	
106.8	KC, Inc.	0	
106.9	Dream, Inc.	0	
119	Merchandise inventory	0	
126	Computer supplies	580	
128	Prepaid insurance	1,665	
131	Prepaid rent	825	
163	Office equipment	8,000	
164	Accumulated depreciation—Office equipment		$ 400
167	Computer equipment	20,000	
168	Accumulated depreciation—Computer equipment		1,250
201	Accounts payable		1,100

No.	Account Title	Dr.	Cr.
210	Wages payable		$ 500
236	Unearned computer services revenue		1,500
301	S. Rey, Capital		80,360
302	S. Rey, Withdrawals	$0	
403	Computer services revenue		0
413	Sales		0
414	Sales returns and allowances	0	
415	Sales discounts	0	
502	Cost of goods sold	0	
612	Depreciation expense—Office equipment	0	
613	Depreciation expense—Computer equipment	0	
623	Wages expense	0	
637	Insurance expense	0	
640	Rent expense	0	
652	Computer supplies expense	0	
655	Advertising expense	0	
676	Mileage expense	0	
677	Miscellaneous expenses	0	
684	Repairs expense—Computer	0	

In response to requests from customers, S. Rey will begin selling computer software. The company will extend credit terms of 1/10, n/30, FOB shipping point, to all customers who purchase this merchandise. However, no cash discount is available on consulting fees. Additional accounts (Nos. 119, 413, 414, 415, and 502) are added to its general ledger to accommodate the company's new merchandising activities. Also, Business Solutions does not use reversing entries and, therefore, all revenue and expense accounts have zero beginning balances as of January 1, 2012. Its transactions for January through March follow:

Jan. 4 The company paid cash to Lyn Addie for five days' work at the rate of $125 per day. Four of the five days relate to wages payable that were accrued in the prior year.

5 Santana Rey invested an additional $25,000 cash in the company.

7 The company purchased $5,800 of merchandise from Kansas Corp. with terms of 1/10, n/30, FOB shipping point, invoice dated January 7.

9 The company received $2,668 cash from Gomez Co. as full payment on its account.

11 The company completed a five-day project for Alex's Engineering Co. and billed it $5,500, which is the total price of $7,000 less the advance payment of $1,500.

Check Jan. 11, Dr. Unearned Computer Services Revenue $1,500

13 The company sold merchandise with a retail value of $5,200 and a cost of $3,560 to Liu Corp., invoice dated January 13.
15 The company paid $600 cash for freight charges on the merchandise purchased on January 7.
16 The company received $4,000 cash from Delta Co. for computer services provided.
17 The company paid Kansas Corp. for the invoice dated January 7, net of the discount.
20 Liu Corp. returned $500 of defective merchandise from its invoice dated January 13. The returned merchandise, which had a $320 cost, is discarded. (The policy of Business Solutions is to leave the cost of defective products in cost of goods sold.)

Check Jan. 20, No entry to Cost of Goods Sold

22 The company received the balance due from Liu Corp., net of both the discount and the credit for the returned merchandise.
24 The company returned defective merchandise to Kansas Corp. and accepted a credit against future purchases. The defective merchandise invoice cost, net of the discount, was $496.
26 The company purchased $9,000 of merchandise from Kansas Corp. with terms of 1/10, n/30, FOB destination, invoice dated January 26.
26 The company sold merchandise with a $4,640 cost for $5,800 on credit to KC, Inc., invoice dated January 26.
29 The company received a $496 credit memorandum from Kansas Corp. concerning the merchandise returned on January 24.
31 The company paid cash to Lyn Addie for 10 days' work at $125 per day.
Feb. 1 The company paid $2,475 cash to Hillside Mall for another three months' rent in advance.
3 The company paid Kansas Corp. for the balance due, net of the cash discount, less the $496 amount in the credit memorandum.
5 The company paid $600 cash to the local newspaper for an advertising insert in today's paper.
11 The company received the balance due from Alex's Engineering Co. for fees billed on January 11.
15 Santana Rey withdrew $4,800 cash from the company for personal use.
23 The company sold merchandise with a $2,660 cost for $3,220 on credit to Delta Co., invoice dated February 23.
26 The company paid cash to Lyn Addie for eight days' work at $125 per day.
27 The company reimbursed Santana Rey for business automobile mileage (600 miles at $0.32 per mile).
Mar. 8 The company purchased $2,730 of computer supplies from Harris Office Products on credit, invoice dated March 8.
9 The company received the balance due from Delta Co. for merchandise sold on February 23.
11 The company paid $960 cash for minor repairs to the company's computer.
16 The company received $5,260 cash from Dream, Inc., for computing services provided.
19 The company paid the full amount due to Harris Office Products, consisting of amounts created on December 15 (of $1,100) and March 8.
24 The company billed Easy Leasing for $9,047 of computing services provided.
25 The company sold merchandise with a $2,002 cost for $2,800 on credit to Wildcat Services, invoice dated March 25.
30 The company sold merchandise with a $1,048 cost for $2,220 on credit to IFM Company, invoice dated March 30.
31 The company reimbursed Santana Rey for business automobile mileage (400 miles at $0.32 per mile).

The following additional facts are available for preparing adjustments on March 31 prior to financial statement preparation:

a. The March 31 amount of computer supplies still available totals $2,005.
b. Three more months have expired since the company purchased its annual insurance policy at a $2,220 cost for 12 months of coverage.
c. Lyn Addie has not been paid for seven days of work at the rate of $125 per day.
d. Three months have passed since any prepaid rent has been transferred to expense. The monthly rent expense is $825.
e. Depreciation on the computer equipment for January 1 through March 31 is $1,250.
f. Depreciation on the office equipment for January 1 through March 31 is $400.
g. The March 31 amount of merchandise inventory still available totals $704.

Required

Check (2) Ending balances at March 31: Cash, $68,057; Sales, $19,240;

(3) Unadj. totals, $151,557; Adj. totals, $154,082;

(4) Net income, $18,833;

(5) S. Rey, Capital (at March 31), $119,393;

(6) Total assets, $120,268

1. Prepare journal entries to record each of the January through March transactions.
2. Post the journal entries in part 1 to the accounts in the company's general ledger. (*Note:* Begin with the ledger's post-closing adjusted balances as of December 31, 2011.)
3. Prepare a partial work sheet consisting of the first six columns (similar to the one shown in Exhibit 5B.1) that includes the unadjusted trial balance, the March 31 adjustments (*a*) through (*g*), and the adjusted trial balance. Do not prepare closing entries and do not journalize the adjustments or post them to the ledger.
4. Prepare an income statement (from the adjusted trial balance in part 3) for the three months ended March 31, 2012. Use a single-step format. List all expenses without differentiating between selling expenses and general and administrative expenses.
5. Prepare a statement of owner's equity (from the adjusted trial balance in part 3) for the three months ended March 31, 2012.
6. Prepare a classified balance sheet (from the adjusted trial balance) as of March 31, 2012.

Beyond the Numbers

REPORTING IN ACTION

A1

RIM

BTN 5-1 Refer to **Research In Motion**'s financial statements in Appendix A to answer the following.

Required

1. Assume that the amounts reported for inventories and cost of sales reflect items purchased in a form ready for resale. Compute the net cost of goods purchased for the fiscal year ended February 27, 2010.
2. Compute the current ratio and acid-test ratio as of February 27, 2010, and February 28, 2009. Interpret and comment on the ratio results. How does Research In Motion compare to the industry average of 2.4 for the current ratio and 1.5 for the acid-test ratio?

Fast Forward

3. Access Research In Motion's financial statements (form 10-K) for fiscal years ending after February 27, 2010, from its Website (**RIM.com**) or the SEC's EDGAR database (**www.SEC.gov**). Recompute and interpret the current ratio and acid-test ratio for these current fiscal years.

COMPARATIVE ANALYSIS

A2 

Apple

BTN 5-2 Key comparative figures for both **Research In Motion** and **Apple** follow.

($ millions)	Research In Motion		Apple	
	Current Year	Prior Year	Current Year	Prior Year
Revenues (net sales)	$14,953	$11,065	$42,905	$37,491
Cost of sales	8,369	5,968	25,683	24,294

Required

1. Compute the dollar amount of gross margin and the gross margin ratio for the two years shown for each of these companies.
2. Which company earns more in gross margin for each dollar of net sales? How do they compare to the industry average of 40.0%?
3. Did the gross margin ratio improve or decline for these companies?

ETHICS CHALLENGE

C1 P2

BTN 5-3 Ashton Martin is a student who plans to attend approximately four professional events a year at her college. Each event necessitates a financial outlay of $100 to $200 for a new suit and accessories. After incurring a major hit to her savings for the first event, Ashton developed a different approach. She buys the suit on credit the week before the event, wears it to the event, and returns it the next week to the store for a full refund on her charge card.

Required

1. Comment on the ethics exhibited by Ashton and possible consequences of her actions.
2. How does the merchandising company account for the suits that Ashton returns?

COMMUNICATING IN PRACTICE

C2 P3 P5  

BTN 5-4 You are the financial officer for Music Plus, a retailer that sells goods for home entertainment needs. The business owner, Jamie Madsen, recently reviewed the annual financial statements you prepared and sent you an e-mail stating that he thinks you overstated net income. He explains that although he has invested a great deal in security, he is sure shoplifting and other forms of inventory shrinkage have occurred, but he does not see any deduction for shrinkage on the income statement. The store uses a perpetual inventory system.

Required

Prepare a brief memorandum that responds to the owner's concerns.

TAKING IT TO THE NET

A2 C1  

BTN 5-5 Access the SEC's EDGAR database (**www.SEC.gov**) and obtain the March 19, 2010, filing of its fiscal 2010 10-K report (for year ended January 30, 2010) for **J. Crew Group, Inc** (ticker: JCG).

Required

Prepare a table that reports the gross margin ratios for J. Crew using the revenues and cost of goods sold data from J. Crew's income statement for each of its most recent three years. Analyze and comment on the trend in its gross margin ratio.

TEAMWORK IN ACTION

C1 C2

BTN 5-6 Best Brands' general ledger and supplementary records at the end of its current period reveal the following.

Sales	$430,000	Merchandise inventory (beginning of period)	$ 49,000
Sales returns	18,000	Invoice cost of merchandise purchases	180,000
Sales discounts	6,600	Purchase discounts received	4,500
Cost of transportation-in	11,000	Purchase returns and allowances	5,500
Operating expenses	20,000	Merchandise inventory (end of period)	42,000

Required

1. *Each* member of the team is to assume responsibility for computing *one* of the following items. You are not to duplicate your teammates' work. Get any necessary amounts to compute your item from the appropriate teammate. Each member is to explain his or her computation to the team in preparation for reporting to the class.
   - **a.** Net sales
   - **b.** Total cost of merchandise purchases
   - **c.** Cost of goods sold
   - **d.** Gross profit
   - **e.** Net income
2. Check your net income with the instructor. If correct, proceed to step 3.
3. Assume that a physical inventory count finds that actual ending inventory is $38,000. Discuss how this affects previously computed amounts in step 1.

Point: In teams of four, assign the same student *a* and *e*. Rotate teams for reporting on a different computation and the analysis in step 3.

ENTREPRENEURIAL DECISION

C1 C2 P4  

BTN 5-7 Refer to the opening feature about **Heritage Link Brands**. Assume that Selena and Khary Cuffe report current annual sales at approximately $10 million and disclose the following income statement.

Heritage Link Brands Income Statement For Year Ended January 31, 2010	
Net sales	$10,000,000
Cost of sales	6,100,000
Expenses (other than cost of sales)	2,000,000
Net income	$ 1,900,000

Selena and Khary Cuffe sell to various individuals and retailers, ranging from small shops to large chains. Assume that they currently offer credit terms of 1/15, n/60, and ship FOB destination. To improve their cash flow, they are considering changing credit terms to 3/10, n/30. In addition, they propose to change shipping terms to FOB shipping point. They expect that the increase in discount rate will increase net sales by 9%, but the gross margin ratio (and ratio of cost of sales divided by net sales) is expected to remain unchanged. They also expect that delivery expenses will be zero under this proposal; thus, expenses other than cost of sales are expected to increase only 6%.

Required

1. Prepare a forecasted income statement for the year ended January 31, 2011, based on the proposal.
2. Based on the forecasted income statement alone (from your part 1 solution), do you recommend that Selena and Khary implement the new sales policies? Explain.
3. What else should Selena and Khary consider before deciding whether or not to implement the new policies? Explain.

HITTING THE ROAD

C1   

Point: This activity complements the Ethics Challenge assignment.

BTN 5-8 Arrange an interview (in person or by phone) with the manager of a retail shop in a mall or in the downtown area of your community. Explain to the manager that you are a student studying merchandising activities and the accounting for sales returns and sales allowances. Ask the manager what the store policy is regarding returns. Also find out if sales allowances are ever negotiated with customers. Inquire whether management perceives that customers are abusing return policies and what actions management takes to counter potential abuses. Be prepared to discuss your findings in class.

GLOBAL DECISION

A2 P4  

NOKIA

RIM

Apple

BTN 5-9 **Nokia** (www.Nokia.com), **Research In Motion**, and **Apple** are competitors in the global marketplace. Key comparative figures for each company follow.

	Net Sales	Cost of Sales
Nokia*	40,984	27,720
Research In Motion†	$14,953	$ 8,369
Apple†	$42,905	$25,683

* EUR millions for Nokia.

† $ millions for Research In Motion and Apple.

Required

1. Rank the three companies (highest to lowest) based on the gross margin ratio.
2. Which of the companies uses a multiple-step income statement format? (These companies' income statements are in Appendix A.)

ANSWERS TO MULTIPLE CHOICE QUIZ

1. c; Gross profit = \$550,000 − \$193,000 = \$357,000
2. d; (\$4,500 − \$250) × (100% − 2%) = \$4,165
3. b; Net sales = \$75,000 + \$320,000 − \$13,700 − \$6,000 = \$375,300
4. b; Acid-test ratio = \$37,500/\$50,000 = 0.750
5. a; Gross margin ratio = (\$675,000 − \$459,000)/\$675,000 = 32%

6 Inventories and Cost of Sales

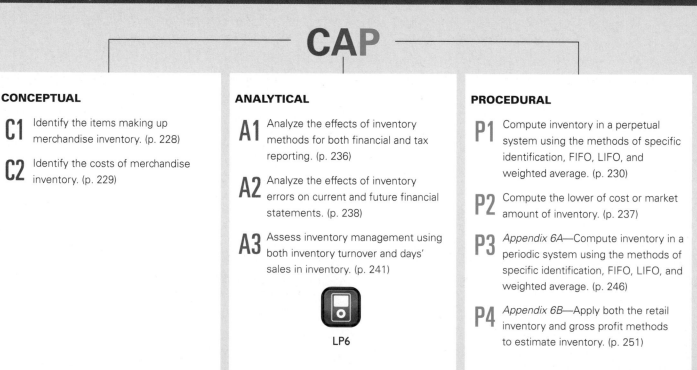

A Look Back

Chapter 5 focused on merchandising activities and how they are reported. We analyzed and recorded purchases and sales and explained accounting adjustments and closing for merchandisers.

A Look at This Chapter

This chapter emphasizes accounting for inventory. We describe methods for assigning costs to inventory and we explain the items and costs making up merchandise inventory. We also discuss methods of estimating and measuring inventory.

A Look Ahead

Chapter 7 emphasizes accounting information systems. We describe system principles, the system components, use of special journals and subsidiary ledgers, and technology-based systems.

Learning Objectives

CONCEPTUAL

C1 Identify the items making up merchandise inventory. (p. 228)

C2 Identify the costs of merchandise inventory. (p. 229)

ANALYTICAL

A1 Analyze the effects of inventory methods for both financial and tax reporting. (p. 236)

A2 Analyze the effects of inventory errors on current and future financial statements. (p. 238)

A3 Assess inventory management using both inventory turnover and days' sales in inventory. (p. 241)

LP6

PROCEDURAL

P1 Compute inventory in a perpetual system using the methods of specific identification, FIFO, LIFO, and weighted average. (p. 230)

P2 Compute the lower of cost or market amount of inventory. (p. 237)

P3 *Appendix 6A*—Compute inventory in a periodic system using the methods of specific identification, FIFO, LIFO, and weighted average. (p. 246)

P4 *Appendix 6B*—Apply both the retail inventory and gross profit methods to estimate inventory. (p. 251)

Decision Insight

The Gizmo!

"I wanted to re-create the SEAL team environment"
—RANDY HETRICK

SAN FRANCISCO—The Navy SEALs call it "the gizmo." This gizmo, created by former Navy SEAL Randy Hetrick, CEO of Fitness Anywhere, Inc and the inventor of Suspension Training®, is a resistance exercise device officially named the TRX Suspension Trainer. It is the hallmark product of Randy's start-up exercise equipment business, **Fitness Anywhere Inc. (FitnessAnywhere.com)**.

Randy explains that to keep himself in shape for clandestine missions, he stitched parachute webbing into straps that he could fasten to almost anything and then use as a pulley system where his own body weight served as resistance. After leaving the Navy, Randy headed to business school and devoted himself to producing and marketing his new invention.

However, the entrepreneurial road was rough. Randy struggled with inventory production and sales planning, and had to deal with discounts, returns, and allowances. A major challenge was maintaining appropriate inventories while controlling costs. Randy admits that mistakes are part of entrepreneurial endeavors, but that he just had to throw himself into it and learn.

And, learn he did. Applying inventory management, and old-fashion trial-and-error, Randy learned to fill orders, collect money, and maintain the right inventory. "I wanted to re-create the SEAL team environment," explains Randy. To help, he set up a perpetual inventory system to account for inventory sales and purchases in real time. Randy insists that it is really important to serve customers' needs, which demands sound inventory accounting.

But business success requires more than good products and perpetual inventory management, explains Randy. It requires commitment, patience, energy, faith, and maybe some luck. "I thought this was a commando tool, pure and simple," laughs Randy. "Man, was I wrong!"

While Randy continues to measure, monitor, and manage inventories and costs, his success and growth are pushing him into new products and opportunities. He explains that he now has a line of portable, resistance exercise devices. Still, Randy demands that his business stay true to "the small, flat, high-performance . . . kind of [SEALs] culture." His inventory procedures and office setting contribute to that lean and mean culture. "Working out [in the office] is not only sanctioned," says Randy, "it almost is required."

[Sources: *FitnessAnywhere Website*, January 2011; *Entrepreneur*, February 2010; *Triathlete Magazine*, December 2009; *Wall Street Journal*, September 2009]

Chapter Preview

Merchandisers' activities include the purchasing and reselling of merchandise. We explained accounting for merchandisers in Chapter 5, including that for purchases and sales. In this chapter, we extend the study and analysis of inventory by explaining the methods used to assign costs to merchandise inventory *and* to cost of goods sold. Retailers, wholesalers, and other merchandising companies that purchase products for resale use the principles and methods described here. Understanding inventory accounting helps in the analysis and interpretation of financial statements and helps people run their businesses.

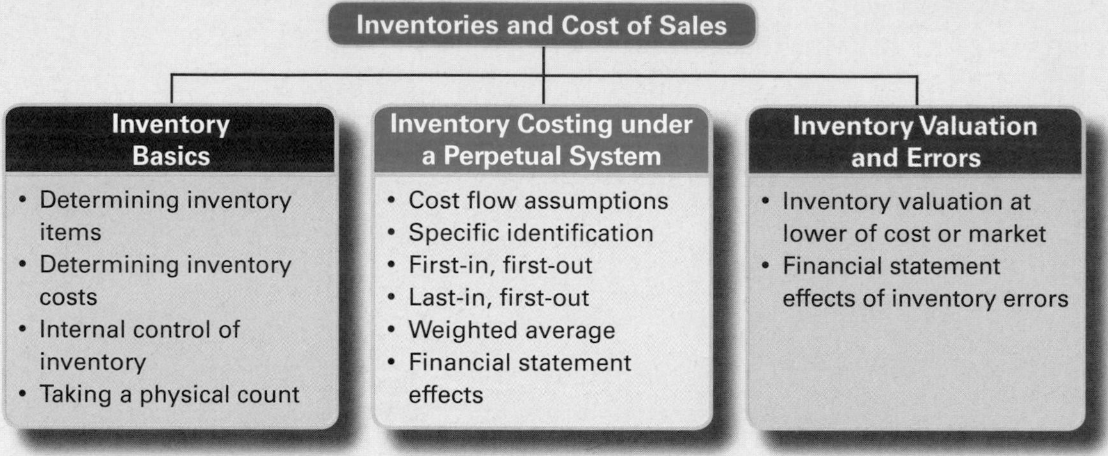

INVENTORY BASICS

This section identifies the items and costs making up merchandise inventory. It also describes the importance of internal controls in taking a physical count of inventory.

Determining Inventory Items

C1 Identify the items making up merchandise inventory.

Merchandise inventory includes all goods that a company owns and holds for sale. This rule holds regardless of where the goods are located when inventory is counted. Certain inventory items require special attention, including goods in transit, goods on consignment, and goods that are damaged or obsolete.

Goods in Transit Does a purchaser's inventory include goods in transit from a supplier? The answer is that if ownership has passed to the purchaser, the goods are included in the purchaser's inventory. We determine this by reviewing the shipping terms: *FOB destination* or *FOB shipping point.* If the purchaser is responsible for paying freight, ownership passes when goods are loaded on the transport vehicle. If the seller is responsible for paying freight, ownership passes when goods arrive at their destination.

Goods on Consignment Goods on consignment are goods shipped by the owner, called the **consignor,** to another party, the **consignee.** A consignee sells goods for the owner. The consignor continues to own the consigned goods and reports them in its inventory. **Upper Deck**, for instance, pays sports celebrities such as Tony Romo of the Dallas Cowboys to sign memorabilia, which are offered to shopping networks on consignment. Upper Deck, the consignor, must report these items in its inventory until sold.

Goods Damaged or Obsolete Damaged and obsolete (and deteriorated) goods are not counted in inventory if they cannot be sold. If these goods can be sold at a reduced price, they are included in inventory at a conservative estimate of their **net realizable value.** Net realizable value is sales price minus the cost of making the sale. The period when damage or obsolescence (or deterioration) occurs is the period when the loss in value is reported.

Decision Insight

A wireless portable device with a two-way radio allows clerks to quickly record inventory by scanning bar codes and to instantly send and receive inventory data. It gives managers access to up-to-date information on inventory and its location. ■

Determining Inventory Costs

C2 Identify the costs of merchandise inventory.

Merchandise inventory includes costs of expenditures necessary, directly or indirectly, to bring an item to a salable condition and location. This means that the cost of an inventory item includes its invoice cost minus any discount, and plus any incidental costs necessary to put it in a place and condition for sale. Incidental costs can include import duties, freight, storage, insurance, and costs incurred in an aging process (for example, aging wine or cheese).

Accounting principles prescribe that incidental costs be added to inventory. Also, the *matching (expense recognition) principle* states that inventory costs should be recorded against revenue in the period when inventory is sold. However, some companies use the *materiality constraint* (*cost-to-benefit constraint*) to avoid assigning some incidental costs of acquiring merchandise to inventory. Instead, they expense them when incurred. These companies argue either that those incidental costs are immaterial or that the effort in assigning them outweighs the benefit.

Internal Controls and Taking a Physical Count

The Inventory account under a perpetual system is updated for each purchase and sale, but events can cause the Inventory account balance to differ from the actual inventory available. Such events include theft, loss, damage, and errors. Thus, nearly all companies take a *physical count of inventory* at least once each year—informally called *taking an inventory.* This often occurs at the end of a fiscal year or when inventory amounts are low. This physical count is used to adjust the Inventory account balance to the actual inventory available.

A company applies internal controls when taking a physical count of inventory that usually include the following:

- *Prenumbered inventory tickets* are prepared and distributed to the *counters*—each ticket must be accounted for.
- Counters of inventory are assigned and do not include those responsible for inventory.
- Counters confirm the validity of inventory, including its existence, amount, and quality.
- A second count is taken by a different counter.
- A manager confirms that all inventories are ticketed once, and only once.

Point: The Inventory account is a controlling account for the inventory subsidiary ledger. This *subsidiary ledger* contains a separate record (units and costs) for each separate product, and it can be in electronic or paper form. Subsidiary records assist managers in planning and monitoring inventory.

Quick Check Answers — p. 253

1. What accounting principle most guides the allocation of cost of goods available for sale between ending inventory and cost of goods sold?
2. If **Skechers** sells goods to **Target** with terms FOB shipping point, which company reports these goods in its inventory while they are in transit?
3. An art gallery purchases a painting for $11,400 on terms FOB shipping point. Additional costs in obtaining and offering the artwork for sale include $130 for transportation-in, $150 for import duties, $100 for insurance during shipment, $180 for advertising, $400 for framing, and $800 for office salaries. For computing inventory, what cost is assigned to the painting?

INVENTORY COSTING UNDER A PERPETUAL SYSTEM

Accounting for inventory affects both the balance sheet and the income statement. A major goal in accounting for inventory is to properly match costs with sales. We use the *matching principle* to decide how much of the cost of the goods available for sale is deducted from sales and how much is carried forward as inventory and matched against future sales.

Management decisions in accounting for inventory involve the following:

- Items included in inventory and their costs.
- Costing method (specific identification, FIFO, LIFO, or weighted average).
- Inventory system (perpetual or periodic).
- Use of market values or other estimates.

The first point was explained on the prior two pages. The second and third points will be addressed now. The fourth point is the focus at the end of this chapter. Decisions on these points affect the reported amounts for inventory, cost of goods sold, gross profit, income, current assets, and other accounts.

One of the most important issues in accounting for inventory is determining the per unit costs assigned to inventory items. When all units are purchased at the same unit cost, this process is simple. When identical items are purchased at different costs, however, a question arises as to which amounts to record in cost of goods sold and which amounts remain in inventory.

Four methods are commonly used to assign costs to inventory and to cost of goods sold: (1) specific identification; (2) first-in, first-out; (3) last-in, first-out; and (4) weighted average. Exhibit 6.1 shows the frequency in the use of these methods.

EXHIBIT 6.1

Frequency in Use of Inventory Methods

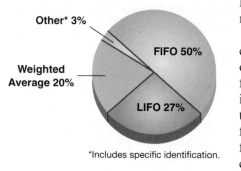

Other* 3%
FIFO 50%
Weighted Average 20%
LIFO 27%

*Includes specific identification.

Each method assumes a particular pattern for how costs flow through inventory. Each of these four methods is acceptable whether or not the actual physical flow of goods follows the cost flow assumption. Physical flow of goods depends on the type of product and the way it is stored. (Perishable goods such as fresh fruit demand that a business attempt to sell them in a first-in, first-out physical flow. Other products such as crude oil and minerals such as coal, gold, and decorative stone can be sold in a last-in, first-out physical flow.) **Physical flow and cost flow need not be the same**.

Inventory Cost Flow Assumptions

P1 Compute inventory in a perpetual system using the methods of specific identification, FIFO, LIFO, and weighted average.

This section introduces inventory cost flow assumptions. For this purpose, assume that three identical units are purchased separately at the following three dates and costs: May 1 at $45, May 3 at $65, and May 6 at $70. One unit is then sold on May 7 for $100. Exhibit 6.2 gives a visual layout of the flow of costs to either the gross profit section of the income statement or the inventory reported on the balance sheet for FIFO, LIFO, and weighted average.

Point: It is helpful to recall the cost flow of inventory from Exhibit 5.4.

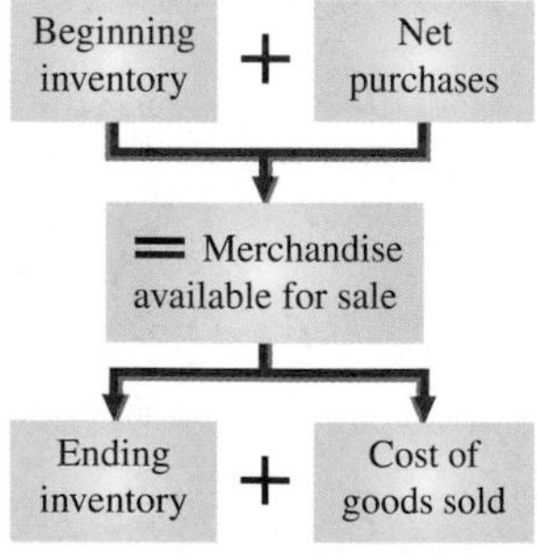

(1) *FIFO assumes costs flow in the order incurred.* The unit purchased on May 1 for $45 is the earliest cost incurred—it is sent to cost of goods sold on the income statement first. The remaining two units ($65 and $70) are reported in inventory on the balance sheet.

(2) *LIFO assumes costs flow in the reverse order incurred.* The unit purchased on May 6 for $70 is the most recent cost incurred—it is sent to cost of goods sold on the income statement. The remaining two units ($45 and $65) are reported in inventory on the balance sheet.

(3) *Weighted average assumes costs flow at an average of the costs available.* The units available at the May 7 sale average $60 in cost, computed as ($45 + $65 + $70)/3. One unit's $60 average cost is sent to cost of goods sold on the income statement. The remaining two units' average costs are reported in inventory at $120 on the balance sheet.

Cost flow assumptions can markedly impact gross profit and inventory numbers. Exhibit 6.2 shows that gross profit as a percent of net sales ranges from 30% to 55% due to nothing else but the cost flow assumption.

The following sections on inventory costing use the perpetual system. Appendix 6A uses the periodic system. An instructor can choose to cover either one or both systems. If the perpetual system is skipped, then read Appendix 6A and return to the section (seven pages ahead) titled "Valuing Inventory at LCM and . . ."

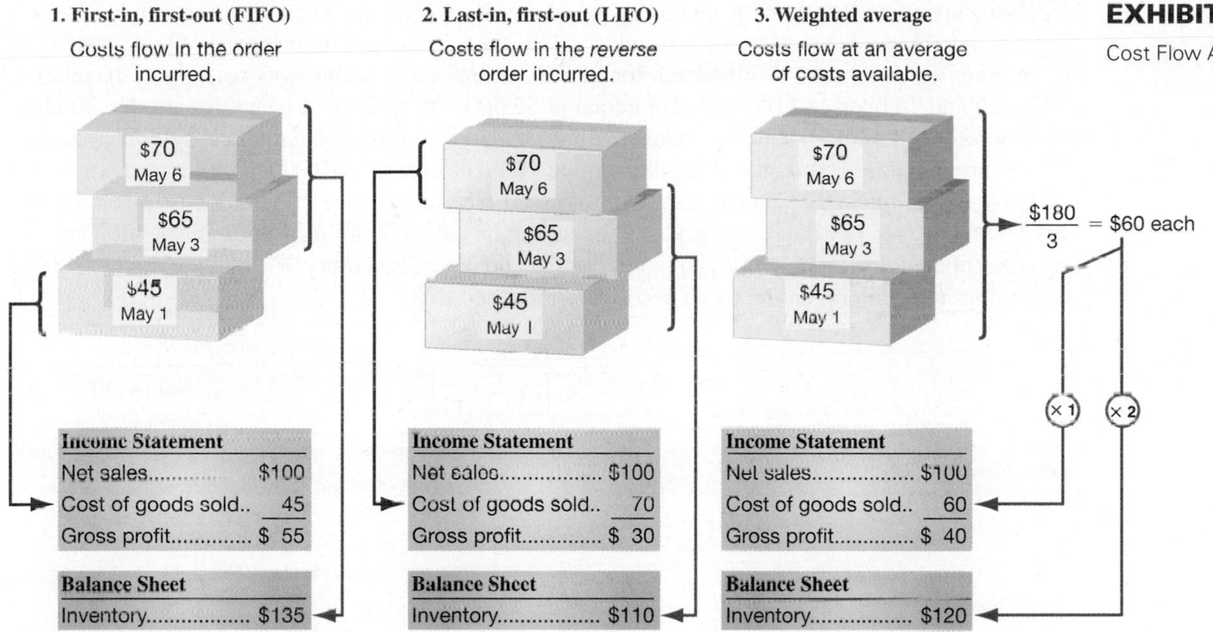

EXHIBIT 6.2
Cost Flow Assumptions

Inventory Costing Illustration

This section provides a comprehensive illustration of inventory costing methods. We use information from Trekking, a sporting goods store. Among its many products, Trekking carries one type of mountain bike whose sales are directed at resorts that provide inexpensive mountain bikes for complimentary guest use. Its customers usually purchase in amounts of 10 or more bikes. We use Trekking's data from August. Its mountain bike (unit) inventory at the beginning of August and its purchases and sales during August are shown in Exhibit 6.3. It ends August with 12 bikes remaining in inventory.

EXHIBIT 6.3
Purchases and Sales of Goods

Date	Activity	Units Acquired at Cost	Units Sold at Retail	Unit Inventory
Aug. 1	Beginning inventory	10 units @ $ 91 = $ 910		10 units
Aug. 3	Purchases	15 units @ $106 = $ 1,590		25 units
Aug. 14	Sales		20 units @ $130	5 units
Aug. 17	Purchases	20 units @ $115 = $ 2,300		25 units
Aug. 28	Purchases	10 units @ $119 = $ 1,190		35 units
Aug. 31	Sales		23 units @ $150	12 units
	Totals	55 units $5,990	43 units	

Trekking uses the perpetual inventory system, which means that its merchandise inventory account is continually updated to reflect purchases and sales. **(Appendix 6A describes the assignment of costs to inventory using a periodic system.)** Regardless of what inventory method or system is used, cost of goods available for sale must be allocated between cost of goods sold and ending inventory.

Point: The perpetual inventory system is now the most dominant system for U.S. businesses.

Point: Cost of goods sold plus ending inventory equals cost of goods available for sale.

Specific Identification

When each item in inventory can be identified with a specific purchase and invoice, we can use **specific identification** (also called *specific invoice inventory pricing*) to assign costs. We also need sales records that identify exactly which items were sold and when. Trekking's internal documents reveal the following specific unit sales:

August 14 Sold 8 bikes costing $91 each and 12 bikes costing $106 each
August 31 Sold 2 bikes costing $91 each, 3 bikes costing $106 each, 15 bikes costing $115 each, and 3 bikes costing $119 each

Point: Three key variables determine the dollar value of ending inventory: (1) inventory quantity, (2) costs of inventory, and (3) cost flow assumption.

Applying specific identification, and using the information above and from Exhibit 6.3, we prepare Exhibit 6.4. This exhibit starts with 10 bikes at $91 each in beginning inventory. On August 3, 15 more bikes are purchased at $106 each for $1,590. Inventory available now consists of 10 bikes at $91 each and 15 bikes at $106 each, for a total of $2,500. On August 14 (see sales above), 20 bikes costing $2,000 are sold—leaving 5 bikes costing $500 in inventory. On August 17, 20 bikes costing $2,300 are purchased, and on August 28, another 10 bikes costing $1,190 are purchased, for a total of 35 bikes costing $3,990 in inventory. On August 31 (see sales above), 23 bikes costing $2,582 are sold, which leaves 12 bikes costing $1,408 in ending inventory. Carefully study this exhibit and the boxed explanations to see the flow of costs both in and out of inventory. Each unit, whether sold or remaining in inventory, has its own specific cost attached to it.

EXHIBIT 6.4

Specific Identification Computations

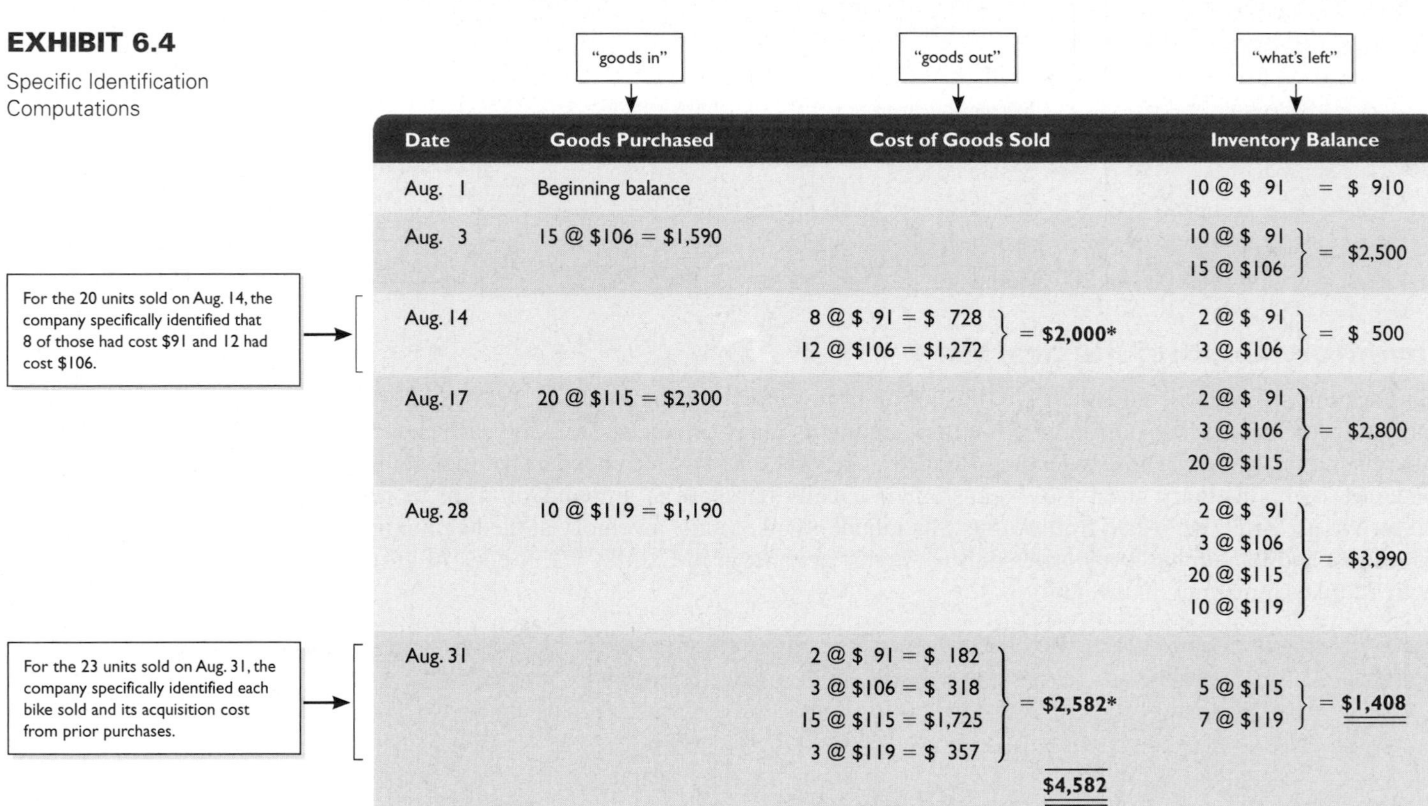

Date	Goods Purchased	Cost of Goods Sold		Inventory Balance	
Aug. 1	Beginning balance			10 @ $ 91	= $ 910
Aug. 3	15 @ $106 = $1,590			10 @ $ 91 15 @ $106	= $2,500
Aug. 14		8 @ $ 91 = $ 728 12 @ $106 = $1,272	= $2,000*	2 @ $ 91 3 @ $106	= $ 500
Aug. 17	20 @ $115 = $2,300			2 @ $ 91 3 @ $106 20 @ $115	= $2,800
Aug. 28	10 @ $119 = $1,190			2 @ $ 91 3 @ $106 20 @ $115 10 @ $119	= $3,990
Aug. 31		2 @ $ 91 = $ 182 3 @ $106 = $ 318 15 @ $115 = $1,725 3 @ $119 = $ 357	= $2,582*	5 @ $115 7 @ $119	= $1,408
			$4,582		

* Identification of items sold (and their costs) is obtained from internal documents that track each unit from its purchase to its sale.

Point: Specific identification is usually practical only for companies with expensive, custom-made inventory.

When using specific identification, Trekking's cost of goods sold reported on the income statement totals **$4,582**, the sum of $2,000 and $2,582 from the third column of Exhibit 6.4. Trekking's ending inventory reported on the balance sheet is **$1,408**, which is the final inventory balance from the fourth column of Exhibit 6.4.

The purchases and sales entries for Exhibit 6.4 follow (the colored boldface numbers are those impacted by the cost flow assumption).

Purchases

Date	Account	Debit	Credit
Aug. 3	Merchandise Inventory	1,590	
	Accounts Payable		1,590
17	Merchandise Inventory	2,300	
	Accounts Payable		2,300
28	Merchandise Inventory	1,190	
	Accounts Payable		1,190

Sales

Date	Account	Debit	Credit
Aug. 14	Accounts Receivable	2,600	
	Sales		2,600
14	Cost of Goods Sold	**2,000**	
	Merchandise Inventory		**2,000**
31	Accounts Receivable	3,450	
	Sales		3,450
31	Cost of Goods Sold	**2,582**	
	Merchandise Inventory		**2,582**

First-In, First-Out

The **first-in, first-out (FIFO)** method of assigning costs to both inventory and cost of goods sold assumes that inventory items are sold in the order acquired. When sales occur, the costs of the earliest units acquired are charged to cost of goods sold. This leaves the costs from the most recent purchases in ending inventory. Use of FIFO for computing the cost of inventory and cost of goods sold is shown in Exhibit 6.5.

Point: The "Goods Purchased" column is identical for all methods. Data are taken from Exhibit 6.3.

This exhibit starts with beginning inventory of 10 bikes at $91 each. On August 3, 15 more bikes costing $106 each are bought for $1,590. Inventory now consists of 10 bikes at $91 each and 15 bikes at $106 each, for a total of $2,500. On August 14, 20 bikes are sold—applying FIFO, the first 10 sold cost $91 each and the next 10 sold cost $106 each, for a total cost of $1,970. This leaves 5 bikes costing $106 each, or $530, in inventory. On August 17, 20 bikes costing $2,300 are purchased, and on August 28, another 10 bikes costing $1,190 are purchased, for a total of 35 bikes costing $4,020 in inventory. On August 31, 23 bikes are sold—applying FIFO, the first 5 bikes sold cost $530 and the next 18 sold cost $2,070, which leaves 12 bikes costing $1,420 in ending inventory.

EXHIBIT 6.5

FIFO Computations—Perpetual System

Date	Goods Purchased	Cost of Goods Sold		Inventory Balance	
Aug. 1	Beginning balance			10 @ $ 91	= $ 910
Aug. 3	15 @ $106 = $1,590			10 @ $ 91 15 @ $106	= $2,500
Aug. 14		10 @ $ 91 = $ 910 10 @ $106 = $1,060	= **$1,970**	5 @ $106	= $ 530
Aug. 17	20 @ $115 = $2,300			5 @ $106 20 @ $115	= $2,830
Aug. 20	10 @ $119 = $1,190			5 @ $106 20 @ $115 10 @ $119	= $4,020
Aug. 31		5 @ $106 = $ 530 18 @ $115 = $2,070	= **$2,600**	2 @ $115 10 @ $119	= **$1,420**
			$4,570		

For the 20 units sold on Aug. 14, the first 10 sold are assigned the earliest cost of $91 (from beg. bal.). The next 10 sold are assigned the next earliest cost of $106.

For the 23 units sold on Aug. 31, the first 5 sold are assigned the earliest available cost of $106 (from Aug. 3 purchase). The next 18 sold are assigned the next earliest cost of $115 (from Aug. 17 purchase).

Trekking's FIFO cost of goods sold reported on its income statement (reflecting the 43 units sold) is **$4,570** ($1,970 + $2,600), and its ending inventory reported on the balance sheet (reflecting the 12 units unsold) is **$1,420**.

Point: Under FIFO, a unit sold is assigned the earliest (oldest) cost from inventory. This leaves the most recent costs in ending inventory.

The purchases and sales entries for Exhibit 6.5 follow (the colored boldface numbers are those affected by the cost flow assumption).

Purchases

Date	Account	Debit	Credit
Aug. 3	Merchandise Inventory	1,590	
	Accounts Payable		1,590
17	Merchandise Inventory	2,300	
	Accounts Payable		2,300
28	Merchandise Inventory	1,190	
	Accounts Payable		1,190

Sales

Date	Account	Debit	Credit
Aug. 14	Accounts Receivable	2,600	
	Sales		2,600
14	Cost of Goods Sold	**1,970**	
	Merchandise Inventory		**1,970**
31	Accounts Receivable	3,450	
	Sales		3,450
31	Cost of Goods Sold	**2,600**	
	Merchandise Inventory		**2,600**

Last-In, First-Out

The **last-in, first-out (LIFO)** method of assigning costs assumes that the most recent purchases are sold first. These more recent costs are charged to the goods sold, and the costs of the earliest purchases are assigned to inventory. As with other methods, LIFO is acceptable even when the

Point: Under LIFO, a unit sold is assigned the most recent (latest) cost from inventory. This leaves the oldest costs in inventory.

physical flow of goods does not follow a last-in, first-out pattern. One appeal of LIFO is that by assigning costs from the most recent purchases to cost of goods sold, LIFO comes closest to matching current costs of goods sold with revenues (compared to FIFO or weighted average).

Exhibit 6.6 shows the LIFO computations. It starts with beginning inventory of 10 bikes at $91 each. On August 3, 15 more bikes costing $106 each are bought for $1,590. Inventory now consists of 10 bikes at $91 each and 15 bikes at $106 each, for a total of $2,500. On August 14, 20 bikes are sold—applying LIFO, the first 15 sold are from the most recent purchase costing $106 each, and the next 5 sold are from the next most recent purchase costing $91 each, for a total cost of $2,045. This leaves 5 bikes costing $91 each, or $455, in inventory. On August 17, 20 bikes costing $2,300 are purchased, and on August 28, another 10 bikes costing $1,190 are purchased, for a total of 35 bikes costing $3,945 in inventory. On August 31, 23 bikes are sold—applying LIFO, the first 10 bikes sold are from the most recent purchase costing $1,190, and the next 13 sold are from the next most recent purchase costing $1,495, which leaves 12 bikes costing $1,260 in ending inventory.

EXHIBIT 6.6

LIFO Computations—Perpetual System

Date	Goods Purchased	Cost of Goods Sold		Inventory Balance	
Aug. 1	Beginning balance			10 @ $ 91	= $ 910
Aug. 3	15 @ $106 = $1,590			10 @ $ 91 15 @ $106	= $ 2,500
Aug. 14		15 @ $106 = $1,590 5 @ $ 91 = $ 455	= **$2,045**	5 @ $ 91	= $ 455
Aug. 17	20 @ $115 = $2,300			5 @ $ 91 20 @ $115	= $ 2,755
Aug. 28	10 @ $119 = $1,190			5 @ $ 91 20 @ $115 10 @ $119	= $ 3,945
Aug. 31		10 @ $119 = $1,190 13 @ $115 = $1,495	= **$2,685**	5 @ $ 91 7 @ $115	= **$1,260**
			$4,730		

For the 20 units sold on Aug. 14, the first 15 sold are assigned the most recent cost of $106. The next 5 sold are assigned the next most recent cost of $91.

For the 23 units sold on Aug. 31, the first 10 sold are assigned the most recent cost of $119. The next 13 sold are assigned the next most recent cost of $115.

Trekking's LIFO cost of goods sold reported on the income statement is **$4,730** ($2,045 + $2,685), and its ending inventory reported on the balance sheet is **$1,260**.

The purchases and sales entries for Exhibit 6.6 follow (the colored boldface numbers are those affected by the cost flow assumption).

Purchases

Aug. 3	Merchandise Inventory	1,590	
	Accounts Payable		1,590
17	Merchandise Inventory	2,300	
	Accounts Payable		2,300
28	Merchandise Inventory	1,190	
	Accounts Payable		1,190

Sales

Aug. 14	Accounts Receivable	2,600	
	Sales		2,600
14	Cost of Goods Sold	**2,045**	
	Merchandise Inventory		**2,045**
31	Accounts Receivable	3,450	
	Sales		3,450
31	Cost of Goods Sold	**2,685**	
	Merchandise Inventory		**2,685**

Weighted Average

The **weighted average** (also called **average cost**) method of assigning cost requires that we use the weighted average cost per unit of inventory at the time of each sale. Weighted average cost per unit at the time of each sale equals the cost of goods available for sale divided by the units available. The results using weighted average (WA) for Trekking are shown in Exhibit 6.7.

This exhibit starts with beginning inventory of 10 bikes at $91 each. On August 3, 15 more bikes costing $106 each are bought for $1,590. Inventory now consists of 10 bikes at $91 each and 15 bikes at $106 each, for a total of $2,500. The average cost per bike for that inventory is $100, computed as $2,500/(10 bikes + 15 bikes). On August 14, 20 bikes are sold—applying

EXHIBIT 6.7

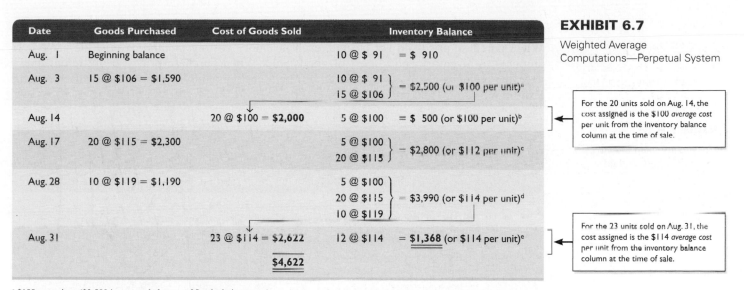

Weighted Average Computations—Perpetual System

Date	Goods Purchased	Cost of Goods Sold	Inventory Balance
Aug. 1	Beginning balance		10 @ $ 91 = $ 910
Aug. 3	15 @ $106 = $1,590		10 @ $ 91, 15 @ $106 } = $2,500 (or $100 per unit)[a]
Aug. 14		20 @ $100 = **$2,000**	5 @ $100 = $ 500 (or $100 per unit)[b]
Aug. 17	20 @ $115 = $2,300		5 @ $100, 20 @ $115 } = $2,800 (or $112 per unit)[c]
Aug. 28	10 @ $119 = $1,190		5 @ $100, 20 @ $115, 10 @ $119 } = $3,990 (or $114 per unit)[d]
Aug. 31		23 @ $114 = **$2,622**	12 @ $114 = **$1,368** (or $114 per unit)[e]
		$4,622	

For the 20 units sold on Aug. 14, the cost assigned is the $100 *average cost* per unit from the inventory balance column at the time of sale.

For the 23 units sold on Aug. 31, the cost assigned is the $114 *average cost* per unit from the inventory balance column at the time of sale.

[a] $100 per unit = ($2,500 inventory balance ÷ 25 units in inventory).
[b] $100 per unit = ($500 inventory balance ÷ 5 units in inventory).
[c] $112 per unit = ($2,800 inventory balance ÷ 25 units in inventory).
[d] $114 per unit = ($3,990 inventory balance ÷ 35 units in inventory).
[e] $114 per unit = ($1,368 inventory balance ÷ 12 units in inventory).

WA, the 20 sold are assigned the $100 average cost, for a total cost of $2,000. This leaves 5 bikes with an average cost of $100 each, or $500, in inventory. On August 17, 20 bikes costing $2,300 are purchased, and on August 28, another 10 bikes costing $1,190 are purchased, for a total of 35 bikes costing $3,990 in inventory at August 28. The average cost per bike for the August 28 inventory is $114, computed as $3,990/(5 bikes + 20 bikes + 10 bikes). On August 31, 23 bikes are sold—applying WA, the 23 sold are assigned the $114 average cost, for a total cost of $2,622. This leaves 12 bikes costing $1,368 in ending inventory.

Trekking's cost of goods sold reported on the income statement (reflecting the 43 units sold) is **$4,622** ($2,000 + $2,622), and its ending inventory reported on the balance sheet (reflecting the 12 units unsold) is **$1,368**.

Point: Under weighted average, a unit sold is assigned the average cost of all items currently available for sale at the date of each sale.

The purchases and sales entries for Exhibit 6.7 follow (the colored boldface numbers are those affected by the cost flow assumption).

Purchases

Date	Account	Debit	Credit
Aug. 3	Merchandise Inventory	1,590	
	Accounts Payable		1,590
17	Merchandise Inventory	2,300	
	Accounts Payable		2,300
28	Merchandise Inventory	1,190	
	Accounts Payable		1,190

Sales

Date	Account	Debit	Credit
Aug. 14	Accounts Receivable	2,600	
	Sales		2,600
14	Cost of Goods Sold	**2,000**	
	Merchandise Inventory		**2,000**
31	Accounts Receivable	3,450	
	Sales		3,450
31	Cost of Goods Sold	**2,622**	
	Merchandise Inventory		**2,622**

This completes computations under the four most common perpetual inventory costing methods. Advances in technology have greatly reduced the cost of a perpetual inventory system. Many companies now ask whether they can afford *not* to have a perpetual inventory system because timely access to inventory information is a competitive advantage and it can help reduce the amount of inventory, which reduces costs.

Decision Insight

Inventory Control SOX demands that companies safeguard inventory and properly report it. Safeguards include restricted access, use of authorized requisitions, security measures, and controlled environments to prevent damage. Proper accounting includes matching inventory received with purchase order terms and quality requirements, preventing misstatements, and controlling access to inventory records. A study reports that 23% of employees in purchasing and procurement observed inappropriate kickbacks or gifts from suppliers (KPMG 2009). Another 23% of employees in production witnessed fabrication of product quality results. ■

Financial Statement Effects of Costing Methods

A1 Analyze the effects of inventory methods for both financial and tax reporting.

When purchase prices do not change, each inventory costing method assigns the same cost amounts to inventory and to cost of goods sold. When purchase prices are different, however, the methods nearly always assign different cost amounts. We show these differences in Exhibit 6.8 using Trekking's data.

EXHIBIT 6.8

Financial Statement Effects of Inventory Costing Methods

TREKKING COMPANY For Month Ended August 31	Specific Identification	FIFO	LIFO	Weighted Average
Income Statement				
Sales	$ 6,050	$ 6,050	$ 6,050	$ 6,050
Cost of goods sold	**4,582**	**4,570**	**4,730**	**4,622**
Gross profit	1,468	1,480	1,320	1,428
Expenses	450	450	450	450
Income before taxes	1,018	1,030	870	978
Income tax expense (30%)	305	309	261	293
Net income	**$ 713**	**$ 721**	**$ 609**	**$ 685**
Balance Sheet				
Inventory	**$1,408**	**$1,420**	**$1,260**	**$1,368**

This exhibit reveals two important results. First, when purchase costs *regularly rise,* as in Trekking's case, the following occurs:

Point: Managers prefer FIFO when costs are rising *and* incentives exist to report higher income for reasons such as bonus plans, job security, and reputation.

- FIFO assigns the lowest amount to cost of goods sold—yielding the highest gross profit and net income.
- LIFO assigns the highest amount to cost of goods sold—yielding the lowest gross profit and net income, which also yields a temporary tax advantage by postponing payment of some income tax.
- Weighted average yields results between FIFO and LIFO.
- Specific identification always yields results that depend on which units are sold.

Point: LIFO inventory is often less than the inventory's replacement cost because LIFO inventory is valued using the oldest inventory purchase costs.

Second, when costs *regularly decline,* the reverse occurs for FIFO and LIFO. Namely, FIFO gives the highest cost of goods sold—yielding the lowest gross profit and income. However, LIFO then gives the lowest cost of goods sold—yielding the highest gross profit and income.

All four inventory costing methods are acceptable. However, a company must disclose the inventory method it uses in its financial statements or notes. Each method offers certain advantages as follows:

- FIFO assigns an amount to inventory on the balance sheet that approximates its current cost; it also mimics the actual flow of goods for most businesses.
- LIFO assigns an amount to cost of goods sold on the income statement that approximates its current cost; it also better matches current costs with revenues in computing gross profit.
- Weighted average tends to smooth out erratic changes in costs.
- Specific identification exactly matches the costs of items with the revenues they generate.

Decision Maker Answer — p. 253 

Financial Planner One of your clients asks if the inventory account of a company using FIFO needs any "adjustments" for analysis purposes in light of recent inflation. What is your advice? Does your advice depend on changes in the costs of these inventories? ■

Tax Effects of Costing Methods Trekking's segment income statement in Exhibit 6.8 includes income tax expense (at a rate of 30%) because it was formed as a corporation. Since inventory costs affect net income, they have potential tax effects. Trekking gains a temporary tax advantage by using LIFO. Many companies use LIFO for this reason.

Companies can and often do use different costing methods for financial reporting and tax reporting. *The only exception is when LIFO is used for tax reporting; in this case, the IRS requires that it also be used in financial statements*—called the LIFO conformity rule.

Consistency in Using Costing Methods

The **consistency concept** prescribes that a company use the same accounting methods period after period so that financial statements are comparable across periods—the only exception is when a change from one method to another will improve its financial reporting. The *full-disclosure principle* prescribes that the notes to the statements report this type of change, its justification, and its effect on income.

The consistency concept does *not* require a company to use one method exclusively. For example, it can use different methods to value different categories of inventory.

Decision Ethics Answer — p. 253

Inventory Manager Your compensation as inventory manager includes a bonus plan based on gross profit. Your superior asks your opinion on changing the inventory costing method from FIFO to LIFO. Since costs are expected to continue to rise, your superior predicts that LIFO would match higher current costs against sales, thereby lowering taxable income (and gross profit). What do you recommend? ■

Quick Check Answers — p. 253

4. Describe one advantage for each of the inventory costing methods: specific identification, FIFO, LIFO, and weighted average.
5. When costs are rising, which method reports higher net income—LIFO or FIFO?
6. When costs are rising, what effect does LIFO have on a balance sheet compared to FIFO?
7. A company takes a physical count of inventory at the end of 2010 and finds that ending inventory is understated by $10,000. Would this error cause cost of goods sold to be overstated or understated in 2010? In year 2011? If so, by how much?

VALUING INVENTORY AT LCM AND THE EFFECTS OF INVENTORY ERRORS

This section examines the role of market costs in determining inventory on the balance sheet and also the financial statement effects of inventory errors.

Lower of Cost or Market

P2 Compute the lower of cost or market amount of inventory

We explained how to assign costs to ending inventory and cost of goods sold using one of four costing methods (FIFO, LIFO, weighted average, or specific identification). However, *accounting principles require that inventory be reported at the market value (cost) of replacing inventory when market value is lower than cost.* Merchandise inventory is then said to be reported on the balance sheet at the **lower of cost or market (LCM).**

Computing the Lower of Cost or Market *Market* in the term *LCM* is defined as the current replacement cost of purchasing the same inventory items in the usual manner. A decline in replacement cost reflects a loss of value in inventory. When the recorded cost of inventory is higher than the replacement cost, a loss is recognized. When the recorded cost is lower, no adjustment is made.

LCM is applied in one of three ways: (1) to each individual item separately, (2) to major categories of items, or (3) to the whole of inventory. The less similar the items that make up inventory, the more likely companies are to apply LCM to individual items or categories. With the increasing application of technology and inventory tracking, companies increasingly apply

EXHIBIT 6.9

Lower of Cost or Market Computations

$140,000 is the lower of $160,000 or $140,000

Market amount of $265,000 is lower than the $295,000 recorded cost

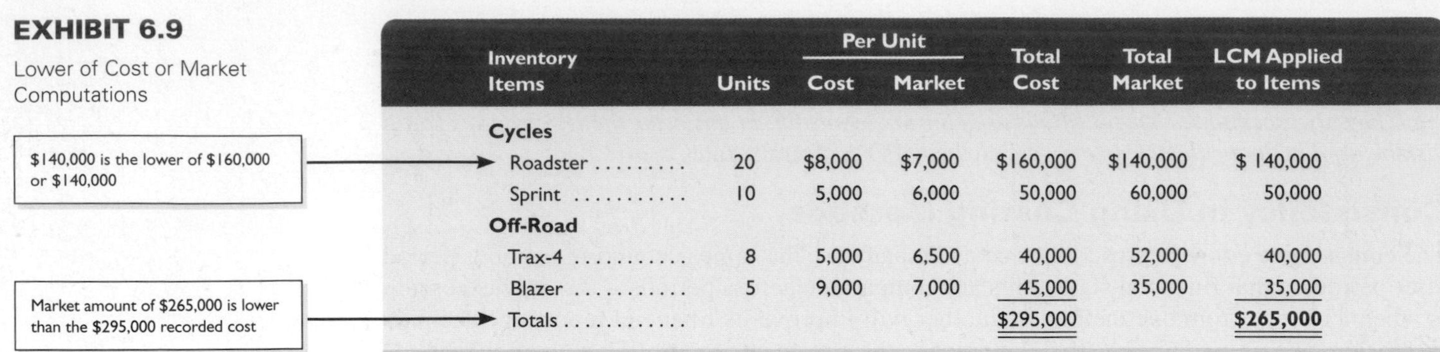

Inventory Items	Units	Per Unit Cost	Per Unit Market	Total Cost	Total Market	LCM Applied to Items
Cycles						
Roadster	20	$8,000	$7,000	$160,000	$140,000	$ 140,000
Sprint	10	5,000	6,000	50,000	60,000	50,000
Off-Road						
Trax-4	8	5,000	6,500	40,000	52,000	40,000
Blazer	5	9,000	7,000	45,000	35,000	35,000
Totals				$295,000		**$265,000**

LCM to each individual item separately. Accordingly, we show that method only; however, advanced courses cover the other two methods. To illustrate LCM, we apply it to the ending inventory of a motorsports retailer in Exhibit 6.9.

LCM Applied to Individual Items When LCM is applied to individual *items* of inventory, the number of comparisons equals the number of items. For Roadster, $140,000 is the lower of the $160,000 cost and the $140,000 market. For Sprint, $50,000 is the lower of the $50,000 cost and the $60,000 market. For Trax-4, $40,000 is the lower of the $40,000 cost and the $52,000 market. For Blazer, $35,000 is the lower of the $45,000 cost and the $35,000 market. This yields a $265,000 reported inventory, computed from $140,000 for Roadster plus $50,000 for Sprint plus $40,000 for Trax-4 plus $35,000 for Blazer.

Point: Advances in technology encourage the individual-item approach for LCM.

The manufacturer **Research In Motion** applies LCM and reports that its "inventories are stated at the lower of cost and net realizable value [or replacement cost]."

Recording the Lower of Cost or Market Inventory must be adjusted downward when market is less than cost. To illustrate, if LCM is applied to the individual items of inventory in Exhibit 6.9, the Merchandise Inventory account must be adjusted from the $295,000 recorded cost down to the $265,000 market amount as follows.

	Debit	Credit
Cost of Goods Sold	30,000	
Merchandise Inventory		30,000
To adjust inventory cost to market.		

Accounting rules require that inventory be adjusted to market when market is less than cost, but inventory normally cannot be written up to market when market exceeds cost. If recording inventory down to market is acceptable, why are companies not allowed to record inventory up to market? One view is that a gain from a market increase should not be realized until a sales transaction verifies the gain. However, this problem also applies when market is less than cost. A second and primary reason is the **conservatism constraint,** which prescribes the use of the less optimistic amount when more than one estimate of the amount to be received or paid exists and these estimates are about equally likely.

Financial Statement Effects of Inventory Errors

A2 Analyze the effects of inventory errors on current and future financial statements.

Companies must take care in both taking a physical count of inventory and in assigning a cost to it. An inventory error causes misstatements in cost of goods sold, gross profit, net income, current assets, and equity. It also causes misstatements in the next period's statements because ending inventory of one period is the beginning inventory of the next. As we consider the financial statement effects in this section, it is helpful if we recall the following *inventory relation.*

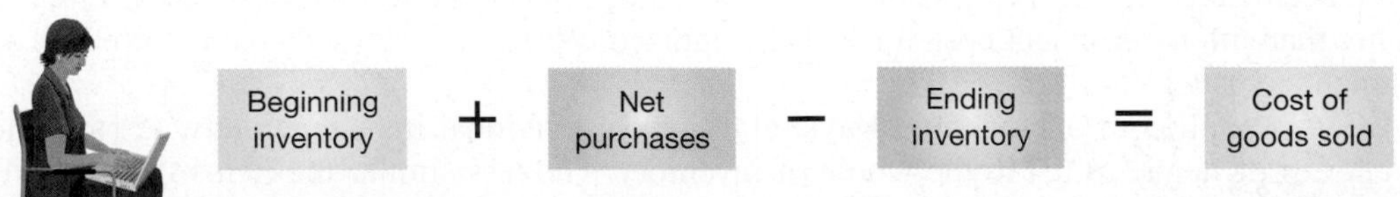

Income Statement Effects Exhibit 6.10 shows the effects of inventory errors on key amounts in the current and next periods' income statements. Let's look at row 1 and year 1. We

see that understating ending inventory overstates cost of goods sold. This can be seen from the above inventory relation where we subtract a smaller ending inventory amount in computing cost of goods sold. Then a higher cost of goods sold yields a lower income.

To understand year 2 of row 1, remember that an understated ending inventory for year 1 becomes an understated beginning inventory for year 2. Using the above inventory relation, we see that if beginning inventory is understated, then cost of goods sold is understated (because we are starting with a smaller amount). A lower cost of goods sold yields a higher income.

Turning to overstatements, let's look at row 2 and year 1. If ending inventory is overstated, we use the inventory relation to see that cost of goods sold is understated. A lower cost of goods sold yields a higher income.

For year 2 of row 2, we again recall that an overstated ending inventory for year 1 becomes an overstated beginning inventory for year 2. If beginning inventory is overstated, we use the inventory relation to see that cost of goods sold is overstated. A higher cost of goods sold yields a lower income.

EXHIBIT 6.10

Effects of Inventory Errors on the Income Statement

	Year 1		Year 2	
Ending Inventory	Cost of Goods Sold	Net Income	Cost of Goods Sold	Net Income
Understated↓	Overstated↑	Understated↓	Understated↓	Overstated↑
Overstated*↑	Understated↓	Overstated↑	Overstated↑	Understated↓

* This error is less likely under a perpetual system because it implies more inventory than is recorded (or less shrinkage than expected). Management will normally follow up and discover and correct this error before it impacts any accounts.

To illustrate, consider an inventory error for a company with $100,000 in sales for each of the years 2010, 2011, and 2012. If this company maintains a steady $20,000 inventory level during this period and makes $60,000 in purchases in each of these years, its cost of goods sold is $60,000 and its gross profit is $40,000 each year.

Ending Inventory Understated—Year 1 Assume that this company errs in computing its 2010 ending inventory and reports $16,000 instead of the correct amount of $20,000. The effects of this error are shown in Exhibit 6.11. The $4,000 understatement of 2010 ending inventory causes a $4,000 overstatement in 2010 cost of goods sold and a $4,000 understatement in both gross profit and net income for 2010. We see that these effects match the effects predicted in Exhibit 6.10.

EXHIBIT 6.11

Effects of Inventory Errors on Three Periods' Income Statements

Income Statements	2010		2011		2012	
Sales		$100,000		$100,000		$100,000
Cost of goods sold						
Beginning inventory	$20,000		→ **$16,000***		→ $20,000	
Cost of goods purchased	60,000		60,000		60,000	
Goods available for sale	80,000		76,000		80,000	
Ending inventory	**16,000***		20,000		20,000	
Cost of goods sold		64,000†		56,000†		60,000
Gross profit		36,000		44,000		40,000
Expenses		10,000		10,000		10,000
Net income		$ 26,000		$ 34,000		$ 30,000 ← Correct income is $30,000 for each year

* Correct amount is $20,000. † Correct amount is $60,000.

Ending Inventory Understated—Year 2 The 2010 understated ending inventory becomes the 2011 understated *beginning* inventory. We see in Exhibit 6.11 that this error causes an understatement in 2011 cost of goods sold and a $4,000 overstatement in both gross profit and net income for 2011.

Ending Inventory Understated—Year 3 Exhibit 6.11 shows that the 2010 ending inventory error affects only that period and the next. It does not affect 2012 results or any period thereafter. An inventory error is said to be *self-correcting* because it always yields an offsetting error in the next period. This does not reduce the severity of inventory errors. Managers, lenders, owners, and others make important decisions from analysis of income and costs.

Example: If 2010 ending inventory in Exhibit 6.11 is overstated by $3,000 (not understated by $4,000), what is the effect on cost of goods sold, gross profit, assets, and equity? *Answer:* Cost of goods sold is understated by $3,000 in 2010 and overstated by $3,000 in 2011. Gross profit and net income are overstated in 2010 and understated in 2011. Assets and equity are overstated in 2010.

Point: A former internal auditor at **Coca-Cola** alleges that just before midnight at a prior calendar year-end, fully loaded Coke trucks were ordered to drive about 2 feet away from the loading dock so that Coke could record millions of dollars in extra sales.

We can also do an analysis of beginning inventory errors. The income statement effects are the opposite of those for ending inventory.

Balance Sheet Effects Balance sheet effects of an inventory error can be seen by considering the accounting equation: Assets = Liabilities + Equity. For example, understating ending inventory understates both current and total assets. An understatement in ending inventory also yields an understatement in equity because of the understatement in net income. Exhibit 6.12 shows the effects of inventory errors on the current period's balance sheet amounts. Errors in *beginning* inventory do not yield misstatements in the end-of-period balance sheet, but they do affect that current period's income statement.

EXHIBIT 6.12

Effects of Inventory Errors on Current Period's Balance Sheet

Ending Inventory	Assets	Equity
Understated ↓	Understated ↓	Understated ↓
Overstated ↑	Overstated ↑	Overstated ↑

Quick Check

Answers — p. 254

8. Use LCM applied separately to the following individual items to compute ending inventory.

Product	Units	Unit Recorded Cost	Unit Market Cost
A	20	$ 6	$ 5
B	40	9	8
C	10	12	15

GLOBAL VIEW

This section discusses differences between U.S. GAAP and IFRS in the items and costs making up merchandise inventory, in the methods to assign costs to inventory, and in the methods to estimate inventory values.

Items and Costs Making Up Inventory Both U.S. GAAP and IFRS include broad and similar guidance for the items and costs making up merchandise inventory. Specifically, under both accounting systems, merchandise inventory includes all items that a company owns and holds for sale. Further, merchandise inventory includes costs of expenditures necessary, directly or indirectly, to bring those items to a salable condition and location.

Assigning Costs to Inventory Both U.S. GAAP and IFRS allow companies to use specific identification in assigning costs to inventory. Further, both systems allow companies to apply a *cost flow assumption.* The usual cost flow assumptions are: FIFO, Weighted Average, and LIFO. However, IFRS does not (currently) allow use of LIFO. As the convergence project progresses, this prohibition may or may not persist.

Estimating Inventory Costs The value of inventory can change while it awaits sale to customers. That value can decrease or increase.

Decreases in Inventory Value Both U.S. GAAP and IFRS require companies to write down (reduce the cost recorded for) inventory when its value falls below the cost recorded. This is referred to as the *lower of cost or market* method explained in this chapter. U.S. GAAP prohibits any later increase in the recorded value of that inventory even if that decline in value is reversed through value increases in later periods. However, IFRS allows reversals of those write downs up to the original acquisition cost. For example, if **Research In Motion** wrote down its 2010 inventory from $622 million to $600 million, it could not reverse this in future periods even if its value increased to more than $622 million. However, if RIM applied IFRS, it could reverse that previous loss. (Another difference is that value refers to *replacement cost* under U.S. GAAP, but *net realizable value* under IFRS.)

RIM

Increases in Inventory Value Neither U.S. GAAP nor IFRS allow inventory to be adjusted upward beyond the original cost. (One exception is that IFRS requires agricultural assets such as animals, forests, and plants to be measured at fair value less point-of-sale costs.)

Nokia provides the following description of its inventory valuation procedures:

NOKIA

> Inventories are stated at the lower of cost or net realizable value. Cost . . . approximates actual cost on a FIFO (First-in First-out) basis. Net realizable value is the amount that can be realized from the sale of the inventory in the normal course of business after allowing for the costs of realization.

Inventory Turnover and Days' Sales in Inventory — Decision Analysis

Inventory Turnover

A3 Assess inventory management using both inventory turnover and days' sales in inventory.

Earlier chapters described two important ratios useful in evaluating a company's short term liquidity: current ratio and acid-test ratio. A merchandiser's ability to pay its short term obligations also depends on how quickly it sells its merchandise inventory. **Inventory turnover,** also called *merchandise inventory turnover,* is one ratio used to assess this and is defined in Exhibit 6.13.

EXHIBIT 6.13

Inventory Turnover

$$\textbf{Inventory turnover} = \frac{\textbf{Cost of goods sold}}{\textbf{Average inventory}}$$

This ratio reveals how many *times* a company turns over (sells) its inventory during a period. If a company's inventory greatly varies within a year, average inventory amounts can be computed from interim periods such as quarters or months.

Point: We must take care when comparing turnover ratios across companies that use different costing methods (such as FIFO and LIFO).

Users apply inventory turnover to help analyze short-term liquidity and to assess whether management is doing a good job controlling the amount of inventory available. A low ratio compared to that of competitors suggests inefficient use of assets. The company may be holding more inventory than it needs to support its sales volume. Similarly, a very high ratio compared to that of competitors suggests inventory might be too low. This can cause lost sales if customers must back-order merchandise. Inventory turnover has no simple rule except to say *a high ratio is preferable provided inventory is adequate to meet demand.*

Days' Sales in Inventory

To better interpret inventory turnover, many users measure the adequacy of inventory to meet sales demand. **Days' sales in inventory,** also called *days' stock on hand,* is a ratio that reveals how much inventory is available in terms of the number of days' sales. It can be interpreted as the number of days one can sell from inventory if no new items are purchased. This ratio is often viewed as a measure of the buffer against out-of-stock inventory and is useful in evaluating liquidity of inventory. It is defined in Exhibit 6.14.

Point: Inventory turnover is higher and days' sales in inventory is lower for industries such as foods and other perishable products. The reverse holds for nonperishable product industries.

EXHIBIT 6.14

Days' Sales in Inventory

$$\textbf{Days' sales in inventory} = \frac{\textbf{Ending inventory}}{\textbf{Cost of goods sold}} \times 365$$

Days' sales in inventory focuses on ending inventory and it estimates how many days it will take to convert inventory at the end of a period into accounts receivable or cash. Days' sales in inventory focuses on *ending* inventory whereas inventory turnover focuses on *average* inventory.

Point: Days' sales in inventory for many Ford models has risen: Freestyle, 122 days; Montego, 109 days; Five Hundred, 118 days. The industry average is 73 days. (*BusinessWeek*)

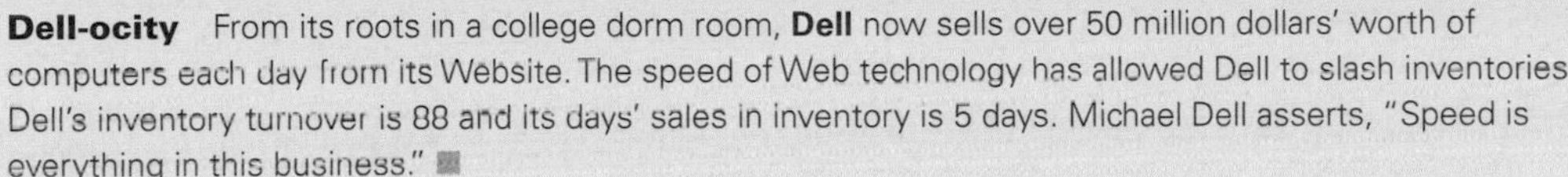

Decision Insight

Dell-ocity From its roots in a college dorm room, **Dell** now sells over 50 million dollars' worth of computers each day from its Website. The speed of Web technology has allowed Dell to slash inventories. Dell's inventory turnover is 88 and its days' sales in inventory is 5 days. Michael Dell asserts, "Speed is everything in this business." ■

Analysis of Inventory Management

Inventory management is a major emphasis for merchandisers. They must both plan and control inventory purchases and sales. **Toys "R" Us** is one of those merchandisers. Its inventory in fiscal year 2009 was $1,781 million. This inventory constituted 59% of its current assets and 21% of its total assets. We apply the analysis tools in this section to Toys "R" Us, as shown in Exhibit 6.15—also see margin graph.

EXHIBIT 6.15

Inventory Turnover and Days' Sales in Inventory for Toys "R" Us

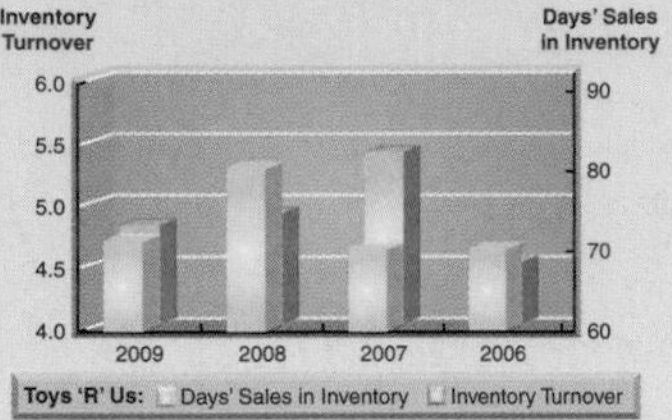

($ millions)	2009	2008	2007	2006
Cost of goods sold	$8,976	$8,987	$8,638	$7,652
Ending inventory	$1,781	$1,998	$1,690	$1,488
Inventory turnover	**4.8** times	**4.9** times	**5.4** times	**4.5** times
Industry inventory turnover	3.2 times	3.4 times	3.0 times	2.8 times
Days' sales in inventory	**72** days	**81** days	**71** days	**71** days
Industry days' sales in inventory	124 days	135 days	129 days	135 days

Its 2009 inventory turnover of 4.8 times means that Toys "R" Us turns over its inventory 4.8 times per year, or once every 76 days (365 days ÷ 4.8). We prefer inventory turnover to be high provided inventory is not out of stock and the company is not losing customers. The second metric, the 2009 days' sales in inventory of 72 days, reveals that it is carrying 72 days of sales in inventory. This inventory buffer seems more than adequate. Toys "R" Us would benefit from further management efforts to increase inventory turnover and reduce inventory levels.

Decision Maker Answer — p. 253

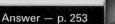

Entrepreneur Analysis of your retail store yields an inventory turnover of 5.0 and a days' sales in inventory of 73 days. The industry norm for inventory turnover is 4.4 and for days' sales in inventory is 74 days. What is your assessment of inventory management? ■

DEMONSTRATION PROBLEM

Craig Company uses a perpetual inventory system for its one product. Its beginning inventory, purchases, and sales during calendar year 2011 follow.

Date	Activity	Units Acquired at Cost	Units Sold at Retail	Unit Inventory
Jan. 1	Beg. Inventory	400 units @ $14 = $ 5,600		400 units
Jan. 15	Sale		200 units @ $30	200 units
March 10	Purchase	200 units @ $15 = $ 3,000		400 units
April 1	Sale		200 units @ $30	200 units
May 9	Purchase	300 units @ $16 = $ 4,800		500 units
Sept. 22	Purchase	250 units @ $20 = $ 5,000		750 units
Nov. 1	Sale		300 units @ $35	450 units
Nov. 28	Purchase	100 units @ $21 = $ 2,100		550 units
	Totals	1,250 units $20,500	700 units	

Additional tracking data for specific identification: (1) January 15 sale—200 units @ $14, (2) April 1 sale—200 units @ $15, and (3) November 1 sale—200 units @ $14 and 100 units @ $20.

Required

1. Calculate the cost of goods available for sale.
2. Apply the four different methods of inventory costing (FIFO, LIFO, weighted average, and specific identification) to calculate ending inventory and cost of goods sold under each method.
3. Compute gross profit earned by the company for each of the four costing methods in part 2. Also, report the inventory amount reported on the balance sheet for each of the four methods.

4. In preparing financial statements for year 2011, the financial officer was instructed to use FIFO but failed to do so and instead computed cost of goods sold according to LIFO. Determine the impact on year 2011's income from the error. Also determine the effect of this error on year 2012's income. Assume no income taxes.
5. Management wants a report that shows how changing from FIFO to another method would change net income. Prepare a table showing (1) the cost of goods sold amount under each of the four methods, (2) the amount by which each cost of goods sold total is different from the FIFO cost of goods sold, and (3) the effect on net income if another method is used instead of FIFO.

PLANNING THE SOLUTION

- Compute cost of goods available for sale by multiplying the units of beginning inventory and each purchase by their unit costs to determine the total cost of goods available for sale.
- Prepare a perpetual FIFO table starting with beginning inventory and showing how inventory changes after each purchase and after each sale (see Exhibit 6.5).
- Prepare a perpetual LIFO table starting with beginning inventory and showing how inventory changes after each purchase and after each sale (see Exhibit 6.6).
- Make a table of purchases and sales recalculating the average cost of inventory prior to each sale to arrive at the weighted average cost of ending inventory. Total the average costs associated with each sale to determine cost of goods sold (see Exhibit 6.7).
- Prepare a table showing the computation of cost of goods sold and ending inventory using the specific identification method (see Exhibit 6.4).
- Compare the year-end 2011 inventory amounts under FIFO and LIFO to determine the misstatement of year 2011 income that results from using LIFO. The errors for year 2011 and 2012 are equal in amount but opposite in effect.
- Create a table showing cost of goods sold under each method and how net income would differ from FIFO net income if an alternate method is adopted.

SOLUTION TO DEMONSTRATION PROBLEM

1. Cost of goods available for sale (this amount is the same for all methods).

Date		Units	Unit Cost	Cost
Jan. 1	Beg. Inventory	400	$14	$ 5,600
March 10	Purchase	200	15	3,000
May 9	Purchase	300	16	4,800
Sept. 22	Purchase	250	20	5,000
Nov. 28	Purchase	100	21	2,100
Total goods available for sale		1,250		$20,500

2a. FIFO perpetual method.

Date	Goods Purchased	Cost of Goods Sold	Inventory Balance	
Jan. 1	Beginning balance		400 @ $14	= $ 5,600
Jan. 15		200 @ $14 = $2,800	200 @ $14	= $ 2,800
Mar. 10	200 @ $15 = $3,000		200 @ $14 200 @ $15	= $ 5,800
April 1		200 @ $14 = $2,800	200 @ $15	= $ 3,000
May 9	300 @ $16 = $4,800		200 @ $15 300 @ $16	= $ 7,800
Sept. 22	250 @ $20 = $5,000		200 @ $15 300 @ $16 250 @ $20	= $12,800
Nov. 1		200 @ $15 = $3,000 100 @ $16 = $1,600	200 @ $16 250 @ $20	= $ 8,200
Nov. 28	100 @ $21 = $2,100		200 @ $16 250 @ $20 100 @ $21	= **$10,300**
Total cost of goods sold		**$10,200**		

Note to students: **In a classroom situation,** once we compute cost of goods available for sale, we can compute the amount for either cost of goods sold or ending inventory—it is a matter of preference. **In practice,** the costs of items sold are identified as sales are made and immediately transferred from the inventory account to the cost of goods sold account. The previous solution showing the line-by-line approach illustrates actual application in practice. The following alternate solutions illustrate that, once the concepts are understood, other solution approaches are available. Although this is only shown for FIFO, it could be shown for all methods.

Alternate Methods to Compute FIFO Perpetual Numbers

[FIFO Alternate No. 1: Computing cost of goods sold first]

Cost of goods available for sale (from part 1)			$ 20,500
Cost of goods sold			
Jan. 15	Sold (200 @ $14)	$2,800	
April 1	Sold (200 @ $14)	2,800	
Nov. 1	Sold (200 @ $15 and 100 @ $16)	4,600	10,200
Ending inventory			**$10,300**

[FIFO Alternate No. 2: Computing ending inventory first]

Cost of goods available for sale (from part 1)			$ 20,500
Ending inventory*			
Nov. 28	Purchase (100 @ $21)	$2,100	
Sept. 22	Purchase (250 @ $20)	5,000	
May 9	Purchase (200 @ $16)	3,200	
Ending inventory			**10,300**
Cost of goods sold			**$10,200**

* Since FIFO assumes that the earlier costs are the first to flow out, we determine ending inventory by assigning the most recent costs to the remaining items.

2b. LIFO perpetual method.

Date	Goods Purchased	Cost of Goods Sold	Inventory Balance	
Jan. 1	Beginning balance		400 @ $14	= $ 5,600
Jan. 15		200 @ $14 = $2,800	200 @ $14	= $ 2,800
Mar. 10	200 @ $15 = $3,000		200 @ $14 200 @ $15	= $ 5,800
April 1		200 @ $15 = $3,000	200 @ $14	= $ 2,800
May 9	300 @ $16 = $4,800		200 @ $14 300 @ $16	= $ 7,600
Sept. 22	250 @ $20 = $5,000		200 @ $14 300 @ $16 250 @ $20	= $12,600
Nov. 1		250 @ $20 = $5,000 50 @ $16 = $ 800	200 @ $14 250 @ $16	= $ 6,800
Nov. 28	100 @ $21 = $2,100		200 @ $14 250 @ $16 100 @ $21	= **$8,900**
Total cost of goods sold		**$11,600**		

2c. Weighted average perpetual method.

Date	Goods Purchased	Cost of Goods Sold	Inventory Balance	
Jan. 1	Beginning balance		400 @ $14	= $ 5,600
Jan. 15		200 @ $14 = $2,800	200 @ $14	= $ 2,800
Mar. 10	200 @ $15 = $3,000		200 @ $14 200 @ $15 (avg. cost is $14.5)	= $ 5,800
April 1		200 @ $14.5 = $2,900	200 @ $14.5	= $ 2,900
May 9	300 @ $16 = $4,800		200 @ $14.5 300 @ $16 (avg. cost is $15.4)	= $ 7,700
Sept. 22	250 @ $20 = $5,000		200 @ $14.5 300 @ $16 250 @ $20 (avg. cost is $16.93)	= $ 12,700
Nov. 1		300 @ $16.93 = $5,079	450 @ $16.93	= $ 7,618.5
Nov. 28	100 @ $21 = $2,100		450 @ $16.93 100 @ $21	= $9,718.5
Total cost of goods sold*		**$10,779**		

* The cost of goods sold ($10,779) plus ending inventory ($9,718.5) is $2.5 less than the cost of goods available for sale ($20,500) due to rounding.

2d. Specific identification method.

Date	Goods Purchased	Cost of Goods Sold	Inventory Balance	
Jan. 1	Beginning balance		400 @ $14	= $ 5,600
Jan. 15		200 @ $14 = $2,800	200 @ $14	= $ 2,800
Mar. 10	200 @ $15 = $3,000		200 @ $14 200 @ $15	= $ 5,800
April 1		200 @ $15 = $3,000	200 @ $14	= $ 2,800
May 9	300 @ $16 = $4,800		200 @ $14 300 @ $16	= $ 7,600
Sept. 22	250 @ $20 = $5,000		200 @ $14 300 @ $16 250 @ $20	= $ 12,600
Nov. 1		200 @ $14 = $2,800 100 @ $20 = $2,000	300 @ $16 150 @ $20	= $ 7,800
Nov. 28	100 @ $21 = $2,100		300 @ $16 150 @ $20 100 @ $21	= $ 9,900
Total cost of goods sold		**$10,600**		

3.

	FIFO	LIFO	Weighted Average	Specific Identification
Income Statement				
Sales*	$ 22,500	$22,500	$ 22,500	$22,500
Cost of goods sold	10,200	11,600	10,779	10,600
Gross profit	$ 12,300	$10,900	$ 11,721	$11,900
Balance Sheet				
Inventory	$10,300	$ 8,900	$9,718.5	$ 9,900

* Sales = (200 units × $30) + (200 units × $30) + (300 units × $35) = $22,500

4. Mistakenly using LIFO when FIFO should have been used overstates cost of goods sold in year 2011 by $1,400, which is the difference between the FIFO and LIFO amounts of ending inventory. It understates income in 2011 by $1,400. In year 2012, income is overstated by $1,400 because of the understatement in beginning inventory.
5. Analysis of the effects of alternative inventory methods.

	Cost of Goods Sold	Difference from FIFO Cost of Goods Sold	Effect on Net Income If Adopted Instead of FIFO
FIFO	$10,200	—	—
LIFO	11,600	+$1,400	$1,400 lower
Weighted average	10,779	+ 579	579 lower
Specific identification	10,600	+ 400	400 lower

APPENDIX

6A Inventory Costing under a Periodic System

P3 Compute inventory in a periodic system using the methods of specific identification, FIFO, LIFO, and weighted average.

The basic aim of the periodic system and the perpetual system is the same: to assign costs to inventory and cost of goods sold. The same four methods are used to assign costs under both systems: specific identification; first-in, first-out; last-in, first-out; and weighted average. We use information from Trekking to show how to assign costs using these four methods with a periodic system. Data for sales and purchases are in Exhibit 6A.1. Also, recall that we explained the accounting entries under a periodic system in Appendix 5A.

EXHIBIT 6A.1

Purchases and Sales of Goods

Date	Activity	Units Acquired at Cost	Units Sold at Retail	Unit Inventory
Aug. 1	Beginning inventory	10 units @ $ 91 = $ 910		10 units
Aug. 3	Purchases	15 units @ $106 = $ 1,590		25 units
Aug. 14	Sales		20 units @ $130	5 units
Aug. 17	Purchases	20 units @ $115 = $ 2,300		25 units
Aug. 28	Purchases	10 units @ $119 = $ 1,190		35 units
Aug. 31	Sales		23 units @ $150	12 units
	Totals	55 units $5,990	43 units	

Specific Identification We use the above sales and purchases information and the specific identification method to assign costs to ending inventory and units sold. Trekking's internal data reveal the following specific unit sales:

August 14	Sold 8 bikes costing $91 each and 12 bikes costing $106 each
August 31	Sold 2 bikes costing $91 each, 3 bikes costing $106 each, 15 bikes costing $115 each, and 3 bikes costing $119 each

Applying specific identification and using the information above, we prepare Exhibit 6A.2. This exhibit starts with 10 bikes at $91 each in beginning inventory. On August 3, 15 more bikes are purchased at $106 each for $1,590. Inventory available now consists of 10 bikes at $91 each and 15 bikes at $106 each, for a total of $2,500. On August 14 (see specific sales data above), 20 bikes costing $2,000 are sold—leaving 5 bikes costing $500 in inventory. On August 17, 20 bikes costing $2,300 are purchased, and on August 28, another 10 bikes costing $1,190 are purchased, for a total of 35 bikes costing $3,990 in inventory. On August 31 (see specific sales above), 23 bikes costing $2,582 are sold, which leaves 12 bikes costing $1,408 in ending inventory. Carefully study Exhibit 6A.2 to see the flow of costs both in and out of inventory. Each unit, whether sold or remaining in inventory, has its own specific cost attached to it.

EXHIBIT 6A.2

Specific Identification Computations

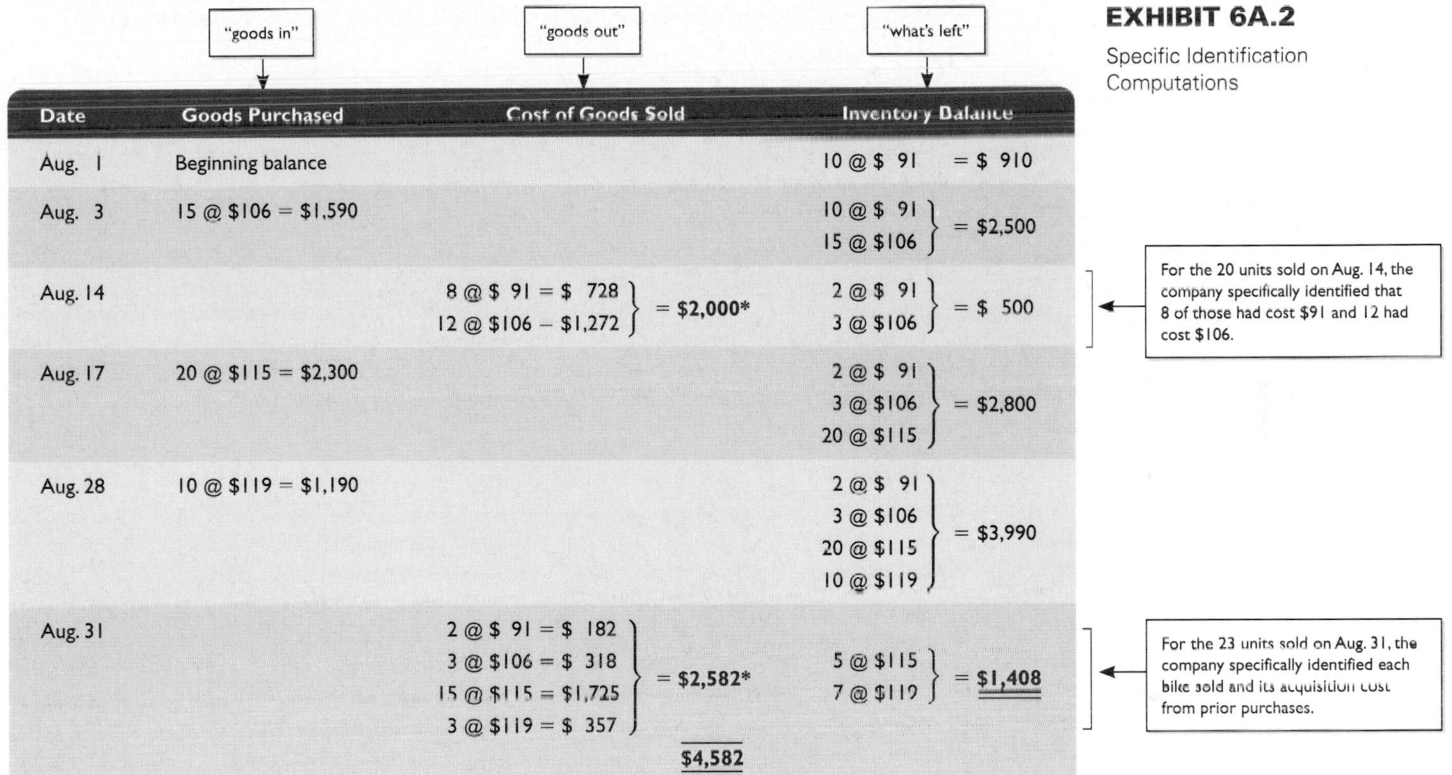

Date	Goods Purchased ("goods in")	Cost of Goods Sold ("goods out")		Inventory Balance ("what's left")	
Aug. 1	Beginning balance			10 @ $ 91	= $ 910
Aug. 3	15 @ $106 = $1,590			10 @ $ 91 15 @ $106	= $2,500
Aug. 14		8 @ $ 91 = $ 728 12 @ $106 = $1,272	= $2,000*	2 @ $ 91 3 @ $106	= $ 500
Aug. 17	20 @ $115 = $2,300			2 @ $ 91 3 @ $106 20 @ $115	= $2,800
Aug. 28	10 @ $119 = $1,190			2 @ $ 91 3 @ $106 20 @ $115 10 @ $119	= $3,990
Aug. 31		2 @ $ 91 = $ 182 3 @ $106 = $ 318 15 @ $115 = $1,725 3 @ $119 = $ 357	= $2,582*	5 @ $115 7 @ $119	= $1,408
			$4,582		

For the 20 units sold on Aug. 14, the company specifically identified that 8 of those had cost $91 and 12 had cost $106.

For the 23 units sold on Aug. 31, the company specifically identified each bike sold and its acquisition cost from prior purchases.

* Identification of items sold (and their costs) is obtained from internal documents that track each unit from its purchase to its sale.

When using specific identification, Trekking's cost of goods sold reported on the income statement totals **$4,582**, the sum of $2,000 and $2,582 from the third column of Exhibit 6A.2. Trekking's ending inventory reported on the balance sheet is **$1,408**, which is the final inventory balance from the fourth column. The purchases and sales entries for Exhibit 6A.2 follow (the colored boldface numbers are those affected by the cost flow assumption).

Point: The assignment of costs to the goods sold and to inventory using specific identification is the same for both the perpetual and periodic systems.

Purchases

Date	Account	Debit	Credit
Aug. 3	Purchases	1,590	
	Accounts Payable		1,590
17	Purchases	2,300	
	Accounts Payable		2,300
28	Purchases	1,190	
	Accounts Payable		1,190

Sales

Date	Account	Debit	Credit
Aug. 14	Accounts Receivable	2,600	
	Sales		2,600
31	Accounts Receivable	3,450	
	Sales		3,450
	Adjusting Entry		
31	Merchandise Inventory	**1,408**	
	Income Summary		498
	Merchandise Inventory		**910**

First-In, First-Out The first-in, first-out (FIFO) method of assigning costs to inventory assumes that inventory items are sold in the order acquired. When sales occur, the costs of the earliest units acquired are charged to cost of goods sold. This leaves the costs from the most recent purchases in ending inventory. Use of FIFO for computing the cost of inventory and cost of goods sold is shown in Exhibit 6A.3.

This exhibit starts with computing $5,990 in total units available for sale—this is given to us at the start of this appendix. Applying FIFO, we know that the 12 units in ending inventory will be reported at the cost of the most recent 12 purchases. Reviewing purchases in reverse order, we assign costs to the 12 bikes in ending inventory as follows: $119 cost to 10 bikes and $115 cost to 2 bikes. This yields 12 bikes costing $1,420 in ending inventory. We then subtract this $1,420 in ending inventory from $5,990 in cost of goods available to get $4,570 in cost of goods sold.

EXHIBIT 6A.3

FIFO Computations—Periodic System

Exhibit 6A.1 shows that the 12 units in ending inventory consist of 10 units from the latest purchase on Aug. 28 and 2 units from the next latest purchase on Aug. 17.

Total cost of 55 units available for sale (from Exhibit 6A.1)		$5,990
Less ending inventory priced using FIFO		
10 units from August 28 purchase at $119 each	$1,190	
2 units from August 17 purchase at $115 each	230	
Ending inventory		1,420
Cost of goods sold		$4,570

Trekking's ending inventory reported on the balance sheet is **$1,420**, and its cost of goods sold reported on the income statement is **$4,570**. These amounts are the same as those computed using the perpetual system. This always occurs because the most recent purchases are in ending inventory under both systems. The purchases and sales entries for Exhibit 6A.3 follow (the colored boldface numbers are those affected by the cost flow assumption).

Point: The assignment of costs to the goods sold and to inventory using FIFO is the same for both the perpetual and periodic systems.

Purchases

Date	Account	Debit	Credit
Aug. 3	Purchases	1,590	
	Accounts Payable		1,590
17	Purchases	2,300	
	Accounts Payable		2,300
28	Purchases	1,190	
	Accounts Payable		1,190

Sales

Date	Account	Debit	Credit
Aug. 14	Accounts Receivable	2,600	
	Sales		2,600
31	Accounts Receivable	3,450	
	Sales		3,450
	Adjusting Entry		
31	Merchandise Inventory	**1,420**	
	Income Summary		510
	Merchandise Inventory		**910**

Last-In, First-Out The last-in, first-out (LIFO) method of assigning costs assumes that the most recent purchases are sold first. These more recent costs are charged to the goods sold, and the costs of the earliest purchases are assigned to inventory. LIFO results in costs of the most recent purchases being assigned to cost of goods sold, which means that LIFO comes close to matching current costs of goods sold with revenues. Use of LIFO for computing cost of inventory and cost of goods sold is shown in Exhibit 6A.4.

This exhibit starts with computing $5,990 in total units available for sale—this is given to us at the start of this appendix. Applying LIFO, we know that the 12 units in ending inventory will be reported at the cost of the earliest 12 purchases. Reviewing the earliest purchases in order, we assign costs to the 12 bikes in ending inventory as follows: $91 cost to 10 bikes and $106 cost to 2 bikes. This yields 12 bikes costing $1,122 in ending inventory. We then subtract this $1,122 in ending inventory from $5,990 in cost of goods available to get $4,868 in cost of goods sold.

EXHIBIT 6A.4

LIFO Computations—Periodic System

Exhibit 6A.1 shows that the 12 units in ending inventory consist of 10 units from the earliest purchase (beg. inv.) and 2 units from the next earliest purchase on Aug. 3.

Total cost of 55 units available for sale (from Exhibit 6A.1)		$5,990
Less ending inventory priced using LIFO		
10 units in beginning inventory at $91 each	$910	
2 units from August 3 purchase at $106 each	212	
Ending inventory		1,122
Cost of goods sold		$4,868

Trekking's ending inventory reported on the balance sheet is **$1,122**, and its cost of goods sold reported on the income statement is **$4,868**. When LIFO is used with the periodic system, cost of goods sold is assigned costs from the most recent purchases for the period. With a perpetual system, cost of goods sold is assigned costs from the most recent purchases at the point of *each sale*. The purchases and sales entries for Exhibit 6A.4 follow (the colored boldface numbers are those affected by the cost flow assumption).

Purchases

Date	Account	Debit	Credit
Aug. 3	Purchases	1,590	
	Accounts Payable		1,590
17	Purchases	2,300	
	Accounts Payable		2,300
28	Purchases	1,190	
	Accounts Payable		1,190

Sales

Date	Account	Debit	Credit
Aug. 14	Accounts Receivable	2,600	
	Sales		2,600
31	Accounts Receivable	3,450	
	Sales		3,450
	Adjusting Entry		
31	Merchandise Inventory	**1,122**	
	Income Summary		212
	Merchandise Inventory		**910**

Weighted Average The **weighted average** or **WA** (also called **average cost**) method of assigning cost requires that we use the average cost per unit of inventory at the end of the period. Weighted average cost per unit equals the cost of goods available for sale divided by the units available. The weighted average method of assigning cost involves three important steps. The first two steps are shown in Exhibit 6A.5. First, multiply the per unit cost for beginning inventory and each particular purchase by the corresponding number of units (from Exhibit 6A.1). Second, add these amounts and divide by the total number of units available for sale to find the weighted average cost per unit.

EXHIBIT 6A.5

Weighted Average Cost per Unit

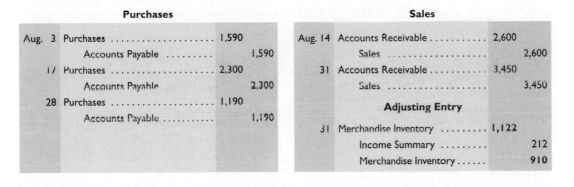

Step 1:	10 units @ $ 91 =	$ 910
	15 units @ $106 =	1,590
	20 units @ $115 =	2,300
	10 units @ $119 =	1,190
	55	$5,990
Step 2:	$5,990/55 units = **$108.91** weighted average cost per unit	

Example: In Exhibit 6A.5, if 5 more units had been purchased at $120 each, what would be the weighted average cost per unit?
Answer: $109.83 ($6,590/60)

The third step is to use the weighted average cost per unit to assign costs to inventory and to the units sold as shown in Exhibit 6A.6.

EXHIBIT 6A.6

Weighted Average Computations—Periodic

Step 3:	Total cost of 55 units available for sale (from Exhibit 6A.1)	$5,990
	Less **ending inventory** priced on a weighted average cost basis: 12 units at $108.91 each (from Exhibit 6A.5)	1,307
	Cost of goods sold	**$4,683**

Trekking's ending inventory reported on the balance sheet is **$1,307**, and its cost of goods sold reported on the income statement is **$4,683** when using the weighted average (periodic) method. The purchases and sales entries for Exhibit 6A.6 follow (the colored boldface numbers are those affected by the cost flow assumption).

Point: Weighted average usually yields different results for the perpetual and the periodic systems because under a perpetual system it recomputes the per unit cost prior to each sale, whereas under a periodic system, the per unit cost is computed only at the end of a period.

Purchases

Date	Account	Debit	Credit
Aug. 3	Purchases	1,590	
	Accounts Payable		1,590
17	Purchases	2,300	
	Accounts Payable		2,300
28	Purchases	1,190	
	Accounts Payable		1,190

Sales

Date	Account	Debit	Credit
Aug. 14	Accounts Receivable	2,600	
	Sales		2,600
31	Accounts Receivable	3,450	
	Sales		3,450
	Adjusting Entry		
31	Merchandise Inventory	**1,307**	
	Income Summary		397
	Merchandise Inventory		**910**

Point: LIFO inventory is often less than the inventory's replacement cost because LIFO inventory is valued using the oldest inventory purchase costs.

Financial Statement Effects When purchase prices do not change, each inventory costing method assigns the same cost amounts to inventory and to cost of goods sold. When purchase prices are different, however, the methods nearly always assign different cost amounts. We show these differences in Exhibit 6A.7 using Trekking's data.

EXHIBIT 6A.7

Financial Statement Effects of Inventory Costing Methods

TREKKING COMPANY For Month Ended August 31	Specific Identification	FIFO	LIFO	Weighted Average
Income Statement				
Sales	$ 6,050	$ 6,050	$ 6,050	$ 6,050
Cost of goods sold	**4,582**	**4,570**	**4,868**	**4,683**
Gross profit	1,468	1,480	1,182	1,367
Expenses	450	450	450	450
Income before taxes	1,018	1,030	732	917
Income tax expense (30%)	305	309	220	275
Net income	**$ 713**	**$ 721**	**$ 512**	**$ 642**
Balance Sheet				
Inventory	**$1,408**	**$1,420**	**$1,122**	**$1,307**

This exhibit reveals two important results. First, when purchase costs *regularly rise,* as in Trekking's case, observe the following:

- FIFO assigns the lowest amount to cost of goods sold—yielding the highest gross profit and net income.
- LIFO assigns the highest amount to cost of goods sold—yielding the lowest gross profit and net income, which also yields a temporary tax advantage by postponing payment of some income tax.
- Weighted average yields results between FIFO and LIFO.
- Specific identification always yields results that depend on which units are sold.

Second, when costs *regularly decline,* the reverse occurs for FIFO and LIFO. FIFO gives the highest cost of goods sold—yielding the lowest gross profit and income. And LIFO gives the lowest cost of goods sold—yielding the highest gross profit and income.

All four inventory costing methods are acceptable in practice. A company must disclose the inventory method it uses. Each method offers certain advantages as follows:

- FIFO assigns an amount to inventory on the balance sheet that approximates its current cost; it also mimics the actual flow of goods for most businesses.
- LIFO assigns an amount to cost of goods sold on the income statement that approximates its current cost; it also better matches current costs with revenues in computing gross profit.
- Weighted average tends to smooth out erratic changes in costs.
- Specific identification exactly matches the costs of items with the revenues they generate.

Quick Check Answers — p. 254

9. A company reports the following beginning inventory and purchases, and it ends the period with 30 units in inventory.

Beginning inventory	100 units at $10 cost per unit
Purchase 1	40 units at $12 cost per unit
Purchase 2	20 units at $14 cost per unit

a. Compute ending inventory using the FIFO periodic system.

b. Compute cost of goods sold using the LIFO periodic system.

APPENDIX

Inventory Estimation Methods 6B

P4 Apply both the retail inventory and gross profit methods to estimate inventory.

Inventory sometimes requires estimation for two reasons. First, companies often require **interim statements** (financial statements prepared for periods of less than one year), but they only annually take a physical count of inventory. Second, companies may require an inventory estimate if some casualty such as fire or flood makes taking a physical count impossible. Estimates are usually only required for companies that use the periodic system. Companies using a perpetual system would presumably have updated inventory data.

This appendix describes two methods to estimate inventory.

Retail Inventory Method To avoid the time-consuming and expensive process of taking a physical inventory each month or quarter, some companies use the **retail inventory method** to estimate cost of goods sold and ending inventory. Some companies even use the retail inventory method to prepare the annual statements. **Home Depot**, for instance, says in its annual report: "Inventories are stated at the lower of cost (first-in, first-out) or market, as determined by the retail inventory method." A company may also estimate inventory for audit purposes or when inventory is damaged or destroyed.

Point: When a retailer takes a physical inventory, it can restate the retail value of inventory to a cost basis by applying the cost-to-retail ratio. It can also estimate the amount of shrinkage by comparing the inventory computed with the amount from a physical inventory.

The retail inventory method uses a three-step process to estimate ending inventory. We need to know the amount of inventory a company had at the beginning of the period in both *cost* and *retail* amounts. We already explained how to compute the cost of inventory. The *retail amount of inventory* refers to its dollar amount measured using selling prices of inventory items. We also need to know the net amount of goods purchased (minus returns, allowances, and discounts) in the period, both at cost and at retail. The amount of net sales at retail is also needed. The process is shown in Exhibit 6B.1.

The reasoning behind the retail inventory method is that if we can get a good estimate of the cost-to-retail ratio, we can multiply ending inventory at retail by this ratio to estimate ending inventory at cost. We show in Exhibit 6B.2 how these steps are applied to estimate ending inventory for a typical company. First, we find that $100,000 of goods (at retail selling prices) were available for sale. We see that $70,000 of these goods were sold, leaving $30,000 (retail value) of merchandise in ending inventory. Second, the cost of these goods is 60% of the $100,000 retail value. Third, since cost for these goods is 60% of retail, the estimated cost of ending inventory is $18,000.

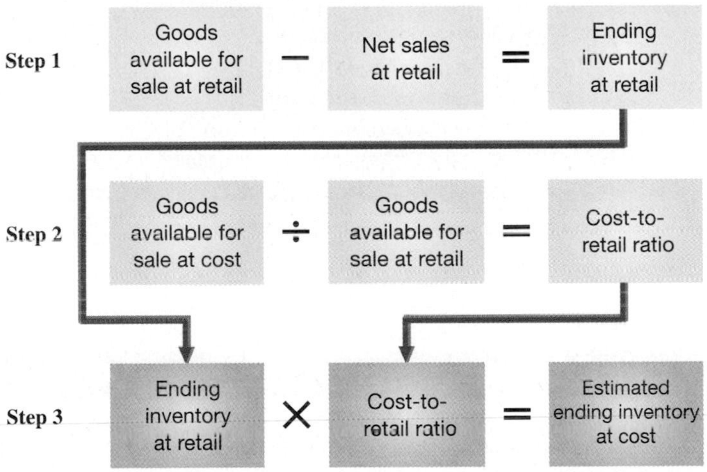

EXHIBIT 6B.1

Retail Inventory Method of Inventory Estimation

Step 1	Goods available for sale at retail	−	Net sales at retail	=	Ending inventory at retail
Step 2	Goods available for sale at cost	÷	Goods available for sale at retail	=	Cost-to-retail ratio
Step 3	Ending inventory at retail	×	Cost-to-retail ratio	=	Estimated ending inventory at cost

Example: What is the cost of ending inventory in Exhibit 6B.2 if the cost of beginning inventory is $22,500 and its retail value is $34,500? *Answer:* $30,000 × 62% = $18,600

EXHIBIT 6B.2

Estimated Inventory Using the Retail Inventory Method

		At Cost	At Retail
	Goods available for sale		
	Beginning inventory	$ 20,500	$ 34,500
	Cost of goods purchased	39,500	65,500
Step 1:	Goods available for sale	60,000	100,000
	Deduct net sales at retail		**70,000**
	Ending inventory at retail		**$ 30,000**
Step 2:	**Cost-to-retail ratio: ($60,000 ÷ $100,000) = 60%**		
Step 3:	**Estimated ending inventory at cost ($30,000 × 60%)**	$18,000	

Gross Profit Method The **gross profit method** estimates the cost of ending inventory by applying the gross profit ratio to net sales (at retail). This type of estimate often is needed when inventory is destroyed, lost, or stolen. These cases require an inventory estimate so that a company can file a claim with its insurer. Users also apply this method to see whether inventory amounts from a physical count are reasonable. This method uses the historical relation between cost of goods sold and net sales to estimate the proportion of cost of goods sold making up current sales. This cost of goods sold estimate is then subtracted from cost of goods available for sale to estimate the ending inventory at cost. These two steps are shown in Exhibit 6B.3.

EXHIBIT 6B.3

Gross Profit Method of Inventory Estimation

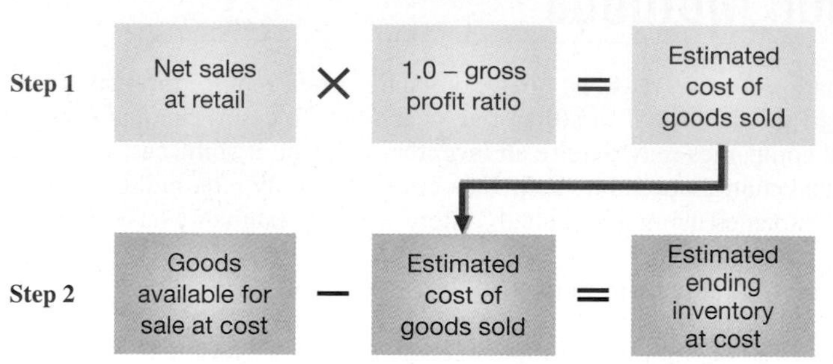

To illustrate, assume that a company's inventory is destroyed by fire in March 2011. When the fire occurs, the company's accounts show the following balances for January through March: sales, $31,500; sales returns, $1,500; inventory (January 1, 2011), $12,000; and cost of goods purchased, $20,500. If this company's gross profit ratio is 30%, then 30% of each net sales dollar is gross profit and 70% is cost of goods sold. We show in Exhibit 6B.4 how this 70% is used to estimate lost inventory of $11,500. To understand this exhibit, think of subtracting the cost of goods sold from the goods available for sale to get the ending inventory.

Point: A fire or other catastrophe can result in an insurance claim for lost inventory or income. Backup and off-site storage of data help ensure coverage for such losses.

Point: Reliability of the gross profit method depends on a good estimate of the gross profit ratio.

EXHIBIT 6B.4

Estimated Inventory Using the Gross Profit Method

	Goods available for sale		
	Inventory, January 1, 2011	$12,000	
	Cost of goods purchased	20,500	
	Goods available for sale (at cost)	32,500	
	Net sales at retail ($31,500 − $1,500)		$30,000
Step 1:	**Estimated cost of goods sold ($30,000 × 70%)**	**(21,000)** ←	× 0.70
Step 2:	**Estimated March inventory at cost**	**$11,500**	

Quick Check Answer — p. 254

10. Using the retail method and the following data, estimate the cost of ending inventory.

	Cost	Retail
Beginning inventory	$324,000	$530,000
Cost of goods purchased	195,000	335,000
Net sales		320,000

Summary

C1 **Identify the items making up merchandise inventory.** Merchandise inventory refers to goods owned by a company and held for resale. Three special cases merit our attention. Goods in transit are reported in inventory of the company that holds ownership rights. Goods on consignment are reported in the consignor's inventory. Goods damaged or obsolete are reported in inventory at their net realizable value.

C2 **Identify the costs of merchandise inventory.** Costs of merchandise inventory include expenditures necessary to bring an item to a salable condition and location. This includes its invoice cost minus any discount plus any added or incidental costs necessary to put it in a place and condition for sale.

A1 **Analyze the effects of inventory methods for both financial and tax reporting.** When purchase costs are rising or falling, the inventory costing methods are likely to assign different costs to inventory. Specific identification exactly matches costs and revenues. Weighted average smooths out cost changes. FIFO assigns an amount to inventory closely approximating current replacement cost. LIFO assigns the most recent costs incurred to cost of goods sold and likely better matches current costs with revenues.

A2 Analyze the effects of inventory errors on current and future financial statements. An error in the amount of ending inventory affects assets (inventory), net income (cost of goods sold), and equity for that period. Since ending inventory is next period's beginning inventory, an error in ending inventory affects next period's cost of goods sold and net income. Inventory errors in one period are offset in the next period.

A3 Assess inventory management using both inventory turnover and days' sales in inventory. We prefer a high inventory turnover, provided that goods are not out of stock and customers are not turned away. We use days' sales in inventory to assess the likelihood of goods being out of stock. We prefer a small number of days' sales in inventory if we can serve customer needs and provide a buffer for uncertainties.

P1 Compute inventory in a perpetual system using the methods of specific identification, FIFO, LIFO, and weighted average. Costs are assigned to the cost of goods sold account *each time* a sale occurs in a perpetual system. Specific identification assigns a cost to each item sold by referring to its actual cost (for example, its net invoice cost). Weighted average assigns a cost to items sold by dividing the current balance in the inventory account by the total items available for sale to determine cost per unit. We then multiply the number of units sold by this cost per unit to get the cost of each sale. FIFO assigns cost to items sold assuming that the earliest units purchased are the first units sold. LIFO assigns cost to items sold assuming that the most recent units purchased are the first units sold.

P2 Compute the lower of cost or market amount of inventory. Inventory is reported at market cost when market is *lower* than recorded cost, called the *lower of cost or market (LCM) inventory.* Market is typically measured as replacement cost. Lower of cost or market can be applied separately to each item, to major categories of items, or to the entire inventory.

P3A Compute inventory in a periodic system using the methods of specific identification, FIFO, LIFO, and weighted average. Periodic inventory systems allocate the cost of goods available for sale between cost of goods sold and ending inventory *at the end of a period.* Specific identification and FIFO give identical results whether the periodic or perpetual system is used. LIFO assigns costs to cost of goods sold assuming the last units purchased for the period are the first units sold. The weighted average cost per unit is computed by dividing the total cost of beginning inventory and net purchases for the period by the total number of units available. Then, it multiplies cost per unit by the number of units sold to give cost of goods sold.

P4B Apply both the retail inventory and gross profit methods to estimate inventory. The retail inventory method involves three steps: (1) goods available at retail minus net sales at retail equals ending inventory at retail, (2) goods available at cost divided by goods available at retail equals the cost-to-retail ratio, and (3) ending inventory at retail multiplied by the cost-to-retail ratio equals estimated ending inventory at cost. The gross profit method involves two steps: (1) net sales at retail multiplied by 1 minus the gross profit ratio equals estimated cost of goods sold, and (2) goods available at cost minus estimated cost of goods sold equals estimated ending inventory at cost.

Guidance Answers to Decision Maker and Decision Ethics

Financial Planner The FIFO method implies that the oldest costs are the first ones assigned to cost of goods sold. This leaves the most recent costs in ending inventory. You report this to your client and note that in most cases, the ending inventory of a company using FIFO is reported at or near its replacement cost. This means that your client need not in most cases adjust the reported value of inventory. Your answer changes only if there are major increases in replacement cost compared to the cost of recent purchases reported in inventory. When major increases in costs occur, your client might wish to adjust inventory (for internal reports) for the difference between the reported cost of inventory and its replacement cost. (*Note:* Decreases in costs of purchases are recognized under the lower of cost or market adjustment.)

Inventory Manager It seems your company can save (or at least postpone) taxes by switching to LIFO, but the switch is likely to reduce bonus money that you think you have earned and deserve. Since the U.S. tax code requires companies that use LIFO for tax reporting also to use it for financial reporting, your options are further constrained. Your best decision is to tell your superior about the tax savings with LIFO. You also should discuss your bonus plan and how this is likely to hurt you unfairly. You might propose to compute inventory under the LIFO method for reporting purposes but use the FIFO method for your bonus calculations. Another solution is to revise the bonus plan to reflect the company's use of the LIFO method.

Entrepreneur Your inventory turnover is markedly higher than the norm, whereas days' sales in inventory approximates the norm. Since your turnover is already 14% better than average, you are probably best served by directing attention to days' sales in inventory. You should see whether you can reduce the level of inventory while maintaining service to customers. Given your higher turnover, you should be able to hold less inventory.

Guidance Answers to Quick Checks

1. The matching principle.
2. Target reports these goods in its inventory.
3. Total cost assigned to the painting is $12,180, computed as $11,400 + $130 + $150 + $100 + $400.
4. Specific identification exactly matches costs and revenues. Weighted average tends to smooth out cost changes. FIFO assigns an amount to inventory that closely approximates current replacement cost. LIFO assigns the most recent costs incurred to cost of goods sold and likely better matches current costs with revenues.
5. FIFO—it gives a lower cost of goods sold, a higher gross profit, and a higher net income when costs are rising.

6. When costs are rising, LIFO gives a lower inventory figure on the balance sheet as compared to FIFO. FIFO's inventory amount approximates current replacement costs.
7. Cost of goods sold would be overstated by $10,000 in 2010 and understated by $10,000 in year 2011.
8. The reported LCM inventory amount (using items) is $540, computed as [(20 × $5) + (40 × $8) + (10 × $12)].
9.[A] **a.** FIFO periodic inventory = (20 × $14) + (10 × $12) = $400

b. LIFO periodic cost of goods sold = (20 × $14) + (40 × $12) + (70 × $10) = $1,460

10.[B] Estimated ending inventory (at cost) is $327,000. It is computed as follows:

Step 1: ($530,000 + $335,000) − $320,000 = $545,000

Step 2: $\frac{\$324{,}000 + \$195{,}000}{\$530{,}000 + \$335{,}000} = 60\%$

Step 3: $545,000 × 60% = $327,000

Key Terms

mhhe.com/wildFAP20e

Average cost (p. 234)
Conservatism constraint (p. 238)
Consignee (p. 228)
Consignor (p. 228)
Consistency concept (p. 237)
Days' sales in inventory (p. 241)
First-in, first-out (FIFO) (p. 233)
Gross profit method (p. 252)
Interim statements (p. 251)
Inventory turnover (p. 241)
Last-in, first-out (LIFO) (p. 233)
Lower of cost or market (LCM) (p. 237)
Net realizable value (p. 228)
Retail inventory method (p. 251)
Specific identification (p. 231)
Weighted average (p. 234)

Multiple Choice Quiz

Answers on p. 269

mhhe.com/wildFAP20e

Additional Quiz Questions are available at the book's Website.

Use the following information from Marvel Company for the month of July to answer questions 1 through 4.

July 1	Beginning inventory	75 units @ $25 each
July 3	Purchase	348 units @ $27 each
July 8	Sale	300 units
July 15	Purchase	257 units @ $28 each
July 23	Sale	275 units

1. Assume that Marvel uses a perpetual FIFO inventory system. What is the dollar value of its ending inventory?
   a. $2,940 **b.** $2,685 **c.** $2,625 **d.** $2,852 **e.** $2,705
2. Assume that Marvel uses a perpetual LIFO inventory system. What is the dollar value of its ending inventory?
   a. $2,940 **b.** $2,685 **c.** $2,625 **d.** $2,852 **e.** $2,705
3. Assume that Marvel uses a perpetual specific identification inventory system. Its ending inventory consists of 20 units from beginning inventory, 40 units from the July 3 purchase, and 45 units from the July 15 purchase. What is the dollar value of its ending inventory?
   a. $2,940 **b.** $2,685 **c.** $2,625 **d.** $2,852 **e.** $2,840
4.[A] Assume that Marvel uses a *periodic* FIFO inventory system. What is the dollar value of its ending inventory?
   a. $2,940 **b.** $2,685 **c.** $2,625 **d.** $2,852 **e.** $2,705
5. A company has cost of goods sold of $85,000 and ending inventory of $18,000. Its days' sales in inventory equals:
   a. 49.32 days **b.** 0.21 days **c.** 4.72 days **d.** 77.29 days **e.** 1,723.61 days

A(B) *Superscript letter A (B) denotes assignments based on Appendix 6A (6B).*
Icon denotes assignments that involve decision making.

Discussion Questions

1. Describe how costs flow from inventory to cost of goods sold for the following methods: (*a*) FIFO and (*b*) LIFO.
2. Where is the amount of merchandise inventory disclosed in the financial statements?
3. Why are incidental costs sometimes ignored in inventory costing? Under what accounting constraint is this permitted?
4. If costs are declining, will the LIFO or FIFO method of inventory valuation yield the lower cost of goods sold? Why?

5. What does the full-disclosure principle prescribe if a company changes from one acceptable accounting method to another?
6. Can a company change its inventory method each accounting period? Explain.
7. Does the accounting concept of consistency preclude any changes from one accounting method to another?
8. If inventory errors are said to correct themselves, why are accounting users concerned when such errors are made?
9. Explain the following statement: "Inventory errors correct themselves."
10. What is the meaning of *market* as it is used in determining the lower of cost or market for inventory?
11. What guidance does the accounting constraint of conservatism offer?
12. What factors contribute to (or cause) inventory shrinkage?
13.[A] What accounts are used in a periodic inventory system but not in a perpetual inventory system?
14. Refer to **Research In Motion**'s financial statements in Appendix A. On February 27, 2010, what percent of current assets are represented by inventory? RIM
15. Refer to **Apple**'s financial statements in Appendix A and compute its cost of goods available for sale for the year ended September 26, 2009. Apple
16. Refer to **Nokia**'s financial statements in Appendix A. Compute its cost of goods available for sale for the year ended December 31, 2009. NOKIA
17. Refer to **Palm**'s financial statements in Appendix A. What percent of its current assets are inventory as of May 31, 2008 and 2009? Palm
18.[D] When preparing interim financial statements, what two methods can companies utilize to estimate cost of goods sold and ending inventory?

connect

QUICK STUDY

QS 6-1
Inventory costing with FIFO perpetual
P1

A company reports the following beginning inventory and purchases for the month of January. On January 26, the company sells 360 units. What is the cost of the 155 units that remain in ending inventory at January 31, assuming costs are assigned based on a perpetual inventory system and use of FIFO? (Round per unit costs to three decimals, but inventory balances to the dollar.)

	Units	Unit Cost
Beginning inventory on January 1	320	$6.00
Purchase on January 9	85	6.40
Purchase on January 25	110	6.60

QS 6-2
Inventory costing with LIFO perpetual P1

Refer to the information in QS 6-1 and assume the perpetual inventory system is used. Determine the costs assigned to ending inventory when costs are assigned based on LIFO. (Round per unit costs to three decimals, but inventory balances to the dollar.)

QS 6-3
Inventory costing with weighted average perpetual P1
Check $960

Refer to the information in QS 6-1 and assume the perpetual inventory system is used. Determine the costs assigned to ending inventory when costs are assigned based on weighted average. (Round per unit costs to three decimals, but inventory balances to the dollar.)

QS 6-4
Computing goods available for sale P1

Segoe Company reports beginning inventory of 10 units at $50 each. Every week for four weeks it purchases an additional 10 units at respective costs of $51, $52, $55 and $60 per unit for weeks 1 through 4. Calculate the cost of goods available for sale and the units available for sale for this four-week period. Assume that no sales occur during those four weeks.

QS 6-5
Assigning costs with FIFO perpetual
P1

Mercedes Brown starts a merchandising business on December 1 and enters into three inventory purchases:

December 7	10 units @ $ 9 cost
December 14	20 units @ $10 cost
December 21	15 units @ $12 cost

Brown sells 18 units for $35 each on December 15. Seven of the sold units are from the December 7 purchase and eleven are from the December 14 purchase. Brown uses a perpetual inventory system. Determine the costs assigned to the December 31 ending inventory based on FIFO. (Round per unit costs to three decimals, but inventory balances to the dollar.)

QS 6-6
Inventory costing with LIFO perpetual P1

Refer to the information in QS 6-5 and assume the perpetual inventory system is used. Determine the costs assigned to ending inventory when costs are assigned based on LIFO. (Round per unit costs to three decimals, but inventory balances to the dollar.)

QS 6-7
Inventory costing with weighted average perpetual P1
Check End. Inv. = $296

Refer to the information in QS 6-5 and assume the perpetual inventory system is used. Determine the costs assigned to ending inventory when costs are assigned based on weighted average. (Round per unit costs to three decimals, but inventory balances to the dollar.)

QS 6-8
Inventory costing with specific identification perpetual P1

Refer to the information in QS 6-5 and assume the perpetual inventory system is used. Determine the costs assigned to ending inventory when costs are assigned based on specific identification. (Round per unit costs to three decimals, but inventory balances to the dollar.)

QS 6-9
Contrasting inventory costing methods
A1 

Identify the inventory costing method best described by each of the following separate statements. Assume a period of increasing costs.

1. The preferred method when each unit of product has unique features that markedly affect cost.
2. Matches recent costs against net sales.
3. Provides a tax advantage (deferral) to a corporation when costs are rising.
4. Yields a balance sheet inventory amount often markedly less than its replacement cost.
5. Results in a balance sheet inventory amount approximating replacement cost.

QS 6-10
Inventory ownership
C1

Crafts Galore, a distributor of handmade gifts, operates out of owner Jenny Finn's house. At the end of the current period, Jenny reports she has 1,500 units (products) in her basement, 30 of which were damaged by water and cannot be sold. She also has another 250 units in her van, ready to deliver per a customer order, terms FOB destination, and another 70 units out on consignment to a friend who owns a retail store. How many units should Jenny include in her company's period-end inventory?

QS 6-11
Inventory costs
C2

A car dealer acquires a used car for $3,000, terms FOB shipping point. Additional costs in obtaining and offering the car for sale include $150 for transportation-in, $200 for import duties, $50 for insurance during shipment, $25 for advertising, and $250 for sales staff salaries. For computing inventory, what cost is assigned to the used car?

QS 6-12
Applying LCM to inventories
P2

Tailspin Trading Co. has the following products in its ending inventory. Compute lower of cost or market for inventory applied separately to each product.

Product	Quantity	Cost per Unit	Market per Unit
Mountain bikes	9	$360	$330
Skateboards	12	210	270
Gliders	25	480	420

QS 6-13
Inventory errors
A2 

In taking a physical inventory at the end of year 2011, Nadir Company forgot to count certain units. Explain how this error affects the following: (*a*) 2011 cost of goods sold, (*b*) 2011 gross profit, (*c*) 2011 net income, (*d*) 2012 net income, (*e*) the combined two-year income, and (*f*) income for years after 2012.

QS 6-14
Analyzing inventory A3

Market Company begins the year with $200,000 of goods in inventory. At year-end, the amount in inventory has increased to $230,000. Cost of goods sold for the year is $1,600,000. Compute Market's inventory turnover and days' sales in inventory. Assume that there are 365 days in the year.

QS 6-15[A]
Assigning costs with FIFO periodic P3

Refer to the information in QS 6-1 and assume the periodic inventory system is used. Determine the costs assigned to the ending inventory when costs are assigned based on FIFO. (Round per unit costs to three decimals, but inventory balances to the dollar.)

QS 6-16A
Inventory costing with LIFO periodic P3

Refer to the information in QS 6-1 and assume the periodic inventory system is used. Determine the costs assigned to ending inventory when costs are assigned based on LIFO. (Round per unit costs to three decimals, but inventory balances to the dollar.)

QS 6-17A
Inventory costing with weighted average periodic P3

Refer to the information in QS 6-1 and assume the periodic inventory system is used. Determine the costs assigned to ending inventory when costs are assigned based on weighted average. (Round per unit costs to three decimals, but inventory balances to the dollar.)

QS 6-18A
Inventory costing with FIFO periodic P3

Refer to the information in QS 6-5 and assume the periodic inventory system is used. Determine the costs assigned to the December 31 ending inventory when costs are assigned based on FIFO. (Round per unit costs to three decimals, but inventory balances to the dollar.)

QS 6-19A
Inventory costing with LIFO periodic P3

Refer to the information in QS 6-5 and assume the periodic inventory system is used. Determine the costs assigned to ending inventory when costs are assigned based on LIFO. (Round per unit costs to three decimals, but inventory balances to the dollar.)

QS 6-20A
Inventory costing with weighted average periodic P3

Refer to the information in QS 6-5 and assume the periodic inventory system is used. Determine the costs assigned to ending inventory when costs are assigned based on weighted average. (Round per unit costs to three decimals, but inventory balances to the dollar.)

QS 6-21A
Inventory costing with specific identification periodic P3

Refer to the information in QS 6-5 and assume the periodic inventory system is used. Determine the costs assigned to ending inventory when costs are assigned based on specific identification. (Round per unit costs to three decimals, but inventory balances to the dollar.)

QS 6-22B
Estimating inventories—gross profit method

P4

Dooling Store's inventory is destroyed by a fire on September 5, 2011. The following data for year 2011 are available from the accounting records. Estimate the cost of the inventory destroyed.

Jan. 1 inventory	$180,000
Jan. 1 through Sept. 5 purchases (net)	$342,000
Jan. 1 through Sept. 5 sales (net)	$675,000
Year 2011 estimated gross profit rate	42%

QS 6-23
International accounting standards

C1 C2 P2 

Answer each of the following questions related to international accounting standards.

a. Explain how the accounting for items and costs making up merchandise inventory is different between IFRS and U.S. GAAP.

b. Can companies reporting under IFRS apply a cost flow assumption in assigning costs to inventory? If yes, identify at least two acceptable cost flow assumptions.

c. Both IFRS and U.S. GAAP apply the lower of cost or market method for reporting inventory values. If inventory is written down from applying the lower of cost or market method, explain in general terms how IFRS and U.S. GAAP differ in accounting for any subsequent period reversal of that reported decline in inventory value.

connect

EXERCISES

Exercise 6-1
Inventory ownership C1

1. Jolie Company has shipped $500 of goods to China Co., and China Co. has arranged to sell the goods for Jolie. Identify the consignor and the consignee. Which company should include any unsold goods as part of its inventory?

2. At year-end, Jolie Co. had shipped $850 of merchandise FOB destination to China Co. Which company should include the $850 of merchandise in transit as part of its year-end inventory?

Exercise 6-2
Inventory costs

C2

Duke Associates, antique dealers, purchased the contents of an estate for $37,500. Terms of the purchase were FOB shipping point, and the cost of transporting the goods to Duke Associates' warehouse was $1,200. Duke Associates insured the shipment at a cost of $150. Prior to putting the goods up for sale, they cleaned and refurbished them at a cost of $490. Determine the cost of the inventory acquired from the estate.

Exercise 6-3
Inventory costing methods—perpetual
P1

Park Company reported the following March purchases and sales data for its only product.

Date	Activities	Units Acquired at Cost		Units Sold at Retail
Mar. 1	Beginning inventory	150 units @ $7.00 =	$1,050	
Mar. 10	Sales			90 units @ $15
Mar. 20	Purchase	220 units @ $6.00 =	1,320	
Mar. 25	Sales			145 units @ $15
Mar. 30	Purchase	90 units @ $5.00 =	450	
	Totals	460 units	$2,820	235 units

Park uses a perpetual inventory system. Determine the cost assigned to ending inventory and to cost of goods sold using (*a*) specific identification, (*b*) weighted average, (*c*) FIFO, and (*d*) LIFO. (Round per unit costs to three decimals, but inventory balances to the dollar.) For specific identification, ending inventory consists of 225 units, where 90 are from the March 30 purchase, 80 are from the March 20 purchase, and 55 are from beginning inventory.

Check Ending inventory: LIFO, $1,320; WA, $1,289

Exercise 6-4
Income effects of inventory methods
A1

Use the data in Exercise 6-3 to prepare comparative income statements for the month of January for Park Company similar to those shown in Exhibit 6.8 for the four inventory methods. Assume expenses are $1,600, and that the applicable income tax rate is 30%.

1. Which method yields the highest net income?
2. Does net income using weighted average fall between that using FIFO and LIFO?
3. If costs were rising instead of falling, which method would yield the highest net income?

Exercise 6-5
Inventory costing methods (perpetual)—FIFO and LIFO
P1

Harold Co. reported the following current-year purchases and sales data for its only product.

Date	Activities	Units Acquired at Cost		Units Sold at Retail
Jan. 1	Beginning inventory	100 units @ $10 =	$ 1,000	
Jan. 10	Sales			90 units @ $40
Mar. 14	Purchase	250 units @ $15 =	3,750	
Mar. 15	Sales			140 units @ $40
July 30	Purchase	400 units @ $20 =	8,000	
Oct. 5	Sales			300 units @ $40
Oct. 26	Purchase	600 units @ $25 =	15,000	
	Totals	1,350 units	$27,750	530 units

Harold uses a perpetual inventory system. Determine the costs assigned to ending inventory and to cost of goods sold using (*a*) FIFO and (*b*) LIFO. Compute the gross margin for each method.

Check Ending inventory: LIFO, $18,750

Exercise 6-6
Specific identification P1

Refer to the data in Exercise 6-5. Assume that ending inventory is made up of 100 units from the March 14 purchase, 120 units from the July 30 purchase, and all 600 units from the October 26 purchase. Using the specific identification method, calculate (*a*) the cost of goods sold and (*b*) the gross profit.

Exercise 6-7
Lower of cost or market
P2

Ripken Company's ending inventory includes the following items. Compute the lower of cost or market for ending inventory applied separately to each product.

		Per Unit	
Product	**Units**	**Cost**	**Market**
Helmets	22	$50	$54
Bats	15	78	72
Shoes	36	95	91
Uniforms	40	36	36

Check LCM = $6,896

Exercise 6-8
Analysis of inventory errors
A2 

Ringo Company had $900,000 of sales in each of three consecutive years 2010–2012, and it purchased merchandise costing $500,000 in each of those years. It also maintained a $200,000 physical inventory from the beginning to the end of that three-year period. In accounting for inventory, it made an error at the end of year 2010 that caused its year-end 2010 inventory to appear on its statements as $180,000 rather than the correct $200,000.

1. Determine the correct amount of the company's gross profit in each of the years 2010–2012.

2. Prepare comparative income statements as in Exhibit 6.11 to show the effect of this error on the company's cost of goods sold and gross profit for each of the years 2010–2012.

Check 2010 reported gross profit, $380,000

Exercise 6-9
Comparing LIFO numbers to FIFO numbers; ratio analysis
A1 A3 

Chess Company uses LIFO for inventory costing and reports the following financial data. It also recomputed inventory and cost of goods sold using FIFO for comparison purposes.

	2011	2010
LIFO inventory	$150	$100
LIFO cost of goods sold	730	670
FIFO inventory	220	125
FIFO cost of goods sold	685	—
Current assets (using LIFO)	210	180
Current liabilities	190	170

1. Compute its current ratio, inventory turnover, and days' sales in inventory for 2011 using (*a*) LIFO numbers and (*b*) FIFO numbers. (Round answers to one decimal.)

2. Comment on and interpret the results of part 1.

Check (1) FIFO: Current ratio, 1.5; Inventory turnover, 4.0 times

Exercise 6-10
Inventory turnover and days' sales in inventory
A3  

Use the following information for Ryder Co. to compute inventory turnover for 2011 and 2010, and its days' sales in inventory at December 31, 2011 and 2010. (Round answers to one decimal.) Comment on Ryder's efficiency in using its assets to increase sales from 2010 to 2011.

	2011	2010	2009
Cost of goods sold	$643,825	$426,650	$391,300
Ending inventory	96,400	86,750	91,500

Exercise 6-11[A]
Inventory costing—periodic system P3

Refer to Exercise 6-3 and assume the periodic inventory system is used. Determine the costs assigned to ending inventory and to cost of goods sold using (*a*) specific identification, (*b*) weighted average, (*c*) FIFO, and (*d*) LIFO. (Round per unit costs to three decimals, but inventory balances to the dollar.)

Exercise 6-12[A]
Inventory costing—periodic system P3

Refer to Exercise 6-5 and assume the periodic inventory system is used. Determine the costs assigned to ending inventory and to cost of goods sold using (*a*) FIFO and (*b*) LIFO. Then (*c*) compute the gross margin for each method.

Exercise 6-13[A]
Alternative cost flow assumptions—periodic
P3

Lopez Co. reported the following current-year data for its only product. The company uses a periodic inventory system, and its ending inventory consists of 300 units—100 from each of the last three purchases. Determine the cost assigned to ending inventory and to cost of goods sold using (*a*) specific identification, (*b*) weighted average, (*c*) FIFO, and (*d*) LIFO. (Round per unit costs to three decimals, but inventory balances to the dollar.) Which method yields the highest net income?

Jan. 1	Beginning inventory	200 units @ $2.00 =	$ 400
Mar. 7	Purchase	440 units @ $2.25 =	990
July 28	Purchase	1080 units @ $2.50 =	2,700
Oct. 3	Purchase	960 units @ $2.80 =	2,688
Dec. 19	Purchase	320 units @ $2.90 =	928
	Totals	3,000 units	$7,706

Check Inventory; LIFO, $625; FIFO, $870

Exercise 6-14[A]
Alternative cost flow assumptions—periodic
P3

Candis Gifts reported the following current-year data for its only product. The company uses a periodic inventory system, and its ending inventory consists of 300 units—100 from each of the last three purchases. Determine the cost assigned to ending inventory and to cost of goods sold using (*a*) specific identification, (*b*) weighted average, (*c*) FIFO, and (*d*) LIFO. (Round per unit costs to three decimals, but inventory balances to the dollar.) Which method yields the lowest net income?

Jan. 1	Beginning inventory	280 units @ $3.00 =	$ 840
Mar. 7	Purchase	600 units @ $2.80 =	1,680
July 28	Purchase	800 units @ $2.50 =	2,000
Oct. 3	Purchase	1,100 units @ $2.30 =	2,530
Dec. 19	Purchase	250 units @ $2.00 =	500
	Totals	3,030 units	$7,550

Check Inventory: LIFO, $896; FIFO, $615

Exercise 6-15[B]
Estimating ending inventory—retail method
P4

In 2011, Wichita Company had net sales (at retail) of $130,000. The following additional information is available from its records at the end of 2011. Use the retail inventory method to estimate Wichita's 2011 ending inventory at cost.

	At Cost	At Retail
Beginning inventory	$ 31,900	$64,200
Cost of goods purchased	57,810	98,400

Check End. Inventory, $17,930

Exercise 6-16[B]
Estimating ending inventory—gross profit method
P4

On March 1, KB Shop had $450,000 of inventory at cost. In the first quarter of the year, it purchased $1,590,000 of merchandise, returned $23,100, and paid freight charges of $37,600 on purchased merchandise, terms FOB shipping point. The company's gross profit averages 30%, and the store had $2,000,000 of net sales (at retail) in the first quarter of the year. Use the gross profit method to estimate its cost of inventory at the end of the first quarter.

Exercise 6-17
Accounting for inventory following IFRS
P2

Samsung Electronics reports the following regarding its accounting for inventories.

> Inventories are stated at the lower of cost or net realizable value. Cost is determined using the average cost method, except for materials-in-transit which are stated at actual cost as determined using the specific identification method. Losses on valuation of inventories and losses on inventory obsolescence are recorded as part of cost of sales. As of December 31, 2008, losses on valuation of inventories amounted to ₩651,296 million (₩ is Korean won).

1. What cost flow assumption(s) does Samsung apply in assigning costs to its inventories?
2. What has Samsung recorded for 2008 as a write-down on valuation of its inventories?
3. If at year-end 2009 there was an increase in the value of its inventories such that there was a reversal of ₩900 million for the 2008 write-down, how would Samsung account for this under IFRS? Would Samsung's accounting be different for this reversal if it reported under U.S. GAAP? Explain.

PROBLEM SET A

Problem 6-1A
Alternative cost flows—perpetual
P1

Anthony Company uses a perpetual inventory system. It entered into the following purchases and sales transactions for March.

Date	Activities	Units Acquired at Cost	Units Sold at Retail
Mar. 1	Beginning inventory	50 units @ $50/unit	
Mar. 5	Purchase	200 units @ $55/unit	
Mar. 9	Sales		210 units @ $85/unit
Mar. 18	Purchase	60 units @ $60/unit	
Mar. 25	Purchase	100 units @ $62/unit	
Mar. 29	Sales		80 units @ $95/unit
	Totals	410 units	290 units

Required

1. Compute cost of goods available for sale and the number of units available for sale.
2. Compute the number of units in ending inventory.
3. Compute the cost assigned to ending inventory using (*a*) FIFO, (*b*) LIFO, (*c*) weighted average, and (*d*) specific identification. (Round per unit costs to three decimals, but inventory balances to the dollar.) For specific identification, the March 9 sale consisted of 40 units from beginning inventory and 170 units from the March 5 purchase; the March 29 sale consisted of 20 units from the March 18 purchase and 60 units from the March 25 purchase.
4. Compute gross profit earned by the company for each of the four costing methods in part 3.

Check (3) Ending Inventory: FIFO, $7,400, LIFO, $6,840, WA, $7,176

(4) LIFO gross profit, $8,000

Problem 6-2A
Alternative cost flows—perpetual
P1

Marlow Company uses a perpetual inventory system. It entered into the following calendar-year 2011 purchases and sales transactions.

Date	Activities	Units Acquired at Cost	Units Sold at Retail
Jan. 1	Beginning inventory	600 units @ $44/unit	
Feb. 10	Purchase	200 units @ $40/unit	
Mar. 13	Purchase	100 units @ $20/unit	
Mar. 15	Sales		400 units @ $75/unit
Aug. 21	Purchase	160 units @ $60/unit	
Sept. 5	Purchase	280 units @ $48/unit	
Sept. 10	Sales		200 units @ $75/unit
	Totals	1,340 units	600 units

Required

1. Compute cost of goods available for sale and the number of units available for sale.
2. Compute the number of units in ending inventory.
3. Compute the cost assigned to ending inventory using (*a*) FIFO, (*b*) LIFO, (*c*) specific identification—units sold consist of 500 units from beginning inventory and 100 units from the March 13 purchase, and (*d*) weighted average. (Round per unit costs to three decimals, but inventory balances to the dollar.)
4. Compute gross profit earned by the company for each of the four costing methods in part 3.

Check (3) Ending inventory: FIFO, $33,040; LIFO, $35,440; WA, $34,055;

(4) LIFO gross profit, $21,000

Analysis Component

5. If the company's manager earns a bonus based on a percent of gross profit, which method of inventory costing will the manager likely prefer?

Problem 6-3A
Lower of cost or market
P2

A physical inventory of Helmke Company taken at December 31 reveals the following.

Item	Units	Per Unit Cost	Per Unit Market
Audio equipment			
Receivers	335	$ 90	$ 98
CD players	250	111	100
MP3 players	316	86	95
Speakers	194	52	41
Video equipment			
Handheld LCDs	470	150	125
VCRs	281	93	84
Camcorders	202	310	322
Car audio equipment			
Satellite radios	175	70	84
CD/MP3 radios	160	97	105

Required

1. Calculate the lower of cost or market for the inventory applied separately to each item.
2. If the market amount is less than the recorded cost of the inventory, then record the LCM adjustment to the Merchandise Inventory account.

Check $263,024

Problem 6-4A
Analysis of inventory errors
A2

mhhe.com/wildFAP20e

Doubletree Company's financial statements show the following. The company recently discovered that in making physical counts of inventory, it had made the following errors: Inventory on December 31, 2010, is understated by $50,000, and inventory on December 31, 2011, is overstated by $20,000.

For Year Ended December 31	2010	2011	2012
(a) Cost of goods sold	$ 725,000	$ 955,000	$ 790,000
(b) Net income.	268,000	275,000	250,000
(c) Total current assets	1,247,000	1,360,000	1,230,000
(d) Total equity	1,387,000	1,580,000	1,245,000

Required

1. For each key financial statement figure—(*a*), (*b*), (*c*), and (*d*) above—prepare a table similar to the following to show the adjustments necessary to correct the reported amounts.

Figure: ________	2010	2011	2012
Reported amount	________	________	________
Adjustments for: 12/31/2010 error	________	________	________
12/31/2011 error	________	________	________
Corrected amount	========	========	========

Check (1) Corrected net income: 2010, $318,000; 2011, $205,000; 2012, $270,000

Analysis Component

2. What is the error in total net income for the combined three-year period resulting from the inventory errors? Explain.

3. Explain why the understatement of inventory by $50,000 at the end of 2010 results in an understatement of equity by the same amount in that year.

Problem 6-5A[A]
Alternative cost flows—periodic
P3

mhhe.com/wildFAP20e

Viper Company began year 2011 with 20,000 units of product in its January 1 inventory costing $15 each. It made successive purchases of its product in year 2011 as follows. The company uses a periodic inventory system. On December 31, 2011, a physical count reveals that 35,000 units of its product remain in inventory.

Mar. 7	28,000 units @ $18 each
May 25	30,000 units @ $22 each
Aug. 1	20,000 units @ $24 each
Nov. 10	33,000 units @ $27 each

Required

1. Compute the number and total cost of the units available for sale in year 2011.

Check (2) Cost of goods sold: FIFO, $1,896,000; LIFO, $2,265,000; WA, $2,077,557

2. Compute the amounts assigned to the 2011 ending inventory and the cost of goods sold using (*a*) FIFO, (*b*) LIFO, and (*c*) weighted average. (Round per unit costs to three decimals, but inventory balances to the dollar.)

Problem 6-6A[A]
Income comparisons and cost flows—periodic
A1 P3

Botch Corp. sold 5,500 units of its product at $45 per unit in year 2011 and incurred operating expenses of $6 per unit in selling the units. It began the year with 600 units in inventory and made successive purchases of its product as follows.

Jan. 1	Beginning inventory	600 units @ $18 per unit
Feb. 20	Purchase	1,500 units @ $19 per unit
May 16	Purchase	700 units @ $20 per unit
Oct. 3	Purchase	400 units @ $21 per unit
Dec. 11	Purchase	3,300 units @ $22 per unit
	Total	6,500 units

Required

Check (1) Net income: FIFO, $71,540; LIFO, $69,020; WA, $70,603

1. Prepare comparative income statements similar to Exhibit 6.8 for the three inventory costing methods of FIFO, LIFO, and weighted average. (Round per unit costs to three decimals, but inventory balances to the dollar.) Include a detailed cost of goods sold section as part of each statement. The company uses a periodic inventory system, and its income tax rate is 30%.

2. How would the financial results from using the three alternative inventory costing methods change if Botch had been experiencing declining costs in its purchases of inventory?
3. What advantages and disadvantages are offered by using (*a*) LIFO and (*b*) FIFO? Assume the continuing trend of increasing costs.

Problem 6-7A^B
Retail inventory method
P4

The records of Nilson Company provide the following information for the year ended December 31.

	At Cost	At Retail
January 1 beginning inventory	$ 471,350	$ 927,150
Cost of goods purchased	3,276,030	6,279,350
Sales		5,495,700
Sales returns		44,600

Required

1. Use the retail inventory method to estimate the company's year-end inventory at cost.
2. A year-end physical inventory at retail prices yields a total inventory of $1,675,800. Prepare a calculation showing the company's loss from shrinkage at cost and at retail.

Check (1) Inventory, $912,808 cost; (2) Inventory shortage at cost, $41,392

Problem 6-8A^B
Gross profit method
P4

Wayman Company wants to prepare interim financial statements for the first quarter. The company wishes to avoid making a physical count of inventory. Wayman's gross profit rate averages 35%. The following information for the first quarter is available from its records.

January 1 beginning inventory	$ 300,260
Cost of goods purchased	939,050
Sales	1,191,150
Sales returns	9,450

Required

Use the gross profit method to estimate the company's first quarter ending inventory.

Check Estimated ending inventory, $471,205

PROBLEM SET B

Problem 6-1B
Alternative cost flows—perpetual
P1

CCO Company uses a perpetual inventory system. It entered into the following purchases and sales transactions for April.

Date	Activities	Units Acquired at Cost	Units Sold at Retail
Apr. 1	Beginning inventory	15 units @ $3,000/unit	
Apr. 6	Purchase	35 units @ $3,500/unit	
Apr. 9	Sales		18 units @ $12,000/unit
Apr. 17	Purchase	8 units @ $4,500/unit	
Apr. 25	Purchase	10 units @ $4,580/unit	
Apr. 30	Sales		30 units @ $14,000/unit
	Total	68 units	48 units

Required

1. Compute cost of goods available for sale and the number of units available for sale.
2. Compute the number of units in ending inventory.
3. Compute the cost assigned to ending inventory using (*a*) FIFO, (*b*) LIFO, (*c*) weighted average, and (*d*) specific identification. (Round per unit costs to three decimals, but inventory balances to the dollar.) For specific identification, the April 9 sale consisted of 8 units from beginning inventory and 10 units from the April 6 purchase; the April 30 sale consisted of 20 units from the April 6 purchase and 10 units from the April 25 purchase.
4. Compute gross profit earned by the company for each of the four costing methods in part 3.

Check (3) Ending inventory: FIFO, $88,800; LIFO, $62,500; WA, $75,600;

(4) LIFO gross profit, $449,200

Problem 6-2B
Alternative cost flows—perpetual
P1 

Venus Company uses a perpetual inventory system. It entered into the following calendar-year 2011 purchases and sales transactions.

Date	Activities	Units Acquired at Cost	Units Sold at Retail
Jan. 1	Beginning inventory	600 units @ $55/unit	
Jan. 10	Purchase	450 units @ $56/unit	
Feb. 13	Purchase	200 units @ $57/unit	
Feb. 15	Sales		430 units @ $90/unit
July 21	Purchase	230 units @ $58/unit	
Aug. 5	Purchase	345 units @ $59/unit	
Aug. 10	Sales		335 units @ $90/unit
	Total	1,825 units	765 units

Required

1. Compute cost of goods available for sale and the number of units available for sale.
2. Compute the number of units in ending inventory.
3. Compute the cost assigned to ending inventory using (*a*) FIFO, (*b*) LIFO, (*c*) specific identification—units sold consist of 600 units from beginning inventory and 165 units from the February 13 purchase, and (*d*) weighted average. (Round per unit costs to three decimals, but inventory balances to the dollar.)
4. Compute gross profit earned by the company for each of the four costing methods in part 3.

Check (3) Ending inventory: FIFO, $61,055; LIFO, $59,250; WA, $60,293;

(4) LIFO gross profit, $24,805

Analysis Component

5. If the company's manager earns a bonus based on a percent of gross profit, which method of inventory costing will the manager likely prefer?

Problem 6-3B
Lower of cost or market
P2

A physical inventory of Office Deals taken at December 31 reveals the following.

Item	Units	Per Unit Cost	Per Unit Market
Office furniture			
Desks	436	$261	$305
Credenzas	295	227	256
Chairs	587	49	43
Bookshelves	321	93	82
Filing cabinets			
Two-drawer	214	81	70
Four-drawer	398	135	122
Lateral	175	104	118
Office equipment			
Fax machines	430	168	200
Copiers	545	317	288
Telephones	352	125	117

Required

Check $584,444

1. Compute the lower of cost or market for the inventory applied separately to each item.
2. If the market amount is less than the recorded cost of the inventory, then record the LCM adjustment to the Merchandise Inventory account.

Problem 6-4B
Analysis of inventory errors
A2

Watson Company's financial statements show the following. The company recently discovered that in making physical counts of inventory, it had made the following errors: Inventory on December 31, 2010, is overstated by $70,000, and inventory on December 31, 2011, is understated by $55,000.

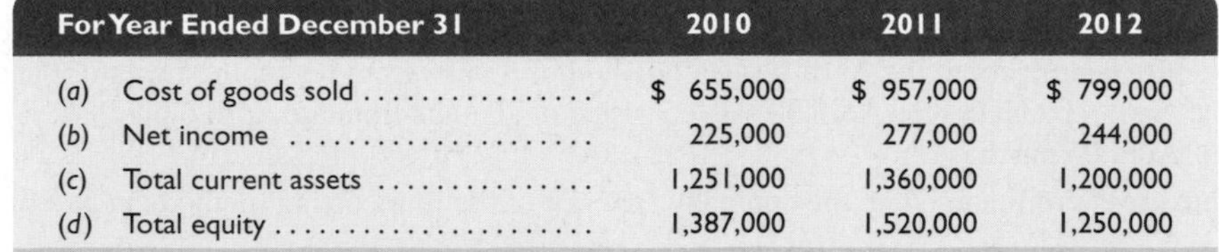

For Year Ended December 31	2010	2011	2012
(*a*) Cost of goods sold	$ 655,000	$ 957,000	$ 799,000
(*b*) Net income	225,000	277,000	244,000
(*c*) Total current assets	1,251,000	1,360,000	1,200,000
(*d*) Total equity	1,387,000	1,520,000	1,250,000

Required

1. For each key financial statement figure—(*a*), (*b*), (*c*), and (*d*) above—prepare a table similar to the following to show the adjustments necessary to correct the reported amounts.

Figure: ______	2010	2011	2012
Reported amount	______	______	______
Adjustments for: 12/31/2010 error	______	______	______
12/31/2011 error	______	______	______
Corrected amount	______	______	______

Check (1) Corrected net income: 2010, $155,000; 2011, $402,000; 2012, $189,000

Analysis Component

2. What is the error in total net income for the combined three-year period resulting from the inventory errors? Explain.

3. Explain why the overstatement of inventory by $70,000 at the end of 2010 results in an overstatement of equity by the same amount in that year.

Problem 6-5B^A
Alternative cost flows—periodic
P3

Solaris Co. began year 2011 with 6,300 units of product in its January 1 inventory costing $35 each. It made successive purchases of its product in year 2011 as follows. The company uses a periodic inventory system. On December 31, 2011, a physical count reveals that 16,500 units of its product remain in inventory.

Jan. 4	10,500 units @ $33 each
May 18	13,000 units @ $32 each
July 9	12,000 units @ $29 each
Nov. 21	15,500 units @ $26 each

Required

1. Compute the number and total cost of the units available for sale in year 2011.

2. Compute the amounts assigned to the 2011 ending inventory and the cost of goods sold using (*a*) FIFO, (*b*) LIFO, and (*c*) weighted average. (Round per unit costs to three decimals, but inventory balances to the dollar.)

Check (2) Cost of goods sold: FIFO, $1,302,000; LIFO, $1,176,900; WA, $1,234,681

Problem 6-6B^A
Income comparisons and cost flows—periodic
A1 P3

Rikkers Company sold 2,500 units of its product at $98 per unit in year 2011 and incurred operating expenses of $14 per unit in selling the units. It began the year with 740 units in inventory and made successive purchases of its product as follows.

Jan. 1	Beginning inventory	740 units @ $58 per unit
April 2	Purchase	700 units @ $59 per unit
June 14	Purchase	600 units @ $61 per unit
Aug. 29	Purchase	500 units @ $64 per unit
Nov. 18	Purchase	800 units @ $65 per unit
	Total	3,340 units

Required

1. Prepare comparative income statements similar to Exhibit 6.8 for the three inventory costing methods of FIFO, LIFO, and weighted average. (Round per unit costs to three decimals, but inventory balances to the dollar.) Include a detailed cost of goods sold section as part of each statement. The company uses a periodic inventory system, and its income tax rate is 25%.

Check (1) Net income: LIFO, $40,500; FIFO, $44,805; WA, $42,519

2. How would the financial results from using the three alternative inventory costing methods change if the company had been experiencing decreasing prices in its purchases of inventory?

3. What advantages and disadvantages are offered by using (*a*) LIFO and (*b*) FIFO? Assume the continuing trend of increasing costs.

Problem 6-7B^B
Retail inventory method
P4

The records of Saturn Co. provide the following information for the year ended December 31.

	At Cost	At Retail
January 1 beginning inventory	$ 81,670	$114,610
Cost of goods purchased	492,250	751,730
Sales		786,120
Sales returns		4,480

Check (1) Inventory, $55,902 cost; (2) Inventory shortage at cost, $4,059

Required

1. Use the retail inventory method to estimate the company's year-end inventory.
2. A year-end physical inventory at retail prices yields a total inventory of $78,550. Prepare a calculation showing the company's loss from shrinkage at cost and at retail.

Problem 6-8B[B]
Gross profit method
P4

Ernst Equipment Co. wants to prepare interim financial statements for the first quarter. The company wishes to avoid making a physical count of inventory. Ernst's gross profit rate averages 30%. The following information for the first quarter is available from its records.

January 1 beginning inventory	$ 752,880
Cost of goods purchased	2,159,630
Sales	3,710,250
Sales returns	74,200

Check Estim. ending inventory, $367,275

Required

Use the gross profit method to estimate the company's first quarter ending inventory.

SERIAL PROBLEM

Business Solutions
P2 A3 

(This serial problem began in Chapter 1 and continues through most of the book. If previous chapter segments were not completed, the serial problem can begin at this point.)

SP 6

Part A

Santana Rey of Business Solutions is evaluating her inventory to determine whether it must be adjusted based on lower of cost or market rules. Business Solutions has three different types of software in its inventory and the following information is available for each.

		Per Unit	
Inventory Items	Units	Cost	Market
Office productivity	3	$ 76	$ 74
Desktop publishing	2	103	100
Accounting	3	90	96

Required

1. Compute the lower of cost or market for ending inventory assuming Rey applies the lower of cost or market rule to inventory as a whole. Must Rey adjust the reported inventory value? Explain.
2. Assume that Rey had instead applied the lower of cost or market rule to each product in inventory. Under this assumption, must Rey adjust the reported inventory value? Explain.

Part B

Selected accounts and balances for the three months ended March 31, 2012, for Business Solutions follow.

January 1 beginning inventory	$ 0
Cost of goods sold	14,052
March 31 ending inventory	704

Required

1. Compute inventory turnover and days' sales in inventory for the three months ended March 31, 2012.
2. Assess the company's performance if competitors average 15 times for inventory turnover and 25 days for days' sales in inventory.

Beyond the Numbers

REPORTING IN ACTION

C2 A3 

RIM

BTN 6-1 Refer to **Research In Motion**'s financial statements in Appendix A to answer the following.

Required

1. What amount of inventories did Research In Motion report as a current asset on February 27, 2010? On February 28, 2009?
2. Inventories represent what percent of total assets on February 27, 2010? On February 28, 2009?

3. Comment on the relative size of Research In Motion's inventories compared to its other types of assets.
4. What accounting method did Research In Motion use to compute inventory amounts on its balance sheet?
5. Compute inventory turnover for fiscal year ended February 27, 2010, and days' sales in inventory as of February 27, 2010.

Fast Forward

6. Access Research In Motion's financial statements for fiscal years ended after February 27, 2010, from its Website (RIM.com) or the SEC's EDGAR database (www.sec.gov). Answer questions 1 through 5 using the current RIM information and compare results to those prior years.

COMPARATIVE ANALYSIS

A3 

RIM

Apple

BTN 6-2 Comparative figures for **Research In Motion** and **Apple** follow.

($ millions)	Research In Motion Current Year	Research In Motion One Year Prior	Research In Motion Two Years Prior	Apple Current Year	Apple One Year Prior	Apple Two Years Prior
Inventory	$ 622	$ 682	$ 396	$ 455	$ 509	$ 346
Cost of sales	8,369	5,968	2,929	25,683	24,294	16,426

Required

1. Compute inventory turnover for each company for the most recent two years shown.
2. Compute days' sales in inventory for each company for the three years shown.
3. Comment on and interpret your findings from parts 1 and 2. Assume an industry average for inventory turnover of 10.

ETHICS CHALLENGE

A1  

BTN 6-3 Golf Mart is a retail sports store carrying golf apparel and equipment. The store is at the end of its second year of operation and is struggling. A major problem is that its cost of inventory has continually increased in the past two years. In the first year of operations, the store assigned inventory costs using LIFO. A loan agreement the store has with its bank, its prime source of financing, requires the store to maintain a certain profit margin and current ratio. The store's owner is currently looking over Golf Mart's preliminary financial statements for its second year. The numbers are not favorable. The only way the store can meet the required financial ratios agreed on with the bank is to change from LIFO to FIFO. The store originally decided on LIFO because of its tax advantages. The owner recalculates ending inventory using FIFO and submits those numbers and statements to the loan officer at the bank for the required bank review. The owner thankfully reflects on the available latitude in choosing the inventory costing method.

Required

1. How does Golf Mart's use of FIFO improve its net profit margin and current ratio?
2. Is the action by Golf Mart's owner ethical? Explain.

COMMUNICATING IN PRACTICE

A1  

BTN 6-4 You are a financial adviser with a client in the wholesale produce business that just completed its first year of operations. Due to weather conditions, the cost of acquiring produce to resell has escalated during the later part of this period. Your client, Raphaela Gonzalez, mentions that because her business sells perishable goods, she has striven to maintain a FIFO flow of goods. Although sales are good, the increasing cost of inventory has put the business in a tight cash position. Gonzalez has expressed concern regarding the ability of the business to meet income tax obligations.

Required

Prepare a memorandum that identifies, explains, and justifies the inventory method you recommend your client, Ms. Gonzalez, adopt.

TAKING IT TO THE NET

A3  

BTN 6-5 Access the 2009 annual 10-K report for **Polaris Industries** (Ticker PII), filed on March 1, 2010, from the EDGAR filings at www.sec.gov.

Required

1. What products are manufactured by Polaris?
2. What inventory method does Polaris use? (*Hint:* See the Note 1 to its financial statements.)

3. Compute its gross margin and gross margin ratio for the 2009 calendar year. Comment on your computations—assume an industry average of 27% for the gross margin ratio.
4. Compute its inventory turnover and days' sales in inventory for the year ended December 31, 2009. Comment on your computations—assume an industry average of 5.9 for inventory turnover and 55 for days' sales in inventory.

TEAMWORK IN ACTION

A1 P1 

Point: Step 1 allows four choices or areas for expertise. Larger teams will have some duplication of choice, but the specific identification method should not be duplicated.

BTN 6-6 Each team member has the responsibility to become an expert on an inventory method. This expertise will be used to facilitate teammates' understanding of the concepts relevant to that method.

1. Each learning team member should select an area for expertise by choosing one of the following inventory methods: specific identification, LIFO, FIFO, or weighted average.
2. Form expert teams made up of students who have selected the same area of expertise. The instructor will identify where each expert team will meet.
3. Using the following data, each expert team must collaborate to develop a presentation that illustrates the relevant concepts and procedures for its inventory method. Each team member must write the presentation in a format that can be shown to the learning team.

Data

The company uses a perpetual inventory system. It had the following beginning inventory and current year purchases of its product.

Jan. 1	Beginning inventory	50 units @ $10 =	$ 500
Jan. 14	Purchase	150 units @ $12 =	1,800
Apr. 30	Purchase	200 units @ $15 =	3,000
Sept. 26	Purchase	300 units @ $20 =	6,000

The company transacted sales on the following dates at a $35 per unit sales price.

Jan. 10	30 units	(specific cost: 30 @ $10)
Feb. 15	100 units	(specific cost: 100 @ $12)
Oct. 5	350 units	(specific cost: 100 @ $15 and 250 @ $20)

Concepts and Procedures to Illustrate in Expert Presentation

a. Identify and compute the costs to assign to the units sold. (Round per unit costs to three decimals.)
b. Identify and compute the costs to assign to the units in ending inventory. (Round inventory balances to the dollar.)
c. How likely is it that this inventory costing method will reflect the actual physical flow of goods? How relevant is that factor in determining whether this is an acceptable method to use?
d. What is the impact of this method versus others in determining net income and income taxes?
e. How closely does the ending inventory amount reflect replacement cost?

4. Re-form learning teams. In rotation, each expert is to present to the team the presentation developed in part 3. Experts are to encourage and respond to questions.

ENTREPRENEURIAL DECISION

A3  

BTN 6-7 Review the chapter's opening feature highlighting Randy Hetrick and his company, **Fitness Anywhere**. Assume that Fitness Anywhere consistently maintains an inventory level of $300,000, meaning that its average and ending inventory levels are the same. Also assume its annual cost of sales is $1,200,000. To cut costs, Randy proposes to slash inventory to a constant level of $150,000 with no impact on cost of sales. He plans to work with suppliers to get quicker deliveries and to order smaller quantities more often.

Required

1. Compute the company's inventory turnover and its days' sales in inventory under (*a*) current conditions and (*b*) proposed conditions.
2. Evaluate and comment on the merits of his proposal given your analysis for part 1. Identify any concerns you might have about the proposal.

HITTING THE ROAD

C1 C2 

BTN 6-8 Visit four retail stores with another classmate. In each store, identify whether the store uses a bar-coding system to help manage its inventory. Try to find at least one store that does not use bar-coding. If a store does not use bar-coding, ask the store's manager or clerk whether he or she knows which type of inventory method the store employs. Create a table that shows columns for the name of store visited, type of merchandise sold, use or nonuse of bar-coding, and the inventory method used if bar-coding is not employed. You might also inquire as to what the store's inventory turnover is and how often physical inventory is taken.

GLOBAL DECISION

A3

NOKIA

RIM

Apple

BTN 6-9 Key figures (EUR millions) for **Nokia** (www.Nokia.com), which is a leading global manufacturer of mobile devices and services, follow.

EUR millions	Current Year	One Year Prior	Two Years Prior
Inventory	1,865	2,533	2,876
Cost of sales	27,720	33,337	33,781

Required

1. Use these data and those from BTN 6-2 to compute (*a*) inventory turnover and (*b*) days' sales in inventory for the most recent two years shown for **Nokia**, **Research In Motion**, and **Apple**.

2. Comment on and interpret your findings from part 1.

ANSWERS TO MULTIPLE CHOICE QUIZ

1. a; FIFO perpetual

Date	Goods Purchased	Cost of Goods Sold	Inventory Balance
July 1			75 units @ $25 = $ 1,875
July 3	348 units @ $27 = $9,396		75 units @ $25 348 units @ $27 } = $ 11,271
July 8		75 units @ $25 225 units @ $27 } = $ 7,950	123 units @ $27 = $ 3,321
July 15	257 units @ $28 = $7,196		123 units @ $27 257 units @ $28 } = $ 10,517
July 23		123 units @ $27 152 units @ $28 } = $ 7,577	105 units @ $28 = **$ 2,940**
		$15,527	

2. b; LIFO perpetual

Date	Goods Purchased	Cost of Goods Sold	Inventory Balance
July 1			75 units @ $25 = $ 1,875
July 3	348 units @ $27 = $9,396		75 units @ $25 348 units @ $27 } = $ 11,271
July 8		300 units @ $27 = $ 8,100	75 units @ $25 48 units @ $27 } = $ 3,171
July 15	257 units @ $28 = $7,196		75 units @ $25 48 units @ $27 257 units @ $28 } = $ 10,367
July 23		257 units @ $28 18 units @ $27 } = $ 7,682	75 units @ $25 30 units @ $27 } = **$ 2,685**
		$15,782	

3. e; Specific identification perpetual—Ending inventory computation.

20 units @ $25	$ 500
40 units @ $27	1,080
45 units @ $28	1,260
105 units	$2,840

4. a; FIFO periodic—Ending inventory computation.
105 units @ $28 each = $2,940; The FIFO periodic inventory computation is identical to the FIFO perpetual inventory computation (see question 1).

5. d; Days' sales in inventory = (Ending inventory/Cost of goods sold × 365)
= ($18,000/$85,000) × 365 = 77.29 days

7 Accounting Information Systems

A Look Back

Chapters 5 and 6 focused on merchandising activities and accounting for inventory. We explained inventory systems, accounting for inventory transactions, and assigning costs to inventory.

A Look at This Chapter

This chapter emphasizes accounting information systems. We describe fundamental system principles, the system's components, use of special journals and subsidiary ledgers, and technology-based systems.

A Look Ahead

Chapter 8 focuses on internal controls and accounting for cash and cash equivalents. We explain good internal control procedures and their importance.

Learning Objectives

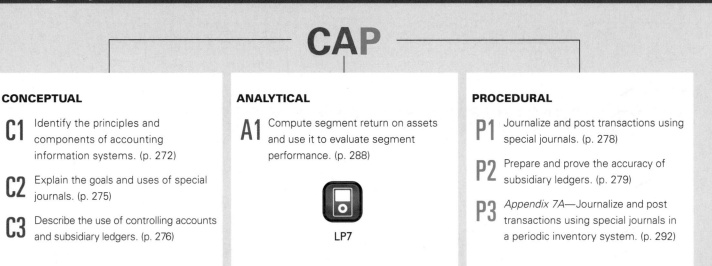

CONCEPTUAL

C1 Identify the principles and components of accounting information systems. (p. 272)

C2 Explain the goals and uses of special journals. (p. 275)

C3 Describe the use of controlling accounts and subsidiary ledgers. (p. 276)

ANALYTICAL

A1 Compute segment return on assets and use it to evaluate segment performance. (p. 288)

LP7

PROCEDURAL

P1 Journalize and post transactions using special journals. (p. 278)

P2 Prepare and prove the accuracy of subsidiary ledgers. (p. 279)

P3 *Appendix 7A*—Journalize and post transactions using special journals in a periodic inventory system. (p. 292)

Decision Insight

Successful Brew

"It's just following your instincts, knowing the basics, and sticking with what's important"

—KIM JORDAN

FORT COLLINS, CO—Kim Jordan's entrepreneurial roots were anything but frothy. "For about eight months, we didn't pay ourselves," explains Kim. "We borrowed money from parents and made payroll . . . looking at the bills, we had to decide which to pay." From those meager beginnings, Kim created **New Belgium Brewing Company (NewBelgium.com),** which is committed to the Belgian brewing tradition of delicious beers with loads of character.

"We did have a set of values, a purpose, and some outcomes that we wanted to achieve," says Kim. "Four things were important to us: to produce world class Belgium-style beers, to promote beer culture, to be environmental stewards, and to have fun!" To achieve those goals, Kim set up an accounting system to measure, track, summarize, and report on operations. "It is important to have the ability to read financial statements," insists Kim. "And, to understand ratios." Those expectations and priorities fundamentally shaped Kim's accounting system and controls.

"There has to be execution," explains Kim. That focus on execution includes applying internal controls, special journals, accounting ledgers, and systems technology. Kim maintains special journals for sales, cash receipts, purchases, and cash disbursements. Developing her accounting system to capture all aspects of her operations is no easy task, but well worth the effort. "Working hard and being dedicated or committed to an outcome are keys," asserts Kim. "Our co-workers [all employees] get to see all of our financials!" Kim explains that this in turn helps shape the special journals for her business, including the control procedures applied in the brewery.

Kim's company is riding high with the right accounting systems and controls for long run success. "Stasis is not an option," says Kim. "If we're all in the same place today that we were five years ago, that wouldn't be very interesting." Kim smiles and adds, "There's something wrong if making beer can't be fun!"

[Sources: *NewBelgium Website,* January 2011; *Entrepreneur,* November 2009; *50entrepreneurs.com,* March 2010; *CNNMoney.com,* June 2009; *Beverage World,* September 2009]

Chapter Preview

With increases in the number and complexity of business activities, the demands placed on accounting information systems increase. Accounting information systems must meet this challenge in an efficient and effective manner. In this chapter, we learn about fundamental principles guiding information systems, and we study components making up these systems. We also explain procedures that use special journals and subsidiary ledgers to make accounting information systems more efficient. An understanding of the details of accounting reports makes us better decision makers when using financial information, and it improves our ability to analyze and interpret financial statements.

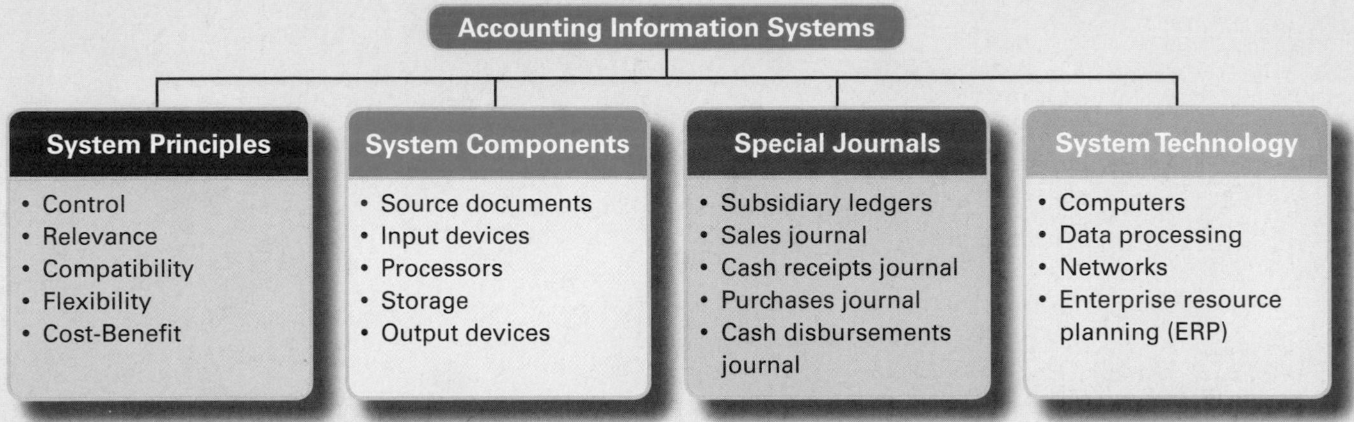

Accounting Information Systems
System Principles
• Control
• Relevance
• Compatibility
• Flexibility
• Cost-Benefit
System Components
• Source documents
• Input devices
• Processors
• Storage
• Output devices
Special Journals
• Subsidiary ledgers
• Sales journal
• Cash receipts journal
• Purchases journal
• Cash disbursements journal
System Technology
• Computers
• Data processing
• Networks
• Enterprise resource planning (ERP)

FUNDAMENTAL SYSTEM PRINCIPLES

C1 Identify the principles and components of accounting information systems.

Accounting information systems collect and process data from transactions and events, organize them in useful reports, and communicate results to decision makers. With the increasing complexity of business and the growing need for information, accounting information systems are more important than ever. All decision makers need to have a basic knowledge of how accounting information systems work. This knowledge gives decision makers a competitive edge as they gain a better understanding of information constraints, measurement limitations, and potential applications. It allows them to make more informed decisions and to better balance the risks and returns of different strategies. This section explains five basic principles of accounting information systems, shown in Exhibit 7.1.

EXHIBIT 7.1

System Principles

Control
Relevance
Compatibility
Flexibility
Cost-Benefit Principle
System Principles

Control Principle

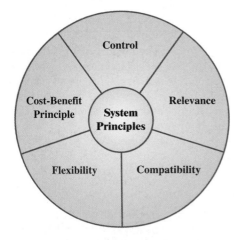

Managers need to control and monitor business activities. The **control principle** prescribes that an accounting information system have internal controls. **Internal controls** are methods and procedures allowing managers to control and monitor business activities. They include policies to direct operations toward common goals, procedures to ensure reliable financial reports, safeguards to protect company assets, and methods to achieve compliance with laws and regulations.

Point: A hacker stole 300,000 credit card numbers from online music retailer CDUniverse due to internal control failure.

Relevance Principle

Decision makers need relevant information to make informed decisions. The **relevance principle** prescribes that an accounting information system report useful, understandable, timely, and pertinent information for effective decision making. The system must be designed to capture data that make a difference in decisions. To ensure this, we must consider all decision makers when identifying relevant information for disclosure.

Compatibility Principle

Accounting information systems must be consistent with the aims of a company. The **compatibility principle** prescribes that an accounting information system conform with a company's activities, personnel, and structure. It also must adapt to a company's unique characteristics. The system must not be intrusive but must work in harmony with and be driven by company goals. Most start-up entrepreneurs require only a simple information system. **Harley-Davidson**, on the other hand, demands both a merchandising and a manufacturing information system able to assemble data from its global operations.

Flexibility Principle

Accounting information systems must be able to adjust to changes. The **flexibility principle** prescribes that an accounting information system be able to adapt to changes in the company, business environment, and needs of decisions makers. Technological advances, competitive pressures, consumer tastes, regulations, and company activities constantly evolve. A system must be designed to adapt to these changes.

Cost-Benefit Principle

The **cost-benefit principle** prescribes that the benefits from an activity in an accounting information system outweigh the costs of that activity. The costs and benefits of an activity such as producing a specific report will impact the decisions of both external and internal users. Decisions regarding other systems principles (control, relevance, compatibility, and flexibility) are also affected by the cost-benefit principle.

Point: Law requires that *all* employers destroy credit-check and other employee records *before* tossing them. A cross-cut shredder is the tool of choice.

Decision Insight

Digital Is Forever E-communications have helped bring down many employees, including the former CEO of **Boeing**. To comply with Sarbanes-Oxley, more and more companies now archive and monitor e-mails, instant messages, blog postings, and Net-based phone calls. Using natural-language software, companies sift through digital communications in milliseconds, checking for trade secrets, bad language, porn, and pirated files. ■

COMPONENTS OF ACCOUNTING SYSTEMS

Accounting information systems consist of people, records, methods, and equipment. The systems are designed to capture information about a company's transactions and to provide output including financial, managerial, and tax reports. All accounting information systems have these same goals, and thus share some basic components. These components apply whether or not a system is heavily computerized, yet the components of computerized systems usually provide more accuracy, speed, efficiency, and convenience than those of manual systems.

The five basic **components of accounting systems** are source documents, input devices, information processors, information storage, and output devices. Exhibit 7.2 shows these components as a series of steps, yet we know that much two-way communication occurs between many of these components. We briefly describe each of these key components in this section.

EXHIBIT 7.2

Accounting System Components

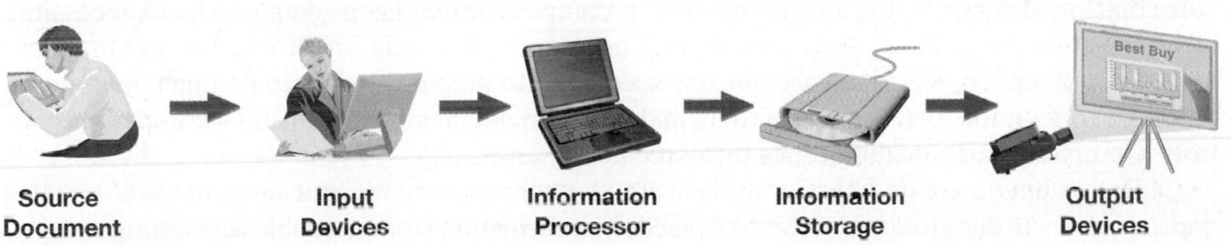

Source Documents

We introduced source documents in Chapters 1 and 2 and explained their importance for both business transactions and information collection. Source documents provide the basic information processed by an accounting system. Examples of source documents include bank statements and checks, invoices from suppliers, billings to customers, cash register files, and employee earnings records. Source documents can be paper, although they increasingly are taking the form of electronic files and Web communications. A growing number of companies are sending documents directly from their systems to their customers' and suppliers' systems. The Web is playing a major role in this transformation from paper-based to *paperless* systems.

Accurate source documents are crucial to accounting information systems. Input of faulty or incomplete information seriously impairs the reliability and relevance of the information system. We commonly refer to this as "garbage in, garbage out." Information systems are set up with attention on control procedures to limit the possibility of entering faulty data in the system.

Input Devices

Input devices capture information from source documents and enable its transfer to the system's information processing component. These devices often involve converting data on source documents from written or electronic form to a form usable for the system. Journal entries, both electronic and paper based, are a type of input device. Keyboards, scanners, and modems are some of the most common input devices in practice today. For example, bar code readers capture code numbers and transfer them to the organization's computer for processing. Moreover, a scanner can capture writing samples and other input directly from source documents.

Point: Understanding a manual accounting system is useful in understanding an electronic system.

Controls are used to ensure that only authorized individuals input data to the system. Controls increase the system's reliability and allow information to be traced back to its source.

Decision Insight

Geek Chic Cyberfashion pioneers are creating geek chic, a kind of wearable computer. Cyberfashion draws on digital cellular phones, lithium batteries, and miniature monitors. Special thread is woven into clothing to carry low-voltage signals from one part of the system to another, and fabric keyboards are sewn into clothes. These creations give new meaning to the term *software*. ■

Information Processors

Information processors are systems that interpret, transform, and summarize information for use in analysis and reporting. An important part of an information processor in accounting systems is professional judgment. Accounting principles are never so structured that they limit the need for professional judgment. Other parts of an information processor include journals, ledgers, working papers, and posting procedures. Each assists in transforming raw data to useful information.

Point: *BusinessWeek* reported that 75% of all e-mail traffic is spam.

Increasingly, computer technology (both computing hardware and software) is assisting manual information processors. This assistance is freeing accounting professionals to take on increased analysis, interpretive, and managerial roles. Web-based application service providers (ASPs) offer another type of information processor.

Information Storage

Information storage is the accounting system component that keeps data in a form accessible to information processors. After being input and processed, data are stored for use in future analyses and reports. The database must be accessible to preparers of periodic financial reports. Auditors rely on this database when they audit both financial statements and a company's controls. Companies also maintain files of source documents.

Point: A financial accounting database can be designed to support a wide range of internal reports for management.

Older systems consisted almost exclusively of paper documents, but most modern systems depend on electronic storage devices. Advances in information storage enable accounting systems to increasingly store more detailed data. This means managers have more data to access and work with in planning and controlling business activities. Information storage can be online, meaning that data can be accessed whenever, and from wherever, it is needed. Off-line storage means access often requires assistance and authorization. Information storage is increasingly augmented by Web sources such as SEC databases, benchmarking services, and financial and product markets.

Decision Insight 

Direct Output A screenless computer display, called *virtual retinal display* (VRD), scans rows of pixels directly onto the user's retina by means of a laser. VRDs can simulate three-dimensional virtual worlds, including 3D financial graphics. ■

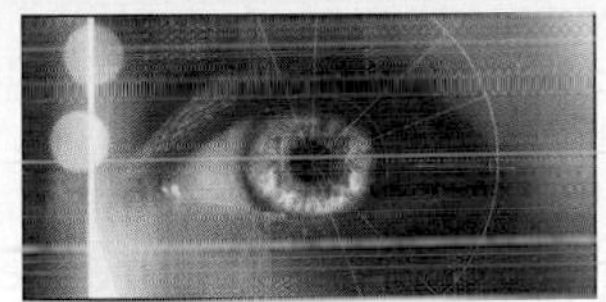

Output Devices

Output devices are the means to take information out of an accounting system and make it available to users. Common output devices are printers, monitors, projectors, and Web communications. Output devices provide users a variety of items including graphics, analysis reports, bills to customers, checks to suppliers, employee paychecks, financial statements, and internal reports. When requests for output occur, an information processor takes the needed data from a database and prepares the necessary report, which is then sent to an output device. A special type of output is an electronic funds transfer (EFT). One example is the transfer of payroll from the company's bank account to its employees' bank accounts. This requires an interface to allow a company's accounting system to send payroll data directly to the bank's accounting system. This interface can involve a company recording its payroll data in an encrypted zip file and forwarding it to the bank. The bank then uses this output to transfer wages earned to employees' accounts.

Decision Ethics  Answer — p. 296 

Accountant Your client requests advice in purchasing software for its accounting system. You have been offered a 10% commission by a software company for each purchase of its system by one of your clients. Does this commission arrangement affect your evaluation of software? Do you tell your client about the commission arrangement? ■

Quick Check Answers — p. 297 

1. Identify the five primary components of an accounting information system.
2. What is the aim of information processors in an accounting system?
3. How are data in the information storage component of an accounting system used?

SPECIAL JOURNALS IN ACCOUNTING

 C2 Explain the goals and uses of special journals.

This section describes the underlying records of accounting information systems. Designed correctly, these records support efficiency in processing transactions and events. They are part of all systems in various forms and are increasingly electronic. Even in technologically advanced systems, a basic understanding of the records we describe in this section aids in using, interpreting, and applying accounting information. It also improves our knowledge of computer-based systems. Remember that all accounting systems have common purposes and internal workings whether or not they depend on technology.

This section focuses on special journals and subsidiary ledgers that are an important part of accounting systems. We describe how special journals are used to capture transactions, and we explain how subsidiary ledgers are set up to capture details of accounts. This section uses a *perpetual* inventory system, and the special journals are set up using this system. Appendix 7A describes the change in special journals required for a *periodic* system. We also include a note at the bottom of each of the special journals explaining the change required if a company uses a periodic system.

Basics of Special Journals

A **general journal** is an all-purpose journal in which we can record any transaction. Use of a general journal for all transactions is usually more costly for a business *and* is a less effective control procedure. Moreover, for less technologically advanced systems, use of a general journal requires that each debit and each credit entered be individually posted to its respective ledger account. To enhance internal control and reduce costs, transactions are organized into common groups. A **special journal** is used to record and post transactions of similar type. Most transactions of a merchandiser, for instance, can be categorized into the journals shown in Exhibit 7.3. This section assumes the use of these four special journals along with the general journal. The general journal continues to be used for transactions not covered by special journals and for adjusting, closing, and correcting entries. We show in the following discussion that special journals are *efficient tools in helping journalize and post transactions.* This is done, for instance, by accumulating debits and credits of similar transactions, which allows posting of amounts as column *totals* rather than as individual amounts. The advantage of this system increases as the number of transactions increases. Special journals allow an *efficient division of labor,* which is also an effective control procedure.

Point: Companies can use as many special journals as necessary given their unique business activities.

Point: A specific transaction is recorded in only *one* journal.

EXHIBIT 7.3

Using Special Journals with a General Journal

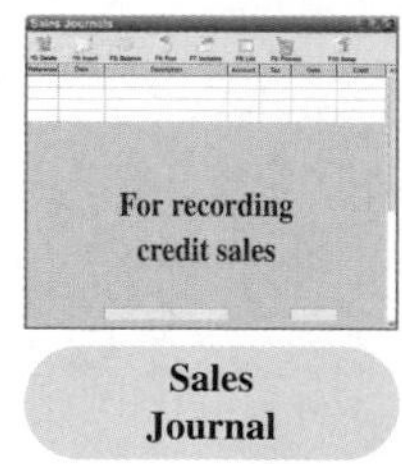

Sales Journal

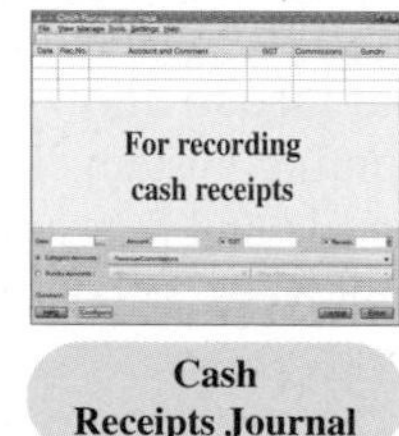

Cash Receipts Journal

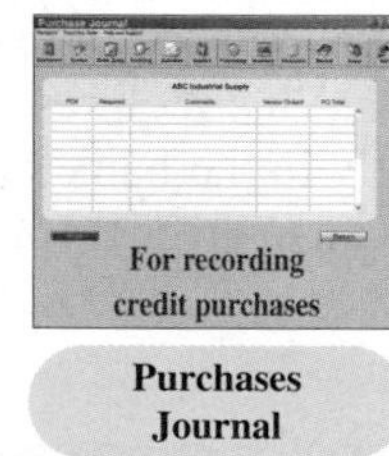

Purchases Journal

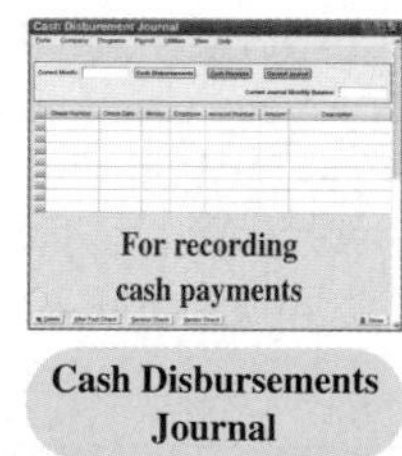

Cash Disbursements Journal

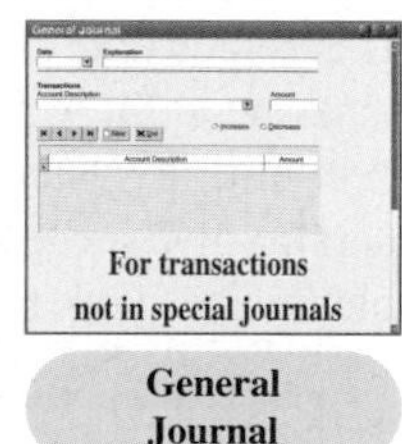

General Journal

It is important to note that special journals and subsidiary ledgers *are designed in a manner that is best suited for each business.* The most likely candidates for special journal status are recurring transactions—for many businesses those are sales, cash receipts, purchases, and cash disbursements. However, good systems design for a business could involve collapsing sales and cash receipts in one journal, or purchases and cash disbursements in another. It could also involve adding more special journals or additional subsidiary ledgers for other recurring transactions. This design decision extends to journal and ledger format. That is, the selection on number of columns, column headings, and so forth is based on what is best suited for each business. Thus, read the following sections as one example of a common systems design, but not the only design.

Subsidiary Ledgers

 Describe the use of controlling accounts and subsidiary ledgers.

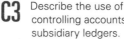

To understand special journals, it is necessary to understand the workings of a **subsidiary ledger,** which is a list of individual accounts with a common characteristic. A subsidiary ledger contains detailed information on specific accounts in the general ledger. Information systems often include several subsidiary ledgers. Two of the most important are:

- *Accounts receivable ledger*—stores transaction data of individual customers.
- *Accounts payable ledger*—stores transaction data of individual suppliers.

Individual accounts in subsidiary ledgers are often arranged alphabetically, which is the approach taken here. We describe accounts receivable and accounts payable ledgers in this section. Our discussion of special journals uses these ledgers.

Accounts Receivable Ledger When we recorded credit sales in prior chapters, we debited (increased) Accounts Receivable. When a company has more than one credit customer, the accounts receivable records must show how much *each* customer purchased, paid, and has yet to pay. This information is collected by keeping a separate account receivable for each credit customer. A separate account for each customer *could* be kept in the general ledger with the other financial statement accounts, but this is uncommon. Instead, the general ledger usually has a single Accounts Receivable account, and a *subsidiary ledger* is set up to keep a separate account for each customer. This subsidiary ledger is called the **accounts receivable ledger** (also called *accounts receivable subsidiary ledger* or *customers ledger*), and it can exist in electronic or paper form.

Exhibit 7.4 shows the relation between the Accounts Receivable account and its individual accounts in the subsidiary ledger. After all items are posted, the balance in the Accounts Receivable account must equal the sum of all balances of its customers' accounts. The Accounts Receivable account is said to control the accounts receivable ledger and is called a **controlling account.** Since the accounts receivable ledger is a supplementary record controlled by an account in the general ledger, it is called a *subsidiary* ledger.

Point: When a general ledger account has a subsidiary ledger, any transaction that impacts one of them also impacts the other—some refer to this as *general and subsidiary ledgers kept in tandem.*

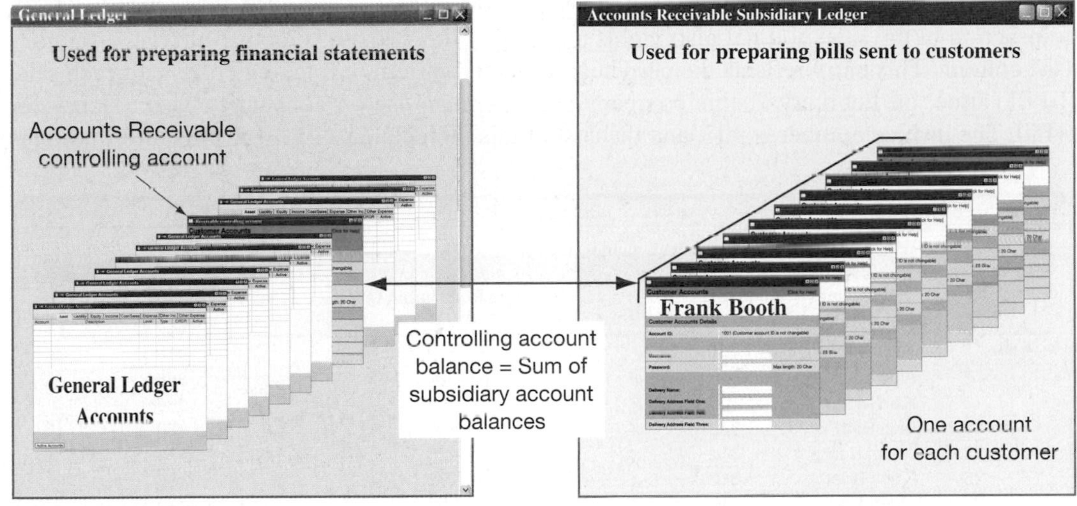

EXHIBIT 7.4

Accounts Receivable Controlling Account and Its Subsidiary Ledger

Point: A control account refers to any general ledger account that summarizes subsidiary ledger data.

Accounts Payable Ledger There are other controlling accounts and subsidiary ledgers. We know, for example, that many companies buy on credit from several suppliers. This means that companies must keep a separate account for each supplier by keeping an Accounts Payable controlling account in the general ledger and a separate account for each supplier (creditor) in an **accounts payable ledger** (also called *accounts payable subsidiary ledger* or *creditors ledger*).

Other Subsidiary Ledgers Subsidiary ledgers are common for several other accounts. A company with many classes of equipment, for example, might keep only one Equipment account in its general ledger, but its Equipment account would control a subsidiary ledger in which each class of equipment is recorded in a separate account. Similar treatment is common for investments, inventory, and any accounts needing separate detailed records. **Genmar Holdings**, which manufactures boats by Champion, Glastron, Four Winns, and Larson, reports sales information by product line in its report. Yet its accounting system keeps much more detailed sales records. Genmar Holdings, for instance, sells hundreds of different products and must be able to analyze the sales performance of each. This detail can be captured by many different general ledger sales accounts but is instead captured by using supplementary records that function like subsidiary ledgers. Overall, subsidiary ledgers are applied in many different ways to ensure that the accounting system captures sufficient details to support analyses that decision makers need. At least four benefits derive from subsidiary ledgers:

1. Removal of excessive details, and detailed accounts, from the general ledger.
2. Up-to-date information readily available on specific customers and suppliers.
3. Aid in error identification for specific accounts.
4. Potential efficiencies in recordkeeping through division of labor in posting.

Sales Journal

P1 Journalize and post transactions using special journals.

A typical **sales journal** is used to record sales of inventory *on credit.* Sales of inventory for cash are not recorded in a sales journal but in a cash receipts journal. Sales of noninventory assets on credit are recorded in the general journal.

Journalizing Credit sale transactions are recorded with information about each sale entered separately in a sales journal. This information is often taken from a copy of the sales ticket or invoice prepared at the time of sale. The top portion of Exhibit 7.5 shows a typical sales journal from a merchandiser. It has columns for recording the date, customer's name, invoice number, posting reference, and the retail and cost amounts of each credit sale. The sales journal in this exhibit is called a **columnar journal,** which is any journal with more than one column.

Point: Each transaction in the sales journal includes a debit to accounts receivable and a credit to sales.

Each transaction recorded in the sales journal yields an entry in the "Accounts Receivable Dr., Sales Cr." column. We usually need only one column for these two accounts. (An exception is when managers need more information about taxes, returns, and other sales details.) Each transaction in the sales journal also yields an entry in the "Cost of Goods Sold Dr., Inventory Cr." column. This entry reflects the perpetual inventory system of tracking costs with each sale. To illustrate, on February 2, this company sold merchandise on account to Jason Henry for $450. The invoice number is 307, and the cost of this merchandise is $315. This information is

EXHIBIT 7.5

Sales Journal with Posting*

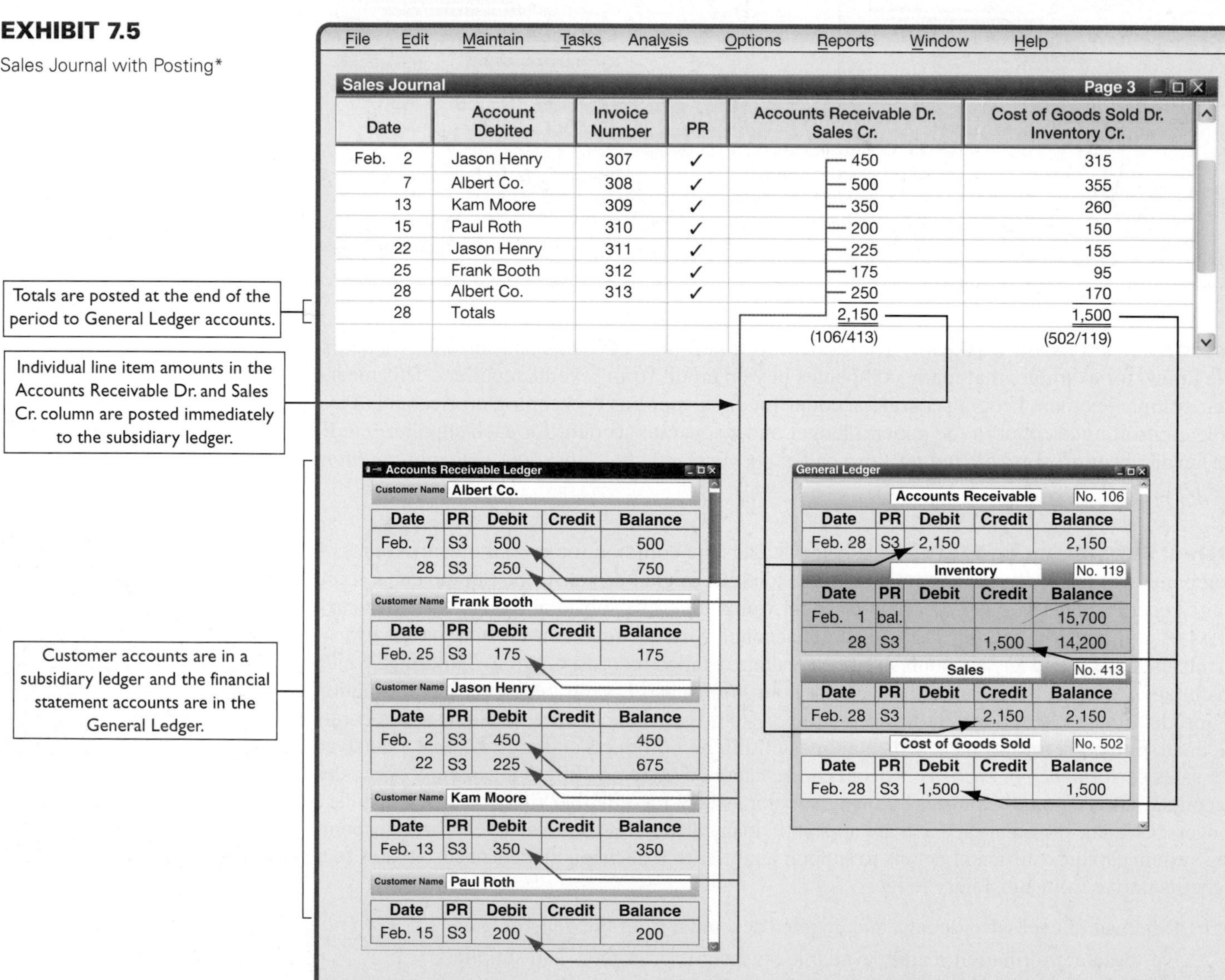

File Edit Maintain Tasks Analysis Options Reports Window Help
Totals are posted at the end of the period to General Ledger accounts.
Individual line item amounts in the Accounts Receivable Dr. and Sales Cr. column are posted immediately to the subsidiary ledger.
Customer accounts are in a subsidiary ledger and the financial statement accounts are in the General Ledger.

Sales Journal — Page 3

Date	Account Debited	Invoice Number	PR	Accounts Receivable Dr. Sales Cr.	Cost of Goods Sold Dr. Inventory Cr.
Feb. 2	Jason Henry	307	✓	450	315
7	Albert Co.	308	✓	500	355
13	Kam Moore	309	✓	350	260
15	Paul Roth	310	✓	200	150
22	Jason Henry	311	✓	225	155
25	Frank Booth	312	✓	175	95
28	Albert Co.	313	✓	250	170
28	Totals			2,150	1,500
				(106/413)	(502/119)

Accounts Receivable Ledger

Customer Name: Albert Co.

Date	PR	Debit	Credit	Balance
Feb. 7	S3	500		500
28	S3	250		750

Customer Name: Frank Booth

Date	PR	Debit	Credit	Balance
Feb. 25	S3	175		175

Customer Name: Jason Henry

Date	PR	Debit	Credit	Balance
Feb. 2	S3	450		450
22	S3	225		675

Customer Name: Kam Moore

Date	PR	Debit	Credit	Balance
Feb. 13	S3	350		350

Customer Name: Paul Roth

Date	PR	Debit	Credit	Balance
Feb. 15	S3	200		200

General Ledger

Accounts Receivable — No. 106

Date	PR	Debit	Credit	Balance
Feb. 28	S3	2,150		2,150

Inventory — No. 119

Date	PR	Debit	Credit	Balance
Feb. 1	bal.			15,700
28	S3		1,500	14,200

Sales — No. 413

Date	PR	Debit	Credit	Balance
Feb. 28	S3		2,150	2,150

Cost of Goods Sold — No. 502

Date	PR	Debit	Credit	Balance
Feb. 28	S3	1,500		1,500

*The Sales Journal in a *periodic* system would exclude the column on the far right titled "Cost of Goods Sold Dr., Inventory Cr." (see Exhibit 7A.1).

captured on one line in the sales journal. No further explanations or entries are necessary, saving time and effort. Moreover, this sales journal is consistent with most inventory systems that use bar codes to record both sales and costs with each sale transaction. Note that the Posting Reference (PR) column is not used when entering transactions but instead is used when posting.

Point: Continuously updated customer accounts provide timely information for customer inquiries on those accounts and on current amounts owed.

Posting A sales journal is posted as reflected in the arrow lines of Exhibit 7.5. Two types of posting can be identified: (1) posting to the subsidiary ledger(s) and (2) posting to the general ledger.

Posting to subsidiary ledger. Individual transactions in the sales journal are posted regularly (typically concurrently) to customer accounts in the accounts receivable ledger. These postings keep customer accounts up-to-date, which is important for the person granting credit to customers. When sales recorded in the sales journal are individually posted to customer accounts in the accounts receivable ledger, check marks are entered in the sales journal's PR column. Check marks are used rather than account numbers because customer accounts usually are arranged alphabetically in the accounts receivable ledger. Note that posting debits to Accounts Receivable twice—once to Accounts Receivable and once to the customer's subsidiary account—does not violate the accounting equation of debits equal credits. The equality of debits and credits is always maintained in the general ledger.

Point: PR column is only checked *after* the amount(s) is posted.

Posting to general ledger. The sales journal's account columns are totaled at the end of each period (the month of February in this case). For the "sales" column, the $2,150 total is debited to Accounts Receivable and credited to Sales in the general ledger (see Exhibit 7.5). For the "cost" column, the $1,500 total is debited to Cost of Goods Sold and credited to Inventory in the general ledger. When totals are posted to accounts in the general ledger, the account numbers are entered below the column total in the sales journal for tracking. For example, we enter (106/413) below the total in the sales column after this amount is posted to account number 106 (Accounts Receivable) and account number 413 (Sales).

Point: Postings are automatic in a computerized system.

A company identifies in the PR column of its subsidiary ledgers the journal and page number from which an amount is taken. We identify a journal by using an initial. Items posted from the sales journal carry the initial ***S*** before their journal page numbers in a PR column. Likewise, items from the cash receipts journal carry the initial ***R***; items from the cash disbursements journal carry the initial ***D***; items from the purchases journal carry the initial ***P***; and items from the general journal carry the initial ***G***.

Proving the Ledgers Account balances in the general ledger and subsidiary ledgers are periodically proved (or reviewed) for accuracy after posting. To do this we first prepare a trial balance of the general ledger to confirm that debits equal credits. Second, we test a subsidiary ledger by preparing a *schedule* of individual accounts and amounts. A **schedule of accounts receivable** lists each customer and the balance owed. If this total equals the balance of the Accounts Receivable controlling account, the accounts in the accounts receivable ledger are assumed correct. Exhibit 7.6 shows a schedule of accounts receivable drawn from the accounts receivable ledger of Exhibit 7.5.

P2 Prepare and prove the accuracy of subsidiary ledgers.

EXHIBIT 7.6

Schedule of Accounts Receivable

Schedule of Accounts Receivable February 28	
Albert Co.	$ 750
Frank Booth	175
Jason Henry	675
Kam Moore	350
Paul Roth	200
Total accounts receivable	$2,150

Additional Issues We consider three additional issues with the sales journal: (1) recording sales taxes, (2) recording sales returns and allowances, and (3) using actual sales invoices as a journal.

Point: In accounting, the word *schedule* generally means a list.

Sales taxes. Governmental agencies such as cities and states often require sellers to collect sales taxes from customers and to periodically send these taxes to the appropriate agency. When using a columnar sales journal, we can keep a record of taxes collected by adding a Sales Taxes Payable column as follows.

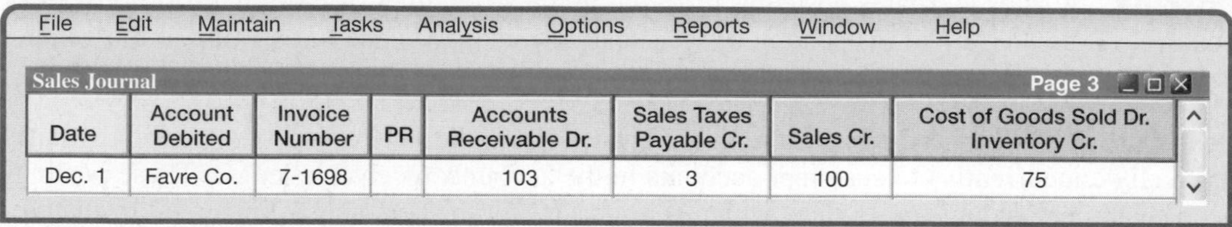

Date	Account Debited	Invoice Number	PR	Accounts Receivable Dr.	Sales Taxes Payable Cr.	Sales Cr.	Cost of Goods Sold Dr. Inventory Cr.
Dec. 1	Favre Co.	7-1698		103	3	100	75

Individual amounts in the Accounts Receivable column would continue to be posted immediately to customer accounts in the accounts receivable ledger. Individual amounts in the Sales Taxes Payable and Sales columns are not posted. Column totals would continue to be posted as usual. (A company that collects sales taxes on its cash sales can also use a Sales Taxes Payable column in its cash receipts journal.)

Sales returns and allowances. A company with only a few sales returns and allowances can record them in a general journal with an entry such as the following:

Assets	=	Liabilities	+	Equity
−175				−175

May 17	Sales Returns and Allowances	414	175	
	Accounts Receivable—Ray Ball	106/✓		175
	Customer returned merchandise.			

The debit in this entry is posted to the Sales Returns and Allowances account (no. 414). The credit is posted to both the Accounts Receivable controlling account (no. 106) and to the customer's account. When we enter the account number and the check mark, 106/✓, in the PR column on the credit line, this means both the Accounts Receivable controlling account in the general ledger and the Ray Ball account in the accounts receivable ledger are credited for $175. [*Note:* If the returned goods can be resold to another customer, the company would debit (increase) the Inventory account and credit (decrease) the Cost of Goods Sold account. If the returned goods are defective (worthless), the company could simply leave their costs in the Cost of Goods Sold account (see Chapter 5).] A company with a large number of sales returns and allowances can save time by recording them in a separate sales returns and allowances journal.

Sales invoices as a sales journal. To save costs, some small companies avoid using a sales journal for credit sales and instead post each sales invoice amount directly to the customer's account in the accounts receivable ledger. They then put copies of invoices in a file. At the end of the period, they total all invoices for that period and make a general journal entry to debit Accounts Receivable and credit Sales for the total amount. The file of invoice copies acts as a sales journal. This is called *direct posting of sales invoices.*

Quick Check Answers — p. 297

4. When special journals are used, where are cash payments by check recorded?
5. How does a columnar journal save posting time and effort?
6. How do debits and credits remain equal when credit sales are posted twice (once to Accounts Receivable and once to the customer's subsidiary account)?
7. How do we identify the journal from which an amount in a ledger account was posted?
8. How are sales taxes recorded in the context of special journals?
9. What is direct posting of sales invoices?

Cash Receipts Journal

A **cash receipts journal** is typically used to record all receipts of cash. Exhibit 7.7 shows one common form of the cash receipts journal.

Journalizing and Posting Cash receipts can be separated into one of three types: (1) cash from credit customers in payment of their accounts, (2) cash from cash sales, and (3) cash from other sources. The cash receipts journal in Exhibit 7.7 has a separate credit

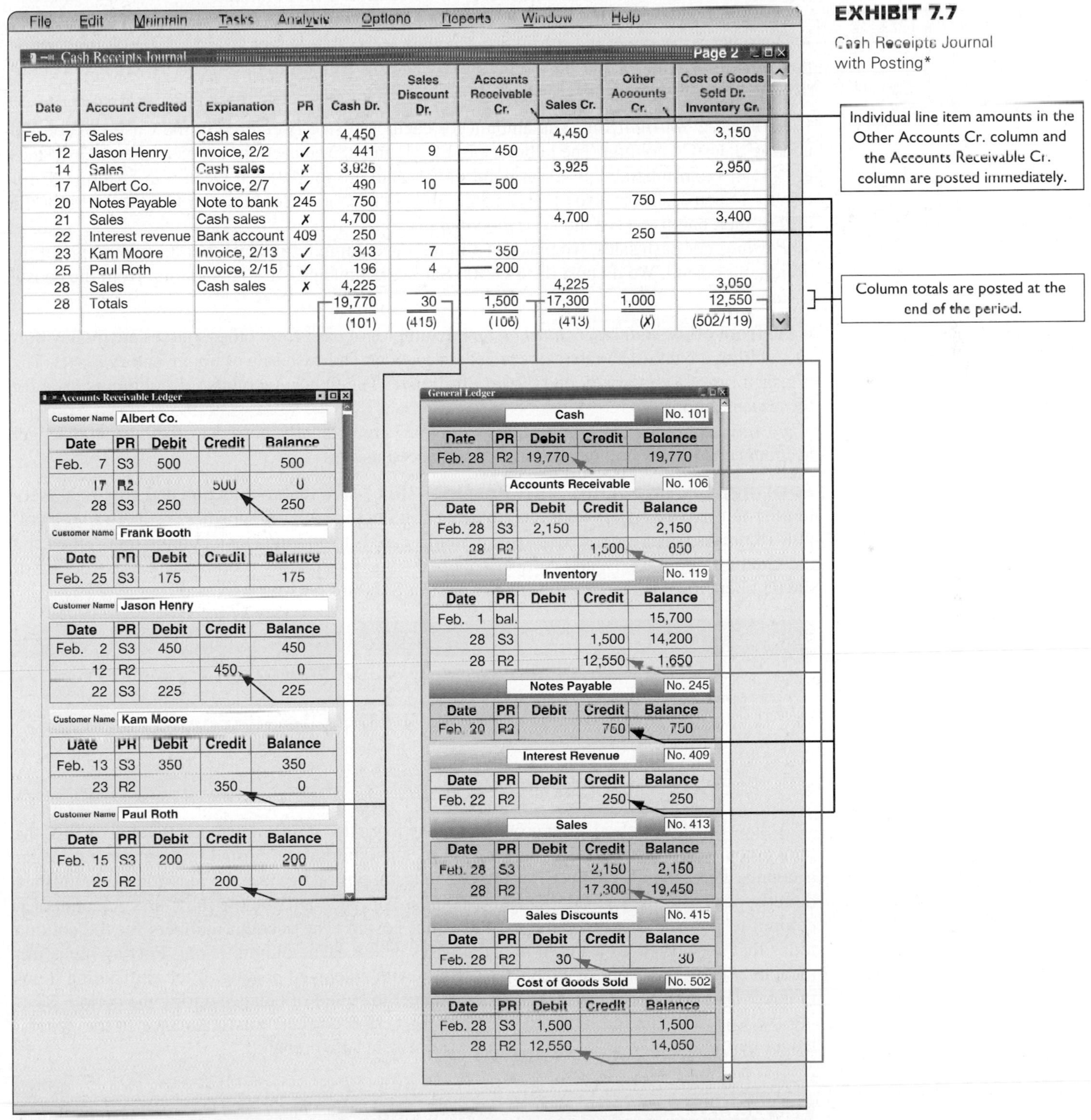

Date	Account Credited	Explanation	PR	Cash Dr.	Sales Discount Dr.	Accounts Receivable Cr.	Sales Cr.	Other Accounts Cr.	Cost of Goods Sold Dr. Inventory Cr.
Feb. 7	Sales	Cash sales	✗	4,450			4,450		3,150
12	Jason Henry	Invoice, 2/2	✓	441	9	450			
14	Sales	Cash sales	✗	3,925			3,925		2,950
17	Albert Co.	Invoice, 2/7	✓	490	10	500			
20	Notes Payable	Note to bank	245	750				750	
21	Sales	Cash sales	✗	4,700			4,700		3,400
22	Interest revenue	Bank account	409	250				250	
23	Kam Moore	Invoice, 2/13	✓	343	7	350			
25	Paul Roth	Invoice, 2/15	✓	196	4	200			
28	Sales	Cash sales	✗	4,225			4,225		3,050
28	Totals			19,770	30	1,500	17,300	1,000	12,550
				(101)	(415)	(106)	(413)	(✗)	(502/119)

Accounts Receivable Ledger

Customer Name: Albert Co.

Date	PR	Debit	Credit	Balance
Feb. 7	S3	500		500
17	R2		500	0
28	S3	250		250

Customer Name: Frank Booth

Date	PR	Debit	Credit	Balance
Feb. 25	S3	175		175

Customer Name: Jason Henry

Date	PR	Debit	Credit	Balance
Feb. 2	S3	450		450
12	R2		450	0
22	S3	225		225

Customer Name: Kam Moore

Date	PR	Debit	Credit	Balance
Feb. 13	S3	350		350
23	R2		350	0

Customer Name: Paul Roth

Date	PR	Debit	Credit	Balance
Feb. 15	S3	200		200
25	R2		200	0

General Ledger

Cash — No. 101

Date	PR	Debit	Credit	Balance
Feb. 28	R2	19,770		19,770

Accounts Receivable — No. 106

Date	PR	Debit	Credit	Balance
Feb. 28	S3	2,150		2,150
28	R2		1,500	650

Inventory — No. 119

Date	PR	Debit	Credit	Balance
Feb. 1	bal.			15,700
28	S3		1,500	14,200
28	R2		12,550	1,650

Notes Payable — No. 245

Date	PR	Debit	Credit	Balance
Feb. 20	R2		750	750

Interest Revenue — No. 409

Date	PR	Debit	Credit	Balance
Feb. 22	R2		250	250

Sales — No. 413

Date	PR	Debit	Credit	Balance
Feb. 28	S3		2,150	2,150
28	R2		17,300	19,450

Sales Discounts — No. 415

Date	PR	Debit	Credit	Balance
Feb. 28	R2	30		30

Cost of Goods Sold — No. 502

Date	PR	Debit	Credit	Balance
Feb. 28	S3	1,500		1,500
28	R2	12,550		14,050

EXHIBIT 7.7

Cash Receipts Journal with Posting*

*The Cash Receipts Journal in a *periodic* system would exclude the column on the far right titled "Cost of Goods Sold Dr., Inventory Cr." (see Exhibit 7A.2).

Point: Each transaction in the cash receipts journal involves a debit to Cash. Credit accounts will vary.

column for each of these three sources. We describe how to journalize transactions from each of these three sources. (An Explanation column is included in the cash receipts journal to identify the source.)

Cash from credit customers. *Journalizing.* To record cash received in payment of a customer's account, the customer's name is first entered in the Account Credited column—see transactions dated February 12, 17, 23, and 25. Then the amounts debited to both Cash and the Sales Discount (if any) are entered in their respective columns, and the amount credited to the customer's account is entered in the Accounts Receivable Cr. column.

Posting. Individual amounts in the Accounts Receivable Cr. column are posted immediately to customer accounts in the subsidiary accounts receivable ledger. The $1,500 column total is posted at the end of the period (month in this case) as a credit to the Accounts Receivable controlling account in the general ledger.

Cash sales. *Journalizing.* The amount for each cash sale is entered in the Cash Dr. column and the Sales Cr. column. The February 7, 14, 21, and 28 transactions are examples. (Cash sales are usually journalized daily or at point of sale, but are journalized weekly in Exhibit 7.7 for brevity.) Each cash sale also yields an entry to Cost of Goods Sold Dr. and Inventory Cr. for the cost of merchandise—see the far right column.

Point: Some software packages put cash sales in the sales journal.

Posting. For cash sales, we place an *x* in the PR column to indicate that its amount is not individually posted. We do post the $17,300 Sales Cr. total and the $12,550 total from the "cost" column.

Example: Record in the cash receipts journal a $700 cash sale of land when the land carries a $700 original cost. *Answer:* Debit the Cash column for $700, and credit the Other Accounts column for $700 (the account credited is Land).

Cash from other sources. *Journalizing.* Examples of cash from other sources are money borrowed from a bank, cash interest received on account, and cash sale of noninventory assets. The transactions of February 20 and 22 are illustrative. The Other Accounts Cr. column is used for these transactions.

Posting. Amounts from these transactions are immediately posted to their general ledger accounts and the PR column identifies those accounts.

Point: Subsidiary ledgers and their controlling accounts are *in balance* only after all posting is complete.

Footing, Crossfooting, and Posting To be sure that total debits and credits in a columnar journal are equal, we often crossfoot column totals before posting them. To *foot* a column of numbers is to add it. To *crossfoot* in this case is to add the Debit column totals, then add the Credit column totals, and compare the two sums for equality. Footing and crossfooting of the numbers in Exhibit 7.7 result in the report in Exhibit 7.8.

EXHIBIT 7.8

Footing and Crossfooting Journal Totals

Debit Columns		Credit Columns	
Cash Dr.	$19,770	Accounts Receivable Cr.	$ 1,500
Sales Discounts Dr.	30	Sales Cr.	17,300
Cost of Goods Sold Dr.	12,550	Other Accounts Cr.	1,000
		Inventory Cr.	12,550
Total	$32,350	Total	$32,350

At the end of the period, after crossfooting the journal to confirm that debits equal credits, the total amounts from the columns of the cash receipts journal are posted to their general ledger accounts. The Other Accounts Cr. column total is not posted because the individual amounts are directly posted to their general ledger accounts. We place an *x* below the Other Accounts Cr. column to indicate that this column total is not posted. The account numbers for the column totals that are posted are entered in parentheses below each column. (*Note:* Posting items immediately from the Other Accounts Cr. column with a delayed posting of their offsetting items in the Cash column total causes the general ledger to be out of balance during the period. Posting the Cash Dr. column total at the end of the period corrects this imbalance in the general ledger before the trial balance and financial statements are prepared.)

Answer — p. 297

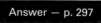

Entrepreneur You want to know how promptly customers are paying their bills. This information can help you decide whether to extend credit and to plan your cash payments. Where do you find this information? ■

Purchases Journal

A **purchases journal** is typically used to record all credit purchases, including those for inventory. Purchases for cash are recorded in the Cash Disbursements Journal.

Journalizing Entries in the purchases journal in Exhibit 7.9 reflect purchase invoices or other source documents. We use the invoice date and terms to compute the date when payment for each purchase is due. The Accounts Payable Cr. column is used to record the amounts owed to each creditor. Inventory purchases are recorded in the Inventory Dr. column.

To illustrate, inventory costing $200 is purchased from Ace Manufacturing on February 5. The creditor's name (Ace) is entered in the Account column, the invoice date is entered in the Date of Invoice column, the purchase terms are entered in the Terms column, and the $200 amount is entered in the Accounts Payable Cr. and the Inventory Dr. columns. When a purchase involves an amount recorded in the Other Accounts Dr. column, we use the Account column to identify the general ledger account debited. For example, the February 28 transaction involves purchases of inventory, office supplies, and store supplies from ITT. The journal has no column for store supplies, so the Other Accounts Dr. column is used. In this case, Store Supplies is entered in the Account column along with the creditor's name (ITT). This purchases journal also includes a separate column for credit purchases of office supplies. A separate column such as this is useful when several transactions involve debits to the same account. Each company uses its own judgment in deciding on the number of separate columns necessary.

Point: The number of special journals and the design of each are based on a company's specific needs.

Point: Each transaction in the purchases journal has a credit to Accounts Payable. Debit accounts will vary.

Point: The Other Accounts Dr. column allows the purchases journal to be used for any purchase on credit.

Posting The amounts in the Accounts Payable Cr. column are immediately posted to individual creditor accounts in the accounts payable subsidiary ledger. Individual amounts in the Other Accounts Dr. column are immediately posted to their general ledger accounts. At the end

EXHIBIT 7.9

Purchases Journal with Posting*

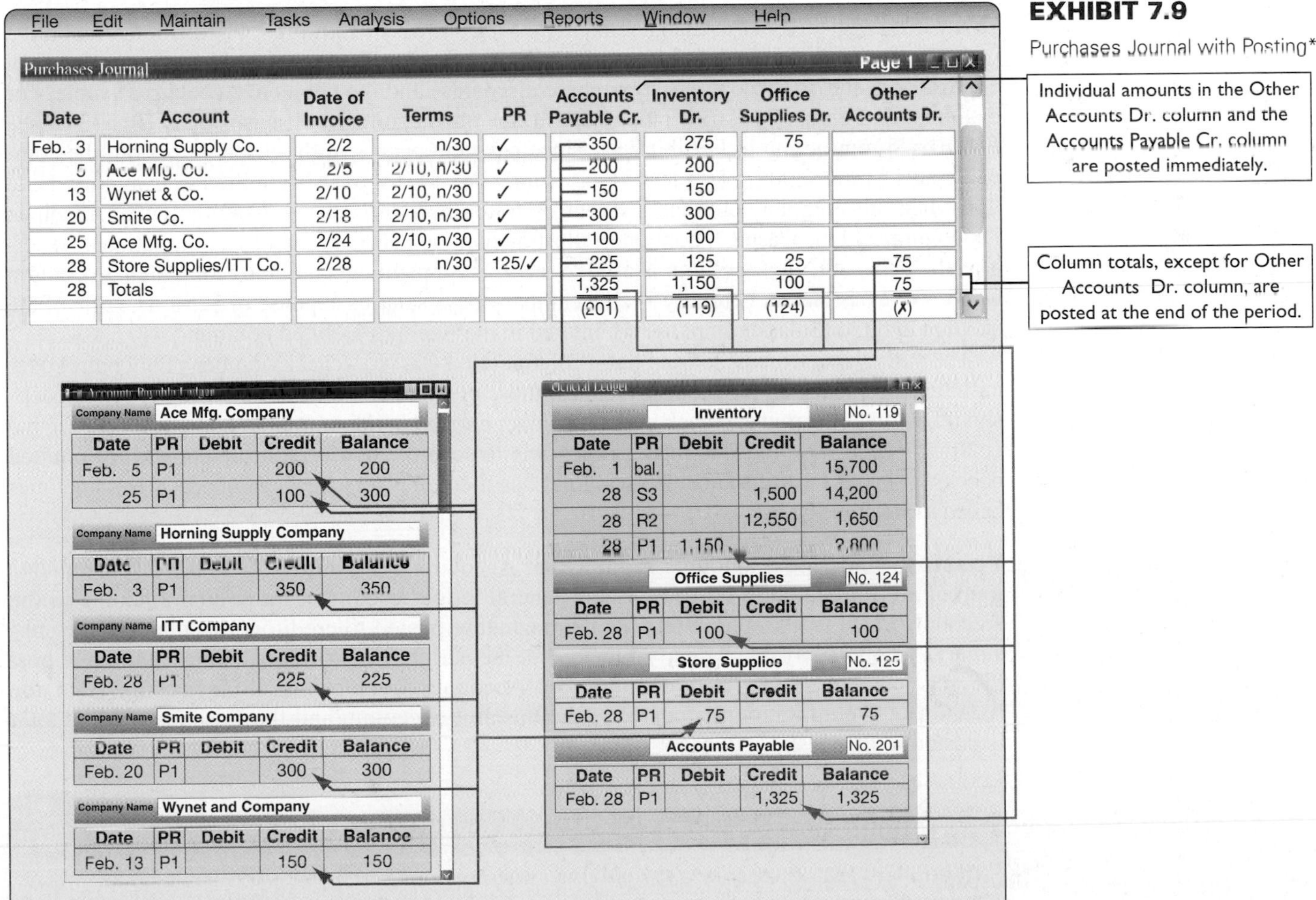

File Edit Maintain Tasks Analysis Options Reports Window Help

Purchases Journal — Page 1

Date	Account	Date of Invoice	Terms	PR	Accounts Payable Cr.	Inventory Dr.	Office Supplies Dr.	Other Accounts Dr.
Feb. 3	Horning Supply Co.	2/2	n/30	✓	350	275	75	
5	Ace Mfg. Co.	2/5	2/10, n/30	✓	200	200		
13	Wynet & Co.	2/10	2/10, n/30	✓	150	150		
20	Smite Co.	2/18	2/10, n/30	✓	300	300		
25	Ace Mfg. Co.	2/24	2/10, n/30	✓	100	100		
28	Store Supplies/ITT Co.	2/28	n/30	125/✓	225	125	25	75
28	Totals				1,325	1,150	100	75
					(201)	(119)	(124)	(✗)

Individual amounts in the Other Accounts Dr. column and the Accounts Payable Cr. column are posted immediately.

Column totals, except for Other Accounts Dr. column, are posted at the end of the period.

Accounts Payable Ledger

Company Name: Ace Mfg. Company

Date	PR	Debit	Credit	Balance
Feb. 5	P1		200	200
25	P1		100	300

Company Name: Horning Supply Company

Date	PR	Debit	Credit	Balance
Feb. 3	P1		350	350

Company Name: ITT Company

Date	PR	Debit	Credit	Balance
Feb. 28	P1		225	225

Company Name: Smite Company

Date	PR	Debit	Credit	Balance
Feb. 20	P1		300	300

Company Name: Wynet and Company

Date	PR	Debit	Credit	Balance
Feb. 13	P1		150	150

General Ledger

Inventory — No. 119

Date	PR	Debit	Credit	Balance
Feb. 1	bal.			15,700
28	S3		1,500	14,200
28	R2		12,550	1,650
28	P1	1,150		2,800

Office Supplies — No. 124

Date	PR	Debit	Credit	Balance
Feb. 28	P1	100		100

Store Supplies — No. 125

Date	PR	Debit	Credit	Balance
Feb. 28	P1	75		75

Accounts Payable — No. 201

Date	PR	Debit	Credit	Balance
Feb. 28	P1		1,325	1,325

*The Purchases Journal in a *periodic* system replaces "Inventory Dr." with "Purchases Dr." (see Exhibit 7A.3).

of the period, all column totals except the Other Accounts Dr. column are posted to their general ledger accounts.

Proving the Ledger Accounts payable balances in the subsidiary ledger can be periodically proved after posting. We prove the subsidiary ledger by preparing a **schedule of accounts payable,** which is a list of accounts from the accounts payable ledger with their balances and the total. If this total of the individual balances equals the balance of the Accounts Payable controlling account, the accounts in the accounts payable ledger are assumed correct. Exhibit 7.10 shows a schedule of accounts payable drawn from the accounts payable ledger of Exhibit 7.9. (This schedule can be done after any posting; for example, we could prepare another schedule of accounts payable after the postings in Exhibit 7.11.)

Point: The balance in the Accounts Payable controlling account must equal the sum of the individual account balances in the accounts payable subsidiary ledger after posting.

EXHIBIT 7.10

Schedule of Accounts Payable

Schedule of Accounts Payable February 28	
Ace Mfg. Company	$ 300
Horning Supply Company	350
ITT Company	225
Smite Company	300
Wynet & Company	150
Total accounts payable	$1,325

Cash Disbursements Journal

A **cash disbursements journal,** also called a *cash payments journal,* is typically used to record all cash payments.

Journalizing The cash disbursements journal shown in Exhibit 7.11 illustrates repetitive entries to the Cash Cr. column of this journal (reflecting cash payments). Also note the frequent credits to Inventory (which reflect purchase discounts) and the debits to Accounts Payable. For example, on February 15, the company pays Ace on account (credit terms of 2/10, n/30—see February 5 transaction in Exhibit 7.9). Since payment occurs in the discount period, the company pays $196 ($200 invoice less $4 discount). The $4 discount is credited to Inventory. Note that when this company purchases inventory for cash, it is recorded using the Other Accounts Dr. column and the Cash Cr. column as illustrated in the February 3 and 12 transactions. Generally, the Other Accounts column is used to record cash payments on items for which no column exists. For example, on February 15, the company pays salaries expense of $250. The title of the account debited (Salaries Expense) is entered in the Account Debited column.

Point: Each transaction in the cash disbursements journal involves a credit to Cash. The debit accounts will vary.

The cash disbursements journal has a column titled Ck. No. (check number). For control over cash disbursements, all payments except for those of small amounts are made by check. Checks should be prenumbered and each check's number entered in the journal in numerical order in the column headed Ck. No. This makes it possible to scan the numbers in the column for omitted checks. When a cash disbursements journal has a column for check numbers, it is sometimes called a **check register.**

Posting Individual amounts in the Other Accounts Dr. column of a cash disbursements journal are immediately posted to their general ledger accounts. Individual amounts in the Accounts Payable Dr. column are also immediately posted to creditors' accounts in the subsidiary Accounts Payable ledger. At the end of the period, we crossfoot column totals and post the Accounts Payable Dr. column total to the Accounts Payable controlling account. Also, the Inventory Cr. column total is posted to the Inventory account, and the Cash Cr. column total is posted to the Cash account.

Answer — p. 297

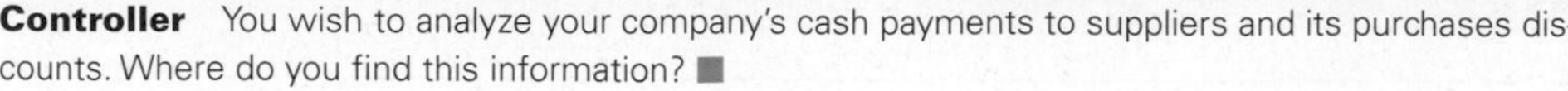

Controller You wish to analyze your company's cash payments to suppliers and its purchases discounts. Where do you find this information? ■

EXHIBIT 7.11

Cash Disbursements Journal with Posting*

File Edit Maintain Tasks Analysis Options Reports Window Help

Cash Disbursements Journal Page 2

Date	Ck. No.	Payee	Account Debited	PR	Cash Cr.	Inventory Cr.	Other Accounts Dr.	Accounts Payable Dr.
Feb. 3	105	L. & N. Railroad	Inventory	119	15		15	
12	106	East Sales Co.	Inventory	119	25		25	
15	107	Ace Mfg. Co.	Ace Mfg. Co.	✓	196	4		200
15	108	Jerry Hale	Salaries Expense	622	250		250	
20	109	Wynet & Co.	Wynet & Co.	✓	147	3		150
28	110	Smite Co.	Smite Co.	✓	294	6		300
28		Totals			927	13	290	650
					(101)	(119)	(X)	(201)

Individual amounts in the Other Accounts Dr. column and the Accounts Payable Dr. column are posted immediately.

Column totals, except for Other Accounts column, are posted at the end of the period.

General Ledger

Cash — No. 101

Date	PR	Debit	Credit	Balance
Feb. 28	R2	19,770		19,770
28	D2		927	18,843

Inventory — No. 119

Date	PR	Debit	Credit	Balance
Feb. 1	bal.			15,700
3	D2	15		15,715
12	D2	25		15,740
28	S3		1,500	14,240
28	R2		12,550	1,690
28	P1	1,150		2,840
28	D2		13	2,827

Accounts Payable — No. 201

Date	PR	Debit	Credit	Balance
Feb. 28	P1		1,325	1,325
28	D2	650		675

Salaries Expense — No. 622

Date	PR	Debit	Credit	Balance
Feb. 15	D2	250		250

Accounts Payable Ledger

Company Name: Ace Mfg. Company

Date	PR	Debit	Credit	Balance
Feb. 5	P1		200	200
15	D2	200		0
25	P1		100	100

Company Name: Horning Supply Company

Date	PR	Debit	Credit	Balance
Feb. 3	P1		350	350

Company Name: ITT Company

Date	PR	Debit	Credit	Balance
Feb. 28	P1		225	225

Company Name: Smite Company

Date	PR	Debit	Credit	Balance
Feb. 20	P1		300	300
28	D2	300		0

Company Name: Wynet & Company

Date	PR	Debit	Credit	Balance
Feb. 13	P1		150	150
20	D2	150		0

*The Cash Disbursements Journal in a *periodic* system replaces "Inventory Cr." with "Purchases Discounts Cr." (see Exhibit 7A.4).

General Journal Transactions

When special journals are used, we still need a general journal for adjusting, closing, and any other transactions for which no special journal has been set up. Examples of these other transactions might include purchases returns and allowances, purchases of plant assets by issuing a note payable, sales returns if a sales returns and allowances journal is not used, and receipt of a note receivable from a customer. We described the recording of transactions in a general journal in Chapters 2 and 3.

Quick Check

Answers — p. 297

10. What are the normal recording and posting procedures when using special journals and controlling accounts with subsidiary ledgers?
11. What is the process for posting to a subsidiary ledger and its controlling account?
12. How do we prove the accuracy of account balances in the general ledger and subsidiary ledgers after posting?
13. Why does a company need a general journal when using special journals for sales, purchases, cash receipts, and cash disbursements?

TECHNOLOGY-BASED ACCOUNTING SYSTEMS

Accounting information systems are supported with technology, which can range from simple calculators to advanced computerized systems. Since technology is increasingly important in accounting information systems, we discuss the impact of computer technology, how data processing works with accounting data, and the role of computer networks.

Computer Technology in Accounting

Computer technology provides accuracy, speed, efficiency, and convenience in performing accounting tasks. A program can be written, for instance, to process customers' merchandise orders. Multipurpose off-the-shelf software applications exist for a variety of business operations. These include familiar accounting programs such as Peachtree® and QuickBooks®. Off-the-shelf programs are designed to be user friendly and menu driven, and many operate more efficiently as *integrated* systems. In an integrated system, actions taken in one part of the system automatically affect related parts. When a credit sale is recorded in an integrated system, for instance, several parts of the system are automatically updated, such as posting.

Point: Companies that have reported missing or stolen employee data such as Social Security numbers include Time Warner, Polo Ralph Lauren, Lexis/Nexis, ChoicePoint, and DSW Shoes.

Computer technology can dramatically reduce the time and effort devoted to recordkeeping. Less effort spent on recordkeeping means more time for accounting professionals to concentrate on analysis and managerial decision making. These advances have created a greater demand for accounting professionals who understand financial reports and can draw insights and information from mountains of processed data. Accounting professionals have expertise in determining relevant and reliable information for decision making. They also can assess the effects of transactions and events on a company and its financial statements.

Decision Insight

Middleware is software allowing different computer programs in a company or across companies to work together. It allows transfer of purchase orders, invoices, and other electronic documents between accounting systems. For example, suppliers can monitor inventory levels of their buyers for production and shipping purposes. ■

Data Processing in Accounting

Accounting systems differ with regard to how input is entered and processed. **Online processing** enters and processes data as soon as source documents are available. This means that databases are immediately updated. **Batch processing** accumulates source documents for a period of time and then processes them all at once such as daily, weekly, or monthly. The advantage of online processing is timeliness. This often requires additional costs related to both software and hardware requirements. Companies such as **Intuit (Intuit.com)** are making online processing of accounting data a reality for many businesses. The advantage of batch processing is that it requires only periodic updating of databases. Records used to send bills to customers, for instance, might require updating only once a month. The disadvantage of batch processing is the lack of updated databases for management to use when making business decisions.

Computer Networks in Accounting

Networking, or linking computers with each other, can create information advantages (and cost efficiencies). **Computer networks** are links among computers giving different users and different computers access to common databases, programs, and hardware. Many college computer labs, for instance, are networked. A small computer network is called a *local area network (LAN);* it links machines with *hard-wire* hookups. Large computer networks extending over long distances often rely on *modem* or *wireless* communication.

Demand for information sometimes requires advanced networks such as the systems **Federal Express** and **UPS** use to track packages and bill customers and the system **Walmart** uses to monitor inventory levels in its stores. These networks include many computers and satellite communications to gather information and to provide ready access to its databases from all locations.

Enterprise Resource Planning Software

Enterprise resource planning (ERP) software includes the programs that manage a company's vital operations. They extend from order taking to manufacturing to accounting. When working properly, these integrated programs can speed decision making, identify costs for reduction, and give managers control over operations with the click of a mouse. For many managers, ERP software allows them to scrutinize business, identify where inventories are piling up, and see what plants are most efficient. The software is designed to link every part of a company's operations. This software allowed **Monsanto** to slash production planning from six weeks to three, trim its inventories, and increase its bargaining power with suppliers. Monsanto estimates that this software saves the company $200 million per year.

ERP has several suppliers. **SAP** leads the market, with **Oracle**, which gobbled up PeopleSoft and J. D. Edwards, a distant second (*AMR Research*). SAP software is used by more than half of the world's 500 largest companies. It links ordering, inventory, production, purchasing, planning, tracking, and human resources. A transaction or event triggers an immediate chain reaction of events throughout the enterprise. It is making companies more efficient and profitable.

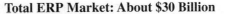

Total ERP Market: About $30 Billion

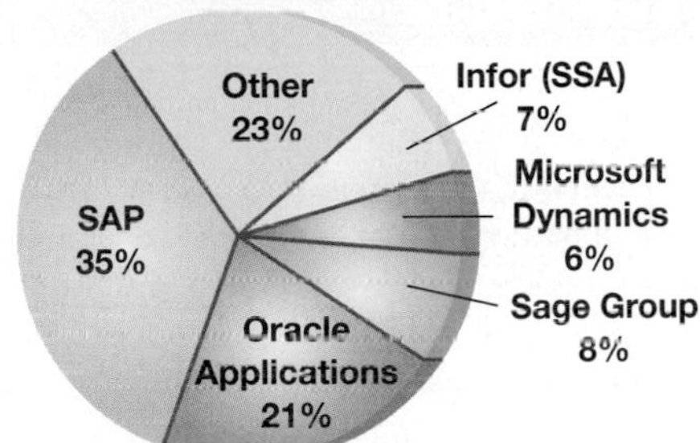

ERP is pushing into cyberspace and customer relationship management (CRM). Now companies can share data with customers and suppliers. Applesauce maker **Mott's** is using SAP so that distributors can check the status of orders and place them over the Net, and the **Coca-Cola Company** uses it to ship soda on time. ERP is also increasingly used by small business. For example, **NetSuite**'s accounting services to small and medium businesses are powered by Oracle's system.

Decision Insight

A new generation of accounting support is available. With the touch of a key, users can create real-time inventory reports showing all payments, charges, and credit limits at any point in the accounting cycle. Many services also include "alert signals" notifying the company when, for example, a large order exceeds a customer's credit limit or when purchases need to be made or when a bank balance is running low. These alerts occur via e-mail, fax, PDA, or phone. ■

Quick Check

Answers — p. 297

14. Identify an advantage of an integrated computer-based accounting system.
15. What advantages do computer systems offer over manual systems?
16. Identify an advantage of computer networks.
17. Describe ERP software and its potential advantages to businesses.

GLOBAL VIEW

This section discusses similarities and differences between U.S. GAAP and IFRS regarding system principles and components, and special journals.

System Principles and Components Both U.S. GAAP and IFRS aim for high-quality financial reporting. That aim implies that sound information system principles and components are applied worldwide.

However, while system principles and components are fundamentally similar across the globe, culture and other realities often mean different emphases are placed on the mix of system controls. **Nokia** provides the following description of its system controls:

Nokia's disclosure controls and procedures . . . are designed to provide reasonable assurance regarding the quality and integrity of the company's financial statements and related disclosures.

Special Journals Accounting systems for recording sales, purchases, cash receipts, and cash disbursements are similar worldwide. Although the exact structure of special journals is unique to each company, the basic structure is identical. Companies desire to apply accounting in an efficient manner. Accordingly, systems that employ special journals are applied worldwide.

Decision Analysis — Segment Return on Assets

A1 Compute segment return on assets and use it to evaluate segment performance.

Good accounting information systems collect financial data for a company's various segments. A *segment* refers to a part of a company that is separately identified by its products or services, or by the geographic market it serves. **Callaway Golf Company** reports that it operates in two business segments: (1) golf clubs and (2) golf balls. Users of financial statements are especially interested in segment information to better understand a company's activities because segments often vary on profitability, risk, and growth.

Companies must report segment information, including their sales, operating income, identifiable assets, capital expenditures, and depreciation. However, managers are reluctant to release information that can harm competitive position. Exhibit 7.12 shows survey results on the number of companies with different (reported) segments.

EXHIBIT 7.12

Companies Reporting Operations by Types of Segments*

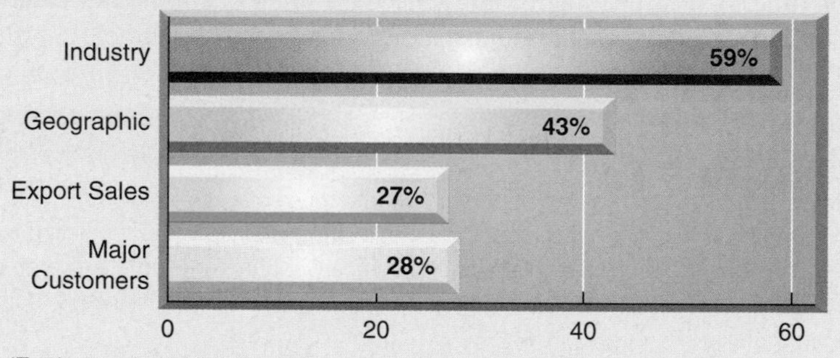

*Total exceeds 100% because companies can report more than one segment.

One measure of success for business segments is the **segment return on assets** ratio defined as follows.

$$\textbf{Segment return on assets} = \frac{\textbf{Segment operating income}}{\textbf{Segment average assets}}$$

EXHIBIT 7.13

Callaway Golf's Segment Return on Assets

This ratio reflects on the profitability of a segment. Exhibit 7.13 shows the segments' operating income, average assets, and return on assets for Callaway Golf Company.

Golf Segment* ($ thousands)	2009		2008		2007		2006	
	Clubs	Balls	Clubs	Balls	Clubs	Balls	Clubs	Balls
Operating income	$ 38,934	$(13,864)	$134,018	$ 6,903	$151,759	$ 902	$101,837	$ (6,396)
Average assets	$406,835	$129,796	$429,170	$146,855	$413,352	$140,730	$419,212	$152,282
Segment return on assets	10%	n.a.	31%	5%	37%	1%	24%	n.a.

* A segment's operating income is usually measured as pretax income, and assets is usually measured as identifiable assets.

The trend in Callaway's segment return on assets is up-and-down for its golf club segment, and similarly mixed for its golf balls segment. Importantly, its golf clubs segment makes up a much greater portion of its operations; for example, 2008 income of $134,018 from golf clubs make up 95% of its total income of $140,921 from both segments. Callaway should continue investments in its golf club segment vis-a-vis its golf balls segment given the greater returns and larger total income from that segment. Analysis can also be extended to geographical segments and any other segments that companies report.

Decision Maker Answer — p. 297 

Banker A bicycle merchandiser requests a loan from you to expand operations. Its net income is $220,000, reflecting a 10% increase over the prior year. You ask about segment results. The owner reports that $160,000 of net income is from Cuban operations, reflecting a 60% increase over the prior year. The remaining $60,000 of net income is from U.S. operations, reflecting a 40% decrease. Does this segment information impact your loan decision? ■

DEMONSTRATION PROBLEM—PERPETUAL SYSTEM

Pepper Company completed the following selected transactions and events during March of this year. (Terms of all credit sales for the company are 2/10, n/30.)

Mar. 4 Sold merchandise on credit to Jennifer Nelson, Invoice No. 954, for $16,800 (cost is $12,200).
6 Purchased $1,220 of office supplies on credit from Mack Company. Invoice dated March 3, terms n/30.
6 Sold merchandise on credit to Dennie Hoskins, Invoice No. 955, for $10,200 (cost is $8,100).
11 Purchased $52,600 of merchandise, invoice dated March 6, terms 2/10, n/30, from Defore Industries.
12 Borrowed $26,000 cash by giving Commerce Bank a long-term promissory note payable.
14 Received cash payment from Jennifer Nelson for the March 4 sale less the discount (Invoice No. 954).
16 Received a $200 credit memorandum from Defore Industries for unsatisfactory merchandise Pepper purchased on March 11 and later returned.
16 Received cash payment from Dennie Hoskins for the March 6 sale less the discount (Invoice No. 955).
18 Purchased $22,850 of store equipment on credit from Schmidt Supply, invoice dated March 15, terms n/30.
20 Sold merchandise on credit to Marjorie Allen, Invoice No. 956, for $5,600 (cost is $3,800).
21 Sent Defore Industries Check No. 516 in payment of its March 6 dated invoice less the return and the discount.
22 Purchased $41,625 of merchandise, invoice dated March 18, terms 2/10, n/30, from Welch Company.
26 Issued a $600 credit memorandum to Marjorie Allen for defective merchandise Pepper sold on March 20 and Allen later returned.
31 Issued Check No. 517, payable to Payroll, in payment of $15,900 sales salaries for the month. Cashed the check and paid the employees.
31 Cash sales for the month are $134,680 (cost is $67,340). (Cash sales are recorded daily but are recorded only once here to reduce repetitive entries.)

Required

1. Open the following selected general ledger accounts: Cash (101), Accounts Receivable (106) Inventory (119), Office Supplies (124), Store Equipment (165), Accounts Payable (201), Long-Term Notes Payable (251), Sales (413), Sales Returns and Allowances (414), Sales Discounts (415), Cost of Goods Sold (502), and Sales Salaries Expense (621). Open the following accounts receivable ledger accounts: Marjorie Allen, Dennie Hoskins, and Jennifer Nelson. Open the following accounts payable ledger accounts: Defore Industries, Mack Company, Schmidt Supply, and Welch Company.
2. Enter the transactions using a sales journal, a purchases journal, a cash receipts journal, a cash disbursements journal, and a general journal similar to the ones illustrated in the chapter. Regularly post to the individual customer and creditor accounts. Also, post any amounts that should be posted as individual amounts to general ledger accounts. Foot and crossfoot the journals and make the month-end postings. *Pepper Co. uses the perpetual inventory system.*

3. Prepare a trial balance for the selected general ledger accounts in part 1 and prove the accuracy of subsidiary ledgers by preparing schedules of accounts receivable and accounts payable.

PLANNING THE SOLUTION

- Set up the required general ledger, the subsidiary ledger accounts, and the five required journals as illustrated in the chapter.
- Read and analyze each transaction and decide in which special journal (or general journal) the transaction is recorded.
- Record each transaction in the proper journal (and post the appropriate individual amounts).
- Once you have recorded all transactions, total the journal columns. Post from each journal to the appropriate ledger accounts.
- Prepare a trial balance to prove the equality of the debit and credit balances in your general ledger.
- Prepare schedules of accounts receivable and accounts payable. Compare the totals of these schedules to the Accounts Receivable and Accounts Payable controlling account balances, making sure that they agree.

SOLUTION TO DEMONSTRATION PROBLEM—PERPETUAL SYSTEM

Sales Journal — Page 2

Date	Account Debited	Invoice Number	PR	Accounts Receivable Dr. Sales Cr.	Cost of Goods Sold Dr. Inventory Cr.
Mar. 4	Jennifer Nelson	954	✓	16,800	12,200
6	Dennie Hoskins	955	✓	10,200	8,100
20	Marjorie Allen	956	✓	5,600	3,800
31	Totals			32,600	24,100
				(106/413)	(502/119)

Cash Receipts Journal — Page 3

Date	Account Credited	Explanation	PR	Cash Dr.	Sales Discount Dr.	Accounts Receivable Cr.	Sales Cr.	Other Accounts Cr.	Cost of Goods Sold Dr. Inventory Cr.
Mar. 12	L.T. Notes Payable	Note to bank	251	26,000				26,000	
14	Jennifer Nelson	Invoice 954, 3/4	✓	16,464	336	16,800			
16	Dennie Hoskins	Invoice 955, 3/6	✓	9,996	204	10,200			
31	Sales	Cash sales	*x*	134,680			134,680		67,340
31	Totals			187,140	540	27,000	134,680	26,000	67,340
				(101)	(415)	(106)	(413)	(*x*)	(502/119)

Purchases Journal — Page 3

Date	Account	Date of Invoice	Terms	PR	Accounts Payable Cr.	Inventory Dr.	Office Supplies Dr.	Other Accounts Dr.
Mar. 6	Office Supplies/Mack Co	3/3	n/30	✓	1,220		1,220	
11	Defore Industries	3/6	2/10, n/30	✓	52,600	52,600		
18	Store Equipment/Schmidt Supp	3/15	n/30	165/✓	22,850			22,850
22	Welch Company	3/18	2/10, n/30	✓	41,625	41,625		
31	Totals				118,295	94,225	1,220	22,850
					(201)	(119)	(124)	(*x*)

Cash Disbursements Journal — Page 3

Date	Ck. No.	Payee	Account Debited	PR	Cash Cr.	Inventory Cr.	Other Accounts Dr.	Accounts Payable Dr.
Mar. 21	516	Defore Industries	Defore Industries	✓	51,352	1,048		52,400
31	517	Payroll	Sales Salaries Expense	621	15,900		15,900	
31		Totals			67,252	1,048	15,900	52,400
					(101)	(119)	(*x*)	(201)

General Journal — Page 2

Date	Account	PR	Debit	Credit
Mar. 16	Accounts Payable—Defore Industries	201/✓	200	
	Inventory	119		200
	To record credit memorandum received.			
26	Sales Returns and Allowances	414	600	
	Accounts Receivable—Marjorie Allen	106/✓		600
	To record credit memorandum issued.			

Accounts Receivable Ledger

Marjorie Allen

Date	PR	Debit	Credit	Balance
Mar. 20	S2	5,600		5,600
26	G2		600	5,000

Dennie Hoskins

Date	PR	Debit	Credit	Balance
Mar. 6	S2	10,200		10,200
16	R3		10,200	0

Jennifer Nelson

Date	PR	Debit	Credit	Balance
Mar. 4	S2	16,800		16,800
14	R3		16,800	0

Accounts Payable Ledger

Defore Industries

Date	PR	Debit	Credit	Balance
Mar. 11	P3		52,600	52,600
16	G2	200		52,400
21	D3	52,400		0

Mack Company

Date	PR	Debit	Credit	Balance
Mar. 6	P3		1,220	1,220

Schmidt Supply

Date	PR	Debit	Credit	Balance
Mar. 18	P3		22,850	22,850

Welch Company

Date	PR	Debit	Credit	Balance
Mar. 22	P3		41,625	41,625

General Ledger (Partial Listing)

Cash Acct. No. 101

Date	PR	Debit	Credit	Balance
Mar. 31	R3	187,140		187,140
31	D3		67,252	119,888

Accounts Receivable Acct. No. 106

Date	PR	Debit	Credit	Balance
Mar. 26	G2		600	(600)
31	S2	32,600		32,000
31	R3		27,000	5,000

Inventory Acct. No. 119

Date	PR	Debit	Credit	Balance
Mar. 16	G2		200	(200)
21	D3		1,048	(1,248)
31	P3	94,225		92,977
31	S2		24,100	68,877
31	R3		67,340	1,537

Office Supplies Acct. No. 124

Date	PR	Debit	Credit	Balance
Mar. 31	P3	1,220		1,220

Store Equipment Acct. No. 165

Date	PR	Debit	Credit	Balance
Mar. 18	P3	22,850		22,850

Accounts Payable Acct. No. 201

Date	PR	Debit	Credit	Balance
Mar. 16	G2	200		(200)
31	P3		118,295	118,095
31	D3	52,400		65,695

Long-Term Notes Payable Acct. No. 251

Date	PR	Debit	Credit	Balance
Mar. 12	R3		26,000	26,000

Sales Acct. No. 413

Date	PR	Debit	Credit	Balance
Mar. 31	S2		32,600	32,600
31	R3		134,680	167,280

Sales Returns and Allowances Acct. No. 414

Date	PR	Debit	Credit	Balance
Mar. 26	G2	600		600

Sales Discounts Acct. No. 415

Date	PR	Debit	Credit	Balance
Mar. 31	R3	540		540

Cost of Goods Sold Acct. No. 502

Date	PR	Debit	Credit	Balance
Mar. 31	R3	67,340		67,340
31	S2	24,100		91,440

Sales Salaries Expense Acct. No. 621

Date	PR	Debit	Credit	Balance
Mar. 31	D3	15,900		15,900

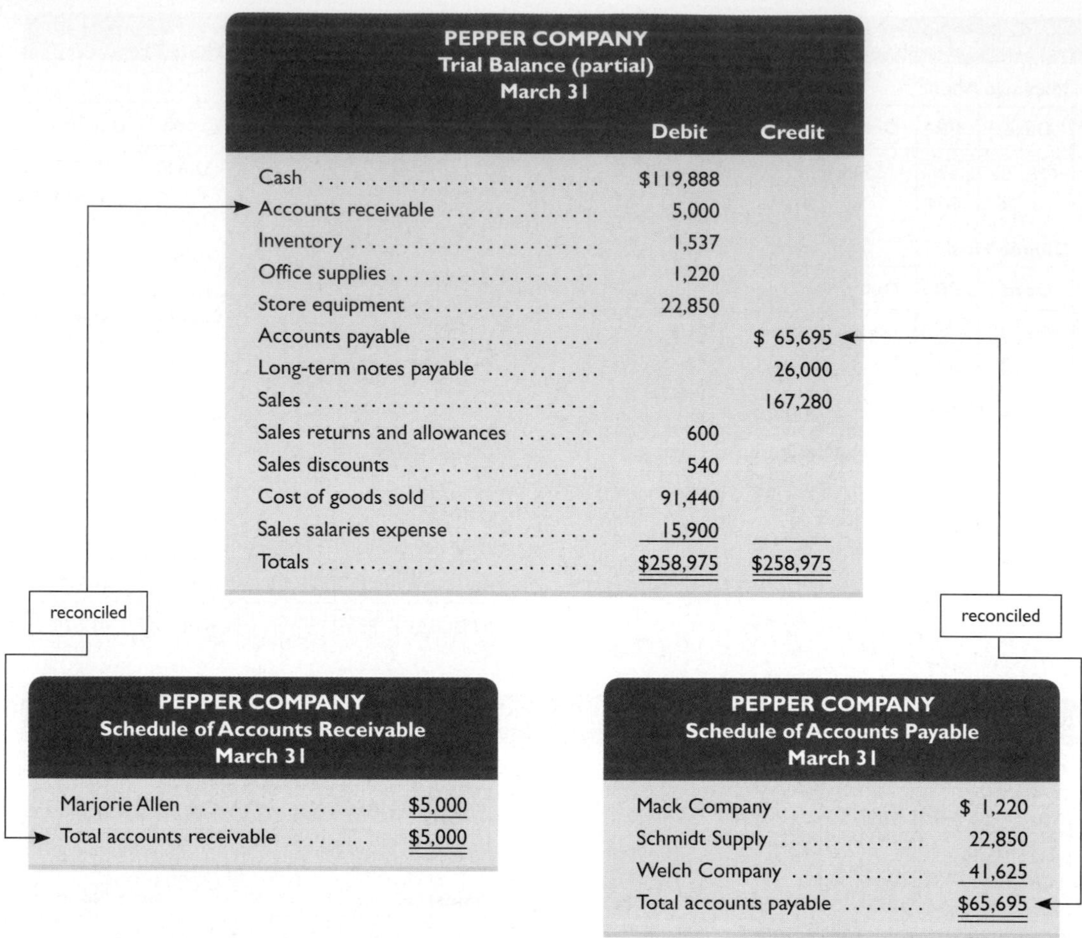

PEPPER COMPANY
Trial Balance (partial)
March 31

	Debit	Credit
Cash	$119,888	
Accounts receivable	5,000	
Inventory	1,537	
Office supplies	1,220	
Store equipment	22,850	
Accounts payable		$ 65,695
Long-term notes payable		26,000
Sales		167,280
Sales returns and allowances	600	
Sales discounts	540	
Cost of goods sold	91,440	
Sales salaries expense	15,900	
Totals	$258,975	$258,975

PEPPER COMPANY
Schedule of Accounts Receivable
March 31

Marjorie Allen	$5,000
Total accounts receivable	$5,000

PEPPER COMPANY
Schedule of Accounts Payable
March 31

Mack Company	$ 1,220
Schmidt Supply	22,850
Welch Company	41,625
Total accounts payable	$65,695

APPENDIX 7A Special Journals under a Periodic System

P3 Journalize and post transactions using special journals in a periodic inventory system.

This appendix describes special journals under a periodic inventory system. Each journal is slightly impacted. The sales journal and the cash receipts journal both require one less column (namely that of Cost of Goods Sold Dr., Inventory Cr.). The Purchases Journal replaces the Inventory Dr. column with a Purchases Dr. column in a periodic system. The cash disbursements journal replaces the Inventory Cr. column with a Purchases Discounts Cr. column in a periodic system. These changes are illustrated.

Sales Journal The sales journal using the periodic inventory system is shown in Exhibit 7A.1. The difference in the sales journal between the perpetual and periodic system is the exclusion of the column to record cost of goods sold and inventory amounts for each sale. The periodic system does *not* record the increase in cost of goods sold and the decrease in inventory at the time of each sale.

EXHIBIT 7A.1

Sales Journal—Periodic System

Sales Journal — Page 3

Date	Account Debited	Invoice Number	PR	Accounts Receivable Dr. Sales Cr.
Feb. 2	Jason Henry	307	✓	450
7	Albert Co.	308	✓	500
13	Kam Moore	309	✓	350
15	Paul Roth	310	✓	200
22	Jason Henry	311	✓	225
25	Frank Booth	312	✓	175
28	Albert Co.	313	✓	250
28	Total			2,150
				(106/413)

Cash Receipts Journal The cash receipts journal using the periodic system is shown in Exhibit 7A.2. Note the absence of the column on the far right side to record debits to Cost of Goods Sold and credits to Inventory for the cost of merchandise sold (seen under the perpetual system). Consistent with the cash receipts journal shown in Exhibit 7.7, we show only the weekly (summary) cash sale entries.

EXHIBIT 7A.2

Cash Receipts Journal—Periodic System

Cash Receipts Journal — Page 2

Date	Account Credited	Explanation	PR	Cash Dr.	Sales Discount Dr.	Accounts Receivable Cr.	Sales Cr.	Other Accounts Cr.
Feb. 7	Sales	Cash sales	x	4,450			4,450	
12	Jason Henry	Invoice 307, 2/2	✓	441	9	450		
14	Sales	Cash sales	x	3,925			3,925	
17	Albert Co.	Invoice 308, 2/7	✓	490	10	500		
20	Notes Payable	Note to bank	245	750				750
21	Sales	Cash sales	x	4,700			4,700	
22	Interest revenue	Bank account	409	250				250
23	Kam Moore	Invoice 309, 2/13	✓	343	7	350		
25	Paul Roth	Invoice 310, 2/15	✓	196	4	200		
28	Sales	Cash sales	x	4,225			4,225	
28	Totals			19,770	30	1,500	17,300	1,000
				(101)	(415)	(106)	(413)	(x)

Purchases Journal The purchases journal using the periodic system is shown in Exhibit 7A.3. This journal under a perpetual system included an Inventory column where the periodic system now has a Purchases column.

EXHIBIT 7A.3

Purchases Journal—Periodic System

Purchases Journal — Page 1

Date	Account	Date of Invoice	Terms	PR	Accounts Payable Cr.	Purchases Dr.	Office Supplies Dr.	Other Accounts Dr.
Feb. 3	Horning Supply Co.	2/2	n/30	✓	350	275	75	
5	Ace Mfg. Co.	2/5	2/10, n/30	✓	200	200		
13	Wynet and Co.	2/10	2/10, n/30	✓	150	150		
20	Smite Co.	2/18	2/10, n/30	✓	300	300		
25	Ace Mfg. Co.	2/24	2/10, n/30	✓	100	100		
28	Store Supplies/ITT Co.	2/28	n/30	125/✓	225	125	25	75
28	Totals				1,325	1,150	100	75
					(201)	(505)	(124)	(x)

Cash Disbursements Journal The cash disbursements journal using a periodic system is shown in Exhibit 7A.4. This journal under the perpetual system included an Inventory column where the periodic system now has the Purchases Discounts column.

EXHIBIT 7A.4

Cash Disbursements Journal—Periodic System

Cash Disbursements Journal — Page 2

Date	Ck. No.	Payee	Account Debited	PR	Cash Cr.	Purchases Discounts Cr.	Other Accounts Dr.	Accounts Payable Dr.
Feb. 3	105	L. and N. Railroad	Purchases	505	15		15	
12	106	East Sales Co.	Purchases	505	25		25	
15	107	Ace Mfg. Co.	Ace Mfg. Co.	✓	196	4		200
15	108	Jerry Hale	Salaries Expense	622	250		250	
20	109	Wynet and Co.	Wynet and Co.	✓	147	3		150
28	110	Smite Co.	Smite Co.	✓	294	6		300
28		Totals			927	13	290	650
					(101)	(507)	(x)	(201)

DEMONSTRATION PROBLEM—PERIODIC SYSTEM

Refer to Pepper Company's selected transactions described under the Demonstration Problem—Perpetual System to fulfill the following requirements.

Required

1. Open the following selected general ledger accounts: Cash (101), Accounts Receivable (106), Office Supplies (124), Store Equipment (165), Accounts Payable (201), Long-Term Notes Payable (251), Sales (413), Sales Returns and Allowances (414), Sales Discounts (415), Purchases (505), Purchases

Returns and Allowances (506), Purchases Discounts (507), and Sales Salaries Expense (621). Open the following accounts receivable ledger accounts: Marjorie Allen, Dennie Hoskins, and Jennifer Nelson. Open the following accounts payable ledger accounts: Defore Industries, Mack Company, Schmidt Supply, and Welch Company.

2. Enter the transactions using a sales journal, a purchases journal, a cash receipts journal, a cash disbursements journal, and a general journal similar to the ones illustrated in Appendix 7A. Regularly post to the individual customer and creditor accounts. Also, post any amounts that should be posted as individual amounts to general ledger accounts. Foot and crossfoot the journals and make the month-end postings. *Pepper Co. uses the periodic inventory system in this problem.*
3. Prepare a trial balance for the selected general ledger accounts in part 1 and prove the accuracy of subsidiary ledgers by preparing schedules of accounts receivable and accounts payable.

SOLUTION TO DEMONSTRATION PROBLEM—PERIODIC SYSTEM

Sales Journal — Page 2

Date	Account Debited	Invoice Number	PR	Accounts Receivable Dr. Sales Cr.
Mar. 4	Jennifer Nelson	954	✓	16,800
6	Dennie Hoskins	955	✓	10,200
20	Marjorie Allen	956	✓	5,600
31	Totals			32,600
				(106/413)

Cash Receipts Journal — Page 3

Date	Account Credited	Explanation	PR	Cash Dr.	Sales Discount Dr.	Accounts Receivable Cr.	Sales Cr.	Other Accounts Cr.
Mar. 12	L.T. Notes Payable	Note to bank	251	26,000				26,000
14	Jennifer Nelson	Invoice 954, 3/4	✓	16,464	336	16,800		
16	Dennie Hoskins	Invoice 955, 3/6	✓	9,996	204	10,200		
31	Sales	Cash sales	x	134,680			134,680	
31	Totals			187,140	540	27,000	134,680	26,000
				(101)	(415)	(106)	(413)	(x)

Purchases Journal — Page 3

Date	Account	Date of Invoice	Terms	PR	Accounts Payable Cr.	Purchases Dr.	Office Supplies Dr.	Other Accounts Dr.
Mar. 6	Office Supplies/Mack Co	3/3	n/30	✓	1,220		1,220	
11	Defore Industries	3/6	2/10, n/30	✓	52,600	52,600		
18	Store Equipment/Schmidt Supp	3/15	n/30	165/✓	22,850			22,850
22	Welch Company	3/18	2/10, n/30	✓	41,625	41,625		
31	Totals				118,295	94,225	1,220	22,850
					(201)	(505)	(124)	(x)

Cash Disbursements Journal — Page 3

Date	Ck. No.	Payee	Account Debited	PR	Cash Cr.	Purchases Discount Cr.	Other Accounts Dr.	Accounts Payable Dr.
Mar. 21	516	Defore Industries	Defore Industries	✓	51,352	1,048		52,400
31	517	Payroll	Sales Salaries Expense	621	15,900		15,900	
31		Totals			67,252	1,048	15,900	52,400
					(101)	(507)	(x)	(201)

General Journal — Page 2

Date	Account	PR	Dr.	Cr.
Mar. 16	Accounts Payable—Defore Industries	201/✓	200	
	Purchases Returns and Allowances	506		200
	To record credit memorandum received.			
26	Sales Returns and Allowances	414	600	
	Accounts Receivable—Marjorie Allen	106/✓		600
	To record credit memorandum issued.			

Accounts Receivable Ledger

Marjorie Allen

Date	PR	Debit	Credit	Balance
Mar. 20	S2	5,600		5,600
26	G2		600	5,000

Dennie Hockins

Date	PR	Debit	Credit	Balance
Mar. 6	S2	10,200		10,200
16	R3		10,200	0

Jennifer Nelson

Date	PR	Debit	Credit	Balance
Mar. 4	S2	16,800		16,800
14	R3		16,800	0

Accounts Payable Ledger

Defore Industries

Date	PR	Debit	Credit	Balance
Mar. 11	P3		52,600	52,600
16	G2	200		52,400
21	D3	52,400		0

Mack Company

Date	PR	Debit	Credit	Balance
Mar. 6	P3		1,220	1,220

Schmidt Supply

Date	PR	Debit	Credit	Balance
Mar. 18	P3		22,850	22,850

Welch Company

Date	PR	Debit	Credit	Balance
Mar. 22	P3		41,625	41,625

General Ledger (Partial Listing)

Cash — **Acct. No. 101**

Date	PR	Debit	Credit	Balance
Mar. 31	R3	187,140		187,140
31	D3		67,252	119,888

Accounts Receivable — **Acct. No. 106**

Date	PR	Debit	Credit	Balance
Mar. 26	G2		600	(600)
31	S2	32,600		32,000
31	R3		27,000	5,000

Office Supplies — **Acct. No. 124**

Date	PR	Debit	Credit	Balance
Mar. 31	P3	1,220		1,220

Store Equipment — **Acct. No. 165**

Date	PR	Debit	Credit	Balance
Mar. 18	P3	22,850		22,850

Accounts Payable — **Acct. No. 201**

Date	PR	Debit	Credit	Balance
Mar. 16	G2	200		(200)
31	P3		118,295	118,095
31	D3	52,400		65,695

Long-Term Notes Payable — **Acct. No. 251**

Date	PR	Debit	Credit	Balance
Mar. 12	R3		26,000	26,000

Sales — **Acct. No. 413**

Date	PR	Debit	Credit	Balance
Mar. 31	S2		32,600	32,600
31	R3		134,680	167,280

Sales Returns and Allowances — **Acct. No. 414**

Date	PR	Debit	Credit	Balance
Mar. 26	G2	600		600

Sales Discounts — **Acct. No. 415**

Date	PR	Debit	Credit	Balance
Mar. 31	R3	540		540

Purchases — **Acct. No. 505**

Date	PR	Debit	Credit	Balance
Mar. 31	P3	94,225		94,225

Purchases Returns and Allowances — **Acct. No. 506**

Date	PR	Debit	Credit	Balance
Mar. 16	G2		200	200

Purchases Discounts — **Acct. No. 507**

Date	PR	Debit	Credit	Balance
Mar. 31	D3		1,048	1,048

Sales Salaries Expense — **Acct. No. 621**

Date	PR	Debit	Credit	Balance
Mar. 31	D3	15,900		15,900

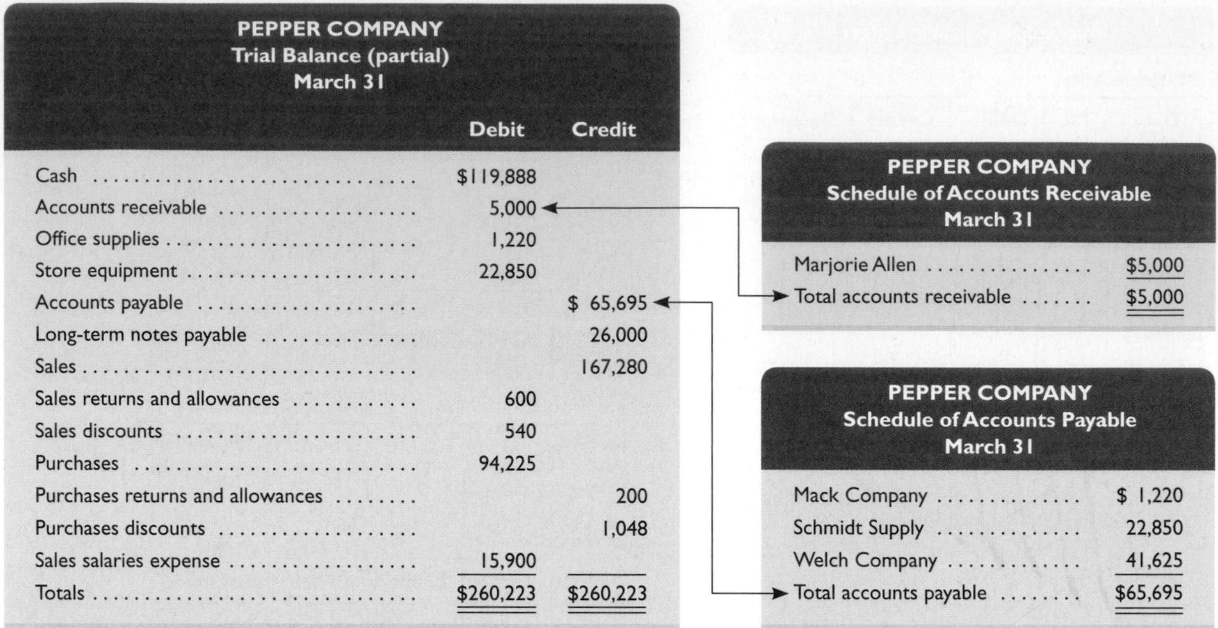

PEPPER COMPANY
Trial Balance (partial)
March 31

	Debit	Credit
Cash	$119,888	
Accounts receivable	5,000	
Office supplies	1,220	
Store equipment	22,850	
Accounts payable		$ 65,695
Long-term notes payable		26,000
Sales		167,280
Sales returns and allowances	600	
Sales discounts	540	
Purchases	94,225	
Purchases returns and allowances		200
Purchases discounts		1,048
Sales salaries expense	15,900	
Totals	$260,223	$260,223

PEPPER COMPANY
Schedule of Accounts Receivable
March 31

Marjorie Allen	$5,000
Total accounts receivable	$5,000

PEPPER COMPANY
Schedule of Accounts Payable
March 31

Mack Company	$ 1,220
Schmidt Supply	22,850
Welch Company	41,625
Total accounts payable	$65,695

Summary

C1 Identify the principles and components of accounting information systems. Accounting information systems are governed by five fundamental principles: control, relevance, compatibility, flexibility, and cost-benefit. The five basic components of an accounting information system are source documents, input devices, information processors, information storage, and output devices.

C2 Explain the goals and uses of special journals. Special journals are used for recording transactions of similar type, each meant to cover one kind of transaction. Four of the most common special journals are the sales journal, cash receipts journal, purchases journal, and cash disbursements journal. Special journals are efficient and cost-effective tools in the journalizing and posting processes.

C3 Describe the use of controlling accounts and subsidiary ledgers. A general ledger keeps controlling accounts such as Accounts Receivable and Accounts Payable, but details on individual accounts making up the controlling account are kept in subsidiary ledgers (such as an accounts receivable ledger). The balance in a controlling account must equal the sum of its subsidiary account balances after posting is complete.

A1 Compute segment return on assets and use it to evaluate segment performance. A business segment is a part of a company that is separately identified by its products or services or by the geographic market it serves. Analysis of a company's segments is aided by the segment return on assets (segment operating income divided by segment average assets).

P1 Journalize and post transactions using special journals. Each special journal is devoted to similar kinds of transactions. Transactions are journalized on one line of a special journal, with columns devoted to specific accounts, dates, names, posting references, explanations, and other necessary information. Posting is threefold: (1) individual amounts in the Other Accounts column are posted to their general ledger accounts on a regular (daily) basis, (2) individual amounts in a column whose total is *not* posted to a controlling account at the end of a period (month) are posted regularly (daily) to their general ledger accounts, and (3) total amounts for all columns except the Other Accounts column are posted at the end of a period (month) to their column's account title in the general ledger.

P2 Prepare and prove the accuracy of subsidiary ledgers. Account balances in the general ledger and its subsidiary ledgers are tested for accuracy after posting is complete. This procedure is twofold: (1) prepare a trial balance of the general ledger to confirm that debits equal credits and (2) prepare a schedule to confirm that the controlling account's balance equals the subsidiary ledger's balance.

P3A Journalize and post transactions using special journals in a periodic inventory system. Transactions are journalized and posted using special journals in a periodic system. The methods are similar to those in a perpetual system; the primary difference is that both cost of goods sold and inventory are not adjusted at the time of each sale. This usually results in the deletion (or renaming) of one or more columns devoted to these accounts in each special journal.

Guidance Answers to Decision Maker and Decision Ethics

Accountant The main issue is whether commissions have an actual or perceived impact on the integrity and objectivity of your advice. You probably should not accept a commission arrangement (the AICPA Code of Ethics prohibits it when you perform the audit or a review). In any event, you should tell the client of your commission arrangement. Also, you need to seriously examine the merits of agreeing to a commission arrangement when you are in a position to exploit it.

Entrepreneur The accounts receivable ledger has much of the information you need. It lists detailed information for each customer's account, including the amounts, dates for transactions, and dates of payments. It can be reorganized into an "aging schedule" to show how long customers wait before paying their bills.

Controller Much of the information you need is in the accounts payable ledger. It contains information for each supplier, the amounts due, and when payments are made. This subsidiary ledger along with information on credit terms should enable you to conduct your analyses.

Banker This merchandiser's segment information is likely to greatly impact your loan decision. The risks associated with the company's two sources of net income are quite different. While net income is up by 10%, U.S. operations are performing poorly and Cuban operations are subject to many uncertainties. These uncertainties depend on political events, legal issues, business relationships, Cuban economic conditions, and a host of other risks. Overall, net income results suggested a low-risk loan opportunity, but the segment information reveals a high-risk situation.

Guidance Answers to Quick Checks

1. The five components are source documents, input devices, information processors, information storage, and output devices.
2. Information processors interpret, transform, and summarize the recorded accounting information so that it can be used in analysis, interpretation, and decision making.
3. Data saved in information storage are used to prepare periodic financial reports and special-purpose internal reports as well as source documentation for auditors.
4. All cash payments by check are recorded in the cash disbursements journal.
5. Columnar journals allow us to accumulate repetitive debits and credits and post them as column totals rather than as individual amounts from each entry.
6. The equality of debits and credits is kept within the general ledger. The subsidiary ledger keeps the customer's individual account and is used only for supplementary information.
7. An initial and the page number of the journal from which the amount was posted are entered in the PR column next to the amount.
8. A separate column for Sales Taxes Payable can be included in both the cash receipts journal and the sales journal.
9. This refers to a procedure of using copies of sales invoices as a sales journal. Each invoice amount is posted directly to the customer's account. All invoices are totaled at period-end for posting to the general ledger accounts.
10. The normal recording and posting procedures are threefold. First, transactions are entered in a special journal if applicable. Second, individual amounts are posted to any subsidiary ledger accounts. Third, column totals are posted to general ledger accounts if not already individually posted.
11. Controlling accounts are debited periodically for an amount or amounts equal to the sum of their respective debits in the subsidiary ledgers (equals journal column totals), and they are credited periodically for an amount or amounts equal to the sum of their respective credits in the subsidiary ledgers (from journal column totals).
12. Tests for accuracy of account balances in the general ledger and subsidiary ledgers are twofold. First, we prepare a trial balance of the general ledger to confirm that debits equal credits. Second, we prove the subsidiary ledgers by preparing schedules of accounts receivable and accounts payable.
13. The general journal is still needed for adjusting, closing, and correcting entries and for special transactions such as sales returns, purchases returns, and certain asset purchases.
14. Integrated systems can save time and minimize errors. This is so because actions taken in one part of the system automatically affect and update related parts.
15. Computer systems offer increased accuracy, speed, efficiency, and convenience.
16. Computer networks can create advantages by linking computers, and giving different users and different computers access to common databases, programs, and hardware.
17. ERP software involves integrated programs, from order taking to manufacturing to accounting. It can speed decision making, help identify costs for reduction, and aid managers in controlling operations.

Key Terms

mhhe.com/wildFAP20e

Accounting information systems (p. 272)
Accounts payable ledger (p. 277)
Accounts receivable ledger (p. 277)
Batch processing (p. 286)
Cash disbursements journal (p. 284)
Cash receipts journal (p. 281)
Check register (p. 284)
Columnar journal (p. 278)
Compatibility principle (p. 273)
Components of accounting systems (p. 273)
Computer network (p. 286)
Control principle (p. 272)
Controlling account (p. 277)
Cost-benefit principle (p. 273)
Enterprise resource planning (ERP) software (p. 287)
Flexibility principle (p. 273)
General journal (p. 276)
Information processor (p. 274)
Information storage (p. 274)
Input device (p. 274)
Internal controls (p. 272)
Online processing (p. 286)
Output devices (p. 275)
Purchases journal (p. 283)
Relevance principle (p. 272)

Sales journal (p. 278)
Schedule of accounts payable (p. 284)
Schedule of accounts receivable (p. 279)
Segment return on assets (p. 288)
Special journal (p. 276)
Subsidiary ledger (p. 276)

Multiple Choice Quiz

Answers on p. 313

mhhe.com/wildFAP20e

Additional Quiz Questions are available at the book's Website.

1. The sales journal is used to record
   a. Credit sales
   b. Cash sales
   c. Cash receipts
   d. Cash purchases
   e. Credit purchases
2. The purchases journal is used to record
   a. Credit sales
   b. Cash sales
   c. Cash receipts
   d. Cash purchases
   e. Credit purchases
3. The ledger that contains the financial statement accounts of a company is the
   a. General journal
   b. Column balance journal
   c. Special ledger
   d. General ledger
   e. Special journal
4. A subsidiary ledger that contains a separate account for each supplier (creditor) to the company is the
   a. Controlling account
   b. Accounts payable ledger
   c. Accounts receivable ledger
   d. General ledger
   e. Special journal
5. Enterprise resource planning software
   a. Refers to programs that help manage company operations.
   b. Is another name for spreadsheet programs.
   c. Uses batch processing of business information.
   d. Is substantially declining in use.
   e. Is another name for database programs.

A Superscript letter A denotes assignments based on Appendix 7A.
Icon denotes assignments that involve decision making.

Discussion Questions

1. What are the five fundamental principles of accounting information systems?
2. What are five basic components of an accounting system?
3. What are source documents? Give two examples.
4. What is the purpose of an input device? Give examples of input devices for computer systems.
5. What is the difference between data that are stored off-line and data that are stored online?
6. What purpose is served by the output devices of an accounting system?
7. When special journals are used, they are usually used to record each of four different types of transactions. What are these four types of transactions?
8. What notations are entered into the Posting Reference column of a ledger account?
9. When a general journal entry is used to record sales returns, the credit of the entry must be posted twice. Does this cause the trial balance to be out of balance? Explain.
10. Describe the procedures involving the use of copies of a company's sales invoices as a sales journal.
11. Credits to customer accounts and credits to Other Accounts are individually posted from a cash receipts journal such as the one in Exhibit 7.7. Why not put both types of credits in the same column and save journal space?
12. Why should sales to and receipts of cash from credit customers be recorded and posted immediately?
13. Locate the note that discusses **Research In Motion**'s operations by segments in Appendix A. In what segment does it predominantly operate? RIM
14. Does the income statement of **Palm** in Appendix A indicate the net income earned by its business segments? If so, list them. Palm
15. Locate the note that discusses **Apple**'s segments from its 2009 annual report on its Website. What five reportable segments does Apple have? Apple
16. Does the balance sheet of **Nokia** in Appendix A indicate the identifiable assets owned by its business segments? If so, list them. NOKIA

connect

For account titles and numbers, use the Chart of Accounts at the end of the book.

QUICK STUDY

QS 7-1
Accounting information system components
C1

Identify the most likely role in an accounting system played by each of the numbered items 1 through 12 by assigning a letter from the list A through E on the left.

A. Source documents
B. Input devices
C. Information processors
D. Information storage
E. Output devices

_____ **1.** Bar code reader
_____ **2.** Filing cabinet
_____ **3.** Bank statement
_____ **4.** Computer scanner
_____ **5.** Computer keyboard
_____ **6.** Zip drive
_____ **7.** Computer monitor
_____ **8.** Invoice from a supplier
_____ **9.** Computer software
_____ **10.** Computer printer
_____ **11.** Digital camera
_____ **12.** MP3 player

QS 7-2
Accounting information system principles
C1

Enter the letter of each system principle in the blank next to its best description.

A. Control principle
B. Relevance principle
C. Compatibility principle
D. Flexibility principle
E. Cost-benefit principle

1. _____ The principle prescribes the accounting information system to change in response to technological advances and competitive pressures.
2. _____ The principle prescribes the accounting information system to help monitor activities.
3. _____ The principle prescribes the accounting information system to provide timely information for effective decision making.
4. _____ The principle prescribes the accounting information system to adapt to the unique characteristics of the company.
5. _____ The principle that affects all other accounting information system principles.

QS 7-3
Accounting information system
C1

Fill in the blanks to complete the following descriptions.

1. _____ _____ _____ software comprises programs that help manage a company's vital operations, from manufacturing to accounting.
2. A computer _____ allows different computer users to share access to data and programs.
3. A _____ is an input device that captures writing and other input directly from source documents.
4. With _____ processing, source documents are accumulated for a period and then processed all at the same time, such as once a day, week, or month.

QS 7-4
Identifying the special journal of entry
C2

General Electronics uses a sales journal, a purchases journal, a cash receipts journal, a cash disbursements journal, and a general journal as illustrated in this chapter. General recently completed the following transactions *a* through *h*. Identify the journal in which each transaction should be recorded.

a. Paid cash to a creditor.
b. Sold merchandise on credit.
c. Purchased shop supplies on credit.
d. Paid an employee's salary in cash.
e. Borrowed cash from the bank.
f. Sold merchandise for cash.
g. Purchased merchandise on credit.
h. Purchased inventory for cash.

QS 7-5
Entries in the general journal
C2

Lue Gifts uses a sales journal, a purchases journal, a cash receipts journal, a cash disbursements journal, and a general journal as illustrated in this chapter. Journalize its March transactions that should be recorded in the general journal. For those not recorded in the general journal, identify the special journal where each should be recorded.

Mar. 2 The company purchased $2,900 of merchandise on credit from the Elko Co., terms 2/10, n/30.
12 The owner, T. Lue, contributed an automobile worth $15,000 to the company.
16 The company sold $1,100 of merchandise (cost is $700) on credit to K. Gould, terms n/30.
19 K. Gould returned $150 of (worthless) merchandise to the company originally purchased on March 16 (assume the cost of this merchandise is left in cost of goods sold).

QS 7-6
Controlling accounts and subsidiary ledgers
C3

Following is information from Thompson Company for its initial month of business. (1) Identify the balances listed in the accounts receivable subsidiary ledger. (2) Identify the accounts receivable balance listed in the general ledger at month's end.

Credit Sales			Cash Collections		
Jan. 10	Boerman Company	$3,000	Jan. 20	Boerman Company	$2,000
19	Lehman Brothers	1,600	28	Lehman Brothers	1,600
23	Finger Company	2,200	31	Finger Company	1,300

QS 7-7
Purchases journal—perpetual
P1

Redmon Company uses a sales journal, a purchases journal, a cash receipts journal, a cash disbursements journal, and a general journal. The following transactions occur in the month of June.

June 1 Purchased $8,100 of merchandise on credit from Krause, Inc., terms n/30.
8 Sold merchandise costing $900 on credit to G. Seles for $1,500 subject to a $30 sales discount if paid by the end of the month.
14 Purchased $240 of store supplies from Chang Company on credit, terms n/30.
17 Purchased $260 of office supplies on credit from Monder Company, terms n/30.
24 Sold merchandise costing $400 to D. Lee for $630 cash.
28 Purchased store supplies from Porter's for $90 cash.
29 Paid Krause, Inc., $8,100 cash for the merchandise purchased on June 1.

Prepare headings for a purchases journal like the one in Exhibit 7.9. Journalize the June transactions that should be recorded in the purchases journal.

QS 7-8
Identifying journal of entry C2

Refer to QS 7-7 and for each of the June transactions identify the journal in which it would be recorded. Assume the company uses a sales journal, purchases journal, cash receipts journal, cash disbursements journal, and general journal as illustrated in this chapter.

QS 7-9A
Purchases journal—periodic P3

Prepare headings for a purchases journal like the one in Exhibit 7A.3. Journalize the June transactions from QS 7-7 that should be recorded in the purchases journal assuming the periodic inventory system is used.

QS 7-10
Accounts receivable ledger; posting from sales journal
P2

Winslow Company posts its sales invoices directly and then binds them into a Sales Journal. Winslow had the following credit sales to these customers during June.

June 2	Joe Mack	$ 3,600
8	Eric Horner	6,100
10	Tess Wilson	13,400
14	Hong Jiang	20,500
20	Tess Wilson	11,200
29	Joe Mack	7,300
	Total credit sales	$62,100

Required

1. Open an accounts receivable subsidiary ledger having a T-account for each customer. Post the invoices to the subsidiary ledger.
2. Open an Accounts Receivable controlling T-account and a Sales T-account to reflect general ledger accounts. Post the end-of-month total from the sales journal to these accounts.
3. Prepare a schedule of accounts receivable and prove that its total equals the Accounts Receivable controlling account balance.

QS 7-11
Analyzing segment reports
A1 
Apple

Apple reports the following operating income (and average assets in parentheses) for each of its geographic segments—$ millions: Americas, $6,637 ($1,882); Europe, $4,296 ($1,352); and Japan, $961 ($483). Apple also reports the following sales (only) by product segments: iPhone, $13,033; iPod, $8,091; Desktops, $4,324; Portables, $9,535; Other, $7,922. Compute Apple's return on assets for each of its geographic segments, and assess the relative performance of these segments. Compute the percentage of total sales for each of its five product segments.

QS 7-12
International accounting and special journals
C2

Nestlé, a Switzerland-based company, uses a sales journal, a purchases journal, a cash receipts journal, a cash disbursements journal, and a general journal in a manner similar to that explained in this chapter. Journalize the following summary transactions of Nestlé transactions that should be recorded in the general journal. For those not recorded in the general journal, identify only the special journal where each should be recorded. (All amounts in millions of Swiss franc, CHF.)

1. Nestlé purchased CHF 8,000 of merchandise on credit from the suppliers.
2. Nestlé sold CHF 100,000 of merchandise (cost is CHF 44,000) on credit to customers.
3. A key customer returned CHF 900 of (worthless) merchandise to Nestlé (assume the cost of this merchandise is left in cost of goods sold).

connect

EXERCISES

For account titles and numbers, use the Chart of Accounts at the end of the book.

Exercise 7-1
Sales journal—perpetual
P1

Hutton Company uses a sales journal, a purchases journal, a cash receipts journal, a cash disbursements journal, and a general journal. The following transactions occur in the month of March.

Mar. 2 Sold merchandise costing $300 to B. Fager for $450 cash, invoice no. 5703.
5 Purchased $2,300 of merchandise on credit from Marsh Corp.
7 Sold merchandise costing $800 to J. Dryer for $1,150, terms 2/10, n/30, invoice no. 5704.
8 Borrowed $8,000 cash by signing a note payable to the bank.
12 Sold merchandise costing $200 to R. Land for $320, terms n/30, invoice no. 5705.
16 Received $1,127 cash from J. Dryer to pay for the purchase of March 7.
19 Sold used store equipment for $900 cash to Malone, Inc.
25 Sold merchandise costing $350 to T. Burton for $550, terms n/30, invoice no. 5706.

Prepare headings for a sales journal like the one in Exhibit 7.5. Journalize the March transactions that should be recorded in this sales journal.

Exercise 7-2
Identifying journal of entry C2

Refer to Exercise 7-1 and for each of the March transactions identify the journal in which it would be recorded. Assume the company uses a sales journal, purchases journal, cash receipts journal, cash disbursements journal, and general journal as illustrated in this chapter.

Exercise 7-3[A]
Sales journal—periodic P3

Prepare headings for a sales journal like the one in Exhibit 7A.1. Journalize the March transactions shown in Exercise 7-1 that should be recorded in the sales journal assuming that the periodic inventory system is used.

Exercise 7-4
Cash receipts journal—perpetual
P1

Moeder Co. uses a sales journal, a purchases journal, a cash receipts journal, a cash disbursements journal, and a general journal. The following transactions occur in the month of November.

Nov. 3 The company purchased $3,100 of merchandise on credit from Hargrave Co., terms n/20.
7 The company sold merchandise costing $840 on credit to J. York for $900, subject to an $18 sales discount if paid by the end of the month.
9 The company borrowed $2,750 cash by signing a note payable to the bank.
13 J. Emling, the owner, contributed $4,000 cash to the company.
18 The company sold merchandise costing $130 to B. Box for $230 cash.
22 The company paid Hargrave Co. $3,100 cash for the merchandise purchased on November 3.
27 The company received $882 cash from J. York in payment of the November 7 purchase.
30 The company paid salaries of $1,600 in cash.

Prepare headings for a cash receipts journal like the one in Exhibit 7.7. Journalize the November transactions that should be recorded in the cash receipts journal.

Exercise 7-5
Identifying journal of entry C2

Refer to Exercise 7-4 and for each of the November transactions identify the journal in which it would be recorded. Assume the company uses a sales journal, purchases journal, cash receipts journal, cash disbursements journal, and general journal as illustrated in this chapter.

Exercise 7-6[A]
Cash receipts journal—periodic
P3

Prepare headings for a cash receipts journal like the one in Exhibit 7A.2. Journalize the November transactions shown in Exercise 7-4 that should be recorded in the cash receipts journal assuming that the periodic inventory system is used.

Exercise 7-7
Controlling accounts and subsidiary ledgers
C3

Following is information from Ryan Company for its initial month of business. (1) Identify the balances listed in the accounts payable subsidiary ledger. (2) Identify the accounts payable balance listed in the general ledger at month's end.

Credit Purchases			Cash Paid		
Jan. 9	Boeder Company	$7,000	Jan. 19	Boeder Company	$5,100
18	Johnson Brothers	6,600	27	Johnson Brothers	6,600
22	Padley Company	4,200	31	Padley Company	3,400

Exercise 7-8
Cash disbursements journal—perpetual
P1

Pebblebrook Supply uses a sales journal, a purchases journal, a cash receipts journal, a cash disbursements journal, and a general journal. The following transactions occur in the month of April.

Apr. 3 Purchased merchandise for $2,750 on credit from Scott, Inc., terms 2/10, n/30.
9 Issued check no. 210 to Kidman Corp. to buy store supplies for $450.
12 Sold merchandise costing $400 on credit to C. Meyers for $670, terms n/30.
17 Issued check no. 211 for $1,500 to pay off a note payable to City Bank.
20 Purchased merchandise for $3,500 on credit from LeBron, terms 2/10, n/30.
28 Issued check no. 212 to LeBron to pay the amount due for the purchase of April 20, less the discount.
29 Paid salary of $1,700 to B. Decker by issuing check no. 213.
30 Issued check no. 214 to Scott, Inc., to pay the amount due for the purchase of April 3.

Prepare headings for a cash disbursements journal like the one in Exhibit 7.11. Journalize the April transactions that should be recorded in the cash disbursements journal.

Exercise 7-9
Identifying journal of entry C2

Refer to Exercise 7-8 and for each of the April transactions identify the journal in which it would be recorded. Assume the company uses a sales journal, purchases journal, cash receipts journal, cash disbursements journal, and general journal as illustrated in this chapter.

Exercise 7-10A
Cash disbursements journal—periodic P3

Prepare headings for a cash disbursements journal like the one in Exhibit 7A.4. Journalize the April transactions from Exercise 7-8 that should be recorded in the cash disbursements journal assuming that the periodic inventory system is used.

Exercise 7-11
Special journal transactions and error discovery
P1 

Porter Pharmacy uses the following journals: sales journal, purchases journal, cash receipts journal, cash disbursements journal, and general journal. On June 5, Porter purchased merchandise priced at $12,000, subject to credit terms of 2/10, n/30. On June 14, the pharmacy paid the net amount due for the merchandise. In journalizing the payment, the pharmacy debited Accounts Payable for $12,000 but failed to record the cash discount on the purchases. Cash was properly credited for the actual $11,760 paid. (*a*) In what journals would the June 5 and the June 14 transactions be recorded? (*b*) What procedure is likely to discover the error in journalizing the June 14 transaction?

Exercise 7-12
Posting to subsidiary ledger accounts; preparing a schedule of accounts receivable
P2

At the end of May, the sales journal of Clear View appears as follows.

Sales Journal — Page 2

Date	Account Debited	Invoice Number	PR	Accounts Receivable Dr. Sales Cr.	Cost of Goods Sold Dr. Inventory Cr.
May 6	Aaron Reckers	190		2,880	2,200
10	Sara Reed	191		1,940	1,600
17	Anna Page	192		850	500
25	Sara Reed	193		340	200
31	Totals			6,010	4,500

Clear View also recorded the return of defective merchandise with the following entry.

May 20	Sales Returns and Allowances	250	
	Accounts Receivable—Anna Page		250
	Customer returned (worthless) merchandise.		

Required

1. Open an accounts receivable subsidiary ledger that has a T-account for each customer listed in the sales journal. Post to the customer accounts the entries in the sales journal and any portion of the general journal entry that affects a customer's account.
2. Open a general ledger that has T-accounts for Accounts Receivable, Inventory, Sales, Sales Returns and Allowances, and Cost of Goods Sold. Post the sales journal and any portion of the general journal entry that affects these accounts.
3. Prepare a schedule of accounts receivable and prove that its total equals the balance in the Accounts Receivable controlling account.

Check (3) Ending Accounts Receivable, $5,760

Exercise 7-13
Purchases journal and error identification
P1 

A company that records credit purchases in a purchases journal and records purchases returns in a general journal made the following errors. Indicate when each error should be discovered.

1. Posted a purchases return to the Accounts Payable account and to the creditor's subsidiary account but did not post the purchases return to the Inventory account.
2. Posted a purchases return to the Inventory account and to the Accounts Payable account but did not post to the creditor's subsidiary account.
3. Correctly recorded a $4,000 purchase in the purchases journal but posted it to the creditor's subsidiary account as a $400 purchase.
4. Made an addition error in determining the balance of a creditor's subsidiary account.
5. Made an addition error in totaling the Office Supplies column of the purchases journal.

Exercise 7-14
Computing and analyzing segment return on assets
A1 

Refer to Exhibit 7.13 and complete the segment return on assets table for Wolfe Company. Analyze your findings and identify the segment with the highest, and that with the lowest, segment return on assets.

	Segment Operating Income (in $ mil.)		Segment Assets (in $ mil.)		Segment Return on Assets
Segment	**2011**	**2010**	**2011**	**2010**	**2011**
Specialty					
Skiing Group	$ 62	$ 58	$ 581	$440	
Skating Group	9	6	53	42	
Specialty Footwear	22	19	155	136	
Other Specialty	11	4	37	24	
Subtotal	104	87	826	642	
General Merchandise					
South America	32	36	305	274	
United States	7	8	52	35	
Europe	5	3	14	12	
Subtotal	44	47	371	321	
Total	$148	$134	$1197	$963	

Check Europe segment return, 38.5%

connect

For account titles and numbers, use the Chart of Accounts at the end of the book.

PROBLEM SET A

Problem 7-1A
Special journals, subsidiary ledgers, and schedule of accounts receivable—perpetual
C3 P1 P2 

Wise Company completes these transactions during April of the current year (the terms of all its credit sales are 2/10, n/30).

Apr. 2 Purchased $13,300 of merchandise on credit from Negi Company, invoice dated April 2, terms 2/10, n/60.

3 Sold merchandise on credit to Brooke Sledd, Invoice No. 760, for $3,000 (cost is $2,000).

3 Purchased $1,380 of office supplies on credit from Madison, Inc. Invoice dated April 2, terms n/10 EOM.

4 Issued Check No. 587 to *U.S. View* for advertising expense, $999.

5 Sold merchandise on credit to Paul Kohr, Invoice No. 761, for $8,000 (cost is $6,500).

6 Received an $85 credit memorandum from Madison, Inc., for the return of some of the office supplies received on April 3.

9 Purchased $11,125 of store equipment on credit from Ned's Supply, invoice dated April 9, terms n/10 EOM.

11 Sold merchandise on credit to Amy Nilson, Invoice No 762, for $9,500 (cost is $7,000).
12 Issued Check No. 588 to Negi Company in payment of its April 2 invoice, less the discount.
13 Received payment from Brooke Sledd for the April 3 sale, less the discount.
13 Sold $4,100 of merchandise on credit to Brooke Sledd (cost is $2,600), Invoice No. 763.
14 Received payment from Paul Kohr for the April 5 sale, less the discount.
16 Issued Check No. 589, payable to Payroll, in payment of sales salaries expense for the first half of the month, $9,750. Cashed the check and paid employees.
16 Cash sales for the first half of the month are $50,840 (cost is $33,880). (Cash sales are recorded daily from cash register data but are recorded only twice in this problem to reduce repetitive entries.)
17 Purchased $12,750 of merchandise on credit from Price Company, invoice dated April 17, terms 2/10, n/30.
18 Borrowed $50,000 cash from First State Bank by signing a long-term note payable.
20 Received payment from Amy Nilson for the April 11 sale, less the discount.
20 Purchased $730 of store supplies on credit from Ned's Supply, invoice dated April 19, terms n/10 EOM.
23 Received a $400 credit memorandum from Price Company for the return of defective merchandise received on April 17.
23 Received payment from Brooke Sledd for the April 13 sale, less the discount.
25 Purchased $10,375 of merchandise on credit from Negi Company, invoice dated April 24, terms 2/10, n/60.
26 Issued Check No. 590 to Price Company in payment of its April 17 invoice, less the return and the discount.
27 Sold $3,070 of merchandise on credit to Paul Kohr, Invoice No. 764 (cost is $2,420).
27 Sold $5,700 of merchandise on credit to Amy Nilson, Invoice No. 765 (cost is $3,305).
30 Issued Check No. 591, payable to Payroll, in payment of the sales salaries expense for the last half of the month, $9,750.
30 Cash sales for the last half of the month are $70,975 (cost is $55,900).

Required

1. Prepare a sales journal like that in Exhibit 7.5 and a cash receipts journal like that in Exhibit 7.7. Number both journal pages as page 3. Then review the transactions of Wise Company and enter those that should be journalized in the sales journal and those that should be journalized in the cash receipts journal. Ignore any transactions that should be journalized in a purchases journal, a cash disbursements journal, or a general journal.
2. Open the following general ledger accounts: Cash, Accounts Receivable, Inventory, Long-Term Notes Payable, B. Wise, Capital, Sales, Sales Discounts, and Cost of Goods Sold. Enter the March 31 balances for Cash ($85,000), Inventory ($125,000), Long-Term Notes Payable ($110,000), and B. Wise, Capital ($100,000). Also open accounts receivable subsidiary ledger accounts for Paul Kohr, Brooke Sledd, and Amy Nilson.
3. Verify that amounts that should be posted as individual amounts from the journals have been posted. (Such items are immediately posted.) Foot and crossfoot the journals and make the month-end postings.
4. Prepare a trial balance of the general ledger and prove the accuracy of the subsidiary ledger by preparing a schedule of accounts receivable.

Check Trial balance totals, $415,185

Analysis Component

5. Assume that the total for the schedule of Accounts Receivable does not equal the balance of the controlling account in the general ledger. Describe steps you would take to discover the error(s).

Problem 7-2A[A]
Special journals, subsidiary ledgers, and schedule of accounts receivable—periodic
C3 P2 P3

Assume that Wise Co. in Problem 7-1A uses the periodic inventory system.

Required

1. Prepare headings for a sales journal like the one in Exhibit 7A.1. Prepare headings for a cash receipts journal like the one in Exhibit 7A.2. Journalize the April transactions shown in Problem 7-1A that should be recorded in the sales journal and the cash receipts journal assuming the *periodic* inventory system is used.
2. Open the general ledger accounts with balances as shown in Problem 7-1A (do not open a Cost of Goods Sold ledger account). Also open accounts receivable subsidiary ledger accounts for

Brooke Sledd, Paul Kohr, and Amy Nilson. Under the periodic system, an Inventory account exists but is inactive until its balance is updated to the correct inventory balance at year-end. In this problem, the Inventory account remains inactive but must be included to correctly complete the trial balance.

3. Complete parts 3, 4, and 5 of Problem 7-1A using the results of parts 1 and 2 of this problem.

Check Trial balance totals, $415,185

Problem 7-3A
Special journals, subsidiary ledgers, and schedule of accounts payable—perpetual
C3 P1 P2

The April transactions of Wise Company are described in Problem 7-1A.

Required

1. Prepare a general journal, a purchases journal like that in Exhibit 7.9, and a cash disbursements journal like that in Exhibit 7.11. Number all journal pages as page 3. Review the April transactions of Wise Company and enter those transactions that should be journalized in the general journal, the purchases journal, or the cash disbursements journal. Ignore any transactions that should be journalized in a sales journal or cash receipts journal.

2. Open the following general ledger accounts: Cash, Inventory, Office Supplies, Store Supplies, Store Equipment, Accounts Payable, Long-Term Notes Payable, B. Wise, Capital, Sales Salaries Expense, and Advertising Expense. Enter the March 31 balances of Cash ($85,000), Inventory ($125,000), Long-Term Notes Payable ($110,000), and B. Wise, Capital ($100,000). Also open accounts payable subsidiary ledger accounts for Ned's Supply, Negi Company, Price Company, and Madison, Inc.

3. Verify that amounts that should be posted as individual amounts from the journals have been posted. (Such items are immediately posted.) Foot and crossfoot the journals and make the month-end postings.

4. Prepare a trial balance of the general ledger and a schedule of accounts payable.

Check Trial balance totals, $233,525

Problem 7-4A[A]
Special journals, subsidiary ledgers, and schedule of accounts payable—periodic
C3 P2 P3

Refer to Problem 7-1A and assume that Wise Co. uses the periodic inventory system.

Required

1. Prepare a general journal, a purchases journal like that in Exhibit 7A.3, and a cash disbursements journal like that in Exhibit 7A.4. Number all journal pages as page 3. Review the April transactions of Wise Company (Problem 7-1A) and enter those transactions that should be journalized in the general journal, the purchases journal, or the cash disbursements journal. Ignore any transaction that should be journalized in a sales journal or cash receipts journal.

2. Open the following general ledger accounts: Cash, Inventory, Office Supplies, Store Supplies, Store Equipment, Accounts Payable, Long-Term Notes Payable, B. Wise, Capital, Purchases, Purchases Returns and Allowances, Purchases Discounts, Sales Salaries Expense, and Advertising Expense. Enter the March 31 balances of Cash ($85,000), Inventory ($125,000), Long-Term Notes Payable ($110,000), and B. Wise, Capital ($100,000). Also open accounts payable subsidiary ledger accounts for Ned's Supply, Negi Company, Price Company, and Madison, Inc.

3. Complete parts 3 and 4 of Problem 7-3A using the results of parts 1 and 2 of this problem.

Check Trial balance totals, $234,438

Problem 7-5A
Special journals, subsidiary ledgers, trial balance—perpetual
C3 P1 P2

mhhe.com/wildFAP20e

Bishop Company completes these transactions and events during March of the current year (terms for all its credit sales are 2/10, n/30).

Mar.	1	Purchased $42,600 of merchandise from Soy Industries, invoice dated March 1, terms 2/15, n/30.
	2	Sold merchandise on credit to Min Cho, Invoice No. 854, for $15,800 (cost is $7,900).
	3	Purchased $1,120 of office supplies on credit from Stacy Company, invoice dated March 3, terms n/10 EOM.
	3	Sold merchandise on credit to Lance Snow, Invoice No. 855, for $9,200 (cost is $4,600).
	6	Borrowed $72,000 cash from Federal Bank by signing a long-term note payable.
	9	Purchased $20,850 of office equipment on credit from Tells Supply, invoice dated March 9, terms n/10 EOM.
	10	Sold merchandise on credit to Taylor Few, Invoice No. 856, for $4,600 (cost is $2,300).
	12	Received payment from Min Cho for the March 2 sale less the discount.
	13	Sent Soy Industries Check No. 416 in payment of the March 1 invoice less the discount.
	13	Received payment from Lance Snow for the March 3 sale less the discount.
	14	Purchased $31,625 of merchandise from the JW Company, invoice dated March 13, terms 2/10, n/30.
	15	Issued Check No. 417, payable to Payroll, in payment of sales salaries expense for the first half of the month, $15,900. Cashed the check and paid the employees.

15 Cash sales for the first half of the month are $164,680 (cost is $138,000). (Cash sales are recorded daily, but are recorded only twice here to reduce repetitive entries.)
16 Purchased $1,670 of store supplies on credit from Stacy Company, invoice dated March 16, terms n/10 EOM.
17 Received a $2,425 credit memorandum from JW Company for the return of unsatisfactory merchandise purchased on March 14.
19 Received a $630 credit memorandum from Tells Supply for office equipment received on March 9 and returned for credit.
20 Received payment from Taylor Few for the sale of March 10 less the discount.
23 Issued Check No. 418 to JW Company in payment of the invoice of March 13 less the March 17 return and the discount.
27 Sold merchandise on credit to Taylor Few, Invoice No. 857, for $13,910 (cost is $6,220).
28 Sold merchandise on credit to Lance Snow, Invoice No. 858, for $5,315 (cost is $2,280).
31 Issued Check No. 419, payable to Payroll, in payment of sales salaries expense for the last half of the month, $15,900. Cashed the check and paid the employees.
31 Cash sales for the last half of the month are $174,590 (cost is $143,000).
31 Verify that amounts impacting customer and creditor accounts were posted and that any amounts that should have been posted as individual amounts to the general ledger accounts were posted. Foot and crossfoot the journals and make the month-end postings.

Required

1. Open the following general ledger accounts: Cash; Accounts Receivable; Inventory (March 1 beg. bal. is $300,000); Office Supplies; Store Supplies; Office Equipment; Accounts Payable; Long-Term Notes Payable; M. Bishop, Capital (March 1 beg. bal. is $300,000); Sales; Sales Discounts; Cost of Goods Sold; and Sales Salaries Expense. Open the following accounts receivable subsidiary ledger accounts: Taylor Few, Min Cho, and Lance Snow. Open the following accounts payable subsidiary ledger accounts: Stacy Company, Soy Industries, Tells Supply, and JW Company.
2. Enter these transactions in a sales journal like Exhibit 7.5, a purchases journal like Exhibit 7.9, a cash receipts journal like Exhibit 7.7, a cash disbursements journal like Exhibit 7.11, or a general journal. Number all journal pages as page 2.

Check Trial balance totals, $783,105

3. Prepare a trial balance of the general ledger and prove the accuracy of the subsidiary ledgers by preparing schedules of both accounts receivable and accounts payable.

Problem 7-6A[A]
Special journals, subsidiary ledgers, trial balance—periodic
C3 P2 P3

mhhe.com/wildFAP20e

Assume that Bishop Company in Problem 7-5A uses the periodic inventory system.

Required

1. Open the following general ledger accounts: Cash; Accounts Receivable; Inventory (March 1 beg. bal. is $300,000); Office Supplies; Store Supplies; Office Equipment; Accounts Payable; Long-Term Notes Payable; M. Bishop, Capital (March 1 beg. bal. is $300,000); Sales; Sales Discounts; Purchases; Purchases Returns and Allowances; Purchases Discounts; and Sales Salaries Expense. Open the following accounts receivable subsidiary ledger accounts: Taylor Few, Min Cho, and Lance Snow. Open the following accounts payable subsidiary ledger accounts: Stacy Company, Soy Industries, Tells Supply, and JW Company.
2. Enter the transactions from Problem 7-5A in a sales journal like that in Exhibit 7A.1, a purchases journal like that in Exhibit 7A.3, a cash receipts journal like that in Exhibit 7A.2, a cash disbursements journal like that in Exhibit 7A.4, or a general journal. Number journal pages as page 2.

Check Trial balance totals, $786,966

3. Prepare a trial balance of the general ledger and prove the accuracy of the subsidiary ledgers by preparing schedules of both accounts receivable and accounts payable.

PROBLEM SET B

For account titles and numbers, use the Chart of Accounts at the end of the book.

Problem 7-1B
Special journals, subsidiary ledgers, schedule of accounts receivable—perpetual
C3 P1 P2 

Alcorn Industries completes these transactions during July of the current year (the terms of all its credit sales are 2/10, n/30).

July 1 Purchased $6,300 of merchandise on credit from Tahoe Company, invoice dated June 30, terms 2/10, n/30.
3 Issued Check No. 300 to *The Weekly* for advertising expense, $575.
5 Sold merchandise on credit to Kim Newsom, Invoice No. 918, for $18,400 (cost is $9,700).

6 Sold merchandise on credit to Ruth Baker, Invoice No. 919, for $7,500 (cost is $4,300).
7 Purchased $1,050 of store supplies on credit from Pryor, Inc., invoice dated July 7, terms n/10 EOM.
8 Received a $150 credit memorandum from Pryor, Inc., for the return of store supplies received on July 7.
9 Purchased $37,710 of store equipment on credit from Caro's Supply, invoice dated July 8, terms n/10 EOM.
10 Issued Check No. 301 to Tahoe Company in payment of its June 30 invoice, less the discount.
13 Sold merchandise on credit to Stephanie Meyer, Invoice No. 920, for $8,350 (cost is $5,030).
14 Sold merchandise on credit to Kim Newsom, Invoice No. 921, for $4,100 (cost is $2,800).
15 Received payment from Kim Newsom for the July 5 sale, less the discount.
15 Issued Check No. 302, payable to Payroll, in payment of sales salaries expense for the first half of the month, $30,620. Cashed the check and paid employees.
15 Cash sales for the first half of the month are $121,370 (cost is $66,330). (Cash sales are recorded daily using data from the cash registers but are recorded only twice in this problem to reduce repetitive entries.)
16 Received payment from Ruth Baker for the July 6 sale, less the discount.
17 Purchased $8,200 of merchandise on credit from Dixon Company, invoice dated July 17, terms 2/10, n/30.
20 Purchased $750 of office supplies on credit from Caro's Supply, invoice dated July 19, terms n/10 EOM.
21 Borrowed $20,000 cash from College Bank by signing a long-term note payable.
23 Received payment from Stephanie Meyer for the July 13 sale, less the discount.
24 Received payment from Kim Newsom for the July 14 sale, less the discount.
24 Received a $2,400 credit memorandum from Dixon Company for the return of defective merchandise received on July 17.
26 Purchased $9,770 of merchandise on credit from Tahoe Company, invoice dated July 26, terms 2/10, n/30.
27 Issued Check No. 303 to Dixon Company in payment of its July 17 invoice, less the return and the discount.
29 Sold merchandise on credit to Ruth Baker, Invoice No. 922, for $28,090 (cost is $22,850).
30 Sold merchandise on credit to Stephanie Meyer, Invoice No. 923, for $15,750 (cost is $9,840).
31 Issued Check No. 304, payable to Payroll, in payment of the sales salaries expense for the last half of the month, $30,620.
31 Cash sales for the last half of the month are $79,020 (cost is $51,855).

Required

1. Prepare a sales journal like that in Exhibit 7.5 and a cash receipts journal like that in Exhibit 7.7. Number both journals as page 3. Then review the transactions of Alcorn Industries and enter those transactions that should be journalized in the sales journal and those that should be journalized in the cash receipts journal. Ignore any transactions that should be journalized in a purchases journal, a cash disbursements journal, or a general journal.

2. Open the following general ledger accounts: Cash, Accounts Receivable, Inventory, Long-Term Notes Payable, R. Alcorn, Capital, Sales, Sales Discounts, and Cost of Goods Sold. Enter the June 30 balances for Cash ($100,000), Inventory ($200,000), Long-Term Notes Payable ($200,000), and R. Alcorn, Capital ($100,000). Also open accounts receivable subsidiary ledger accounts for Kim Newsom, Stephanie Meyer, and Ruth Baker.

3. Verify that amounts that should be posted as individual amounts from the journals have been posted. (Such items are immediately posted.) Foot and crossfoot the journals and make the month-end postings.

4. Prepare a trial balance of the general ledger and prove the accuracy of the subsidiary ledger by preparing a schedule of accounts receivable.

Check Trial balance totals, $602,580

Analysis Component

5. Assume that the total for the schedule of Accounts Receivable does not equal the balance of the controlling account in the general ledger. Describe steps you would take to discover the error(s).

Problem 7-2B[A]
Special journals, subsidiary ledgers, and schedule of accounts receivable—periodic
C3 P2 P3

Assume that Alcorn Industries in Problem 7-1B uses the periodic inventory system.

Required

1. Prepare headings for a sales journal like the one in Exhibit 7A.1. Prepare headings for a cash receipts journal like the one in Exhibit 7A.2. Journalize the July transactions shown in Problem 7-1B that should be recorded in the sales journal and the cash receipts journal assuming the periodic inventory system is used.
2. Open the general ledger accounts with balances as shown in Problem 7-1B (do not open a Cost of Goods Sold ledger account). Also open accounts receivable subsidiary ledger accounts for Ruth Baker, Stephanie Meyer, and Kim Newsom. Under the periodic system, an Inventory account exists but is inactive until its balance is updated to the correct inventory balance at year-end. In this problem, the Inventory account remains inactive but must be included to correctly complete the trial balance.
3. Complete parts 3, 4, and 5 of Problem 7-1B using the results of parts 1 and 2 of this problem.

Check Trial balance totals, $602,580

Problem 7-3B
Special journals, subsidiary ledgers, and schedule of accounts payable—perpetual
C3 P1 P2

The July transactions of Alcorn Industries are described in Problem 7-1B.

Required

1. Prepare a general journal, a purchases journal like that in Exhibit 7.9, and a cash disbursements journal like that in Exhibit 7.11. Number all journal pages as page 3. Review the July transactions of Alcorn Industries and enter those transactions that should be journalized in the general journal, the purchases journal, or the cash disbursements journal. Ignore any transactions that should be journalized in a sales journal or cash receipts journal.
2. Open the following general ledger accounts: Cash, Inventory, Office Supplies, Store Supplies, Store Equipment, Accounts Payable, Long-Term Notes Payable, R. Alcorn, Capital, Sales Salaries Expense, and Advertising Expense. Enter the June 30 balances of Cash ($100,000), Inventory ($200,000), Long-Term Notes Payable ($200,000), and R. Alcorn, Capital ($100,000). Also open accounts payable subsidiary ledger accounts for Caro's Supply, Tahoe Company, Dixon Company, and Pryor, Inc.
3. Verify that amounts that should be posted as individual amounts from the journals have been posted. (Such items are immediately posted.) Foot and crossfoot the journals and make the month-end postings.
4. Prepare a trial balance of the general ledger and a schedule of accounts payable.

Check Trial balance totals, $349,130

Problem 7-4B[A]
Special journals, subsidiary ledgers, and schedule of accounts payable—periodic
C3 P2 P3

Refer to Problem 7-1B and assume that Alcorn uses the periodic inventory system.

Required

1. Prepare a general journal, a purchases journal like that in Exhibit 7A.3, and a cash disbursements journal like that in Exhibit 7A.4. Number all journal pages as page 3. Review the July transactions of Alcorn Company (Problem 7-1B) and enter those transactions that should be journalized in the general journal, the purchases journal, or the cash disbursements journal. Ignore any transaction that should be journalized in a sales journal or cash receipts journal.
2. Open the following general ledger accounts: Cash, Inventory, Office Supplies, Store Supplies, Store Equipment, Accounts Payable, Long-Term Notes Payable, R. Alcorn, Capital, Purchases, Purchases Returns and Allowances, Purchases Discounts, Sales Salaries Expense, and Advertising Expense. Enter the June 30 balances of Cash ($100,000), Inventory ($200,000), Long-Term Notes Payable ($200,000), and R. Alcorn, Capital ($100,000). Also open accounts payable subsidiary ledger accounts for Tahoe Company, Pryor, Inc., Caro's Supply, and Dixon Company.
3. Complete parts 3 and 4 of Problem 7-3B using the results of parts 1 and 2 of this problem.

Check Trial balance totals, $351,772

Problem 7-5B
Special journals, subsidiary ledgers, trial balance—perpetual
C3 P2 P3

Suppan Company completes these transactions during November of the current year (terms for all its credit sales are 2/10, n/30).

Nov. 1 Purchased $5,062 of office equipment on credit from Blix Supply, invoice dated November 1, terms n/10 EOM.
2 Borrowed $86,250 cash from Kansas Bank by signing a long-term note payable.
4 Purchased $11,400 of merchandise from ATM Industries, invoice dated November 3, terms 2/10, n/30.
5 Purchased $1,020 of store supplies on credit from Globe Company, invoice dated November 5, terms n/10 EOM.

8 Sold merchandise on credit to Sid Ragan, Invoice No. 439, for $6,350 (cost is $3,710).
10 Sold merchandise on credit to Carlos Mane, Invoice No. 440, for $12,500 (cost is $7,500).
11 Purchased $2,887 of merchandise from Xu Company, invoice dated November 10, terms 2/10, n/30.
12 Sent ATM Industries Check No. 633 in payment of its November 3 invoice less the discount.
15 Issued Check No. 634, payable to Payroll, in payment of sales salaries expense for the first half of the month, $8,435. Cashed the check and paid the employees.
15 Cash sales for the first half of the month are $27,170 (cost is $17,000). (Cash sales are recorded daily but are recorded only twice in this problem to reduce repetitive entries.)
15 Sold merchandise on credit to Tony Timmons, Invoice No. 441, for $4,250 (cost is $1,450).
16 Purchased $559 of office supplies on credit from Globe Company, invoice dated November 16, terms n/10 EOM.
17 Received a $487 credit memorandum from Xu Company for the return of unsatisfactory merchandise purchased on November 11.
18 Received payment from Sid Ragan for the November 8 sale less the discount.
19 Received payment from Carlos Mane for the November 10 sale less the discount.
19 Issued Check No. 635 to Xu Company in payment of its invoice of November 10 less the return and the discount.
22 Sold merchandise on credit to Carlos Mane, Invoice No. 442, for $2,595 (cost is $1,060).
24 Sold merchandise on credit to Tony Timmons, Invoice No. 443, for $3,240 (cost is $1,090).
25 Received payment from Tony Timmons for the sale of November 15 less the discount.
26 Received a $922 credit memorandum from Blix Supply for the return of office equipment purchased on November 1.
30 Issued Check No. 636, payable to Payroll, in payment of sales salaries expense for the last half of the month, $8,435. Cashed the check and paid the employees.
30 Cash sales for the last half of the month are $35,703 (cost is $20,400).
30 Verify that amounts impacting customer and creditor accounts were posted and that any amounts that should have been posted as individual amounts to the general ledger accounts were posted. Foot and crossfoot the journals and make the month end postings.

Required

1. Open the following general ledger accounts: Cash; Accounts Receivable; Inventory (November 1 beg. bal. is $40,000); Office Supplies; Store Supplies; Office Equipment; Accounts Payable; Long-Term Notes Payable; J. Suppan, Capital (Nov. 1 beg. bal. is $40,000); Sales; Sales Discounts; Cost of Goods Sold; and Sales Salaries Expense. Open the following accounts receivable subsidiary ledger accounts: Carlos Mane, Tony Timmons, and Sid Ragan. Open the following accounts payable subsidiary ledger accounts: Globe Company, ATM Industries, Blix Supply, and Xu Company.
2. Enter these transactions in a sales journal like that in Exhibit 7.5, a purchases journal like that in Exhibit 7.9, a cash receipts journal like that in Exhibit 7.7, a cash disbursements journal like that in Exhibit 7.11, or a general journal. Number all journal pages as page 2.
3. Prepare a trial balance of the general ledger and prove the accuracy of the subsidiary ledgers by preparing schedules of both accounts receivable and accounts payable.

Check Trial balance totals, $229,777

Problem 7-6B^A
Special journals, subsidiary ledgers, trial balance—periodic
C3 P2 P3

Assume that Suppan Company in Problem 7-5B uses the periodic inventory system.

Required

1. Open the following general ledger accounts: Cash; Accounts Receivable; Inventory (November 1 beg. bal. is $40,000); Office Supplies; Store Supplies; Office Equipment; Accounts Payable; Long-Term Notes Payable; J. Suppan, Capital (Nov. 1 beg. bal. is $40,000); Sales; Sales Discounts; Purchases; Purchases Returns and Allowances; Purchases Discounts; and Sales Salaries Expense. Open the following accounts receivable subsidiary ledger accounts: Carlos Mane, Tony Timmons, and Sid Ragan. Open the following accounts payable subsidiary ledger accounts: Globe Company, ATM Industries, Blix Supply, and Xu Company.
2. Enter the transactions from Problem 7-5B in a sales journal like that in Exhibit 7A.1, a purchases journal like that in Exhibit 7A.3, a cash receipts journal like that in Exhibit 7A.2, a cash disbursements journal like that in Exhibit 7A.4, or a general journal. Number journal pages as page 2.
3. Prepare a trial balance of the general ledger and prove the accuracy of the subsidiary ledgers by preparing schedules of both accounts receivable and accounts payable.

Check Trial balance totals, $224,540

SERIAL PROBLEM

Business Solutions P1

(This serial problem began in Chapter 1 and continues through most of the book. If previous chapter segments were not completed, the serial problem can begin at this point. It is helpful, but not necessary, to use the Working Papers that accompany the book.)

SP 7 Assume that Santana Rey expands Business Solutions' accounting system to include special journals.

Required

1. Locate the transactions related to January through March 2012 for Business Solutions in Chapter 5.
2. Enter the Business Solutions transactions for January through March in a sales journal like that in Exhibit 7.5 (insert "n/a" in the Invoice column), a cash receipts journal like that in Exhibit 7.7, a purchases journal like that in Exhibit 7.9 (use Computer Supplies heading instead of Office Supplies), and a cash disbursements journal like that in Exhibit 7.11 (insert "n/a" in the Check Number column), or a general journal. Number journal pages as page 2. If the transaction does not specify the name of the payee, state "not specified" in the Payee column of the cash disbursements journal.
3. The transactions on the following dates should be journalized in the general journal: January 5, 11, 20, 24, and 29 (no entry required) and March 24. Do not record and post the adjusting entries for the end of March.

COMPREHENSIVE PROBLEM

Colo Company

mhhe.com/wildFAP20e

(If the Working Papers that accompany this book are not available, omit this comprehensive problem.) Assume it is Monday, May 1, the first business day of the month, and you have just been hired as the accountant for Colo Company, which operates with monthly accounting periods. All of the company's accounting work is completed through the end of April and its ledgers show April 30 balances. During your first month on the job, the company experiences the following transactions and events (terms for all its credit sales are 2/10, n/30 unless stated differently):

May 1 Issued Check No. 3410 to S&P Management Co. in payment of the May rent, $3,710. (Use two lines to record the transaction. Charge 80% of the rent to Rent Expense—Selling Space and the balance to Rent Expense—Office Space.)

2 Sold merchandise on credit to Hensel Company, Invoice No. 8785, for $6,100 (cost is $4,100).

2 Issued a $175 credit memorandum to Knox Co., for defective (worthless) merchandise sold on April 28 and returned for credit. The total selling price (gross) was $4,725.

3 Received a $798 credit memorandum from Peyton Products for the return of merchandise purchased on April 29.

4 Purchased the following on credit from Gear Supply Co.: merchandise, $37,072; store supplies, $574; and office supplies, $83. Invoice dated May 4, terms n/10 EOM.

5 Received payment from Knox Co., for the balance from the April 28 sale less the May 2 return and the discount.

8 Issued Check No. 3411 to Peyton Products to pay for the $7,098 of merchandise purchased on April 29 less the May 3 return and a 2% discount.

9 Sold store supplies to the merchant next door at their cost of $350 cash.

10 Purchased $4,074 of office equipment on credit from Gear Supply Co., invoice dated May 10, terms n/10 EOM.

11 Received payment from Hensel Company for the May 2 sale less the discount.

11 Purchased $8,800 of merchandise from Garcia, Inc., invoice dated May 10, terms 2/10, n/30.

12 Received an $854 credit memorandum from Gear Supply Co. for the return of defective office equipment received on May 10.

15 Issued Check No. 3412, payable to Payroll, in payment of sales salaries, $5,320, and office salaries, $3,150. Cashed the check and paid the employees.

15 Cash sales for the first half of the month are $59,220 (cost is $38,200). (Cash sales are recorded daily but are recorded only twice here to reduce repetitive entries.)

15 Post to the customer and creditor accounts. Also post individual items that are not included in column totals at the end of the month to the general ledger accounts. (Such items are posted daily but are posted only twice each month because they are few in number.)

16 Sold merchandise on credit to Hensel Company, Invoice No. 8786, for $3,990 (cost is $1,890).

17 Purchased $13,650 of merchandise from Fink Corp., invoice dated May 14, terms 2/10, n/60.

19 Issued Check No. 3413 to Garcia, Inc., in payment of its May 10 invoice less the discount.

22 Sold merchandise to Lee Services, Invoice No. 8787, for $6,850 (cost is $4,990), terms 2/10, n/60.

23 Issued Check No. 3414 to Fink Corp. in payment of its May 14 invoice less the discount.

24 Purchased the following on credit from Gear Supply Co.: merchandise, $8,120; store supplies, $630; and office supplies, $280. Invoice dated May 24, terms n/10 EOM.

25 Purchased $3,080 of merchandise from Peyton Products, invoice dated May 23, terms 2/10, n/30.
26 Sold merchandise on credit to Crane Corp., Invoice No. 8788, for $14,210 (cost is $8,230).
26 Issued Check No. 3415 to Perennial Power in payment of the May electric bill, $1,283.
29 The owner of Colo Company, Jenny Colo, used Check No. 3416 to withdraw $7,000 cash from the business for personal use.
30 Received payment from Lee Services for the May 22 sale less the discount.
30 Issued Check No. 3417, payable to Payroll, in payment of sales salaries, $5,320, and office salaries, $3,150. Cashed the check and paid the employees.
31 Cash sales for the last half of the month are $66,052 (cost is $42,500).
31 Post to the customer and creditor accounts. Also post individual items that are not included in column totals at the end of the month to the general ledger accounts. Foot and crossfoot the journals and make the month-end postings.

Required

1. Enter these transactions in a sales journal, a purchases journal, a cash receipts journal, a cash disbursements journal, or a general journal as illustrated in this chapter (number all journal pages as page 2). Post when instructed to do so. Assume a perpetual inventory system.
2. Prepare a trial balance in the Trial Balance columns of the work sheet form provided with the working papers. Complete the work sheet using the following information for accounting adjustments.
   a. Expired insurance, $553.
   b. Ending store supplies inventory, $2,632.
   c. Ending office supplies inventory, $504.
   d. Depreciation of store equipment, $567.
   e. Depreciation of office equipment, $329.

   Prepare and post adjusting and closing entries.
3. Prepare a May 2011 multiple-step income statement, a May 2011 statement of owner's equity, and a May 31, 2011, classified balance sheet.
4. Prepare a post-closing trial balance. Also prove the accuracy of subsidiary ledgers by preparing schedules of both accounts receivable and accounts payable.

Check (2) Unadjusted trial balance totals, $545,020; Adjustments column totals, $2,407

(3) Net income, $31,647; Total assets, $385,791

Beyond the Numbers

REPORTING IN ACTION
A1
RIM

BTN 7-1 Refer to **Research In Motion**'s financial statements in Appendix A to answer the following.

1. Identify the note that reports on Research In Motion's business segments.
2. Describe the focus and activities of each of Research In Motion's business segments.

Fast Forward

3. Access Research In Motion's annual report for fiscal years ending after February 27, 2010, from its Website (**RIM.com**) or the SEC's EDGAR database (**www.SEC.gov**). Has Research In Motion changed its reporting policy regarding segment information? Explain.

COMPARATIVE ANALYSIS
A1
RIM
Apple

BTN 7-2 Key figures for **Research In Motion** and **Apple** follow ($ millions).

	Current Year		One Year Prior		Two Years Prior	
RIM Segment	Segment Revenue	Segment Assets	Segment Revenue	Segment Assets	Segment Revenue	Segment Assets
Domestic	$8,620	$4,059	$6,968	$2,647	$3,529	$1,739
International	6,333	6,145	4,097	5,454	2,480	3,772

	Current Year		One Year Prior		Two Years Prior	
Apple Segment	Segment Revenue	Segment Assets	Segment Revenue	Segment Assets	Segment Revenue	Segment Assets
Domestic	$22,325	$2,698	$20,893	$2,269	$14,683	$1,752
International	20,580	495	16,598	410	9,895	260

Required

1. Compute the ratio of segment revenue divided by segment assets for each of the segments of Research In Motion and Apple for each of the two most recent years shown. (We do not compute the segment return on assets as these companies did not report their segment income.)
2. Interpret and comment on your results of part 1.

ETHICS CHALLENGE

C1   

BTN 7-3 Erica Gray, CPA, is a sole practitioner. She has been practicing as an auditor for 10 years. Recently a long-standing audit client asked Gray to design and implement an integrated computer-based accounting information system. The fees associated with this additional engagement with the client are very attractive. However, Gray wonders if she can remain objective on subsequent audits in her evaluation of the client's accounting system and its records if she was responsible for its design and implementation. Gray knows that professional auditing standards require her to remain independent in fact and appearance from her auditing clients.

Required

1. What do you believe auditing standards are mainly concerned with when they require independence in fact? In appearance?
2. Why is it important that auditors remain independent of their clients?
3. Do you think Gray can accept this engagement and remain independent? Justify your response.

COMMUNICATING IN PRACTICE

C2 C3   

BTN 7-4 Your friend, Wendy Geiger, owns a small retail store that sells candies and nuts. Geiger acquires her goods from a few select vendors. She generally makes purchase orders by phone and on credit. Sales are primarily for cash. Geiger keeps her own manual accounting system using a general journal and a general ledger. At the end of each business day, she records one summary entry for cash sales. Geiger recently began offering items in creative gift packages. This has increased sales substantially, and she is now receiving orders from corporate and other clients who order large quantities and prefer to buy on credit. As a result of increased credit transactions in both purchases and sales, keeping the accounting records has become extremely time consuming. Geiger wants to continue to maintain her own manual system and calls you for advice. Write a memo to her advising how she might modify her current manual accounting system to accommodate the expanded business activities. Geiger is accustomed to checking her ledger by using a trial balance. Your memo should explain the advantages of what you propose and of any other verification techniques you recommend.

TAKING IT TO THE NET

A1   

BTN 7-5 Access the March 18, 2010, filing of the fiscal 2010 10-K report for **Dell** (ticker DELL) at www.SEC.gov. Read its Note 14 that details Dell's segment information and answer the following.

1. Dell's operations are divided among which four global business segments?
2. In fiscal year 2010, which segment had the largest dollar amount of operating income? Which had the largest amount of assets?
3. Compute the return on assets for each segment for fiscal year 2010. Use operating income and average total assets by segment for your calculation. Which segment has the highest return on assets?
4. For what product groups does Dell provide segment data? What percent of Dell's net revenue is earned by each product group?

TEAMWORK IN ACTION

C3 P1 P2

BTN 7-6 Each member of the team is to assume responsibility for one of the following tasks:

a. Journalizing in the purchases journal.
b. Journalizing in the cash disbursements journal.
c. Maintaining and verifying the Accounts Payable ledger.
d. Journalizing in the sales journal and the general journal.
e. Journalizing in the cash receipts journal.
f. Maintaining and verifying the Accounts Receivable ledger.

The team should abide by the following procedures in carrying out responsibilities.

Required

1. After tasks *a–f* are assigned, each team member is to quickly read the list of transactions in Problem 7-5A, identifying with initials the journal in which each transaction is to be recorded. Upon completion,

the team leader is to read transaction dates, and the appropriate team member is to vocalize responsibility. Any disagreement between teammates must be resolved.

2. Journalize and continually update subsidiary ledgers. Journal recorders should alert teammates assigned to subsidiary ledgers when an entry must be posted to their subsidiary.
3. Team members responsible for tasks *a*, *b*, *d*, and *e* are to summarize and prove journals; members responsible for tasks *c* and *f* are to prepare both payables and receivables schedules.
4. The team leader is to take charge of the general ledger, rotating team members to obtain amounts to be posted. The person responsible for a journal must complete posting references in that journal. Other team members should verify the accuracy of account balance computations. To avoid any abnormal account balances, post in the following order: P, S, G, R, D. (*Note:* Posting any necessary individual general ledger amounts is also done at this time.)
5. The team leader is to read out general ledger account balances while another team member fills in the trial balance form. Concurrently, one member should keep a running balance of debit account balance totals and another credit account balance totals. Verify the final total of the trial balance and the schedules. If necessary, the team must resolve any errors. Turn in the trial balance and schedules to the instructor.

ENTREPRENEURIAL DECISION

P1 

BTN 7-7 Refer to the chapter's opening feature about Kim Jordan and her company, **New Belgium Brewing Company**. Her manufacturing company deals with numerous suppliers and customers.

Required

1. Identify the special journals that New Belgium Brewing would be likely to use in its operations. Also identify any subsidiary ledgers that it would likely use.
2. New Belgium Brewing hopes to double yearly sales within five years hence from its current $100 million annual amount. Assume that its sales growth projections are as follows.

Year	One Year Hence	Two Years Hence	Three Years Hence	Four Years Hence	Five Years Hence
Projected growth in sales (from the preceding year)	0%	20%	15%	25%	20%

Estimate New Belgium Brewing's projected sales for each year (round to the nearest dollar). If this pattern of sales growth holds, will New Belgium Brewing achieve its goal of doubling sales in five years?

GLOBAL DECISION

A1  

NOKIA

BTN 7-8 Access and refer to the December 31, 2009, annual report for **Nokia** at www.Nokia.com.

Required

1. Identify its Note 2 (Segmental Information) to its financial statements and locate its information relating to Nokia's operating and reportable segments. Identify those three segments.
2. What financial figures does it disclose for each segment?
3. Does Nokia have a dominant segment? Explain.

ANSWERS TO MULTIPLE CHOICE QUIZ

1. a
2. e
3. d
4. b
5. a

8 Cash and Internal Controls

A Look Back

Chapter 7 focused on accounting information systems. We explained the principles and components of information systems, the use of special journals and subsidiary ledgers, and technology-based systems.

A Look at This Chapter

This chapter extends our study of accounting to internal control and the analysis of cash. We describe procedures that are good for internal control. We also explain the control of and the accounting for cash, including control features of banking activities.

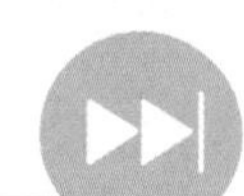

A Look Ahead

Chapter 9 focuses on receivables. We explain how to account and report on receivables and their related accounts. This includes estimating uncollectible receivables and computing interest earned.

Learning Objectives

CONCEPTUAL

C1 Define internal control and identify its purpose and principles. (p. 316)

C2 Define cash and cash equivalents and explain how to report them. (p. 321)

ANALYTICAL

A1 Compute the days' sales uncollected ratio and use it to assess liquidity. (p. 335)

LP8

PROCEDURAL

P1 Apply internal control to cash receipts and disbursements. (p. 322)

P2 Explain and record petty cash fund transactions. (p. 326)

P3 Prepare a bank reconciliation. (p. 331)

P4 *Appendix 8A*—Describe the use of documentation and verification to control cash disbursements. (p. 338)

P5 *Appendix 8B—Apply the net method to control purchase discounts.* (p. 341)

Decision Insight

Candyland Biz

"It's a creative outlet for me . . . it doesn't feel like work"
—DYLAN LAUREN

NEW YORK—A 10-foot chocolate bunny greets you as you enter the store—that should be warning enough! This elite designer candy store, christened **Dylan's Candy Bar (DylansCandyBar.com),** is the brainchild of co-founder Dylan Lauren. Explains Dylan, "I got a business plan together and set out to make candy my livelihood."

This sweet-lovers' heaven offers more than 5,000 different choices of sweets from all over the world. It has become a hip hangout for locals and tourists—and it has made candy cool. Says Dylan, "Park Avenue women come in, and the first thing they ask for is Gummi bears. They love that it's very childhood, nostalgic."

Although marketing is an important part of its success, Dylan's management of internal controls and cash is equally impressive. Several control procedures monitor its business activities and safeguard its assets. An example is the biometric time and attendance control system using fingerprint characteristics. Says Dylan, "There's no fooling the system! It is going to help us remotely manage our employees while eliminating human error and dishonesty. [It] is a cost-effective and important business management tool." Similar controls are applied throughout the store. Dylan explains that such controls raise productivity and cut expenses.

The store's cash management practices are equally impressive, including controls over cash receipts, disbursements, and petty cash. The use of bank reconciliations further helps with the store's control and management of cash. Dylan explains that she takes advantage of available banking services to enhance controls over cash.

Internal controls are crucial when on a busy day its stores bring in thousands of customers, and their cash. They have already expanded to three stores in New York, and one each in Houston and Orlando. Through it all, Dylan says it is "totally fun."

[Sources: *Dylan's Candy Bar Website,* January 2011; *Entrepreneur,* June 2005; *NYC Official City Guide,* July 2009; *The New York Times,* June & March 2009; *Dolce Vita Magazine,* June 2009; *Luxury Insider,* March 2009.]

Chapter Preview

We all are aware of theft and fraud. They affect us in several ways: We lock doors, chain bikes, review sales receipts, and acquire alarm systems. A company also takes actions to safeguard, control, and manage what it owns. Experience tells us that small companies are most vulnerable, usually due to weak internal controls. It is management's responsibility to set up policies and procedures to safeguard a company's assets, especially cash. To do so, management *and* employees must understand and apply principles of internal control. This chapter describes these principles and how to apply them. It focuses special attention on cash because it is easily transferable and is often at high risk of loss.

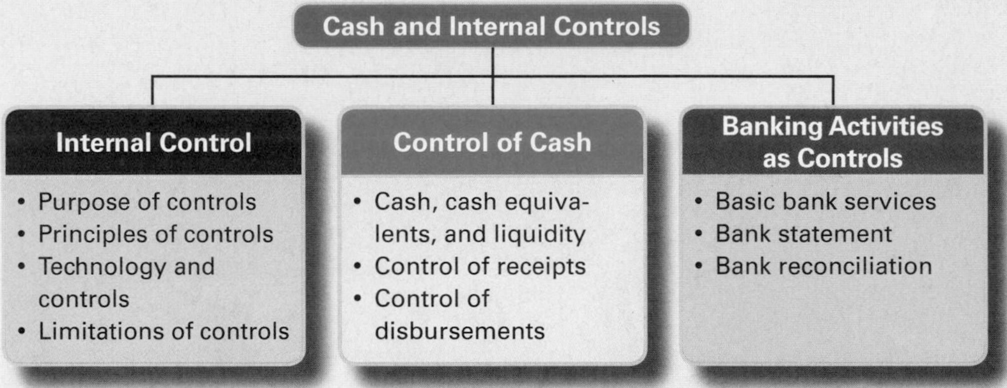

INTERNAL CONTROL

This section describes internal control and its fundamental principles. We also discuss the impact of technology on internal control and the limitations of control procedures.

Purpose of Internal Control

C1 Define internal control and identify its purpose and principles.

Managers (or owners) of small businesses often control the entire operation. These managers usually purchase all assets, hire and manage employees, negotiate all contracts, and sign all checks. They know from personal contact and observation whether the business is actually receiving the assets and services paid for. Most companies, however, cannot maintain this close personal supervision. They must delegate responsibilities and rely on formal procedures rather than personal contact in controlling business activities.

Internal Control System Managers use an internal control system to monitor and control business activities. An **internal control system** consists of the policies and procedures managers use to

- Protect assets.
- Ensure reliable accounting.
- Promote efficient operations.
- Urge adherence to company policies.

A properly designed internal control system is a key part of systems design, analysis, and performance. Managers place a high priority on internal control systems because they can prevent avoidable losses, help managers plan operations, and monitor company and employee performance. Internal controls do not provide guarantees, but they lower the company's risk of loss.

Sarbanes-Oxley Act (SOX) The **Sarbanes-Oxley Act (SOX)** requires the managers and auditors of companies whose stock is traded on an exchange (called *public companies*) to document and certify the system of internal controls. Following are some of the specific requirements:

- Auditors must evaluate internal controls and issue an internal control report.
- Auditors of a client are restricted as to what consulting services they can provide that client.
- The person leading an audit can serve no more than seven years without a two-year break.
- Auditors' work is overseen by the *Public Company Accounting Oversight Board* (PCAOB).
- Harsh penalties exist for violators—sentences up to 25 years in prison with severe fines.

SOX has markedly impacted companies, and the costs of its implementation are high. Importantly, **Section 404** of SOX requires that managers document and assess the effectiveness of all internal control processes that can impact financial reporting. The benefits include greater confidence in accounting systems and their related reports. However, the public continues to debate the costs versus the benefits of SOX as nearly all business activities of these companies are impacted by SOX. Section 404 of SOX requires that managers document and assess their internal controls *and* that auditors provide an opinion on managers' documentation and assessment. Costs of complying with Section 404 for companies is reported to average $4 million (source: Financial Executives Institute).

Principles of Internal Control

Internal control policies and procedures vary from company to company according to such factors as the nature of the business and its size. Certain fundamental internal control principles apply to all companies. The **principles of internal control** are to

1. Establish responsibilities.
2. Maintain adequate records.
3. Insure assets and bond key employees.
4. Separate recordkeeping from custody of assets.
5. Divide responsibility for related transactions.
6. Apply technological controls.
7. Perform regular and independent reviews.

This section explains these seven principles and describes how internal control procedures minimize the risk of fraud and theft. These procedures also increase the reliability and accuracy of accounting records. A framework for how these seven principles improve the quality of financial reporting is provided by the **Committee of Sponsoring Organizations (COSO)** (**www.COSO.org**). Specifically, these principles link to five aspects of internal control: control activities, control environment, risk assessment, monitoring, and communication.

Point: Sarbanes-Oxley Act (SOX) requires that each annual report contain an *internal control report*, which must: (1) state managers' responsibility for establishing and maintaining adequate internal controls for financial reporting; and (2) assess the effectiveness of those controls.

Establish Responsibilities Proper internal control means that responsibility for a task is clearly established and assigned to one person. When a problem occurs in a company where responsibility is not identified, determining who is at fault is difficult. For instance, if two salesclerks share the same cash register and there is a cash shortage, neither clerk can be held accountable. To prevent this problem, one clerk might be given responsibility for handling all cash sales. Alternately, a company can use a register with separate cash drawers for each clerk. Most of us have waited at a retail counter during a shift change while employees swap cash drawers.

Point: Many companies have a mandatory vacation policy for employees who handle cash. When another employee must cover for the one on vacation, it is more difficult to hide cash frauds.

Maintain Adequate Records Good recordkeeping is part of an internal control system. It helps protect assets and ensures that employees use prescribed procedures. Reliable records are also a source of information that managers use to monitor company activities. When detailed records of equipment are kept, for instance, items are unlikely to be lost or stolen without detection. Similarly, transactions are less likely to be entered in wrong accounts if a chart of accounts is set up and carefully used. Many preprinted forms and internal documents are also designed for use in a good internal control system. When sales slips are properly designed, for instance, sales personnel can record needed information efficiently with less chance of errors or delays to customers. When sales slips are prenumbered and controlled, each one issued is the responsibility of one salesperson, preventing the salesperson from pocketing cash by making a sale and destroying the sales slip. Computerized point-of-sale systems achieve the same control results.

Insure Assets and Bond Key Employees Good internal control means that assets are adequately insured against casualty and that employees handling large amounts of cash and easily transferable assets are bonded. An employee is *bonded* when a company purchases an insurance policy, or a bond, against losses from theft by that employee. Bonding reduces the risk of loss. It also discourages theft because bonded employees know an independent bonding company will be involved when theft is uncovered and is unlikely to be sympathetic with an employee involved in theft.

Point: The Association of Certified Fraud Examiners (**cfenet.com**) estimates that employee fraud costs small companies more than $100,000 per incident.

Decision Insight

Tag Control A novel technique exists for marking physical assets. It involves embedding a less than one-inch-square tag of fibers that creates a unique optical signature recordable by scanners. Manufacturers hope to embed tags in everything from compact discs and credit cards to designer clothes for purposes of internal control and efficiency. ■

Separate Recordkeeping from Custody of Assets A person who controls or has access to an asset must not keep that asset's accounting records. This principle reduces the risk of theft or waste of an asset because the person with control over it knows that another person keeps its records. Also, a recordkeeper who does not have access to the asset has no reason to falsify records. This means that to steal an asset and hide the theft from the records, two or more people must *collude*—or agree in secret to commit the fraud.

Divide Responsibility for Related Transactions Good internal control divides responsibility for a transaction or a series of related transactions between two or more individuals or departments. This is to ensure that the work of one individual acts as a check on the other. This principle, often called *separation of duties,* is not a call for duplication of work. Each employee or department should perform unduplicated effort. Examples of transactions with divided responsibility are placing purchase orders, receiving merchandise, and paying vendors. These tasks should not be given to one individual or department. Assigning responsibility for two or more of these tasks to one party increases mistakes and perhaps fraud. Having an independent person, for example, check incoming goods for quality and quantity encourages more care and attention to detail than having the person who placed the order do the checking. Added protection can result from identifying a third person to approve payment of the invoice. A company can even designate a fourth person with authority to write checks as another protective measure.

Point: There's a new security device—a person's ECG (electrocardiogram) reading—that is as unique as a fingerprint and a lot harder to lose or steal than a PIN. ECGs can be read through fingertip touches. An ECG also shows that a living person is actually there, whereas fingerprint and facial recognition software can be fooled.

Apply Technological Controls Cash registers, check protectors, time clocks, and personal identification scanners are examples of devices that can improve internal control. Technology often improves the effectiveness of controls. A cash register with a locked-in tape or electronic file makes a record of each cash sale. A check protector perforates the amount of a check into its face and makes it difficult to alter the amount. A time clock registers the exact time an employee both arrives at and departs from the job. Mechanical change and currency counters quickly and accurately count amounts, and personal scanners limit access to only authorized individuals. Each of these and other technological controls are an effective part of many internal control systems.

Decision Insight

About Face Face-recognition software snaps a digital picture of the face and converts key facial features—say, the distance between the eyes—into a series of numerical values. These can be stored on an ID or ATM card as a simple bar code to prohibit unauthorized access. ■

Perform Regular and Independent Reviews Changes in personnel, stress of time pressures, and technological advances present opportunities for shortcuts and lapses. To counter these factors, regular reviews of internal control systems are needed to ensure that procedures are followed. These reviews are preferably done by internal auditors not directly involved in the activities. Their impartial perspective encourages an evaluation of the efficiency as well as the effectiveness of the internal control system. Many companies also pay for audits by independent, external auditors. These external auditors test the company's financial records to give an opinion as to whether its financial statements are presented fairly. Before external auditors decide on how much testing is needed, they evaluate the effectiveness of the internal control system. This evaluation is often helpful to a client.

Decision Maker

Answer — p. 343

Entrepreneur As owner of a start-up information services company, you hire a systems analyst. One of her first recommendations is to require all employees to take at least one week of vacation per year. Why would she recommend a "forced vacation" policy? ■

Technology and Internal Control

The fundamental principles of internal control are relevant no matter what the technological state of the accounting system, from purely manual to fully automated systems. Technology impacts an internal control system in several important ways. Perhaps the most obvious is that technology allows us quicker access to databases and information. Used effectively, technology greatly improves managers' abilities to monitor and control business activities. This section describes some technological impacts we must be alert to.

Point: Information on Internet fraud can be found at these Websites:
sec.gov/investor/pubs/cyberfraud.htm
ftc.gov/bcp/consumer.shtm
www.fraud.org

Reduced Processing Errors Technologically advanced systems reduce the number of errors in processing information. Provided the software and data entry are correct, the risk of mechanical and mathematical errors is nearly eliminated. However, we must remember that erroneous software or data entry does exist. Also, less human involvement in data processing can cause data entry errors to go undiscovered. Moreover, errors in software can produce consistent but erroneous processing of transactions. Continually checking and monitoring all types of systems are important.

Point: Evidence of any internal control failure for a company reduces user confidence in its financial statements.

More Extensive Testing of Records A company's review and audit of electronic records can include more extensive testing when information is easily and rapidly accessed. When accounting records are kept manually, auditors and others likely select only small samples of data to test. When data are accessible with computer technology, however, auditors can quickly analyze large samples or even the entire database.

Limited Evidence of Processing Many data processing steps are increasingly done by computer. Accordingly, fewer hard-copy items of documentary evidence are available for review. Yet technologically advanced systems can provide new evidence. They can, for instance, record who made the entries, the date and time, the source of the entry, and so on. Technology can also be designed to require the use of passwords or other identification before access to the system is granted. This means that internal control depends more on the design and operation of the information system and less on the analysis of its resulting documents.

Point: We look to several sources when assessing a company's internal controls. Sources include the auditor's report, management report on controls (if available), management discussion and analysis, and financial press.

Crucial Separation of Duties Technological advances in accounting information systems often yield some job eliminations or consolidations. While those who remain have the special skills necessary to operate advanced programs and equipment, a company with a reduced workforce risks losing its crucial separation of duties. The company must establish ways to control and monitor employees to minimize risk of error and fraud. For instance, the person who designs and programs the information system must not be the one who operates it. The company must also separate control over programs and files from the activities related to cash receipts and disbursements. For instance, a computer operator should not control check-writing activities. Achieving acceptable separation of duties can be especially difficult and costly in small companies with few employees.

Point: COSO organizes control components into five types:
- Control environment
- Control activities
- Risk assessment
- Monitoring
- Information and communication

Increased E-Commerce Technology has encouraged the growth of e-commerce. **Amazon.com** and **eBay** are examples of companies that have successfully exploited e-commerce. Most companies have some e-commerce transactions. All such transactions involve at least three risks. (1) *Credit card number theft* is a risk of using, transmitting, and storing such data online. This increases the cost of e-commerce. (2) *Computer viruses* are malicious programs that attach themselves to innocent files for purposes of infecting and harming other files and programs. (3) *Impersonation* online can result in charges of sales to bogus accounts, purchases of inappropriate materials, and the unknowing giving up of confidential information to hackers. Companies use both firewalls and encryption to

"Worst case of identity theft I've ever seen!"

combat some of these risks—firewalls are points of entry to a system that require passwords to continue, and encryption is a mathematical process to rearrange contents that cannot be read without the process code. Nearly 5% of Americans already report being victims of identity theft, and roughly 10 million say their privacy has been compromised.

Decision Insight

Cheery Fraud Victim Certified Fraud Examiners Website reports the following: Andrew Cameron stole Jacqueline Boanson's credit card. Cameron headed to the racetrack and promptly charged two bets for $150 on the credit card—winning $400. Unfortunately for Cameron the racetrack refused to pay him cash as its internal control policy is to credit winnings from bets made on a credit card to that same card. Cameron was later nabbed; and the racetrack let Ms. Boanson keep the winnings. ■

Limitations of Internal Control

All internal control policies and procedures have limitations that usually arise from either (1) the human element or (2) the cost–benefit principle.

Internal control policies and procedures are applied by people. This human element creates several potential limitations that we can categorize as either (1) human error or (2) human fraud. *Human error* can occur from negligence, fatigue, misjudgment, or confusion. *Human fraud* involves intent by people to defeat internal controls, such as *management override,* for personal gain. Fraud also includes collusion to thwart the separation of duties. The human element highlights the importance of establishing an *internal control environment* to convey management's commitment to internal control policies and procedures. Human fraud is driven by the *triple-threat* of fraud:

- **Opportunity**—refers to internal control deficiencies in the workplace.
- **Pressure**—refers to financial, family, society, and other stresses to succeed.
- **Rationalization**—refers to employees justifying fraudulent behavior.

Point: Cybercrime.gov pursues computer and intellectual property crimes, including that of e-commerce.

The second major limitation on internal control is the *cost–benefit principle,* which dictates that the costs of internal controls must not exceed their benefits. Analysis of costs and benefits must consider all factors, including the impact on morale. Most companies, for instance, have a legal right to read employees' e-mails, yet companies seldom exercise that right unless they are confronted with evidence of potential harm to the company. The same holds for drug testing, phone tapping, and hidden cameras. The bottom line is that managers must establish internal control policies and procedures with a net benefit to the company.

Address www.hacker'sguidetocyberspace.com GO

Hacker's Guide to Cyberspace

Pharming Viruses attached to e-mails and Websites load software onto your PC that monitors keystrokes; when you sign on to financial Websites, it steals your passwords.

Phishing Hackers send e-mails to you posing as banks; you are asked for information using fake Websites where they reel in your passwords and personal data.

WI-Phishing Cybercrooks set up wireless networks hoping you use them to connect to the Web; your passwords and data are stolen as you use their network.

Bot-Networking Hackers send remote-control programs to your PC that take control to send out spam and viruses; they even rent your bot to other cybercrooks.

Typo-Squatting Hackers set up Websites with addresses similar to legit outfits; when you make a typo and hit their sites, they infect your PC with viruses or take them over as bots.

Quick Check Answers — p. 343 

1. Principles of internal control suggest that (choose one): (*a*) Responsibility for a series of related transactions (such as placing orders, receiving and paying for merchandise) should be assigned to one employee; (*b*) Responsibility for individual tasks should be shared by more than one employee so that one serves as a check on the other; or (*c*) Employees who handle considerable cash and easily transferable assets should be bonded.
2. What are some impacts of computing technology on internal control?

CONTROL OF CASH

Cash is a necessary asset of every company. Most companies also own *cash equivalents* (defined below), which are assets similar to cash. Cash and cash equivalents are the most liquid of all assets and are easily hidden and moved. An effective system of internal controls protects these assets and it should meet three basic guidelines:

1. Handling cash is separate from recordkeeping of cash.
2. Cash receipts are promptly deposited in a bank.
3. Cash disbursements are made by check.

The first guideline applies separation of duties to minimize errors and fraud. When duties are separated, two or more people must collude to steal cash and conceal this action in the accounting records. The second guideline uses immediate (say, daily) deposits of all cash receipts to produce a timely independent record of the cash received. It also reduces the likelihood of cash theft (or loss) and the risk that an employee could personally use the money before depositing it. The third guideline uses payments by check to develop an independent bank record of cash disbursements. This guideline also reduces the risk of cash theft (or loss).

This section begins with definitions of cash and cash equivalents. Discussion then focuses on controls and accounting for both cash receipts and disbursements. The exact procedures used to achieve control over cash vary across companies. They depend on factors such as company size, number of employees, volume of cash transactions, and sources of cash.

Cash, Cash Equivalents, and Liquidity

C2 Define cash and cash equivalents and explain how to report them.

Good accounting systems help in managing the amount of cash and controlling who has access to it. Cash is the usual means of payment when paying for assets, services, or liabilities. **Liquidity** refers to a company's ability to pay for its near-term obligations. Cash and similar assets are called **liquid assets** because they can be readily used to settle such obligations. A company needs liquid assets to effectively operate.

Cash includes currency and coins along with the amounts on deposit in bank accounts, checking accounts (called *demand deposits*), and many savings accounts (called *time deposits*). Cash also includes items that are acceptable for deposit in these accounts such as customer checks, cashier's checks, certified checks, and money orders. **Cash equivalents** are short-term, highly liquid investment assets meeting two criteria: (1) readily convertible to a known cash amount and (2) sufficiently close to their due date so that their market value is not sensitive to interest rate changes. Only investments purchased within three months of their due date usually satisfy these criteria. Examples of cash equivalents are short-term investments in assets such as U.S. Treasury bills and money market funds. To increase their return, many companies invest idle cash in cash equivalents. Most companies combine cash equivalents with cash as a single item on the balance sheet.

Point: The most liquid assets are usually reported first on a balance sheet; the least liquid assets are reported last.

Point: Google reports cash and cash equivalents of $10,198 million in its balance sheet. This amount makes up nearly 25% of its total assets.

Cash Management

When companies fail, one of the most common causes is their inability to manage cash. Companies must plan both cash receipts and cash payments. The goals of cash management are twofold:

1. Plan cash receipts to meet cash payments when due.
2. Keep a minimum level of cash necessary to operate.

The *treasurer* of the company is responsible for cash management. Effective cash management involves applying the following cash management principles.

- **Encourage collection of receivables.** The more quickly customers and others pay the company, the more quickly that company can use the money. Some companies have cash-only sales policies. Others might offer discounts for payments received early.
- **Delay payment of liabilities.** The more delayed a company is in paying others, the more time it has to use the money. Some companies regularly wait to pay their bills until the last possible day allowed—although, a company must take care not to hurt its credit standing.
- **Keep only necessary levels of assets.** The less money tied up in idle assets, the more money to invest in productive assets. Some companies maintain *just-in-time* inventory; meaning they plan inventory to be available at the same time orders are filled. Others might lease out excess warehouse space or rent equipment instead of buying it.
- **Plan expenditures.** Money should be spent only when it is available. Companies must look at seasonal and business cycles to plan expenditures.
- **Invest excess cash.** Excess cash earns no return and should be invested. Excess cash from seasonal cycles can be placed in a bank account or other short-term investment for income. Excess cash beyond what's needed for regular business should be invested in productive assets like factories and inventories.

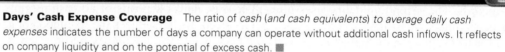

Decision Insight

Days' Cash Expense Coverage The ratio of *cash (and cash equivalents) to average daily cash expenses* indicates the number of days a company can operate without additional cash inflows. It reflects on company liquidity and on the potential of excess cash. ■

Control of Cash Receipts

P1 Apply internal control to cash receipts and disbursements.

Internal control of cash receipts ensures that cash received is properly recorded and deposited. Cash receipts can arise from transactions such as cash sales, collections of customer accounts, receipts of interest earned, bank loans, sales of assets, and owner investments. This section explains internal control over two important types of cash receipts: over-the-counter and by mail.

Over-the-Counter Cash Receipts For purposes of internal control, over-the-counter cash receipts from sales should be recorded on a cash register at the time of each sale. To help ensure that correct amounts are entered, each register should be located so customers can read the amounts entered. Clerks also should be required to enter each sale before wrapping merchandise and to give the customer a receipt for each sale. The design of each cash register should provide a permanent, locked-in record of each transaction. In many systems, the register is directly linked with computing and accounting services. Less advanced registers simply print a record of each transaction on a paper tape or electronic file locked inside the register.

Proper internal control prescribes that custody over cash should be separate from its recordkeeping. For over-the-counter cash receipts, this separation begins with the cash sale. The clerk who has access to cash in the register should not have access to its locked-in record. At the end of the clerk's work period, the clerk should count the cash in the register, record the amount, and turn over the cash and a record of its amount to the company cashier. The cashier, like the clerk, has access to the cash but should not have access to accounting records (or the register tape or file). A third employee, often a supervisor, compares the record of total register transactions (or the register tape or file) with the cash receipts reported by the cashier. This record is the basis for a journal entry recording over-the-counter cash receipts. The third employee has access to the records for cash but not to the actual cash. The clerk and the cashier have access to cash but not to the accounting records. None of them can make a mistake or divert cash without the difference being revealed—see the following diagram.

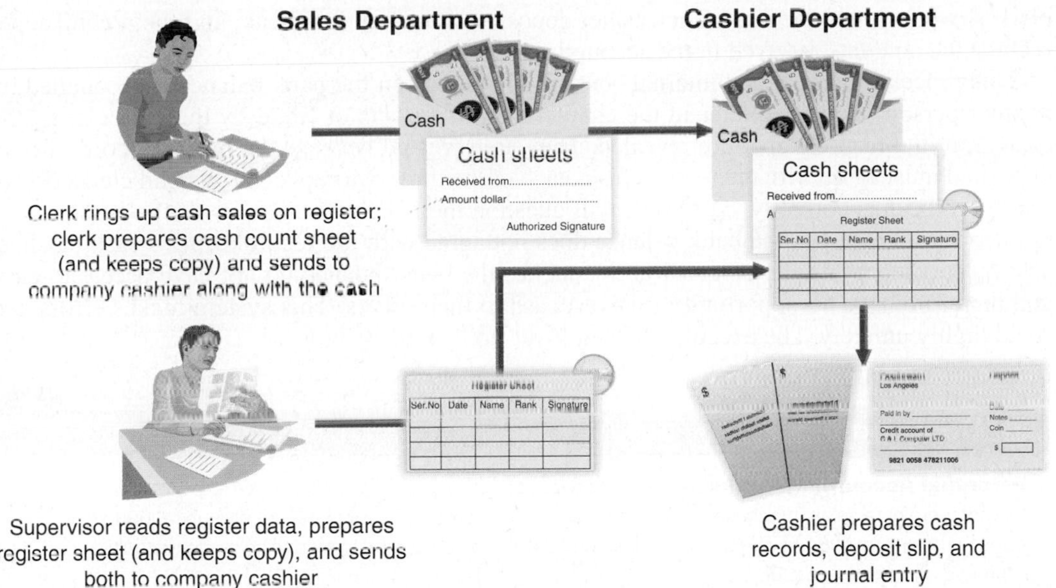
Sales Department
Cashier Department
Cash
Cash sheets
Received from
Amount dollar
Authorized Signature
Cash
Cash sheets
Received from
Register Sheet
Ser.No | Date | Name | Rank | Signature
Clerk rings up cash sales on register; clerk prepares cash count sheet (and keeps copy) and sends to company cashier along with the cash
Register Sheet
Ser.No | Date | Name | Rank | Signature
Supervisor reads register data, prepares register sheet (and keeps copy), and sends both to company cashier
Cashier prepares cash records, deposit slip, and journal entry

Cash over and short. Sometimes errors in making change are discovered from differences between the cash in a cash register and the record of the amount of cash receipts. Although a clerk is careful, one or more customers can be given too much or too little change. This means that at the end of a work period, the cash in a cash register might not equal the record of cash receipts. This difference is reported in the **Cash Over and Short** account, also called *Cash Short and Over,* which is an income statement account recording the income effects of cash overages and cash shortages. To illustrate, if a cash register's record shows $550 but the count of cash in the register is $555, the entry to record cash sales and its overage is

Point: Retailers often require cashiers to restrictively endorse checks immediately on receipt by stamping them "For deposit only."

	Debit	Credit
Cash	555	
Cash Over and Short		5
Sales		550
To record cash sales and a cash overage.		

Assets	=	Liabilities	+	Equity
+555				+ 5
				+550

On the other hand, if a cash register's record shows $625 but the count of cash in the register is $621, the entry to record cash sales and its shortage is

	Debit	Credit
Cash	621	
Cash Over and Short	4	
Sales		625
To record cash sales and a cash shortage.		

Assets	=	Liabilities	+	Equity
+621				4
				+625

Since customers are more likely to dispute being shortchanged than being given too much change, the Cash Over and Short account usually has a debit balance at the end of an accounting period. A debit balance reflects an expense. It is reported on the income statement as part of general and administrative expenses. (Since the amount is usually small, it is often combined with other small expenses and reported as part of *miscellaneous expenses*—or as part of *miscellaneous revenues* if it has a credit balance.)

Point: Merchants begin a business day with a *change fund* in their cash register. The accounting for a change fund is similar to that for petty cash, including that for cash shortages or overages.

Cash Receipts by Mail Control of cash receipts that arrive through the mail starts with the person who opens the mail. Preferably, two people are assigned the task of, and are present for, opening the mail. In this case, theft of cash receipts by mail requires collusion between these two employees. Specifically, the person(s) opening the mail enters a list (in triplicate) of money received. This list should contain a record of each sender's name, the amount, and an explanation of why the money is sent. The first copy is sent with the money to the cashier. A second copy is sent to the recordkeeper in the accounting area. A third copy is kept by the

Point: Collusion implies that two or more individuals are knowledgeable or involved with the activities of the other(s).

clerk(s) who opened the mail. The cashier deposits the money in a bank, and the recordkeeper records the amounts received in the accounting records.

This process reflects good internal control. That is, when the bank balance is reconciled by another person (explained later in the chapter), errors or acts of fraud by the mail clerks, the cashier, or the recordkeeper are revealed. They are revealed because the bank's record of cash deposited must agree with the records from each of the three. Moreover, if the mail clerks do not report all receipts correctly, customers will question their account balances. If the cashier does not deposit all receipts, the bank balance does not agree with the recordkeeper's cash balance. The recordkeeper and the person who reconciles the bank balance do not have access to cash and therefore have no opportunity to divert cash to themselves. This system makes errors and fraud highly unlikely. The exception is employee collusion.

Decision Insight

Perpetual Accounting **Walmart** uses a network of information links with its point-of-sale cash registers to coordinate sales, purchases, and distribution. Its supercenters, for instance, ring up 15,000 separate sales on heavy days. By using cash register information, the company can fix pricing mistakes quickly and capitalize on sales trends. ■

Control of Cash Disbursements

Control of cash disbursements is especially important as most large thefts occur from payment of fictitious invoices. One key to controlling cash disbursements is to require all expenditures to be made by check. The only exception is small payments made from petty cash. Another key is to deny access to the accounting records to anyone other than the owner who has the authority to sign checks. A small business owner often signs checks and knows from personal contact that the items being paid for are actually received. This arrangement is impossible in large businesses. Instead, internal control procedures must be substituted for personal contact. Such procedures are designed to assure the check signer that the obligations recorded are properly incurred and should be paid. This section describes these and other internal control procedures, including the voucher system and petty cash system. A method for management of cash disbursements for purchases is described in Appendix 8B.

Decision Insight

Cash Budget Projected cash receipts and cash disbursements are often summarized in a *cash budget*. Provided that sufficient cash exists for effective operations, companies wish to minimize the cash they hold because of its risk of theft and its low return versus other investment opportunities. ■

Voucher System of Control A **voucher system** is a set of procedures and approvals designed to control cash disbursements and the acceptance of obligations. The voucher system of control establishes procedures for

- Verifying, approving, and recording obligations for eventual cash disbursement.
- Issuing checks for payment of verified, approved, and recorded obligations.

A reliable voucher system follows standard procedures for every transaction. This applies even when multiple purchases are made from the same supplier.

A voucher system's control over cash disbursements begins when a company incurs an obligation that will result in payment of cash. A key factor in this system is that only approved departments and individuals are authorized to incur such obligations. The system often limits the type of obligations that a department or individual can incur. In a large retail store, for instance, only a purchasing department should be authorized to incur obligations for merchandise inventory. Another key factor is that procedures for purchasing, receiving, and paying for merchandise are divided among several departments (or individuals). These departments include the one requesting the purchase, the purchasing department, the receiving department, and the accounting department. To coordinate and control responsibilities of these departments, a company uses

Point: MCI, formerly WorldCom, paid a whopping $500 million in SEC fines for accounting fraud. Among the charges were that it inflated earnings by as much as $10 billion. Its CEO, Bernard Ebbers, was sentenced to 25 years.

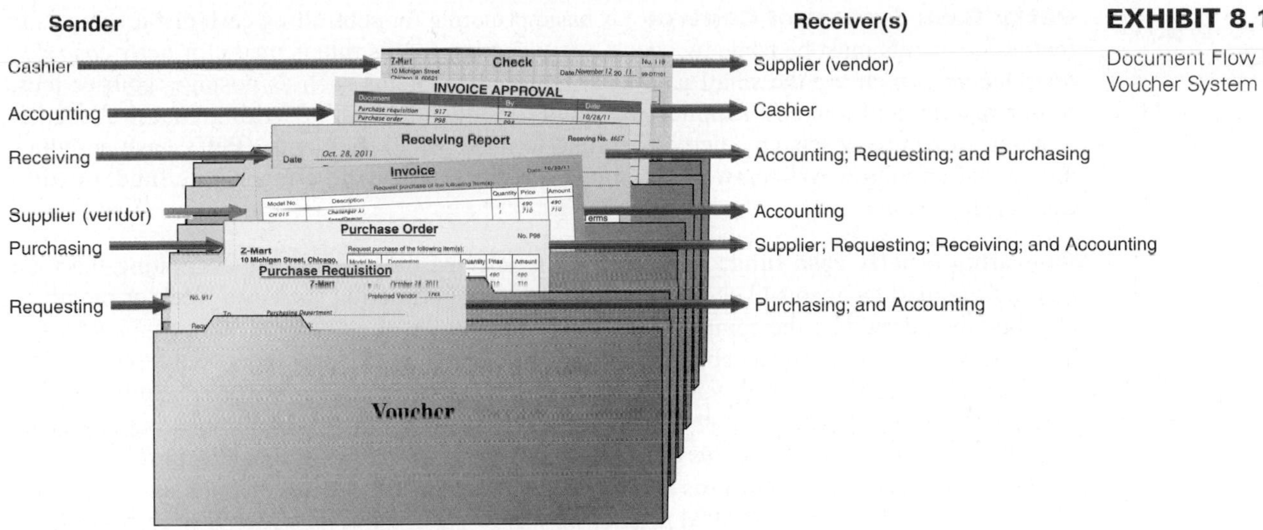

EXHIBIT 8.1

Document Flow in a Voucher System

several different business documents. Exhibit 8.1 shows how documents are accumulated in a **voucher,** which is an internal document (or file) used to accumulate information to control cash disbursements and to ensure that a transaction is properly recorded. This specific example begins with a *purchase requisition* and concludes with a *check* drawn against cash. Appendix 8A describes the documentation and verification necessary for a voucher system of control. It also describes the internal control objective served by each document.

A voucher system should be applied not only to purchases of inventory but to all expenditures. To illustrate, when a company receives a monthly telephone bill, it should review and verify the charges, prepare a voucher (file), and insert the bill. This transaction is then recorded with a journal entry. If the amount is currently due, a check is issued. If not, the voucher is filed for payment on its due date. If no voucher is prepared, verifying the invoice and its amount after several days or weeks can be difficult. Also, without records, a dishonest employee could collude with a dishonest supplier to get more than one payment for an obligation, payment for excessive amounts, or payment for goods and services not received. An effective voucher system helps prevent such frauds.

Point: A *voucher* is an internal document (or file).

Point: The basic purposes of paper and electronic documents are similar. However, the internal control system must change to reflect different risks, including confidential and competitive-sensitive information that is at greater risk in electronic systems.

Decision Insight

Cyber Setup The FTC is on the cutting edge of cybersleuthing. Opportunists in search of easy money are lured to WeMarket4U.net/SundaeStation and WeMarket4U.net/FatFoe. Take the bait and you get warned. The top 5 fraud complaints as compiled by the Bureau of Consumer Protection are shown to the right.

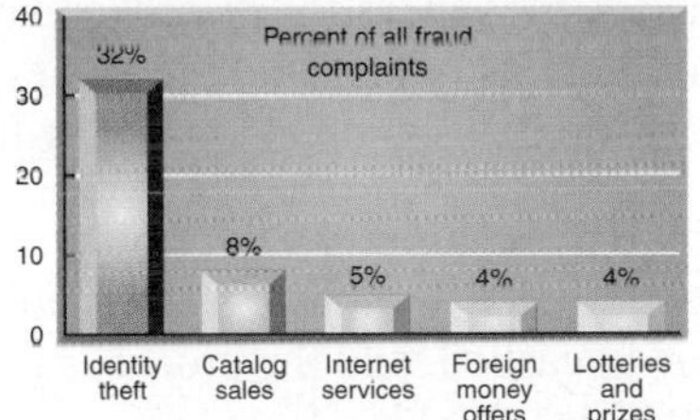

Quick Check

Answers — p. 343

3. Why must a company hold liquid assets?
4. Why does a company hold cash equivalent assets in addition to cash?
5. Identify at least two assets that are classified as cash equivalents.
6. Good internal control procedures for cash include which of the following? (*a*) All cash disbursements, other than those for very small amounts, are made by check; (*b*) One employee counts cash received from sales and promptly deposits cash receipts; or (*c*) Cash receipts by mail are opened by one employee who is then responsible for recording and depositing them.
7. Should all companies require a voucher system? At what point in a company's growth would you recommend a voucher system?

P2 Explain and record petty cash fund transactions.

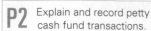

Petty Cash System of Control A basic principle for controlling cash disbursements is that all payments must be made by check. An exception to this rule is made for *petty cash disbursements,* which are the small payments required for items such as postage, courier fees, minor repairs, and low-cost supplies. To avoid the time and cost of writing checks for small amounts, a company sets up a petty cash fund to make small payments. (**Petty cash** activities are part of an *imprest system,* which designates advance money to establish the fund, to withdraw from the fund, and to reimburse the fund.)

Operating a petty cash fund. Establishing a petty cash fund requires estimating the total amount of small payments likely to be made during a short period such as a week or month. A check is then drawn by the company cashier for an amount slightly in excess of this estimate. This check is recorded with a debit to the Petty Cash account (an asset) and a credit to Cash. The check is cashed, and the currency is given to an employee designated as the *petty cashier* or *petty cash custodian*. The petty cashier is responsible for keeping this cash safe, making payments from the fund, and keeping records of it in a secure place referred to as the *petty cashbox*.

When each cash disbursement is made, the person receiving payment should sign a prenumbered *petty cash receipt,* also called *petty cash ticket*—see Exhibit 8.2. The petty cash receipt is then placed in the petty cashbox with the remaining money. Under this system, the sum of all receipts plus the remaining cash equals the total fund amount. A $100 petty cash fund, for instance, contains any combination of cash and petty cash receipts that totals $100 (examples are $80 cash plus $20 in receipts, or $10 cash plus $90 in receipts). Each disbursement reduces cash and increases the amount of receipts in the petty cashbox.

Point: A petty cash fund is used only for business expenses.

EXHIBIT 8.2

Petty Cash Receipt

Z-Mart No. 9

PETTY CASH RECEIPT

For *Freight charges*
Date *November 5, 2009*
Charge to *Merchandise Inventory*
Amount *$6.75*
Approved by [signature]
Received by [signature]

The petty cash fund should be reimbursed when it is nearing zero and at the end of an accounting period when financial statements are prepared. For this purpose, the petty cashier sorts the paid receipts by the type of expense or account and then totals the receipts. The petty cashier presents all paid receipts to the company cashier, who stamps all receipts *paid* so they cannot be reused, files them for recordkeeping, and gives the petty cashier a check for their sum. When this check is cashed and the money placed in the cashbox, the total money in the cashbox is restored to its original amount. The fund is now ready for a new cycle of petty cash payments.

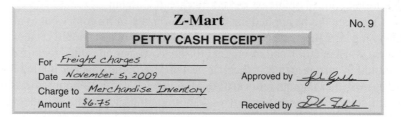

Point: Petty cash receipts with either no signature or a forged signature usually indicate misuse of petty cash. Companies respond with surprise petty cash counts for verification.

Illustrating a petty cash fund. To illustrate, assume Z-Mart establishes a petty cash fund on November 1 and designates one of its office employees as the petty cashier. A $75 check is drawn, cashed, and the proceeds given to the petty cashier. The entry to record the setup of this petty cash fund is

Assets = Liabilities + Equity
+75
−75

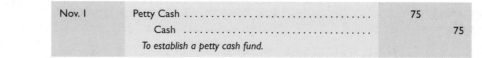

Nov. 1	Petty Cash	75	
	Cash		75
	To establish a petty cash fund.		

After the petty cash fund is established, the Petty Cash account is not debited or credited again unless the amount of the fund is changed. (A fund should be increased if it requires reimbursement too frequently. On the other hand, if the fund is too large, some of its money should be redeposited in the Cash account.)

Next, assume that Z-Mart's petty cashier makes several November payments from petty cash. Each person who received payment is required to sign a receipt. On November 27, after making a $26.50 cash payment for tile cleaning, only $3.70 cash remains in the fund. The petty cashier then summarizes and totals the petty cash receipts as shown in Exhibit 8.3.

Point: Reducing or eliminating a petty cash fund requires a credit to Petty Cash.

Point: Although *individual* petty cash disbursements are not evidenced by a check, the initial petty cash fund is evidenced by a check, and later petty cash expenditures are evidenced by a check to replenish them *in total.*

Z-MART Petty Cash Payments Report			
Miscellaneous Expenses			
Nov. 2	Cleaning of LCD panels	$20.00	
Nov. 27	Tile cleaning	26.50	$ 46.50
Merchandise Inventory (transportation-in)			
Nov. 5	Transport of merchandise purchased	6.75	
Nov. 20	Transport of merchandise purchased	8.30	15.05
Delivery Expense			
Nov. 18	Customer's package delivered		5.00
Office Supplies Expense			
Nov. 15	Purchase of office supplies immediately used		4.75
Total			**$71.30**

EXHIBIT 8.3

Petty Cash Payments Report

Point: This report can also include receipt number and names of those who approved and received cash payment (see Demo Problem 2).

The petty cash payments report and all receipts are given to the company cashier in exchange for a $71.30 check to reimburse the fund. The petty cashier cashes the check and puts the $71.30 cash in the petty cashbox. The company records this reimbursement as follows.

Nov. 27	Miscellaneous Expenses	46.50	
	Merchandise Inventory	15.05	
	Delivery Expense	5.00	
	Office Supplies Expense	4.75	
	Cash		71.30
	To reimburse petty cash.		

Assets	=	Liabilities	+	Equity
−71.30				−46.50
				−15.05
				− 5.00
				− 4.75

A petty cash fund is usually reimbursed at the end of an accounting period so that expenses are recorded in the proper period, even if the fund is not low on money. If the fund is not reimbursed at the end of a period, the financial statements would show both an overstated cash asset and understated expenses (or assets) that were paid out of petty cash. Some companies do not reimburse the petty cash fund at the end of each period under the notion that this amount is immaterial to users of financial statements.

Point: To avoid errors in recording petty cash reimbursement, follow these steps: (1) prepare payments report, (2) compute cash needed by subtracting cash remaining from total fund amount, (3) record entry, and (4) check "Dr. = Cr." in entry. Any difference is Cash Over and Short.

Increasing or decreasing a petty cash fund. A decision to increase or decrease a petty cash fund is often made when reimbursing it. To illustrate, assume Z-Mart decides to *increase* its petty cash fund from $75 to $100 on November 27 when it reimburses the fund. The entries required are to (1) reimburse the fund as usual (see the preceding November 27 entry) and (2) increase the fund amount as follows.

Nov. 27	Petty Cash	25	
	Cash		25
	To increase the petty cash fund amount.		

Alternatively, if Z-Mart *decreases* the petty cash fund from $75 to $55 on November 27, the entry is to (1) credit Petty Cash for $20 (decreasing the fund from $75 to $55) and (2) debit Cash for $20 (reflecting the $20 transfer from Petty Cash to Cash).

Cash over and short. Sometimes a petty cashier fails to get a receipt for payment or overpays for the amount due. When this occurs and the fund is later reimbursed, the petty cash payments report plus the cash remaining will not total to the fund balance. This mistake causes the fund to be *short*. This shortage is recorded as an expense in the reimbursing entry with a debit to the Cash Over and Short account. (An overage in the petty cash fund is recorded with a credit to Cash Over and Short in the reimbursing entry.) To illustrate, prepare the June 1 entry

Summary of Petty Cash Accounting

Event	Petty Cash	Cash	Expenses
Set up fund	Dr.	Cr.	—
Reimburse fund	—	Cr.	Dr.
Increase fund	Dr.	Cr.	—
Decrease fund	Cr.	Dr.	—

to reimburse a $200 petty cash fund when its payments report shows $178 in miscellaneous expenses and $15 cash remains.

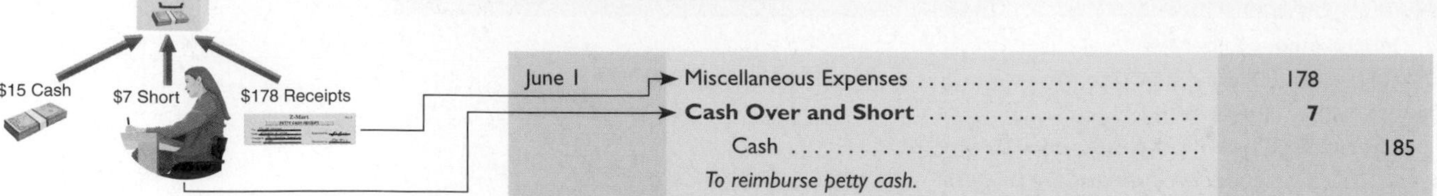

June 1	Miscellaneous Expenses	178	
	Cash Over and Short	7	
	Cash		185
	To reimburse petty cash.		

Decision Insight

Warning Signs There are clues to internal control violations. Warning signs from accounting include (1) an increase in customer refunds—could be fake, (2) missing documents—could be used for fraud, (3) differences between bank deposits and cash receipts—could be cash embezzled, and (4) delayed recording—could reflect fraudulent records. Warning signs from employees include (1) lifestyle change—could be embezzlement, (2) too close with suppliers—could signal fraudulent transactions, and (3) failure to leave job, even for vacations—could conceal fraudulent activities. ■

Quick Check

Answers – p. 343

8. Why are some cash payments made from a petty cash fund and not by check?

9. Why should a petty cash fund be reimbursed at the end of an accounting period?

10. Identify at least two results of reimbursing a petty cash fund.

BANKING ACTIVITIES AS CONTROLS

Banks (and other financial institutions) provide many services, including helping companies control cash. Banks safeguard cash, provide detailed and independent records of cash transactions, and are a source of cash financing. This section describes these services and the documents provided by banking activities that increase managers' control over cash.

Basic Bank Services

This section explains basic bank services—such as the bank account, the bank deposit, and checking—that contribute to the control of cash.

Bank Account, Deposit, and Check A *bank account* is a record set up by a bank for a customer. It permits a customer to deposit money for safekeeping and helps control withdrawals. To limit access to a bank account, all persons authorized to write checks on the account must sign a **signature card,** which bank employees use to verify signatures on checks. Many companies have more than one bank account to serve different needs and to handle special transactions such as payroll.

Point: Online banking services include the ability to stop payment on a check, move money between accounts, get up-to-date balances, and identify cleared checks and deposits.

Each bank deposit is supported by a **deposit ticket,** which lists items such as currency, coins, and checks deposited along with their corresponding dollar amounts. The bank gives the customer a copy of the deposit ticket or a deposit receipt as proof of the deposit. Exhibit 8.4 shows one type of deposit ticket.

To withdraw money from an account, the depositor can use a **check,** which is a document signed by the depositor instructing the bank to pay a specified amount of money to a designated recipient. A check involves three parties: a *maker* who signs the check, a *payee* who is the recipient, and a *bank* (or *payer*) on which the check is drawn. The bank provides a depositor the checks that are serially numbered and imprinted with the name and address of both the depositor and bank. Both checks and deposit tickets are imprinted with identification codes in magnetic ink

EXHIBIT 8.4

Deposit Ticket

Front

DEPOSIT TICKET

Date October 2 20 11

VideoBuster Company
901 Main Street
Hillcrest, NY 11749

CASH	CURRENCY	36	50
	COIN		
LIST CHECKS SINGLY			
TOTAL FROM OTHER SIDE		203	50
TOTAL		240	00
NET DEPOSIT		240	00

USE OTHER SIDE FOR ADDITIONAL LISTINGS. BE SURE EACH ITEM IS PROPERLY ENDORSED

Deposit checks
(Memo)

00 DT/101

FN First National
Hillcrest, New York 11750

Checks and other items are received for deposit subject to the provisions of the uniform commercial code or any applicable collection agreement

ı:0124ı04ı97ı: ı457923 · 02 75

Back

	CHECKS LIST SINGLY	DOLLARS	CENTS
1	14-287/939	90	50
2	82-759/339	82	80
3	76-907/919	30	20
4			
5			
6			
7			
8			
9			
10			
11			
12			
13			
14			
15			
16			
17			
18			
19			
20			
21			
22			
	TOTAL	203	50

ENTER TOTAL ON THE FRONT OF THIS TICKET

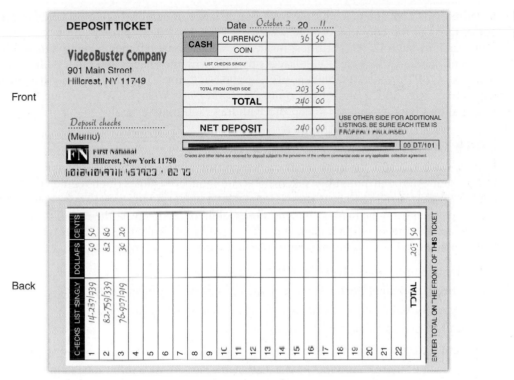

for computer processing. Exhibit 8.5 shows one type of check. It is accompanied with an optional *remittance advice* explaining the payment. When a remittance advice is unavailable, the *memo* line is often used for a brief explanation.

Electronic Funds Transfer **Electronic funds transfer (EFT)** is the electronic transfer of cash from one party to another. No paper documents are necessary. Banks simply transfer cash from one account to another with a journal entry. Companies are increasingly using EFT

EXHIBIT 8.5

Check with Remittance Advice

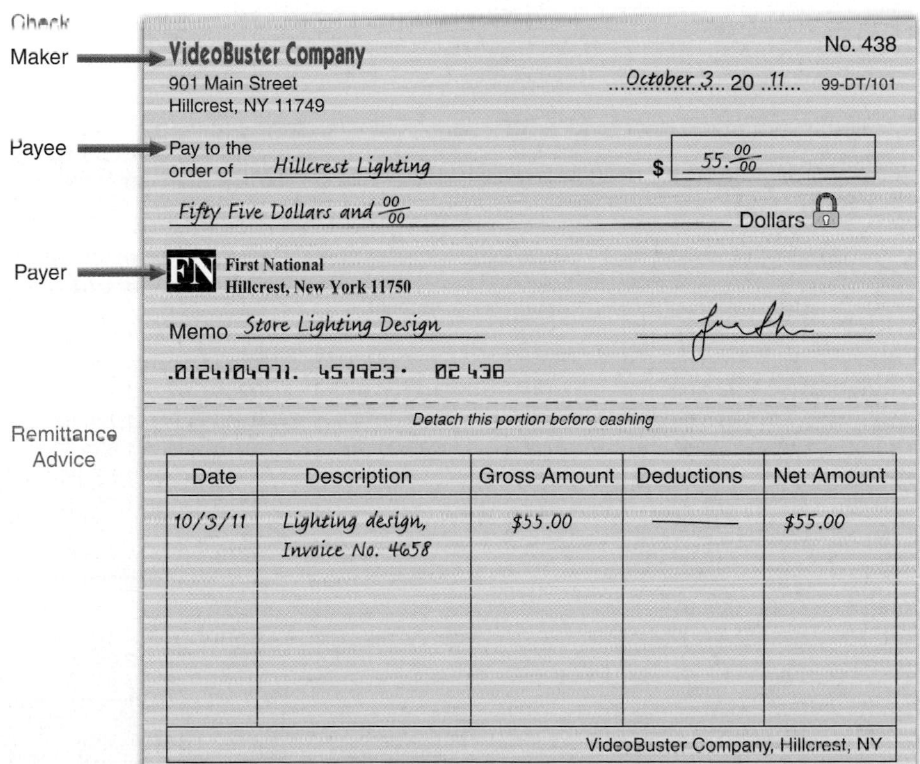

Check Maker → VideoBuster Company
901 Main Street
Hillcrest, NY 11749

No. 438

October 3 20 11 99-DT/101

Payee → Pay to the order of Hillcrest Lighting $ 55.00/00

Fifty Five Dollars and 00/00 Dollars

Payer → FN First National
Hillcrest, New York 11750

Memo Store Lighting Design

.0124104971. 457923· 02 438

Detach this portion before cashing

Remittance Advice

Date	Description	Gross Amount	Deductions	Net Amount
10/3/11	Lighting design, Invoice No. 4658	$55.00	———	$55.00

VideoBuster Company, Hillcrest, NY

because of its convenience and low cost. For instance, it can cost up to 50 cents to process a check through the banking system, whereas EFT cost is near zero. We now commonly see items such as payroll, rent, utilities, insurance, and interest payments being handled by EFT. The bank statement lists cash withdrawals by EFT with the checks and other deductions. Cash receipts by EFT are listed with deposits and other additions. A bank statement is sometimes a depositor's only notice of an EFT. *Automated teller machines (ATMs)* are one form of EFT, which allows bank customers to deposit, withdraw, and transfer cash.

Bank Statement

Point: Good internal control is to deposit all cash receipts daily and make all payments for goods and services by check. This controls access to cash and creates an independent record of all cash activities.

Usually once a month, the bank sends each depositor a **bank statement** showing the activity in the account. Although a monthly statement is common, companies often regularly access information on their banking transactions. (Companies can choose to record any accounting adjustments required from the bank statement immediately or later, say, at the end of each day, week, month, or when reconciling a bank statement.) Different banks use different formats for their bank statements, but all of them include the following items of information:

1. Beginning-of-period balance of the depositor's account.
2. Checks and other debits decreasing the account during the period.
3. Deposits and other credits increasing the account during the period.
4. End-of-period balance of the depositor's account.

This information reflects the bank's records. Exhibit 8.6 shows one type of bank statement. Identify each of these four items in that statement. Part Ⓐ of Exhibit 8.6 summarizes changes in the account. Part Ⓑ lists paid checks along with other debits. Part Ⓒ lists deposits and credits to the account, and part Ⓓ shows the daily account balances.

In reading a bank statement note that a depositor's account is a liability on the bank's records. This is so because the money belongs to the depositor, not the bank. When a depositor increases

EXHIBIT 8.6

Bank Statement

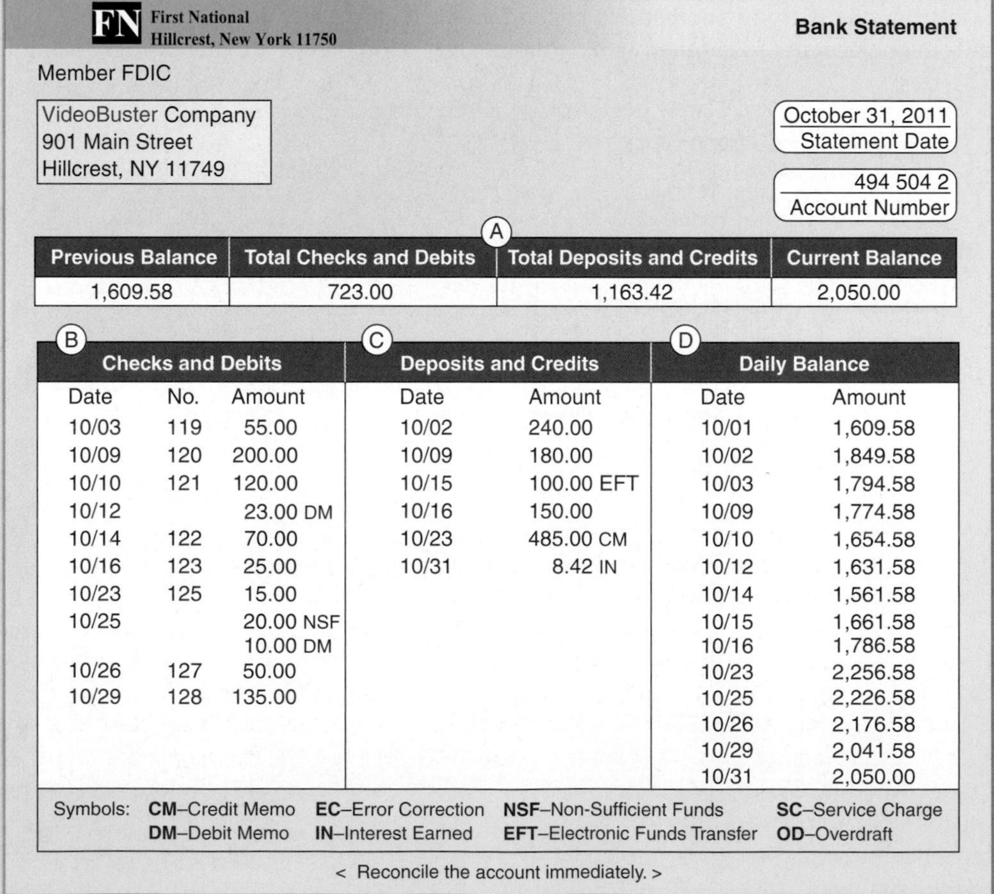

FN First National
Hillcrest, New York 11750

Bank Statement

Member FDIC

VideoBuster Company
901 Main Street
Hillcrest, NY 11749

October 31, 2011
Statement Date

494 504 2
Account Number

Ⓐ

Previous Balance	Total Checks and Debits	Total Deposits and Credits	Current Balance
1,609.58	723.00	1,163.42	2,050.00

Ⓑ Checks and Debits			Ⓒ Deposits and Credits		Ⓓ Daily Balance	
Date	No.	Amount	Date	Amount	Date	Amount
10/03	119	55.00	10/02	240.00	10/01	1,609.58
10/09	120	200.00	10/09	180.00	10/02	1,849.58
10/10	121	120.00	10/15	100.00 EFT	10/03	1,794.58
10/12		23.00 DM	10/16	150.00	10/09	1,774.58
10/14	122	70.00	10/23	485.00 CM	10/10	1,654.58
10/16	123	25.00	10/31	8.42 IN	10/12	1,631.58
10/23	125	15.00			10/14	1,561.58
10/25		20.00 NSF			10/15	1,661.58
		10.00 DM			10/16	1,786.58
10/26	127	50.00			10/23	2,256.58
10/29	128	135.00			10/25	2,226.58
					10/26	2,176.58
					10/29	2,041.58
					10/31	2,050.00

Symbols: **CM**–Credit Memo **DM**–Debit Memo **EC**–Error Correction **IN**–Interest Earned **NSF**–Non-Sufficient Funds **EFT**–Electronic Funds Transfer **SC**–Service Charge **OD**–Overdraft

< Reconcile the account immediately. >

Point: Many banks separately report other debits and credits apart from checks and deposits.

the account balance, the bank records it with a *credit* to that liability account. This means that debit memos from the bank produce *credits* on the depositor's books, and credit memos from the bank produce *debits* on the depositor's books.

Enclosed with a bank statement is a list of the depositor's canceled checks (or the actual canceled checks) along with any debit or credit memoranda affecting the account. Increasingly, banks are showing canceled checks electronically via online access to accounts. **Canceled checks** are checks the bank has paid and deducted from the customer's account during the period. Other deductions that can appear on a bank statement include (1) service charges and fees assessed by the bank, (2) checks deposited that are uncollectible, (3) corrections of previous errors, (4) withdrawals through automated teller machines (ATMs), and (5) periodic payments arranged in advance by a depositor. (Most company checking accounts do not allow ATM withdrawals because of the company's desire to make all disbursements by check.) Except for service charges, the bank notifies the depositor of each deduction with a debit memorandum when the bank reduces the balance. A copy of each debit memorandum is usually sent with the statement (again, this information is often available earlier via online access and notifications).

Global: If cash is in more than one currency, a company usually translates these amounts into U.S. dollars using the exchange rate as of the balance sheet date. Also, a company must disclose any restrictions on cash accounts located outside the U.S.

Transactions that increase the depositor's account include amounts the bank collects on behalf of the depositor and the corrections of previous errors. Credit memoranda notify the depositor of all increases when they are recorded. A copy of each credit memorandum is often sent with the bank statement. Banks that pay interest on checking accounts often compute the amount of interest earned on the average cash balance and credit it to the depositor's account each period. In Exhibit 8.6, the bank credits $8.42 of interest to the account.

Bank Reconciliation

P3 Prepare a bank reconciliation.

When a company deposits all cash receipts and makes all cash payments (except petty cash) by check, it can use the bank statement for proving the accuracy of its cash records. This is done using a **bank reconciliation,** which is a report explaining any differences between the checking account balance according to the depositor's records and the balance reported on the bank statement. The figure below reflects this process, which we describe in the following sections.

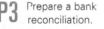

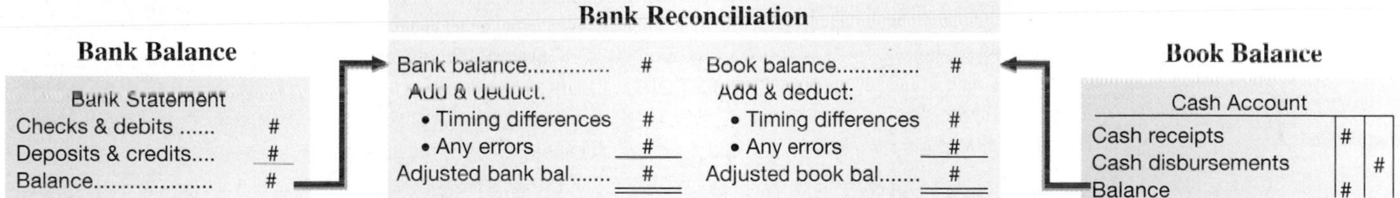

Purpose of Bank Reconciliation The balance of a checking account reported on the bank statement rarely equals the balance in the depositor's accounting records. This is usually due to information that one party has that the other does not. We must therefore prove the accuracy of both the depositor's records and those of the bank. This means we must *reconcile* the two balances and explain or account for any differences in them. Among the factors causing the bank statement balance to differ from the depositor's book balance are these:

- **Outstanding checks. Outstanding checks** are checks written (or drawn) by the depositor, deducted on the depositor's records, and sent to the payees but not yet received by the bank for payment at the bank statement date.
- **Deposits in transit** (also called **outstanding deposits**). **Deposits in transit** are deposits made and recorded by the depositor but not yet recorded on the bank statement. For example, companies can make deposits (in the night depository) at the end of a business day after the bank is closed. If such a deposit occurred on a bank statement date, it would not appear on this period's statement. The bank would record such a deposit on the next business day, and it would appear on the next period's bank statement. Deposits mailed to the bank near the end of a period also can be in transit and unrecorded when the statement is prepared.
- **Deductions for uncollectible items and for services.** A company sometimes deposits another party's check that is uncollectible (usually meaning the balance in that party's account is not large enough to cover the check). This check is called a *non-sufficient funds (NSF)* check. The bank would have initially credited the depositor's account for the amount of the

Forms of Check Fraud (CkFraud.org)

- Forged signatures—legitimate blank checks with fake payer signature
- Forged endorsements—stolen check that is endorsed and cashed by someone other than the payee
- Counterfeit checks—fraudulent checks with fake payer signature
- Altered checks—legitimate check altered (such as changed payee or amount) to benefit perpetrator
- Check kiting—deposit check from one bank account (without sufficient funds) into a second bank account

check. When the bank learns the check is uncollectible, it debits (reduces) the depositor's account for the amount of that check. The bank may also charge the depositor a fee for processing an uncollectible check and notify the depositor of the deduction by sending a debit memorandum. The depositor should record each deduction when a debit memorandum is received, but an entry is sometimes not made until the bank reconciliation is prepared. Other possible bank charges to a depositor's account that are first reported on a bank statement include printing new checks and service fees.

- **Additions for collections and for interest.** Banks sometimes act as collection agents for their depositors by collecting notes and other items. Banks can also receive electronic funds transfers to the depositor's account. When a bank collects an item, it is added to the depositor's account, less any service fee. The bank also sends a credit memorandum to notify the depositor of the transaction. When the memorandum is received, the depositor should record it; yet it sometimes remains unrecorded until the bank reconciliation is prepared. The bank statement also includes a credit for any interest earned.
- **Errors.** Both banks and depositors can make errors. Bank errors might not be discovered until the depositor prepares the bank reconciliation. Also, depositor errors are sometimes discovered when the bank balance is reconciled. Error testing includes: (a) comparing deposits on the bank statement with deposits in the accounting records and (b) comparing canceled checks on the bank statement with checks recorded in the accounting records.

Point: Small businesses with few employees often allow recordkeepers to both write checks and keep the general ledger. If this is done, it is essential that the owner do the bank reconciliation.

Point: The person preparing the bank reconciliation should not be responsible for processing cash receipts, managing checks, or maintaining cash records.

Illustration of a Bank Reconciliation We follow nine steps in preparing the bank reconciliation. It is helpful to refer to the bank reconciliation in Exhibit 8.7 when studying steps 1 through 9.

EXHIBIT 8.7

Bank Reconciliation

VIDEOBUSTER
Bank Reconciliation
October 31, 2011

①	Bank statement balance		$ 2,050.00	⑤	Book balance		$ 1,404.58
②	Add			⑥	Add		
	Deposit of Oct. 31 in transit		145.00		Collect $500 note less $15 fee	$485.00	
			2,195.00		Interest earned	8.42	493.42
③	Deduct						1,898.00
	Outstanding checks			⑦	Deduct		
	No. 124	$150.00			Check printing charge	23.00	
	No. 126	200.00	350.00		NSF check plus service fee	30.00	53.00
④	**Adjusted bank balance**		**$1,845.00**	⑧	**Adjusted book balance**		**$1,845.00**

⑨ Balances are equal (reconciled)

1 Identify the bank statement balance of the cash account (*balance per bank*). VideoBuster's bank balance is $2,050.

2 Identify and list any unrecorded deposits and any bank errors understating the bank balance. Add them to the bank balance. VideoBuster's $145 deposit placed in the bank's night depository on October 31 is not recorded on its bank statement.

3 Identify and list any outstanding checks and any bank errors overstating the bank balance. Deduct them from the bank balance. VideoBuster's comparison of canceled checks with its books shows two checks outstanding: No. 124 for $150 and No. 126 for $200.

4 Compute the *adjusted bank balance,* also called the *corrected* or *reconciled balance*.

5 Identify the company's book balance of the cash account (*balance per book*). VideoBuster's book balance is $1,404.58.

6 Identify and list any unrecorded credit memoranda from the bank, any interest earned, and errors understating the book balance. Add them to the book balance. VideoBuster's bank statement includes a credit memorandum showing the bank collected a note receivable for the

Point: Outstanding checks are identified by comparing canceled checks on the bank statement with checks recorded. This includes identifying any outstanding checks listed on the *previous* period's bank reconciliation that are not included in the canceled checks on this period's bank statement.

company on October 23. The note's proceeds of $500 (minus a $15 collection fee) are credited to the company's account. VideoBuster's bank statement also shows a credit of $8.42 for interest earned on the average cash balance. There was no prior notification of this item, and it is not yet recorded.

7 Identify and list any unrecorded debit memoranda from the bank, any service charges, and errors overstating the book balance. Deduct them from the book balance. Debits on VideoBuster's bank statement that are not yet recorded include (a) a $23 charge for check printing and (b) an NSF check for $20 plus a related $10 processing fee. (The NSF check is dated October 16 and was included in the book balance.)

8 Compute the *adjusted book balance,* also called *corrected* or *reconciled balance.*

9 Verify that the two adjusted balances from steps 4 and 8 are equal. If so, they are reconciled. If not, check for accuracy and missing data to achieve reconciliation.

Point: Adjusting entries can be combined into one compound entry.

Adjusting Entries from a Bank Reconciliation A bank reconciliation often identifies unrecorded items that need recording by the company. In VideoBuster's reconciliation, the adjusted balance of $1,845 is the correct balance as of October 31. But the company's accounting records show a $1,404.58 balance. We must prepare journal entries to adjust the book balance to the correct balance. It is important to remember that only the items reconciling the *book balance* require adjustment. A review of Exhibit 8.7 indicates that four entries are required for VideoBuster.

Collection of note. The first entry is to record the proceeds of its note receivable collected by the bank less the expense of having the bank perform that service.

Oct. 31	Cash	485	
	Collection Expense	15	
	Notes Receivable		500
	To record the collection fee and proceeds for a note collected by the bank.		

Assets = Liabilities + Equity
+485 −15
−500

Interest earned. The second entry records interest credited to its account by the bank.

Oct. 31	Cash	8.42	
	Interest Revenue		8.42
	To record interest earned on the cash balance in the checking account.		

Assets = Liabilities + Equity
+8.42 +8.42

Check printing. The third entry records expenses for the check printing charge.

Oct. 31	Miscellaneous Expenses	23	
	Cash		23
	Check printing charge.		

Assets = Liabilities + Equity
−23 −23

NSF check. The fourth entry records the NSF check that is returned as uncollectible. The $20 check was originally received from T. Woods in payment of his account and then deposited. The bank charged $10 for handling the NSF check and deducted $30 total from VideoBuster's account. This means the entry must reverse the effects of the original entry made when the check was received and must record (add) the $10 bank fee.

Point: The company will try to collect the entire NSF amount of $30 from customer.

Oct. 31	Accounts Receivable—T. Woods	30	
	Cash		30
	To charge Woods' account for $20 NSF check and $10 bank fee.		

Assets = Liabilities + Equity
+30
−30

Point: The Demo Problem 1 shows an adjusting entry for an error correction.

Cash			
Unadj. bal.	1,404.58		
⑥	485.00	⑦	23.00
⑥	8.42	⑦	30.00
Adj. bal.	1,845.00		

After these four entries are recorded, the book balance of cash is adjusted to the correct amount of $1,845 (computed as $1,404.58 + $485 + $8.42 − $23 − $30). The Cash T-account to the side shows the same computation, where entries are keyed to the numerical codes in Exhibit 8.7.

Decision Insight

Fraud A survey reports that 74% of employees had 'personally seen' or had 'firsthand knowledge of' fraud or misconduct in their company within the past year. These employees also identified factors that would drive employees and managers to engage in misconduct. They cited pressures to meet targets, lack of standards, and other root causes—see graphic (KPMG 2009). ■

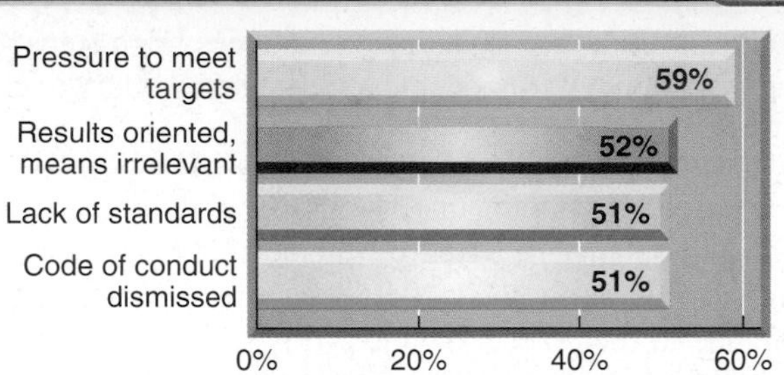

Quick Check

Answers — p. 344

11. What is a bank statement?
12. What is the meaning of the phrase *to reconcile a bank balance?*
13. Why do we reconcile the bank statement balance of cash and the depositor's book balance of cash?
14. List at least two items affecting the *bank balance* side of a bank reconciliation and indicate whether the items are added or subtracted.
15. List at least three items affecting the *book balance* side of a bank reconciliation and indicate whether the items are added or subtracted.

GLOBAL VIEW

This section discusses similarities and differences between U.S. GAAP and IFRS regarding internal controls and in the accounting and reporting of cash.

Internal Control Purposes, Principles, and Procedures Both U.S. GAAP and IFRS aim for high-quality financial reporting. That aim translates into enhanced internal controls worldwide. Specifically, the purposes and principles of internal control systems are fundamentally the same across the globe. However, culture and other realities suggest different emphases on the mix of control procedures, and some sensitivity to different customs and environments when establishing that mix. Nevertheless, the discussion in this chapter applies internationally. **Nokia** provides the following description of its control activities.

NOKIA

> Nokia has an internal audit function that acts as an independent appraisal function by examining and evaluating the adequacy and effectiveness of the company's system of internal control.

Control of Cash Accounting definitions for cash are similar for U.S. GAAP and IFRS. The need for control of cash is universal and applies globally. This means that companies worldwide desire to apply cash management procedures as explained in this chapter and aim to control both cash receipts and disbursements. Accordingly, systems that employ tools such as cash monitoring mechanisms, verification of documents, and petty cash processes are applied worldwide. The basic techniques explained in this chapter are part of those control procedures.

Banking Activities as Controls There is a global demand for banking services, bank statements, and bank reconciliations. To the extent feasible, companies utilize banking services as part of their effective control procedures. Further, bank statements are similarly used along with bank reconciliations to control and monitor cash.

 **IFRS**

Internal controls are crucial to companies that convert from U.S. GAAP to IFRS. Major risks include misstatement of financial information and fraud. Other risks are ineffective communication of the impact of this change for investors, creditors and others, and management's inability to certify the effectiveness of controls over financial reporting. ■

Days' Sales Uncollected

 **Decision Analysis** 

A1 Compute the days' sales uncollected ratio and use it to assess liquidity.

An important part of cash management is monitoring the receipt of cash from receivables. If customers and others who owe money to a company are delayed in payment, then that company can find it difficult to pay its obligations when they are due. A company's customers are crucial partners in its cash management. Many companies attract customers by selling to them on credit. This means that cash receipts from customers are delayed until accounts receivable are collected.

One measure of how quickly a company can convert its accounts receivable into cash is the **days' sales uncollected,** also called *days' sales in receivables*. This measure is computed by dividing the current balance of receivables by net credit sales over the year just completed and then multiplying by 365 (number of days in a year). Since net credit sales usually are not reported to external users, the net sales (or revenues) figure is commonly used in the computation as in Exhibit 8.8.

EXHIBIT 8.8

Days' Sales Uncollected

$$\textbf{Days' sales uncollected} = \frac{\textbf{Accounts receivable}}{\textbf{Net sales}} \times 365$$

We use days' sales uncollected to estimate how much time is likely to pass before the current amount of accounts receivable is received in cash. For evaluation purposes, we need to compare this estimate to that for other companies in the same industry. We also make comparisons between current and prior periods.

To illustrate, we select data from the annual reports of two toy manufacturers, **Hasbro** and **Mattel**. Their days' sales uncollected figures are shown in Exhibit 8.9.

EXHIBIT 8.9

Analysis Using Days' Sales Uncollected

Company	Figure ($ millions)	2009	2008	2007	2006	2005
Hasbro	Accounts receivable	$1,039	$612	$655	$556	$523
	Net sales	$4,068	$4,022	$3,838	$3,151	$3,088
	Days' sales uncollected	**93 days**	**56 days**	**62 days**	**64 days**	**62 days**
Mattel	Accounts receivable	$749	$874	$991	$944	$761
	Net sales	$5,431	$5,918	$5,970	$5,650	$5,179
	Days' sales uncollected	**50 days**	**54 days**	**61 days**	**61 days**	**54 days**

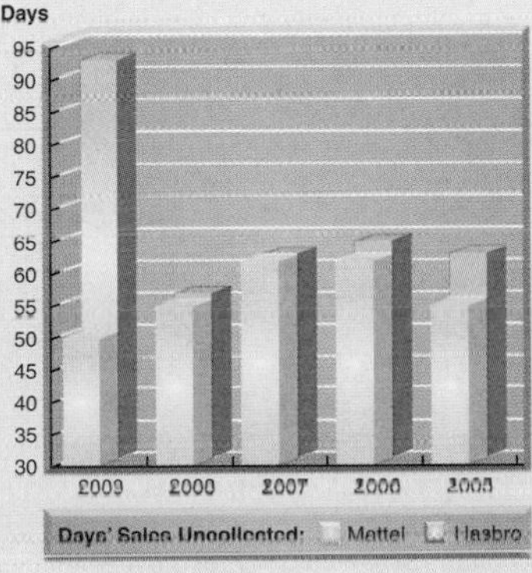

Days' sales uncollected for Hasbro in 2009 is computed as ($1,039/$4,068) × 365 days = 93 days. This means that it will take about 93 days to collect cash from ending accounts receivable. This number reflects one or more of the following factors: a company's ability to collect receivables, customer financial health, customer payment strategies, and discount terms. To further assess days' sales uncollected for Hasbro, we compare it to four prior years and to those of Mattel. We see that Hasbro's days' sales uncollected has worsened in 2009 as it takes much longer to collect its receivables relative to the prior four years. In comparison, Mattel fluctuated on days' sales uncollected for each of those years—from 54 days, to 61 days for two years, then back down to 54 days, and then down to the current 50 days. For all years, Mattel is superior to Hasbro on this measure of cash management. The less time that money is tied up in receivables often translates into increased profitability.

Decision Maker Answer — p. 343 

Sales Representative The sales staff is told to take action to help reduce days' sales uncollected for cash management purposes. What can you, a salesperson, do to reduce days' sales uncollected? ■

DEMONSTRATION PROBLEM 1

Prepare a bank reconciliation for Jamboree Enterprises for the month ended November 30, 2011. The following information is available to reconcile Jamboree Enterprises' book balance of cash with its bank statement balance as of November 30, 2011:

a. After all posting is complete on November 30, the company's book balance of Cash has a $16,380 debit balance, but its bank statement shows a $38,520 balance.

b. Checks No. 2024 for $4,810 and No. 2026 for $5,000 are outstanding.

c. In comparing the canceled checks on the bank statement with the entries in the accounting records, it is found that Check No. 2025 in payment of rent is correctly drawn for $1,000 but is erroneously entered in the accounting records as $880.

d. The November 30 deposit of $17,150 was placed in the night depository after banking hours on that date, and this amount does not appear on the bank statement.

e. In reviewing the bank statement, a check written by Jumbo Enterprises in the amount of $160 was erroneously drawn against Jamboree's account.

f. A credit memorandum enclosed with the bank statement indicates that the bank collected a $30,000 note and $900 of related interest on Jamboree's behalf. This transaction was not recorded by Jamboree prior to receiving the statement.

g. A debit memorandum for $1,100 lists a $1,100 NSF check received from a customer, Marilyn Welch. Jamboree had not recorded the return of this check before receiving the statement.

h. Bank service charges for November total $40. These charges were not recorded by Jamboree before receiving the statement.

PLANNING THE SOLUTION

- Set up a bank reconciliation with a bank side and a book side (as in Exhibit 8.7). Leave room to both add and deduct items. Each column will result in a reconciled, equal balance.
- Examine each item *a* through *h* to determine whether it affects the book or the bank balance and whether it should be added or deducted from the bank or book balance.
- After all items are analyzed, complete the reconciliation and arrive at a reconciled balance between the bank side and the book side.
- For each reconciling item on the book side, prepare an adjusting entry. Additions to the book side require an adjusting entry that debits Cash. Deductions on the book side require an adjusting entry that credits Cash.

SOLUTION TO DEMONSTRATION PROBLEM 1

JAMBOREE ENTERPRISES
Bank Reconciliation
November 30, 2011

Bank statement balance		$ 38,520	Book balance		$ 16,380
Add			Add		
Deposit of Nov. 30	$17,150		Collection of note	$30,000	
Bank error (Jumbo)	160	17,310	Interest earned	900	30,900
		55,830			47,280
Deduct			Deduct		
Outstanding checks			NSF check (M. Welch)	1,100	
No. 2024	4,810		Recording error (# 2025)	120	
No. 2026	5,000	9,810	Service charge	40	1,260
Adjusted bank balance		**$46,020**	**Adjusted book balance**		**$46,020**

Required Adjusting Entries for Jamboree

Nov. 30	Cash	30,900	
	Notes Receivable		30,000
	Interest Earned		900
	To record collection of note with interest.		
Nov. 30	Accounts Receivable—M. Welch	1,100	
	Cash		1,100
	To reinstate account due from an NSF check.		
Nov. 30	Rent Expense	120	
	Cash		120
	To correct recording error on check no. 2025.		
Nov. 30	Bank Service Charges	40	
	Cash		40
	To record bank service charges.		

Point: Error correction can alternatively involve (1) reversing the error entry, and (2) recording the correct entry.

DEMONSTRATION PROBLEM 2

Bacardi Company established a $150 petty cash fund with Dean Martin as the petty cashier. When the fund balance reached $19 cash, Martin prepared a petty cash payment report, which follows.

Petty Cash Payments Report

Receipt No.	Account Charged		Approved by	Received by
12	Delivery Expense	$ 29	Martin	A. Smirnoff
13	Merchandise Inventory	18	Martin	J. Daniels
15	(Omitted)	32	Martin	C. Carlsberg
16	Miscellaneous Expense	41	(Omitted)	J. Walker
	Total	$120		

Required

1. Identify four internal control weaknesses from the payment report.
2. Prepare general journal entries to record:
   a. Establishment of the petty cash fund.
   b. Reimbursement of the fund. (Assume for this part only that petty cash receipt no. 15 was issued for miscellaneous expenses.)
3. What is the Petty Cash account balance immediately before reimbursement? Immediately after reimbursement?

SOLUTION TO DEMONSTRATION PROBLEM 2

1. Four internal control weaknesses are
   a. Petty cash ticket no. 14 is missing. Its omission raises questions about the petty cashier's management of the fund.
   b. The $19 cash balance means that $131 has been withdrawn ($150 − $19 = $131). However, the total amount of the petty cash receipts is only $120 ($29 + $18 + $32 + $41). The fund is $11 short of cash ($131 − $120 = $11). Was petty cash receipt no. 14 issued for $11? Management should investigate.
   c. The petty cashier (Martin) did not sign petty cash receipt no. 16. This omission could have been an oversight on his part or he might not have authorized the payment. Management should investigate.
   d. Petty cash receipt no. 15 does not indicate which account to charge. This omission could have been an oversight on the petty cashier's part. Management could check with C. Carlsberg and the petty cashier (Martin) about the transaction. Without further information, debit Miscellaneous Expense.

2. Petty cash general journal entries.

a. Entry to establish the petty cash fund.

Petty Cash	150	
Cash		150

b. Entry to reimburse the fund.

Delivery Expense	29	
Merchandise Inventory	18	
Miscellaneous Expense ($41 + $32)	73	
Cash Over and Short	11	
Cash		131

3. The Petty Cash account balance *always* equals its fund balance, in this case $150. This account balance does not change unless the fund is increased or decreased.

APPENDIX

8A Documentation and Verification

This appendix describes the important business documents of a voucher system of control.

P4 Describe the use of documentation and verification to control cash disbursements.

Purchase Requisition Department managers are usually not allowed to place orders directly with suppliers for control purposes. Instead, a department manager must inform the purchasing department of its needs by preparing and signing a **purchase requisition,** which lists the merchandise needed and requests that it be purchased—see Exhibit 8A.1. Two copies of the purchase requisition are sent to the purchasing department, which then sends one copy to the accounting department. When the accounting department receives a purchase requisition, it creates and maintains a voucher for this transaction. The requesting department keeps the third copy.

EXHIBIT 8A.1

Purchase Requisition

Z-Mart

PURCHASE REQUISITION No. 917

From *Sporting Goods Department*
To *Purchasing Department*

Date *October 28, 2011*
Preferred Vendor *Trex*

Request purchase of the following item(s):

MODEL NO.	DESCRIPTION	QUANTITY
CH 015	*Challenger X7*	*1*
SD 099	*SpeedDemon*	*1*

Reason for Request *Replenish inventory*
Approval for Request *J.Z.*

For Purchasing Department use only: Order Date *10/30/11* P.O. No. *P98*

Point: A voucher system is designed to uniquely meet the needs of a specific business. Thus, we should read this appendix as one example of a common voucher system design, but *not* the only design.

Purchase Order A **purchase order** is a document the purchasing department uses to place an order with a **vendor** (seller or supplier). A purchase order authorizes a vendor to ship ordered merchandise at the stated price and terms—see Exhibit 8A.2. When the purchasing department receives a purchase requisition, it prepares at least five copies of a purchase order. The copies are distributed as follows: *copy 1* to the vendor as a purchase request and as authority to ship merchandise; *copy 2,* along with a copy of the purchase requisition, to the accounting department, where it is entered in the voucher and used in approving payment of the invoice; *copy 3* to the requesting department to inform its manager that action is being taken; *copy 4* to the receiving department without order quantity so it can compare with goods received and provide independent count of goods received; and *copy 5* retained on file by the purchasing department.

EXHIBIT 8A.2

Purchase Order

Z-Mart
10 Michigan Street
Chicago, Illinois 60521

PURCHASE ORDER

No. P98

To: Trex
W9797 Cherry Road
Antigo, Wisconsin 54409

Date	10/30/11
FOB	Destination
Ship by	As soon as possible
Terms	2/15, n/30

Request shipment of the following item(s):

Model No.	Description	Quantity	Price	Amount
CH 015	Challenger X7	1	490	490
SD 099	SpeedDemon	1	710	710

All shipments and invoices must include purchase order number

J.W.
ORDERED BY

Invoice An **invoice** is an itemized statement of goods prepared by the vendor listing the customer's name, items sold, sales prices, and terms of sale. An invoice is also a bill sent to the buyer from the supplier. From the vendor's point of view, it is a *sales invoice*. The buyer, or **vendee,** treats it as a *purchase invoice*. When receiving a purchase order, the vendor ships the ordered merchandise to the buyer and includes or mails a copy of the invoice covering the shipment to the buyer. The invoice is sent to the buyer's accounting department where it is placed in the voucher. (Refer back to Exhibit 5.5, which shows Z-Mart's purchase invoice.)

Receiving Report Many companies maintain a separate department to receive all merchandise and purchased assets. When each shipment arrives, this receiving department counts the goods and checks them for damage and agreement with the purchase order. It then prepares four or more copies of a **receiving report,** which is used within the company to notify the appropriate persons that ordered goods have been received and to describe the quantities and condition of the goods. One copy is sent to accounting and placed in the voucher. Copies are also sent to the requesting department and the purchasing department to notify them that the goods have arrived. The receiving department retains a copy in its files.

Invoice Approval When a receiving report arrives, the accounting department should have copies of the following documents in the voucher: purchase requisition, purchase order, and invoice. With the information in these documents, the accounting department can record the purchase and approve its payment. In approving an invoice for payment, it checks and compares information across all documents. To facilitate this checking and to ensure that no step is omitted, it often uses an **invoice approval,** also called *check authorization*—see Exhibit 8A.3. An invoice approval is a checklist of steps necessary for approving an invoice for recording and payment. It is a separate document either filed in the voucher or preprinted (or stamped) on the voucher.

EXHIBIT 8A.3

Invoice Approval

INVOICE APPROVAL

DOCUMENT		BY	DATE
Purchase requisition	917	TZ	10/28/11
Purchase order	P98	JW	10/30/11
Receiving report	R85	SK	11/03/11
Invoice:	4657		11/12/11
Price		JK	11/12/11
Calculations		JK	11/12/11
Terms		JK	11/12/11
Approved for payment		BC	

Point: Recording a purchase is initiated by an invoice approval, not an invoice. An invoice approval verifies that the amount is consistent with that requested, ordered, and received. This controls and verifies purchases and related liabilities.

As each step in the checklist is approved, the person initials the invoice approval and records the current date. Final approval implies the following steps have occurred:

1. **Requisition check:** Items on invoice are requested per purchase requisition.
2. **Purchase order check:** Items on invoice are ordered per purchase order.
3. **Receiving report check:** Items on invoice are received per receiving report.
4. **Invoice check: Price:** Invoice prices are as agreed with the vendor.
   Calculations: Invoice has no mathematical errors.
   Terms: Terms are as agreed with the vendor.

Voucher Once an invoice has been checked and approved, the voucher is complete. A complete voucher is a record summarizing a transaction. Once the voucher certifies a transaction, it authorizes recording an obligation. A voucher also contains approval for paying the obligation on an appropriate date. The physical form of a voucher varies across companies. Many are designed so that the invoice and other related source documents are placed inside the voucher, which can be a folder.

Completion of a voucher usually requires a person to enter certain information on both the inside and outside of the voucher. Typical information required on the inside of a voucher is shown in Exhibit 8A.4, and that for the outside is shown in Exhibit 8A.5. This information is taken from the invoice and the supporting documents filed in the voucher. A complete voucher is sent to an authorized individual (often called an *auditor*). This person performs a final review, approves the accounts and amounts for debiting (called the *accounting distribution*), and authorizes recording of the voucher.

EXHIBIT 8A.4

Inside of a Voucher

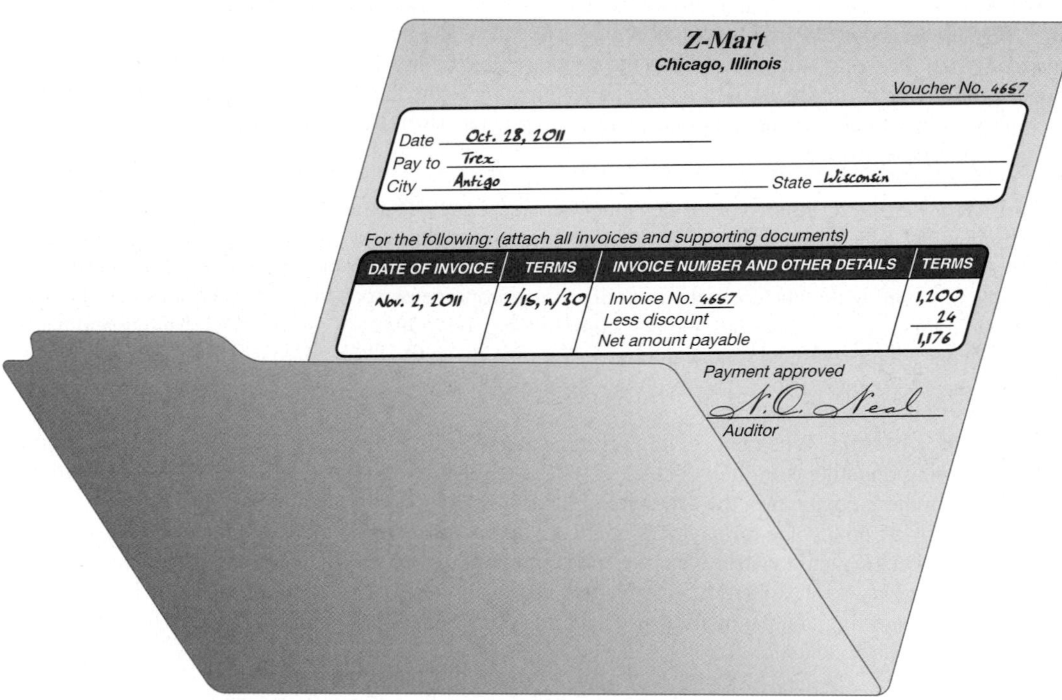

Z-Mart
Chicago, Illinois
Voucher No. 4657

Date Oct. 28, 2011
Pay to Trex
City Antigo State Wisconsin

For the following: (attach all invoices and supporting documents)

DATE OF INVOICE	TERMS	INVOICE NUMBER AND OTHER DETAILS	TERMS
Nov. 2, 2011	2/15, n/30	Invoice No. 4657	1,200
		Less discount	24
		Net amount payable	1,176

Payment approved
N.O. Neal
Auditor

After a voucher is approved and recorded (in a journal called a **voucher register**), it is filed by its due date. A check is then sent on the payment date from the cashier, the voucher is marked "paid," and the voucher is sent to the accounting department and recorded (in a journal called the **check register**). The person issuing checks relies on the approved voucher and its signed supporting documents as proof that an obligation has been incurred and must be paid. The purchase requisition and purchase order confirm the purchase was authorized. The receiving report shows that items have been received, and the invoice approval form verifies that the invoice has been checked for errors. There is little chance for error and even less chance for fraud without collusion unless all the documents and signatures are forged.

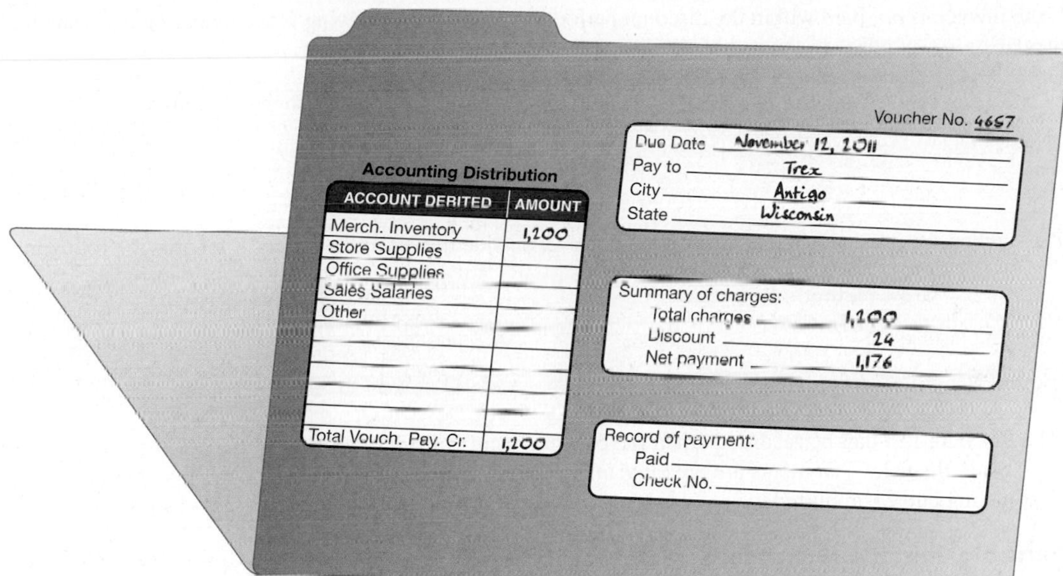

Voucher No. 4657
Due Date November 12, 2011
Pay to Trex
City Antigo
State Wisconsin
Accounting Distribution
ACCOUNT DEBITED
AMOUNT
Merch. Inventory 1,200
Store Supplies
Office Supplies
Sales Salaries
Other
Total Vouch. Pay. Cr. 1,200
Summary of charges:
Total charges 1,200
Discount 24
Net payment 1,176
Record of payment:
Paid
Check No.

EXHIBIT 8A.5

Outside of a Voucher

APPENDIX

Control of Purchase Discounts 8B

This appendix explains how a company can better control its cash *disbursements* to take advantage of favorable purchases discounts. Chapter 5 described the entries to record the receipt and payment of an invoice for a merchandise purchase with and without discount terms. Those entries were prepared under what is called the **gross method** of recording purchases, which initially records the invoice at its *gross* amount ignoring any cash discount.

P5 Apply the net method to control purchase discounts.

The **net method** is another means of recording purchases, which initially records the invoice at its *net* amount of any cash discount. The net method gives management an advantage in controlling and monitoring cash payments involving purchase discounts.

To explain, when invoices are recorded at *gross* amounts, the amount of any discounts taken is deducted from the balance of the Merchandise Inventory account when cash payment is made. This means that the amount of any discounts lost is not reported in any account or on the income statement. Lost discounts recorded in this way are unlikely to come to the attention of management. When purchases are recorded at *net* amounts, a **Discounts Lost** expense account is recorded and brought to management's attention. Management can then seek to identify the reason for discounts lost such as oversight, carelessness, or unfavorable terms. (Chapter 5 explains how managers assess whether a discount is favorable or not.)

Perpetual Inventory System To illustrate, assume that a company purchases merchandise on November 2 at a $1,200 invoice price with terms of 2/10, n/30. Its November 2 entries under the gross and net methods are

Gross Method—Perpetual

Merchandise Inventory	1,200	
Accounts Payable		1,200

Net Method—Perpetual

Merchandise Inventory	1,176	
Accounts Payable		1,176

If the invoice is paid on November 12 within the discount period, it records the following:

Gross Method—Perpetual

Accounts Payable	1,200	
Merchandise Inventory		24
Cash		1,176

Net Method—Perpetual

Accounts Payable	1,176	
Cash		1,176

If the invoice is *not* paid within the discount period, it records the following November 12 entry (which is the date corresponding to the end of the discount period):

Gross Method—Perpetual

Account	Debit	Credit
No entry		

Net Method—Perpetual

Account	Debit	Credit
Discounts Lost	24	
Accounts Payable		24

Then, when the invoice is later paid on December 2, outside the discount period, it records the following:

Gross Method—Perpetual

Account	Debit	Credit
Accounts Payable	1,200	
Cash		1,200

Net Method—Perpetual

Account	Debit	Credit
Accounts Payable	1,200	
Cash		1,200

(The discount lost can be recorded when the cash payment is made with a single entry. However, in this case, when financial statements are prepared after a discount is lost and before the cash payment is made, an adjusting entry is required to recognize any unrecorded discount lost in the period when incurred.)

Periodic Inventory System The preceding entries assume a perpetual inventory system. If a company is using a periodic system, its November 2 entries under the gross and net methods are

Gross Method—Periodic

Account	Debit	Credit
Purchases	1,200	
Accounts Payable		1,200

Net Method—Periodic

Account	Debit	Credit
Purchases	1,176	
Accounts Payable		1,176

If the invoice is paid on November 12 within the discount period, it records the following:

Gross Method—Periodic

Account	Debit	Credit
Accounts Payable	1,200	
Purchases Discounts		24
Cash		1,176

Net Method—Periodic

Account	Debit	Credit
Accounts Payable	1,176	
Cash		1,176

If the invoice is *not* paid within the discount period, it records the following November 12 entry:

Gross Method—Periodic

Account	Debit	Credit
No entry		

Net Method—Periodic

Account	Debit	Credit
Discounts Lost	24	
Accounts Payable		24

Then, when the invoice is later paid on December 2, outside the discount period, it records the following:

Gross Method—Periodic

Account	Debit	Credit
Accounts Payable	1,200	
Cash		1,200

Net Method—Periodic

Account	Debit	Credit
Accounts Payable	1,200	
Cash		1,200

Summary

C1 Define internal control and identify its purpose and principles. An internal control system consists of the policies and procedures managers use to protect assets, ensure reliable accounting, promote efficient operations, and urge adherence to company policies. It can prevent avoidable losses and help managers both plan operations and monitor company and human performance. Principles of good internal control include establishing responsibilities, maintaining adequate records, insuring assets and bonding employees, separating recordkeeping from custody of assets, dividing responsibilities for related transactions, applying technological controls, and performing regular independent reviews.

C2 Define cash and cash equivalents and explain how to report them. Cash includes currency, coins, and amounts on (or acceptable for) deposit in checking and savings accounts. Cash equivalents are short-term, highly liquid investment assets readily convertible to a known cash amount and sufficiently close to their maturity date so that market value is not sensitive to interest rate changes. Cash and cash equivalents are liquid assets because they are readily converted into other assets or can be used to pay for goods, services, or liabilities.

A1 Compute the days' sales uncollected ratio and use it to assess liquidity. Many companies attract customers by selling to them on credit. This means that cash receipts from customers are delayed until accounts receivable are collected. Users want to know how quickly a company can convert its accounts receivable into cash. The days' sales uncollected ratio, one measure reflecting company liquidity, is computed by dividing the ending balance of receivables by annual net sales, and then multiplying by 365.

P1 Apply internal control to cash receipts and disbursements. Internal control of cash receipts ensures that all cash received is properly recorded and deposited. Attention focuses on two important types of cash receipts: over-the-counter and by mail. Good internal control for over-the-counter cash receipts includes use of a cash register, customer review, use of receipts, a permanent transaction record, and separation of the custody of cash from its recordkeeping. Good internal control for cash receipts by mail includes at least two people assigned to open mail and a listing of each sender's name, amount, and explanation. (Banks offer several services that promote the control and safeguarding of cash.)

P2 Explain and record petty cash fund transactions. Petty cash disbursements are payments of small amounts for items such as postage, courier fees, minor repairs, and supplies. A company usually sets up one or more petty cash funds. A petty cash fund cashier is responsible for safekeeping the cash, making payments from this fund, and keeping receipts and records. A Petty Cash account is debited only when the fund is established or increased in amount. When the fund is replenished, petty cash disbursements are recorded with debits to expense (or asset) accounts and a credit to cash.

P3 Prepare a bank reconciliation. A bank reconciliation proves the accuracy of the depositor's and the bank's records. The bank statement balance is adjusted for items such as outstanding checks and unrecorded deposits made on or before the bank statement date but not reflected on the statement. The book balance is adjusted for items such as service charges, bank collections for the depositor, and interest earned on the account.

P4^A Describe the use of documentation and verification to control cash disbursements. A voucher system is a set of procedures and approvals designed to control cash disbursements and acceptance of obligations. The voucher system of control relies on several important documents, including the voucher and its supporting files. A key factor in this system is that only approved departments and individuals are authorized to incur certain obligations.

P5^B Apply the net method to control purchase discounts. The net method aids management in monitoring and controlling purchase discounts. When invoices are recorded at gross amounts, the amount of discounts taken is deducted from the balance of the Inventory account. This means that the amount of any discounts lost is not reported in any account and is unlikely to come to the attention of management. When purchases are recorded at net amounts, a Discounts Lost account is brought to management's attention as an operating expense. Management can then seek to identify the reason for discounts lost, such as oversight, carelessness, or unfavorable terms.

Guidance Answers to Decision Maker and Decision Ethics

Entrepreneur A forced vacation policy is part of a good system of internal controls. When employees are forced to take vacations, their ability to hide any fraudulent behavior decreases because others must perform the vacationers' duties. A replacement employee potentially can uncover fraudulent behavior or falsified records. A forced vacation policy is especially important for employees in sensitive positions of handling money or in control of easily transferable assets.

Sales Representative A salesperson can take several steps to reduce days' sales uncollected. These include (1) decreasing the ratio of sales on account to total sales by encouraging more cash sales, (2) identifying customers most delayed in their payments and encouraging earlier payments or cash sales, and (3) applying stricter credit policies to eliminate credit sales to customers that never pay.

Guidance Answers to Quick Checks

1. (*c*)
2. Technology reduces processing errors. It also allows more extensive testing of records, limits the amount of hard evidence, and highlights the importance of separation of duties.
3. A company holds liquid assets so that it can purchase other assets, buy services, and pay obligations.
4. It owns cash equivalents because they yield a return greater than what cash earns (and are readily exchanged for cash).
5. Examples of cash equivalents are 90-day (or less) U.S. Treasury bills, money market funds, and commercial paper (notes).
6. (*a*)
7. A voucher system is used when an owner/manager can no longer control purchasing procedures through personal supervision and direct participation.
8. If all cash payments are made by check, numerous checks for small amounts must be written. Since this practice is expensive and time-consuming, a petty cash fund is often established for making small (immaterial) cash payments.
9. If the petty cash fund is not reimbursed at the end of an accounting period, the transactions involving petty cash are not yet recorded and the petty cash asset is overstated.
10. First, petty cash transactions are recorded when the petty cash fund is reimbursed. Second, reimbursement provides cash to allow the fund to continue being used. Third, reimbursement identifies any cash shortage or overage in the fund.
11. A bank statement is a report prepared by the bank describing the activities in a depositor's account.

12. To reconcile a bank balance means to explain the difference between the cash balance in the depositor's accounting records and the cash balance on the bank statement.
13. The purpose of the bank reconciliation is to determine whether the bank or the depositor has made any errors and whether the bank has entered any transactions affecting the account that the depositor has not recorded.
14. Unrecorded deposits—added
Outstanding checks—subtracted
15. Interest earned—added
Credit memos—added
Debit memos—subtracted
NSF checks—subtracted
Bank service charges—subtracted

Key Terms

mhhe.com/wildFAP20e

Bank reconciliation (p. 331)
Bank statement (p. 330)
Canceled checks (p. 331)
Cash (p. 321)
Cash equivalents (p. 321)
Cash Over and Short (p. 323)
Check (p. 328)
Check register (p. 340)
Committee of Sponsoring Organizations (COSO) (p. 317)
Days' sales uncollected (p. 335)
Deposit ticket (p. 328)
Deposits in transit (p. 331)
Discounts lost (p. 341)
Electronic funds transfer (EFT) (p. 329)
Gross method (p. 341)
Internal control system (p. 316)
Invoice (p. 339)
Invoice approval (p. 339)
Liquid assets (p. 321)
Liquidity (p. 321)
Net method (p. 341)
Outstanding checks (p. 331)
Petty cash (p. 326)
Principles of internal control (p. 317)
Purchase order (p. 338)
Purchase requisition (p. 338)
Receiving report (p. 339)
Sarbanes-Oxley Act (p. 316)
Section 404 (of SOX) (p. 317)
Signature card (p. 328)
Vendee (p. 339)
Vendor (p. 338)
Voucher (p. 325)
Voucher register (p. 340)
Voucher system (p. 324)

Multiple Choice Quiz

Answers on p. 391

mhhe.com/wildFAP20e

Additional Quiz Questions are available at the book's Website.

1. A company needs to replenish its $500 petty cash fund. Its petty cash box has $75 cash and petty cash receipts of $420. The journal entry to replenish the fund includes
   a. A debit to Cash for $75.
   b. A credit to Cash for $75.
   c. A credit to Petty Cash for $420.
   d. A credit to Cash Over and Short for $5.
   e. A debit to Cash Over and Short for $5.
2. The following information is available for Hapley Company:
   - The November 30 bank statement shows a $1,895 balance.
   - The general ledger shows a $1,742 balance at November 30.
   - A $795 deposit placed in the bank's night depository on November 30 does not appear on the November 30 bank statement.
   - Outstanding checks amount to $638 at November 30.
   - A customer's $335 note was collected by the bank in November. A collection fee of $15 was deducted by the bank and the difference deposited in Hapley's account.
   - A bank service charge of $10 is deducted by the bank and appears on the November 30 bank statement.

   How will the customer's note appear on Hapley's November 30 bank reconciliation?
   a. $320 appears as an addition to the book balance of cash.
   b. $320 appears as a deduction from the book balance of cash.
   c. $320 appears as an addition to the bank balance of cash.
   d. $320 appears as a deduction from the bank balance of cash.
   e. $335 appears as an addition to the bank balance of cash.
3. Using the information from question 2, what is the reconciled balance on Hapley's November 30 bank reconciliation?
   a. $2,052
   b. $1,895
   c. $1,742
   d. $2,201
   e. $1,184
4. A company had net sales of $84,000 and accounts receivable of $6,720. Its days' sales uncollected is
   a. 3.2 days
   b. 18.4 days
   c. 230.0 days
   d. 29.2 days
   e. 12.5 days
5.[B] A company records its purchases using the net method. On August 1, it purchases merchandise on account for $6,000 with terms of 2/10, n/30. The August 1 journal entry to record this transaction includes a
   a. Debit to Merchandise Inventory for $6,000.
   b. Debit to Merchandise Inventory for $5,880.
   c. Debit to Merchandise Inventory for $120.
   d. Debit to Accounts Payable for $5,880.
   e. Credit to Accounts Payable for $6,000.

A(B) *Superscript letter A(B) denotes assignments based on Appendix 8A (8B).*
Icon denotes assignments that involve decision making.

Discussion Questions

1. List the seven broad principles of internal control.
2. Internal control procedures are important in every business, but at what stage in the development of a business do they become especially critical?
3. Why should responsibility for related transactions be divided among different departments or individuals?
4. Why should the person who keeps the records of an asset not be the person responsible for its custody?
5. When a store purchases merchandise, why are individual departments not allowed to directly deal with suppliers?
6. What are the limitations of internal controls?
7. Which of the following assets is most liquid? Which is least liquid? Inventory, building, accounts receivable, or cash.
8. What is a petty cash receipt? Who should sign it?
9. Why should cash receipts be deposited on the day of receipt?
10. **Research In Motion**'s statement of cash flows in Appendix A describes changes in cash and cash equivalents for the year ended February 27, 2010. What total amount is provided (used) by investing activities? What amount is provided (used) by financing activities? **RIM**
11. Refer to **Apple**'s financial statements in Appendix A. Identify Apple's net income for the year ended December 31, 2009. Is its net income equal to the increase in cash and cash equivalents for the year? Explain the difference between net income and the increase in cash and cash equivalents. **Apple**
12. Refer to **Nokia**'s balance sheet in Appendix A. How does its cash (titled "bank and cash") compare with its other current assets (both in amount and percent) as of December 31, 2009? Compare and assess its cash at December 31, 2009, with its cash at December 31, 2008. **NOKIA**
13. **Palm**'s balance sheet in Appendix A reports that cash and equivalents decreased during the fiscal year ended May, 31, 2009. Identify the cash generated (or used) by operating activities, by investing activities, and by financing activities. **Palm**

connect

QUICK STUDY

QS 8-1
Internal control objectives
C1 

An internal control system consists of all policies and procedures used to protect assets, ensure reliable accounting, promote efficient operations, and urge adherence to company policies.

1. What is the main objective of internal control procedures? How is that objective achieved?
2. Why should recordkeeping for assets be separated from custody over those assets?
3. Why should the responsibility for a transaction be divided between two or more individuals or departments?

QS 8-2
Internal control for cash
P1  

A good system of internal control for cash provides adequate procedures for protecting both cash receipts and cash disbursements.

1. What are three basic guidelines that help achieve this protection?
2. Identify two control systems or procedures for cash disbursements.

QS 8-3
Cash and equivalents
C2

Good accounting systems help in managing cash and controlling who has access to it.

1. What items are included in the category of cash?
2. What items are included in the category of cash equivalents?
3. What does the term *liquidity* refer to?

QS 8-4
Petty cash accounting
P2

1. The petty cash fund of the Rio Agency is established at $75. At the end of the current period, the fund contained $14 and had the following receipts: film rentals, $19, refreshments for meetings, $23 (both expenditures to be classified as Entertainment Expense); postage, $6; and printing, $13. Prepare journal entries to record (*a*) establishment of the fund and (*b*) reimbursement of the fund at the end of the current period.
2. Identify the two events that cause a Petty Cash account to be credited in a journal entry.

QS 8-5
Bank reconciliation
P3

1. For each of the following items, indicate whether its amount (i) affects the bank or book side of a bank reconciliation and (ii) represents an addition or a subtraction in a bank reconciliation.
   a. Outstanding checks
   b. Debit memos
   c. NSF checks
   d. Unrecorded deposits
   e. Interest on cash balance
   f. Credit memos
   g. Bank service charges
2. Which of the items in part 1 require an adjusting journal entry?

QS 8-6
Bank reconciliation
P3

Practice

Cruz Company deposits all cash receipts on the day when they are received and it makes all cash payments by check. At the close of business on June 30, 2011, its Cash account shows an $11,352 debit balance. Cruz's June 30 bank statement shows $10,332 on deposit in the bank. Prepare a bank reconciliation for Cruz Company using the following information.

a. Outstanding checks as of June 30 total $1,713.
b. The June 30 bank statement included a $23 debit memorandum for bank services; Cruz has not yet recorded the cost of these services.
c. In reviewing the bank statement, a $90 check written by Cruz Company was mistakenly recorded in Cruz Company's books at $99.
d. June 30 cash receipts of $2,724 were placed in the bank's night depository after banking hours and were not recorded on the June 30 bank statement.
e. The bank statement included a $5 credit for interest earned on the cash in the bank.

QS 8-7
Days' sales uncollected
A1 

The following annual account balances are taken from ProTeam Sports at December 31.

	2011	2010
Accounts receivable	$ 75,692	$ 70,484
Net sales	2,591,933	2,296,673

What is the change in the number of days' sales uncollected between years 2010 and 2011? According to this analysis, is the company's collection of receivables improving? Explain.

QS 8-8A
Documents in a voucher system
P4

Management uses a voucher system to help control and monitor cash disbursements. Identify and describe at least four key documents that are part of a voucher system of control.

QS 8-9B
Purchase discounts P5 

An important part of cash management is knowing when, and if, to take purchase discounts.

a. Which accounting method uses a Discounts Lost account?
b. What is the advantage of this method for management?

QS 8-10
International accounting and internal controls
C1 P1 

Answer each of the following related to international accounting standards.

a. Explain how the purposes and principles of internal controls are different between accounting systems reporting under IFRS versus U.S. GAAP.
b. Cash presents special internal control challenges. How do internal controls for cash differ for accounting systems reporting under IFRS versus U.S. GAAP? How do the procedures applied differ across those two accounting systems?

QS 8-11
Reviewing bank statements
P3

An entrepreneur commented that a bank reconciliation may not be necessary as she regularly reviews her online bank statement for any unusual items and errors.

a. Describe how a bank reconciliation and an online review (or reading) of the bank statement are not equivalent.
b. Identify and explain at least two frauds or errors that would be uncovered through a bank reconciliation and that would *not* be uncovered through an online review of the bank statement.

EXERCISES

Exercise 8-1
Internal control recommendations
C1 

What internal control procedures would you recommend in each of the following situations?

1. A concession company has one employee who sells towels, coolers, and sunglasses at the beach. Each day, the employee is given enough towels, coolers, and sunglasses to last through the day and enough cash to make change. The money is kept in a box at the stand.
2. An antique store has one employee who is given cash and sent to garage sales each weekend. The employee pays cash for any merchandise acquired that the antique store resells.

Exercise 8-2
Analyzing internal control
C1 

Cantu Company is a rapidly growing start-up business. Its recordkeeper, who was hired nine months ago, left town after the company's manager discovered that a large sum of money had disappeared over the past three months. An audit disclosed that the recordkeeper had written and signed several checks made payable to her fiancé and then recorded the checks as salaries expense. The fiancé, who cashed the checks but never worked for the company, left town with the recordkeeper. As a result, the company incurred an uninsured loss of $84,000. Evaluate Cantu's internal control system and indicate which principles of internal control appear to have been ignored.

Exercise 8-3
Control of cash receipts by mail
P1 

Some of Chester Company's cash receipts from customers are received by the company with the regular mail. Chester's recordkeeper opens these letters and deposits the cash received each day. (*a*) Identify any internal control problem(s) in this arrangement. (*b*) What changes to its internal control system do you recommend?

Exercise 8-4
Cash, liquidity, and return
C2

Good accounting systems help with the management and control of cash and cash equivalents.

1. Define and contrast the terms *liquid asset* and *cash equivalent.*
2. Why would companies invest their idle cash in cash equivalents?
3. Identify five principles of effective cash management.

Exercise 8-5
Petty cash fund with a shortage
P2

Hawk Company establishes a $400 petty cash fund on September 9. On September 30, the fund shows $166 in cash along with receipts for the following expenditures: transportation-in, $32; postage expenses, $113; and miscellaneous expenses, $87. The petty cashier could not account for a $2 shortage in the fund. Hawk uses the perpetual system in accounting for merchandise inventory. Prepare (1) the September 9 entry to establish the fund, (2) the September 30 entry to reimburse the fund, and (3) an October 1 entry to decrease the fund to $300.

Check (2) Cr. Cash $234 and (3) Dr. Cash $100

Exercise 8-6
Petty cash fund accounting
P2

NetPerks Co. establishes a $200 petty cash fund on January 1. On January 8, the fund shows $28 in cash along with receipts for the following expenditures: postage, $64; transportation-in, $19; delivery expenses, $36; and miscellaneous expenses, $53. NetPerks uses the perpetual system in accounting for merchandise inventory. Prepare journal entries to (1) establish the fund on January 1, (2) reimburse it on January 8, and (3) both reimburse the fund and increase it to $500 on January 8, assuming no entry in part 2. (*Hint*: Make two separate entries for part 3.)

Check (3) Cr. Cash $472 (total)

Exercise 8-7
Bank reconciliation and adjusting entries
P3

Prepare a table with the following headings for a monthly bank reconciliation dated September 30.

Bank Balance		Book Balance			Not Shown on the Reconciliation
Add	Deduct	Add	Deduct	Adjust	

For each item 1 through 12, place an *x* in the appropriate column to indicate whether the item should be added to or deducted from the book or bank balance, or whether it should not appear on the reconciliation. If the book balance is to be adjusted, place a *Dr.* or *Cr.* in the Adjust column to indicate whether the Cash balance should be debited or credited. At the left side of your table, number the items to correspond to the following list.

1. Bank service charge for September.
2. Checks written and mailed to payees on October 2.
3. Checks written by another depositor but charged against this company's account.
4. Principal and interest on a note receivable to this company is collected by the bank but not yet recorded by the company.
5. Special bank charge for collection of note in part 4 on this company's behalf.
6. Check written against the company's account and cleared by the bank; erroneously not recorded by the company's recordkeeper.
7. Interest earned on the September cash balance in the bank.
8. Night deposit made on September 30 after the bank closed.
9. Checks outstanding on August 31 that cleared the bank in September.
10. NSF check from customer is returned on September 25 but not yet recorded by this company.
11. Checks written by the company and mailed to payees on September 30.
12. Deposit made on September 5 and processed by the bank on September 6.

Exercise 8-8
Voucher system
P1

The voucher system of control is designed to control cash disbursements and the acceptance of obligations.

1. The voucher system of control establishes procedures for what two processes?
2. What types of expenditures should be overseen by a voucher system of control?
3. When is the voucher initially prepared? Explain.

Exercise 8-9
Bank reconciliation
P3

Frederick Clinic deposits all cash receipts on the day when they are received and it makes all cash payments by check. At the close of business on June 30, 2011, its Cash account shows a $15,141 debit balance. Frederick Clinic's June 30 bank statement shows $14,275 on deposit in the bank. Prepare a bank reconciliation for Frederick Clinic using the following information:

a. Outstanding checks as of June 30 total $2,500.
b. The June 30 bank statement included a $125 debit memorandum for bank services.
c. Check No. 919, listed with the canceled checks, was correctly drawn for $645 in payment of a utility bill on June 15. Frederick Clinic mistakenly recorded it with a debit to Utilities Expense and a credit to Cash in the amount of $654.
d. The June 30 cash receipts of $3,250 were placed in the bank's night depository after banking hours and were not recorded on the June 30 bank statement.

Check Reconciled bal., $15,025

Exercise 8-10
Adjusting entries from bank reconciliation P3

Prepare the adjusting journal entries that Frederick Clinic must record as a result of preparing the bank reconciliation in Exercise 8-9.

Exercise 8-11
Bank reconciliation
P3

Chung Company deposits all cash receipts on the day when they are received and it makes all cash payments by check. At the close of business on May 31, 2011, its Cash account shows a $15,500 debit balance. Chung's May 31 bank statement shows $13,800 on deposit in the bank. Prepare a bank reconciliation for Chung Company using the following information:

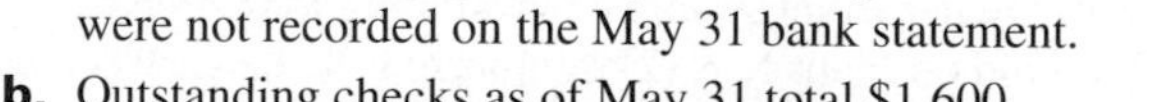

a. May 31 cash receipts of $2,200 were placed in the bank's night depository after banking hours and were not recorded on the May 31 bank statement.
b. Outstanding checks as of May 31 total $1,600.
c. The May 31 bank statement included a $100 debit memorandum for bank services; Chung has not yet recorded the cost of these services.
d. In reviewing the bank statement, a $400 check written by Wald Company was mistakenly drawn against Chung's account.
e. A debit memorandum for $600 refers to a $600 NSF check from a customer; Chung has not yet recorded this NSF check.

Check Reconciled bal., $14,800

Exercise 8-12
Liquid assets and accounts receivable
A1 

Deacon Co. reported annual net sales for 2010 and 2011 of $565,000 and $647,000, respectively. Its year-end balances of accounts receivable follow: December 31, 2010, $51,000; and December 31, 2011, $83,000. (*a*) Calculate its days' sales uncollected at the end of each year. (*b*) Evaluate and comment on any changes in the amount of liquid assets tied up in receivables.

Exercise 8-13[A]
Documents in a voucher system
P4

Match each document in a voucher system in column one with its description in column two.

Document	Description
1. Voucher	A. A document used to notify the appropriate persons that ordered goods have arrived, including a description of the quantities and condition of goods.
2. Invoice approval	B. An internal file used to store documents and information to control cash disbursements and to ensure that a transaction is properly authorized and recorded.
3. Receiving report	C. A document used to place an order with a vendor that authorizes the vendor to ship ordered merchandise at the stated price and terms.
4. Invoice	D. A checklist of steps necessary for the approval of an invoice for recording and payment; also known as a check authorization.
5. Purchase order	E. A document used by department managers to inform the purchasing department to place an order with a vendor.
6. Purchase requisition	F. An itemized statement of goods prepared by the vendor listing the customer's name, items sold, sales prices, and terms of sale.

Exercise 8-14[B]
Record invoices at gross or net amounts
P5

USA Imports uses the perpetual system in accounting for merchandise inventory and had the following transactions during the month of October. Prepare entries to record these transactions assuming that USA Imports records invoices (*a*) at gross amounts and (*b*) at net amounts.

Oct. 2 Purchased merchandise at a $4,000 price, invoice dated October 2, terms 2/10, n/30.
10 Received a $400 credit memorandum (at full invoice price) for the return of merchandise that it purchased on October 2.
17 Purchased merchandise at a $4,400 price, invoice dated October 16, terms 2/10, n/30.
26 Paid for the merchandise purchased on October 17, less the discount.
31 Paid for the merchandise purchased on October 2. Payment was delayed because the invoice was mistakenly filed for payment today. This error caused the discount to be lost.

connect

PROBLEM SET A

Problem 8-1A
Analyzing internal control
C1 

For each of these five separate cases, identify the principle(s) of internal control that is violated. Recommend what the business should do to ensure adherence to principles of internal control.

1. Heather Flat records all incoming customer cash receipts for her employer and posts the customer payments to their respective accounts.
2. At Netco Company, Jeff and Jose alternate lunch hours. Jeff is the petty cash custodian, but if someone needs petty cash when he is at lunch, Jose fills in as custodian.
3. Nadine Cox posts all patient charges and payments at the Dole Medical Clinic. Each night Nadine backs up the computerized accounting system to a tape and stores the tape in a locked file at her desk.
4. Barto Sayles prides himself on hiring quality workers who require little supervision. As office manager, Barto gives his employees full discretion over their tasks and for years has seen no reason to perform independent reviews of their work.
5. Desi West's manager has told her to reduce costs. Desi decides to raise the deductible on the plant's property insurance from $5,000 to $10,000. This cuts the property insurance premium in half. In a related move, she decides that bonding the plant's employees is a waste of money since the company has not experienced any losses due to employee theft. Desi saves the entire amount of the bonding insurance premium by dropping the bonding insurance.

Problem 8-2A
Establish, reimburse, and adjust petty cash
P2

Shawnee Co. set up a petty cash fund for payments of small amounts. The following transactions involving the petty cash fund occurred in May (the last month of the company's fiscal year).

May 1 Prepared a company check for $250 to establish the petty cash fund.
15 Prepared a company check to replenish the fund for the following expenditures made since May 1.
a. Paid $78 for janitorial services.
b. Paid $63.68 for miscellaneous expenses.
c. Paid postage expenses of $43.50.
d. Paid $57.15 to *The County Gazette* (the local newspaper) for an advertisement.
e. Counted $11.15 remaining in the petty cash box.
16 Prepared a company check for $200 to increase the fund to $450.
31 The petty cashier reports that $293.39 cash remains in the fund. A company check is drawn to replenish the fund for the following expenditures made since May 15.
f. Paid postage expenses of $48.36.
g. Reimbursed the office manager for business mileage, $38.50.
h. Paid $39.75 to deliver merchandise to a customer, terms FOB destination.
31 The company decides that the May 16 increase in the fund was too large. It reduces the fund by $50, leaving a total of $400.

Required

1. Prepare journal entries to establish the fund on May 1, to replenish it on May 15 and on May 31, and to reflect any increase or decrease in the fund balance on May 16 and May 31.

Check (1) Cr. to Cash: May 15, $238.85; May 16, $200.00

Analysis Component

2. Explain how the company's financial statements are affected if the petty cash fund is not replenished and no entry is made on May 31.

Problem 8-3A
Establish, reimburse, and increase petty cash
P2

Shelton Gallery had the following petty cash transactions in February of the current year.

Feb. 2 Wrote a $300 check, cashed it, and gave the proceeds and the petty cashbox to Bo Brown, the petty cashier.
5 Purchased bond paper for the copier for $10.13 that is immediately used.
9 Paid $22.50 COD shipping charges on merchandise purchased for resale, terms FOB shipping point. Shelton uses the perpetual system to account for merchandise inventory.
12 Paid $9.95 postage to express mail a contract to a client.
14 Reimbursed Alli Buck, the manager, $58 for business mileage on her car.
20 Purchased stationery for $77.76 that is immediately used.
23 Paid a courier $18 to deliver merchandise sold to a customer, terms FOB destination.
25 Paid $15.10 COD shipping charges on merchandise purchased for resale, terms FOB shipping point.
27 Paid $64 for postage expenses.
28 The fund had $21.23 remaining in the petty cash box. Sorted the petty cash receipts by accounts affected and exchanged them for a check to reimburse the fund for expenditures.
28 The petty cash fund amount is increased by $100 to a total of $400.

Required

1. Prepare the journal entry to establish the petty cash fund.

2. Prepare a petty cash payments report for February with these categories: delivery expense, mileage expense, postage expense, merchandise inventory (for transportation-in), and office supplies expense. Sort the payments into the appropriate categories and total the expenditures in each category.

3. Prepare the journal entries for part 2 to both (*a*) reimburse and (*b*) increase the fund amount.

Check (3a & 3b) Total Cr. to Cash $378.77

Problem 8-4A
Prepare a bank reconciliation and record adjustments
P3

mhhe.com/wildFAP20e

Homework

The following information is available to reconcile Clark Company's book balance of cash with its bank statement cash balance as of July 31, 2011.

a. On July 31, the company's Cash account has a $26,193 debit balance, but its July bank statement shows a $28,020 cash balance.

b. Check No. 3031 for $1,380 and Check No. 3040 for $552 were outstanding on the June 30 bank reconciliation. Check No. 3040 is listed with the July canceled checks, but Check No. 3031 is not. Also, Check No. 3065 for $336 and Check No. 3069 for $2,148, both written in July, are not among the canceled checks on the July 31 statement.

c. In comparing the canceled checks on the bank statement with the entries in the accounting records, it is found that Check No. 3056 for July rent was correctly written and drawn for $1,250 but was erroneously entered in the accounting records as $1,230.

d. A credit memorandum enclosed with the July bank statement indicates the bank collected $9,000 cash on a non-interest-bearing note for Clark, deducted a $45 collection fee, and credited the remainder to its account. Clark had not recorded this event before receiving the statement.

e. A debit memorandum for $805 lists a $795 NSF check plus a $10 NSF charge. The check had been received from a customer, Jim Shaw. Clark has not yet recorded this check as NSF.

f. Enclosed with the July statement is a $15 debit memorandum for bank services. It has not yet been recorded because no previous notification had been received.

g. Clark's July 31 daily cash receipts of $10,152 were placed in the bank's night depository on that date, but do not appear on the July 31 bank statement.

Required

1. Prepare the bank reconciliation for this company as of July 31, 2011.

2. Prepare the journal entries necessary to bring the company's book balance of cash into conformity with the reconciled cash balance as of July 31, 2011.

Check (1) Reconciled balance, $34,308; (2) Cr. Note Receivable $9,000

Analysis Component

3. Assume that the July 31, 2011, bank reconciliation for this company is prepared and some items are treated incorrectly. For each of the following errors, explain the effect of the error on (i) the adjusted bank statement cash balance and (ii) the adjusted cash account book balance.

a. The company's unadjusted cash account balance of $26,193 is listed on the reconciliation as $26,139.

b. The bank's collection of the $9,000 note less the $45 collection fee is added to the bank statement cash balance on the reconciliation.

Problem 8-5A
Prepare a bank reconciliation and record adjustments
P3

mhhe.com/wildFAP20e

Els Company most recently reconciled its bank statement and book balances of cash on August 31 and it reported two checks outstanding, No. 5888 for $1,038.05 and No. 5893 for $484.25. The following information is available for its September 30, 2011, reconciliation.

From the September 30 Bank Statement

PREVIOUS BALANCE	TOTAL CHECKS AND DEBITS	TOTAL DEPOSITS AND CREDITS	CURRENT BALANCE
16,800.45	9,620.05	11,182.85	18,363.25

CHECKS AND DEBITS			DEPOSITS AND CREDITS		DAILY BALANCE	
Date	No.	Amount	Date	Amount	Date	Amount
09/03	5888	1,038.05	09/05	1,103.75	08/31	16,800.45
09/04	5902	731.90	09/12	2,226.90	09/03	15,762.40
09/07	5901	1,824.25	09/21	4,093.00	09/04	15,030.50
09/17		588.25 NSF	09/25	2,351.70	09/05	16,134.25
09/20	5905	937.00	09/30	22.50 IN	09/07	14,310.00
09/22	5903	399.10	09/30	1,385.00 CM	09/12	16,536.90
09/22	5904	2,080.00			09/17	15,948.65
09/28	5907	213.85			09/20	15,011.65
09/29	5909	1,807.65			09/21	19,104.65
					09/22	16,625.55
					09/25	18,977.25
					09/28	18,763.40
					09/29	16,955.75
					09/30	18,363.25

From Els Company's Accounting Records

Cash Receipts Deposited

Date			Cash Debit
Sept.	5		1,103.75
	12		2,226.90
	21		4,093.00
	25		2,351.70
	30		1,582.75
			11,358.10

Cash Disbursements

Check No.		Cash Credit
5901		1,824.25
5902		731.90
5903		399.10
5904		2,050.00
5905		937.00
5906		859.30
5907		213.85
5908		276.00
5909		1,807.65
		9,099.05

Cash — Acct. No. 101

Date		Explanation	PR	Debit	Credit	Balance
Aug.	31	Balance				15,278.15
Sept.	30	Total receipts	R12	11,358.10		26,636.25
	30	Total disbursements	D23		9,099.05	17,537.20

Additional Information

Check No. 5904 is correctly drawn for $2,080 to pay for computer equipment; however, the recordkeeper misread the amount and entered it in the accounting records with a debit to Computer Equipment and a credit to Cash of $2,050. The NSF check shown in the statement was originally received from a customer, S. Nilson, in payment of her account. Its return has not yet been recorded by the company. The credit memorandum is from the collection of a $1,400 note for Els Company by the bank. The bank deducted a $15 collection fee. The collection and fee are not yet recorded.

Required

Check (1) Reconciled balance, $18,326.45 (2) Cr. Note Receivable $1,400

1. Prepare the September 30, 2011, bank reconciliation for this company.
2. Prepare the journal entries to adjust the book balance of cash to the reconciled balance.

Analysis Component

3. The bank statement reveals that some of the prenumbered checks in the sequence are missing. Describe three situations that could explain this.

PROBLEM SET B

Problem 8-1B
Analyzing internal control
C1 

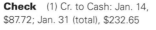

For each of these five separate cases, identify the principle(s) of internal control that is violated. Recommend what the business should do to ensure adherence to principles of internal control.

1. Latoya Tally is the company's computer specialist and oversees its computerized payroll system. Her boss recently asked her to put password protection on all office computers. Latoya has put a password in place that allows only the boss access to the file where pay rates are changed and personnel are added or deleted from the payroll.
2. Lake Theater has a computerized order-taking system for its tickets. The system is active all week and backed up every Friday night.
3. X2U Company has two employees handling acquisitions of inventory. One employee places purchase orders and pays vendors. The second employee receives the merchandise.
4. The owner of Super-Aid Pharmacy uses a check protector to perforate checks, making it difficult for anyone to alter the amount of the check. The check protector is on the owner's desk in an office that contains company checks and is normally unlocked.
5. LeAnn Company is a small business that has separated the duties of cash receipts and cash disbursements. The employee responsible for cash disbursements reconciles the bank account monthly.

Problem 8-2B
Establishing, reimbursing, and adjusting petty cash
P2

Pepco Co. establishes a petty cash fund for payments of small amounts. The following transactions involving the petty cash fund occurred in January (the last month of the company's fiscal year).

Jan. 3 A company check for $150 is written and made payable to the petty cashier to establish the petty cash fund.

14 A company check is written to replenish the fund for the following expenditures made since January 3.

a. Purchased office supplies for $16.29 that are immediately used up.
b. Paid $17.60 COD shipping charges on merchandise purchased for resale, terms FOB shipping point. Pepco uses the perpetual system to account for inventory.
c. Paid $36.57 to All-Tech for minor repairs to a computer.
d. Paid $14.82 for items classified as miscellaneous expenses.
e. Counted $62.28 remaining in the petty cash box.

15 Prepared a company check for $25 to increase the fund to $175.

31 The petty cashier reports that $17.35 remains in the fund. A company check is written to replenish the fund for the following expenditures made since January 14.

f. Paid $40 to *The Smart Shopper* for an advertisement in January's newsletter.
g. Paid $38.19 for postage expenses.
h. Paid $58 to Take-You-There for delivery of merchandise, terms FOB destination.

31 The company decides that the January 15 increase in the fund was too little. It increases the fund by another $75, leaving a total of $250.

Required

Check (1) Cr. to Cash: Jan. 14, $87.72; Jan. 31 (total), $232.65

1. Prepare journal entries to establish the fund on January 3, to replenish it on January 14 and January 31, and to reflect any increase or decrease in the fund balance on January 15 and 31.

Analysis Component

2. Explain how the company's financial statements are affected if the petty cash fund is not replenished and no entry is made on January 31.

Problem 8-3B
Establish, reimburse, and increase petty cash
P2

RPM Music Center had the following petty cash transactions in March of the current year.

March 5 Wrote a $200 check, cashed it, and gave the proceeds and the petty cashbox to Liz Buck, the petty cashier.
6 Paid $14.50 COD shipping charges on merchandise purchased for resale, terms FOB shipping point. RPM uses the perpetual system to account for merchandise inventory.
11 Paid $8.75 delivery charges on merchandise sold to a customer, terms FOB destination.
12 Purchased file folders for $12.13 that are immediately used.
14 Reimbursed Will Nelson, the manager, $9.65 for office supplies purchased and used.
18 Purchased printer paper for $22.54 that is immediately used.
27 Paid $47.10 COD shipping charges on merchandise purchased for resale, terms FOB shipping point.
28 Paid postage expenses of $16.
30 Reimbursed Nelson $58.80 for business car mileage.
31 Cash of $11.53 remained in the fund. Sorted the petty cash receipts by accounts affected and exchanged them for a check to reimburse the fund for expenditures.
31 The petty cash fund amount is increased by $50 to a total of $250.

Required

1. Prepare the journal entry to establish the petty cash fund.
2. Prepare a petty cash payments report for March with these categories: delivery expense, mileage expense, postage expense, merchandise inventory (for transportation-in), and office supplies expense. Sort the payments into the appropriate categories and total the expenses in each category.
3. Prepare the journal entries for part 2 to both (*a*) reimburse and (*b*) increase the fund amount.

Check (2) Total expenses $189.47

(3a & 3b) Total Cr. to Cash $238.47

Problem 8-4B
Prepare a bank reconciliation and record adjustments
P3

The following information is available to reconcile Style Co.'s book balance of cash with its bank statement cash balance as of December 31, 2011.

a. The December 31 cash balance according to the accounting records is $31,743.70, and the bank statement cash balance for that date is $45,091.80.

b. Check No. 1273 for $1,084.20 and Check No. 1282 for $390, both written and entered in the accounting records in December, are not among the canceled checks. Two checks, No. 1231 for $2,289 and No. 1242 for $370.50, were outstanding on the most recent November 30 reconciliation. Check No. 1231 is listed with the December canceled checks, but Check No. 1242 is not.

c. When the December checks are compared with entries in the accounting records, it is found that Check No. 1267 had been correctly drawn for $2,435 to pay for office supplies but was erroneously entered in the accounting records as $2,453.

d. Two debit memoranda are enclosed with the statement and are unrecorded at the time of the reconciliation. One debit memorandum is for $749.50 and dealt with an NSF check for $732 received from a customer, Titus Industries, in payment of its account. The bank assessed a $17.50 fee for processing it. The second debit memorandum is a $79 charge for check printing. Style did not record these transactions before receiving the statement.

e. A credit memorandum indicates that the bank collected $20,000 cash on a note receivable for the company, deducted a $20 collection fee, and credited the balance to the company's Cash account. Style did not record this transaction before receiving the statement.

f. Style's December 31 daily cash receipts of $7,666.10 were placed in the bank's night depository on that date, but do not appear on the December 31 bank statement.

Required

1. Prepare the bank reconciliation for this company as of December 31, 2011.
2. Prepare the journal entries necessary to bring the company's book balance of cash into conformity with the reconciled cash balance as of December 31, 2011.

Check (1) Reconciled balance, $50,913.20; (2) Cr. Note Receivable $20,000

Analysis Component

3. Explain the nature of the communications conveyed by a bank when the bank sends the depositor (*a*) a debit memorandum and (*b*) a credit memorandum.

Problem 8-5B
Prepare a bank reconciliation and record adjustments
P3

Safe Systems most recently reconciled its bank balance on April 30 and reported two checks outstanding at that time, No. 1771 for $781 and No. 1780 for $1,325.90. The following information is available for its May 31, 2011, reconciliation.

Practice

From the May 31 Bank Statement

PREVIOUS BALANCE	TOTAL CHECKS AND DEBITS	TOTAL DEPOSITS AND CREDITS	CURRENT BALANCE
18,290.70	12,898.90	16,416.80	21,808.60

CHECKS AND DEBITS			DEPOSITS AND CREDITS		DAILY BALANCE	
Date	No.	Amount	Date	Amount	Date	Amount
05/01	1771	781.00	05/04	2,438.00	04/30	18,290.70
05/02	1783	195.30	05/14	2,898.00	05/01	17,509.70
05/04	1782	1,285.50	05/22	1,801.80	05/02	17,314.40
05/11	1784	1,449.60	05/25	7,200.00 CM	05/04	18,466.90
05/18		431.80 NSF	05/26	2,079.00	05/11	17,017.30
05/25	1787	8,032.50			05/14	19,915.30
05/26	1785	157.20			05/18	19,483.50
05/29	1788	554.00			05/22	21,285.30
05/31		12.00 SC			05/25	20,452.80
					05/26	22,374.60
					05/29	21,820.60
					05/31	21,808.60

From Safe Systems' Accounting Records

Cash Receipts Deposited

Date			Cash Debit
May	4		2,438.00
	14		2,898.00
	22		1,801.80
	26		2,079.00
	31		2,526.30
			11,743.10

Cash Disbursements

Check No.		Cash Credit
1782		1,285.50
1783		195.30
1784		1,449.60
1785		157.20
1786		353.10
1787		8,032.50
1788		544.00
1789		639.50
		12,656.70

Cash — Acct. No. 101

Date		Explanation	PR	Debit	Credit	Balance
Apr.	30	Balance				16,183.80
May	31	Total receipts	R7	11,743.10		27,926.90
	31	Total disbursements	D8		12,656.70	15,270.20

Additional Information

Check No. 1788 is correctly drawn for $554 to pay for May utilities; however, the recordkeeper misread the amount and entered it in the accounting records with a debit to Utilities Expense and a credit to Cash for $544. The bank paid and deducted the correct amount. The NSF check shown in the statement was originally received from a customer, S. Bax, in payment of her account. The company has not yet recorded its return. The credit memorandum is from a $7,300 note that the bank collected for the company. The bank deducted a $100 collection fee and deposited the remainder in the company's account. The collection and fee have not yet been recorded.

Required

1. Prepare the May 31, 2011, bank reconciliation for Safe Systems.
2. Prepare the journal entries to adjust the book balance of cash to the reconciled balance.

Check (1) Reconciled balance, $22,016.40; (2) Cr. Note Receivable $7,300

Analysis Component

3. The bank statement reveals that some of the prenumbered checks in the sequence are missing. Describe three possible situations to explain this.

SERIAL PROBLEM

Business Solutions

P3

(This serial problem began in Chapter 1 and continues through most of the book. If previous chapter segments were not completed, the serial problem can begin at this point. It is helpful, but not necessary, to use the Working Papers that accompany the book.)

SP 8 Santana Rey receives the March bank statement for Business Solutions on April 11, 2012. The March 31 bank statement shows an ending cash balance of $67,566. A comparison of the bank statement with the general ledger Cash account, No. 101, reveals the following.

a. S. Rey notices that the bank erroneously cleared a $500 check against her account in March that she did not issue. The check documentation included with the bank statement shows that this check was actually issued by a company named Business Systems.

b. On March 25, the bank issued a $50 debit memorandum for the safety deposit box that Business Solutions agreed to rent from the bank beginning March 25.

c. On March 26, the bank issued a $102 debit memorandum for printed checks that Business Solutions ordered from the bank.

d. On March 31, the bank issued a credit memorandum for $33 interest earned on Business Solutions' checking account for the month of March.

e. S. Rey notices that the check she issued for $128 on March 31, 2012, has not yet cleared the bank.

f. S. Rey verifies that all deposits made in March do appear on the March bank statement.

g. The general ledger Cash account, No. 101, shows an ending cash balance per books of $68,057 as of March 31 (prior to any reconciliation).

Required

1. Prepare a bank reconciliation for Business Solutions for the month ended March 31, 2012.
2. Prepare any necessary adjusting entries. Use Miscellaneous Expenses, No. 677, for any bank charges. Use Interest Revenue, No. 404, for any interest earned on the checking account for the month of March.

Check (1) Adj. bank bal. $67,938

Beyond the Numbers

REPORTING IN ACTION

C2 A1 

RIM

BTN 8-1 Refer to **Research In Motion**'s financial statements in Appendix A to answer the following.

1. For both fiscal year-ends February 27, 2010, and February 28, 2009, identify the total amount of cash and cash equivalents. Determine the percent this amount represents of total current assets, total current liabilities, total shareholders' equity, and total assets for both years. Comment on any trends.
2. For fiscal years ended February 27, 2010, and February 28, 2009, use the information in the statement of cash flows to determine the percent change between the beginning and ending year amounts of cash and cash equivalents.
3. Compute the days' sales uncollected as of February 27, 2010, and February 28, 2009. Has the collection of receivables improved? Are accounts receivable an important asset for Research In Motion? Explain.

Fast Forward

4. Access Research In Motion's financial statements for fiscal years ending after February 27, 2010, from its Website (**RIM.com**) or the SEC's EDGAR database (**www.SEC.gov**). Recompute its days' sales uncollected for fiscal years ending after February 27, 2010. Compare this to the days' sales uncollected for 2010 and 2009.

COMPARATIVE ANALYSIS

A1 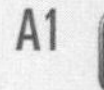

RIM

Apple

BTN 8-2 Key comparative figures for **Research In Motion** and **Apple** follow.

($ millions)	Research In Motion Current Year	Research In Motion Prior Year	Apple Current Year	Apple Prior Year
Accounts receivable	$ 2,594	$ 2,112	$ 3,361	$ 2,422
Net sales	14,953	11,065	42,905	37,491

Required

Compute days' sales uncollected for these companies for each of the two years shown. Comment on any trends for the companies. Which company has the largest percent change in days' sales uncollected?

ETHICS CHALLENGE

C1

BTN 8-3 Carol Benton, Sue Knox, and Marcia Diamond work for a family physician, Dr. Gwen Conrad, who is in private practice. Dr. Conrad is knowledgeable about office management practices and has segregated the cash receipt duties as follows. Benton opens the mail and prepares a triplicate list of money received. She sends one copy of the list to Knox, the cashier, who deposits the receipts daily in the bank. Diamond, the recordkeeper, receives a copy of the list and posts payments to patients' accounts. About once a month the office clerks have an expensive lunch they pay for as follows. First, Knox endorses a patient's check in Dr. Conrad's name and cashes it at the bank. Benton then destroys the remittance advice accompanying the check. Finally, Diamond posts payment to the customer's account as a miscellaneous credit. The three justify their actions by their relatively low pay and knowledge that Dr. Conrad will likely never miss the money.

Required

1. Who is the best person in Dr. Conrad's office to reconcile the bank statement?
2. Would a bank reconciliation uncover this office fraud?
3. What are some procedures to detect this type of fraud?
4. Suggest additional internal controls that Dr. Conrad could implement.

COMMUNICATING IN PRACTICE

P5

BTN 8-4[B] Assume you are a business consultant. The owner of a company sends you an e-mail expressing concern that the company is not taking advantage of its discounts offered by vendors. The company currently uses the gross method of recording purchases. The owner is considering a review of all invoices and payments from the previous period. Due to the volume of purchases, however, the owner recognizes that this is time-consuming and costly. The owner seeks your advice about monitoring purchase discounts in the future. Provide a response in memorandum form.

TAKING IT TO THE NET

C1 P1

BTN 8-5 Visit the Association of Certified Fraud Examiners Website at **cfenet.com**. Find and open the file "2008 Report to the Nation." Read the two-page Executive Summary and fill in the following blanks. (The report is under its *Fraud Resources* tab or under its *About the ACFE* tab [under Press Room]; we can also use the *Search* tab.)

1. The median loss caused by occupational frauds was $________.
2. More than __________ of fraud cases caused at least $1 million in losses.
3. Companies lose ___% of their annual revenues to fraud; this figure translates to $______ billion in fraud losses.
4. The typical length of fraud schemes was ____ years from the time the fraud began until it was detected.
5. Companies that conducted surprise audits suffered a median loss of $_______, whereas those without surprise audits had a median loss of $_______.
6. The median loss suffered by companies with fewer than 100 employees was $_______ per scheme.
7. ____________ and ____________ were the most common small business fraud schemes.
8. ___% of respondents cited inadequate internal controls as the primary contributing factor in the frauds investigated.
9. Only ___% of the perpetrators had convictions prior to committing their frauds.

TEAMWORK IN ACTION
C1

BTN 8-6 Organize the class into teams. Each team must prepare a list of 10 internal controls a consumer could observe in a typical retail department store. When called upon, the team's spokesperson must be prepared to share controls identified by the team that have not been shared by another team's spokesperson.

ENTREPRENEURIAL DECISION
C1 P1   

BTN 8-7 Review the opening feature of this chapter that highlights Dylan Lauren and her company **Dylan's Candy Bar**.

Required

1. List the seven principles of internal control and explain how Dylan could implement each of them in her retail stores.
2. Do you believe that Dylan will need to add controls as her business expands? Explain.

HITTING THE ROAD
C1 

BTN 8-8 Visit an area of your college that serves the student community with either products or services. Some examples are food services, libraries, and bookstores. Identify and describe between four and eight internal controls being implemented.

GLOBAL DECISION
C2 A1 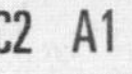 

NOKIA

BTN 8-9 The following information is from **Nokia (www.Nokia.com)**, which is a leading global manufacturer of mobile devices and services.

EUR millions	Current Year	Prior Year
Cash	1,142	1,706
Accounts receivable	7,981	9,444
Current assets	23,613	24,470
Total assets	35,738	39,582
Current liabilities	15,188	20,355
Shareholders' equity	14,749	16,510
Net sales	40,984	50,710

Required

1. For each year, compute the percentage that cash represents of current assets, total assets, current liabilities, and shareholders' equity. Comment on any trends in these percentages.
2. Determine the percentage change between the current and prior year cash balances.
3. Compute the days' sales uncollected at the end of both the current year and the prior year. Has the collection of receivables improved? Explain.

ANSWERS TO MULTIPLE CHOICE QUIZ

1. e; The entry follows.

Debits to expenses (or assets)	420	
Cash Over and Short	5	
Cash		425

2. a; recognizes cash collection of note by bank.
3. a; the bank reconciliation follows.

Bank Reconciliation November 30			
Balance per bank statement	$1,895	Balance per books	$1,742
Add: Deposit in transit	795	Add: Note collected less fee	320
Deduct: Outstanding checks	(638)	Deduct: Service charge	(10)
Reconciled balance	$2,052	Reconciled balance	$2,052

4. d; ($6,720/$84,000) × 365 = 29.2 days
5. b; The entry follows.

Merchandise Inventory*	5,880	
Accounts Payable		5,880

*$6,000 × 98%

Accounting for Receivables

A Look Back

Chapter 8 focused on internal control and reporting for cash. We described internal control procedures and the accounting for and management of cash.

A Look at This Chapter

This chapter emphasizes receivables. We explain that they are liquid assets and describe how companies account for and report them. We also discuss the importance of estimating uncollectibles.

A Look Ahead

Chapter 10 focuses on plant assets, natural resources, and intangible assets. We explain how to account for, report, and analyze these long-term assets.

Learning Objectives

CAP

CONCEPTUAL

C1 Describe accounts receivable and how they occur and are recorded. (p. 360)

C2 Describe a note receivable, the computation of its maturity date, and the recording of its existence. (p. 370)

C3 Explain how receivables can be converted to cash before maturity. (p. 373)

ANALYTICAL

A1 Compute accounts receivable turnover and use it to help assess financial condition. (p. 375)

LP9

PROCEDURAL

P1 Apply the direct write-off method to account for accounts receivable. (p. 363)

P2 Apply the allowance method and estimate uncollectibles based on sales and accounts receivable. (p. 366)

P3 Record the honoring and dishonoring of a note and adjustments for interest. (p. 372)

Decision Insight

Monk E-Business

"We are not wearing bling . . . I mean, we are still monks"
—BROTHER BERNARD MCCOY

SPARTA, WI—"My printer ran out of toner," recalls Brother Bernard McCoy. "I was just appalled at the cost of the black dust . . . the markup on toner is sinfully high!" So, Bernard, who is part of a handful of monks living at and trying to keep a remote monastery in rural Wisconsin going, started thinking. "Nine hundred years ago, my brothers were copying manuscripts and making their own paper and ink," explains Bernard. His response was to launch **LaserMonks (LaserMonks.com)**, a supplier of toner and ink products (and other goods).

Sales quickly soared, and Bernard, along with what he calls his monk-helper angels, had to contend with accounting activities, receivables management, and other day-to-day record-keeping needs. Special attention was focused on monitoring receivables. Decisions on credit sales and policies for extending credit can make or break a start-up, and Bernard was determined to succeed in spite of the demands of a monk's life. "We spend about five hours a day in Gregorian chant, and another couple of hours in prayers," explains Bernard. "We're monks . . . we do monk things!"

Nevertheless, Bernard and his angels ensured that credit sales were extended to customers in good credit standing. Further, his team knows their customers, including who pays and when. Explains Bernard, we understand our customers—inside and out—including cash payment patterns that allow them to estimate uncollectibles and minimize bad debts. Bernard points out, however, that "we use the money for good works and to support monks who dedicate their lives to serving God and neighbor."

A commitment to quality customers and products is propelling LaserMonks' sales and shattering Bernard's most optimistic goals. "The results have been beyond anything we could imagine," affirms Bernard. Both accounts and notes receivables receive his attention. Bernard and his team's financial focus includes reviewing the allowance for doubtful accounts monthly. "We're scrambling to keep up with growth," adds Bernard. "[We're] continuing to negotiate with suppliers . . . processing orders between our times of prayer."

Bernard's focus on serving people is unwavering. "Our customer service is following our order's tradition of hospitality," explains Bernard. "We try to transfer monastic hospitality into commerce hospitality . . . we try to treat every single customer with kid gloves." Bernard says he wishes that all customers "be abundantly blessed with prosperity of soul."

[Sources: *LaserMonks Website,* January 2011; *Entrepreneur,* September 2009; *CBS Broadcasting,* August 2006; *Religion & Ethics Newsweekly,* September 2009; *Consumer Reports,* February 2010]

Chapter Preview

This chapter focuses on accounts receivable and short-term notes receivable. We describe each of these assets, their uses, and how they are accounted for and reported in financial statements. This knowledge helps us use accounting information to make better business decisions. It can also help in predicting future company performance and financial condition as well as in managing one's own business.

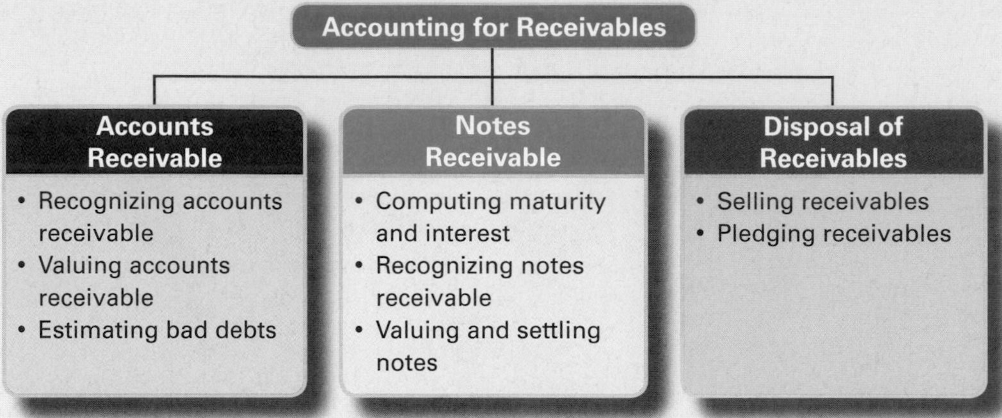

ACCOUNTS RECEIVABLE

A *receivable* is an amount due from another party. The two most common receivables are accounts receivable and notes receivable. Other receivables include interest receivable, rent receivable, tax refund receivable, and receivables from employees. **Accounts receivable** are amounts due from customers for credit sales. This section begins by describing how accounts receivable occur. It includes receivables that occur when customers use credit cards issued by third parties and when a company gives credit directly to customers. When a company does extend credit directly to customers, it (1) maintains a separate account receivable for each customer and (2) accounts for bad debts from credit sales.

Recognizing Accounts Receivable

C1 Describe accounts receivable and how they occur and are recorded.

Accounts receivable occur from credit sales to customers. The amount of credit sales has increased in recent years, reflecting several factors including an efficient financial system. Retailers such as **Costco** and **Best Buy** hold millions of dollars in accounts receivable. Similar amounts are held by wholesalers such as **SUPERVALU** and **SYSCO**. Exhibit 9.1 shows recent dollar amounts of receivables and their percent of total assets for four well-known companies.

EXHIBIT 9.1

Accounts Receivable for Selected Companies

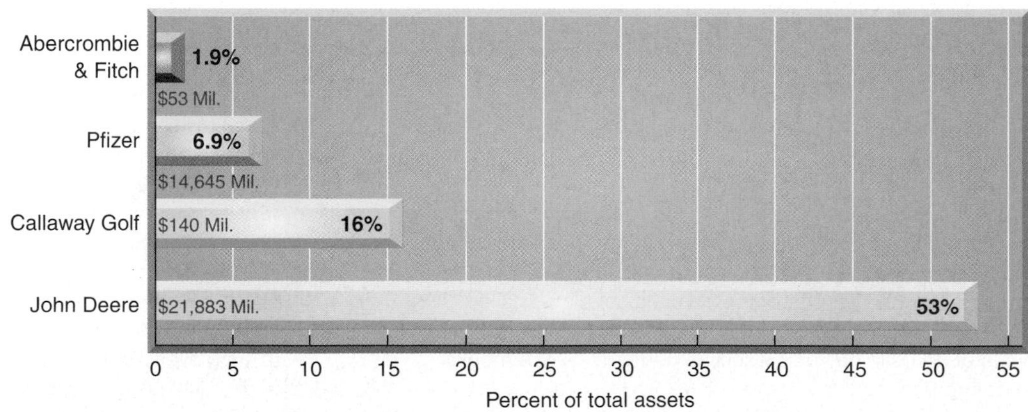

Sales on Credit Credit sales are recorded by increasing (debiting) Accounts Receivable. A company must also maintain a separate account for each customer that tracks how much that customer purchases, has already paid, and still owes. This information provides the basis for sending bills to customers and for other business analyses. To maintain this information, companies that extend credit directly to their customers keep a separate account receivable for each one of them. The general ledger continues to have a single Accounts Receivable account along with the other financial statement accounts, but a supplementary record is created to maintain a separate account for each customer. This supplementary record is called the *accounts receivable ledger*.

Exhibit 9.2 shows the relation between the Accounts Receivable account in the general ledger and its individual customer accounts in the accounts receivable ledger for TechCom, a small electronics wholesaler. This exhibit reports a $3,000 ending balance of TechCom's accounts receivable for June 30. TechCom's transactions are mainly in cash, but it has two major credit customers: CompStore and RDA Electronics. Its *schedule of accounts receivable* shows that the $3,000 balance of the Accounts Receivable account in the general ledger equals the total of its two customers' balances in the accounts receivable ledger.

EXHIBIT 9.2

General Ledger and the Accounts Receivable Ledger (before July 1 transactions)

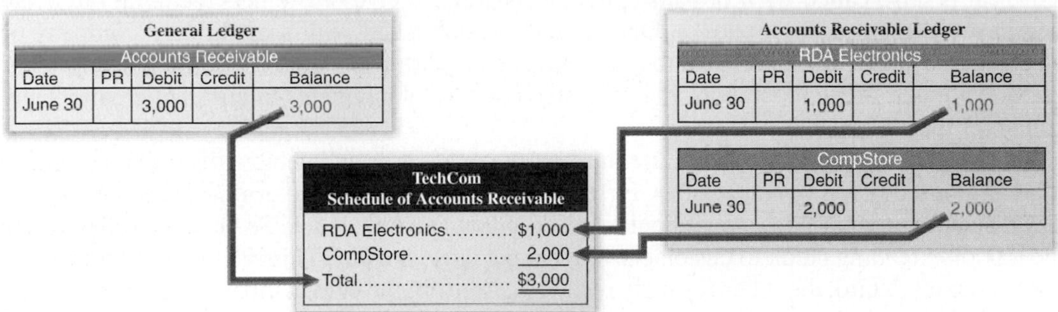

To see how accounts receivable from credit sales are recognized in the accounting records, we look at two transactions on July 1 between TechCom and its credit customers—see Exhibit 9.3. The first is a credit sale of $950 to CompStore. A credit sale is posted with both a debit to the Accounts Receivable account in the general ledger and a debit to the customer account in the accounts receivable ledger. The second transaction is a collection of $720 from RDA Electronics from a prior credit sale. Cash receipts from a credit customer are posted with a credit to the Accounts Receivable account in the general ledger and flow through to credit the customer account in the accounts receivable ledger. (Posting debits or credits to Accounts Receivable in two separate ledgers does not violate the requirement that debits equal credits. The equality of debits and credits is maintained in the general ledger. The accounts receivable ledger is a *supplementary* record providing information on each customer.)

EXHIBIT 9.3

Accounts Receivable Transactions

July 1	Accounts Receivable—CompStore	950	
	Sales		950
	*To record credit sales**		
July 1	Cash	720	
	Accounts Receivable—RDA Electronics		720
	To record collection of credit sales.		

Assets = Liabilities + Equity
+950 +950

Assets = Liabilities + Equity
+720
−720

* We omit the entry to Dr. Cost of Sales and Cr. Merchandise Inventory to focus on sales and receivables.

Exhibit 9.4 shows the general ledger and the accounts receivable ledger after recording the two July 1 transactions. The general ledger shows the effects of the sale, the collection, and the resulting balance of $3,230. These events are also reflected in the individual customer accounts: RDA Electronics has an ending balance of $280, and CompStore's ending balance is $2,950.

EXHIBIT 9.4

General Ledger and the Accounts Receivable Ledger (after July 1 transactions)

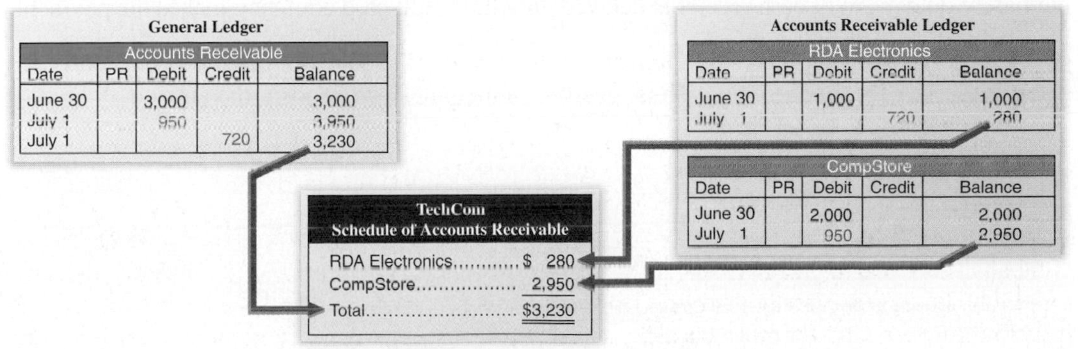

The $3,230 sum of the individual accounts equals the debit balance of the Accounts Receivable account in the general ledger.

Like TechCom, many large retailers such as **Sears** and **JCPenney** sell on credit. Many also maintain their own credit cards to grant credit to approved customers and to earn interest on any balance not paid within a specified period of time. This allows them to avoid the fee charged by credit card companies. The entries in this case are the same as those for TechCom except for the possibility of added interest revenue. If a customer owes interest on a bill, we debit Interest Receivable and credit Interest Revenue for that amount.

Point: **Visa USA** now transacts more than $1 trillion from its credit, debit, and prepaid cards.

Credit Card Sales Many companies allow their customers to pay for products and services using third-party credit cards such as **Visa**, **MasterCard**, or **American Express**, and debit cards (also called ATM or bank cards). This practice gives customers the ability to make purchases without cash or checks. Once credit is established with a credit card company or bank, the customer does not have to open an account with each store. Customers using these cards can make single monthly payments instead of several payments to different creditors and can defer their payments.

Many sellers allow customers to use third-party credit cards and debit cards instead of granting credit directly for several reasons. First, the seller does not have to evaluate each customer's credit standing or make decisions about who gets credit and how much. Second, the seller avoids the risk of extending credit to customers who cannot or do not pay. This risk is transferred to the card company. Third, the seller typically receives cash from the card company sooner than had it granted credit directly to customers. Fourth, a variety of credit options for customers offers a potential increase in sales volume. **Sears** historically offered credit only to customers using a Sears card but later changed its policy to permit customers to charge purchases to third-party credit card companies in a desire to increase sales. It reported: "SearsCharge increased its share of Sears retail sales even as the company expanded the payment options available to its customers with the acceptance . . . of Visa, MasterCard, and American Express in addition to the [Sears] Card."

There are guidelines in how companies account for credit card and debit card sales. Some credit cards, but nearly all debit cards, credit a seller's Cash account immediately upon deposit. In this case the seller deposits a copy of each card sales receipt in its bank account just as it deposits a customer's check. The majority of credit cards, however, require the seller to remit a copy (often electronically) of each receipt to the card company. Until payment is received, the seller has an account receivable from the card company. In both cases, the seller pays a fee for services provided by the card company, often ranging from 1% to 5% of card sales. This charge is deducted from the credit to the seller's account or the cash payment to the seller.

Decision Insight

Debit Card vs. Credit Card A buyer's debit card purchase reduces the buyer's cash account balance at the card company, which is often a bank. Since the buyer's cash account balance is a liability (with a credit balance) for the card company to the buyer, the card company would debit that account for a buyer's purchase—hence, the term *debit card.* A credit card reflects authorization by the card company of a line of credit for the buyer with preset interest rates and payment terms—hence, the term *credit card.* Most card companies waive interest charges if the buyer pays its balance each month. ■

Point: Web merchants pay twice as much in credit card association fees as other retailers because they suffer 10 times as much fraud.

The procedures used in accounting for credit card sales depend on whether cash is received immediately on deposit or cash receipt is delayed until the credit card company makes the payment.

Cash Received Immediately on Deposit To illustrate, if TechCom has $100 of credit card sales with a 4% fee, and its $96 cash is received immediately on deposit, the entry is

Assets	=	Liabilities	+	Equity
+96				+100
				−4

July 15	Cash	96	
	Credit Card Expense	4	
	Sales		100
	*To record credit card sales less a 4% credit card expense.**		

* We omit the entry to Dr. Cost of Sales and Cr. Merchandise Inventory to focus on credit card expense.

Cash Received Some Time after Deposit However, if instead TechCom must remit electronically the credit card sales receipts to the credit card company and wait for the $96 cash payment, the entry on the date of sale is

July 15	Accounts Receivable—Credit Card Co.	96	
	Credit Card Expense	4	
	Sales		100
	*To record credit card sales less 4% credit card expense.**		

* We omit the entry to Dr. Cost of Sales and Cr. Merchandise Inventory to focus on credit card expense.

Assets = Liabilities + Equity
+96 +100
−4

When cash is later received from the credit card company, usually through electronic funds transfer, the entry is

July 20	Cash	96	
	Accounts Receivable—Credit Card Co.		96
	To record cash receipt.		

Assets = Liabilities + Equity
+96
−96

Some firms report credit card expense in the income statement as a type of discount deducted from sales to get net sales. Other companies classify it as a selling expense or even as an administrative expense. Arguments can be made for each approach.

Point: Third-party credit card costs can be large. JCPenney reported third-party credit card costs exceeding $10 million.

Installment Sales and Receivables Many companies allow their credit customers to make periodic payments over several months. For example, **Ford Motor Company** reports more than $75 billion in installment receivables. The seller refers to such assets as *installment accounts* (or *finance*) *receivable,* which are amounts owed by customers from credit sales for which payment is required in periodic amounts over an extended time period. Source documents for installment accounts receivable include sales slips or invoices describing the sales transactions. The customer is usually charged interest. Although installment accounts receivable can have credit periods of more than one year, they are classified as current assets if the seller regularly offers customers such terms.

Decision Maker Answer — p. 378

Entrepreneur As a small retailer, you are considering allowing customers to buy merchandise using credit cards. Until now, your store accepted only cash and checks. What analysis do you use to make this decision? ■

Quick Check Answers — p. 379

1. In recording credit card sales, when do you debit Accounts Receivable and when do you debit Cash?
2. A company accumulates sales receipts and remits them to the credit card company for payment. When are the credit card expenses recorded? When are these expenses incurred?

Valuing Accounts Receivable—Direct Write-Off Method

P1 Apply the direct write-off method to account for accounts receivable.

When a company directly grants credit to its customers, it expects that some customers will not pay what they promised. The accounts of these customers are *uncollectible accounts,* commonly called **bad debts.** The total amount of uncollectible accounts is an expense of selling on credit. Why do companies sell on credit if they expect some accounts to be uncollectible? The answer is that companies believe that granting credit will increase total sales and net income enough to offset bad debts. Companies use two methods to account for uncollectible accounts: (1) direct write-off method and (2) allowance method. We describe both.

Point: Managers realize that some portion of credit sales will be uncollectible, but which credit sales are uncollectible is unknown.

Recording and Writing Off Bad Debts The **direct write-off method** of accounting for bad debts records the loss from an uncollectible account receivable when it is determined to be uncollectible. No attempt is made to predict bad debts expense. To illustrate, if TechCom determines on January 23 that it cannot collect $520 owed to it by its customer J. Kent, it recognizes the loss using the direct write-off method as follows:

Assets = Liabilities + Equity
−520 −520

Jan. 23	Bad Debts Expense	520	
	Accounts Receivable—J. Kent		520
	To write off an uncollectible account.		

The debit in this entry charges the uncollectible amount directly to the current period's Bad Debts Expense account. The credit removes its balance from the Accounts Receivable account in the general ledger (and its subsidiary ledger).

Point: If a customer fails to pay within the credit period, most companies send out repeated billings and make other efforts to collect.

Recovering a Bad Debt Although uncommon, sometimes an account written off is later collected. This can be due to factors such as continual collection efforts or a customer's good fortune. If the account of J. Kent that was written off directly to Bad Debts Expense is later collected in full, the following two entries record this recovery.

Assets = Liabilities + Equity
+520 +520

Assets = Liabilities + Equity
+520
−520

Mar. 11	Accounts Receivable—J. Kent	520	
	Bad Debts Expense		520
	To reinstate account previously written off.		
Mar. 11	Cash	520	
	Accounts Receivable—J. Kent		520
	To record full payment of account.		

Assessing the Direct Write-Off Method Examples of companies that use the direct write-off method include **Rand Medical Billing**, **Gateway Distributors**, **Microwave Satellite Technologies**, **First Industrial Realty**, **New Frontier Energy**, and **Sub Surface Waste Management**. The following disclosure by **Pharma-Bio Serv** is typical of the justification for this method: Bad debts are accounted for using the direct write-off method whereby an expense is recognized only when a specific account is determined to be uncollectible. The effect of using this method approximates that of the allowance method. Companies must weigh at least two accounting concepts when considering the use of the direct write-off method: the (1) matching principle and (2) materiality constraint.

Matching principle applied to bad debts. The **matching (expense recognition) principle** requires expenses to be reported in the same accounting period as the sales they helped produce. This means that if extending credit to customers helped produce sales, the bad debts expense linked to those sales is matched and reported in the same period. The direct write-off method usually does *not* best match sales and expenses because bad debts expense is not recorded until an account becomes uncollectible, which often occurs in a period after that of the credit sale. To match bad debts expense with the sales it produces therefore requires a company to estimate future uncollectibles.

Point: **Harley-Davidson** reports $169 million of credit losses matched against $4,782 million of total revenues.

Materiality constraint applied to bad debts. The **materiality constraint** states that an amount can be ignored if its effect on the financial statements is unimportant to users' business decisions. The materiality constraint permits the use of the direct write-off method when bad debts expenses are very small in relation to a company's other financial statement items such as sales and net income.

Valuing Accounts Receivable—Allowance Method

The **allowance method** of accounting for bad debts matches the *estimated* loss from uncollectible accounts receivable against the sales they helped produce. We must use estimated losses because when sales occur, management does not know which customers will not pay their bills. This means that at the end of each period, the allowance method requires an estimate of the total bad debts expected to result from that period's sales. This method has two advantages over the direct write-off method: (1) it records estimated bad debts expense in the period when the related sales are recorded and (2) it reports accounts receivable on the balance sheet at the estimated amount of cash to be collected.

Point: Under direct write-off, expense is recorded each time an account is written off. Under the allowance method, expense is recorded with an adjusting entry equal to the total estimated uncollectibles for that period's sales.

Recording Bad Debts Expense The allowance method estimates bad debts expense at the end of each accounting period and records it with an adjusting entry. TechCom, for instance, had credit sales of $300,000 during its first year of operations. At the end of the first year, $20,000 of credit sales remained uncollected. Based on the experience of similar businesses, TechCom estimated that $1,500 of its accounts receivable would be uncollectible. This estimated expense is recorded with the following adjusting entry.

Dec. 31	Bad Debts Expense	1,500	
	Allowance for Doubtful Accounts		1,500
	To record estimated bad debts.		

Assets = Liabilities + Equity
−1,500 −1,500

The estimated Bad Debts Expense of $1,500 is reported on the income statement (as either a selling expense or an administrative expense) and offsets the $300,000 credit sales it helped produce. The **Allowance for Doubtful Accounts** is a contra asset account. A contra account is used instead of reducing accounts receivable directly because at the time of the adjusting entry, the company does not know which customers will not pay. After the bad debts adjusting entry is posted, TechCom's account balances (in T-account form) for Accounts Receivable and its Allowance for Doubtful Accounts are as shown in Exhibit 9.5.

Point: Credit approval is usually not assigned to the selling dept. because its goal is to increase sales, and it may approve customers at the cost of increased bad debts. Instead, approval is assigned to a separate credit-granting or administrative dept.

EXHIBIT 9.5

General Ledger Entries after Bad Debts Adjusting Entry

Accounts Receivable				Allowance for Doubtful Accounts			
Dec. 31	20,000					Dec. 31	1,500

The Allowance for Doubtful Accounts credit balance of $1,500 has the effect of reducing accounts receivable to its estimated realizable value. **Realizable value** refers to the expected proceeds from converting an asset into cash. Although credit customers owe $20,000 to TechCom, only $18,500 is expected to be realized in cash collections from these customers. In the balance sheet, the Allowance for Doubtful Accounts is subtracted from Accounts Receivable and is often reported as shown in Exhibit 9.6.

Point: Bad Debts Expense is also called *Uncollectible Accounts Expense*. The Allowance for Doubtful Accounts is also called *Allowance for Uncollectible Accounts*.

EXHIBIT 9.6

Balance Sheet Presentation of the Allowance for Doubtful Accounts

Current assets		
Accounts receivable	**$20,000**	
Less allowance for doubtful accounts	**1,500**	**$18,500**

Sometimes the Allowance for Doubtful Accounts is not reported separately. This alternative presentation is shown in Exhibit 9.7 (also see Appendix A).

EXHIBIT 9.7

Alternative Presentation of the Allowance for Doubtful Accounts

Current assets	
Accounts receivable (net of $1,500 doubtful accounts)	**$18,500**

Writing Off a Bad Debt When specific accounts are identified as uncollectible, they are written off against the Allowance for Doubtful Accounts. To illustrate, TechCom decides that J. Kent's $520 account is uncollectible and makes the following entry to write it off.

Jan. 23	Allowance for Doubtful Accounts	520	
	Accounts Receivable—J. Kent		520
	To write off an uncollectible account.		

Assets = Liabilities + Equity
+520
−520

Posting this write-off entry to the Accounts Receivable account removes the amount of the bad debt from the general ledger (it is also posted to the accounts receivable subsidiary ledger). The general ledger accounts now appear as in Exhibit 9.8 (assuming no other transactions affecting these accounts).

Point: The Bad Debts Expense account is not debited in the write-off entry because it was recorded in the period when sales occurred.

EXHIBIT 9.8

General Ledger Entries after Write-Off

Accounts Receivable				Allowance for Doubtful Accounts			
Dec. 31	20,000					Dec. 31	1,500
		Jan. 23	520	Jan. 23	520		

Point: In posting a write-off, the ledger's Explanation column indicates the reason for this credit so it is not misinterpreted as payment in full.

The write-off does *not* affect the realizable value of accounts receivable as shown in Exhibit 9.9. Neither total assets nor net income is affected by the write-off of a specific account. Instead, both assets and net income are affected in the period when bad debts expense is predicted and recorded with an adjusting entry.

EXHIBIT 9.9

Realizable Value before and after Write-Off of a Bad Debt

	Before Write-Off	After Write-Off
Accounts receivable	$ 20,000	$ 19,480
Less allowance for doubtful accounts	1,500	980
Estimated realizable accounts receivable	**$18,500**	**$18,500**

Recovering a Bad Debt When a customer fails to pay and the account is written off as uncollectible, his or her credit standing is jeopardized. To help restore credit standing, a customer sometimes volunteers to pay all or part of the amount owed. A company makes two entries when collecting an account previously written off by the allowance method. The first is to reverse the write-off and reinstate the customer's account. The second entry records the collection of the reinstated account. To illustrate, if on March 11 Kent pays in full his account previously written off, the entries are

Assets = Liabilities + Equity
+520
−520

Assets = Liabilities + Equity
+520
−520

Date	Account	Debit	Credit
Mar. 11	Accounts Receivable—J. Kent	520	
	Allowance for Doubtful Accounts		520
	To reinstate account previously written off.		
Mar. 11	Cash	520	
	Accounts Receivable—J. Kent		520
	To record full payment of account.		

Example: If TechCom used a collection agency and paid a 35% commission on $520 collected from Kent, how is this recorded? *Answer:*

Cash	338	
Collection Expense	182	
Accts. Recble.—J. Kent		520

In this illustration, Kent paid the entire amount previously written off, but sometimes a customer pays only a portion of the amount owed. A question then arises as to whether the entire balance of the account or just the amount paid is returned to accounts receivable. This is a matter of judgment. If we believe this customer will later pay in full, we return the entire amount owed to accounts receivable, but if we expect no further collection, we return only the amount paid.

Decision Insight

PayPal PayPal is legally just a money transfer agent, but it is increasingly challenging big credit card brands—see chart. PayPal is successful because: (1) online credit card processing fees often exceed $0.15 per dollar, but PayPal's fees are under $0.10 per dollar. (2) PayPal's merchant fraud losses are under 0.2% of revenues, which compares to nearly 2% for online merchants using credit cards. ■

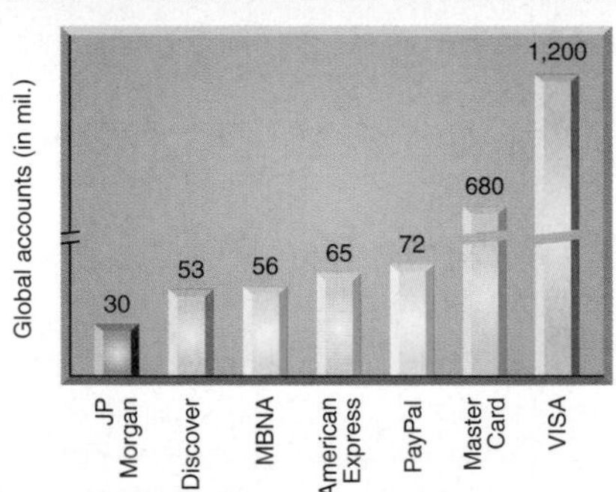

Estimating Bad Debts—Percent of Sales Method

P2 Apply the allowance method and estimate uncollectibles based on sales and accounts receivable.

The allowance method requires an estimate of bad debts expense to prepare an adjusting entry at the end of each accounting period. There are two common methods. One is based on the income statement relation between bad debts expense and sales. The second is based on the balance sheet relation between accounts receivable and the allowance for doubtful accounts.

The *percent of sales method,* also referred to as the *income statement method,* is based on the idea that a given percent of a company's credit sales for the period is uncollectible. To illustrate, assume that Musicland has credit sales of $400,000 in year 2011. Based on past experience,

Musicland estimates 0.6% of credit sales to be uncollectible. This implies that Musicland expects $2,400 of bad debts expense from its sales (computed as $400,000 × 0.006). The adjusting entry to record this estimated expense is

Point: Focus is on *credit* sales because cash sales do not produce bad debts. If cash sales are a small or stable percent of credit sales, total sales can be used.

Dec. 31	Bad Debts Expense	2,400	
	Allowance for Doubtful Accounts		2,400
	To record estimated bad debts.		

Assets = Liabilities + Equity
−2,400 −2,400

The allowance account ending balance on the balance sheet for this method would rarely equal the bad debts expense on the income statement. This is so because unless a company is in its first period of operations, its allowance account has a zero balance only if the prior amounts written off as uncollectible *exactly* equal the prior estimated bad debts expenses. (When computing bad debts expense as a percent of sales, managers monitor and adjust the percent so it is not too high or too low.)

Point: When using the *percent of sales method* for estimating uncollectibles, the estimate of bad debts is the number used in the adjusting entry.

Estimating Bad Debts—Percent of Receivables Method

The *accounts receivable methods,* also referred to as *balance sheet methods,* use balance sheet relations to estimate bad debts—mainly the relation between accounts receivable and the allowance amount. The goal of the bad debts adjusting entry for these methods is to make the Allowance for Doubtful Accounts balance equal to the portion of accounts receivable that is estimated to be uncollectible. The estimated balance for the allowance account is obtained in one of two ways: (1) computing the percent uncollectible from the total accounts receivable or (2) aging accounts receivable.

The *percent of accounts receivable method* assumes that a given percent of a company's receivables is uncollectible. This percent is based on past experience and is impacted by current conditions such as economic trends and customer difficulties. The total dollar amount of all receivables is multiplied by this percent to get the estimated dollar amount of uncollectible accounts—reported in the balance sheet as the Allowance for Doubtful Accounts.

To illustrate, assume that Musicland has $50,000 of accounts receivable on December 31, 2011. Experience suggests 5% of its receivables is uncollectible. This means that *after* the adjusting entry is posted, we want the Allowance for Doubtful Accounts to show a $2,500 credit balance (5% of $50,000). We are also told that its beginning balance is $2,200, which is 5% of the $44,000 accounts receivable on December 31, 2010—see Exhibit 9.10.

Point: When using an accounts receivable method for estimating uncollectibles, the allowance account balance is adjusted to equal the estimate of uncollectibles.

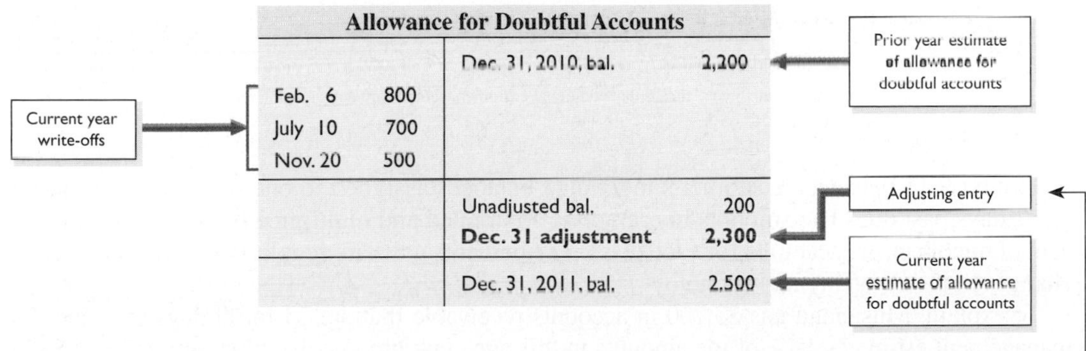

EXHIBIT 9.10

Allowance for Doubtful Accounts after Bad Debts Adjusting Entry

During 2011, accounts of customers are written off on February 6, July 10, and November 20. Thus, the account has a $200 credit balance *before* the December 31, 2011, adjustment. The adjusting entry to give the allowance account the estimated $2,500 balance is

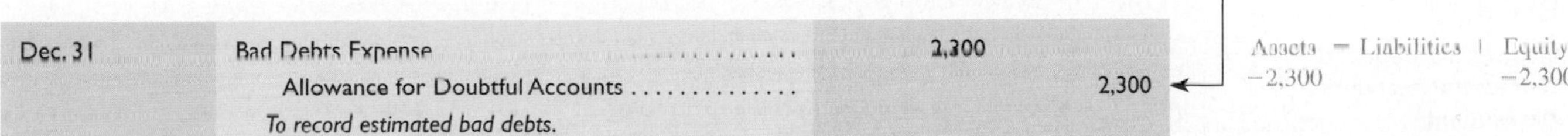

Dec. 31	Bad Debts Expense	2,300	
	Allowance for Doubtful Accounts		2,300
	To record estimated bad debts.		

Assets = Liabilities + Equity
−2,300 −2,300

Decision Insight

Aging Pains Experience shows that the longer a receivable is past due, the lower is the likelihood of its collection. An *aging schedule* uses this knowledge to estimate bad debts. The chart here is from a survey that reported estimates of bad debts for receivables grouped by how long they were past their due dates. Each company sets its own estimates based on its customers and its experiences with those customers' payment patterns. ■

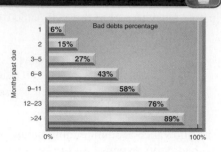

Bad debts percentage

Months past due	Bad debts percentage
1	6%
2	15%
3–5	27%
6–8	43%
9–11	58%
12–23	76%
>24	89%

0% 100%

Estimating Bad Debts—Aging of Receivables Method

The **aging of accounts receivable** method uses both past and current receivables information to estimate the allowance amount. Specifically, each receivable is classified by how long it is past its due date. Then estimates of uncollectible amounts are made assuming that the longer an amount is past due, the more likely it is to be uncollectible. Classifications are often based on 30-day periods. After the amounts are classified (or aged), experience is used to estimate the percent of each uncollectible class. These percents are applied to the amounts in each class and then totaled to get the estimated balance of the Allowance for Doubtful Accounts. This computation is performed by setting up a schedule such as Exhibit 9.11.

EXHIBIT 9.11

Aging of Accounts Receivable

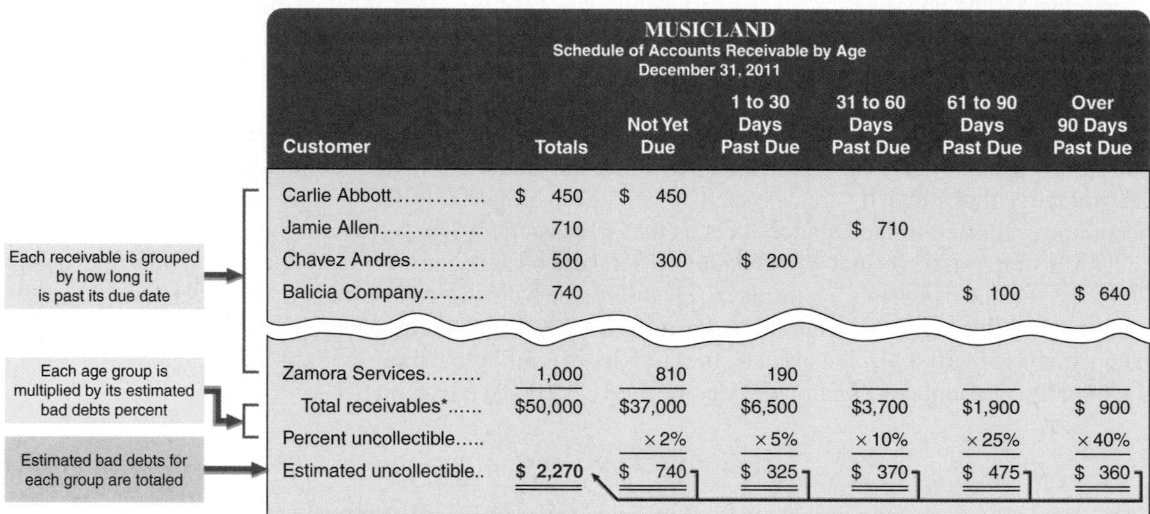

MUSICLAND
Schedule of Accounts Receivable by Age
December 31, 2011

Customer	Totals	Not Yet Due	1 to 30 Days Past Due	31 to 60 Days Past Due	61 to 90 Days Past Due	Over 90 Days Past Due
Carlie Abbott..............	$ 450	$ 450				
Jamie Allen................	710			$ 710		
Chavez Andres...........	500	300	$ 200			
Balicia Company..........	740				$ 100	$ 640
Zamora Services.........	1,000	810	190			
Total receivables*......	$50,000	$37,000	$6,500	$3,700	$1,900	$ 900
Percent uncollectible.....		× 2%	× 5%	× 10%	× 25%	× 40%
Estimated uncollectible..	$ 2,270	$ 740	$ 325	$ 370	$ 475	$ 360

Each receivable is grouped by how long it is past its due date
Each age group is multiplied by its estimated bad debts percent
Estimated bad debts for each group are totaled

*The "white line break" means that additional customer accounts are not shown in the table but are included in each column's total.

Exhibit 9.11 lists each customer's individual balances assigned to one of five classes based on its days past due. The amounts in each class are totaled and multiplied by the estimated percent of uncollectible accounts for each class. The percents used are regularly reviewed to reflect changes in the company and economy.

To explain, Musicland has $3,700 in accounts receivable that are 31 to 60 days past due. Its management estimates 10% of the amounts in this age class are uncollectible, or a total of $370 (computed as $3,700 × 10%). Similar analysis is done for each of the other four classes. The final total of $2,270 ($740 + $325 + 370 + $475 + $360) shown in the first column is the estimated balance for the Allowance for Doubtful Accounts. Exhibit 9.12 shows that since the allowance

EXHIBIT 9.12

Computation of the Required Adjustment for the Accounts Receivable Method

Unadjusted balance	$ 200 credit
Estimated balance	2,270 credit
Required adjustment	**$2,070 credit**

account has an unadjusted credit balance of $200, the required adjustment to the Allowance for Doubtful Accounts is $2,070. (We could also use a T-account for this analysis as shown in the margin.) This yields the following end-of-period adjusting entry.

Allowance for Doubtful Accounts	
	Unadj. bal. 200
	Req. adj. 2,070
	Estim. bal. 2,270

Dec. 31	Bad Debts Expense	2,070	
	Allowance for Doubtful Accounts		2,070
	To record estimated bad debts.		

Assets = Liabilities + Equity
−2,070 −2,070

Alternatively, if the allowance account had an unadjusted *debit* balance of $500 (instead of the $200 credit balance), its required adjustment would be computed as follows. (Again, a T-account can be used for this analysis as shown in the margin.)

Point: A debit balance implies that write-offs for that period exceed the total allowance.

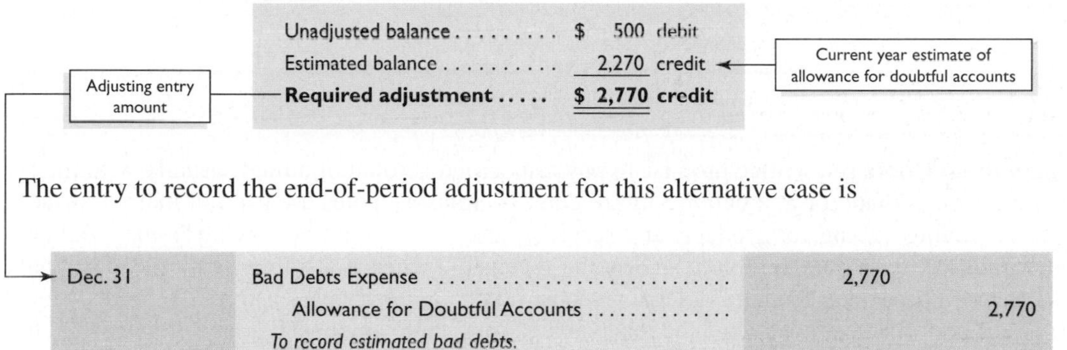

Unadjusted balance	$ 500 debit
Estimated balance	2,270 credit
Required adjustment	**$ 2,770 credit**

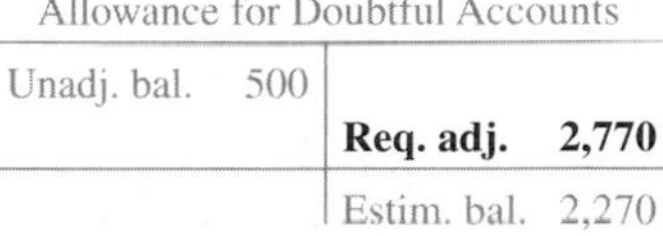

Allowance for Doubtful Accounts	
Unadj. bal. 500	
	Req. adj. 2,770
	Estim. bal. 2,270

The entry to record the end-of-period adjustment for this alternative case is

Dec. 31	Bad Debts Expense	2,770	
	Allowance for Doubtful Accounts		2,770
	To record estimated bad debts.		

Assets = Liabilities + Equity
−2,770 −2,770

The aging of accounts receivable method is an examination of specific accounts and is usually the most reliable of the estimation methods.

Estimating Bad Debts—Summary of Methods Exhibit 9.13 summarizes the principles guiding all three estimation methods and their focus of analysis. Percent of sales, with its income statement focus, does a good job at matching bad debts expense with sales. The accounts receivable methods, with their balance sheet focus, do a better job at reporting accounts receivable at realizable value.

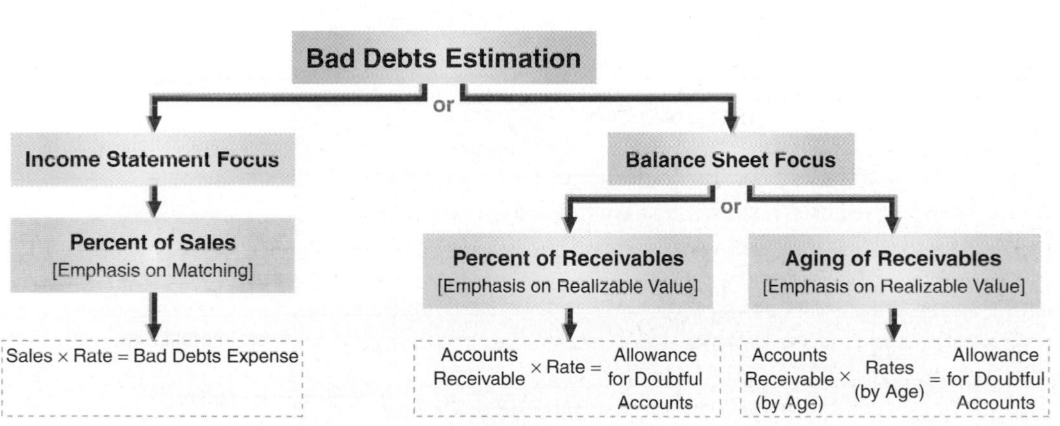

EXHIBIT 9.13

Methods to Estimate Bad Debts

Decision Maker Answer — p. 379

Labor Union Chief One week prior to labor contract negotiations, financial statements are released showing no income growth. A 10% growth was predicted. Your analysis finds that the company increased its allowance for uncollectibles from 1.5% to 4.5% of receivables. Without this change, income would show a 9% growth. Does this analysis impact negotiations? ■

Quick Check Answers — p. 379 

3. Why must bad debts expense be estimated if such an estimate is possible?
4. What term describes the balance sheet valuation of Accounts Receivable less the Allowance for Doubtful Accounts?
5. Why is estimated bad debts expense credited to a contra account (Allowance for Doubtful Accounts) rather than to the Accounts Receivable account?
6. SnoBoard Company's year-end balance in its Allowance for Doubtful Accounts is a credit of $440. By aging accounts receivable, it estimates that $6,142 is uncollectible. Prepare SnoBoard's year-end adjusting entry for bad debts.
7. Record entries for these transactions assuming the allowance method is used:

   Jan. 10 The $300 account of customer Cool Jam is determined uncollectible.

   April 12 Cool Jam unexpectedly pays in full the account deemed uncollectible on Jan. 10.

NOTES RECEIVABLE

C2 Describe a note receivable, the computation of its maturity date, and the recording of its existence.

A **promissory note** is a written promise to pay a specified amount of money, usually with interest, either on demand or at a definite future date. Promissory notes are used in many transactions, including paying for products and services, and lending and borrowing money. Sellers sometimes ask for a note to replace an account receivable when a customer requests additional time to pay a past-due account. For legal reasons, sellers generally prefer to receive notes when the credit period is long and when the receivable is for a large amount. If a lawsuit is needed to collect from a customer, a note is the buyer's written acknowledgment of the debt, its amount, and its terms.

Exhibit 9.14 shows a simple promissory note dated July 10, 2011. For this note, Julia Browne promises to pay TechCom or to its order (according to TechCom's instructions) a specified amount of money ($1,000), called the **principal of a note,** at a definite future date (October 8, 2011). As the one who signed the note and promised to pay it at maturity, Browne is the **maker of the note.** As the person to whom the note is payable, TechCom is the **payee of the note.** To Browne, the note is a liability called a *note payable*. To TechCom, the same note is an asset called a *note receivable*. This note bears interest at 12%, as written on the note. **Interest** is the charge for using the money until its due date. To a borrower, interest is an expense. To a lender, it is revenue.

EXHIBIT 9.14

Promissory Note

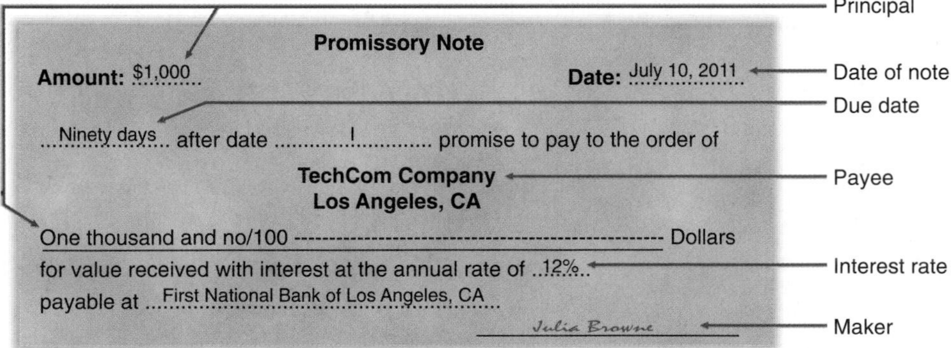
Promissory Note

Amount: $1,000 Date: July 10, 2011

Ninety days after date ....I........ promise to pay to the order of

TechCom Company
Los Angeles, CA

One thousand and no/100 ---------- Dollars

for value received with interest at the annual rate of 12%

payable at First National Bank of Los Angeles, CA

Julia Browne

Computing Maturity and Interest

This section describes key computations for notes including the determination of maturity date, period covered, and interest computation.

Maturity Date and Period The **maturity date of a note** is the day the note (principal and interest) must be repaid. The *period* of a note is the time from the note's (contract) date to its maturity date. Many notes mature in less than a full year, and the period they cover is often expressed in days. When the time of a note is expressed in days, its maturity date is the specified number of days after the note's date. As an example, a five-day note dated June 15 matures and is due on June 20. A 90-day note dated July 10 matures on October 8. This October 8 due date is computed as shown in Exhibit 9.15. The period of a note is sometimes expressed in months or years. When months are used, the note matures and is payable in the month of its maturity on the *same day of the month* as its original date. A nine-month note dated July 10, for instance, is payable on April 10. The same analysis applies when years are used.

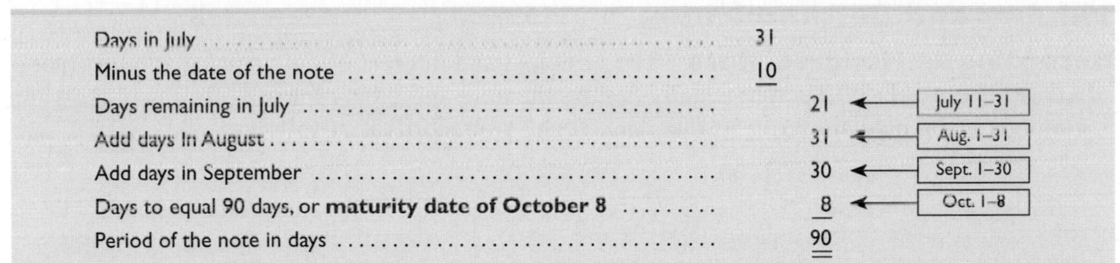

Days in July	31		
Minus the date of the note	10		
Days remaining in July		21	← July 11–31
Add days in August		31	← Aug. 1–31
Add days in September		30	← Sept. 1–30
Days to equal 90 days, or **maturity date of October 8**		8	← Oct. 1–8
Period of the note in days		90	

EXHIBIT 9.15

Maturity Date Computation

Interest Computation *Interest* is the cost of borrowing money for the borrower or, alternatively, the profit from lending money for the lender. Unless otherwise stated, the rate of interest on a note is the rate charged for the use of the principal for one year. The formula for computing interest on a note is shown in Exhibit 9.16.

Principal of the note × **Annual interest rate** × **Time expressed in fraction of year** = **Interest**

EXHIBIT 9.16

Computation of Interest Formula

To simplify interest computations, a year is commonly treated as having 360 days (called the *banker's rule* in the business world and widely used in commercial transactions). **We treat a year as having 360 days for interest computations in the examples and assignments.** Using the promissory note in Exhibit 9.14 where we have a 90-day, 12%, $1,000 note, the total interest is computed as follows.

$$\$1{,}000 \times 12\% \times \frac{90}{360} = \$1{,}000 \times 0.12 \times 0.25 = \$30$$

Recognizing Notes Receivable

Notes receivable are usually recorded in a single Notes Receivable account to simplify recordkeeping. The original notes are kept on file, including information on the maker, rate of interest, and due date. (When a company holds a large number of notes, it sometimes sets up a controlling account and a subsidiary ledger for notes. This is similar to the handling of accounts receivable.) To illustrate the recording for the receipt of a note, we use the $1,000, 90-day, 12% promissory note in Exhibit 9.14. TechCom received this note at the time of a product sale to Julia Browne. This transaction is recorded as follows.

July 10*	Notes Receivable	1,000	
	Sales		1,000
	Sold goods in exchange for a 90-day, 12% note.		

Assets = Liabilities + Equity
+1,000 +1,000

* We omit the entry to Dr. Cost of Sales and Cr. Merchandise Inventory to focus on sales and receivables.

When a seller accepts a note from an overdue customer as a way to grant a time extension on a past-due account receivable, it will often collect part of the past-due balance in cash. This partial payment forces a concession from the customer, reduces the customer's debt (and the seller's risk), and produces a note for a smaller amount. To illustrate, assume that TechCom agreed to accept $232 in cash along with a $600, 60-day, 15% note from Jo Cook to

Point: Notes receivable often are a major part of a company's assets. Likewise, notes payable often are a large part of a company's liabilities.

settle her $832 past-due account. TechCom made the following entry to record receipt of this cash and note.

Assets = Liabilities + Equity
+232
+600
−832

Oct. 5	Cash	232	
	Notes Receivable	600	
	Accounts Receivable—J. Cook		832
	Received cash and note to settle account.		

Valuing and Settling Notes

P3 Record the honoring and dishonoring of a note and adjustments for interest.

Recording an Honored Note The principal and interest of a note are due on its maturity date. The maker of the note usually *honors* the note and pays it in full. To illustrate, when J. Cook pays the note above on its due date, TechCom records it as follows.

Assets = Liabilities + Equity
+615 +15
−600

Dec. 4	Cash	615	
	Notes Receivable		600
	Interest Revenue		15
	Collect note with interest of $600 × 15% × 60/360.		

Interest Revenue, also called *Interest Earned,* is reported on the income statement.

Recording a Dishonored Note When a note's maker is unable or refuses to pay at maturity, the note is *dishonored.* The act of dishonoring a note does not relieve the maker of the obligation to pay. The payee should use every legitimate means to collect. How do companies report this event? The balance of the Notes Receivable account should include only those notes that have not matured. Thus, when a note is dishonored, we remove the amount of this note from the Notes Receivable account and charge it back to an account receivable from its maker. To illustrate, TechCom holds an $800, 12%, 60-day note of Greg Hart. At maturity, Hart dishonors the note. TechCom records this dishonoring of the note as follows.

Point: When posting a dishonored note to a customer's account, an explanation is included so as not to misinterpret the debit as a sale on account.

Assets = Liabilities + Equity
+816 +16
−800

Oct. 14	Accounts Receivable—G. Hart	816	
	Interest Revenue		16
	Notes Receivable		800
	To charge account of G. Hart for a dishonored note and interest of $800 × 12% × 60/360.		

Point: Reporting the details of notes is consistent with the **full disclosure principle,** which requires financial statements (including footnotes) to report all relevant information.

Charging a dishonored note back to the account of its maker serves two purposes. First, it removes the amount of the note from the Notes Receivable account and records the dishonored note in the maker's account. Second, and more important, if the maker of the dishonored note applies for credit in the future, his or her account will reveal all past dealings, including the dishonored note. Restoring the account also reminds the company to continue collection efforts from Hart for both principal and interest. The entry records the full amount, including interest, to ensure that it is included in collection efforts.

Recording End-of-Period Interest Adjustment When notes receivable are outstanding at the end of a period, any accrued interest earned is computed and recorded. To illustrate, on December 16, TechCom accepts a $3,000, 60-day, 12% note from a customer in granting an extension on a past-due account. When TechCom's accounting period ends on December 31, $15 of interest has accrued on this note ($3,000 × 12% × 15/360). The following adjusting entry records this revenue.

Assets = Liabilities + Equity
+15 +15

Dec. 31	Interest Receivable	15	
	Interest Revenue		15
	To record accrued interest earned.		

Interest Revenue appears on the income statement, and Interest Receivable appears on the balance sheet as a current asset. When the December 16 note is collected on February 14, TechCom's entry to record the cash receipt is

Feb. 14	Cash	3,060	
	Interest Revenue		45
	Interest Receivable		15
	Notes Receivable		3,000
	Received payment of note and its interest.		

Assets = Liabilities + Equity
+3,060 +45
−15
−3,000

Total interest earned on the 60-day note is $60. The $15 credit to Interest Receivable on February 14 reflects the collection of the interest accrued from the December 31 adjusting entry. The $45 interest earned reflects TechCom's revenue from holding the note from January 1 to February 14 of the current period.

Quick Check Answers — p. 379

8. Irwin purchases $7,000 of merchandise from Stamford on December 16, 2011. Stamford accepts Irwin's $7,000, 90-day, 12% note as payment. Stamford's accounting period ends on December 31, and it does not make reversing entries. Prepare entries for Stamford on December 16, 2011, and December 31, 2011.
9. Using the information in Quick Check 8, prepare Stamford's March 16, 2012, entry if Irwin dishonors the note.

DISPOSAL OF RECEIVABLES

Companies can convert receivables to cash before they are due. Reasons for this include the need for cash or the desire not to be involved in collection activities. Converting receivables is usually done either by (1) selling them or (2) using them as security for a loan. A recent survey shows that about 20% of companies obtain cash from either selling receivables or pledging them as security. In some industries such as textiles, apparel and furniture, this is common practice.

C3 Explain how receivables can be converted to cash before maturity.

Selling Receivables

A company can sell all or a portion of its receivables to a finance company or bank. The buyer, called a *factor,* charges the seller a *factoring fee* and then the buyer takes ownership of the receivables and receives cash when they come due. By incurring a factoring fee, the seller receives cash earlier and can pass the risk of bad debts to the factor. The seller can also choose to avoid costs of billing and accounting for the receivables. To illustrate, if TechCom sells $20,000 of its accounts receivable and is charged a 4% factoring fee, it records this sale as follows.

Global: Firms in export sales increasingly sell their receivables to factors.

Aug. 15	Cash	19,200	
	Factoring Fee Expense	800	
	Accounts Receivable		20,000
	Sold accounts receivable for cash, less 4% fee.		

Assets = Liabilities + Equity
+19,200 −800
−20,000

The accounting for sales of notes receivable is similar to that for accounts receivable. The detailed entries are covered in advanced courses.

Pledging Receivables

A company can raise cash by borrowing money and *pledging* its receivables as security for the loan. Pledging receivables does not transfer the risk of bad debts to the lender because the borrower retains ownership of the receivables. If the borrower defaults on the loan, the lender has a right to be paid from the cash receipts of the receivable when collected. To illustrate, when TechCom borrows $35,000 and pledges its receivables as security, it records this transaction as follows.

Assets = Liabilities + Equity
+35,000 +35,000

Aug. 20	Cash	35,000	
	Notes Payable		35,000
	Borrowed money with a note secured by pledging receivables.		

Since pledged receivables are committed as security for a specific loan, the borrower's financial statements disclose the pledging of them. TechCom, for instance, includes the following note with its statements: Accounts receivable of $40,000 are pledged as security for a $35,000 note payable.

Decision Insight

What's the Proper Allowance? How can we assess whether a company has properly estimated its allowance for uncollectibles? One way is to compute the ratio of the allowance account to the gross accounts receivable. When this ratio is analyzed over several consecutive periods, trends often emerge that reflect on the adequacy of the allowance amount. ■

GLOBAL VIEW

This section discusses similarities and differences between U.S. GAAP and IFRS regarding the recognition, measurement, and disposition of receivables.

Recognition of Receivables Both U.S. GAAP and IFRS have similar asset criteria that apply to recognition of receivables. Further, receivables that arise from revenue-generating activities are subject to broadly similar criteria for U.S. GAAP and IFRS. Specifically, both refer to the realization principle and an earnings process. The realization principle under U.S. GAAP implies an *arm's-length transaction* occurs, whereas under IFRS this notion is applied in terms of reliable measurement and likelihood of economic benefits. Regarding U.S. GAAP's reference to an earnings process, IFRS instead refers to risk transfer and ownership reward. While these criteria are broadly similar, differences do exist, and they arise mainly from industry-specific guidance under U.S. GAAP, which is very limited under IFRS.

Valuation of Receivables Both U.S. GAAP and IFRS require that receivables be reported net of estimated uncollectibles. Further, both systems require that the expense for estimated uncollectibles be recorded in the same period when any revenues from those receivables are recorded. This means that for accounts receivable, both U.S. GAAP and IFRS require the allowance method for uncollectibles (unless uncollectibles are immaterial). The allowance method using percent of sales, percent of receivables, and aging was explained in this chapter. **Nokia** reports the following for its allowance for uncollectibles:

NOKIA

Management specifically analyzes accounts receivables and historical bad debt, customer concentrations, customer creditworthiness, current economic trends and changes in our customer payment terms when evaluating the adequacy of the allowance.

Disposition of Receivables Both U.S. GAAP and IFRS apply broadly similar rules in recording dispositions of receivables. Those rules are discussed in this chapter. We should be aware of an important difference in terminology. Companies reporting under U.S. GAAP disclose Bad Debts Expense, which is also referred to as Provision for Bad Debts or the Provision for Uncollectible Accounts. For U.S. GAAP, *provision* here refers to expense. Under IFRS, the term *provision* usually refers to a liability whose amount or timing (or both) is uncertain.

Accounts Receivable Turnover — Decision Analysis

A1 Compute accounts receivable turnover and use it to help assess financial condition.

For a company selling on credit, we want to assess both the quality and liquidity of its accounts receivable. *Quality* of receivables refers to the likelihood of collection without loss. Experience shows that the longer receivables are outstanding beyond their due date, the lower the likelihood of collection. *Liquidity* of receivables refers to the speed of collection. **Accounts receivable turnover** is a measure of both the quality and liquidity of accounts receivable. It indicates how often, on average, receivables are received and collected during the period. The formula for this ratio is shown in Exhibit 9.17.

EXHIBIT 9.17

Accounts Receivable Turnover

$$\textbf{Accounts receivable turnover} = \frac{\textbf{Net sales}}{\textbf{Average accounts receivable, net}}$$

We prefer to use net *credit* sales in the numerator because cash sales do not create receivables. However, since financial statements rarely report net credit sales, our analysis uses net sales. The denominator is the *average* accounts receivable balance, computed as (Beginning balance + Ending balance) ÷ 2. TechCom has an accounts receivable turnover of 5.1. This indicates its average accounts receivable balance is converted into cash 5.1 times during the period. Exhibit 9.18 shows graphically this turnover activity for TechCom.

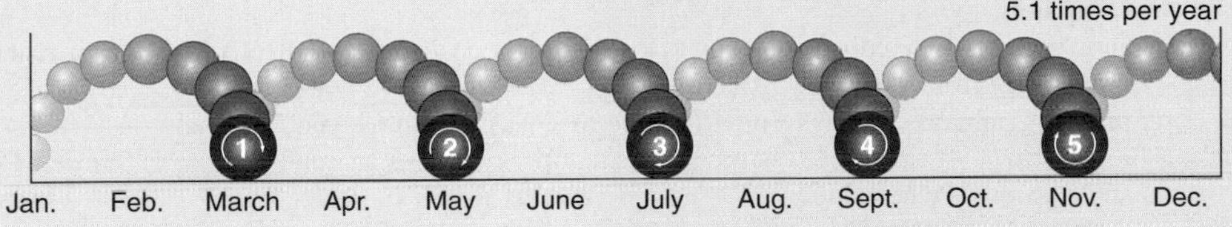

EXHIBIT 9.18

Rate of Accounts Receivable Turnover for TechCom

Accounts receivable turnover also reflects how well management is doing in granting credit to customers in a desire to increase sales. A high turnover in comparison with competitors suggests that management should consider using more liberal credit terms to increase sales. A low turnover suggests management should consider stricter credit terms and more aggressive collection efforts to avoid having its resources tied up in accounts receivable.

To illustrate, we take fiscal year data from two competitors: **Dell** and **Apple**. Exhibit 9.19 shows accounts receivable turnover for both companies.

Point: **Credit risk ratio** is computed by dividing the Allowance for Doubtful Accounts by Accounts Receivable. The higher this ratio, the higher is credit risk.

EXHIBIT 9.19

Analysis Using Accounts Receivable Turnover

Company	Figure ($ millions)	2008	2007	2006	2005
Dell	Net sales	$61,101	$61,133	$57,420	$55,788
	Average accounts receivable, net	$ 5,346	$ 5,292	$ 4,352	$ 3,826
	Accounts receivable turnover	**11.4**	**11.6**	**13.2**	**14.6**
Apple	Net sales	$32,479	$24,006	$19,315	$13,931
	Average accounts receivable, net	$ 2,030	$ 1,445	$ 1,074	$ 835
	Accounts receivable turnover	**16.0**	**16.6**	**18.0**	**16.7**

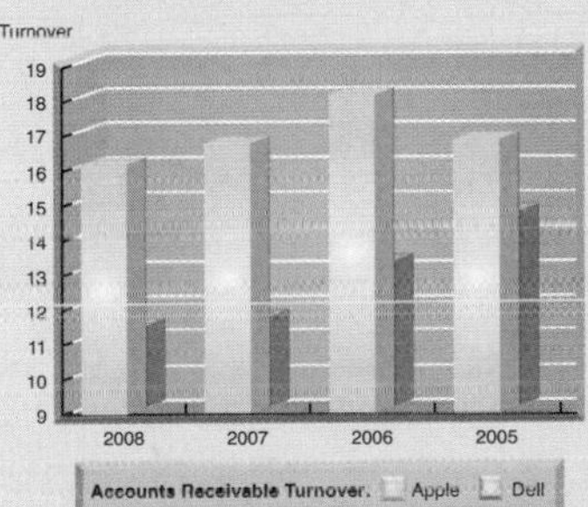

Dell's 2008 turnover is 11.4, computed as $61,101/$5,346 ($ millions). This means that Dell's average accounts receivable balance was converted into cash 11.4 times in 2008. Its turnover declined in 2008, as it has for each of the past 3 years. Apple's turnover exceeds that for Dell in each of the past 4 years. Is either company's turnover too high? Since sales are stable or markedly growing over this time period, each company's turnover rate does not appear to be too high. Instead, both Dell and Apple seem to be doing well in managing receivables. This is especially true given the recessionary period of 2008 and 2009. Turnover for competitors is generally in the range of 7 to 12 for this same period.[1]

Decision Maker Answer — p. 379

Family Physician Your medical practice is barely profitable, so you hire a health care analyst. The analyst highlights several points including the following: *"Accounts receivable turnover is too low. Tighter credit policies are recommended along with discontinuing service to those most delayed in payments."* How do you interpret these recommendations? What actions do you take? ■

DEMONSTRATION PROBLEM

Clayco Company completes the following selected transactions during year 2011.

July 14	Writes off a $750 account receivable arising from a sale to Briggs Company that dates to 10 months ago. (Clayco Company uses the allowance method.)
30	Clayco Company receives a $1,000, 90-day, 10% note in exchange for merchandise sold to Sumrell Company (the merchandise cost $600).
Aug. 15	Receives $2,000 cash plus a $10,000 note from JT Co. in exchange for merchandise that sells for $12,000 (its cost is $8,000). The note is dated August 15, bears 12% interest, and matures in 120 days.
Nov. 1	Completed a $200 credit card sale with a 4% fee (the cost of sales is $150). The cash is received immediately from the credit card company.
3	Sumrell Company refuses to pay the note that was due to Clayco Company on October 28. Prepare the journal entry to charge the dishonored note plus accrued interest to Sumrell Company's accounts receivable.
5	Completed a $500 credit card sale with a 5% fee (the cost of sales is $300). The payment from the credit card company is received on Nov. 9.
15	Received the full amount of $750 from Briggs Company that was previously written off on July 14. Record the bad debts recovery.
Dec. 13	Received payment of principal plus interest from JT for the August 15 note.

Required

1. Prepare journal entries to record these transactions on Clayco Company's books.
2. Prepare an adjusting journal entry as of December 31, 2011, assuming the following:
   a. Bad debts are estimated to be $20,400 by aging accounts receivable. The unadjusted balance of the Allowance for Doubtful Accounts is $1,000 debit.
   b. Alternatively, assume that bad debts are estimated using the percent of sales method. The Allowance for Doubtful Accounts had a $1,000 debit balance before adjustment, and the company estimates bad debts to be 1% of its credit sales of $2,000,000.

PLANNING THE SOLUTION

- Examine each transaction to determine the accounts affected, and then record the entries.
- For the year-end adjustment, record the bad debts expense for the two approaches.

[1] As an estimate of *average days' sales uncollected,* we compute how many days (*on average*) it takes to collect receivables as follows: 365 days ÷ accounts receivable turnover. An increase in this *average collection period* can signal a decline in customers' financial condition.

SOLUTION TO DEMONSTRATION PROBLEM

1.

July 14	Allowance for Doubtful Accounts	750	
	Accounts Receivable—Briggs Co.		750
	Wrote off an uncollectible account.		
July 30	Notes Receivable—Sumrell Co.	1,000	
	Sales		1,000
	Sold merchandise for a 90-day, 10% note.		
July 30	Cost of Goods Sold	600	
	Merchandise Inventory		600
	To record the cost of July 30 sale.		
Aug. 15	Cash	2,000	
	Notes Receivable—JT Co.	10,000	
	Sales		12,000
	Sold merchandise to customer for $2,000 cash and $10,000 note.		
Aug. 15	Cost of Goods Sold	8,000	
	Merchandise Inventory		8,000
	To record the cost of Aug. 15 sale.		
Nov. 1	Cash	192	
	Credit Card Expense	8	
	Sales		200
	To record credit card sale less a 4% credit card expense.		
Nov. 1	Cost of Goods Sold	150	
	Merchandise Inventory		150
	To record the cost of Nov. 1 sale.		
Nov. 3	Accounts Receivable—Sumrell Co.	1,025	
	Interest Revenue		25
	Notes Receivable—Sumrell Co.		1,000
	To charge account of Sumrell Company for a $1,000 dishonored note and interest of $1,000 × 10% × 90/360.		
Nov. 5	Accounts Receivable—Credit Card Co.	475	
	Credit Card Expense	25	
	Sales		500
	To record credit card sale less a 5% credit card expense.		
Nov. 5	Cost of Goods Sold	300	
	Merchandise Inventory		300
	To record the cost of Nov. 5 sale.		
Nov. 9	Cash	475	
	Accounts Receivable—Credit Card Co.		475
	To record cash receipt from Nov. 5 sale.		
Nov. 15	Accounts Receivable—Briggs Co.	750	
	Allowance for Doubtful Accounts		750
	To reinstate the account of Briggs Company previously written off.		
Nov. 15	Cash	750	
	Accounts Receivable—Briggs Co.		750
	Cash received in full payment of account.		
Dec. 13	Cash	10,400	
	Interest Revenue		400
	Note Receivable—JT Co.		10,000
	Collect note with interest of $10,000 × 12% × 120/360.		

2a. Aging of accounts receivable method.

Dec. 31	Bad Debts Expense	21,400	
	Allowance for Doubtful Accounts		21,400
	To adjust allowance account from a $1,000 debit balance to a $20,400 credit balance.		

2b. Percent of sales method.*

Dec. 31	Bad Debts Expense	20,000	
	Allowance for Doubtful Accounts		20,000
	To provide for bad debts as 1% × $2,000,000 in credit sales.		

* For the income statement approach, which requires estimating bad debts as a percent of sales or credit sales, the Allowance account balance is *not* considered when making the adjusting entry.

Summary

C1 Describe accounts receivable and how they occur and are recorded. Accounts receivable are amounts due from customers for credit sales. A subsidiary ledger lists amounts owed by each customer. Credit sales arise from at least two sources: (1) sales on credit and (2) credit card sales. *Sales on credit* refers to a company's granting credit directly to customers. Credit card sales involve customers' use of third-party credit cards.

C2 Describe a note receivable, the computation of its maturity date, and the recording of its existence. A note receivable is a written promise to pay a specified amount of money at a definite future date. The maturity date is the day the note (principal and interest) must be repaid. Interest rates are normally stated in annual terms. The amount of interest on the note is computed by expressing time as a fraction of one year and multiplying the note's principal by this fraction and the annual interest rate. A note received is recorded at its principal amount by debiting the Notes Receivable account. The credit amount is to the asset, product, or service provided in return for the note.

C3 Explain how receivables can be converted to cash before maturity. Receivables can be converted to cash before maturity in three ways. First, a company can sell accounts receivable to a factor, who charges a factoring fee. Second, a company can borrow money by signing a note payable that is secured by pledging the accounts receivable. Third, notes receivable can be discounted at (sold to) a financial institution.

A1 Compute accounts receivable turnover and use it to help assess financial condition. Accounts receivable turnover is a measure of both the quality and liquidity of accounts receivable. The accounts receivable turnover measure indicates how often, on average, receivables are received and collected during the period. Accounts receivable turnover is computed as net sales divided by average accounts receivable.

P1 Apply the direct write-off method to account for accounts receivable. The direct write-off method charges Bad Debts Expense when accounts are written off as uncollectible. This method is acceptable only when the amount of bad debts expense is immaterial.

P2 Apply the allowance method and estimate uncollectibles based on sales and accounts receivable. Under the allowance method, bad debts expense is recorded with an adjustment at the end of each accounting period that debits the Bad Debts Expense account and credits the Allowance for Doubtful Accounts. The uncollectible accounts are later written off with a debit to the Allowance for Doubtful Accounts. Uncollectibles are estimated by focusing on either (1) the income statement relation between bad debts expense and credit sales or (2) the balance sheet relation between accounts receivable and the allowance for doubtful accounts. The first approach emphasizes the matching principle using the income statement. The second approach emphasizes realizable value of accounts receivable using the balance sheet.

P3 Record the honoring and dishonoring of a note and adjustments for interest. When a note is honored, the payee debits the money received and credits both Notes Receivable and Interest Revenue. Dishonored notes are credited to Notes Receivable and debited to Accounts Receivable (to the account of the maker in an attempt to collect), and Interest Revenue is recorded for interest earned for the time the note is held.

Guidance Answers to Decision Maker and Decision Ethics

Entrepreneur Analysis of credit card sales should weigh the benefits against the costs. The primary benefit is the potential to increase sales by attracting customers who prefer the convenience of credit cards. The primary cost is the fee charged by the credit card company for providing this service. Analysis should therefore estimate the expected increase in dollar sales from allowing credit card sales and then subtract (1) the normal costs and expenses and (2) the credit card fees associated with this expected increase in dollar sales. If your analysis shows an increase in profit from allowing credit card sales, your store should probably accept them.

Labor Union Chief Yes, this information is likely to impact your negotiations. The obvious question is why the company markedly increased this allowance. The large increase in this allowance means a substantial increase in bad debts expense *and* a decrease in earnings. This change (coming immediately prior to labor contract discussions) also raises concerns since it reduces the union's bargaining power for increased compensation. You want to ask management for supporting documentation justifying this increase. You also want data for two or three prior years and similar data from competitors. These data should give you some sense of whether the change in the allowance for uncollectibles is justified.

Family Physician The recommendations are twofold. First, the analyst suggests more stringent screening of patients' credit standing. Second, the analyst suggests dropping patients who are most overdue in payments. You are likely bothered by both suggestions. They are probably financially wise recommendations, but you are troubled by eliminating services to those less able to pay. One alternative is to follow the recommendations while implementing a care program directed at patients less able to pay for services. This allows you to continue services to patients less able to pay and lets you discontinue services to patients able but unwilling to pay.

Guidance Answers to Quick Checks

1. If cash is immediately received when credit card sales receipts are deposited, the company debits Cash at the time of sale. If the company does not receive payment until after it submits receipts to the credit card company, it debits Accounts Receivable at the time of sale. (Cash is later debited when payment is received from the credit card company.)
2. Credit card expenses are usually *recorded* and *incurred* at the time of their related sales, not when cash is received from the credit card company.
3. If possible, bad debts expense must be matched with the sales that gave rise to the accounts receivable. This requires that companies estimate future bad debts at the end of each period before they learn which accounts are uncollectible.
4. Realizable value (also called *net realizable value*).
5. The estimated amount of bad debts expense cannot be credited to the Accounts Receivable account because the specific customer accounts that will prove uncollectible cannot yet be identified and removed from the accounts receivable subsidiary ledger. Moreover, if only the Accounts Receivable account is credited, its balance would not equal the sum of its subsidiary account balances.
6.

Dec. 31	Bad Debts Expense	5,702	
	Allowance for Doubtful Accounts		5,702

7.

Jan. 10	Allowance for Doubtful Accounts	300	
	Accounts Receivable—Cool Jam		300
Apr. 12	Accounts Receivable—Cool Jam	300	
	Allowance for Doubtful Accounts		300
Apr. 12	Cash	300	
	Accounts Receivable—Cool Jam		300

8.

Dec. 16	Note Receivable—Irwin	7,000	
	Sales		7,000
Dec. 31	Interest Receivable	35	
	Interest Revenue		35
	($7,000 × 12% × 15/360)		

9.

Mar. 16	Accounts Receivable—Irwin	7,210	
	Interest Revenue		175
	Interest Receivable		35
	Notes Receivable—Irwin		7,000

Key Terms

mhhe.com/wildFAP20e

Accounts receivable (p. 360)
Accounts receivable turnover (p. 375)
Aging of accounts receivable (p. 368)
Allowance for Doubtful Accounts (p. 365)
Allowance method (p. 364)
Bad debts (p. 363)
Direct write-off method (p. 363)
Interest (p. 370)
Maker of the note (p. 370)
Matching (expense recognition) principle (p. 364)
Materiality constraint (p. 364)
Maturity date of a note (p. 370)
Payee of the note (p. 370)
Principal of a note (p. 370)
Promissory note (or note) (p. 370)
Realizable value (p. 365)

Multiple Choice Quiz

Answers on p. 391

mhhe.com/wildFAP20e

Additional Quiz Questions are available at the book's Website.

1. A company's Accounts Receivable balance at its December 31 year-end is $125,650, and its Allowance for Doubtful Accounts has a credit balance of $328 before year-end adjustment. Its net sales are $572,300. It estimates that 4% of outstanding accounts receivable are uncollectible. What amount of Bad Debts Expense is recorded at December 31?
   a. $5,354
   b. $328
   c. $5,026
   d. $4,698
   e. $34,338
2. A company's Accounts Receivable balance at its December 31 year-end is $489,300, and its Allowance for Doubtful Accounts has a debit balance of $554 before year-end adjustment. Its net sales are $1,300,000. It estimates that 6% of outstanding accounts receivable are uncollectible. What amount of Bad Debts Expense is recorded at December 31?
   a. $29,912
   b. $28,804
   c. $78,000
   d. $29,358
   e. $554
3. Total interest to be earned on a $7,500, 5%, 90-day note is
   a. $93.75
   b. $375.00
   c. $1,125.00
   d. $31.25
   e. $125.00
4. A company receives a $9,000, 8%, 60-day note. The maturity value of the note is
   a. $120
   b. $9,000
   c. $9,120
   d. $720
   e. $9,720
5. A company has net sales of $489,600 and average accounts receivable of $40,800. What is its accounts receivable turnover?
   a. 0.08
   b. 30.41
   c. 1,341.00
   d. 12.00
   e. 111.78

[I] Icon denotes assignments that involve decision making.

Discussion Questions

1. [I] How do sellers benefit from allowing their customers to use credit cards?
2. [I] Why does the direct write-off method of accounting for bad debts usually fail to match revenues and expenses?
3. Explain the accounting constraint of materiality.
4. Explain why writing off a bad debt against the Allowance for Doubtful Accounts does not reduce the estimated realizable value of a company's accounts receivable.
5. [I] Why does the Bad Debts Expense account usually not have the same adjusted balance as the Allowance for Doubtful Accounts?
6. Why might a business prefer a note receivable to an account receivable?
7. [I] Refer to the financial statements and notes of **Research In Motion** in Appendix A. In its presentation of accounts receivable on the balance sheet, how does it title accounts receivable? What does it report for its allowance as of February 27, 2010? RIM
8. [I] Refer to the balance sheet of **Apple** in Appendix A. Does it use the direct write-off method or allowance method in accounting for its Accounts Receivable? What is the realizable value of its receivable's balance as of September 26, 2009? Apple
9. Refer to the financial statements of **Palm** in Appendix A. What are Palm's gross accounts receivable at May 31, 2009? What percentage of its accounts receivable does it believe to be uncollectible at this date? Palm
10. Refer to the December 31, 2009, financial statements of **Nokia** in Appendix A. What does it title its accounts receivable on its statement of financial position? What percent of its accounts receivable does it believe to be uncollectible? NOKIA

connect

QUICK STUDY

QS 9-1
Credit card sales
C1

Prepare journal entries for the following credit card sales transactions (the company uses the perpetual inventory system).

1. Sold $10,000 of merchandise, that cost $7,500, on MasterCard credit cards. The net cash receipts from sales are immediately deposited in the seller's bank account. MasterCard charges a 5% fee.
2. Sold $3,000 of merchandise, that cost $1,500, on an assortment of credit cards. Net cash receipts are received 7 days later, and a 4% fee is charged.

QS 9-2
Allowance method for bad debts
P2

Milner Corp. uses the allowance method to account for uncollectibles. On October 31, it wrote off a $1,000 account of a customer, C. Schaub. On December 9, it receives a $200 payment from Schaub.

1. Prepare the journal entry or entries for October 31.
2. Prepare the journal entry or entries for December 9; assume no additional money is expected from Schaub.

QS 9-3
Percent of accounts receivable method
P2

Wecker Company's year-end unadjusted trial balance shows accounts receivable of $89,000, allowance for doubtful accounts of $500 (credit), and sales of $270,000. Uncollectibles are estimated to be 1.5% of accounts receivable.

1. Prepare the December 31 year-end adjusting entry for uncollectibles.
2. What amount would have been used in the year-end adjusting entry if the allowance account had a year-end unadjusted debit balance of $200?

QS 9-4
Percent of sales method P2

Assume the same facts as in QS 9-3, except that Wecker estimates uncollectibles as 1.0% of sales. Prepare the December 31 year-end adjusting entry for uncollectibles.

QS 9-5
Note receivable C2

On August 2, 2011, JLK Co. receives a $5,500, 90-day, 12% note from customer Tom Menke as payment on his $9,000 account. (1) Compute the maturity date for this note. (2) Prepare JLK's journal entry for August 2.

QS 9-6
Note receivable P3

Refer to the information in QS 9-5 and prepare the journal entry assuming the note is honored by the customer on October 31, 2011.

QS 9-7
Note receivable P3

Dekon Company's December 31 year-end unadjusted trial balance shows a $8,000 balance in Notes Receivable. This balance is from one 6% note dated December 1, with a period of 45 days. Prepare any necessary journal entries for December 31 and for the note's maturity date assuming it is honored.

QS 9-8
Disposing receivables C3

Record the sale by Kroll Company of $1,000 in accounts receivable on May 1. Kroll is charged a 3% factoring fee.

QS 9-9
Direct write-off method P1

Krugg Company determines on May 1 that it cannot collect $1,000 of its accounts receivable from its customer P. Carroll. Apply the direct write-off method to record this loss as of May 1.

QS 9-10
Recovering a bad debt P1

Refer to the information in QS 9-9. On May 30, P. Carroll unexpectedly paid his account in full to Krugg Company. Record Krugg's entry(ies) to reflect this recovery of this bad debt.

QS 9-11
Accounts receivable turnover
A1 

The following data are taken from the comparative balance sheets of Fulton Company. Compute and interpret its accounts receivable turnover for year 2011 (competitors average a turnover of 7.5).

	2011	2010
Accounts receivable, net	$152,900	$133,700
Net sales	754,200	810,600

QS 9-12
International accounting standards
C1 

Answer each of the following related to international accounting standards.

a. Explain (in general terms) how the accounting for recognition of receivables is different between IFRS and U.S. GAAP.
b. Explain (in general terms) how the accounting for valuation of receivables is different between IFRS and U.S. GAAP.

connect

EXERCISES

Exercise 9-1
Accounting for credit card sales
C1

Petri Company uses the perpetual inventory system and allows customers to use two credit cards in charging purchases. With the Omni Bank Card, Petri receives an immediate credit to its account when it deposits sales receipts. Omni assesses a 4% service charge for credit card sales. The second credit card that Petri accepts is the Continental Card. Petri sends its accumulated receipts to Continental on a weekly basis and is paid by Continental about a week later. Continental assesses a 2.5% charge on sales for using its card. Prepare journal entries to record the following selected credit card transactions of Petri Company.

Apr. 8 Sold merchandise for $9,200 (that had cost $6,800) and accepted the customer's Omni Bank Card. The Omni receipts are immediately deposited in Petri's bank account.
12 Sold merchandise for $5,400 (that had cost $3,500) and accepted the customer's Continental Card. Transferred $5,400 of credit card receipts to Continental, requesting payment.
20 Received Continental's check for the April 12 billing, less the service charge.

Exercise 9-2
Accounts receivable subsidiary ledger; schedule of accounts receivable
C1

Sami Company recorded the following selected transactions during November 2011.

Date	Account	Debit	Credit
Nov. 5	Accounts Receivable—Surf Shop	4,417	
	Sales		4,417
10	Accounts Receivable—Yum Enterprises	1,250	
	Sales		1,250
13	Accounts Receivable—Matt Albin	733	
	Sales		733
21	Sales Returns and Allowances	189	
	Accounts Receivable—Matt Albin		189
30	Accounts Receivable—Surf Shop	2,606	
	Sales		2,606

1. Open a general ledger having T-accounts for Accounts Receivable, Sales, and Sales Returns and Allowances. Also open an accounts receivable subsidiary ledger having a T-account for each customer. Post these entries to both the general ledger and the accounts receivable ledger.
2. Prepare a schedule of accounts receivable (see Exhibit 9.4) and compare its total with the balance of the Accounts Receivable controlling account as of November 30.

Check Accounts Receivable ending balance, $8,817

Exercise 9-3
Direct write-off method
P1

Diablo Company applies the direct write-off method in accounting for uncollectible accounts. Prepare journal entries to record the following selected transactions of Diablo.

June 11 Diablo determines that it cannot collect $9,000 of its accounts receivable from its customer Chaffey Company.
29 Chaffey Company unexpectedly pays its account in full to Diablo Company. Diablo records its recovery of this bad debt.

Exercise 9-4
Percent of sales method; write-off
P2

At year-end (December 31), Alvare Company estimates its bad debts as 0.5% of its annual credit sales of $875,000. Alvare records its Bad Debts Expense for that estimate. On the following February 1, Alvare decides that the $420 account of P. Coble is uncollectible and writes it off as a bad debt. On June 5, Coble unexpectedly pays the amount previously written off. Prepare the journal entries of Alvare to record these transactions and events of December 31, February 1, and June 5.

Exercise 9-5
Percent of accounts receivable method
P2

At each calendar year-end, Cabool Supply Co. uses the percent of accounts receivable method to estimate bad debts. On December 31, 2011, it has outstanding accounts receivable of $53,000, and it estimates that 4% will be uncollectible. Prepare the adjusting entry to record bad debts expense for year 2011 under the assumption that the Allowance for Doubtful Accounts has (*a*) a $915 credit balance before the adjustment and (*b*) a $1,332 debit balance before the adjustment.

Exercise 9-6
Aging of receivables method
P2

Hecter Company estimates uncollectible accounts using the allowance method at December 31. It prepared the following aging of receivables analysis.

		Days Past Due				
	Total	0	1 to 30	31 to 60	61 to 90	Over 90
Accounts receivable	$190,000	$132,000	$30,000	$12,000	$6,000	$10,000
Percent uncollectible		1%	2%	4%	7%	12%

a. Estimate the balance of the Allowance for Doubtful Accounts using the aging of accounts receivable method.

b. Prepare the adjusting entry to record Bad Debts Expense using the estimate from part *a*. Assume the unadjusted balance in the Allowance for Doubtful Accounts is a $600 credit.

c. Prepare the adjusting entry to record Bad Debts Expense using the estimate from part *a*. Assume the unadjusted balance in the Allowance for Doubtful Accounts is a $400 debit.

Exercise 9-7
Percent of receivables method
P2

Refer to the information in Exercise 9-6 to complete the following requirements.

a. Estimate the balance of the Allowance for Doubtful Accounts assuming the company uses 3.5% of total accounts receivable to estimate uncollectibles, instead of the aging of receivables method.

b. Prepare the adjusting entry to record Bad Debts Expense using the estimate from part *a*. Assume the unadjusted balance in the Allowance for Doubtful Accounts is a $300 credit.

c. Prepare the adjusting entry to record Bad Debts Expense using the estimate from part *a*. Assume the unadjusted balance in the Allowance for Doubtful Accounts is a $200 debit.

Exercise 9-8
Writing off receivables
P2

Refer to the information in Exercise 9-6 to complete the following requirements.

a. On February 1 of the next period, the company determined that $1,900 in customer accounts is uncollectible; specifically, $400 for Oxford Co. and $1,500 for Brookes Co. Prepare the journal entry to write off those accounts.

b. On June 5 of that next period, the company unexpectedly received a $400 payment on a customer account, Oxford Company, that had previously been written off in part *a*. Prepare the entries necessary to reinstate the account and to record the cash received.

Exercise 9-9
Estimating bad debts
P2

At December 31, GreenTea Company reports the following results for its calendar-year.

Cash sales	$1,200,000
Credit sales	900,000

Its year-end unadjusted trial balance includes the following items.

Accounts receivable	$195,000 debit
Allowance for doubtful accounts	3,000 debit

a. Prepare the adjusting entry to record Bad Debts Expense assuming uncollectibles are estimated to be 1.5% of credit sales.

Check Dr. Bad Debts Expense: (*a*) $13,500

b. Prepare the adjusting entry to record Bad Debts Expense assuming uncollectibles are estimated to be 0.5% of total sales.

c. Prepare the adjusting entry to record Bad Debts Expense assuming uncollectibles are estimated to be 6% of year-end accounts receivable.

(*c*) $14,700

Exercise 9-10
Selling and pledging accounts receivable
C3

On June 30, Roman Co. has $125,900 of accounts receivable. Prepare journal entries to record the following selected July transactions. Also prepare any footnotes to the July 31 financial statements that result from these transactions. (The company uses the perpetual inventory system.)

July	4	Sold $6,295 of merchandise (that had cost $4,000) to customers on credit.
	9	Sold $18,000 of accounts receivable to Center Bank. Center charges a 4% factoring fee.
	17	Received $3,436 cash from customers in payment on their accounts.
	27	Borrowed $10,000 cash from Center Bank, pledging $13,000 of accounts receivable as security for the loan.

Exercise 9-11
Honoring a note
P3

Prepare journal entries to record these selected transactions for Eduardo Company.

Nov.	1	Accepted a $5,000, 180-day, 6% note dated November 1 from Melosa Allen in granting a time extension on her past-due account receivable.
Dec.	31	Adjusted the year-end accounts for the accrued interest earned on the Allen note.
Apr.	30	Allen honors her note when presented for payment; February has 28 days for the current year.

Exercise 9-12
Dishonoring a note
P3

Prepare journal entries to record the following selected transactions of Paloma Company.

Mar. 21	Accepted a $3,100, 180-day, 10% note dated March 21 from Salma Hernandez in granting a time extension on her past-due account receivable.
Sept. 17	Hernandez dishonors her note when it is presented for payment.
Dec. 31	After exhausting all legal means of collection, Paloma Company writes off Hernandez's account against the Allowance for Doubtful Accounts.

Exercise 9-13
Notes receivable transactions
C2

Check Dec. 31, Cr. Interest Revenue $40

Prepare journal entries for the following selected transactions of Deshawn Company for 2010.

2010

Dec. 13	Accepted a $10,000, 45-day, 8% note dated December 13 in granting Latisha Clark a time extension on her past-due account receivable.
31	Prepared an adjusting entry to record the accrued interest on the Clark note.

Exercise 9-14
Notes receivable transactions
P3

Check Jan. 27, Dr. Cash $10,100
June 1, Dr. Cash $4,100

Refer to the information in Exercise 9-13 and prepare the journal entries for the following selected transactions of Deshawn Company for 2011.

2011

Jan. 27	Received Clark's payment for principal and interest on the note dated December 13.
Mar. 3	Accepted a $4,000, 10%, 90-day note dated March 3 in granting a time extension on the past-due account receivable of Shandi Company.
17	Accepted a $2,000, 30-day, 9% note dated March 17 in granting Juan Torres a time extension on his past-due account receivable.
Apr. 16	Torres dishonors his note when presented for payment.
May 1	Wrote off the Torres account against the Allowance for Doubtful Accounts.
June 1	Received the Shandi payment for principal and interest on the note dated March 3.

Exercise 9-15
Accounts receivable turnover
A1

The following information is from the annual financial statements of Waseem Company. Compute its accounts receivable turnover for 2010 and 2011. Compare the two years results and give a possible explanation for any change (competitors average a turnover of 11).

	2011	2010	2009
Net sales	$305,000	$236,000	$288,000
Accounts receivable, net (year-end)	22,900	20,700	17,400

Exercise 9-16
Accounting for bad debts following IFRS
P2

Hitachi, Ltd., reports total revenues of ¥10,000,369 million for its fiscal year ending March 31, 2009, and its March 31, 2009, unadjusted trial balance reports a debit balance for trade receivables (gross) of ¥2,179,764 million.

a. Prepare the adjusting entry to record its Bad Debts Expense assuming uncollectibles are estimated to be 0.4% of total revenues and its unadjusted trial balance reports a credit balance of ¥10,000 million.

b. Prepare the adjusting entry to record Bad Debts Expense assuming uncollectibles are estimated to be 2.1% of year-end trade receivables (gross) and its unadjusted trial balance reports a credit balance of ¥10,000 million.

connect

PROBLEM SET A

Problem 9-1A
Sales on account and credit card sales
C1

Atlas Co. allows select customers to make purchases on credit. Its other customers can use either of two credit cards: Zisa or Access. Zisa deducts a 3% service charge for sales on its credit card and credits the bank account of Atlas immediately when credit card receipts are deposited. Atlas deposits the Zisa credit card receipts each business day. When customers use Access credit cards, Atlas accumulates the receipts for several days before submitting them to Access for payment. Access deducts a 2% service charge and usually pays within one week of being billed. Atlas completes the following transactions in June. (The terms of all credit sales are 2/15, n/30, and all sales are recorded at the gross price.)

June 4	Sold $750 of merchandise (that had cost $500) on credit to Anne Cianci.
5	Sold $5,900 of merchandise (that had cost $3,200) to customers who used their Zisa cards.

6 Sold $4,800 of merchandise (that had cost $2,800) to customers who used their Access cards.
8 Sold $3,200 of merchandise (that had cost $1,900) to customers who used their Access cards.
10 Submitted Access card receipts accumulated since June 6 to the credit card company for payment.
13 Wrote off the account of Nakia Wells against the Allowance for Doubtful Accounts. The $329 balance in Wells's account stemmed from a credit sale in October of last year.
17 Received the amount due from Access.
18 Received Cianci's check in full payment for the purchase of June 4.

Check June 17, Dr. Cash $7,840

Required

Prepare journal entries to record the preceding transactions and events. (The company uses the perpetual inventory system. Round amounts to the nearest dollar.)

Problem 9-2A
Accounts receivable transactions and bad debts adjustments
C1 P2

Lopez Company began operations on January 1, 2010. During its first two years, the company completed a number of transactions involving sales on credit, accounts receivable collections, and bad debts. These transactions are summarized as follows.

2010

a. Sold $1,803,750 of merchandise (that had cost $1,475,000) on credit, terms n/30.
b. Wrote off $20,300 of uncollectible accounts receivable.
c. Received $789,200 cash in payment of accounts receivable.
d. In adjusting the accounts on December 31, the company estimated that 1.5% of accounts receivable will be uncollectible.

Check (*d*) Dr. Bad Debts Expense $35,214

2011

e. Sold $1,825,700 of merchandise (that had cost $1,450,000) on credit, terms n/30.
f. Wrote off $28,800 of uncollectible accounts receivable.
g. Received $1,304,800 cash in payment of accounts receivable.
h. In adjusting the accounts on December 31, the company estimated that 1.5% of accounts receivable will be uncollectible.

(*h*) Dr. Bad Debts Expense $36,181

Required

Prepare journal entries to record Lopez's 2010 and 2011 summarized transactions and its year-end adjustments to record bad debts expense. (The company uses the perpetual inventory system. Round amounts to the nearest dollar.)

Problem 9-3A
Estimating and reporting bad debts
P2 

At December 31, 2011, Ethan Company reports the following results for its calendar-year.

Cash sales	$1,803,750
Credit sales	3,534,000

In addition, its unadjusted trial balance includes the following items.

Accounts receivable	$1,070,100 debit
Allowance for doubtful accounts	15,750 debit

Required

1. Prepare the adjusting entry for this company to recognize bad debts under each of the following independent assumptions.
   a. Bad debts are estimated to be 2% of credit sales.
   b. Bad debts are estimated to be 1% of total sales.
   c. An aging analysis estimates that 5% of year-end accounts receivable are uncollectible.
2. Show how Accounts Receivable and the Allowance for Doubtful Accounts appear on its December 31, 2011, balance sheet given the facts in part 1*a*.
3. Show how Accounts Receivable and the Allowance for Doubtful Accounts appear on its December 31, 2011, balance sheet given the facts in part 1*c*.

Check Bad Debts Expense: (1*a*) $70,680, (1*c*) $69,255

Problem 9-4A
Aging accounts receivable and accounting for bad debts
P2 

Carmack Company has credit sales of $2.6 million for year 2011. On December 31, 2011, the company's Allowance for Doubtful Accounts has an unadjusted credit balance of $13,400. Carmack prepares a schedule of its December 31, 2011, accounts receivable by age. On the basis of past experience, it estimates the percent of receivables in each age category that will become uncollectible. This information is summarized here.

December 31, 2011 Accounts Receivable	Age of Accounts Receivable	Expected Percent Uncollectible
$730,000	Not yet due	1.25%
354,000	1 to 30 days past due	2.00
76,000	31 to 60 days past due	6.50
48,000	61 to 90 days past due	32.75
12,000	Over 90 days past due	68.00

Required

1. Estimate the required balance of the Allowance for Doubtful Accounts at December 31, 2011, using the aging of accounts receivable method.
2. Prepare the adjusting entry to record bad debts expense at December 31, 2011.

Check (2) Dr. Bad Debts Expense $31,625

Analysis Component

3. On June 30, 2012, Carmack Company concludes that a customer's $3,750 receivable (created in 2011) is uncollectible and that the account should be written off. What effect will this action have on Carmack's 2012 net income? Explain.

Problem 9-5A
Analyzing and journalizing notes receivable transactions
C2 C3 P3

The following selected transactions are from Ohlde Company.

2010

Dec. 16 Accepted a $9,600, 60-day, 9% note dated this day in granting Todd Duke a time extension on his past-due account receivable.
31 Made an adjusting entry to record the accrued interest on the Duke note.

2011

Feb. 14 Received Duke's payment of principal and interest on the note dated December 16.
Mar. 2 Accepted an $4,120, 8%, 90-day note dated this day in granting a time extension on the past-due account receivable from Mare Co.
17 Accepted a $2,400, 30-day, 7% note dated this day in granting Jolene Halaam a time extension on her past-due account receivable.
Apr. 16 Halaam dishonored her note when presented for payment.
June 2 Mare Co. refuses to pay the note that was due to Ohlde Co. on May 31. Prepare the journal entry to charge the dishonored note plus accrued interest to Mare Co.'s accounts receivable.
July 17 Received payment from Mare Co. for the maturity value of its dishonored note plus interest for 46 days beyond maturity at 8%.
Aug. 7 Accepted an $5,440, 90-day, 10% note dated this day in granting a time extension on the past-due account receivable of Birch and Byer Co.
Sept. 3 Accepted a $2,080, 60-day, 10% note dated this day in granting Kevin York a time extension on his past-due account receivable.
Nov. 2 Received payment of principal plus interest from York for the September 3 note.
Nov. 5 Received payment of principal plus interest from Birch and Byer for the August 7 note.
Dec. 1 Wrote off the Jolene Halaam account against Allowance for Doubtful Accounts.

Check Feb. 14, Cr. Interest Revenue $108

June 2, Cr. Interest Revenue $82

Nov. 2, Cr. Interest Revenue $35

Required

1. Prepare journal entries to record these transactions and events. (Round amounts to the nearest dollar.)

Analysis Component

2. What reporting is necessary when a business pledges receivables as security for a loan and the loan is still outstanding at the end of the period? Explain the reason for this requirement and the accounting principle being satisfied.

PROBLEM SET B

Problem 9-1B
Sales on account and credit card sales
C1

Able Co. allows select customers to make purchases on credit. Its other customers can use either of two credit cards: Commerce Bank or Aztec. Commerce Bank deducts a 3% service charge for sales on its credit card and immediately credits the bank account of Able when credit card receipts are deposited. Able deposits the Commerce Bank credit card receipts each business day. When customers use the Aztec card, Able accumulates the receipts for several days and then submits them to Aztec for payment. Aztec deducts a 2% service charge and usually pays within one week of being billed. Able completed the following transactions in August (terms of all credit sales are 2/10, n/30; and all sales are recorded at the gross price).

Aug. 4 Sold $2,780 of merchandise (that had cost $1,750) on credit to Stacy Dalton.
10 Sold $3,248 of merchandise (that had cost $2,456) to customers who used their Commerce Bank credit cards.
11 Sold $1,575 of merchandise (that had cost $1,150) to customers who used their Aztec cards.
14 Received Dalton's check in full payment for the purchase of August 4.
15 Sold $2,960 of merchandise (that had cost $1,758) to customers who used their Aztec cards.
18 Submitted Aztec card receipts accumulated since August 11 to the credit card company for payment.
22 Wrote off the account of Ness City against the Allowance for Doubtful Accounts. The $398 balance in Ness City's account stemmed from a credit sale in November of last year.
25 Received the amount due from Aztec.

Check Aug. 25, Dr. Cash $4,444

Required

Prepare journal entries to record the preceding transactions and events. (The company uses the perpetual inventory system. Round amounts to the nearest dollar.)

Problem 9-2B
Accounts receivable transactions and bad debts adjustments
C1 P2

Practice

Crist Co. began operations on January 1, 2010, and completed several transactions during 2010 and 2011 that involved sales on credit, accounts receivable collections, and bad debts. These transactions are summarized as follows.

2010

a. Sold $673,490 of merchandise (that had cost $500,000) on credit, terms n/30.
b. Received $437,250 cash in payment of accounts receivable.
c. Wrote off $8,330 of uncollectible accounts receivable.
d. In adjusting the accounts on December 31, the company estimated that 1% of accounts receivable will be uncollectible.

Check (*d*) Dr. Bad Debts Expense $10,609

2011

e. Sold $930,100 of merchandise (that had cost $650,000) on credit, terms n/30.
f. Received $890,220 cash in payment of accounts receivable.
g. Wrote off $10,090 of uncollectible accounts receivable.
h. In adjusting the accounts on December 31, the company estimated that 1% of accounts receivable will be uncollectible.

(*h*) Dr. Bad Debts Expense $10,388

Required

Prepare journal entries to record Crist's 2010 and 2011 summarized transactions and its year-end adjusting entry to record bad debts expense. (The company uses the perpetual inventory system. Round amounts to the nearest dollar.)

Problem 9-3B
Estimating and reporting bad debts
P2  

At December 31, 2011, Klimck Company reports the following results for the year.

Cash sales	$1,015,000
Credit sales	1,241,000

In addition, its unadjusted trial balance includes the following items.

Accounts receivable	$475,000 debit
Allowance for doubtful accounts	5,200 credit

Required

1. Prepare the adjusting entry for Klimek Co. to recognize bad debts under each of the following independent assumptions.
   a. Bad debts are estimated to be 2.5% of credit sales.
   b. Bad debts are estimated to be 1.5% of total sales.
   c. An aging analysis estimates that 6% of year-end accounts receivable are uncollectible.
2. Show how Accounts Receivable and the Allowance for Doubtful Accounts appear on its December 31, 2011, balance sheet given the facts in part 1*a*.
3. Show how Accounts Receivable and the Allowance for Doubtful Accounts appear on its December 31, 2011, balance sheet given the facts in part 1*c*.

Check Bad debts expense: (1*b*) $33,840, (1*c*) $23,300

Problem 9-4B
Aging accounts receivable and accounting for bad debts
P2 

Quisp Company has credit sales of $3.5 million for year 2011. At December 31, 2011, the company's Allowance for Doubtful Accounts has an unadjusted debit balance of $4,100. Quisp prepares a schedule of its December 31, 2011, accounts receivable by age. On the basis of past experience, it estimates the percent of receivables in each age category that will become uncollectible. This information is summarized here.

December 31, 2011 Accounts Receivable	Age of Accounts Receivable	Expected Percent Uncollectible
$296,400	Not yet due	2.0%
177,800	1 to 30 days past due	4.0
58,000	31 to 60 days past due	8.5
7,600	61 to 90 days past due	39.0
3,700	Over 90 days past due	82.0

Required

1. Compute the required balance of the Allowance for Doubtful Accounts at December 31, 2011, using the aging of accounts receivable method.
2. Prepare the adjusting entry to record bad debts expense at December 31, 2011.

Check (2) Dr. Bad Debts Expense $28,068

Analysis Component

3. On July 31, 2012, Quisp concludes that a customer's $2,345 receivable (created in 2011) is uncollectible and that the account should be written off. What effect will this action have on Quisp's 2012 net income? Explain.

Problem 9-5B
Analyzing and journalizing notes receivable transactions

The following selected transactions are from Seeker Company.

2010

Nov.	1	Accepted a $4,800, 90-day, 8% note dated this day in granting Julie Stephens a time extension on her past-due account receivable.
Dec.	31	Made an adjusting entry to record the accrued interest on the Stephens note.

2011

Jan.	30	Received Stephens's payment for principal and interest on the note dated November 1.
Feb.	28	Accepted a $12,600, 6%, 30-day note dated this day in granting a time extension on the past-due account receivable from Kramer Co.
Mar.	1	Accepted a $6,200, 60-day, 8% note dated this day in granting Shelly Myers a time extension on her past-due account receivable.
	30	The Kramer Co. dishonored its note when presented for payment.
April	30	Received payment of principal plus interest from Myers for the March 1 note.
June	15	Accepted a $2,000, 60-day, 10% note dated this day in granting a time extension on the past-due account receivable of Rhonda Rye.
	21	Accepted a $9,500, 90-day, 12% note dated this day in granting J. Striker a time extension on his past-due account receivable.
Aug.	14	Received payment of principal plus interest from R. Rye for the note of June 15.
Sep.	19	Received payment of principal plus interest from J. Striker for the June 21 note.
Nov.	30	Wrote off Kramer's account against Allowance for Doubtful Accounts.

Check Jan. 30, Cr. Interest Revenue $32

April 30, Cr. Interest Revenue $83

Sep. 19, Cr. Interest Revenue $285

Required

1. Prepare journal entries to record these transactions and events. (Round amounts to the nearest dollar.)

Analysis Component

2. What reporting is necessary when a business pledges receivables as security for a loan and the loan is still outstanding at the end of the period? Explain the reason for this requirement and the accounting principle being satisfied.

SERIAL PROBLEM

Business Solutions

P1 P2

(This serial problem began in Chapter 1 and continues through most of the book. If previous chapter segments were not completed, the serial problem can begin at this point. It is helpful, but not necessary, to use the Working Papers that accompany the book.)

SP 9 Santana Rey, owner of Business Solutions, realizes that she needs to begin accounting for bad debts expense. Assume that Business Solutions has total revenues of $44,000 during the first three months of 2012, and that the Accounts Receivable balance on March 31, 2012, is $22,867.

Required

1. Prepare the adjusting entry needed for Business Solutions to recognize bad debts expense on March 31, 2012, under each of the following independent assumptions (assume a zero unadjusted balance in the Allowance for Doubtful Accounts at March 31).
   - **a.** Bad debts are estimated to be 1% of total revenues. (Round amounts to the dollar.)
   - **b.** Bad debts are estimated to be 2% of accounts receivable. (Round amounts to the dollar.)
2. Assume that Business Solutions' Accounts Receivable balance at June 30, 2012, is $20,250 and that one account of $100 has been written off against the Allowance for Doubtful Accounts since March 31, 2012. If S. Rey uses the method prescribed in Part 1*b*, what adjusting journal entry must be made to recognize bad debts expense on June 30, 2012?
3. Should S. Rey consider adopting the direct write-off method of accounting for bad debts expense rather than one of the allowance methods considered in part 1? Explain.

Check (2) Bad Debts Expense, $48

Beyond the Numbers

REPORTING IN ACTION

A1

RIM

BTN 9-1 Refer to **Research In Motion**'s financial statements in Appendix A to answer the following.

1. What is the amount of Research In Motion's accounts receivable as of February 27, 2010?
2. Compute Research In Motion's accounts receivable turnover as of February 27, 2010.
3. How long does it take, *on average*, for the company to collect receivables? Do you believe that customers actually pay the amounts due within this short period? Explain.
4. Research In Motion's most liquid assets include (*a*) cash and cash equivalents, (*b*) short-term investments, and (*c*) receivables. Compute the percentage that these liquid assets make up of current liabilities as of February 27, 2010. Do the same computations for February 28, 2009. Comment on the company's ability to satisfy its current liabilities as of its 2010 fiscal year-end compared to its 2009 fiscal year-end.
5. What criteria did Research In Motion use to classify items as cash equivalents?

Fast Forward

6. Access Research In Motion's financial statements for fiscal years after February 27, 2010, at its Website (www.RIM.com) or the SEC's EDGAR database (www.SEC.gov). Recompute parts 2 and 4 and comment on any changes since February 27, 2010.

COMPARATIVE ANALYSIS

A1 P2 

RIM

Apple

BTN 9-2 Comparative figures for **Research In Motion** and **Apple** follow.

	Research In Motion			Apple		
($ millions)	Current Year	One Year Prior	Two Years Prior	Current Year	One Year Prior	Two Years Prior
Accounts receivable, net	$ 2,594	$ 2,112	$1,175	$ 3,361	$ 2,422	$ 1,637
Net sales	14,953	11,065	6,009	42,905	37,491	24,578

Required

1. Compute the accounts receivable turnover for Research In Motion and Apple for each of the two most recent years using the data shown.
2. Using results from part 1, compute how many days it takes each company, *on average,* to collect receivables. Compare the collection periods for RIM and Apple, and suggest at least one explanation for the difference.
3. Which company is more efficient in collecting its accounts receivable? Explain.

Hint: Average collection period equals 365 divided by the accounts receivable turnover.

ETHICS CHALLENGE

P2 

BTN 9-3 Kelly Steinman is the manager of a medium-size company. A few years ago, Steinman persuaded the owner to base a part of her compensation on the net income the company earns each year. Each December she estimates year-end financial figures in anticipation of the bonus she will receive. If the bonus is not as high as she would like, she offers several recommendations to the accountant for year-end adjustments. One of her favorite recommendations is for the controller to reduce the estimate of doubtful accounts.

Required

1. What effect does lowering the estimate for doubtful accounts have on the income statement and balance sheet?
2. Do you believe Steinman's recommendation to adjust the allowance for doubtful accounts is within her right as manager, or do you believe this action is an ethics violation? Justify your response.
3. What type of internal control(s) might be useful for this company in overseeing the manager's recommendations for accounting changes?

COMMUNICATING IN PRACTICE

P2 

BTN 9-4 As the accountant for Pure-Air Distributing, you attend a sales managers' meeting devoted to a discussion of credit policies. At the meeting, you report that bad debts expense is estimated to be $59,000 and accounts receivable at year-end amount to $1,750,000 less a $43,000 allowance for doubtful accounts. Sid Omar, a sales manager, expresses confusion over why bad debts expense and the allowance for doubtful accounts are different amounts. Write a one-page memorandum to him explaining why a difference in bad debts expense and the allowance for doubtful accounts is not unusual. The company estimates bad debts expense as 2% of sales.

TAKING IT TO THE NET

C1 

BTN 9-5 Access **eBay**'s, February 17, 2010, filing of its 10-K report for the year ended December 31, 2009, at www.SEC.gov.

Required

1. What is the amount of eBay's net accounts receivable at December 31, 2009, and at December 31, 2008?
2. "Financial Statement Schedule II" to its financial statements lists eBay's allowance for doubtful accounts (including authorized credits). For the two years ended December 31, 2009 and 2008, compute its allowance for doubtful accounts (including authorized credits) as a percent of gross accounts receivable.
3. Do you believe that these percentages are reasonable based on what you know about eBay? Explain.

TEAMWORK IN ACTION

P2

BTN 9-6 Each member of a team is to participate in estimating uncollectibles using the aging schedule and percents shown in Problem 9-4A. The division of labor is up to the team. Your goal is to accurately complete this task as soon as possible. After estimating uncollectibles, check your estimate with the instructor. If the estimate is correct, the team then should prepare the adjusting entry and the presentation of accounts receivable (net) for the December 31, 2011, balance sheet.

ENTREPRENEURIAL DECISION

C1  

BTN 9-7 Bernard McCoy of **LaserMonks** is introduced in the chapter's opening feature. Bernard currently sells his products through multiple outlets. Assume that he is considering two new selling options.

Plan A. LaserMonks would begin selling additional products online directly to customers, which are only currently sold directly to outlet stores. These new online customers would use their credit cards. It currently has the capability of selling through its Website with no additional investment in hardware or software. Credit sales are expected to increase by $250,000 per year. Costs associated with this plan are: cost of these sales will be $135,500, credit card fees will be 4.75% of sales, and additional recordkeeping and shipping costs will be 6% of sales. These online sales will reduce the sales to stores by $35,000 because some customers will now purchase items online. Sales to stores have a 25% gross margin percentage.

Plan B. LaserMonks would expand its market to more outlet stores. It would make additional credit sales of $500,000 to those stores. Costs associated with those sales are: cost of sales will be $375,000, additional recordkeeping and shipping will be 4% of sales, and uncollectible accounts will be 6.2% of sales.

Required

1. Compute the additional annual net income or loss expected under (a) Plan A and (b) Plan B.
2. Should LaserMonks pursue either plan? Discuss both the financial and nonfinancial factors relevant to this decision.

Check (1*b*) Net income, $74,000

BTN 9-8 Many commercials include comments similar to the following: "We accept **VISA**" or "We do not accept **American Express**." Conduct your own research by contacting at least five companies via interviews, phone calls, or the Internet to determine the reason(s) companies discriminate in their use of credit cards. Collect information on the fees charged by the different cards for the companies contacted. (The instructor can assign this as a team activity.)

HITTING THE ROAD
C1  

BTN 9-9 Key information from **Nokia** (www.Nokia.com), which is a leading global manufacturer of mobile devices and services, follows.

GLOBAL DECISION
C1 P2

NOKIA
RIM
Apple

EUR millions	Current Year	Prior Year
Accounts receivable, net*	7,981	9,444
Sales	40,984	50,710

*Nokia refers to it as "Accounts receivable, net of allowance for doubtful accounts."

1. Compute the accounts receivable turnover for the current year.
2. How long does it take on average for Nokia to collect receivables?
3. Refer to BTN 9-2. How does Nokia compare to Research In Motion and Apple in terms of its accounts receivable turnover and its collection period?
4. Nokia reports an aging analysis of its receivables, based on due dates, as follows (in EUR millions) as of December 31, 2009. Compute the percent of receivables in each category.

EUR millions	Total Receivables
Current	7,302
Past due 1–30 days	393
Past due 31–180 days	170
More than 180 days	116

ANSWERS TO MULTIPLE CHOICE QUIZ

1. d; Desired balance in Allowance for Doubtful Accounts = $ 5,026 cr. ($125,650 × 0.04)
   Current balance in Allowance for Doubtful Accounts = (328) cr.
   Bad Debts Expense to be recorded = $ 4,698
2. a; Desired balance in Allowance for Doubtful Accounts = $29,358 cr. ($489,300 × 0.06)
   Current balance in Allowance for Doubtful Accounts = 554 dr.
   Bad Debts Expense to be recorded = $29,912
3. a; $7,500 × 0.05 × 90/360 = $93.75
4. c; Principal amount . . . $9,000
   Interest accrued . . . 120 ($9,000 × 0.08 × 60/360)
   Maturity value . . . $9,120
5. d; $489,600/$40,800 = 12

Plant Assets, Natural Resources, and Intangibles

A Look Back

Chapters 8 and 9 focused on short-term assets: cash, cash equivalents, and receivables. We explained why they are known as liquid assets and described how companies account and report for them.

A Look at This Chapter

This chapter introduces us to long-term assets. We explain how to account for a long-term asset's cost, the allocation of an asset's cost to periods benefiting from it, the recording of additional costs after an asset is purchased, and the disposal of an asset.

A Look Ahead

Chapter 11 focuses on current liabilities. We explain how they are computed, recorded, and reported in financial statements. We also explain the accounting for company payroll and contingencies.

Learning Objectives

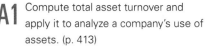

CONCEPTUAL

C1 Explain the cost principle for computing the cost of plant assets. (p. 395)

C2 Explain depreciation for partial years and changes in estimates. (p. 402)

C3 Distinguish between revenue and capital expenditures, and account for them. (p. 404)

ANALYTICAL

A1 Compute total asset turnover and apply it to analyze a company's use of assets. (p. 413)

LP10

PROCEDURAL

P1 Compute and record depreciation using the straight-line, units-of-production, and declining-balance methods. (p. 398)

P2 Account for asset disposal through discarding or selling an asset. (p. 406)

P3 Account for natural resource assets and their depletion. (p. 408)

P4 Account for intangible assets. (p. 409)

P5 *Appendix 10A*—Account for asset exchanges. (p. 416)

Decision Insight

Gaming Assets

"We want the average kid to have a party like a rock star"
—DAVID PIKOFF

AUSTIN, TX—Fun and games are the common bond for brothers Stuart and David Pikoff. That bond was also the driving force for an excursion into business. "We're both fun guys, we love kids, and we love games," explains David. "So we thought, 'Why not create our own game franchise?'" What they did was create **Games2U (Games2U.com)**, a business focused on bringing fun and games to children and adults, using vans and trailers outfitted with state-of-the-art games and activities.

The brothers started operations by scraping up just enough money. However, long-term assets such as mobile vehicles outfitted with video games, large flat-screen displays, high-quality sound systems, and laser-light and fog machines for effects, are very expensive. David explains that financing such equipment, machinery, and similar assets is a struggle. "We would be much bigger, much quicker, if we didn't have that challenge." The owners had to work out depreciation schedules and estimate payback for different games and accessories.

Games2U is now rocking—employing nearly 20 workers, offering franchise agreements to others interested in mimicking their fun and games business, and generating several million in annual sales. Still, a constant challenge for the brothers is maintaining the right kind and amount of assets to meet people's demands and be profitable. "That made us hone in on product development," explains David. "How do we provide unique entertainment at your doorstep?" Games2U's success depends on monitoring and controlling those asset costs, which range from a mobile 4-D movie theater to decked-out trailers to a patented seven-foot tall kid-controlled robot.

Each of these tangible and intangible assets commands Stuart and David's attention. The brothers account for, manage, and focus on recovering all costs of these long-term assets. "We're never done," says David. "We're always challenging ourselves." Their success in asset management permits them to pursue further expansion and new ideas for gaming experiences. They have expanded into outdoor laser tag, human gyros, air cannons, and a version of capture-the-flag called "Booger Wars." "We have a unique concept, a solid infrastructure," explains David. "We provide unique entertainment."

[Sources: *Games2U Website,* January 2011; *Entrepreneur,* June 2009; *The Wall Street Journal,* March 2010; *Inc.com* October 2009; *The Monitor,* September 2009; *Franchise Update,* August 2009]

Chapter Preview

This chapter focuses on long-term assets, which can be grouped into plant assets, natural resource assets, and intangible assets. Plant assets make up a large part of assets on most balance sheets, and they yield depreciation, often one of the largest expenses on income statements. The acquisition or building of a plant asset is often referred to as a *capital expenditure.* Capital expenditures are important events because they impact both the short- and long-term success of a company. Natural resource assets and intangible assets have similar impacts. This chapter describes the purchase and use of these assets. We also explain what distinguishes these assets from other types of assets, how to determine their cost, how to allocate their costs to periods benefiting from their use, and how to dispose of them.

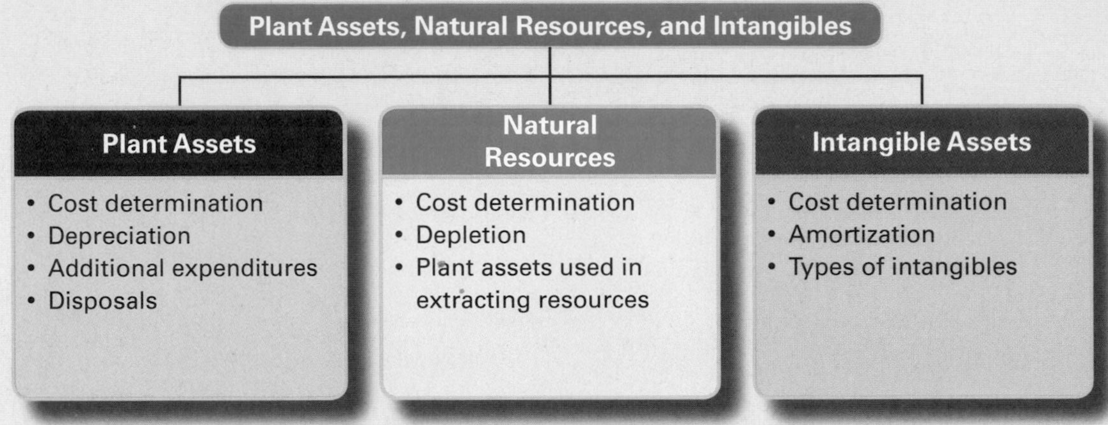

Plant Assets, Natural Resources, and Intangibles
Plant Assets
• Cost determination
• Depreciation
• Additional expenditures
• Disposals
Natural Resources
• Cost determination
• Depletion
• Plant assets used in extracting resources
Intangible Assets
• Cost determination
• Amortization
• Types of intangibles

Section 1—Plant Assets

Plant assets are tangible assets used in a company's operations that have a useful life of more than one accounting period. Plant assets are also called *plant and equipment; property, plant, and equipment;* or *fixed assets.* For many companies, plant assets make up the single largest class of assets they own. Exhibit 10.1 shows plant assets as a percent of total assets for several companies. Not only do they make up a large percent of many companies' assets, but their dollar values are large. **McDonald's** plant assets, for instance, are reported at more than $20 billion, and **Walmart** reports plant assets of more than $92 billion.

EXHIBIT 10.1

Plant Assets of Selected Companies

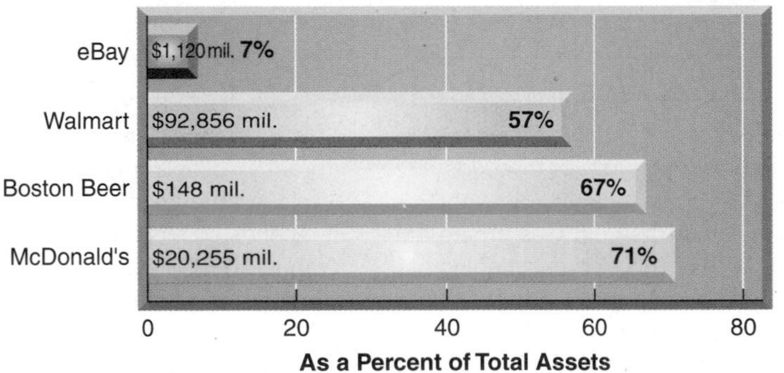

Plant assets are set apart from other assets by two important features. First, *plant assets are used in operations.* This makes them different from, for instance, inventory that is held for sale and not used in operations. The distinctive feature here is use, not type of asset. A company that purchases a computer to resell it reports it on the balance sheet as inventory. If the same company purchases this computer to use in operations, however, it is a plant asset. Another example is land held for future expansion, which is reported as a long-term investment. However, if this land holds a factory used in operations, the land is part of plant assets. Another example is equipment held for use in the event of a breakdown or for peak periods of production, which is reported in plant assets. If this same equipment is removed from use and held for sale, however, it is not reported in plant assets.

The second important feature is that *plant assets have useful lives extending over more than one accounting period.* This makes plant assets different from current assets such as supplies that are normally consumed in a short time period after they are placed in use.

The accounting for plant assets reflects these two features. Since plant assets are used in operations, we try to match their costs against the revenues they generate. Also, since their useful lives extend over more than one period, our matching of costs and revenues must extend over several periods. Specifically, we value plant assets (balance sheet effect) and then, for many of them, we allocate their costs to periods benefiting from their use (income statement effect). An important exception is land; land cost is not allocated to expense when we expect it to have an indefinite life.

Point: It can help to view plant assets as prepaid expenses that benefit several future accounting periods.

Exhibit 10.2 shows four main issues in accounting for plant assets: (1) computing the costs of plant assets, (2) allocating the costs of most plant assets (less any salvage amounts) against revenues for the periods they benefit, (3) accounting for expenditures such as repairs and improvements to plant assets, and (4) recording the disposal of plant assets. The following sections discuss these issues.

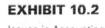

EXHIBIT 10.2

Issues in Accounting for Plant Assets

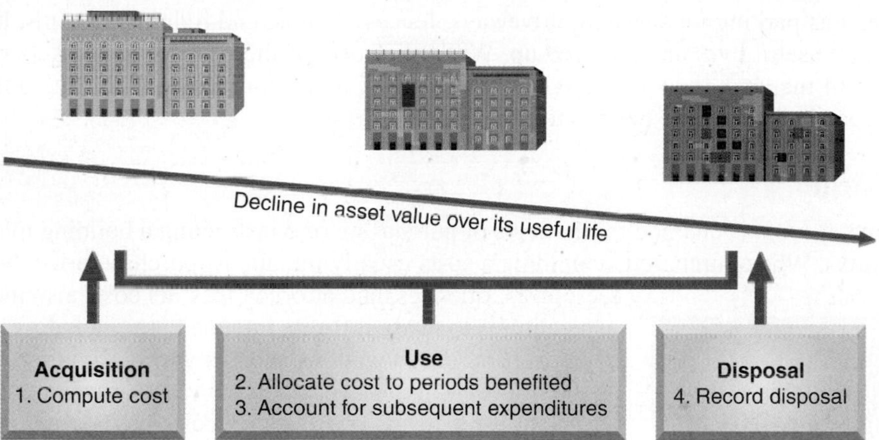

COST DETERMINATION

C1 Explain the cost principle for computing the cost of plant assets.

Plant assets are recorded at cost when acquired. This is consistent with the *cost principle.* **Cost** includes all normal and reasonable expenditures necessary to get the asset in place and ready for its intended use. The cost of a factory machine, for instance, includes its invoice cost less any cash discount for early payment, plus any necessary freight, unpacking, assembling, installing, and testing costs. Examples are the costs of building a base or foundation for a machine, providing electrical hookups, and testing the asset before using it in operations.

To be recorded as part of the cost of a plant asset, an expenditure must be normal, reasonable, and necessary in preparing it for its intended use. If an asset is damaged during unpacking, the repairs are not added to its cost. Instead, they are charged to an expense account. Nor is a paid traffic fine for moving heavy machinery on city streets without a proper permit part of the machinery's cost; but payment for a proper permit is included in the cost of machinery. Charges are sometimes incurred to modify or customize a new plant asset. These charges are added to the asset's cost. We explain in this section how to determine the cost of plant assets for each of its four major classes.

Land

When land is purchased for a building site, its cost includes the total amount paid for the land, including any real estate commissions, title insurance fees, legal fees, and any accrued property taxes paid by the purchaser. Payments for surveying, clearing, grading, and draining also are included in the cost of land. Other costs include government assessments, whether incurred at the time of purchase or later, for items such as public roadways, sewers, and sidewalks. These assessments are included because they permanently add to the land's value. Land purchased as a building site sometimes includes structures that must be removed. In such cases, the total purchase price is charged to the Land account as is the cost of removing the structures, less any amounts recovered through sale of salvaged materials. To illustrate, assume that **Starbucks** paid $167,000 cash to acquire land for a retail store. This land had an old service garage that was removed at a net cost of

EXHIBIT 10.3
Computing Cost of Land

Cash price of land	$ 167,000
Net cost of garage removal	13,000
Closing costs	10,000
Cost of land	**$190,000**

$13,000 ($15,000 in costs less $2,000 proceeds from salvaged materials). Additional closing costs total $10,000, consisting of brokerage fees ($8,000), legal fees ($1,500), and title costs ($500). The cost of this land to Starbucks is $190,000 and is computed as shown in Exhibit 10.3.

Land Improvements

Land has an indefinite (unlimited) life and is not usually used up over time. **Land improvements** such as parking lot surfaces, driveways, fences, shrubs, and lighting systems, however, have limited useful lives and are used up. While the costs of these improvements increase the usefulness of the land, they are charged to a separate Land Improvement account so that their costs can be allocated to the periods they benefit.

Buildings

A Building account is charged for the costs of purchasing or constructing a building that is used in operations. When purchased, a building's costs usually include its purchase price, brokerage fees, taxes, title fees, and attorney fees. Its costs also include all expenditures to ready it for its intended use, including any necessary repairs or renovations such as wiring, lighting, flooring, and wall coverings. When a company constructs a building or any plant asset for its own use, its costs include materials and labor plus a reasonable amount of indirect overhead cost. Overhead includes the costs of items such as heat, lighting, power, and depreciation on machinery used to construct the asset. Costs of construction also include design fees, building permits, and insurance during construction. However, costs such as insurance to cover the asset *after* it is placed in use are operating expenses.

Machinery and Equipment

The costs of machinery and equipment consist of all costs normal and necessary to purchase them and prepare them for their intended use. These include the purchase price, taxes, transportation charges, insurance while in transit, and the installing, assembling, and testing of the machinery and equipment.

Lump-Sum Purchase

Example: If appraised values in Exhibit 10.4 are land, $24,000; land improvements, $12,000; and building, $84,000, what cost is assigned to the building? *Answer:*
(1) $24,000 + $12,000 + $84,000 = $120,000 (total appraisal)
(2) $84,000/$120,000 = 70% (building's percent of total)
(3) 70% × $90,000 = $63,000 (building's apportioned cost)

Plant assets sometimes are purchased as a group in a single transaction for a lump-sum price. This transaction is called a *lump-sum purchase,* or *group, bulk,* or *basket purchase.* When this occurs, we allocate the cost of the purchase among the different types of assets acquired based on their *relative market values,* which can be estimated by appraisal or by using the tax-assessed valuations of the assets. To illustrate, assume **CarMax** paid $90,000 cash to acquire a group of items consisting of land appraised at $30,000, land improvements appraised at $10,000, and a building appraised at $60,000. The $90,000 cost is allocated on the basis of these appraised values as shown in Exhibit 10.4.

EXHIBIT 10.4
Computing Costs in a Lump-Sum Purchase

	Appraised Value	Percent of Total	Apportioned Cost
Land	$ 30,000	30% ($30,000/$100,000)	**$27,000** ($90,000 × 30%)
Land improvements	10,000	10 ($10,000/$100,000)	**9,000** ($90,000 × 10%)
Building	60,000	60 ($60,000/$100,000)	**54,000** ($90,000 × 60%)
Totals	$100,000	100%	$ 90,000

Quick Check

Answers — p. 419 

1. Identify the asset class for each of the following: (*a*) supplies, (*b*) office equipment, (*c*) inventory, (*d*) land for future expansion, and (*e*) trucks used in operations.
2. Identify the account charged for each of the following: (*a*) the purchase price of a vacant lot to be used in operations and (*b*) the cost of paving that same vacant lot.
3. Compute the amount recorded as the cost of a new machine given the following payments related to its purchase: gross purchase price, $700,000; sales tax, $49,000; purchase discount taken, $21,000; freight cost—terms FOB shipping point, $3,500, normal assembly costs, $3,000; cost of necessary machine platform, $2,500; cost of parts used in maintaining machine, $4,200.

DEPRECIATION

Depreciation is the process of allocating the cost of a plant asset to expense in the accounting periods benefiting from its use. Depreciation does not measure the decline in the asset's market value each period, nor does it measure the asset's physical deterioration. Since depreciation reflects the cost of using a plant asset, depreciation charges are only recorded when the asset is actually in service. This section describes the factors we must consider in computing depreciation, the depreciation methods used, revisions in depreciation, and depreciation for partial periods.

Factors in Computing Depreciation

Factors that determine depreciation are (1) cost, (2) salvage value, and (3) useful life.

Cost The **cost** of a plant asset consists of all necessary and reasonable expenditures to acquire it and to prepare it for its intended use.

Salvage Value The total amount of depreciation to be charged off over an asset's benefit period equals the asset's cost minus its salvage value. **Salvage value,** also called *residual value* or *scrap value,* is an estimate of the asset's value at the end of its benefit period. This is the amount the owner expects to receive from disposing of the asset at the end of its benefit period. If the asset is expected to be traded in on a new asset, its salvage value is the expected trade-in value.

Point: If we expect additional costs in preparing a plant asset for disposal, the salvage value equals the expected amount from disposal less any disposal costs.

Useful Life The **useful life** of a plant asset is the length of time it is productively used in a company's operations. Useful life, also called *service life,* might not be as long as the asset's total productive life. For example, the productive life of a computer can be eight years or more. Some companies, however, trade in old computers for new ones every two years. In this case, these computers have a two-year useful life, meaning the cost of these computers (less their expected trade-in values) is charged to depreciation expense over a two-year period.

Point: Useful life and salvage value are estimates. Estimates require judgment based on all available information.

Several variables often make the useful life of a plant asset difficult to predict. A major variable is the wear and tear from use in operations. Two other variables, inadequacy and obsolescence, also require consideration. **Inadequacy** refers to the insufficient capacity of a company's plant assets to meet its growing productive demands. **Obsolescence** refers to the condition of a plant asset that is no longer useful in producing goods or services with a competitive advantage because of new inventions and improvements. Both inadequacy and obsolescence are difficult to predict because of demand changes, new inventions, and improvements. A company usually disposes of an inadequate or obsolete asset before it wears out.

A company is often able to better predict a new asset's useful life when it has past experience with a similar asset. When it has no such experience, a company relies on the experience of others or on engineering studies and judgment. In note 1 of its annual report, **Tootsie Roll**, a snack food manufacturer, reports the following useful lives:

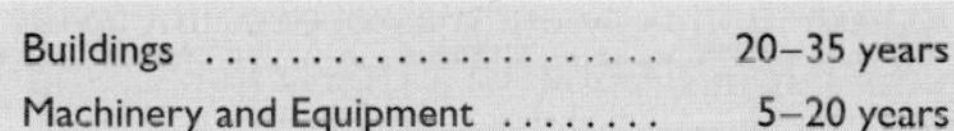

Buildings	20–35 years
Machinery and Equipment	5–20 years

Decision Insight

Life Line Life expectancy of plant assets is often in the eye of the beholder. For instance, **Hershey Foods** and **Tootsie Roll** are competitors and apply similar manufacturing processes, yet their equipment's life expectancies are different. Hershey depreciates equipment over 3 to 15 years, but Tootsie Roll depreciates them over 5 to 20 years. Such differences markedly impact financial statements. ■

Depreciation Methods

P1 Compute and record depreciation using the straight-line, units-of-production, and declining-balance methods.

Depreciation methods are used to allocate a plant asset's cost over the accounting periods in its useful life. The most frequently used method of depreciation is the straight-line method. Another common depreciation method is the units-of-production method. We explain both of these methods in this section. This section also describes accelerated depreciation methods, with a focus on the declining-balance method.

The computations in this section use information about a machine that inspects athletic shoes before packaging. Manufacturers such as **Converse**, **Reebok**, **adidas**, and **Fila** use this machine. Data for this machine are in Exhibit 10.5.

EXHIBIT 10.5

Data for Athletic Shoe-Inspecting Machine

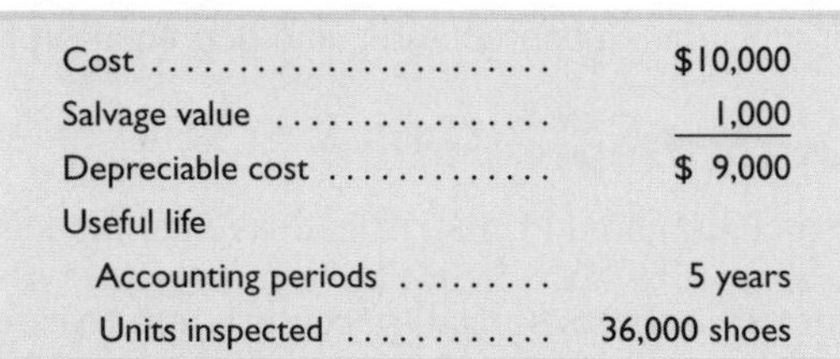

Cost	$10,000
Salvage value	1,000
Depreciable cost	$ 9,000
Useful life	
Accounting periods	5 years
Units inspected	36,000 shoes

Straight-Line Method **Straight-line depreciation** charges the same amount of expense to each period of the asset's useful life. A two-step process is used. We first compute the *depreciable cost* of the asset, also called the *cost to be depreciated.* It is computed by subtracting the asset's salvage value from its total cost. Second, depreciable cost is divided by the number of accounting periods in the asset's useful life. The formula for straight-line depreciation, along with its computation for the inspection machine just described, is shown in Exhibit 10.6.

EXHIBIT 10.6

Straight-Line Depreciation Formula and Example

$$\frac{\textbf{Cost} - \textbf{Salvage value}}{\textbf{Useful life in periods}} = \frac{\$10{,}000 - \$1{,}000}{5 \text{ years}} = \$1{,}800 \text{ per year}$$

If this machine is purchased on December 31, 2010, and used throughout its predicted useful life of five years, the straight-line method allocates an equal amount of depreciation to each of the years 2011 through 2015. We make the following adjusting entry at the end of each of the five years to record straight-line depreciation of this machine.

Assets	=	Liabilities	+	Equity
−1,800				−1,800

Dec. 31	Depreciation Expense	1,800	
	Accumulated Depreciation—Machinery		1,800
	To record annual depreciation.		

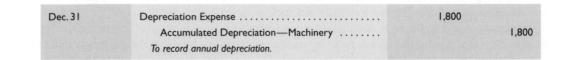

Example: If the salvage value of the machine is $2,500, what is the annual depreciation? *Answer:* ($10,000 − $2,500)/5 years = $1,500

The $1,800 Depreciation Expense is reported on the income statement among operating expenses. The $1,800 Accumulated Depreciation is a contra asset account to the Machinery account in the balance sheet. The graph on the left in Exhibit 10.7 shows the $1,800 per year expenses reported in each of the five years. The graph on the right shows the amounts reported on each of the six December 31 balance sheets.

EXHIBIT 10.7

Financial Statement Effects of Straight-Line Depreciation

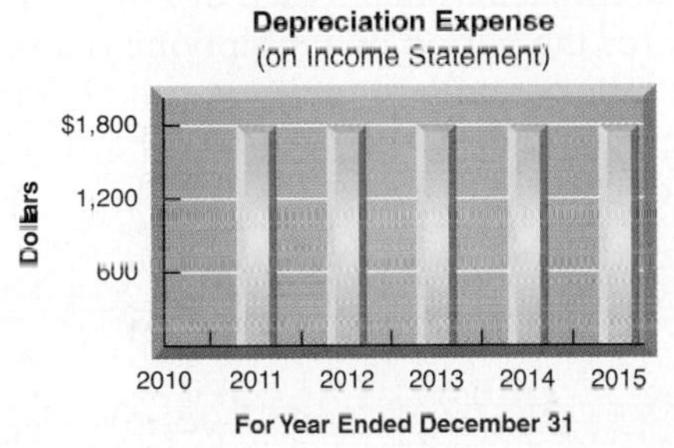

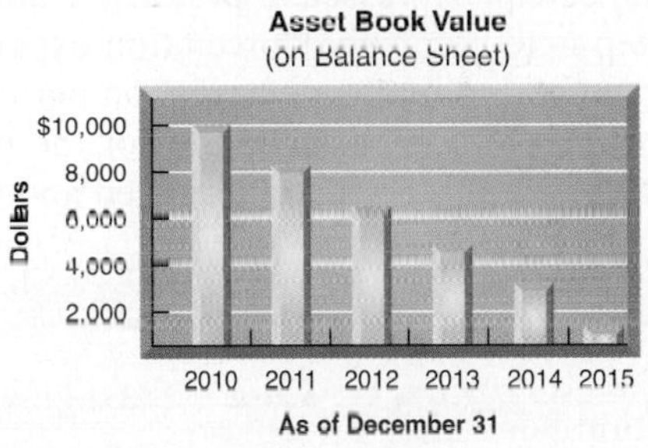

The net balance sheet amount is the **asset book value,** or simply *book value,* and is computed as the asset's total cost less its accumulated depreciation. For example, at the end of year 2 (December 31, 2012), its book value is $6,400 and is reported in the balance sheet as follows:

Machinery	$10,000	
Less accumulated depreciation	3,600	$6,400

The book value of this machine declines by $1,800 each year due to depreciation. From the graphs in Exhibit 10.7 we can see why this method is called straight-line.

We also can compute the *straight-line depreciation rate,* defined as 100% divided by the number of periods in the asset's useful life. For the inspection machine, this rate is 20% (100% ÷ 5 years, or 1/5 per period). We use this rate, along with other information, to compute the machine's *straight-line depreciation schedule* shown in Exhibit 10.8. Note three points in this exhibit. First, depreciation expense is the same each period. Second, accumulated depreciation is the sum of current and prior periods' depreciation expense. Third, book value declines each period until it equals salvage value at the end of the machine's useful life.

Point: Depreciation requires estimates for salvage value and useful life. Ethics are relevant when managers might be tempted to choose estimates to achieve desired results on financial statements.

EXHIBIT 10.8

Straight-Line Depreciation Schedule

	Depreciation for the Period			End of Period	
Annual Period	Depreciable Cost*	Depreciation Rate	Depreciation Expense	Accumulated Depreciation	Book Value†
2010	—	—	—	—	$10,000
2011	$9,000	20%	$1,800	$1,800	8,200
2012	9,000	20	1,800	3,600	6,400
2013	9,000	20	1,800	5,400	4,600
2014	9,000	20	1,800	7,200	2,800
2015	9,000	20	1,800	9,000	**1,000**

* $10,000 − $1,000. † Book value is total cost minus accumulated depreciation.

Units-of-Production Method The straight-line method charges an equal share of an asset's cost to each period. If plant assets are used up in about equal amounts each accounting period, this method produces a reasonable matching of expenses with revenues. However, the use of some plant assets varies greatly from one period to the next. A builder, for instance, might use a piece of construction equipment for a month and then not use it again for several months. When equipment use varies from period to period, the units-of-production depreciation method can better match expenses with revenues. **Units-of-production depreciation** charges a varying amount to expense for each period of an asset's useful life depending on its usage.

A two-step process is used to compute units-of-production depreciation. We first compute *depreciation per unit* by subtracting the asset's salvage value from its total cost and then dividing by the total number of units expected to be produced during its useful life. Units of production can be expressed in product or other units such as hours used or miles driven. The second step is to compute depreciation expense for the period by multiplying the units produced in the period by the depreciation per unit. The formula for units-of-production depreciation, along with its computation for the machine described in Exhibit 10.5, is shown in Exhibit 10.9. (7,000 shoes are inspected and sold in its first year.)

EXHIBIT 10.9

Units-of-Production Depreciation Formula and Example

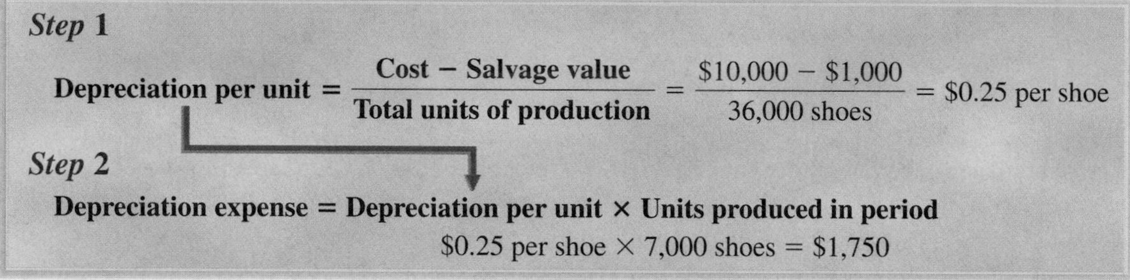

Step 1
Depreciation per unit = Cost − Salvage value / Total units of production = $10,000 − $1,000 / 36,000 shoes = $0.25 per shoe
Step 2
Depreciation expense = Depreciation per unit × Units produced in period
$0.25 per shoe × 7,000 shoes = $1,750

Using data on the number of shoes inspected by the machine, we can compute the *units-of-production depreciation schedule* shown in Exhibit 10.10. For example, depreciation for the first year is $1,750 (7,000 shoes at $0.25 per shoe). Depreciation for the second year is $2,000 (8,000 shoes at $0.25 per shoe). Other years are similarly computed. Exhibit 10.10 shows that (1) depreciation expense depends on unit output, (2) accumulated depreciation is the sum of current and prior periods' depreciation expense, and (3) book value declines each period until it equals salvage value at the end of the asset's useful life. **Deltic Timber** is one of many companies using the units-of-production depreciation method. It reports that depreciation "is calculated over the estimated useful lives of the assets by using the units of production method for machinery and equipment."

Example: Refer to Exhibit 10.10. If the number of shoes inspected in 2015 is 5,500, what is depreciation for 2015? *Answer:* $1,250 (never depreciate below salvage value)

EXHIBIT 10.10

Units-of-Production Depreciation Schedule

	Depreciation for the Period			End of Period	
Annual Period	Number of Units	Depreciation per Unit	Depreciation Expense	Accumulated Depreciation	Book Value
2010	—	—	—	—	$10,000
2011	7,000	$0.25	**$1,750**	$1,750	8,250
2012	8,000	0.25	**2,000**	3,750	6,250
2013	9,000	0.25	**2,250**	6,000	4,000
2014	7,000	0.25	**1,750**	7,750	2,250
2015	5,000	0.25	**1,250**	9,000	**1,000**

Declining-Balance Method An **accelerated depreciation method** yields larger depreciation expenses in the early years of an asset's life and less depreciation in later years. The most common accelerated method is the **declining-balance method** of depreciation, which uses a depreciation rate that is a multiple of the straight-line rate and applies it to the asset's beginning-of-period book value. The amount of depreciation declines each period because book value declines each period.

A common depreciation rate for the declining-balance method is double the straight-line rate. This is called the *double-declining-balance (DDB)* method. This method is applied in three steps: (1) compute the asset's straight-line depreciation rate, (2) double the straight-line rate, and (3) compute depreciation expense by multiplying this rate by the asset's beginning-of-period book value. To illustrate, let's return to the machine in Exhibit 10.5 and apply the double-declining-balance method to compute depreciation expense. Exhibit 10.11 shows the first-year depreciation computation for the machine. The three-step process is to (1) divide 100% by five years to determine the straight-line rate of 20%, or 1/5, per year, (2) double this 20% rate to get the

Point: In the DDB method, *double* refers to the rate and *declining balance* refers to book value. The rate is applied to beginning book value each period.

declining-balance rate of 40%, or 2/5, per year, and (3) compute depreciation expense as 40%, or 2/5, multiplied by the beginning-of-period book value.

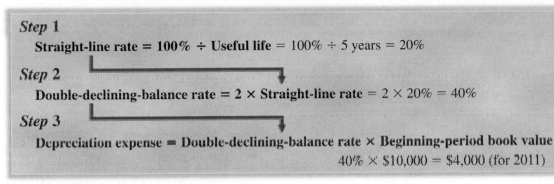

EXHIBIT 10.11

Double Declining Balance Depreciation Formula*

Step 1
Straight-line rate = 100% ÷ Useful life = 100% ÷ 5 years = 20%

Step 2
Double-declining-balance rate = 2 × Straight-line rate = 2 × 20% = 40%

Step 3
Depreciation expense = Double-declining-balance rate × Beginning-period book value
40% × $10,000 = $4,000 (for 2011)

* To simplify: DDB depreciation = (2 × Beginning period book value)/Useful life.

The *double-declining-balance depreciation schedule* is shown in Exhibit 10.12. The schedule follows the formula except for year 2015, when depreciation expense is $296. This $296 is not equal to 40% × $1,296, or $518.40. If we had used the $518.40 for depreciation expense in 2015, the ending book value would equal $777.60, which is less than the $1,000 salvage value. Instead, the $296 is computed by subtracting the $1,000 salvage value from the $1,296 book value at the beginning of the fifth year (the year when DDB depreciation cuts into salvage value).

Example: What is the DDB depreciation expense in year 2014 if the salvage value is $2,000?
Answer: $2,160 − $2,000 = $160

EXHIBIT 10.12

Double-Declining-Balance Depreciation Schedule

	Depreciation for the Period			End of Period	
Annual Period	**Beginning of Period Book Value**	**Depreciation Rate**	**Depreciation Expense**	**Accumulated Depreciation**	**Book Value**
2010	—	—	—	—	$10,000
2011	$10,000	40%	**$4,000**	$4,000	6,000
2012	6,000	40	**2,400**	6,400	3,600
2013	3,600	40	**1,440**	7,840	2,160
2014	2,160	40	**864**	8,704	1,296
2015	1,296	40	**296***	9,000	**1,000**

* Year 2015 depreciation is $1,296 − $1,000 = $296 (never depreciate book value below salvage value).

Comparing Depreciation Methods Exhibit 10.13 shows depreciation expense for each year of the machine's useful life under each of the three depreciation methods. While depreciation expense per period differs for different methods, total depreciation expense of $9,000 is the same over the machine's useful life.

EXHIBIT 10.13

Depreciation Expense for the Different Methods

Period	Straight-Line	Units-of-Production	Double-Declining-Balance
2011	$1,800	$1,750	$4,000
2012	1,800	2,000	2,400
2013	1,800	2,250	1,440
2014	1,800	1,750	864
2015	1,800	1,250	296
Totals	**$9,000**	**$9,000**	**$9,000**

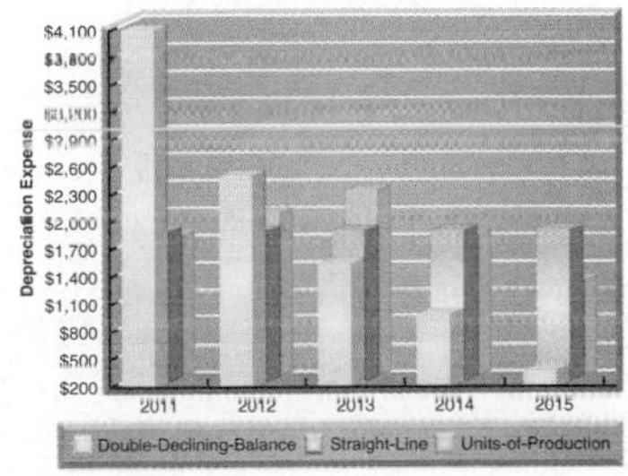

Each method starts with a total cost of $10,000 and ends with a salvage value of $1,000. The difference is the pattern in depreciation expense over the useful life. The book value of the asset when using straight-line is always greater than the book value from using double declining balance, except at the beginning and end of the asset's useful life, when it is the same. Also,

Point: Depreciation is higher and income lower in the short run when using accelerated versus straight-line methods.

the straight-line method yields a steady pattern of depreciation expense while the units-of-production depreciation depends on the number of units produced. Each of these methods is acceptable because it allocates cost in a systematic and rational manner.

Decision Insight

In Vogue About 87% of companies use straight-line depreciation for plant assets, 4% use units-of-production, and 4% use declining-balance. Another 5% use an unspecified accelerated method—most likely declining-balance. ■

Straight-line, 87%
Accelerated and other, 5%
Declining-balance, 4%
Units-of-production, 4%

Depreciation for Tax Reporting The records a company keeps for financial accounting purposes are usually separate from the records it keeps for tax accounting purposes. This is so because financial accounting aims to report useful information on financial performance and position, whereas tax accounting reflects government objectives in raising revenues. Differences between these two accounting systems are normal and expected. Depreciation is a common example of how the records differ. For example, many companies use accelerated depreciation in computing taxable income. Reporting higher depreciation expense in the early years of an asset's life reduces the company's taxable income in those years and increases it in later years, when the depreciation expense is lower. The company's goal here is to *postpone* its tax payments.

Point: Understanding depreciation for financial accounting will help in learning MACRS for tax accounting. Rules for MACRS are available from www.IRS.gov.

The U.S. federal income tax law has rules for depreciating assets. These rules include the **Modified Accelerated Cost Recovery System (MACRS),** which allows straight-line depreciation for some assets but requires accelerated depreciation for most kinds of assets. MACRS separates depreciable assets into different classes and defines the depreciable life and rate for each class. MACRS is *not* acceptable for financial reporting because it often allocates costs over an arbitrary period that is less than the asset's useful life and it fails to estimate salvage value. Details of MACRS are covered in tax accounting courses.

Partial-Year Depreciation

C2 Explain depreciation for partial years and changes in estimates.

Plant assets are purchased and disposed of at various times. When an asset is purchased (or disposed of) at a time other than the beginning or end of an accounting period, depreciation is recorded for part of a year. This is done so that the year of purchase or the year of disposal is charged with its share of the asset's depreciation.

To illustrate, assume that the machine in Exhibit 10.5 is purchased and placed in service on October 8, 2010, and the annual accounting period ends on December 31. Since this machine is purchased and used for nearly three months in 2010, the calendar-year income statement should report depreciation expense on the machine for that part of the year. Normally, depreciation assumes that the asset is purchased on the first day of the month nearest the actual date of purchase. In this case, since the purchase occurred on October 8, we assume an October 1 purchase date. This means that three months' depreciation is recorded in 2010. Using straight-line depreciation, we compute three months' depreciation of $450 as follows.

$$\frac{\$10{,}000 - \$1{,}000}{5 \text{ years}} \times \frac{3}{12} = \$450$$

A similar computation is necessary when an asset disposal occurs during a period. To illustrate, assume that the machine is sold on June 24, 2015. Depreciation is recorded for the period January 1 through June 24 when it is disposed of. This partial year's depreciation, computed to the nearest whole month, is

$$\frac{\$10{,}000 - \$1{,}000}{5 \text{ years}} \times \frac{6}{12} = \$900$$

Example: If the machine's salvage value is zero and purchase occurs on Oct. 8, 2010, how much depreciation is recorded at Dec. 31, 2010?
Answer: $10,000/5 × 3/12 = $500

Change in Estimates for Depreciation

Depreciation is based on estimates of salvage value and useful life. During the useful life of an asset, new information may indicate that these estimates are inaccurate. If our estimate of an asset's useful life and/or salvage value changes, what should we do? The answer is to use the new estimate to compute depreciation for current and future periods. This means that we revise the depreciation expense computation by spreading the cost yet to be depreciated over the remaining useful life. This approach is used for all depreciation methods.

Point: Remaining depreciable cost equals book value less revised salvage value at the point of revision.

Let's return to the machine described in Exhibit 10.8 using straight-line depreciation. At the beginning of this asset's third year, its book value is $6,400, computed as $10,000 minus $3,600. Assume that at the beginning of its third year, the estimated number of years remaining in its useful life changes from three to four years *and* its estimate of salvage value changes from $1,000 to $400. Straight-line depreciation for each of the four remaining years is computed as shown in Exhibit 10.14.

Point: Income is overstated (and depreciation understated) when useful life is too high; when useful life is too low, the opposite results.

EXHIBIT 10.14

Computing Revised Straight-Line Depreciation

$$\frac{\textbf{Book value} - \textbf{Revised salvage value}}{\textbf{Revised remaining useful life}} = \frac{\$6{,}400 - \$400}{4 \text{ years}} = \$1{,}500 \text{ per year}$$

Thus, $1,500 of depreciation expense is recorded for the machine at the end of the third through sixth years—each year of its remaining useful life. Since this asset was depreciated at $1,800 per year for the first two years, it is tempting to conclude that depreciation expense was overstated in the first two years. However, these expenses reflected the best information available at that time. We do not go back and restate prior years' financial statements for this type of new information. Instead, we adjust the current and future periods' statements to reflect this new information. Revising an estimate of the useful life or salvage value of a plant asset is referred to as a **change in an accounting estimate** and is reflected in current and future financial statements, not in prior statements.

Example: If at the beginning of its second year the machine's remaining useful life changes from four to three years and salvage value from $1,000 to $400, how much straight-line depreciation is recorded in remaining years?
Answer: Revised depreciation = ($8,200 − $400)/3 = $2,600.

Reporting Depreciation

Both the cost and accumulated depreciation of plant assets are reported on the balance sheet or in its notes. **Dale Jarrett Racing Adventure**, for instance, reports the following.

Office furniture and equipment	$ 54,593
Shop and track equipment	202,973
Race vehicles and other	975,084
Property and equipment, gross	1,232,650
Less accumulated depreciation	628,355
Property and equipment, net	$ 604,295

Many companies also show plant assets on one line with the net amount of cost less accumulated depreciation. When this is done, the amount of accumulated depreciation is disclosed in a note. **Apple** reports only the net amount of its property, plant and equipment in its balance sheet in Appendix A. To satisfy the full-disclosure principle, Apple describes its depreciation methods in its Note 1 and the amounts comprising plant assets in its Note 5—see its 10-K at **www.SEC.gov**.

Point: A company usually keeps records for each asset showing its cost and depreciation to date. The combined records for individual assets are a type of *plant asset subsidiary ledger.*

Reporting both the cost and accumulated depreciation of plant assets helps users compare the assets of different companies. For example, a company holding assets costing $50,000 and accumulated depreciation of $40,000 is likely in a situation different from a company with new assets costing $10,000. While the net undepreciated cost of $10,000 is the same in both cases, the first company may have more productive capacity available but likely is facing the need to replace older assets. These insights are not provided if the two balance sheets report only the $10,000 book values.

Users must remember that plant assets are reported on a balance sheet at their undepreciated costs (book value), not at fair (market) values. This emphasis on costs rather than fair values is based on the *going-concern assumption* described in Chapter 1. This assumption states that, unless there is evidence to the contrary, we assume that a company continues in business. This implies that plant assets are held and used long enough to recover their cost through the sale of products and services. Because plant assets are not for sale, their fair values are not reported. An exception is when there is a *permanent decline* in the fair value of an asset relative to its book value, called an asset **impairment.** In this case the company writes the asset down to this fair value (details for the two-step process for assessing and computing the impairment loss are in advanced courses).

Example: Assume equipment carries a book value of $800 ($900 cost less $100 accumulated depreciation) and a fair (market) value of $750, *and* this $50 decline in value meets the 2-step impairment test. The entry to record this impairment is:

Impairment Loss	$50	
Accum Depr-Equip.		$50

Accumulated Depreciation is a contra asset account with a normal credit balance. It does *not* reflect funds accumulated to buy new assets when the assets currently owned are replaced. If a company has funds available to buy assets, the funds are shown on the balance sheet among liquid assets such as Cash or Investments.

Decision Ethics Answer — p. 418

Controller You are the controller for a struggling company. Its operations require regular investments in equipment, and depreciation is its largest expense. Its competitors frequently replace equipment—often depreciated over three years. The company president instructs you to revise useful lives of equipment from three to six years and to use a six-year life on all new equipment. What actions do you take? ■

Quick Check Answers — p. 419

4. On January 1, 2011, a company pays $77,000 to purchase office furniture with a zero salvage value. The furniture's useful life is somewhere between 7 and 10 years. What is the year 2011 straight-line depreciation on the furniture using (*a*) a 7-year useful life and (*b*) a 10-year useful life?
5. What does the term *depreciation* mean in accounting?
6. A company purchases a machine for $96,000 on January 1, 2011. Its useful life is five years or 100,000 units of product, and its salvage value is $8,000. During 2011, 10,000 units of product are produced. Compute the book value of this machine on December 31, 2011, assuming (*a*) straight-line depreciation and (*b*) units-of-production depreciation.
7. In early January 2011, a company acquires equipment for $3,800. The company estimates this equipment to have a useful life of three years and a salvage value of $200. Early in 2013, the company changes its estimates to a total four-year useful life and zero salvage value. Using the straight-line method, what is depreciation for the year ended 2013?

ADDITIONAL EXPENDITURES

C3 Distinguish between revenue and capital expenditures, and account for them.

After a company acquires a plant asset and puts it into service, it often makes additional expenditures for that asset's operation, maintenance, repair, and improvement. In recording these expenditures, it must decide whether to capitalize or expense them (to capitalize an expenditure is to debit the asset account). The issue is whether these expenditures are reported as current period expenses or added to the plant asset's cost and depreciated over its remaining useful life.

Revenue expenditures, also called *income statement expenditures,* are additional costs of plant assets that do not materially increase the asset's life or productive capabilities. They are recorded as expenses and deducted from revenues in the current period's income statement. Examples of revenue expenditures are cleaning, repainting, adjustments, and lubricants. **Capital expenditures,** also called *balance sheet expenditures,* are additional costs of plant assets that provide benefits extending beyond the current period. They are debited to asset accounts and reported on the balance sheet. Capital expenditures increase or improve the type or amount of service an asset provides. Examples are roofing replacement, plant expansion, and major overhauls of machinery and equipment.

	Financial Statement Effect	
	Accounting	**Expense Timing**
Revenue expenditure	Income stmt. account debited	Expensed currently
Capital expenditure	Balance sheet account debited	Expensed in future

Financial statements are affected for several years by the accounting choice of recording costs as either revenue expenditures or capital expenditures. This decision is based on whether the expenditures are identified as ordinary repairs or as betterments and extraordinary repairs.

Ordinary Repairs

Ordinary repairs are expenditures to keep an asset in normal, good operating condition. They are necessary if an asset is to perform to expectations over its useful life. Ordinary repairs do not extend an asset's useful life beyond its original estimate or increase its productivity beyond original expectations. Examples are normal costs of cleaning, lubricating, adjusting, and replacing small parts of a machine. Ordinary repairs are treated as *revenue expenditures.* This means their costs are reported as expenses on the current period income statement. Following this rule, **Brunswick** reports that "maintenance and repair costs are expensed as incurred." If Brunswick's current year repair costs are $9,500, it makes the following entry.

Point: Many companies apply the *materiality constraint* to treat *low-cost plant assets* (say, less than $500) as revenue expenditures. This practice is referred to as a "capitalization policy."

Dec. 31	Repairs Expense	9,500	
	Cash		9,500
	To record ordinary repairs of equipment.		

Assets = Liabilities + Equity
9,500 −9,500

Betterments and Extraordinary Repairs

Accounting for betterments and extraordinary repairs is similar—both are treated as *capital expenditures.*

Betterments (Improvements) **Betterments,** also called *improvements,* are expenditures that make a plant asset more efficient or productive. A betterment often involves adding a component to an asset or replacing one of its old components with a better one, and does not always increase an asset's useful life. An example is replacing manual controls on a machine with automatic controls. One special type of betterment is an *addition,* such as adding a new wing or dock to a warehouse. Since a betterment benefits future periods, it is debited to the asset account as a capital expenditure. The new book value (less salvage value) is then depreciated over the asset's remaining useful life. To illustrate, suppose a company pays $8,000 for a machine with an eight-year useful life and no salvage value. After three years and $3,000 of depreciation, it adds an automated control system to the machine at a cost of $1,800. This results in reduced labor costs in future periods. The cost of the betterment is added to the Machinery account with this entry.

Example: Assume a firm owns a Web server. Identify each cost as a revenue or capital expenditure: (1) purchase price, (2) necessary wiring, (3) platform for operation, (4) circuits to increase capacity, (5) cleaning after each month of use, (6) repair of a faulty switch, and (7) replaced a worn fan. *Answer:* Capital expenditures: 1, 2, 3, 4; revenue expenditures: 5, 6, 7.

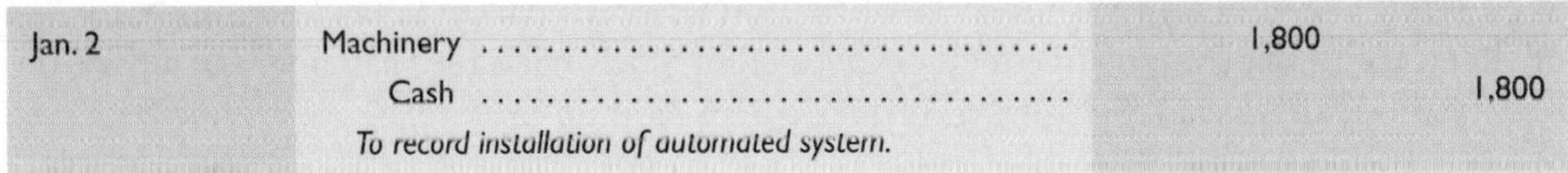

Jan. 2	Machinery	1,800	
	Cash		1,800
	To record installation of automated system.		

Assets = Liabilities + Equity
+1,800
−1,800

After the betterment is recorded, the remaining cost to be depreciated is $6,800, computed as $8,000 − $3,000 + $1,800. Depreciation expense for the remaining five years is $1,360 per year, computed as $6,800/5 years.

Point: Both extraordinary repairs and betterments require revising future depreciation.

Extraordinary Repairs (Replacements) **Extraordinary repairs** are expenditures extending the asset's useful life beyond its original estimate. Extraordinary repairs are *capital expenditures* because they benefit future periods. Their costs are debited to the asset account (or to accumulated depreciation). For example, **Delta Air Lines** reports, "modifications that . . . extend the useful lives of airframes or engines are capitalized and amortized [depreciated] over the remaining estimated useful life of the asset."

Decision Maker Answer — p. 419 

Entrepreneur Your start-up Internet services company needs cash, and you are preparing financial statements to apply for a short-term loan. A friend suggests that you treat as many expenses as possible as capital expenditures. What are the impacts on financial statements of this suggestion? What do you think is the aim of this suggestion? ■

DISPOSALS OF PLANT ASSETS

Plant assets are disposed of for several reasons. Some are discarded because they wear out or become obsolete. Others are sold because of changing business plans. Regardless of the reason, disposals of plant assets occur in one of three basic ways: discarding, sale, or exchange. The general steps in accounting for a disposal of plant assets are described in Exhibit 10.15.

EXHIBIT 10.15

Accounting for Disposals of Plant Assets

1. Record depreciation up to the date of disposal—this also updates Accumulated Depreciation.
2. Record the removal of the disposed asset's account balances—including its Accumulated Depreciation.
3. Record any cash (and/or other assets) received or paid in the disposal.
4. Record any gain or loss—computed by comparing the disposed asset's book value with the market value of any assets received.*

* An exception to step 4 is the case of an exchange that lacks *commercial substance*—see Appendix 10A.

Discarding Plant Assets

P2 Account for asset disposal through discarding or selling an asset.

A plant asset is *discarded* when it is no longer useful to the company and it has no market value. To illustrate, assume that a machine costing $9,000 with accumulated depreciation of $9,000 is discarded. When accumulated depreciation equals the asset's cost, it is said to be *fully depreciated* (zero book value). The entry to record the discarding of this asset is

Assets	=	Liabilities	+	Equity
+9,000				
−9,000				

June 5	Accumulated Depreciation—Machinery	9,000	
	Machinery		9,000
	To discard fully depreciated machinery.		

This entry reflects all four steps of Exhibit 10.15. Step 1 is unnecessary since the machine is fully depreciated. Step 2 is reflected in the debit to Accumulated Depreciation and credit to Machinery. Since no other asset is involved, step 3 is irrelevant. Finally, since book value is zero and no other asset is involved, no gain or loss is recorded in step 4.

How do we account for discarding an asset that is not fully depreciated or one whose depreciation is not up-to-date? To answer this, consider equipment costing $8,000 with accumulated depreciation of $6,000 on December 31 of the prior fiscal year-end. This equipment is being depreciated using the straight-line method over eight years with zero salvage. On July 1 of the current year it is discarded. Step 1 is to bring depreciation up-to-date.

Point: Recording depreciation expense up-to-date gives an up-to-date book value for determining gain or loss.

Assets	=	Liabilities	+	Equity
−500				−500

July 1	Depreciation Expense	500	
	Accumulated Depreciation—Equipment		500
	To record 6 months' depreciation ($1,000 × 6/12).		

Steps 2 through 4 of Exhibit 10.15 are reflected in the second (and final) entry.

Assets	=	Liabilities	+	Equity
+6,500				−1,500
−8,000				

July 1	Accumulated Depreciation—Equipment	6,500	
	Loss on Disposal of Equipment	1,500	
	Equipment		8,000
	To discard equipment with a $1,500 book value.		

Point: Gain or loss is determined by comparing "value given" (book value) to "value received."

This loss is computed by comparing the equipment's $1,500 book value ($8,000 − $6,000 − $500) with the zero net cash proceeds. The loss is reported in the Other Expenses and Losses section of the income statement. Discarding an asset can sometimes require a cash payment that would increase the loss.

Selling Plant Assets

Companies often sell plant assets when they restructure or downsize operations. To illustrate the accounting for selling plant assets, we consider BTO's March 31 sale of equipment that cost $16,000 and has accumulated depreciation of $12,000 at December 31 of the prior calendar year-end. Annual depreciation on this equipment is $4,000 computed using straight-line depreciation. Step 1 of this sale is to record depreciation expense and update accumulated depreciation to March 31 of the current year.

March 31	Depreciation Expense	1,000	
	Accumulated Depreciation—Equipment		1,000
	To record 3 months' depreciation ($4,000 × 3/12).		

Assets = Liabilities + Equity
−1,000 −1,000

Steps 2 through 4 of Exhibit 10.15 can be reflected in one final entry that depends on the amount received from the asset's sale. We consider three different possibilities.

Sale at Book Value If BTO receives $3,000 cash, an amount equal to the equipment's book value as of March 31 (book value = $16,000 − $12,000 − $1,000), no gain or loss occurs on disposal. The entry is

Sale price = Book value → No gain or loss

March 31	Cash	3,000	
	Accumulated Depreciation—Equipment	13,000	
	Equipment		16,000
	To record sale of equipment for no gain or loss.		

Assets = Liabilities + Equity
+3,000
+13,000
−16,000

Sale above Book Value If BTO receives $7,000, an amount that is $4,000 above the equipment's $3,000 book value as of March 31, a gain on disposal occurs. The entry is

Sale price > Book value → Gain

March 31	Cash	7,000	
	Accumulated Depreciation—Equipment	13,000	
	Gain on Disposal of Equipment		4,000
	Equipment		16,000
	To record sale of equipment for a $4,000 gain.		

Assets = Liabilities + Equity
+7,000 +4,000
+13,000
−16,000

Sale below Book Value If BTO receives $2,500, an amount that is $500 below the equipment's $3,000 book value as of March 31, a loss on disposal occurs. The entry is

Sale price < Book value → Loss

March 31	Cash	2,500	
	Loss on Disposal of Equipment	500	
	Accumulated Depreciation—Equipment	13,000	
	Equipment		16,000
	To record sale of equipment for a $500 loss.		

Assets = Liabilities + Equity
+2,500 −500
+13,000
16,000

IFRS

Unlike U.S. GAAP, IFRS requires an annual review of useful life and salvage value estimates. IFRS also permits revaluation of plant assets to market value if market value is reliably determined. ■

Quick Check

Answers — p. 419

8. Early in the fifth year of a machine's six-year useful life, it is overhauled, and its useful life is extended to nine years. This machine originally cost $108,000 and the overhaul cost is $12,000. Prepare the entry to record the overhaul cost.

9. Explain the difference between revenue expenditures and capital expenditures and how both are recorded.

10. What is a betterment? How is a betterment recorded?

11. A company acquires equipment on January 10, 2011, at a cost of $42,000. Straight-line depreciation is used with a five-year life and $7,000 salvage value. On June 27, 2012, the company sells this equipment for $32,000. Prepare the entry(ies) for June 27, 2012.

Section 2—Natural Resources

P3 Account for natural resource assets and their depletion.

Natural resources are assets that are physically consumed when used. Examples are standing timber, mineral deposits, and oil and gas fields. Since they are consumed when used, they are often called *wasting assets*. These assets represent soon-to-be inventories of raw materials that will be converted into one or more products by cutting, mining, or pumping. Until that conversion takes place, they are noncurrent assets and are shown in a balance sheet using titles such as timberlands, mineral deposits, or oil reserves. Natural resources are reported under either plant assets or their own separate category. **Alcoa**, for instance, reports its natural resources under the balance sheet title *Properties, plants and equipment.* In a note to its financial statements, Alcoa reports a separate amount for *Land and land rights, including mines.* **Weyerhaeuser**, on the other hand, reports its timber holdings in a separate balance sheet category titled *Timber and timberlands.*

Cost Determination and Depletion

Natural resources are recorded at cost, which includes all expenditures necessary to acquire the resource and prepare it for its intended use. **Depletion** is the process of allocating the cost of a natural resource to the period when it is consumed. Natural resources are reported on the balance sheet at cost less *accumulated depletion.* The depletion expense per period is usually based on units extracted from cutting, mining, or pumping. This is similar to units-of-production depreciation. **Exxon Mobil** uses this approach to amortize the costs of discovering and operating its oil wells.

To illustrate depletion of natural resources, let's consider a mineral deposit with an estimated 250,000 tons of available ore. It is purchased for \$500,000, and we expect zero salvage value. The depletion charge per ton of ore mined is \$2, computed as \$500,000 ÷ 250,000 tons. If 85,000 tons are mined and sold in the first year, the depletion charge for that year is \$170,000. These computations are detailed in Exhibit 10.16.

EXHIBIT 10.16

Depletion Formula and Example

Step 1

$$\textbf{Depletion per unit} = \frac{\textbf{Cost} - \textbf{Salvage value}}{\textbf{Total units of capacity}} = \frac{\$500{,}000 - \$0}{250{,}000 \text{ tons}} = \$2 \text{ per ton}$$

Step 2

$$\textbf{Depletion expense} = \textbf{Depletion per unit} \times \textbf{Units extracted and sold in period}$$
$$= \$2 \times 85{,}000 = \$170{,}000$$

Depletion expense for the first year is recorded as follows.

Assets	= Liabilities	+ Equity
−170,000		−170,000

Dec. 31	Depletion Expense—Mineral Deposit	170,000	
	Accumulated Depletion—Mineral Deposit		170,000
	To record depletion of the mineral deposit.		

The period-end balance sheet reports the mineral deposit as shown in Exhibit 10.17.

EXHIBIT 10.17

Balance Sheet Presentation of Natural Resources

Mineral deposit	\$500,000	
Less accumulated depletion	**170,000**	\$330,000

Since all 85,000 tons of the mined ore are sold during the year, the entire \$170,000 of depletion is reported on the income statement. If some of the ore remains unsold at year-end, however, the depletion related to the unsold ore is carried forward on the balance sheet and reported as

Ore Inventory, a current asset. To illustrate, and continuing with our example, assume that 40,000 tons are mined in the second year, but only 34,000 tons are sold. We record depletion of $68,000 (34,000 tons × $2 depletion per unit) and the remaining Ore Inventory of $12,000 (6,000 tons × $2 depletion per unit) as follows.

Dec. 31	Depletion Expense—Mineral Deposit	68,000	
	Ore Inventory	12,000	
	Accumulated Depletion—Mineral Deposit		80,000
	To record depletion and inventory of mineral deposit.		

Assets	=	Liabilities	+	Equity
−80,000				−68,000
+12,000				

Plant Assets Used in Extracting

The conversion of natural resources by mining, cutting, or pumping usually requires machinery, equipment, and buildings. When the usefulness of these plant assets is directly related to the depletion of a natural resource, their costs are depreciated using the units-of-production method in proportion to the depletion of the natural resource. For example, if a machine is permanently installed in a mine and 10% of the ore is mined and sold in the period, then 10% of the machine's cost (less any salvage value) is allocated to depreciation expense. The same procedure is used when a machine is abandoned once resources have been extracted. If, however, a machine will be moved to and used at another site when extraction is complete, the machine is depreciated over its own useful life.

Decision Insight

Asset Control Long-term assets must be safeguarded against theft, misuse, and other damages. Controls take many forms depending on the asset, including use of security tags, the legal monitoring of rights infringements, and approvals of all asset disposals. A study reports that 44% of employees in operations and service areas witnessed the wasting, mismanaging, or abusing of assets in the past year (KPMG 2009). Another 21% in general management and administration observed stealing or misappropriation of assets. ■

Section 3—Intangible Assets

P4 Account for intangible assets.

Intangible assets are nonphysical assets (used in operations) that confer on their owners long-term rights, privileges, or competitive advantages. Examples are patents, copyrights, licenses, leaseholds, franchises, goodwill, and trademarks. Lack of physical substance does not necessarily imply an intangible asset. Notes and accounts receivable, for instance, lack physical substance, but they are not intangibles. This section identifies the more common types of intangible assets and explains the accounting for them.

Cost Determination and Amortization

An intangible asset is recorded at cost when purchased. Intangibles are then separated into those with limited lives or indefinite lives. If an intangible has a **limited life,** its cost is systematically allocated to expense over its estimated useful life through the process of **amortization.** If an intangible asset has an **indefinite life**—meaning that no legal, regulatory, contractual, competitive, economic, or other factors limit its useful life—it should not be amortized. (If an intangible with an indefinite life is later judged to have a limited life, it is amortized over that limited life.) Amortization of intangible assets is similar to depreciation of plant assets and the depletion of natural resources in that it is a process of cost allocation. However, only the straight-line method is used for amortizing intangibles *unless* the company can show that another method is preferred. The effects of amortization are recorded in a contra account (Accumulated Amortization). The gross acquisition cost of intangible assets is disclosed in the balance sheet along with their accumulated amortization (these disclosures are new). The eventual disposal of an intangible asset involves removing its book value, recording any other asset(s) received or given up, and recognizing any gain or loss for the difference.

Point: The cost to acquire a Website address is an intangible asset.

Point: Goodwill is not amortized; instead, it is annually tested for impairment.

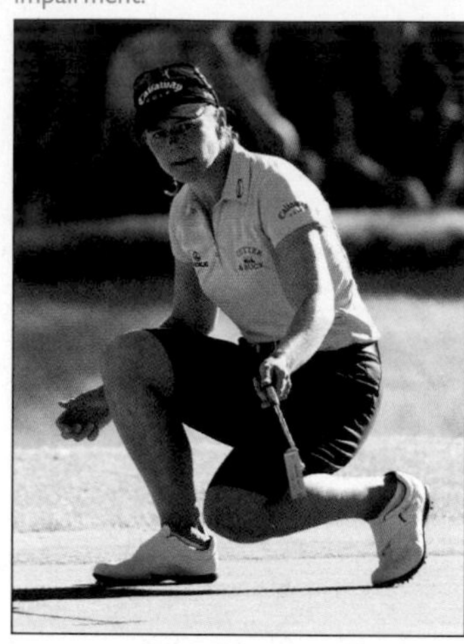

Many intangibles have limited lives due to laws, contracts, or other asset characteristics. Examples are patents, copyrights, and leaseholds. Other intangibles such as goodwill, trademarks, and trade names have lives that cannot be easily determined. The cost of intangible assets is amortized over the periods expected to benefit by their use, but in no case can this period be longer than the asset's legal existence. The values of some intangible assets such as goodwill continue indefinitely into the future and are not amortized. (An intangible asset that is not amortized is tested annually for **impairment**—if necessary, an impairment loss is recorded. Details for this test are in advanced courses.)

Intangible assets are often shown in a separate section of the balance sheet immediately after plant assets. **Callaway Golf**, for instance, follows this approach in reporting nearly $150 million of intangible assets in its balance sheet. Companies usually disclose their amortization periods for intangibles. The remainder of our discussion focuses on accounting for specific types of intangible assets.

Types of Intangibles

Patents The federal government grants patents to encourage the invention of new technology, mechanical devices, and production processes. A **patent** is an exclusive right granted to its owner to manufacture and sell a patented item or to use a process for 20 years. When patent rights are purchased, the cost to acquire the rights is debited to an account called Patents. If the owner engages in lawsuits to successfully defend a patent, the cost of lawsuits is debited to the Patents account. However, the costs of research and development leading to a new patent are expensed when incurred.

A patent's cost is amortized over its estimated useful life (not to exceed 20 years). If we purchase a patent costing $25,000 with a useful life of 10 years, we make the following adjusting entry at the end of each of the 10 years to amortize one-tenth of its cost.

Assets	=	Liabilities	+	Equity
−2,500				−2,500

Dec. 31	Amortization Expense—Patents	2,500	
	Accumulated Amortization—Patents		2,500
	To amortize patent costs over its useful life.		

The $2,500 debit to Amortization Expense appears on the income statement as a cost of the product or service provided under protection of the patent. The Accumulated Amortization—Patents account is a contra asset account to Patents.

Decision Insight

Mention "drug war" and most people think of illegal drug trade. But another drug war is under way: Brand-name drugmakers are fighting to stop generic copies of their products from hitting the market once patents expire. Delaying a generic rival can yield millions in extra sales. ■

Percent of Prescriptions That Specify Generics

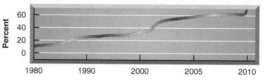

Copyrights A **copyright** gives its owner the exclusive right to publish and sell a musical, literary, or artistic work during the life of the creator plus 70 years, although the useful life of most copyrights is much shorter. The costs of a copyright are amortized over its useful life. The only identifiable cost of many copyrights is the fee paid to the Copyright Office of the federal government or international agency granting the copyright. If this fee is immaterial, it is charged directly to an expense account; but if the identifiable costs of a copyright are material, they are capitalized (recorded in an asset account) and periodically amortized by debiting an account called Amortization Expense—Copyrights.

Franchises and Licenses **Franchises** and **licenses** are rights that a company or government grants an entity to deliver a product or service under specified conditions. Many organizations grant franchise and license rights—**McDonald's**, **Pizza Hut**, and **Major**

League Baseball are just a few examples. The costs of franchises and licenses are debited to a Franchises and Licenses asset account and are amortized over the lives of the agreements. If an agreement is for an indefinite or perpetual period, those costs are not amortized.

Trademarks and Trade Names Companies often adopt unique symbols or select unique names and brands in marketing their products. A **trademark** or **trade (brand) name** is a symbol, name, phrase, or jingle identified with a company, product, or service. Examples are Nike swoosh, Marlboro Man, Big Mac, Coca-Cola, and Corvette. Ownership and exclusive right to use a trademark or trade name is often established by showing that one company used it before another. Ownership is best established by registering a trademark or trade name with the government's Patent Office. The cost of developing, maintaining, or enhancing the value of a trademark or trade name (such as advertising) is charged to expense when incurred. If a trademark or trade name is purchased, however, its cost is debited to an asset account and then amortized over its expected life. If the company plans to renew indefinitely its right to the trademark or trade name, the cost is not amortized.

Point: McDonald's "golden arches" are one of the world's most valuable trademarks, yet this asset is not shown on McDonald's balance sheet.

Goodwill **Goodwill** has a specific meaning in accounting. Goodwill is the amount by which a company's value exceeds the value of its individual assets and liabilities. This usually implies that the company as a whole has certain valuable attributes not measured among its individual assets and liabilities. These can include superior management, skilled workforce, good supplier or customer relations, quality products or services, good location, or other competitive advantages.

To keep accounting information from being too subjective, goodwill is not recorded unless an entire company or business segment is purchased. Purchased goodwill is measured by taking the purchase price of the company and subtracting the market value of its individual net assets (excluding goodwill). For instance, **Yahoo!** paid nearly $3.0 billion to acquire **GeoCities**; about $2.8 of the $3.0 billion was for goodwill and other intangibles.

Goodwill is measured as the excess of the cost of an acquired entity over the value of the acquired net assets. Goodwill is recorded as an asset, and it is *not* amortized. Instead, goodwill is annually tested for impairment. If the book value of goodwill does not exceed its fair (market) value, goodwill is not impaired. However, if the book value of goodwill does exceed its fair value, an impairment loss is recorded equal to that excess. (Details of this test are in advanced courses.)

Point: Amortization of goodwill is different for financial accounting and tax accounting. The IRS requires the amortization of goodwill over 15 years.

Example: Assume goodwill carries a book value of $500 and has an implied fair value of $475, *and* this $25 decline in value meets the 2-step impairment test. The entry to record this impairment is:

Impairment Loss	$25	
Goodwill		$25

Leaseholds Property is rented under a contract called a **lease.** The property's owner, called the **lessor,** grants the lease. The one who secures the right to possess and use the property is called the **lessee.** A **leasehold** refers to the rights the lessor grants to the lessee under the terms of the lease. A leasehold is an intangible asset for the lessee.

Certain leases require no advance payment from the lessee but require monthly rent payments. In this case, we do not set up a Leasehold account. Instead, the monthly payments are debited to a Rent Expense account. If a long-term lease requires the lessee to pay the final period's rent in advance when the lease is signed, the lessee records this advance payment with a debit to the Leasehold account. Since the advance payment is not used until the final period, the Leasehold account balance remains intact until that final period when its balance is transferred to Rent Expense. (Some long-term leases give the lessee essentially the same rights as a purchaser. This results in a tangible asset and a liability reported by the lessee. Chapter 14 describes these so-called *capital leases.*)

A long-term lease can increase in value when current rental rates for similar property rise while the required payments under the lease remain constant. This increase in value of a lease is not reported on the lessee's balance sheet. However, if the property is subleased and the new tenant makes a cash payment to the original lessee for the rights under the old lease, the new tenant debits this payment to a Leasehold account, which is amortized to Rent Expense over the remaining life of the lease.

Point: A leasehold account implies existence of future benefits that the lessee controls because of a prepayment. It also meets the definition of an asset.

Leasehold Improvements A lessee sometimes pays for alterations or improvements to the leased property such as partitions, painting, and storefronts. These alterations and improvements are called **leasehold improvements,** and the lessee debits these costs to a Leasehold Improvements account. Since leasehold improvements become part of the property and revert to the lessor at the end of the lease, the lessee amortizes these costs over the life of the lease or the life of the improvements, whichever is shorter. The amortization entry debits

Amortization Expense—Leasehold Improvements and credits Accumulated Amortization—Leasehold Improvements.

Other Intangibles There are other types of intangible assets such as *software, noncompete covenants, customer lists,* and so forth. Our accounting for them is the same. First, we record the intangible asset's costs. Second, we determine whether the asset has a limited or indefinite life. If limited, we allocate its costs over that period. If indefinite, its costs are not amortized.

Quick Check Answers — p. 419

12. Give an example of a natural resource and of an intangible asset.
13. A company pays $650,000 for an ore deposit. The deposit is estimated to have 325,000 tons of ore that will be mined over the next 10 years. During the first year, it mined, processed, and sold 91,000 tons. What is that year's depletion expense?
14. On January 6, 2011, a company pays $120,000 for a patent with a remaining 17-year legal life to produce a toy expected to be marketable for three years. Prepare entries to record its acquisition and the December 31, 2011, amortization entry.

GLOBAL VIEW

This section discusses similarities and differences between U.S. GAAP and IFRS in accounting and reporting for plant assets and intangible assets.

Accounting for Plant Assets Issues involving cost determination, depreciation, additional expenditures, and disposals of plant assets are subject to broadly similar guidance for both U.S. GAAP and IFRS. Although differences exist, the similarities vastly outweigh the differences. **Nokia** describes its accounting for plant assets as follows:

NOKIA

> Property, plant and equipment are stated at cost less accumulated depreciation. Depreciation is recorded on a straight-line basis over the expected useful lives of the assets. Maintenance, repairs and renewals are generally charged to expense during the financial period in which they are incurred. However, major renovations are capitalized and included in the carrying amount of the asset . . . Major renovations are depreciated over the remaining useful life of the related asset.

One area where notable differences exist is in accounting for changes in the value of plant assets (between the time they are acquired and when disposed of). Namely, how does IFRS and U.S. GAAP treat decreases and increases in the value of plant assets subsequent to acquisition?

Decreases in the Value of Plant Assets When the value of plant assets declines after acquisition, but before disposition, both U.S. GAAP and IFRS require companies to record those decreases as *impairment losses*. While the *test for impairment* uses a different base between U.S. GAAP and IFRS, a more fundamental difference is that U.S. GAAP revalues impaired plant assets to *fair value* whereas IFRS revalues them to a *recoverable amount* (defined as fair value less costs to sell).

Increases in the Value of Plant Assets U.S. GAAP prohibits companies from recording increases in the value of plant assets. However, IFRS permits upward *asset revaluations*. Namely, under IFRS, if an impairment was previously recorded, a company would reverse that impairment to the extent necessary and record that increase in income. If the increase is beyond the original cost, that increase is recorded in comprehensive income.

Accounting for Intangible Assets For intangible assets, the accounting for cost determination, amortization, additional expenditures, and disposals is subject to broadly similar guidance for U.S. GAAP and IFRS. Although differences exist, the similarities vastly outweigh differences. Again, and consistent with the accounting for plant assets, U.S. GAAP and IFRS handle decreases and increases in the value of intangible assets differently. However, IFRS requirements for recording increases in the value of intangible assets are so restrictive that such increases are rare. **Nokia** describes its accounting for intangible assets as follows:

> [Intangible assets] are capitalized and amortized using the straight-line method over their useful lives. Where an indication of impairment exists, the carrying amount of any intangible asset is assessed and written down to its recoverable amount.

NOKIA

Total Asset Turnover

Decision Analysis

A1 Compute total asset turnover and apply it to analyze a company's use of assets.

A company's assets are important in determining its ability to generate sales and earn income. Managers devote much attention to deciding what assets a company acquires, how much it invests in assets, and how to use assets most efficiently and effectively. One important measure of a company's ability to use its assets is **total asset turnover,** defined in Exhibit 10.18.

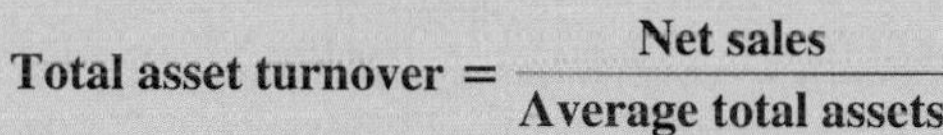

$$\textbf{Total asset turnover} = \frac{\textbf{Net sales}}{\textbf{Average total assets}}$$

EXHIBIT 10.18

Total Asset Turnover

The numerator reflects the net amounts earned from the sale of products and services. The denominator reflects the average total resources devoted to operating the company and generating sales.

To illustrate, let's look at total asset turnover in Exhibit 10.19 for two competing companies: **Molson Coors** and **Boston Beer**.

EXHIBIT 10.19

Analysis Using Total Asset Turnover

Company	Figure ($ millions)	2009	2008	2007	2006	2005
Molson Coors	Net sales	$ 3,032.4	$ 4,774.3	$ 6,190.6	$ 5,845.0	$ 5,506.9
	Average total assets	$11,203.9	$11,934.1	$12,527.5	$11,701.4	$ 8,228.4
	Total asset turnover	**0.27**	**0.40**	**0.49**	**0.50**	**0.67**
Boston Beer	Net sales	$ 415.053	$ 398.400	$ 341.647	$ 285.431	$238.304
	Average total assets	$ 241.347	$ 208.856	$ 176.215	$ 136.765	$113.258
	Total asset turnover	**1.72**	**1.91**	**1.94**	**2.09**	**2.10**

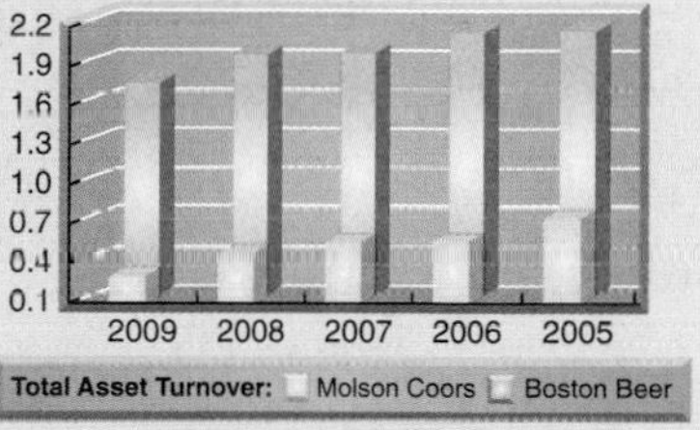

To show how we use total asset turnover, let's look at Molson Coors. We express Molson Coors's use of assets in generating net sales by saying "it turned its assets over 0.27 times during 2009." This means that each $1.00 of assets produced $0.27 of net sales. Is a total asset turnover of 0.27 good or bad? It is safe to say that all companies desire a high total asset turnover. Like many ratio analyses, however, a company's total asset turnover must be interpreted in comparison with those of prior years and of its competitors. Interpreting the total asset turnover also requires an understanding of the company's operations. Some operations are capital intensive, meaning that a relatively large amount is invested in assets to generate sales. This suggests a relatively lower total asset turnover. Other companies' operations are labor intensive, meaning that they generate sales more by the efforts of people than the use of assets. In that case, we expect a higher total asset turnover. Companies with low total asset turnover require higher profit margins (examples are hotels and real estate); companies with high total asset turnover can succeed with lower profit margins (examples are food stores and toy merchandisers). Molson Coors's turnover recently declined and is now much lower than that for Boston Beer and many other competitors. Total asset turnover for Molson Coors's competitors, available in industry publications such as Dun & Bradstreet, is generally in the range of 0.5 to 1.0 over this same period. Overall, Molson Coors must improve relative to its competitors on total asset turnover.

Point: An estimate of **plant asset useful life** equals the plant asset cost divided by depreciation expense.

Point: The **plant asset age** is estimated by dividing accumulated depreciation by depreciation expense. Older plant assets can signal needed asset replacements; they may also signal less efficient assets.

Decision Maker

Answer — p. 419

Environmentalist A paper manufacturer claims it cannot afford more environmental controls. It points to its low total asset turnover of 1.9 and argues that it cannot compete with companies whose total asset turnover is much higher. Examples cited are food stores (5.5) and auto dealers (3.8). How do you respond? ■

DEMONSTRATION PROBLEM

On July 14, 2011, Tulsa Company pays $600,000 to acquire a fully equipped factory. The purchase involves the following assets and information.

Asset	Appraised Value	Salvage Value	Useful Life	Depreciation Method
Land	$160,000			Not depreciated
Land improvements	80,000	$ 0	10 years	Straight-line
Building	320,000	100,000	10 years	Double-declining-balance
Machinery	240,000	20,000	10,000 units	Units-of-production*
Total	$800,000			

* The machinery is used to produce 700 units in 2011 and 1,800 units in 2012.

Required

1. Allocate the total $600,000 purchase cost among the separate assets.
2. Compute the 2011 (six months) and 2012 depreciation expense for each asset, and compute the company's total depreciation expense for both years.
3. On the last day of calendar year 2013, Tulsa discarded machinery that had been on its books for five years. The machinery's original cost was $12,000 (estimated life of five years) and its salvage value was $2,000. No depreciation had been recorded for the fifth year when the disposal occurred. Journalize the fifth year of depreciation (straight-line method) and the asset's disposal.
4. At the beginning of year 2013, Tulsa purchased a patent for $100,000 cash. The company estimated the patent's useful life to be 10 years. Journalize the patent acquisition and its amortization for the year 2013.
5. Late in the year 2013, Tulsa acquired an ore deposit for $600,000 cash. It added roads and built mine shafts for an additional cost of $80,000. Salvage value of the mine is estimated to be $20,000. The company estimated 330,000 tons of available ore. In year 2013, Tulsa mined and sold 10,000 tons of ore. Journalize the mine's acquisition and its first year's depletion.

6.[A] On the first day of 2013, Tulsa exchanged the machinery that was acquired on July 14, 2011, along with $5,000 cash for machinery with a $210,000 market value. Journalize the exchange of these assets assuming the exchange lacked commercial substance. (Refer to background information in parts 1 and 2.)

PLANNING THE SOLUTION

- Complete a three-column table showing the following amounts for each asset: appraised value, percent of total value, and apportioned cost.
- Using allocated costs, compute depreciation for 2011 (only one-half year) and 2012 (full year) for each asset. Summarize those computations in a table showing total depreciation for each year.
- Remember that depreciation must be recorded up-to-date before discarding an asset. Calculate and record depreciation expense for the fifth year using the straight-line method. Since salvage value is not received at the end of a discarded asset's life, the amount of any salvage value becomes a loss on disposal. Record the loss on the disposal as well as the removal of the discarded asset and its related accumulated depreciation.
- Record the patent (an intangible asset) at its purchase price. Use straight-line amortization over its useful life to calculate amortization expense.
- Record the ore deposit (a natural resource asset) at its cost, including any added costs to ready the mine for use. Calculate depletion per ton using the depletion formula. Multiply the depletion per ton by the amount of tons mined and sold to calculate depletion expense for the year.
- Remember that gains and losses on asset exchanges that lack commercial substance are not recognized. Make a journal entry to add the acquired machinery to the books and to remove the old machinery, along with its accumulated depreciation, and to record the cash given in the exchange.

SOLUTION TO DEMONSTRATION PROBLEM

1. Allocation of the total cost of $600,000 among the separate assets.

Asset	Appraised Value	Percent of Total Value	Apportioned Cost
Land	$160,000	20%	**$120,000** ($600,000 × 20%)
Land improvements	80,000	10	**60,000** ($600,000 × 10%)
Building	320,000	40	**240,000** ($600,000 × 40%)
Machinery	240,000	30	**180,000** ($600,000 × 30%)
Total	$800,000	100%	$ 600,000

2. Depreciation for each asset. (Land is not depreciated.)

Land Improvements	
Cost	$ 60,000
Salvage value	0
Depreciable cost	$ 60,000
Useful life	10 years
Annual depreciation expense ($60,000/10 years)	$ 6,000
2011 depreciation ($6,000 × 6/12)	**$ 3,000**
2012 depreciation	**$ 6,000**
Building	
Straight-line rate = 100%/10 years = 10%	
Double-declining-balance rate = 10% × 2 = 20%	
2011 depreciation ($240,000 × 20% × 6/12)	**$ 24,000**
2012 depreciation [($240,000 − $24,000) × 20%]	**$ 43,200**
Machinery	
Cost	$180,000
Salvage value	20,000
Depreciable cost	$160,000
Total expected units of production	10,000 units
Depreciation per unit ($160,000/10,000 units)	$ 16
2011 depreciation ($16 × 700 units)	**$ 11,200**
2012 depreciation ($16 × 1,800 units)	**$ 28,800**

Total depreciation expense for each year:

	2011	2012
Land improvements	$ 3,000	$ 6,000
Building	24,000	43,200
Machinery	11,200	28,800
Total	$38,200	$78,000

3. Record the depreciation up-to-date on the discarded asset.

Depreciation Expense—Machinery	2,000	
Accumulated Depreciation—Machinery		2,000
To record depreciation on date of disposal: ($12,000 − $2,000)/5		

Record the removal of the discarded asset and its loss on disposal.

Accumulated Depreciation—Machinery	10,000	
Loss on Disposal of Machinery	2,000	
Machinery		12,000
To record the discarding of machinery with a $2,000 book value.		

4.

Patent	100,000	
Cash		100,000
To record patent acquisition.		

Amortization Expense—Patent	10,000	
Accumulated Amortization—Patent		10,000
To record amortization expense: $100,000/10 years = $10,000.		

5.

Ore Deposit	680,000	
Cash		680,000
To record ore deposit acquisition and its related costs.		

Depletion Expense—Ore Deposit	20,000	
Accumulated Depletion—Ore Deposit		20,000
To record depletion expense: ($680,000 − $20,000)/330,000 tons = $2 per ton. 10,000 tons mined and sold × $2 = $20,000 depletion.		

6. Record the asset exchange: The book value on the exchange date is $180,000 (cost) − $40,000 (accumulated depreciation). The book value of the machinery given up in the exchange ($140,000) plus the $5,000 cash paid is less than the $210,000 value of the machine acquired. The entry to record this exchange of assets that lacks commercial substance does not recognize the $65,000 "gain."

Machinery (new)	145,000*	
Accumulated Depreciation—Machinery (old)	40,000	
Machinery (old)		180,000
Cash		5,000
To record asset exchange that lacks commercial substance.		

* Market value of the acquired asset of $210,000 minus $65,000 "gain."

APPENDIX

10A Exchanging Plant Assets

P5A Account for asset exchanges.

Many plant assets such as machinery, automobiles, and office equipment are disposed of by exchanging them for newer assets. In a typical exchange of plant assets, a *trade-in allowance* is received on the old asset and the balance is paid in cash. Accounting for the exchange of assets depends on whether the transaction has *commercial substance* (per *SFAS 153,* commercial substance implies that it alters the company's future cash flows). If an asset exchange has commercial substance, a gain or loss is recorded based on the difference between the book value of the asset(s) given up and the market value of the asset(s) received. If an asset exchange lacks commercial substance, no gain or loss is recorded, and the asset(s) received is recorded based on the book value of the asset(s) given up. An exchange has commercial substance if the company's future cash flows change as a result of the transaction. This section describes the accounting for the exchange of assets.

Exchange with Commercial Substance: A Loss A company acquires $42,000 in new equipment. In exchange, the company pays $33,000 cash and trades in old equipment. The old equipment originally cost $36,000 and has accumulated depreciation of $20,000, which implies a $16,000 book value at the time of exchange. We are told this exchange has commercial substance and that the old equipment has a trade-in allowance of $9,000. This exchange yields a loss as computed in the middle (Loss) columns of Exhibit 10A.1; the loss is computed as Asset received − Assets given = $42,000 − $49,000 = $(7,000). We can also compute the loss as Trade-in allowance − Book value of asset given = $9,000 − $16,000 = $(7,000).

EXHIBIT 10A.1

Computing Gain or Loss on Asset Exchange with Commercial Substance

Asset Exchange Has Commercial Substance	Loss		Gain	
Market value of asset received		$42,000		$52,000
Book value of assets given:				
Equipment ($36,000 − $20,000)	$16,000		$16,000	
Cash	33,000	49,000	33,000	49,000
Gain (loss) on exchange		**$(7,000)**		**$ 3,000**

The entry to record this asset exchange is

Jan. 3	Equipment (**new**)	42,000	
	Loss on Exchange of Assets	7,000	
	Accumulated Depreciation—Equipment (**old**)	20,000	
	Equipment (**old**)		36,000
	Cash		33,000
	To record exchange (with commercial substance) of old equipment and cash for new equipment.		

Assets = Liabilities + Equity
+42,000 −7,000
+20,000
−36,000
−33,000

Point: Parenthetical notes to "new" and "old" equipment are for illustration only. Both the debit and credit are to the same Equipment account.

Exchange with Commercial Substance: A Gain Let's assume the same facts as in the preceding asset exchange *except* that the new equipment received has a market value of $52,000 instead of $42,000. We are told that this exchange has commercial substance and that the old equipment has a trade-in allowance of $19,000. This exchange yields a gain as computed in the right-most (Gain) columns of Exhibit 10A.1; the gain is computed as Asset received − Assets given = $52,000 − $49,000 = $3,000. We can also compute the gain as Trade-in allowance − Book value of asset given = $19,000 − $16,000 = $3,000. The entry to record this asset exchange is

Jan. 3	Equipment (**new**)	52,000	
	Accumulated Depreciation—Equipment (**old**)	20,000	
	Equipment (**old**)		36,000
	Cash		33,000
	Gain on Exchange of Assets		3,000
	To record exchange (with commercial substance) of old equipment and cash for new equipment.		

Assets = Liabilities + Equity
+52,000 +3,000
+20,000
−36,000
−33,000

Exchanges without Commercial Substance Let's assume the same facts as in the preceding asset exchange involving new equipment received with a market value of $52,000, but let's instead assume the transaction *lacks commercial substance.* The entry to record this asset exchange is

Jan. 3	Equipment (**new**)	49,000	
	Accumulated Depreciation—Equipment (**old**)	20,000	
	Equipment (**old**)		36,000
	Cash		33,000
	To record exchange (without commercial substance) of old equipment and cash for new equipment.		

Assets = Liabilities + Equity
+49,000
+20,000
−36,000
−33,000

The $3,000 gain recorded when the transaction has commercial substance is *not* recognized in this entry because of the rule prohibiting recording a gain or loss on asset exchanges without commercial substance. The $49,000 recorded for the new equipment equals its cash price ($52,000) less the unrecognized gain ($3,000) on the exchange. The $49,000 cost recorded is called the *cost basis* of the new machine. This cost basis is the amount we use to compute depreciation and its book value. The cost basis of the new asset also can be computed by summing the book values of the assets given up as shown in Exhibit 10A.2. The same analysis and approach are taken for a loss on an asset exchange without commercial substance.

Point: No gain or loss is recorded for exchanges *without* commercial substance.

EXHIBIT 10A.2

Cost Basis of New Asset When Gain Not Recorded on Asset Exchange without Commercial Substance

Cost of old equipment	$ 36,000
Less accumulated depreciation	20,000
Book value of old equipment	16,000
Cash paid in the exchange	33,000
Cost recorded for new equipment	**$49,000**

Quick Check

Answer — p. 419

15. A company trades an old Web server for a new one. The cost of the old server is $30,000, and its accumulated depreciation at the time of the trade is $23,400. The new server has a cash price of $45,000. Prepare entries to record the trade under two different assumptions where the company receives a trade-in allowance of (*a*) $3,000 and the exchange has commercial substance, and (*b*) $7,000 and the exchange lacks commercial substance.

Summary

C1 Explain the cost principle for computing the cost of plant assets. Plant assets are set apart from other tangible assets by two important features: use in operations and useful lives longer than one period. Plant assets are recorded at cost when purchased. Cost includes all normal and reasonable expenditures necessary to get the asset in place and ready for its intended use. The cost of a lump-sum purchase is allocated among its individual assets.

C2 Explain depreciation for partial years and changes in estimates. Partial-year depreciation is often required because assets are bought and sold throughout the year. Depreciation is revised when changes in estimates such as salvage value and useful life occur. If the useful life of a plant asset changes, for instance, the remaining cost to be depreciated is spread over the remaining (revised) useful life of the asset.

C3 Distinguish between revenue and capital expenditures, and account for them. Revenue expenditures expire in the current period and are debited to expense accounts and matched with current revenues. Ordinary repairs are an example of revenue expenditures. Capital expenditures benefit future periods and are debited to asset accounts. Examples of capital expenditures are extraordinary repairs and betterments.

A1 Compute total asset turnover and apply it to analyze a company's use of assets. Total asset turnover measures a company's ability to use its assets to generate sales. It is defined as net sales divided by average total assets. While all companies desire a high total asset turnover, it must be interpreted in comparison with those for prior years and its competitors.

P1 Compute and record depreciation using the straight-line, units-of-production, and declining-balance methods. *Depreciation* is the process of allocating to expense the cost of a plant asset over the accounting periods that benefit from its use. Depreciation does not measure the decline in a plant asset's market value or its physical deterioration. Three factors determine depreciation: cost, salvage value, and useful life. Salvage value is an estimate of the asset's value at the end of its benefit period. Useful (service) life is the length of time an asset is productively used. The straight-line method divides cost less salvage value by the asset's useful life to determine depreciation expense per period. The units-of-production method divides cost less salvage value by the estimated number of units the asset will produce over its life to determine depreciation per unit. The declining-balance method multiplies the asset's beginning-of-period book value by a factor that is often double the straight-line rate.

P2 Account for asset disposal through discarding or selling an asset. When a plant asset is discarded or sold, its cost and accumulated depreciation are removed from the accounts. Any cash proceeds from discarding or selling an asset are recorded and compared to the asset's book value to determine gain or loss.

P3 Account for natural resource assets and their depletion. The cost of a natural resource is recorded in a noncurrent asset account. Depletion of a natural resource is recorded by allocating its cost to depletion expense using the units-of-production method. Depletion is credited to an Accumulated Depletion account.

P4 Account for intangible assets. An intangible asset is recorded at the cost incurred to purchase it. The cost of an intangible asset with a definite useful life is allocated to expense using the straight-line method, and is called *amortization*. Goodwill and intangible assets with an indefinite useful life are not amortized—they are annually tested for impairment. Intangible assets include patents, copyrights, leaseholds, goodwill, and trademarks.

P5A Account for asset exchanges. For an asset exchange with commercial substance, a gain or loss is recorded based on the difference between the book value of the asset given up and the market value of the asset received. For an asset exchange without commercial substance, no gain or loss is recorded, and the asset received is recorded based on the book value of the asset given up.

Guidance Answers to Decision Maker and Decision Ethics

Controller The president's instructions may reflect an honest and reasonable prediction of the future. Since the company is struggling financially, the president may have concluded that the normal pattern of replacing assets every three years cannot continue. Perhaps the strategy is to avoid costs of frequent replacements and stretch use of equipment a few years longer until financial conditions improve. However, if you believe the president's decision is unprincipled, you might confront the president with your opinion that it is unethical to change the estimate to increase income. Another possibility is to wait and see whether the auditor will prohibit this change in estimate. In either case, you should insist that the statements be based on reasonable estimates.

Entrepreneur Treating an expense as a capital expenditure means that reported expenses will be lower and income higher in the short run. This is so because a capital expenditure is not expensed immediately but is spread over the asset's useful life. Treating an expense as a capital expenditure also means that asset and equity totals are reported at larger amounts in the short run. This continues until the asset is fully depreciated. Your friend is probably trying to help, but the suggestion is misguided. Only an expenditure benefiting future periods is a capital expenditure.

Environmentalist The paper manufacturer's comparison of its total asset turnover with food stores and auto dealers is misdirected. These other industries' turnovers are higher because their profit margins are lower (about 2%). Profit margins for the paper industry are usually 3% to 3.5%. You need to collect data from competitors in the paper industry to show that a 1.9 total asset turnover is about the norm for this industry. You might also want to collect data on this company's revenues and expenses, along with compensation data for its high-ranking officers and employees.

Guidance Answers to Quick Checks

1. **a.** Supplies—current assets
   b. Office equipment—plant assets
   c. Inventory—current assets
   d. Land for future expansion—long-term investments
   e. Trucks used in operations—plant assets
2. **a.** Land **b.** Land Improvements
3. $700,000 + $49,000 − $21,000 + $3,500 + $3,000 + $2,500 = $737,000
4. **a.** Straight-line with 7-year life: ($77,000/7) = $11,000
   b. Straight-line with 10-year life: ($77,000/10) = $7,700
5. Depreciation is a process of allocating the cost of plant assets to the accounting periods that benefit from the assets' use.
6. **a.** Book value using straight-line depreciation: $96,000 − [($96,000 − $8,000)/5] = $78,400
   b. Book value using units of production: $96,000 − [($96,000 − $8,000) × (10,000/100,000)] = $87,200
7. ($3,800 − $200)/3 = $1,200 (original depreciation per year)
   $1,200 × 2 = $2,400 (accumulated depreciation)
   ($3,800 − $2,400)/2 = $700 (revised depreciation)
8.

Machinery	12,000	
Cash		12,000

9. A revenue expenditure benefits only the current period and should be charged to expense in the current period. A capital expenditure yields benefits that extend beyond the end of the current period and should be charged to an asset.
10. A betterment involves modifying an existing plant asset to make it more efficient, usually by replacing part of the asset with an improved or superior part. The cost of a betterment is debited to the asset account.
11.

Depreciation Expense	3,500	
Accumulated Depreciation		3,500
Cash	32,000	
Accumulated Depreciation	10,500	
Gain on Sale of Equipment		500
Equipment		42,000

12. Examples of natural resources are timberlands, mineral deposits, and oil reserves. Examples of intangible assets are patents, copyrights, leaseholds, leasehold improvements, goodwill, trademarks, and licenses.
13. ($650,000/325,000 tons) × 91,000 tons = $182,000
14.

Jan. 6	Patents	120,000	
	Cash		120,000
Dec. 31	Amortization Expense	40,000*	
	Accumulated Amortization—Patents		40,000

* $120,000/3 years = $40,000

15.

(a) Equipment (new)	45,000	
Loss on Exchange of Assets	3,600	
Accumulated Depreciation—Equipment (old)	23,100	
Equipment (old)		30,000
Cash ($45,000 − $3,000)		42,000

(b) Equipment (new)*	44,600	
Accumulated Depreciation—Equipment (old)	23,400	
Equipment (old)		30,000
Cash ($45,000 − $7,000)		38,000

* Includes $400 unrecognized gain.

Key Terms

mhhe.com/wildFAP20e

Land improvements (p. 396)
Lease (p. 411)
Leasehold (p. 411)
Leasehold improvements (p. 411)
Lessee (p. 411)
Lessor (p. 411)
Licenses (p. 410)
Limited life (p. 409)
Modified Accelerated Cost Recovery System (MACRS) (p. 402)
Natural resources (p. 408)
Obsolescence (p. 397)
Ordinary repairs (p. 404)
Patent (p. 410)
Plant asset age (p. 413)
Plant assets (p. 394)
Revenue expenditures (p. 404)
Salvage value (p. 397)
Straight-line depreciation (p. 398)
Total asset turnover (p. 413)
Trademark or **trade (brand) name** (p. 411)
Units-of-production depreciation (p. 399)
Useful life (p. 397)

Multiple Choice Quiz

Answers on p. 433 mhhe.com/wildFAP20e

Additional Quiz Questions are available at the book's Website.

1. A company paid $326,000 for property that included land, land improvements, and a building. The land was appraised at $175,000, the land improvements were appraised at $70,000, and the building was appraised at $105,000. What is the allocation of property costs to the three assets purchased?
   - **a.** Land, $150,000; Land Improvements, $60,000; Building, $90,000
   - **b.** Land, $163,000; Land Improvements, $65,200; Building, $97,800
   - **c.** Land, $150,000; Land Improvements, $61,600; Building, $92,400
   - **d.** Land, $159,000; Land Improvements, $65,200; Building, $95,400
   - **e.** Land, $175,000; Land Improvements, $70,000; Building, $105,000
2. A company purchased a truck for $35,000 on January 1, 2011. The truck is estimated to have a useful life of four years and an estimated salvage value of $1,000. Assuming that the company uses straight-line depreciation, what is the depreciation expense on the truck for the year ended December 31, 2012?
   - **a.** $8,750
   - **b.** $17,500
   - **c.** $8,500
   - **d.** $17,000
   - **e.** $25,500
3. A company purchased machinery for $10,800,000 on January 1, 2011. The machinery has a useful life of 10 years and an estimated salvage value of $800,000. What is the depreciation expense on the machinery for the year ended December 31, 2012, assuming that the double-declining-balance method is used?
   - **a.** $2,160,000
   - **b.** $3,888,000
   - **c.** $1,728,000
   - **d.** $2,000,000
   - **e.** $1,600,000
4. A company sold a machine that originally cost $250,000 for $120,000 when accumulated depreciation on the machine was $100,000. The gain or loss recorded on the sale of this machine is
   - **a.** $0 gain or loss.
   - **b.** $120,000 gain.
   - **c.** $30,000 loss.
   - **d.** $30,000 gain.
   - **e.** $150,000 loss.
5. A company had average total assets of $500,000, gross sales of $575,000, and net sales of $550,000. The company's total asset turnover is
   - **a.** 1.15
   - **b.** 1.10
   - **c.** 0.91
   - **d.** 0.87
   - **e.** 1.05

A *Superscript letter A denotes assignments based on Appendix 10A.*
Icon denotes assignments that involve decision making.

Discussion Questions

1. What characteristics of a plant asset make it different from other assets?
2. What is the general rule for cost inclusion for plant assets?
3. What is different between land and land improvements?
4. Why is the cost of a lump-sum purchase allocated to the individual assets acquired?
5. Does the balance in the Accumulated Depreciation—Machinery account represent funds to replace the machinery when it wears out? If not, what does it represent?
6. Why is the Modified Accelerated Cost Recovery System not generally accepted for financial accounting purposes?

7. What accounting concept justifies charging low-cost plant asset purchases immediately to an expense account?
8. What is the difference between ordinary repairs and extraordinary repairs? How should each be recorded?
9. Identify events that might lead to disposal of a plant asset.
10. What is the process of allocating the cost of natural resources to expense as they are used?
11. Is the declining-balance method an acceptable way to compute depletion of natural resources? Explain.
12. What are the characteristics of an intangible asset?
13. What general procedures are applied in accounting for the acquisition and potential cost allocation of intangible assets?
14. When do we know that a company has goodwill? When can goodwill appear in a company's balance sheet?
15. Assume that a company buys another business and pays for its goodwill. If the company plans to incur costs each year to maintain the value of the goodwill, must it also amortize this goodwill?
16. How is total asset turnover computed? Why would a financial statement user be interested in total asset turnover?
17. Refer to **Research In Motion**'s balance sheet in Appendix A. What property, plant and equipment assets does RIM list on its balance sheet? What is the book value of its total net property, plant and equipment assets at February 27, 2010? **RIM**
18. **Apple** lists its plant assets as "Property, plant and equipment, net." What does "net" mean in this title? Apple
19. Refer to **Nokia**'s balance sheet in Appendix A. What does it title its plant assets? What is the book value of its plant assets at December 31, 2009? **NOKIA**
20. Refer to the May 31, 2009, balance sheet of **Palm** in Appendix A. What long-term assets discussed in this chapter are reported by the company? **Palm**

connect

QUICK STUDY

QS 10-1
Cost of plant assets C1 

Strike Bowling installs automatic scorekeeping equipment with an invoice cost of $180,000. The electrical work required for the installation costs $8,000. Additional costs are $3,000 for delivery and $12,600 for sales tax. During the installation, a component of the equipment is carelessly left on a lane and hit by the automatic lane-cleaning machine. The cost of repairing the component is $2,250. What is the total recorded cost of the automatic scorekeeping equipment?

QS 10-2
Defining assets C1 

Identify the main difference between (1) plant assets and inventory, (2) plant assets and current assets, and (3) plant assets and long-term investments.

QS 10-3
Straight-line depreciation P1

On January 2, 2011, the Crossover Band acquires sound equipment for concert performances at a cost of $55,900. The band estimates it will use this equipment for four years, during which time it anticipates performing about 120 concerts. It estimates that after four years it can sell the equipment for $1,900. During year 2011, the band performs 40 concerts. Compute the year 2011 depreciation using the straight-line method.

QS 10-4
Units-of-production depreciation P1

Refer to the information in QS 10-3. Compute the year 2011 depreciation using the units-of-production method.

QS 10-5
Computing revised depreciation C2

Refer to the facts in QS 10-3. Assume that the Crossover Band uses straight-line depreciation but realizes at the start of the second year that due to concert bookings beyond expectations, this equipment will last only a total of three years. The salvage value remains unchanged. Compute the revised depreciation for both the second and third years.

QS 10-6
Double-declining-balance method P1

A fleet of refrigerated delivery trucks is acquired on January 5, 2011, at a cost of $930,000 with an estimated useful life of eight years and an estimated salvage value of $150,000. Compute the depreciation expense for the first three years using the double-declining-balance method.

QS 10-7
Recording plant asset impairment C2

Assume a company's equipment carries a book value of $4,000 ($4,500 cost less $500 accumulated depreciation) and a fair value of $3,750, *and* that the $250 decline in fair value in comparison to the book value meets the 2-step impairment test. Prepare the entry to record this $250 impairment.

QS 10-8
Revenue and capital expenditures
C3 

1. Classify the following as either revenue or capital expenditures.
   - **a.** Completed an addition to an office building for $250,000 cash.
   - **b.** Paid $160 for the monthly cost of replacement filters on an air-conditioning system.
   - **c.** Paid $300 cash per truck for the cost of their annual tune-ups.
   - **d.** Paid $50,000 cash to replace a compressor on a refrigeration system that extends its useful life by four years.
2. Prepare the journal entries to record transactions *a* and *d* of part 1.

QS 10-9
Disposal of assets P2

Horizon Co. owns equipment that cost $138,750, with accumulated depreciation of $81,000. Horizon sells the equipment for cash. Record the sale of the equipment assuming Horizon sells the equipment for (1) $63,000 cash, (2) $57,750 cash, and (3) $46,500 cash.

QS 10-10
Natural resources and depletion
P3

Diamond Company acquires an ore mine at a cost of $1,300,000. It incurs additional costs of $200,000 to access the mine, which is estimated to hold 500,000 tons of ore. The estimated value of the land after the ore is removed is $150,000.

1. Prepare the entry(ies) to record the cost of the ore mine.
2. Prepare the year-end adjusting entry if 90,000 tons of ore are mined and sold the first year.

QS 10-11
Classify assets
P3 P4 

Which of the following assets are reported on the balance sheet as intangible assets? Which are reported as natural resources? (*a*) timberland, (*b*) patent, (*c*) leasehold, (*d*) Oil well, (*e*) equipment, (*f*) copyright, (*g*) franchise, (*h*) gold mine.

QS 10-12
Intangible assets and amortization P4

On January 4 of this year, Larsen Boutique incurs a $95,000 cost to modernize its store. Improvements include new floors, ceilings, wiring, and wall coverings. These improvements are estimated to yield benefits for 10 years. Larsen leases its store and has eight years remaining on the lease. Prepare the entry to record (1) the cost of modernization and (2) amortization at the end of this current year.

QS 10-13
Computing total asset turnover
A1

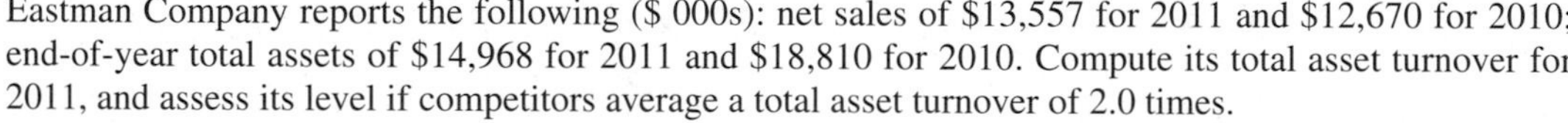

Eastman Company reports the following ($ 000s): net sales of $13,557 for 2011 and $12,670 for 2010; end-of-year total assets of $14,968 for 2011 and $18,810 for 2010. Compute its total asset turnover for 2011, and assess its level if competitors average a total asset turnover of 2.0 times.

QS 10-14[A]
Asset exchange
P5

Esteban Co. owns a machine that costs $38,400 with accumulated depreciation of $20,400. Esteban exchanges the machine for a newer model that has a market value of $48,000. (1) Record the exchange assuming Esteban paid $32,000 cash and the exchange has commercial substance. (2) Record the exchange assuming Esteban pays $24,000 cash and the exchange lacks commercial substance.

QS 10-15
International accounting standards
C1 C3 

Answer each of the following related to international accounting standards.

- **a.** Accounting for plant assets involves cost determination, depreciation, additional expenditures, and disposals. Is plant asset accounting broadly similar or dissimilar between IFRS and U.S. GAAP? Identify one notable difference between IFRS and U.S. GAAP in accounting for plant assets.
- **b.** Describe how IFRS and U.S. GAAP treat increases in the value of plant assets subsequent to their acquisition (but before their disposition).

EXERCISES

Exercise 10-1
Cost of plant assets
 C1 

Farha Co. purchases a machine for $11,500, terms 2/10, n/60, FOB shipping point. The seller prepaid the $260 freight charges, adding the amount to the invoice and bringing its total to $11,760. The machine requires special steel mounting and power connections costing $795. Another $375 is paid to assemble the machine and get it into operation. In moving the machine to its steel mounting, $190 in damages occurred. Materials costing $30 are used in adjusting the machine to produce a satisfactory product. The adjustments are normal for this machine and are not the result of the damages. Compute the cost recorded for this machine. (Farha pays for this machine within the cash discount period.)

Exercise 10-2
Recording costs of assets C1

Cerner Manufacturing purchases a large lot on which an old building is located as part of its plans to build a new plant. The negotiated purchase price is $225,000 for the lot plus $120,000 for the old building. The company pays $34,500 to tear down the old building and $51,000 to fill and level the lot. It also pays a total of $1,440,000 in construction costs—this amount consists of $1,354,500 for the new building and $85,500 for lighting and paving a parking area next to the building. Prepare a single journal entry to record these costs incurred by Cerner, all of which are paid in cash.

Exercise 10-3
Lump-sum purchase of plant assets C1

Ming Yue Company pays $368,250 for real estate plus $19,600 in closing costs. The real estate consists of land appraised at $166,320; land improvements appraised at $55,440; and a building appraised at $174,240. Allocate the total cost among the three purchased assets and prepare the journal entry to record the purchase.

Exercise 10-4
Straight-line depreciation P1

In early January 2011, LabTech purchases computer equipment for $147,000 to use in operating activities for the next four years. It estimates the equipment's salvage value at $30,000. Prepare a table showing depreciation and book value for each of the four years assuming straight-line depreciation.

Exercise 10-5
Double-declining-balance depreciation P1

Refer to the information in Exercise 10-4. Prepare a table showing depreciation and book value for each of the four years assuming double-declining-balance depreciation.

Exercise 10-6
Straight-line depreciation P1

Feng Company installs a computerized manufacturing machine in its factory at the beginning of the year at a cost of $42,300. The machine's useful life is estimated at 10 years, or 363,000 units of product, with a $6,000 salvage value. During its second year, the machine produces 35,000 units of product. Determine the machine's second-year depreciation under the straight-line method.

Exercise 10-7
Units-of-production depreciation P1

Refer to the information in Exercise 10-6. Determine the machine's second-year depreciation using the units-of-production method.

Exercise 10-8
Double-declining-balance depreciation P1

Refer to the information in Exercise 10-6. Determine the machine's second-year depreciation using the double-declining-balance method.

Exercise 10-9
Straight-line, partial-year depreciation C2

On April 1, 2010, Stone's Backhoe Co. purchases a trencher for $250,000. The machine is expected to last five years and have a salvage value of $25,000. Compute depreciation expense for both 2010 and 2011 assuming the company uses the straight-line method.

Exercise 10-10
Double-declining-balance, partial-year depreciation C2

Refer to the information in Exercise 10-9. Compute depreciation expense for both 2010 and 2011 assuming the company uses the double-declining-balance method.

Exercise 10-11
Revising depreciation C2

Supreme Fitness Club uses straight-line depreciation for a machine costing $21,750, with an estimated four-year life and a $2,250 salvage value. At the beginning of the third year, Supreme determines that the machine has three more years of remaining useful life, after which it will have an estimated $1,800 salvage value. Compute (1) the machine's book value at the end of its second year and (2) the amount of depreciation for each of the final three years given the revised estimates.

Check (2) $3,400

Exercise 10-12
Straight-line depreciation and income effects P1

Mulan Enterprises pays $235,200 for equipment that will last five years and have a $52,500 salvage value. By using the equipment in its operations for five years, the company expects to earn $85,500 annually, after deducting all expenses except depreciation. Prepare a table showing income before depreciation, depreciation expense, and net (pretax) income for each year and for the total five-year period, assuming straight-line depreciation.

Exercise 10-13
Double-declining-balance depreciation P1

Refer to the information in Exercise 10-12. Prepare a table showing income before depreciation, depreciation expense, and net (pretax) income for each year and for the total five-year period, assuming double-declining-balance depreciation is used.

Check Year 3 NI, $53,328

Exercise 10-14
Extraordinary repairs; plant asset age
C3 

Passat Company owns a building that appears on its prior year-end balance sheet at its original $561,000 cost less $420,750 accumulated depreciation. The building is depreciated on a straight-line basis assuming a 20-year life and no salvage value. During the first week in January of the current calendar year, major structural repairs are completed on the building at a $67,200 cost. The repairs extend its useful life for 7 years beyond the 20 years originally estimated.

1. Determine the building's age (plant asset age) as of the prior year-end balance sheet date.
2. Prepare the entry to record the cost of the structural repairs that are paid in cash.
3. Determine the book value of the building immediately after the repairs are recorded.
4. Prepare the entry to record the current calendar year's depreciation.

Check (3) $207,450

Exercise 10-15
Ordinary repairs, extraordinary repairs and betterments
C3

Patterson Company pays $262,500 for equipment expected to last four years and have a $30,000 salvage value. Prepare journal entries to record the following costs related to the equipment.

1. During the second year of the equipment's life, $21,000 cash is paid for a new component expected to increase the equipment's productivity by 10% a year.
2. During the third year, $5,250 cash is paid for normal repairs necessary to keep the equipment in good working order.
3. During the fourth year, $13,950 is paid for repairs expected to increase the useful life of the equipment from four to five years.

Exercise 10–16
Disposal of assets
P2

Millworks Company owns a milling machine that cost $125,000 and has accumulated depreciation of $91,000. Prepare the entry to record the disposal of the milling machine on January 5 under each of the following independent situations.

1. The machine needed extensive repairs, and it was not worth repairing. Millworks disposed of the machine, receiving nothing in return.
2. Millworks sold the machine for $17,500 cash.
3. Millworks sold the machine for $34,000 cash.
4. Millworks sold the machine for $40,000 cash.

Exercise 10-17
Partial-year depreciation; disposal of plant asset
P2

Finesse Co. purchases and installs a machine on January 1, 2011, at a total cost of $92,750. Straight-line depreciation is taken each year for four years assuming a seven-year life and no salvage value. The machine is disposed of on July 1, 2015, during its fifth year of service. Prepare entries to record the partial year's depreciation on July 1, 2015, and to record the disposal under the following separate assumptions: (1) the machine is sold for $35,000 cash and (2) Finesse receives an insurance settlement of $30,000 resulting from the total destruction of the machine in a fire.

Exercise 10-18
Depletion of natural resources
P1 P3

On April 2, 2011, Idaho Mining Co. pays $3,633,750 for an ore deposit containing 1,425,000 tons. The company installs machinery in the mine costing $171,000, with an estimated seven-year life and no salvage value. The machinery will be abandoned when the ore is completely mined. Idaho begins mining on May 1, 2011, and mines and sells 156,200 tons of ore during the remaining eight months of 2011. Prepare the December 31, 2011, entries to record both the ore deposit depletion and the mining machinery depreciation. Mining machinery depreciation should be in proportion to the mine's depletion.

Exercise 10-19
Amortization of intangible assets
P4

Busch Gallery purchases the copyright on an oil painting for $236,700 on January 1, 2011. The copyright legally protects its owner for 12 more years. The company plans to market and sell prints of the original for 15 years. Prepare entries to record the purchase of the copyright on January 1, 2011, and its annual amortization on December 31, 2011.

Exercise 10-20
Goodwill
P4

On January 1, 2011, Timothy Company purchased Macys Company at a price of $3,750,000. The fair market value of the net assets purchased equals $2,700,000.

1. What is the amount of goodwill that Timothy records at the purchase date?
2. Explain how Timothy would determine the amount of goodwill amortization for the year ended December 31, 2011.
3. Timothy Company believes that its employees provide superior customer service, and through their efforts, Timothy Company believes it has created $1,350,000 of goodwill. How would Timothy Company record this goodwill?

Exercise 10-21
Cash flows related to assets
C1
Apple

Refer to the statement of cash flows for **Apple** in Appendix A for the fiscal year ended September 26, 2009, to answer the following.

1. What amount of cash is used to purchase property, plant, and equipment?
2. How much depreciation, amortization, and accretion are recorded?
3. What total amount of net cash is used in investing activities?

Exercise 10-22
Evaluating efficient use of assets
A1

Joy Co. reports net sales of $4,862,000 for 2010 and $7,542,000 for 2011. End-of-year balances for total assets are 2009, $1,586,000; 2010, $1,700,000; and 2011, $1,882,000. (*a*) Compute Joy's total asset turnover for 2010 and 2011. (*b*) Comment on Joy's efficiency in using its assets if its competitors average a total asset turnover of 3.0.

Exercise 10-23[A]
Exchanging assets
P5

Ramond Construction trades in an old tractor for a new tractor, receiving a $31,850 trade-in allowance and paying the remaining $93,275 in cash. The old tractor had cost $107,900, and straight-line accumulated depreciation of $58,500 had been recorded to date under the assumption that it would last eight years and have a $14,300 salvage value. Answer the following questions assuming the exchange has commercial substance.

1. What is the book value of the old tractor at the time of exchange?
2. What is the loss on this asset exchange?
3. What amount should be recorded (debited) in the asset account for the new tractor?

Check (2) $17,550

Exercise 10-24[A]
Recording plant asset disposals
P2 P5

On January 5, 2011, Holstrom Co. disposes of a machine costing $65,500 with accumulated depreciation of $35,284. Prepare the entries to record the disposal under each of the following separate assumptions.

1. The machine is sold for $25,343 cash.
2. The machine is traded in for a newer machine having an $86,125 cash price. A $31,912 trade-in allowance is received, and the balance is paid in cash. Assume the asset exchange lacks commercial substance.
3. The machine is traded in for a newer machine having an $86,125 cash price. A $23,393 trade-in allowance is received, and the balance is paid in cash. Assume the asset exchange has commercial substance.

Check (2) Dr. Machinery (new), $84,429

Exercise 10-25
Accounting for plant assets under IFRS
C2 P1 P2

Volkswagen Group reports the following information for property, plant and equipment as of December 31, 2008, along with additions, disposals, depreciation, and impairments for the year ended December 31, 2008 (euros in millions):

Property, plant and equipment, net	€23,121
Additions to property, plant and equipment	6,651
Disposals of property, plant and equipment	2,322
Depreciation on property, plant and equipment	4,625
Impairments to property, plant and equipment	184

1. Prepare Volkswagen's journal entry to record its depreciation for 2008.
2. Prepare Volkswagen's journal entry to record its additions for 2008 assuming they are paid in cash and are treated as "betterments (improvements)" to the assets.
3. Prepare Volkswagen's journal entry to record its €2,322 in disposals for 2008 assuming it receives €700 cash in return and the accumulated depreciation on the disposed assets totals €1,322.
4. Volkswagen reports €184 of impairments. Do these impairments increase or decrease the property, plant and equipment account? And, by what amount?

connect

PROBLEM SET A

Problem 10-1A
Plant asset costs; depreciation methods C1 P1

mhhe.com/wildFAP20e

Xavier Construction negotiates a lump-sum purchase of several assets from a company that is going out of business. The purchase is completed on January 1, 2011, at a total cash price of $787,500 for a building, land, land improvements, and four vehicles. The estimated market values of the assets are building, $408,000; land, $289,000; land improvements, $42,500; and four vehicles, $110,500. The company's fiscal year ends on December 31.

Required

1. Prepare a table to allocate the lump-sum purchase price to the separate assets purchased (round percents to the nearest 1%). Prepare the journal entry to record the purchase.

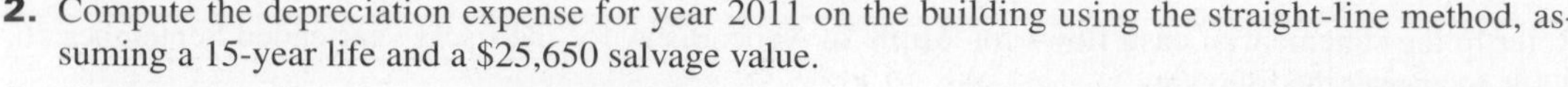

Check (2) $23,490

2. Compute the depreciation expense for year 2011 on the building using the straight-line method, assuming a 15-year life and a $25,650 salvage value.

(3) $15,750

3. Compute the depreciation expense for year 2011 on the land improvements assuming a five-year life and double-declining-balance depreciation.

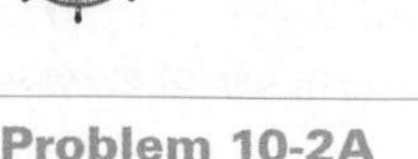

Analysis Component

4. Defend or refute this statement: Accelerated depreciation results in payment of less taxes over the asset's life.

Problem 10-2A
Asset cost allocation; straight-line depreciation
C1 P1

mhhe.com/wildFAP20e

In January 2011, Keona Co. pays $2,800,000 for a tract of land with two buildings on it. It plans to demolish Building 1 and build a new store in its place. Building 2 will be a company office; it is appraised at $641,300, with a useful life of 20 years and an $80,000 salvage value. A lighted parking lot near Building 1 has improvements (Land Improvements 1) valued at $408,100 that are expected to last another 14 years with no salvage value. Without the buildings and improvements, the tract of land is valued at $1,865,600. The company also incurs the following additional costs:

Cost to demolish Building 1	$ 422,600
Cost of additional land grading	167,200
Cost to construct new building (Building 3), having a useful life of 25 years and a $390,100 salvage value	2,019,000
Cost of new land improvements (Land Improvements 2) near Building 2 having a 20-year useful life and no salvage value	158,000

Required

Check (1) Land costs, $2,381,800; Building 2 costs, $616,000

1. Prepare a table with the following column headings: Land, Building 2, Building 3, Land Improvements 1, and Land Improvements 2. Allocate the costs incurred by Keona to the appropriate columns and total each column (round percents to the nearest 1%).
2. Prepare a single journal entry to record all the incurred costs assuming they are paid in cash on January 1, 2011.

(3) Depr.—Land Improv. 1 and 2, $28,000 and $7,900

3. Using the straight-line method, prepare the December 31 adjusting entries to record depreciation for the 12 months of 2011 when these assets were in use.

Problem 10-3A
Computing and revising depreciation; revenue and capital expenditures
C1 C2 C3

Clarion Contractors completed the following transactions and events involving the purchase and operation of equipment in its business.

2010

Jan. 1 Paid $255,440 cash plus $15,200 in sales tax and $2,500 in transportation (FOB shipping point) for a new loader. The loader is estimated to have a four-year life and a $34,740 salvage value. Loader costs are recorded in the Equipment account.

Jan. 3 Paid $3,660 to enclose the cab and install air conditioning in the loader to enable operations under harsher conditions. This increased the estimated salvage value of the loader by another $1,110.

Check Dec. 31, 2010, Dr. Depr. Expense—Equip., $60,238

Dec. 31 Recorded annual straight-line depreciation on the loader.

2011

Jan. 1 Paid $4,500 to overhaul the loader's engine, which increased the loader's estimated useful life by two years.

Feb. 17 Paid $920 to repair the loader after the operator backed it into a tree.

Check Dec. 31, 2011, Dr. Depr. Expense—Equip., $37,042

Dec. 31 Recorded annual straight-line depreciation on the loader.

Required

Prepare journal entries to record these transactions and events.

Problem 10-4A
Computing and revising depreciation; selling plant assets
C2 P1 P2

Chen Company completed the following transactions and events involving its delivery trucks.

2010

Jan. 1 Paid $19,415 cash plus $1,165 in sales tax for a new delivery truck estimated to have a five-year life and a $3,000 salvage value. Delivery truck costs are recorded in the Trucks account.

Dec. 31 Recorded annual straight-line depreciation on the truck.

2011

Dec. 31 Due to new information obtained earlier in the year, the truck's estimated useful life was changed from five to four years, and the estimated salvage value was increased to $3,500. Recorded annual straight-line depreciation on the truck.

Check Dec. 31, 2011, Dr. Depr. Expense—Trucks, $4,521

2012

Dec. 31 Recorded annual straight-line depreciation on the truck.
Dec. 31 Sold the truck for $6,200 cash.

Dec. 31, 2012, Dr. Loss on Disposal of Trucks, $1,822

Required

Prepare journal entries to record these transactions and events.

Problem 10-5A
Depreciation methods
P1

A machine costing $210,000 with a four-year life and an estimated $20,000 salvage value is installed in Calhoon Company's factory on January 1. The factory manager estimates the machine will produce 475,000 units of product during its life. It actually produces the following units: year 1, 121,400; year 2, 122,400; year 3, 119,600; and year 4, 118,200. The total number of units produced by the end of year 4 exceeds the original estimate—this difference was not predicted. (The machine must not be depreciated below its estimated salvage value.)

Required

Prepare a table with the following column headings and compute depreciation for each year (and total depreciation of all years combined) for the machine under each depreciation method.

Year	Straight-Line	Units-of-Production	Double-Declining-Balance

Check Year 4: units-of-production depreciation, $44,640; DDB depreciation, $6,250

Problem 10-6A
Disposal of plant assets
C1 P1 P2

Saturn Co. purchases a used machine for $167,000 cash on January 2 and readies it for use the next day at an $3,420 cost. On January 3, it is installed on a required operating platform costing $1,080, and it is further readied for operations. The company predicts the machine will be used for six years and have a $14,600 salvage value. Depreciation is to be charged on a straight-line basis. On December 31, at the end of its fifth year in operations, it is disposed of.

Required

1. Prepare journal entries to record the machine's purchase and the costs to ready and install it. Cash is paid for all costs incurred.
2. Prepare journal entries to record depreciation of the machine at December 31 of (*a*) its first year in operations and (*b*) the year of its disposal.
3. Prepare journal entries to record the machine's disposal under each of the following separate assumptions: (*a*) it is sold for $13,500 cash; (*b*) it is sold for $45,000 cash; and (*c*) it is destroyed in a fire and the insurance company pays $24,000 cash to settle the loss claim.

Check (2*b*) Depr. Exp., $26,150

(3*c*) Dr. Loss from Fire, $16,750

Problem 10-7A
Natural resources
P3

On July 23 of the current year, Dakota Mining Co. pays $4,836,000 for land estimated to contain 7,800,000 tons of recoverable ore. It installs machinery costing $390,000 that has a 10-year life and no salvage value and is capable of mining the ore deposit in eight years. The machinery is paid for on July 25, seven days before mining operations begin. The company removes and sells 400,000 tons of ore during its first five months of operations ending on December 31. Depreciation of the machinery is in proportion to the mine's depletion as the machinery will be abandoned after the ore is mined.

Required

Prepare entries to record (*a*) the purchase of the land, (*b*) the cost and installation of machinery, (*c*) the first five months' depletion assuming the land has a net salvage value of zero after the ore is mined, and (*d*) the first five months' depreciation on the machinery.

Check (*c*) Depletion, $248,000
(*d*) Depreciation, $20,000

Analysis Component

Describe both the similarities and differences in amortization, depletion, and depreciation.

Problem 10-8A
Intangible assets
P4 

On July 1, 2006, Sweetman Company signed a contract to lease space in a building for 15 years. The lease contract calls for annual (prepaid) rental payments of $70,000 on each July 1 throughout the life of the lease and for the lessee to pay for all additions and improvements to the leased property. On June 25, 2011, Sweetman decides to sublease the space to Kirk & Associates for the remaining 10 years of the lease—Kirk pays $185,000 to Sweetman for the right to sublease and it agrees to assume the obligation to pay the $70,000 annual rent to the building owner beginning July 1, 2011. After taking possession of the leased space, Kirk pays for improving the office portion of the leased space at a $129,840 cost. The improvements are paid for by Kirk on July 5, 2011, and are estimated to have a useful life equal to the 16 years remaining in the life of the building.

Required

1. Prepare entries for Kirk to record (*a*) its payment to Sweetman for the right to sublease the building space, (*b*) its payment of the 2011 annual rent to the building owner, and (*c*) its payment for the office improvements.
2. Prepare Kirk's year-end adjusting entries required at December 31, 2011, to (*a*) amortize the $185,000 cost of the sublease, (*b*) amortize the office improvements, and (*c*) record rent expense.

Check Dr. Rent Expense for (2*a*) $9,250, (2*c*) $35,000

PROBLEM SET B

Problem 10-1B
Plant asset costs; depreciation methods
C1 P1 

Racerback Company negotiates a lump-sum purchase of several assets from a contractor who is relocating. The purchase is completed on January 1, 2011, at a total cash price of $1,610,000 for a building, land, land improvements, and six trucks. The estimated market values of the assets are building, $784,800; land, $540,640; land improvements, $226,720; and six trucks, $191,840. The company's fiscal year ends on December 31.

Required

1. Prepare a table to allocate the lump-sum purchase price to the separate assets purchased (round percents to the nearest 1%). Prepare the journal entry to record the purchase.
2. Compute the depreciation expense for year 2011 on the building using the straight-line method, assuming a 12-year life and a $100,500 salvage value.
3. Compute the depreciation expense for year 2011 on the land improvements assuming a 10-year life and double-declining-balance depreciation.

Check (2) $52,000

(3) $41,860

Analysis Component

4. Defend or refute this statement: Accelerated depreciation results in payment of more taxes over the asset's life.

Problem 10-2B
Asset cost allocation; straight-line depreciation
C1 P1

In January 2011, InTech Co. pays $1,350,000 for a tract of land with two buildings. It plans to demolish Building A and build a new shop in its place. Building B will be a company office; it is appraised at $472,770, with a useful life of 15 years and a $90,000 salvage value. A lighted parking lot near Building B has improvements (Land Improvements B) valued at $125,145 that are expected to last another six years with no salvage value. Without the buildings and improvements, the tract of land is valued at $792,585. The company also incurs the following additional costs.

Cost to demolish Building A	$ 117,000
Cost of additional land grading	172,500
Cost to construct new building (Building C), having a useful life of 20 years and a $295,500 salvage value	1,356,000
Cost of new land improvements (Land Improvements C) near Building C, having a 10-year useful life and no salvage value	101,250

Required

1. Prepare a table with the following column headings: Land, Building B, Building C, Land Improvements B, and Land Improvements C. Allocate the costs incurred by InTech to the appropriate columns and total each column (round percents to the nearest 1%).
2. Prepare a single journal entry to record all incurred costs assuming they are paid in cash on January 1, 2011.
3. Using the straight-line method, prepare the December 31 adjusting entries to record depreciation for the 12 months of 2011 when these assets were in use.

Check (1) Land costs, $1,059,000; Building B costs, $459,000

(3) Depr.—Land Improv. B and C, $20,250 and $10,125

Problem 10-3B
Computing and revising depreciation; revenue and capital expenditures
C1 C2 C3

Xpress Delivery Service completed the following transactions and events involving the purchase and operation of equipment for its business.

2010

Jan. 1 Paid $24,950 cash plus $1,950 in sales tax for a new delivery van that was estimated to have a five-year life and a $3,400 salvage value. Van costs are recorded in the Equipment account.

Jan. 3 Paid $1,550 to install sorting racks in the van for more accurate and quicker delivery of packages. This increases the estimated salvage value of the van by another $200.

Dec. 31 Recorded annual straight-line depreciation on the van.

Check Dec. 31, 2010, Dr. Depr. Expense—Equip., $4,970

2011

Jan. 1 Paid $1,970 to overhaul the van's engine, which increased the van's estimated useful life by two years.

May 10 Paid $600 to repair the van after the driver backed it into a loading dock.

Dec. 31 Record annual straight-line depreciation on the van. (Round to the nearest dollar.)

Check Dec. 31, 2011, Dr. Depr. Expense—Equip., $3,642

Required

Prepare journal entries to record these transactions and events.

Problem 10-4B
Computing and revising depreciation; selling plant assets
C2 P1 P2

Field Instruments completed the following transactions and events involving its machinery.

2010

Jan. 1 Paid $106,600 cash plus $6,400 in sales tax for a new machine. The machine is estimated to have a six-year life and a $9,800 salvage value.

Dec. 31 Recorded annual straight-line depreciation on the machinery.

2011

Dec. 31 Due to new information obtained earlier in the year, the machine's estimated useful life was changed from six to four years, and the estimated salvage value was increased to $13,050. Recorded annual straight-line depreciation on the machinery.

Check Dec. 31, 2011, Dr. Depr. Expense—Machinery, $27,583

2012

Dec. 31 Recorded annual straight-line depreciation on the machinery.

Dec. 31 Sold the machine for $25,240 cash.

Dec. 31, 2012, Dr. Loss on Disposal of Machinery, $15,394

Required

Prepare journal entries to record these transactions and events.

Problem 10-5B
Depreciation methods
P1

On January 2, Gannon Co. purchases and installs a new machine costing $312,000 with a five-year life and an estimated $28,000 salvage value. Management estimates the machine will produce 1,136,000 units of product during its life. Actual production of units is as follows: year 1, 245,600; year 2, 230,400; year 3, 227,000; year 4, 232,600; and year 5, 211,200. The total number of units produced by the end of year 5 exceeds the original estimate—this difference was not predicted. (The machine must not be depreciated below its estimated salvage value.)

Required

Prepare a table with the following column headings and compute depreciation for each year (and total depreciation of all years combined) for the machine under each depreciation method.

Year	Straight-Line	Units-of-Production	Double-Declining-Balance

Check DDB Depreciation, Year 3, $44,928; U of P Depreciation, Year 4, $58,150

Problem 10-6B
Disposal of plant assets
C1 P1 P2

On January 1, Jefferson purchases a used machine for $130,000 and readies it for use the next day at a cost of $3,390. On January 4, it is mounted on a required operating platform costing $4,800, and it is further readied for operations. Management estimates the machine will be used for seven years and have an $18,000 salvage value. Depreciation is to be charged on a straight-line basis. On December 31, at the end of its sixth year of use, the machine is disposed of.

Required

1. Prepare journal entries to record the machine's purchase and the costs to ready and install it. Cash is paid for all costs incurred.

Check (2*b*) Depr. Exp., $17,170

2. Prepare journal entries to record depreciation of the machine at December 31 of (*a*) its first year in operations and (*b*) the year of its disposal.

(3*c*) Dr. Loss from Fire, $15,170

3. Prepare journal entries to record the machine's disposal under each of the following separate assumptions: (*a*) it is sold for $30,000 cash; (*b*) it is sold for $50,000 cash; and (*c*) it is destroyed in a fire and the insurance company pays $20,000 cash to settle the loss claim.

Problem 10-7B
Natural resources
P3

On February 19 of the current year, Rock Chalk Co. pays $4,450,000 for land estimated to contain 5 million tons of recoverable ore. It installs machinery costing $200,000 that has a 16-year life and no salvage value and is capable of mining the ore deposit in 12 years. The machinery is paid for on March 21, eleven days before mining operations begin. The company removes and sells 352,000 tons of ore during its first nine months of operations ending on December 31. Depreciation of the machinery is in proportion to the mine's depletion as the machinery will be abandoned after the ore is mined.

Required

Check (*c*) Depletion, $313,280; (*d*) Depreciation, $14,080

Prepare entries to record (*a*) the purchase of the land, (*b*) the cost and installation of the machinery, (*c*) the first nine months' depletion assuming the land has a net salvage value of zero after the ore is mined, and (*d*) the first nine months' depreciation on the machinery.

Analysis Component

Describe both the similarities and differences in amortization, depletion, and depreciation.

Problem 10-8B
Intangible assets
P4 

On January 1, 2004, Liberty Co. entered into a 12-year lease on a building. The lease contract requires (1) annual (prepaid) rental payments of $26,400 each January 1 throughout the life of the lease and (2) for the lessee to pay for all additions and improvements to the leased property. On January 1, 2011, Liberty decides to sublease the space to Moberly Co. for the remaining five years of the lease—Moberly pays $30,000 to Liberty for the right to sublease and agrees to assume the obligation to pay the $26,400 annual rent to the building owner beginning January 1, 2011. After taking possession of the leased space, Moberly pays for improving the office portion of the leased space at an $18,000 cost. The improvements are paid for by Moberly on January 3, 2011, and are estimated to have a useful life equal to the 13 years remaining in the life of the building.

Required

1. Prepare entries for Moberly to record (*a*) its payment to Liberty for the right to sublease the building space, (*b*) its payment of the 2011 annual rent to the building owner, and (*c*) its payment for the office improvements.

Check Dr. Rent Expense: (2*a*) $6,000, (2*c*) $26,400

2. Prepare Moberly's year-end adjusting entries required on December 31, 2011, to (*a*) amortize the $30,000 cost of the sublease, (*b*) amortize the office improvements, and (*c*) record rent expense.

SERIAL PROBLEM
Business Solutions
P1 A1

(This serial problem began in Chapter 1 and continues through most of the book. If previous chapter segments were not completed, the serial problem can begin at this point. It is helpful, but not necessary, to use the Working Papers that accompany the book.)

SP 10 Selected ledger account balances for Business Solutions follow.

	For Three Months Ended December 31, 2011	For Three Months Ended March 31, 2012
Office equipment	$ 8,000	$ 8,000
Accumulated depreciation—Office equipment	400	800
Computer equipment	20,000	20,000
Accumulated depreciation—Computer equipment	1,250	2,500
Total revenue	31,284	44,000
Total assets	83,460	120,268

Required

1. Assume that Business Solutions does not acquire additional office equipment or computer equipment in 2012. Compute amounts for *the year ended* December 31, 2012, for Depreciation Expense—Office Equipment and for Depreciation Expense—Computer Equipment (assume use of the straight-line method).
2. Given the assumptions in part 1, what is the book value of both the office equipment and the computer equipment as of December 31, 2012?
3. Compute the three-month total asset turnover for Business Solutions as of March 31, 2012. Use total revenue for the numerator and average the December 31, 2011, total assets and the March 31, 2012, total assets for the denominator. Interpret its total asset turnover if competitors average 2.5 for annual periods. (Round turnover to two decimals.)

Check (3) Three-month (annual) turnover = 0.43 (1.73 annual)

Beyond the Numbers

REPORTING IN ACTION

A1 

RIM

BTN 10-1 Refer to the financial statements of **Research In Motion** in Appendix A to answer the following.

1. What percent of the original cost of RIM's property, plant and equipment remains to be depreciated as of February 27, 2010, and at February 28, 2009? Assume these assets have no salvage value.
2. Over what length(s) of time is RIM depreciating its major categories of property, plant and equipment?
3. What is the change in total property, plant and equipment (before accumulated depreciation) for the year ended February 27, 2010? What is the amount of cash provided (used) by investing activities for property, plant and equipment for the year ended February 27, 2010? What is one possible explanation for the difference between these two amounts?
4. Compute its total asset turnover for the year ended February 27, 2010, and the year ended February 28, 2009. Assume total assets at March 1, 2008, are $5,511 ($ millions).

Fast Forward

5. Access RIM's financial statements for fiscal years ending after February 27, 2010, at its Website (**RIM.com**) or the SEC's EDGAR database (**www.SEC.gov**). Recompute RIM's total asset turnover for the additional years' data you collect. Comment on any differences relative to the turnover computed in part 4.

COMPARATIVE ANALYSIS

A1

RIM

Apple

BTN 10-2 Comparative figures for **Research In Motion** and **Apple** follow.

	Research In Motion			Apple		
($ millions)	Current Year	One Year Prior	Two Years Prior	Current Year	One Year Prior	Two Years Prior
Total assets	$10,204	$ 8,101	$5,511	$47,501	$36,171	$25,347
Net sales	14,953	11,065	6,009	42,905	37,491	24,578

Required

1. Compute total asset turnover for the most recent two years for Research In Motion and Apple using the data shown.
2. Which company is more efficient in generating net sales given the total assets it employs? Assume an industry average of 1.0 for asset turnover.

ETHICS CHALLENGE

C1  

BTN 10-3 Flo Choi owns a small business and manages its accounting. Her company just finished a year in which a large amount of borrowed funds was invested in a new building addition as well as in equipment and fixture additions. Choi's banker requires her to submit semiannual financial statements so he can monitor the financial health of her business. He has warned her that if profit margins erode, he might raise the interest rate on the borrowed funds to reflect the increased loan risk from the bank's point of view. Choi knows profit margin is likely to decline this year. As she prepares year-end adjusting entries, she decides to apply the following depreciation rule: All asset additions are considered to be in use on the first day of the following month. (The previous rule assumed assets are in use on the first day of the month nearest to the purchase date.)

Required

1. Identify decisions that managers like Choi must make in applying depreciation methods.
2. Is Choi's rule an ethical violation, or is it a legitimate decision in computing depreciation?
3. How will Choi's new depreciation rule affect the profit margin of her business?

COMMUNICATING IN PRACTICE

A1 

BTN 10-4 Teams are to select an industry, and each team member is to select a different company in that industry. Each team member is to acquire the financial statements (Form 10-K) of the company selected—see the company's Website or the SEC's EDGAR database (www.SEC.gov). Use the financial statements to compute total asset turnover. Communicate with teammates via a meeting, e-mail, or telephone to discuss the meaning of this ratio, how different companies compare to each other, and the industry norm. The team must prepare a one-page report that describes the ratios for each company and identifies the conclusions reached during the team's discussion.

TAKING IT TO THE NET

P4 

BTN 10-5 Access the **Yahoo!** (ticker: YHOO) 10-K report for the year ended December 31, 2009, filed on February 26, 2010, at www.SEC.gov.

Required

1. What amount of goodwill is reported on Yahoo!'s balance sheet? What percentage of total assets does its goodwill represent? Is goodwill a major asset for Yahoo!? Explain.
2. Locate Note 5 to its financial statements. Identify the change in goodwill from December 31, 2008, to December 31, 2009. Comment on the change in goodwill over this period.
3. Locate Note 6 to its financial statements. What are the three categories of intangible assets that Yahoo! reports at December 31, 2009? What proportion of total assets do the intangibles represent?
4. What does Yahoo! indicate is the life of "Trade names, trademarks, and domain names" according to its Note 6? Comment on the difference between the estimated useful life and the legal life of Yahoo!'s trademark.

TEAMWORK IN ACTION

P1 

BTN 10-6 Each team member is to become an expert on one depreciation method to facilitate teammates' understanding of that method. Follow these procedures:

a. Each team member is to select an area for expertise from one of the following depreciation methods: straight-line, units-of-production, or double-declining-balance.
b. Expert teams are to be formed from those who have selected the same area of expertise. The instructor will identify the location where each expert team meets.
c. Using the following data, expert teams are to collaborate and develop a presentation answering the requirements. Expert team members must write the presentation in a format they can show to their learning teams.

Point: This activity can follow an overview of each method. Step 1 allows for three areas of expertise. Larger teams will have some duplication of areas, but the straight-line choice should not be duplicated. Expert teams can use the book and consult with the instructor.

Data and Requirements On January 8, 2009, Waverly Riders purchases a van to transport rafters back to the point of departure at the conclusion of the rafting adventures they operate. The cost of the van is $44,000. It has an estimated salvage value of $2,000 and is expected to be used for four years and driven 60,000 miles. The van is driven 12,000 miles in 2009, 18,000 miles in 2010, 21,000 in 2011, and 10,000 in 2012.

1. Compute the annual depreciation expense for each year of the van's estimated useful life.
2. Explain when and how annual depreciation is recorded.
3. Explain the impact on income of this depreciation method versus others over the van's life.
4. Identify the van's book value for each year of its life and illustrate the reporting of this amount for any one year.

d. Re-form original learning teams. In rotation, experts are to present to their teams the results from part *c*. Experts are to encourage and respond to questions.

ENTREPRENEURIAL DECISION

A1  

BTN 10-7 Review the chapter's opening feature involving **Games2U**. Assume that the company currently has net sales of $8,000,000, and that it is planning an expansion that will increase net sales by $4,000,000. To accomplish this expansion, Games2U must increase its average total assets from $2,500,000 to $3,000,000.

Required

1. Compute the company's total asset turnover under (*a*) current conditions and (*b*) proposed conditions.
2. Evaluate and comment on the merits of the proposal given your analysis in part 1. Identify any concerns you would express about the proposal.

HITTING THE ROAD

P3 P4

BTN 10-8 Team up with one or more classmates for this activity. Identify companies in your community or area that must account for at least one of the following assets: natural resource; patent; lease; leasehold improvement; copyright; trademark; or goodwill. You might find a company having more than one type of asset. Once you identify a company with a specific asset, describe the accounting this company uses to allocate the cost of that asset to the periods benefited from its use.

GLOBAL DECISION

A1

NOKIA

RIM

Apple

BTN 10-9 **Nokia** (www.Nokia.com), **Research In Motion**, and **Apple** are all competitors in the global marketplace. Comparative figures for these companies' recent annual accounting periods follow.

(in millions, except turnover)	Nokia (EUR millions)			Research In Motion		Apple	
	Current Year	Prior Year	Two Years Prior	Current Year	Prior Year	Current Year	Prior Year
Total assets	35,738	39,582	37,599	$10,204	$ 8,101	$47,501	$36,171
Net sales	40,984	50,710	51,058	14,953	11,065	42,905	37,491
Total asset turnover	?	?	—	1.63	1.63	1.03	1.22

Required

1. Compute total asset turnover for the most recent two years for Nokia using the data shown.
2. Which company is most efficient in generating net sales given the total assets it employs?

ANSWERS TO MULTIPLE CHOICE QUIZ

1. b;

	Appraisal Value	%	Total Cost	Allocated
Land	$175,000	50%	$326,000	$163,000
Land improvements	70,000	20	326,000	65,200
Building	105,000	30	326,000	97,800
Totals	$350,000			$326,000

2. c; ($35,000 − $1,000)/4 years = $8,500 per year.
3. c; 2011: $10,800,000 × (2 × 10%) = $2,160,000
   2012: ($10,800,000 − $2,160,000) × (2 × 10%) = $1,728,000
4. c;

Cost of machine	$250,000
Accumulated depreciation	100,000
Book value	150,000
Cash received	120,000
Loss on sale	$ 30,000

5. b; $550,000/$500,000 = 1.10

11

Current Liabilities and Payroll Accounting

A Look Back

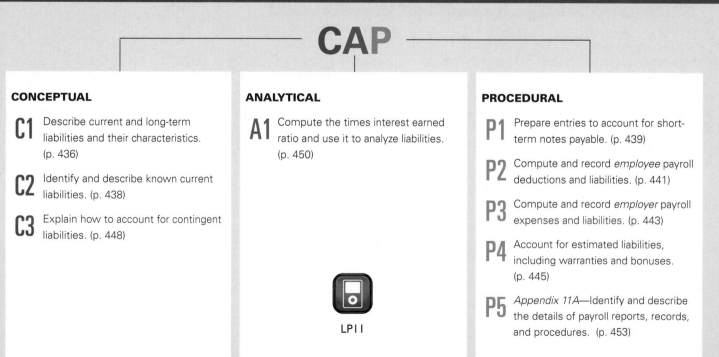

Chapter 10 focused on long-term assets including plant assets, natural resources, and intangibles. We showed how to account for and analyze those assets.

A Look at This Chapter

This chapter explains how to identify, compute, record, and report current liabilities in financial statements. We also analyze and interpret these liabilities, including those related to employee costs.

A Look Ahead

Chapter 12 explains the partnership form of organization. It also describes the accounting concepts and procedures for partnership transactions.

Learning Objectives

CAP

CONCEPTUAL

C1 Describe current and long-term liabilities and their characteristics. (p. 436)

C2 Identify and describe known current liabilities. (p. 438)

C3 Explain how to account for contingent liabilities. (p. 448)

ANALYTICAL

A1 Compute the times interest earned ratio and use it to analyze liabilities. (p. 450)

LP11

PROCEDURAL

P1 Prepare entries to account for short-term notes payable. (p. 439)

P2 Compute and record *employee* payroll deductions and liabilities. (p. 441)

P3 Compute and record *employer* payroll expenses and liabilities. (p. 443)

P4 Account for estimated liabilities, including warranties and bonuses. (p. 445)

P5 *Appendix 11A*—Identify and describe the details of payroll reports, records, and procedures. (p. 453)

Decision Insight

No Stuffed Shirts

"Part of the fun is the journey . . . working til 2 am every day"
—MATT WALLS

ATLANTA, GA—Brothers Matt and Bryan Walls never planned to be entrepreneurs in the T-shirt business. "[It was] an idea we had while hanging out in our parents' basement," explains Matt. "We were naive and, like many first-time entrepreneurs, just dove right in." Matt and Bryan's plans involved making T-shirts with visual humor and pop culture themes. Their company, **SnorgTees (SnorgTees.com),** had a shaky start but soon found its groove with best-selling T-shirts such as "With a shirt like this, who needs pants?" "Don't act like you're not impressed," and "I'm kind of a big deal."

"We dreamed it would be successful overnight," recalls Matt. "But when things first started we had a huge reality check, and at that point I don't know if I believed." Today their business is thriving. Their commitment to success carries over to the financial side. They especially focus on the important task of managing liabilities for payroll, supplies, employee wages, training, and taxes. Both insist that effective management of liabilities, especially payroll and employee benefits, is crucial. They stress that monitoring and controlling liabilities are a must.

To help control liabilities, Matt and Bryan describe how they began by working out of their parents' home to reduce liabilities. "Most people think all we do is sit around and think up funny ideas," explains Matt. "In reality most of the time is spent on executing projects and managing the business . . . [including] order fulfillment, supply chain management, marketing, and accounting." In short, creative reduction of liabilities can mean success or failure.

The two continue to monitor liabilities and their payment patterns. "I'm pretty conservative about spending money," admits Matt. "If you want to run a successful company, you can't forget all the details." The two insist that accounting for and monitoring liabilities are one key to a successful start-up. Their company now generates sufficient income to pay for liabilities and produces revenue growth for expansion. "We plan to keep having fun," insists Matt. "We do business with people all over the world."

Sources: *SnorgTees Website,* January 2011; *Entrepreneur,* September 2009; *RetireAt21.com,* October 2008; *Business to Business,* January 2008; *WannaBeMogul.com,* November 2007.

Chapter Preview

Previous chapters introduced liabilities such as accounts payable, notes payable, wages payable, and unearned revenues. This chapter further explains these liabilities and additional ones such as warranties, taxes, payroll, vacation pay, and bonuses. It also describes contingent liabilities and introduces long-term liabilities. The focus is on how to define, classify, measure, report, and analyze these liabilities so that this information is useful to business decision makers.

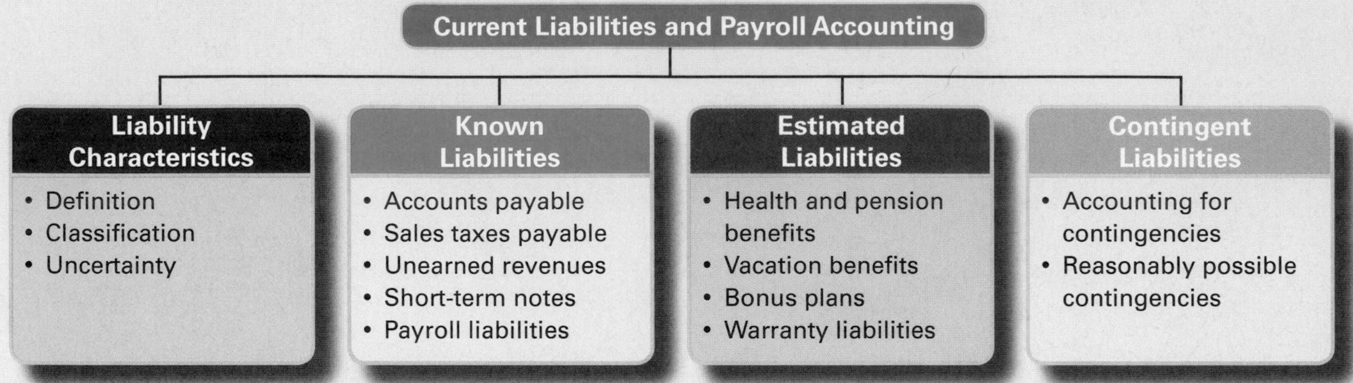

Current Liabilities and Payroll Accounting
Liability Characteristics
• Definition
• Classification
• Uncertainty
Known Liabilities
• Accounts payable
• Sales taxes payable
• Unearned revenues
• Short-term notes
• Payroll liabilities
Estimated Liabilities
• Health and pension benefits
• Vacation benefits
• Bonus plans
• Warranty liabilities
Contingent Liabilities
• Accounting for contingencies
• Reasonably possible contingencies

CHARACTERISTICS OF LIABILITIES

This section discusses important characteristics of liabilities and how liabilities are classified and reported.

Defining Liabilities

C1 Describe current and long-term liabilities and their characteristics.

A *liability* is a probable future payment of assets or services that a company is presently obligated to make as a result of past transactions or events. This definition includes three crucial factors:

1. A past transaction or event.
2. A present obligation.
3. A future payment of assets or services.

These three important elements are portrayed visually in Exhibit 11.1. Liabilities reported in financial statements exhibit those characteristics. No liability is reported when one or more of those characteristics is absent. For example, most companies expect to pay wages to their employees in upcoming months and years, but these future payments are *not* liabilities because no past event such as employee work resulted in a present obligation. Instead, such liabilities arise when employees perform their work and earn the wages.

EXHIBIT 11.1

Characteristics of a Liability

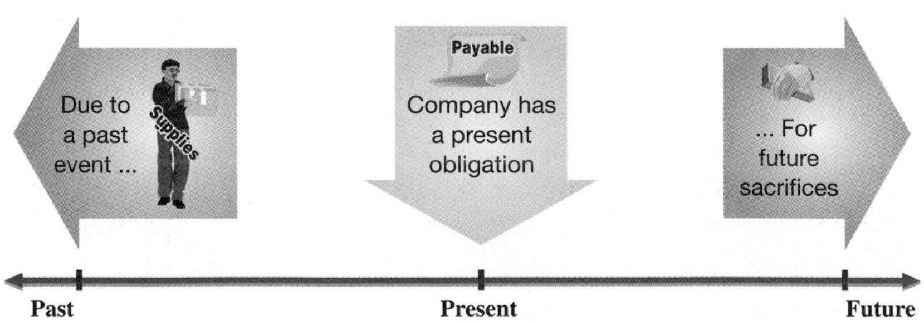

Classifying Liabilities

Information about liabilities is more useful when the balance sheet identifies them as either current or long term. Decision makers need to know when obligations are due so they can plan for them and take appropriate action.

Current Liabilities **Current liabilities,** also called *short-term liabilities,* are obligations due within one year or the company's operating cycle, whichever is longer. They are expected to be paid using current assets or by creating other current liabilities. Common examples of current liabilities are accounts payable, short-term notes payable, wages payable, warranty liabilities, lease liabilities, taxes payable, and unearned revenues.

Point: Improper classification of liabilities can distort ratios used in financial statement analysis and business decisions.

Current liabilities differ across companies because they depend on the type of company operations. **MGM Mirage**, for instance, included the following current liabilities related to its gaming, hospitality and entertainment operations ($000s):

Advance deposits and ticket sales	$104,911
Casino outstanding chip liability	83,957
Casino front money deposits	80,944

Harley-Davidson reports a much different set of current liabilities. It discloses current liabilities made up of items such as warranty, recall, and dealer incentive liabilities.

Long-Term Liabilities A company's obligations not expected to be paid within the longer of one year or the company's operating cycle are reported as **long-term liabilities.** They can include long-term notes payable, warranty liabilities, lease liabilities, and bonds payable. They are sometimes reported on the balance sheet in a single long-term liabilities total or in multiple categories. **Domino's Pizza**, for instance, reports long-term liabilities of $1,555 million. They are reported after current liabilities. A single liability also can be divided between the current and noncurrent sections if a company expects to make payments toward it in both the short and long term. Domino's reports ($ millions) long-term debt, $1,522; and current portion of long-term debt, $50. The second item is reported in current liabilities. We sometimes see liabilities that do not have a fixed due date but instead are payable on the creditor's demand. These are reported as current liabilities because of the possibility of payment in the near term. Exhibit 11.2 shows amounts of current liabilities and as a percent of total liabilities for selected companies.

Point: The current ratio is overstated if a company fails to classify any portion of long-term debt due next period as a current liability.

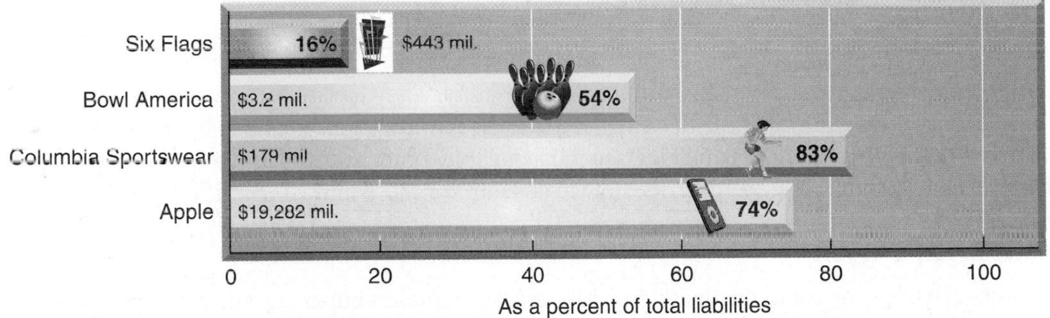

EXHIBIT 11.2

Current Liabilities of Selected Companies

Uncertainty in Liabilities

Accounting for liabilities involves addressing three important questions: Whom to pay? When to pay? How much to pay? Answers to these questions are often decided when a liability is incurred. For example, if a company has a $100 account payable to a specific individual, payable on March 15, the answers are clear. The company knows whom to pay, when to pay, and how much to pay. However, the answers to one or more of these questions are uncertain for some liabilities.

Uncertainty in Whom to Pay Liabilities can involve uncertainty in whom to pay. For instance, a company can create a liability with a known amount when issuing a note that is payable to its holder. In this case, a specific amount is payable to the note's holder at a specified date, but the company does not know who the holder is until that date. Despite this uncertainty, the company reports this liability on its balance sheet.

Point: An *accrued expense* is an unpaid expense, and is also called an *accrued liability.*

Uncertainty in When to Pay A company can have an obligation of a known amount to a known creditor but not know when it must be paid. For example, a legal services firm can accept fees in advance from a client who plans to use the firm's services in the future. This means that the firm has a liability that it settles by providing services at an unknown future date. Although this uncertainty exists, the legal firm's balance sheet must report this liability. These types of obligations are reported as current liabilities because they are likely to be settled in the short term.

Uncertainty in How Much to Pay A company can be aware of an obligation but not know how much will be required to settle it. For example, a company using electrical power is billed only after the meter has been read. This cost is incurred and the liability created before a bill is received. A liability to the power company is reported as an estimated amount if the balance sheet is prepared before a bill arrives.

 **IFRS**

IFRS records a contingent liability when an obligation exists from a past event if there is a 'probable' outflow of resources and the amount can be estimated reliably. However, IFRS defines probable as 'more likely than not' while U.S. GAAP defines it as 'likely to occur.' ■

Quick Check Answers — p. 461 

1. What is a liability? Identify its crucial characteristics.
2. Is every expected future payment a liability?
3. If a liability is payable in 15 months, is it classified as current or long term?

KNOWN LIABILITIES

C2 Identify and describe known current liabilities.

Most liabilities arise from situations with little uncertainty. They are set by agreements, contracts, or laws and are measurable. These liabilities are **known liabilities,** also called *definitely determinable liabilities.* Known liabilities include accounts payable, notes payable, payroll, sales taxes, unearned revenues, and leases. We describe how to account for these known liabilities in this section.

Accounts Payable

Accounts payable, or trade accounts payable, are amounts owed to suppliers for products or services purchased on credit. Accounting for accounts payable is primarily explained and illustrated in our discussion of merchandising activities in Chapters 5 and 6.

Sales Taxes Payable

Nearly all states and many cities levy taxes on retail sales. Sales taxes are stated as a percent of selling prices. The seller collects sales taxes from customers when sales occur and remits these collections (often monthly) to the proper government agency. Since sellers currently owe these collections to the government, this amount is a current liability. **Home Depot**, for instance, reports sales taxes payable of $362 million in its recent annual report. To illustrate, if Home Depot sells materials on August 31 for $6,000 cash that are subject to a 5% sales tax, the revenue portion of this transaction is recorded as follows:

Assets	=	Liabilities	+	Equity
+6,300		+300		+6,000

Date	Account	Debit	Credit
Aug. 31	Cash	6,300	
	Sales		6,000
	Sales Taxes Payable ($6,000 × 0.05)		300
	To record cash sales and 5% sales tax.		

Sales Taxes Payable is debited and Cash credited when it remits these collections to the government. Sales Taxes Payable is not an expense. It arises because laws require sellers to collect this cash from customers for the government.[1]

Unearned Revenues

Unearned revenues (also called *deferred revenues, collections in advance,* and *prepayments*) are amounts received in advance from customers for future products or services. Advance ticket sales for sporting events or music concerts are examples. **Beyonce**, for instance, has "deferred revenues" from advance ticket sales. To illustrate, assume that Beyonce sells $5 million in tickets for eight concerts; the entry is

Point: To *defer* a revenue means to postpone recognition of a revenue collected in advance until it is earned. Sport teams must defer recognition of ticket sales until games are played.

June 30	Cash	5,000,000	
	Unearned Ticket Revenue		5,000,000
	To record sale of concert tickets.		

Assets = Liabilities + Equity
+5,000,000 +5,000,000

When a concert is played, Beyonce would record revenue for the portion earned.

Oct. 31	Unearned Ticket Revenue	625,000	
	Ticket Revenue		625,000
	To record concert ticket revenues earned.		

Assets = Liabilities + Equity
−625,000 +625,000

Unearned Ticket Revenue is an unearned revenue account and is reported as a current liability. Unearned revenues also arise with airline ticket sales, magazine subscriptions, construction projects, hotel reservations, and custom orders.

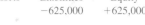

Decision Insight

Reward Programs Gift card sales now exceed $100 billion annually, and reward (also called loyalty) programs are growing. There are no exact rules for how retailers account for rewards. When **Best Buy** launched its "Reward Zone," shoppers earned $5 on each $125 spent and had 90 days to spend it. Retailers make assumptions about how many reward program dollars will be spent and how to report it. Best Buy sets up a liability and reduces revenue by the same amount. **Talbots** does not reduce revenue but instead increases selling expense. **Men's Wearhouse** records rewards in cost of goods sold, whereas **Neiman Marcus** subtracts them from revenue. The FASB continues to review reward programs. ■

Short-Term Notes Payable

A **short-term note payable** is a written promise to pay a specified amount on a definite future date within one year or the company's operating cycle, whichever is longer. These promissory notes are negotiable (as are checks), meaning they can be transferred from party to party by endorsement. The written documentation provided by notes is helpful in resolving disputes and for pursuing legal actions involving these liabilities. Most notes payable bear interest to compensate for use of the money until payment is made. Short-term notes payable can arise from many transactions. A company that purchases merchandise on credit can sometimes extend the credit period by signing a note to replace an account payable. Such notes also can arise when money is borrowed from a bank. We describe both of these cases.

P1 Prepare entries to account for short-term notes payable.

Point: Required characteristics for negotiability of a note: (1) unconditional promise, (2) in writing, (3) specific amount, and (4) definite due date.

[1] Sales taxes can be computed from total sales receipts when sales taxes are not separately identified on the register. To illustrate, assume a 5% sales tax and $420 in total sales receipts (which includes sales taxes). Sales are computed as follows:

$$\text{Sales} = \text{Total sales receipts}/(1 + \text{Sales tax percentage}) = \$420/1.05 = \$400$$

Thus, the sales tax amount equals total sales receipts minus sales, or $420 − $400 = $20.

Note Given to Extend Credit Period A company can replace an account payable with a note payable. A common example is a creditor that requires the substitution of an interest-bearing note for an overdue account payable that does not bear interest. A less common situation occurs when a debtor's weak financial condition motivates the creditor to accept a note, sometimes for a lesser amount, and to close the account to ensure that this customer makes no additional credit purchases.

To illustrate, let's assume that on August 23, Brady Company asks to extend its past-due $600 account payable to McGraw. After some negotiations, McGraw agrees to accept $100 cash and a 60-day, 12%, $500 note payable to replace the account payable. Brady records the transaction with this entry:

Assets	=	Liabilities	+	Equity
−100		−600		
		+500		

Aug. 23	Accounts Payable—McGraw	600	
	Cash		100
	Notes Payable—McGraw		500
	Gave $100 cash and a 60-day, 12% note for payment on account.		

Point: Accounts payable are detailed in a subsidiary ledger, but notes payable are sometimes not. A file with copies of notes can serve as a subsidiary ledger.

Signing the note does not resolve Brady's debt. Instead, the form of debt is changed from an account payable to a note payable. McGraw prefers the note payable over the account payable because it earns interest and it is written documentation of the debt's existence, term, and amount. When the note comes due, Brady pays the note and interest by giving McGraw a check for $510. Brady records that payment with this entry:

Assets	=	Liabilities	+	Equity
−510		−500		−10

Oct. 22	Notes Payable—McGraw	500	
	Interest Expense	10	
	Cash		510
	Paid note with interest ($500 × 12% × 60/360).		

Point: Commercial companies commonly compute interest using a 360-day year. This is known as the *banker's rule.*

Interest expense is computed by multiplying the principal of the note ($500) by the annual interest rate (12%) for the fraction of the year the note is outstanding (60 days/360 days).

Note Given to Borrow from Bank A bank nearly always requires a borrower to sign a promissory note when making a loan. When the note matures, the borrower repays the note with an amount larger than the amount borrowed. The difference between the amount borrowed and the amount repaid is *interest*. This section considers a type of note whose signer promises to pay *principal* (the amount borrowed) plus interest. In this case, the *face value* of the note equals principal. Face value is the value shown on the face (front) of the note. To illustrate, assume that a company needs $2,000 for a project and borrows this money from a bank at 12% annual interest. The loan is made on September 30, 2011, and is due in 60 days. Specifically, the borrowing company signs a note with a face value equal to the amount borrowed. The note includes a statement similar to this: *"I promise to pay $2,000 plus interest at 12% within 60 days after September 30."* This simple note is shown in Exhibit 11.3.

Point: When money is borrowed from a bank, the loan is reported as an asset (receivable) on the bank's balance sheet.

EXHIBIT 11.3

Note with Face Value Equal to Amount Borrowed

Promissory Note

$2,000 — Face Value   Sept. 30, 2011 — Date

Sixty days after date, I promise to pay to the order of

National Bank
Boston, MA

Two thousand and no/100 ------------------------- Dollars

plus interest at the annual rate of 12%.

Janet Lee

The borrower records its receipt of cash and the new liability with this entry:

Sept. 30	Cash	2,000	
	Notes Payable		2,000
	Borrowed $2,000 cash with a 60-day, 12%, $2,000 note.		

Assets = Liabilities + Equity
+2,000 +2,000

When principal and interest are paid, the borrower records payment with this entry:

Nov. 29	Notes Payable	2,000	
	Interest Expense	40	
	Cash		2,040
	Paid note with interest ($2,000 × 12% × 60/360).		

Assets = Liabilities + Equity
−2,040 −2,000 −40

End-of-period interest adjustment. When the end of an accounting period occurs between the signing of a note payable and its maturity date, the *matching principle* requires us to record the accrued but unpaid interest on the note. To illustrate, let's return to the note in Exhibit 11.3, but assume that the company borrows $2,000 cash on December 16, 2011, instead of September 30. This 60-day note matures on February 14, 2012, and the company's fiscal year ends on December 31. Thus, we need to record interest expense for the final 15 days in December. This means that one-fourth (15 days/60 days) of the $40 total interest is an expense of year 2011. The borrower records this expense with the following adjusting entry:

2011			
Dec. 31	Interest Expense	10	
	Interest Payable		10
	To record accrued interest on note ($2,000 × 12% × 15/360).		

Assets = Liabilities + Equity
+10 −10

Example: If this note is dated Dec. 1 instead of Dec. 16, how much expense is recorded on Dec. 31? *Answer:* $2,000 × 12% × 30/360 = $20

When this note matures on February 14, the borrower must recognize 45 days of interest expense for year 2012 and remove the balances of the two liability accounts:

2012			
Feb. 14	Interest Expense*	30	
	Interest Payable	10	
	Notes Payable	2,000	
	Cash		2,040
	*Paid note with interest. *($2,000 × 12% × 45/360)*		

Assets = Liabilities + Equity
−2,040 −10 −30
−2,000

Decision Insight

Many franchisors such as **Baskin-Robbins**, **Dunkin' Donuts**, and **Cold Stone Creamery**, use notes to help entrepreneurs acquire their own franchises, including using notes to pay for the franchise fee and any equipment. Payments on these notes are usually collected monthly and often are secured by the franchisees' assets. ■

Payroll Liabilities

An employer incurs several expenses and liabilities from having employees. These expenses and liabilities are often large and arise from salaries and wages earned, from employee benefits, and from payroll taxes levied on the employer. **Boston Beer**, for instance, reports payroll-related current liabilities of more than $6.6 million from accrued "employee wages, benefits and reimbursements." We discuss payroll liabilities and related accounts in this section. Appendix 11A describes details about payroll reports, records, and procedures.

P2 Compute and record *employee* payroll deductions and liabilities.

Employee Payroll Deductions **Gross pay** is the total compensation an employee earns including wages, salaries, commissions, bonuses, and any compensation earned before deductions such as taxes. (*Wages* usually refer to payments to employees at an hourly rate. *Salaries* usually refer to payments to employees at a monthly or yearly rate.) **Net pay,** also called *take-home pay,* is gross pay less all deductions. **Payroll deductions,** commonly called *withholdings,* are amounts withheld from an employee's gross pay, either required or voluntary. Required deductions result from laws and include income taxes and Social Security taxes. Voluntary deductions, at an employee's option, include pension and health contributions, health and life insurance premiums, union dues, and charitable giving. Exhibit 11.4 shows the typical payroll deductions of an employee. The employer withholds payroll deductions from employees' pay and is obligated to transmit this money to the designated organization. The employer records payroll deductions as current liabilities until these amounts are transmitted. This section discusses the major payroll deductions.

Point: Deductions at some companies, such as those for insurance coverage, are "required" under its own labor contracts.

EXHIBIT 11.4

Payroll Deductions

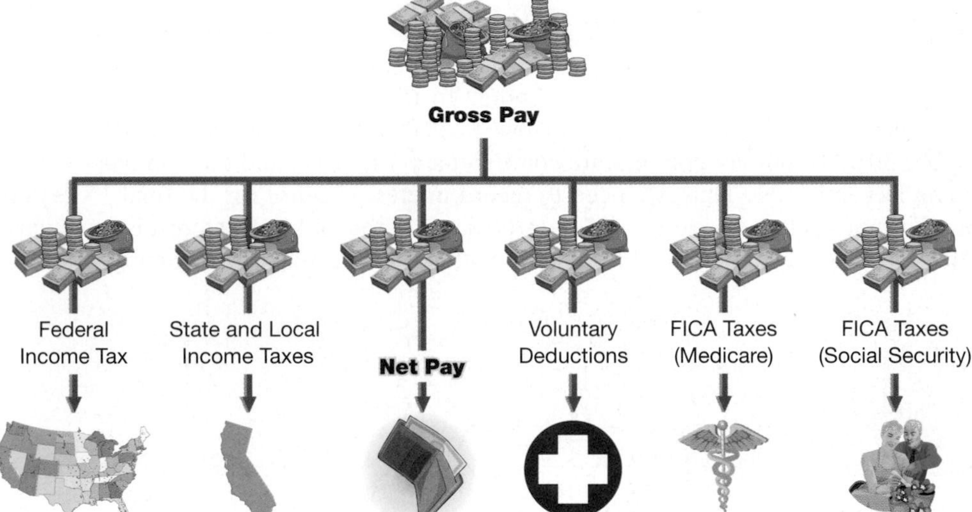

Employee FICA taxes. The federal Social Security system provides retirement, disability, survivorship, and medical benefits to qualified workers. Laws *require* employers to withhold **Federal Insurance Contributions Act (FICA) taxes** from employees' pay to cover costs of the system. Employers usually separate FICA taxes into two groups: (1) retirement, disability, and survivorship and (2) medical. For the first group, the Social Security system provides monthly cash payments to qualified retired workers for the rest of their lives. These payments are often called *Social Security benefits.* Taxes related to this group are often called *Social Security taxes.* For the second group, the system provides monthly payments to deceased workers' surviving families and to disabled workers who qualify for assistance. These payments are commonly called *Medicare benefits;* like those in the first group, they are paid with *Medicare taxes* (part of FICA taxes).

Law requires employers to withhold FICA taxes from each employee's salary or wages on each payday. The taxes for Social Security and Medicare are computed separately. For example, for the year 2010, the amount withheld from each employee's pay for Social Security tax was 6.2% of the first $106,800 the employee earns in the calendar year, or a maximum of $6,621.60. The Medicare tax was 1.45% of *all* amounts the employee earns; there is no maximum limit to Medicare tax.

Employers must pay withheld taxes to the Internal Revenue Service (IRS) on specific filing dates during the year. Employers who fail to send the withheld taxes to the IRS on time can be assessed substantial penalties. Until all the taxes are sent to the IRS, they are included in employers' current liabilities. For any changes in rates or with the maximum earnings level, check the IRS Website at **www.IRS.gov** or the SSA Website at **www.SSA.gov**.

Point: The sources of U.S. tax receipts are roughly as follows:

50%	Personal income tax
35	FICA and FUTA taxes
10	Corporate income tax
5	Other taxes

Employee income tax. Most employers are required to withhold federal income tax from each employee's paycheck. The amount withheld is computed using tables published by the IRS. The amount depends on the employee's annual earnings rate and the number of *withholding allowances* the employee claims. Allowances reduce the amount of taxes one owes the government. The more allowances one claims, the less tax the employer will withhold. Employees

Point: Part-time employees may claim "exempt from withholding" if they did not have any income tax liability in the prior year and do not expect any in the current year.

can claim allowances for themselves and their dependents. They also can claim additional allowances if they expect major declines in their taxable income for medical expenses. (An employee who claims more allowances than appropriate is subject to a fine.) Most states and many local governments require employers to withhold income taxes from employees' pay and to remit them promptly to the proper government agency. Until they are paid, withholdings are reported as a current liability on the employer's balance sheet.

Point: IRS withholding tables are based on projecting weekly (or other period) pay into an annual figure.

Employee voluntary deductions. Beyond Social Security, Medicare, and income taxes, employers often withhold other amounts from employees' earnings. These withholdings arise from employee requests, contracts, unions, or other agreements. They can include amounts for charitable giving, medical and life insurance premiums, pension contributions, and union dues. Until they are paid, such withholdings are reported as part of employers' current liabilities.

Recording employee payroll deductions. Employers must accrue payroll expenses and liabilities at the end of each pay period. To illustrate, assume that an employee earns a salary of $2,000 per month. At the end of January, the employer's entry to accrue payroll expenses and liabilities for this employee is

Jan. 31	Salaries Expense	2,000	
	FICA—Social Security Taxes Payable (6.2%)		124
	FICA—Medicare Taxes Payable (1.45%)		29
	Employee Federal Income Taxes Payable*		213
	Employee Medical Insurance Payable*		85
	Employee Union Dues Payable*		25
	Salaries Payable		1,524
	To record accrued payroll for January.		

* Amounts taken from employer's accounting records.

Assets	=	Liabilities	+	Equity
		+124		−2,000
		+29		
		+213		
		+85		
		+25		
		+1,524		

Salaries Expense (debit) shows that the employee earns a gross salary of $2,000. The first five payables (credits) show the liabilities the employer owes on behalf of this employee to cover FICA taxes, income taxes, medical insurance, and union dues. The Salaries Payable account (credit) records the $1,524 net pay the employee receives from the $2,000 gross pay earned. When the employee is paid, another entry (or a series of entries) is required to record the check written and distributed (or funds transferred). The entry to record cash payment to this employee is to debit Salaries Payable and credit Cash for $1,524.

Salaries Payable	1,524	
Cash		1,524

Decision Insight

A company's delay or failure to pay withholding taxes to the government has severe consequences. For example, a 100% penalty can be levied, with interest, on the unpaid balance. The government can even close a company, take its assets, and pursue legal actions against those involved. ■

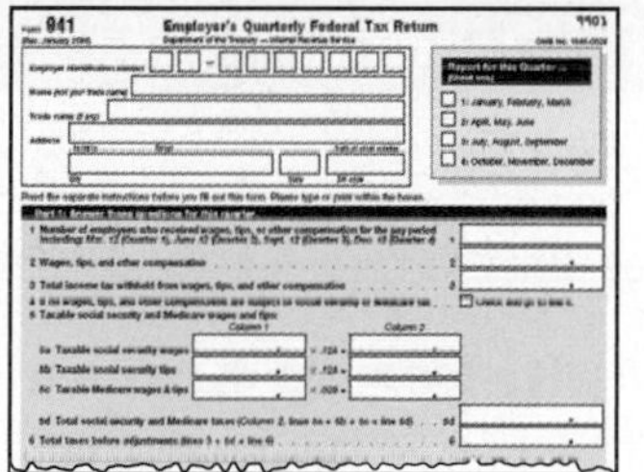
941 Employer's Quarterly Federal Tax Return

Employer Payroll Taxes Employers must pay payroll taxes in addition to those required of employees. Employer taxes include FICA and unemployment taxes.

P3 Compute and record *employer* payroll expenses and liabilities.

Employer FICA tax. Employers must pay FICA taxes *equal in amount to* the FICA taxes withheld from their employees. An employer's tax is credited to the same FICA Taxes Payable accounts used to record the Social Security and Medicare taxes withheld from employees. (A self-employed person must pay both the employee and employer FICA taxes.)

Federal and state unemployment taxes. The federal government participates with states in a joint federal and state unemployment insurance program. Each state administers its program. These programs provide unemployment benefits to qualified workers. The federal government approves state programs and pays a portion of their administrative expenses.

Federal Unemployment Taxes (FUTA). Employers are subject to a federal unemployment tax on wages and salaries paid to their employees. For the year 2010, employers were required to pay FUTA taxes of as much as 6.2% of the first $7,000 earned by each employee. This federal tax can be reduced by a credit of up to 5.4% for taxes paid to a state program. As a result, the net federal unemployment tax is often only 0.8%.

State Unemployment Taxes (SUTA). All states support their unemployment insurance programs by placing a payroll tax on employers. (A few states require employees to make a contribution. In the book's assignments, we assume that this tax is only on the employer.) In most states, the base rate for SUTA taxes is 5.4% of the first $7,000 paid each employee. This base rate is adjusted according to an employer's merit rating. The state assigns a **merit rating** that reflects a company's stability or instability in employing workers. A good rating reflects stability in employment and means an employer can pay less than the 5.4% base rate. A low rating reflects high turnover or seasonal hirings and layoffs. To illustrate, an employer with 50 employees each of whom earns $7,000 or more per year saves $15,400 annually if it has a merit rating of 1.0% versus 5.4%. This is computed by comparing taxes of $18,900 at the 5.4% rate to only $3,500 at the 1.0% rate.

Recording employer payroll taxes. Employer payroll taxes are an added expense beyond the wages and salaries earned by employees. These taxes are often recorded in an entry separate from the one recording payroll expenses and deductions. To illustrate, assume that the $2,000 recorded salaries expense from the previous example is earned by an employee whose earnings have not yet reached $5,000 for the year. This means the entire salaries expense for this period is subject to tax because year-to-date pay is under $7,000. Also assume that the federal unemployment tax rate is 0.8% and the state unemployment tax rate is 5.4%. Consequently, the FICA portion of the employer's tax is $153, computed by multiplying both the 6.2% and 1.45% by the $2,000 gross pay. Moreover, state unemployment (SUTA) taxes are $108 (5.4% of the $2,000 gross pay), and federal unemployment (FUTA) taxes are $16 (0.8% of $2,000). The entry to record the employer's payroll tax expense and related liabilities is

Example: If the employer's merit rating in this example reduces its SUTA rate to 2.9%, what is its SUTA liability? *Answer:* SUTA payable = $2,000 × 2.9% = $58

Assets	=	Liabilities	+	Equity
		+124		−277
		+29		
		+108		
		+16		

Jan. 31	Payroll Taxes Expense	277	
	FICA—Social Security Taxes Payable (6.2%)		124
	FICA—Medicare Taxes Payable (1.45%)		29
	State Unemployment Taxes Payable		108
	Federal Unemployment Taxes Payable		16
	To record employer payroll taxes.		

Point: Internal control is important for payroll accounting. Managers must monitor (1) employee hiring, (2) timekeeping, (3) payroll listings, and (4) payroll payments. Poor controls led the U.S. Army to pay nearly $10 million to deserters, fictitious soldiers, and other unauthorized entities.

Decision Ethics Answer — p. 460

Web Designer You take a summer job working for a family friend who runs a small IT service. On your first payday, the owner slaps you on the back, gives you full payment in cash, winks, and adds: "No need to pay those high taxes, eh." What action, if any, do you take? ■

Multi-Period Known Liabilities

Many known liabilities extend over multiple periods. These often include unearned revenues and notes payable. For example, if **Sports Illustrated** sells a four-year magazine subscription, it records amounts received for this subscription in an Unearned Subscription Revenues account. Amounts in this account are liabilities, but are they current or long term? They are *both.* The portion of the Unearned Subscription Revenues account that will be fulfilled in the next year is reported as a current liability. The remaining portion is reported as a long-term liability.

The same analysis applies to notes payable. For example, a borrower reports a three-year note payable as a long-term liability in the first two years it is outstanding. In the third year, the borrower reclassifies this note as a current liability since it is due within one year or the operating cycle, whichever is longer. The **current portion of long-term debt** refers to that part of long-term debt due within one year or the operating cycle, whichever is longer. Long-term debt is reported under long-term liabilities, but the *current portion due* is reported under current liabilities. To illustrate, assume that a $7,500 debt is paid in installments of $1,500 per year for five years. The $1,500 due within the year is reported as a current liability. No journal entry is necessary for this reclassification. Instead, we simply classify the amounts for debt as either current or long term when the balance sheet is prepared.

Point: Some accounting systems do make an entry to transfer the current amount due out of Long-Term Debt and into the Current Portion of Long-Term Debt as follows:

Long-Term Debt	1,500	
Current Portion of L-T Debt...		1,500

Some known liabilities are rarely reported in long-term liabilities. These include accounts payable, sales taxes, and wages and salaries.

Decision Insight

Liability Limits Probably the greatest number of frauds involve payroll. Companies must safeguard payroll activities. Controls include proper approvals and processes for employee additions, deletions, and pay rate changes. A common fraud is a manager adding a fictitious employee to the payroll and then cashing the fictitious employee's check. A study reports that 28% of employees in operations and service areas witnessed violations of employee wage, overtime, or benefit rules in the past year (KPMG 2009). Another 21% observed falsifying of time and expense reports. ■

Quick Check

Answers — p. 461

4. Why does a creditor prefer a note payable to a past-due account payable?
5. A company pays its one employee $3,000 per month. This company's FUTA rate is 0.8% on the first $7,000 earned; its SUTA rate is 4.0% on the first $7,000; its Social Security tax rate is 6.2% of the first $106,800; and its Medicare tax rate is 1.45% of all amounts earned. The entry to record this company's March payroll includes what amount for total payroll taxes expense?
6. Identify whether the employer or employee or both incurs each of the following: (*a*) FICA taxes, (*b*) FUTA taxes, (*c*) SUTA taxes, and (*d*) withheld income taxes.

ESTIMATED LIABILITIES

P4 Account for estimated liabilities, including warranties and bonuses.

An **estimated liability** is a known obligation that is of an uncertain amount but that can be reasonably estimated. Common examples are employee benefits such as pensions, health care and vacation pay, and warranties offered by a seller. We discuss each of these in this section. Other examples of estimated liabilities include property taxes and certain contracts to provide future services.

Health and Pension Benefits

Many companies provide **employee benefits** beyond salaries and wages. An employer often pays all or part of medical, dental, life, and disability insurance. Many employers also contribute to *pension plans,* which are agreements by employers to provide benefits (payments) to employees after retirement. Many companies also provide medical care and insurance benefits to their retirees. When payroll taxes and charges for employee benefits are totaled, payroll cost often exceeds employees' gross earnings by 25% or more.

To illustrate, assume that an employer agrees to (1) pay an amount for medical insurance equal to $8,000 and (2) contribute an additional 10% of the employees' $120,000 gross salary to a retirement program. The entry to record these accrued benefits is

Dec. 31	Employee Benefits Expense	20,000	
	Employee Medical Insurance Payable		8,000
	Employee Retirement Program Payable		12,000
	To record costs of employee benefits.		

Assets	=	Liabilities	+	Equity
		+8,000		−20,000
		+12,000		

Decision Insight

Postgame Spoils Baseball was the first pro sport to set up a pension, originally up to $100 per month depending on years played. Many former players now take home six-figure pensions. Cal Ripken Jr.'s pension when he reaches 62 is estimated at $160,000 per year (he played 21 seasons). The requirement is only 43 games for a full pension and just one game for full medical benefits. ■

Vacation Benefits

Many employers offer paid vacation benefits, also called *paid absences*. To illustrate, assume that salaried employees earn 2 weeks' vacation per year. This benefit increases employers' payroll expenses because employees are paid for 52 weeks but work for only 50 weeks. Total annual salary is the same, but the cost per week worked is greater than the amount paid per week. For example, if an employee is paid $20,800 for 52 weeks but works only 50 weeks, the total weekly expense to the employer is $416 ($20,800/50 weeks) instead of the $400 cash paid weekly to the employee ($20,800/52 weeks). The $16 difference between these two amounts is recorded weekly as follows:

Assets	=	Liabilities	+	Equity
		+16		−16

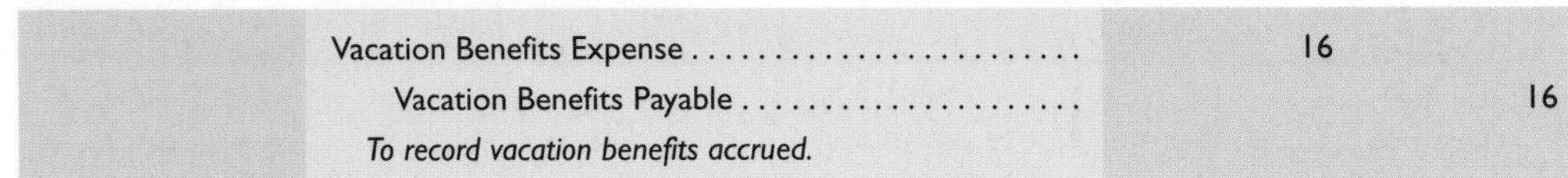

		Debit	Credit
	Vacation Benefits Expense	16	
	Vacation Benefits Payable		16
	To record vacation benefits accrued.		

Vacation Benefits Payable	#	
Cash		#

Vacation Benefits Expense is an operating expense, and Vacation Benefits Payable is a current liability. When the employee takes a vacation, the employer reduces (debits) the Vacation Benefits Payable and credits Cash (no additional expense is recorded).

Bonus Plans

Many companies offer bonuses to employees, and many of the bonuses depend on net income. To illustrate, assume that an employer offers a bonus to its employees equal to 5% of the company's annual net income (to be equally shared by all). The company's expected annual net income is $210,000. The year-end adjusting entry to record this benefit is

Assets	=	Liabilities	+	Equity
		+10,000		−10,000

		Debit	Credit
Dec. 31	Employee Bonus Expense*	10,000	
	Bonus Payable		10,000
	To record expected bonus costs.		

* Bonus Expense (B) equals 5% of net income, which equals $210,000 minus the bonus; this is computed as:

$$B = 0.05\,(\$210{,}000 - B)$$
$$B = \$10{,}500 - 0.05B$$
$$1.05B = \$10{,}500$$
$$\mathbf{B = \$10{,}500/1.05 = \$10{,}000}$$

When the bonus is paid, Bonus Payable is debited and Cash is credited for $10,000.

Warranty Liabilities

Point: **Kodak** recently reported $60 million in warranty obligations.

A **warranty** is a seller's obligation to replace or correct a product (or service) that fails to perform as expected within a specified period. Most new cars, for instance, are sold with a warranty covering parts for a specified period of time. **Ford Motor Company** reported more than $15 billion in "dealer and customer allowances and claims" in its annual report. To comply with the *full disclosure* and *matching principles,* the seller reports the expected warranty expense in the period when revenue from the sale of the product or service is reported. The seller reports this warranty obligation as a liability, although the existence, amount, payee, and date of future sacrifices are uncertain. This is because such warranty costs are probable and the amount can be estimated using, for instance, past experience with warranties.

To illustrate, a dealer sells a used car for $16,000 on December 1, 2011, with a maximum one-year or 12,000-mile warranty covering parts. This dealer's experience shows that warranty expense averages about 4% of a car's selling price, or $640 in this case ($16,000 × 4%). The dealer records the estimated expense and liability related to this sale with this entry:

2011			
Dec. 1	Warranty Expense	640	
	Estimated Warranty Liability		640
	To record estimated warranty expense.		

Assets = Liabilities + Equity
+640 −640

This entry alternatively could be made as part of end-of-period adjustments. Either way, the estimated warranty expense is reported on the 2011 income statement and the warranty liability on the 2011 balance sheet. To further extend this example, suppose the customer returns the car for warranty repairs on January 9, 2012. The dealer performs this work by replacing parts costing $200. The entry to record partial settlement of the estimated warranty liability is

Point: Recognition of warranty liabilities is necessary to comply with the matching and full disclosure principles.

2012			
Jan. 9	Estimated Warranty Liability	200	
	Auto Parts Inventory		200
	To record costs of warranty repairs.		

Assets = Liabilities + Equity
−200 −200

This entry reduces the balance of the estimated warranty liability. Warranty expense was previously recorded in 2011, the year the car was sold with the warranty. Finally, what happens if total warranty expenses are more or less than the estimated 4%, or $640? The answer is that management should monitor actual warranty expenses to see whether the 4% rate is accurate. If experience reveals a large difference from the estimate, the rate for current and future sales should be changed. Differences are expected, but they should be small.

Point: Both U.S. GAAP and IFRS account for restructuring costs in a manner similar to accounting for warranties.

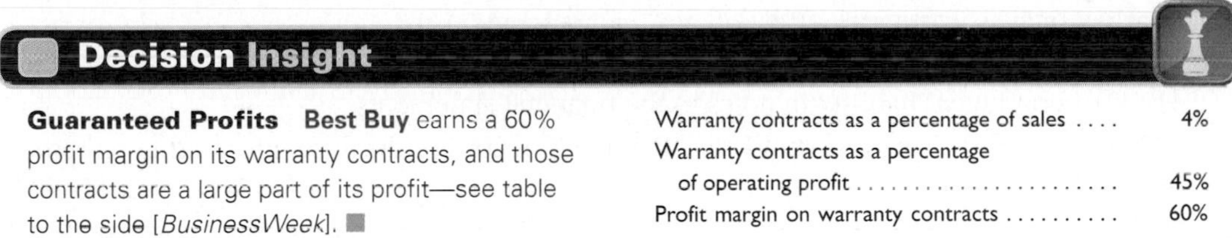

Decision Insight

Guaranteed Profits **Best Buy** earns a 60% profit margin on its warranty contracts, and those contracts are a large part of its profit—see table to the side [*BusinessWeek*]. ■

Warranty contracts as a percentage of sales	4%
Warranty contracts as a percentage of operating profit	45%
Profit margin on warranty contracts	60%

Multi-Period Estimated Liabilities

Estimated liabilities can be both current and long term. For example, pension liabilities to employees are long term to workers who will not retire within the next period. For employees who are retired or will retire within the next period, a portion of pension liabilities is current. Other examples include employee health benefits and warranties. Specifically, many warranties are for 30 or 60 days in length. Estimated costs under these warranties are properly reported in current liabilities. Many other automobile warranties are for three years or 36,000 miles. A portion of these warranties is reported as long term.

Quick Check Answers — p. 461

7. Estimated liabilities involve an obligation to pay which of these? (*a*) An uncertain but reasonably estimated amount owed on a known obligation or (*b*) A known amount to a specific entity on an uncertain due date.
8. A car is sold for $15,000 on June 1, 2011, with a one-year warranty on parts. Warranty expense is estimated at 1.5% of selling price at each calendar year-end. On March 1, 2012, the car is returned for warranty repairs costing $135. The amount recorded as warranty expense on March 1 is (*a*) $0; (*b*) $60; (*c*) $75; (*d*) $135; (*e*) $225.

CONTINGENT LIABILITIES

C3 Explain how to account for contingent liabilities.

A **contingent liability** is a potential obligation that depends on a future event arising from a past transaction or event. An example is a pending lawsuit. Here, a past transaction or event leads to a lawsuit whose result depends on the outcome of the suit. Future payment of a contingent liability depends on whether an uncertain future event occurs.

Accounting for Contingent Liabilities

Accounting for contingent liabilities depends on the likelihood that a future event will occur and the ability to estimate the future amount owed if this event occurs. Three different possibilities are identified in the following chart: record liability, disclose in notes, or no disclosure.

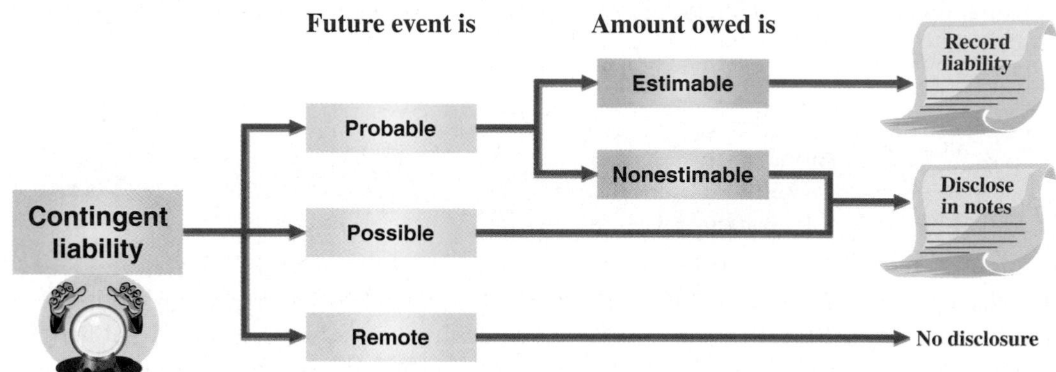

The conditions that determine each of these three possibilities follow:

1. The future event is *probable* (likely) and the amount owed can be *reasonably estimated.* We then record this amount as a liability. Examples are the estimated liabilities described earlier such as warranties, vacation pay, and income taxes.
2. The future event is *reasonably possible* (could occur). We disclose information about this type of contingent liability in notes to the financial statements.
3. The future event is *remote* (unlikely). We do not record or disclose information on remote contingent liabilities.

Point: A contingency is an *if.* Namely, if a future event occurs, then financial consequences are likely for the entity.

Reasonably Possible Contingent Liabilities

This section identifies and discusses contingent liabilities that commonly fall in the second category—when the future event is reasonably possible. Disclosing information about contingencies in this category is motivated by the *full-disclosure principle,* which requires information relevant to decision makers be reported and not ignored.

Potential Legal Claims Many companies are sued or at risk of being sued. The accounting issue is whether the defendant should recognize a liability on its balance sheet or disclose a contingent liability in its notes while a lawsuit is outstanding and not yet settled. The answer is that a potential claim is recorded in the accounts *only* if payment for damages is probable and the amount can be reasonably estimated. If the potential claim cannot be reasonably estimated or is less than probable but reasonably possible, it is disclosed. **Ford Motor Company**, for example, includes the following note in its annual report: "Various legal actions, governmental investigations and proceedings and claims are pending . . . arising out of alleged defects in our products."

Point: A sale of a note receivable is often a contingent liability. It becomes a liability if the original signer of the note fails to pay it at maturity.

Debt Guarantees Sometimes a company guarantees the payment of debt owed by a supplier, customer, or another company. The guarantor usually discloses the guarantee in its financial statement notes as a contingent liability. If it is probable that the debtor will default, the guarantor needs to record and report the guarantee in its financial statements as a liability. The **Boston Celtics** report a unique guarantee when it comes to coaches and players: "Certain of the contracts provide for guaranteed payments which must be paid even if the employee [player] is injured or terminated."

Other Contingencies Other examples of contingencies include environmental damages, possible tax assessments, insurance losses, and government investigations. **Sunoco**, for instance, reports that "federal, state and local laws . . . result in liabilities and loss contingencies. Sunoco accrues . . . cleanup costs [that] are probable and reasonably estimable. Management believes it is reasonably possible (i.e., less than probable but greater than remote) that additional . . . losses will be incurred." Many of Sunoco's contingencies are revealed only in notes.

Point: Auditors and managers often have different views about whether a contingency is recorded, disclosed, or omitted.

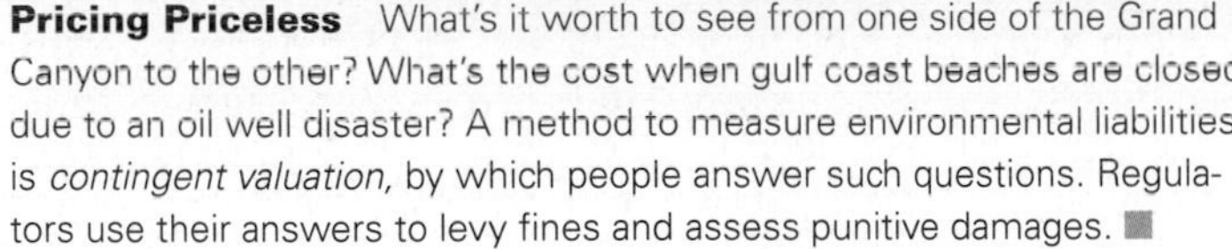

Decision Insight

Pricing Priceless What's it worth to see from one side of the Grand Canyon to the other? What's the cost when gulf coast beaches are closed due to an oil well disaster? A method to measure environmental liabilities is *contingent valuation*, by which people answer such questions. Regulators use their answers to levy fines and assess punitive damages. ■

Uncertainties that Are Not Contingencies

All organizations face uncertainties from future events such as natural disasters and the development of new competing products or services. These uncertainties are not contingent liabilities because they are future events *not* arising from past transactions. Accordingly, they are not disclosed.

Quick Check Answers — p. 461

9. A future payment is reported as a liability on the balance sheet if payment is contingent on a future event that (*a*) is reasonably possible but the payment cannot be reasonably estimated; (*b*) is probable and the payment can be reasonably estimated; or (*c*) is not probable but the payment is known.
10. Under what circumstances is a future payment reported in the notes to the financial statements as a contingent liability?

GLOBAL VIEW

This section discusses similarities and differences between U.S. GAAP and IFRS in accounting and reporting for current liabilities.

Characteristics of Liabilities The definitions and characteristics of current liabilities are broadly similar for both U.S. GAAP and IFRS. Although differences exist, the similarities vastly outweigh any differences. Remembering that "provision" is typically used under IFRS to refer to what is titled "liability" under U.S. GAAP, **Nokia** describes its recognition of liabilities as follows:

> Provisions are recognized when the Group has a present legal or constructive obligation as a result of past events, it is probable that an outflow of resources will be required to settle the obligation and a reliable estimate of the amount can be made.

NOKIA

Known (Determinable) Liabilities When there is little uncertainty surrounding current liabilities, both U.S. GAAP and IFRS require companies to record them in a similar manner. This correspondence in accounting applies to accounts payable, sales taxes payable, unearned revenues, short-term notes, and payroll liabilities. Of course, tax regulatory systems of countries are different, which implies use of different rates and levels. Still, the basic approach is the same.

Estimated Liabilities When there is a known current obligation that involves an uncertain amount, but one that can be reasonably estimated, both U.S. GAAP and IFRS require similar treatment. This treatment extends to many obligations such as those arising from vacations, warranties, restructurings, pensions, and health care. Both accounting systems require that companies record estimated expenses related to these obligations when they can reasonably estimate the amounts. **Nokia** reports wages, salaries and bonuses of €5,658 million. It also reports pension expenses of €427 million.

Decision Analysis — Times Interest Earned Ratio

A1 Compute the times interest earned ratio and use it to analyze liabilities.

A company incurs interest expense on many of its current and long-term liabilities. Examples extend from its short-term notes and the current portion of long-term liabilities to its long-term notes and bonds. Interest expense is often viewed as a *fixed expense* because the amount of these liabilities is likely to remain in one form or another for a substantial period of time. This means that the amount of interest is unlikely to vary due to changes in sales or other operating activities. While fixed expenses can be advantageous when a company is growing, they create risk. This risk stems from the possibility that a company might be unable to pay fixed expenses if sales decline. To illustrate, consider Diego Co.'s results for 2011 and two possible outcomes for year 2012 in Exhibit 11.5.

EXHIBIT 11.5
Actual and Projected Results

($ thousands)	2011	2012 Projections: Sales Increase	2012 Projections: Sales Decrease
Sales	$600	$900	$300
Expenses (75% of sales)	450	675	225
Income before interest	150	225	75
Interest expense (fixed)	60	60	60
Net income	$ 90	$165	$ 15

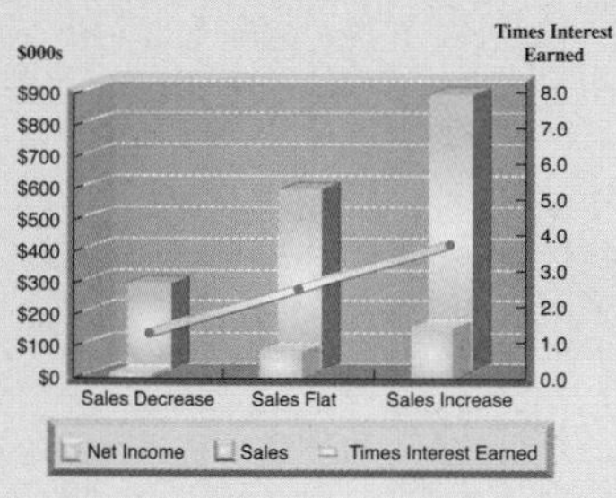

Expenses excluding interest are at, and expected to remain at, 75% of sales. Expenses such as these that change with sales volume are called *variable expenses.* However, interest expense is at, and expected to remain at, $60,000 per year due to its fixed nature.

The middle numerical column of Exhibit 11.5 shows that Diego's income increases by 83% to $165,000 if sales increase by 50% to $900,000. In contrast, the far right column shows that income decreases by 83% if sales decline by 50%. These results reveal that the amount of fixed interest expense affects a company's risk of its ability to pay interest, which is numerically reflected in the **times interest earned** ratio in Exhibit 11.6.

EXHIBIT 11.6
Times Interest Earned

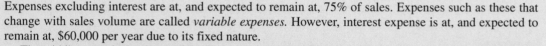

$$\textbf{Times interest earned} = \frac{\textbf{Income before interest expense and income taxes}}{\textbf{Interest expense}}$$

For 2011, Diego's times interest earned is computed as $150,000/$60,000, or 2.5 times. This ratio suggests that Diego faces low to moderate risk because its sales must decline sharply before it would be unable to cover its interest expenses. (Diego is an LLC and does not pay income taxes.)

Experience shows that when times interest earned falls below 1.5 to 2.0 and remains at that level or lower for several periods, the default rate on liabilities increases sharply. This reflects increased risk for companies and their creditors. We also must interpret the times interest earned ratio in light of information about the variability of a company's income before interest. If income is stable from year to year or if it is growing, the company can afford to take on added risk by borrowing. If its income greatly varies from year to year, fixed interest expense can increase the risk that it will not earn enough income to pay interest.

Answer — p. 461

Entrepreneur You wish to invest in a franchise for either one of two national chains. Each franchise has an expected annual net income *after* interest and taxes of $100,000. Net income for the first franchise includes a regular fixed interest charge of $200,000. The fixed interest charge for the second franchise is $40,000. Which franchise is riskier to you if sales forecasts are not met? Does your decision change if the first franchise has more variability in its income stream? ■

DEMONSTRATION PROBLEM

The following transactions and events took place at Kern Company during its recent calendar-year reporting period (Kern does not use reversing entries).

a. In September 2011, Kern sold $140,000 of merchandise covered by a 180-day warranty. Prior experience shows that costs of the warranty equal 5% of sales. Compute September's warranty expense and prepare the adjusting journal entry for the warranty liability as recorded at September 30. Also prepare the journal entry on October 8 to record a $300 cash expenditure to provide warranty service on an item sold in September.

b. On October 12, 2011, Kern arranged with a supplier to replace Kern's overdue $10,000 account payable by paying $2,500 cash and signing a note for the remainder. The note matures in 90 days and has a 12% interest rate. Prepare the entries recorded on October 12, December 31, and January 10, 2012, related to this transaction.

c. In late December, Kern learns it is facing a product liability suit filed by an unhappy customer. Kern's lawyer advises that although it will probably suffer a loss from the lawsuit, it is not possible to estimate the amount of damages at this time.

d. Sally Bline works for Kern. For the pay period ended November 30, her gross earnings are $3,000. Bline has $800 deducted for federal income taxes and $200 for state income taxes from each paycheck. Additionally, a $35 premium for her health care insurance and a $10 donation for the United Way are deducted. Bline pays FICA Social Security taxes at a rate of 6.2% and FICA Medicare taxes at a rate of 1.45%. She has not earned enough this year to be exempt from any FICA taxes. Journalize the accrual of salaries expense of Bline's wages by Kern.

e. On November 1, Kern borrows $5,000 cash from a bank in return for a 60-day, 12%, $5,000 note. Record the note's issuance on November 1 and its repayment with interest on December 31.

f.[B] Kern has estimated and recorded its quarterly income tax payments. In reviewing its year-end tax adjustments, it identifies an additional $5,000 of income tax expense that should be recorded. A portion of this additional expense, $1,000, is deferrable to future years. Record this year-end income taxes expense adjusting entry.

g. For this calendar-year, Kern's net income is $1,000,000, its interest expense is $275,000, and its income taxes expense is $225,000. Calculate Kern's times interest earned ratio.

PLANNING THE SOLUTION

- For *a,* compute the warranty expense for September and record it with an estimated liability. Record the October expenditure as a decrease in the liability.
- For *b,* eliminate the liability for the account payable and create the liability for the note payable. Compute interest expense for the 80 days that the note is outstanding in 2011 and record it as an additional liability. Record the payment of the note, being sure to include the interest for the 10 days in 2012.
- For *c,* decide whether the company's contingent liability needs to be disclosed or accrued (recorded) according to the two necessary criteria: probable loss and reasonably estimable.
- For *d,* set up payable accounts for all items in Bline's paycheck that require deductions. After deducting all necessary items, credit the remaining amount to Salaries Payable.
- For *e,* record the issuance of the note. Calculate 60 days' interest due using the 360-day convention in the interest formula.
- For *f,* determine how much of the income taxes expense is payable in the current year and how much needs to be deferred.
- For *g,* apply and compute times interest earned.

SOLUTION TO DEMONSTRATION PROBLEM

a. Warranty expense = 5% × $140,000 = $7,000

Sept. 30	Warranty Expense	7,000	
	Estimated Warranty Liability		7,000
	To record warranty expense for the month.		
Oct. 8	Estimated Warranty Liability	300	
	Cash		300
	To record the cost of the warranty service.		

b. Interest expense for 2011 = 12% × $7,500 × 80/360 = $200
Interest expense for 2012 = 12% × $7,500 × 10/360 = $25

Oct. 12	Accounts Payable	10,000	
	Notes Payable		7,500
	Cash		2,500
	Paid $2,500 cash and gave a 90-day, 12% note to extend the due date on the account.		
Dec. 31	Interest Expense	200	
	Interest Payable		200
	To accrue interest on note payable.		
Jan. 10	Interest Expense	25	
	Interest Payable	200	
	Notes Payable	7,500	
	Cash		7,725
	Paid note with interest, including the accrued interest payable.		

c. Disclose the pending lawsuit in the financial statement notes. Although the loss is probable, no liability can be accrued since the loss cannot be reasonably estimated.

d.

Nov. 30	Salaries Expense	3,000.00	
	FICA—Social Security Taxes Payable (6.2%)		186.00
	FICA—Medicare Taxes Payable (1.45%)		43.50
	Employee Federal Income Taxes Payable		800.00
	Employee State Income Taxes Payable		200.00
	Employee Medical Insurance Payable		35.00
	Employee United Way Payable		10.00
	Salaries Payable		1,725.50
	To record Bline's accrued payroll.		

e.

Nov. 1	Cash	5,000	
	Notes Payable		5,000
	Borrowed cash with a 60-day, 12% note.		

When the note and interest are paid 60 days later, Kern Company records this entry:

Dec. 31	Notes Payable	5,000	
	Interest Expense	100	
	Cash		5,100
	Paid note with interest ($5,000 × 12% × 60/360).		

f.

Dec. 31	Income Taxes Expense	5,000	
	Income Taxes Payable		4,000
	Deferred Income Tax Liability		1,000
	To record added income taxes expense and the deferred tax liability.		

g. Times interest earned $= \frac{\$1{,}000{,}000 + \$275{,}000 + \$225{,}000}{\$275{,}000} = \underline{\underline{5.45 \text{ times}}}$

APPENDIX

Payroll Reports, Records, and Procedures 11A

Understanding payroll procedures and keeping adequate payroll reports and records are essential to a company's success. This appendix focuses on payroll accounting and its reports, records, and procedures.

P5 Identify and describe the details of payroll reports, records, and procedures.

Payroll Reports Most employees and employers are required to pay local, state, and federal payroll taxes. Payroll expenses involve liabilities to individual employees, to federal and state governments, and to other organizations such as insurance companies. Beyond paying these liabilities, employers are required to prepare and submit reports explaining how they computed these payments.

Reporting FICA Taxes and Income Taxes The Federal Insurance Contributions Act (FICA) requires each employer to file an Internal Revenue Service (IRS) **Form 941,** the *Employer's Quarterly Federal Tax Return,* within one month after the end of each calendar quarter. A sample Form 941 is shown in Exhibit 11A.1 for Phoenix Sales & Service, a landscape design company. Accounting information and software are helpful in tracking payroll transactions and reporting the accumulated information on Form 941. Specifically, the employer reports total wages subject to income tax withholding on line 2 of Form 941. (For simplicity, this appendix uses *wages* to refer to both wages and salaries.) The income tax withheld is reported on line 3. The combined amount of employee and employer FICA (Social Security) taxes for Phoenix Sales & Service is reported on line 5a (taxable Social Security wages, $36,599 × 12.4% = $4,538.28). The 12.4% is the sum of the Social Security tax withheld, computed as 6.2% tax withheld from the employee wages for the quarter plus the 6.2% tax levied on the employer. The combined amount of employee Medicare wages is reported on line 5c. The 2.9% is the sum of 1.45% withheld from employee wages for the quarter plus 1.45% tax levied on the employer. Total FICA taxes are reported on line 5d and are added to the total income taxes withheld of $3,056.47 to yield a total of $8,656.12. For this year, assume that income up to $106,800 is subject to Social Security tax. There is no income limit on amounts subject to Medicare tax. Congress sets annual limits on the amount owed for Social Security tax.

Federal depository banks are authorized to accept deposits of amounts payable to the federal government. Deposit requirements depend on the amount of tax owed. For example, when the sum of FICA taxes plus the employee income taxes is less than $2,500 for a quarter, the taxes can be paid when Form 941 is filed. Companies with large payrolls are often required to pay monthly or even semiweekly.

Reporting FUTA Taxes and SUTA Taxes An employer's federal unemployment taxes (FUTA) are reported on an annual basis by filing an *Annual Federal Unemployment Tax Return,* IRS **Form 940.** It must be mailed on or before January 31 following the end of each tax year. Ten more days are allowed if all required tax deposits are filed on a timely basis and the full amount of tax is paid on or before January 31. FUTA payments are made quarterly to a federal depository bank if the total amount due exceeds $500. If $500 or less is due, the taxes are remitted annually. Requirements for paying and reporting state unemployment taxes (SUTA) vary depending on the laws of each state. Most states require quarterly payments and reports.

EXHIBIT 11A.1

Form 941

Form **941** **Employer's QUARTERLY Federal Tax Return**

Department of the Treasury — Internal Revenue Service

(EIN) Employer identification number: 8 6 – 3 2 1 4 5 8 7

Name (not your trade name): Phoenix Sales & Service

Trade name (if any):

Address: 1214 Mill Road (Number, Street, Suite or room number)

Phoenix AZ 85621 (City, State, ZIP code)

Report for this Quarter ... (Check one.)

- [ ] 1: January, February, March
- [ ] 2: April, May, June
- [ ] 3: July, August, September
- [X] 4: October, November, December

Part 1: Answer these questions for this quarter.

1	Number of employees who received wages, tips, or other compensation for the pay period including: *Mar. 12* (Quarter 1), *June 12* (Quarter 2), *Sept. 12* (Quarter 3), *Dec. 12* (Quarter 4)	1
2	Wages, tips, and other compensation	36,599.00
3	Total income tax withheld from wages, tips, and other compensation	3,056.47
4	If no wages, tips, and other compensation are subject to social security or Medicare tax ☐ Check and go to line 6.	

5 Taxable social security and Medicare wages and tips:

	Column 1		Column 2
5a Taxable social security wages	36,599.00	× .124 =	4,538.28
5b Taxable social security tips	.	× .124 =	.
5c Taxable Medicare wages & tips	36,599.00	× .029 =	1,061.37

5d	Total social security and Medicare taxes (*Column 2*, lines 5a + 5b + 5c = line 5d)	5,599.65
6	Total taxes before adjustments (lines 3 + 5d = line 6)	8,656.12
7	TAX ADJUSTMENTS (Read the instructions for line 7 before completing lines 7a through 7h.):	
7a	Current quarter's fractions of cents	.
7b	Current quarter's sick pay	.
7c	Current quarter's adjustments for tips and group-term life insurance	.
7d	Current year's income tax withholding (attach Form 941c)	.
7e	Prior quarters' social security and Medicare taxes (attach Form 941c)	.
7f	Special additions to federal income tax (attach Form 941c)	.
7g	Special additions to social security and Medicare (attach Form 941c)	.
7h	TOTAL ADJUSTMENTS (Combine all amounts: lines 7a through 7g.)	0.00
8	Total taxes after adjustments (Combine lines 6 and 7h.)	8,656.12
9	Advance earned income credit (EIC) payments made to employees	.
10	Total taxes after adjustment for advance EIC (lines 8 – line 9 = line 10)	8,656.12
11	Total deposits for this quarter, including overpayment applied from a prior quarter	8,656.12
12	Balance due (If line 10 is more than line 11, write the difference here.) Make checks payable to *United States Treasury.*	0.00
13	Overpayment (If line 11 is more than line 10, write the difference here.) Check one ☐ Apply to next return. ☐ Send a refund.	0.00

Part 2: Tell us about your deposit schedule and tax liability for this quarter.

If you are unsure about whether you are a monthly schedule depositor or a semiweekly schedule depositor, see *Pub. 15 (Circular E)*, section 11.

14 A Z Write the state abbreviation for the state where you made your deposits OR write "MU" if you made your deposits in *multiple* states.

15 Check one:

- [ ] Line 10 is less than $2,500. Go to Part 3.
- [X] You were a monthly schedule depositor for the entire quarter. Fill out your tax liability for each month. Then go to Part 3.

Tax liability:	
Month 1	3,079.11
Month 2	2,049.77
Month 3	3,527.24
Total liability for quarter	8,656.12

Total must equal line 10.

- [ ] You were a semiweekly schedule depositor for any part of this quarter. Fill out *Schedule B (Form 941): Report of Tax Liability for Semiweekly Schedule Depositors*, and attach it to this form.

Part 3: Tell us about your business. If a question does NOT apply to your business, leave it blank.

16 If your business has closed or you stopped paying wages ☐ Check here, and enter the final date you paid wages __/__/__.

17 If you are a seasonal employer and you do not have to file a return for every quarter of the year. ☐ Check here.

Part 4: May we speak with your third-party designee?

Do you want to allow an employee, a paid tax preparer, or another person to discuss this return with the IRS? See the instructions for details.

☐ Yes. Designee's name

Phone ( ) – Personal Identification Number (PIN)

☒ No.

Part 5: Sign here. You MUST fill out both sides of this form and SIGN it.

Under penalties of perjury, I declare that I have examined this return, including accompanying schedules and statements, and to the best of my knowledge and belief, it is true, correct, and complete.

✗ Sign your name here

Print name and title

Date / / Phone ( ) –

Reporting Wages and Salaries Employers are required to give each employee an annual report of his or her wages subject to FICA and federal income taxes along with the amounts of these taxes withheld. This report is called a *Wage and Tax Statement,* or **Form W-2.** It must be given to employees before January 31 following the year covered by the report. Exhibit 11A.2 shows Form W-2 for one of the employees at Phoenix Sales & Service. Copies of the W-2 Form must be sent to the Social Security Administration, where the amount of the employee's wages subject to FICA taxes and FICA taxes withheld are posted to each employee's Social Security account. These posted amounts become the basis for determining an employee's retirement and survivors' benefits. The Social Security Administration also transmits to the IRS the amount of each employee's wages subject to federal income taxes and the amount of taxes withheld.

EXHIBIT 11A.2

Form W-2

Form **W-2** Wage and Tax Statement
Department of the Treasury—Internal Revenue Service
Copy 1—For State, City, or Local Tax Department

a Control number: AR101	22222	OMB No. 1545-0008
b Employer identification number (EIN): 86-3214587	1 Wages, tips, other compensation: 4,910.00	2 Federal income tax withheld: 333.37
c Employer's name, address and ZIP code: Phoenix Sales & Service, 1214 Mill Road, Phoenix, AZ 85621	3 Social security wages: 4,910.00	4 Social security tax withheld: 304.42
	5 Medicare wages and tips: 4,910.00	6 Medicare tax withheld: 71.20
	7 Social security tips	8 Allocated tips
d Employee's social security number: 333-22-9999	9 Advance EIC payment	10 Dependent care benefits
e Employee's first name and initial: Robert J. Last name: Austin	11 Nonqualified plans	12a Code
f Employee's address and ZIP code: 18 Roosevelt Blvd., Apt. C, Tempe, AZ 86322	13 Statutory employee / Retirement plan / Third-party sick pay	12b Code
	14 Other	12c Code
		12d Code

15 State	Employer's state ID number	16 State wages, tips, etc.	17 State income tax	18 Local wages, tips, etc.	19 Local income tax	20 Locality name
AZ	13-902319	4,910.00	26.68			

Payroll Records Employers must keep payroll records in addition to reporting and paying taxes. These records usually include a payroll register and an individual earnings report for each employee.

Payroll Register A **payroll register** usually shows the pay period dates, hours worked, gross pay, deductions, and net pay of each employee for each pay period. Exhibit 11A.3 shows a payroll register for Phoenix Sales & Service. It is organized into nine columns:

Col. 1 Employee identification (ID); Employee name; Social Security number (SS No.); Reference (check number); and Date (date check issued)
Col. 2 Pay Type (regular and overtime)
Col. 3 Pay Hours (number of hours worked as regular and overtime)
Col. 4 Gross Pay (amount of gross pay)[2]
Col. 5 FIT (federal income taxes withheld); FUTA (federal unemployment taxes)
Col. 6 SIT (state income taxes withheld); SUTA (state unemployment taxes)
Col. 7 FICA-SS_EE (social security taxes withheld, employee); FICA-SS_ER (social security taxes, employer)
Col. 8 FICA-Med_EE (medicare tax withheld, employee); FICA-Med_ER (medicare tax, employer)
Col. 9 Net pay (Gross pay less amounts withheld from employees)

[2] The Gross Pay column shows regular hours worked on the first line multiplied by the regular pay rate—this equals regular pay. Overtime hours multiplied by the overtime premium rate equals overtime premium pay reported on the second line. If employers are engaged in interstate commerce, federal law sets a minimum overtime rate of pay to employees. For this company, workers earn 150% of their regular rate for hours in excess of 40 per week.

EXHIBIT 11A.3
Payroll Register

Accounting System: Exhibit A.3

File Edit Maintain Tasks Analysis Options Reports Window Help

Phoenix Sales & Service
Payroll Register
For Week Ended Oct. 8, 2011

Employee ID Employee SS No. Refer., Date	Gross Pay Pay Type	 Pay Hours	 Gross Pay	FIT [blank] FUTA	SIT [blank] SUTA	FICA-SS_EE [blank] FICA-SS_ER	FICA-Med_EE [blank] FICA-Med_ER	Net Pay
AR101	Regular	40.00	400.00	−28.99	−2.32	−24.80	−5.80	338.09
Robert Austin	Overtime	0.00	0.00					
333-22-9999			400.00	−3.20	−10.80	−24.80	−5.80	
9001, 10/8/11								
CJ102	Regular	40.00	560.00	−52.97	−4.24	−36.02	−8.42	479.35
Judy Cross	Overtime	1.00	21.00					
299-11-9201			581.00	−4.65	−15.69	−36.02	−8.42	
9002, 10/8/11								
DJ103	Regular	40.00	560.00	−48.33	−3.87	−37.32	−8.73	503.75
John Diaz	Overtime	2.00	42.00					
444-11-9090			602.00	−4.82	−16.25	−37.32	−8.73	
9003, 10/8/11								
KK104	Regular	40.00	560.00	−68.57	−5.49	−34.72	−8.12	443.10
Kay Keife	Overtime	0.00	0.00					
909-11-3344			560.00	−4.48	−15.12	−34.72	−8.12	
9004, 10/8/11								
ML105	Regular	40.00	560.00	−34.24	−2.74	−34.72	−8.12	480.18
Lee Miller	Overtime	0.00	0.00					
444-56-3211			560.00	−4.48	−15.12	−34.72	−8.12	
9005, 10/8/11								
SD106	Regular	40.00	560.00	−68.57	−5.49	−34.72	−8.12	443.10
Dale Sears	Overtime	0.00	0.00					
909-33-1234			560.00	−4.48	−15.12	−34.72	−8.12	
9006, 10/8/11								
Totals	Regular	240.00	3,200.00	−301.67	−24.15	−202.30	−47.31	2,687.57
	Overtime	3.00	63.00					
			3,263.00	−26.11	−88.10	−202.30	−47.31	

Sales Purchases General Ledger Payroll Inventory Company Analysis

Net pay for each employee is computed as gross pay minus the items on the first line of columns 5–8. The employer's payroll tax for each employee is computed as the sum of items on the third line of columns 5–8. A payroll register includes all data necessary to record payroll. In some software programs the entries to record payroll are made in a special *payroll journal.*

Payroll Check Payment of payroll is usually done by check or electronic funds transfer. Exhibit 11A.4 shows a *payroll check* for a Phoenix employee. This check is accompanied with a detachable *statement of earnings* (at top) showing gross pay, deductions, and net pay.

Employee Earnings Report An **employee earnings report** is a cumulative record of an employee's hours worked, gross earnings, deductions, and net pay. Payroll information on this report is taken from the payroll register. The employee earnings report for R. Austin at Phoenix Sales & Service is shown in Exhibit 11A.5. An employee earnings report accumulates information that can show when an employee's earnings reach the tax-exempt points for FICA, FUTA, and SUTA taxes. It also gives data an employer needs to prepare Form W-2.

Payroll Procedures

Employers must be able to compute federal income tax for payroll purposes. This section explains how we compute this tax and how to use a payroll bank account.

Computing Federal Income Taxes To compute the amount of taxes withheld from each employee's wages, we need to determine both the employee's wages earned and the employee's number of *withholding*

EXHIBIT 11A.4

Check and Statement of Earnings

EMPLOYEE NO.	EMPLOYEE NAME	SOCIAL SECURITY NO.	PAY PERIOD END	CHECK DATE
AR101	Robert Austin	333-22-9999	10/8/11	10/8/11

ITEM	RATE	HOURS	TOTAL	ITEM	THIS CHECK	YEAR TO DATE
Regular	10.00	40.00	400.00	Gross	400.00	400.00
Overtime	15.00			Fed. Income tax	-28.99	-28.99
				FICA-Soc. Sec.	-24.80	-24.80
				FICA-Medicare	-5.80	-5.80
				State Income tax	-2.32	-2.32

HOURS WORKED	GROSS THIS PERIOD	GROSS YEAR TO DATE	NET CHECK	CHECK No.
40.00	400.00	400.00	$338.09	9001

(Detach and retain for your records)

PHOENIX SALES & SERVICE
1214 Mill Road
Phoenix, AZ 85621
602-555-8900

Phoenix Bank and Trust
Phoenix, AZ 85621
3312-87044

No. 9001

DATE October 8, 20 11

Check No. 9001

Amount Three Hundred Thirty-Eight and 9/100 Dollars $ **************$338.09*

Pay to the order of Robert Austin
18 Roosevelt Blvd., Apt C
Tempe, AZ 86322

Mary Wills
AUTHORIZED SIGNATURE

EXHIBIT 11A.5

Employee Earnings Report

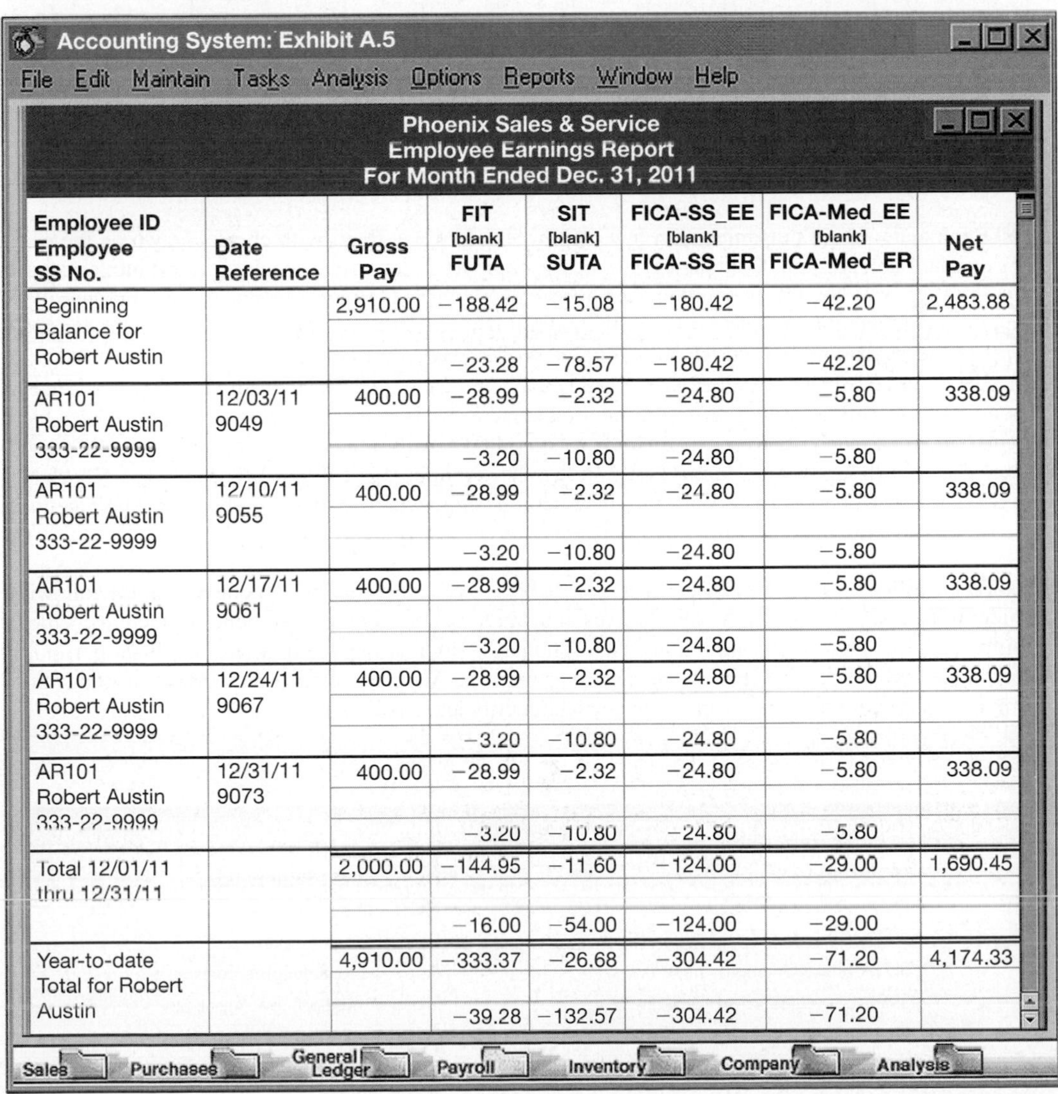

Accounting System: Exhibit A.5

File Edit Maintain Tasks Analysis Options Reports Window Help

Phoenix Sales & Service
Employee Earnings Report
For Month Ended Dec. 31, 2011

Employee ID Employee SS No.	Date Reference	Gross Pay	FIT [blank] FUTA	SIT [blank] SUTA	FICA-SS_EE [blank] FICA-SS_ER	FICA-Med_EE [blank] FICA-Med_ER	Net Pay
Beginning		2,910.00	−188.42	−15.08	−180.42	−42.20	2,483.88
Balance for							
Robert Austin			−23.28	−78.57	−180.42	−42.20	
AR101	12/03/11	400.00	−28.99	−2.32	−24.80	−5.80	338.09
Robert Austin	9049						
333-22-9999			−3.20	−10.80	−24.80	−5.80	
AR101	12/10/11	400.00	−28.99	−2.32	−24.80	−5.80	338.09
Robert Austin	9055						
333-22-9999			−3.20	−10.80	−24.80	−5.80	
AR101	12/17/11	400.00	−28.99	−2.32	−24.80	−5.80	338.09
Robert Austin	9061						
333-22-9999			−3.20	−10.80	−24.80	−5.80	
AR101	12/24/11	400.00	−28.99	−2.32	−24.80	−5.80	338.09
Robert Austin	9067						
333-22-9999			−3.20	−10.80	−24.80	−5.80	
AR101	12/31/11	400.00	−28.99	−2.32	−24.80	−5.80	338.09
Robert Austin	9073						
333-22-9999			−3.20	−10.80	−24.80	−5.80	
Total 12/01/11		2,000.00	−144.95	−11.60	−124.00	−29.00	1,690.45
thru 12/31/11							
			−16.00	−54.00	−124.00	−29.00	
Year-to-date		4,910.00	−333.37	−26.68	−304.42	−71.20	4,174.33
Total for Robert							
Austin			−39.28	−132.57	−304.42	−71.20	

Sales Purchases General Ledger Payroll Inventory Company Analysis *allowances.* Each employee records the number of withholding allowances claimed on a withholding allowance certificate, **Form W-4,** filed with the employer. When the number of withholding allowances increases, the amount of income taxes withheld decreases.

Employers often use a **wage bracket withholding table** similar to the one shown in Exhibit 11A.6 to compute the federal income taxes withheld from each employee's gross pay. The table in Exhibit 11A.6 is for a single employee paid weekly. Tables are also provided for married employees and for biweekly, semimonthly, and monthly pay periods (most payroll software includes these tables). When using a wage bracket withholding table to compute federal income tax withheld from an employee's gross wages, we need to locate an employee's wage bracket within the first two columns. We then find the amount withheld by looking in the withholding allowance column for that employee.

EXHIBIT 11A.6

Wage Bracket Withholding Table

SINGLE Persons—WEEKLY Payroll Period

If the wages are–		And the number of withholding allowances claimed is—										
At least	But less than	0	1	2	3	4	5	6	7	8	9	10
		The amount of income tax to be withheld is—										
$600	$610	$76	$67	$58	$49	$39	$30	$21	$12	$6	$0	$0
610	620	79	69	59	50	41	32	22	13	7	1	0
620	630	81	70	61	52	42	33	24	15	8	2	0
630	640	84	72	62	53	44	35	25	16	9	3	0
640	650	86	73	64	55	45	36	27	18	10	4	0
650	660	89	75	65	56	47	38	28	19	11	5	0
660	670	91	76	67	58	48	39	30	21	12	6	0
670	680	94	78	68	59	50	41	31	22	13	7	1
680	690	96	81	70	61	51	42	33	24	14	8	2
690	700	99	83	71	62	53	44	34	25	16	9	3
700	710	101	86	73	64	54	45	35	27	17	10	4
710	720	104	88	74	65	56	47	37	28	19	11	5
720	730	106	91	76	67	57	48	39	30	20	12	6
730	740	109	93	78	68	59	50	40	31	22	13	7
740	750	111	96	80	70	60	51	42	33	23	14	8

Payroll Bank Account Companies with few employees often pay them with checks drawn on the company's regular bank account. Companies with many employees often use a special **payroll bank account** to pay employees. When this account is used, a company either (1) draws one check for total payroll on the regular bank account and deposits it in the payroll bank account or (2) executes an *electronic funds transfer* to the payroll bank account. Individual payroll checks are then drawn on this payroll bank account. Since only one check for the total payroll is drawn on the regular bank account each payday, use of a special payroll bank account helps with internal control. It also helps in reconciling the regular bank account. When companies use a payroll bank account, they usually include check numbers in the payroll register. The payroll register in Exhibit 11A.3 shows check numbers in column 1. For instance, Check No. 9001 is issued to Robert Austin. With this information, the payroll register serves as a supplementary record of wages earned by and paid to employees.

Who Pays What Payroll Taxes and Benefits We conclude this appendix with the following table identifying who pays which payroll taxes and which common employee benefits such as medical, disability, pension, charitable, and union costs. Who pays which employee benefits, and what portion, is subject to agreements between companies and their workers. Also, self-employed workers must pay both the employer and employee FICA taxes for Social Security and Medicare.

Employer Payroll Taxes and Costs	Employee Payroll Deductions
• FICA—Social Security Taxes	• FICA—Social Security taxes
• FICA—Medicare Taxes	• FICA—Medicare taxes
• FUTA (Federal Unemployment Taxes)	• Federal Income taxes
• SUTA (State Unemployment Taxes)	• State and local income taxes
• Share of medical coverage, if any	• Share of medical coverage, if any
• Share of pension coverage, if any	• Share of pension coverage, if any
• Share of other benefits, if any	• Share of other benefits, if any

Quick Check Answers — p. 461 

11. What three items determine the amount deducted from an employee's wages for federal income taxes?
12. What amount of income tax is withheld from the salary of an employee who is single with three withholding allowances and earnings of $675 in a week? (*Hint:* Use the wage bracket withholding table in Exhibit 11A.6.)
13. Which of the following steps are executed when a company draws one check for total payroll and deposits it in a special payroll bank account? (*a*) Write a check to the payroll bank account for the total payroll and record it with a debit to Salaries Payable and a credit to Cash. (*b*) Deposit a check (or transfer funds) for the total payroll in the payroll bank account. (*c*) Issue individual payroll checks drawn on the payroll bank account. (*d*) All of the above.

APPENDIX

Corporate Income Taxes 11B

This appendix explains current liabilities involving income taxes for corporations.

Income Tax Liabilities Corporations are subject to income taxes and must estimate their income tax liability when preparing financial statements. Since income tax expense is created by earning income, a liability is incurred when income is earned. This tax must be paid quarterly under federal regulations. To illustrate, consider a corporation that prepares monthly financial statements. Based on its income in January 2011, this corporation estimates that it owes income taxes of $12,100. The following adjusting entry records this estimate:

Jan. 31	Income Taxes Expense	12,100	
	Income Taxes Payable		12,100
	To accrue January income taxes.		

Assets	=	Liabilities	+	Equity
		+12,100		−12,100

The tax liability is recorded each month until the first quarterly payment is made. If the company's estimated taxes for this first quarter total $30,000, the entry to record its payment is

Apr. 10	Income Taxes Payable	30,000	
	Cash		30,000
	Paid estimated quarterly income taxes based on first quarter income.		

Assets	=	Liabilities	+	Equity
−30,000		−30,000		

This process of accruing and then paying estimated income taxes continues through the year. When annual financial statements are prepared at year-end, the corporation knows its actual total income and the actual amount of income taxes it must pay. This information allows it to properly record income taxes expense for the fourth quarter so that the total of the four quarters' expense amounts equals the actual taxes paid to the government.

Deferred Income Tax Liabilities An income tax liability for corporations can arise when the amount of income before taxes that the corporation reports on its income statement is not the same as the amount of income reported on its income tax return. This difference occurs because income tax laws and GAAP measure income differently. (Differences between tax laws and GAAP arise because Congress uses tax laws to generate receipts, stimulate the economy, and influence behavior, whereas GAAP are intended to provide financial information useful for business decisions. Also, tax accounting often follows the cash basis, whereas GAAP follows the accrual basis.)

Some differences between tax laws and GAAP are temporary. *Temporary differences* arise when the tax return and the income statement report a revenue or expense in different years. As an example, companies are often able to deduct higher amounts of depreciation in the early years of an asset's life and smaller amounts in later years for tax reporting in comparison to GAAP. This means that in the early years, depreciation for tax reporting is often more than depreciation on the income statement. In later years, depreciation for tax reporting is often less than depreciation on the income statement. When temporary differences exist between taxable income on the tax return and the income before taxes on the income statement, corporations compute income taxes expense based on the income reported on the income statement. The result is that income taxes expense reported in the income statement is often different from the amount of income taxes payable to the government. This difference is the **deferred income tax liability.**

To illustrate, assume that in recording its usual quarterly income tax payments, a corporation computes $25,000 of income taxes expense. It also determines that only $21,000 is currently due and $4,000 is deferred to future years (a timing difference). The entry to record this end-of-period adjustment is

Assets	=	Liabilities	+	Equity
		+21,000		−25,000
		+4,000		

Dec. 31	Income Taxes Expense	25,000	
	Income Taxes Payable		21,000
	Deferred Income Tax Liability		4,000
	To record tax expense and deferred tax liability.		

The credit to Income Taxes Payable reflects the amount currently due to be paid. The credit to Deferred Income Tax Liability reflects tax payments deferred until future years when the temporary difference reverses.

Temporary differences also can cause a company to pay income taxes *before* they are reported on the income statement as expense. If so, the company reports a *Deferred Income Tax Asset* on its balance sheet.

Summary

C1 Describe current and long-term liabilities and their characteristics. Liabilities are probable future payments of assets or services that past transactions or events obligate an entity to make. Current liabilities are due within one year or the operating cycle, whichever is longer. All other liabilities are long term.

C2 Identify and describe known current liabilities. Known (determinable) current liabilities are set by agreements or laws and are measurable with little uncertainty. They include accounts payable, sales taxes payable, unearned revenues, notes payable, payroll liabilities, and the current portion of long-term debt.

C3 Explain how to account for contingent liabilities. If an uncertain future payment depends on a probable future event and the amount can be reasonably estimated, the payment is recorded as a liability. The uncertain future payment is reported as a contingent liability (in the notes) if (*a*) the future event is reasonably possible but not probable or (*b*) the event is probable but the payment amount cannot be reasonably estimated.

A1 Compute the times interest earned ratio and use it to analyze liabilities. Times interest earned is computed by dividing a company's net income before interest expense and income taxes by the amount of interest expense. The times interest earned ratio reflects a company's ability to pay interest obligations.

P1 Prepare entries to account for short-term notes payable. Short-term notes payable are current liabilities; most bear interest. When a short-term note's face value equals the amount borrowed, it identifies a rate of interest to be paid at maturity.

P2 Compute and record *employee* payroll deductions and liabilities. Employee payroll deductions include FICA taxes, income taxes, and voluntary deductions such as for pensions and charities. They make up the difference between gross and net pay.

P3 Compute and record *employer* payroll expenses and liabilities. An employer's payroll expenses include employees' gross earnings, any employee benefits, and the payroll taxes levied on the employer. Payroll liabilities include employees' net pay amounts, withholdings from employee wages, any employer-promised benefits, and the employer's payroll taxes.

P4 Account for estimated liabilities, including warranties and bonuses. Liabilities for health and pension benefits, warranties, and bonuses are recorded with estimated amounts. These items are recognized as expenses when incurred and matched with revenues generated.

P5A Identify and describe the details of payroll reports, records, and procedures. Employers report FICA taxes and federal income tax withholdings using Form 941. FUTA taxes are reported on Form 940. Earnings and deductions are reported to each employee and the federal government on Form W-2. An employer's payroll records often include a payroll register for each pay period, payroll checks and statements of earnings, and individual employee earnings reports.

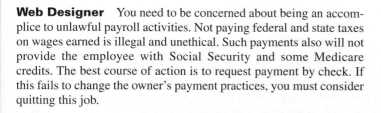

Guidance Answers to Decision Maker and Decision Ethics

Web Designer You need to be concerned about being an accomplice to unlawful payroll activities. Not paying federal and state taxes on wages earned is illegal and unethical. Such payments also will not provide the employee with Social Security and some Medicare credits. The best course of action is to request payment by check. If this fails to change the owner's payment practices, you must consider quitting this job.

Entrepreneur Risk is partly reflected by the times interest earned ratio. This ratio for the first franchise is 1.5 [($100,000 + $200,000)/$200,000], whereas the ratio for the second franchise is 3.5 [($100,000 + $40,000)/$40,000]. This analysis shows that the first franchise is more at risk of incurring a loss if its sales decline. The second question asks about variability of income. If income greatly varies, this increases the risk an owner will not earn sufficient income to cover interest. Since the first franchise has the greater variability, it is a riskier investment.

Guidance Answers to Quick Checks

1. A liability involves a probable future payment of assets or services that an entity is presently obligated to make as a result of past transactions or events.
2. No, an expected future payment is not a liability unless an existing obligation was created by a past event or transaction.
3. In most cases, a liability due in 15 months is classified as long term. It is classified as a current liability if the company's operating cycle is 15 months or longer.
4. A creditor prefers a note payable instead of a past-due account payable so as to (*a*) charge interest and/or (*b*) have evidence of the debt and its terms for potential litigation or disputes.
5. \$1,000* × (.008) + \$1,000* × (.04) + \$3,000 × (.062) + \$3,000 × (.0145) = \$277.50

* \$1,000 of the \$3,000 March pay is subject to FUTA and SUTA—the entire \$6,000 pay from January and February was subject to them.

6. (*a*) FICA taxes are incurred by both employee and employer. (*b*) FUTA taxes are incurred by the employer. (*c*) SUTA taxes are incurred by the employer. (*d*) Withheld income taxes are incurred by the employee.
7. (*a*)
8. (*a*) Warranty expense was previously estimated and recorded.
9. (*b*)
10. A future payment is reported in the notes as a contingent liability if (*a*) the uncertain future event is probable but the amount of payment cannot be reasonably estimated or (*b*) the uncertain future event is not probable but has a reasonable possibility of occurring.
11. An employee's marital status, gross earnings and number of withholding allowances determine the deduction for federal income taxes.
12. \$59
13. (*d*)

Key Terms

mhhe.com/wildFAP20e

Contingent liability (p. 448)
Current liabilities (p. 437)
Current portion of long-term debt (p. 445)
Deferred income tax liability (p. 460)
Employee benefits (p. 445)
Employee earnings report (p. 456)
Estimated liability (p. 445)
Federal depository bank (p. 453)
Federal Insurance Contributions Act (FICA) Taxes (p. 442)
Federal Unemployment Taxes (FUTA) (p. 444)
Form 940 (p. 453)
Form 941 (p. 453)
Form W-2 (p. 455)
Form W-4 (p. 458)
Gross pay (p. 442)
Known liabilities (p. 438)
Long-term liabilities (p. 437)
Merit rating (p. 444)
Net pay (p. 442)
Payroll bank account (p. 458)
Payroll deductions (p. 442)
Payroll register (p. 455)
Short-term note payable (p. 439)
State Unemployment Taxes (SUTA) (p. 444)
Times interest earned (p. 450)
Wage bracket withholding table (p. 458)
Warranty (p. 446)

Multiple Choice Quiz

Answers on p. 477

mhhe.com/wildFAP20e

Additional Quiz Questions are available at the book's Website.

1. On December 1, a company signed a \$6,000, 90-day, 5% note payable, with principal plus interest due on March 1 of the following year. What amount of interest expense should be accrued at December 31 on the note?
   - **a.** \$300
   - **b.** \$25
   - **c.** \$100
   - **d.** \$75
   - **e.** \$0
2. An employee earned \$50,000 during the year. FICA tax for social security is 6.2% and FICA tax for Medicare is 1.45%. The employer's share of FICA taxes is
   - **a.** Zero, since the employee's pay exceeds the FICA limit.
   - **b.** Zero, since FICA is not an employer tax.
   - **c.** \$3,100
   - **d.** \$725
   - **e.** \$3,825
3. Assume the FUTA tax rate is 0.8% and the SUTA tax rate is 5.4%. Both taxes are applied to the first \$7,000 of an employee's pay. What is the total unemployment tax an employer must pay on an employee's annual wages of \$40,000?
   - **a.** \$2,480
   - **b.** \$434
   - **c.** \$56
   - **d.** \$378
   - **e.** Zero; the employee's wages exceed the \$7,000 maximum.
4. A company sells big screen televisions for \$3,000 each. Each television has a two-year warranty that covers the replacement of defective parts. It is estimated that 1% of all televisions sold will be returned under warranty at an average cost of \$250 each. During July, the company sold 10,000 big screen televisions, and 80 were serviced under the warranty during July at a total cost of \$18,000. The credit balance in the Estimated

Warranty Liability account at July 1 was $26,000. What is the company's warranty expense for the month of July?

a. $51,000
b. $1,000
c. $25,000
d. $33,000
e. $18,000

5. Employees earn vacation pay at the rate of 1 day per month. During October, 150 employees qualify for one vacation day each. Their average daily wage is $175 per day. What is the amount of vacation benefit expense for October?

a. $26,250
b. $175
c. $2,100
d. $63,875
e. $150

A(B) *Superscript letter A (B) denotes assignments based on Appendix 11A (11B).*
Icon denotes assignments that involve decision making.

Discussion Questions

1. What are the three important questions concerning the uncertainty of liabilities?
2. What is the difference between a current and a long-term liability?
3. What is an estimated liability?
4. If $988 is the total of a sale that includes its sales tax of 4%, what is the selling price of the item only?
5. What is the combined amount (in percent) of the employee and employer Social Security tax rate?
6. What is the current Medicare tax rate? This rate is applied to what maximum level of salary and wages?
7. What determines the amount deducted from an employee's wages for federal income taxes?
8. Which payroll taxes are the employee's responsibility and which are the employer's responsibility?
9. What is an employer's unemployment merit rating? How are these ratings assigned to employers?
10. Why are warranty liabilities usually recognized on the balance sheet as liabilities even when they are uncertain?
11. Suppose that a company has a facility located where disastrous weather conditions often occur. Should it report a probable loss from a future disaster as a liability on its balance sheet? Explain.
12.[A] What is a wage bracket withholding table?
13.[A] What amount of income tax is withheld from the salary of an employee who is single with two withholding allowances and earning $725 per week? What if the employee earned $625 and has no withholding allowances? (Use Exhibit 11A.6.)
14. Refer to **Research In Motion**'s balance sheet in Appendix A. What revenue-related liability does Research In Motion report at February 27, 2010? *RIM*
15. Refer to **Apple**'s balance sheet in Appendix A. What is the amount of Apple's accounts payable as of September 26, 2009? Apple
16. Refer to **Nokia**'s balance sheet in Appendix A. List Nokia's current liabilities as of December 31, 2009. **NOKIA**
17. Refer to **Palm**'s balance sheet in Appendix A. What current liabilities related to income taxes are on its balance sheet? Explain the meaning of each income tax account identified. **Palm**

connect

QUICK STUDY

QS 11-1
Classifying liabilities C1 

Which of the following items are normally classified as a current liability for a company that has a 15-month operating cycle?

1. Salaries payable.
2. Note payable due in 19 months.
3. FICA taxes payable.
4. Note payable maturing in 3 years.
5. Note payable due in 10 months.
6. Portion of long-term note due in 15 months.

QS 11-2
Accounting for sales taxes
C2

Wrecker Computing sells merchandise for $5,000 cash on September 30 (cost of merchandise is $2,900). The sales tax law requires Wrecker to collect 4% sales tax on every dollar of merchandise sold. Record the entry for the $5,000 sale and its applicable sales tax. Also record the entry that shows the remittance of the 4% tax on this sale to the state government on October 15.

QS 11-3
Unearned revenue C2

Tickets, Inc., receives $5,500,000 cash in advance ticket sales for a four-date tour of Bruce Springsteen. Record the advance ticket sales on October 31. Record the revenue earned for the first concert date of November 8, assuming it represents one-fourth of the advance ticket sales.

QS 11-4
Accounting for contingent liabilities
C3

The following legal claims exist for Kalamazoo Co. Identify the accounting treatment for each claim as either (*a*) a liability that is recorded or (*b*) an item described in notes to its financial statements.

1. Kalamazoo (defendant) estimates that a pending lawsuit could result in damages of $1,000,000; it is reasonably possible that the plaintiff will win the case.
2. Kalamazoo faces a probable loss on a pending lawsuit; the amount is not reasonably estimable.
3. Kalamazoo estimates damages in a case at $2,500,000 with a high probability of losing the case.

QS 11-5
Interest-bearing note transactions P1

On November 7, 2011, Ortez Company borrows $150,000 cash by signing a 90-day, 8% note payable with a face value of $150,000. (1) Compute the accrued interest payable on December 31, 2011, (2) prepare the journal entry to record the accrued interest expense at December 31, 2011, and (3) prepare the journal entry to record payment of the note at maturity.

QS 11-6
Record employee payroll taxes
P2

On January 14, the end of the first bi-weekly pay period of the year, Rockin Company's payroll register showed that its employees earned $14,000 of sales salaries. Withholdings from the employees' salaries include FICA Social Security taxes at the rate of 6.2%, FICA Medicare taxes at the rate of 1.45%, $2,600 of federal income taxes, $309 of medical insurance deductions, and $120 of union dues. No employee earned more than $7,000 in this first period. Prepare the journal entry to record Rockin Company's January 14 (employee) payroll expenses and liabilities.

QS 11-7
Record employer payroll taxes
P3

Merger Co. has ten employees, each of whom earns $2,000 per month and has been employed since January 1. FICA Social Security taxes are 6.2% of the first $106,800 paid to each employee, and FICA Medicare taxes are 1.45% of gross pay. FUTA taxes are 0.8% and SUTA taxes are 5.4% of the first $7,000 paid to each employee. Prepare the March 31 journal entry to record the March payroll taxes expense.

QS 11-8
Recording warranty repairs
P4

On September 11, 2010, Home Store sells a mower for $400 with a one-year warranty that covers parts. Warranty expense is estimated at 5% of sales. On July 24, 2011, the mower is brought in for repairs covered under the warranty requiring $35 in materials taken from the Repair Parts Inventory. Prepare the July 24, 2011, entry to record the warranty repairs.

QS 11-9
Accounting for bonuses P4

Paris Company offers an annual bonus to employees if the company meets certain net income goals. Prepare the journal entry to record a $10,000 bonus owed to its workers (to be shared equally) at calendar year-end.

QS 11-10
Accounting for vacations
P4

Chester Co.'s salaried employees earn four weeks vacation per year. It pays $192,000.12 in total employee salaries for 52 weeks but its employees work only 48 weeks. This means Chester's total weekly expense is $4,000 ($192,000/48 weeks) instead of the $3,692.31 cash paid weekly to the employees ($192,000/52 weeks). Record Chester's weekly vacation benefits expense.

QS 11-11
Times interest earned A1 

Compute the times interest earned for Weltin Company, which reports income before interest expense and income taxes of $2,044,000, and interest expense of $350,000. Interpret its times interest earned (assume that its competitors average a times interest earned of 4.0).

QS 11-12[A]
Net pay and tax computations
P5

The payroll records of Clix Software show the following information about Trish Farqua, an employee, for the weekly pay period ending September 30, 2011. Farqua is single and claims one allowance. Compute her Social Security tax (6.2%), Medicare tax (1.45%), federal income tax withholding, state income tax (1.0%), and net pay for the current pay period. (Use the withholding table in Exhibit 11A.6 and round tax amounts to the nearest cent.)

Total (gross) earnings for current pay period	$ 735
Cumulative earnings of previous pay periods	9,700

Check Net pay, $578.42

QS 11-13[B]
Record deferred income tax liability P4

Cather Corporation has made and recorded its quarterly income tax payments. After a final review of taxes for the year, the company identifies an additional $30,000 of income tax expense that should be recorded. A portion of this additional expense, $8,000, is deferred for payment in future years. Record Cather's year-end adjusting entry for income tax expense.

QS 11-14
International accounting standards
C1 C2 

Answer each of the following related to international accounting standards.

a. In general, how similar or different are the definitions and characteristics of current liabilities between IFRS and U.S. GAAP?

b. Companies reporting under IFRS often reference a set of current liabilities with the title *financial liabilities.* Identify two current liabilities that would be classified under financial liabilities per IFRS. (*Hint:* **Nokia** provides examples in this chapter and in Appendix A.)

connect

EXERCISES

Exercise 11-1
Classifying liabilities
C1 

The following items appear on the balance sheet of a company with a two-month operating cycle. Identify the proper classification of each item as follows: *C* if it is a current liability, *L* if it is a long-term liability, or *N* if it is not a liability.

_____ **1.** Sales taxes payable.
_____ **2.** FUTA taxes payable.
_____ **3.** Accounts receivable.
_____ **4.** Wages payable.
_____ **5.** Salaries payable.
_____ **6.** Notes payable (due in 6 to 12 months).
_____ **7.** Notes payable (due in 120 days).
_____ **8.** Current portion of long-term debt.
_____ **9.** Notes payable (mature in five years).
_____ **10.** Notes payable (due in 13 to 24 months).

Exercise 11-2
Recording known current liabilities
C2

Prepare any necessary adjusting entries at December 31, 2011, for Yacht Company's year-end financial statements for each of the following separate transactions and events.

1. Yacht Company records an adjusting entry for $2,000,000 of previously unrecorded cash sales (costing $1,000,000) and its sales taxes at a rate of 5%.
2. The company earned $40,000 of $100,000 previously received in advance for services.

Exercise 11-3
Accounting for contingent liabilities
C3

Prepare any necessary adjusting entries at December 31, 2011, for Moor Company's year-end financial statements for each of the following separate transactions and events.

1. A disgruntled employee is suing Moor Company. Legal advisers believe that the company will probably need to pay damages, but the amount cannot be reasonably estimated.
2. Moor Company guarantees the $5,000 debt of a supplier. The supplier will probably not default on the debt.

Exercise 11-4
Accounting for note payable
P1

Check (2b) Interest expense, $1,880

Perfect Systems borrows $94,000 cash on May 15, 2011, by signing a 60-day, 12% note.

1. On what date does this note mature?
2. Suppose the face value of the note equals $94,000, the principal of the loan. Prepare the journal entries to record (*a*) issuance of the note and (*b*) payment of the note at maturity.

Exercise 11-5
Interest-bearing notes payable with year-end adjustments
P1

Check (2) $2,250
(3) $1,125

Kwon Co. borrows $150,000 cash on November 1, 2011, by signing a 90-day, 9% note with a face value of $150,000.

1. On what date does this note mature? (Assume that February of 2011 has 28 days.)
2. How much interest expense results from this note in 2011? (Assume a 360-day year.)
3. How much interest expense results from this note in 2012? (Assume a 360-day year.)
4. Prepare journal entries to record (*a*) issuance of the note, (*b*) accrual of interest at the end of 2011, and (*c*) payment of the note at maturity.

Exercise 11-6
Computing payroll taxes
P2 P3

Check (*a*) FUTA, $4.80; SUTA, $17.40

MRI Company has one employee. FICA Social Security taxes are 6.2% of the first $106,800 paid to its employee, and FICA Medicare taxes are 1.45% of gross pay. For MRI, its FUTA taxes are 0.8% and SUTA taxes are 2.9% of the first $7,000 paid to its employee. Compute MRI's amounts for each of these four taxes as applied to the employee's gross earnings for September under each of three separate situations (*a*), (*b*), and (*c*).

	Gross Pay through August	Gross Pay for September
a.	$ 6,400	$ 800
b.	18,200	2,100
c.	100,500	8,000

Exercise 11-7
Payroll-related journal entries P2

Using the data in situation *a* of Exercise 11-6, prepare the employer's September 30 journal entries to record salary expense and its related payroll liabilities for this employee. The employee's federal income taxes withheld by the employer are $135 for this pay period.

Exercise 11-8
Payroll-related journal entries P3

Using the data in situation *a* of Exercise 11-6, prepare the employer's September 30 journal entries to record the *employer's* payroll taxes expense and its related liabilities.

Exercise 11-9
Computing and recording bonuses P4

For the year ended December 31, 2011, Winter Company has implemented an employee bonus program equal to 3% of Winter's net income, which employees will share equally. Winter's net income (prebonus) is expected to be $1,000,000, and bonus expense is deducted in computing net income.

1. Compute the amount of the bonus payable to the employees at year-end (use the method described in the chapter and round to the nearest dollar).
2. Prepare the journal entry at December 31, 2011, to record the bonus due the employees.
3. Prepare the journal entry at January 19, 2012, to record payment of the bonus to employees.

Check (1) $29,126

Exercise 11-10
Accounting for estimated liabilities
P4

Prepare any necessary adjusting entries at December 31, 2011, for Jester Company's year-end financial statements for each of the following separate transactions and events.

1. During December, Jester Company sold 3,000 units of a product that carries a 60-day warranty. December sales for this product total $120,000. The company expects 8% of the units to need warranty repairs, and it estimates the average repair cost per unit will be $15.
2. Employees earn vacation pay at a rate of one day per month. During December, 20 employees qualify for one vacation day each. Their average daily wage is $120 per employee.

Exercise 11-11
Warranty expense and liability computations and entries
P4

Chang Co. sold a copier costing $3,800 with a two-year parts warranty to a customer on August 16, 2011, for $5,500 cash. Chang uses the perpetual inventory system. On November 22, 2012, the copier requires on-site repairs that are completed the same day. The repairs cost $199 for materials taken from the Repair Parts Inventory. These are the only repairs required in 2012 for this copier. Based on experience, Chang expects to incur warranty costs equal to 4% of dollar sales. It records warranty expense with an adjusting entry at the end of each year.

1. How much warranty expense does the company report in 2011 for this copier?
2. How much is the estimated warranty liability for this copier as of December 31, 2011?
3. How much warranty expense does the company report in 2012 for this copier?
4. How much is the estimated warranty liability for this copier as of December 31, 2012?
5. Prepare journal entries to record (*a*) the copier's sale; (*b*) the adjustment on December 31, 2011, to recognize the warranty expense; and (*c*) the repairs that occur in November 2012.

Check (1) $220

(4) $21

Exercise 11-12
Computing and interpreting times interest earned
A1 

Use the following information from separate companies *a* through *f* to compute times interest earned. Which company indicates the strongest ability to pay interest expense as it comes due?

	Net Income (Loss)	Interest Expense	Income Taxes
a.	$140,000	$48,000	$ 35,000
b.	140,000	15,000	50,000
c.	140,000	8,000	70,000
d.	265,000	12,000	130,000
e.	79,000	12,000	30,000
f.	(4,000)	12,000	0

Check (b) 13.67

Exercise 11-13[A]
Gross and net pay computation
P5

Tony Newbern, an unmarried employee, works 48 hours in the week ended January 12. His pay rate is $12 per hour, and his wages are subject to no deductions other than FICA—Social Security, FICA— Medicare, and federal income taxes. He claims two withholding allowances. Compute his regular pay, overtime pay (for this company, workers earn 150% of their regular rate for hours in excess of 40 per week), and gross pay. Then compute his FICA tax deduction (use 6.2% for the Social Security portion and 1.45% for the Medicare portion), income tax deduction (use the wage bracket withholding table of Exhibit 11A.6), total deductions, and net pay. (Round tax amounts to the nearest cent.)

Check Net pay, $515.26

Exercise 11-14[B]
Accounting for income taxes
P4

Ming Corporation prepares financial statements for each month-end. As part of its accounting process, estimated income taxes are accrued each month for 30% of the current month's net income. The income taxes are paid in the first month of each quarter for the amount accrued for the prior quarter. The following information is available for the fourth quarter of year 2011. When tax computations are completed on January 20, 2012, Ming determines that the quarter's Income Taxes Payable account balance should be $29,100 on December 31, 2011 (its unadjusted balance is $23,640).

October 2011 net income	$27,900
November 2011 net income	18,200
December 2011 net income	32,700

Check (1) $5,460

1. Determine the amount of the accounting adjustment (dated as of December 31, 2011) to produce the proper ending balance in the Income Taxes Payable account.
2. Prepare journal entries to record (*a*) the December 31, 2011, adjustment to the Income Taxes Payable account and (*b*) the January 20, 2012, payment of the fourth-quarter taxes.

Exercise 11-15
Accounting for current liabilities under IFRS
P4 

Volvo Group reports the following information for its product warranty costs as of December 31, 2008, along with provisions and utilizations of warranty liabilities for the year ended December 31, 2008 (SEK in millions).

Product warranty costs

Estimated costs for product warranties are charged to cost of sales when the products are sold. Estimated warranty costs include contractual warranty and goodwill warranty. Warranty provisions are estimated with consideration of historical claims statistics, the warranty period, the average time-lag between faults occurring and claims to the company, and anticipated changes in quality indexes. Differences between actual warranty claims and the estimated claims generally affect the recognized expense and provisions in future periods. At December 31, 2008, warranty cost provisions amounted to 10,354.

Product warranty liabilities, December 31, 2007	SEK 9,373
Additional provisions to product warranty liabilities	6,201
Utilizations and reductions of product warranty liabilities	(5,220)
Product warranty liabilities, December 31, 2008	10,354

1. Prepare Volvo's journal entry to record its estimated warranty liabilities (provisions) for 2008.
2. Prepare Volvo's journal entry to record its costs (utilizations) related to its warranty program for 2008. Assume those costs involve replacements taken out of Inventory, with no cash involved.
3. How much warranty expense does Volvo report for 2008?

Exercise 11-16
Recording payroll
P2 P3

The following monthly data are taken from Nunez Company at July 31: Sales salaries, $120,000; Office salaries, $60,000; Federal income taxes withheld, $45,000; State income taxes withheld, $10,000; Social security taxes withheld, $11,160; Medicare taxes withheld, $2,610; Medical insurance premiums, $7,000; Life insurance premiums, $4,000; Union dues deducted, $1,000; and Salaries subject to unemployment taxes, $50,000. The employee pays forty percent of medical and life insurance premiums.

Prepare journal entries to record: (1) accrued payroll, including employee deductions, for July; (2) cash payment of the net payroll (salaries payable) for July; (3) accrued employer payroll taxes, and other related employment expenses, for July—assume that FICA taxes are identical to those on employees and that SUTA taxes are 5.4% and FUTA taxes are 0.8%; and (4) cash payment of all liabilities related to the July payroll.

Exercise 11-17
Computing payroll taxes
P2 P3

Madison Company has nine employees. FICA Social Security taxes are 6.2% of the first $106,800 paid to each employee, and FICA Medicare taxes are 1.45% of gross pay. FUTA taxes are 0.8% and SUTA taxes are 5.4% of the first $7,000 paid to each employee. Cumulative pay for the current year for each of its employees follows.

Employee	Cumulative Pay	Employee	Cumulative Pay	Employee	Cumulative Pay
Steve S.	$ 6,000	Christina S.	$156,800	Dana W.	$116,800
Tim V.	60,000	Michelle H.	106,800	Stewart M.	36,800
Brent G.	87,000	Kathleen K.	110,000	Sankha B.	4,000

a. Prepare a table with the following column headings: Employee; Cumulative Pay; Pay Subject to FICA Social Security Taxes; Pay Subject to FICA Medicare Taxes; Pay Subject to FUTA Taxes; Pay Subject to SUTA Taxes. Compute the amounts in this table for each employee and total the columns.
b. For the company, compute each total for: FICA Social Security taxes, FICA Medicare taxes, FUTA taxes, and SUTA taxes. (*Hint:* Remember to include in those totals any employee share of taxes that the company must collect.)

Exercise 11-18
Preparing payroll register and related entries P5

SP Company has five employees. Employees paid by the hour receive a $10 per hour pay rate for the regular 40-hour work week plus one and one-half times the hourly rate for each overtime hour beyond the 40-hours per week. Hourly employees are paid every two weeks, but salaried employees are paid monthly on the last biweekly payday of each month. FICA Social Security taxes are 6.2% of the first $106,800 paid to each employee, and FICA Medicare taxes are 1.45% of gross pay. FUTA taxes are 0.8% and SUTA taxes are 5.4% of the first $7,000 paid to each employee. The company has a benefits plan that includes medical insurance, life insurance, and retirement funding for employees. Under this plan, employees must contribute 5 percent of their gross income as a payroll withholding, which the company matches with double the amount. Following is the partially completed payroll register for the biweekly period ending August 31, which is the last payday of August.

Employee	Cumulative Pay (Excludes Current Period)	Current Period Gross Pay			FIT	FUTA	FICA-SS_EE	FICA-Med_EE	EE-Ben Plan Withholding	Employee Net Pay
		Pay Type	Pay Hours	Gross Pay	SIT	SUTA	FICA-SS_ER	FICA-Med_ER	ER-Ben Plan Withholding	
Kathleen	$105,000.00	Salary	---	$7,000.00	$2,000.00					
					300.00					
Nicholas	6,800.00	Salary	---	500.00	80.00					
					20.00					
Anthony	15,000.00	Regular	80		110.00					
		Overtime	8		25.00					
Zoey	6,500.00	Regular	80		100.00					
		Overtime	4		22.00					
Gracie	5,000.00	Regular	74	740.00	90.00					
		Overtime	0	0.00	21.00					
Totals	138,300.00				2,380.00					
					388.00					

* Table abbreviations follow those in Exhibit 11A.3 (see pages 455–456); and, "Ben_Plan" refers to employee (EE) or employer (ER) withholding for the benefits plan.

a. Complete this payroll register by filling in all cells for the pay period ended August 31. *Hint:* See Exhibit 11A.3 for guidance. (Round amounts to cents.)

b. Prepare the August 31 journal entry to record the accrued biweekly payroll and related liabilities for deductions.

c. Prepare the August 31 journal entry to record the employer's cash payment of the net payroll of part *b*.

d. Prepare the August 31 journal entry to record the employer's payroll taxes including the contribution to the benefits plan.

e. Prepare the August 31 journal entry to pay all liabilities (expect net payroll in part *c*) for this biweekly period.

connect

PROBLEM SET A

Problem 11-1A
Short-term notes payable transactions and entries
P1

mhhe.com/wildFAP20e

Tytus Co. entered into the following transactions involving short-term liabilities in 2010 and 2011.

2010

Apr. 20 Purchased $38,500 of merchandise on credit from Frier, terms are 1/10, n/30. Tytus uses the perpetual inventory system.

May 19 Replaced the April 20 account payable to Frier with a 90-day, $30,000 note bearing 9% annual interest along with paying $8,500 in cash.

July 8 Borrowed $60,000 cash from Community Bank by signing a 120-day, 10% interest-bearing note with a face value of $60,000.

__?__ Paid the amount due on the note to Frier at the maturity date.

__?__ Paid the amount due on the note to Community Bank at the maturity date.

Nov. 28 Borrowed $21,000 cash from UMB Bank by signing a 60-day, 8% interest-bearing note with a face value of $21,000.

Dec. 31 Recorded an adjusting entry for accrued interest on the note to UMB Bank.

2011

__?__ Paid the amount due on the note to UMB Bank at the maturity date.

Required

1. Determine the maturity date for each of the three notes described.

2. Determine the interest due at maturity for each of the three notes. (Assume a 360-day year.)

3. Determine the interest expense to be recorded in the adjusting entry at the end of 2010.

4. Determine the interest expense to be recorded in 2011.

5. Prepare journal entries for all the preceding transactions and events for years 2010 and 2011.

Check (2) Frier, $675
(3) $154
(4) $126

Problem 11-2A
Warranty expense and liability estimation
P4

On October 29, 2010, Lue Co. began operations by purchasing razors for resale. Lue uses the perpetual inventory method. The razors have a 90-day warranty that requires the company to replace any nonworking razor. When a razor is returned, the company discards it and mails a new one from Merchandise Inventory to the customer. The company's cost per new razor is $18 and its retail selling price is $80 in both 2010 and 2011. The manufacturer has advised the company to expect warranty costs to equal 7% of dollar sales. The following transactions and events occurred.

2010

Nov.	11	Sold 75 razors for $6,000 cash.
	30	Recognized warranty expense related to November sales with an adjusting entry.
Dec.	9	Replaced 15 razors that were returned under the warranty.
	16	Sold 210 razors for $16,800 cash.
	29	Replaced 30 razors that were returned under the warranty.
	31	Recognized warranty expense related to December sales with an adjusting entry.

2011

Jan.	5	Sold 130 razors for $10,400 cash.
	17	Replaced 50 razors that were returned under the warranty.
	31	Recognized warranty expense related to January sales with an adjusting entry.

Required

1. Prepare journal entries to record these transactions and adjustments for 2010 and 2011.
2. How much warranty expense is reported for November 2010 and for December 2010?
3. How much warranty expense is reported for January 2011?
4. What is the balance of the Estimated Warranty Liability account as of December 31, 2010?
5. What is the balance of the Estimated Warranty Liability account as of January 31, 2011?

Check (3) $728
(4) $786 Cr.
(5) $614 Cr.

Problem 11-3A
Computing and analyzing times interest earned
A1 

Shown here are condensed income statements for two different companies (both are organized as LLCs and pay no income taxes).

Ace Company	
Sales	$500,000
Variable expenses (80%)	400,000
Income before interest	100,000
Interest expense (fixed)	30,000
Net income	$ 70,000

Deuce Company	
Sales	$500,000
Variable expenses (60%)	300,000
Income before interest	200,000
Interest expense (fixed)	130,000
Net income	$ 70,000

Required

1. Compute times interest earned for Ace Company.
2. Compute times interest earned for Deuce Company.
3. What happens to each company's net income if sales increase by 30%?
4. What happens to each company's net income if sales increase by 50%?
5. What happens to each company's net income if sales increase by 80%?
6. What happens to each company's net income if sales decrease by 10%?
7. What happens to each company's net income if sales decrease by 20%?
8. What happens to each company's net income if sales decrease by 40%?

Check (3) Ace net income, $100,000 (43% increase)

(6) Deuce net income, $50,000 (29% decrease)

Analysis Component

9. Comment on the results from parts 3 through 8 in relation to the fixed-cost strategies of the two companies and the ratio values you computed in parts 1 and 2.

Problem 11-4A
Payroll expenses, withholdings, and taxes
P2 P3

Legal Stars has four employees. FICA Social Security taxes are 6.2% of the first $106,800 paid to each employee, and FICA Medicare taxes are 1.45% of gross pay. Also, its FUTA taxes are 0.8% and SUTA taxes are 2.15% of the first $7,000 paid to each employee. The company is preparing its payroll calculations for the week ended August 25. Payroll records show the following information for the company's four employees.

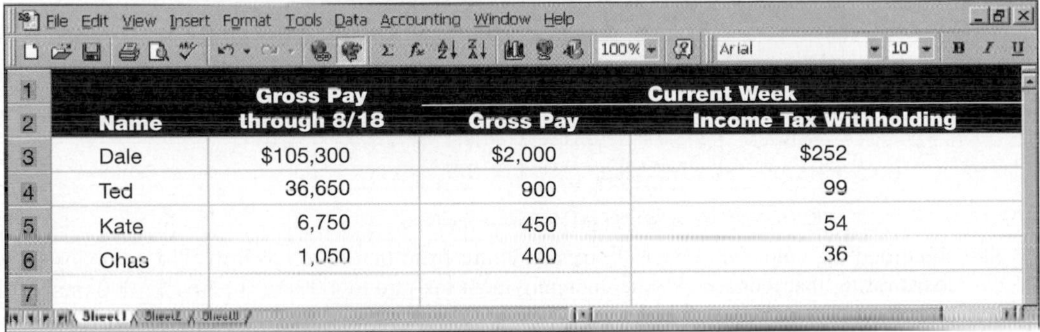

	Name	Gross Pay through 8/18	Current Week Gross Pay	Current Week Income Tax Withholding
3	Dale	$105,300	$2,000	$252
4	Ted	36,650	900	99
5	Kate	6,750	450	54
6	Chas	1,050	400	36

mhhe.com/wildFAP20e

In addition to gross pay, the company must pay one-half of the $32 per employee weekly health insurance; each employee pays the remaining one-half. The company also contributes an extra 8% of each employee's gross pay (at no cost to employees) to a pension fund.

Required

Compute the following for the week ended August 25 (round amounts to the nearest cent):

1. Each employee's FICA withholdings for Social Security.
2. Each employee's FICA withholdings for Medicare.
3. Employer's FICA taxes for Social Security.
4. Employer's FICA taxes for Medicare.
5. Employer's FUTA taxes.
6. Employer's SUTA taxes.
7. Each employee's net (take-home) pay.
8. Employer's total payroll-related expense for each employee.

Check (3) $201.50
(4) $54.38
(5) $5.20
(7) Total net pay, $2,989.12

Problem 11-5A
Entries for payroll transactions
P2 P3

On January 8, the end of the first weekly pay period of the year, Royal Company's payroll register showed that its employees earned $11,380 of office salaries and $32,920 of sales salaries. Withholdings from the employees' salaries include FICA Social Security taxes at the rate of 6.2%, FICA Medicare taxes at the rate of 1.45%, $6,340 of federal income taxes, $670 of medical insurance deductions, and $420 of union dues. No employee earned more than $7,000 in this first period.

Required

1. Calculate FICA Social Security taxes payable and FICA Medicare taxes payable. Prepare the journal entry to record Royal Company's January 8 (employee) payroll expenses and liabilities.
2. Prepare the journal entry to record Royal's (employer) payroll taxes resulting from the January 8 payroll. Royal's merit rating reduces its state unemployment tax rate to 4% of the first $7,000 paid each employee. The federal unemployment tax rate is 0.8%.

Check (1) Cr. Salaries Payable, $33,481.05
(2) Dr. Payroll Taxes Expense, $5,515.35

Problem 11-6A[A]
Entries for payroll transactions
P2 P3 P5

Polo Company has 10 employees, each of whom earns $2,600 per month and is paid on the last day of each month. All 10 have been employed continuously at this amount since January 1. Polo uses a payroll bank account and special payroll checks to pay its employees. On March 1, the following accounts and balances exist in its general ledger:

a. FICA—Social Security Taxes Payable, $3,224; FICA—Medicare Taxes Payable, $754. (The balances of these accounts represent total liabilities for *both* the employer's and employees' FICA taxes for the February payroll only.)
b. Employees' Federal Income Taxes Payable, $3,900 (liability for February only).
c. Federal Unemployment Taxes Payable, $416 (liability for January and February together).
d. State Unemployment Taxes Payable, $2,080 (liability for January and February together).

During March and April, the company had the following payroll transactions.

Mar. 15 Issued check payable to Fleet Bank, a federal depository bank authorized to accept employers' payments of FICA taxes and employee income tax withholdings. The $7,878 check is in payment of the February FICA and employee income taxes.

31 Recorded the March payroll and transferred funds from the regular bank account to the payroll bank account. Issued checks payable to each employee in payment of the March payroll. The payroll register shows the following summary totals for the March pay period.

Check March 31: Cr. Salaries Payable, $20,111

Salaries and Wages				Federal	
Office Salaries	Shop Wages	Gross Pay	FICA Taxes*	Income Taxes	Net Pay
$10,400	$15,600	$26,000	$1,612 $ 377	$3,900	$20,111

* FICA taxes are Social Security and Medicare, respectively.

March 31: Dr. Payroll Taxes Expenses, $2,853

April 15: Cr. Cash, $7,878 (Fleet Bank)

31 Recorded the employer's payroll taxes resulting from the March payroll. The company has a merit rating that reduces its state unemployment tax rate to 4.0% of the first $7,000 paid each employee. The federal rate is 0.8%.

Apr. 15 Issued check to Fleet Bank in payment of the March FICA and employee income taxes.

15 Issued check to the State Tax Commission for the January, February, and March state unemployment taxes. Mailed the check and the first quarter tax return to the Commission.

30 Issued check payable to Fleet Bank in payment of the employer's FUTA taxes for the first quarter of the year.

30 Mailed Form 941 to the IRS, reporting the FICA taxes and the employees' federal income tax withholdings for the first quarter.

Required

Prepare journal entries to record the transactions and events for both March and April.

PROBLEM SET B

Problem 11-1B
Short-term notes payable transactions and entries
P1

Bargen Co. entered into the following transactions involving short-term liabilities in 2010 and 2011.

2010

Apr. 22 Purchased $4,000 of merchandise on credit from Quinn Products, terms are 1/10, n/30. Bargen uses the perpetual inventory system.

May 23 Replaced the April 22 account payable to Quinn Products with a 60-day, $3,600 note bearing 15% annual interest along with paying $400 in cash.

July 15 Borrowed $9,000 cash from Blackhawk Bank by signing a 120-day, 10% interest-bearing note with a face value of $9,000.

__?__ Paid the amount due on the note to Quinn Products at maturity.

__?__ Paid the amount due on the note to Blackhawk Bank at maturity.

Dec. 6 Borrowed $16,000 cash from City Bank by signing a 45-day, 9% interest-bearing note with a face value of $16,000.

31 Recorded an adjusting entry for accrued interest on the note to City Bank.

2011

__?__ Paid the amount due on the note to City Bank at maturity.

Required

1. Determine the maturity date for each of the three notes described.
2. Determine the interest due at maturity for each of the three notes. (Assume a 360-day year.)
3. Determine the interest expense to be recorded in the adjusting entry at the end of 2010.
4. Determine the interest expense to be recorded in 2011.
5. Prepare journal entries for all the preceding transactions and events for years 2010 and 2011.

Check (2) Quinn, $90
(3) $100
(4) $80

Problem 11-2B
Warranty expense and liability estimation
P4

On November 10, 2011, Byung Co. began operations by purchasing coffee grinders for resale. Byung uses the perpetual inventory method. The grinders have a 60-day warranty that requires the company to replace any nonworking grinder. When a grinder is returned, the company discards it and mails a new one from Merchandise Inventory to the customer. The company's cost per new grinder is $14 and its retail selling price is $35 in both 2011 and 2012. The manufacturer has advised the company to expect warranty costs to equal 10% of dollar sales. The following transactions and events occurred.

2011

Nov. 16 Sold 50 grinders for $1,750 cash.

30 Recognized warranty expense related to November sales with an adjusting entry.

Dec. 12 Replaced six grinders that were returned under the warranty.

18 Sold 150 grinders for $5,250 cash.

28 Replaced 17 grinders that were returned under the warranty.

31 Recognized warranty expense related to December sales with an adjusting entry.

2012

Jan. 7 Sold 60 grinders for $2,100 cash.
21 Replaced 38 grinders that were returned under the warranty.
31 Recognized warranty expense related to January sales with an adjusting entry.

Required

1. Prepare journal entries to record these transactions and adjustments for 2011 and 2012.
2. How much warranty expense is reported for November 2011 and for December 2011?
3. How much warranty expense is reported for January 2012?
4. What is the balance of the Estimated Warranty Liability account as of December 31, 2011?
5. What is the balance of the Estimated Warranty Liability account as of January 31, 2012?

Check (3) $210
(4) $378 Cr.
(5) $56 Cr.

Problem 11-3B
Computing and analyzing times interest earned
A1 

Shown here are condensed income statements for two different companies (both are organized as LLCs and pay no income taxes).

Virgo Company	
Sales	$120,000
Variable expenses (50%)	60,000
Income before interest	60,000
Interest expense (fixed)	45,000
Net income	$ 15,000

Zodiac Company	
Sales	$120,000
Variable expenses (75%)	90,000
Income before interest	30,000
Interest expense (fixed)	15,000
Net income	$ 15,000

Required

1. Compute times interest earned for Virgo Company.
2. Compute times interest earned for Zodiac Company.
3. What happens to each company's net income if sales increase by 10%?
4. What happens to each company's net income if sales increase by 40%?
5. What happens to each company's net income if sales increase by 90%?
6. What happens to each company's net income if sales decrease by 20%?
7. What happens to each company's net income if sales decrease by 50%?
8. What happens to each company's net income if sales decrease by 80%?

Check (4) Virgo net income, $39,000 (160% increase)

(6) Zodiac net income, $9,000 (40% decrease)

Analysis Component

9. Comment on the results from parts 3 through 8 in relation to the fixed cost strategies of the two companies and the ratio values you computed in parts 1 and 2.

Problem 11-4B
Payroll expenses, withholdings, and taxes
P2 P3

Sea Biz Co. has four employees. FICA Social Security taxes are 6.2% of the first $106,800 paid to each employee, and FICA Medicare taxes are 1.45% of gross pay. Also, its FUTA taxes are 0.8% and SUTA taxes are 1.75% of the first $7,000 paid to each employee. The company is preparing its payroll calculations for the week ended September 30. Payroll records show the following information for the company's four employees.

Name	Gross Pay through 9/23	Current Week Gross Pay	Current Week Income Tax Withholding
Alli	$104,300	$2,500	$198
Eve	36,650	1,515	182
Hong	6,650	475	52
Juan	22,200	600	48

In addition to gross pay, the company must pay one-half of the $44 per employee weekly health insurance; each employee pays the remaining one-half. The company also contributes an extra 5% of each employee's gross pay (at no cost to employees) to a pension fund.

Required

Compute the following for the week ended September 30 (round amounts to the nearest cent):

Check (3) $315.58
(4) $73.81
(5) $2.80
(7) Total net pay, $4,132.61

1. Each employee's FICA withholdings for Social Security.
2. Each employee's FICA withholdings for Medicare.
3. Employer's FICA taxes for Social Security.
4. Employer's FICA taxes for Medicare.
5. Employer's FUTA taxes.
6. Employer's SUTA taxes.
7. Each employee's net (take-home) pay.
8. Employer's total payroll-related expense for each employee.

Problem 11-5B
Entries for payroll transactions
P2 P3

Palmer Company's first weekly pay period of the year ends on January 8. On that date, the column totals in Palmer's payroll register indicate its sales employees earned $69,490, its office employees earned $42,450, and its delivery employees earned $2,060. The employees are to have withheld from their wages FICA Social Security taxes at the rate of 6.2%, FICA Medicare taxes at the rate of 1.45%, $17,250 of federal income taxes, $2,320 of medical insurance deductions, and $275 of union dues. No employee earned more than $7,000 in the first pay period.

Required

Check (1) Cr. Salaries Payable, $85,434

(2) Dr. Payroll Taxes Expense, $13,509

1. Calculate FICA Social Security taxes payable and FICA Medicare taxes payable. Prepare the journal entry to record Palmer Company's January 8 (employee) payroll expenses and liabilities.
2. Prepare the journal entry to record Palmer's (employer) payroll taxes resulting from the January 8 payroll. Palmer's merit rating reduces its state unemployment tax rate to 3.4% of the first $7,000 paid each employee. The federal unemployment tax rate is 0.8%.

Problem 11-6B[A]
Entries for payroll transactions
P2 P3 P5

JLK Company has five employees, each of whom earns $1,200 per month and is paid on the last day of each month. All five have been employed continuously at this amount since January 1. JLK uses a payroll bank account and special payroll checks to pay its employees. On June 1, the following accounts and balances exist in its general ledger:

a. FICA—Social Security Taxes Payable, $744; FICA—Medicare Taxes Payable, $174. (The balances of these accounts represent total liabilities for *both* the employer's and employees' FICA taxes for the May payroll only.)
b. Employees' Federal Income Taxes Payable, $900 (liability for May only).
c. Federal Unemployment Taxes Payable, $96 (liability for April and May together).
d. State Unemployment Taxes Payable, $480 (liability for April and May together).

During June and July, the company had the following payroll transactions.

June 15 Issued check payable to Security Bank, a federal depository bank authorized to accept employers' payments of FICA taxes and employee income tax withholdings. The $1,818 check is in payment of the May FICA and employee income taxes.

Check June 30: Cr. Salaries Payable, $4,641

30 Recorded the June payroll and transferred funds from the regular bank account to the payroll bank account. Issued checks payable to each employee in payment of the June payroll. The payroll register shows the following summary totals for the June pay period.

Salaries and Wages					
Office Salaries	Shop Wages	Gross Pay	FICA Taxes*	Federal Income Taxes	Net Pay
$2,000	$4,000	$6,000	$372 $ 87	$900	$4,641

* FICA taxes are Social Security and Medicare, respectively.

Check June 30: Dr. Payroll Taxes Expenses, $699

July 15: Cr. Cash $1,818 (Security Bank)

30 Recorded the employer's payroll taxes resulting from the June payroll. The company has a merit rating that reduces its state unemployment tax rate to 4.0% of the first $7,000 paid each employee. The federal rate is 0.8%.

July 15 Issued check payable to Security Bank in payment of the June FICA and employee income taxes.

15 Issued check to the State Tax Commission for the April, May and June state unemployment taxes. Mailed the check and the second quarter tax return to the State Tax Commission.

31 Issued check payable to Security Bank in payment of the employer's FUTA taxes for the first quarter of the year.

31 Mailed Form 941 to the IRS, reporting the FICA taxes and the employees' federal income tax withholdings for the second quarter.

Required

Prepare journal entries to record the transactions and events for both June and July.

SERIAL PROBLEM

Business Solutions

P2 P3 C2

(This serial problem began in Chapter 1 and continues through most of the book. If previous chapter segments were not completed, the serial problem can begin at this point. It is helpful, but not necessary, to use the Working Papers that accompany the book.)

SP 11 Review the February 26 and March 25 transactions for Business Solutions (SP 5) from Chapter 5.

Required

1. Assume that Lyn Addie is an unmarried employee. Her $1,000 of wages are subject to no deductions other than FICA Social Security taxes, FICA Medicare taxes, and federal income taxes. Her federal income taxes for this pay period total $159. Compute her net pay for the eight days' work paid on February 26. (Round amounts to the nearest cent.)
2. Record the journal entry to reflect the payroll payment to Lyn Addie as computed in part 1.
3. Record the journal entry to reflect the (employer) payroll tax expenses for the February 26 payroll payment. Assume Lyn Addie has not met earnings limits for FUTA and SUTA—the FUTA rate is 0.8% and the SUTA rate is 4% for Business Solutions. (Round amounts to the nearest cent.)
4. Record the entry(ies) for the merchandise sold on March 25 if a 4% sales tax rate applies.

COMPREHENSIVE PROBLEM

Bug-Off Exterminators

(Review of Chapters 1–11)

CP 11 Bug-Off Exterminators provides pest control services and sells extermination products manufactured by other companies. The following six-column table contains the company's unadjusted trial balance as of December 31, 2011.

BUG-OFF EXTERMINATORS
December 31, 2011

	Unadjusted Trial Balance		Adjustments		Adjusted Trial Balance	
Cash	$ 17,000					
Accounts receivable	4,000					
Allowance for doubtful accounts		$ 828				
Merchandise inventory	11,700					
Trucks	32,000					
Accum. depreciation—Trucks		0				
Equipment	45,000					
Accum. depreciation—Equipment		12,200				
Accounts payable		5,000				
Estimated warranty liability		1,400				
Unearned services revenue		0				
Interest payable		0				
Long-term notes payable		15,000				
D. Buggs, Capital		59,700				
D. Buggs, Withdrawals	10,000					
Extermination services revenue		60,000				
Interest revenue		872				
Sales (of merchandise)		71,026				
Cost of goods sold	46,300					
Depreciation expense—Trucks	0					
Depreciation expense—Equipment	0					
Wages expense	35,000					
Interest expense	0					
Rent expense	9,000					
Bad debts expense	0					
Miscellaneous expense	1,226					
Repairs expense	8,000					
Utilities expense	6,800					
Warranty expense	0					
Totals	$226,026	$226,026				

The following information in *a* through *h* applies to the company at the end of the current year.

a. The bank reconciliation as of December 31, 2011, includes the following facts.

Cash balance per bank	$15,100
Cash balance per books	17,000
Outstanding checks	1,800
Deposit in transit	2,450
Interest earned (on bank account)	52
Bank service charges (miscellaneous expense)	15

Reported on the bank statement is a canceled check that the company failed to record. (Information from the bank reconciliation allows you to determine the amount of this check, which is a payment on an account payable.)

b. An examination of customers' accounts shows that accounts totaling $679 should be written off as uncollectible. Using an aging of receivables, the company determines that the ending balance of the Allowance for Doubtful Accounts should be $700.

c. A truck is purchased and placed in service on January 1, 2011. Its cost is being depreciated with the straight-line method using the following facts and estimates.

Original cost	$32,000
Expected salvage value	8,000
Useful life (years)	4

d. Two items of equipment (a sprayer and an injector) were purchased and put into service in early January 2009. They are being depreciated with the straight-line method using these facts and estimates.

	Sprayer	Injector
Original cost	$27,000	$18,000
Expected salvage value	3,000	2,500
Useful life (years)	8	5

e. On August 1, 2011, the company is paid $3,840 cash in advance to provide monthly service for an apartment complex for one year. The company began providing the services in August. When the cash was received, the full amount was credited to the Extermination Services Revenue account.

f. The company offers a warranty for the services it sells. The expected cost of providing warranty service is 2.5% of the extermination services revenue of $57,760 for 2011. No warranty expense has been recorded for 2011. All costs of servicing warranties in 2011 were properly debited to the Estimated Warranty Liability account.

g. The $15,000 long-term note is an 8%, five-year, interest-bearing note with interest payable annually on December 31. The note was signed with First National Bank on December 31, 2011.

h. The ending inventory of merchandise is counted and determined to have a cost of $11,700. Bug-Off uses a perpetual inventory system.

Required

1. Use the preceding information to determine amounts for the following items.

Check (1*a*) Cash bal. $15,750
(1*b*) $551 credit

a. Correct (reconciled) ending balance of Cash, and the amount of the omitted check.

b. Adjustment needed to obtain the correct ending balance of the Allowance for Doubtful Accounts.

c. Depreciation expense for the truck used during year 2011.

d. Depreciation expense for the two items of equipment used during year 2011.

e. The adjusted 2011 ending balances of the Extermination Services Revenue and Unearned Services Revenue accounts.

(1*f*) Estim. warranty liability, $2,844 Cr.

f. The adjusted 2011 ending balances of the accounts for Warranty Expense and Estimated Warranty Liability.

g. The adjusted 2011 ending balances of the accounts for Interest Expense and Interest Payable. (Round amounts to nearest whole dollar.)

2. Use the results of part 1 to complete the six-column table by first entering the appropriate adjustments for items *a* through *g* and then completing the adjusted trial balance columns. (*Hint:* Item *b* requires two adjustments.)
3. Prepare journal entries to record the adjustments entered on the six-column table. Assume Bug-Off's adjusted balance for Merchandise Inventory matches the year-end physical count.
4. Prepare a single-step income statement, a statement of owner's equity (cash withdrawals during 2011 were $10,000), and a classified balance sheet.

(2) Adjusted trial balance totals, $238,207

(4) Net income, $9,274; Total assets, $82,771

Beyond the Numbers

REPORTING IN ACTION
A1 P4

RIM

BTN 11-1 Refer to the financial statements of **Research In Motion** in Appendix A to answer the following.

1. Compute times interest earned for the fiscal years ended 2010, 2009, and 2008. Comment on RIM's ability to cover its interest expense for this period. Assume interest expense of $1, $502, and $31 for fiscal years ended 2010, 2009, and 2008 ($ thousands); and, assume an industry average of 18.1 for times interest earned.
2. RIM's current liabilities include "deferred revenue"; assume that this account reflects "Unredeemed gift card liabilities." Explain how this liability is created and how RIM satisfies this liability.
3. Does RIM have any commitments or contingencies? Briefly explain them.

Fast Forward

4. Access RIM's financial statements for fiscal years ending after February 27, 2010, at its Website (RIM.com) or the SEC's EDGAR database (www.SEC.gov). Compute its times interest earned for years ending after February 27, 2010, and compare your results to those in part 1.

COMPARATIVE ANALYSIS
A1

RIM
Apple

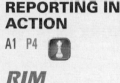

BTN 11-2 Key figures for **Research In Motion** and **Apple** follow. (Interest expense figures for Apple are assumed as it has no interest expense for these years.)

	Research In Motion			Apple		
($ millions)	Current Year	One Year Prior	Two Years Prior	Current Year	One Year Prior	Two Years Prior
Net income	$2,457.144	$1,892.616	$1,293.867	$8,235	$6,119	$3,495
Income taxes	809.366	907.747	516.653	3,831	2,828	1,511
Interest expense	.001	.502	.031	3	2	1

Required

1. Compute times interest earned for the three years' data shown for each company.
2. Comment on which company appears stronger in its ability to pay interest obligations if income should decline. Assume an industry average of 18.1.

ETHICS CHALLENGE
P4

BTN 11-3 Connor Bly is a sales manager for an automobile dealership. He earns a bonus each year based on revenue from the number of autos sold in the year less related warranty expenses. Actual warranty expenses have varied over the prior 10 years from a low of 3% of an automobile's selling price to a high of 10%. In the past, Bly has tended to estimate warranty expenses on the high end to be conservative. He must work with the dealership's accountant at year-end to arrive at the warranty expense accrual for cars sold each year.

1. Does the warranty accrual decision create any ethical dilemma for Bly?
2. Since warranty expenses vary, what percent do you think Bly should choose for the current year? Justify your response.

COMMUNICATING IN PRACTICE
C3

BTN 11-4 Dustin Clemens is the accounting and finance manager for a manufacturer. At year-end, he must determine how to account for the company's contingencies. His manager, Madeline Pretti, objects to Clemens's proposal to recognize an expense and a liability for warranty service on units of a new product introduced in the fourth quarter. Pretti comments, "There's no way we can estimate this warranty cost. We don't owe anyone anything until a product fails and it is returned. Let's report an expense if and when we do any warranty work."

Required

Prepare a one-page memorandum for Clemens to send to Pretti defending his proposal.

TAKING IT TO THE NET

C1 A1

BTN 11-5 Access the February 26, 2010, filing of the December 31, 2009, annual 10-K report of **McDonald's Corporation** (Ticker: MCD), which is available from www.SEC.gov.

Required

1. Identify the current liabilities on McDonald's balance sheet as of December 31, 2009.
2. What portion (in percent) of McDonald's long-term debt matures within the next 12 months?
3. Use the consolidated statement of income for the year ended December 31, 2009, to compute McDonald's times interest earned ratio. Comment on the result. Assume an industry average of 12.0.

TEAMWORK IN ACTION

C2 P1

BTN 11-6 Assume that your team is in business and you must borrow $6,000 cash for short-term needs. You have been shopping banks for a loan, and you have the following two options.

A. Sign a $6,000, 90-day, 10% interest-bearing note dated June 1.

B. Sign a $6,000, 120-day, 8% interest-bearing note dated June 1.

Required

1. Discuss these two options and determine the best choice. Ensure that all teammates concur with the decision and understand the rationale.
2. Each member of the team is to prepare *one* of the following journal entries.
   a. Option A—at date of issuance.
   b. Option B—at date of issuance.
   c. Option A—at maturity date.
   d. Option B—at maturity date.
3. In rotation, each member is to explain the entry he or she prepared in part 2 to the team. Ensure that all team members concur with and understand the entries.
4. Assume that the funds are borrowed on December 1 (instead of June 1) and your business operates on a calendar-year reporting period. Each member of the team is to prepare *one* of the following entries.
   a. Option A—the year-end adjustment.
   b. Option B—the year-end adjustment.
   c. Option A—at maturity date.
   d. Option B—at maturity date.
5. In rotation, each member is to explain the entry he or she prepared in part 4 to the team. Ensure that all team members concur with and understand the entries.

ENTREPRENEURIAL DECISION

A1

BTN 11-7 Review the chapter's opening feature about Matt and Bryan Walls, and their start-up company, **SnorgTees**. Assume that these young entrepreneurs are considering expanding their business to open an outlet in Europe. Assume their current income statement is as follows.

SNORGTEES Income Statement For Year Ended December 31, 2011	
Sales	$1,000,000
Cost of goods sold (30%)	300,000
Gross profit	700,000
Operating expenses (25%)	250,000
Net income	$ 450,000

SnorgTees currently has no interest-bearing debt. If it expands to open a European location, it will require a $300,000 loan. SnorgTees has found a bank that will loan it the money on a 7% note payable. The company believes that, at least for the first few years, sales at its European location will be $250,000, and that all expenses (including cost of goods sold) will follow the same patterns as its current locations.

Required

1. Prepare an income statement (showing three separate columns for current operations, European, and total) for SnorgTees assuming that it borrows the funds and expands to Europe. Annual revenues for current operations are expected to remain at $1,000,000.
2. Compute SnorgTees' times interest earned under the expansion assumptions in part 1.
3. Assume sales at its European location are $400,000. Prepare an income statement (with columns for current operations, European, and total) for the company and compute times interest earned.
4. Assume sales at its European location are $100,000. Prepare an income statement (with columns for current operations, European, and total) for the company and compute times interest earned.
5. Comment on your results from parts 1 through 4.

HITTING THE ROAD

P2

BTN 11-8 Check your phone book or the Social Security Administration Website (www.SSA.gov) to locate the Social Security office near you. Visit the office to request a personal earnings and estimate form. Fill out the form and mail according to the instructions. You will receive a statement from the Social Security Administration regarding your earnings history and future Social Security benefits you can receive. (Formerly the request could be made online. The online service has been discontinued and is now under review by the Social Security Administration due to security concerns.) It is good to request an earnings and benefit statement every 5 to 10 years to make sure you have received credit for all wages earned and for which you and your employer have paid taxes into the system.

GLOBAL DECISION

A1 

NOKIA

RIM

Apple

BTN 11-9 **Nokia, Research In Motion,** and **Apple** are all competitors in the global marketplace. Comparative figures for Nokia (www.Nokia.com), along with selected figures from Research In Motion and Apple, follow.

	Nokia (EUR millions)		Research In Motion		Apple	
Key Figures	**Current Year**	**Prior Year**	**Current Year**	**Prior Year**	**Current Year**	**Prior Year**
Net income	260	3,889	—	—	—	—
Income taxes	702	1,081	—	—	—	—
Interest expense	243	185	—	—	—	—
Times interest earned	?	?	3,267	5,579	4,023	4,475

Required

1. Compute the times interest earned ratio for the most recent two years for Nokia using the data shown.
2. Which company of the three presented provides the best coverage of interest expense? Explain.

ANSWERS TO MULTIPLE CHOICE QUIZ

1. b; $6,000 × 0.05 × 30/360 = $25
2. e; $50,000 × (.062 + .0145) = $3,825
3. b; $7,000 × (.008 + .054) = $434
4. c; 10,000 television sets × .01 × $250 = $25,000
5. a; 150 employees × $175 per day × 1 vacation day earned = $26,250

12 Accounting for Partnerships

A Look Back

Chapter 11 focused on how current liabilities are identified, computed, recorded, and reported. Attention was directed at notes, payroll, sales taxes, warranties, employee benefits, and contingencies.

A Look at This Chapter

This chapter explains the partnership form of organization. Important partnership characteristics are described along with the accounting concepts and procedures for its most fundamental transactions.

A Look Ahead

Chapter 13 extends our discussion to the corporate form of organization. We describe the accounting and reporting for stock issuances, dividends, and other equity transactions.

Learning Objectives

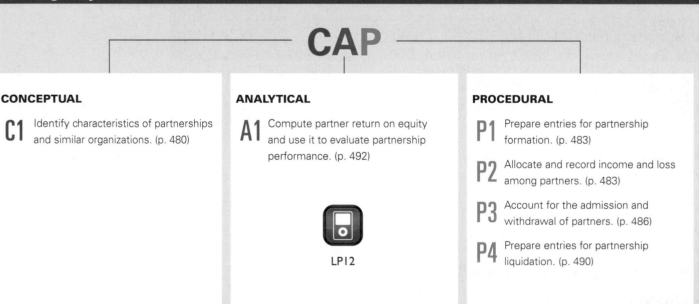

CONCEPTUAL

C1 Identify characteristics of partnerships and similar organizations. (p. 480)

ANALYTICAL

A1 Compute partner return on equity and use it to evaluate partnership performance. (p. 492)

LP12

PROCEDURAL

P1 Prepare entries for partnership formation. (p. 483)

P2 Allocate and record income and loss among partners. (p. 483)

P3 Account for the admission and withdrawal of partners. (p. 486)

P4 Prepare entries for partnership liquidation. (p. 490)

Decision Insight

Let's Do Eco-Lunch

"We are making a difference"

—CHANCE CLAXTON AND LYNN JULIAN

PHOENIX—Believe it or not, nearly 20,000 pounds of trash is generated annually from the typical elementary school. "When we researched it," explains Chance Claxton, "We discovered that 67 pounds of lunchtime trash is created by each schoolage child each school year." Armed with that evidence, and as mothers of young children, Chance, along with partner Lynn Julian, felt an urgent need to respond. The result is **Kids Konserve (KidsKonserve.com)**, a start-up partnership that sells reusable and recycled food kits. "With waste from snack and lunch breaks at an all-time high," says Chance, "Kids Konserve is empowering parents and kids with information and a reusable product that will help . . . decrease waste in community landfills."

While Chance focuses on the design and sales side, Lynn's focus is on the accounting, marketing, and financial side of Kids Konserve. Her knowledge of partnerships and their financial implications are important to Kid Konserve's success. Lynn explains that she is working on a model for fund-raising opportunities to further expand their product opportunities. Both partners stress the importance of attending to partnership formation, partnership agreements, and financial reports to stay afloat. They refer to the partners' return on equity and establishing the proper organizational form as key inputs to partnership strategies and decisions.

Success is causing their partnership to evolve, but the partners adhere to an eco-focused mentality. "The best part of being a 'mompreneur' is that I am doing something for myself, for others, for my family, and for the earth," insists Chance. "It is a great feeling to have my children watch me work."

The partners continue to apply strict accounting fundamentals. Lynn explains that their partnership cannot survive unless the business is profitable, even with their noble agenda. To that end, both partners review their accounting results and regularly assess the partnership's costs and revenues. Nevertheless, Lynn emphasizes their greater goal: "We're delivering a program that reduces waste on campus. I'd say that deserves an A+."

[Sources: *Kids Konserve Website,* January 2011; *Entrepreneur,* October 2009; *MomBites.com,* September 2009; *Daily Grommet,* September 2009]

Chapter Preview

The three basic types of business organizations are proprietorships, partnerships, and corporations. Partnerships are similar to proprietorships, except they have more than one owner. This chapter explains partnerships and looks at several variations of them such as limited partnerships, limited liability partnerships, S corporations, and limited liability companies. Understanding the advantages and disadvantages of the partnership form of business organization is important for making informed business decisions.

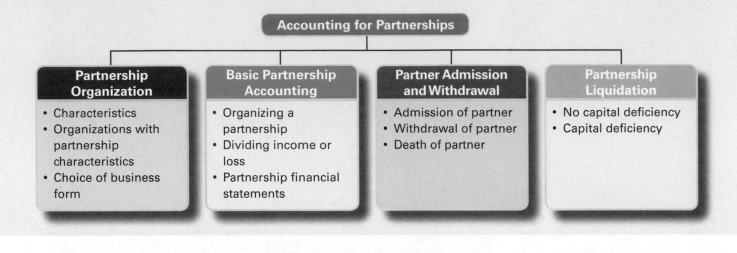

Accounting for Partnerships

Partnership Organization
- Characteristics
- Organizations with partnership characteristics
- Choice of business form

Basic Partnership Accounting
- Organizing a partnership
- Dividing income or loss
- Partnership financial statements

Partner Admission and Withdrawal
- Admission of partner
- Withdrawal of partner
- Death of partner

Partnership Liquidation
- No capital deficiency
- Capital deficiency

PARTNERSHIP FORM OF ORGANIZATION

C1 Identify characteristics of partnerships and similar organizations.

A **partnership** is an unincorporated association of two or more people to pursue a business for profit as co-owners. Many businesses are organized as partnerships. They are especially common in small retail and service businesses. Many professional practitioners, including physicians, lawyers, investors, and accountants, also organize their practices as partnerships.

Characteristics of Partnerships

Partnerships are an important type of organization because they offer certain advantages with their unique characteristics. We describe these characteristics in this section.

Voluntary Association A partnership is a voluntary association between partners. Joining a partnership increases the risk to one's personal financial position. Some courts have ruled that partnerships are created by the actions of individuals even when there is no *express agreement* to form one.

Partnership Agreement Forming a partnership requires that two or more legally competent people (who are of age and of sound mental capacity) agree to be partners. Their agreement becomes a **partnership contract,** also called *articles of copartnership.* Although it should be in writing, the contract is binding even if it is only expressed verbally. Partnership agreements normally include details of the partners' (1) names and contributions, (2) rights and duties, (3) sharing of income and losses, (4) withdrawal arrangement, (5) dispute procedures, (6) admission and withdrawal of partners, and (7) rights and duties in the event a partner dies.

Point: When a new partner is admitted, all parties usually must agree to the admission.

Limited Life The life of a partnership is limited. Death, bankruptcy, or any event taking away the ability of a partner to enter into or fulfill a contract ends a partnership. Any one of the partners can also terminate a partnership at will.

Point: The end of a partnership is referred to as its *dissolution.*

Taxation A partnership is not subject to taxes on its income. The income or loss of a partnership is allocated to the partners according to the partnership agreement, and it is included in determining the taxable income for each partner's tax return. Partnership income or loss is allocated each year whether or not cash is distributed to partners.

Point: Partners are taxed on their share of partnership income, not on their withdrawals.

Mutual Agency **Mutual agency** implies that each partner is a fully authorized agent of the partnership. As its agent, a partner can commit or bind the partnership to any contract within the scope of the partnership business. For instance, a partner in a merchandising business can sign contracts binding the partnership to buy merchandise, lease a store building, borrow money, or hire employees. These activities are all within the scope of a merchandising firm. A partner in a law firm, acting alone, however, cannot bind the other partners to a contract to buy snowboards for resale or rent an apartment for parties. These actions are outside the normal scope of a law firm's business. Partners also can agree to limit the power of any one or more of the partners to negotiate contracts for the partnership. This agreement is binding on the partners and on outsiders who know it exists. It is not binding on outsiders who do not know it exists. Outsiders unaware of the agreement have the right to assume each partner has normal agency powers for the partnership. Mutual agency exposes partners to the risk of unwise actions by any one partner.

Point: The majority of states adhere to the Uniform Partnership Act for the basic rules of partnership formation, operation, and dissolution.

Unlimited Liability **Unlimited liability** implies that each partner can be called on to pay a partnership's debts. When a partnership cannot pay its debts, creditors usually can apply their claims to partners' *personal* assets. If a partner does not have enough assets to meet his or her share of the partnership debt, the creditors can apply their claims to the assets of the other partners. A partnership in which all partners have *mutual agency* and *unlimited liability* is called a **general partnership.** Mutual agency and unlimited liability are two main reasons that most general partnerships have only a few members.

Point: Limited life, mutual agency, and unlimited liability are disadvantages of a partnership.

Co-Ownership of Property Partnership assets are owned jointly by all partners. Any investment by a partner becomes the joint property of all partners. Partners have a claim on partnership assets based on their capital account and the partnership contract.

Organizations with Partnership Characteristics

Organizations exist that combine certain characteristics of partnerships with other forms of organizations. We discuss several of these forms in this section.

Limited Partnerships Some individuals who want to invest in a partnership are unwilling to accept the risk of unlimited liability. Their needs can be met with a **limited partnership.** This type of organization is identified in its name with the words "Limited Partnership" or "Ltd." or "LP." A limited partnership has two classes of partners, general and limited. At least one partner must be a **general partner,** who assumes management duties and unlimited liability for the debts of the partnership. The **limited partners** have no personal liability beyond the amounts they invest in the partnership. Limited partners have no active role except as specified in the partnership agreement. A limited partnership agreement often specifies unique procedures for allocating income and losses between general and limited partners. The accounting procedures are similar for both limited and general partnerships.

Decision Insight

Nutty Partners The Hawaii-based **ML Macadamia Orchards LP** is one of the world's largest growers of macadamia nuts. It reported the following partners' capital balances ($ 000s) in its balance sheet: ■

General Partner	$ 81
Limited Partners	$43,560

Limited Liability Partnerships Most states allow individuals to form a **limited liability partnership.** This is identified in its name with the words "Limited Liability Partnership" or by "LLP." This type of partnership is designed to protect innocent partners from malpractice or negligence claims resulting from the acts of another partner. When a partner provides service resulting in a malpractice claim, that partner has personal liability for the claim. The remaining partners who were not responsible for the actions resulting in the claim are not personally liable for it. However, most states hold all partners personally liable for other partnership debts. Accounting for a limited liability partnership is the same as for a general partnership.

Point: Many accounting services firms are set up as LLPs.

S Corporations Certain corporations with 100 or fewer stockholders can elect to be treated as a partnership for income tax purposes. These corporations are called *Sub-Chapter S* or simply **S corporations.** This distinguishes them from other corporations, called *Sub-Chapter C* or simply **C corporations.** S corporations provide stockholders the same limited liability feature that C corporations do. The advantage of an S corporation is that it does not pay income taxes. If stockholders work for an S corporation, their salaries are treated as expenses of the corporation. The remaining income or loss of the corporation is allocated to stockholders for inclusion on their personal tax returns. Except for C corporations having to account for income tax expenses and liabilities, the accounting procedures are the same for both S and C corporations.

Point: The majority of proprietorships and partnerships that are organized today are set up as LLCs.

Limited Liability Companies A relatively new form of business organization is the **limited liability company.** The names of these businesses usually include the words "Limited Liability Company" or an abbreviation such as "LLC" or "LC." This form of business has certain features similar to a corporation and others similar to a limited partnership. The owners, who are called *members,* are protected with the same limited liability feature as owners of corporations. While limited partners cannot actively participate in the management of a limited partnership, the members of a limited liability company can assume an active management role. A limited liability company usually has a limited life. For income tax purposes, a limited liability company is typically treated as a partnership. This treatment depends on factors such as whether the members' equity interests are freely transferable and whether the company has continuity of life. A limited liability company's accounting system is designed to help management comply with the dictates of the articles of organization and company regulations adopted by its members. The accounting system also must provide information to support the company's compliance with state and federal laws, including taxation.

Point: Accounting for LLCs is similar to that for partnerships (and proprietorships). One difference is that Owner (Partner), Capital is usually called *Members, Capital* for LLCs.

Choosing a Business Form

Choosing the proper business form is crucial. Many factors should be considered, including taxes, liability risk, tax and fiscal year-end, ownership structure, estate planning, business risks, and earnings and property distributions. The following table summarizes several important characteristics of business organizations:

	Proprietorship	Partnership	LLP	LLC	S Corp.	Corporation
Business entity	Yes	Yes	Yes	Yes	Yes	Yes
Legal entity	No	No	No	Yes	Yes	Yes
Limited liability	No	No	Limited*	Yes	Yes	Yes
Business taxed	No	No	No	No	No	Yes
One owner allowed	Yes	No	No	Yes	Yes	Yes

* A partner's personal liability for LLP debts is limited. Most LLPs carry insurance to protect against malpractice.

Point: The Small Business Administration provides suggestions and information on setting up the proper form for your organization—see **SBA.gov**.

We must remember that this table is a summary, not a detailed list. Many details underlie each of these business forms, and several details differ across states. Also, state and federal laws change, and a body of law is still developing around LLCs. Business owners should look at these details and consider unique business arrangements such as organizing various parts of their businesses in different forms.

Quick Check Answers – p. 495 

1. A partnership is terminated in the event (*a*) a partnership agreement is not in writing, (*b*) a partner dies, (*c*) a partner exercises mutual agency.
2. What does the term *unlimited liability* mean when applied to a general partnership?
3. Which of the following forms of organization do not provide limited liability to *all* of its owners? (*a*) S corporation, (*b*) limited liability company, (*c*) limited partnership.

BASIC PARTNERSHIP ACCOUNTING

Since ownership rights in a partnership are divided among partners, partnership accounting

- Uses a capital account for each partner.
- Uses a withdrawals account for each partner.
- Allocates net income or loss to partners according to the partnership agreement.

This section describes partnership accounting for organizing a partnership, distributing income and loss, and preparing financial statements.

Organizing a Partnership

P1 Prepare entries for partnership formation.

When partners invest in a partnership, their capital accounts are credited for the invested amounts. Partners can invest both assets and liabilities. Each partner's investment is recorded at an agreed-on value, normally the market values of the contributed assets and liabilities at the date of contribution. To illustrate, Kayla Zayn and Hector Perez organize a partnership on January 11 called BOARDS that offers year-round facilities for skateboarding and snowboarding. Zayn's initial net investment in BOARDS is $30,000, made up of cash ($7,000), boarding facilities ($33,000), and a note payable reflecting a bank loan for the new business ($10,000). Perez's initial investment is cash of $10,000. These amounts are the values agreed on by both partners. The entries to record these investments follow.

Zayn's Investment

Jan. 11	Cash	7,000	
	Boarding facilities	33,000	
	Note payable		10,000
	K. Zayn, Capital		30,000
	To record the investment of Zayn.		

Assets	=	Liabilities	+	Equity
+7,000		+10,000		+30,000
+33,000				

Perez's Investment

Jan. 11	Cash	10,000	
	H. Perez, Capital		10,000
	To record the investment of Perez.		

Assets	=	Liabilities	+	Equity
+10,000				+10,000

In accounting for a partnership, the following additional relations hold true: (1) Partners' withdrawals are debited to their own separate withdrawals accounts. (2) Partners' capital accounts are credited (or debited) for their shares of net income (or net loss) when closing the accounts at the end of a period. (3) Each partner's withdrawals account is closed to that partner's capital account. Separate capital and withdrawals accounts are kept for each partner.

Point: Both equity and cash are reduced when a partner withdraws cash from a partnership.

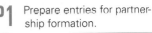

Decision Insight

Broadway Partners **Big River Productions** is a partnership that owns the rights to the play *Big River*. The play is performed on tour and periodically on Broadway. For a recent year-end, its Partners' Capital was approximately $300,000, and it was distributed in its entirety to the partners. ■

Dividing Income or Loss

P2 Allocate and record income and loss among partners.

Partners are not employees of the partnership but are its owners. If partners devote their time and services to their partnership, they are understood to do so for profit, not for salary. This means there are no salaries to partners that are reported as expenses on the partnership income statement. However, when net income or loss of a partnership is allocated among partners, the partners can agree to allocate "salary allowances" reflecting the relative value of services provided. Partners also can agree to allocate "interest allowances" based on the amount invested. For instance, since Zayn contributes three times the investment of Perez, it is only fair that this be considered when allocating income between them. Like salary allowances, these interest allowances are not expenses on the income statement.

Partners can agree to any method of dividing income or loss. In the absence of an agreement, the law says that the partners share income or loss of a partnership equally. If partners agree on how to share income but say nothing about losses, they share losses the same way they share income. Three common methods to divide income or loss use (1) a stated ratio basis, (2) the ratio of capital balances, or (3) salary and interest allowances and any remainder according to a fixed ratio. We explain each of these methods in this section.

Point: Partners can agree on a ratio to divide income and another ratio to divide a loss.

Allocation on Stated Ratios The *stated ratio* (also called the *income-and-loss-sharing ratio,* the *profit and loss ratio,* or the *P&L ratio*) method of allocating partnership income or loss gives each partner a fraction of the total. Partners must agree on the fractional share each receives. To illustrate, assume the partnership agreement of K. Zayn and H. Perez says Zayn receives two-thirds and Perez one-third of partnership income and loss. If their partnership's net income is $60,000, it is allocated to the partners when the Income Summary account is closed as follows.

Point: The fractional basis can be stated as a proportion, ratio, or percent. For example, a 3:2 basis is the same as 3/5 and 2/5, or 60% and 40%.

Assets = Liabilities + Equity
−60,000
+40,000
+20,000

Dec. 31	Income Summary	60,000	
	K. Zayn, Capital		40,000
	H. Perez, Capital		20,000
	To allocate income and close Income Summary.		

Allocation on Capital Balances The *capital balances* method of allocating partnership income or loss assigns an amount based on the ratio of each partner's relative capital balance. If Zayn and Perez agree to share income and loss on the ratio of their beginning capital balances—Zayn's $30,000 and Perez's $10,000—Zayn receives three-fourths of any income or loss ($30,000/$40,000) and Perez receives one-fourth ($10,000/$40,000). The journal entry follows the same format as that using stated ratios (see the preceding entries).

Point: To determine the percent of income received by each partner, divide an individual partner's share by total net income.

Allocation on Services, Capital, and Stated Ratios The *services, capital, and stated ratio* method of allocating partnership income or loss recognizes that service and capital contributions of partners often are not equal. Salary allowances can make up for differences in service contributions. Interest allowances can make up for unequal capital contributions. Also, the allocation of income and loss can include *both* salary and interest allowances. To illustrate, assume that the partnership agreement of K. Zayn and H. Perez reflects differences in service and capital contributions as follows: (1) annual salary allowances of $36,000 to Zayn and $24,000 to Perez, (2) annual interest allowances of 10% of a partner's beginning-year capital balance, and (3) equal share of any remaining balance of income or loss. These salaries and interest allowances are *not* reported as expenses on the income statement. They are simply a means of dividing partnership income or loss. The remainder of this section provides two illustrations using this three-point allocation agreement.

Illustration when income exceeds allowance. If BOARDS has first-year net income of $70,000, and Zayn and Perez apply the three-point partnership agreement described in the prior paragraph, income is allocated as shown in Exhibit 12.1. Zayn gets $42,000 and Perez gets $28,000 of the $70,000 total.

Point: When allowances exceed income, the amount of this negative balance often is referred to as a *sharing agreement loss* or *deficit.*

Illustration when allowances exceed income. The sharing agreement between Zayn and Perez must be followed even if net income is less than the total of the allowances. For example, if BOARDS' first-year net income is $50,000 instead of $70,000, it is allocated to the partners as shown in Exhibit 12.2. Computations for salaries and interest are identical to those in Exhibit 12.1. However, when we apply the total allowances against income, the balance of income is negative. This $(14,000) negative balance is allocated equally to the partners per their sharing agreement. This means that a negative $(7,000) is allocated to each partner. In this case, Zayn ends up with $32,000 and Perez with $18,000. If BOARDS had experienced a net loss, Zayn and Perez would share it in the same manner as the $50,000 income. The only difference is that they would have begun with a negative amount because of the loss. Specifically, the partners would still have been

Point: Check to make sure the sum of the dollar amounts allocated to each partner equals net income or loss.

EXHIBIT 12.1

Dividing Income When Income Exceeds Allowances

	Zayn	Perez	Total
Net income			$70,000
Salary allowances			
Zayn	$ 36,000		
Perez		$ 24,000	
Interest allowances			
Zayn (10% × $30,000)	3,000		
Perez (10% × $10,000)		1,000	
Total salaries and interest	39,000	25,000	64,000
Balance of income			**6,000**
Balance allocated equally			
Zayn	3,000		
Perez		3,000	
Total allocated			6,000
Balance of income			**$ 0**
Income of each partner	**$42,000**	**$28,000**	

EXHIBIT 12.2

Dividing Income When Allowances Exceed Income

	Zayn	Perez	Total
Net income			$50,000
Salary allowances			
Zayn	$ 36,000		
Perez		$ 24,000	
Interest allowances			
Zayn (10% × $30,000)	3,000		
Perez (10% × $10,000)		1,000	
Total salaries and interest	39,000	25,000	64,000
Balance of income			**(14,000)**
Balance allocated equally			
Zayn	(7,000)		
Perez		(7,000)	
Total allocated			(14,000)
Balance of income			**$ 0**
Income of each partner	**$32,000**	**$18,000**	

allocated their salary and interest allowances, further adding to the negative balance of the loss. This *total* negative balance *after* salary and interest allowances would have been allocated equally between the partners. These allocations would have been applied against the positive numbers from any allowances to determine each partner's share of the loss.

Point: When a loss occurs, it is possible for a specific partner's capital to increase (when closing income summary) if that partner's allowance is in excess of his or her share of the negative balance. This implies that decreases to the capital balances of other partners exceed the partnership's loss amount.

Quick Check Answer — p. 495 

4. Denzel and Shantell form a partnership by contributing $70,000 and $35,000, respectively. They agree to an interest allowance equal to 10% of each partner's capital balance at the beginning of the year, with the remaining income shared equally. Allocate first-year income of $40,000 to each partner.

Partnership Financial Statements

Partnership financial statements are similar to those of other organizations. The **statement of partners' equity,** also called *statement of partners' capital,* is one exception. It shows *each* partner's beginning capital balance, additional investments, allocated income or loss, withdrawals, and ending capital balance. To illustrate, Exhibit 12.3 shows the statement of partners' equity for BOARDS prepared using the sharing agreement of Exhibit 12.1. Recall that BOARDS' income was $70,000; also, assume that Zayn withdrew $20,000 and Perez $12,000 at year-end.

EXHIBIT 12.3

Statement of Partners' Equity

BOARDS Statement of Partners' Equity For Year Ended December 31, 2011		Zayn		Perez	Total
Beginning capital balances		$ 0		$ 0	$ 0
Plus					
Investments by owners		30,000		10,000	40,000
Net income					
Salary allowances	$36,000		$24,000		
Interest allowances	3,000		1,000		
Balance allocated	3,000		3,000		
Total net income		42,000		28,000	70,000
		72,000		38,000	110,000
Less partners' withdrawals		(20,000)		(12,000)	(32,000)
Ending capital balances		**$52,000**		**$26,000**	**$78,000**

The equity section of the balance sheet of a partnership usually shows the separate capital account balance of each partner. In the case of BOARDS, both K. Zayn, Capital, and H. Perez, Capital, are listed in the equity section along with their balances of $52,000 and $26,000, respectively.

Decision Insight

Gambling Partners **Trump Entertainment Resorts LP** and subsidiaries operate three casino hotel properties in Atlantic City: Trump Taj Mahal Casino Resort ("Trump Taj Mahal"), Trump Plaza Hotel and Casino ("Trump Plaza"), and Trump Marina Hotel Casino ("Trump Marina"). Its recent statement of partners' equity reports $1,020,000 in partners' withdrawals, leaving $605,314,000 in partners' capital balances. ■

ADMISSION AND WITHDRAWAL OF PARTNERS

P3 Account for the admission and withdrawal of partners.

A partnership is based on a contract between individuals. When a partner is admitted or withdraws, the present partnership ends. Still, the business can continue to operate as a new partnership consisting of the remaining partners. This section considers how to account for the admission and withdrawal of partners.

Admission of a Partner

A new partner is admitted in one of two ways: by purchasing an interest from one or more current partners or by investing cash or other assets in the partnership.

Purchase of Partnership Interest The purchase of partnership interest is a *personal transaction between one or more current partners and the new partner.* To become a partner, the current partners must accept the purchaser. Accounting for the purchase of partnership interest involves reallocating current partners' capital to reflect the transaction. To illustrate, at the end of BOARDS' first year, H. Perez sells one-half of his partnership interest to Tyrell Rasheed for $18,000. This means that Perez gives up a $13,000 recorded interest ($26,000 × 1/2) in the partnership (see the ending capital balance in Exhibit 12.3). The partnership records this January 4 transaction as follows.

Assets = Liabilities + Equity
−13,000
+13,000

Jan. 4	H. Perez, Capital	13,000	
	T. Rasheed, Capital		13,000
	To record admission of Rasheed by purchase.		

After this entry is posted, BOARDS' equity shows K. Zayn, Capital; H. Perez, Capital; and T. Rasheed, Capital, and their respective balances of $52,000, $13,000, and $13,000.

Two aspects of this transaction are important. First, the partnership does *not* record the $18,000 Rasheed paid Perez. The partnership's assets, liabilities, and *total equity* are unaffected by this transaction among partners. Second, Zayn and Perez must agree that Rasheed is to become a partner. If they agree to accept Rasheed, a new partnership is formed and a new contract with a new income-and-loss-sharing agreement is prepared. If Zayn or Perez refuses to accept Rasheed as a partner, then (under the Uniform Partnership Act) Rasheed gets Perez's sold share of partnership income and loss. If the partnership is liquidated, Rasheed gets Perez's sold share of partnership assets. Rasheed gets no voice in managing the company unless Rasheed is admitted as a partner.

Point: Partners' withdrawals are not constrained by the partnership's annual income or loss.

Investing Assets in a Partnership Admitting a partner by accepting assets is a *transaction between the new partner and the partnership.* The invested assets become partnership property. To illustrate, if Zayn (with a $52,000 interest) and Perez (with a $26,000 interest) agree to accept Rasheed as a partner in BOARDS after an investment of $22,000 cash, this is recorded as follows.

Jan. 4	Cash	22,000	
	T. Rasheed, Capital		22,000
	To record admission of Rasheed by investment.		

Assets	= Liabilities +	Equity
+22,000		+22,000

After this entry is posted, both assets (cash) and equity (T. Rasheed, Capital) increase by $22,000. Rasheed now has a 22% equity in the assets of the business, computed as $22,000 divided by the entire partnership equity ($52,000 + $26,000 + $22,000). Rasheed does not necessarily have a right to 22% of income. Dividing income and loss is a separate matter on which partners must agree.

Bonus to old partners. When the current value of a partnership is greater than the recorded amounts of equity, the partners usually require a new partner to pay a bonus for the privilege of joining. To illustrate, assume that Zayn and Perez agree to accept Rasheed as a partner with a 25% interest in BOARDS if Rasheed invests $42,000. Recall that the partnership's accounting records show that Zayn's recorded equity in the business is $52,000 and Perez's recorded equity is $26,000 (see Exhibit 12.3). Rasheed's equity is determined as follows.

Equities of existing partners ($52,000 + $26,000)	$ 78,000
Investment of new partner	42,000
Total partnership equity	$120,000
Equity of Rasheed (25% × $120,000)	$ 30,000

Although Rasheed invests $42,000, the equity attributed to Rasheed in the new partnership is only $30,000. The $12,000 difference is called a *bonus* and is allocated to existing partners (Zayn and Perez) according to their income-and-loss-sharing agreement. A bonus is shared in this way because it is viewed as reflecting a higher value of the partnership that is not yet reflected in income. The entry to record this transaction follows.

Jan. 4	Cash	42,000	
	T. Rasheed, Capital		30,000
	K. Zayn, Capital ($12,000 × ½)		6,000
	H. Perez, Capital ($12,000 × ½)		6,000
	To record admission of Rasheed and bonus.		

Assets	= Liabilities +	Equity
+42,000		+30,000
		+6,000
		+6,000

Bonus to new partner. Alternatively, existing partners can grant a bonus to a new partner. This usually occurs when they need additional cash or the new partner has exceptional talents. The bonus to the new partner is in the form of a larger share of equity than the amount invested. To illustrate, assume that Zayn and Perez agree to accept Rasheed as a partner with a

25% interest in the partnership, but they require Rasheed to invest only $18,000. Rasheed's equity is determined as follows.

Equities of existing partners ($52,000 + $26,000)	$78,000
Investment of new partner	18,000
Total partnership equity	$96,000
Equity of Rasheed (25% × $96,000)	$24,000

The old partners contribute the $6,000 bonus (computed as $24,000 minus $18,000) to Rasheed according to their income-and-loss-sharing ratio. Moreover, Rasheed's 25% equity does not necessarily entitle Rasheed to 25% of future income or loss. This is a separate matter for agreement by the partners. The entry to record the admission and investment of Rasheed is

Assets	= Liabilities +	Equity
+18,000		−3,000
		−3,000
		+24,000

Jan. 4	Cash	18,000	
	K. Zayn, Capital ($6,000 × ½)	3,000	
	H. Perez, Capital ($6,000 × ½)	3,000	
	T. Rasheed, Capital		24,000
	To record Rasheed's admission and bonus.		

Withdrawal of a Partner

A partner generally withdraws from a partnership in one of two ways. (1) First, the withdrawing partner can sell his or her interest to another person who pays for it in cash or other assets. For this, we need only debit the withdrawing partner's capital account and credit the new partner's capital account. (2) The second case is when cash or other assets of the partnership are distributed to the withdrawing partner in settlement of his or her interest. To illustrate these cases, assume that Perez withdraws from the partnership of BOARDS in some future period. The partnership shows the following capital balances at the date of Perez's withdrawal: K. Zayn, $84,000; H. Perez, $38,000; and T. Rasheed, $38,000. The partners (Zayn, Perez, and Rasheed) share income and loss equally. Accounting for Perez's withdrawal depends on whether a bonus is paid. We describe three possibilities.

No Bonus If Perez withdraws and takes cash equal to Perez's capital balance, the entry is

Assets	= Liabilities +	Equity
−38,000		−38,000

Oct. 31	H. Perez, Capital	38,000	
	Cash		38,000
	To record withdrawal of Perez from partnership with no bonus.		

Perez can take any combination of assets to which the partners agree to settle Perez's equity. Perez's withdrawal creates a new partnership between the remaining partners. A new partnership contract and a new income-and-loss-sharing agreement are required.

Bonus to Remaining Partners A withdrawing partner is sometimes willing to take less than the recorded value of his or her equity to get out of the partnership or because the recorded value is overstated. Whatever the reason, when this occurs, the withdrawing partner in effect gives the remaining partners a bonus equal to the equity left behind. The remaining partners share this unwithdrawn equity according to their income-and-loss-sharing ratio. To illustrate, if Perez withdraws and agrees to take $34,000 cash in settlement of Perez's capital balance, the entry is

Assets	= Liabilities +	Equity
−34,000		−38,000
		+2,000
		+2,000

Oct. 31	H. Perez, Capital	38,000	
	Cash		34,000
	K. Zayn, Capital		2,000
	T. Rasheed, Capital		2,000
	To record withdrawal of Perez and bonus to remaining partners.		

Perez withdrew $4,000 less than Perez's recorded equity of $38,000. This $4,000 is divided between Zayn and Rasheed according to their income-and-loss-sharing ratio.

Bonus to Withdrawing Partner A withdrawing partner may be able to receive more than his or her recorded equity for at least two reasons. First, the recorded equity may be understated. Second, the remaining partners may agree to remove this partner by giving assets of greater value than this partner's recorded equity. In either case, the withdrawing partner receives a bonus. The remaining partners reduce their equity by the amount of this bonus according to their income-and-loss-sharing ratio. To illustrate, if Perez withdraws and receives $40,000 cash in settlement of Perez's capital balance, the entry is

Oct. 31	H. Perez, Capital	38,000	
	K. Zayn, Capital	1,000	
	T. Rasheed, Capital	1,000	
	Cash		40,000
	To record Perez's withdrawal from partnership with a bonus to Perez.		

Assets	=	Liabilities	+	Equity
−40,000				−38,000
				−1,000
				−1,000

Falcon Cable Communications set up a partnership withdrawal agreement. Falcon owns and operates cable television systems and had two managing general partners. The partnership agreement stated that either partner "can offer to sell to the other partner the offering partner's entire partnership interest . . . for a negotiated price. If the partner receiving such an offer rejects it, the offering partner may elect to cause [the partnership] . . . to be liquidated and dissolved."

Death of a Partner

A partner's death dissolves a partnership. A deceased partner's estate is entitled to receive his or her equity. The partnership contract should contain provisions for settlement in this case. These provisions usually require (1) closing the books to determine income or loss since the end of the previous period and (2) determining and recording current market values for both assets and liabilities. The remaining partners and the deceased partner's estate then must agree to a settlement of the deceased partner's equity. This can involve selling the equity to remaining partners or to an outsider, or it can involve withdrawing assets.

Decision Ethics

Answer — p. 495

Financial Planner You are hired by the two remaining partners of a three-member partnership after the third partner's death. The partnership agreement states that a deceased partner's estate is entitled to a "share of partnership assets equal to the partner's relative equity balance" (partners' equity balances are equal). The estate argues that it is entitled to one-third of the current value of partnership assets. The remaining partners say the distribution should use asset book values, which are 75% of current value. They also point to partnership liabilities, which equal 40% of total asset book value and 30% of current value. How would you resolve this situation? ■

LIQUIDATION OF A PARTNERSHIP

P4 Prepare entries for partnership liquidation.

When a partnership is liquidated, its business ends and four concluding steps are required.

1. Record the sale of noncash assets for cash and any gain or loss from their liquidation.
2. Allocate any gain or loss from liquidation of the assets in step 1 to the partners *using their income-and-loss-sharing ratio.*
3. Pay or settle all partner liabilities.
4. Distribute any remaining cash to partners *based on their capital balances.*

Partnership liquidation usually falls into one of two cases, as described in this section.

No Capital Deficiency

No capital deficiency means that all partners have a zero or credit balance in their capital accounts for final distribution of cash. To illustrate, assume that Zayn, Perez, and Rasheed operate their partnership in BOARDS for several years, sharing income and loss equally. The partners then decide to liquidate. On the liquidation date, the current period's income or loss is transferred to the partners' capital accounts according to the sharing agreement. After that transfer, assume the partners' recorded account balances (immediately prior to liquidation) are:

Cash	$178,000	Accounts payable	$20,000	H. Perez, Capital	$66,000
Land	40,000	K. Zayn, Capital	70,000	T. Rasheed, Capital	62,000

We apply three steps for liquidation. ① *The partnership sells its noncash assets, and any losses or gains from liquidation are shared among partners according to their income-and-loss-sharing agreement* (equal for these partners). Assume that BOARDS sells its noncash assets consisting of $40,000 in land for $46,000 cash, yielding a net gain of $6,000. In a liquidation, gains or losses usually result from the sale of noncash assets, which are called *losses and gains from liquidation*. The entry to sell its assets for $46,000 follows.

Assets = Liabilities + Equity
−40,000 +6,000
+46,000

Jan. 15	Cash	46,000	
	Land		40,000
	Gain from Liquidation		6,000
	Sold noncash assets at a gain.		

Allocation of the gain from liquidation per the partners' income-and-loss-sharing agreement follows.

Assets = Liabilities + Equity
−6,000
+2,000
+2,000
+2,000

Jan. 15	Gain from Liquidation	6,000	
	K. Zayn, Capital		2,000
	H. Perez, Capital		2,000
	T. Rasheed, Capital		2,000
	To allocate liquidation gain to partners.		

② *The partnership pays its liabilities, and any losses or gains from liquidation of liabilities are shared among partners according to their income-and-loss-sharing agreement.* BOARDS' only liability is $20,000 in accounts payable, and no gain or loss occurred.

Assets = Liabilities + Equity
−20,000 −20,000

Jan. 15	Accounts Payable	20,000	
	Cash		20,000
	To pay claims of creditors.		

After step 2, we have the following capital balances along with the remaining cash balance.

K. Zayn

	Bal.	70,000
	(2)	2,000
	Bal.	72,000

H. Perez, Capital

	Bal.	66,000
	(2)	2,000
	Bal.	68,000

T. Rasheed, Capital

	Bal.	62,000
	(2)	2,000
	Bal.	64,000

Cash

Bal.	178,000	(3)	20,000
(1)	46,000		
Bal.	204,000		

③ *Any remaining cash is divided among the partners* ***according to their capital account balances.*** The entry to record the final distribution of cash to partners follows.

Assets = Liabilities + Equity
−204,000 −72,000
−68,000
−64,000

Jan. 15	K. Zayn, Capital	72,000	
	H. Perez, Capital	68,000	
	T. Rasheed, Capital	64,000	
	Cash		204,000
	To distribute remaining cash to partners.		

It is important to remember that the final cash payment is distributed to partners according to their capital account balances, whereas gains and losses from liquidation are allocated according to the income-and-loss-sharing ratio. The following *statement of liquidation* summarizes the three steps in this section.

Statement of Liquidation	Cash	Noncash Assets	=	Liabilities	K. Zayn, Capital	H. Perez, Capital	T. Rasheed, Capital
Balances prior to liquidation. . . .	$178,000	$ 40,000		$ 20,000	$ 70,000	$66,000	$62,000
① Sale of noncash assets	46,000	(40,000)			2,000	2,000	2,000
② Payment of liabilities	(20,000)			(20,000)	0	0	0
Balances for distribution	204,000				72,000	68,000	64,000
③ Distribution of cash to partners	(204,000)				(72,000)	(68,000)	(64,000)

Capital Deficiency

Capital deficiency means that at least one partner has a debit balance in his or her capital account at the point of final cash distribution (during step ③ as explained in the prior section). This can arise from liquidation losses, excessive withdrawals before liquidation, or recurring losses in prior periods. A partner with a capital deficiency must, if possible, cover the deficit by paying cash into the partnership.

To illustrate, assume that Zayn, Perez, and Rasheed operate their partnership in BOARDS for several years, sharing income and losses equally. The partners then decide to liquidate. Immediately prior to the final distribution of cash, the partners' recorded capital balances are Zayn, $19,000; Perez, $8,000; and Rasheed, $(3,000). Rasheed's capital deficiency means that Rasheed owes the partnership $3,000. Both Zayn and Perez have a legal claim against Rasheed's personal assets. The final distribution of cash in this case depends on how this capital deficiency is handled. Two possibilities exist: the partner pays the deficiency or the partner cannot pay the deficiency.

Partner Pays Deficiency Rasheed is obligated to pay $3,000 into the partnership to cover the deficiency. If Rasheed is willing and able to pay, the entry to record receipt of payment from Rasheed follows.

		Debit	Credit
Jan. 15	Cash	3,000	
	T. Rasheed, Capital		3,000
	To record payment of deficiency by Rasheed.		

Assets = Liabilities + Equity
+3,000 +3,000

After the $3,000 payment, the partners' capital balances are Zayn, $19,000; Perez, $8,000; and Rasheed, $0. The entry to record the final cash distributions to partners is

		Debit	Credit
Jan. 15	K. Zayn, Capital	19,000	
	H. Perez, Capital	8,000	
	Cash		27,000
	To distribute remaining cash to partners.		

Assets = Liabilities + Equity
−27,000 −19,000
−8,000

Partner Cannot Pay Deficiency The remaining partners with credit balances absorb any partner's unpaid deficiency according to their income-and-loss-sharing ratio. To illustrate, if Rasheed is unable to pay the $3,000 deficiency, Zayn and Perez absorb it. Since they share income and loss equally, Zayn and Perez each absorb $1,500 of the deficiency. This is recorded as follows.

		Debit	Credit
Jan. 15	K. Zayn, Capital	1,500	
	H. Perez, Capital	1,500	
	T. Rasheed, Capital		3,000
	To transfer Rasheed deficiency to Zayn and Perez.		

Assets = Liabilities + Equity
−1,500
−1,500
+3,000

After Zayn and Perez absorb Rasheed's deficiency, the capital accounts of the partners are Zayn, $17,500; Perez, $6,500; and Rasheed, $0. The entry to record the final cash distribution to the partners is

		Debit	Credit
Jan. 15	K. Zayn, Capital	17,500	
	H. Perez, Capital	6,500	
	Cash		24,000
	To distribute remaining cash to partners.		

Assets = Liabilities + Equity
−24,000 −17,500
−6,500

Rasheed's inability to cover this deficiency does not relieve Rasheed of the liability. If Rasheed becomes able to pay at a future date, Zayn and Perez can each collect $1,500 from Rasheed.

GLOBAL VIEW

Partnership accounting according to U.S. GAAP is similar, but not identical, to that under IFRS. This section discusses broad differences in partnership accounting, organization, admission, withdrawal, and liquidation.

Both U.S. GAAP and IFRS include broad and similar guidance for partnership accounting. Further, partnership organization is similar worldwide; however, different legal and tax systems dictate different implications and motivations for how a partnership is effectively set up.

The accounting for partnership admission, withdrawal, and liquidation is likewise similar worldwide. Specifically, procedures for admission, withdrawal, and liquidation depend on the partnership agreements constructed by all parties involved. However, different legal and tax systems impact those agreements and their implications to the parties.

Decision Analysis

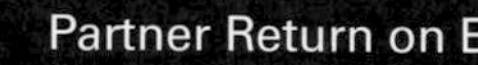

Partner Return on Equity

A1 Compute partner return on equity and use it to evaluate partnership performance.

An important role of partnership financial statements is to aid current and potential partners in evaluating partnership success compared with other opportunities. One measure of this success is the **partner return on equity** ratio:

$$\textbf{Partner return on equity} = \frac{\textbf{Partner net income}}{\textbf{Average partner equity}}$$

This measure is separately computed for each partner. To illustrate, Exhibit 12.4 reports selected data from the **Boston Celtics LP**. The return on equity for the *total* partnership is computed as $216/[($85 + $253)/2] = 127.8%. However, return on equity is quite different across the partners. For example, the **Boston Celtics LP I** partner return on equity is computed as $44/[($122 + $166)/2] = 30.6%, whereas the **Celtics LP** partner return on equity is computed as $111/[($270 + $333)/2] = 36.8%. Partner return on equity provides *each* partner an assessment of its return on its equity invested in the partnership. A specific partner often uses this return to decide whether additional investment or withdrawal of resources is best for that partner. Exhibit 12.4 reveals that the year shown produced good returns for all partners (the Boston Celtics LP II return is not computed because its average equity is negative due to an unusual and large distribution in the prior year).

EXHIBIT 12.4

Selected Data from Boston Celtics LP

($ thousands)	Total*	Boston Celtics LP I	Boston Celtics LP II	Celtics LP
Beginning-year balance	$ 85	$122	$(307)	$270
Net income (loss) for year	216	44	61	111
Cash distribution	(48)	—	—	(48)
Ending-year balance	$253	$166	$(246)	$333
Partner return on equity	**127.8%**	**30.6%**	**n.a.**	**36.8%**

* Totals may not add up due to rounding.

DEMONSTRATION PROBLEM

The following transactions and events affect the partners' capital accounts in several successive partnerships. Prepare a table with six columns, one for each of the five partners along with a total column to show the effects of the following events on the five partners' capital accounts.

Part 1

4/13/2009 Ries and Bax create R&B Company. Each invests $10,000, and they agree to share income and losses equally.

12/31/2009 R&B Co. earns $15,000 in income for its first year. Ries withdraws $4,000 from the partnership, and Bax withdraws $7,000.

1/1/2010 Royce is made a partner in RB&R Company after contributing $12,000 cash. The partners agree that a 10% interest allowance will be given on each partner's beginning-year capital balance. In addition, Bax and Royce are to receive $5,000 salary allowances. The remainder of the income or loss is to be divided evenly.

12/31/2010 The partnership's income for the year is $40,000, and withdrawals at year-end are Ries, $5,000; Bax, $12,500; and Royce, $11,000.

1/1/2011 Ries sells her interest for $20,000 to Murdock, whom Bax and Royce accept as a partner in the new BR&M Co. Income or loss is to be shared equally after Bax and Royce receive $25,000 salary allowances.

12/31/2011 The partnership's income for the year is $35,000, and year-end withdrawals are Bax, $2,500, and Royce, $2,000.

1/1/2012 Elway is admitted as a partner after investing $60,000 cash in the new Elway & Associates partnership. He is given a 50% interest in capital after the other partners transfer $3,000 to his account from each of theirs. A 20% interest allowance (on the beginning-year capital balances) will be used in sharing any income or loss, there will be no salary allowances, and Elway will receive 40% of the remaining balance—the other three partners will each get 20%.

12/31/2012 Elway & Associates earns $127,600 in income for the year, and year-end withdrawals are Bax, $25,000; Royce, $27,000; Murdock, $15,000; and Elway, $40,000.

1/1/2013 Elway buys out Bax and Royce for the balances of their capital accounts after a revaluation of the partnership assets. The revaluation gain is $50,000, which is divided in using a 1:1:1:2 ratio (Bax:Royce:Murdock:Elway). Elway pays the others from personal funds. Murdock and Elway will share income on a 1:9 ratio.

2/28/2013 The partnership earns $10,000 of income since the beginning of the year. Murdock retires and receives partnership cash equal to her capital balance. Elway takes possession of the partnership assets in his own name, and the partnership is dissolved.

Part 2

Journalize the events affecting the partnership for the year ended December 31, 2010.

PLANNING THE SOLUTION

- Evaluate each transaction's effects on the capital accounts of the partners.
- Each time a new partner is admitted or a partner withdraws, allocate any bonus based on the income-or-loss-sharing agreement.
- Each time a new partner is admitted or a partner withdraws, allocate subsequent net income or loss in accordance with the new partnership agreement.
- Prepare entries to (1) record Royce's initial investment; (2) record the allocation of interest, salaries, and remainder; (3) show the cash withdrawals from the partnership; and (4) close the withdrawal accounts on December 31, 2010.

SOLUTION TO DEMONSTRATION PROBLEM

Part 1

Event	Ries	Bax	Royce	Murdock	Elway	Total
4/13/2009						
Initial investment	$10,000	$10,000				$ 20,000
12/31/2009						
Income (equal)	7,500	7,500				15,000
Withdrawals	(4,000)	(7,000)				(11,000)
Ending balance	$13,500	$10,500				$ 24,000
1/1/2010						
New investment			$12,000			$ 12,000
12/31/2010						
10% interest	1,350	1,050	1,200			3,600
Salaries		5,000	5,000			10,000
Remainder (equal)	8,800	8,800	8,800			26,400
Withdrawals	(5,000)	(12,500)	(11,000)			(28,500)
Ending balance	$18,650	$12,850	$16,000			$ 47,500

[continued on next page]

[continued from previous page]

Event	Ries	Bax	Royce	Murdock	Elway	Total
1/1/2011						
Transfer interest	(18,650)			$18,650		$ 0
12/31/2011						
Salaries		25,000	25,000			50,000
Remainder (equal)		(5,000)	(5,000)	(5,000)		(15,000)
Withdrawals		(2,500)	(2,000)			(4,500)
Ending balance	$ 0	$30,350	$34,000	$13,650		$ 78,000
1/1/2012						
New investment					$ 60,000	60,000
Bonuses to Elway		(3,000)	(3,000)	(3,000)	9,000	0
Adjusted balance		$27,350	$31,000	$10,650	$ 69,000	$138,000
12/31/2012						
20% interest		5,470	6,200	2,130	13,800	27,600
Remainder (1:1:1:2)		20,000	20,000	20,000	40,000	100,000
Withdrawals		(25,000)	(27,000)	(15,000)	(40,000)	(107,000)
Ending balance		$27,820	$30,200	$17,780	$ 82,800	$158,600
1/1/2013						
Gain (1:1:1:2)		10,000	10,000	10,000	20,000	50,000
Adjusted balance		$37,820	$40,200	$27,780	$102,800	$208,600
Transfer interests		(37,820)	(40,200)		78,020	0
Adjusted balance		$ 0	$ 0	$27,780	$180,820	$208,600
2/28/2013						
Income (1:9)				1,000	9,000	10,000
Adjusted balance				$28,780	$189,820	$218,600
Settlements				(28,780)	(189,820)	(218,600)
Final balance				$ 0	$ 0	$ 0

Part 2

Date	Account	Debit	Credit
2010			
Jan. 1	Cash	12,000	
	Royce, Capital		12,000
	To record investment of Royce.		
Dec. 31	Income Summary	40,000	
	Ries, Capital		10,150
	Bax, Capital		14,850
	Royce, Capital		15,000
	To allocate interest, salaries, and remainders.		
Dec. 31	Ries, Withdrawals	5,000	
	Bax, Withdrawals	12,500	
	Royce, Withdrawals	11,000	
	Cash		28,500
	To record cash withdrawals by partners.		
Dec. 31	Ries, Capital	5,000	
	Bax, Capital	12,500	
	Royce, Capital	11,000	
	Ries, Withdrawals		5,000
	Bax, Withdrawals		12,500
	Royce, Withdrawals		11,000
	To close withdrawal accounts.		

Summary

C1 Identify characteristics of partnerships and similar organizations. Partnerships are voluntary associations, involve partnership agreements, have limited life, are not subject to income tax, include mutual agency, and have unlimited liability. Organizations that combine selected characteristics of partnerships and corporations include limited partnerships, limited liability partnerships, S corporations, and limited liability companies.

A1 Compute partner return on equity and use it to evaluate partnership performance. Partner return on equity provides each partner an assessment of his or her return on equity invested in the partnership.

P1 Prepare entries for partnership formation. A partner's initial investment is recorded at the market value of the assets contributed to the partnership.

P2 Allocate and record income and loss among partners. A partnership agreement should specify how to allocate partnership income or loss among partners. Allocation can be based on a stated ratio, capital balances, or salary and interest allowances to compensate partners for differences in their service and capital contributions.

P3 Account for the admission and withdrawal of partners. When a new partner buys a partnership interest directly from one or more existing partners, the amount of cash paid from one partner to another does not affect the partnership total recorded equity. When a new partner purchases equity by investing additional assets in the partnership, the new partner's investment can yield a bonus either to existing partners or to the new partner. The entry to record a withdrawal can involve payment from either (1) the existing partners' personal assets or (2) partnership assets. The latter can yield a bonus to either the withdrawing or remaining partners.

P4 Prepare entries for partnership liquidation. When a partnership is liquidated, losses and gains from selling partnership assets are allocated to the partners according to their income-and-loss-sharing ratio. If a partner's capital account has a deficiency that the partner cannot pay, the other partners share the deficit according to their relative income-and-loss-sharing ratio.

Guidance Answers to Decision Ethics

Financial Planner The partnership agreement apparently fails to mention liabilities or use the term *net assets.* To give the estate one-third of total assets is not fair to the remaining partners because if the partner had lived and the partners had decided to liquidate, the liabilities would need to be paid out of assets before any liquidation. Also, a settlement based on the deceased partner's recorded equity would fail to recognize excess of current value over book value. This value increase would be realized if the partnership were liquidated. A fair settlement would seem to be a payment to the estate for the balance of the deceased partner's equity based on the *current value of net assets.*

Guidance Answers to Quick Checks

1. (*b*)
2. *Unlimited liability* means that the creditors of a partnership require each partner to be personally responsible for all partnership debts.
3. (*c*)
4.

	Denzel	Shantell	Total
Net income			$40,000
Interest allowance (10%)	$ 7,000	$ 3,500	10,500
Balance of income	↓	↓	**$29,500**
Balance allocated equally	14,750	14,750	29,500
Balance of income			$ 0
Income of partners	**$21,750**	**$18,250**	

Key Terms

mhhe.com/wildFAP20e

C corporation (p. 482)
General partner (p. 481)
General partnership (p. 481)
Limited liability company (LLC) (p. 482)
Limited liability partnership (p. 481)
Limited partners (p. 481)
Limited partnership (p. 481)
Mutual agency (p. 480)
Partner return on equity (p. 492)
Partnership (p. 480)
Partnership contract (p. 480)
Partnership liquidation (p. 489)
S corporation (p. 482)
Statement of partners' equity (p. 485)
Unlimited liability (p. 481)

Multiple Choice Quiz

Answers on p. 505

mhhe.com/wildFAP20e

Additional Quiz Questions are available at the book's Website.

1. Stokely and Leder are forming a partnership. Stokely invests a building that has a market value of $250,000; and the partnership assumes responsibility for a $50,000 note secured by a mortgage on that building. Leder invests $100,000 cash. For the partnership, the amounts recorded for the building and for Stokely's Capital account are these:
   a. Building, $250,000; Stokely, Capital, $250,000.
   b. Building, $200,000; Stokely, Capital, $200,000.
   c. Building, $200,000; Stokely, Capital, $100,000.
   d. Building, $200,000; Stokely, Capital, $250,000.
   e. Building, $250,000; Stokely, Capital, $200,000.
2. Katherine, Alliah, and Paulina form a partnership. Katherine contributes $150,000, Alliah contributes $150,000, and Paulina contributes $100,000. Their partnership agreement calls for the income or loss division to be based on the ratio of capital invested. If the partnership reports income of $90,000 for its first year of operations, what amount of income is credited to Paulina's capital account?
   a. $22,500
   b. $25,000
   c. $45,000
   d. $30,000
   e. $90,000
3. Jamison and Blue form a partnership with capital contributions of $600,000 and $800,000, respectively. Their partnership agreement calls for Jamison to receive $120,000 per year in salary. Also, each partner is to receive an interest allowance equal to 10% of the partner's beginning capital contributions, with any remaining income or loss divided equally. If net income for its initial year is $270,000, then Jamison's and Blue's respective shares are
   a. $135,000; $135,000.
   b. $154,286; $115,714.
   c. $120,000; $150,000.
   d. $185,000; $85,000.
   e. $85,000; $185,000.
4. Hansen and Fleming are partners and share equally in income or loss. Hansen's current capital balance in the partnership is $125,000 and Fleming's is $124,000. Hansen and Fleming agree to accept Black with a 20% interest. Black invests $75,000 in the partnership. The bonus granted to Hansen and Fleming equals
   a. $13,000 each.
   b. $5,100 each.
   c. $4,000 each.
   d. $5,285 to Hansen; $4,915 to Fleming.
   e. $0; Hansen and Fleming grant a bonus to Black.
5. Mee Su is a partner in Hartford Partners, LLC. Her partnership capital balance at the beginning of the current year was $110,000, and her ending balance was $124,000. Her share of the partnership income is $10,500. What is her partner return on equity?
   a. 8.97%
   b. 1060.00%
   c. 9.54%
   d. 1047.00%
   e. 8.47%

Icon denotes assignments that involve decision making.

Discussion Questions

1. If a partnership contract does not state the period of time the partnership is to exist, when does the partnership end?
2. What does the term *mutual agency* mean when applied to a partnership?
3. Can partners limit the right of a partner to commit their partnership to contracts? Would such an agreement be binding (*a*) on the partners and (*b*) on outsiders?
4. Assume that Amey and Lacey are partners. Lacey dies, and her son claims the right to take his mother's place in the partnership. Does he have this right? Why or why not?
5. Assume that the Barnes and Ardmore partnership agreement provides for a two-third/one-third sharing of income but says nothing about losses. The first year of partnership operation resulted in a loss, and Barnes argues that the loss should be shared equally because the partnership agreement said nothing about sharing losses. Is Barnes correct? Explain.
6. Allocation of partnership income among the partners appears on what financial statement?
7. What does the term *unlimited liability* mean when it is applied to partnership members?
8. How does a general partnership differ from a limited partnership?
9. George, Burton, and Dillman have been partners for three years. The partnership is being dissolved. George is leaving the firm, but Burton and Dillman plan to carry on the business. In the final settlement, George places a $75,000 salary claim against the partnership. He contends that he has a claim for a salary of $25,000 for each year because he devoted all of his time for three years to the affairs of the partnership. Is his claim valid? Why or why not?
10. Kay, Kat, and Kim are partners. In a liquidation, Kay's share of partnership losses exceeds her capital account balance. Moreover, she is unable to meet the deficit from her personal assets, and her partners shared the excess losses. Does this relieve Kay of liability?
11. After all partnership assets have been converted to cash and all liabilities paid, the remaining cash should equal the sum of the balances of the partners' capital accounts. Why?
12. Assume a partner withdraws from a partnership and receives assets of greater value than the book value of his equity. Should the remaining partners share the resulting reduction in their equities in the ratio of their relative capital balances or according to their income-and-loss-sharing ratio?

connect

QUICK STUDY

QS 12-1
Partnership liability
C1 

Kent and Davis are partners in operating a store. Without consulting Kent, Davis enters into a contract to purchase merchandise for the store. Kent contends that he did not authorize the order and refuses to pay for it. The vendor sues the partners for the contract price of the merchandise. (*a*) Must the partnership pay for the merchandise? Why? (*b*) Does your answer differ if Kent and Davis are partners in a public accounting firm? Explain.

QS 12-2
Liability in limited partnerships
P1 

Lamb organized a limited partnership and is the only general partner. Maxi invested $20,000 in the partnership and was admitted as a limited partner with the understanding that she would receive 10% of the profits. After two unprofitable years, the partnership ceased doing business. At that point, partnership liabilities were $85,000 larger than partnership assets. How much money can the partnership's creditors obtain from Maxi's personal assets to satisfy the unpaid partnership debts?

QS 12-3
Partnership income allocation
P2

Ann Keeley and Susie Norton are partners in a business they started two years ago. The partnership agreement states that Keeley should receive a salary allowance of $40,000 and that Norton should receive a $30,000 salary allowance. Any remaining income or loss is to be shared equally. Determine each partner's share of the current year's net income of $210,000.

QS 12-4
Partnership income allocation
P2 

Jake and Ness are partners who agree that Jake will receive a $60,000 salary allowance and that any remaining income or loss will be shared equally. If Ness's capital account is credited for $1,000 as his share of the net income in a given period, how much net income did the partnership earn in that period?

QS 12-5
Admission of a partner
P3

Jones and Bordan are partners, each with $30,000 in their partnership capital accounts. Holly is admitted to the partnership by investing $30,000 cash. Make the entry to show Holly's admission to the partnership.

QS 12-6
Partner admission through purchase of interest
P3

Mintz agrees to pay Bogg and Heyer $10,000 each for a one-third (33⅓%) interest in the Bogg and Heyer partnership. Immediately prior to Mintz's admission, each partner had a $30,000 capital balance. Make the journal entry to record Mintz's purchase of the partners' interest.

QS 12-7
Liquidation of partnership
P4

The Red, White & Blue partnership was begun with investments by the partners as follows: Red, $175,000; White, $220,000; and Blue, $205,000. The operations did not go well, and the partners eventually decided to liquidate the partnership, sharing all losses equally. On August 31, after all assets were converted to cash and all creditors were paid, only $60,000 in partnership cash remained.

1. Compute the capital account balance of each partner after the liquidation of assets and the payment of creditors.

2. Assume that any partner with a deficit agrees to pay cash to the partnership to cover the deficit. Present the journal entries on August 31 to record (*a*) the cash receipt from the deficient partner(s) and (*b*) the final disbursement of cash to the partners.

3. Assume that any partner with a deficit is not able to reimburse the partnership. Present journal entries (*a*) to transfer the deficit of any deficient partners to the other partners and (*b*) to record the final disbursement of cash to the partners.

Check (1) Red, $(5,000)

QS 12-8
Partner return on equity
A1

Gilson and Lott's company is organized as a partnership. At the prior year-end, partnership equity totaled $300,000 ($200,000 from Gilson and $100,000 from Lott). For the current year, partnership net income is $50,000 ($40,000 allocated to Gilson and $10,000 allocated to Lott), and year-end total partnership equity is $400,000 ($280,000 from Gilson and $120,000 from Lott). Compute the total partnership return on equity *and* the individual partner return on equity ratios.

connect

EXERCISES

Exercise 12-1
Forms of organization
C1  

For each of the following separate cases, recommend a form of business organization. With each recommendation, explain how business income would be taxed if the owners adopt the form of organization recommended. Also list several advantages that the owners will enjoy from the form of business organization that you recommend.

a. Milan has been out of school for about six years and has become quite knowledgeable about the residential real estate market. He would like to organize a company that buys and sells real estate. Milan believes he has the expertise to manage the company but needs funds to invest in residential property.

b. Dr. Langholz and Dr. Clark are recent graduates from medical residency programs. Both are family practice physicians and would like to open a clinic in an underserved rural area. Although neither has any funds to bring to the new venture, an investor has expressed interest in making a loan to provide start-up funds for their practice.

c. Ross, Jenks and Keim are recent college graduates in computer science. They want to start a Website development company. They all have college debts and currently do not own any substantial computer equipment needed to get the company started.

Exercise 12-2
Characteristics of partnerships
C1

Next to the following list of eight characteristics of business organizations, enter a brief description of how each characteristic applies to general partnerships.

Characteristic	Application to General Partnerships
1. Ease of formation	
2. Transferability of ownership	
3. Ability to raise large amounts of capital	
4. Life	
5. Owners' liability	
6. Legal status	
7. Tax status of income	
8. Owners' authority	

Exercise 12-3
Journalizing partnership formation
P2

Anita Kroll and Aaron Rogers organize a partnership on January 1. Kroll's initial net investment is $60,000, consisting of cash ($14,000), equipment ($66,000), and a note payable reflecting a bank loan for the new business ($20,000). Rogers's initial investment is cash of $25,000. These amounts are the values agreed on by both partners. Prepare journal entries to record (1) Kroll's investment and (2) Rogers's investment.

Exercise 12-4
Journalizing partnership transactions
P2

On March 1, 2011, Abbey and Dames formed a partnership. Abbey contributed $88,000 cash and Dames contributed land valued at $70,000 and a building valued at $100,000. The partnership also assumed responsibility for Dames's $80,000 long-term note payable associated with the land and building. The partners agreed to share income as follows: Abbey is to receive an annual salary allowance of $30,000, both are to receive an annual interest allowance of 10% of their beginning-year capital investment, and any remaining income or loss is to be shared equally. On October 20, 2011, Abbey withdrew $32,000 cash and Dames withdrew $25,000 cash. After the adjusting and closing entries are made to the revenue and expense accounts at December 31, 2011, the Income Summary account had a credit balance of $79,000.

1. Prepare journal entries to record (*a*) the partners' initial capital investments, (*b*) their cash withdrawals, and (*c*) the December 31 closing of both the Withdrawals and Income Summary accounts.

2. Determine the balances of the partners' capital accounts as of December 31, 2011.

Check (2) Dames, $89,600

Exercise 12-5
Income allocation in a partnership
P2

Cosmo and Ellis began a partnership by investing $50,000 and $75,000, respectively. During its first year, the partnership earned $165,000. Prepare calculations showing how the $165,000 income should be allocated to the partners under each of the following three separate plans for sharing income and loss: (1) the partners failed to agree on a method to share income; (2) the partners agreed to share income and loss in proportion to their initial investments (round amounts to the nearest dollar); and (3) the partners agreed to share income by granting a $55,000 per year salary allowance to Cosmo, a $45,000 per year salary allowance to Ellis, 10% interest on their initial capital investments, and the remaining balance shared equally.

Check Plan 3, Cosmo, $86,250

Exercise 12-6
Income allocation in a partnership
P2

Assume that the partners of Exercise 12-5 agreed to share net income and loss by granting annual salary allowances of $55,000 to Cosmo and $45,000 to Ellis, 10% interest allowances on their investments, and any remaining balance shared equally.

1. Determine the partners' shares of Cosmo and Ellis given a first-year net income of $94,400.
2. Determine the partners' shares of Cosmo and Ellis given a first-year net loss of $15,700.

Check (2) Cosmo, $(4,100)

Exercise 12-7
Sale of partnership interest
P3

The partners in the Biz Partnership have agreed that partner Mona may sell her $90,000 equity in the partnership to Seal, for which Seal will pay Mona $75,000. Present the partnership's journal entry to record the sale of Mona's interest to Seal on September 30.

Exercise 12-8
Admission of new partner
P3

The Treed Partnership has total partners' equity of $510,000, which is made up of Elm, Capital, $400,000, and Oak, Capital, $110,000. The partners share net income and loss in a ratio of 80% to Elm and 20% to Oak. On November 1, Ash is admitted to the partnership and given a 15% interest in equity and a 15% share in any income and loss. Prepare the journal entry to record the admission of Ash under each of the following separate assumptions: Ash invests cash of (1) $90,000; (2) $125,000; and (3) $60,000.

Exercise 12-9
Retirement of partner
P3

Holland, Flowers, and Tulip have been partners while sharing net income and loss in a 5:3:2 ratio. On January 31, the date Tulip retires from the partnership, the equities of the partners are Holland, $350,000; Flowers, $240,000; and Tulip, $180,000. Present journal entries to record Tulip's retirement under each of the following separate assumptions: Tulip is paid for her equity using partnership cash of (1) $180,000; (2) $200,000; and (3) $150,000.

Exercise 12-10
Liquidation of partnership
P4

Tuttle, Ritter, and Lee are partners who share income and loss in a 1:4:5 ratio. After lengthy disagreements among the partners and several unprofitable periods, the partners decide to liquidate the partnership. Immediately before liquidation, the partnership balance sheet shows total assets, $116,000; total liabilities, $88,000; Tuttle, Capital, $1,200; Ritter, Capital, $11,700; and Lee, Capital, $15,100. The cash proceeds from selling the assets were sufficient to repay all but $24,000 to the creditors. (*a*) Calculate the loss from selling the assets. (*b*) Allocate the loss to the partners. (*c*) Determine how much of the remaining liability should be paid by each partner.

Check (b) Lee, Capital after allocation, $(10,900)

Exercise 12-11
Liquidation of limited partnership
P4

Assume that the Tuttle, Ritter, and Lee partnership of Exercise 12-10 is a limited partnership. Tuttle and Ritter are general partners and Lee is a limited partner. How much of the remaining $24,000 liability should be paid by each partner? (Round amounts to the nearest dollar.)

Exercise 12-12
Partner return on equity
A1

Hunt Sports Enterprises LP is organized as a limited partnership consisting of two individual partners: Soccer LP and Football LP. Both partners separately operate a minor league soccer team and a semipro football team. Compute partner return on equity for each limited partnership (and the total) for the year ended June 30, 2011, using the following selected data on partner capital balances from Hunt Sports Enterprises LP.

	Soccer LP	Football LP	Total
Balance at 6/30/2010	$378,000	$1,516,000	$1,894,000
Annual net income	44,268	891,796	936,064
Cash distribution	—	(100,000)	(100,000)
Balance at 6/30/2011	$422,268	$2,307,796	$2,730,064

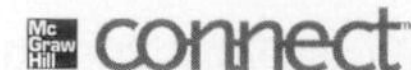

PROBLEM SET A

Problem 12-1A
Allocating partnership income
P2

Kim Ries, Tere Bax, and Josh Thomas invested $40,000, $56,000, and $64,000, respectively, in a partnership. During its first calendar year, the firm earned $124,500.

Required

Prepare the entry to close the firm's Income Summary account as of its December 31 year-end and to allocate the $124,500 net income to the partners under each of the following separate assumptions: The partners (1) have no agreement on the method of sharing income and loss; (2) agreed to share income and loss in the ratio of their beginning capital investments; and (3) agreed to share income and loss by providing annual salary allowances of $33,000 to Ries, $28,000 to Bax, and $40,000 to Thomas; granting 10% interest on the partners' beginning capital investments; and sharing the remainder equally.

Check (3) Thomas, Capital, $48,900

Problem 12-2A
Allocating partnership income and loss; sequential years
P2

mhhe.com/wildFAP20e

Rex Baker and Ty Farney are forming a partnership to which Baker will devote one-half time and Farney will devote full time. They have discussed the following alternative plans for sharing income and loss: (*a*) in the ratio of their initial capital investments, which they have agreed will be $21,000 for Baker and $31,500 for Farney; (*b*) in proportion to the time devoted to the business; (*c*) a salary allowance of $3,000 per month to Farney and the balance in accordance with the ratio of their initial capital investments; or (*d*) a salary allowance of $3,000 per month to Farney, 10% interest on their initial capital investments, and the balance shared equally. The partners expect the business to perform as follows: year 1, $18,000 net loss; year 2, $45,000 net income; and year 3, $75,000 net income.

Required

Prepare three tables with the following column headings.

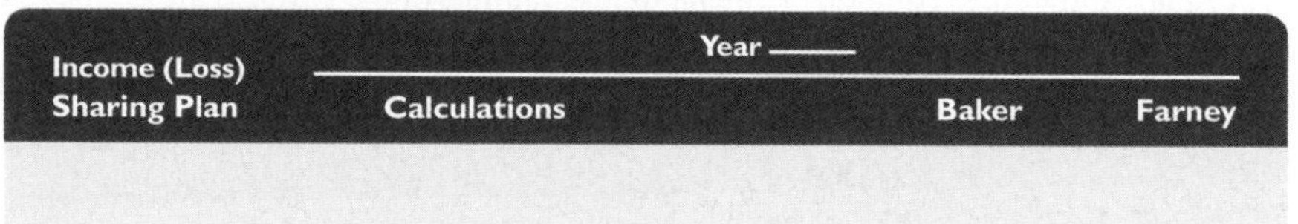

Income (Loss) Sharing Plan	Year ____		
	Calculations	Baker	Farney

Complete the tables, one for each of the first three years, by showing how to allocate partnership income or loss to the partners under each of the four plans being considered. (Round answers to the nearest whole dollar.)

Check Plan d, year 1, Farney's share, $9,525

Problem 12-3A
Partnership income allocation, statement of partners' equity, and closing entries
P2

mhhe.com/wildFAP20e

Will Beck, Ron Beck, and Barb Beck formed the BBB Partnership by making capital contributions of $183,750, $131,250, and $210,000, respectively. They predict annual partnership net income of $225,000 and are considering the following alternative plans of sharing income and loss: (*a*) equally; (*b*) in the ratio of their initial capital investments; or (*c*) salary allowances of $40,000 to Will, $30,000 to Ron, and $45,000 to Barb; interest allowances of 10% on their initial capital investments; and the balance shared equally.

Required

1. Prepare a table with the following column headings.

Income (Loss) Sharing Plan	Calculations	Will	Ron	Barb	Total

Use the table to show how to distribute net income of $225,000 for the calendar year under each of the alternative plans being considered. (Round answers to the nearest whole dollar.)

2. Prepare a statement of partners' equity showing the allocation of income to the partners assuming they agree to use plan (*c*), that income earned is $104,500, and that Will, Ron, and Barb withdraw $17,000, $24,000, and $32,000, respectively, at year-end.
3. Prepare the December 31 journal entry to close Income Summary assuming they agree to use plan (*c*) and that net income is $104,500. Also close the withdrawals accounts.

Check (2) Barb, Ending Capital, $223,000

Problem 12-4A
Partner withdrawal and admission
P3

Part 1. Goering, Zarcus, and Schmit are partners and share income and loss in a 3:2:5 ratio. The partnership's capital balances are as follows: Goering, $84,000; Zarcus, $69,000; and Schmit, $147,000. Zarcus decides to withdraw from the partnership, and the partners agree to not have the assets revalued upon Zarcus's retirement. Prepare journal entries to record Zarcus's February 1 withdrawal from the partnership under each of the following separate assumptions: Zarcus (*a*) sells her interest to Getz for $80,000 after Goering and Schmit approve the entry of Getz as a partner; (*b*) gives her interest to a son-in-law, Swanson, and thereafter Goering and Schmit accept Swanson as a partner; (*c*) is paid $69,000 in partnership cash for her equity; (*d*) is paid $107,000 in partnership cash for her equity; and (*e*) is paid $15,000 in partnership cash plus equipment recorded on the partnership books at $35,000 less its accumulated depreciation of $11,600.

Check (1*e*) Cr. Schmit, Capital, $19,125

Part 2. Assume that Zarcus does not retire from the partnership described in Part 1. Instead, Ford is admitted to the partnership on February 1 with a 25% equity. Prepare journal entries to record Ford's entry into the partnership under each of the following separate assumptions: Ford invests (*a*) $100,000; (*b*) $74,000; and (*c*) $131,000.

(2*c*) Cr. Zarcus, Capital, $4,650

Problem 12-5A
Liquidation of a partnership
P4

Quick, Drake, and Sage share income and loss in a 3:2:1 ratio. The partners have decided to liquidate their partnership. On the day of liquidation their balance sheet appears as follows.

QUICK, DRAKE, AND SAGE
Balance Sheet
May 31

Assets		Liabilities and Equity	
Cash	$ 90,400	Accounts payable	$122,750
Inventory	268,600	Quick, Capital	46,500
		Drake, Capital	106,250
		Sage, Capital	83,500
Total assets	$359,000	Total liabilities and equity	$359,000

Required

Prepare journal entries for (*a*) the sale of inventory, (*b*) the allocation of its gain or loss, (*c*) the payment of liabilities at book value, and (*d*) the distribution of cash in each of the following separate cases: Inventory is sold for (1) $300,000; (2) $250,000; (3) $160,000 and any partners with capital deficits pay in the amount of their deficits; and (4) $125,000 and the partners have no assets other than those invested in the partnership. (Round to the nearest dollar.)

Check (4) Cash distribution: Sage, $51,134

PROBLEM SET B

Problem 12-1B
Allocating partnership income
P2

Matt Albin, Ryan Peters and Seth Ramsey invested $82,000, $49,200 and $32,800, respectively, in a partnership. During its first calendar year, the firm earned $135,000.

Required

Prepare the entry to close the firm's Income Summary account as of its December 31 year-end and to allocate the $135,000 net income to the partners under each of the following separate assumptions. (Round answers to whole dollars.) The partners (1) have no agreement on the method of sharing income and loss; (2) agreed to share income and loss in the ratio of their beginning capital investments; and (3) agreed to share income and loss by providing annual salary allowances of $48,000 to Albin, $36,000 to Peters, and $25,000 to Ramsey; granting 10% interest on the partners' beginning capital investments; and sharing the remainder equally.

Check (3) Ramsey, Capital, $31,480

Problem 12-2B
Allocating partnership income and loss; sequential years
P2

Maria Karto and J.R. Black are forming a partnership to which Karto will devote one-third time and Black will devote full time. They have discussed the following alternative plans for sharing income and loss: (*a*) in the ratio of their initial capital investments, which they have agreed will be $52,000 for Karto and $78,000 for Black; (*b*) in proportion to the time devoted to the business; (*c*) a salary allowance of $2,000 per month to Black and the balance in accordance with the ratio of their initial capital investments; or (*d*) a salary allowance of $2,000 per month to Black, 10% interest on their initial capital investments, and the balance shared equally. The partners expect the business to perform as follows: year 1, $18,000 net loss; year 2, $38,000 net income; and year 3, $94,000 net income.

Required

Prepare three tables with the following column headings.

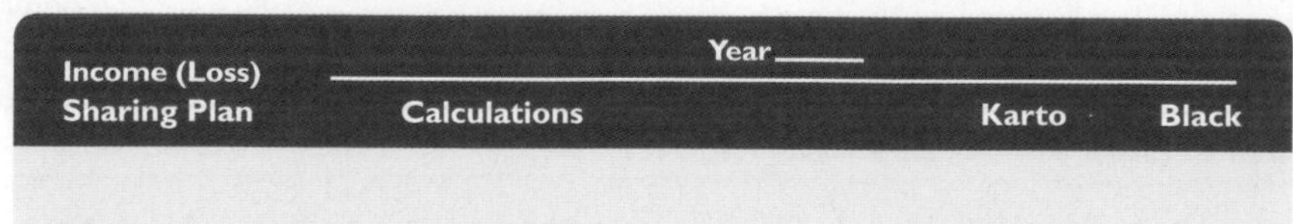

Income (Loss) Sharing Plan	Calculations	Year ____ Karto	Black

Check Plan d, year 1, Black's share, $4,300

Complete the tables, one for each of the first three years, by showing how to allocate partnership income or loss to the partners under each of the four plans being considered. (Round answers to the nearest whole dollar.)

Problem 12-3B
Partnership income allocation, statement of partners' equity, and closing entries
P2

Staci Cook, Lin Xi, and Kevin Schwartz formed the CXS Partnership by making capital contributions of $72,000, $108,000, and $60,000, respectively. They predict annual partnership net income of $120,000 and are considering the following alternative plans of sharing income and loss: (*a*) equally; (*b*) in the ratio of their initial capital investments; or (*c*) salary allowances of $20,000 to Cook, $15,000 to Xi, and $40,000 to Schwartz; interest allowances of 12% on their initial capital investments; and the balance shared equally.

Required

1. Prepare a table with the following column headings.

Income (Loss) Sharing Plan	Calculations	Cook	Xi	Schwartz	Total

Use the table to show how to distribute net income of $120,000 for the calendar year under each of the alternative plans being considered. (Round answers to the nearest whole dollar.)

Check (2) Schwartz, Ending Capital, $75,200

2. Prepare a statement of partners' equity showing the allocation of income to the partners assuming they agree to use plan (*c*), that income earned is $43,800, and that Cook, Xi, and Schwartz withdraw $9,000, $19,000, and $12,000, respectively, at year-end.

3. Prepare the December 31 journal entry to close Income Summary assuming they agree to use plan (*c*) and that net income is $43,800. Also close the withdrawals accounts.

Problem 12-4B
Partner withdrawal and admission
P3

Part 1. Gibbs, Mier, and Hill are partners and share income and loss in a 5:1:4 ratio. The partnership's capital balances are as follows: Gibbs, $303,000; Mier, $74,000; and Hill, $223,000. Gibbs decides to withdraw from the partnership, and the partners agree not to have the assets revalued upon Gibbs's retirement. Prepare journal entries to record Gibbs's April 30 withdrawal from the partnership under each of the following separate assumptions: Gibbs (*a*) sells her interest to Brady for $250,000 after Mier and Hill approve the entry of Brady as a partner; (*b*) gives her interest to a daughter-in-law, Cannon, and thereafter Mier and Hill accept Cannon as a partner; (*c*) is paid $303,000 in partnership cash for her equity; (*d*) is paid $175,000 in partnership cash for her equity; and (*e*) is paid $100,000 in partnership cash plus manufacturing equipment recorded on the partnership books at $269,000 less its accumulated depreciation of $168,000.

Check (1*e*) Cr. Hill, Capital, $81,600

Part 2. Assume that Gibbs does not retire from the partnership described in Part 1. Instead, Brise is admitted to the partnership on April 30 with a 20% equity. Prepare journal entries to record the entry of Brise under each of the following separate assumptions: Brise invests (*a*) $150,000; (*b*) $98,000; and (*c*) $213,000.

Check (2*c*) Cr. Mier, Capital, $5,040

Problem 12-5B
Liquidation of a partnership
P4

Asure, Ramirez, and Soney, who share income and loss in a 2:1:2 ratio, plan to liquidate their partnership. At liquidation, their balance sheet appears as follows.

ASURE, RAMIREZ, AND SONEY Balance Sheet January 18			
Assets		**Liabilities and Equity**	
Cash	$174,300	Accounts payable	$171,300
Equipment	308,600	Asure, Capital	150,200
		Ramirez, Capital	97,900
		Soney, Capital	63,500
Total assets	$482,900	Total liabilities and equity	$482,900

Required

Prepare journal entries for (*a*) the sale of equipment, (*b*) the allocation of its gain or loss, (*c*) the payment of liabilities at book value, and (*d*) the distribution of cash in each of the following separate cases: Equipment is sold for (1) $325,000; (2) $265,000; (3) $100,000 and any partners with capital deficits pay in the amount of their deficits; and (4) $75,000 and the partners have no assets other than those invested in the partnership. (Round amounts to the nearest dollar.)

Check (4) Cash distribution: Asure, $36,800

SERIAL PROBLEM

Business Solutions
P3

(This serial problem began in Chapter 1 and continues through most of the book. If previous chapter segments were not completed, the serial problem can begin at this point. It is helpful, but not necessary, to use the Working Papers that accompany the book.)

SP 12 At the start of 2012, Santana Rey is considering adding a partner to her business. She envisions the new partner taking the lead in generating sales of both services and merchandise for Business Solutions. S. Rey's equity in Business Solutions as of January 1, 2012, is reflected in the following capital balance.

S. Rey, Capital	$80,360

Required

1. S. Rey is evaluating whether the prospective partner should be an equal partner with respect to capital investment and profit sharing (1:1) or whether the agreement should be 4:1 with Rey retaining four-fifths interest with rights to four-fifths of the net income or loss. What factors should she consider in deciding which partnership agreement to offer?
2. Prepare the January 1, 2012, journal entry(ies) necessary to admit a new partner to Business Solutions through the purchase of a partnership interest for each of the following two separate cases: (*a*) 1:1 sharing agreement and (*b*) 4:1 sharing agreement.
3. Prepare the January 1, 2012, journal entry(ies) required to admit a new partner if the new partner invests cash of $20,090.
4. After posting the entry in part 3, what would be the new partner's equity percentage?

Beyond the Numbers

REPORTING IN ACTION

C1 

RIM

BTN 12-1 Take a step back in time and imagine **Research In Motion** in its infancy as a company. The year is 1984.

Required

1. Read the history of Research In Motion at www.RIM.com. Identify the two partners that founded the company.
2. Assume that Research In Motion was originally organized as a partnership. RIM's income statement in Appendix A varies in several key ways from what it would look like for a partnership. Identify at least two ways in which a corporate income statement differs from a partnership income statement.
3. Compare the Research In Motion balance sheet in Appendix A to what a partnership balance sheet would have shown. Identify and explain any account differences we would anticipate.

COMPARATIVE ANALYSIS

C1 

RIM

Apple

BTN 12-2 Over the years **Research In Motion** and **Apple** have evolved into large corporations. Today it is difficult to imagine them as fledgling start-ups. Research each company's history online.

Required

1. Which company is older?
2. In what years did each company first achieve $1,000,000,000 in sales?
3. In what years did each company have its first public offering of stock?

ETHICS CHALLENGE

P2   

BTN 12-3 Doctors Maben, Orlando, and Clark have been in a group practice for several years. Maben and Orlando are family practice physicians, and Clark is a general surgeon. Clark receives many referrals for surgery from his family practice partners. Upon the partnership's original formation, the three doctors agreed to a two-part formula to share income. Every month each doctor receives a salary allowance of $3,000. Additional income is divided according to a percent of patient charges the doctors generate for the month. In the current month, Maben generated 10% of the billings, Orlando 30%, and Clark 60%. The group's income for this month is $50,000. Clark has expressed dissatisfaction with the income-sharing formula and asks that income be split entirely on patient charge percents.

Required

1. Compute the income allocation for the current month using the original agreement.
2. Compute the income allocation for the current month using Clark's proposed agreement.
3. Identify the ethical components of this partnership decision for the doctors.

COMMUNICATING IN PRACTICE

C1

BTN 12-4 Assume that you are studying for an upcoming accounting exam with a good friend. Your friend says that she has a solid understanding of general partnerships but is less sure that she understands organizations that combine certain characteristics of partnerships with other forms of business organization. You offer to make some study notes for your friend to help her learn about limited partnerships, limited liability partnerships, S corporations, and limited liability companies. Prepare a one-page set of well-organized, complete study notes on these four forms of business organization.

TAKING IT TO THE NET

P1 P2 

BTN 12-5 Access the March 29, 2010, filing of the December 31, 2009, 10-K of **America First Tax Exempt Investors LP**. This company deals with tax-exempt mortgage revenue bonds that, among other things, finance student housing properties.

1. Locate its December 31, 2009, balance sheet and list the account titles reported in the equity section of the balance sheet.
2. Locate its statement of partners' capital and comprehensive income (loss). How many units of limited partnership (known as "beneficial unit certificate holders") are outstanding at December 31, 2009?
3. What is the partnership's largest asset and its amount at December 31, 2009?

TEAMWORK IN ACTION

P2

BTN 12-6 This activity requires teamwork to reinforce understanding of accounting for partnerships.

Required

1. Assume that Baker, Warner, and Rice form the BWR Partnership by making capital contributions of $200,000, $300,000, and $500,000, respectively. BWR predicts annual partnership net income of $600,000. The partners are considering various plans for sharing income and loss. Assign a different team member to compute how the projected $600,000 income would be shared under each of the following separate plans:
   - **a.** Shared equally.
   - **b.** In the ratio of the partners' initial capital investments.
   - **c.** Salary allowances of $50,000 to Baker, $60,000 to Warner, and $70,000 to Rice, with the remaining balance shared equally.
   - **d.** Interest allowances of 10% on the partners' initial capital investments, with the remaining balance shared equally.

2. In sequence, each member is to present his or her income-sharing calculations with the team.
3. As a team, identify and discuss at least one other possible way that income could be shared.

ENTREPRENEURIAL DECISION

C1  

BTN 12-7 Recall the chapter's opening feature involving Chance Claxton and Lynn Julian, and their company, **Kids Konserve**. Assume that Chance and Lynn, partners in Kids Konserve, decide to expand their business with the help of general partners.

Required

1. What details should Chance, Lynn, and their future partners specify in the general partnership agreements?
2. What advantages should Chance, Lynn, and their future partners be aware of with respect to organizing as a general partnership?
3. What disadvantages should Chance, Lynn, and their future partners be aware of with respect to organizing as a general partnership?

GLOBAL DECISION

C1  

BTN 12-8 Access **Nokia**'s Website (**www.Nokia.com**) and research the company's history.

1. When was the company founded?
2. What three companies merged to create Nokia Corporation?
3. What are some of the companies that are part of Nokia?

ANSWERS TO MULTIPLE CHOICE QUIZ

1. e; Capital = $250,000 − $50,000
2. a; $90,000 × [$100,000/($150,000 + $150,000 + $100,000)] = $22,500
3. d;

	Jamison	Blue	Total
Net income			$ 270,000
Salary allowance	$120,000		(120,000)
Interest allowance	60,000	$80,000	(140,000)
Balance of income			10,000
Balance divided equally	5,000	5,000	(10,000)
Totals	$185,000	$85,000	$ 0

4. b; Total partnership equity = $125,000 + $124,000 + $75,000 = $324,000
   Equity of Black = $324,000 × 20% = $64,800
   Bonus to old partners = $75,000 − $64,800 = $10,200, split equally
5. a; $10,500/[($110,000 + $124,000)/2] = 8.97%

Appendix

Financial Statement Information

This appendix includes financial information for (1) **Research In Motion**, (2) **Apple**, (3) **Palm**, and (4) **Nokia**. This information is taken from their annual 10-K reports (20-F for Nokia) filed with the SEC. An **annual report** is a summary of a company's financial results for the year along with its current financial condition and future plans. This report is directed to external users of financial information, but it also affects the actions and decisions of internal users.

A company often uses an annual report to showcase itself and its products. Many annual reports include photos, diagrams, and illustrations related to the company. The primary objective of annual reports, however, is the *financial section*, which communicates much information about a company, with most data drawn from the accounting information system. The layout of an annual report's financial section is fairly established and typically includes the following:

- Letter to Shareholders
- Financial History and Highlights
- Management Discussion and Analysis
- Management's Report on Financial Statements and on Internal Controls
- Report of Independent Accountants (Auditor's Report) and on Internal Controls
- Financial Statements
- Notes to Financial Statements
- List of Directors and Officers

This appendix provides the financial statements for Research In Motion (plus selected notes), Apple, Palm, and Nokia. The appendix is organized as follows:

- **Research In Motion A-2** through **A-18**
- **Apple A-19** through **A-23**
- **Palm A-24** through **A-28**
- **Nokia A-29** through **A-33**

RIM
Apple
Palm
NOKIA

Many assignments at the end of each chapter refer to information in this appendix. We encourage readers to spend time with these assignments; they are especially useful in showing the relevance and diversity of financial accounting and reporting.

Special note: The SEC maintains the EDGAR (**E**lectronic **D**ata **G**athering, **A**nalysis, and **R**etrieval) database at **www.SEC.gov**. (Over the next few years, the SEC will be moving to IDEA, short for Interactive Data Electronic Applications, which will eventually replace the EDGAR system.) The **Form 10-K** is the annual report form for most companies. It provides electronically accessible information. The **Form 10-KSB** is the annual report form filed by small businesses. It requires slightly less information than the Form 10-K. One of these forms must be filed within 90 days after the company's fiscal year-end. (Forms 10-K405, 10-KT, 10-KT405, and 10-KSB405 are slight variations of the usual form due to certain regulations or rules.)

RESEARCH IN MOTION

Research In Motion Financial Report

Research In Motion Limited
Summary Data—Management's Discussion and Analysis of Financial Condition and Results of Operations

As at and for the Fiscal Year Ended	February 27, 2010	February 28, 2009	March 1, 2008	March 3, 2007	March 4, 2006
	(In thousands, except for per share amounts)				
Revenue	**$ 14,953,224**	$ 11,065,186	$ 6,009,395	$ 3,037,103	$ 2,065,845
Cost of sales	**8,368,958**	5,967,888	2,928,814	1,379,301	925,598
Gross margin	**6,584,266**	5,097,298	3,080,581	1,657,802	1,140,247
Operating expenses					
Research and development	**964,841**	684,702	359,828	236,173	158,887
Selling, marketing and administration	**1,907,398**	1,495,697	881,482	537,922	314,317
Amortization	**310,357**	194,803	108,112	76,879	49,951
Litigation	**163,800**	—	—	—	201,791
Total operating expenses	**3,346,396**	2,375,202	1,349,422	850,974	724,946
Income from operations	**3,237,870**	2,722,096	1,731,159	806,828	415,301
Investment income	**28,640**	78,267	79,361	52,117	66,218
Income before income taxes	**3,266,510**	2,800,363	1,810,520	858,945	481,519
Provision for income taxes	**809,366**	907,747	516,653	227,373	106,863
Net income	**$ 2,457,144**	$ 1,892,616	$ 1,293,867	$ 631,572	$ 374,656
Earnings per share					
Basic	**$ 4.35**	$ 3.35	$ 2.31	$ 1.14	$ 0.66
Diluted	**$ 4.31**	$ 3.30	$ 2.26	$ 1.10	$ 0.64
Weighted-average number of shares outstanding (000's)					
Basic	**564,492**	565,059	559,778	556,059	566,742
Diluted	**569,759**	574,156	572,830	571,809	588,468
Total asset	**$ 10,204,409**	$ 8,101,372	$ 5,511,187	$ 3,088,949	$ 2,314,349
Total liabilities	**$ 2,601,746**	$ 2,227,244	$ 1,577,621	$ 605,449	$ 318,934
Total long-term liabilities	**$ 169,969**	$ 111,893	$ 103,190	$ 58,874	$ 34,709
Shareholders' equity	**$ 7,602,663**	$ 5,874,128	$ 3,933,566	$ 2,483,500	$ 1,995,415

REPORT OF INDEPENDENT REGISTERED PUBLIC ACCOUNTING FIRM

To the Shareholders of **Research In Motion Limited**

We have audited the accompanying consolidated balance sheets of **Research In Motion Limited** [the "Company"] as at February 27, 2010 and February 28, 2009, and the related consolidated statements of operations, shareholders' equity and cash flows for the years ended February 27, 2010, February 28, 2009 and March 1, 2008. These financial statements are the responsibility of the Company's management. Our responsibility is to express an opinion on these financial statements based on our audits.

We conducted our audits in accordance with Canadian generally accepted auditing standards and the standards of the Public Company Accounting Oversight Board (United States). Those standards require that we plan and perform the audit to obtain reasonable assurance about whether the financial statements are free of material misstatement. An audit includes examining, on a test basis, evidence supporting the amounts and disclosures in the financial statements. An audit also includes assessing the accounting principles used and significant estimates made by management, as well as evaluating the overall financial statement presentation. We believe that our audits provide a reasonable basis for our opinion.

In our opinion, the consolidated financial statements referred to above present fairly, in all material respects, the financial position of the Company as at February 27, 2010 and February 28, 2009, and the results of its operations and its cash flows for the years ended February 27, 2010, February 28, 2009 and March 1, 2008, in conformity with United States generally accepted accounting principles.

We also have audited, in accordance with the standards of the Public Company Accounting Oversight Board (United States), the Company's internal control over financial reporting as of February 27, 2010, based on criteria established in Internal Control-Integrated Framework issued by the Committee of Sponsoring Organizations of the Treadway Commission and our report dated April 1, 2010 expressed an unqualified opinion thereon.

Ernst & Young LLP

Kitchener, Canada,
April 1, 2010

Chartered Accountants
Licensed Public Accountants

REPORT OF INDEPENDENT REGISTERED PUBLIC ACCOUNTING FIRM ON INTERNAL CONTROL OVER FINANCIAL REPORTING

To the Shareholders of **Research In Motion Limited**

We have audited **Research In Motion Limited's** [the "Company"] internal control over financial reporting as of February 27, 2010, based on criteria established in Internal Control — Integrated Framework issued by the Committee of Sponsoring Organizations of the Treadway Commission ["the COSO criteria"]. The Company's management is responsible for maintaining effective internal control over financial reporting, and for its assessment of the effectiveness of internal control over financial reporting. Our responsibility is to express an opinion on the Company's internal control over financial reporting based on our audit.

We conducted our audit in accordance with the standards of the Public Company Accounting Oversight Board (United States). Those standards require that we plan and perform the audit to obtain reasonable assurance about whether effective internal control over financial reporting was maintained in all material respects. Our audit included obtaining an understanding of internal control over financial reporting, assessing the risk that a material weakness exists, testing and evaluating the design and operating effectiveness of internal control based on the assessed risk, and performing such other procedures as we considered necessary in the circumstances. We believe that our audit provides a reasonable basis for our opinion.

A company's internal control over financial reporting is a process designed to provide reasonable assurance regarding the reliability of financial reporting and the preparation of financial statements for external purposes in accordance with generally accepted accounting principles. A company's internal control over financial reporting includes those policies and procedures that [1] pertain to the maintenance of records that, in reasonable detail, accurately and fairly reflect the transactions and dispositions of the assets of the company; [2] provide reasonable assurance that transactions are recorded as necessary to permit preparation of financial statements in accordance with generally accepted accounting principles, and that receipts and expenditures of the company are being made only in accordance with authorizations of management and directors of the company; and [3] provide reasonable assurance regarding prevention or timely detection of unauthorized acquisition, use or disposition of the company's assets that could have a material effect on the financial statements.

Because of its inherent limitations, internal control over financial reporting may not prevent or detect misstatements. Also, projections of any evaluation of effectiveness to future periods are subject to the risk that controls may become inadequate because of changes in conditions, or that the degree of compliance with the policies or procedures may deteriorate.

In our opinion, the Company maintained, in all material respects, effective internal control over financial reporting as of February 27, 2010, based on the COSO criteria.

We also have audited, in accordance with the standards of the Public Company Accounting Oversight Board (United States), the consolidated balance sheets of the Company as at February 27, 2010 and February 28, 2009, and the consolidated statements of operations, shareholders' equity and cash flows for the years ended February 27, 2010, February 28, 2009 and March 1, 2008 of the Company and our report dated April 1, 2010 expressed an unqualified opinion thereon.

Ernst & Young LLP

Chartered Accountants
Licensed Public Accountants

Kitchener, Canada,
April 1, 2010.

Research In Motion Limited
Consolidated Balance Sheets

($US, in thousands)	February 27, 2010	February 28, 2009
Assets		
Current		
Cash and cash equivalents	$ 1,550,861	$ 835,546
Short-term investments	360,614	682,666
Accounts receivable, net	2,593,742	2,112,117
Other receivables	206,373	157,728
Inventories	621,611	682,400
Other current assets	285,539	187,257
Deferred income tax asset	193,916	183,872
Total current assets	5,812,656	4,841,586
Long-term investments	958,248	720,635
Property, plant and equipment, net	1,956,581	1,334,648
Intangible assets, net	1,326,363	1,066,527
Goodwill	150,561	137,572
Deferred income tax asset	—	404
Total assets	$10,204,409	$8,101,372
Liabilities		
Current		
Accounts payable	$ 615,620	$ 448,339
Accrued liabilities	1,638,260	1,238,602
Income taxes payable	95,650	361,460
Deferred revenue	67,573	53,834
Deferred income tax liability	14,674	13,116
Total current liabilities	2,431,777	2,115,351
Deferred income tax liability	141,382	87,917
Income taxes payable	28,587	23,976
Total liabilities	2,601,746	2,227,244
Shareholders' Equity		
Capital stock		
Preferred shares, authorized unlimited number of non-voting, cumulative, redeemable and retractable	—	—
Common shares, authorized unlimited number of non-voting, redeemable, retractable Class A common shares and unlimited number of voting common shares. Issued — 557,328,394 voting common shares (February 28, 2009 — 566,218,819)	2,207,609	2,208,235
Treasury stock		
February 27, 2010 — 1,458,950 (February 28, 2009 — nil)	(94,463)	—
Retained earnings	5,274,365	3,545,710
Additional paid-in capital	164,060	119,726
Accumulated other comprehensive income	51,092	457
Total shareholders equity	7,602,663	5,874,128
Total liabilities and shareholders' equity	$10,204,409	$8,101,372

Research In Motion Limited
Consolidated Statements of Operations

($US, in thousands, except per share data) For the Year Ended	February 27, 2010	February 28, 2009	March 1, 2008
Revenue			
Devices and other	$12,535,998	$ 9,410,755	$4,914,366
Service and software	2,417,226	1,654,431	1,095,029
Total revenue	$14,953,224	11,065,186	6,009,395
Cost of sales			
Devices and other	7,979,163	5,718,041	2,758,250
Service and software	389,795	249,847	170,564
Total cost of sales	8,368,958	5,967,888	2,928,814
Gross margin	6,584,266	5,097,298	3,080,581
Operating expenses			
Research and development	964,841	684,702	359,828
Selling, marketing and administration	1,907,398	1,495,697	881,482
Amortization	310,357	194,803	108,112
Litigation	163,800	—	—
Total operating expenses	3,346,396	2,375,202	1,349,422
Income from operations	3,237,870	2,722,096	1,731,159
Investment income	28,640	78,267	79,361
Income before income taxes	3,266,510	2,800,363	1,810,520
Provision for income taxes	809,366	907,747	516,653
Net income	$ 2,457,144	$ 1,892,616	$1,293,867
Earnings per share			
Basic	$ 4.35	$ 3.35	$ 2.31
Diluted	$ 4.31	$ 3.30	$ 2.26

Research In Motion Limited

Consolidated Statements of Shareholders' Equity

($US, in thousands)	Capital Stock	Additional Paid-In Capital	Treasury Stock	Retained Earnings	Accumulated Other Comprehensive Income (Loss)	Total
Balance as at March 3, 2007	$2,099,696	$ 36,093	$ —	$ 359,227	$(11,516)	$2,483,500
Comprehensive income (loss):						
Net income	—	—	—	1,293,867	—	1,293,867
Net change in unrealized gains on available-for-sale investments	—	—	—	—	13,467	13,467
Net change in fair value of derivatives designated as cash flow hedges during the year	—	—	—	—	37,564	37,564
Amounts reclassified to earnings during the year	—	—	—	—	(9,232)	(9,232)
Other paid-in capital	—	9,626	—	—	—	9,626
Shares issued:						
Exercise of stock options	62,889	—	—	—	—	62,889
Transfers to capital stock from stock option exercises	7,271	(7,271)	—	—	—	—
Stock-based compensation	—	33,700	—	—	—	33,700
Excess tax benefits from stock-based compensation	—	8,185	—	—	—	8,185
Balance as at March 1, 2008	$2,169,856	$ 80,333	$ —	$1,653,094	$ 30,283	$3,933,566
Comprehensive income (loss):						
Net income	—	—	—	1,892,616	—	1,892,616
Net change in unrealized gains on available-for-sale investments	—	—	—	—	(7,161)	(7,161)
Net change in fair value of derivatives designated as cash flow hedges during the year	—	—	—	—	(6,168)	(6,168)
Amounts reclassified to earnings during the year	—	—	—	—	(16,497)	(16,497)
Shares issued:						
Exercise of stock options	27,024	—	—	—	—	27,024
Transfers to capital stock from stock option exercises	11,355	(11,355)	—	—	—	—
Stock-based compensation	—	38,100	—	—	—	38,100
Excess tax benefits from stock-based compensation	—	12,648	—	—	—	12,648
Balance as at February 28, 2009	$2,208,233	$119,726	$	$3,545,710	$ 457	$5,874,128
Comprehensive income:						
Net income	—	—	—	2,457,144	—	2,457,144
Net change in unrealized gains on available-for-sale investments	—	—	—	—	6,803	6,803
Net change in fair value of derivatives designated as cash flow hedges during the year	—	—	—	—	28,324	28,324
Amounts reclassified to earnings during the year	—	—	—	—	15,508	15,508
Shares issued:						
Exercise of stock options	30,246	—	—	—	—	30,246
Transfers to capital stock from stock option exercises	15,647	(15,647)	—	—	—	—
Stock-based compensation	—	58,038	—	—	—	58,038
Excess tax benefits from stock-based compensation	—	1,943	—	—	—	1,943
Purchase of treasury stock	—	—	(94,463)	—	—	(94,463)
Common shares repurchased	(46,519)			(728,489)		(775,008)
Balance as at February 27, 2010	$2,207,609	$164,060	$(94,463)	$5,274,365	$ 51,092	$7,602,663

Research In Motion Limited
Consolidated Statements of Cash Flows

For the Year Ended ($US, in thousands)	February 27, 2010	February 28, 2009	March 1, 2008
Cash flows from operating activities			
Net income	$ 2,457,144	$ 1,892,616	$ 1,293,867
Adjustments to reconcile net income to net cash provided by operating activities:			
Amortization	615,621	327,896	177,366
Deferred income taxes	51,363	(36,623)	(67,244)
Income taxes payable	4,611	(6,897)	4,973
Stock-based compensation	58,038	38,100	33,700
Other	8,806	5,867	3,303
Net changes in working capital items	(160,709)	(769,114)	130,794
Net cash provided by operating activities	3,034,874	1,451,845	1,576,759
Cash flows from investing activities			
Acquisition of long-term investments	(862,977)	(507,082)	(757,656)
Proceeds on sale or maturity of long-term investments	473,476	431,713	260,393
Acquisition of property, plant and equipment	(1,009,416)	(833,521)	(351,914)
Acquisition of intangible assets	(421,400)	(687,913)	(374,128)
Business acquisitions, net of cash acquired	(143,375)	(48,425)	(6,200)
Acquisition of short-term investments	(476,956)	(917,316)	(1,249,919)
Proceeds on sale or maturity of short-term investments	970,521	739,021	1,325,487
Net cash used in investing activities	(1,470,127)	(1,823,523)	(1,153,937)
Cash flows from financing activities			
Issuance of common shares	30,246	27,024	62,889
Additional paid-in capital	—	—	9,626
Excess tax benefits from stock-based compensation	1,943	12,648	8,185
Purchase of treasury stock	(94,463)	—	—
Common shares repurchased	(775,008)	—	—
Repayment of debt	(6,099)	(14,305)	(302)
Net cash provided by (used in) financing activities	(843,381)	25,367	80,398
Effect of foreign exchange gain (loss) on cash and cash equivalents	(6,051)	(2,541)	4,034
Net increase (decrease) in cash and cash equivalents for the year	715,315	(348,852)	507,254
Cash and cash equivalents, beginning of year	835,546	1,184,398	677,144
Cash and cash equivalents, end of year	$ 1,550,861	$ 835,546	$ 1,184,398

RIM—SELECTED Notes to the Consolidated Financial Statements

$US in thousands, except share and per share data, and where otherwise indicated

1. RESEARCH IN MOTION LIMITED AND SUMMARY OF SIGNIFICANT ACCOUNTING POLICIES

Research In Motion Limited ("RIM" or the "Company") is a leading designer, manufacturer and marketer of innovative wireless solutions for the worldwide mobile communications market. Through the development of integrated hardware, software and services that support multiple wireless network standards, RIM provides platforms and solutions for seamless access to time-sensitive information including email, phone, short messaging service (SMS), Internet and intranet-based applications. RIM technology also enables a broad array of third party developers and manufacturers to enhance their products and services with wireless connectivity to data. RIM's portfolio of award-winning products, services and embedded technologies are used by thousands of organizations and millions of consumers around the world and include the BlackBerry wireless solution, and other software and hardware. The Company's sales and marketing efforts include collaboration with strategic partners and distribution channels, as well as its own supporting sales and marketing teams, to promote the sale of its products and services.

Basis of presentation and preparation

The consolidated financial statements include the accounts of all subsidiaries of the Company with intercompany transactions and balances eliminated on consolidation. All of the Company's subsidiaries are wholly-owned. These consolidated financial statements have been prepared by management in accordance with United States generally accepted accounting principles ("U.S. GAAP") on a basis consistent for all periods presented except as described in note 2. Certain of the comparative figures have been reclassified to conform to the current year presentation. The Company's fiscal year end date is the 52 or 53 weeks ending on the last Saturday of February, or the first Saturday of March. The fiscal years ended February 27, 2010, February 28, 2009, and March 1, 2008 comprise 52 weeks.

The significant accounting policies used in these U.S. GAAP consolidated financial statements are as follows:

Use of estimates

The preparation of the consolidated financial statements requires management to make estimates and assumptions with respect to the reported amounts of assets, liabilities, revenues and expenses and the disclosure of contingent assets and liabilities. Significant areas requiring the use of management estimates relate to the determination of reserves for various litigation claims, provisions for excess and obsolete inventories and liabilities for purchase commitments with contract manufacturers and suppliers, fair values of assets acquired and liabilities assumed in business combinations, royalties, amortization expense, implied fair value of goodwill, provision for income taxes, realization of deferred income tax assets and the related components of the valuation allowance, provisions for warranty and the fair values of financial instruments. Actual results could differ from these estimates.

Foreign currency translation

The U.S. dollar is the functional and reporting currency of the Company. Foreign currency denominated assets and liabilities of the Company and all of its subsidiaries are translated into U.S. dollars. Accordingly, monetary assets and liabilities are translated using the exchange rates in effect at the consolidated balance sheet date and revenues and expenses at the rates of exchange prevailing when the transactions occurred. Remeasurement adjustments are included in income. Non-monetary assets and liabilities are translated at historical exchange rates.

Cash and cash equivalents

Cash and cash equivalents consist of balances with banks and liquid investments with maturities of three months or less at the date of acquisition.

Accounts receivable, net

The accounts receivable balance which reflects invoiced and accrued revenue is presented net of an allowance for doubtful accounts. The allowance for doubtful accounts reflects estimates of probable losses in accounts receivables. The Company is dependent on a number of significant customers and on large complex contracts with respect to sales of the majority of its products, software and services. The Company expects the majority of its accounts receivable balances to continue to come from large customers as it sells the majority of its devices and software products and service relay access through network carriers and resellers rather than directly.

The Company evaluates the collectability of its accounts receivables based upon a combination of factors on a periodic basis such as specific credit risk of its customers, historical trends and economic circumstances. The Company, in the normal course of business, monitors the financial condition of its customers and reviews the credit history of each new

$US in thousands, except share and per share data, and where otherwise indicated

customer. When the Company becomes aware of a specific customer's inability to meet its financial obligations to the Company (such as in the case of bankruptcy filings or material deterioration in the customer's operating results or financial position, and payment experiences), RIM records a specific bad debt provision to reduce the customer's related accounts receivable to its estimated net realizable value. If circumstances related to specific customers change, the Company's estimates of the recoverability of accounts receivables balances could be further adjusted. The allowance for doubtful accounts as at February 27, 2010 is $2.0 million (February 28, 2009- $2.1 million).

Investments

The Company's investments, other than cost method investments of $2.5 million and equity method investments of $4.1 million, consist of money market and other debt securities, and are classified as available-for-sale for accounting purposes. The Company does not exercise significant influence with respect to any of these investments.

Investments with maturities one year or less, as well as any investments that management intends to hold for less than one year, are classified as short-term investments. Investments with maturities in excess of one year are classified as long-term investments.

The Company determines the appropriate classification of investments at the time of purchase and subsequently reassesses the classification of such investments at each balance sheet date. Investments classified as available-for-sale are carried at fair value with unrealized gains and losses recorded in accumulated other comprehensive income (loss) until such investments mature or are sold. The Company uses the specific identification method of determining the cost basis in computing realized gains or losses on available-for-sale investments which are recorded in investment income.

The Company assesses individual investments in an unrealized loss position to determine whether the unrealized loss is other-than-temporary. The Company makes this assessment by considering available evidence, including changes in general market conditions, specific industry and individual company data, the length of time and the extent to which the fair value has been less than cost, the financial condition, the near-term prospects of the individual investment and the Company's intent and ability to hold the investments. In the event that a decline in the fair value of an investment occurs and the decline in value is considered to be other-than-temporary, an impairment charge is recorded in investment income equal to the difference between the cost basis and the fair value of the individual investment at the balance sheet date of the reporting period for which the assessment was made. The fair value of the investment then becomes the new cost basis of the investment.

Effective in the second quarter of fiscal 2010, if a debt security's market value is below its amortized cost and the Company either intends to sell the security or it is more likely than not that the Company will be required to sell the security before its anticipated recovery, the Company records an other-than-temporary impairment charge to investment income for the entire amount of the impairment. For other-than-temporary impairments on debt securities that the Company does not intend to sell and it is not more likely than not that the entity will be required to sell the security before its anticipated recovery, the Company would separate the other-than-temporary impairment into the amount representing the credit loss and the amount related to all other factors. The Company would record the other-than-temporary impairment related to the credit loss as a charge to investment income and the remaining other-than-temporary impairment would be recorded as a component of accumulated other comprehensive income.

Derivative financial instruments

The Company uses derivative financial instruments, including forward contracts and options, to hedge certain foreign currency exposures. The Company does not use derivative financial instruments for speculative purposes.

Inventories

Raw materials are stated at the lower of cost and replacement cost. Work in process and finished goods inventories are stated at the lower of cost and net realizable value. Cost includes the cost of materials plus direct labour applied to the product and the applicable share of manufacturing overhead. Cost is determined on a first-in-first-out basis.

Property, plant and equipment, net

Property, plant and equipment is stated at cost less accumulated amortization. No amortization is provided for construction in progress until the assets are ready for use. Amortization is provided using the following rates and methods:

Buildings, leaseholds and other	Straight-line over terms between 5 and 40 years
BlackBerry operations and other information technology	Straight-line over terms between 3 and 5 years
Manufacturing equipment, R&D equipment and tooling	Straight-line over terms between 2 and 8 years
Furniture and fixtures	Declining balance at 20% per annum

$US in thousands, except share and per share data, and where otherwise indicated

Intangible assets, net

Intangible assets are stated at cost less accumulated amortization and are comprised of acquired technology, licenses, and patents. Acquired technology consists of purchased developed technology arising from the Company's business acquisitions. Licenses include licenses or agreements that the Company has negotiated with third parties upon use of third parties' technology. Patents comprise trademarks, internally developed patents, as well as individual patents or portfolios of patents acquired from third parties. Costs capitalized and subsequently amortized include all costs necessary to acquire intellectual property, such as patents and trademarks, as well as legal defense costs arising out of the assertion of any Company-owned patents.

Intangible assets are amortized as follows:

Acquired technology	Straight-line over 2 to 5 years
Licenses	Straight-line over terms of the license agreements or on a per unit basis based upon the anticipated number of units sold during the terms, subject to a maximum of 5 years
Patents	Straight-line over 17 years or over estimated useful life

Goodwill

Goodwill represents the excess of the purchase price of business acquisitions over the fair value of identifiable net assets acquired. Goodwill is allocated as at the date of the business combination. Goodwill is not amortized, but is tested for impairment annually, or more frequently if events or changes in circumstances indicate the asset may be impaired.

Impairment of long-lived assets

The Company reviews long-lived assets such as property, plant and equipment and intangible assets with finite useful lives for impairment whenever events or changes in circumstances indicate that the carrying amount may not be recoverable. If the total of the expected undiscounted future cash flows is less than the carrying amount of the asset, a loss is recognized for the excess of the carrying amount over the fair value of the asset.

Income taxes

The Company uses the liability method of tax allocation to account for income taxes. Deferred income tax assets and liabilities are recognized based upon temporary differences between the financial reporting and tax bases of assets and liabilities, and measured using enacted tax rates and laws that will be in effect when the differences are expected to reverse. The Company records a valuation allowance to reduce deferred income tax assets to the amount that is more likely than not to be realized. The Company considers both positive evidence and negative evidence, to determine whether, based upon the weight of that evidence, a valuation allowance is required. Judgment is required in considering the relative impact of negative and positive evidence.

Revenue recognition

The Company recognizes revenue when it is realized or realizable and earned. The Company considers revenue realized or realizable and earned when it has persuasive evidence of an arrangement, the product has been delivered or the services have been provided to the customer, the sales price is fixed or determinable and collectability is reasonably assured. In addition to this general policy, the following paragraphs describe the specific revenue recognition policies for each major category of revenue.

Devices

Revenue from the sales of BlackBerry devices is recognized when title is transferred to the customer and all significant contractual obligations that affect the customer's final acceptance have been fulfilled. For hardware products for which software is deemed not to be incidental, the Company recognizes revenue in accordance with industry specific software revenue recognition guidance. The Company records reductions to revenue for estimated commitments related to price protection and for customer incentive programs, including reseller and end-user rebates. The estimated cost of the incentive programs are accrued based on historical experience, as a reduction to revenue in the period the Company has sold the product and committed to a plan. Price protection is accrued as a reduction to revenue based on estimates of future price reductions and certain agreed customer inventories at the date of the price adjustment. In addition, provisions are made at the time of sale for warranties and royalties.

Service

Revenue from service is recognized rateably on a monthly basis when the service is provided. In instances where the Company bills the customer prior to performing the service, the prebilling is recorded as deferred revenue.

Software

Revenue from licensed software is recognized at the inception of the license term and in accordance with industry

$US in thousands, except share and per share data, and where otherwise indicated

specific software revenue recognition guidance. When the fair value of a delivered element has not been established, the Company uses the residual method to recognize revenue if the fair value of undelivered elements is determinable. Revenue from software maintenance, unspecified upgrades and technical support contracts is recognized over the period that such items are delivered or that services are provided.

Other

Revenue from the sale of accessories is recognized when title is transferred to the customer and all significant contractual obligations that affect the customer's final acceptance have been fulfilled. Technical support ("T-Support") contracts extending beyond the current period are recorded as deferred revenue. Revenue from repair and maintenance programs is recognized when the service is delivered which is when the title is transferred to the customer and all significant contractual obligations that affect the customer's final acceptance have been fulfilled. Revenue for non-recurring engineering contracts is recognized as specific contract milestones are met. The attainment of milestones approximates actual performance.

Shipping and handling costs

Shipping and handling costs charged to income are included in cost of sales where they can be reasonably attributed to certain revenue; otherwise they are included in selling, marketing and administration.

Multiple-element arrangements

The Company enters into transactions that represent multiple-element arrangements which may include any combination of hardware and/or service or software and T-Support. These multiple-element arrangements are assessed to determine whether they can be separated into more than one unit of accounting or element for the purpose of revenue recognition. When the appropriate criteria for separating revenue into more than one unit of accounting is met and there is vendor specific objective evidence of fair value for all units of accounting or elements in an arrangement, the arrangement consideration is allocated to the separate units of accounting or elements based on each unit's relative fair value. When the fair value of a delivered element has not been established, the Company uses the residual method to recognize revenue if the fair value of undelivered elements is determinable. This vendor specific objective evidence of fair value is established through prices charged for each revenue element when that element is sold separately. The revenue recognition policies described above are then applied to each unit of accounting.

Research and development

Research costs are expensed as incurred. Development costs for BlackBerry devices and licensed software to be sold, leased or otherwise marketed are subject to capitalization beginning when a product's technological feasibility has been established and ending when a product is available for general release to customers. The Company's products are generally released soon after technological feasibility has been established and therefore costs incurred subsequent to achievement of technological feasibility are not significant and have been expensed as incurred.

Comprehensive income (loss)

Comprehensive income (loss) is defined as the change in net assets of a business enterprise during a period from transactions and other events and circumstances from non-owner sources and includes all changes in equity during a period except those resulting from investments by owners and distributions to owners. The Company's reportable items of comprehensive income are cash flow hedges and changes in the fair value of available-for-sale investments. Realized gains or losses on available-for-sale investments are reclassified into investment income using the specific identification basis.

Earnings per share

Earnings per share is calculated based on the weighted-average number of shares outstanding during the year. The treasury stock method is used for the calculation of the dilutive effect of stock options.

Stock-based compensation plans

The Company has stock-based compensation plans.

Warranty

The Company provides for the estimated costs of product warranties at the time revenue is recognized. BlackBerry devices are generally covered by a time-limited warranty for varying periods of time. The Company's warranty obligation is affected by product failure rates, differences in warranty periods, regulatory developments with respect to warranty obligations in the countries in which the Company carries on business, freight expense, and material usage and other related repair costs. The Company's estimates of costs are based upon historical experience and expectations of future return rates and unit warranty repair cost. If the Company experiences increased or decreased warranty activity, or increased or decreased costs associated with servicing those obligations, revisions to the estimated warranty liability would be recognized in the reporting period when such revisions are made.

Advertising costs

The Company expenses all advertising costs as incurred. These costs are included in selling, marketing and administration.

$US in thousands, except share and per share data, and where otherwise indicated

4. CASH, CASH EQUIVALENTS AND INVESTMENTS

The components of cash, cash equivalents and investments were as follows:

	Cost Basis	Unrealized Gains	Unrealized Losses	Recorded Basis	Cash and Cash Equivalents	Short-term Investments	Long-term Investments
As at February 27, 2010							
Bank balances	$ 535,445	$ —	$	$ 535,445	$ 535,445	$ —	$ —
Money market fund	3,278	—	—	3,278	3,278	—	—
Bankers acceptances and term deposits/certificates	377,596	—	—	377,596	377,596	—	—
Commercial paper and corporate notes/bonds	855,145	6,528	(49)	861,624	472,312	187,369	201,943
Treasury bills/notes	203,514	129	(12)	203,631	92,272	50,786	60,573
Government sponsored enterprise notes	447,131	2,590	(13)	449,708	69,958	111,977	267,773
Asset-backed securities	393,751	5,280	(50)	398,981	—	10,482	388,499
Auction-rate securities	40,527	—	(7,688)	32,839	—	—	32,839
Other investments	6,621	—	—	6,621	—		6,621
	$2,863,008	$14,527	$ (7,812)	$2,869,723	$1,550,861	$360,614	$958,248

Realized gains and losses on available-for-sale securities comprise the following:

For the year ended	February 27, 2010	February 28, 2009	March 1, 2008
Realized gains	$439	$ 158	$ 10
Realized losses	(17)	(1,801)	(410)
Net realized gains (losses)	$422	$(1,643)	$(400)

The contractual maturities of available-for-sale investments at February 27, 2010 were as follows:

	Cost Basis	Fair Value
Due in one year or less	$1,371,047	$1,372,752
Due in one to five years	773,471	783,451
Due after five years	173,146	168,176
No fixed maturity date	3,278	3,278
	$2,320,942	$2,327,657

5. FAIR VALUE MEASUREMENTS

The Company defines fair value as the price that would be received to sell an asset or paid to transfer a liability in an orderly transaction between market participants at the measurement date. When determining the fair value measurements for assets and liabilities required to be recorded at fair value, the Company considers the principal or most advantageous market in which it would transact and considers assumptions that market participants would use in pricing the asset or liability such as inherent risk, non-performance risk and credit risk. The Company applies the following fair value hierarchy, which prioritizes the inputs used in the valuation methodologies in measuring fair value into three levels:

- Level 1 — Unadjusted quoted prices at the measurement date for identical assets or liabilities in active markets.
- Level 2 — Observable inputs other than quoted prices included in Level 1, such as quoted prices for similar assets and liabilities in active markets; quoted prices for identical or similar assets and liabilities in markets that are not active; or other inputs that are observable or can be corroborated by observable market data.
- Level 3 — Significant unobservable inputs which are supported by little or no market activity.

The fair value hierarchy also requires the Company to maximize the use of observable inputs and minimize the use of unobservable inputs when measuring fair value. The carrying amounts of the Company's cash and cash equivalents, accounts receivable, other receivables, accounts payable and accrued liabilities, approximate fair value due to their short maturities. When determining the fair value of its investments held, the Company primarily relies on an independent third party valuator for the fair valuation of securities.

$US in thousands, except share and per share data, and where otherwise indicated

6. INVENTORIES

Inventories were comprised as follows:

	February 27, 2010	February 28, 2009
Raw materials	$ 490,063	$464,497
Work in process	231,939	250,728
Finished goods	17,068	35,264
Provision for excess and obsolete inventories	(117,459)	(68,089)
	$ 621,611	$682,400

7. PROPERTY, PLANT AND EQUIPMENT, NET

Property, plant and equipment were comprised of the following:

February 27, 2010	Cost	Accumulated amortization	Net book value
Land	$ 104,254	$ —	$ 104,254
Buildings, leaseholds and other	926,747	115,216	811,531
BlackBerry operations and other information technology	1,152,637	484,180	668,457
Manufacturing equipment, research and development equipment, and tooling	347,692	182,228	165,464
Furniture and fixtures	346,641	139,766	206,875
	$2,877,971	$921,390	$1,956,581

As at February 27, 2010, the carrying amount of assets under construction was $254.3 million (February 28, 2009 — $88.9 million). Of this amount, $110.9 million (February 28, 2009 — $50.0 million) was included in buildings, leaseholds and other; $102.5 million (February 28, 2009 - $35.8 million) was included in BlackBerry operations and other information technology; and $40.9 million (February 28, 2009 — $3.2 million) was included in manufacturing equipment, research and development equipment, and tooling. As at February 27, 2010, $31.7 million has been classified as an asset held for sale and accordingly has been reclassified from property, plant and equipment to other current assets. For the year ended February 27, 2010, amortization expense related to property, plant and equipment was $344.5 million (February 28, 2009 — $203.4 million; March 1, 2008 — $133.1 million).

8. INTANGIBLE ASSETS, NET

Intangible assets were comprised of the following:

February 27, 2010	Cost	Accumulated amortization	Net book value
Acquired technology	$ 165,791	$ 70,777	$ 95,014
Licenses	711,969	196,618	515,351
Patents	889,467	173,469	715,998
	$1,767,227	$440,864	$1,326,363

For the year ended February 27, 2010, amortization expense related to intangible assets was $271.1 million (February 28, 2009 — $124.5 million; March 1, 2008 — $44.3 million). Total additions to intangible assets in fiscal 2010 were $531.0 million (2009 — $721.1 million). Based on the carrying value of the identified intangible assets as at February 27, 2010 and assuming no subsequent impairment of the underlying assets, the annual amortization expense for the next five fiscal years is expected to be as follows: 2011 — $324 million; 2012 — $275 million; 2013 — $227 million; 2014 — $139 million; and 2015 — $61 million. The weighted-average remaining useful life of the acquired technology is 3.4 years (2009 – 3.7 years).

$US in thousands, except share and per share data, and where otherwise indicated

10. INCOME TAXES

The difference between the amount of the provision for income taxes and the amount computed by multiplying income before income taxes by the statutory Canadian tax rate is reconciled as follows:

For the year ended	February 27, 2010	February 28, 2009
Statutory Canadian tax rate	32.8%	33.4%
Expected income tax provision	$1,072,395	$935,881
Differences in income taxes resulting from:		
Impact of Canadian U.S. dollar functional currency election	(145,000)	—
Investment tax credits	(101,214)	(81,173)
Manufacturing and processing activities	(52,053)	(49,808)
Foreign exchange	2,837	99,575
Foreign tax rate differences	5,291	(16,273)
Non deductible stock compensation	9,600	10,500
Adjustments to deferred tax balances for enacted changes in tax laws and rates	7,927	1,260
Other differences	9,583	7,785
	$ 809,366	$907,747

11. CAPITAL STOCK

(a) Capital stock

The Company is authorized to issue an unlimited number of non-voting, redeemable, retractable Class A common shares, an unlimited number of voting common shares and an unlimited number of non-voting, cumulative, redeemable, retractable preferred shares. At February 27, 2010 and February 28, 2009, there were no Class A common shares or preferred shares outstanding. The Company declared a 3-for-1 stock split of the Company's outstanding common shares on June 28, 2007. The stock split was implemented by way of a stock dividend. Shareholders received an additional two common shares of the Company for each common share held. The stock dividend was paid on August 20, 2007 to common shareholders of record at the close of business on August 17, 2007. All share, earnings per share and stock option data have been adjusted to reflect this stock dividend.

The following details the changes in issued and outstanding common shares for the year ended February 27, 2010:

	Capital Stock		Treasury Stock	
	Stock Outstanding (000's)	Amount	Stock Outstanding (000's)	Amount
Common shares outstanding as at February 28, 2009	566,219	2,208,235	—	—
Exercise of stock options	3,408	30,246	—	—
Conversion of restricted share units	2	—	—	—
Transfers to capital stock resulting from stock option exercises	—	15,647	—	—
Restricted share unit plan purchase of shares	—	—	1,459	(94,463)
Common shares repurchased	(12,300)	(46,519)	—	—
Common shares outstanding as at February 27, 2010	557,329	$2,207,609	1,459	$(94,463)

On November 4, 2009, the Company's Board of Directors authorized a Common Share Repurchase Program for the repurchase and cancellation, through the facilities of the NASDAQ Stock Market, common shares having an aggregate purchase price of up to $1.2 billion, or approximately 21 million common shares based on trading prices at the time of the authorization. This represents approximately 3.6% of the outstanding common shares of the Company at the time of the authorization. All common shares repurchased by the Company pursuant to the Common Share Repurchase Program have been cancelled. The Common Share Repurchase Program will remain in place for up to 12 months from November 4, 2009 or until the purchases are completed or the program is terminated by the Company.

(b) Stock-based compensation

Stock Option Plan

The Company recorded a charge to income and a credit to paid-in-capital of $37.0 million in fiscal 2010 (fiscal 2009 — $38.1 million; fiscal 2008 — $33.7 million) in relation to stock-based compensation expense.

The Company has not paid a dividend in the previous twelve fiscal years and has no current expectation of paying cash dividends on its common shares.

Restricted Share Unit Plan

During fiscal 2010, the trustee purchased 1,458,950 common shares for total consideration of approximately $94.5 million

$US in thousands, except share and per share data, and where otherwise indicated

to comply with its obligations to deliver shares upon vesting. These purchased shares are classified as treasury stock for accounting purposes and included in the shareholders' equity section of the Company's consolidated balance sheet. The Company recorded compensation expense with respect to RSUs of $21.0 million in the year ended February 27, 2010 (February 28, 2009 — $196; March 1, 2008 — $33).

Deferred Share Unit Plan

The Company issued 14,593 DSUs in the year ended February 27, 2010. There are 34,801 DSUs outstanding as at February 27, 2010 (February 28, 2009 — 20,208). The Company had a liability of $2.5 million in relation to the DSU plan as at February 27, 2010 (February 28, 2009 — $834).

12. COMMITMENTS AND CONTINGENCIES

(a) Credit Facility

The Company has $150.0 million in unsecured demand credit facilities (the "Facilities") to support and secure operating and financing requirements. As at February 27, 2010, the Company has utilized $6.9 million of the Facilities for outstanding letters of credit, and $143.1 million of the Facilities are unused.

(b) Lease commitments

The Company is committed to future minimum annual lease payments under operating leases as follows:

	Real Estate	Equipment and other	Total
For the years ending			
2011	$ 35,088	$1,917	$ 37,005
2012	30,611	1,202	31,813
2013	27,841	163	28,004
2014	26,178	—	26,178
2015	21,755	—	21,755
Thereafter	63,631	—	63,631
	$205,104	$3,282	$208,386

For the year ended February 27, 2010, the Company incurred rental expense of $39.6 million (February 28, 2009 — $22.7 million; March 1, 2008 — $15.5 million).

(c) Litigation

The Company is involved in litigation in the normal course of its business, both as a defendant and as a plaintiff. The Company may be subject to claims (including claims related to patent infringement, purported class actions and derivative actions) either directly or through indemnities against these claims that it provides to certain of it partners.

13. PRODUCT WARRANTY

The Company estimates its warranty costs at the time of revenue recognition based on historical warranty claims experience and records the expense in cost of sales. The warranty accrual balance is reviewed quarterly to establish that it materially reflects the remaining obligation based on the anticipated future expenditures over the balance of the obligation period. Adjustments are made when the actual warranty claim experience differs from estimates. The change in the Company's warranty expense and actual warranty experience from March 3, 2007 to February 27, 2010 as well as the accrued warranty obligations as at February 27, 2010 are set forth in the following table:

Accrued warranty obligations as at March 3, 2007	$ 36,669
Actual warranty experience during fiscal 2008	(68,166)
Fiscal 2008 warranty provision	116,045
Accrued warranty obligations as at March 1, 2008	84,548
Actual warranty experience during fiscal 2009	(146,434)
Fiscal 2009 warranty provision	258,757
Adjustments for changes in estimate	(12,536)
Accrued warranty obligations as at February 28, 2009	184,335
Actual warranty experience during fiscal 2010	(416,393)
Fiscal 2010 warranty provision	462,834
Adjustments for changes in estimate	21,541
Accrued warranty obligations as at February 27, 2010	$ 252,317

$US in thousands, except share and per share data, and where otherwise indicated

14. EARNINGS PER SHARE

The following table sets forth the computation of basic and diluted earnings per share:

For the year ended	February 27, 2010	February 28, 2009	March 1, 2008
Net income for basic and diluted earnings per share available to common shareholders	$2,457,144	$1,892,616	$1,293,867
Weighted-average number of shares outstanding (000's) — basic	564,492	565,059	559,778
Effect of dilutive securities (000's) — stock-based compensation	5,267	9,097	13,052
Weighted-average number of shares and assumed conversions (000's) — diluted	569,759	574,156	572,830
Earnings per share — reported			
Basic	$ 4.35	$ 3.35	$ 2.31
Diluted	$ 4.31	$ 3.30	$ 2.26

15. COMPREHENSIVE INCOME (LOSS)

The components of comprehensive income (loss) are shown in the following table:

For the year ended	February 27, 2010	February 28, 2009	March 1, 2008
Net income	$2,457,144	$1,892,616	$1,293,867
Net change in unrealized gains (losses) on available-for-sale investments	6,803	(7,161)	13,467
Net change in fair value of derivatives designated as cash flow hedges during the year, net of income taxes of $13,190 (February 28, 2009 tax recovery of $8,641; March 1, 2008 - income taxes of $19,238)	28,324	(6,168)	37,564
Amounts reclassified to earnings during the year, net of income tax recovery of $6,079 (February 28, 2009 - income taxes of $4,644; March 1, 2008 - income taxes of $5,142)	15,508	(16,497)	(9,232)
Comprehensive income	$2,507,779	$1,862,790	$1,335,666

The components of accumulated other comprehensive income (loss) are as follows:

	February 27, 2010	February 28, 2009	March 1, 2008
Accumulated net unrealized gains (losses) on available- for-sale investments	$ 6,715	$ (88)	$ 7,073
Accumulated net unrealized gains on derivative instruments designated as cash flow hedges	44,377	545	23,210
Total accumulated other comprehensive income	$51,092	$457	$30,283

16. SUPPLEMENTAL INFORMATION

(a) Cash flows resulting from net changes in working capital items are as follows:

For the year ended	February 27, 2010	February 28, 2009	March 1, 2008
Accounts receivable	$(480,610)	$(936,514)	$(602,055)
Other receivables	(44,719)	(83,039)	(34,515)
Inventories	60,789	(286,133)	(140,360)
Other current assets	(52,737)	(50,280)	(26,161)
Accounts payable	167,281	177,263	140,806
Accrued liabilities	442,065	506,859	383,020
Income taxes payable	(266,517)	(113,868)	401,270
Deferred revenue	13,739	16,598	8,789
	$(160,709)	$(769,114)	$ 130,794

(b) Certain statement of cash flow information related to interest and income taxes paid is summarized as follows:

For the year ended	February 27, 2010	February 28, 2009	March 1, 2008
Interest paid during the year	$ —	$ 502	$ 518
Income taxes paid during the year	$1,081,720	$946,237	$216,095

$US in thousands, except share and per share data, and where otherwise indicated

(c) The following items are included in the accrued liabilities balance:

	February 27, 2010	February 28, 2009
Marketing costs	$ 91,554	$ 91,160
Vendor inventory liabilities	125,761	18,000
Warranty	252,316	184,335
Royalties	383,939	279,476
Rebates	146,304	134,788
Other	638,386	530,843
	$1,638,260	$1,238,602

Other accrued liabilities as noted in the above chart, include, among other things, salaries, payroll withholding taxes and incentive accruals, none of which are greater than 5% of the current liability balance.

(d) Additional information

Advertising expense, which includes media, agency and promotional expenses totalling $790.8 million (February 28, 2009 — $718.9 million; March 1, 2008 — $336.0 million) is included in selling, marketing and administration expense.

Selling, marketing and administration expense for the fiscal year includes $58.4 million with respect to foreign exchange losses (February 28, 2009 – loss of $6.1 million; March 1, 2008 – loss of $5.3 million). For the year ended February 27, 2010, the Company recorded a $54.3 million charge primarily relating to the reversal of foreign exchange gains previously recorded in fiscal 2009 on the revaluation of Canadian dollar denominated tax liability balances.

17. DERIVATIVE FINANCIAL INSTRUMENTS

The Company uses derivative instruments to manage exposures to foreign exchange risk resulting from transactions in currencies other than its functional currency, the U.S. dollar. The Company's risk management objective in holding derivative instruments is to reduce the volatility of current and future income as a result of changes in foreign currency. To limit its exposure to adverse movements in foreign currency exchange rates, the Company enters into foreign currency forward and option contracts.

18. SEGMENT DISCLOSURES

The Company is organized and managed as a single reportable business segment. The Company's operations are substantially all related to the research, design, manufacture and sales of wireless communications products, services and software. Selected financial information is as follows:

Revenue, classified by major geographic segments in which our customers are located, was as follows:

For the year ended	February 27, 2010	February 28, 2009	March 1, 2008
Revenue			
Canada	$ 843,762	$ 887,005	$ 438,302
United States	8,619,762	6,967,598	3,528,858
United Kingdom	1,447,417	711,536	461,592
Other	4,042,283	2,499,047	1,580,643
	$14,953,224	$11,065,186	$6,009,395

	February 27, 2010	February 28, 2009
Total assets		
Canada	$ 4,502,522	$3,218,640
United States	4,059,174	2,646,783
United Kingdom	1,195,534	1,931,387
Other	447,179	304,562
	$10,204,409	$8,101,372

Apple Financial Report

APPLE INC.
CONSOLIDATED BALANCE SHEETS
(in millions, except share amounts)

	September 26, 2009	September 27, 2008
ASSETS		
Current assets		
Cash and cash equivalents	$ 5,263	$11,875
Short-term marketable securities	18,201	10,236
Accounts receivable, less allowances of $52 and $47, respectively	3,361	2,422
Inventories	455	509
Deferred tax assets	1,135	1,044
Other current assets	3,140	3,920
Total current assets	31,555	30,006
Long-term marketable securities	10,528	2,379
Property, plant and equipment, net	2,954	2,455
Goodwill	206	207
Acquired intangible assets, net	247	285
Other assets	2,011	839
Total assets	$47,501	$36,171
LIABILITIES AND SHAREHOLDERS' EQUITY		
Current liabilities		
Accounts payable	$ 5,601	$ 5,520
Accrued expenses	3,852	4,224
Deferred revenue	2,053	1,617
Total current liabilities	11,506	11,361
Deferred revenue – non-current	853	768
Other non-current liabilities	3,502	1,745
Total liabilities	15,861	13,874
Shareholders' equity		
Common stock, no par value; 1,800,000,000 shares authorized; 899,805,500 and 888,325,973 shares issued and outstanding, respectively	8,210	7,177
Retained earnings	23,353	15,129
Accumulated other comprehensive income/(loss)	77	(9)
Total shareholders' equity	31,640	22,297
Total liabilities and shareholders' equity	$47,501	$36,171

APPLE INC.
CONSOLIDATED STATEMENTS OF OPERATIONS
(in millions, except share amounts which are reflected in thousands and per share amounts)

For fiscal year ended	September 26, 2009	September 27, 2008	September 29, 2007
Net sales	$ 42,905	$ 37,491	$ 24,578
Cost of sales	25,683	24,294	16,426
Gross margin	17,222	13,197	8,152
Operating expenses			
Research and development	1,333	1,109	782
Selling, general and administrative	4,149	3,761	2,963
Total operating expenses	5,482	4,870	3,745
Operating income	11,740	8,327	4,407
Other income and expense	326	620	599
Income before provision for income taxes	12,066	8,947	5,006
Provision for income taxes	3,831	2,828	1,511
Net income	$ 8,235	$ 6,119	$ 3,495
Earnings per common share:			
Basic	$ 9.22	$ 6.94	$ 4.04
Diluted	$ 9.08	$ 6.78	$ 3.93
Shares used in computing earnings per share:			
Basic	893,016	881,592	864,595
Diluted	907,005	902,139	889,292

APPLE

APPLE INC.
CONSOLIDATED STATEMENTS OF SHAREHOLDERS' EQUITY
(in millions, except share amounts which are reflected in thousands)

	Common Stock		Retained Earnings	Accumulated Other Comprehensive Income	Total Shareholders' Equity
	Shares	Amount			
Balances as of September 30, 2006	855,263	$ 4,355	$ 5,607	$ 22	$ 9,984
Components of comprehensive income:					
Net income	—	—	3,495	—	3,495
Change in foreign currency translation	—	—	—	51	51
Change in unrealized loss on available-for-sale securities, net of tax	—	—	—	(7)	(7)
Change in unrealized gain on derivative instruments, net of tax	—	—	—	(3)	(3)
Total comprehensive income					3,536
Stock-based compensation	—	251	—	—	251
Common stock issued under stock plans, net of shares withheld for employee taxes	17,066	364	(2)	—	362
Tax benefit from employee stock plan awards	—	398	—	—	398
Balances as of September 29, 2007	872,329	5,368	9,100	63	14,531
Cumulative effect of change in accounting principle	—	45	11	—	56
Components of comprehensive income:					
Net income	—	—	6,119		6,119
Change in foreign currency translation	—	—	—	(28)	(28)
Change in unrealized loss on available-for-sale securities, net of tax	—	—	—	(63)	(63)
Change in unrealized gain on derivative instruments, net of tax		—	—	19	19
Total comprehensive income					6,047
Stock-based compensation	—	513	—	—	513
Common stock issued under stock plans, net of shares withheld for employee taxes	15,888	460	(101)	—	359
Issuance of common stock in connection with an asset acquisition	109	21	—	—	21
Tax benefit from employee stock plan awards	—	770	—	—	770
Balances as of September 27, 2008	888,326	7,177	15,129	(9)	22,297
Components of comprehensive income:					
Net income	—	—	8,235	—	8,235
Change in foreign currency translation	—	—	—	(14)	(14)
Change in unrealized loss on available-for-sale securities, net of tax	—	—	—	118	118
Change in unrealized gain on derivative instruments, net of tax	—	—	—	(18)	(18)
Total comprehensive income					8,321
Stock-based compensation	—	707	—	—	707
Common stock issued under stock plans, net of shares withheld for employee taxes	11,480	404	(11)		393
Tax benefit from employee stock plan awards, including transfer pricing adjustments	—	(78)	—	—	(78)
Balances as of September 26, 2009	899,806	$ 8,210	$23,353	$ 77	$31,640

APPLE INC.
CONSOLIDATED STATEMENTS OF CASH FLOWS
(in millions)

For fiscal year ended	September 26, 2009	September 27, 2008	September 29, 2007
Cash and cash equivalents, beginning of the year	$ 11,875	$ 9,352	$ 6,392
Operating Activities			
Net income	8,235	6,119	3,495
Adjustments to reconcile net income to cash generated by operating activities			
Depreciation, amortization and accretion	734	496	327
Stock-based compensation expense	710	516	242
Deferred income tax expense	1,040	398	73
Loss on disposition of property, plant and equipment	26	22	12
Changes in operating assets and liabilities			
Accounts receivable, net	(939)	(785)	(385)
Inventories	54	(163)	(76)
Other current assets	749	(274)	(1,279)
Other assets	(902)	289	285
Accounts payable	92	596	1,494
Deferred revenue	521	718	566
Other liabilities	(161)	1,664	716
Cash generated by operating activities	10,159	9,596	5,470
Investing Activities			
Purchases of marketable securities	(46,724)	(22,965)	(11,719)
Proceeds from maturities of marketable securities	19,790	11,804	6,483
Proceeds from sales of marketable securities	10,888	4,439	2,941
Purchases of other long-term investments	(101)	(38)	(17)
Payments made in connection with business acquisitions, net of cash acquired	—	(220)	—
Payment for acquisition of property, plant and equipment	(1,144)	(1,091)	(735)
Payment for acquisition of intangible assets	(69)	(108)	(251)
Other	(74)	(10)	49
Cash used in investing activities	(17,434)	(8,189)	(3,249)
Financing Activities			
Proceeds from issuance of common stock	475	483	365
Excess tax benefits from stock-based compensation	270	757	377
Cash used to net share settle equity awards	(82)	(124)	(3)
Cash generated by financing activities	663	1,116	739
(Decrease)/increase in cash and cash equivalents	(6,612)	2,523	2,960
Cash and cash equivalents, end of the year	$ 5,263	$11,875	$ 9,352
Supplemental cash flow disclosures:			
Cash paid for income taxes, net	$ 2,997	$ 1,267	$ 863

APPLE

Palm Financial Report

PALM

Palm, Inc.

Consolidated Balance Sheets

(In thousands, except par value amounts)

	May 31, 2009	May 31, 2008
ASSETS		
Current assets		
Cash and cash equivalents	$ 152,400	$ 176,918
Short-term investments	102,733	81,830
Accounts receivable, net of allowance for doubtful accounts of $350 and $1,169, respectively	66,452	116,430
Inventories	19,716	67,461
Deferred income taxes	174	82,011
Prepaids and other	12,104	15,436
Total current assets	353,579	540,086
Restricted investments	9,496	8,620
Non-current auction rate securities	6,105	29,944
Deferred costs	14,896	—
Property and equipment, net	31,167	39,636
Goodwill	166,320	166,332
Intangible assets, net	48,914	61,048
Deferred income taxes	331	318,850
Other assets	12,428	15,746
Total assets	$ 643,236	$1,180,262
LIABILITIES AND STOCKHOLDERS' EQUITY (DEFICIT)		
Current liabilities		
Accounts payable	$ 105,628	$ 161,642
Income taxes payable	475	1,088
Deferred revenues	18,429	4,080
Accrued restructuring	6,090	8,058
Current portion of long-term debt	4,000	4,000
Other accrued liabilities	207,820	232,478
Total current liabilities	342,442	411,346
Non-current liabilities		
Long-term debt	390,000	394,000
Non-current deferred revenues	13,077	—
Non-current tax liabilities	5,783	6,127
Other non-current liabilities	—	2,098
Series B redeemable convertible preferred stock, $0.001 par value, 325 shares authorized and outstanding; aggregate liquidation value: $325,000	265,412	255,671
Series C redeemable convertible preferred stock, $0.001 par value, 100 shares authorized; outstanding: 51 shares and 0 shares, respectively; aggregate liquidation value: $51,000 and $0, respectively	40,387	—
Stockholders' equity (deficit)		
Preferred stock, $0.001 par value, 125,000 shares authorized:		
Series A: 2,000 shares authorized, none outstanding	—	—
Common stock, $0.001 par value, 2,000,000 shares authorized; outstanding: 139,687 shares and 108,369 shares, respectively	140	108
Additional paid-in capital	854,649	659,141
Accumulated deficit	(1,269,672)	(537,484)
Accumulated other comprehensive income (loss)	1,018	(10,745)
Total stockholders' equity (deficit)	(413,865)	111,020
Total liabilities and stockholders' equity (deficit)	$ 643,236	$1,180,262

Palm, Inc.

Consolidated Statements of Operations
(In thousands, except per share amounts)

Years Ended May 31	2009	2008	2007
Revenues	$ 735,872	$1,318,691	$1,560,507
Cost of revenues	576,113	916,810	985,369
Gross profit	159,759	401,881	575,138
Operating expenses			
Sales and marketing	174,052	229,702	248,685
Research and development	177,210	202,764	190,952
General and administrative	55,923	60,778	59,762
Amortization of intangible assets	3,054	3,775	1,981
Restructuring charges	16,134	30,353	—
Casualty recovery	(268)	—	—
Patent acquisition cost (refund)	(1,537)	5,000	—
Gain on sale of land	—	(4,446)	—
In-process research and development	—	—	3,700
Total operating expenses	424,568	527,926	505,080
Operating income (loss)	(264,809)	(126,045)	70,058
Impairment of non-current auction rate securities	(35,885)	(32,175)	—
Interest (expense)	(25,299)	(20,397)	(1,970)
Interest income	5,840	21,860	25,958
Loss on series C derivative	(2,515)	—	—
Other income (expense), net	(5,255)	(1,471)	(1,619)
Income (loss) before income taxes	(327,923)	(158,228)	92,427
Income tax provision (benefit)	404,265	(52,809)	36,044
Net income (loss)	(732,188)	(105,419)	56,383
Accretion of series B and series C redeemable convertible preferred stock	21,285	5,516	—
Net income (loss) applicable to common shareholders	$(753,473)	$ (110,935)	$ 56,383
Net income (loss) per common share:			
Basic	$ (6.51)	$ (1.05)	$ 0.55
Diluted	$ (6.51)	$ (1.05)	$ 0.54
Shares used to compute net income (loss) per common share:			
Basic	115,725	105,891	102,757
Diluted	115,725	105,891	104,442

PALM

Palm, Inc.

Consolidated Statements of Stockholders' Equity (Deficit) and Comprehensive Income (Loss)

(In thousands)

	Common Stock	Additional Paid-In Capital	Unamortized Deferred Stock-Based Compensation	Accumulated Deficit	Accumulated Other Comprehensive Income (Loss)	Total
Balances, May 31, 2006	$ 103	$1,475,319	$ (2,752)	$ (488,081)	$ (684)	$ 983,905
Components of comprehensive income:						
Net income	—	—	—	56,383	—	56,383
Net unrealized gains on available-for-sale investments	—	—	—	—	1,522	1,522
Recognized gains included in results of operations	—	—	—	—	(110)	(110)
Accumulated translation adjustments	—	—	—	—	915	915
Total comprehensive income	—	—	—	—	—	58,710
Common stock issued under stock plans, net	3	21,923	—	—	—	21,926
Stock-based compensation expense	—	21,503	2,752	—	—	24,255
Tax benefit from employee stock options	—	4,578	—	—	—	4,578
Shares repurchased and retired	(2)	(30,961)				(30,963)
Balances, May 31, 2007	104	1,492,362	—	(431,698)	1,643	1,062,411
Components of comprehensive loss:						
Net loss	—	—	—	(105,419)	—	(105,419)
Net unrealized losses on available-for-sale investments	—	—	—	—	(1,261)	(1,261)
Net unrealized losses in value of non-current auction rate securities	—	—	—	—	(44,706)	(44,706)
Net recognized losses on non-current auction rate securities included in results of operations	—	—	—	—	32,175	32,175
Net recognized gains on available-for-sale investments included in results of operations	—	—	—	—	(68)	(68)
Accumulated translation adjustments	—	—	—	—	1,472	1,472
Total comprehensive loss	—	—	—	—	—	(117,807)
Common stock issued under stock plans, net	4	28,433	—	—	—	28,437
Stock-based compensation expense	—	32,181	—	—	—	32,181
Tax deficiency from employee stock options	—	(3,663)	—	—	—	(3,663)
Cash distribution to stockholders	—	(949,691)	—	—	—	(949,691)
Discount recognized on issuance of series B redeemable convertible preferred stock	—	65,035	—	—	—	65,035
Accretion of series B redeemable convertible preferred stock	—	(5,516)	—	—	—	(5,516)
Adjustment to accumulated deficit due to adoption of FIN No. 48 (see Note 16)	—	—	—	(367)	—	(367)
Balances, May 31, 2008	108	659,141	—	(537,484)	(10,745)	111,020
Components of comprehensive loss:						
Net loss	—	—	—	(732,188)	—	(732,188)
Net unrealized losses on available-for-sale investments	—	—	—	—	(1,649)	(1,649)
Net unrealized losses in value of non-current auction rate securities	—	—	—	—	(23,354)	(23,354)
Net recognized losses on non-current auction rate securities included in results of operations	—	—	—	—	35,885	35,885
Net recognized losses on available-for-sale investments included in results of operations	—	—	—	—	3,594	3,594
Accumulated translation adjustments	—	—	—	—	(2,713)	(2,713)
Total comprehensive loss	—	—	—	—	—	(720,425)
Common stock issued under stock plans, net	5	15,531	—	—	—	15,536
Stock-based compensation expense	—	23,853	—	—	—	23,853
Tax benefit from employee stock options	—	1,924	—	—	—	1,924
Distribution liability related to canceled shares of restricted stock	—	34	—	—	—	34
Accretion of series B and series C redeemable convertible preferred stock	—	(21,285)	—	—	—	(21,285)
Warrants recorded in connection with issuance of series C units	—	21,966	—	—	—	21,966
Conversion of series C units and issuance of additional common stock, net	27	101,544	—	—	—	101,571
Discount recognized on issuance of series C redeemable convertible preferred stock	—	51,941	—	—	—	51,941
Balances, May 31, 2009	$ 140	$ 854,649	$ —	$ (1,269,672)	$ 1,018	$ (413,865)

Palm, Inc.

Consolidated Statements of Cash Flows
(In thousands)

Years Ended May 31	2009	2008	2007
Cash flows from operating activities			
Net income (loss)	$(732,188)	$(105,419)	$ 56,383
Adjustments to reconcile net income (loss) to net cash flows from operating activities			
Depreciation	19,677	19,699	13,316
Stock-based compensation	23,853	32,181	24,255
Amortization of intangible assets	12,134	16,510	8,315
Amortization of debt issuance costs	3,139	1,834	—
In-process research and development	—	—	3,700
Deferred income taxes	401,670	(58,227)	11,313
Realized (gain) loss on short-term investments	3,594	(68)	(110)
Excess tax benefit related to stock-based compensation	(142)	(40)	(5,241)
Realized loss (gain) on disposition of property and equipment and sale of land	619	(4,446)	—
Impairment of non-current auction rate securities	35,885	32,175	—
Loss on series C derivative	2,515	—	—
Changes in assets and liabilities			
Accounts receivable	48,425	89,312	2
Inventories	47,571	(28,147)	18,842
Prepaids and other	4,542	736	1,790
Accounts payable	(54,883)	(35,840)	11,654
Income taxes payable	(346)	3,033	16,421
Accrued restructuring	(361)	6,303	(1,803)
Deferred revenues/costs, net	12,530	—	—
Other accrued liabilities	(16,746)	12,866	9,354
Net cash provided by (used in) operating activities	(188,512)	(17,538)	168,191
Cash flows from investing activities			
Purchase of brand name intangible asset	—	(1,500)	(44,000)
Purchase of property and equipment	(13,452)	(22,999)	(24,651)
Proceeds from sale of land	—	64,446	—
Cash paid for business acquisitions	—	(495)	(19,000)
Purchase of short-term investments	(112,385)	(517,104)	(682,882)
Sales/maturities of short-term investments	88,109	777,917	671,623
Purchase of restricted investments	(2,000)	(8,951)	—
Sale of restricted investments	1,124	331	—
Proceeds related to investments in non-current auction rate securities	485	250	—
Net cash provided by (used in) investing activities	(38,119)	291,895	(98,910)
Cash flows from financing activities			
Proceeds from issuance of common stock, net	104,049	—	—
Proceeds from issuance of common stock, employee stock plans	15,536	28,437	21,926
Purchase and subsequent retirement of common stock	—	—	(30,963)
Excess tax benefit related to stock-based compensation	142	40	5,241
Proceeds from issuance of redeemable convertible preferred stock and series C units, net	99,173	315,190	—
Proceeds from issuance of debt, net	—	381,107	—
Repayment of debt	(14,446)	(3,089)	(50,816)
Cash distribution to stockholders	(439)	(948,949)	—
Net cash provided by (used in) financing activities	204,015	(227,264)	(54,612)
Effects of exchange rate changes on cash and cash equivalents	(1,902)	1,695	—
Change in cash and cash equivalents	(24,518)	48,788	14,669
Cash and cash equivalents, beginning of period	176,918	128,130	113,461
Cash and cash equivalents, end of period	$ 152,400	$ 176,918	$ 128,130
Supplemental cash flow information:			
Cash paid for income taxes	$ 3,402	$ 3,391	$ 8,900
Cash paid for interest	$ 21,828	$ 18,042	$ 1,741
Non-cash investing and financing activities:			
Liability for property and equipment acquired	$ —	$ 3,334	$ 2,309

Nokia Financial Report

Nokia Corporation and Subsidiaries
Consolidated Statements of Financial Position

December 31	2009 EURm	2008 EURm
ASSETS		
Non-current assets		
Capitalized development costs	**143**	244
Goodwill	**5 171**	6 257
Other intangible assets	**2 762**	3 913
Property, plant and equipment	**1 867**	2 090
Investments in associated companies	**69**	96
Available-for-sale investments	**554**	512
Deferred tax assets	**1 507**	1 963
Long-term loans receivable	**46**	27
Other non-current assets	**6**	10
	12 125	15 112
Current assets		
Inventories	**1 865**	2 533
Accounts receivable, net of allowances for doubtful accounts (2009: EUR 391 million, 2008: EUR 415 million)	**7 981**	9 444
Prepaid expenses and accrued income	**4 551**	4 538
Current portion of long-term loans receivable	**14**	101
Other financial assets	**329**	1 034
Investments at fair value through profit and loss, liquid assets	**580**	—
Available-for-sale investments, liquid assets	**2 367**	1 272
Available-for-sale investments, cash equivalents	**4 784**	3 842
Bank and cash	**1 142**	1 706
	23 613	24 470
Total assets	**35 738**	39 582
SHAREHOLDERS' EQUITY AND LIABILITIES		
Capital and reserves attributable to equity holders of the parent		
Share capital	**246**	246
Share issue premium	**279**	442
Treasury shares, at cost	**(681)**	(1 881)
Translation differences	**(127)**	341
Fair value and other reserves	**69**	62
Reserve for invested non-restricted equity	**3 170**	3 306
Retained earnings	**10 132**	11 692
	13 088	14 208
Minority interests	**1 661**	2 302
Total equity	**14 749**	16 510
Non-current liabilities		
Long-term interest-bearing liabilities	**4 432**	861
Deferred tax liabilities	**1 303**	1 787
Other long-term liabilities	**66**	69
	5 801	2 717
Current liabilities		
Current portion of long-term loans	**44**	13
Short-term borrowings	**727**	3 578
Other financial liabilities	**245**	924
Accounts payable	**4 950**	5 225
Accrued expenses	**6 504**	7 023
Provisions	**2 718**	3 592
	15 188	20 355
Total shareholders' equity and liabilities	**35 738**	39 582

NOKIA

Nokia Corporation and Subsidiaries
Consolidated Income Statements

Financial Year Ended December 31	2009 EURm	2008 EURm	2007 EURm
Net sales	**40 984**	50 710	51 058
Cost of sales	**(27 720)**	(33 337)	(33 781)
Gross profit	**13 264**	17 373	17 277
Research and development expenses	**(5 909)**	(5 968)	(5 636)
Selling and marketing expenses	**(3 933)**	(4 380)	(4 379)
Administrative and general expenses	**(1 145)**	(1 284)	(1 165)
Impairment of goodwill	**(908)**	—	—
Other income	**338**	420	2 312
Other expenses	**(510)**	(1 195)	(424)
Operating profit	**1 197**	4 966	7 985
Share of results of associated companies	**30**	6	44
Financial income and expenses	**(265)**	(2)	239
Profit before tax	**962**	4 970	8 268
Tax	**(702)**	(1 081)	(1 522)
Profit	**260**	3 889	6 746
Profit attributable to equity holders of the parent	**891**	3 988	7 205
Loss attributable to minority interests	**(631)**	(99)	(459)
	260	3 889	6 746

	2009 EUR	2008 EUR	2007 EUR
Earnings per share			
(for profit attributable to the equity holders of the parent)			
Basic	**0.24**	1.07	1.85
Diluted	**0.24**	1.05	1.83

	2009	2008	2007
Average number of shares (000's shares)			
Basic	**3 705 116**	3 743 622	3 885 408
Diluted	**3 721 072**	3 780 363	3 932 008

Nokia Corporation and Subsidiaries
Consolidated Statements of Comprehensive Income

Financial Year Ended December 31	2009 EURm	2008 EURm	2007 EURm
Profit	**260**	3 889	6 746
Other comprehensive income			
Translation differences	**(563)**	595	(151)
Net investment hedge gains (losses)	**114**	(123)	51
Cash flow hedges	**25**	(40)	(7)
Available-for-sale investments	**48**	(15)	49
Other increase (decrease), net	**(7)**	28	(46)
Income tax related to components of other comprehensive income	**(44)**	58	(12)
Other comprehensive income (expense), net of tax	**(427)**	503	(116)
Total comprehensive income (expense)	**(167)**	4 392	6 630
Total comprehensive income (expense) attributable to:			
Equity holders of the parent	**429**	4 577	7 073
Minority interests	**(596)**	(185)	(443)
	(167)	4 392	6 630

Nokia Corporation and Subsidiaries
Consolidated Statements of Changes in Shareholders' Equity

	Number of shares (000's)	Share capital	Share issue premium	Treasury shares	Translation differences	Fair value and other reserves	Reserve for invested non-restrict. equity	Retained earnings	Before minority interests	Minority interests	Total
Balance at December 31, 2007	**3 845 950**	**246**	**644**	**(3 146)**	**(163)**	**23**	**3 299**	**13 870**	**14 773**	**2 565**	**17 338**
Translation differences					595				595		595
Net investment hedge gains, net of tax					(91)				(91)		(91)
Cash flow hedges, net of tax						42			42	(67)	(25)
Available-for-sale investments, net of tax						(3)			(3)	(2)	(5)
Other increase, net								46	46	(17)	29
Profit								3 988	3 988	(99)	3 889
Total comprehensive income		—	—	—	**504**	**39**	—	**4 034**	**4 577**	(185)	**4 392**
Stock options exercised	3 547						51		51		51
Stock options exercised related to acquisitions			1						1		1
Share-based compensation			74						74		74
Excess tax benefit on share-based compensation			(117)						(117)	(6)	(124)
Settlement of performance and restricted shares	5 622		(179)	154			(44)		(69)		(69)
Acquisition of treasury shares	(157 390)			(3 123)					(3 123)		(3 123)
Reissuance of treasury shares	143			2					2		2
Cancellation of treasury shares			0	4 232				(4 232)	—		—
Dividend								(1 992)	(1 992)	(35)	(2 027)
Acquisitions and other change in minority interests										(37)	(37)
Vested portion of share-based payment awards related to acquisitions			19						19		19
Acquisition of Symbian								12	12		12
Total of other equity movements		—	**(202)**	**1 265**	—	—	**7**	**(6 212)**	**(5 142)**	**(78)**	**(5 220)**
Balance at December 31, 2008	**3 697 872**	**246**	**442**	**(1 881)**	**341**	**62**	**3 306**	**11 692**	**14 208**	**2 302**	**16 510**
Translation differences					(552)				(552)	(9)	(561)
Net investment hedge gains, net of tax					84				84		84
Cash flow hedges, net of tax						(35)			(35)	49	14
Available-for-sale investments, net of tax						42			42	2	44
Other decrease, net								(1)	(1)	(7)	(8)
Profit								891	891	(631)	260
Total comprehensive income		—	—	—	**(468)**	**7**	—	**890**	**429**	**(596)**	**(167)**
Stock options exercised	7						—				—
Stock options exercised related to acquisitions			(1)						(1)		(1)
Share-based compensation			16						16		16
Excess tax benefit on share-based compensation			(12)						(12)	(1)	(13)
Settlement of performance and restricted shares	10 352		(166)	230			(136)		(72)		(72)
Acquisition of treasury shares									—		—
Reissuance of treasury shares	31			1					1		1
Cancellation of treasury shares				969				(969)	—		—
Dividend								(1 481)	(1 481)	(44)	(1 525)
Total of other equity movements		—	**(163)**	**1 200**	—	—	**(136)**	**(2 450)**	**(1 549)**	**(45)**	**(1 594)**
Balance at December 31, 2009	**3 708 262**	**246**	**279**	**(681)**	**(127)**	**69**	**3 170**	**10 132**	**13 088**	**1 661**	**14 749**

Dividends declared per share were EUR 0.40 for 2009 (EUR 0.40 for 2008 and EUR 0.53 for 2007), subject to shareholders' approval.

NOKIA

Nokia Corporation and Subsidiaries
Consolidated Statements of Cash Flows

Financial Year Ended December 31	2009 EURm	2008 EURm	2007 EURm
Cash flow from operating activities			
Profit attributable to equity holders of the parent	**891**	3 988	7 205
Adjustments, total	**3 390**	3 024	1 159
Change in net working capital	**140**	(2 546)	605
Cash generated from operations	**4 421**	4 466	8 969
Interest received	**125**	416	362
Interest paid	**(256)**	(155)	(59)
Other financial income and expenses, net received	**(128)**	250	67
Income taxes paid, net received	**(915)**	(1 780)	(1 457)
Net cash from operating activities	**3 247**	3 197	7 882
Cash flow from investing activities			
Acquisition of Group companies, net of acquired cash	**(29)**	(5 962)	253
Purchase of current available-for-sale investments, liquid assets	**(2 800)**	(669)	(4 798)
Purchase of investments at fair value through profit and loss, liquid assets	**(695)**	—	—
Purchase of non-current available-for-sale investments	**(95)**	(121)	(126)
Purchase of shares in associated companies	**(30)**	(24)	(25)
Additions to capitalized development costs	**(27)**	(131)	(157)
Long-term loans made to customers	—	—	(261)
Proceeds from repayment and sale of long-term loans receivable	—	129	163
Proceeds from (+) / payment of (-) other long-term receivables	**2**	(1)	5
Proceeds from (+) / payment of (-) short-term loans receivable	**2**	(15)	(119)
Capital expenditures	**(531)**	(889)	(715)
Proceeds from disposal of shares in associated companies	**40**	3	6
Proceeds from disposal of businesses	**61**	41	—
Proceeds from maturities and sale of current available-for-sale investments, liquid assets	**1 730**	4 664	4 930
Proceeds from maturities and sale of investments at fair value through profit and loss, liquid assets	**108**	—	—
Proceeds from sale of non-current available-for-sale investments	**14**	10	50
Proceeds from sale of fixed assets	**100**	54	72
Dividends received	**2**	6	12
Net cash used in investing activities	**(2 148)**	(2 905)	(710)
Cash flow from financing activities			
Proceeds from stock option exercises	—	53	987
Purchase of treasury shares	—	(3 121)	(3 819)
Proceeds from long-term borrowings	**3 901**	714	115
Repayment of long-term borrowings	**(209)**	(34)	(16)
Proceeds from (+) / repayment of (-) short-term borrowings	**(2 842)**	2 891	661
Dividends paid	**(1 546)**	(2 048)	(1 760)
Net cash used in financing activities	**(696)**	(1 545)	(3 832)
Foreign exchange adjustment	**(25)**	(49)	(15)
Net increase (+) / decrease (-) in cash and cash equivalents	**378**	(1 302)	3 325
Cash and cash equivalents at beginning of period	**5 548**	6 850	3 525
Cash and cash equivalents at end of period	**5 926**	5 548	6 850
Cash and cash equivalents comprise of:			
Bank and cash	**1 142**	1 706	2 125
Current available-for-sale investments, cash equivalents	**4 784**	3 842	4 725
	5 926	5 548	6 850

NOKIA

Appendix

B

Time Value of Money

Learning Objectives

CAP

CONCEPTUAL

C1 Describe the earning of interest and the concepts of present and future values. (p. B-1)

PROCEDURAL

P1 Apply present value concepts to a single amount by using interest tables. (p. B-3)

P2 Apply future value concepts to a single amount by using interest tables. (p. B-4)

P3 Apply present value concepts to an annuity by using interest tables. (p. B-5)

P4 Apply future value concepts to an annuity by using interest tables. (p. B-6)

Appendix Preview

The concepts of present and future values are important to modern business, including the preparation and analysis of financial statements. The purpose of this appendix is to explain, illustrate, and compute present and future values. This appendix applies these concepts with reference to both business and everyday activities.

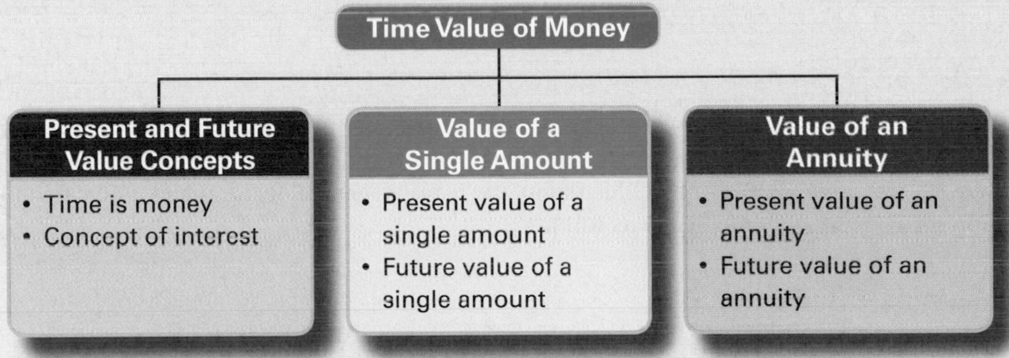

PRESENT AND FUTURE VALUE CONCEPTS

C1 Describe the earning of interest and the concepts of present and future values.

The old saying "Time is money" reflects the notion that as time passes, the values of our assets and liabilities change. This change is due to *interest,* which is a borrower's payment to the owner of an asset for its use. The most common example of interest is a savings account asset. As we keep a balance of cash in the account, it earns interest that the financial institution pays us. An example of a liability is a car loan. As we carry the balance of the loan, we accumulate interest costs on it. We must ultimately repay this loan with interest.

Present and future value computations enable us to measure or estimate the interest component of holding assets or liabilities over time. The present value computation is important when we want to know the value of future-day assets *today.* The future value computation is important when we want to know the value of present-day assets *at a future date.* The first section focuses on the present value of a single amount. The second section focuses on the future value of a single amount. Then both the present and future values of a series of amounts (called an *annuity*) are defined and explained.

Decision Insight

Keep That Job Lottery winners often never work again. Kenny Dukes, a recent Georgia lottery winner, doesn't have that option. He is serving parole for burglary charges, and Georgia requires its parolees to be employed (or in school). For his lottery winnings, Dukes had to choose between $31 million in 30 annual payments or $16 million in one lump sum ($10.6 million after-tax); he chose the latter. ■

PRESENT VALUE OF A SINGLE AMOUNT

We graphically express the present value, called p, of a single future amount, called f, that is received or paid at a future date in Exhibit B.1.

EXHIBIT B.1

Present Value of a Single Amount Diagram

The formula to compute the present value of a single amount is shown in Exhibit B.2, where p = present value; f = future value; i = rate of interest per period; and n = number of periods. (Interest is also called the *discount,* and an interest rate is also called the *discount rate.*)

EXHIBIT B.2

Present Value of a Single Amount Formula

$$p = \frac{f}{(1 + i)^n}$$

To illustrate present value concepts, assume that we need $220 one period from today. We want to know how much we must invest now, for one period, at an interest rate of 10% to provide for this $220. For this illustration, the p, or present value, is the unknown amount—the specifics are shown graphically as follows:

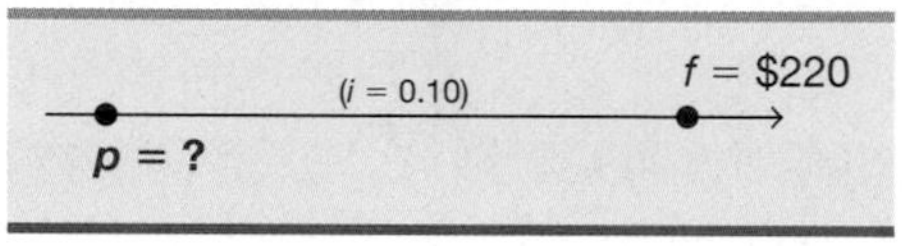

(i = 0.10) f = $220

p = ?

Conceptually, we know p must be less than $220. This is obvious from the answer to this question: Would we rather have $220 today or $220 at some future date? If we had $220 today, we could invest it and see it grow to something more than $220 in the future. Therefore, we would prefer the $220 today. This means that if we were promised $220 in the future, we would take less than $220 today. But how much less? To answer that question, we compute an estimate of the present value of the $220 to be received one period from now using the formula in Exhibit B.2 as follows:

$$p = \frac{f}{(1 + i)^n} = \frac{\$220}{(1 + 0.10)^1} = \$200$$

We interpret this result to say that given an interest rate of 10%, we are indifferent between $200 today or $220 at the end of one period.

We can also use this formula to compute the present value for *any number of periods.* To illustrate, consider a payment of $242 at the end of two periods at 10% interest. The present value of this $242 to be received two periods from now is computed as follows:

$$p = \frac{f}{(1 + i)^n} = \frac{\$242}{(1 + 0.10)^2} = \$200$$

Together, these results tell us we are indifferent between $200 today, or $220 one period from today, or $242 two periods from today given a 10% interest rate per period.

The number of periods (n) in the present value formula does not have to be expressed in years. Any period of time such as a day, a month, a quarter, or a year can be used. Whatever period is used, the interest rate (i) must be compounded for the same period. This means that if a situation expresses n in months and i equals 12% per year, then i is transformed into interest earned per month (or 1%). In this case, interest is said to be *compounded monthly.*

A present value table helps us with present value computations. It gives us present values (factors) for a variety of both interest rates (i) and periods (n). Each present value in a present value table assumes that the future value (f) equals 1. When the future value (f) is different from 1, we simply multiply the present value (p) from the table by that future value to give us the estimate. The formula used to construct a table of present values for a single future amount of 1 is shown in Exhibit B.3.

EXHIBIT B.3

Present Value of 1 Formula

$$p = \frac{1}{(1 + i)^n}$$

This formula is identical to that in Exhibit B.2 except that f equals 1. Table B.1 at the end of this appendix is such a present value table. It is often called a **present value of 1 table**. A present value table involves three factors: p, i, and n. Knowing two of these three factors allows us to compute the third. (A fourth is f, but as already explained, we need only multiply the 1 used in the formula by f.) To illustrate the use of a present value table, consider three cases.

P1 Apply present value concepts to a single amount by using interest tables.

Case 1 (solve for p when knowing i and n). To show how we use a present value table, let's look again at how we estimate the present value of $220 (the f value) at the end of one period ($n = 1$) where the interest rate (i) is 10%. To solve this case, we go to the present value table (Table B.1) and look in the row for 1 period and in the column for 10% interest. Here we find a present value (p) of 0.9091 based on a future value of 1. This means, for instance, that $1 to be received one period from today at 10% interest is worth $0.9091 today. Since the future value in this case is not $1 but $220, we multiply the 0.9091 by $220 to get an answer of $200.

Case 2 (solve for n when knowing p and i). To illustrate, assume a $100,000 future value ($f$) that is worth $13,000 today ($p$) using an interest rate of 12% (i) but where n is unknown. In particular, we want to know how many periods (n) there are between the present value and the future value. To put this in context, it would fit a situation in which we want to retire with $100,000 but currently have only $13,000 that is earning a 12% return and we will be unable to save any additional money. How long will it be before we can retire? To answer this, we go to Table B.1 and look in the 12% interest column. Here we find a column of present values (p) based on a future value of 1. To use the present value table for this solution, we must divide $13,000 ($p$) by $100,000 ($f$), which equals 0.1300. This is necessary because *a present value table defines* f *equal to 1, and* p *as a fraction of 1.* We look for a value nearest to 0.1300 (p), which we find in the row for 18 periods (n). This means that the present value of $100,000 at the end of 18 periods at 12% interest is $13,000; alternatively stated, we must work 18 more years.

Case 3 (solve for i when knowing p and n). In this case, we have, say, a $120,000 future value ($f$) worth $60,000 today ($p$) when there are nine periods (n) between the present and future values, but the interest rate is unknown. As an example, suppose we want to retire with $120,000, but we have only $60,000 and we will be unable to save any additional money, yet we hope to retire in nine years. What interest rate must we earn to retire with $120,000 in nine years? To answer this, we go to the present value table (Table B.1) and look in the row for nine periods. To use the present value table, we must divide $60,000 ($p$) by $120,000 ($f$), which equals 0.5000. Recall that this step is necessary because a present value table defines f equal to 1 and p as a fraction of 1. We look for a value in the row for nine periods that is nearest to 0.5000 (p), which we find in the column for 8% interest (i). This means that the present value of $120,000 at the end of nine periods at 8% interest is $60,000 or, in our example, we must earn 8% annual interest to retire in nine years.

Quick Check Answer — p. B-7 

1. A company is considering an investment expected to yield $70,000 after six years. If this company demands an 8% return, how much is it willing to pay for this investment?

FUTURE VALUE OF A SINGLE AMOUNT

We must modify the formula for the present value of a single amount to obtain the formula for the future value of a single amount. In particular, we multiply both sides of the equation in Exhibit B.2 by $(1 + i)^n$ to get the result shown in Exhibit B.4.

$$f = p \times (1 + i)^n$$

EXHIBIT B.4

Future Value of a Single Amount Formula

The future value (f) is defined in terms of p, i, and n. We can use this formula to determine that \$200 (p) invested for 1 (n) period at an interest rate of 10% (i) yields a future value of \$220 as follows:

$$
\begin{aligned}
f &= p \times (1 + i)^n \\
&= \$200 \times (1 + 0.10)^1 \\
&= \$220
\end{aligned}
$$

P2 Apply future value concepts to a single amount by using interest tables.

This formula can also be used to compute the future value of an amount for *any number of periods* into the future. To illustrate, assume that \$200 is invested for three periods at 10%. The future value of this \$200 is \$266.20, computed as follows:

$$
\begin{aligned}
f &= p \times (1 + i)^n \\
&= \$200 \times (1 + 0.10)^3 \\
&= \$266.20
\end{aligned}
$$

A future value table makes it easier for us to compute future values (f) for many different combinations of interest rates (i) and time periods (n). Each future value in a future value table assumes the present value (p) is 1. As with a present value table, if the future amount is something other than 1, we simply multiply our answer by that amount. The formula used to construct a table of future values (factors) for a single amount of 1 is in Exhibit B.5.

EXHIBIT B.5

Future Value of 1 Formula

$$f = (1 + i)^n$$

Table B.2 at the end of this appendix shows a table of future values for a current amount of 1. This type of table is called a **future value of 1 table**.

There are some important relations between Tables B.1 and B.2. In Table B.2, for the row where $n = 0$, the future value is 1 for each interest rate. This is so because no interest is earned when time does not pass. We also see that Tables B.1 and B.2 report the same information but in a different manner. In particular, one table is simply the *inverse* of the other. To illustrate this inverse relation, let's say we invest \$100 for a period of five years at 12% per year. How much do we expect to have after five years? We can answer this question using Table B.2 by finding the future value (f) of 1, for five periods from now, compounded at 12%. From that table we find $f = 1.7623$. If we start with \$100, the amount it accumulates to after five years is \$176.23 (\$100 × 1.7623). We can alternatively use Table B.1. Here we find that the present value (p) of 1, discounted five periods at 12%, is 0.5674. Recall the inverse relation between present value and future value. This means that $p = 1/f$ (or equivalently, $f = 1/p$). We can compute the future value of \$100 invested for five periods at 12% as follows: $f = \$100 \times (1/0.5674) = \$176.24$ (which equals the \$176.23 just computed, except for a 1 cent rounding difference).

A future value table involves three factors: f, i, and n. Knowing two of these three factors allows us to compute the third. To illustrate, consider these three possible cases.

Case 1 (solve for f when knowing i and n). Our preceding example fits this case. We found that \$100 invested for five periods at 12% interest accumulates to \$176.24.

Case 2 (solve for n when knowing f and i). In this case, we have, say, \$2,000 (p) and we want to know how many periods (n) it will take to accumulate to \$3,000 (f) at 7% (i) interest. To answer this, we go to the future value table (Table B.2) and look in the 7% interest column. Here we find a column of future values (f) based on a present value of 1. To use a future value table, we must divide \$3,000 (f) by \$2,000 (p), which equals 1.500. This is necessary because *a future value table defines* p *equal to 1, and* f *as a multiple of 1.* We look for a value nearest to 1.50 (f), which we find in the row for six periods (n). This means that \$2,000 invested for six periods at 7% interest accumulates to \$3,000.

Case 3 (solve for i when knowing f and n). In this case, we have, say, \$2,001 (p), and in nine years (n) we want to have \$4,000 (f). What rate of interest must we earn to accomplish this? To answer that, we go to Table B.2 and search in the row for nine periods. To use a future value table, we must divide \$4,000 (f) by \$2,001 (p), which equals 1.9990. Recall that this is necessary because a future value table defines p equal to 1 and f as a multiple of 1. We look for a value nearest to 1.9990 (f), which we find in the column for 8% interest (i). This means that \$2,001 invested for nine periods at 8% interest accumulates to \$4,000.

Quick Check Answer — p. B-7 

2. Assume that you win a \$150,000 cash sweepstakes. You decide to deposit this cash in an account earning 8% annual interest, and you plan to quit your job when the account equals \$555,000. How many years will it be before you can quit working?

PRESENT VALUE OF AN ANNUITY

An *annuity* is a series of equal payments occurring at equal intervals. One example is a series of three annual payments of \$100 each. An *ordinary annuity* is defined as equal end-of-period payments at equal intervals. An ordinary annuity of \$100 for three periods and its present value (p) are illustrated in Exhibit B.6.

EXHIBIT B.6

Present Value of an Ordinary Annuity Diagram

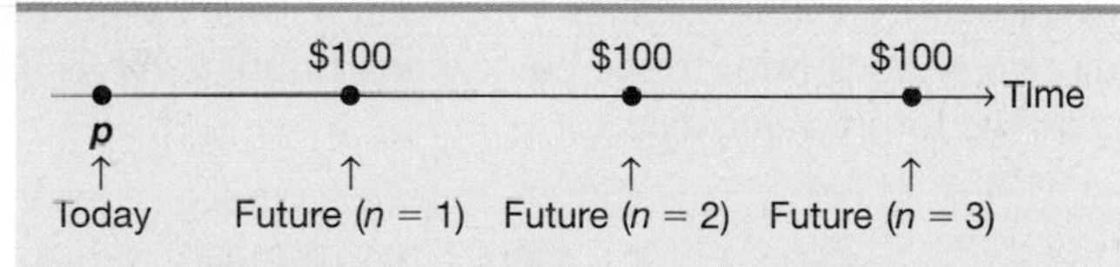

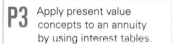

P3 Apply present value concepts to an annuity by using interest tables.

One way to compute the present value of an ordinary annuity is to find the present value of each payment using our present value formula from Exhibit B.3. We then add each of the three present values. To illustrate, let's look at three \$100 payments at the end of each of the next three periods with an interest rate of 15%. Our present value computations are

$$p = \frac{\$100}{(1 + 0.15)^1} + \frac{\$100}{(1 + 0.15)^2} + \frac{\$100}{(1 + 0.15)^3} = \$228.32$$

This computation is identical to computing the present value of each payment (from Table B.1) and taking their sum or, alternatively, adding the values from Table B.1 for each of the three payments and multiplying their sum by the \$100 annuity payment.

A more direct way is to use a present value of annuity table. Table B.3 at the end of this appendix is one such table. This table is called a **present value of an annuity of 1 table.** If we look at Table B.3 where $n = 3$ and $i = 15\%$, we see the present value is 2.2832. This means that the present value of an annuity of 1 for three periods, with a 15% interest rate, equals 2.2832.

A present value of an annuity formula is used to construct Table B.3. It can also be constructed by adding the amounts in a present value of 1 table. To illustrate, we use Tables B.1 and B.3 to confirm this relation for the prior example:

From Table B.1		From Table B.3	
i = 15%, n = 1	0.8696		
i = 15%, n = 2	0.7561		
i = 15%, n = 3	0.6575		
Total	2.2832	i = 15%, n = 3	2.2832

We can also use business calculators or spreadsheet programs to find the present value of an annuity.

Decision Insight

Better Lucky Than Good "I don't have good luck—I'm blessed," proclaimed Andrew "Jack" Whittaker, 55, a sewage treatment contractor, after winning the largest ever undivided jackpot in a U.S. lottery. Whittaker had to choose between $315 million in 30 annual installments or $170 million in one lump sum ($112 million after-tax). ■

Quick Check Answer — p. B-7

3. A company is considering an investment paying $10,000 every six months for three years. The first payment would be received in six months. If this company requires an 8% annual return, what is the maximum amount it is willing to pay for this investment?

FUTURE VALUE OF AN ANNUITY

The future value of an *ordinary annuity* is the accumulated value of each annuity payment with interest as of the date of the final payment. To illustrate, let's consider the earlier annuity of three annual payments of $100. Exhibit B.7 shows the point in time for the future value (f). The first payment is made two periods prior to the point when future value is determined, and the final payment occurs on the future value date.

EXHIBIT B.7

Future Value of an Ordinary Annuity Diagram

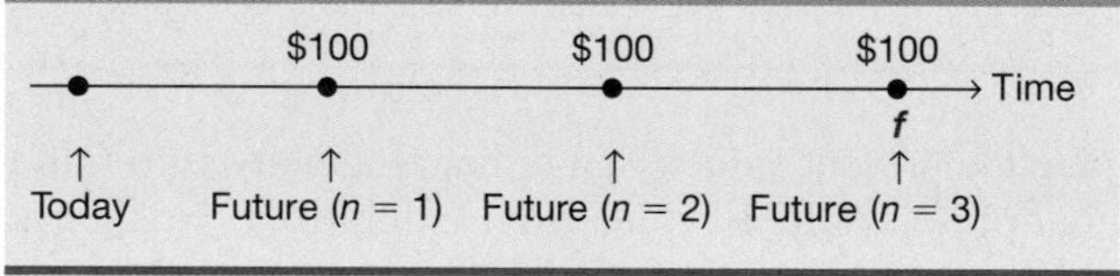

One way to compute the future value of an annuity is to use the formula to find the future value of *each* payment and add them. If we assume an interest rate of 15%, our calculation is

$$f = \$100 \times (1 + 0.15)^2 + \$100 \times (1 + 0.15)^1 + \$100 \times (1 + 0.15)^0 = \$347.25$$

This is identical to using Table B.2 and summing the future values of each payment, or adding the future values of the three payments of 1 and multiplying the sum by $100.

P4 Apply future value concepts to an annuity by using interest tables.

A more direct way is to use a table showing future values of annuities. Such a table is called a **future value of an annuity of 1 table**. Table B.4 at the end of this appendix is one such table. Note that in Table B.4 when $n = 1$, the future values equal 1 ($f = 1$) for all rates of interest. This is so because such an annuity consists of only one payment and the future value is determined on the date of that payment—no time passes between the payment and its future value. The future value of an annuity formula is used to construct Table B.4. We can also construct it by adding the amounts from a future value of 1 table. To illustrate, we use Tables B.2 and B.4 to confirm this relation for the prior example:

From Table B.2		From Table B.4	
i = 15%, n = 0	1.0000		
i = 15%, n = 1	1.1500		
i = 15%, n = 2	1.3225		
Total	3.4725	i = 15%, n = 3	3.4725

Note that the future value in Table B.2 is 1.0000 when $n = 0$, but the future value in Table B.4 is 1.0000 when $n = 1$. Is this a contradiction? No. When $n = 0$ in Table B.2, the future value is determined on the date when a single payment occurs. This means that no interest is earned because no time has passed, and the future value equals the payment. Table B.4 describes annuities with equal payments occurring at the end of each period. When $n = 1$, the annuity has one payment, and its future value equals 1 on the date of its final and only payment. Again, no time passes between the payment and its future value date.

Quick Check Answer — p. B-7

4. A company invests $45,000 per year for five years at 12% annual interest. Compute the value of this annuity investment at the end of five years.

Summary

C1 Describe the earning of interest and the concepts of present and future values. Interest is payment by a borrower to the owner of an asset for its use. Present and future value computations are a way for us to estimate the interest component of holding assets or liabilities over a period of time.

P1 Apply present value concepts to a single amount by using interest tables. The present value of a single amount received at a future date is the amount that can be invested now at the specified interest rate to yield that future value.

P2 Apply future value concepts to a single amount by using interest tables. The future value of a single amount invested at a specified rate of interest is the amount that would accumulate by the future date.

P3 Apply present value concepts to an annuity by using interest tables. The present value of an annuity is the amount that can be invested now at the specified interest rate to yield that series of equal periodic payments.

P4 Apply future value concepts to an annuity by using interest tables. The future value of an annuity invested at a specific rate of interest is the amount that would accumulate by the date of the final payment.

Guidance Answers to Quick Checks

1. $70,000 × 0.6302 = $44,114 (use Table B.1, $i = 8\%$, $n = 6$).
2. $555,000/$150,000 = 3.7000; Table B.2 shows this value is not achieved until after 17 years at 8% interest.
3. $10,000 × 5.2421 = $52,421 (use Table B.3, $i = 4\%$, $n = 6$).
4. $45,000 × 6.3528 = $285,876 (use Table B.4, $i = 12\%$, $n = 5$).

connect

QUICK STUDY

QS B-1
Identifying interest rates in tables
C1

Assume that you must make future value estimates using the *future value of 1 table* (Table B.2). Which interest rate column do you use when working with the following rates?

1. 8% compounded quarterly
2. 12% compounded annually
3. 6% compounded semiannually
4. 12% compounded monthly

QS B-2
Interest rate on an investment P1

Ken Francis is offered the possibility of investing $2,745 today and in return to receive $10,000 after 15 years. What is the annual rate of interest for this investment? (Use Table B.1.)

QS B-3
Number of periods of an investment P1

Megan Brink is offered the possibility of investing $6,651 today at 6% interest per year in a desire to accumulate $10,000. How many years must Brink wait to accumulate $10,000? (Use Table B.1.)

QS B-4
Present value of an amount P1

Flaherty is considering an investment that, if paid for immediately, is expected to return $140,000 five years from now. If Flaherty demands a 9% return, how much is she willing to pay for this investment?

QS B-5
Future value of an amount P2

CII, Inc., invests $630,000 in a project expected to earn a 12% annual rate of return. The earnings will be reinvested in the project each year until the entire investment is liquidated 10 years later. What will the cash proceeds be when the project is liquidated?

QS B-6
Present value of an annuity P3

Beene Distributing is considering a project that will return $150,000 annually at the end of each year for six years. If Beene demands an annual return of 7% and pays for the project immediately, how much is it willing to pay for the project?

QS B-7
Future value of an annuity P4

Claire Fitch is planning to begin an individual retirement program in which she will invest $1,500 at the end of each year. Fitch plans to retire after making 30 annual investments in the program earning a return of 10%. What is the value of the program on the date of the last payment?

EXERCISES

Exercise B-1
Number of periods of an investment P2

Bill Thompson expects to invest $10,000 at 12% and, at the end of a certain period, receive $96,463. How many years will it be before Thompson receives the payment? (Use Table B.2.)

Exercise B-2
Interest rate on an investment P2

Ed Summers expects to invest $10,000 for 25 years, after which he wants to receive $108,347. What rate of interest must Summers earn? (Use Table B.2.)

Exercise B-3
Interest rate on an investment P3

Jones expects an immediate investment of $57,466 to return $10,000 annually for eight years, with the first payment to be received one year from now. What rate of interest must Jones earn? (Use Table B.3.)

Exercise B-4
Number of periods of an investment P3

Keith Riggins expects an investment of $82,014 to return $10,000 annually for several years. If Riggins earns a return of 10%, how many annual payments will he receive? (Use Table B.3.)

Exercise B-5
Interest rate on an investment P4

Algoe expects to invest $1,000 annually for 40 years to yield an accumulated value of $154,762 on the date of the last investment. For this to occur, what rate of interest must Algoe earn? (Use Table B.4.)

Exercise B-6
Number of periods of an investment P4

Kate Beckwith expects to invest $10,000 annually that will earn 8%. How many annual investments must Beckwith make to accumulate $303,243 on the date of the last investment? (Use Table B.4.)

Exercise B-7
Present value of an annuity P3

Sam Weber finances a new automobile by paying $6,500 cash and agreeing to make 40 monthly payments of $500 each, the first payment to be made one month after the purchase. The loan bears interest at an annual rate of 12%. What is the cost of the automobile?

Exercise B-8
Present value of bonds P1 P3

Spiller Corp. plans to issue 10%, 15-year, $500,000 par value bonds payable that pay interest semiannually on June 30 and December 31. The bonds are dated December 31, 2011, and are issued on that date. If the market rate of interest for the bonds is 8% on the date of issue, what will be the total cash proceeds from the bond issue?

Exercise B-9
Present value of an amount P1

McAdams Company expects to earn 10% per year on an investment that will pay $606,773 six years from now. Use Table B.1 to compute the present value of this investment. (Round the amount to the nearest dollar.)

Exercise B-10
Present value of an amount and of an annuity P1 P3

Compute the amount that can be borrowed under each of the following circumstances:

1. A promise to repay $90,000 seven years from now at an interest rate of 6%.
2. An agreement made on February 1, 2011, to make three separate payments of $20,000 on February 1 of 2012, 2013, and 2014. The annual interest rate is 10%.

Exercise B-11
Present value of an amount P1

On January 1, 2011, a company agrees to pay $20,000 in three years. If the annual interest rate is 10%, determine how much cash the company can borrow with this agreement.

Exercise B-12
Present value of an amount P1

Find the amount of money that can be borrowed today with each of the following separate debt agreements *a* through *f*. (Round amounts to the nearest dollar.)

Case	Single Future Payment	Number of Periods	Interest Rate
a.	$40,000	3	4%
b.	75,000	7	8
c.	52,000	9	10
d.	18,000	2	4
e.	63,000	8	6
f.	89,000	5	2

Exercise B-13
Present values of annuities
P3

C&H Ski Club recently borrowed money and agrees to pay it back with a series of six annual payments of $5,000 each. C&H subsequently borrows more money and agrees to pay it back with a series of four annual payments of $7,500 each. The annual interest rate for both loans is 6%.

1. Use Table B.1 to find the present value of these two separate annuities. (Round amounts to the nearest dollar.)
2. Use Table B.3 to find the present value of these two separate annuities. (Round amounts to the nearest dollar.)

Exercise B-14
Present value with semiannual compounding
C1 P3

Otto Co. borrows money on April 30, 2011, by promising to make four payments of $13,000 each on November 1, 2011; May 1, 2012; November 1, 2012; and May 1, 2013.

1. How much money is Otto able to borrow if the interest rate is 8%, compounded semiannually?
2. How much money is Otto able to borrow if the interest rate is 12%, compounded semiannually?
3. How much money is Otto able to borrow if the interest rate is 16%, compounded semiannually?

Exercise B-15
Future value of an amount P2

Mark Welsch deposits $7,200 in an account that earns interest at an annual rate of 8%, compounded quarterly. The $7,200 plus earned interest must remain in the account 10 years before it can be withdrawn. How much money will be in the account at the end of 10 years?

Exercise B-16
Future value of an annuity P4

Kelly Malone plans to have $50 withheld from her monthly paycheck and deposited in a savings account that earns 12% annually, compounded monthly. If Malone continues with her plan for two and one-half years, how much will be accumulated in the account on the date of the last deposit?

Exercise B-17
Future value of an amount plus an annuity P2 P4

Starr Company decides to establish a fund that it will use 10 years from now to replace an aging production facility. The company will make a $100,000 initial contribution to the fund and plans to make quarterly contributions of $50,000 beginning in three months. The fund earns 12%, compounded quarterly. What will be the value of the fund 10 years from now?

Exercise B-18
Future value of an amount P2

Catten, Inc., invests $163,170 today earning 7% per year for nine years. Use Table B.2 to compute the future value of the investment nine years from now. (Round the amount to the nearest dollar.)

Exercise B-19
Using present and future value tables
C1 P1 P2 P3 P4

For each of the following situations, identify (1) the case as either (*a*) a present or a future value and (*b*) a single amount or an annuity, (2) the table you would use in your computations (but do not solve the problem), and (3) the interest rate and time periods you would use.

a. You need to accumulate $10,000 for a trip you wish to take in four years. You are able to earn 8% compounded semiannually on your savings. You plan to make only one deposit and let the money accumulate for four years. How would you determine the amount of the one-time deposit?
b. Assume the same facts as in part (*a*) except that you will make semiannual deposits to your savings account.
c. You want to retire after working 40 years with savings in excess of $1,000,000. You expect to save $4,000 a year for 40 years and earn an annual rate of interest of 8%. Will you be able to retire with more than $1,000,000 in 40 years? Explain.
d. A sweepstakes agency names you a grand prize winner. You can take $225,000 immediately or elect to receive annual installments of $30,000 for 20 years. You can earn 10% annually on any investments you make. Which prize do you choose to receive?

TABLE B.1

Present Value of 1

$$p = 1/(1 + i)^n$$

Periods	Rate 1%	2%	3%	4%	5%	6%	7%	8%	9%	10%	12%	15%
1	0.9901	0.9804	0.9709	0.9615	0.9524	0.9434	0.9346	0.9259	0.9174	0.9091	0.8929	0.8696
2	0.9803	0.9612	0.9426	0.9246	0.9070	0.8900	0.8734	0.8573	0.8417	0.8264	0.7972	0.7561
3	0.9706	0.9423	0.9151	0.8890	0.8638	0.8396	0.8163	0.7938	0.7722	0.7513	0.7118	0.6575
4	0.9610	0.9238	0.8885	0.8548	0.8227	0.7921	0.7629	0.7350	0.7084	0.6830	0.6355	0.5718
5	0.9515	0.9057	0.8626	0.8219	0.7835	0.7473	0.7130	0.6806	0.6499	0.6209	0.5674	0.4972
6	0.9420	0.8880	0.8375	0.7903	0.7462	0.7050	0.6663	0.6302	0.5963	0.5645	0.5066	0.4323
7	0.9327	0.8706	0.8131	0.7599	0.7107	0.6651	0.6227	0.5835	0.5470	0.5132	0.4523	0.3759
8	0.9235	0.8535	0.7894	0.7307	0.6768	0.6274	0.5820	0.5403	0.5019	0.4665	0.4039	0.3269
9	0.9143	0.8368	0.7664	0.7026	0.6446	0.5919	0.5439	0.5002	0.4604	0.4241	0.3606	0.2843
10	0.9053	0.8203	0.7441	0.6756	0.6139	0.5584	0.5083	0.4632	0.4224	0.3855	0.3220	0.2472
11	0.8963	0.8043	0.7224	0.6496	0.5847	0.5268	0.4751	0.4289	0.3875	0.3505	0.2875	0.2149
12	0.8874	0.7885	0.7014	0.6246	0.5568	0.4970	0.4440	0.3971	0.3555	0.3186	0.2567	0.1869
13	0.8787	0.7730	0.6810	0.6006	0.5303	0.4688	0.4150	0.3677	0.3262	0.2897	0.2292	0.1625
14	0.8700	0.7579	0.6611	0.5775	0.5051	0.4423	0.3878	0.3405	0.2992	0.2633	0.2046	0.1413
15	0.8613	0.7430	0.6419	0.5553	0.4810	0.4173	0.3624	0.3152	0.2745	0.2394	0.1827	0.1229
16	0.8528	0.7284	0.6232	0.5339	0.4581	0.3936	0.3387	0.2919	0.2519	0.2176	0.1631	0.1069
17	0.8444	0.7142	0.6050	0.5134	0.4363	0.3714	0.3166	0.2703	0.2311	0.1978	0.1456	0.0929
18	0.8360	0.7002	0.5874	0.4936	0.4155	0.3503	0.2959	0.2502	0.2120	0.1799	0.1300	0.0808
19	0.8277	0.6864	0.5703	0.4746	0.3957	0.3305	0.2765	0.2317	0.1945	0.1635	0.1161	0.0703
20	0.8195	0.6730	0.5537	0.4564	0.3769	0.3118	0.2584	0.2145	0.1784	0.1486	0.1037	0.0611
25	0.7798	0.6095	0.4776	0.3751	0.2953	0.2330	0.1842	0.1460	0.1160	0.0923	0.0588	0.0304
30	0.7419	0.5521	0.4120	0.3083	0.2314	0.1741	0.1314	0.0994	0.0754	0.0573	0.0334	0.0151
35	0.7059	0.5000	0.3554	0.2534	0.1813	0.1301	0.0937	0.0676	0.0490	0.0356	0.0189	0.0075
40	0.6717	0.4529	0.3066	0.2083	0.1420	0.0972	0.0668	0.0460	0.0318	0.0221	0.0107	0.0037

TABLE B.2

Future Value of 1

$$f = (1 + i)^n$$

Periods	Rate 1%	2%	3%	4%	5%	6%	7%	8%	9%	10%	12%	15%
0	1.0000	1.0000	1.0000	1.0000	1.0000	1.0000	1.0000	1.0000	1.0000	1.0000	1.0000	1.0000
1	1.0100	1.0200	1.0300	1.0400	1.0500	1.0600	1.0700	1.0800	1.0900	1.1000	1.1200	1.1500
2	1.0201	1.0404	1.0609	1.0816	1.1025	1.1236	1.1449	1.1664	1.1881	1.2100	1.2544	1.3225
3	1.0303	1.0612	1.0927	1.1249	1.1576	1.1910	1.2250	1.2597	1.2950	1.3310	1.4049	1.5209
4	1.0406	1.0824	1.1255	1.1699	1.2155	1.2625	1.3108	1.3605	1.4116	1.4641	1.5735	1.7490
5	1.0510	1.1041	1.1593	1.2167	1.2763	1.3382	1.4026	1.4693	1.5386	1.6105	1.7623	2.0114
6	1.0615	1.1262	1.1941	1.2653	1.3401	1.4185	1.5007	1.5869	1.6771	1.7716	1.9738	2.3131
7	1.0721	1.1487	1.2299	1.3159	1.4071	1.5036	1.6058	1.7138	1.8280	1.9487	2.2107	2.6600
8	1.0829	1.1717	1.2668	1.3686	1.4775	1.5938	1.7182	1.8509	1.9926	2.1436	2.4760	3.0590
9	1.0937	1.1951	1.3048	1.4233	1.5513	1.6895	1.8385	1.9990	2.1719	2.3579	2.7731	3.5179
10	1.1046	1.2190	1.3439	1.4802	1.6289	1.7908	1.9672	2.1589	2.3674	2.5937	3.1058	4.0456
11	1.1157	1.2434	1.3842	1.5395	1.7103	1.8983	2.1049	2.3316	2.5804	2.8531	3.4785	4.6524
12	1.1268	1.2682	1.4258	1.6010	1.7959	2.0122	2.2522	2.5182	2.8127	3.1384	3.8960	5.3503
13	1.1381	1.2936	1.4685	1.6651	1.8856	2.1329	2.4098	2.7196	3.0658	3.4523	4.3635	6.1528
14	1.1495	1.3195	1.5126	1.7317	1.9799	2.2609	2.5785	2.9372	3.3417	3.7975	4.8871	7.0757
15	1.1610	1.3459	1.5580	1.8009	2.0789	2.3966	2.7590	3.1722	3.6425	4.1772	5.4736	8.1371
16	1.1726	1.3728	1.6047	1.8730	2.1829	2.5404	2.9522	3.4259	3.9703	4.5950	6.1304	9.3576
17	1.1843	1.4002	1.6528	1.9479	2.2920	2.6928	3.1588	3.7000	4.3276	5.0545	6.8660	10.7613
18	1.1961	1.4282	1.7024	2.0258	2.4066	2.8543	3.3799	3.9960	4.7171	5.5599	7.6900	12.3755
19	1.2081	1.4568	1.7535	2.1068	2.5270	3.0256	3.6165	4.3157	5.1417	6.1159	8.6128	14.2318
20	1.2202	1.4859	1.8061	2.1911	2.6533	3.2071	3.8697	4.6610	5.6044	6.7275	9.6463	16.3665
25	1.2824	1.6406	2.0938	2.6658	3.3864	4.2919	5.4274	6.8485	8.6231	10.8347	17.0001	32.9190
30	1.3478	1.8114	2.4273	3.2434	4.3219	5.7435	7.6123	10.0627	13.2677	17.4494	29.9599	66.2118
35	1.4166	1.9999	2.8139	3.9461	5.5160	7.6861	10.6766	14.7853	20.4140	28.1024	52.7996	133.1755
40	1.4889	2.2080	3.2620	4.8010	7.0400	10.2857	14.9745	21.7245	31.4094	45.2593	93.0510	267.8635

$$p = \left[1 - \frac{1}{(1+i)^n}\right] / i$$

TABLE B.3

Present Value of an Annuity of 1

Periods	Rate 1%	2%	3%	4%	5%	6%	7%	8%	9%	10%	12%	15%
1	0.9901	0.9804	0.9709	0.9615	0.9524	0.9434	0.9346	0.9259	0.9174	0.9091	0.8929	0.8696
2	1.9704	1.9416	1.9135	1.8861	1.8594	1.8334	1.8080	1.7833	1.7591	1.7355	1.6901	1.6257
3	2.9410	2.8839	2.8286	2.7751	2.7232	2.6730	2.6243	2.5771	2.5313	2.4869	2.4018	2.2832
4	3.9020	3.8077	3.7171	3.6299	3.5460	3.4651	3.3872	3.3121	3.2397	3.1699	3.0373	2.8550
5	4.8534	4.7135	4.5797	4.4518	4.3295	4.2124	4.1002	3.9927	3.8897	3.7908	3.6048	3.3522
6	5.7955	5.6014	5.4172	5.2421	5.0757	4.9173	4.7665	4.6229	4.4859	4.3553	4.1114	3.7845
7	6.7282	6.4720	6.2303	6.0021	5.7864	5.5824	5.3893	5.2064	5.0330	4.8684	4.5638	4.1604
8	7.6517	7.3255	7.0197	6.7327	6.4632	6.2098	5.9713	5.7466	5.5348	5.3349	4.9676	4.4873
9	8.5660	8.1622	7.7861	7.4353	7.1078	6.8017	6.5152	6.2469	5.9952	5.7590	5.3282	4.7716
10	9.4713	8.9826	8.5302	8.1109	7.7217	7.3601	7.0236	6.7101	6.4177	6.1446	5.6502	5.0188
11	10.3676	9.7868	9.2526	8.7605	8.3064	7.8869	7.4987	7.1390	6.8052	6.4951	5.9377	5.2337
12	11.2551	10.5753	9.9540	9.3851	8.8633	8.3838	7.9427	7.5361	7.1607	6.8137	6.1944	5.4206
13	12.1337	11.3484	10.6350	9.9856	9.3936	8.8527	8.3577	7.9038	7.4869	7.1034	6.4235	5.5831
14	13.0037	12.1062	11.2961	10.5631	9.8986	9.2950	8.7455	8.2442	7.7862	7.3667	6.6282	5.7245
15	13.8651	12.8493	11.9379	11.1184	10.3797	9.7122	9.1079	8.5595	8.0607	7.6061	6.8109	5.8474
16	14.7179	13.5777	12.5611	11.6523	10.8378	10.1059	9.4466	8.8514	8.3126	7.8237	6.9740	5.9542
17	15.5623	14.2919	13.1661	12.1657	11.2741	10.4773	9.7632	9.1216	8.5436	8.0216	7.1196	6.0472
18	16.3983	14.9920	13.7535	12.6593	11.6896	10.8276	10.0591	9.3719	8.7556	8.2014	7.2497	6.1280
19	17.2260	15.6785	14.3238	13.1339	12.0853	11.1581	10.3356	9.6036	8.9501	8.3649	7.3658	6.1982
20	18.0456	16.3514	14.8775	13.5903	12.4622	11.4699	10.5940	9.8181	9.1285	8.5136	7.4694	6.2593
25	22.0232	19.5235	17.4131	15.6221	14.0939	12.7834	11.6536	10.6748	9.8226	9.0770	7.8431	6.4641
30	25.8077	22.3965	19.6004	17.2920	15.3725	13.7648	12.4090	11.2578	10.2737	9.4269	8.0552	6.5660
35	29.4086	24.9986	21.4872	18.6646	16.3742	14.4982	12.9477	11.6546	10.5668	9.6442	8.1755	6.6166
40	32.8347	27.3555	23.1148	19.7928	17.1591	15.0463	13.3317	11.9246	10.7574	9.7791	8.2438	6.6418

$$f = [(1+i)^n - 1]/i$$

TABLE B.4

Future Value of an Annuity of 1

Periods	Rate 1%	2%	3%	4%	5%	6%	7%	8%	9%	10%	12%	15%
1	1.0000	1.0000	1.0000	1.0000	1.0000	1.0000	1.0000	1.0000	1.0000	1.0000	1.0000	1.0000
2	2.0100	2.0200	2.0300	2.0400	2.0500	2.0600	2.0700	2.0800	2.0900	2.1000	2.1200	2.1500
3	3.0301	3.0604	3.0909	3.1216	3.1525	3.1836	3.2149	3.2464	3.2781	3.3100	3.3744	3.4725
4	4.0604	4.1216	4.1836	4.2465	4.3101	4.3746	4.4399	4.5061	4.5731	4.6410	4.7793	4.9934
5	5.1010	5.2040	5.3091	5.4163	5.5256	5.6371	5.7507	5.8666	5.9847	6.1051	6.3528	6.7424
6	6.1520	6.3081	6.4684	6.6330	6.8019	6.9753	7.1533	7.3359	7.5233	7.7156	8.1152	8.7537
7	7.2135	7.4343	7.6625	7.8983	8.1420	8.3938	8.6540	8.9228	9.2004	9.4872	10.0890	11.0668
8	8.2857	8.5830	8.8923	9.2142	9.5491	9.8975	10.2598	10.6366	11.0285	11.4359	12.2997	13.7268
9	9.3685	9.7546	10.1591	10.5828	11.0266	11.4913	11.9780	12.4876	13.0210	13.5795	14.7757	16.7858
10	10.4622	10.9497	11.4639	12.0061	12.5779	13.1808	13.8164	14.4866	15.1929	15.9374	17.5487	20.3037
11	11.5668	12.1687	12.8078	13.4864	14.2068	14.9716	15.7836	16.6455	17.5603	18.5312	20.6546	24.3493
12	12.6825	13.4121	14.1920	15.0258	15.9171	16.8699	17.8885	18.9771	20.1407	21.3843	24.1331	29.0017
13	13.8093	14.6803	15.6178	16.6268	17.7130	18.8821	20.1406	21.4953	22.9534	24.5227	28.0291	34.3519
14	14.9474	15.9739	17.0863	18.2919	19.5986	21.0151	22.5505	24.2149	26.0192	27.9750	32.3926	40.5047
15	16.0969	17.2934	18.5989	20.0236	21.5786	23.2760	25.1290	27.1521	29.3609	31.7725	37.2797	47.5804
16	17.2579	18.6393	20.1569	21.8245	23.6575	25.6725	27.8881	30.3243	33.0034	35.9497	42.7533	55.7175
17	18.4304	20.0121	21.7616	23.6975	25.8404	28.2129	30.8402	33.7502	36.9737	40.5447	48.8837	65.0751
18	19.6147	21.4123	23.4144	25.6454	28.1324	30.9057	33.9990	37.4502	41.3013	45.5992	55.7497	75.8364
19	20.8109	22.8406	25.1169	27.6712	30.5390	33.7600	37.3790	41.4463	46.0185	51.1591	63.4397	88.2118
20	22.0190	24.2974	26.8704	29.7781	33.0660	36.7856	40.9955	45.7620	51.1601	57.2750	72.0524	102.4436
25	28.2432	32.0303	36.4593	41.6459	47.7271	54.8645	63.2490	73.1059	84.7009	98.3471	133.3339	212.7930
30	34.7849	40.5681	47.5754	56.0849	66.4388	79.0582	94.4608	113.2832	136.3075	164.4940	241.3327	434.7451
35	41.6603	49.9945	60.4621	73.6522	90.3203	111.4348	138.2369	172.3168	215.7108	271.0244	431.6635	881.1702
40	48.8864	60.4020	75.4013	95.0255	120.7998	154.7620	199.6351	259.0565	337.8824	442.5926	767.0914	1,779.0903

Glossary

Absorption costing Costing method that assigns both variable and fixed costs to products. *(p. 915)*

Accelerated depreciation method Method that produces larger depreciation charges in the early years of an asset's life and smaller charges in its later years. *(p. 400)*

Account Record within an accounting system in which increases and decreases are entered and stored in a specific asset, liability, equity, revenue, or expense. *(p. 51)*

Account balance Difference between total debits and total credits (including the beginning balance) for an account. *(p. 55)*

Account form balance sheet Balance sheet that lists assets on the left side and liabilities and equity on the right. *(p. 18)*

Account payable Liability created by buying goods or services on credit; backed by the buyer's general credit standing. *(p. 50)*

Accounting Information and measurement system that identifies, records, and communicates relevant information about a company's business activities. *(p. 4)*

Accounting cycle Recurring steps performed each accounting period, starting with analyzing transactions and continuing through the post-closing trial balance (or reversing entries). *(p. 146)*

Accounting equation Equality involving a company's assets, liabilities, and equity; Assets = Liabilities + Equity; also called *balance sheet equation*. *(p. 14)*

Accounting information system People, records, and methods that collect and process data from transactions and events, organize them in useful forms, and communicate results to decision makers. *(p. 272)*

Accounting period Length of time covered by financial statements; also called *reporting period*. *(p. 94)*

Accounting rate of return Rate used to evaluate the acceptability of an investment; equals the after-tax periodic income from a project divided by the average investment in the asset; also called *rate of return on average investment*. *(p. 1039)*

Accounts payable ledger Subsidiary ledger listing individual creditor (supplier) accounts. *(p. 277)*

Accounts receivable Amounts due from customers for credit sales; backed by the customer's general credit standing. *(p. 360)*

Accounts receivable ledger Subsidiary ledger listing individual customer accounts. *(p. 277)*

Accounts receivable turnover Measure of both the quality and liquidity of accounts receivable; indicates how often receivables are received and collected during the period; computed by dividing net sales by average accounts receivable. *(p. 375)*

Accrual basis accounting Accounting system that recognizes revenues when earned and expenses when incurred; the basis for GAAP. *(p. 95)*

Accrued expenses Costs incurred in a period that are both unpaid and unrecorded; adjusting entries for recording accrued expenses involve increasing expenses and increasing liabilities. *(p. 101)*

Accrued revenues Revenues earned in a period that are both unrecorded and not yet received in cash (or other assets); adjusting entries for recording accrued revenues involve increasing assets and increasing revenues. *(pp. 103 & 960)*

Accumulated depreciation Cumulative sum of all depreciation expense recorded for an asset. *(p. 97)*

Acid-test ratio Ratio used to assess a company's ability to settle its current debts with its most liquid assets; defined as quick assets (cash, short-term investments, and current receivables) divided by current liabilities. *(p. 196)*

Activity-based budgeting (ABB) Budget system based on expected activities. *(p. 960)*

Activity-based costing (ABC) Cost allocation method that focuses on activities performed; traces costs to activities and then assigns them to cost objects. *(p. 861)*

Activity cost driver Variable that causes an activity's cost to go up or down; a causal factor. *(p. 861)*

Activity cost pool Temporary account that accumulates costs a company incurs to support an activity. *(p. 861)*

Adjusted trial balance List of accounts and balances prepared after period-end adjustments are recorded and posted. *(p. 106)*

Adjusting entry Journal entry at the end of an accounting period to bring an asset or liability account to its proper amount and update the related expense or revenue account. *(p. 96)*

Aging of accounts receivable Process of classifying accounts receivable by how long they are past due for purposes of estimating uncollectible accounts. *(p. 368)*

Allowance for Doubtful Accounts Contra asset account with a balance approximating uncollectible accounts receivable; also called *Allowance for Uncollectible Accounts*. *(p. 365)*

Allowance method Procedure that (a) estimates and matches bad debts expense with its sales for the period and/or (b) reports accounts receivable at estimated realizable value. *(p. 364)*

Amortization Process of allocating the cost of an intangible asset to expense over its estimated useful life. *(p. 409)*

Annual financial statements Financial statements covering a one-year period; often based on a calendar year, but any consecutive 12-month (or 52-week) period is acceptable. *(p. 94)*

Annual report Summary of a company's financial results for the year with its current financial condition and future plans; directed to external users of financial information. *(p. A-1)*

Annuity Series of equal payments at equal intervals. *(p. 571)*

Appropriated retained earnings Retained earnings separately reported to inform stockholders of funding needs. *(p. 525)*

Asset book value (See *book value*.)

Assets Resources a business owns or controls that are expected to provide current and future benefits to the business. *(p. 14)*

Audit Analysis and report of an organization's accounting system, its records, and its reports using various tests. *(p. 12)*

Auditors Individuals hired to review financial reports and information systems. *Internal auditors* of a company are employed to assess and evaluate its system of internal controls, including the resulting reports. *External auditors* are independent of a company and are hired to assess and evaluate the "fairness" of financial statements (or to perform other contracted financial services) *(p. 13)*.

Authorized stock Total amount of stock that a corporation's charter authorizes it to issue. *(p. 511)*

Available-for-sale (AFS) securities Investments in debt and equity securities that are not classified as trading securities or held-to-maturity securities. *(p. 600)*

Average cost See *weighted average*.

Avoidable expense Expense (or cost) that is relevant for decision making; expense that is not incurred if a department, product, or service is eliminated. *(p. 1053)*

Bad debts Accounts of customers who do not pay what they have promised to pay; an expense of selling on credit; also called *uncollectible accounts*. *(p. 363)*

Balance column account Account with debit and credit columns for recording entries and another column for showing the balance of the account after each entry. *(p. 58)*

Balance sheet Financial statement that lists types and dollar amounts of assets, liabilities, and equity at a specific date. *(p. 19)*

Balance sheet equation (See *accounting equation*.)

Balanced scorecard A system of performance measurement that collects information on several key performance indicators within each of four perspectives: customer, internal processes, innovation and learning, and financial. *(p. 874)*

Bank reconciliation Report that explains the difference between the book (company) balance of cash and the cash balance reported on the bank statement. *(p. 331)*

Bank statement Bank report on the depositor's beginning and ending cash balances, and a listing of its changes, for a period. *(p. 330)*

Basic earnings per share Net income less any preferred dividends and then divided by weighted-average common shares outstanding. *(p. 527)*

Batch processing Accumulating source documents for a period of time and then processing them all at once such as once a day, week, or month. *(p. 286)*

Bearer bonds Bonds made payable to whoever holds them (the *bearer*); also called *unregistered bonds*. *(p. 566)*

Benchmarking Practice of comparing and analyzing company financial performance or position with other companies or standards. *(p. 1002)*

Betterments Expenditures to make a plant asset more efficient or productive; also called *improvements*. *(p. 405)*

Bond Written promise to pay the bond's par (or face) value and interest at a stated contract rate; often issued in denominations of $1,000. *(p. 552)*

Bond certificate Document containing bond specifics such as issuer's name, bond par value, contract interest rate, and maturity date. *(p. 554)*

Bond indenture Contract between the bond issuer and the bondholders; identifies the parties' rights and obligations. *(p. 554)*

Book value Asset's acquisition costs less its accumulated depreciation (or depletion, or amortization); also sometimes used synonymously as the *carrying value* of an account. *(p. 100)*

Book value per common share Recorded amount of equity applicable to common shares divided by the number of common shares outstanding. *(p. 528)*

Book value per preferred share Equity applicable to preferred shares (equals its call price [or par value if it is not callable] plus any cumulative dividends in arrears) divided by the number of preferred shares outstanding. *(p. 528)*

Bookkeeping (See *recordkeeping*.)

Break-even point Output level at which sales equals fixed plus variable costs; where income equals zero. *(p. 915)*

Break-even time (BET) Time-based measurement used to evaluate the acceptability of an investment; equals the time expected to pass before the present value of the net cash flows from an investment equals its initial cost. *(p. 1055)*

Budget Formal statement of future plans, usually expressed in monetary terms. *(p. 946)*

Budget report Report comparing actual results to planned objectives; sometimes used as a progress report. *(p. 990)*

Budgetary control Management use of budgets to monitor and control company operations. *(p. 990)*

Budgeted balance sheet Accounting report that presents predicted amounts of the company's assets, liabilities, and equity balances as of the end of the budget period. *(p. 958)*

Budgeted income statement Accounting report that presents predicted amounts of the company's revenues and expenses for the budget period. *(p. 958)*

Budgeting Process of planning future business actions and expressing them as formal plans. *(p. 946)*

Business An organization of one or more individuals selling products and/or services for profit. *(p. 10)*

Business entity assumption Principle that requires a business to be accounted for separately from its owner(s) and from any other entity. *(p. 11)*

Business segment Part of a company that can be separately identified by the products or services that it provides or by the geographic markets that it serves; also called *segment.* *(p. 710)*

C corporation Corporation that does not qualify for nor elect to be treated as a proprietorship or partnership for income tax purposes and therefore is subject to income taxes; also called *C corp.* *(p. 482)*

Call price Amount that must be paid to call and retire a callable preferred stock or a callable bond. *(p. 521)*

Callable bonds Bonds that give the issuer the option to retire them at a stated amount prior to maturity. *(p. 566)*

Callable preferred stock Preferred stock that the issuing corporation, at its option, may retire by paying the call price plus any dividends in arrears. *(p. 521)*

Canceled checks Checks that the bank has paid and deducted from the depositor's account. *(p. 331)*

Capital budgeting Process of analyzing alternative investments and deciding which assets to acquire or sell. *(p. 1036)*

Capital expenditures Additional costs of plant assets that provide material benefits extending beyond the current period; also called *balance sheet expenditures.* *(p. 404)*

Capital expenditures budget Plan that lists dollar amounts to be both received from disposal of plant assets and spent to purchase plant assets. *(p. 956)*

Capital leases Long-term leases in which the lessor transfers substantially all risk and rewards of ownership to the lessee. *(p. 577)*

Capital stock General term referring to a corporation's stock used in obtaining capital (owner financing). *(p. 511)*

Capitalize Record the cost as part of a permanent account and allocate it over later periods.

Carrying (book) value of bonds Net amount at which bonds are reported on the balance sheet; equals the par value of the bonds less any unamortized discount or plus any unamortized premium; also called *carrying amount or book value.* *(p. 556)*

Cash Includes currency, coins, and amounts on deposit in bank checking or savings accounts. *(p. 321)*

Cash basis accounting Accounting system that recognizes revenues when cash is received and records expenses when cash is paid. *(p. 95)*

Cash budget Plan that shows expected cash inflows and outflows during the budget period, including receipts from loans needed to maintain a minimum cash balance and repayments of such loans. *(p. 956)*

Cash disbursements journal Special journal normally used to record all payments of cash; also called *cash payments journal.* *(p. 284)*

Cash discount Reduction in the price of merchandise granted by a seller to a buyer when payment is made within the discount period. *(p. 183)*

Cash equivalents Short-term, investment assets that are readily convertible to a known cash amount or sufficiently close to their maturity date (usually within 90 days) so that market value is not sensitive to interest rate changes. *(p. 321)*

Cash flow on total assets Ratio of operating cash flows to average total assets; not sensitive to income recognition and measurement; partly reflects earnings quality. *(p. 650)*

Cash Over and Short Income statement account used to record cash overages and cash shortages arising from errors in cash receipts or payments. *(p. 323)*

Cash receipts journal Special journal normally used to record all receipts of cash. *(p. 281)*

Change in an accounting estimate Change in an accounting estimate that results from new information, subsequent developments, or improved judgment that impacts current and future periods. *(pp. 403 & 525)*

Chart of accounts List of accounts used by a company; includes an identification number for each account. *(p. 54)*

Check Document signed by a depositor instructing the bank to pay a specified amount to a designated recipient. *(p. 328)*

Check register Another name for a cash disbursements journal when the journal has a column for check numbers. *(pp. 284 & 340)*

Classified balance sheet Balance sheet that presents assets and liabilities in relevant subgroups, including current and noncurrent classifications. *(p. 147)*

Clock card Source document used to record the number of hours an employee works and to determine the total labor cost for each pay period. *(p. 782)*

Closing entries Entries recorded at the end of each accounting period to transfer end-of-period balances in revenue, gain, expense, loss, and withdrawal (dividend for a corporation) accounts to the capital account (to retained earnings for a corporation). *(p. 143)*

Closing process Necessary end-of-period steps to prepare the accounts for recording the transactions of the next period. *(p. 142)*

Columnar journal Journal with more than one column. *(p. 278)*

Committee on Sponsoring Organizations (COSO) Committee devoted to improving the quality of financial reporting through effective internal controls, consisting of five interrelated components, along with other mechanisms (www.COSO.org). *(p. 315)*

Common stock Corporation's basic ownership share; also generically called *capital stock.* *(pp. 12 & 510)*

Common-size financial statement Statement that expresses each amount as a percent of a base amount. In the balance sheet, total assets is usually the base and is expressed as 100%. In the income statement, net sales is usually the base. *(p. 693)*

Comparative financial statement Statement with data for two or more successive periods placed in side-by-side columns, often with changes shown in dollar amounts and percents. *(p. 688)*

Compatibility principle Information system principle that prescribes an accounting system to conform with a company's activities, personnel, and structure. *(p. 273)*

Complex capital structure Capital structure that includes outstanding rights or options to purchase common stock, or securities that are convertible into common stock. *(p. 527)*

Components of accounting systems Five basic components of accounting systems are source documents, input devices, information processors, information storage, and output devices. *(p. 273)*

Composite unit Generic unit consisting of a specific number of units of each product; unit comprised in proportion to the expected sales mix of its products. *(p. 922)*

Compound journal entry Journal entry that affects at least three accounts. *(p. 61)*

Comprehensive income Net change in equity for a period, excluding owner investments and distributions. *(p. 604)*

Computer hardware Physical equipment in a computerized accounting information system.

Computer network Linkage giving different users and different computers access to common databases and programs. *(p. 286)*

Computer software Programs that direct operations of computer hardware.

Conceptual framework A written framework to guide the development, preparation, and interpretation of financial accounting information. *(p. 9)*

Conservatism constraint Principle that prescribes the less optimistic estimate when two estimates are about equally likely. *(p. 238)*

Consignee Receiver of goods owned by another who holds them for purposes of selling them for the owner. *(p. 228)*

Consignor Owner of goods who ships them to another party who will sell them for the owner. *(p. 228)*

Consistency concept Principle that prescribes use of the same accounting method(s) over time so that financial statements are comparable across periods. *(p. 237)*

Consolidated financial statements Financial statements that show all (combined) activities under the parent's control, including those of any subsidiaries. *(p. 603)*

Contingent liability Obligation to make a future payment if, and only if, an uncertain future event occurs. *(p. 448)*

Continuous budgeting Practice of preparing budgets for a selected number of future periods and revising those budgets as each period is completed. *(p. 949)*

Continuous improvement Concept requiring every manager and employee continually to look to improve operations. *(p. 748)*

Contra account Account linked with another account and having an opposite normal balance; reported as a subtraction from the other account's balance. *(p. 99)*

Contract rate Interest rate specified in a bond indenture (or note); multiplied by the par value to determine the interest paid each period; also called *coupon rate, stated rate,* or *nominal rate*. *(p. 555)*

Contributed capital Total amount of cash and other assets received from stockholders in exchange for stock; also called *paid-in capital*. *(p. 13)*

Contributed capital in excess of par value Difference between the par value of stock and its issue price when issued at a price above par.

Contribution margin Sales revenue less total variable costs.

Contribution margin income statement Income statement that separates variable and fixed costs; highlights the contribution margin, which is sales less variable expenses.

Contribution margin per unit Amount that the sale of one unit contributes toward recovering fixed costs and earning profit; defined as sales price per unit minus variable expense per unit. *(p. 914)*

Contribution margin ratio Product's contribution margin divided by its sale price. *(p. 914)*

Control Process of monitoring planning decisions and evaluating the organization's activities and employees. *(p. 733)*

Control principle Information system principle that prescribes an accounting system to aid managers in controlling and monitoring business activities. *(p. 272)*

Controllable costs Costs that a manager has the power to control or at least strongly influence. *(pp. 737 & 875)*

Controllable variance Combination of both overhead spending variances (variable and fixed) and the variable overhead efficiency variance. *(p. 1003)*

Controlling account General ledger account, the balance of which (after posting) equals the sum of the balances in its related subsidiary ledger. *(p. 277)*

Conversion costs Expenditures incurred in converting raw materials to finished goods; includes direct labor costs and overhead costs. *(p. 743)*

Conversion costs per equivalent unit The combined costs of direct labor and factory overhead per equivalent unit. *(p. 829)*

Convertible bonds Bonds that bondholders can exchange for a set number of the issuer's shares. *(p. 566)*

Convertible preferred stock Preferred stock with an option to exchange it for common stock at a specified rate. *(p. 520)*

Copyright Right giving the owner the exclusive privilege to publish and sell musical, literary, or artistic work during the creator's life plus 70 years. *(p. 410)*

Corporation Business that is a separate legal entity under state or federal laws with owners called *shareholders* or *stockholders*. *(pp. 12 & 508)*

Cost All normal and reasonable expenditures necessary to get an asset in place and ready for its intended use. *(p. 395)*

Cost accounting system Accounting system for manufacturing activities based on the perpetual inventory system. *(p. 776)*

Cost-based transfer pricing A form of pricing transfers between divisions of the same company based on costs to the transferring division; typically used when the transferring division has excess capacity. *(p. 883)*

Cost-benefit constraint Notion that only information with benefits of disclosure greater than the costs of disclosure need be disclosed. *(p. 12)*

Cost-benefit principle Information system principle that prescribes the benefits from an activity in an accounting system to outweigh the costs of that activity. *(p. 273)*

Cost center Department that incurs costs but generates no revenues; common example is the accounting or legal department. *(p. 865)*

Cost object Product, process, department, or customer to which costs are assigned. *(p. 737)*

Cost of capital Rate the company must pay to its long-term creditors and shareholders; also called *hurdle rate*. *(p. 1041)*

Cost of goods available for sale Consists of beginning inventory plus net purchases of a period.

Cost of goods manufactured Total manufacturing costs (direct materials, direct labor, and factory overhead) for the period plus beginning goods in process less ending goods in process; also called *net cost of goods manufactured* and *cost of goods completed*. *(p. 827)*

Cost of goods sold Cost of inventory sold to customers during a period; also called *cost of sales*. *(p. 180)*

Cost principle Accounting principle that prescribes financial statement information to be based on actual costs incurred in business transactions. *(p. 10)*

Cost variance Difference between the actual incurred cost and the standard cost. *(p. 997)*

Cost-volume-profit (CVP) analysis Planning method that includes predicting the volume of activity, the costs incurred, sales earned, and profits received. *(p. 908)*

Cost-volume-profit (CVP) chart Graphic representation of cost-volume-profit relations. *(p. 916)*

Coupon bonds Bonds with interest coupons attached to their certificates; bondholders detach coupons when they mature and present them to a bank or broker for collection. *(p. 566)*

Credit Recorded on the right side; an entry that decreases asset and expense accounts, and increases liability, revenue, and most equity accounts; abbreviated Cr. *(p. 55)*

Credit memorandum Notification that the sender has credited the recipient's account in the sender's records. *(p. 189)*

Credit period Time period that can pass before a customer's payment is due. *(p. 183)*

Credit terms Description of the amounts and timing of payments that a buyer (debtor) agrees to make in the future. *(p. 183)*

Creditors Individuals or organizations entitled to receive payments. *(p. 52)*

Cumulative preferred stock Preferred stock on which undeclared dividends accumulate until paid; common stockholders cannot receive dividends until cumulative dividends are paid. *(p. 519)*

Current assets Cash and other assets expected to be sold, collected, or used within one year or the company's operating cycle, whichever is longer. *(p. 148)*

Current liabilities Obligations due to be paid or settled within one year or the company's operating cycle, whichever is longer. *(p. 149 & 437)*

Current portion of long-term debt Portion of long-term debt due within one year or the operating cycle, whichever is longer; reported under current liabilities. *(p. 445)*

Current ratio Ratio used to evaluate a company's ability to pay its short-term obligations, calculated by dividing current assets by current liabilities. *(p. 150)*

Curvilinear cost Cost that changes with volume but not at a constant rate. *(p. 910)*

Customer orientation Company position that its managers and employees be in tune with the changing wants and needs of consumers. *(p. 747)*

Cycle efficiency (CE) A measure of production efficiency, which is defined as value-added (process) time divided by total cycle time. *(p. 750)*

Cycle time (CT) A measure of the time to produce a product or service, which is the sum of process time, inspection time, move time, and wait time; also called *throughput time*. *(p. 749)*

Date of declaration Date the directors vote to pay a dividend. *(p. 515)*

Date of payment Date the corporation makes the dividend payment. *(p. 515)*

Date of record Date directors specify for identifying stockholders to receive dividends. *(p. 515)*

Days' sales in inventory Estimate of number of days needed to convert inventory into receivables or cash; equals ending inventory divided by cost of goods sold and then multiplied by 365; also called days' *stock on hand.* *(p. 241)*

Days' sales uncollected Measure of the liquidity of receivables computed by dividing the current balance of receivables by the annual credit (or net) sales and then multiplying by 365; also called *days' sales in receivables*. *(p. 335)*

Debit Recorded on the left side; an entry that increases asset and expense accounts, and decreases liability, revenue, and most equity accounts; abbreviated Dr. *(p. 55)*

Debit memorandum Notification that the sender has debited the recipient's account in the sender's records. *(p. 184)*

Debt ratio Ratio of total liabilities to total assets; used to reflect risk associated with a company's debts. *(p. 69)*

Debt-to-equity ratio Defined as total liabilities divided by total equity; shows the proportion of a company financed by non-owners (creditors) in comparison with that financed by owners. *(p. 567)*

Debtors Individuals or organizations that owe money. *(p. 51)*

Declining-balance method Method that determines depreciation charge for the period by multiplying a depreciation rate (often twice the straight-line rate) by the asset's beginning-period book value. *(p. 400)*

Deferred income tax liability Corporation income taxes that are deferred until future years because of temporary differences between GAAP and tax rules. *(p. 460)*

Degree of operating leverage (DOL) Ratio of contribution margin divided by pretax income; used to assess the effect on income of changes in sales. *(p. 924)*

Departmental accounting system Accounting system that provides information useful in evaluating the profitability or cost effectiveness of a department. *(p. 864)*

Departmental contribution to overhead Amount by which a department's revenues exceed its direct expenses. *(p. 871)*

Depletion Process of allocating the cost of natural resources to periods when they are consumed and sold. *(p. 408)*

Deposit ticket Lists items such as currency, coins, and checks deposited and their corresponding dollar amounts. *(p. 328)*

Deposits in transit Deposits recorded by the company but not yet recorded by its bank. *(p. 331)*

Depreciable cost Cost of a plant asset less its salvage value.

Depreciation Expense created by allocating the cost of plant and equipment to periods in which they are used; represents the expense of using the asset. *(pp. 99 & 397)*

Diluted earnings per share Earnings per share calculation that requires dilutive securities be added to the denominator of the basic EPS calculation. *(p. 527)*

Dilutive securities Securities having the potential to increase common shares outstanding; examples are options, rights, convertible bonds, and convertible preferred stock. *(p. 527)*

Direct costs Costs incurred for the benefit of one specific cost object. *(p. 737)*

Direct expenses Expenses traced to a specific department (object) that are incurred for the sole benefit of that department. *(p. 865)*

Direct labor Efforts of employees who physically convert materials to finished product. *(p. 742)*

Direct labor costs Wages and salaries for direct labor that are separately and readily traced through the production process to finished goods. *(p. 742)*

Direct material Raw material that physically becomes part of the product and is clearly identified with specific products or batches of product. *(p. 742)*

Direct material costs Expenditures for direct material that are separately and readily traced through the production process to finished goods. *(p. 742)*

Direct method Presentation of net cash from operating activities for the statement of cash flows that lists major operating cash receipts less major operating cash payments. *(p. 638)*

Direct write-off method Method that records the loss from an uncollectible account receivable at the time it is determined to be uncollectible; no attempt is made to estimate bad debts. *(p. 363)*

Discount on bonds payable Difference between a bond's par value and its lower issue price or carrying value; occurs when the contract rate is less than the market rate. *(p. 555)*

Discount on note payable Difference between the face value of a note payable and the (lesser) amount borrowed; reflects the added interest to be paid on the note over its life.

Discount on stock Difference between the par value of stock and its issue price when issued at a price below par value. *(p. 513)*

Discount period Time period in which a cash discount is available and the buyer can make a reduced payment. *(p. 183)*

Discount rate Expected rate of return on investments; also called *cost of capital, hurdle rate,* or *required rate of return.* *(p. B-2)*

Discounts lost Expenses resulting from not taking advantage of cash discounts on purchases. *(p. 341)*

Dividend in arrears Unpaid dividend on cumulative preferred stock; must be paid before any regular dividends on preferred stock and before any dividends on common stock. *(p. 519)*

Dividends Corporation's distributions of assets to its owners.

Dividend yield Ratio of the annual amount of cash dividends distributed to common shareholders relative to the common stock's market value (price). *(p. 528)*

Double-declining-balance (DDB) depreciation Depreciation equals beginning book value multiplied by 2 times the straight-line rate.

Double taxation Corporate income is taxed and then its later distribution through dividends is normally taxed again for shareholders.

Double-entry accounting Accounting system in which each transaction affects at least two accounts and has at least one debit and one credit. *(p. 55)*

Earnings (See *net income.*)

Earnings per share (EPS) Amount of income earned by each share of a company's outstanding common stock; also called *net income per share.* *(p. 527)*

Effective interest method Allocates interest expense over the bond life to yield a constant rate of interest; interest expense for a period is found by multiplying the balance of the liability at the beginning of the period by the bond market rate at issuance; also called *interest method.* *(p. 572)*

Efficiency Company's productivity in using its assets; usually measured relative to how much revenue a certain level of assets generates. *(p. 687)*

Efficiency variance Difference between the actual quantity of an input and the standard quantity of that input. *(p. 1010)*

Electronic funds transfer (EFT) Use of electronic communication to transfer cash from one party to another. *(p. 329)*

Employee benefits Additional compensation paid to or on behalf of employees, such as premiums for medical, dental, life, and disability insurance, and contributions to pension plans. *(p. 445)*

Employee earnings report Record of an employee's net pay, gross pay, deductions, and year-to-date payroll information. *(p. 456)*

Enterprise resource planning (ERP) software Programs that manage a company's vital operations, which range from order taking to production to accounting. *(p. 287)*

Entity Organization that, for accounting purposes, is separate from other organizations and individuals.

EOM Abbreviation for *end of month;* used to describe credit terms for credit transactions. *(p. 183)*

Equity Owner's claim on the assets of a business; equals the residual interest in an entity's assets after deducting liabilities; also called *net assets.* *(p. 14)*

Equity method Accounting method used for long-term investments when the investor has "significant influence" over the investee. *(p. 602)*

Equity ratio Portion of total assets provided by equity, computed as total equity divided by total assets. *(p. 701)*

Equity securities with controlling influence Long-term investment when the investor is able to exert controlling influence over the investee; investors owning 50% or more of voting stock are presumed to exert controlling influence. *(p. 603)*

Equity securities with significant influence Long-term investment when the investor is able to exert significant influence over the investee; investors owning 20 percent or more (but less than 50 percent) of voting stock are presumed to exert significant influence. *(p. 602)*

Equivalent units of production (EUP) Number of units that would be completed if all effort during a period had been applied to units that were started and finished. *(p. 821)*

Estimated liability Obligation of an uncertain amount that can be reasonably estimated. *(p. 445)*

Estimated line of cost behavior Line drawn on a graph to visually fit the relation between cost and sales. *(p. 912)*

Ethics Codes of conduct by which actions are judged as right or wrong, fair or unfair, honest or dishonest. *(pp. 8 & 736)*

Events Happenings that both affect an organization's financial position and can be reliably measured. *(p. 15)*

Expanded accounting equation Assets = Liabilities + Equity; Equity equals [Owner capital − Owner withdrawals + Revenues − Expenses] for a noncorporation; Equity equals [Contributed capital + Retained earnings + Revenues − Expenses] for a corporation where dividends are subtracted from retained earnings. *(p. 14)*

Expense recognition (or matching) principle (See *matching principle.*) *(pp. 11 & 96)*

Expenses Outflows or using up of assets as part of operations of a business to generate sales. *(p. 14)*

External transactions Exchanges of economic value between one entity and another entity. *(p. 15)*

External users Persons using accounting information who are not directly involved in running the organization. *(p. 5)*

Extraordinary gains or losses Gains or losses reported separately from continuing operations because they are both unusual and infrequent. *(p. 710)*

Extraordinary repairs Major repairs that extend the useful life of a plant asset beyond prior expectations; treated as a capital expenditure. *(p. 405)*

Factory overhead Factory activities supporting the production process that are not direct material or direct labor; also called *overhead and manufacturing overhead. (p. 742)*

Factory overhead costs Expenditures for factory overhead that cannot be separately or readily traced to finished goods; also called *overhead costs. (p. 742)*

Fair value option Reporting option that permits a company to use fair value in reporting certain assets and liabilities, which is presently based on a 3-level system to determine fair value. *(p. 565)*

Favorable variance Difference in actual revenues or expenses from the budgeted amount that contributes to a higher income. *(p. 991)*

Federal depository bank Bank authorized to accept deposits of amounts payable to the federal government. *(p. 453)*

Federal Insurance Contributions Act (FICA) Taxes Taxes assessed on both employers and employees; for Social Security and Medicare programs. *(p. 442)*

Federal Unemployment Taxes (FUTA) Payroll taxes on employers assessed by the federal government to support its unemployment insurance program. *(p. 444)*

FIFO method (See *first-in, first-out.*) *(pp. 233 & 833)*

Financial accounting Area of accounting aimed mainly at serving external users. *(p. 5)*

Financial Accounting Standards Board (FASB) Independent group of full-time members responsible for setting accounting rules. *(p. 9)*

Financial leverage Earning a higher return on equity by paying dividends on preferred stock or interest on debt at a rate lower than the return earned with the assets from issuing preferred stock or debt; also called *trading on the equity. (p. 521)*

Financial reporting Process of communicating information relevant to investors, creditors, and others in making investment, credit, and business decisions. *(p. 687)*

Financial statement analysis Application of analytical tools to general-purpose financial statements and related data for making business decisions. *(p. 686)*

Financial statements Includes the balance sheet, income statement, statement of owner's (or stockholders') equity, and statement of cash flows.

Financing activities Transactions with owners and creditors that include obtaining cash from issuing debt, repaying amounts borrowed, and obtaining cash from or distributing cash to owners. *(p. 634)*

Finished goods inventory Account that controls the finished goods files, which acts as a subsidiary ledger (of the Inventory account) in which the costs of finished goods that are ready for sale are recorded. *(pp. 741 & 779)*

First-in, first-out (FIFO) Method to assign cost to inventory that assumes items are sold in the order acquired; earliest items purchased are the first sold. *(p. 233)*

Fiscal year Consecutive 12-month (or 52-week) period chosen as the organization's annual accounting period. *(p. 95)*

Fixed budget Planning budget based on a single predicted amount of volume; unsuitable for evaluations if the actual volume differs from predicted volume. *(p. 991)*

Fixed budget performance report Report that compares actual revenues and costs with fixed budgeted amounts and identifies the differences as favorable or unfavorable variances. *(p. 991)*

Fixed cost Cost that does not change with changes in the volume of activity. *(p. 736)*

Flexibility principle Information system principle that prescribes an accounting system be able to adapt to changes in the company, its operations, and needs of decision makers. *(p. 273)*

Flexible budget Budget prepared (using actual volume) once a period is complete that helps managers evaluate past performance; uses fixed and variable costs in determining total costs. *(p. 992)*

Flexible budget performance report Report that compares actual revenues and costs with their variable budgeted amounts based on actual sales volume (or other level of activity) and identifies the differences as variances. *(p. 994)*

FOB Abbreviation for *free on board;* the point when ownership of goods passes to the buyer; *FOB shipping point* (or *factory*) means the buyer pays shipping costs and accepts ownership of goods when the seller transfers goods to carrier; *FOB destination* means the seller pays shipping costs and buyer accepts ownership of goods at the buyer's place of business. *(p. 185)*

Foreign exchange rate Price of one currency stated in terms of another currency. *(p. 610)*

Form 940 IRS form used to report an employer's federal unemployment taxes (FUTA) on an annual filing basis. *(p. 453)*

Form 941 IRS form filed to report FICA taxes owed and remitted. *(p. 453)*

Form 10-K (or 10-KSB) Annual report form filed with SEC by businesses (small businesses) with publicly traded securities. *(p. A-1)*

Form W-2 Annual report by an employer to each employee showing the employee's wages subject to FICA and federal income taxes along with amounts withheld. *(p. 455)*

Form W-4 Withholding allowance certificate, filed with the employer, identifying the number of withholding allowances claimed. *(p. 458)*

Franchises Privileges granted by a company or government to sell a product or service under specified conditions. *(p. 410)*

Full disclosure principle Principle that prescribes financial statements (including notes) to report all relevant information about an entity's operations and financial condition. *(p. 11)*

GAAP (See *generally accepted accounting principles.*)

General accounting system Accounting system for manufacturing activities based on the *periodic* inventory system. *(p. 776)*

General and administrative expenses Expenses that support the operating activities of a business. *(p. 193)*

General and administrative expense budget Plan that shows predicted operating expenses not included in the selling expenses budget. *(p. 955)*

General journal All-purpose journal for recording the debits and credits of transactions and events. *(pp. 56 & 276)*

General ledger (See *ledger*.) *(p. 51)*

General partner Partner who assumes unlimited liability for the debts of the partnership; responsible for partnership management. *(p. 481)*

General partnership Partnership in which all partners have mutual agency and unlimited liability for partnership debts. *(p. 481)*

Generally accepted accounting principles (GAAP) Rules that specify acceptable accounting practices. *(p. 8)*

Generally accepted auditing standards (GAAS) Rules that specify auditing practices.

General-purpose financial statements Statements published periodically for use by a variety of interested parties; includes the income statement, balance sheet, statement of owner's equity (or statement of retained earnings for a corporation), statement of cash flows, and notes to these statements. *(p. 687)*

Going-concern assumption Principle that prescribes financial statements to reflect the assumption that the business will continue operating. *(p. 11)*

Goods in process inventory Account in which costs are accumulated for products that are in the process of being produced but are not yet complete; also called *work in process inventory*. *(pp. 741 & 778)*

Goodwill Amount by which a company's (or a segment's) value exceeds the value of its individual assets less its liabilities. *(p. 411)*

Gross margin (See *gross profit*.)

Gross margin ratio Gross margin (net sales minus cost of goods sold) divided by net sales; also called *gross profit ratio*. *(p. 196)*

Gross method Method of recording purchases at the full invoice price without deducting any cash discounts. *(p. 341)*

Gross pay Total compensation earned by an employee. *(p. 442)*

Gross profit Net sales minus cost of goods sold; also called *gross margin*. *(p. 180)*

Gross profit method Procedure to estimate inventory when the past gross profit rate is used to estimate cost of goods sold, which is then subtracted from the cost of goods available for sale. *(p. 252)*

Held-to-maturity (HTM) securities Debt securities that a company has the intent and ability to hold until they mature. *(p. 600)*

High-low method Procedure that yields an estimated line of cost behavior by graphically connecting costs associated with the highest and lowest sales volume. *(p. 912)*

Horizontal analysis Comparison of a company's financial condition and performance across time. *(p. 688)*

Hurdle rate Minimum acceptable rate of return (set by management) for an investment. *(pp. 873 & 1045)*

Impairment Diminishment of an asset value. *(pp. 404 & 410)*

Imprest system Method to account for petty cash; maintains a constant balance in the fund, which equals cash plus petty cash receipts.

Inadequacy Condition in which the capacity of plant assets is too small to meet the company's production demands. *(p. 397)*

Income (See *net income*.)

Income statement Financial statement that subtracts expenses from revenues to yield a net income or loss over a specified period of time; also includes any gains or losses. *(p. 19)*

Income Summary Temporary account used only in the closing process to which the balances of revenue and expense accounts (including any gains or losses) are transferred; its balance is transferred to the capital account (or retained earnings for a corporation). *(p. 143)*

Incremental cost Additional cost incurred only if a company pursues a specific course of action. *(p. 1048)*

Indefinite life Asset life that is not limited by legal, regulatory, contractual, competitive, economic, or other factors. *(p. 409)*

Indirect costs Costs incurred for the benefit of more than one cost object. *(p. 737)*

Indirect expenses Expenses incurred for the joint benefit of more than one department (or cost object). *(p. 865)*

Indirect labor Efforts of production employees who do not work specifically on converting direct materials into finished products and who are not clearly identified with specific units or batches of product. *(p. 742)*

Indirect labor costs Labor costs that cannot be physically traced to production of a product or service; included as part of overhead. *(p. 742)*

Indirect material Material used to support the production process but not clearly identified with products or batches of product. *(p. 740)*

Indirect method Presentation that reports net income and then adjusts it by adding and subtracting items to yield net cash from operating activities on the statement of cash flows. *(p. 638)*

Information processor Component of an accounting system that interprets, transforms, and summarizes information for use in analysis and reporting. *(p. 274)*

Information storage Component of an accounting system that keeps data in a form accessible to information processors. *(p. 274)*

Infrequent gain or loss Gain or loss not expected to recur given the operating environment of the business. *(p. 710)*

Input device Means of capturing information from source documents that enables its transfer to information processors. *(p. 274)*

Installment note Liability requiring a series of periodic payments to the lender. *(p. 562)*

Institute of Management Accountants (IMA) A professional association of management accountants. *(p. 736)*

Intangible assets Long-term assets (resources) used to produce or sell products or services; usually lack physical form and have uncertain benefits. *(pp. 149 & 409)*

Interest Charge for using money (or other assets) loaned from one entity to another. *(p. 370)*

Interim financial statements Financial statements covering periods of less than one year; usually based on one-, three-, or six-month periods. *(pp. 94 & 251)*

Internal controls or **Internal control system** All policies and procedures used to protect assets, ensure reliable accounting, promote efficient operations, and urge adherence to company policies. *(pp. 272 & 736)*

Internal rate of return (IRR) Rate used to evaluate the acceptability of an investment; equals the rate that yields a net present value of zero for an investment. *(p. 1043)*

Internal transactions Activities within an organization that can affect the accounting equation. *(p. 15)*

Internal users Persons using accounting information who are directly involved in managing the organization. *(p. 6)*

International Accounting Standards Board (IASB) Group that identifies preferred accounting practices and encourages global acceptance; issues International Financial Reporting Standards (IFRS). *(p. 9)*

International Financial Reporting Standards (IFRS) International Financial Reporting Standards (IFRS) are required or allowed by over 100 countries; IFRS is set by the International Accounting Standards Board (IASB), which aims to develop a single set of global standards, to promote those standards, and to converge national and international standards globally. *(p. 9)*

Inventory Goods a company owns and expects to sell in its normal operations. *(p. 181)*

Inventory turnover Number of times a company's average inventory is sold during a period; computed by dividing cost of goods sold by average inventory; also called *merchandise turnover. (p. 241)*

Investing activities Transactions that involve purchasing and selling of long-term assets, includes making and collecting notes receivable and investments in other than cash equivalents. *(p. 634)*

Investment center Center of which a manager is responsible for revenues, costs, and asset investments. *(p. 865)*

Investment center residual income The net income an investment center earns above a target return on average invested assets. *(p. 873)*

Investment center return on total assets Center net income divided by average total assets for the center. *(p. 873)*

Investment turnover The efficiency with which a company generates sales from its available assets; computed as sales divided by average invested assets. *(p. 878)*

Invoice Itemized record of goods prepared by the vendor that lists the customer's name, items sold, sales prices, and terms of sale. *(p. 339)*

Invoice approval Document containing a checklist of steps necessary for approving the recording and payment of an invoice; also called *check authorization. (p. 339)*

Job Production of a customized product or service. *(p. 776)*

Job cost sheet Separate record maintained for each job. *(p. 778)*

Job lot Production of more than one unit of a customized product or service. *(p. 777)*

Job order cost accounting system Cost accounting system to determine the cost of producing each job or job lot. *(pp. 778 & 817)*

Job order production Production of special-order products; also called *customized production. (p. 776)*

Joint cost Cost incurred to produce or purchase two or more products at the same time. *(p. 883)*

Journal Record in which transactions are entered before they are posted to ledger accounts; also called *book of original entry. (p. 56)*

Journalizing Process of recording transactions in a journal. *(p. 56)*

Just-in-time (JIT) manufacturing Process of acquiring or producing inventory only when needed. *(p. 748)*

Known liabilities Obligations of a company with little uncertainty; set by agreements, contracts, or laws; also called *definitely determinable liabilities. (p. 438)*

Land improvements Assets that increase the benefits of land, have a limited useful life, and are depreciated. *(p. 396)*

Large stock dividend Stock dividend that is more than 25% of the previously outstanding shares. *(p. 516)*

Last-in, first-out (LIFO) Method to assign cost to inventory that assumes costs for the most recent items purchased are sold first and charged to cost of goods sold. *(p. 233)*

Lean business model Practice of eliminating waste while meeting customer needs and yielding positive company returns. *(p. 747)*

Lease Contract specifying the rental of property. *(pp. 411 & 576)*

Leasehold Rights the lessor grants to the lessee under the terms of a lease. *(p. 411)*

Leasehold improvements Alterations or improvements to leased property such as partitions and storefronts. *(p. 411)*

Least-squares regression Statistical method for deriving an estimated line of cost behavior that is more precise than the high-low method and the scatter diagram. *(p. 913)*

Ledger Record containing all accounts (with amounts) for a business; also called *general ledger. (p. 51)*

Lessee Party to a lease who secures the right to possess and use the property from another party (the lessor). *(p. 411)*

Lessor Party to a lease who grants another party (the lessee) the right to possess and use its property. *(p. 411)*

Liabilities Creditors' claims on an organization's assets; involves a probable future payment of assets, products, or services that a company is obligated to make due to past transactions or events. *(p. 14)*

Licenses (See *franchises.*) *(p. 410)*

Limited liability Owner can lose no more than the amount invested. *(p. 11)*

Limited liability company Organization form that combines select features of a corporation and a limited partnership; provides limited liability to its members (owners), is free of business tax, and allows members to actively participate in management. *(p. 482)*

Limited liability partnership Partnership in which a partner is not personally liable for malpractice or negligence unless that partner is responsible for providing the service that resulted in the claim. *(p. 481)*

Limited life (See *useful life.*)

Limited partners Partners who have no personal liability for partnership debts beyond the amounts they invested in the partnership. *(p. 481)*

Limited partnership Partnership that has two classes of partners, limited partners and general partners. *(p. 481)*

Liquid assets Resources such as cash that are easily converted into other assets or used to pay for goods, services, or liabilities. *(p. 321)*

Liquidating cash dividend Distribution of assets that returns part of the original investment to stockholders; deducted from contributed capital accounts. *(p. 516)*

Liquidation Process of going out of business; involves selling assets, paying liabilities, and distributing remainder to owners.

Liquidity Availability of resources to meet short-term cash requirements. *(pp. 321 & 687)*

List price Catalog (full) price of an item before any trade discount is deducted. *(p. 182)*

Long-term investments Long-term assets not used in operating activities such as notes receivable and investments in stocks and bonds. *(pp. 149 & 596)*

Long-term liabilities Obligations not due to be paid within one year or the operating cycle, whichever is longer. *(pp. 149 & 437)*

Lower of cost or market (LCM) Required method to report inventory at market replacement cost when that market cost is lower than recorded cost. *(p. 237)*

Maker of the note Entity who signs a note and promises to pay it at maturity. *(p. 370)*

Management by exception Management process to focus on significant variances and give less attention to areas where performance is close to the standard. *(p. 995)*

Managerial accounting Area of accounting aimed mainly at serving the decision-making needs of internal users; also called *management accounting*. *(pp. 6 & 732)*

Manufacturer Company that uses labor and operating assets to convert raw materials to finished goods.

Manufacturing budget Plan that shows the predicted costs for direct materials, direct labor, and overhead to be incurred in manufacturing units in the production budget. *(p. 966)*

Manufacturing statement Report that summarizes the types and amounts of costs incurred in a company's production process for a period; also called *cost of goods manufacturing statement*. *(p. 745)*

Margin of safety Excess of expected sales over the level of break-even sales. *(p. 920)*

Market-based transfer price The market price of a good or service being transferred between divisions within a company; typically used when the transferring division does not have excess capacity. *(p. 883)*

Market prospects Expectations (both good and bad) about a company's future performance as assessed by users and other interested parties. *(p. 687)*

Market rate Interest rate that borrowers are willing to pay and lenders are willing to accept for a specific lending agreement given the borrowers' risk level. *(p. 555)*

Market value per share Price at which stock is bought or sold. *(p. 511)*

Master budget Comprehensive business plan that includes specific plans for expected sales, product units to be produced, merchandise (or materials) to be purchased, expenses to be incurred, plant assets to be purchased, and amounts of cash to be borrowed or loans to be repaid, as well as a budgeted income statement and balance sheet. *(p. 950)*

Matching (or expense recognition) principle Prescribes expenses to be reported in the same period as the revenues that were earned as a result of the expenses. *(pp. 11 & 364)*

Materiality constraint Prescribes that accounting for items that significantly impact financial statement and any inferences from them adhere strictly to GAAP. *(pp. 12 & 364)*

Materials consumption report Document that summarizes the materials a department uses during a reporting period; replaces materials requisitions. *(p. 818)*

Materials ledger card Perpetual record updated each time units are purchased or issued for production use. *(p. 780)*

Materials requisition Source document production managers use to request materials for production; used to assign materials costs to specific jobs or overhead. *(p. 781)*

Maturity date of a note Date when a note's principal and interest are due. *(p. 370)*

Measurement principle Accounting information is based on cost with potential subsequent adjustments to fair value; see also *cost principle*. *(p. 10)*

Merchandise (See *merchandise inventory*.) *(p. 180)*

Merchandise inventory Goods that a company owns and expects to sell to customers; also called *merchandise* or *inventory*. *(p. 181)*

Merchandise purchases budget Plan that shows the units or costs of merchandise to be purchased by a merchandising company during the budget period. *(p. 953)*

Merchandiser Entity that earns net income by buying and selling merchandise. *(p. 180)*

Merit rating Rating assigned to an employer by a state based on the employer's record of employment. *(p. 444)*

Minimum legal capital Amount of assets defined by law that stockholders must (potentially) invest in a corporation; usually defined as par value of the stock; intended to protect creditors. *(p. 511)*

Mixed cost Cost that behaves like a combination of fixed and variable costs. *(p. 909)*

Modified Accelerated Cost Recovery System (MACRS) Depreciation system required by federal income tax law. *(p. 402)*

Monetary unit assumption Principle that assumes transactions and events can be expressed in money units. *(p. 11)*

Mortgage Legal loan agreement that protects a lender by giving the lender the right to be paid from the cash proceeds from the sale of a borrower's assets identified in the mortgage. *(p. 564)*

Multinational Company that operates in several countries. *(p. 610)*

Multiple-step income statement Income statement format that shows subtotals between sales and net income, categorizes expenses, and often reports the details of net sales and expenses. *(p. 192)*

Mutual agency Legal relationship among partners whereby each partner is an agent of the partnership and is able to bind the partnership to contracts within the scope of the partnership's business. *(p. 480)*

Natural business year Twelve-month period that ends when a company's sales activities are at their lowest point. *(p. 95)*

Natural resources Assets physically consumed when used; examples are timber, mineral deposits, and oil and gas fields; also called *wasting assets*. *(p. 408)*

Negotiated transfer price A price, determined by negotiation between division managers, to record transfers between divisions; typically lies between the variable cost and the market price of the item transferred. *(p. 883)*

Net assets (See *equity*.)

Net income Amount earned after subtracting all expenses necessary for and matched with sales for a period; also called *income, profit,* or *earnings. (p. 14)*

Net loss Excess of expenses over revenues for a period. *(p. 14)*

Net method Method of recording purchases at the full invoice price less any cash discounts. *(p. 341)*

Net pay Gross pay less all deductions; also called *take-home pay. (p. 442)*

Net present value (NPV) Dollar estimate of an asset's value that is used to evaluate the acceptability of an investment; computed by discounting future cash flows from the investment at a satisfactory rate and then subtracting the initial cost of the investment. *(p. 1041)*

Net realizable value Expected selling price (value) of an item minus the cost of making the sale. *(p. 228)*

Noncumulative preferred stock Preferred stock on which the right to receive dividends is lost for any period when dividends are not declared. *(p. 519)*

Noninterest-bearing note Note with no stated (contract) rate of interest; interest is implicitly included in the note's face value.

Nonparticipating preferred stock Preferred stock on which dividends are limited to a maximum amount each year. *(p. 520)*

Nonsufficient funds (NSF) check Maker's bank account has insufficient money to pay the check; also called *hot check.*

Non-value-added time The portion of cycle time that is not directed at producing a product or service; equals the sum of inspection time, move time, and wait time. *(p. 750)*

No-par value stock Stock class that has not been assigned a par (or stated) value by the corporate charter. *(p. 511)*

Not controllable costs Costs that a manager does not have the power to control or strongly influence. *(p. 737)*

Note (See *promissory note*.)

Note payable Liability expressed by a written promise to pay a definite sum of money on demand or on a specific future date(s).

Note receivable Asset consisting of a written promise to receive a definite sum of money on demand or on a specific future date(s).

Objectivity principle Principle that prescribes independent, unbiased evidence to support financial statement information. *(p. 9)*

Obsolescence Condition in which, because of new inventions and improvements, a plant asset can no longer be used to produce goods or services with a competitive advantage. *(p. 397)*

Off-balance-sheet financing Acquisition of assets by agreeing to liabilities not reported on the balance sheet. *(p. 577)*

Online processing Approach to inputting data from source documents as soon as the information is available. *(p. 286)*

Operating activities Activities that involve the production or purchase of merchandise and the sale of goods or services to customers, including expenditures related to administering the business. *(p. 633)*

Operating cycle Normal time between paying cash for merchandise or employee services and receiving cash from customers. *(p. 147)*

Operating leases Short-term (or cancelable) leases in which the lessor retains risks and rewards of ownership. *(p. 576)*

Operating leverage Extent, or relative size, of fixed costs in the total cost structure. *(p. 924)*

Opportunity cost Potential benefit lost by choosing a specific action from two or more alternatives. *(p. 738)*

Ordinary repairs Repairs to keep a plant asset in normal, good operating condition; treated as a revenue expenditure and immediately expensed. *(p. 404)*

Organization expenses (costs) Costs such as legal fees and promoter fees to bring an entity into existence. *(pp. 509 & 514)*

Other comprehensive income Equals net income less comprehensive income; includes unrealized gains and losses on available-for-sale securities, foreign currency adjustments, and pension adjustments. *(p. 604)*

Out-of-pocket cost Cost incurred or avoided as a result of management's decisions. *(p. 738)*

Output devices Means by which information is taken out of the accounting system and made available for use. *(p. 275)*

Outsourcing Manager decision to buy a product or service from another part of a *make-or-buy* decision; also called *make or buy.*

Outstanding checks Checks written and recorded by the depositor but not yet paid by the bank at the bank statement date. *(p. 331)*

Outstanding stock Corporation's stock held by its shareholders.

Overapplied overhead Amount by which the overhead applied to production in a period using the predetermined overhead rate exceeds the actual overhead incurred in a period. *(p. 787)*

Overhead cost variance Difference between the total overhead cost applied to products and the total overhead cost actually incurred. *(p. 1002)*

Owner, Capital Account showing the owner's claim on company assets; equals owner investments plus net income (or less net losses) minus owner withdrawals since the company's inception; also referred to as *equity. (p. 14)*

Owner investment Assets put into the business by the owner. *(p. 14)*

Owner's equity (See *equity.*)

Owner, withdrawals Account used to record asset distributions to the owner. (See also *withdrawals.*) *(p. 14)*

Paid-in capital (See *contributed capital.*) *(p. 512)*

Paid-in capital in excess of par value Amount received from issuance of stock that is in excess of the stock's par value. *(p. 513)*

Par value Value assigned a share of stock by the corporate charter when the stock is authorized. *(p. 511)*

Par value of a bond Amount the bond issuer agrees to pay at maturity and the amount on which cash interest payments are based; also called *face amount* or *face value* of a bond. *(p. 552)*

Par value stock Class of stock assigned a par value by the corporate charter. *(p. 511)*

Parent Company that owns a controlling interest in a corporation (requires more than 50% of voting stock). *(p. 603)*

Participating preferred stock Preferred stock that shares with common stockholders any dividends paid in excess of the percent stated on preferred stock. *(p. 520)*

Partner return on equity Partner net income divided by average partner equity for the period. *(p. 492)*

Partnership Unincorporated association of two or more persons to pursue a business for profit as co-owners. *(pp. 11 & 480)*

Partnership contract Agreement among partners that sets terms under which the affairs of the partnership are conducted; also called *articles of partnership*. *(p. 480)*

Partnership liquidation Dissolution of a partnership by (1) selling noncash assets and allocating any gain or loss according to partners' income-and-loss ratio, (2) paying liabilities, and (3) distributing any remaining cash according to partners' capital balances. *(p. 489)*

Patent Exclusive right granted to its owner to produce and sell an item or to use a process for 20 years. *(p. 410)*

Payback period (PBP) Time-based measurement used to evaluate the acceptability of an investment; equals the time expected to pass before an investment's net cash flows equal its initial cost. *(p. 1037)*

Payee of the note Entity to whom a note is made payable. *(p. 370)*

Payroll bank account Bank account used solely for paying employees; each pay period an amount equal to the total employees' net pay is deposited in it and the payroll checks are drawn on it. *(p. 458)*

Payroll deductions Amounts withheld from an employee's gross pay; also called *withholdings*. *(p. 442)*

Payroll register Record for a pay period that shows the pay period dates, regular and overtime hours worked, gross pay, net pay, and deductions. *(p. 455)*

Pension plan Contractual agreement between an employer and its employees for the employer to provide benefits to employees after they retire; expensed when incurred. *(p. 578)*

Period costs Expenditures identified more with a time period than with finished products costs; includes selling and general administrative expenses. *(p. 738)*

Periodic inventory system Method that records the cost of inventory purchased but does not continuously track the quantity available or sold to customers; records are updated at the end of each period to reflect the physical count and costs of goods available. *(p. 182)*

Permanent accounts Accounts that reflect activities related to one or more future periods; balance sheet accounts whose balances are not closed; also called *real accounts*. *(p. 142)*

Perpetual inventory system Method that maintains continuous records of the cost of inventory available and the cost of goods sold. *(p. 182)*

Petty cash Small amount of cash in a fund to pay minor expenses; accounted for using an imprest system. *(p. 326)*

Planning Process of setting goals and preparing to achieve them. *(p. 732)*

Plant asset age Estimate of the age of a company's plant assets, computed by dividing accumulated depreciation by depreciation expense. *(p. 413)*

Plant assets Tangible long-lived assets used to produce or sell products and services; also called *property, plant and equipment (PP&E)* or *fixed assets*. *(pp. 99 & 394)*

Pledged assets to secured liabilities Ratio of the book value of a company's pledged assets to the book value of its secured liabilities.

Post-closing trial balance List of permanent accounts and their balances from the ledger after all closing entries are journalized and posted. *(p. 146)*

Posting Process of transferring journal entry information to the ledger; computerized systems automate this process. *(p. 56)*

Posting reference (PR) column A column in journals in which individual ledger account numbers are entered when entries are posted to those ledger accounts. *(p. 58)*

Predetermined overhead rate Rate established prior to the beginning of a period that relates estimated overhead to another variable, such as estimated direct labor, and is used to assign overhead cost to production. *(p. 784)*

Preemptive right Stockholders' right to maintain their proportionate interest in a corporation with any additional shares issued. *(p. 510)*

Preferred stock Stock with a priority status over common stockholders in one or more ways, such as paying dividends or distributing assets. *(p. 518)*

Premium on bonds Difference between a bond's par value and its higher carrying value; occurs when the contract rate is higher than the market rate; also called *bond premium*. *(p. 558)*

Premium on stock (See *contributed capital in excess of par value*.) *(p. 513)*

Prepaid expenses Items paid for in advance of receiving their benefits; classified as assets. *(p. 97)*

Price-earnings (PE) ratio Ratio of a company's current market value per share to its earnings per share; also called *price-to-earnings*. *(p. 527)*

Price variance Difference between actual and budgeted revenue or cost caused by the difference between the actual price per unit and the budgeted price per unit. *(p. 995)*

Prime costs Expenditures directly identified with the production of finished goods; include direct materials costs and direct labor costs. *(p. 743)*

Principal of a note Amount that the signer of a note agrees to pay back when it matures, not including interest. *(p. 370)*

Principles of internal control Principles prescribing management to establish responsibility, maintain records, insure assets, separate recordkeeping from custody of assets, divide responsibility for related transactions, apply technological controls, and perform reviews. *(p. 317)*

Prior period adjustment Correction of an error in a prior year that is reported in the statement of retained earnings (or statement of stockholders' equity) net of any income tax effects. *(p. 525)*

Pro forma financial statements Statements that show the effects of proposed transactions and events as if they had occurred. *(p. 142)*

Process cost accounting system System of assigning direct materials, direct labor, and overhead to specific processes; total costs associated with each process are then divided by the number of units passing through that process to determine the cost per equivalent unit. *(p. 817)*

Process cost summary Report of costs charged to a department, its equivalent units of production achieved, and the costs assigned to its output. *(p. 826)*

Process operations Processing of products in a continuous (sequential) flow of steps; also called *process manufacturing* or *process production.* *(p. 814)*

Product costs Costs that are capitalized as inventory because they produce benefits expected to have future value; include direct materials, direct labor, and overhead. *(p. 738)*

Production budget Plan that shows the units to be produced each period. *(p. 966)*

Profit (See *net income.*)

Profit center Business unit that incurs costs and generates revenues. *(p. 865)*

Profit margin Ratio of a company's net income to its net sales; the percent of income in each dollar of revenue; also called *net profit margin.* *(pp. 109 & 878)*

Profitability Company's ability to generate an adequate return on invested capital. *(p. 687)*

Profitability index A measure of the relation between the expected benefits of a project and its investment, computed as the present value of expected future cash flows from the investment divided by the cost of the investment; a higher value indicates a more desirable investment, and a value below 1 indicates an unacceptable project. *(p. 1043)*

Promissory note (or **note**) Written promise to pay a specified amount either on demand or at a definite future date; is a *note receivable* for the lender but a *note payable* for the lendee. *(p. 370)*

Proprietorship (See *sole proprietorship.*) *(p. 11)*

Proxy Legal document giving a stockholder's agent the power to exercise the stockholder's voting rights. *(p. 509)*

Purchase discount Term used by a purchaser to describe a cash discount granted to the purchaser for paying within the discount period. *(p. 183)*

Purchase order Document used by the purchasing department to place an order with a seller (vendor). *(p. 338)*

Purchase requisition Document listing merchandise needed by a department and requesting it be purchased. *(p. 338)*

Purchases journal Journal normally used to record all purchases on credit. *(p. 283)*

Quantity variance Difference between actual and budgeted revenue or cost caused by the difference between the actual number of units and the budgeted number of units. *(p. 995)*

Ratio analysis Determination of key relations between financial statement items as reflected in numerical measures. *(p. 688)*

Raw materials inventory Goods a company acquires to use in making products. *(p. 740)*

Realizable value Expected proceeds from converting an asset into cash. *(p. 365)*

Receiving report Form used to report that ordered goods are received and to describe their quantity and condition. *(p. 339)*

Recordkeeping Part of accounting that involves recording transactions and events, either manually or electronically; also called *bookkeeping.* *(p. 4)*

Registered bonds Bonds owned by investors whose names and addresses are recorded by the issuer; interest payments are made to the registered owners. *(p. 566)*

Relevance principle Information system principle prescribing that its reports be useful, understandable, timely, and pertinent for decision making. *(p. 272)*

Relevant benefits Additional or incremental revenue generated by selecting a particular course of action over another. *(p. 1047)*

Relevant range of operations Company's normal operating range; excludes extremely high and low volumes not likely to occur. *(p. 917)*

Report form balance sheet Balance sheet that lists accounts vertically in the order of assets, liabilities, and equity.

Responsibility accounting budget Report of expected costs and expenses under a manager's control. *(p. 876)*

Responsibility accounting performance report Responsibility report that compares actual costs and expenses for a department with budgeted amounts. *(p. 876)*

Responsibility accounting system System that provides information that management can use to evaluate the performance of a department's manager. *(p. 864)*

Restricted retained earnings Retained earnings not available for dividends because of legal or contractual limitations. *(p. 524)*

Retail inventory method Method to estimate ending inventory based on the ratio of the amount of goods for sale at cost to the amount of goods for sale at retail. *(p. 251)*

Retailer Intermediary that buys products from manufacturers or wholesalers and sells them to consumers. *(p. 180)*

Retained earnings Cumulative income less cumulative losses and dividends. *(p. 512)*

Retained earnings deficit Debit (abnormal) balance in Retained Earnings; occurs when cumulative losses and dividends exceed cumulative income; also called *accumulated deficit.* *(p. 515)*

Return Monies received from an investment; often in percent form. *(p. 26)*

Return on assets (See *return on total assets*) *(p. 22)*

Return on equity Ratio of net income to average equity for the period.

Return on total assets Ratio reflecting operating efficiency; defined as net income divided by average total assets for the period; also called *return on assets* or *return on investment.* *(p. 605)*

Revenue expenditures Expenditures reported on the current income statement as an expense because they do not provide benefits in future periods. *(p. 404)*

Revenue recognition principle The principle prescribing that revenue is recognized when earned. *(p. 10)*

Revenues Gross increase in equity from a company's business activities that earn income; also called *sales.* *(p. 14)*

Reverse stock split Occurs when a corporation calls in its stock and replaces each share with less than one new share; increases both market value per share and any par or stated value per share. *(p. 518)*

Reversing entries Optional entries recorded at the beginning of a period that prepare the accounts for the usual journal entries as if adjusting entries had not occurred in the prior period. *(p. 154)*

Risk Uncertainty about an expected return. *(p. 26)*

Rolling budget New set of budgets a firm adds for the next period (with revisions) to replace the ones that have lapsed. *(p. 949)*

S corporation Corporation that meets special tax qualifications so as to be treated like a partnership for income tax purposes. *(p. 482)*

Safety stock Quantity of inventory or materials over the minimum needed to satisfy budgeted demand. *(p. 953)*

Sales (See *revenues.*)

Sales budget Plan showing the units of goods to be sold or services to be provided; the starting point in the budgeting process for most departments. *(p. 952)*

Sales discount Term used by a seller to describe a cash discount granted to buyers who pay within the discount period. *(p. 183)*

Sales journal Journal normally used to record sales of goods on credit. *(p. 278)*

Sales mix Ratio of sales volumes for the various products sold by a company. *(p. 921)*

Salvage value Estimate of amount to be recovered at the end of an asset's useful life; also called *residual value* or *scrap value*. *(p. 397)*

Sarbanes-Oxley Act (SOX) Created the *Public Company Accounting Oversight Board,* regulates analyst conflicts, imposes corporate governance requirements, enhances accounting and control disclosures, impacts insider transactions and executive loans, establishes new types of criminal conduct, and expands penalties for violations of federal securities laws. *(pp. 12 & 316)*

Scatter diagram Graph used to display data about past cost behavior and sales as points on a diagram. *(p. 911)*

Schedule of accounts payable List of the balances of all accounts in the accounts payable ledger and their totals. *(p. 284)*

Schedule of accounts receivable List of the balances of all accounts in the accounts receivable ledger and their totals. *(p. 279)*

Section 404 (of SOX) Section 404 of SOX requires that company management document and assess the effectiveness of all internal control processes that can affect financial reporting; company auditors express an opinion on whether management's assessment of the effectiveness of internal controls is fairly stated. *(p. 317)*

Secured bonds Bonds that have specific assets of the issuer pledged as collateral. *(p. 566)*

Securities and Exchange Commission (SEC) Federal agency Congress has charged to set reporting rules for organizations that sell ownership shares to the public. *(p. 9)*

Segment return on assets Segment operating income divided by segment average (identifiable) assets for the period. *(p. 288)*

Selling expense budget Plan that lists the types and amounts of selling expenses expected in the budget period. *(p. 954)*

Selling expenses Expenses of promoting sales, such as displaying and advertising merchandise, making sales, and delivering goods to customers. *(p. 193)*

Serial bonds Bonds consisting of separate amounts that mature at different dates. *(p. 566)*

Service company Organization that provides services instead of tangible products.

Shareholders Owners of a corporation; also called *stockholders.* *(p. 12)*

Shares Equity of a corporation divided into ownership units; also called *stock.* *(p. 12)*

Short-term investments Debt and equity securities that management expects to convert to cash within the next 3 to 12 months (or the operating cycle if longer); also called *temporary investments* or *marketable securities.* *(p. 596)*

Short-term note payable Current obligation in the form of a written promissory note. *(p. 439)*

Shrinkage Inventory losses that occur as a result of theft or deterioration. *(p. 190)*

Signature card Includes the signatures of each person authorized to sign checks on the bank account. *(p. 328)*

Simple capital structure Capital structure that consists of only common stock and nonconvertible preferred stock; consists of no dilutive securities. *(p. 527)*

Single-step income statement Income statement format that includes cost of goods sold as an expense and shows only one subtotal for total expenses. *(p. 193)*

Sinking fund bonds Bonds that require the issuer to make deposits to a separate account; bondholders are repaid at maturity from that account. *(p. 566)*

Small stock dividend Stock dividend that is 25% or less of a corporation's previously outstanding shares. *(p. 516)*

Social responsibility Being accountable for the impact that one's actions might have on society. *(p. 8)*

Sole proprietorship Business owned by one person that is not organized as a corporation; also called *proprietorship.* *(p. 11)*

Solvency Company's long-run financial viability and its ability to cover long-term obligations. *(p. 687)*

Source documents Source of information for accounting entries that can be in either paper or electronic form; also called *business papers.* *(p. 50)*

Special journal Any journal used for recording and posting transactions of a similar type. *(p. 276)*

Specific identification Method to assign cost to inventory when the purchase cost of each item in inventory is identified and used to compute cost of inventory. *(p. 231)*

Spending variance Difference between the actual price of an item and its standard price. *(p. 1010)*

Spreadsheet Computer program that organizes data by means of formulas and format; also called *electronic work sheet.*

Standard costs Costs that should be incurred under normal conditions to produce a product or component or to perform a service. *(p. 995)*

State Unemployment Taxes (SUTA) State payroll taxes on employers to support its unemployment programs. *(p. 444)*

Stated value stock No-par stock assigned a stated value per share; this amount is recorded in the stock account when the stock is issued. *(p. 512)*

Statement of cash flows A financial statement that lists cash inflows (receipts) and cash outflows (payments) during a period; arranged by operating, investing, and financing. *(pp. 19 & 632)*

Statement of owner's equity Report of changes in equity over a period; adjusted for increases (owner investment and net income) and for decreases (withdrawals and net loss). *(p. 19)*

Statement of partners' equity Financial statement that shows total capital balances at the beginning of the period, any additional investment by partners, the income or loss of the period, the partners' withdrawals, and the partners' ending capital balances; also called *statement of partners' capital. (p. 485)*

Statement of retained earnings Report of changes in retained earnings over a period; adjusted for increases (net income), for decreases (dividends and net loss), and for any prior period adjustment.

Statement of stockholders' equity Financial statement that lists the beginning and ending balances of each major equity account and describes all changes in those accounts. *(p. 525)*

Statements of Financial Accounting Standards (SFAS) FASB publications that establish U.S. GAAP.

Step-wise cost Cost that remains fixed over limited ranges of volumes but changes by a lump sum when volume changes occur outside these limited ranges. *(p. 910).*

Stock (See *shares.*) *(p. 12)*

Stock dividend Corporation's distribution of its own stock to its stockholders without the receipt of any payment. *(p. 516)*

Stock options Rights to purchase common stock at a fixed price over a specified period of time. *(p. 525)*

Stock split Occurs when a corporation calls in its stock and replaces each share with more than one new share; decreases both the market value per share and any par or stated value per share. *(p. 518)*

Stock subscription Investor's contractual commitment to purchase unissued shares at future dates and prices.

Stockholders (See *shareholders.*) *(p. 12)*

Stockholders' equity A corporation's equity; also called *shareholders' equity* or *corporate capital. (p. 512)*

Straight-line depreciation Method that allocates an equal portion of the depreciable cost of plant asset (cost minus salvage) to each accounting period in its useful life. *(pp. 99 & 398)*

Straight-line bond amortization Method allocating an equal amount of bond interest expense to each period of the bond life. *(p. 556)*

Subsidiary Entity controlled by another entity (parent) in which the parent owns more than 50% of the subsidiary's voting stock. *(p. 603)*

Subsidiary ledger List of individual subaccounts and amounts with a common characteristic; linked to a controlling account in the general ledger. *(p. 276)*

Sunk cost Cost already incurred and cannot be avoided or changed. *(p. 738)*

Supplementary records Information outside the usual accounting records; also called *supplemental records. (p. 186)*

Supply chain Linkages of services or goods extending from suppliers, to the company itself, and on to customers.

T-account Tool used to show the effects of transactions and events on individual accounts. *(p. 55)*

Target cost Maximum allowable cost for a product or service; defined as expected selling price less the desired profit. *(p. 777)*

Temporary accounts Accounts used to record revenues, expenses, and withdrawals (dividends for a corporation); they are closed at the end of each period; also called *nominal accounts. (p. 142)*

Term bonds Bonds scheduled for payment (maturity) at a single specified date. *(p. 566)*

Throughput time (See *cycle time.*)

Time period assumption Assumption that an organization's activities can be divided into specific time periods such as months, quarters, or years. *(pp. 11 & 94)*

Time ticket Source document used to report the time an employee spent working on a job or on overhead activities and then to determine the amount of direct labor to charge to the job or the amount of indirect labor to charge to overhead. *(p. 782)*

Times interest earned Ratio of income before interest expense (and any income taxes) divided by interest expense; reflects risk of covering interest commitments when income varies. *(p. 450)*

Total asset turnover Measure of a company's ability to use its assets to generate sales; computed by dividing net sales by average total assets. *(p. 413)*

Total quality management (TQM) Concept calling for all managers and employees at all stages of operations to strive toward higher standards and reduce number of defects. *(p. 748)*

Trade discount Reduction from a list or catalog price that can vary for wholesalers, retailers, and consumers. *(p. 182)*

Trademark or **trade (brand) name** Symbol, name, phrase, or jingle identified with a company, product, or service. *(p. 411)*

Trading on the equity (See *financial leverage.*)

Trading securities Investments in debt and equity securities that the company intends to actively trade for profit. *(p. 599)*

Transfer price The price used to record transfers of goods or services between divisions in the same company. *(p. 882)*

Transaction Exchange of economic consideration affecting an entity's financial position that can be reliably measured.

Treasury stock Corporation's own stock that it reacquired and still holds. *(p. 522)*

Trial balance List of accounts and their balances at a point in time; total debit balances equal total credit balances. *(p. 65)*

Unadjusted trial balance List of accounts and balances prepared before accounting adjustments are recorded and posted. *(p. 106)*

Unavoidable expense Expense (or cost) that is not relevant for business decisions; an expense that would continue even if a department, product, or service is eliminated. *(p. 1053)*

Unclassified balance sheet Balance sheet that broadly groups assets, liabilities, and equity accounts. *(p. 147)*

Uncontrollable costs Costs that a manager does not have the power to determine or strongly influence. *(p. 875)*

Underapplied overhead Amount by which overhead incurred in a period exceeds the overhead applied to that period's production using the predetermined overhead rate. *(p. 787)*

Unearned revenue Liability created when customers pay in advance for products or services; earned when the products or services are later delivered. *(pp. 52 & 100)*

Unfavorable variance Difference in revenues or costs, when the actual amount is compared to the budgeted amount, that contributes to a lower income.

Unit contribution margin Amount a product's unit selling price exceeds its total unit variable cost.

Units-of-production depreciation Method that charges a varying amount to depreciation expense for each period of an asset's useful life depending on its usage. *(p. 399)*

Unlimited liability Legal relationship among general partners that makes each of them responsible for partnership debts if the other partners are unable to pay their shares. *(p. 481)*

Unrealized gain (loss) Gain (loss) not yet realized by an actual transaction or event such as a sale. *(p. 599)*

Unsecured bonds Bonds backed only by the issuer's credit standing; almost always riskier than secured bonds; also called *debentures*. *(p. 566)*

Unusual gain or loss Gain or loss that is abnormal or unrelated to the company's ordinary activities and environment. *(p. 710)*

Useful life Length of time an asset will be productively used in the operations of a business; also called *service life* or *limited life*. *(p. 397)*

Value-added time The portion of cycle time that is directed at producing a product or service; equals process time. *(p. 750)*

Value chain Sequential activities that add value to an entity's products or services; includes design, production, marketing, distribution, and service. *(p. 748)*

Variable cost Cost that changes in proportion to changes in the activity output volume. *(p. 736)*

Variable costing income statement An income statement which reports variable costs and fixed costs separately; also called a *contribution margin income statement*. *(p. 915)*

Variance analysis Process of examining differences between actual and budgeted revenues or costs and describing them in terms of price and quantity differences. *(p. 995)*

Vendee Buyer of goods or services. *(p. 339)*

Vendor Seller of goods or services. *(p. 338)*

Vertical analysis Evaluation of each financial statement item or group of items in terms of a specific base amount. *(p. 688)*

Volume variance Difference between two dollar amounts of fixed overhead cost; one amount is the total budgeted overhead cost, and the other is the overhead cost allocated to products using the predetermined fixed overhead rate. *(p. 1003)*

Voucher Internal file used to store documents and information to control cash disbursements and to ensure that a transaction is properly authorized and recorded. *(p. 325)*

Voucher register Journal (referred to as *book of original entry*) in which all vouchers are recorded after they have been approved. *(p. 340)*

Voucher system Procedures and approvals designed to control cash disbursements and acceptance of obligations. *(p. 324)*

Wage bracket withholding table Table of the amounts of income tax withheld from employees' wages. *(p. 458)*

Warranty Agreement that obligates the seller to correct or replace a product or service when it fails to perform properly within a specified period. *(p. 446)*

Weighted average Method to assign inventory cost to sales; the cost of available-for-sale units is divided by the number of units available to determine per unit cost prior to each sale that is then multiplied by the units sold to yield the cost of that sale. *(pp. 234 & 824)*

Weighted-average contribution margin Contribution margin for a multiproduct company; computed based on each products' percentage of the company's sales mix. *(p. 922)*

Weighted-average method (See *weighted average*.)

Wholesaler Intermediary that buys products from manufacturers or other wholesalers and sells them to retailers or other wholesalers. *(p. 180)*

Withdrawals Payment of cash or other assets from a proprietorship or partnership to its owner or owners. *(p. 14)*

Work sheet Spreadsheet used to draft an unadjusted trial balance, adjusting entries, adjusted trial balance, and financial statements. *(p. 138)*

Working capital Current assets minus current liabilities at a point in time. *(p. 697)*

Working papers Analyses and other informal reports prepared by accountants and managers when organizing information for formal reports and financial statements. *(p. 138)*

Credits

Chapter 1
Page 3 AP Images/Paul Sakuma
Page 8 ©Mario Tama/Getty Images
Page 10 ©Martin Shields/Getty Images/Photographer's Choice
Page 11 ©Scott Boehm/Getty Images
Page 15 ©PAUL J. RICHARDS/AFP/Getty Images

Chapter 2
Page 49 Laura Boyd/ Courtesy of CitySlips
Page 52 Laura Boyd/ Courtesy of CitySlips
Page 53 ©Sports Illustrated/Getty Images
Page 54 ©Jed Jacobsohn/Getty Images

Chapter 3
Page 93 AP Images/Jason DeCrow
Page 95 EZIO PETERSEN/UPI/Landov

Chapter 4
Page 137 Courtesy of Gamer Grub
Page 147 ©Cameron Spencer/Getty Images

Chapter 5
Page 179 ©Asia Kepka Photography
Page 185 ©Christie & Cole/photolibrary
Page 189 ©Michael Newman/PhotoEdit

Chapter 6
Page 227 ©2010 Fitness Anywhere, Inc. Used under license
Page 229 © Blend Images/Alamy

Chapter 7
Page 271 Courtesy of New Belgium Brewing Company
Page 274 AP Images/Eric Risberg
Page 275 ©Royalty-Free/CORBIS
Page 277 ©Jody Dole/Getty Images/The Image Bank
Page 286 ©Nick Koudis/Getty Images/PhotoDisc

Chapter 8
Page 315 Courtesy of Dylan's Candy Bar
Page 318 ©Lawrence Lawry/Getty Images/Photodisc

Chapter 9
Page 359 AP Images/Morry Gash
Page 362 ©Ken Reid/Getty Images/Photographer's Choice
Page 363 ©STAN HONDA/AFP/Getty Images

Chapter 10
Page 393 Courtesy Emily O'Brien/Games2U
Page 396 ©Getty Images
Page 398 ©Bradley C. Bower/Bloomberg via Getty Images
Page 403 ©Streeter Lecka/Getty Images
Page 408 ©Digital Vision/Getty Images
Page 410 ©Hunter Martin/Getty Images

Chapter 11
Page 435 Courtesy of Snorg Tees
Page 439 ©Dove Shore/Getty Images
Page 441 ©Adam Gault/Getty Images/OJO Images
Page 446 ©Jeff Zelevansky/Getty Images
Page 449 ©John Burcham/National Geographic/Getty Images

Chapter 12
Page 479 "images by Kay Photography"
Page 481 ©Martin Harvey/Getty Images/Photodisc
Page 483 AP Images/Frank Franklin II, f
Page 486 ©Royalty Free/Corbis

Index

Note: Page numbers followed by *n* indicate information found in footnotes; **bold-face** entries indicate defined terms.

A Rose by Any Other Name

The same financial statement sometimes receives different titles. Following are some of the more common aliases.*

Balance Sheet	Statement of Financial Position Statement of Financial Condition
Income Statement	Statement of Income Operating Statement Statement of Operations Statement of Operating Activity Earnings Statement Statement of Earnings Profit and Loss (P&L) Statement
Statement of Cash Flows	Statement of Cash Flow Cash Flows Statement Statement of Changes in Cash Position Statement of Changes in Financial Position
Statement of Owner's Equity	Statement of Changes in Owner's Equity Statement of Changes in Owner's Capital Statement of Shareholders' Equity† Statement of Changes in Shareholders' Equity† Statement of Stockholders' Equity and Comprehensive Income† Statement of Changes in Capital Accounts†

* The term **Consolidated** often precedes or follows these statement titles to reflect the combination of different entities, such as a parent company and its subsidiaries.

† For corporations only.

We thank Dr. Louella Moore from Arkansas State University for suggesting this listing.

Chart of Accounts

Following is a typical chart of accounts, which is used in several assignments. Every company has its own unique accounts and numbering system.

Assets

Current Assets

101 Cash
102 Petty cash
103 Cash equivalents
104 Short-term investments
105 Fair value adjustment, _______ securities (S-T)
106 Accounts receivable
107 Allowance for doubtful accounts
108 Legal fees receivable
109 Interest receivable
110 Rent receivable
111 Notes receivable
119 Merchandise inventory
120 __________ inventory
121 __________ inventory
124 Office supplies
125 Store supplies
126 _______ supplies
128 Prepaid insurance
129 Prepaid interest
131 Prepaid rent
132 Raw materials inventory
133 Goods in process inventory, _______
134 Goods in process inventory, _______
135 Finished goods inventory

Long-Term Investments

141 Long-term investments
142 Fair value adjustment, _______ securities (L-T)
144 Investment in _______
145 Bond sinking fund

Plant Assets

151 Automobiles
152 Accumulated depreciation—Automobiles
153 Trucks
154 Accumulated depreciation—Trucks
155 Boats
156 Accumulated depreciation—Boats
157 Professional library
158 Accumulated depreciation—Professional library
159 Law library
160 Accumulated depreciation—Law library
161 Furniture
162 Accumulated depreciation—Furniture
163 Office equipment
164 Accumulated depreciation—Office equipment
165 Store equipment
166 Accumulated depreciation—Store equipment
167 _______ equipment
168 Accumulated depreciation—_______ equipment
169 Machinery
170 Accumulated depreciation—Machinery
173 Building _______
174 Accumulated depreciation—Building _______
175 Building _______
176 Accumulated depreciation—Building _______
179 Land improvements _______
180 Accumulated depreciation—Land improvements _______
181 Land improvements _______
182 Accumulated depreciation—Land improvements _______
183 Land

Natural Resources

185 Mineral deposit
186 Accumulated depletion—Mineral deposit

Intangible Assets

191 Patents
192 Leasehold
193 Franchise
194 Copyrights
195 Leasehold improvements
196 Licenses
197 Accumulated amortization—_______

Liabilities

Current Liabilities

201 Accounts payable
202 Insurance payable
203 Interest payable
204 Legal fees payable
207 Office salaries payable
208 Rent payable
209 Salaries payable
210 Wages payable
211 Accrued payroll payable
214 Estimated warranty liability
215 Income taxes payable
216 Common dividend payable
217 Preferred dividend payable
218 State unemployment taxes payable
219 Employee federal income taxes payable
221 Employee medical insurance payable
222 Employee retirement program payable
223 Employee union dues payable
224 Federal unemployment taxes payable
225 FICA taxes payable
226 Estimated vacation pay liability

Unearned Revenues

230 Unearned consulting fees
231 Unearned legal fees
232 Unearned property management fees
233 Unearned _______ fees
234 Unearned _______ fees
235 Unearned janitorial revenue
236 Unearned _______ revenue
238 Unearned rent

Notes Payable

240 Short-term notes payable
241 Discount on short-term notes payable
245 Notes payable
251 Long-term notes payable
252 Discount on long-term notes payable

Long-Term Liabilities

253 Long-term lease liability
255 Bonds payable
256 Discount on bonds payable
257 Premium on bonds payable
258 Deferred income tax liability

Equity

Owner's Equity

301 _____________, Capital
302 _____________, Withdrawals
303 _____________, Capital
304 _____________, Withdrawals
305 _____________, Capital
306 _____________, Withdrawals

Paid-In Capital

307 Common stock, $ _______ par value
308 Common stock, no-par value
309 Common stock, $ _______ stated value
310 Common stock dividend distributable
311 Paid-in capital in excess of par value, Common stock

312 Paid-in capital in excess of stated value, No-par common stock
313 Paid-in capital from retirement of common stock
314 Paid-in capital, Treasury stock
315 Preferred stock
316 Paid-in capital in excess of par value, Preferred stock

Retained Earnings

318 Retained earnings
319 Cash dividends (or Dividends)
320 Stock dividends

Other Equity Accounts

321 Treasury stock, Common
322 Unrealized gain—Equity
323 Unrealized loss—Equity

Revenues

401 ______ fees earned
402 ______ fees earned
403 ______ services revenue
404 ______ services revenue
405 Commissions earned
406 Rent revenue (or Rent earned)
407 Dividends revenue (or Dividend earned)
408 Earnings from investment in ______
409 Interest revenue (or Interest earned)
410 Sinking fund earnings
413 Sales
414 Sales returns and allowances
415 Sales discounts

Cost of Sales

Cost of Goods Sold

502 Cost of goods sold
505 Purchases
506 Purchases returns and allowances
507 Purchases discounts
508 Transportation-in

Manufacturing

520 Raw materials purchases
521 Freight-in on raw materials
530 Factory payroll
531 Direct labor
540 Factory overhead
541 Indirect materials
542 Indirect labor
543 Factory insurance expired
544 Factory supervision
545 Factory supplies used
546 Factory utilities
547 Miscellaneous production costs
548 Property taxes on factory building
549 Property taxes on factory equipment
550 Rent on factory building
551 Repairs, factory equipment
552 Small tools written off
560 Depreciation of factory equipment
561 Depreciation of factory building

Standard Cost Variance

580 Direct material quantity variance
581 Direct material price variance
582 Direct labor quantity variance
583 Direct labor price variance
584 Factory overhead volume variance
585 Factory overhead controllable variance

Expenses

Amortization, Depletion, and Depreciation

601 Amortization expense—______
602 Amortization expense—______
603 Depletion expense—______
604 Depreciation expense—Boats
605 Depreciation expense—Automobiles
606 Depreciation expense—Building ______
607 Depreciation expense—Building ______
608 Depreciation expense—Land improvements ______
609 Depreciation expense—Land improvements ______
610 Depreciation expense—Law library
611 Depreciation expense—Trucks
612 Depreciation expense—______ equipment
613 Depreciation expense—______ equipment
614 Depreciation expense—______
615 Depreciation expense—______

Employee-Related Expenses

620 Office salaries expense
621 Sales salaries expense
622 Salaries expense
623 ______ wages expense
624 Employees' benefits expense
625 Payroll taxes expense

Financial Expenses

630 Cash over and short
631 Discounts lost
632 Factoring fee expense
633 Interest expense

Insurance Expenses

635 Insurance expense—Delivery equipment
636 Insurance expense—Office equipment
637 Insurance expense—______

Rental Expenses

640 Rent expense
641 Rent expense—Office space
642 Rent expense—Selling space
643 Press rental expense
644 Truck rental expense
645 ______ rental expense

Supplies Expenses

650 Office supplies expense
651 Store supplies expense
652 ______ supplies expense
653 ______ supplies expense

Miscellaneous Expenses

655 Advertising expense
656 Bad debts expense
657 Blueprinting expense
658 Boat expense
659 Collection expense
661 Concessions expense
662 Credit card expense
663 Delivery expense
664 Dumping expense
667 Equipment expense
668 Food and drinks expense
671 Gas and oil expense
672 General and administrative expense
673 Janitorial expense
674 Legal fees expense
676 Mileage expense
677 Miscellaneous expenses
678 Mower and tools expense
679 Operating expense
680 Organization expense
681 Permits expense
682 Postage expense
683 Property taxes expense
684 Repairs expense—______
685 Repairs expense—______
687 Selling expense
688 Telephone expense
689 Travel and entertainment expense
690 Utilities expense
691 Warranty expense
695 Income taxes expense

Gains and Losses

701 Gain on retirement of bonds
702 Gain on sale of machinery
703 Gain on sale of investments
704 Gain on sale of trucks
705 Gain on ______
706 Foreign exchange gain or loss
801 Loss on disposal of machinery
802 Loss on exchange of equipment
803 Loss on exchange of ______
804 Loss on sale of notes
805 Loss on retirement of bonds
806 Loss on sale of investments
807 Loss on sale of machinery
808 Loss on ______
809 Unrealized gain—Income
810 Unrealized loss—Income
811 Impairment gain
812 Impairment loss

Clearing Accounts

901 Income summary
902 Manufacturing summary

SELECTED TRANSACTIONS AND RELATIONS

① Merchandising Transactions Summary

	Merchandising Transactions	Merchandising Entries	Dr.	Cr.
Purchases	Purchasing merchandise for resale.	• Merchandise Inventory	#	
		Cash or Accounts Payable		#
	Paying freight costs on purchases; FOB shipping point.	• Merchandise Inventory	#	
		Cash		#
	Paying within discount period.	• Accounts Payable	#	
		Merchandise Inventory		#
		Cash		#
	Recording purchase returns or allowances.	• Cash or Accounts Payable	#	
		Merchandise Inventory		#
Sales	Selling merchandise.	• Cash or Accounts Receivable	#	
		Sales		#
		• Cost of Goods Sold..................	#	
		Merchandise Inventory		#
	Receiving payment within discount period.	• Cash	#	
		Sales Discounts	#	
		Accounts Receivable		#
	Granting sales returns or allowances.	• Sales Returns and Allowances...........	#	
		Cash or Accounts Receivable		#
		• Merchandise Inventory	#	
		Cost of Goods Sold		#
	Paying freight costs on sales; FOB destination.	• Delivery Expense	#	
		Cash		#

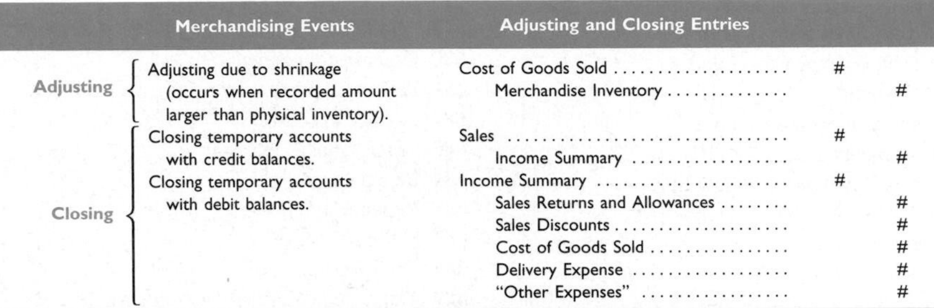

	Merchandising Events	Adjusting and Closing Entries	Dr.	Cr.
Adjusting	Adjusting due to shrinkage (occurs when recorded amount larger than physical inventory).	Cost of Goods Sold	#	
		Merchandise Inventory		#
Closing	Closing temporary accounts with credit balances.	Sales	#	
		Income Summary		#
	Closing temporary accounts with debit balances.	Income Summary	#	
		Sales Returns and Allowances		#
		Sales Discounts		#
		Cost of Goods Sold		#
		Delivery Expense		#
		"Other Expenses"		#

② Merchandising Cash Flows

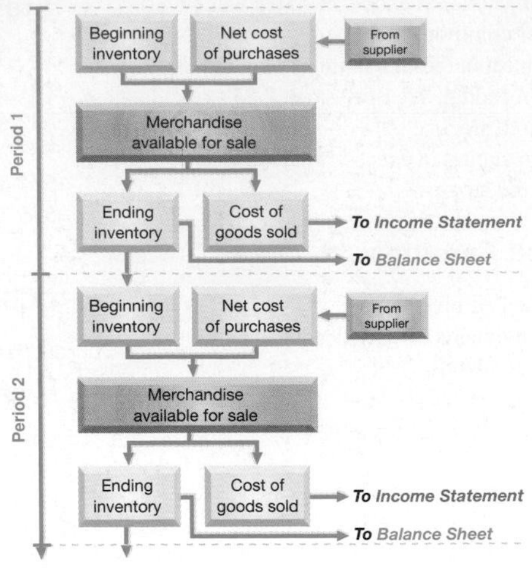

③ Credit Terms and Amounts

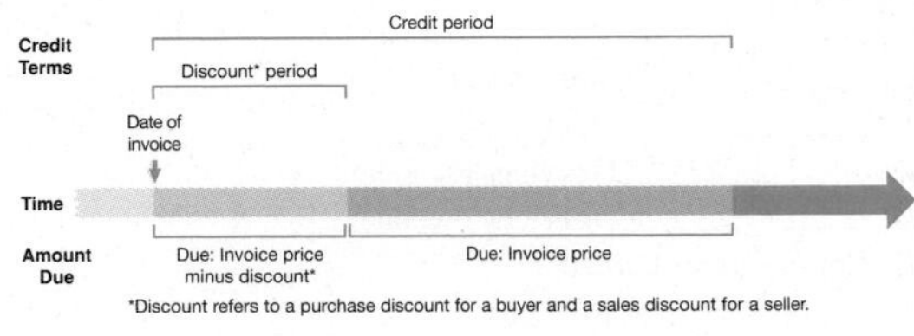

④ Bad Debts Estimation

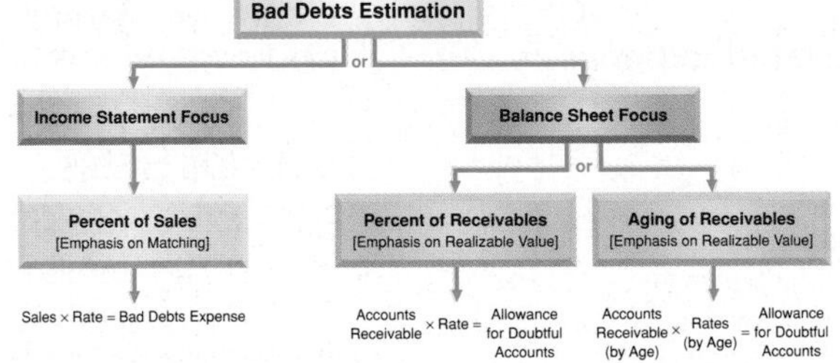

⑤ Bond Valuation

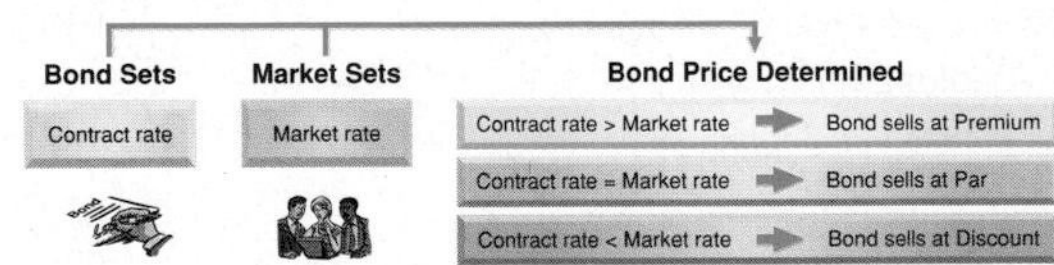

⑥ Stock Transactions Summary

	Stock Transactions	Stock Entries	Dr.	Cr.
Issue Common Stock	Issue par value common stock at par (par stock recorded at par).	Cash	#	
		Common Stock		#
	Issue par value common stock at premium (par stock recorded at par).	Cash	#	
		Common Stock		#
		Paid-In Capital in Excess of Par Value, Common Stock		#
	Issue no-par value common stock (no-par stock recorded at amount received).	Cash	#	
		Common Stock		#
	Issue stated value common stock at stated value (stated stock recorded at stated value).	Cash	#	
		Common stock		#
	Issue stated value common stock at premium (stated stock recorded at stated value).	Cash	#	
		Common stock		#
		Paid-In Capital in Excess of Stated Value, Common Stock		#
Issue Preferred Stock	Issue par value preferred stock at par (par stock recorded at par).	Cash	#	
		Preferred Stock		#
	Issue par value preferred stock at premium (par stock recorded at par).	Cash	#	
		Preferred Stock		#
		Paid-In Capital in Excess of Par Value, Preferred Stock		#
Reacquire Common Stock	Reacquire its own common stock (treasury stock recorded at cost).	Treasury Stock, Common	#	
		Cash		#
Reissue Common Stock	Reissue its treasury stock at cost (treasury stock removed at cost).	Cash	#	
		Treasury Stock, Common		#
	Reissue its treasury stock above cost (treasury stock removed at cost).	Cash	#	
		Treasury Stock, Common........		#
		Paid-In Capital, Treasury		#
	Reissue its treasury stock below cost (treasury stock removed at cost; if paid-in capital is insufficient to cover amount below cost, retained earnings is debited for remainder).	Cash	#	
		Paid-In Capital, Treasury		#
		Treasury Stock, Common		#
		Retained Earnings (if necessary) ...		#

⑦ Dividend Transactions

Account Affected	Type of Dividend: Cash Dividend	Stock Dividend	Stock Split
Cash............	Decrease	—	—
Common Stock....	—	Increase	—
Retained Earnings ..	Decrease	Decrease	—

⑧ A Rose by Any Other Name

The same financial statement sometimes receives different titles. Following are some of the more common aliases.*

Balance Sheet	Statement of Financial Position Statement of Financial Condition
Income Statement	Statement of Income Operating Statement Statement of Operations Statement of Operating Activity Earnings Statement Statement of Earnings Profit and Loss (P&L) Statement
Statement of Cash Flows	Statement of Cash Flow Cash Flows Statement Statement of Changes in Cash Position Statement of Changes in Financial Position
Statement of Owner's Equity	Statement of Changes in Owner's Equity Statement of Changes in Owner's Capital Statement of Shareholders' Equity† Statement of Changes in Shareholders' Equity† Statement of Stockholders' Equity and Comprehensive Income† Statement of Changes in Capital Accounts†

* The term **Consolidated** often precedes or follows these statement titles to reflect the combination of different entities, such as a parent company and its subsidiaries.
† Corporation only.

MANAGERIAL ANALYSES AND REPORTS

① Cost Types

Variable costs: Total cost changes in proportion to volume of activity
Fixed costs: Total cost does not change in proportion to volume of activity
Mixed costs: Cost consists of both a variable and a fixed element

② Cost Sources

Direct materials: Raw materials costs directly linked to finished product
Direct labor: Employee costs directly linked to finished product
Overhead: Costs indirectly linked to finished product

③ Costing Systems

Job order costing: Costs assigned to each unique unit or batch of units
Process costing: Costs assigned to similar products that are mass-produced in a continuous manner

④ Costing Ratios

Contribution margin ratio = (Net sales − Variable costs)/Net sales
Predetermined overhead rate = Estimated overhead costs/Estimated activity base
Break-even point in units = Total fixed costs/Contribution margin per unit

⑤ Planning and Control Metrics

Cost variance = Actual cost − Standard (budgeted) cost
Sales (revenue) variance = Actual sales − Standard (budgeted) sales

⑥ Capital Budgeting

Payback period = Time expected to recover investment cost
Accounting rate of return = Expected annual net income/Average annual investment
Net present value (NPV) = Present value of future cash flows − Investment cost
NPV rule: 1. Compute net present value (NPV in $)
2. If NPV ≥ 0, then accept project; If NPV < 0, then reject project
Internal rate of return rule: 1. Compute internal rate of return (IRR in %)
2. If IRR ≥ hurdle rate, accept project; If IRR < hurdle rate, reject project

⑦ Costing Terminology

Relevant range: Organization's normal range of operating activity.
Direct cost: Cost incurred for the benefit of one cost object.
Indirect cost: Cost incurred for the benefit of more than one cost object.
Product cost: Cost that is necessary and integral to finished products.
Period cost: Cost identified more with a time period than with finished products.
Overhead cost: Cost not separately or directly traceable to a cost object.
Relevant cost: Cost that is pertinent to a decision.
Opportunity cost: Benefit lost by choosing an action from two or more alternatives.
Sunk cost: Cost already incurred that cannot be avoided or changed.
Standard cost: Cost computed using standard price and standard quantity.
Budget: Formal statement of an organization's future plans.
Break-even point: Sales level at which an organization earns zero profit.
Incremental cost: Cost incurred only if the organization undertakes a certain action.
Transfer price: Price on transactions between divisions within a company.

⑧ Standard Cost Variances

Total materials variance = Materials price variance + Materials quantity variance

Total labor variance = Labor (rate) variance + Labor efficiency (quantity) variance

Total overhead variance = Overhead controllable variance + Fixed overhead volume variance

Overhead controllable variance = Actual total overhead − Applied total overhead from flexible budget
Fixed overhead volume variance = Budgeted fixed overhead − Applied fixed overhead
Variable overhead variance = Variable overhead spending variance + Variable overhead efficiency variance
Fixed overhead variance = Fixed overhead spending variance + Fixed overhead volume variance
(Variable overhead variance + Fixed overhead variance = Total overhead variance)

Materials price variance = [AQ × AP] − [AQ × SP]
Materials quantity variance = [AQ × SP] − [SQ × SP]
Labor (rate) variance = [AH × AR] − [AH × SR]
Labor efficiency (quantity) variance = [AH × SR] − [SH × SR]

Variable overhead spending variance = [AH × AVR] − [AH × SVR]
Variable overhead efficiency variance = [AH × SVR] − [SH × SVR]
Fixed overhead spending variance = Actual fixed overhead − Budgeted fixed overhead

where AQ is actual quantity of materials; AP is actual price of materials; AH is actual hours of labor; AR is actual rate of wages; AVR is actual variable rate of overhead; SQ is standard quantity of materials; SP is standard price of materials; SH is standard hours of labor; SR is standard rate of wages; SVR is standard variable rate of overhead.

⑨ Sales Variances

Sales price variance = [AS × AP] − [AS × BP]
Sales volume variance = [AS × BP] − [BS × BP]

where AS = actual sales units; AP = actual sales price; BP = budgeted sales price; BS = budgeted sales units (fixed budget)

Manufacturing Statement
For *period* Ended *date*

Direct materials	
Raw materials inventory, Beginning	$ #
Raw materials purchases	#
Raw materials available for use	#
Raw materials inventory, Ending	(#)
Direct materials used	#
Direct labor	#
Overhead costs	
Total overhead costs	#
Total manufacturing costs	#
Add goods in process inventory, Beginning	#
Total cost of goods in process	#
Deduct goods in process inventory, Ending	(#)
Cost of goods manufactured	$ #

Contribution Margin Income Statement
For *period* Ended *date*

Net sales (revenues)	$ #
Total variable costs	#
Contribution margin	#
Total fixed costs	#
Net income	$ #

Flexible Budget
For *period* Ended *date*

	Flexible Budget: Variable Amount per Unit	Flexible Budget: Fixed Cost	Flexible Budget for Unit Sales of #
Sales (revenues)	$ #		$ #
Variable costs			
Examples: Direct materials, Direct labor, Other variable costs	#		#
Total variable costs	#		#
Contribution margin	$ #		#
Fixed costs			
Examples: Depreciation, Manager		$ #	#
salaries, Administrative salaries		#	#
Total fixed costs		$ #	#
Income from operations			$ #

Fixed Budget Performance Report
For *period* Ended *date*

	Fixed Budget	Actual Performance	Variances[†]
Sales: In units	#	#	
In dollars	$ #	$ #	$ # F or U
Cost of sales			
Direct costs	#	#	# F or U
Indirect costs	#	#	# F or U
Selling expenses			
Examples: Commissions,	#	#	# F or U
Shipping expenses	#	#	# F or U
General and administrative expenses			
Examples: Administrative salaries	#	#	# F or U
Total expenses	$ #	$ #	$ # F or U
Income from operations	$ #	$ #	$ # F or U

[†]F = Favorable variance; U = Unfavorable variance.

Master Budget Sequence

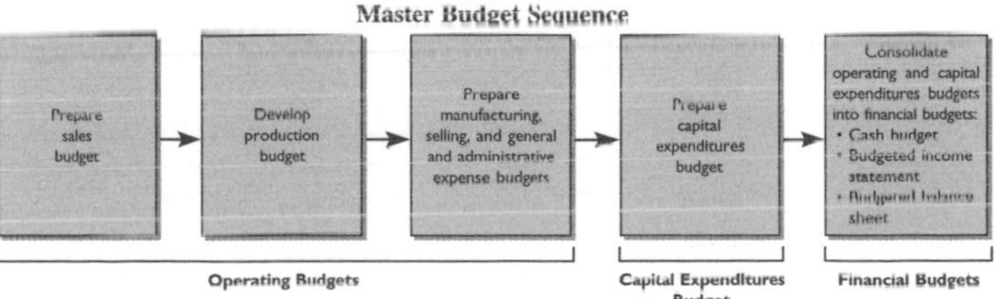

FUNDAMENTALS

① Accounting Equation

Assets		=	Liabilities		+	Equity	
↑ Debit for increases	↓ Credit for decreases		↓ Debit for decreases	↑ Credit for increases		↓ Debit for decreases	↑ Credit for increases

Owner's Capital*		−	Owner's Withdrawals*		+	Revenues		−	Expenses	
↓ Dr. for decreases	↑ Cr. for increases		↑ Dr. for increases	↓ Cr. for decreases		↓ Dr. for decreases	↑ Cr. for increases		↑ Dr. for increases	↓ Cr. for decreases

[shaded] Indicates normal balance.

*Comparable corporate accounts are Common Stock (Paid-In Capital) and Dividends.

② Accounting Cycle

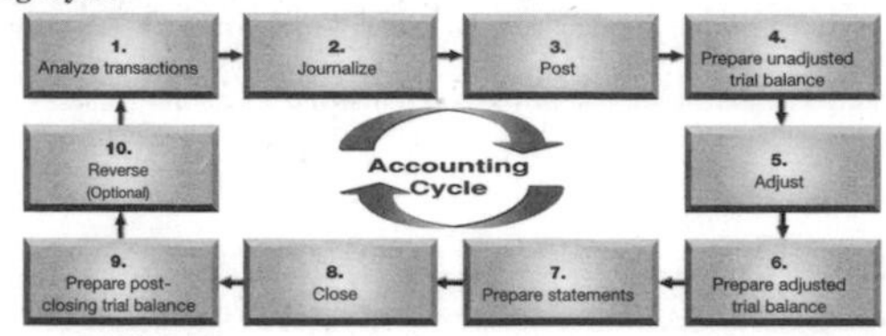

③ Adjustments and Entries

Type	Adjusting Entry	
Prepaid Expenses	Dr. Expense	Cr. Asset*
Unearned Revenues	Dr. Liability	Cr. Revenue
Accrued Expenses	Dr. Expense	Cr. Liability
Accrued Revenues	Dr. Asset	Cr. Revenue

*For depreciation, credit Accumulated Depreciation (contra asset).

④ 4-Step Closing Process

1. Transfer revenue and gain account balances to Income Summary.
2. Transfer expense and loss account balances to Income Summary.
3. Transfer Income Summary balance to Owner's Capital.
4. Transfer Withdrawals balance to Owner's Capital.

⑤ Accounting Concepts

Characteristics	Assumptions	Principles	Constraints
Relevance	Business entity	Historical cost	Cost-benefit
Reliability	Going concern	Revenue recognition	Materiality
Comparability	Monetary unit	Expense recognition	Industry practice
Consistency	Periodicity	Full disclosure	Conservatism

⑥ Ownership of Inventory

	Ownership Transfers When Goods Passed To	Transportation Costs Paid By
FOB Shipping Point	Carrier	Buyer
FOB Destination	Buyer	Seller

⑦ Inventory Costing Methods

- Specific Identification
- First-In, First-Out (FIFO)
- Weighted-Average
- Last-In, First-Out (LIFO)

⑧ Depreciation and Depletion

Straight-Line: $$\frac{\text{Cost} - \text{Salvage value}}{\text{Useful life in periods}} \times \text{Periods expired}$$

Units-of-Production: $$\frac{\text{Cost} - \text{Salvage value}}{\text{Useful life in units}} \times \text{Units produced}$$

Declining-Balance: Rate* × Beginning-of-period book value

*Rate is often double the straight-line rate, or 2 × (1/Useful life)

Depletion: $$\frac{\text{Cost} - \text{Salvage value}}{\text{Total capacity in units}} \times \text{Units extracted}$$

⑨ Interest Computation

Interest = Principal (face) × Rate × Time

⑩ Accounting for Investment Securities

Classification*	Accounting
Short-Term Investment in Securities	
Held-to-maturity (debt) securities	**Cost** (without any discount or premium amortization)
Trading (debt and equity) securities	**Fair value** (with fair value adjustment to income)
Available-for-sale (debt and equity) securities	**Fair value** (with fair value adjustment to equity)
Long-Term Investment in Securities	
Held-to-maturity (debt) securities	**Cost** (with any discount or premium amortization)
Available-for-sale (debt and equity) securities	**Fair value** (with fair value adjustment to equity)
Equity securities with significant influence	Equity method
Equity securities with controlling influence	Equity method (with consolidation)

*A *fair value option* allows companies to report HTM and AFS securities much like trading securities.

ANALYSES

① Liquidity and Efficiency

Current ratio $= \frac{\text{Current assets}}{\text{Current liabilities}}$ — p. 148

Working capital = Current assets − Current liabilities — p. 697

Acid-test ratio $= \frac{\text{Cash + Short-term investments + Current receivables}}{\text{Current liabilities}}$ — p. 196

Accounts receivable turnover $= \frac{\text{Net sales}}{\text{Average accounts receivable, net}}$ — p. 375

Credit risk ratio $= \frac{\text{Allowance for doubtful accounts}}{\text{Accounts receivable, net}}$ — p. 375

Inventory turnover $= \frac{\text{Cost of goods sold}}{\text{Average inventory}}$ — p. 241

Days' sales uncollected $= \frac{\text{Accounts receivable, net}}{\text{Net sales}} \times 365^*$ — p. 335

Days' sales in inventory $= \frac{\text{Ending inventory}}{\text{Cost of goods sold}} \times 365^*$ — p. 241

Total asset turnover $= \frac{\text{Net sales}}{\text{Average total assets}}$ — p. 413

Plant asset useful life $= \frac{\text{Plant asset cost}}{\text{Depreciation expense}}$ — p. 413

Plant asset age $= \frac{\text{Accumulated depreciation}}{\text{Depreciation expense}}$ — p. 413

Days' cash expense coverage $= \frac{\text{Cash and cash equivalents}}{\text{Average daily cash expenses}}$ — p. 322

*360 days is also commonly used.

② Solvency

Debt ratio $= \frac{\text{Total liabilities}}{\text{Total assets}}$ Equity ratio $= \frac{\text{Total equity}}{\text{Total assets}}$ — pp. 69 & 701

Debt-to-equity $= \frac{\text{Total liabilities}}{\text{Total equity}}$ — p. 567

Times interest earned $= \frac{\text{Income before interest expense and income taxes}}{\text{Interest expense}}$ — p. 450

Cash coverage of growth $= \frac{\text{Cash flow from operations}}{\text{Cash outflow for plant assets}}$ — p. 651

Cash coverage of debt $= \frac{\text{Cash flow from operations}}{\text{Total noncurrent liabilities}}$ — p. 646

③ Profitability

Profit margin ratio $= \frac{\text{Net income}}{\text{Net sales}}$ — p. 109

Gross margin ratio $= \frac{\text{Net sales} - \text{Cost of goods sold}}{\text{Net sales}}$ — p. 196

Return on total assets $= \frac{\text{Net income}}{\text{Average total assets}}$ — p. 22

= Profit margin ratio × Total asset turnover — p. 703

Return on common stockholders' equity $= \frac{\text{Net income} - \text{Preferred dividends}}{\text{Average common stockholders' equity}}$ — p. 703

Book value per common share $= \frac{\text{Stockholders' equity applicable to common shares}}{\text{Number of common shares outstanding}}$ — p. 528

Basic earnings per share $= \frac{\text{Net income} - \text{Preferred dividends}}{\text{Weighted-average common shares outstanding}}$ — p. 527

Cash flow on total assets $= \frac{\text{Cash flow from operations}}{\text{Average total assets}}$ — p. 650

Payout ratio $= \frac{\text{Cash dividends declared on common stock}}{\text{Net income}}$ — p. 528

④ Market

Price-earnings ratio $= \frac{\text{Market value (price) per share}}{\text{Earnings per share}}$ — p. 527

Dividend yield $= \frac{\text{Annual cash dividends per share}}{\text{Market price per share}}$ — p. 528

Residual income = Net income − Target net income